Lecture Notes in Computer Science 3491

Commenced Publication in 1973
Founding and Former Series Editors:
Gerhard Goos, Juris Hartmanis, and Jan van Leeuwen

Carol Peters Paul Clough
Julio Gonzalo Gareth J.F. Jones
Michael Kluck Bernardo Magnini (Eds.)

Multilingual Information Access for Text, Speech and Images

5th Workshop of the
Cross-Language Evaluation Forum, CLEF 2004
Bath, UK, September 15-17, 2004
Revised Selected Papers

Volume Editors

Carol Peters
Istituto di Scienza e Tecnologie dell'Informazione
Consiglio Nazionale delle Ricerche (ISTI-CNR)
Via G. Moruzzi 1, 56124 Pisa, Italy
E-mail: carol.peters@isti.cnr.it

Paul Clough
University of Sheffield, Department of Information Studies
Western Bank, Sheffield, S10 2TN, UK
E-mail: p.d.clough@sheffield.ac.uk

Julio Gonzalo
Universidad Nacional de Educación a Distancia
Departamento de Lenguajes y Sistemas Infomáticos
Juan del Rosal, 16, 28040 Madrid, Spain
E-mail: julio@lsi.uned.es

Gareth J.F. Jones
Dublin City University, School of Computing
Glasnevin, Dublin 9, Ireland, UK
E-mail: gareth.jones@computing.dcu.ie

Michael Kluck
Informationszentrum Sozialwissenschaften (IZ)
Lennéstr. 30, 53113 Bonn, Germany
E-mail: michaelkluck@web.de

Bernardo Magnini
Centro per la Ricerca Scientifica e Tecnologica (ITC-Irst)
Via Sommarive 18, 38050 Povo (TN), Italy
E-mail: magnini@itc.it

Library of Congress Control Number: 2005928950

CR Subject Classification (1998): H.3, I.2, H.4

ISSN 0302-9743
ISBN-10 3-540-27420-0 Springer Berlin Heidelberg New York
ISBN-13 978-3-540-27420-9 Springer Berlin Heidelberg New York

Springer is a part of Springer Science+Business Media

springeronline.com

Printed in Germany

Typesetting: Camera-ready by author, data conversion by Scientific Publishing Services, Chennai, India
Printed on acid-free paper SPIN: 11519645 06/3142 5 4 3 2 1 0

Preface

The fifth campaign of the Cross-Language Evaluation Forum (CLEF) for European languages was held from January to September 2004. Participation in the CLEF campaigns has increased each year and CLEF 2004 was no exception: 55 groups submitted results for one or more of the different tracks compared with 42 groups in the previous year. CLEF 2004 also marked a breaking point with respect to previous campaigns. The focus was no longer mainly concentrated on multilingual document retrieval as in previous years but was diversified to include different kinds of text retrieval across languages (e.g., exact answers in the question-answering track) and retrieval on different kinds of media (i.e., not just plain text but collections containing image and speech as well). In addition, increasing attention was given to issues that regard system usability and user satisfaction with tasks to measure the effectiveness of interactive systems or system components being included in both the cross-language question answering and image retrieval tasks with the collaboration of the coordinators of the interactive track.

The campaign culminated in a two-and-a-half-day workshop held in Bath, UK, 15–17 September, immediately following the 8th European Conference on Digital Libraries. The workshop was attended by nearly 100 researchers and system developers. In addition to presentations by participants in the campaign, talks included reports on the activities of the NTCIR evaluation initiative for Asian languages, and on industrial experience in building cross-language applications. The final session consisted of a panel in which the members attempted to analyze the current organization of the CLEF campaigns in depth, discussing whether CLEF is working on the right problems, choosing its investments wisely, and giving sufficient attention to the user perspective. Suggestions for the CLEF 2005 campaign included multilingual Web retrieval and a cross-language Geographic Information Retrieval track.

CLEF 2004 was conducted as an activity of the DELOS Network of Excellence on Digital Libraries, within the framework of the Information Society Technologies programme of the European Commission. These post-campaign proceedings were prepared with the assistance of the Center for the Evaluation of Language and Communication Technologies (CELCT), Trento, Italy. The support of DELOS and CELCT is gratefully acknowledged. We should also like to thank the other members of the CLEF Steering Committee for their assistance in the coordination of this event.

April 2005

Carol Peters
Paul Clough
Julio Gonzalo
Gareth J.F. Jones
Michael Kluck
Bernardo Magnini

CLEF 2004 Coordination

CLEF is coordinated by the Istituto di Scienza e Tecnologie dell'Informazione, Consiglio Nazionale delle Ricerche, ISTI-CNR, Pisa.

The following institutions contributed to the organization of the different tracks of the CLEF 2004 campaign:

- Center for the Evaluation of Language and Communication Technologies (CELCT), Trento, Italy
- Centro per la Ricerca Scientifica e Tecnologica, Istituto Trentino di Cultura, Trento, Italy
- College of Information Studies and Institute for Advanced Computer Studies, University of Maryland, USA
- Department of Computer Science and Information Systems, University of Limerick, Ireland
- Department of Information Studies, University of Sheffield, UK
- Department of Information Studies, University of Tampere, Finland
- Eurospider Information Technology AG, Zürich, Switzerland
- Evaluations and Language Resources Distribution Agency, ELDA, Paris, France
- German Research Centre for Artificial Intelligence, DFKI, Saarbrücken, Germany
- Information and Language Processing Systems, University of Amsterdam, Netherlands
- Informationszentrum Sozialwissenschaften, Bonn, Germany
- Lenguajes y Sistemás Informáticos, Universidad Nacional de Educación a Distancia, Madrid, Spain
- Linguateca, Sintef, Oslo, Norway
- Linguistic Modelling Laboratory, Bulgarian Academy of Sciences, Sofia, Bulgaria
- National Institute of Standards and Technology, Gaithersburg MD, USA
- School of Computing, Dublin City University, Ireland
- University and University Hospitals of Geneva, Switzerland

CLEF 2004 Steering Committee

- Maristella Agosti, University of Padua, Italy
- Eija Airio, University of Tampere, Finland
- Martin Braschler, Eurospider Information Technologies, Switzerland
- Hsin-Hsi Chen, National Taiwan University, Taipei, Taiwan
- Khalid Choukri, Evaluations and Language Resources Distribution Agency, ELDA, Paris, France
- Paul Clough, University of Sheffield, UK
- David A. Evans, Clairvoyance Corporation, USA
- Marcello Federico, ITC-irst, Trento, Italy
- Christian Fluhr, CEA-LIST, Fontenay-aux-Roses, France
- Norbert Fuhr, University of Duisburg, Germany
- Frederic C. Gey, UC Berkeley, USA
- Julio Gonzalo, LSI-UNED, Madrid, Spain
- Donna Harman, National Institute of Standards and Technology, USA
- Gareth Jones, Dublin City University, Ireland
- Franciska de Jong, University of Twente, Netherlands
- Noriko Kando, National Institute of Informatics, Tokyo, Japan
- Jussi Karlgren, Swedish Institute of Computer Science, Sweden
- Michael Kluck, Informationszentrum Sozialwissenschaften Bonn, Germany
- Natalia Loukachevitch, Moscow State University, Russia
- Bernardo Magnini, ITC-irst, Trento, Italy
- Paul McNamee, Johns Hopkins University, USA
- Henning Müller, University and University Hospitals, Geneva, Switzerland
- Douglas W. Oard, University of Maryland, USA
- Maarten de Rijke, University of Amsterdam, Netherlands
- Jacques Savoy, University of Neuchâtel, Switzerland
- Peter Schäuble, Eurospider Information Technologies, Switzerland
- Richard Sutcliffe, University of Limerick, Ireland
- Hans Uszkoreit, German Research Center for Artificial Intelligence (DFKI), Germany
- Felisa Verdejo, LSI-UNED, Madrid, Spain
- José Luis Vicedo, University of Alicante, Spain
- Ellen Voorhees, National Institute of Standards and Technology, USA
- Christa Womser-Hacker, University of Hildesheim, Germany

Table of Contents

Part III. Interactive Cross-Language Information Retrieval

Part IV. Multiple Language Question Answering

Part V. Cross-Language Retrieval in Image Collections

Part VI. Cross-Language Spoken Document Retrieval

Part VII. Issues in CLIR and in Evaluation

What Happened in CLEF 2004?

Carol Peters

Istituto di Scienza e Tecnologie dell'Informazione (ISTI-CNR), Pisa, Italy
carol.peters@isti.cnr.it

Abstract. The organization of the CLEF 2004 evaluation campaign is described and details are provided concerning the tracks, test collections and participation. Information on new activities for CLEF 2005 is also given.

1 Introduction

This volume reports the results of the fifth in a series of annual system evaluation campaigns organised by the Cross-Language Evaluation Forum (CLEF)[1]. The main objectives of CLEF are (i) to provide an infrastructure that facilitates testing of all kinds of multilingual information access systems – from monolingual retrieval for multiple languages to the implementation of complete multilingual multimedia search services, and (ii) to construct test-suites of reusable data that can be used for benchmarking purposes. These objectives are achieved through the organisation of evaluation campaigns that culminate each year in a workshop in which the groups that participated in the campaign can report and discuss their experiments. An additional aim of CLEF is to encourage contacts between the R&D and the application communities and promote the industrial take-up of research results.

The main features of the 2004 campaign are briefly outlined below in order to provide the necessary background to the experiments reported in these post-campaign proceedings.

2 Tracks and Tasks in CLEF 2004

In recent years, CLEF distinguished between the core tracks, which were those offered regularly each campaign (the monolingual, bilingual, multilingual and domain-specific tracks), and additional tracks, which were organised on an experimental basis with the objective of identifying new requirements and appropriate methodologies for their testing in a cross-language context. This distinction no longer held in 2004. The interactive track, run since 2001, was finally recognised as part of the main activity, and the great success of the pilot tracks in CLEF 2003, and in particular the cross-language question answering and image retrieval activities, led to their inclusion as regular tracks. This meant that the scope of CLEF 2004 was considerably widened with respect to previous years, with much attention being given to tasks involving information extraction (question answering) and retrieval from multimedia.

---

[1] CLEF 2004 is included in the activities of the DELOS Network of Excellence on Digital Libraries, funded by the Sixth Framework Programme of the European Commission. DELOS is an "old" friend of CLEF, having promoted the first two campaigns in 2000 and 2001. For information on DELOS, see www.delos.info.

C. Peters et al. (Eds.): CLEF 2004, LNCS 3491, pp. 1–9, 2005.

CLEF 2004 thus offered six tracks designed to evaluate the performance of systems for:

- mono-, bi- and multilingual document retrieval on news collections (Ad hoc)
- mono- and cross-language domain-specific retrieval (GIRT)
- interactive cross-language retrieval (iCLEF)
- multiple language question answering (QA@CLEF)
- cross-language retrieval on image collections (ImageCLEF)
- cross-language spoken document retrieval (CL-SDR)

The organisation of each of these tracks and the results obtained are described and commented in the track overviews at the beginning of each section of this volume.

3 CLEF 2004 Test Collections

CLEF campaigns adopt a comparative evaluation approach in which system performance is measured using appropriate test collections. The test collections consist of sets of sample query statements often called "topics", document collections, and relevance judgments determining the set of relevant documents in a collection for a given query statement. All language dependent tasks such as topic/question creation and relevance assessment are performed in a distributed setting by native speakers. Rules are established and a tight central coordination is maintained in order to ensure consistency and coherency of topic and relevance judgment sets over the different collections, languages and tracks.

Five separate document collections were used in CLEF 2004:

- CLEF multilingual comparable corpus
- GIRT social science database
- St Andrews historical photographic archive
- CasImage radiological medical database
- Speech transcriptions supplied by TREC

The main CLEF collection is the multilingual comparable corpus of newspaper and news agency documents. In 2004, this collection was used by the Ad hoc, iCLEF and QA@CLEF tracks. The multilingual corpus increases in size and coverage every year as new collections and languages are added. In 2004 it contained nearly 1.8 million news documents from the same time period (1994-1995) in ten languages: Dutch, English, Finnish, French, German, Italian, Portuguese[2], Russian, Spanish and Swedish. Table 1 gives the main specifics of this collection and Table 2 shows which part of this collection was used in which track in 2004.

However, news media have characteristics which may not hold true for other genres: e.g. wide use of proper nouns (names and places), association of date stamps, particular style of writing and a rapid evolution of general-purpose vocabulary. Certain features may facilitate access and retrieval, others may hinder it. For this reason, a separate document collection is included for systems tuned for domain-specific tasks.

---

[2] Portuguese was a new addition in 2004; Hungarian and Bulgarian newspaper collections are being added for 2005.

Table 1. Sources and dimensions of the main CLEF 2004 multilingual document collection

Collection	Added in	Size (MB)	No. of Docs	Median Size of Docs. (Bytes)	Median Size of Docs. (Tokens)[3]	Median Size of Docs. (Features)
Dutch: Algemeen Dagblad 94/95	2001	241	106483	1282	166	112
Dutch: NRC Handelsblad 94/95	2001	299	84121	2153	354	203
English: LA Times 94	2000	425	113005	2204	421	246
English: Glasgow Herald 95	2003	154	56472	2219	343	202
Finnish: Aamulehti late 94/95	2002	137	55344	1712	217	150
French: Le Monde 94	2000	158	44013	1994	361	213
French: ATS 94	2001	86	43178	1683	227	137
French: ATS 95	2003	88	42615	1715	234	140
German: Frankfurter Rundschau94	2000	320	139715	1598	225	161
German: Der Spiegel 94/9	2000	63	13979	1324	213	160
German: SDA 94	2001	144	71677	1672	186	131
German: SDA 95	2003	144	69438	1693	188	132
Italian: La Stampa 94	2000	193	58051	1915	435	268
Italian: AGZ 94	2001	86	50527	1454	187	129
Italian: AGZ 95	2003	85	48980	1474	192	132
Portuguese: Público 94	2004	164	51751	NA	NA	NA
Portuguese: Público 95	2004	176	55070	NA	NA	NA
Russian: Izvestia 95	2003	68	16761	NA	NA	NA
Spanish: EFE 94	2001	511	215738	2172	290	171
Spanish: EFE 95	2003	577	238307	2221	299	175
Swedish: TT 94/95	2002	352	142819	2171	183	121

SDA/ATS/AGZ = Schweizerische Depeschenagentur (Swiss News Agency)
EFE = Agencia EFE S.A (Spanish News Agency)
TT = Tidningarnas Telegrambyrå (Swedish newspaper)
NA = Not Available at this moment

[3] The number of tokens extracted from each document can vary slightly across systems, depending on the respective definition of what constitutes a token. Consequently, the number of tokens and features given in this table are approximations and may differ from actual implemented systems.

Table 2. Data collections used in CLEF 2004 Ad hoc, iCLEF and QA tracks

TRACK/TASK	DE	Brit-EN	US-EN	ES	FI	FR	IT	NL	PT	RU	SV
Multilingual: 95 data only		X			X	X				X	
Bilingual: 95 data only – according to task		only newcomer			X	X			X	X	
Monolingual: 95 data only – according to task					X	X			X	X	
iCLEF: 94 & 95 data according to task		X	X	X		X					
QA@CLEF: 94 & 95 data according to task	X	X	X	X		X	X	X	X		

The domain-specific track in CLEF is mainly based on the German Indexing and Retrieval Test (GIRT) corpus of structured social science data. GIRT includes an associated social science thesaurus in German-English and a German-Russian wordlist, both prepared by IZ-Bonn, Germany. UC Berkeley has made an XML version available to CLEF participants. Since the first CLEF campaign in 2000, the GIRT corpus has been enlarged several times. CLEF 2004 used the GIRT4 corpus, which contains about 150,000 documents in German and English and is called pseudo-parallel because the original documents are in German and the English part consists of translations of these German documents into English; the English part is actually considerably smaller than the German.

The ImageCLEF track in CLEF 2004 used two distinct collections: a collection of approximately 30,000 historic photographs complete with short captions provided by St Andrews University, Scotland, and the CasImage collection of about 9000 radiological medical images with French and English case notes made available by the University Hospitals, Geneva.

The cross-language spoken document retrieval track (CL-SDR) used speech transcriptions in English from the TREC-8 and TREC-9 SDR tracks, supplied by the National Institute of Standards and Technology (NIST), USA.

Each track was responsible for preparing its own topic/query statements and for performing the relevance assessments of the results submitted by participating groups. The number of different topic languages used varied from track to track, from a minimum of three in the GIRT track to a maximum of fourteen in the Ad hoc track. Details and descriptions are given in the individual track overviews.

ELDA (Evaluations and Language resources Distribution Agency) is currently preparing a test-suite containing the test collections created by the ad hoc and domain-specific tracks from CLEF 2000 to 2004. This is due to be released shortly on the ELDA catalogue. The aim is to make the valuable collections built up by CLEF over the years publicly available to researchers and system developers for benchmarking purposes.

4 Participation

A total of 55 groups submitted results in CLEF 2004: 37 from Europe, 13 from N.America; 4 from Asia and one mixed European/Asian group. This is a considerable increase on the 42 groups of CLEF 2003. 11 groups consisted of a collaboration between researchers from different institutions. A disappointment was that only six groups this year included representatives from industry – down from nine in 2003. Many groups participated in more than one track. The breakdown of participation of groups per track/task is as follows: Ad hoc: 26 with multilingual 9; bilingual 16; monolingual 19; GIRT: 4; iCLEF: 5; QA@CLEF: 18; ImageCLEF: 18. Unfortunately, the CL-SDR track had problems this year and few participants. For this reason, these proceedings just contain one overview paper presenting the activity of this track.

As in previous years, participating groups consisted of a nice mix of new-comers (23) and groups that had participated in one or more previous editions (32). The introduction of fully-fledged question answering and image retrieval tracks had a big impact on participation in CLEF 2004, not just with respect to the numbers but also regarding the skills and expertise involved. The popularity of question answering has meant that a growing number of participants now have a natural language processing background while the image retrieval tasks have brought in groups with experience in new areas including image processing and medical informatics – making CLEF an increasingly multidisciplinary forum.

Table 3 lists the groups that participated in CLEF 2004 – the asterisks indicate the number of times a group has participated in previous editions of CLEF. The six groups with four asterisks have taken part in all editions. The full affiliation of each group can be seen in their papers in this volume. Figure 1 shows how the focus of CLEF has shifted and diversified over the years.

Table 3. CLEF 2004 Participating Groups

Acad. Sci. /ITC-irst (BG/IT)	Nat.Taiwan U. (TW) ***	U.Lisbon (PT)
CEA/LIC2M (FR) *	KIDS - NCTU/ISU (TW)	U.Maryland (US) ****
CLIPS-IMAG/IPAL-CNRS (FR/SG)*	Ricoh (JP) *	U. Michigan (US)
Clairvoyance Corp. (US) **	SICS/Connexor (SV/FI) ***	U.Montreal (CA) ****
Daedalus/Madrid Universities (ES) *	SUNY at Buffalo (US) *	U.Neuchâtel (CH) ***
DFKI (DE) *	Thomson Legal (US)***	U.Oregon (US)
Dublin City U. (IE)	U.Alicante (ES) ***	U.Oviedo (ES) *
Hummingbird (CA) ***	U.Amsterdam (NL) ***	U.Padova (IT) **
ILC-CNR/U.Pisa (IT)	U.Chicago (US)	U.Salamanca (ES) **
Imperial College London (UK)	U.Evora (PT)	U.Sheffield (UK) ****
INAOE (MX)	U.Edinburgh (UK)	U.Stockholm/SICS (SV)
IRIT-Toulouse (FR) **	U.Glasgow (UK)	U.Surugadai/NII/NTU (JP/TW) *
ITC-irst (IT) ****	U.Hagen (DE) *	RWTH Aachen Comp.Sci (DE)
Johns Hopkins U. (US) ****	U.Helsinki (FI)	RWTH Aachen Medicine (DE)
Linguateca SINTEF (NO)	U.Hildesheim (DE) **	U.Tilburg/U.Maastricht (NL)
LMSI-CNRS (FR)	U.Hospitals Geneva/LITH (CH)	U.Twente/CWI (NL) ***
Nat. Res. Council – ILTG (CA)	U.Jaen (ES) ***	UC Berkeley (US) ****
	U.La Coruna (ES) **	UNED-LSI (ES) ***
	U.Limerick (IE) *	UP Catalunya (ES)

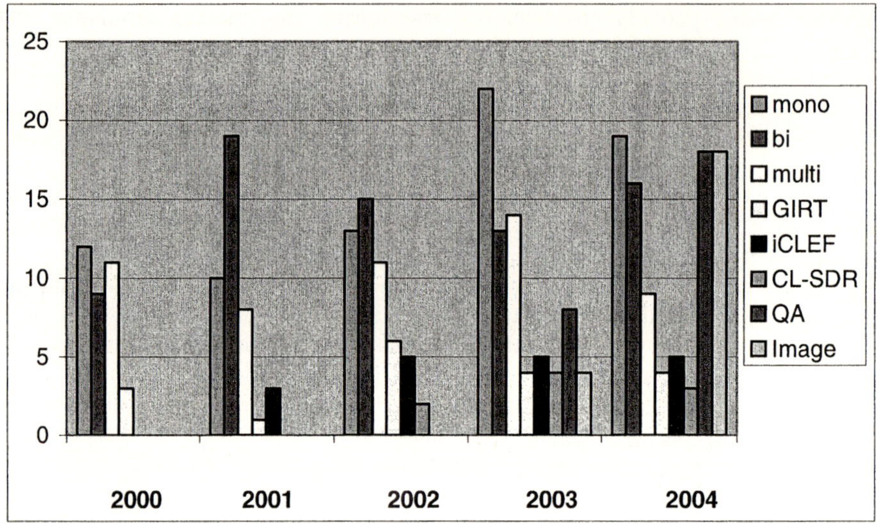

The mono-, bi-, and multilingual ad hoc tasks are listed separately; in 2002 the GIRT track also included the Amaryllis database.

Fig. 1. CLEF 2000 – 2004 - numbers of participants per track

5 The CLEF 2004 Experiments

This volume is organized into separate sections for each of the main evaluation tracks listed above. Each section begins with an overview paper by the track coordinators describing the track objectives, setup, tasks and main results. The majority of the papers are thoroughly revised and expanded versions of the reports presented at the Workshop held in Bath, UK, September 2004. Many also include descriptions of additional experiments and results, as groups often further optimise their systems or try out new ideas as a consequence of discussions at the workshop.

Part I is dedicated to the ad hoc text retrieval track and has two subsections. The first reports on cross-language document retrieval – both multilingual and bilingual - while the second contains papers describing the monolingual-only experiments. Most of the state-of-the-art approaches to cross-language and monolingual retrieval in the multiple language context are covered and new ideas are also presented. A question often asked is whether there is demonstrable improvement in ad hoc cross-language system performance over the years. The overview paper to this section discusses this question – and provides some interesting confirmation.

Part II presents mono- and cross-language experiments in domain-specific retrieval on the GIRT collection of social science documents. The first paper by Michael Kluck analyses the results obtained in this track and provides a detailed description of the test corpus. The other four papers report the individual experiences of participants. Part III contains five papers describing the interactive experiments. This track was proposed in CLEF 2004 as the interactive counterpart to the automatic cross-language question answering track. The task given to the users was to find specific answers to narrowly focused questions. The aim of the track was to develop a methodology to study user-inclusive aspects of cross-language question answering. In their overview paper, the coordinators, Gonzalo and Oard, discuss the preliminary results of this exercise.

The experiments performed by participants in the multilingual question answering track are presented in Part IV. Following the success of the pilot experiment in 2003, this track was very ambitious in scope. Almost all the cross-language combinations between nine query languages and seven target languages were exploited to set up more than fifty different tasks, both monolingual and bilingual. Although this meant that it was not very easy to compare results between different systems, for the first time many groups were able to test a question answering system on a language other than English. The overview paper gives a complete run down of results, language by language. The results of a pilot task for Spanish, which tested systems on different question types than those proposed in the main track, are also included.

Parts V and VI of this volume are dedicated to cross-language experiments on collections with other media: image and speech. The ImageCLEF track aimed at exploring the use of both text and content-based retrieval methods from cross-language retrieval in image collections. Three tasks were offered: automatic ad hoc retrieval and interactive retrieval on a collection of historical photographs with captions and metadata, and retrieval from a medical collection of radiological images. The results are analysed in the overview paper. The main finding was that the best performances were obtained by groups that used a combination of visual and textual retrieval methods. The cross-language spoken document retrieval task was not a great success this year. Only two groups submitted results, probably because the text collections used had already been studied in depth in TREC and the task did not appear particularly challenging. The results are summarised in a single overview paper. An entirely new task will be offered in CLEF 2005.

The final section contains two papers presenting issues involved in cross-language system evaluation. The first paper, by Santos and Rocha, discusses in detail the work involved in adding a new language to the CLEF test collections. Portuguese was included as a target language this year in both the ad hoc and the question answering tracks. This paper not only describes the considerable workload but also provides some interesting comments on the problems that arose and makes some suggestions for changes in the future. The last paper, by Mandl and Womser-Hacker, analyses the extent to which the presence of named entities in topic statements can contribute to system performance.

6 CLEF 2005

The CLEF 2005 campaign is now well under way and eight tracks are being offered. These include the six tracks of CLEF 2004, which have been restructured and expanded with new tasks and/or new collections. The ad hoc track has added two new languages – Bulgarian and Hungarian – and a multilingual task that reuses the CLEF 2003 multilingual-8 test collection and focuses, in particular, on results merging strategies. The domain-specific track now also includes the RSSC (Russian Social Science Corpus) collection in addition to the GIRT database. iCLEF in 2005 studies problems of both cross-language question answering and image retrieval from a user-inclusive perspective. The QA@CLEF track is offering to evaluate cross-language experiments against eight different target languages and is encouraging experiments that do not include English as one of the language pair. ImageCLEF offers four different tasks and includes two totally new collections (as well as expanded versions of those used last year). The cross-language spoken document retrieval track has been completely remodelled: mono- and cross-language retrieval experiments will be assessed on the Malach collection of spontaneous conversational speech from the Shoah archives.

In addition, following proposals made during the CLEF 2004 workshop, two experimental pilot tracks are being organised: WebCLEF and GeoCLEF. In its first year, WebCLEF will evaluate multilingual navigational tasks such as home page and named page finding. The track will use the EuroGOV collection built by University of Amsterdam and consisting of documents from European governmental sites in a large number of languages. The other pilot track in 2005, GeoCLEF, aims at evaluating the development of systems for cross-language geographical retrieval. Given a statement describing a spatial user need, the task will be to find relevant documents from target collections of English or German news documents. Through the organization of these new and challenging tracks, CLEF continues in its mission of stimulating the development of systems for multilingual information access that respond to the emerging needs of the application communities. Further information can be found on the CLEF website at: http://www.clef-campaign.org/

Acknowledgements

CLEF is organised on a distributed basis, with different research groups being responsible for the running of the various tracks. My gratitude goes to all those who have contributed to the coordination of the 2004 campaigns and the organisation of the Workshop. Without their assistance, this initiative would be impossible. A list of the principle institutions involved is given at the beginning of this volume. Here below, let me thank the main track coordinators:

- Martin Braschler, Eurospider Information Technologies, Switzerland, for the Ad hoc Track
- Michael Kluck, IZ-Bonn, Germany, for the GIRT track
- Julio Gonzalo, LSI-UNED, Madrid, Spain, and Douglas W. Oard, U. Maryland, USA, for iCLEF
- Bernardo Magnini, ITC-irst, Trento, Italy, for QA@CLEF
- Paul Clough, U. Sheffield, UK , and Henning Müller, University and U. Hospitals of Geneva, Switzerland, for ImageCLEF
- Marcello Federico, ITC-irst, Trento, Italy, and Gareth Jones, DCU, Ireland, for CL-SDR

In addition, I must thank colleagues from the Natural Language Processing Lab, Department of Computer Science and Information Engineering, National Taiwan University and the National Institute of Informatics, Tokyo, for preparing Chinese and Japanese topics. I also thank the European Language Resources Association for its sponsorship of the workshop.

I should also like to express my gratitude to the members of the CLEF Steering Committee who have assisted me with their advice and suggestions throughout this campaign.

Furthermore, I gratefully acknowledge the support of all the data providers and copyright holders, and in particular:

- The Los Angeles Times, for the American English data collection;
- Le Monde S.A. and ELDA: Evaluations and Language resources Distribution Agency, for the French data.
- Frankfurter Rundschau, Druck und Verlagshaus Frankfurt am Main; Der Spiegel, Spiegel Verlag, Hamburg, for the German newspaper collections.
- InformationsZentrum Sozialwissenschaften, Bonn, for the GIRT database.
- Hypersystems Srl, Torino and La Stampa, for the Italian newspaper data.
- Agencia EFE S.A. for the Spanish newswire data.
- NRC Handelsblad, Algemeen Dagblad and PCM Landelijke dagbladen/Het Parool for the Dutch newspaper data.
- Aamulehti Oyj for the Finnish newspaper documents
- Tidningarnas Telegrambyrå for the Swedish newspapers
- The Herald 1995, SMG Newspapers, for the British English newspaper data
- Público and Linguateca for the Portuguese newspaper collection
- Schweizerische Depeschenagentur, Switzerland, for the French, German and Italian Swiss news agency data.
- Russika-Izvestia for the Russian collection
- St Andrews University Library for the image collection
- Radiology Dept. University Hospitals, Geneva, Switzerland for the Medical Images Database
- NIST for access to the TREC-8 and TREC-9 SDR transcripts.

Without their Ohelp, this evaluation activity would be impossible.

CLEF is an activity of the DELOS Network of Excellence and we are very grateful for the sponsorship and assistance provided by the Network. Particular thanks go to Francesca Borri, ISTI-CNR, whose efforts have done much to ensuring the smooth running of the day-by-day organisation of CLEF 2004.

Last but not least, I would like to thank Danilo Giampiccolo and Alessandro Vallin of the Center for the Evaluation of Language and Communication Technologies (CELCT) for their cheerful and efficient assistance in preparing this volume.

CLEF 2004: Ad Hoc Track Overview and Results Analysis

Martin Braschler[1], Giorgio M. Di Nunzio[2], Nicola Ferro[2], and Carol Peters[3]

[1] Eurospider Information Technology AG, 8006 Zurich, Switzerland
martin_braschler@yahoo.com
[2] Department of Information Engineering, University of Padua, Italy
{dinunzio, ferro}@dei.unipd.it
[3] ISTI-CNR, Area di Ricerca, 56124 Pisa, Italy
carol.peters@isti.cnr.it

Abstract. We describe the objectives and organization of the CLEF 2004 ad hoc track and discuss the main characteristics of the experiments. The results are analyzed and commented and their statistical significance is investigated. The paper concludes with some observations on the impact of the CLEF campaign on the state-of-the-art in cross-language information retrieval.

1 Introduction

The first four CLEF campaigns, held from 2000 through 2003, focused heavily on the ad hoc text retrieval track. One of the main goals of CLEF has been to help participating groups to scale their systems successively to be able to tackle the ambitious problem presented in this track: that of simultaneous retrieval from documents written in many different languages. For this reason, the ad hoc track is structured in three tasks, testing systems for monolingual (querying and retrieving documents in one language), bilingual (querying in one language and retrieving documents in another language) and multilingual (querying in one language and retrieving documents in multiple languages) retrieval, thus helping groups to make the progression from simple to more complex tasks. However, as mentioned in the first paper in this volume [1], the emergence of new tracks in recent CLEF campaigns has changed that emphasis somewhat. CLEF today houses more diverse activities than ever, dealing with issues such as retrieval on semi-structured data, interactive retrieval, speech retrieval, image retrieval and question answering. As a consequence, the ad hoc track has been restructured, both in order to make room for these new activities, but more importantly also to present new challenging research questions, especially for those participants that submitted CLEF experiments in previous years.

On the one hand, the CLEF 2004 multilingual track was “trimmed” to four languages: English, Finnish, French and Russian (in 2003, participants had the choice of working with either four or eight languages). On the other hand, these languages were chosen not according to their political/economic influence or their global distribution (as was done in earlier campaigns), but with respect to their distinct

C. Peters et al. (Eds.): CLEF 2004, LNCS 3491, pp. 10 – 26, 2005.

linguistic characteristics[1]. The assumption was that simultaneous retrieval from such a diverse group of languages would pose (unexpected) new challenges, not least when weighting the languages against each other during retrieval. We felt that this shift, and the resulting omission of some "popular languages", was possible due to the good and stable test collections that had already been built in previous campaigns for the languages omitted this year. The bilingual and monolingual tasks reflected the choice of languages for multilingual with the addition of Portuguese, a new acquisition to the main CLEF multilingual comparable corpus[2].

In this paper we will describe the track setup, the evaluation methodology and the participation in the different tasks (Section 2), present the main characteristics of the experiments (Section 3), provide an analysis of the results (Section 4), and investigate their statistical significance (Section 5). The paper closes with some observations on the impact of the CLEF campaigns on the state-of-the-art in the cross-language information retrieval (CLIR) field.

2 Track Setup

The ad hoc track in CLEF adopts a corpus-based, automatic scoring method for the assessment of system performance, based on ideas first introduced in the Cranfield experiments [2] in the late 1960s. This methodology is widely employed and accepted by the information retrieval community. The test collection used consists of a set of "topics" describing information needs and a collection of documents to be searched to find those documents that satisfy the information needs. Evaluation of system performance is then done by judging the documents retrieved in response to a topic with respect to their relevance, and computing the measures recall and precision. The implications of adopting the Cranfield paradigm are discussed in detail in [3].

The distinguishing feature of CLEF is that it applies this evaluation paradigm in a multilingual setting. This means that the criteria normally adopted to create a test collection, consisting of suitable documents, sample queries and relevance assessments, have been adapted to satisfy the particular requirements of the multilingual context. All language dependent tasks such as topic creation and relevance judgment are performed in a distributed setting by native speakers. Rules are established and a tight central coordination is maintained in order to ensure consistency and coherency of topic and relevance judgment sets over the different collections, languages and tracks.

2.1 Tasks

The document collection used in the CLEF 2004 ad hoc track contains English, Finnish, French, Russian and Portuguese texts. As stated above, the multilingual task

[1] English: Germanic language, global distribution, well studied; French: Romance language, very good linguistic resources, rich morphology; Finnish: Finno-Ugric language group, little shared vocabulary with the other languages, complex morphology, few resources for CLIR; Russian: Cyrillic character set, few resources for CLIR.

[2] In CLEF 2004, the multilingual comparable corpus consisted of collections of news documents for the same time period for ten languages. See [1] for details.

solicited experiments retrieving documents from a collection containing documents in four of these languages (Portuguese excluded). Using a selected topic language, the goal for systems was to retrieve relevant documents for all languages in the collection, listing the results in a single, ranked list.

Similarly to CLEF 2003, the bilingual track imposed particular conditions on some of the source → target language pairs accepted. The aim was to encourage – where possible – experiments with language pairs for which existing bilingual resources are difficult to find. The following combinations were allowed:

- Italian/French/Spanish/Russian queries → Finnish target collection
- German/Dutch/Finnish/Swedish queries → French target collection
- Any query language → Russian target collection
- Any query language → Portuguese target collection

As always, newcomers to a CLEF cross-language task or groups using a new topic language were allowed to submit runs to the English target collection.

The monolingual track offered testing for four languages: Finnish, French, Russian and Portuguese.

2.2 Topics

For each of the above tasks, the participating systems constructed their queries (automatically or manually) from a common set of topics, created to simulate user information needs. Each topic consisted of three parts: a brief "title" statement; a one-sentence "description"; a more complex "narrative" specifying the relevance assessment criteria. For CLEF 2004, 50 such topics were produced on the basis of the contents of the five target collections and were then translated additionally into Amharic, Bulgarian, Chinese, Dutch, German, Italian, Japanese, Spanish and Swedish. As in previous years, for each task attempted, a mandatory run using the title and description fields had to be submitted. The objective is to facilitate comparison between the results of different systems. Here below we give the English version of a typical topic from CLEF 2004:

```
<top>
<num> C217 </num>
<EN-title> AIDS in Africa </EN-title>
<EN-desc> Find documents discussing the increase of AIDS in Africa.</EN-
desc>
<EN-narr> There has been an explosive increase of AIDS in Africa.
Relevant documents will discuss this problem. Of particular interest are
documents mentioning humanitarian organisations fighting AIDS in Africa.
</EN-narr>
</top>
```

The motivation behind using structured topics is to simulate query input for a range of different IR applications, ranging from very short ("title" field) to elaborate query formulations ("description" and "narrative" fields), and representing keyword-style input as well as natural language formulations. The latter potentially allows sophisticated systems to make use of morphological analysis, parsing, query expansion and similar features. In the cross-language context, the transfer component must also be considered, whether dictionary or corpus-based, a fully-fledged MT system or other. Different query structures may be more appropriate for testing one or another approach.

2.3 Relevance Assessment

Relevance assessment was performed by native speakers. The practice of assessing the results on the basis of the longest, most elaborate formulation of the topic (the narrative) means that only using shorter formulations (title and/or description) implicitly assumes a particular interpretation of the user's information need that is not (explicitly) contained in the actual query that is run in the experiment. The fact that such additional interpretations are possible has influence only on the absolute values of the evaluation measures, which in general are inherently difficult to interpret. However, comparative results across systems are usually stable regardless of different interpretations. These considerations are important when using the topics to construct very short queries to evaluate a system in a web-style scenario.

The number of documents in large test collections such as CLEF makes it impractical to judge every document for relevance. Instead approximate recall values are calculated using pooling techniques. The results submitted by the participating groups were used to form a pool of documents for each topic and language by collecting the highly ranked documents from all submissions. This pool was used for subsequent relevance judgment. After calculating the effectiveness measures, the results were analyzed and run statistics produced and distributed. A discussion of the results is given in Section 4. The individual results for all official ad hoc experiments in CLEF 2004 can be found on the CLEF website in the CLEF 2004 Working Notes [4]. The stability of pools constructed in this way and their reliability for post-campaign experiments is discussed in [5] with respect to the CLEF 2003 pools.

2.4 Participation Guidelines

To carry out the retrieval tasks of the CLEF campaign, systems have to build supporting data structures. Allowable data structures include any new structures built automatically (such as inverted files, thesauri, conceptual networks, etc.) or manually (such as thesauri, synonym lists, knowledge bases, rules, etc.) from the documents. They may not, however, be modified in response to the topics, e.g. by adding topic words that are not already in the dictionaries used by their systems in order to extend coverage.

Some CLEF data collections contain manually assigned, controlled or uncontrolled index terms. The use of such terms has been limited to specific experiments that have to be declared as "manual" runs.

Topics can be converted into queries that a system can execute in many different ways. Participants submitting more than one set of results have used both different query construction methods and variants within the same method. CLEF strongly encourages groups to determine what constitutes a base run for their experiments and to include these runs (officially or unofficially) to allow useful interpretations of the results. Unofficial runs are those not submitted to CLEF but evaluated using the trec_eval package available from Cornell University[3].

---

[3] See ftp://ftp.cs.cornell.edu/pub/smart/

As a consequence of limited evaluation resources, a maximum of 5 runs for each multilingual task and a maximum of 10 runs overall for the bilingual tasks, including all language combinations, was accepted. The number of runs for the monolingual task was limited to 12 runs. No more than 4 runs were allowed for any individual language combination. Overall, participants were allowed to submit at most 25 runs in total for the multilingual, bilingual and monolingual tasks (higher if other tasks were attempted).

2.5 Result Calculation

The effectiveness of IR systems can be objectively evaluated by an analysis of a representative set of sample search results. For this, effectiveness measures are calculated based on the results submitted by the participant and the relevance assessments. Popular measures usually adopted for exercises of this type are Recall and Precision. Details on how they are calculated for CLEF are given in [6].

2.6 Participants and Experiments

As shown in Table 1, a total of 26 groups from 14 different countries submitted results for one or more of the ad hoc tasks. A total of 250 experiments were submitted, 40% less than in 2003 due to the reduction in size of the track plus the expansion of other tracks offered by CLEF 2004.

Table 1. CLEF 2004 ad hoc participants

CEA/LIC2M (FR) *	UC Berkeley (US) ****
CLIPS-IMAG/IPAL-CNRS (FR/SG) *	U Chicago (US) *
Daedalus/Madrid Universities (ES) *	U Evora (PT)
Dublin City U. (IE) *** (before as U.Exeter)	U Glasgow (UK) *
Hummingbird (CA) ***	U. Hagen (DE) *
IRIT-Toulouse (FR) ***	U Hildesheim (DE) **
Johns Hopkins U./APL (US) ****	U Jaen (ES) ***
Nat. Research Council - ILTG (CA)	U. Lisbon (PT)
Ricoh (JP) *	U Neuchâtel (CH) ***
SUNY Buffalo (US) *	U Oviedo (ES) *
Thomson Legal (US) ***	U Padua (IT) **
U Alicante (ES) ***	U.Stockholm/SICS (SE) ***
U Amsterdam (NL) ***	U.Surugadai/NII/NTU (JP/TW) *

* = number of previous participations in CLEF

13 different topic languages were used for experiments. As always, the most popular language for queries was English, but this year French came a fairly close second. A breakdown into the separate tasks is shown in Table 2 and of the runs per topic language in Table 3.

Table 2. CLEF 2004 ad hoc experiments

Track	# Participants	# Runs/Experiments
Multilingual	9	35
Bilingual X → FI	2	4
Bilingual X → FR	7	30
Bilingual X → PT	4	15
Bilingual X → RU	8	28
Bilingual X→ EN (restricted)	4	11
Monolingual FI	11	30
Monolingual FR	13	38
Monolingual PT	8	23
Monolingual RU	14	36

Table 3. List of experiments by topic language

Language[4]	# Runs
AM Amharic	1
BG Bulgarian	5
ZH Chinese	2
NL Dutch	7
EN English	65
FI Finnish	30
FR French	48
DE German	22
JP Japanese	2
PT Portuguese	23
ES Spanish	8
SV Swedish	1
RU Russian	36

As stated, participants were required to submit at least one title+description ("TD") run per task in order to increase comparability between experiments. In fact, the large majority of runs (205 out of 250) used this combination of topic fields, 31 used all fields and only 14 used the title field. The majority of experiments were conducted using automatic query construction. Manual runs tend to be a resource-intensive undertaking and it is likely that most participants interested in this type of work concentrated their efforts on the interactive track.

[4] Throughout the paper, language names are sometimes shortened by using their ISO-639 2-letter equivalent.

3 Characteristics of the Experiments

As expected, the choice of our target languages this year for the multilingual task seemed to pose challenges for the participants. As we had hoped to see, various approaches to tackling these challenges were proposed [7, 8, 9]. As already mentioned, the monolingual track saw the introduction of Portuguese this year, and consequently adaptations of existing approaches to this language, as well as to the previously little used Finnish and Russian, were also proposed [10, 11].

An additional consequence of the extra spotlight that the languages used in this year's multilingual track have received is the substantial work on splitting of Finnish compound words (decompounding), e.g. by [10, 12, 13].

The value of stemming and decompounding are issues that were hotly debated in previous campaigns but have now lost some attention. With the exception of the work on Finnish decompounding, the pros and cons of stemming and decompounding were not widely discussed in the participants' descriptions of their work. It could be concluded that this silent acceptance of stemmers and decompounding components as an integral part of most systems demonstrates that, in general, the value of such components for richly inflected languages is recognized by CLEF participants.

To complement these mainly linguistically motivated developments, we can discern a growing interest in new(er) weighting schemes, differing from the classical SMART Lnu.ltn [14] and OKAPI BM25 [15] weighting formulas. Some of the approaches explored by participants include deviation from randomness [12, 16, 17] and language models [13, 18].

Merging, i.e. the weighting of the different subcollections (both inter- and intra-language) from which the systems retrieve relevant documents, remains an unsolved problem from previous campaigns. Many approaches used by participants "reduce" multilingual retrieval to a sequence of bilingual retrieval runs, the results of which are then combined into a single, multilingual result. If retrieval scores are not comparable across these subcollections, the merging (combination) step proves to be difficult. It has been shown that much potential in terms of improving retrieval effectiveness lies in a better solution to the merging problem [19, 20]. Some of the merging experiments conducted this year are included in [18, 21, 22].

Information Retrieval (IR) technology has come a long way in recent years in terms of being incorporated into commercial products. Web search services based on IR approaches gain much attention, but a number of commercial enterprise IR software packages have also successfully entered the market. A different trend emerging in the last few years in the field of computer software is the successful development of "open source software", i.e. software that has liberal usage policies (often free of charge), comes with full source code, and is frequently developed by a volunteer community. The two trends start to produce collaborative results with the arrival of open source IR software. This year, in CLEF, the use of commercial and open source IR software as the basis of experiments has become more prominent, as opposed to using purely experimental tools developed during research work. Groups such as [23, 24] discuss their choice of commercial and open source systems.

In the bilingual task, participants were presented with the same target languages as in the multilingual task, plus Portuguese. It is interesting to note how similar were the performances of different groups for experiments in retrieving documents from the French document collection. French was introduced as a document language in the CLEF campaigns from the very beginning in 2000, meaning that returning participating groups, in particular, have had ample time to gain experience with this language for CLIR. It has been noticed before that the open spirit of the CLEF workshops, where participants freely share experiences and ideas, leads to a substantial pick-up of successful ideas by different groups [25]. This may explain the similarities in performance. It also underscores the value of new participants coming into the campaigns with "exotic" ideas, which minimize the danger of developing monocultures of CLIR approaches (see also [25]). A similar effect was discernible in the French monolingual track this year.

Generally speaking, both for the multilingual and bilingual tracks, query translation, as opposed to document translation, remains the method of choice for most participants. Document translation has clear advantages in terms of avoiding the merging problem, but seems to be judged as too "expensive" in terms of translation effort. Experiments in document translation have been conducted by [13, 26].

4 Results

The individual results of the participants are reported in detail in this volume and in the CLEF 2004 Working Notes [4] which were distributed to participants in the Workshop and are available on the CLEF website. In the following, we briefly summarize the main results for the multilingual, bilingual and monolingual tasks.

4.1 Multilingual Retrieval

This year, nine groups submitted 35 experiments for the multilingual task. This can be compared to the total of fourteen groups in the previous year when the ad hoc track was still the major focus of CLEF and two multilingual tasks were offered. Figure 1 shows the best entries of the top five performing groups in terms of average precision figures. Only entries using the title+description topic field were used for this comparison. Not surprisingly, the groups with the best results for this task were all veteran CLEF participants (with the exception of SUNY Buffalo) that had participated regularly in CLEF since 2001.

The top groups tended to focus a lot of attention on the merging problem [8, 18, 21, 27]. The group with the best result [13] also experimented with combination methods using runs made on various types of indexes, applying both language-dependent and language-independent tokenization techniques. Several of the groups participating in this task mentioned problems in processing and finding appropriate translation resources for the newer and less familiar CLEF languages – Finnish and Russian [17, 24].

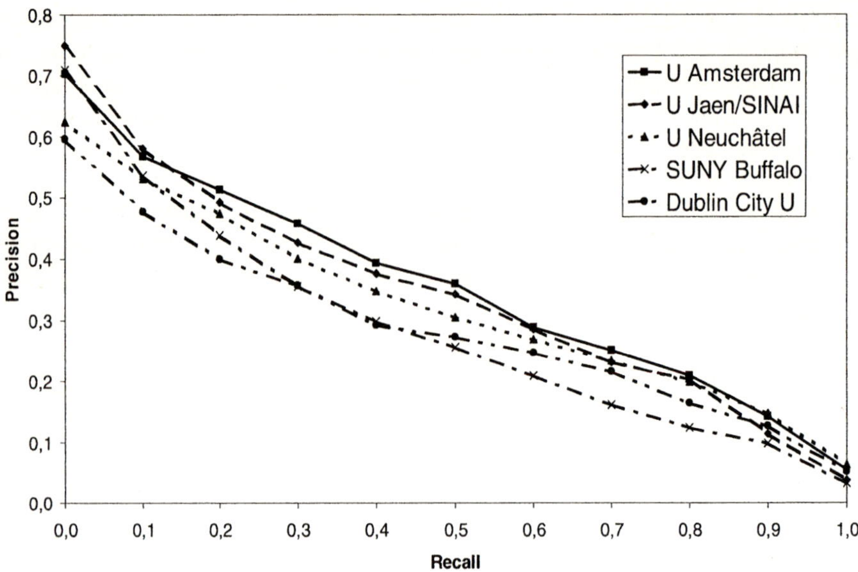

Fig. 1. Best performing entries of the top five participants in the multilingual task. The precision/recall curve, giving precision values at varying levels of recall, is shown. Only experiments using title+description topic fields are included

4.2 Bilingual Retrieval

The bilingual task was structured in four subtasks (X → FI, FR, RU or PT target collection) plus, as usual, an additional subtask with English as a target language – this last task was restricted to newcomers in a CLEF cross-language task or to groups using unusual or new topic languages (in CLEF 2004 Amharic and Bulgarian). Table 4 shows the best results for this task.

As shown in Section 2 above, some restrictions were placed on the topic languages that could be used to query the French and Finnish collections. The aim was to stimulate experiments for language pairs for which bilingual resources are scarce or non-existent. Unfortunately, this may have led to low participation in these two tracks. Only two groups tried the official bilingual to Finnish task, using French and Spanish topics. The effectiveness of these experiments was limited, with the best run scoring at only 47% of the average precision of best monolingual Finnish run. The bilingual to French task, with a choice of topic language between Dutch, Finnish, German and Swedish, was more popular with seven groups submitting a total of 30 runs. By far the most favoured topic language was German (6 groups and 22 runs), next came Dutch (3 groups and 7 runs) and finally a Swedish group contributed just one Swedish to French run. Performance was higher for this task: the best two runs (one using German and the other using Dutch topics) had a performance that was approximately 76% in terms of average precision of the monolingual results for French.

There were no restrictions on the bilingual to Russian and Portuguese target collections. This was because these languages are new additions to CLEF (Russian in 2003 and Portuguese in 2004). All groups that tried these two tasks used English as a topic language; in addition two groups also tried Spanish topics for the Portuguese target, and three different groups also used Chinese, French or Spanish topics to query the Russian target. For both languages, the group with the best monolingual results also provided the best bilingual performance. In each case, these results were obtained using English as the topic language. The difference in performance compared with monolingual was 70% in terms of average precision for Russian and a high 91% for Portuguese. From a first glance at these results, it would seem that certain target languages yield lower cross-language retrieval results. Specifically, cross-language retrieval of Finnish text, with its extremely complex morphology, and Russian text, which uses a different alphabet and encoding system from the other languages in the CLEF collection, appears to pose as yet unsolved difficulties compared to CLIR on French and Portuguese text, respectively.

Table 4. Best entries for the bilingual task (title+description topic fields only). Where applicable, the performance difference between the best and the fifth placed group is given (in terms of average precision)

Trg.	**1st**	**2nd**	**3rd**	**4th**	**5th**	**Δ1st/5th**
FI	JHU/APL	CLIPS				
FR	JHU/APL	Thomson	Daedalus	NII group	DublinCity	+12.4%
PT	U.Neuchâtel	JHU/APL	U.Amsterd.	U.Alicante		
RU	U.Alicante	U.Berkeley	DublinCity	U.Neuchâtel	JHU/APL	+138.6%
EN	U.Amsterd.	U.Oviedo				

4.3 Monolingual Retrieval

Monolingual retrieval was offered for all target collections (Finnish, French, Russian, Portuguese) with the exception of English. As can be seen from Table 2, the number of participants and runs for each language was quite similar, with the exception of Portuguese, which was added when the campaign was already well under way, leading to a somewhat smaller participation. This year just three groups submitted

Table 5. Best entries for the monolingual track (title+description topic fields only). Additionally, the performance difference between the best and the fifth placed group is given (in terms of average precision)

Trg.	**1st**	**2nd**	**3rd**	**4th**	**5th**	**Δ1st/5th**
FI	Hummingb.	Thomson LR	U.Neuchâtel	JHU/APL	U.Amsterd.	+22.4%
FR	Hummingb.	U.Neuchâtel	Daedalus	SUNY	JHU/APL	+7.5%
PT	U.Neuchâtel	Hummingb.	JHU/APL	Thomson	U.Amsterd.	+19.9%
RU	U.Alicante	Hummingb.	U.Amsterd.	U Berkeley	Dublin CU	+26.9%

monolingual runs only (down from ten groups last year), two newcomers and one veteran group [10]. Most of the groups submitting monolingual runs were doing this as part of their bilingual or multilingual system testing activity. All the groups in the top five were veteran CLEF participants (see Table 5).

One of the findings of CLEF over the years has been that successful cross-language retrieval systems are based on effective and robust monolingual processing procedures [25]. Again this year, in confirmation of a trend already observed in the past, we noted that there was very little statistical difference between the results of most of the monolingual submissions (see Table 7 below).

5 Statistical Testing

For reasons of practicality, the CLEF ad hoc track uses a limited number of queries (50 in 2004), which are intended to represent a more or less appropriate sample of all possible queries that users would want to ask from the collection. When the goal is to validate how well results can be expected to hold beyond this particular set of queries, statistical testing can help to determine what differences between runs appear to be real as opposed to differences that are due to sampling issues. We aim to identify runs with results that are significantly different from the results of other runs. "Significantly different" in this context means that the difference between the performance scores for the runs in question appears greater than what might be expected by pure chance. As with all statistical testing, conclusions will be qualified by an error probability, which was chosen to be 0.05 in the following. We have designed our analysis to follow closely the methodology used by similar analyses carried out for TREC [28].

A statistical analysis tool named IR-STAT-PAK [29] was used for the statistical analyses on the ad hoc track for the 2001 – 2003 campaigns. However, as this tool seems to be no longer supported or available on the Web, we have used the MATLAB Statistics Toolbox 5.0.1 this year, which provides the necessary functionality plus some additional functions and utilities. We continue to use the ANOVA test (Analysis of Variance). ANOVA makes some assumptions concerning the data be checked. Hull [28] provides details of these; in particular, the scores in question should be approximately normally distributed and their variance has to be approximately the same for all runs. IR-STAT-PAK uses the Hartley test to verify the equality of variances. This year two tests for goodness of fit to a normal distribution were chosen using the MATLAB statistical toolbox: the Lilliefors test [30] and the Jarque-Bera test [31]. In the case of the CLEF multilingual collection, both tests indicate that the assumption of normality is violated for most of the data samples (in this case the runs for each participant); in particular, the Lilliefors test shows that for 34 out of 35 runs the hypothesis of normality should be rejected, and the Jarque-Bera shows that the same hypothesis should be rejected for 18 runs. In such cases, a transformation of data should be performed. The transformation for measures that range from 0 to 1 is the arcsin-root transformation:

$$f(x) = \arcsin\left(\sqrt{x}\right)$$

which Tague-Sutcliffe [32] recommends for use with precision/recall measures. After the transformation the analysis of the normality of samples distribution improves significantly: the Lilliefors test claims that 15 runs are still non-normally distributed while the Jaque-Bera test indicates that only two samples are non-normally distributed. The difficulty to transform the data into normally distributed samples derives from the original distribution of run performances, which tend towards zero within the interval [0,1].

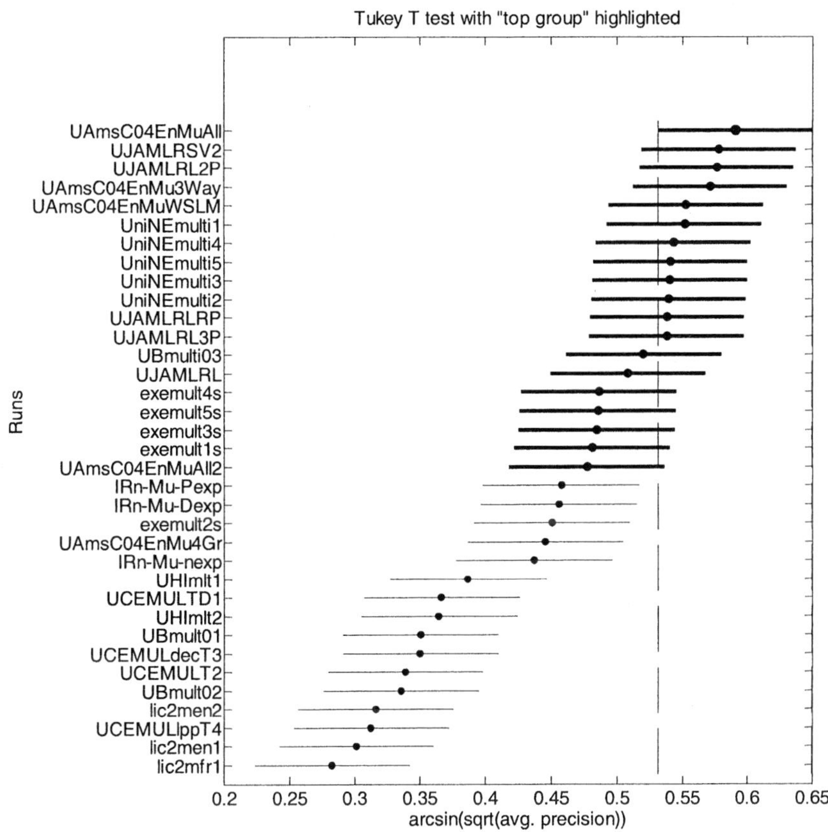

Fig. 2. Tukey T test for the multilingual track

In any case, the situation after the arcsin-root transformation allows us to perform a two-way ANOVA test that determines if there is at least one pair of runs that exhibit a statistical difference. Following a significant two-way ANOVA, various comparison procedures can be employed to investigate significant differences. The Tukey T test was used to find the statistically significant differences between participants' performances and to group runs. In particular, we used the MATLAB *multcompare* function with an *honestly significant difference* (hsd) setup for the Tukey T test.

Table 6. Results of statistical analysis (two-way ANOVA) on the experiments submitted for the multilingual task. All experiments, regardless of topic language or topic fields, are included. Results are therefore only valid for comparison of individual pairs of runs, and not in terms of absolute performance

Arcsin-transformed average precision values	**Run Ids**	**Groups**								
0.5905	UAmsC04EnMuAll	X								
0.5778	UJAMLRSV2	X								
0.5764	UJAMLRL2P	X								
0.5713	UAmsC04EnMu3Way	X	X							
0.5527	UAmsC04EnMuWSLM	X	X	X						
0.5515	UniNEmulti1	X	X	X						
0.5431	UniNEmulti4	X	X	X						
0.5404	UniNEmulti3	X	X	X						
0.5407	UniNEmulti5	X	X	X						
0.5394	UniNEmulti2	X	X	X						
0.5381	UJAMLRLRP	X	X	X						
0.5379	UJAMLRL3P	X	X	X						
0.5203	UBmulti03	X	X	X						
0.5083	UJAMLRL	X	X	X						
0.4863	exemult4s	X	X	X	X					
0.4854	exemult5s	X	X	X	X					
0.4845	exemult3s	X	X	X	X	X				
0.4812	exemult1s	X	X	X	X	X	X			
0.4771	UAmsC04EnMuAll2	X	X	X	X	X	X			
0.4575	IRn-Mu-Pexp		X	X	X	X	X	X		
0.4558	IRn-Mu-Dexp		X	X	X	X	X	X		
0.4505	exemult2s			X	X	X	X	X	X	
0.4455	UAmsC04EnMu4Gr			X	X	X	X	X	X	
0.4367	IRn-Mu-nexp			X	X	X	X	X	X	
0.3866	UHImlt1				X	X	X	X	X	X
0.3666	UCEMULTD1				X	X	X	X	X	X
0.3646	UHImlt2					X	X	X	X	X
0.3505	UBmult01						X	X	X	X
0.3504	UCEMULdecT3							X	X	X
0.3391	UCEMULT2							X	X	X
0.3355	UBmult02							X	X	X
0.3162	lic2men2								X	X
0.3127	UCEMULlppT4									X
0.3014	lic2men1									X
0.2829	lic2mfr1									X

Two different graphs are presented to summarize the results of this test: Figure 2 shows participants' runs (y axis) and performance obtained (x axis). The circle indicates the average performance (in terms of Precision) while the segment shows the interval in which the difference in performance is not statistically significant.

Alternatively, the overall results are presented in Table 6, where all the runs that are included in the same group do not have a significantly different performance. All runs scoring below a certain group perform significantly worse than at least the top entry of that group. Likewise, all the runs scoring above a certain group perform significantly better than at least the bottom entry in that group. To determine all runs that perform significantly worse than a certain run, determine the rightmost group that includes the run. All runs scoring below the bottom entry of that group are significantly worse. Conversely, to determine all runs that perform significantly better than a given run, determine the leftmost group that includes the run. All runs that score better than the top entry of that group perform significantly better.

It is well known that it is fairly difficult to detect statistically significant differences between retrieval results based on 50 queries [32, 33]. While 50 queries remains a good choice based on practicality for doing relevance assessments, statistical testing would be the one of the areas to benefit most from having additional topics.

This fact is addressed by the measures taken to ensure stability of at least part of the document collection across different campaigns, which allows participants to run their system on aggregate sets of queries for post-hoc experiments.

For the 2004 campaign, we conducted a statistical analysis of the "pools of experiments" for all target languages. It seems that each year it is increasingly difficult to identify clearly significant differences in participants' performances. For example, in the multilingual task, the first group identified by the Tukey T test, contains a total of 19 runs submitted by 5 different participants: University of Amsterdam, University of Jaen, Université de Neuchâtel, State University New York at Buffalo, Dublin City University. From these results, it is only possible to state that this first group of participants performed significantly better than the other groups, but it is not possible to identify the top performer with any statistical validity.

Table 7. Results of statistical analysis (ANOVA) on the monolingual experiments. The table shows the number of participants submitting at least one experiment with a performance that is not statistically different to the top performance against the total number of participants submitting experiment for that target collection

Target collection	# of participants in the top group / total # of participants
Finnish	9/12
French	14/15
Portuguese	6/8
Russian	12/15

In addition to the multilingual task, we also examined non-English mono- and bilingual target collections. The analyses included both monolingual runs, and also the bilingual runs to the same target language (i.e. the French analysis contains both French monolingual and German → French bilingual experiments). Like in CLEF 2003, the monolingual tasks were very competitive. Many groups submitted experiments with very similar performances, and almost all groups that submitted at least one run are present in the top performing group (see Table 7). It should be noted, however, that experiments of very different character are mixed in this analysis.

A complete listing and the individual results (statistics and graphs) of all the official experiments for the ad hoc track can be found in the Appendix to the CLEF Working Notes [4].

6 Impact of CLEF

This paper summarizes and analyses the results of the ad hoc track in the CLEF 2004 campaign. The size and scope of the ad hoc track in CLEF 2004 was limited somewhat in order to leave more space for new tracks addressing other issues in CLIR. However, even if the number of experiments submitted is significantly below that of 2003, the track has promoted interesting and novel work (e.g. on the problem of merging results from different collections, and experiments with different weighting formulas).

An important question is what impact the CLEF campaigns have on the current state-of-the-art in CLIR research. As test collections and tasks vary over years, it is not easy to document improvements in system performance. One common method for bilingual retrieval evaluation is to compare results against monolingual baselines. We can observe the following indications with respect to progress in bilingual retrieval over the years:

In 1997, at TREC-6, the best CLIR systems had the following results:

- EN → FR: 49% of best monolingual French IR system
- EN → DE: 64% of best monolingual German IR system

In 2002, at CLEF, with no restriction on topic and target language, the best systems obtained:

- EN →FR: 83% of best monolingual French IR system
- EN → DE: 86% of best monolingual German IR system

However, CLEF 2003 enforced the use of previously "unusual" language pairs, with the following impressive results:

- IT → ES: 83% of best monolingual Spanish IR system
- DE → IT: 87% of best monolingual Italian IR system
- FR → NL: 82% of best monolingual Dutch IR system

CLEF 2004 presented participants with a mixed set of limitations according to the respective target languages. Results include:

- ES → FI: 47% of best monolingual Finnish IR system
- DE/NL → FR: 76% of best monolingual French IR system
- EN → RU: 70% of best monolingual Russian IR system
- EN → PT: 91% of best monolingual Portuguese IR system

Again, comparisons are difficult due to increasingly complex tasks. However, it appears that a steady trend of overall improvement in CLIR performance can be recognized as gradually systems begin to be capable of handling different and previously unusual languages pairs, finding and exploiting translation mechanisms between pairs of languages that do not include English.

It is even harder to measure progress with respect to the multilingual retrieval task. Partly for this reason, in CLEF 2005, we are proposing the CLEF 2003 multilingual-8 task again ("Multi-8 Two-years-on") The aim is to see whether there is an improvement in performance over time. In any case, CLIR systems that tackle this many languages simultaneously are clearly a great testament to the development of the field over the past years.

References

1. Peters, C.: What happened in CLEF 2004? In this volume.
2. Cleverdon, C.: The Cranfield Tests on Index Language Devices. In: Sparck-Jones, K., Willett, P. (eds.): Readings in Information Retrieval, Morgan Kaufmann (1997) 47-59.
3. Harman, D.: The TREC Conferences. In Kuhlen, R., Rittberger, M. (eds.): Hypertext - Information Retrieval - Multimedia: Synergieeffekte Elektronischer Informationssysteme, Proceedings of HIM '95, Universitätsverlag Konstanz, 9-28.
4. CLEF 2004 Working Notes. http://clef.isti.cnr.it/2004/working_notes/CLEF2004WN.
5. Braschler, M.: CLEF 2003 – Overview of results. In: Fourth Workshop of the Cross-Language Evaluation Forum, CLEF 2003, Trondheim, Norway, 2003. Revised papers. Lecture Notes in Computer Science 3237, Springer 2004, 44-63.
6. Braschler, M., Peters, C.: CLEF 2003 Methodology and Metrics. In: Fourth Workshop of the Cross-Language Evaluation Forum, CLEF 2003, Trondheim, Norway, 2003. Revised papers. Lecture Notes in Computer Science 3237, Springer 2004, 7-20.
7. Besançon, R., Ferre, O., Fluhr, C.: LIC2M Experiments at CLEF 2004. In this volume.
8. Martínez-Santiago, F., García-Cumbreras, M.A., Díaz-Galiano, M.C., Ureña, L.A. : SINAI at CLEF 2004: Using Machine Translation Resources with a Mixed 2-Step RSV Merging Algorithm. In this volume.
9. Levow, G.-A., Matveeva, I.: University of Chicago at CLEF2004: Cross-language Text and Spoken Document Retrieval. In this volume.
10. Tomlinson, S.: Portuguese and Russian Retrieval with Hummingbird SearchServer™ at CLEF 2004. In this volume.
11. Di Nunzio, G.M., Ferro, N., Orio, N.: Experiments on Statistical Approaches to Compensate for Limited Linguistic Resources. In this volume.
12. Savoy, J.: Data Fusion for Effective European Monolingual Information Retrieval. In this volume.
13. Kamps, J., Adafre, S.F., de Rijke, M.: Effective Translation, Tokenization and Combination for Cross-Lingual Retrieval. In this volume.
14. Singhal A., Buckley C., Mitra M.: Pivoted Document Length Normalization. In Frei, H.P., Harman, D., Schäuble P., Wilkinson, R., eds.: Proceedings of the 19th Annual International ACM SIGIR Conference on Research and Development in Information Retrieval (SIGIR 1996), Zurich, Switzerland, ACM, 1996, 21-29.
15. Robertson, S.E., Walker, S., Jones, S., Hancock-Beaulieu, M. M., Gatford, M.: Okapi at TREC-3. In: Overview of the Third Text Retrieval Conference (TREC-3), NIST Special Publication 500-225, 1995, 109-126.
16. Lioma, C., He, B., Plachouras, V., Ounis, I.: The University of Glasgow at CLEF 2004: French Monolingual Information Retrieval with Terrier. In this volume.

17. Serasset, G., Chevallet, J.-P.: Using Surface-Syntactic Parser and Derivation from Randomness: X-IOTA IR System used for CLIPS Mono & Bilingual Experiments for CLEF 2004. In this volume.
18. Ruiz, ME., Srikanth, M.: UB at CLEF2004: Cross-language Information Retrieval using Statistical Language Models. In this volume.
19. Chen A.: Cross-Language Retrieval Experiments at CLEF 2002. In Working Notes for the CLEF 2002 Workshop, 2002, 5-20.
20. Braschler, M.: Combination Approaches for Multilingual Text Retrieval, In Information Retrieval, Kluwer Academic Publishers, Vol. 7(1-2), 183-204.
21. Savoy, J., Berger, P.-Y.: Selection and Merging Strategies for Multilingual Information Retrieval. In this volume.
22. Goñi-Menoyo, J.M., González, J.C., Martínez-Fernández, J.L., Villena-Román, J.: MIRACLE's Hybrid Approach to Bilingual and Monolingual Information Retrieval. In this volume.
23. Nadeau, D., Jarmasz, M., Barrière, C., Foster, G., St-Jacques, C.: Using COTS Search Engines and Custom Query Strategies at CLEF. In this volume.
24. Hackl, R., Mandl, T., Womser-Hacker, C.: Mono- and Crosslingual Retrieval Experiments at the University of Hildesheim. In this volume.
25. Braschler, M., Peters, C.: Cross-Language Evaluation Forum: Objectives, Results, Achievements, Information Retrieval, Vol.7 (1-2) 5-29.
26. Gey, F.C.: Searching a Russian Document Collection using English, Chinese and Japanese Queries. In this volume.
27. Jones,G.J.F., Burke, M., Judge,J., Khasin, A., Lam-Adesina, A., Wagner, J.: Dublin City University at CLEF 2004: Experiments in Monolingual, Bilingual and Multilingual Retrieval. In this volume.
28. Hull, D.: Using Statistical Testing in the Evaluation of Retrieval Experiments. In Korfhage, R., Rasmussen, E., Willett, P., eds.: Proc. 16th Annual International ACM SIGIR Conference on Research and Development in Information Retrieval (SIGIR 1993), ACM Press, New York, USA (1993) 329–338.
29. Blustein, J.: IR STAT PAK. URL: http://www.csd.uwo.ca/~jamie/IRSP-overview.html.
30. Conover, W.J.: Practical Nonparametric Statistics, (1st Ed.), John Wiley and Sons, New York, 1971.
31. Judge, G. G., R. C. Hill, W. E. Griffiths, H. Lütkepohl, and T.C. Lee: Introduction to the Theory and Practice of Econometrics, (2nd ed.), John Wiley and Sons, New York, 1988.
32. Tague-Sutcliffe, J.: The Pragmatics of Information Retrieval Experimentation, Revisited. In: Reading in Information Retrieval, Morgan Kaufmann Publishers, San Francisco, CA, USA (1997), 205-216.
33. Voorhees, E., Buckley, C.: The Effect of Topic Set Size on Retrieval Experiment Error. In: Proc. of the 25th Annual International ACM SIGIR Conference on Research and Development in Information Retrieval (1998) 307-314.

Selection and Merging Strategies for Multilingual Information Retrieval

Jacques Savoy and Pierre-Yves Berger

Institut interfacultaire d'informatique, Université de Neuchâtel,
Pierre-à-Mazel 7, 2001 Neuchâtel, Switzerland
{Jacques.Savoy, Pierre-Yves.Berger}@unine.ch

Abstract. In our fourth participation in the CLEF evaluation campaigns, our objective was to verify whether our combined query translation approach would work well with new requests and new languages (Russian and Portuguese in this case). As a second objective, we were to suggest a selection procedure able to extract a smaller number of documents from collections that seemed to contain no or only a few relevant items for the current request. We also applied different merging strategies in order to obtain more evidence about their respective relative merits.

1 Introduction

Based on our bilingual and multilingual experiments of the last years [1], [2], we conducted additional experiments involving various bilingual and multilingual test-collections. Based on a request written in English, we retrieved documents written in English, French, Finnish and Russian. As with previous experiments [2], we adopted a combined query translation strategy capable of submitting queries to documents written in various European languages, based on an original request written in English. Once the query translation phase was completed, we searched in the corresponding document collection using our retrieval scheme (bilingual). In Section 3, we carried out multilingual information retrieval, investigating various merging strategies based on the results obtained during our bilingual searches.

2 Bilingual Information Retrieval

In our experiments, we chose English as the language for submitting queries to be automatically translated into four different languages, using nine different machine translation (MT) systems and one bilingual dictionary ("Babylon"). The following freely available translation tools were used in our experiments:

1. SYSTRAN www.systranlinks.com
2. GOOGLE www.google.com/language_tools
3. FREETRANSLATION www.freetranslation.com
4. INTERTRAN intertran.tranexp.com/

C. Peters et al. (Eds.): CLEF 2004, LNCS 3491, pp. 27–37, 2005.

5. Reverso Online www.reverso.fr/url_translation.asp
6. WorldLingo www.worldlingo.com/
7. BabelFish babelfish.altavista.com/
8. Prompt webtranslation.paralink.com/
9. Online www.online-translator.com/
10. Babylon www.babylon.com.

When using the Babylon bilingual dictionary to translate an English request word-by-word, usually more than one translation is provided, in an unspecified order. We decided to pick only the first translation available (labeled "Babylon 1"), the first two terms (labeled "Babylon 2") or the first three available translations (labeled "Babylon 3").

Table 1. Mean average precision of various single translation devices (TD queries, Okapi model)

	Mean average precision (% of monolingual search)			
TD queries Index	French word 49 queries	Finnish 4-gram 45 queries	Russian word 34 queries	Portuguese word 46 queries
Manual	<u>0.4685</u>	<u>0.5385</u>	0.3800	<u>0.4835</u>
Systran	0.3729 (79.6%)	N/A	<u>0.2077</u> (54.7%)	0.3329 (68.9%)
Google	0.3680 (78.5%)	N/A	N/A	0.3375 (69.8%)
FreeTrans.	**0.3845** (82.1%)	N/A	**0.3067** (80.7%)	**0.4057** (83.9%)
InterTran	<u>0.2664</u> (56.9%)	**0.2653** (49.3%)	<u>0.1216</u> (32.0%)	0.3277 (67.8%)
Reverso	0.3830 (81.8%)	N/A	N/A	N/A
WorldLingo	0.3728 (79.6%)	N/A	<u>0.2077</u> (54.7%)	0.3311 (68.5%)
BabelFish	0.3729 (79.6%)	N/A	<u>0.2077</u> (54.7%)	0.3329 (68.9%)
Prompt	N/A	N/A	0.2960 (77.9%)	N/A
Online	N/A	N/A	0.2888 (76.0%)	0.3879 (80.2%)
Babylon 1	0.3706 (79.1%)	0.1965 (36.5%)	0.2209 (58.1%)	<u>0.3071</u> (63.5%)
Babylon 2	<u>0.3356</u> (71.6%)	N/A	0.2245 (59.1%)	<u>0.2892</u> (59.8%)
Babylon 3	<u>0.3378</u> (72.1%)	N/A	0.2243 (59.0%)	<u>0.2858</u> (59.1%)

Table 1 shows the mean average precision obtained using the various translation tools and the Okapi probabilistic model (see [3] for implementation details). Of course, not all tools can be used for each language, and thus as shown in Table 1, various entries are missing (indicated with the label "N/A"). From this data, we can see that the results from the FreeTranslation MT system usually obtain satisfactory retrieval performances (around 82% of the mean average precision obtained by the corresponding monolingual search). As another good translation systems, we found that Reverso, BabelFish or WorldLingo worked well for French, Prompt for Russian or Online for both the Russian and Portuguese languages. For Finnish we found only two translation tools, but unfortunately their overall performance levels were not very good (similar to low

Table 2. Mean average precision of various combined translation devices (Okapi)

	Mean average precision			
TD queries Index Model	French word 49 queries	Finnish 4-gram 45 queries	Russian word 34 queries	Portuguese word 46 queries
Comb 1	Bab2+Free	Bab1+Inter	Bab1+Free	Free+Online
Comb 2	Bab2+Reverso		Free+Prompt	Bab1+Systran
Comb 3	Reverso+Systran		Prompt+Online	Bab1+Free+Onl
Comb 4	Free+Reverso		Free+Online	Bab1+Free+Sys
Comb 5	Bab2+Free+ Reverso		Bab1+Free+ Online	Bab1+Free+ Online+Systran
Best single	0.3845	0.2653	0.3067	0.4057
Comb 1	0.3784	**0.3042**	**0.3888**	0.4072
Comb 2	0.3857		0.3032	0.3713
Comb 3	0.3858		0.2964	**0.4204**
Comb 4	**0.4066**		0.3043	0.3996
Comb 5	0.3962		0.3324	0.4070

Table 3. Mean average precision of automatically translated queries (without automatic query expansion)

	Mean average precision			
TD queries Index Model	French word 49 queries Comb 4	Finnish 4-gram 45 queries Comb 1	Russian word 34 queries Comb 1	Portuguese word 46 queries Comb 3
Okapi	0.4066	**0.3042**	**0.3888**	**0.4204**
Prosit	0.4111	0.2853	0.3050	0.4085
Round-robin	**0.4129**	<u>0.2969</u>	<u>0.3237</u>	0.4129
Sum RSV	0.4111	<u>0.2965</u>	0.3707	0.4134
Norm Max	0.4096	<u>0.2936</u>	0.3610	0.4152
Norm RSV (Eq. 1)	0.4102	<u>0.2937</u>	0.3617	0.4152
Z-score (Eq. 3)	0.4098	<u>0.2937</u>	0.3618	0.4152
Z-scoreW (Eq. 3)	0.4100	<u>0.2965</u>	0.3645	0.4043

performance levels found when translating English topics into various Asian languages [4]). Not surprisingly we found that there were certain similarities and dissimilarities between the various translation tools. For example, the Systran, BabelFish, and WorldLingo MT systems appeared to be nearly identical MT systems.

To determine whether or not a given search strategy was better than another, we developed a decision rule. This was based on statistical validation using the bootstrap approach [5]. Thus, in the tables presented in this paper we underlined statistically significant differences based on a two-sided non-parametric boot-

Table 4. Mean average precision of automatically translated queries (after blind query expansion)

	Mean average precision			
TD queries	French	Finnish	Russian	Portuguese
Index	word	4-gram	word	word
	49 queries	45 queries	34 queries	46 queries
Model	Comb 4	Comb 1	Comb 1	Comb 3
Okapi (#d/#t)	0.4197 (5/15)	0.3225 (5/150)	0.3888 (0/0)	0.4373 (10/75)
Prosit (#d/#t)	0.4251 (10/15)	0.2960 (5/40)	**0.3945 (5/20)**	0.4805 (10/30)
Round-robin	0.4275	**0.3308**	0.3152	0.4767
Sum RSV	0.4307	0.2970	0.3713	**0.4854**
Norm Max	0.4320	0.3035	0.3174	0.4815
Norm RSV (Eq. 1)	0.4325	0.3041	0.3139	0.4788
Z-score (Eq. 3)	0.4323	0.3001	0.3068	0.4840
Z-scoreW (Eq. 3)	**0.4330**	0.3007	0.3088	0.4851

Table 5. Description and mean average precision of our official bilingual runs

	Russian 34 queries	Russian 34 queries	Portuguese 46 queries	Portuguese 46 queries
IR 1 (#d/#t)	Prosit (3/15)	Prosit (3/15)	Prosit (10/20)	Okapi (0/0)
IR 2 (#d/#t)	Okapi (3/15)	Okapi (3/10)	Okapi (5/15)	Prosit (0/0)
Data fusion	Round-robin	Round-robin	Norm RSV	Norm RSV
Translation	Free-Reverso	Pro-Free-Rever	Onl-Free-Bab1	Onl-Free-Sys-Bab1
MAP	**0.3007**	0.2962	**0.4704**	0.4491
Run name	UniNEBru1	UniNEBru2	UniNEBpt1	UniNEBpt2

strap test, for any means that had a significance level fixed at 5%. As shown in Table 1, we used the best translation system (depicted in bold) as the baseline. As depicted, differences in mean average precision between the manually translated queries and the best automatic translation tools are always statistically significant, except for the Russian collection. On the other hand, differences between the various translation tools are usually not statistically significant, except for a few such as "Babylon 2" and "Babylon 3" for both French and Portuguese, or "InterTran" for French and Russian.

It is known that although a given translation tool may produce acceptable translations for a given set of requests, it may perform poorly for other queries [1], [2]. To date we have not been able to detect with much precision when a given translation will produce satisfactory retrieval performance and when it will fail. In this vein, Kishida *et al.* [6] suggest using a linear regression model to predict the average precision of the current query, based on both manual evaluations of translation quality and the underlying topic difficulty.

In order to hopefully improve retrieval performance, in this study we chose to concatenate two or more translations before submitting a query for translation.

Table 2 shows the retrieval effectiveness for such combinations, using the Okapi probabilistic model. The top part of the table indicates the exact query translation combination used while the bottom part shows the mean average precision achieved by our combined query translation approach. When selecting the query translations to be combined, a priori we considered the best translation tools.

The resulting retrieval performances shown in Table 2 are sometimes better than the best single translation scheme, as indicated in the row labeled "Best single" (e.g., the strategies "Comb 4" or "Comb 5" for French, or "Comb 1" for Russian, and "Comb 3" for Portuguese). Statistically however none of these combined query translation approaches performs better than the best single translation tool.

Of course, the main difficulty in this bilingual search was the translation of English topics into Finnish, due to the limited number of free translation tools available. When handling any languages from around the world that are less frequently used, it seems it would be worthwhile considering other translation alternatives, such as probabilistic translation based on parallel corpora [7], [8].

As described in [3], for monolingual searches we used a data fusion search strategy that combined the Okapi and Prosit probabilistic models. As shown in Table 3, in the current context our data fusion approaches do not improve retrieval effectiveness. However, differences in mean average precision are usually not statistically significant, except for the Finnish corpus where all data fusion approaches used significantly decrease retrieval performance.

Of course before combining the result lists we could also automatically expand the translated queries, using a pseudo-relevance feedback method (Rocchio's approach in the present case). As shown in Table 4, the resulting mean average precision after combining the two IR models (after pseudo-relevance feedback) did not always improve retrieval effectiveness, when compared to the best single approach. Moreover, the statistical tests did not reveal any significant differences. In Tables 3 and 4, under the heading "Z-scoreW", we attached a weight of 1.5 to the best single IR model, and 1 to the other.

Finally, Table 5 lists the parameter settings used for our official runs in the bilingual task. Each experiment uses queries written in English to retrieve documents written either in Russian or in Portuguese.

3 Multilingual Information Retrieval

Our multilingual information retrieval system is based on the use of a query translation strategy instead of either translating all documents into a common language (e.g., English), combining both query and document translations [9] or ignoring the translation phase [10], [8]. For a general overview of these issues, see [11]). In our approach, when a request was received (in English in this study), we automatically translated it into the desired target languages and then searched for pertinent items within each of the four corpora (English, French, Finnish and Russian). We then applied a merging procedure to take each result list received from the search engines, thus providing a single ranked result. As a first solution to this procedure, we considered the round-robin approach whereby we took one document in turn from each individual list [12].

To account for the document score computed for each retrieved item (denoted RSV_k for document D_k), we might formulate the hypothesis that each collection is searched by the same or a very similar search engine and that the similarity values are therefore directly comparable [13]. Such a strategy is called raw-score merging and produces a final list sorted by the document score computed by each collection. When using the same IR model (with the same or very similar parameter settings) to search all collections, such a merging strategy should result in good retrieval performance (e.g., with a logistic regression IR model in [14]).

Unfortunately, the document scores cannot always be directly compared and thus we introduced a third merging strategy by normalizing the document scores within each collection. This was done by dividing the scores by the maximum score (i.e. the document score of the retrieved record in the first position) and denoted them "Norm Max". As a variant of this normalized score merging scheme (denoted "Norm RSV"), we could normalize the document RSV_k scores within the ith result list, according to the following formula:

$$Norm\ RSV_k = \frac{RSV_k - MinRSV^i}{MaxRSV^i - MinRSV^i} \quad (1)$$

As a fifth merging strategy, we might use logistic regression to predict the probability of a binary outcome variable, according to a set of explanatory variables [15]. In our current case, we predicted the probability of relevance for document D_k, given both the logarithm of its rank (indicated by $ln(Rank_k)$) and the original document score RSV_k as indicated in Equation 2. Based on these estimated relevance probabilities (computed independently for each language using S+ software), we sorted the records retrieved from separate collections in order to obtain a single ranked list. This approach requires that a training set is available, in order to estimate the underlying parameters. To achieve this, we used the CLEF-2003 topics and their relevance assessments in our evaluations.

$$Prob\left[D_k\ is\ rel \mid Rank_k,\ RSV_k\right] = \frac{e^{\alpha+\beta_1\cdot ln(Rank_k)+\beta_2\cdot RSV_k}}{1+e^{\alpha+\beta_1\cdot ln(Rank_k)+\beta_2\cdot RSV_k}} \quad (2)$$

As a final strategy we suggest merging the retrieved documents according to the Z-score, calculated on the basis of their document scores [2]. Within this scheme, for the ith result list, we needed to compute average for the RSV_k (denoted μRSV^i) and the standard deviation (denoted σRSV^i). Based on these values, we can normalize the retrieval status value of each document D_k provided by the ith result list, by applying the following formula:

$$Zscore\ RSV_k = \alpha_i \cdot \left[\frac{RSV_k - \mu RSV^i}{\sigma RSV^i} + \delta_i\right] \ \delta_i = \frac{\mu RSV_k - MinRSV^i}{\sigma RSV^i} \quad (3)$$

where the value of δ^i is used to generate only positive values, and α_i (usually fixed at 1) is used to reflect the retrieval performance of the underlying retrieval model and to account for the fact that pertinent items are not uniformly distributed across all collections.

Table 6 lists the exact parameters used to query the four different collections. For the Russian collection, we only considered the word-based indexing strategy while for the Finnish language we only used the 4-gram indexing scheme. The top part of Table 6 shows how we used a combined query translation strategy for French, Finnish and Russian languages (Condition A). As described in our monolingual experiments [3], we might also apply a data fusion phase before merging the result lists. Thus, when searching the English or French corpus, we combined the Okapi and Prosit result lists (both with blind query expansion). In a second multilingual experiment (denoted Condition B), we applied a data fusion approach for all bilingual searches (descriptions given in the middle part of Table 6). Finally, we decided to search through all corpora using the same retrieval model, Prosit in this case, as shown in the bottom part of Table 6 (and corresponding to Condition C).

Table 7 lists the retrieval effectiveness of various merging strategies using three different bilingual search parameter settings. In this table, the round-robin scheme was used as a baseline. On the one hand, when different search engines were merged (Condition A and Condition B), the raw-score merging strategy resulted in very poor mean average precision and differences with the round-robin approach are statistically significant. On the other hand, when the same search engine is used (Condition C), the resulting performance of the raw score merg-

Table 6. Description of various runs done separately on each corpus (descriptions listed at top form Condition A, the middle Condition B, and bottom Condition C)

	Parameters of each single run according to each language			
TD queries	English 42 queries	French 49 queries	Finnish (4-gram) 45 queries	Russian (word) 34 queries
Condition A				
IR 1 (#d/#t)	Okapi (3/15)	Prosit (5/15)	Okapi (5/30)	Prosit (3/15)
IR 2 (#d/#t)	Prosit (3/10)	Okapi (5/10)		
Data fusion	Z-score	Z-scoreW		
Translation		Bab2-Free-Rev	Bab1-Inter	Rev-Free
MAP	0.5580	0.4098	0.2956	0.2914
Condition B				
IR 1 (#d/#t)	Okapi (3/15)	Prosit (5/15)	Okapi (5/30)	Prosit (3/15)
IR 2 (#d/#t)	Prosit (3/10)	Okapi (5/10)	Lnu-ltc (3/40)	Okapi (3/15)
Data fusion	Z-score	Z-scoreW	Round-robin	Round-robin
Translation		Bab2-Free-Rev	Bab1-Inter	Rev-Free
MAP	0.5580	0.4098	0.3080	0.3007
Condition C				
IR (#d/#t)	Prosit (3/10)	Prosit (5/15)	Prosit (10/30)	Prosit (3/15)
Translation		Bab2-Fre-Rev	Bab1-Inter	Rev-Free
MAP	0.5633	0.4055	0.2909	0.2914

Table 7. Mean average precision of various merging strategies (TD queries)

Parameter setting Merging Strategy	Mean average precision (% change) Condition A 50 queries	 Condition B 50 queries	 Condition C 50 queries
Round-robin (baseline)	0.2386	0.2430	0.2358
Raw-score	0.0642 (-73.1%)	0.0650 (-73.2%)	0.3067 (+30.1%)
Norm Max	0.2552 (+7.0%)	0.1044 (-57.0%)	0.2484 (+5.3%)
Norm RSV (Eq. 1)	0.2899 (+21.5%)	0.1042 (-57.1%)	0.2646 (+12.2%)
Log. reg. (ln(rank),RSV)	**0.3090** (+29.5%)	**0.3111** (+28.0%)	**0.3393** (+43.9%)
Biased round-robin	0.2639 (+10.6%)	0.2683 (+10.4%)	0.2613 (+10.8%)
Z-score (Eq. 3)	0.2677 (+12.2%)	0.2903 (+19.5%)	0.2555 (+8.4%)
Z-score (Eq. 3) α_i=1.5	0.2669 (+11.9%)	0.3019 (+24.2%)	0.2867 (+21.6%)
Log. reg. & Select. (0)	0.2957 (+23.9%)	0.2959 (+21.8%)	0.3405 (+44.4%)
Log. reg. & Select. (3)	0.2953 (+23.8%)	0.2982 (+22.7%)	0.3378 (+43.3%)
Log. reg. & Select. (10)	0.2990 (+25.3%)	0.3008 (+23.8%)	0.3381 (+43.4%)
Log. reg. & Select. (20)	0.3010 (+26.1%)	0.3029 (+24.7%)	0.3384 (+43.5%)
Log. reg. & Select. (50)	0.3044 (+27.6%)	0.3064 (+26.1%)	0.3388 (+43.7%)
Log. reg. & OptSelect.	**0.3234** (+35.5%)	**0.3261** (+34.2%)	**0.3558** (+50.9%)

ing is statistically better than the baseline. Normalized score merging based on Equation 1 results in statistically significant degradation compared to the simple round-robin approach when using the parameter settings of Condition B (0.1042 vs. 0.2430, or -57.2% in relative performance). By applying our logistic model using both the rank and the document score as explanatory variables, the resulting mean average precision is statistically better than the round-robin merging strategy, and better than the other merging approaches. Under Condition B however, the difference between our logistic model and the Z-score merging strategy is rather small (0.3111 vs. 0.3019, or 3% in relative performance).

As a simple alternative, we could also suggest a biased round-robin approach which extracts not one document per collection per round, but one document for the Russian corpus and two from the English, French and Finnish collections (because the last three represent larger corpora). This merging strategy provides good retrieval performance, better that of the simple round-robin approach. Finally, the Z-score merging approach seems result in generally satisfactory performance. Moreover, we may multiply the Z-score by an α value (performance under the label "$\alpha_i = 1.5$" where the α_i values set as follows: EN: 1.5, FR: 1.5, FI: 1.0, and RU: 1.0).

It cannot be expected however that each result list would always contain pertinent items, in response to a given request. In fact, a given corpus may contain no relevant information regarding the submitted request or the pertinent articles could not be found by the search engine. In the cross-lingual environment we discovered an additional problem: important facets of the original request were translated with inappropriate words or expressions. In all these cases, it is not useful to include items provided by such collections (or such search engines) in the final result list. In addition, the number of pertinent documents is usually

Table 8. Description and mean average precision of our official automatic multilingual runs

Run name	Query	Language	Merging	Parameters	MAP
UniNEmulti1	TD	English	Logistic	Condition A	**0.3090**
UniNEmulti2	TD	English	Z-scoreW	Cond. A, $\alpha_i = 1.5$	0.2969
UniNEmulti3	TD	English	raw-score	Condition C	0.3067
UniNEmulti4	TD	English	Log. & select	Cond. A, $m = 20$	0.3010
UniNEmulti5	TD	English	Z-scoreW	Condition B	0.3019

not uniformly distributed across all four collections. For a given request (e.g., related to a regional or a national event), only one or two collections may contain relevant documents describing this particular event.

To account for these phenomena, we designed a selection procedure that works as follows. First, for each result list we normalize the document score according to our logistic regression method (given in Equation 2). After this step, each document score represents the probability that the underlying article is relevant (with respect to the query submitted and the collection). It is also interesting to note that these probabilities are obtained after a blind query expansion and therefore the number of search terms are more or less the same across queries.

In the second step, for each result list (or language), we sum the document scores of the top 15 ranked documents. If this sum exceeded a given threshold (depending on the collection or search engine), we could thus assume that the corresponding collection contained many pertinent documents. Otherwise, we might only include the m best ranking retrieved items from the corpus (with a relatively small m value). This allows us to limit the number of items extracted from a given corpus while also taking account of the fact that each collection usually contains few pertinent items. Table 7 lists the mean average precision achieved using this selection strategy under the label "Log. reg. & Select. (m)," where the value m indicates that we always include the m best retrieved items from each corpus in our final result list. Of course, when we set $m = 0$, the system will not extract any documents from a collection having a poor overall score. Finally under the label "Log. reg. & OptSelect.", we computed the mean average precision that could be achieved when selection occurs without any errors (with $m = 0$). When using such an ideal selection system, the mean average precision is clearly better than all other merging strategies (e.g, under Condition C, the mean average precision is 0.3558 vs. 0.3393 with the logistic regression without selection).

Table 8 contains the descriptions of our official runs for the multilingual tracks. In the row entitled "UniNEmulti3", all searches were based on the Prosit retrieval model in order to obtain more comparable document score across the various collections. In this context, the raw-score merging strategy provides good overall performance levels.

4 Conclusion

In this fifth CLEF evaluation campaign, we assessed various query translation tools (see Table 1) used together with a combined translation strategy (see Table 2), that usually resulted in better levels of retrieval performance. However, the differences between the best single query translation tool and the various combinations of query translation strategies were not statistically significant. On the other hand, while a bilingual search can be viewed as easier for some language pairs (e.g., English query of a French document collection, or English of a Portuguese), this task is clearly more complex for other language pairs (e.g., English to Finnish). From combining various result lists (see Table 3 or 4), we cannot always obtain better retrieval effectiveness, where compared to isolated runs and the differences with the best single IR model are usually not statistically significant.

In multilingual tasks, searching documents written in different languages represents a real challenge. In this case we proposed a new simple selecting strategy which would avoid extracting a relatively large number of documents from collections containing many documents seeming to have no or little interest with respect to the current query (see Table 7). In this multilingual task, it was also interesting to mention that combining the result lists provided by the same search engine (Condition C in Table 7) may sometimes produce good retrieval effectiveness, as compared to combining different search models (Condition A in Table 7). If in our implementation combining different IR models did not present a statistically significant difference (see Table 4 and evaluations under Condition B in Table 7), the best multilingual system [16] of this evaluation campaign would be based on this combining approach.

Acknowledgments. The author would like to also thank the CLEF-2004 task organizers for their efforts in developing various European language test-collections. The author would also like to thank C. Buckley from SabIR for giving us the opportunity to use the SMART system, together with Samir Abdou for his help in translating the English topics. This research was supported by the Swiss National Science Foundation under Grant #21-66 742.01.

References

1. Savoy, J.: Combining Multiple Strategies for Effective Monolingual and Cross-Lingual Retrieval. IR Journal, **7** (2004) 121–148
2. Savoy, J.: Report on CLEF-2003 Multilingual Tracks. In: Peters, C., Gonzalo, J., Braschler, M., Kluck, M. (Eds.): Comparative Evaluation of Multilingual Information Access Systems. Lecture Notes in Computer Science 3237. Springer, Heidelberg (2004)
3. Savoy, J.: Data Fusion for Effective European Monolingual Information Retrieval. In this volume.
4. Savoy, J.: Report on CLIR task for the NTCIR-4 Evaluation Campaign. In Proceedings NTCIR-4. Tokyo (2004) 178–185

5. Savoy, J.: Statistical Inference in Retrieval Effectiveness Evaluation. Information Processing & Management, **33** (1997) 495–512
6. Kishida, K., Kuriyama, K., Kando, N., Eguchi, K.: Prediction of Performance on Cross-Lingual Information Retrieval by Regression Models. In Proceedings NTCIR-4. Tokyo (2004) 219–224
7. Nie, J.Y., Simard, M., Isabelle, P., Durand, R.: Cross-Language Information Retrieval based on Parallel Texts and Automatic Mining of Parallel Texts from the Web. In Proceedings of the ACM-SIGIR'99. The ACM Press, New York (1993) 74–81
8. MacNamee, P., Mayfield, J.: JHU/APL Experiments in Tokenization and Non-Word Translation. In: Peters, C., Gonzalo, J., Braschler, M., Kluck, M. (Eds.): Comparative Evaluation of Multilingual Information Access Systems. Lecture Notes in Computer Science 3237. Springer, Heidelberg (2004)
9. Chen, A., Gey, F.: Combining Query Translation and Document Translation in Cross-Language Retrieval. In: Peters, C., Braschler, M., Gonzalo, J., Kluck, M. (Eds.): Advances in Cross-Language Information Retrieval. Lecture Notes in Computer Science. Springer, Heidelberg (2004), to appear
10. Buckley, C., Mitra, M., Waltz, J., Cardie, C.: Using Clustering and Superconcepts within SMART. In Proceedings TREC-6. NIST Publication #500-240, Gaithersburg (1998) 107–124
11. Braschler, M., Peters, C.: Cross-Language Evaluation Forum: Objectives, Results and Achievements. IR Journal, **7** (2004) 7–31
12. Voorhees, E.M., Gupta, N.K., Johnson-Laird, B.: The Collection Fusion Problem. In Proceedings TREC-3. NIST Publication #500-225, Gaithersburg (1995) 95–104
13. Kwok, K.L., Grunfeld, L., Lewis, D.D.: TREC-3 Ad-hoc, Routing Retrieval and Thresholding Experiments using PIRCS. In Proceedings TREC-3. NIST Publication #500-225, Gaithersburg (1995) 247–255
14. Chen, A.: Cross-language Retrieval Experiments at CLEF 2002. In: Peters, C., Braschler, M., Gonzalo, J., Kluck, M. (Eds.): Advances in Cross-Language Information Retrieval. Lecture Notes in Computer Science: Vol. 2785. Springer, Heidelberg (2003), 28–48
15. Le Calvé, A., Savoy, J.: Database Merging strategy based on Logistic Regression. Information Processing & Management, **36** (2000) 341–359
16. Adafre, S.F., van Hage, W.R., Kamps, J., de Melo, G.L., de Rijke, M.: The University of Amsterdam at at CLEF 2004. In this volume.

Using Surface-Syntactic Parser and Deviation from Randomness

X-IOTA IR System Used for CLIPS Mono and Bilingual Experiments in CLEF 2004

Jean-Pierre Chevallet[1] and Gilles Sérasset[2]

[1] IPAL-CNRS, I2R A*STAR, National University of Singapore
viscjp@i2r.a-star.edu.sg
[2] Laboratoire CLIPS-IMAG*, Grenoble, France
Gilles.Serasset@imag.fr

Abstract. This document presents the experiments we performed for our CLEF 2004 participation. We have tested the use of surface-syntactic parsing to extract indexing terms. We have also studied the Deviation From Randomness weighting. For the bilingual part, we have experimented reinforcement query weighting using an association thesaurus.

1 Introduction

In our previous participation at CLEF in 2003 [1], we tested the use of an association thesaurus to enhance query translation. However, we only used the association thesaurus to add some new terms to the proposed translation terms. In our current participation, we have tried another use of such a thesaurus: we do not expand the query, but rather use it to modify the weighting of a given translated query. Our basic idea is the selection of the best term translation using query context and an association thesaurus derived from the corpus. Last year, we neglected the study of the matching function and the influence of the weighting scheme. For this participation we will also focus on this aspect: we have tested the Deviation From Randomness (DFR) against the Okapi measure and some other classical IR weighting. We have also experimented the use of a surface-syntactic parser. All documents are first transformed by the parser. The stemming is then proposed by the parser. Finnish is an agglutinative language, and using such an NL parsing makes it possible to correctly split the compound words into separate correct indexing terms.

This paper first presents the training experiments performed on the 2003 collection. In Section 3, we discuss the monolingual results and, in Section 4, we present the technique used for bilingual results and present hypotheses based on them.

---

* This work is part of the PRISM-IMAG project devoted to high level indexing representation using inter-lingual graph formalism.

C. Peters et al. (Eds.): CLEF 2004, LNCS 3491, pp. 38–49, 2005.

2 Training on Monolingual Runs

In this section, we present some training performed using the monolingual corpora of CLEF 2003. We have mainly used the Finnish and French corpora. The purpose of this training is to select the best weighting scheme for the given CLEF document collection.

2.1 The Underlying IR Model

All experiments are based on the classic vector space model. The goal of the experiment is to compare the statistical Okapi model with the Deviation From Randomness model, versus more classical weightings. This comparison will be done on two different languages.

Basically, the final matching process is achieved by a product of the query vector and document matrix, which computes the Relevant Status Value (RSV) of all documents against the query. For a query vector $Q = (q_i)$ with a dimension of t terms $i \in [1..t]$, and an index document matrix of n documents $D_j = (d_{ij})$, $j \in [1..n]$, the RSV is computed by

$$RSV(Q, D_j) = \sum_{i \in [1..t]} q_i * d_{ij} \tag{1}$$

We keep this matching process for all tests, the changes are in the documents and query processing to select indexing terms, and in the weighting scheme. We note here that the scheme is inspired by the SMART system. We suppose the previous processing steps have produced a matrix $D = (d_{i,j})$. Usually, the value $d_{i,j}$ is only the result of term t_i counting in the document D_j, called term frequency tf_{ij}. Each weighting scheme can be decomposed into three steps: a local, a global and a normalization step. The local step is related to only one vector. All these transformations are listed in Table 1. For all measures we use the following symbols:

n	number of document in the corpus
t	number of unique indexing terms in the corpus
tf_{ij}	frequency of term i in document j
f_i	frequency of term i in the corpus: $f_i = \sum_{j \in [1..n]} tf_{ij}$
S	the corpus size: $S = \sum_{i \in [1..t]} f_i$
d_{ij}	current value in the matrix (initialy tf_{ij})
w_{ij}	new value in the matrix
d^*_{ij}	a normalization of d_{ij} (see below)
λ_i	the fraction f_i/S
df_i	number of documents indexed by term i (document frequency)
c, k_1, b	constants for DFR and Okapi
L_j	the length of document j: $L_j = \sum_{i \in [1..t]} d_{ij}$
$awrL$	mean document length: $awrL = (\sum_{k \in [1..n]} L_k)/n$
q_i	weight of term i of query q

Table 1. Local weighting

Letter	Formula	Meaning
n	$w_{ij} = d_{ij}$	none, no change
b	$w_{ij} = 1$	binary
a	$w_{ij} = \frac{0.5+0.5*d_{ij}}{max_i(d_{ij})}$	local max
l	$w_{ij} = ln(d_{ij} + 1)$	natural log
d	$w_{ij} = ln(ln(d_{ij} + 1) + 1)$	double natural log

The global weighting is related to the matrix, and is a weighing which takes into account the relative importance of a term regarding the whole document collection. The most famous is the Inverse Document Frequency : Idf. Table 2 lists the global weighting we have tested. Okapi and DFR are not global weightings per se but rather complete the weighting scheme. In our X-IOTA system, they are computed at the same time as the global weighting, and it is technically feasible to use them with a local and the final normalization. DFR is presented in the next section.

Table 2. Global weighting

Letter	Formula	Meaning
n	$w_{ij} = d_{ij}$	none, no global change
t	$w_{ij} = d_{ij} * log\frac{n}{df_i}$	Idf
p	$w_{ij} = d_{ij} * log\frac{n-df_i}{df_i}$	Idf variant for Okapi
O	$w_{ij} = \frac{(k_1+1)*d_{ij}}{k_1*[(1-b)+b*\frac{L_j}{awrL}]+d_{ij}}$	Okapi
R	(see below)	DFR

The Okapi measure described in [2, 3], uses the length of the document j, L_j, and also a normalization by the average length $awrL$ of all documents in the corpus. This length is related to the number of indexing terms in a document. The Okapi measure uses 2 constant values called k_1 and b. The last treatment is the normalization of the final vector.

Table 3. Final normalization

Letter	Formula	Meaning
n	$w_{ij} = d_{ij}$	none, no normalization
c	$w_{ij} = \frac{d_{ij}}{\sqrt{\sum_i d_{ij}^2}}$	cosine

A weighting scheme is composed by the combination of the local, global and final weighting. We represent a weighting scheme by 3 letters. For example, nnn is only the raw term frequency. The scheme bnn for both documents and queries leads to a sort of Boolean model where every term in the query is considered connected by a conjunction. In that case the RSV counts the term intersection between documents and queries. The c normalization applied to both document and query vector leads to the computation of the cosine between these two vectors. This is the classical vector space model if we use the `ltc` scheme for document and queries. The scheme nOn for the documents, and npn with the queries, is the Okapi model, and the use of nRn for document and nnn for the queries is the DFR model. For these two models, a constant has to be defined.

Notice that the c normalization of the queries divides the RSV for this query by $\sqrt{\sum_i q_i^2}$. For each query this is a constant value which does not influence the relative order of retrieved document list. It follows that this normalization is useless for queries and should not be used. In the next section we briefly present the Deviation from Randomness weighting that seems to give best results, and that we have used for the submitted runs.

2.2 Deviation from Randomness (DFR)

This weighting scheme has been proposed by Gianni Amati in [5]. Theoretical discussions about this approach can be found in [4]. The formula is given by:

$$w_{ij} = (\log_2(1+\lambda_i) + d^*_{ij} * \log_2 \frac{1+\lambda_i}{\lambda_i}) * \frac{f_i + 1}{df_i * (d^*_{ij} + 1)} \quad . \tag{2}$$

The value d^*_{ij} is a normalization by the length L_j of the document j regarding the average size of all documents in the corpus: $awrL$. A constant value c adjusts the effect of the document length in the weighting.

$$d^*_{i,j} = d_{ij} * \log_2(1 + c * \frac{awrL}{L_j}) \quad . \tag{3}$$

For this participation at CLEF, we have tested this weighting scheme against others. We present these results for the Finnish and French collections.

2.3 Finnish IR

In these experiments, we have first tested the influence of stop words (SW) and stemming. Table 4 sums up the results we obtain using this weighting scheme on the CLEF 2003 queries using the formula described in [5]. As the stemming and stopword removal enhance the results, we use these procedures for the rest of the experiments.

We have not tested the influence of the surface syntactic parser, because the parsing was not available at the time we made these tests. The test performed here is done on the Finnish collection with 2003 queries. As the best results are obtained with stop words and stemming, we have then tested the influence of the c constant in order to find out when we reach the optimum.

The treatment we apply to both documents and queries consists in filtering out the XML tags, transforming XML special characters to their ISO counterpart, deleting all diacritic characters, and changing others to lower case. At this

Table 4. Test weighting nRn nnn

run	nRn nnn c=2	ret_rel (483)
raw	29.89	388
SW	35.39	429
stem SW	39.26	452

Table 5. Variation of c for nRn nnn (stem SW)

c	precision	ret_rel (483)
0.00	4.89	286
0.10	30.24	436
0.50	39.63	448
0.70	40.40	448
0.75	40.90	449
0.80	40.97	449
0.81	41.04	449
0.82	41.06	449
0.83	41.07	449
0.84	41.07	449

c	precision	ret_rel (483)
0.85	41.02	449
0.86	41.01	449
0.87	41.02	450
0.90	40.16	450
0.95	39.98	450
1.00	39.86	450
1.50	39.41	451
2.00	39.26	452
5.00	39.03	449
10.0	37.96	447

stage we still have special Finnish characters and accents. We eliminate common words using a list provided by J. Savoy[1] and then suppress all accents. We apply a Finnish stemmer also proposed by J. Savoy modified to accept XML input/output to produce the final vectors.

Table 5 shows the results of DFR test with the nnn query weighting scheme. When c is zero, the equation becomes (4), where term weights are all equal for all documents.

$$w_{t,d} = \log_2(1 + \lambda_t).\frac{f_t + 1}{df_i} \tag{4}$$

When we examine the DFR formula, we see that when a term does not appear in document d, then only $d_{i,j}$ is null, as well as $d^*_{i,j}$. If we strictly apply the formula in that case, the weight of the term is still not null and is equal to (4). For practical reasons, we have replaced this residual value by zero. This approximation reduces the size of the inverse file, as we do not store null values. In fact we have applied the following weighting:

$$w'_{i,j} = \begin{cases} w_{i,j} & \text{if } d_{i,j} \neq 0 \\ 0 & \text{if } d_{i,j} = 0 \end{cases} \tag{5}$$

Table 5 shows results for some variation in the constant c. Optimum value is around $c = 0.84$. This optimization gains 1.21 points when compared to the

[1] http://www.unine.ch/info/clef

neutral value $c = 1$. We can also notice that we obtain more documents in the first 1000 answers for $c = 2$, but the average precision is lower, which means that they are not well sorted. The conclusion for this weighting is that a good constant c value seems to be 0.83. In the rest of the test, we used the approximated value $c = 0.8$. For the Okapi weighting, we have used the same value as in [5], that is $k_1 = 1.2$, and $b = 0.75$.

Testing Query Weighting. We have tested all combinations of the following weights:

nnn: Only the term frequency is used.
bnn: This is the binary model. Occurring terms are given the value 1, others 0.
lnc: The cosine is the final normalization. When used both for documents and queries, it ensures true vector space model matching, i.e. only the angle between the query and document vector is used. This weighting assumes a log distribution of frequency.
ntc: This is the classical tf*idf measure. When used for queries, the idf is taken from the document collection, not the query collection.
ltc: The same classical measure using log on term frequency.
ltn: The log tf*idf without cosine normalization.
atn: Normalization with the local maximum term frequency is used with idf.
dtn: The double natural log is used instead of the simple one in ltn.
npn: The idf variant used for the Okapi system.
nRn: Deviation from randomness.
nOn: The Okapi probabilistic weighting.

Table 6. Query weighting (stem SW c= 0.83)

	query weighting								
Doc.	nnn	bnn	lnc	ntc	ltc	ltn	atn	dtn	npn
nnn	13.16	9.80	12.22	19.54	19.55	19.55	19.44	19.16	19.82
bnn	28.64	16.61	25.54	34.30	33.67	33.67	33.94	32.50	34.41
atn	26.77	22.65	25.87	28.35	28.02	28.02	28.11	27.85	28.31
ntc	25.72	26.38	25.95	29.26	29.39	29.39	29.60	29.57	29.25
lnc	29.57	23.88	29.75	34.06	35.35	35.35	35.38	25.44	33.99
ltc	32.22	27.84	32.22	32.63	33.00	33.00	32.90	32.44	32.63
ltn	37.71	32.37	37.91	35.99	37.85	37.85	37.86	37.65	36.01
nRn	**41.07**	**36.99**	**40.08**	40.02	**41.29**	**41.29**	**41.05**	**41.92**	40.00
nOn	37.16	29.35	35.95	**40.39**	40.12	40.12	40.32	40.68	**40.12**

Table 6 sums up the results. We notice that the Deviation from Randomness model is very stable against the query weighting and that it has the best results in the majority of query weightings. Hence, we decided to use it in CLEF 2004 in all tests.

2.4 French IR

For training, we have used the French corpus of CLEF 2003. We have used our own stemmer, and our own list for removal of common French terms. In this collection, there are 3 sets of documents. For each collection we have selected the following fields: TITLE TEXT for lemonde94, and TI KW LD TX ST for sda 94 and 95. For the queries, we have selected the fields FR-title FR-desc FR-narr. We have tested the same combination of weighting schemes, tested in the Finnish collection. The results are given in Tables 7 and 8.

Table 7. French average precision 1

	Query weighting			
Doc.	nnn	bnn	lnn	ntn
nnn	7.72	2.78	5.71	16.71
bnn	16.01	4.25	13.19	29.73
atn	31.02	27.03	31.16	29.91
ntc	33.53	34.68	35.86	32.09
lnc	36.20	32.22	36.74	39.06
ltc	35.39	35.37	37.40	34.38
ltn	35.65	22.36	32.68	37.87
nRn	**46.98**	**38.15**	**45.01**	**49.06**
nOn	42.25	33.02	40.39	49.01

Table 8. French average precision 2

	Query weighting			
Doc.	ltn	atn	dtn	npn
nnn	15.86	15.53	14.47	17.49
bnn	25.13	24.97	23.30	29.15
atn	29.76	30.28	29.47	29.95
ntc	33.89	33.99	33.08	31.98
lnc	40.69	40.82	39.37	38.77
ltc	34.17	34.29	34.73	33.40
ltn	36.64	36.99	35.44	37.89
nRn	**48.16**	**48.76**	**47.03**	**48.78**
nOn	47.07	47.36	45.65	48.38

Finally, we have taken the best weighting query scheme for the Okapi model (nOn) and we have computed some variations of the two constant k_1 and b. The results are in Table 9. The best values are obtained with the couple $(1, 0.75)$ which confirms the values presented in [5]. In this language, we also demonstrated the stability of the DFR measure (nRn) which performs better than other query weightings, except with binary queries (bnn). We obtained the best average precision with the inverse document frequency (ntn).

Table 9. k_1 and b variation for nOn ntn

	b				
k_1	0.25	0.5	0.75	1	1.25
0.5	42.83	45.83	47.04	46.95	46.43
1	46.01	47.96	**49.48**	47.86	44.67
1.5	46.95	48.69	49.36	45.08	41.92
2	46.97	48.56	49.01	43.98	39.04
2.5	46.76	48.19	46.31	43.18	11.81

We have not performed any special treatments for the queries, like removing terms that are not related to the theme (ex: document, retrieve, etc). We think that a natural language analysis of the query to remove these empty words should improve the results.

3 Monolingual Results

In this section, we comment the results obtained at CLEF 2004. We participated in the monolingual track on French, Finnish and Russian. As we support the use of syntactic parsing, all submitted monolingual runs use syntactic parsing. Because of time constraints, we have not trained the system with the parsed collection. So we can only compare with CLEF 2003 without parsing.

We used the *Xerox Incremental Parser (XIP)* to parse English and French documents, the *ETAP* analyser for Russian and *Connexor's Machinese Syntax* for Finnish. All parsed documents were transformed into a common XML format. In these experiments, the main interest in using a natural language parser was the correct normalization of words, the correct detection of compound nouns and correct filtering using lexical categories. For all runs, we have chosen the Deviation from Randomness weighting with the constant value fixed to $c = 0.8$, according to the training experiments. Queries were also parsed.

For all languages, we only kept nouns, proper nouns, verbs and adjectives and then removed some terms using a stopword list. The French queries are weighted using *ntn*. The average precision is 44%, which is not a good result on absolute terms. This value is slightly lower than that obtained during our training.

When we examine more closely the results, we discover a big discrepancy between queries. Fig. 1, shows the histogram repartitions of 29 queries in two monolingual runs. For French, there are a lot of queries that have either very low precision level (18 queries under 20%) or very high (13 queries over 80%).

For the Finnish monolingual run, we obtained an average precision of 53%, which is better than the results obtained for CLEF 2003. The Finnish histogram shows that 10 queries are above 90%. In fact exactly 5 queries reach 100% of precision.

For Russian, we cannot compare yet with a more simple raw term indexing, because we do not have a Russian stemmer and stop list. The average results of 35% is the lowest for all three languages. Query precision repartition for Russian shows that a lot of queries (12) have very low precision (under 10%).

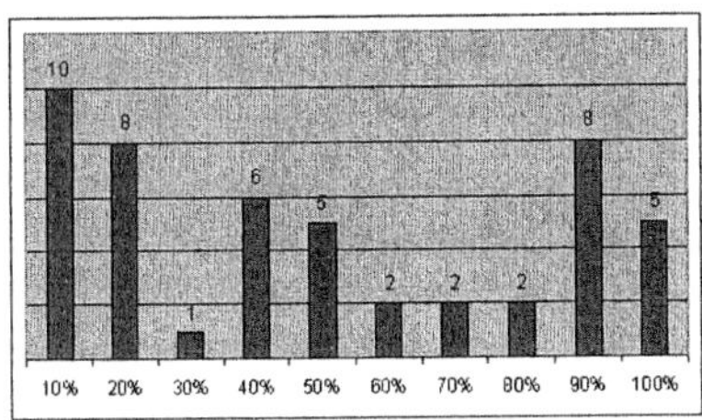

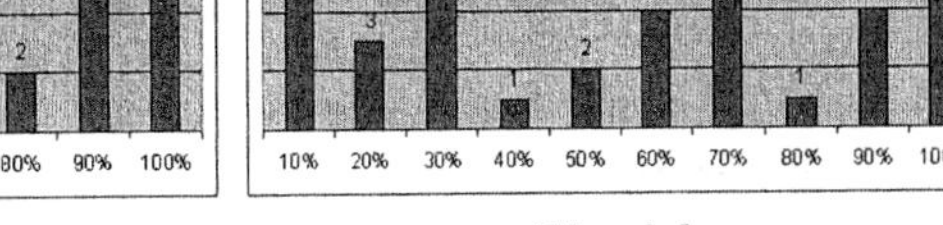

French **Finnish**

Fig. 1. Monolingual precision histograms

The conclusion we can draw, is the good behavior of DFR weighting, and probably the benefit of using a surface parsing on Finnish. In this language, the parser is able to "unglue" terms, and so could achieve better results. We cannot investigate our results further, because we should compare the use of syntactic surface parsing on the same collection.

4 Topic Translation

Bilingual results are obtained by translating the topics using general dictionaries built by compiling several bilingual dictionaries available online (see Section 4.1). Then, we experimented 2 methods of translation (see sections 4.2). Both methods take the topic vectors as input and output a new translated topic vector.

4.1 Construction of the Dictionaries

We compiled 6 bilingual translation dictionaries (see Table 10) using several resources available in house or from Internet. Each resulting dictionary associates a word form with a set of translations and is stored as an XML file.

Table 10. Size of the resulting compiled dictionaries

Dictionary	nb of entry	av. nb of translations per entry	max nb of translations per entry
fr - en	21417	1.92417	22
fr - fi	791	1.06574	4
fr - ru	604	1.06126	3
en - fr	24542	1.67916	25
en - fi	867	1.11649	5
en - ru	15331	2.09901	30

These dictionaries were compiled from the following sources:

- the Bilingual French-English dictionary from the university of Rennes 1, freely available at `http://sun-recomgen.med.univ-rennes1.fr/Dico/`,
- the FeM dictionary (French-English-Malay), freely accessible at `http://www-clips.imag.fr/cgi-bin/geta/fem/fem.pl?lang=fr`,
- the French-English dictionary available on the CLEF web site,
- dictionary entries from the Logos website (`http://www.logos.it/`),
- the "engrus" English-Russian dictionary available on many web sites[2].

As for the French-Russian, French-Finnish and English-Finnish dictionaries, the only available online resource we used is the Logos web site. As it is the

[2] See list of mirrors at http://sinyagin.pp.ru/engrus-mirrors.html

only online service we used (other data were available off-line), we chose to only extract entries that were present in the topics to be translated in order to avoid high loads on a public web site. This explains the very small size of these dictionaries.

As French and English were our chosen topic languages, we also reverted the merged French-English dictionaries.

4.2 Topic Translation

For each bilingual task in which we participated, we experimented 2 methods of translation. Both methods take the topic vectors as input and output a new translated topic vector.

Simple Topic Translation. The first method substitutes each term by all of its available translations. The weight associated with each translation is equal to the weight of the original term divided by the number of available translations (e.g. interest (1) → ИНТЕРЕС (.25), ВЫГОДА (.25), ИНТЕРЕСОВАТЬ (.25), ЗАИНТЕРЕСОВЫВАТЬ (.25)).

Filtering by Means of an Association Thesaurus. As shown in Table 10, many different translations can be found for a single term. Hence, we tried to develop a strategy to give more importance to the "correct" translation(s). For this, we tried to take some context into account, without changing anything in the available lexical resource.

As we needed contextual information in each language, we automatically built an association thesaurus (as described in [1]) for each language from the available monolingual documents (see Table 11).

Table 11. Size of the association thesaurii

Corpus	nb of term in the corpus	nb of arcs in the thesaurus	nb of terms left in the thesaurus
LeMonde95	134786	21717	4247
GH95	151595	23605	4891
Izvestia95	43346	23992	2466
Aamu95	271860	19138	9000

Each association thesaurus is interpreted as a graph linking terms. Each arc in the graph links 2 terms that "regularly"[3] appear in the same context. For this experiment, 2 terms are said to be *in the same context* when they appear in the same document.

[3] In this experiment, we filtered out arcs that had a confidence score lower than 20% or higher than 90%.

For our experiment, we assume that terms that are close to each other share some common semantic. We also assume that their "correct" translations should also share the same semantics. Hence, we used these association thesaurii to know if terms and translations share some semantics. We chose to associate each translation $t_{i,j}$ of a term c_j with a weight $w_{t_{i,j}}$ (see (7)) depending on its distance ($d_{t_{i,j}}$) to the translated context. The distance of a translation to the translated context is given by (6).

$$\begin{array}{c} d_{t_{i,j}} = Min(d(t_{i,j}, t_{k,l}); \forall l, k \mid l \neq j, 1 \leq k \leq [T_l|) \\ \text{where } t_{k,l} \in T_l \\ \text{and } T_l \text{ is the set of translations of the term } c_l \\ \text{and } d(t_{i,j}, t_{k,l}) \text{ is the min. distance in target thesaurus} \end{array} \tag{6}$$

$$w_{t_{i,j}} = \begin{cases} w_j / d_{i,j} \text{ if } d_{i,j} \neq 0 \\ w_j / |T_j| \text{ if } d_{i,j} = 0 \end{cases} \tag{7}$$

where w_j is the weight of the source term c_j in the source vector

This method give a greater weight to translations that share a bigger context with the rest of the query (1) → **ИНТЕРЕС** (.5), ВЫГОДА (.25), ИНТЕРЕСОВАТЬ (.25), ЗАИНТЕРЕСОВЫВАТЬ (.25) in topic 250).

4.3 Discussion

CLIPS results on the bilingual tasks are rather disappointing, with the starting interpolated recall-precision curve dropping from 57.68% (Monolingual Russian) to 17.1% with simple topic translation and even to 8.59% with filtered topic translation (both for Bilingual English-Russian).

The main reason for this drop is certainly due to the lack of wide coverage bilingual lexical resources. The dictionaries we used were very small and did not provide translations for many terms of the topics. This is especially true for French to Russian and Finnish lexical resources where 60% to 70% of the source terms are not translated. English to Russian lexicon was a little better, and about 18% of the terms remain without translation.

However, this does not explain the drop in interpolated recall-precision averages when filtering the translations through the association thesaurii, as it does not change the set of translations, but only the weight of those translations. Moreover, when manually evaluating the weighted translation, one usually agrees with the translations that are chosen. We think that 2 factors explains these drops:

- First, in the simple topic translation method, the weight of each translation is divided by the number of translations for the source term. This lowers the relative importance of terms that bear many translations, (which is usually the case of general nouns or support verbs).
- Second, when raising the weight of "correct" translations by means of the association thesaurii, we also raise the weight of such general terms. Hence, we give more importance to terms that do not bear any thematic closeness to

the requested documents (and this is especially the case with CLEF topics that are instructions usually containing "find documents reporting on..." or "find information on...").

5 Conclusion

All runs were performed on the collection parsed, using a syntactic parser. Best monolingual results are obtained for the Finnish collection, probably because of the correct word splitting. We must redo the test with no analyzer in order to draw a strong conclusion on its use in an IR context. Bilingual results are disappointing but they are partly explained by the difficulty in finding wide coverage lexical resources for languages in which we previously had no experience whatsoever.

The filtering of translations through association thesaurii appears interesting, even if we did not have enough time to use it appropriately. This technique may also be interesting in translation selection tasks or, with adaptation, in lexical disambiguation tasks. Its main interest in such tasks comes from the fact that it does not require any special training data (like parallel documents or manually disambiguated corpora) as association thesaurii may be computed automatically from the corpus. Hence such techniques may easily give some results in those tasks in any language, provided that monolingual data is available as well as an automatic process to lemmatize such corpora.

References

1. Sérasset, Gilles, Chevallet, Jean-Pierre : Simple Translations of Monolingual Queries Expanded Through an Association Thesaurus. X-IOTA IR System used for CLIPS Bilingual Experiment. In Comparative Evaluation of Multilingual Information Access Systems. CLEF 2003. LNCS 3237. Springer, Heidelberg (2004) 242–252.
2. Robertson, S.E., Walker, S., Beaulieu, M.: Okapi at TREC-7: Automatic ad hoc, filtering, VLC and interactive track. Pr0oceedings of TREC-7 (1998) 253–264.
3. Robertson, S.E.: Overview of the Okapi projects. Journal of Documentation. Vol 53(1)(1997)3–7.
4. Amati, G., van Rijsbergen, C.J.: Probabilistic Models of Information Retrieval Based on Measuring the Divergence from Randomness. ACM Transaction on Information Systems Vol 20(4)(2002) 357-389.
5. Amati, G, Carpineto, C., Romano, G.: Comparing weighting models for monolingual information retrieval. In Comparative Evaluation of Multilingual Information Access Systems. CLEF 2003. LNCS 3237. Springer, Heidelberg (2004) 310-318.

Cross-Language Retrieval Using HAIRCUT at CLEF 2004

Paul McNamee and James Mayfield

The Johns Hopkins University Applied Physics Laboratory,
11100 Johns Hopkins Road,
Laurel, MD 20723-6099, USA
{Paul.mcnamee, James.mayfield}@jhuapl.edu

Abstract. JHU/APL continued to explore the use of knowledge-light methods for multilingual retrieval during the CLEF 2004 evaluation. We relied on the language-neutral techniques of character n-gram tokenization, pre-translation query expansion, statistical translation using aligned parallel corpora, fusion from disparate retrievals, and reliance on language similarity when resources are scarce. We participated in the monolingual and bilingual evaluations. Our results support the claims that n-gram based retrieval is highly effective; that fusion of multiple retrievals is helpful in bilingual retrieval; and, that reliance on language similarity in lieu of translation can outperform a high performing system using abundant translation resources and a less similar query language.

1 Introduction

As in the past, JHU/APL's work with the HAIRCUT retrieval system for CLEF 2004 was based on language-neutral methods. In particular, we favor techniques that can be readily applied to any language or language pair. We believe that such methods are at least as effective as approaches that rely on language-specific processing, and perhaps more so. Our principal monolingual techniques include character n-gram tokenization, use of a statistical language model of retrieval, and fusion from multiple retrievals. For bilingual retrieval we focus on pre-translation query expansion using comparable collections, statistical translation from aligned parallel collections, and when translation resources are scarce, reliance on language similarity alone. We also rely on a technique that we first explored in the CLEF 2003 evaluation: direct n-gram translation, a new method of translating queries that uses n-grams rather than words as the elements to be translated [8]. This method does not suffer from certain obstacles in dictionary-based translation, such as word lemmatization, matching of multiple word expressions, and inability to handle out-of-vocabulary words such as common surnames [12].

We submitted official runs for the monolingual and bilingual tracks. For all of our runs we used the HAIRCUT system and a statistical language model similarity calculation. Some of our official runs were based solely on either n-gram processing or the use of stemmed words; however, we believe by using a combination of n-grams and words or stemmed words better performance can often be obtained.

C. Peters et al. (Eds.): CLEF 2004, LNCS 3491, pp. 50 – 59, 2005.

2 Methods

HAIRCUT supports several ways of representing documents using a bag-of-terms assumption. (We emphasize that we frequently use character n-grams, not words as indexing terms.) Our general approach is to process the text of each document, reducing all terms to lower-case. Words were deemed to be white-space delimited tokens in the text; however, we preserve only the first 4 digits of a number and we truncate any particularly long tokens (those greater than 35 characters in length). We make no attempt at compound splitting. Once words are identified we optionally perform transformations on the words to create indexing terms (*e.g.*, stemming). We also remove diacritical marks, believing that they are of little importance. So-called stopwords are retained in our index and the dictionary is created from all words present in the corpus. At query time we ignore high frequency terms for reasons of run-time efficiency, and because such terms typically add little to query semantics. (By default, query terms occurring in greater than 20% of documents are ignored.)

We continue to use a statistical language model for retrieval akin to those presented by Miller et al. [10] and Hiemstra [4] with Jelinek-Mercer smoothing [5]. In this model, relevance is defined as

$$P(D \mid Q) = \prod_{q \in Q} [\alpha P(q \mid D) + (1-\alpha) P(q \mid C)],$$

where Q is a query, D is a document, C is the collection as a whole, and α is a smoothing parameter. The probabilities on the right side of the equation are replaced by their maximum likelihood estimates when scoring a document. The language model has the advantage that term weights are mediated by the corpus. Our experience has been that this type of probabilistic model outperforms a vector-based cosine model or a binary independence model.

For the monolingual task our submitted runs were based on a combination of several base runs using different options for tokenization. JHU/APL's official bilingual submissions were based solely on stemmed words, although we had hoped to submit composite runs. Our method for combination is to normalize scores by probability mass and to then merge documents by score. All of our submitted runs were automatic runs and used only the title and description topic fields.

3 Monolingual Task

For our monolingual work we created several indexes for each language using the permissible document fields appropriate to each collection. (Peters et al. describe the guidelines for the monolingual and bilingual tasks [11]). We indexed the full language collection, making use of documents from 1994 and 1995, despite the fact that only half the collection was used in the evaluation. Prior to submission we discarded retrieved documents from the wrong time period. Our reasons for using the larger collection were to improve corpus statistics, pseudo relevance feedback, and for the bilingual task, pre-translation expansion. Our four basic methods for tokenization were unnormalized words, stemmed words obtained through the use of the Snowball stemmer, 4-grams, and 5-grams. We were unable to get the Snowball stemmer to work with Russian text, and we had some difficulty with it while processing Portuguese queries – many query terms were discarded. Information about each index is shown in Table 1.

Table 1. Summary information about the test collection and index data structures

language	#docs	#rel	index size (MB) / unique terms (1000s)			
			words	stems	4-grams	5-grams
EN	166754	375	143 / 302	123 / 236	504 / 166	827 / 916
FI	55344	413	90 / 978	60 / 521	136 / 138	228 / 707
FR	177450	915	129 / 328	107 / 226	393 / 159	628 / 838
PT	106821	678	101 / 303	77 / 178	292 / 152	492 / 735
RU	16715	123	26 / 253	26 / 253	44 / 136	86 / 569

Our use of 4-grams and 5-grams as indexing terms represents a departure from earlier studies using 6-grams that we justify based on recent findings [9]. The 4-grams and 5-grams seem to work equally well for monolingual retrieval. Our language model requires a single smoothing constant; we used α=0.3 with both words and stems, and α=0.8 with 4-grams and 5-grams. Each of our base runs used blind relevance feedback (queries expanded to 60 terms; terms selected using 20 top-ranked and 75 low-ranked documents). Figure 1 charts performance using our four different term indexing strategies, in isolation. The relative advantage we have previously observed n-grams to have over words is less apparent on the CLEF 2004 data.

Our official submissions were produced by fusing several base runs. We submitted three runs for each language and we report results on the English document set since the relevance judgments are available. Runs were labeled *aplmoxxa*, *aplmoxxb*, or *aplmoxxc*, where *xx* denotes the language of interest. Runs whose names end with a terminal 'a' were produced by combining a 4-gram base run with a stemmed word base run; a terminal 'b' indicates fusion of a 5-grams and stemmed words; terminal 'c' is used for runs that used both 4-grams and 5-grams. Monolingual performance based on mean average precision is reported in Table 2.

4 Bilingual Task

We spent a rather considerable amount of time this year in an effort to improve our translation resources. We have had consistent success using aligned parallel corpora to extract statistical translations. We have relied on this technique for single word translation; however, we recently demonstrated significant improvements in bilingual performance by translating character n-grams directly [8]. We call this 'direct n-gram translation'. Additionally we also translated stemmed words and words.

There is a consensus that lexical coverage is essential for good cross-language retrieval performance. Several studies have sought to understand the relationship between lexical coverage of translation resources and CLIR performance [2,3,7,13]. We believe that the relationship between translation coverage and performance is approximately linear. Accordingly, we sought to grow the size of our parallel collection. However, due to the nature of corpus statistics, doubling the size of a parallel collection will not necessarily double the coverage of a statistically produced translation.

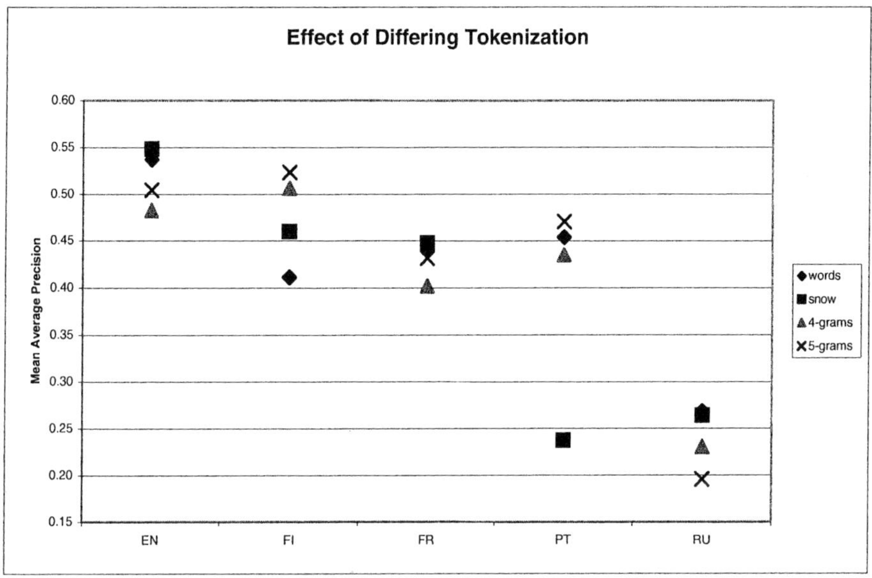

Fig. 1. Relative efficacy of different tokenization methods using the CLEF 2004 test set

Table 2. Official results for monolingual task. The shaded rows are for unofficial English runs The maximal performing run for each language is emboldened

run id	Terms	MAP	= Best	>= Median	Rel. Found	Relevant	# topics
aplmoena	4+snow	0.5414			363	375	42
aplmoenb	5+snow	0.5417			364	375	42
aplmoenc	4+5	0.5070			295	375	42
aplmofia	4+snow	0.5393	8	34	395	413	45
aplmofib	5+snow	0.5443	6	29	394	413	45
aplmofic	4+5	0.5336	8	33	392	413	45
aplmofra	4+snow	0.4284	1	29	888	915	49
aplmofrb	5+snow	0.4581	4	32	891	915	49
aplmofrc	4+5	0.4249	2	25	810	915	49
aplmopta	4+snow	0.4230	8	27	582	678	46
aplmoptb	5+snow	0.4445	10	30	604	678	46
aplmoptc	4+5	0.4690	11	34	589	678	46
aplmorua	4+snow	0.2974	4	18	98	123	34
aplmorub	5+snow	0.3076	6	19	100	123	34
aplmoruc	4+5	0.2604	5	14	97	123	34

For the 2002 and 2003 campaigns we relied on a single source for parallel texts, the Official Journal of the E.U. [14], which is published in the official languages (20 languages as of May 2004). The Journal is available in each of the E.U. languages and consists mainly of governmental topics, for example, trade and foreign relations. For the CLEF 2003 evaluation we had obtained 33 GB of PDF files that we distilled into approximately 300 MB of alignable text, per language. In December 2003 we began the process of mining archival issues of the Journal, beginning with 1998. This process took nearly five months. We obtained data from January 1998 through April 2004 – over six years of data. This is nearly 80 GB of PDF files, or roughly 750 MB of plain text per language. We extracted text using the *pdftotext* program; however this software cannot extract the Greek data set; we were left with data in ten languages, from which 45 possible alignments are possible. Though focused on European topics, the time span is three to ten years after the CLEF 2004 document collection. Though aware of smaller, but aligned parallel data (*e.g.*, Philip Koehn's Europarl corpus [6]) we did not utilize additional data for reasons of homogeneity and convenience.

To align data between two languages, we would:

- convert the data from PDF format to plain text (this introduced some errors, especially when processing diacritical marks in the earlier years);
- apply rules for splitting the text into sections (the data was page-aligned, we desired paragraph-sized chunks);
- and, align files using char_align [1]

To indouce a translation for a given source language term, we proceed by:

- identifying documents (*i.e.*, approximately paragraphs) containing the source language term;
- examining the set of corresponding documents from the target language portion of the aligned collection;
- producing a score for each term that occurs in at least one of the target language paragraphs (more on this below);
- and finally, selecting the single term with the largest translation score for the source language term.

Our method for scoring candidate translations does not require translation model software such as GIZA++. Rather, we rely on information theoretic scores to rank terms. We adopt the same technique we rely on for pseudo relevance feedback – a method we have developed called *affinity sets*. Terms are weighted based on their inverse document frequency (IDF) and the difference between their relative frequency in the set of documents under consideration and the global set of documents. This measure is related to mutual information; however, we believe our technique is more general as it permits the set of documents to be identified through any means, including potentially, query-specific attempts at translation (though we do not attempt this in the experiments we report on here).

We performed pairwise alignments between languages pairs, for example, between Dutch and French. Once aligned, we indexed each pairwise-aligned collection using the technique described for the CLEF 2004 document collections. That is, we created four indexes per sub-collection, per language – one each of words, stems, 4-grams and 5-grams. This year, rather than create a translation dictionary for every term in a source language index, we translated terms on demand using the algorithm presented above. Of course, one could generate multiple translations rather than simply identifying a single one. We have not found this necessary as techniques such as pre-translation query expansion are capable of generating many terms related to a query; thus the harm introduced by a dubious translation is lessened.

We created aligned collections for the following pairs:

- Dutch and French;
- English and Finnish;
- English and French;
- English and Portuguese;
- Spanish and Finnish;
- Spanish and Portuguese;
- French and Finnish;
- and, German and French.

We had envisioned using English as a source language for the multilingual task, but did not produce a submission.

At this point we should mention that the 'proper' translation of an n-gram is decidedly elusive concept –there is typically no single, correct answer. Nonetheless, we simply relied on the large volume of n-grams to smooth topic translation. For example, the central 5-grams of the English phrase 'prime minister' include 'ime_m', 'me_mi', and 'e_min'. The derived 'translations' of these English 5-grams into French are 'er_mi', '_mini', and 'er_mi', respectively. This seems to work as expected for the French phrase 'premier ministre', although the method is not foolproof. Consider n-gram translations from the phrase 'communist party' (parti communiste): '_commu' (mmuna), 'commu' (munau), 'ommun' (munau), 'mmuni' (munau), 'munis' (munis), 'unist' (unist), 'nist_' (unist), 'ist_p' (ist_p), 'st_pa' (1_re_), 't_par' (rtie_), '_part' (_part), 'party' (rtie_), and 'arty_' (rtie_). The word-spanning n-grams in this multiword phrase do not seem to be translated appropriately.

The lexical coverage of translation resources is a critical factor for good CLIR performance, so the fact that almost any n-gram has a 'translation' should improve performance. The direct translation of n-grams may offer a solution to several key obstacles in dictionary-based translation. Word normalization is not essential since sub-word strings will be compared. Translation of multiword expressions can sometimes be approximated by translation of word-spanning n-grams. Out-of-vocabulary words, particularly proper nouns, can be partially translated by common n-gram fragments or left untranslated in close languages.

Our experience on the CLEF 2002 and 2003 bilingual tasks led us to believe that direct translation of 5-grams would likely be the most effective single technique, but that combination using runs generated by translating multiple term types would yield an improvement (see Fig. 2). It was our intent to submit such composite runs for this year's evaluation; however, we could not complete the processing required prior to the submission deadline; it required eight indexes and runs per language pair (48 in total). Instead, we submitted runs for six language pairs using stemmed words as the sole type of token that was translated. We also submitted two runs that made no use of translation whatsoever for the language pairs Spanish to Portuguese and Bulgarian to Russian. We regret to report that we were not able to utilize the Amharic topics.

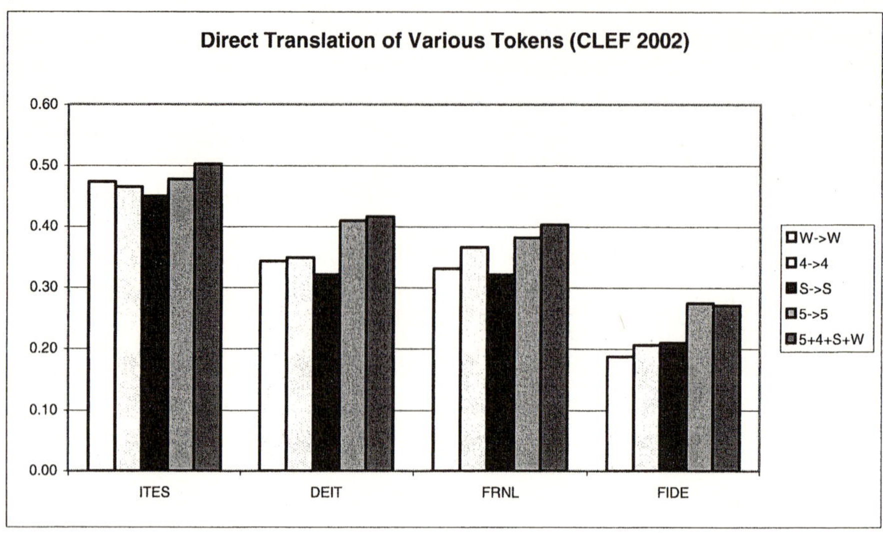

Fig. 2. Relative performance of individual runs using direct translation of words, stems, and n-grams. Fusion of all four yielded the best performance in three of four cases using the CLEF 2002 bilingual test set

The performance of APL's official bilingual runs is summarized in Table 3. A terminal 'a' in the run id indicates the use of translation; a 'b' indicates no translation was attempted. The first six rows report performance against the Finnish, French, and Portuguese sub collections, using two source languages each. For these runs pre-translation expansion was incorporated by using a monolingual run based on 4-grams and stems; from these monolingual runs (against the full source language collection) 60 words were extracted. To produce our bilingual submissions, these words were stemmed and then the stems were translated into corresponding stems using parallel data for the language pair. This expanded, translated query was run against the full target language collection and retrieved documents from the wrong period were omitted.

Table 3. JHU/APL's official results for bilingual task

run id	Terms	MAP	% mono	= Best	>= Median	Rel. Found	Relevant	# topics
aplbidefra	4+s / s	0.3030	66.14	5	28	770	915	49
aplbienpta	4+s / s	0.3414	76.91	10	23	423	678	46
aplbiesfia	4+s / s	0.2982	54.79	17	36	310	413	45
aplbiespta	4+s / s	0.4537	102.08	12	35	546	678	46
aplbifrfia	4+s / s	0.2899	53.26	20	32	322	413	45
aplbinlfra	4+s / s	0.3753	81.93	8	33	845	915	49
aplbibgrub	4	0.1407	45.75	3	18	81	123	34
aplbiesptb	4	0.3825	86.06	9	34	439	678	46

Generally, performance for the Portuguese collection was higher than for the French and Finnish collections. We observed that translation from a very closely related language resulted in exceptional performance; for the Spanish to Portuguese run, we obtained performance 102% of a monolingual Portuguese baseline. We attribute this to the additional query expansion step that occurred (*i.e.,* pre-translation expansion). We also noted that our method of not translating queries between very closely related languages, but relying only on partial n-gram matches (*i.e.,* using 4-grams), was highly effective. This technique was so effective, that Spanish to Portuguese retrieval using 4-grams and no translation (*aplbiesptb*) outperformed translation of English queries (*aplbienpta*). Run *aplbiesptb* did at or better than median on 34 of the 46 topics. Even for language pairs with significant translation resources, language similarity should not be ignored.

We did not have adequate opportunity to develop translation resources for Russian. Thus, we used the Bulgarian topic statements which are also in Cyrillic and hoped 'no-translation' would be effective. We report bilingual retrieval performance 45% of that of a monolingual Russian baseline, which while not as effective as between Spanish and Portuguese, might be serviceable to an end-user.

Fusion of multiple bilingual runs using translation of different token types did, in fact, confer an improvement on this year's data, as it had in previous years. Relative performance increased from between 4% and 33%, depending on the language pair, when runs using words, stems, and 4-grams and 5-grams were combined (see Fig. 3). We observed that the improvement due to this additional fusion seemed inversely proportional to the baseline monolingual performance using our official submissions.

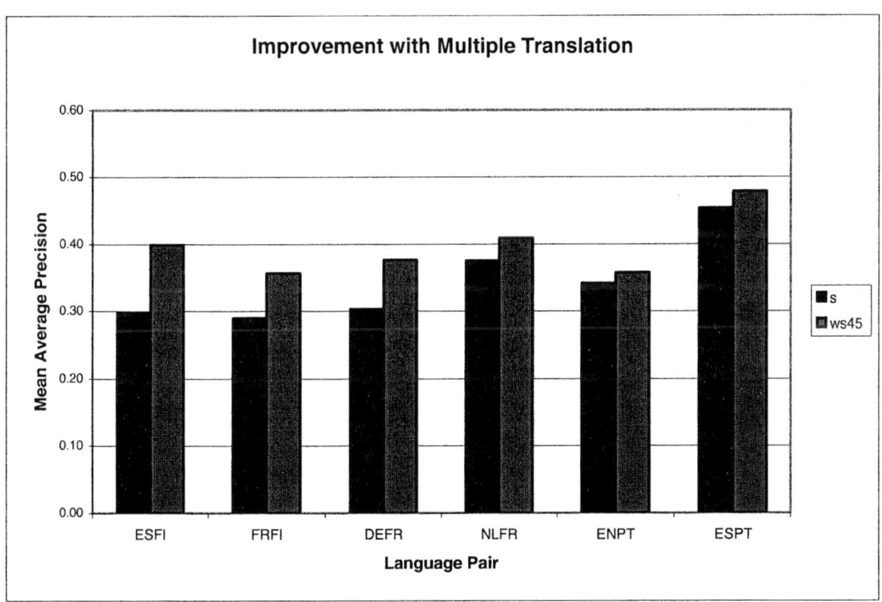

Fig. 3. Improvement observed through combining multiple term translations on the CLEF 2004 Bilingual Task. The improved runs were not official submissions

5 Conclusion

JHU/APL continued its language-neutral approach to multilingual retrieval for the CLEF 2004 evaluation. For monolingual retrieval we compared words, a popular suffix stemmer, and n-grams of lengths four and five, all using the same retrieval engine and language model similarity metric. We found that n-grams continued to perform well for monolingual retrieval; however, their relative advantage compared to ordinary words appeared to be less for the CLEF 2004 data than that previously reported. We continued to combine runs produced through disparate retrievals, which we believe yields a modest improvement.

For bilingual retrieval we used direct translation of n-grams in addition to words and stems. We also found that not translating queries between closely related languages, when n-grams are used, can outperform retrieval with translation from a less similar language, even when large translation resources are available.

We will continue our work in exploring knowledge-light, language neutral approaches for retrieval. We have found the use of character n-grams, pre-translation query expansion, statistical translation using aligned parallel corpora, fusion from disparate retrievals, and reliance on language similarity when resources are scarce, all highly effective. In the future we hope to examine the identification and translation of multi-word phrases to see if such compounds can be used to improve retrieval quality.

References

1. K.W. Church, 'Char_align: A program for aligning parallel texts at the character level.' *Proceedings of the 31st Annual Meeting of the Association for Computational Linguistics*, pp. 1-8, 1993.
2. D. Demner-Fushman and D. W. Oard, 'The effect of bilingual term list size on dictionary-based cross-language information retrieval.' *Proceedings of the 36th Hawaii International Conference on System Sciences*, 2003.
3. M. Franz, J. S. McCarley, T. Ward, and W. Zhu, 'Quantifying the Utility of Parallel Corpora.' *Proceedings of the 24th International ACM SIGIR Conference on Research and Development in Information Retrieval (SIGIR-01)*, pp. 398-399, 2001.
4. D. Hiemstra, *Using Language Models for Information Retrieval.* Ph. D. Thesis, Center for Telematics and Information Technology, The Netherlands, 2000.
5. F. Jelinek and R. Mercer, 'Interpolated Estimation of Markov Source Parameters from Sparse Data'. In Gelsema ES and Kanal LN eds., *Pattern Recognition in Practice*, North Holland, pp. 381-402, 1980.
6. P. Koehn, 'Europarl: A multilingual corpus for evaluation of machine translation.' Unpublished, http://www.isi.edu/ koehn/ publications/europarl/ .
7. P. McNamee and J. Mayfield, 'Comparing Cross-Language Query Expansion Techniques by Degrading Translation Resources'. In the *Proceedings of the 25th Annual International Conference on Research and Development in Information Retrieval*, Tampere, Finland, pp. 159-166, 2002.
8. P. McNamee and J. Mayfield, 'JHU/APL Experiments in Tokenization and Non-Word Translation.' *Working Notes of the CLEF 2003 Workshop*, pp. 19-28, 2003.
9. P. McNamee and J. Mayfield, 'Character N-gram Tokenization for European Language Text Retrieval'. *Information Retrieval*, 7(1-2):73-97, 2004

10. D. Miller, T. Leek, and R. Schwartz, 'A hidden Markov model information retrieval system'. In *Proceedings of the 22nd Annual International ACM SIGIR Conference on Research and Development in Information Retrieval*, Berkeley, California, pp. 214-221, 1999.
11. C. Peters, M. Braschler, G. Di Nunzio, and N. Ferro, 'CLEF 2004: Ad-Hoc Track Overview and Results Analysis.' In this volume.
12. A. Pirkola, T. Hedlund, H. Keskusalo, and K. Järvelin, 'Dictionary-Based Cross-Language Information Retrieval: Problems, Methods, and Research Findings', *Information Retrieval*, 4:209-230, 2001.
13. J. Xu and R. Weischedel, 'Cross-lingual Information Retrieval Using Hidden Markov Models.' In the *Proceedings of the Joint SIGDAT Conference on Empirical Methods in Natural Language Processing and Very Large Corpora (EMNLP/VLC-2000)*, 2000.
14. http://europa.eu.int/

Experiments on Statistical Approaches to Compensate for Limited Linguistic Resources

G.M. Di Nunzio, N. Ferro, and N. Orio

Department of Information Engineering, University of Padua
{dinunzio, nf76,orio}@dei.unipd.it

Abstract. Information Retrieval systems can benefit from advanced linguistic resources when carrying out tasks such as word-stemming or query translation. The main goal of our experiments has been the development of methodologies that minimize the human labor needed for creating linguistic resources for new languages. For this purpose, we have applied statistical techniques to extract information directly from the collections.

1 Introduction

We participated in the monolingual of CLEF 2004 track using a Hidden Markov Model approach for stemmer generation. Our main objective was to study the problem of managing two completely unknown and, for us, non-understandable languages like Finnish and Russian. Building on our experience gained in the campaign of the previous year, we also participated in the bilingual track (German-to-French) to test a new solution for the problem of query expansion/translation from one language to another, especially when linguistic resources are low.

2 Monolingual Track Experiments

The main goal of our monolingual experiments has been the development of methodologies and techniques that do not require, or minimize, the human labor needed when applying information retrieval (IR) techniques to new languages. In this respect, languages such as Finnish and Russian are particularly suitable because they are very different from the languages known by the members of our research group – i.e. Italian, French, and obviously English. French can be considered as a reference language for comparing the system performances.

We focused our attention on the development and test of stemming algorithms, the component of an information retrieval system (IRS) which is most related to the structure of a given language. With the goal of minimizing manual work, we continuedin this evaluation campaign the development of a set of stemmers based on Hidden Markov Models (HMMs). According to our approach, HMMs do not require any previous knowledge about the morphology of the language to be stemmed and can be trained simply using a set of words automatically extracted from the test collection.

C. Peters et al. (Eds.): CLEF 2004, LNCS 3491, pp. 60–72, 2005.

2.1 Hidden Markov Models to Generate Words

Hidden Markov Models (HMMs) are finite-state automata where transitions between states are ruled by probability functions [5]. At each transition, the new state emits a symbol with a given probability. HMMs are called *hidden* because states cannot be directly observed; only the symbols they emit can be observed. The parameters that completely define an HMM are, for each state: the probability of being the initial or the final state, the probabilities of transition to any other state, and the probability of emitting a given symbol.

HMMs are particularly suitable to model processes that are unknown but can be observed through a sequence of symbols. For instance, the sequence of letters that forms a word in a given language can be considered as a sequence of symbols emitted by an HMM. The HMM starts in an initial state and performs a sequence of transitions between states emitting a new letter at each transition, until it stops in a final state. In general, several state sequences, or *paths*, can correspond to a single word. It is possible to compute the probability of each path, and hence to compute the most probable path corresponding to a word. This problem is addressed as *decoding* and solved using the Viterbi algorithm.

In order to apply HMMs to the stemming problem, a sequence of letters that forms a word can be considered the result of a concatenation of two subsequences: a prefix and a suffix. A way to model this process is through an HMM where states are divided in two disjoint sets: states in the *stem-set* generate the first part of the word and states in the *suffix-set* generate the last part, if the word has a suffix. For many Indo-European languages, there are some assumptions that can be made on the model: 1) Initial states belong only to the stem-set – a word always starts with a stem; 2) Transitions from states of the suffix-set to states of the stem-set always have a null probability – a word can be only a concatenation of a stem and a suffix; 3) Final states belong to both sets – a stem can have a number of different derivations, but it may also have no suffix.

Once a complete HMM is available for a given language, stemming can be carried out straightforwardly considering a word as a sequence of symbols emitted by the HMM. As a first step, the most probable path that corresponds to the observed word is computed using decoding. The analysis of this path highlights the transition from a state of the stem-set to a state of the suffix-set. We call this transition the *split-point*. If there is no split-point then the word has no suffix, otherwise the sequence of letters observed before the split-point is taken as the stem and the one observed after it is taken as the suffix.

2.2 Training the HMM

The proposed topology defines the number of states, their labels indicating the sets to which they belong, the initial and final states, and the allowable transitions. Yet all the probability functions that constitute the HMM parameters need to be computed. The computation of these parameters is normally achieved through *training*, which is based on the Expectation-Maximization (EM) [5] algorithm. It is important to stress that our goal is to develop fully automatic stemmers that do not require previous manual work. This means that we con-

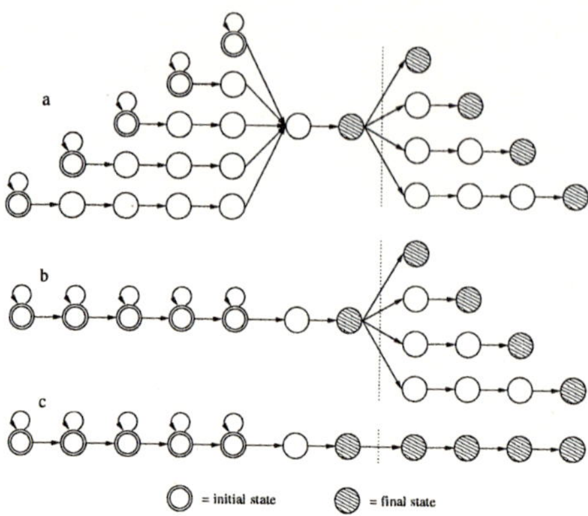

Fig. 1. Three topologies of the HMM that have been tested

sider that neither a formalization of morphological rules nor a training set of manually stemmed words is available.

We propose to perform an unsupervised training of the HMM using only a sample of the words of the considered language. The training set can be built at random by documents that are available at indexing time. It can be noted that an unsupervised training does not guarantee that the split-point of the most probable path has a direct relationship with the stem and the suffix of a given word. In order to create such a relationship, we add some more knowledge about the general rules for the creation of word inflections. Thus, we make the reasonable assumption that, for each language, the number of different suffixes is limited compared to the number of different stems. Suffixes are a set of letter sequences that can be modelled by chains of states of the HMM. This assumption suggests a particular topology for the states in the suffix-set, which can be made by a number of state chains with different lengths, where: transitions from the stem-set are allowed only to the first state of each chain; the transition from one state to the next has probability one; each chain terminates with a final state. The maximum length of state chains gives the maximum length of a possible suffix. Analogously, also the stem-set topology can be modelled by a number of state chains, with the difference that a state can have non-zero self-transition probability. The minimum length of a chain gives the minimum length of a stem. Some examples of topologies for the suffix-set are depicted in Figure 1, where the maximum length of a suffix is set to four letters, and the minimum length of a stem is set to three letters.

After the redefinition of the suffix-set topology, the HMM can be trained using the EM algorithm on a set of words. Given the previous assumption, it is likely that a sequence of letters that corresponds to a suffix will be frequently present in the training set. For this reason, the EM algorithm will assign a higher probability of emitting the letters of frequent suffixes to the states in the suffix-set. For example, considering the suffix-set chains, the state in the one-state chain will emit the last letter of each word with the highest probability, the states in the two-states chain will respectively emit the most frequent couple of ending letters of each word, and so on. Once the model has been trained, for each word the corresponding path that terminates with the most frequent sequence of letters is expected to have a high probability of being selected as the most probable path, giving a correct stemming of the word.

The STON Algorithm. We developed an algorithm, named STON, to test the methodology and the variations in retrieval effectiveness depending on some of its parameters. STON receives as input a sequence of letters corresponding to a word and gives as output the position of the split-point. As explained in the previous sections, STON needs to be trained off-line using a subset of the words of the collection. Stemming can then be carried out on-line for any new word, also for words that are not present in the training set. The algorithm can be divided in three main steps:

1. *Training/off-line*: given a set of words $w \in W_L$, taken from a collection of documents written in a language L, and an HMM with parameters λ which define the number of states and the set of allowable transitions, STON computes through the Expectation-Maximization algorithm: $\lambda_L^* = \arg\max_\lambda \prod_{w \in W_L} Pr(w \mid \lambda)$.
2. *Decoding/on-line*: given a word w_L, written in language L, and a trained model λ_L, STON computes the most probable path q across the states corresponding to w_L by Viterbi decoding: $q^* = \arg\max_q Pr(q \mid w_L, \lambda_L)$.
3. *Stemming/on-line*: once the most probable path q^* for word w_L is computed using model λ_L, the split-point can be computed by a simple inspection of the path, i.e. when the state sequence enters the suffix-set.

3 Bilingual Track Experiments

The main goal of our bilingual experiments was to test the effectiveness of an IRS when advanced tools for query or document translations are not available. This situation applies each time an existing IRS has to be extended to a set of new languages, when it is not possible to acquire reliable translators for each language couple – or for each language from/to a single language (e.g. English). It may even be the case that advanced translators are completely unavailable from/to languages that are spoken by a reduced amount of the world population – or that are spoken in countries where economic and technological growth is still slow. We argue that an IRS should have reasonable performance even when linguistic resources are minimal.

In our approach we only considered simple word-by-word translations, such as the ones provided by most of the free translation services on the Web, as tools for the bilingual experiments in the evaluation campaign. As is well known, word-by-word translations have a number of drawbacks, mainly due to the absence of a context for word disambiguation and because of the need to deal with synonyms and antonyms. Clearly these drawbacks can have a negative impact on the performance of a bilingual IRS. In order to obtain a base translator, we used the Web translation service offered by the Google Web search engine, using the translation of single words in order to not take advantage of the possible use of linguistic cues by the Google translator. It should be noted that this choice imposed an additional constraint, there was no control on the size of the vocabulary.

The methodology that we propose to partially overcome the problems arising from a simple word-to-word translator is based on the use of two collections, the one in the language of the topic and the one in the language of the relevant documents. The source collection is used to expand the query terms that are to be translated. The methodology is presented in the following sections.

3.1 Almost Comparable Corpora

There has been extensive research on the combination of documents collections written in different languages for bilingual information retrieval. Usually the assumption is that two collections of documents, written in two different languages, allow the coupling of documents. The two collections are normally referred to as *parallel corpora* [4] when they can be exactly aligned. This may be the case of transcriptions of legal documents for bilingual countries such as Canada, or when one collection is the translation (made by human experts) of the other one. The two collections are normally referred as *comparable corpora* [6] when documents are independently written in the two languages, but it is possible to couple a subset of the documents, which have the same topic. The coupling can be done using external information such as metadata. An example of this situation is a bi- or multilingual newspaper, where news articles that are potentially of interest for the whole population are independently written in all of the languages, while more local news is reported in articles written in only one language; the GIRT collection, which is available for this evaluation campaign, can be considered an example of comparable corpora.

Unfortunately, parallel and/or comparable corpora are not available for all language couples. Yet there are a number of collections written in different languages that, though not really comparable, have documents that share similar subjects. As an example, we can considered the collections of news articles used for the CLEF campaign. Newspapers in Europe are independently written, yet there are a number of events, for instance of political, social, or economic nature, that are of interest for most European citizens. These events are likely to be the subject of a set of news articles in all of the different newspapers. Clearly, the number of news articles that each newspaper dedicates to a given subject may dramatically vary, depending on political choices, on the locality of the event, and so on. Also the time span in which a given subject is treated can be different. In any case, it is likely that important events give rise to *threads* of news articles, and that threads in different languages can be coupled. We refer to this situation as *almost comparable corpora*.

3.2 Automatic Thread Identification

We propose to use news threads in almost comparable corpora to improve the performance of a bilingual IRS. In particular, if we assume that a topic has been the subject of threads in both the source and the target languages, the automatic identification of a thread in the former can help to retrieve relevant documents in the latter.

The first step in our methodology hence regards the automatic identification of news threads in the source language. We propose to apply *hierarchical clustering* [3] to the documents retrieved by querying a monolingual IRS using the topic of interest. To reduce computational load, clustering is applied only to the first K retrieved documents, that is the ones which are potentially more relevant to the topic. The distance measure used to highlight clusters is based on the classic $tf \times idf$ weighting scheme and computed using the cosine of the angle between retrieved documents. The *inverse document frequency idf* used to calculate the distance between documents is not the same as the original *idf* computed in the first retrieval. The new inverse document frequency is computed on the first K documents chosen for the query expansion. With this approach we try to discover those words less frequent in the first K documents that may give an added value to the ones of the original query.

The clustering step gives a partition of the set of retrieved documents. We made the assumption that clusters are strictly correlated to news threads. The choice of the most relevant threads for the topic can be based on different strategies. For instance, threads with highest average rank can be chosen, as well as threads that contain the documents with the top 5 or top 10 documents. In our experiments, we chose to select only one thread, the one that contained the document with the highest rank, and to stop the clustering step when the number of clusters is 10 or the present distance between documents belonging to different clusters is less than 0.9. This choice allows us to get a good agglomeration of documents without forcing documents or clusters that are distant, in the sense of the cosine angle, for each other to merge together. On the other hand, it is possible that the cluster that contains the document with the highest rank consists of only that document.

3.3 Topic Translation

Once the potentially most relevant thread in the source language has been highlighted, it can be used to retrieve potentially relevant documents in the target language. We are still investigating the possibility of directly coupling threads in the source and the target languages. For the purpose of the present evaluation campaign, our interest was more focused on the use of thread identification to partially overcome the drawbacks of simple word-by-word translators.

We thus applied query expansion techniques to the topic in the source language, by enriching the bag of words of the topic with a set of words taken from the highlighted thread. In particular, we chose to add words that were more discriminating of the thread, that is the ones with high average tf inside the thread and high *idf* inside the set of retrieved documents. It is likely that this additional set of words gives a more complete description of the topic of interest, and also that it contains synonyms of the words in the topic that may allow for a more effective translation.

This expanded set of words can be translated word-by-word, possibly applying stemming, to obtain a set of tokens to be used by an IRS in the target language. The resulting ranked list of documents can be taken as the final result of a run on a given topic. Moreover, the same principle of thread identification can be applied to the target language, in order to rerank the documents according to the threads to which they are potentially relevant. Threads are then highlighted in both source and target language, a coupling between threads might help to refine the results of the run. These steps have not been investigated in detail yet, and are left as future work.

3.4 The Thread-Based Algorithm

According to the methodology outlined above, we developed an algorithm that has been implemented in our IRS. The main step can be described as follows.

1. The topic in the source language is used to query an IRS in the same language. A ranked list of potentially relevant documents is obtained. At this step stemming can be carried out on the source language to possibly improve the performance of the IRS.
2. The first K documents, where K is an integer that has been tested within the range $50 \leq K \leq 100$, are used as the initial set of singletons for hierarchical clustering. The distance between pairs of documents is computed as the cosine of the angle between documents.
3. The merging of clusters stops when the number of created clusters is 10 or when the current distance between documents is 0.9. The cluster that contains the top ranked document is taken as the news thread that is most likely to be relevant to the topic in the source language.
4. The H words that are good candidates to improve query translation are used to expand the initial query in the source language, obtaining an extended set of tokens. A maximum of 10 words for the title of the query and 100 words for the description of the query have been used to expand queries during tests. The algorithm for choosing these words is described in the following section.
5. All the tokens in the extended set are translated singly, using an on-line translation Web service, obtaining an extended set of translated tokens. These tokens are added to the word-by-word translation of the topic in the source language. We used the Google translation Web service.
6. All of the tokens in the target language are used to query an IRS in the same target language. Also at this step, stemming can be carried out in order to improve the system performances.

Finding Good Candidate Words of a Cluster. Once the news *thread* has been found in the first K retrieved documents, how do we choose the words that are going to expand the original query? We propose the following approach: we use a (tf $\times$ idf)-like weighting scheme to weight terms of a cluster. In particular, we consider the documents of the cluster as boolean vectors, thus we do not make an explicit use of term frequency. For each word w we count how many documents contain w and name it *cluster frequency* CF, and use it in a (tf $\times$ idf)-like formula.

The following steps describe the algorithm used to choose the terms of the cluster. The algorithm is repeated both for the words of the title of a document and the words of the body of a document. In this way, we can add specific title terms to the title of the query, and specific body terms to the description or narrative of a query.

1. Get the cluster that contains the first ranked document in the original retrieval; let N be the number of documents of the cluster, and n be the number of documents in which the word w appears.
2. Let the *Cluster Frequency* CF of w be equal to n, and let *relative Cluster Frequency* rCF be n/N.
3. Calculate the weight of each word as the product $(1+log(CF))\times(-log(rCF))$.
4. At this point, cluster words according to their weights, that is to say create sets of words with the same weights and order these sets by decreasing order.
5. Add the first set of terms to the query; continue to add sets of words until the number of words that has been added exceeds a predefined threshold.

4 Experiments

We ran a set of experiments in both the monolingual and bilingual tracks using a prototype system that has been developed in our research group. The experimental information retrieval system, called IRON (Information Retrieval ON) was used for the first time in the CLEF 2002 evaluation campaign; it was completely re-engineered for CLEF 2003, and has been further expanded for CLEF 2004 to support different character sets and to include the proposed approach for news thread identification.

IRON is a java multi-threaded program, which provides IR functionalities and enables concurrent indexing and searching of document collections for both monolingual and bilingual tracks. It provides a modular environment suitable for testing the performance of different IR components, and allowing us to easily plug-in the components under examination, such as lexical analyzers (lexers) or stemmers, at runtime. IRON consists of the following components: a Lexer, an IR engine, a Monolingual Track Manager, a Bilingual Track Manager, and a Logger. IRON is partnered with two other tools: WebIRON, a Java Servlet based Web interface, and IRON-SAT, a Matlab program that interacts with IRON in order to carry the statistical analysis of the experimental results.

A description of the experimental results is presented in the following sections.

4.1 Monolingual Experiments

The aim of the experiments for the monolingual track was to compare the retrieval effectiveness of the language independent stemmer, illustrated in Section 2, with that of an algorithm based on a-priori linguistic knowledge – we have chosen the widely used Porter's stemmers. The hypothesis was that the proposed probabilistic approach generates stemmers that perform as effectively as Porter's stemmers. In order to evaluate stemming algorithms, we have compared the performances of different IR systems by only changing the stemming algorithms for different runs, all other things being equal. Our aim was to test the following hypotheses: H' – stemming does not hurt and can enhance the effectiveness of retrieval, H'' – the proposed statistical stemmers perform as effectively as those of Porter. Experiments were conducted for the following languages: Finnish, French, and Russian. For each track the following stemming algorithms were tested:

- **No Stem**: no stemming algorithm was applied;
- **Porter**: the stemming algorithms freely available at the Snowball Web site edited by Martin Porter for different languages have been used. Russian is an exception, because the java implementation for the Russian stemmer seems not to properly process Unicode strings and so we were unable to produce runs with this stemmer;
- **STON**: the stemming algorithm based on HMMs has been used.

Tables 1 and 1 report the general figures for the 2004 monolingual topics. Both these tables show that stemming improves all the performances figures for all the considered languages. These figures thus give a positive answer to both hypotheses H' and H'' because stemming improves the performance of an IRS. Moreover, the experimental evidence confirms the hypothesis that it is possible to generate stemmers using probabilistic models without or with very little knowledge about the language. However the degree to which the observed differences are significant has to be measured using statistical testing methods. We used the Wilcoxon signed ranks test [2], which is a non parametric statistical test for paired samples. The runs have been compared query-by-query using the same figures reported in Table 1 with a significance level $\alpha = 5\%$.

Tables 2 and 3 allow us to answer question H' for both Porter and STON. For Finnish, the Porter stemmer exhibits an impact on the performances for all the considered measures; STON shows significant differences with respect to the case of no stemming in terms of number of relevant retrieved documents, but not for the other measures. For French, both stemmers show significant differences with respect to the case of no stemming in terms of number of relevant retrieved documents and average precision. Finally for Russian, STON shows significant differences with respect to the case of no stemming in terms of number of relevant retrieved documents, but not for the other measures. Thus, in general, the hypothesis that stemming influences the performances of an IRS cannot be rejected. The impact of the stemming depends on both the language and the measure considered . Table 4 allows us to answer to hypothesis H'' for the

Table 1. General figures for 2004 monolingual topics

(a) Relevant retrieved document number (recall)

Algorithm	Relevant Retrieved (Recall %)		
	Finnish	French	Russian
No Stem	258 (62.46)	763 (83.38)	82 (66.66)
STON	305 (73.84)	809 (88.41)	94 (76.42)
Porter	346 (83.77)	832 (90.92)	–
Total Relevant Docs	413	915	123

(b) Precision

Algorithm	Average Precision (%)			Exact R-Precision (%)		
	Finnish	French	Russian	Finnish	French	Russian
No Stem	39.62	38.64	28.40	36.12	38.64	28.45
STON	40.70	41.53	34.06	36.75	39.55	30.56
Porter	46.31	42.53	–	43.71	38.71	–

Table 2. Comparison of monolingual No Stem and Porter runs for different measures

Measure		Finnish	French	Russian
Rel. Retr.	No Stem > Porter	0	1	–
	No Stem = Porter	34	33	–
	No Stem < Porter	11	15	–
	Signed Rank Test (p–value)	0.10%	0.08%	–
Avg. Prec.	No Stem > Porter	12	14	–
	No Stem = Porter	10	5	–
	No Stem < Porter	23	30	–
	Signed Rank Test (p–value)	3.06%	0.53%	–
Exact R-Prec.	No Stem > Porter	7	8	–
	No Stem = Porter	22	28	–
	No Stem < Porter	16	13	–
	Signed Rank Test (p–value)	4.97%	49.79%	–

STON algorithm. The results show that in general the hypothesis that STON is as effective as Porter's algorithm cannot be rejected. However, for Finnish and French there are significant differences between STON and Porter's stemmers in terms of number of relevant retrieved documents, where Porter's algorithm performed better than STON.

4.2 Bilingual Experiments

As soon as we received the results for the CLEF bilingual track, we discovered an anomalous behavior of the system. In particular, some of the translated queries were completely empty. We found the error in the following point: when a word is translated from German to French, an apostrophe may appear. Since IRON

Table 3. Comparison of monolingual No Stem and STON runs for different measures

Measure		Finnish	French	Russian
Rel. Retr.	No Stem > STON	1	3	0
	No Stem = STON	35	34	25
	No Stem < STON	9	12	9
	Signed Rank Test (p–value)	1.37%	0.54%	0.39%
Avg. Prec.	No Stem > STON	17	14	11
	No Stem = STON	10	5	7
	No Stem < STON	18	30	16
	Signed Rank Test (p–value)	65.83%	2.15%	6.79%
Exact R-Prec.	No Stem > STON	8	8	2
	No Stem = STON	25	25	27
	No Stem < STON	12	16	5
	Signed Rank Test (p–value)	56.28%	20.86%	57.81%

Table 4. Comparison of monolingual STON and Porter runs for different measures

		Finnish	French	Russian
Rel. Retr.	STON > Porter	2	1	–
	STON = Porter	36	40	–
	STON < Porter	7	8	–
	Signed Rank Test (p–value)	1.95%	2.73%	–
Avg. Prec.	STON > Porter	15	20	–
	STON = Porter	9	5	–
	STON < Porter	21	24	–
	Signed Rank Test (p–value)	11.44%	19.92%	–
Exact R-Prec.	STON > Porter	7	11	–
	STON = Porter	24	31	–
	STON < Porter	14	7	–
	Signed Rank Test (p–value)	10.59%	51.35%	–

reads a query with the `StreamTokenizer` Java class, we discovered that this class contains a method (namely `quoteChar()`) that is used when a quote character is encountered. If a string quote character (in our case the apostrophe) is encountered, then a *quotation* string is recognized, consisting of all characters after the string quote character, up to the next occurrence of that same string quote character, or a line terminator, or end of file. This causes IRON to discard parts of (or even whole) queries and consequently to perform badly (around 13% of average precision). When the error was fixed the general performances of the system improved significantly (up to 23% of average precision).

Table 5 presents the correct results of the bilingual track. As can be noted, this time the differences between stem and no-stem is very subtle. Also the difference between using the first 50 or the first 100 documents is small, although the runs using the first 50 documents obtain a better recall than those using the

Table 5. General figures for bilingual German → French

Algorithm	Recall %	Avg. Prec. (%)	Exact R-Prec. (%)
No Stem, first 50 docs	61.85	22.15	21.38
No Stem, first 100 docs	56.50	22.25	21.57
STON, first 50 docs	61.20	22.50	22.36
STON, first 100 docs	53.11	22.41	21.92
Porter, first 50 docs	63.38	23.17	23.00
Porter, first 100 docs	53.22	22.83	22.73
Total Relevant Docs	915	–	–

first 100 documents. We performed the same statistical analysis as described in the previous section, but it does not give any significative difference between stem and no stem, and between using 50 or 100 documents for clustering. There is an exception to this general trend: Porter, first 50 docs, shows a better average precision ($p = 3.57\%$) than No Stem, first 50 docs.

5 Conclusions and Future Work

The idea of minimizing human labor and computing resources was the main point of the many experiments that were carried out this year by the IMS research group. The automatic stemmer generation using Hidden Markov Models was confirmed as a valid alternative to language dependent stemmers such as Porter's. Statistical tests on the monolingual track gave evidence against rejecting the hypothesis that, in general, STON is as effective as Porter's algorithm and that stemming does not hurt and can even enhance retrieval performances. Automatic identification of news threads together with hierarchical clustering was used for query expansion/translation for the bilingual track, results are encouraging. Further experiments and refinements may make performances obtained with this approach comparable to state-of-the-art systems.

References

1. Di Nunzio, G. M., Ferro, N., Melucci, M. and Orio, N.: The University of Padova at CLEF 2003: Experiments to Evaluate Probabilistic Models for Automatic Stemmer Generation and Query Word Translation. In Peters, C., ed.: Working Notes for the CLEF 2003 Workshop, pp. 211–223, 2003.
2. Gibbons, J. D.: Nonparametric Statistical Inference. Marcel Dekker, Inc., New York, USA, 2nd edition, 1985.
3. Johnson, S. C.: Hierarchical Clustering Schemes. Psychometrika, 32, pp. 241–254, 1967.
4. Nie, J.-Y., Simard, M., Isabelle, P. and Durand, R.: Cross-language Information Retrieval Based on Parallel Texts and Automatic Mining of Parallel Texts from the Web. Proc. of the 22nd ACM SIGIR Conference, pp. 74–81, Berkeley, CA, 1999.

5. Rabiner, L. and Juang, B. H.: Fundamentals of speech recognition. Prentice Hall, Englewood Cliffs, NJ, pp. 321–389, 1993.
6. Sheridan, P. and Ballerini, J. P.: Experiments in Multilingual Information Retrieval Using the SPIDER System. Proc. of the 19th ACM SIGIR Conference, pp. 58–65, Zurich, Switzerland, 1996.

Application of Variable Length *N*-Gram Vectors to Monolingual and Bilingual Information Retrieval

Daniel Gayo-Avello, Darío Álvarez-Gutiérrez, and José Gayo-Avello

Department of Informatics, University of Oviedo, Calvo Sotelo
s/n 33007 Oviedo Spain
dani@uniovi.es

Abstract. Our group in the Department of Informatics at the University of Oviedo has participated, for the first time, in two tasks at CLEF: monolingual (Russian) and bilingual (Spanish-to-English) information retrieval. Our main goal was to test the application to IR of a modified version of the *n*-gram vector space model (codenamed blindLight). This new approach has been successfully applied to other NLP tasks such as language identification or text summarization and the results achieved at CLEF 2004, although not exceptional, are encouraging. There are two major differences between the blindLight approach and classical techniques: (1) relative frequencies are no longer used as vector weights but are replaced by n-gram significances, and (2) cosine distance is abandoned in favor of a new metric inspired by sequence alignment techniques, not so computationally expensive. In order to perform cross-language IR we have developed a naive n-gram pseudo-translator similar to those described by McNamee and Mayfield or Pirkola *et al.*

1 Introduction

The vector model is a classic approach in text retrieval [1]. In this model any document (or query) can be represented as a vector of terms and, thus, the similarity between text objects can be determined by a distance in the vector space (often, the cosine of the angle between the vectors). This model does not specify how to set vector weights although there are common elements to any term weighting approach: (1) term weight within a particular document, (2) term weight within the document corpus and, (3) document length normalization. Index terms are usually words or word stems, although *n*-grams have been also successfully used (e.g., D'Amore and Mah [2] or Kimbrell [3]).

Although this model is widely used it shows two major drawbacks. First, since documents are represented by *D* dimensional vectors of weights, where *D* is the total amount of different terms in the whole document set, such vectors are not document representations by themselves but representations according to a bigger, potentially growing, "contextual" corpus. Secondly, cosine similarities (the metric most often used) between high dimensional vectors tend to be zero[1], so, to avoid this "curse of

[1] That is, two random documents have a high probability of being orthogonal to each other.

C. Peters et al. (Eds.): CLEF 2004, LNCS 3491, pp. 73–82, 2005.

dimensionality" problem it is necessary to reduce the number of features (i.e. terms). When using *n*-grams, this is usually done by setting arbitrary weight thresholds.

blindLight is a new approach differing in two aspects from the classical vector space model: (1) every document is assigned to a unique document vector with no regards to any corpus (so, in fact, there is no vector space!) and, (2), another measure, suitable to compare different length vectors is used.

2 Foundations of the blindLight Approach

blindLight, like other *n*-gram vector space solutions, maps every document to a vector of weights; however, such document vectors are rather different from classical ones. On the one hand, any two document vectors obtained through this technique are not necessarily of equal dimensions, thus, there is no actual "vector space" in this proposal. On the other hand, weights used in these vectors are not relative frequencies but represent the significance of each *n*-gram within the document.

Computing a measure of the relation between elements inside *n*-grams, and thus the importance of the whole *n*-gram, is a problem with a long history of research, however, we will focus on just a few references. In 1993 Dunning described a method based on likelihood ratio tests to detect keywords and domain-specific terms [4]. However, his technique worked only for word bigrams. Later Ferreira da Silva and Pereira Lopes [5] presented a generalization of different statistical measures so that these could be applied to arbitrary length word *n*-grams. In addition to this, they also introduced a new measure, Symmetrical Conditional Probability [6] (equations 1 and 2 where $(w_1...w_n)$ is an *n*-gram), which overcomes other statistically-based measures. According to Pereira Lopes, their approach obtains better results than those achieved by Dunning.

blindLight implements the technique described by da Silva and Lopes although applied to character *n*-grams rather than word *n*-grams. It measures the relations between characters inside each *n*-gram and, thus, measures the significance of every *n*-gram or, what is the same, the weight for the components in a document vector.

$$Avp = \frac{1}{n-1} \sum_{i=1}^{i=n-1} p(w_1...w_i) \cdot p(w_{i+1}...w_n) \tag{1}$$

$$SCP\_f((w_1...w_n)) = \frac{p(w_1...w_n)^2}{Avp} \tag{2}$$

With regard to comparisons between vectors, a simple similarity measure such as the cosine distance cannot be straightforwardly applied when using vectors of different dimensions. Of course, it could be considered as a temporary vector space of dimension d_1+d_2, with d_1 and d_2 the respective dimensions of the document vectors to be compared, assigning a null weight to the *n*-grams of one vector that are not present in the other and vice versa. However, we consider the absence of a particular *n*-gram within a document as distinct from its presence with null significance.

Eventually, comparing two vectors with different dimensions can be seen as a pairwise alignment problem. There are two sequences with different lengths and some (or none) elements in common that must be aligned, that is, the highest number of columns of identical pairs must be obtained by only inserting gaps, changing or deleting elements in both sequences.

One of the simplest models of distance for pairwise alignment is the so-called Levenshtein or edit distance [7] which can be defined as the smallest number of insertions, deletions, and substitutions required to change one string into another (e.g. the distance between `"accommodate"` and `"aconmodate"` is 2).

However, there are two noticeable differences between pairwise-alignning text strings and comparing different length vectors, no matter that the previous ones can be seen as vectors of characters. The first difference is important, namely, the order of components is central in pairwise alignment (e.g., DNA analysis or spell checking) while unsuitable within a vector-space model. The second is also highly significant: although not taking into account the order of the components, "weights" in pairwise alignment are integer values while in vector-space models they are real.

Thus, distance functions for pairwise alignment, although inspiring, cannot be applied to the problem under examination. Instead, a new distance measure is needed and, in fact, two are provided. Classical vector-space based approaches assume that the distance, and so the similarity, between two document vectors is commutative (e.g., cosine distance). blindLight, however, proposes two similarity measures when comparing document vectors. For the sake of clarity, we will call them the query (Q) and target (T) documents although these similarity functions can be equally applied to any pair of documents, not only for information retrieval purposes.

Let Q and T be two blindLight document vectors with dimensions m and n:

$$Q = \{(k_{1Q}, w_{1Q}) \ (k_{2Q}, w_{2Q}) \ \ldots \ (k_{mQ}, w_{mQ})\} \tag{3}$$

$$T = \{(k_{1T}, w_{1T}) \ (k_{2T}, w_{2T}) \ \ldots \ (k_{nT}, w_{nT})\} \tag{4}$$

k_{ij} is the i-th n-gram in document j while w_{ij} is the significance (computed using SCP [6]) of the n-gram k_{ij} within the same document j.

We define the total significance for document vectors Q and T, S_Q and S_T respectively, as:

$$S_Q = \sum_{i=1}^{m} w_{iQ} \tag{5}$$

$$S_T = \sum_{i=1}^{n} w_{iT} \tag{6}$$

Then, the pseudo-alignment operator, Ω, is defined as follows:

$$Q\Omega T = \left\{ (k_x, w_x) \middle/ \begin{array}{l} (k_x = k_{iQ} = k_{jT}) \wedge (w_x = \min(w_{iQ}, w_{jT})), \\ (k_{iQ}, w_{iQ}) \in Q, 0 \le i < m, \\ (k_{jT}, w_{jT}) \in T, 0 \le j < n \end{array} \right\} \tag{7}$$

Similarly to equations 5 and 6 we can define the total significance for $Q\Omega T$:

$$S_{Q\Omega T} = \sum w_{iQ\Omega T} \tag{8}$$

Finally, we can define two similarity measures, one to compare Q vs. T, Π (uppercase Pi), and a second one to compare T vs. Q, P (uppercase Rho), which can be seen as analogous to precision and recall measures:

$$\Pi = S_{Q\Omega T} / S_Q \tag{9}$$

$$\mathrm{P} = S_{Q\Omega T} / S_T \tag{10}$$

To clarify these concepts we will show a simple example based on (one of) the shortest stories ever written. We will compare the original version of Monterroso's Dinosaur with a Portuguese translation; the first one will play the query role and the second one the target, the n-grams will be quad-grams.

Cuando despertó, el dinosaurio todavía estaba allí. (Query)

Quando acordou, o dinossauro ainda estava lá. (Target)

Fig. 1. "El dinosaurio" by Augusto Monterroso, Spanish original and Portuguese translation

Q vector (45 elements)

n-gram	weight
Cuan	2.489
l_di	2.392
stab	2.392
...	
saur	2.313
desp	2.313
...	
ndo_	2.137
nosa	2.137
...	
ando	2.012
avía	1.945
_all	1.915

T vector (39 elements)

n-gram	weight
va_l	2.545
rdou	2.323
stav	2.323
...	
saur	2.244
noss	2.177
...	
a_lá	2.022
o_ac	2.022
...	
auro	1.908
ando	1.876
do_a	1.767

QΩT (10 elements)

n-gram	weight
saur	2.244
inos	2.177
uand	2.119
_est	2.091
dino	2.022
_din	2.022
esta	2.012
ndo_	1.981
a_es	1.943
ando	1.876

Π: 0.209 P: 0.253

Fig. 2. blindLight document vectors for both documents in Fig.1 (truncated to show ten elements, blanks have been replaced by underscores). QΩT intersection vector is shown plus Π and P values indicating the similarities between both documents

So, the blindLight technique, although vector-based, does not need a predefined document collection and thus, it can perform IR over ever-growing document sets. Relative frequencies are abandoned as vector weights in favor of a measure of the importance of each n-gram. In addition to this, similarity measures are analogous to those used in pairwise-alignment although computationally inexpensive and, also, non commutative which allows us to "tune" both measures, Π and P, into any linear combination.

3 Information Retrieval Using blindLight

blindLight has been used to extract key phrases and summaries from single documents [8] and to perform language identification and classification of natural languages [9]. At this moment we are interested in the evaluation of this technique applied to information retrieval; this is the reason why we developed a "quick and dirty" prototype to take part in CLEF 2004.

As with any other application of blindLight, a similarity measure to compare queries and documents is needed. At this moment just two have been tested: Π and a more complex one (see equation 11) which provides rather satisfactory results.

$$\frac{\Pi + norm(\Pi \mathrm{P})}{2} \tag{11}$$

The goal of the *norm* function shown in previous equation is just to translate the range of $\Pi \cdot P$ values into the range of Π values, thus making possible a comprehensive combination of both (otherwise, P, and thus $\Pi \cdot$P values, are negligible when compared to Π).

The operation of the blindLight IR system is really simple:

- For each document in the database an *n*-gram vector is obtained and stored.
- When a query is submitted to the system this computes an *n*-gram vector and compares it with every document obtaining Π and P values.
- From these values a ranking measure is worked out, and a reverse ordered list of documents is returned as a response to the query.

This way of operation has both advantages and disadvantages: documents may be added to the database at any moment because there is no indexing process; however, comparing a query with every document in the database can be rather time consuming and not feasible with very large datasets. In order to reduce the number of document-to-query comparisons a clustering phase may be done in advance, in a similar way to the language tree used within the language identifier. Of course, by doing this working over the ever-growing datasets is no longer possible because the system must be shut down periodically to perform indexing. Thorough performance analysis is needed to determine what database size requires this previous clustering.

Before performing CLEF experiments, we tested the blindLight IR prototype on two very small standard collections with encouraging results. These collections were CACM (3204 documents and 64 queries) and CISI (1460 documents and 112 queries). Figure 3 shows the interpolated precision-recall graphs for both collections and ranking measures (namely, pi and piro).

These results are similar to those obtained by several systems but not as good as those achieved by others; for instance, 11-pt. average precision was 16.73% and 13.41% for CACM and CISI, respectively, while the SMART IR system achieves 37.78% and 19.45% for the same collections. However, it must be said that these experiments were performed over the documents and the queries just as they are, that is, common techniques such as stop-word removal, stemming, or query term

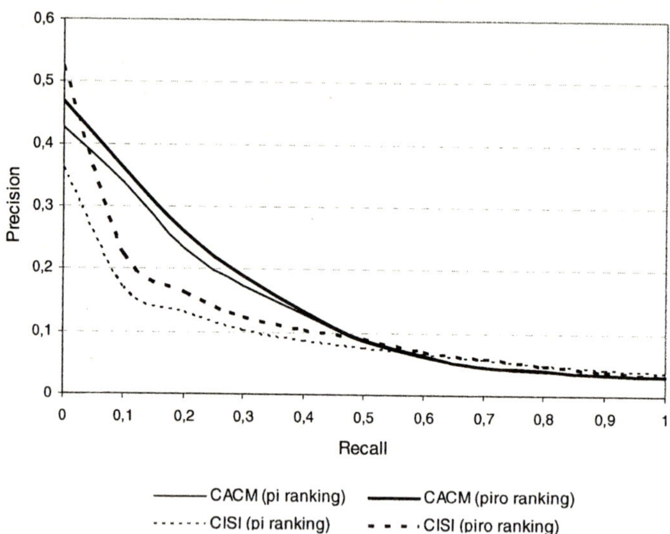

Fig. 3. Interpolated precision-recall graphs for the blindLight IR system applied to CACM and CISI test collections. Top-10 average precision for CACM and CISI was 19.8% and 19.6% respectively, in both cases using `piro` ranking

weighting were not applied to the document set and the queries were provided to the system in a literal fashion[2], as if they were actually submitted by real users. By avoiding such techniques, the system is totally language independent, at least for non ideographic languages, although performance must be improved. One obvious area for future work is represented by the similarity measures; we are planning to use genetic programming in order to test new measures.

4 CLEF 2004 Tasks

4.1 Information Retrieval Method

We applied our prototype to two "ad hoc" tasks [10] from CLEF 2004 [11]: monolingual and bilingual IR. Specifically, we queried the Russian collection with the Russian topics and the English collection with the Spanish topics. All the queries were automatically built from the topics using both title and description fields.

The method employed to obtain the results was the following one:

1. Every SGML file from a collection was parsed to extract individual pieces of news.

---

[2] An example query from the CACM collection: `#64 List all articles on EL1 and ECL (EL1 may be given as EL/1; I don't remember how they did it)`. The blindLight IR prototype processes queries like this one in an "as is" manner.

2. For each piece of news a quad-gram vector was computed, as described above, from the permitted fields (typically, TEXT and TITLE or HEADLINE) and stored.
3. Once the entire collection was processed the topics to query it were also parsed, computing for every topic another quad-gram vector from title and description fields.
4. After parsing the topics file, queries (i.e., their corresponding vectors) were submitted to the prototype in batch mode obtaining ranked lists of one thousand documents. The similarity measure employed to rank the results was the so-called piro since this was the one that performed the best when applied to CACM and CISI collections; however, as has been explained this measure is far from being good and this area needs to be studied in much more depth.

4.2 Pseudo-Translation of Queries

For bilingual information retrieval, the above method needs minor changes with respect to how the query vectors are obtained. This was done without performing actual machine translation using a sentence aligned corpus of source (S) and target (T) languages.

A query written in the source language, *QS*, is split into word chunks (from one word to the whole query). The *S* corpus is searched looking for sentences containing any of these chunks. Every sentence (up to ten) found in *S* is replaced by its counterpart in the *T* corpus. For every sentence found in *T* an *n*-gram vector is computed and then all these vectors are Ω-intersected. Since such *T* sentences contain, allegedly, the translation of some words from language *S* into language *T*, it can be supposed that the Ω intersection of their vectors would contain a kind of "translated" *n*-grams (see Figure 4). Those word chunks that do not appear in the S corpus are incorporated without "translation". Thus, we obtain a vector which is similar, in theory, to that which could be computed from a real translation from the original query.

The European Parliament Proceedings Parallel Corpus 1996-2003 [12] has been used as the sentence aligned corpus and the results obtained have been really interesting. In average terms, 38.59% of the *n*-grams from pseudo-translated query vectors are present within the vectors from actual translated queries and, in turn, 28.31% of the *n*-grams from the actual translated query vectors correspond to n-grams within the pseudo translated ones. In order to check this we have compared vectors obtained through pseudo translation of Spanish queries into English with the vectors computed from actual English topics. This constitutes another area for future work employing different parallel corpora (e.g., OPUS, `http://logos.uio.no/opus`) and improving the "translation" method.

This technique is related to those described by Pirkola *et al* [13] to find cross-lingual spelling variants or by McNamee and Mayfield [14] to "translate" individual *n*-grams. The difference between such techniques and ours is that we do not attempt to obtain word translations nor individual *n*-gram translations but a pseudo-translation for a whole *n*-gram vector containing *n*-grams from the target language that would likely appear in actual query translations. Such a vector can then be straightforwardly submitted to the IR system.

Topic 206 written in language S (Spanish)

Encontrar documentos en los que se habla de las discusiones sobre la reforma de instituciones financieras y, en particular, del Banco Mundial y del FMI durante la cumbre de los G7 que se celebró en Halifax en 1995.

Some sentences from corpus S (Europarl Spanish)

(1315) ...mantiene excelentes relaciones con las instituciones financieras internacionales.
(5865) ...el fortalecimiento de las instituciones financieras internacionales...
(6145) La Comisión deberá estudiar un mecanismo transparente para que las instituciones financieras europeas...

Counterpart sentences from corpus T (Europarl English)

(1315) ...has excellent relationships with the international financial institutions..
(5865) ...strengthening international financial institutions...
(6145) The Commission will have to look at a transparent mechanism so that the European financial institutions...

Pseudo-translated query vector (Ω-intersection of previous T sentences)

(al_i, anci, atio, cial, _fin, fina, ial_, inan, _ins, inst, ions,
itut, l_in, nanc, ncia, nsti, stit, tion, titu, tuti, utio)

Fig. 4. Procedure to pseudo translate a query written originally in a source language (in this case Spanish) onto a vector containing appropriate n grams from the target language (English in this example). Blanks have been replaced by underscores, just one chunk from the query has been pseudo translated (shown underlined)

5 Results Obtained by blindLight IR

As we said before our group submitted results for just two tasks: monolingual retrieval on the Russian collection and bilingual retrieval querying the English

Table 1. Top-5 and bottom-5 performing topics for monolingual and bilingual tasks. Top 5 are those with highest precision at 5 documents. Bottom-5 topics are those which do not provide any relevant result; the more relevant documents available within the collection, the worse the query performs. As can be seen, focused topics related to people, places and/or particular events are the best performers within blindLight IR prototype while broad queries are poorly managed by our system

Top-5 performing topics (ES-EN)	Top-5 performing topics (RU)
218 Andreotti and the Mafia	230 Atlantis-Mir Docking
248 Macedonia Name Dispute	209 Tour de France Winner
202 Nick Leeson's Arrest	210 Nobel Peace Prize Candidates
224 Woman solos Everest	211 Peru-Ecuador Border Conflict
205 Tamil Suicide Attacks	202 Nick Leeson's Arrest
Bottom-5 performing topics (ES-EN)	**Bottom-5 performing topics (RU)**
212 Sportswomen and Doping	227 Altai Ice Maiden
235 Seal-hunting	203 East Timor Guerrillas
241 New political parties	207 Fireworks Injuries
214 Multi-billionaires	228 Prehistorical Art
216 Glue-sniffing Youngsters	250 Rabies in Humans

collection using Spanish as query language. For the Russian task our prototype returned 72 of the 123 relevant documents with an average precision of 0.1433. With regards to the bilingual task we obtained 145 of the 375 relevant documents showing an average precision of 0.0644.

Such results are far from being good but we found them kind of encouraging. Firstly, it is our first participation in CLEF. Secondly, although average results are rather poor we can clearly separate classes of topics that obtain good results from other types which perform poorly (e.g., broad queries) showing us a future line of work.

6 Conclusions and Future Work

blindLight is a new technique related to classical *n*-gram vector space models and developed to perform several natural language processing tasks. We have shown that it is well-suited to extract keyphrases and automatic summaries from single documents [8] in addition to performing language identification and classification of natural languages [9]. At this moment we are testing its applicability to information retrieval since we totally agree with McNamee and Mayfield when they say that "knowledge-light methods can be quite effective" [14]. With regards to this goal, it must be said that partial results are not outstanding but we feel optimistic about this issue since poor performance is mostly constrained to broad topics and focused queries usually achieved reasonable precision.

Three areas require further work: (1) Similarity measures between queries and documents must be improved, perhaps with genetic programming. (2) Different parallel corpora should be used to enhance the n-gram pseudo-translator employed to perform bilingual IR. And (3) thorough research is needed to improve precision when broad topics are submitted to the system.

References

1. Salton, G., Wong, A. and Yang, C.S.: A vector space model for information retrieval. Communications of the ACM, 18(11), pp. 613-620 (1975)
2. D'Amore, R., Mah, C.P.: One-time complete indexing of text: Theory and practice. Proc. of SIGIR 1985, pp. 155-164 (1985)
3. Kimbrell, R.E.: Searching for text? Send an n-gram! Byte, 13(5), pp. 297-312 (1988)
4. Dunning, T.: Accurate methods for the statistics of surprise and coincidence. Computational Linguistics, 19(1), pp. 61-74 (1993)
5. Ferreira da Silva, J., Pereira Lopes, G.: A Local Maxima method and a Fair Dispersion Normalization for extracting multi-word units from corpora. In Proc. of MOL6 (1999)
6. Ferreira da Silva, J., Pereira Lopes, G.: Extracting Multiword Terms from Document Collections. Proc. of VExTAL, Venice, Italy (1999)
7. Levenshtein, V.I.: Binary codes capable of correcting deletions, insertions, and reversals, (English translation from Russian), Soviet Physics Doklady, 10(8), pp. 707-710 (1966).

8. Gayo-Avello, D., Álvarez-Gutiérrez, D., Gayo-Avello, J.: Naive Algorithms for Key phrase Extraction and Text Summarization from a Single Document inspired by the Protein Biosynthesis Process, in Biologically Inspired Approaches to Advanced Information Technology: 1st International Workshop, BioADIT 2004, A.J. Ijspeert, M. Masayuki, and N. Wakamiya (Eds), LNCS 3141, pp. 440-455, (2004)
9. Gayo-Avello, D., Álvarez-Gutiérrez, D., Gayo-Avello, J.: One Size Fits All? A Simple Technique to Perform Several NLP Tasks, in 4th International Conference, EsTAL 2004, J.L. Vicedo *et al* (Eds), LNAI 3230, pp. 267-278, (2004)
10. Peters, C. and Braschler, M. and Di Nunzio, G., and Ferro, N.: CLEF 2004: Ad Hoc Track Overview and Results Analysis, in 5th Workshop of the Cross-Language Evaluation Forum (CLEF 2004), Peters, C. *et al* (Eds), LNCS (in print).
11. Peters, C.; What happened in CLEF 2004, in 5th Workshop of the Cross-Language Evaluation Forum (CLEF 2004), Peters, C. *et al* (Eds), LNCS (in print).
12. Koehn, P.: Europarl: A Multilingual Corpus for Evaluation of Machine Translation, Draft, Unpublished, `http://www.isi.edu/~koehn/publications/europarl.ps`
13. Pirkola, A, Keskustalo, H., Leppänen, E., Känsälä, A. and Järvelin, K. (2002) Targeted *s*-gram matching: a novel *n*-gram matching technique for cross- and monolingual word form variants. Information Research, 7(2) (2002)
14. McNamee, P., Mayfield, J.: JHU/APL Experiments in Tokenization and Non-Word Translation. Working Notes for the CLEF 2003 Workshop. 21-22 August, Trondheim, Norway

Integrating New Languages in a Multilingual Search System Based on a Deep Linguistic Analysis

Romaric Besançon, Olivier Ferret, and Christian Fluhr

CEA-LIST, LIC2M (Multilingual Multimedia Knowledge Engineering Laboratory),
B.P.6 - F92265 Fontenay-aux-Roses Cedex, France
{romaric.besancon, olivier.ferret, christian.fluhr}@cea.fr

Abstract. The LIC2M has designed a cross-lingual search engine based on a deep linguistic analysis of documents and queries that works on French, English, Spanish, German, Arabic and Chinese. For our participation in the CLEF 2004 campaign, we tested the integration in our system of Russian and Finnish, based on a simplified processing. The results we obtained are not good on the new languages introduced, which shows that our system strongly depends on a correct linguistic analysis of the documents. However, integrating more processing steps in the simplified analysis of new languages so that the results of this analysis are more comparable with the results of the complete linguistic analysis seems to be a good direction for improvements.

1 Introduction

The cross-language retrieval system developed at the LIC2M is based on a deep linguistic analysis of both documents and queries. It is currently designed to work on French, English, Spanish, German, Arabic and Chinese. Rather than testing our system on various bilingual tasks on the languages for which we have linguistic resources and processing available, we decided to test, in our CLEF 2004 participation, the possibility of a simple integration, in a limited time, of two new languages: Russian and Finnish. The time factor forced us to use simple strategies for these new languages and try to merge the results obtained with these strategies with the results obtained with the current system.

In section 2, we present the LIC2M multilingual retrieval system: the document and query processing are described, as well as the strategies used for bilingual searches and the merge of the results. We present and discuss in section 3 the results obtained on the different target languages.

2 Multilingual Information Retrieval

The LIC2M cross-language retrieval system is a weighted boolean search engine based on a linguistic analysis of the query and the documents. This system has

C. Peters et al. (Eds.): CLEF 2004, LNCS 3491, pp. 83–89, 2005.

already been used in the small multilingual task of the CLEF 2003 campaign [1]. We present in this section its basic principles.

2.1 Document Processing

The documents are processed to extract informative linguistic elements from their text parts. The processing includes part-of-speech tagging and lemmatization of the words and the extraction of compounds and named entities. After part-of-speech tagging, only content-bearing words (nouns, verbs and adjectives) are kept as informative elements of the documents and stored in indexes. This linguistic processing requires the definition of a set of resources for each language:

- a full form dictionary, containing for each word form its possible part-of-speech tags and linguistic features (gender, number, etc);
- a tagged corpus, from which a set of trigrams and bigrams of part-of-speech categories and their frequencies are learned. These trigrams and bigrams are used for the part-of-speech tagging;
- a set of rules for the shallow parsing of sentences. These rules identify the syntactic relations used to extract compounds from the sentences;
- a set of rules for the identification of named entities. These rules are composed of gazetteers and contextual rules that use specific triggers to identify named entities and their type.

The introduction of Russian and Finnish in the multilingual task raised a difficulty concerning this linguistic processing. For Russian, we used a language dictionary that allowed us to simply associate the words with their possible part-of-speech. We had no time to train a part-of-speech tagger nor to develop sets of rules for syntactic analysis or named entities. The processing of Russian just consisted in keeping all possible normalized forms of nouns, verbs and adjectives, with their categories.

For Finnish, since we did not have a full form dictionary, we used a simple stemmer (Porter Snowball stemmer [2]) and no part-of-speech. We also used the stoplist provided by Jacques Savoy [3] to filter out function words and common words. A basic algorithm for decompounding has also been tested. This algorithm considers every word (with a minimum length l) that appears in the Finnish corpus as a base word, and splits every word (with minimum length $2 \times l$) that can be decomposed into several base words (all candidate decompositions are kept).

2.2 Query Processing

The processing of queries is automatic. Each query is first processed through the linguistic analyzer corresponding to the query language. We kept for this analysis either the three fields of the topic (*title* (T), *description* (D) and *narrative* (N)) or only the two first (T+D).

When using the narrative field in the query processing, a stoplist containing meta-words is used to filter out non-relevant words (words used in the narrative to describe what are relevant documents, such as : "document", "relevant" etc.).

These meta-words stoplists were built on the basis of a manual analysis of the CLEF 2002 topics.

The result of this analysis is a list of linguistic elements that we call the *concepts* of the query. Each concept is reformulated into a set of *search terms* in the language of the considered index, either using bilingual dictionaries or, in the case of monolingual search, using monolingual reformulation dictionaries (adding synonyms and related words) and/or a topical expansion.

This topical expansion is performed by the same method as the one described in [1]. This method relies on the detection, in a large network of lexical cooccurrences built from a corpus, of the strongly connected components that include the words of the query. The detection is performed in an iterative way by a kind of flow simulation algorithm : a flow starts from the words of the query and is propagated towards their neighbors in the network of lexical cooccurrences to select the words that are the most strongly connected to them. The flow then comes back towards the words of the query to discard those that are not directly linked to the global topic of the query. Finally, it is sent again from the words of the query to select the final expansion words, i.e. the words of the network that are part of the components delimited by the flow and that are not already part of the query.

For translation, we had bilingual dictionaries for French-English and English-Russian pairs. The dictionary we used for the reformulation into Finnish language is the FreeLang bilingual English-Finnish dictionary [4]. Other translations (French-Russian, French-Finnish) were performed through a multi-step translation, using English as a pivot language.

2.3 Searching and Merging Strategy

During the query processing, the original topic is associated with four different sets of search terms, one for each target language. Each search term set is used as an independent query against the index of the corresponding language. N documents are retrieved for each language. The $4 \times N$ retrieved documents from the four corpora are then merged and sorted by their relevance to the topic. Only the first 1000 are kept.

For each language, our system retrieves, for each search term, the documents containing the term (until N documents are retrieved). A *concept profile* is associated with each document, each component of which indicates the presence or absence of a query concept in the document (a concept is present in a document if one of its reformulated search terms is present). Retrieved documents sharing the same concept profile are clustered together. This clustering allows a straightforward merging strategy that takes into account the original query concepts and the way they have been reformulated: since the concepts are in the original query language, the concept profiles associated with the clusters formed for different target languages are comparable, and the clusters having the same profile are simply merged.

To compute the relevance weight of each cluster, we first compute a cross-lingual pseudo-*idf* weight of each concept, using only the corpus composed of the $4 \times N$ documents kept as the result of the search. This weight is computed by the formula $idf(c) = \log \frac{4 \times N}{df(c)}$, where $df(c)$ is the number of documents containing the concept c. The weight associated with a cluster is then the sum of the weights of the concepts present in its concept profile.

The clusters are then sorted by their weights: all documents in a cluster are given the weight of the cluster (the documents are not sorted inside the clusters). The list of the first 1000 documents from the best clusters is then built and used for the evaluation.

3 Results

We tested the system for English and French topics, using N=1000 documents retrieved for each language. The result tables present the mean average precision and the number of relevant documents found for each language of the corpus. The average precision for each language is computed only on the subpart of the multilingual search corresponding to the considered language and only on the queries that actually have relevant documents for this language.

3.1 Multilingual Results

Table 1 presents the results obtained with English topics using either T+D fields for the analysis of the query or T+D+N, and the results obtained with French topics, using T+D+N fields for the analysis of the query and topical expansion.

Table 1. Average precision (avg_p) and number of relevant documents retrieved (relret) for all target languages, using English and French topics

eng T+D	all	eng	fin	fre	rus
avg_p	0.128	0.355	0.0133	0.183	0.054
relret	736 (40.3%)	235 (62.7%)	54 (13.5%)	405 (44.3%)	42 (34.1%)
eng T+D+N	**all**	**eng**	**fin**	**fre**	**rus**
avg_p	0.136	0.351	0.0304	0.182	0.067
relret	777 (42.6%)	240 (64%)	77 (20%)	424 (46.3%)	36 (29.3%)
fre T+D+N	**all**	**eng**	**fin**	**fre**	**rus**
avg_p	0.126	0.18	0.0099	0.27	0.0301
relret	753 (41.2%)	157 (41.9%)	18 (4.5%)	542 (59.2%)	36 (29.3%)

Clearly, our system is weak for Russian and Finnish, the two languages where we did not have a complete linguistic processing and backup solutions were adopted. These solutions are not sufficient to get reasonable results because with its present configuration, our system requires a robust linguistic analysis of the target languages. In particular, the bilingual dictionaries we used for translation are based on lemmas and parts-of-speech. We should integrate in our system some default processing for the different steps of linguistic processing that would not require the complete definition of linguistic resources but would rely on basic schemas and training data. This would allow to better integrate new languages in the existing design of our system. Another possible improvement is to enrich the reformulation by techniques such as transliteration or approximate matching (for proper names in particular), or use reformulation data automatically learned from aligned corpora.

The results presented in Table 1 also show that our system seems to work better when using all information available in the query (title, description and narrative). The narrative seems to introduce some relevant information by giving different formulations of the topic and without adding much noise after the basic filtering of meta-words by a specialized stop-list. A more precise analysis of the results should be performed to also study the effect of the negative formulations in the narrative ("*documents that contain ... are not relevant*").

3.2 Improved Multilingual Results on English and French

Table 2 presents the results obtained for English topics, using T+D+N, only on French and English corpus, after some adjustments of the system that appear to improve the results after a quick analysis of the previous results:

- monolingual reformulation introduces too many rare synonyms (or synonyms of too rare senses of the words) that cause non-relevant documents to be retrieved. For the new test, we simply deactivated this monolingual reformulation (in the future, the monolingual reformulation dictionaries will be checked to improve the relevance of added terms).
- the importance of named entities was neglected in the runs we submitted. Giving a special importance to named entities, relatively to the other words of the query, improves the results. For the new test, we set a double weight for named entities, relatively to the other words of the query.
- the value of N (number of documents retrieved for one language) is also important. Indeed, the documents are retrieved until the number of documents N is reached: if this number is too small, all search terms may not be exploited (search terms are used in the decreasing order of their importance in the collection). For the new test, we set this number at 5000. Notice that the improvement obtained by this adjustment is a trick to improve results in this evaluation framework: using a larger number of documents per language actually helps retrieving new documents at the end of the list, but does not change the first documents retrieved. There are chances that this improvement would not be noticed by a user of a real system.

These results show a significant improvement: the average precision for each language is increased by 25% and 90% of the relevant documents are retrieved.

3.3 Finnish Decompounding

The basic decompounding algorithm for Finnish has been tested independently on the Finnish corpus using English topics and T+D fields. Table 3 presents

Table 2. Average precision (avg_p) and number of relevant documents retrieved (relret) for French and English corpus, using English topics

eng T+D+N	fre/eng	eng	fre
avg_p	0.243	0.44	0.238
relret	1168 (90.5%)	362 (96.5%)	806 (88.1%)

Table 3. Average precision (avg_p) and number of relevant documents retrieved (relret) for Finnish corpus, using English topics, for different values of minimum length l used for decompounding

eng T+D	$l = 3$	$l = 4$	$l = 5$	no decompounding
avg_p	0.144	0.147	0.146	0.123
relret	205 (49.6%)	190 (46%)	192 (46.5%)	181 (43.8%)

the results obtained[1] with a decompounding using different values of minimum length for base words ($l = 3, l = 3, l = 5$).

These results show that basic decompounding on Finnish tends to improve the results (the gain for mean average precision is 19% but the value is still small) and the best value for minimum length seems to be 4 (though the difference is not important using 3 or 5).

This basic decompounding process is a first step in the design of a more complete simplified linguistic processing for Finnish that could be more compatible with our search system. For instance, we should try to match compounds obtained with this Finnish decompounding algorithm with compounds obtained by a complete syntactic analysis in French and English.

4 Conclusion

These experiments in the multilingual track of CLEF 2004 show some improved results of our system, relatively to the CLEF 2003 campaign, on French and English corpora. On the other hand, the poor results obtained for Russian and Finnish show that the introduction of new languages in our system with simplified linguistic processing or stemming/stoplist approaches does not perform well. This integration should be made easier by defining robust default processing for some steps of linguistic analysis so that the results of the simplified processing can be more comparable with the results of the linguistic analysis: the integration of a simple decompounding algorithm for Finnish is a first step in this direction and shows a small improvement of the results. Another direction

---

[1] These results are not directly comparable with the previous results since they are true bilingual results (not part of multilingual results), and have been obtained with a different version of the search system (that includes a different linguistic analysis for the English queries).

would be to allow the search system to take as input the result of a completely different approach for new languages (for instance, a simple linguistic analysis combined with a reformulation based on statistical translation lexicons learned from aligned corpora). In this case, we would have to tackle the difficulty of merging the results obtained with different processing. Finally, we would also be interested in testing another kind of query expansion based on word senses that are automatically derived from a corpus. We hope that such a resource is more suitable for query expansion than a lexical network such as WordNet that was mainly built by hand.

References

1. Besançon, R., de Chalendar, G., Ferret, O., Fluhr, C., Mesnard, O., Naets, H.: The LIC2M's CLEF 2003 System. In: Working Notes for the CLEF 2003 Workshop, Trondheim, Norway (2003)
2. Porter, M.: Finnish Snowball Stemmer. http://snowball.tartarus.org/finnish/stemmer.html (2002)
3. Savoy, J.: A Stopword List for Finnish. (http://www.unine.ch/info/clef/)
4. Hämäläinen, K., Kivirinta, T.: Freelang Finnish-English Dictionary. (http://www.kasvua.org/ kphamala/dict.html)

IR-n r2: Using Normalized Passages

Fernando Llopis, Rafael Muñoz, Rafael M. Terol, and Elisa Noguera

Departamento de Lenguajes y Sistemas Informáticos,
Universidad de Alicante
{llopis, rafael, rafamt, elisa}@dlsi.ua.es

Abstract. This paper describes the fourth participation of the IR-n system (Alicante University) at the CLEF evaluation campaigns. For CLEF 2004, we modified our similarity measure and query expansion model. For the similarity measure, we now use normalization based on the number of words for each of the passages. We tested two different approaches for query expansion: the first one is based on documents and the second on passages.

1 Introduction

In line with our participation in the previous CLEF campaigns, the IR-n system was used in several tasks in CLEF 2004: in the monolingual, bilingual and multilingual tasks. The IR-n system has been considerably changed since last year. The system has been re-programmed in order to improve the response times. The new version can also use different similarity measures by adapting a parameter. Several other changes have been made in order to improve both the similarity measures and the query expansion.

This paper is organized as follows. The next section describes the IR-n system and the changes that have been made to it. We then describe the tasks that we tackled in CLEF 2004 using this system. Finally, we present the results obtained and draw some conclusions.

2 The IR-n System

Information Retrieval (IR) systems have to find the relevant documents in a collection for a given user query. The literature reports different kinds of IR systems. If the document collection and the user query are written in the same language then the IR system can be defined as a monolingual IR system. However, if the document collection and the user query are written in different languages then the IR system can be defined as a bilingual (two different languages) or multilingual (more than two languages) system. Obviously, the document collection for multilingual systems is in at least two different languages. The IR-n system is a monolingual, bilingual and multilingual IR system based on passage retrieval.

C. Peters et al. (Eds.): CLEF 2004, LNCS 3491, pp. 90–99, 2005.

Passage Retrieval (PR) systems are information retrieval systems that determine the similarity of a document with respect to a user query according to the similarity of fragments of the document (passages) to the same query.

There are many proposals [1, 6] concerning the best way to derive the passages in order to obtain better results.

2.1 IR-n System r1 (2000-2003)

The IR-n system was originally developed using the C++ program language and running under Linux with no excessive requirements. IR-n is a PR system that uses the sentences as atoms with the aim of defining the passages. Each passage is thus composed of a specific number of sentences. This number depends to a great degree on the collection used. For this reason, the system requires a training phase to improve its results. IR-n uses overlapping passages in order to avoid some documents being considered not relevant if query terms appear in adjacent passages.

From the beginning, the IR-n system used the traditional cosine measure [14]. However, further experiments were performed using other similarity measures which gave better results. The similarity measures used by IR-n differ from traditional IR systems. For example, IR-n does not use normalization factors related to the passage or document size. This is due to the fact that passage size is the same for all documents. So, the IR-n system calculates the similarity between a passage P and the user query q in the following way:

$$sim(Q,P) = \sum_{t \in Q \wedge P} (w_{Q,t} \cdot w_{P,t}) \quad (1)$$

where:

$$w_{Q,t} = freq_{q,t} \cdot \log_e\left(\frac{N - freq_t}{freq_t}\right) \quad (2)$$

$$w_{P,t} = 1 + \log_e(1 + \log_e(freq_{p,t} + 1)) \quad (3)$$

where $freq_{Y,t}$ is the number of appearances or the frequency of term t in the passage or in the query Y. N is the total number of documents in the collection, and $freq_t$ is the number of different documents that contain term t.

Once the system has calculated this score for each of the passages, it is necessary to determine the similarity of the document that contains these passages. All PR systems calculate the similarity measure of the document according to the similarity measure of their passages using the sum of similarity measures for each passage or using the best passage similarity measures for each one of the documents. The experiments performed in [5] have been re-run by IR-n, obtaining better results when the best passage similarity measures were used as the similarity measure of the document.

Our approach is based on the fact that if a passage is relevant then the document is also relevant. In fact, if a PR system uses the sum of every passage similarity measure then the system has the same behaviour as a document-based IR system adding proximity concepts.

Moreover, the use of the best passage similarity measure makes it possible to retrieve the best passage, thus further improving the search process.

The IR-n system calculates the similarity measure of the document based on the best passage similarity measure in the following way:

$$sim(Q, D) = \max_{\forall i: P_i \in D} sim(Q, P_i) \tag{4}$$

Similarly to most IR systems, IR-n also uses techniques of query expansion. Originally, the first release of the IR-n system [9] incorporated synonyms in the original query obtaining poorer scores than the model without query expansion. After that, we incorporated the model proposed in [3], but the terms that were added to the original query were the most frequent terms of the most relevant passages instead of the most frequent terms of the most relevant documents. The use of these techniques permitted us to improve our results in practically all our experiments.

2.2 IR-n System r2 (2004)

A set of changes have been made to our system in order to improve performance. These changes are the following:

1. First, we modified the similarity measure in order to take into account the size of the passages in addition to the number of sentences used in the first release (IR-n r1). For each word, IR-n r1 stored the document and the sentences in which it was found, but did not store the size of each of the sentences. In this way, it was not possible to compare similarities between passages using the size of passages. This change has comported important modifications to the index task and the search process. We did some experiments with pivoted cosine and Okapi measures, and obtained better results with Okapi.
2. The system was also updated in order to consider different similarity measures in the Okapi system. In this way, we can test the best setup for each document collection.
3. This new release applies document-based query expansion techniques. The first release IR-n took the most frequent terms in the passages found and added them to the original query. The new IR-n release uses a new approach based on adding the most frequent terms in the documents instead of passages.
4. One of the most important factors for an information retrieval system is the speed. Although the first release of IR-n had a low response time, the system was slow when writing the most relevant passages. This meant that if the system used query expansion then the response times increased.

In order to improve our system performance, we decided to re-develop the IR-n system r2 practically from the beginning. We used an object-oriented approach with C++ as language for implementation. Moreover, in parallel, an IR-n r3 version has been developed using the ".net" technology [4]. This release is still in an early phase of development, but it has achieved better results for XML documents.

This year, we also developed the web search engine for the University of Alicante using IR-n. This can be accessed from the website of the University of Alicante (www.ua.es) or directly at (www.tabarca.com).

3 IR-n r2 at CLEF 2004

This year our system participated in the following tasks:

- monolingual tasks:
  - French
  - Portuguese
  - Finnish
  - Russian
- bilingual tasks:
  - Spanish-Russian
  - English-Russian
  - Spanish-Portuguese
  - English-Portuguese
- multilingual tasks:
  - English-French-Finnish-Russian

3.1 Monolingual Tasks

We used the main resources available at http://www.unine.ch/info/clef/. We took stemmers and stop-word lists for each language from this website. Moreover, we used the program provided to convert Cyrillic characters into ASCII characters in order to process Russian documents.

However, no Portuguese stemmer was available. For this reason, we decide to develop one. We changed the Spanish endings using appropriate Portuguese ones.

Finnish presents an additional feature: compound nouns. A compound noun is usually composed by the combination of two or more free elements, which are morphemes that can stand on their own and have their own meaning but together form another word with a modified meaning. We have developed an algorithm for splitting compound nouns into several words. This has permitted us to improve our results in the training phase. According to [7], the split process consists in splitting words over 6 letters into known words. Obviously, we can split a word in different ways. For this reason, we use a frequency list extracted from the same corpus. We choose the known words combination that provides the highest frequency with a minimum number of words using the following formula:

$$argmin_S(\prod_{p_i \epsilon S} count(p_i)))^{1/n} \quad (5)$$

The similarity measure used for all languages in the monolingual task was the Okapi measure obtaining the best scores. We made several experiments with and without normalization using the passage size. Different scores were obtained according to the language used as shown in Table 1.

Table 1. AvgP without query expansion

	Passage size using number of sentences	
Similarity measure	**Normalized Okapi**	**Non-normalized Okapi**
Finnish	0.4968	0.5011
Russian	0.4179	0.4180
French	0.4263	0.4939
English	0.5233	0.4827

Similar scores were obtained for Finnish and Russian indifferently of normalization. However, for English the system obtained the best scores using a normalized measures whereas for French the best scores were obtained without normalization. This is due to the fact that we have not chosen the same parameters for the Okapi system or perhaps that in this case it is preferable to use other similarity measures.

Different experiments were performed in order to determine the best approach to query expansion. For each experiment, we tested whether better results could be obtained using 5 or 10 words and 5 or 10 documents/passages. The results obtained in the testing phase were similar to those obtained in the final experiments.

3.2 The Bilingual Task

The participation of the IR-n r2 system in the bilingual task this year has been focused on the following language pairs:

- English-Russian
- Spanish-Russian
- English-Portuguese and
- Spanish-Portuguese.

Following the strategy used last year by IR-n r1, the bilingual task has been performed merging several translations proposed by on-line translators. This strategy is based on the idea that the words that appears in different translations have more relevancy that those that only appear in one translation.

Two translators were used for all languages: Freetanslation[1] and Babel Fish[2]. An additional on-line translator was used for Russian. This translator was IM-Translator[3]. Freetranslator and Babel Fish do not translate directly from Spanish to Russian. For this reason we used English as an intermediate language.

[1] www.freetranslation.com

[2] http://world.altavista.com/

[3] http://translation.paralink.com/translation.asp

3.3 The Multilingual Task

We use the formula described in [2] ir order to merge the different lists of relevant documents for each language.

$$rsv'_j = (rsv_j - rsv_{min})/(rsv_{max} - rsv_{min}) \quad (6)$$

We could not test the merging procedure during the training phase because we only concluded its implementation just before submitting the our results.

4 Results

4.1 Monolingual Tasks

The results obtained in the monolingual task are, to say the least, peculiar. In general, all results excluding the Russian results are below average. We consider the results acceptable because our experiment only uses the title and the description fields. However, and in agreement with the training phase, the Russian scores are impressively over the average. We do not know anything about the Russian language; for this reason we are unable to understand why the results for this language, which use the same release of IR, are above average.

Table 2. CLEF 2004 official results: Monolingual tasks

Language	Run	AvgP	Dif.
Russian	CLEF Average	0.3700	
	nexp	0.4809	**+29.97%**
	pexp	0.4733	
	dexp	0.4796	
French	CLEF Average	0.4370	
	nexp	0.4086	
	pexp	0.4251	**-2.72%**
	dexp	0.4217	
Finish	CLEF Average	0.5096	
	nexp	0.4533	
	pexp	0.4908	
	dexp	0.4914	**-3.57%**
Portuguese	CLEF Average	0.4024	
	nexp	0.3532	
	pexp	0.3750	
	dexp	0.3909	**-2.85%**

Table 2 shows the results for each language using the model without expansion (nexp), the model with expansion based on documents (dexp) and the model with expansion based on passages (pexp). In each case, the best results are compared with the CLEF average.

4.2 Bilingual Results

Obviously, the results obtained in our bilingual experiments were affected by the results for the monolingual track. In fact, the English-Russian and the Spanish-Russian scores are over the average whereas the results for English-Portuguese and Spanish-Portuguese are worse than the average. Table 3 shows the scores obtained for each pair of languages with and without query expansion.

Table 3. CLEF 2004 official results: Monolingual tasks

Language	Run	AvgP	Dif.
	CLEF Average	0.1741	
Spanish-Rusian	nexp	0.3044	
	pexp	0.3087	**+77.31%**
English-Rusian	nexp	0.3296	
	exp	0.3357	**+92.82%**
	CLEF Average	0.3316	
	Free-translator		
English-Portuguese	nexp	0.2379	**-28.25%**
	pexp	0.2173	
Spanish-Portuguese	nexp	0.2977	
	exp	0.3243	**-2.2%**
	Free-translator-Google-BabelFish		
English-Portuguese	nexp	0.2975	
	pexp	0.3123	**-5.83%**

4.3 Multilingual Results

Table 4 shows the scores obtained in the multilingual task without using query expansion (nexp). The table presents the scores obtained using two different types of query expansion: the first one uses the passage-based model (pexp) and the second uses the document-based model (dexp). The best scores obtained for each pair of language was compared against the CLEF average as shown in the *Dif.* column.

4.4 Comparative Evaluation

After the evaluation made by CLEF 2004 organizers, comparing the scores achieve by IR-n v2 with those of other participants, we focus on the high scores

Table 4. CLEF 2004 official results: Multilingual tasks

Language	Run	AvgP	Dif.
	CLEF Average	0.2339	
English	nexp	0.2204	
	pexp	0.2353	**+0.6%**
	dexp	0.2330	

Table 5. CLEF 2004: Monolingual Russian results

Systems	Scores
U. Alicante	0.4809
Hummingbird	0.4431
U. Amsterdam	0.4412
UC. Berkeley	0.4204
Dublin City U.	0.3790

Table 6. CLEF 2004: Bilingual Russian results

Systems	Scores
U. Alicante	0.3357
UC. Berkeley	0.3291
Dublin City U.	0.3210
U. Neuchâtel	0.3007
JHU/APL	0.1407

obtained by our system in the Russian monolingual and bilingual task (Tables 5 and 6).

We need to analyze these scores because we just do not know the reasons that allowed us to obtain good scores for Russian with respect to other languages using the same Information Retrieval engine. Probably, the problem was the setup of the system for each language.

5 Conclusions and Future Work

This year, our impressions are somewhat contradictory. We did not have enough time to develop a new system architecture and to train it satisfactorily. We needed two more weeks to be able to tune our system in order to increase the scores.

First of all, the excellent scores obtained in the bilingual task with Russian as target language were a surprise for us. We did not have any previous experience with this language and the system used was the same for every task. For this reason, we cannot explain why the scores are better in Russian language than in other languages.

An additional aspect to be considered is the use of normalization. We could not demonstrate that normalization improved the scores in all cases. We want to run additional experiments in order to study this issue.

We have presented a comparison between two different query expansion models. Both models obtained similar scores but the passage-based model is faster than the document-based one. However, we want to check the efficiency of this model using larger documents than those in the CLEF collection.

With respect to the bilingual task, and in accordance with our experience of last year, we continue to obtain the best scores by merging the results of different translators rather than by using all the translations. Another conclusion is that using English as source (query) language gives the best results (see bilingual experiments for Russian) at least if both languages are very different. Quite the opposite occurs if both languages have the same root: Romance, Slav, etc. (see bilingual experiments Spanish - Portuguese).

The results obtained for the multilingual task were worse than those of last year although they are slightly above the average of the CLEF 2004 participating systems. We already know that the model used to merge document lists is very dependent on the number of queries that have answers in each language. For the next campaign, we hope to count on a new merging model which we were unable to finish in this edition. Due to the results obtained in the first experiments we think that this model will improve our results.

Finally, we want observe that the time spent on developing the IR-n r2 system has been worth while as we can now make updates easily. We should also like to note that this version of the IR-n system is much faster in displaying the relevant passages.

Acknowledgments

This work has been partially supported by the Spanish Government (CICYT) with grant TIC2003-07158-C04-01.

References

1. Callan, J. P.: Passage-Level Evidence in Document Retrieval. In Proceedings of the 17th Annual International Conference on Research and Development in Information Retrieval, London, UK. Springer Verlag (1994) 302–310,
2. Chen, A.: Cross-Language Retrieval Experiments at CLEF-2002. In Peters et al. [13], 5–20.
3. Chen, J., Diekema, A., Taffet, M., McCracken, N., Ozgencil, N., Yilmazel, O., Liddy, E.: Question Answering: CNLP at the TREC-10 Question Answering Track. In Tenth Text REtrieval Conference (Notebook), Vol. 500-250 of NIST Special Publication, Gaithersburg, USA, Nov 2001.
4. García-PuigCerver, H., Llopis, F., Cano, M., Toral, A., Espí, H.: IR-n system, a Passage Retrieval Architecture. Proceedings of Text Speech and Dialogue 2004. Brno, September 2004
5. Hearst, M., Plaunt, C.: Subtopic structuring for full-length document access. In Sixteenth International ACM SIGIR Conference on Research and Development in Information Retrieval, Pittsburgh, PA, June 1993, 59–68.
6. Kaszkiel, M., Zobel, J.: Effective Ranking with Arbitrary Passages. Journal of the American Society for Information Science and Technology (JASIST), 52(4)(2001) 344–364.
7. Koehn, P., Knight, K.: Empirical Methods for Compond Splitting. Proceding of EACL 2003.
8. Lernout & Hauspie Educational Software Power Translator. Software.
9. Llopis, F., Vicedo, J.L.: IR-n system at CLEF 2002. In Peters et al. [13], 169–176.

10. Llopis, F. and Vicedo, J.L.: IR-n system, a passage retrieval system at CLEF 2001. In Proceedings of the Cross-Language Evaluation Forum (CLEF 2001). LNCS 2406. Springer-Verlag (2002) 244–252.
11. Llopis, F.: IR-n un sistema de Recuperación de Información basado en pasajes. PhD thesis. Universidad de Alicante (2003).
12. Muñoz, R. and Palomar, M.: Sentence Boundary and Named Entity Recognition in EXIT System: Information Extraction System of Notarial Texts. In Emerging Technologies in Accounting and Finance (1999) 129–142.
13. Peters, C., Braschler, M., Gonzalo, J., Kluck, M. (eds.): Proceedings of the Cross-Language Evaluation Forum (CLEF 2002)., Lecture Notes in Computer Science, LNCS 2785. Springer-Verlag 2003.
14. Salton, G., Buckley, C.: Term-weighting Approaches in Automatic Text Retrieval. Information Processing and Management 24(5) (1988) 513–123.

Using COTS Search Engines and Custom Query Strategies at CLEF

David Nadeau, Mario Jarmasz, Caroline Barrière, George Foster, and Claude St-Jacques

Language Technologies Research Centre, Interactive Language Technologies Group, National Research Council of Canada, Gatineau, Québec, Canada, K1A 0R6
{David.Nadeau, Mario.Jarmasz, Caroline.Barriere, George.Foster, Claude.St-Jacques}@cnrc-nrc.gc.ca

Abstract. This paper presents a system for bilingual information retrieval using commercial off-the-shelf search engines (COTS). Several custom query construction, expansion and translation strategies are compared. We present the experiments and the corresponding results for the CLEF 2004 event.

1 Introduction

In our first participation in the Cross-Language Evaluation Forum (CLEF) we entered the French monolingual task as well as the newcomer French to English bilingual tasks. This report is mainly for the latter task although some experimental results are discussed using data from the former. Our research consists in the use of two commercial off-the-shelf (COTS) search engines which we use to perform boolean queries. These search engines do not allow us to perform weighted queries; we attempt to overcome this weakness by developing innovative query strategies. We test our query construction techniques which vary the ways in which the terms are extracted from the topics. We then experiment with various approaches for querying the search engines by combining the terms using the boolean operators. We briefly explore a query expansion approach based on fuzzy logic. Finally, we investigate three different word-for-word translation methods.

We begin by presenting Copernic Enterprise Search (CES) and AltaVista Enterprise Search (AVES), the two COTS search engines used for the 2004 event. Section 3 describes the query term selection process and section 4 describes the steps for constructing the query, i.e. the manner in which the terms and operators are combined. The subsequent sections discuss the query expansion and translation approaches. We end our discussion by stating our conclusions and future work items.

2 Commercial Off-the-Shelf Search Engines

Two commercial search engines were used for our participation at CLEF. Both offer boolean query syntax rather than weighted queries. We realize that this may be a

C. Peters et al. (Eds.): CLEF 2004, LNCS 3491, pp. 100 – 109, 2005.

handicap in CLEF-like competitions. Researchers have found strict binary queries to be limiting (Cöster *et al.*, 2003), and most of the best results from previous years rely on systems where each term in a query can be assigned a weight. UC Berkeley performed very well at CLEF 2003 using such a search engine (Chen, 2002). Yet the availability and quality of commercial search engines make them interesting resources which we feel merit proper investigation.

The first search engine that we use is Copernic Enterprise Search (CES), a system which ranked third in the topic distillation task of the Text Retrieval Conference (TREC) held in 2003 (Craswell *et al.*, 2003). Copernic's ranking is based on term frequency, term adjacency and inclusion of terms in automatically generated document summaries and keywords. It performs stemming using a multilingual algorithm akin to Porter's (1980). Copernic also has the ability to handle meta-data and to take it into consideration when performing its ranking calculations. In our experiments we provided CES with the title meta-data which is found in the *TITLE*, *TI* or *HEADLINE* tags depending on the corpus.

The second search engine used is AltaVista Enterprise Search (AVES) which implements algorithms from the renowned AltaVista company. AVES ranking is based on term frequencies and term adjacency. It performs stemming but the exact algorithm is not documented. Meta-data was not taken into consideration for the searches performed with AVES.

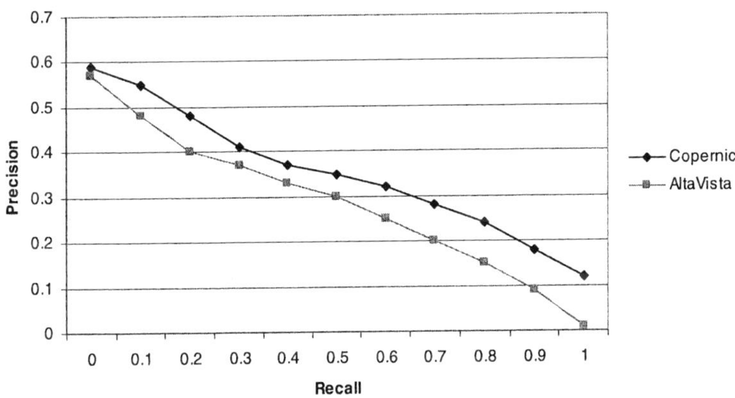

Fig. 1. Precision and recall values for the two search engines using our baseline strategy

Copernic retrieves more relevant documents than AltaVista for the majority of the configurations which we tested on the 2003 data. This observation holds for the CLEF 2004 data. Figure 1 plots the precision-recall curves for both search engines using the 2004 Monolingual French data. The queries consist of a disjunction of the terms in the topic title. This simple strategy serves as our baseline. Our query strategies are explained in detail in the following sections.

An analysis of the 2003 data allows us to observe that the use of the title meta-data, meaning that the search engine assigns a better score to documents in which query terms are found in the title, accounts for about 20% of the difference between the two systems. It is a reasonable assumption that the remaining 80% difference is due to the different ranking algorithms. Since CES and AVES are commercial products, we use them as black boxes and cannot explain the difference in detail.

3 Query Term Selection

The query term selection step consists in extracting important keywords from the topic. Each topic consists of a title, a description and a narrative field. Here is an example of a French topic:

```
<top>
<num> C201 </num>
<FR-title> Incendies domestiques </FR-title>
<FR-desc> Quelles sont les principales causes
d'incendie à la maison ? </FR-desc>
<FR-narr> Les documents pertinents devront mentionner
au moins une des causes possibles d'incendie en général
ou en référence à un exemple particulier. </FR-narr>
</top>
```

We investigated various methods for exploiting these fields. Our research focused on the following strategies:

S1. the use of the title in isolation (this is our baseline);
S2. the use of the description in isolation;
S3. the use of the combination of the title and the description;
S4. the use of Extractor (Turney, 2000) keyphrases extracted from all fields;
S5. the use of the title plus the best Extractor keyphrases.

In all cases we removed the words *trouvez*, *documents*, *pertinents* and *informations* from the French topics. These words are not stop words but are commonly used in CLEF topics. Stop words are later discarded as explained in the Query Construction section. Comparison of methods can be found in Figure 2.

We have established that it is not efficient to use the narrative in isolation due to the presence of many unrelated words and because the narrative often contains a sentence explaining what not to find, for example *"Les plans de réformes futures ne sont pas pertinents"*. More sophisticated natural language processing techniques are required to take advantage of these explanations.

Using the information contained in the topics, queries can consist of as little as two words, when using the title in isolation, or tens of words, when Extractor is used to select salient terms from the entire topic.

Exhaustive results are given in the next section but it is worth noting some interesting observations. First, the title in isolation performs well, even if it only contains a few words. Titles are indeed made of highly relevant words. All our best runs are obtained using the words in the title. Furthermore, Extractor is useful for selecting pertinent words from the description and narrative parts. The best term selection strategy we found is the use of title words combined with a number of Extractor keyphrases.

Extractor can select noun phrases from a text. In our experiments, a noun phrase containing *n* words is considered as *n* independent words instead of one lexical unit. It would be worthwhile to investigate if any gains can be obtained by searching for exact matches of these multi-word-units.

4 Query Construction

We perform three major tasks when building our queries. (1) First, we remove stop words from the list of terms based on their frequency in the corresponding CLEF corpus. (2) Then, the terms are again sorted based on their frequency in order to create a query where the rarest word comes first. (3) Finally, we combine words using the boolean *AND* and *OR* operators. Some of our search strategies require several variants of the queries to be sent to the search engines. In this scenario, the first query usually returns a small number of documents. Then, a larger number of documents is obtained by appending the results of a second query, and so on.

Let's study the term filtering step in greater detail. First, the words that do not appear in the corpus are removed. Then, we remove terms that occur above a specified threshold. We determined this threshold, as a percentage of the total number of documents. For example, the very frequent French stop word "*le*" appears in about 95% of documents, while the less frequent stop word "*avec*" appears in about 47% of the documents. We trained our system using the 2003 CLEF data and tested it using the 2002 data. Using these corpora we set our threshold for the exclusion of terms in a query at about 25%.

The second step involves sorting the terms according to their frequencies in the corpora, from least frequent to most frequent. This decision is based on the TF-IDF idea (Salton & Buckley, 1988) which states that a rare, infrequent term is more informative that a common, frequent term. These informative terms allow obtaining precise results. Sorting is useful with the strategy described next.

The last step is to issue the query to the search engine. Here we experimented with two variants. The first, which we use as baseline, is a simple disjunction of all terms. The second, which we call *Successive Constraint Relaxation* (SCR) consists in sending successive queries to the search engine starting with a conjunction of all terms and ending with a disjunction of all terms. The constraints, which are represented by the conjunctions, are replaced with disjunctions term by term, starting by the last term, meaning the least informative, in the query. When necessary, a query containing the previously removed terms is issued to obtain a list of 1000 documents for our results. Here's a sample query for which the constraints are successively relaxed, given the following words with their frequency in the corpus: *incendies* (394), *domestiques* (194), *causes* (1694) and *maison* (4651), SCR issues:

Query 1: domestiques AND incendies AND causes AND maison
Query 2: domestiques AND incendies AND (causes OR maison)
Query 3: domestiques AND (incendies OR causes OR maison)
Query 4: domestiques OR incendies OR causes OR maison

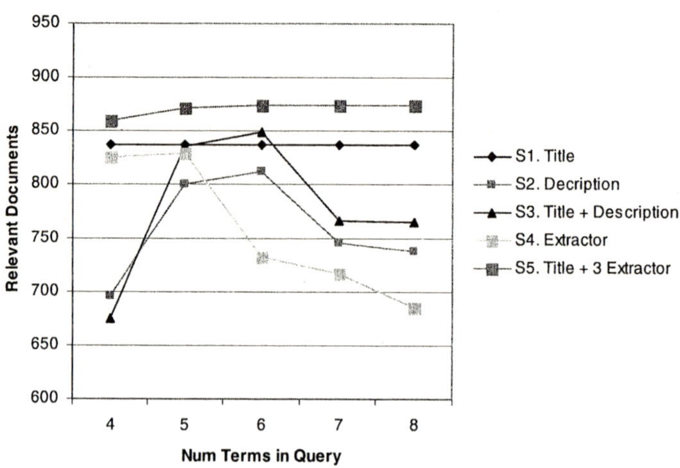

Fig. 2. Results of various term selection strategies using a disjunction

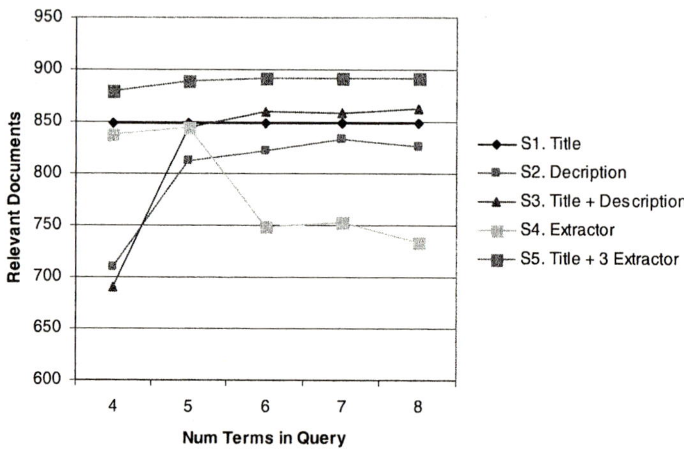

Fig. 3. Results of various term selection strategies using SCR

On Clef 2004 data, SCR produces 4% more relevant documents than a simple disjunction. Figure 2 shows the results of our query construction strategies using a disjunction of four to eight terms. Figure 3 shows the same experiments but using SCR. The results are plotted using the CLEF 2003 monolingual-French data. Precision is not plotted here, since experiment is conducted using a fixed (1000) number of documents.

We developed our strategies and trained our system using the CLEF 2003 data. We tested all combinations of preceding approaches on the 2002 data. We identified the following methods as being the best query term selection and query construction strategy:

- Use terms from the title plus the three best Extractor keyphrases from the entire topic.
- Remove any words that appear in more than 25% of documents.
- Sort low-frequency first.
- Keep at most 8 terms.
- Issue queries using successive constraint relaxation.

In the bilingual track, all our runs use this combination of strategies.

5 Query Expansion

It has been reported that query expansion using pseudo-relevance feedback generally improves results for Information Retrieval (Buckey and Salton, 1995) and is very effective in CLEF-like settings (Lam-Adesina, 2002). In our experiments, our query expansion strategy relies on a *Pseudo-Thesaurus* construction approach (Miyamoto, 1990) making use of the fuzzy logic operator of *max-min* composition (Klir & Yuan, 1995).

The approach is to take the N-best search engine results (hereafter *N-best corpus*), to extend our initial query with other pertinent words from that corpus as determined by evaluating their fuzzy similarity to the query words. Texts from *N-best corpus* are segmented into sentences and a term set (*W*) of single words is extracted after filtering prepositions, conjunctions and adverbs from the vocabulary of the DAFLES dictionary (Verlinde et al., 2003). The number of occurrences per sentence for all words is determined. The association between every word pairs is then calculated using the following fuzzy similarity measure:

Let $f(w_{ik})$ be the frequency of the word $w_i \in W$ in the sentence k from the *N-best corpus*.

$$sim(w_i, w_j) = \frac{\sum_k \min\left(f(w_{ik}), f(w_{jk})\right)}{\sum_k \max\left(f(w_{ik}), f(w_{jk})\right)} \quad (1)$$

Among all words, the ones which are closer to the original query terms were added to our query. We tried adding 1 to 10 terms when building the *N-best corpus* with 5, 10, 25 and 50 documents. This did not improve results, when tested on CLEF 2002 data. The same conclusion holds for 2004.

A possible explanation of the lack of improvement with our query expansion algorithm may be that search engines using only boolean queries may not be able to take advantage of these expanded terms. The extra words added to the queries can be unrelated to the topic, and should have a smaller weight than the initial query terms. The *Pseudo-Thesaurus* gives confidence levels for its expanded list of terms, but we were not able to incorporate this information into our final queries. More investigation is needed to understand why our query expansion attempt failed.

6 Query Translation

A critical part of bilingual information retrieval is the translation of queries, or conversely the translation of the target documents. In our experiments we decided to translate the queries using three different methods. As a baseline we use the free Babel Fish translation service (Babel Fish, 2004). We compare this to (1) an automatic translation method which relies on TERMIUM Plus ® (Termium, 2004), an English-French-Spanish terminological knowledge base which contains more than 3 500 000 terms recommended by the Translation Bureau of Canada and (2) a statistical machine translation technique inspired by IBM Model 1 (Brown *et al.*, 1993), which we call BagTrans. BagTrans has been trained on part of the Europarl Corpus and the Canadian Hansard. The following sections present Termium, BagTrans and, finally, the results obtained by all systems.

The terms stored in Termium are arranged in records, each record containing all the information in the database pertaining to one concept, and each record dealing with only one concept alone (Leonhardt, 2004). Thus the translation task becomes one of word sense disambiguation, where a term must be matched to its most relevant record; this record in turn offers us standardized and alternative translations. A record contains a list of subject fields and entries, all of which are in English and French, and some of which are in Spanish as well. Entries include the main term, synonyms and abbreviations. The translation procedure attempts to find an overlap between the subject fields of the terms in the query so as to select the correct record of the word which is being translated. If none is found, then the most general term is selected. Generality is determined by the number of times a term appears across all records for a given word, or, if the records themselves do not provide adequate information, generality is determined by the term frequency in a terabyte-sized corpus of unlabeled text (Terra and Clarke, 2003). When a word is not contained in Termium, then its translation is obtained using Babel Fish. More details about the translation procedure using Termium can be found in (Jarmasz and Barrière, 2004).

Given a French word, BagTrans assigns probabilities to individual English words that reflect their likelihood of being the translation of that word and then uses the most probable word in the English query. The probability of an English word e is then calculated as the average over all French tokens f in the query of the probability $p(e|f)$ that e is the translation of f. Translation probabilities $p(e|f)$ are derived from the standard bag-of-words translation IBM Model 1, and estimated from parallel corpora using the EM algorithm. Two different parallel corpora were used in our experiments: the Europarl corpus, containing approximately 1M sentence pairs and 60M words;

and a segment of the Hansard corpus, containing approximately 150,000 sentence pairs and 6.5M words.

Figure 4 shows the precision and recall curves for the three translation techniques as measured using the CLEF 2004 data. The automatic translations strategies with Babel Fish and BagTrans do not perform any word sense disambiguation, whereas the ones using Termium attempt to disambiguate the senses by determining the context from the other terms in the query. Note that Termium found more relevant documents than Babel Fish but its precision-recall curve is lower.

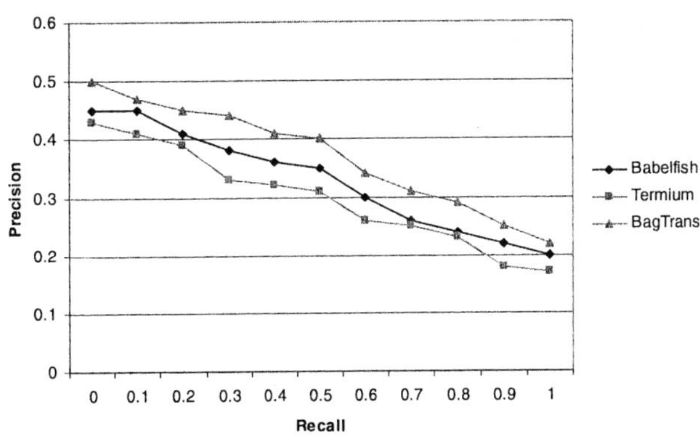

Fig. 4. Comparison of the three translation strategies

There are many ways in which our Termium and BagTrans translation systems can be improved. None have been customized or trained in particular for this CLEF competition. Since our search engines use boolean operators, an incorrect translation can have a big impact on the results. As we do not take context into consideration when using Babel Fish or BagTrans, it is not surprising that the translations are often incorrect. Termium, on the other hand, is a governmental terminological database and it may contain only specific senses of a word, which might be more correct in some official sense, yet less popular. Termium suffers from being normative. We will continue to pursue automatic machine translation methods which can be trained on specific corpora like BagTrans and which take into account the correct word senses for our future participations at CLEF.

7 Conclusion and Future Work

In our first participation in the Cross-Language Evaluation Forum (CLEF) we participated in the French monolingual and French to English bilingual tasks. We use two COTS search engines and implement various query strategies. The best setup we found is creating a query using all words of the topic title plus the 3 best keyphrases of Extractor. We filter stop words based on their frequency in the corpus. Then we sort terms from the rarest to the most frequent. We retrieved documents by issuing successive queries to the search engine, starting with a conjunction of all terms and gradually relaxing constraint by adding disjunction of terms. For the bilingual aspect, BagTrans, a statistical model based on IBM Model 1, yields the best results.

Two main points need more investigation. The first one is our unsuccessful use of the pseudo-relevance feedback. We believe that a strict boolean search engine may be problematic for this kind of algorithm. Indeed, the insertion of only one irrelevant term may lead to irrelevant documents. A weighted query may be the key to smoothen the impact of those terms, especially when our pseudo-relevance feedback algorithm has the ability to output confidence values.

Another pending question is why Termium found many more documents than Babel Fish while the latter present a higher precision-recall curve. We believe it means that Termium did not rank the relevant documents as well as the other strategies did. The explanation, though, remains unclear.

For our next participation, we plan to use a search engine which can perform weighted queries. We'll concentrate on pseudo-relevance feedback, known to be useful at CLEF. We should also add a third language to our translation models to participate in another bilingual track.

Acknowledgements

Thanks to Roland Kuhn and Peter Turney for thorough reading and helpful comments.

References

Babel Fish, (2004), *Babel Fish Translation.* http://babelfish.altavista.com/ [Source checked August 2004].

Brown, P. F., Della Pietra, S. A., Della Pietra, V. J., and Mercer, R. L. (1993). The Mathematics of Statistical Machine Translation: Parameter Estimation. *Computational Linguistics, 19(2)*:263-311.

Buckley, C. and Salton, G. (1995), Optimization of relevance feedback weights, *Proceedings of the 18th annual international ACM SIGIR conference on research and development in information retrieval*, 351-357.

Chen, A. (2002), *Cross*-Language Retrieval Experiments at CLEF 2002, *CLEF 2002, Cross-Language Evaluation Forum.*

Cöster, R., Sahlgren, M. and Karlgren, J. (2003), Selective compound splitting of Swedish queries for Boolean combinations of truncated terms, *CLEF 2003, Cross-Language Evaluation Forum.*

Craswell, N., Hawking, D., Wilkinson R. and Wu M. (2003), Overview of the TREC 2003 Web Track, *The Twelfth Text Retrieval Conference, TREC-2003*, Washington, D. C.

Jarmasz, M. and Barrière, C. (2004), *A Terminological Resource and a Terabyte-Sized Corpus for Automatic Keyphrase in Context Translation*, Technical Report, National Research Council of Canada.

Klir, G. J. and Yuan B. (1995), *Fuzzy Sets and Fuzzy Logic*, Prentice Hall: Upper Saddle River, NJ.

Lam-Adesina, A.M., Jones, G.J.H. (2002), Exeter at CLEF 2001: Experiments with Machine Translation for bilingual retrieval, *CLEF 2001, LNCS 2406*, Peters, C., Braschler, M., Gonzalo, J. and Kluck, M. (Eds.), Springer, Germany.

Leonhardt, C. (2004). *Termium ® History*. http://www.termium.gc.ca/site/histo_e.html [Source checked August 2004].

Miyamoto, S. (1990). *Fuzzy Sets in Information Retrieval and Cluster Analysis*. Dordrecht, Netherlands: Kluwer Academic Publishers.

Porter, M. F. (1980). An Algorithm for Suffix Stripping. *Program,* 14(3): 130-127.

Salton, G. and Buckley, C. (1988), Term-weighting approaches in automatic text retrieval, *Information Processing and Management: an International Journal*, 24 (5): 513-523

Termium (2004), *The Government of Canada's Terminology and Linguistic Database.* http://www.termium.com/ [Source checked August 2004].

Terra, E. and Clarke, C.L.A.. (2003), Frequency estimates for statistical word similarity measures. *In Proceedings of the Human Language Technology and North American Chapter of Association of Computational Linguistics Conference 2003* (HLT/NAACL 2003), Edmonton, Canada, 244 – 251.

Turney, P.D. (2000), Learning Algorithms for Keyphrase Extraction, *Information Retrieval*, 2 (4): 303-336.

Verlinde, S., Selva, T. & GRELEP (Groupe de Recherche en Lexicographie Pédagogique) (2003). *Dafles*

Report on Thomson Legal and Regulatory Experiments at CLEF-2004

Isabelle Moulinier and Ken Williams

Thomson Legal and Regulatory, 610 Opperman Drive,
Eagan, MN 55123, USA
{Isabelle.Moulinier, Ken.Williams}@thomson.com

Abstract. Thomson Legal and Regulatory participated in the CLEF-2004 monolingual and bilingual tracks. Monolingual experiments included Portuguese, Russian and Finnish. We investigated a new query structure to handle Finnish compounds. Our main focus was bilingual search from German to French. Our approach used query translation and post-translation pseudo-relevance feedback. We compared two translation models for query translation, and captured compound translations through fertility probabilities. While the fertility-based approach picks good terms, it does not help improve bilingual retrieval. Pseudo-relevance feedback, on the other hand, resulted in improved average precision.

1 Introduction

During the 2004 CLEF campaign, Thomson Legal and Regulatory participated in monolingual and bilingual information retrieval. With our monolingual experiments, we revisited our approach to handling compounds for Finnish retrieval. Previously, we would attempt to match on compounds and phrases. Our new approach restricts matches to compounds only.

Removing stopwords is generally beneficial. With no language expertise in Finnish, Russian, and Portuguese, we investigated building stopword lists using collection and query log statistics, with no manual editing. Our experiments measured the effect of these lists on retrieval.

Our effort, however, was mainly concentrated on bilingual search. We relied on query translation and investigated building bilingual lexicons from corpora using statistical machine translation. Researchers at IBM [1] have proposed several statistical models of increasing complexity. Through our experiments, we were particularly interested in assessing whether a more sophisticated model (IBM Model 3) would outperform a simpler model (IBM Model 1). Specifically, we focused on the notion of fertility introduced by Model 3, which allows a source term to translate to zero or more target terms. In the case of German to French translations, we used fertilities to capture translating German compounds into French phrases.

In addition to investigating translation approaches, we introduced post-translation pseudo-relevance feedback in our runs. That lead to improved average

C. Peters et al. (Eds.): CLEF 2004, LNCS 3491, pp. 110–122, 2005.

precision. As reported in prior research, we observed a great variability on a per-query basis.

We present our experimental platform and some background in Sect. 2. Section 3 presents our bilingual effort, while monolingual experiments are described in Sect. 4.

2 Background

We briefly describe the retrieval system we used during our CLEF participation, and the pseudo-relevance feedback approach we adopted.

2.1 The WIN System

The WIN system is a full-text natural language search engine, and corresponds to TLR/West Group's implementation of the inference network retrieval model. While based on the same retrieval model as the INQUERY system [2], WIN has evolved separately and focused on the retrieval of legal material in large collections in a commercial environment that supports both Boolean and natural language searches [3].

Indexing. Indexing of European languages considers tokens (words) as indexing units. Tokens are identified by localized tokenization rules (e.g. detecting apostrophes in French). Tokens are also stemmed using a morphological stemmer[1] which also identifies compounds and their parts for compound-rich languages such as Finnish or German.

Document Retrieval. Document retrieval in WIN can be decomposed into two components: query formulation and document scoring. Query formulation identifies query concepts, while scoring find matches for such concepts in documents.

Query formulation identifies "concepts" in natural language text, and imposes a Bayesian belief structure on these concepts. In many cases, each term in the natural language text represents a concept, and a flat structure gives the same weight to all concepts. However, phrases, compounds or misspellings can introduce more complex concepts, using operators such as "natural phrase," "compound," or "synonym."

We used a standard *tf-idf* scheme for computing term beliefs in all our runs. The belief of a single concept is given by:

$$bel_{\text{term}}(Q) = 0.4 + 0.6 * tf_{\text{norm}} * idf_{\text{norm}}$$

where

$$tf_{\text{norm}} = \frac{\log(tf + 0.5)}{\log(tf_{\max} + 1.0)} \quad \text{and} \quad idf_{\text{norm}} = \frac{log(C + 0.5) - log(df)}{log(C + 1.0)}$$

[1] We are using the stemmer commercialized by Inxight within the LinguistX platform.

and tf is the number of occurrences of the term within the document, $tf_{\max}$ is the maximum number of occurrences of any term within the document, df is the number of documents containing the term and C the total number of documents in the collection. $tf_{\max}$ is a weak approximation for document length.

The final document score is an average of the document score as a whole and the score of the best portion, where the best portion is dynamically computed based on query concept occurrences.

2.2 Pseudo-Relevance Feedback

Past research has reported on the benefits of pseudo-relevance feedback. For example, the relevance feedback incorporated in OKAPI BM-25 model has been quite successful at CLEF [4]. Recently, alternative approaches to selecting relevant documents have been introduced; for example, Sakai and Sparck-Jones [5] investigated using document summaries to support pseudo-relevance feedback.

Our approach follows the work outlined by Haines and Croft [6] where feedback was added to INQUERY.

Term Selection. We use a Rocchio-like formula to select terms for expansion:

$$sw = \frac{\beta}{|R|} \sum_{d \in R} (tf_{\text{norm}} * idf_{\text{norm}}) - \frac{\gamma}{|\overline{R}|} \sum_{d \in \overline{R}} (tf_{\text{norm}} * idf_{\text{norm}}) \tag{1}$$

where R is the set of documents considered relevant, $\overline{R}$ the set of documents considered not relevant, and $|X|$ denotes the cardinality of set X. tf_{norm} and idf_{norm} are defined in the previous section. The β and γ weights are set experimentally. Equation 1 reflects that we select terms for expansion solely on the basis of documents.

Reformulated Query. We append N selected terms to the query, eliminating any terms already present in the original query. In addition, each added term is weighted by the tf_{norm} part of the selection weight. Weights of original query terms remain unchanged.

3 Bilingual Experiments

Our approach to bilingual search relies on word-by-word query translation using bilingual lexicons. We build our lexicons from parallel corpora using a statistical machine translation toolkit. In particular, we investigate how parameters from the translation models can be leveraged for selecting translations for German compounds.

3.1 Background

In a cross-lingual search system, user queries and documents may not share the same language. Before matching between documents and queries can happen, some level of translation is required. Conventional approaches separate the translation and retrieval processes, with translation occurring prior to retrieval. However, recent efforts use language modeling [7] to integrate translation and retrieval in a unified model.

We focused on query translation rather than document translation or the translation of both queries and documents. Query translation can be performed using machine translation tools [4] such as Systran, machine readable dictionaries [8], and bilingual lexicons learned from parallel or comparable corpora. Such bilingual lexicons include similarity thesauri [9] which capture the notion of translation and related terms at once; and probability tables from statistical machine translation [7] which attempt to encode exact translations only.

With queries being translated term-by-term using bilingual lexicons, a term may have multiple possible translations. By taking advantage of query structures available in INQUERY, Pirkola [10] has shown that grouping translations for a given term is a better technique than allowing all translations to contribute equally.

3.2 German to French Translation: Translating Compounds

Our experiments focused on leverage statistical Machine Translation (MT) models for information retrieval. We chose to translate queries term-by-term rather than as natural language sentences.

Translation Models 1 and 3. Brown, *et al.* [1] introduced five models of increasing complexity. We chose to compare Model 1 and Model 3. Model 1 is intended to capture individual word translations, while Model 3 introduces modeling of local alignments and fertilities. We were particularly interested in the notion of fertility, which allows a source term to translate to zero or more target terms. In the case of German to French translations, we hoped that fertilities would capture translating German compounds into French phrases.

Using Translation and Fertility Probabilities. We trained Models 1 and 3 on a parallel corpus aligned at the sentence level. Since we chose to translate queries term-by-term, we did not need the decoding phase typically associated with statistical MT. We simply used translation and fertility probabilities for each source term d and target term f:

- $t^1(f|d)$, translation probabilities for Model 1,
- $t^3(f|d)$, translation probabilities for Model 3,
- $n(\phi|d)$ where $\phi = 0 \dots 9$, fertility probabilities for Model 3, and
- p_0, the fertility probability for the empty notion.

We defined two translation methods: a word-based method and a fertility-based method.

The word-based method `lex` selects the n most probable translations of each source term d using the translation probabilities. To limit adding spurious translations, we threshold translation probilities to a fixed value $p_{\min}$. Consequently, the `lex` method may select 0 to n translations for a given term.

The fertility-based approach `fert` represents our attempt at capturing the translation of German compounds. With this approach, we select one translation per source term, but each translation may include multiple terms. The `fert` model generates for each source term d a translation set of the m most probable target terms $f_1, \ldots, f_m$, ranked according to their translation probabilities $t^3(f_i|d)$. The number of selected terms m is given by

$$\underset{\phi}{\text{ArgMax}} \begin{cases} n(\phi|d) * p_0 & \text{if } \phi = 0 \\ n(\phi|d) * \sum_{i=1}^{\phi} t^3(f_i|d) & \text{if } \phi > 0 \end{cases}$$

Examples. Examples of selected translations are reported in Table 1. The first three examples capture the adequate translation for the German term. The last example, *Lawinenunglücken,* is only partially translated to *avalanches* (the disaster aspect is missing). In addition, the `fert` method selects far too many terms because the mass of translation probabilities outweighs the fertility factor.

Additional Processing of Non-translated Terms. We performed some additional processing for non-translated terms, i.e. terms with no entry in the bilingual lexicons. In particular, we focused on compounds that did not appear in the parallel corpus.

When no translation was found for a German term, we first stemmed the German term. If translations were found for the stemmed term, we associated these translations to the original term. If still no translation was found and the stemmed term was identified as a compound, we applied the translation process to each stemmed part. The original term was associated with the translations of the compound parts. Finally, when no translation was found, the original German term was kept as the translation. Examples of compounds translated via this additional processing are given in Table 2.

Query Formulation. We followed Pirkola [10] and others in structuring translated queries to give the same importance to each original term, regardless of the number of translations. We grouped multiple translations under a weighted #SUM node. The weight associated with each translation is its translation probability.

We also investigated using a proximity operator when translating compound terms. When the original German term was a compound, we grouped all translations under the #NPHR operator[2].

3.3 Results and Discussion

We trained Models 1 and 3 using the GIZA++ toolkit [11] on the Europarl corpus [12].

---

[2] The WIN #NPHR operator corresponds to INQUERY phrase operator, and includes partial credit. Partial credit enables both the operator and its children to contribute to document belief scores.

Table 1. Examples of German to French translations. We used the probabilities $t^3(.|.)$ to select translations in the `lex` method. We used both $t^3(.|.)$, the translation probabilities, and $n(\phi|.)$, the fertilities from Model 3 to generate translation in the `fert` approach

Term: **globale**

f	$t^3(f\|d)$	ϕ	$n(\phi\|d)$	`lex` translation	`fert` translation
globale	0.306778	1	0.746871	globale	globale
mondiale	0.152177	0	0.165741	mondiale	
global	0.115814	2	0.0617001	global	
mondial	0.0928475	3	0.0207158		
échelle	0.0456918		...		

Term: **Klimaveränderungen**

f	$t^3(f\|d)$	ϕ	$n(\phi\|d)$	`lex` translation	`fert` translation
climatiques	0.269569	2	0.589625	climatiques	climatiques
changements	0.258488	1	0.105312	changements	changements
changement	0.105622	3	0.0936477	changement	
climatique	0.103034	4	0.07117		
climat	0.0250892		...		

Term: **Treibhauseffektes**

f	$t^3(f\|d)$	ϕ	$n(\phi\|d)$	`lex` translation	`fert` translation
effet	0.265273	2	0.283692	effet	effet
serre	0.26525	1	0.246126	serre	serre
venir	0.0380016	3	0.174969		
mes	0.0191118	9	0.0651408		

Term: **Lawinenunglücken**

f	$t^3(f\|d)$	ϕ	$n(\phi\|d)$	`lex` translation	`fert` translation
avalanches	0.10976	1	0.404492	avalanches	avalanches
programmer	0.10976	2	0.231625	programmer	programmer
servir	0.10976	3	0.1003	servir	servir
court	0.10976	0	0.0752761		court
interventions	0.10976	9	0.0611943		interventions
diverses	0.109759	4	0.0435146		diverses
série	0.109759				série
pourquoi	0.109759		⋮		pourquoi
zones	0.109624				zones

Base Runs. We ran our first set of experiments set to determine whether the more sophisticated translation model (Model 3) improves retrieval performance over the simpler Model 1. We compared Model 1 (t^1) and Model 3 (t^3) with the `lex` translation selection. Results are reported in Table 3. Model 3 with `lex` provided a strong baseline with the #SUM operator. The `lex` method using Model 3 outperforms the `lex` method using Model 1, although the difference is not statistically significant. We found that many queries improved by a noticeable margin when Model 3 was introduced, and that some of that queries that degraded were affected by poor post-translation stopword removal.

Table 2. Examples of compounds translated through additional processing for terms outside the lexicon. Translation is performed using `lex`, $n = 3$, $p_{\min} = 0.1$ and Model 3 translation probabilities

Compound term	Identified Translations	($t(f\|d)$)
Wohnungsbrände	logement	(0.453006)
	incendie	(0.319306)
	au	(0.256685)
	feu	(0.153006)
Weltmeisterin	du	(0.172959)
	champions	(0.135024)
	monde	(0.135023)

Table 3. Comparisons between bilingual base runs. The `lex` approach using Models 1 (t^1) and 3 (t^3) used $n = 3$ and $p_{\min} = 0.1$

Run	Avg. Prec,	R-Prec.	Prec. at 20 doc.
t^1, `lex`, #SUM	0.2934	0.2951	0.2224
t^3, `lex`, #SUM	0.3225	0.3250	0.2541
t^3, `fert`, #SUM	0.2717	0.2868	0.2133

Fertility Runs. Our attempt to capture the translation of compounds using fertilities had limited success. We find the `fert` method promising inasmuch as it is able to identify adequate compound translations but suffers from selecting a single, possibly multi-term translation. The difference between runs `lex` and `fert` using Model 3 (cf. Table 3) is statistically significant[3]. We have already noted (*Lawinenunglücken*) that the `fert` approach may select too many terms when the probability mass of the candidate set outweighs the fertility probability factor. This behavior, however, was observed only three times in the CLEF 2004 query set. The main factor hindering the `fert` approach is the selection of a single, possibly multi-term translation. This limits the effectiveness of retrieval. To confirm this hypothesis, we evaluated the `lex` approach selecting a single translation ($n = 1$). In that experiment, the average precision dropped to 0.2641, and the difference was found to be statistically significant.

Additional Processing of Non-translated Terms. The results reported above include the additional processing of non-translated terms. We found the additional processing beneficial (cf. Table 4), although the gain is not statistically significant. About half of the queries were impacted. Average precision increased by more that 10% for ten queries, but decreased in the same amount for six queries. For example, performance of query 209 dramatically increased by the addition of the term *vainqueurs* as a translation part of the compound *Tour-de-France-Sieger*. On the other hand, performance of queries 205 and 230 was degraded because compounds were only partially translated, missing the

[3] We used the Wilcoxon signed-rank test, with $\alpha = 0.05$.

Table 4. Effect of additional processing of non-translated terms. All runs use #SUM to group translations. The `lex` approach uses Model 3, $n = 3$ and $p_{\min} = 0.1$

Run	Avg. Prec.	R-Prec.	Prec. at 20 doc.
`lex`, no additional processing	0.3042	0.3150	0.2367
`lex`, additional processing	0.3225	0.3250	0.2541
`fert`, no additional processing	0.2496	0.2603	0.1827
`fert`, additional processing	0.2717	0.2868	0.2133

Table 5. Capturing the translation of German compounds. Comparison between the #SUM and the #NPHR operators

Run	Avg Prec.	R-Prec.	Prec. at 20 doc.
t^3, `fert`, #SUM	0.2717	0.2868	0.2133
t^3, `fert`, #NPHR	0.2708	0.2779	0.2153

core meaning: the term *Kamikazeaktionen* was translated to only the term *action*, while the translation of *US-Raumfähre* (US-space shuttle) did not capture the aspect *navette* (shuttle).

Translated Compounds as Phrases. Next we studied the impact of query formulation with the `fert` approach. The `fert` approach captures the translation of German compounds into multiple French terms. We expected that introducing the #NPHR operator would positively impact retrieval, since French phrases were a better representation of German compounds. The results reported in Table 5 did not support our intuition: the #NPHR operator did not improve average precision. We think that partial credit diluted results, because with partial credit the children of a phrase contribute independently as concepts to document scores. In future work, we will explore alternative scoring approaches for the phrase proximity to retain the translations of a source term as a single concept.

Seeding Translation Models. We also investigated seeding the translation models with a machine-readable dictionary. We tested only with Model 3 and found no differences between the two translation probability tables.

Runs Using Pseudo-Relevance Feedback. Finally we report on experiments using post-translation pseudo-relevance feedback (PRF). After the initial retrieval, we selected the five highest-ranked documents as relevant documents. We also selected the twenty lowest-ranked documents as non-relevant. We use the non-relevant documents as a filter to prevent common words from being selected by PRF.

As can be observed in Table 6, the introduction of PRF was beneficial. We observed the typical behavior when comparing base runs and PRF. In the best case (run "t^3, `lex`"), PRF helps improve the performance of 59% of queries and

Table 6. Experimental results using post-translation pseudo-relevance feedback. All runs with PRF used $N = 20$, $n = 5$, $m = 20$, $\beta = 1$. $\star$ indicates that PRF improves over the base run, and the difference is statistically significant with $\alpha = 0.01$ using the Wilcoxon signed-rank test

Run	Avg Prec.	R-Prec.	Prec. at 20 doc.	Above/equal/below Median
t^1, `lex`, nd, NoPRF	0.2934	0.2951	0.2224	–
t^1, `lex`, nd, $\gamma = 4$ (tlrde2fr4)	0.3289	0.3005	0.2531	23 / 1 / 24
t^3, `lex`, nd, NoPRF (tlrde2fr2)	0.3225	0.3250	0.2541	32 / 2 / 14
t^3, `lex`, nd, $\gamma = 1$ (tlrde2fr3)	0.3750$\star$	0.3409	0.3000	31 / 2 / 15
t^3, `fert`, d (tlrde2fr1)	0.2723	0.2877	0.2153	25 / 1 / 22
t^3, `fert`, d, $\gamma = 1$	0.3250	0.2915	0.2571	–

degrade 38% of the queries. In the two other runs, PRF is helpful for 50% of queries, and not so helpful for 44% of queries.

A point of interest is the comparison to the median. There is a significant difference in average precision between the base run and the PRF run using `lex` and Model 3; however each run compares similarly to the median of all runs. After analysis, we observed the well-documented seesaw effect of pseudo-relevance feedback: 10 queries fell below the median when PRF was added, while 8 queries rose above the median.

4 Monolingual Experiments

We participated in the monolingual track with three new languages: Finnish, Portuguese and Russian. We revisited our approach to compound handling and experimented with the creation of stopword lists.

4.1 Compound Handling in Finnish Retrieval

Prior Research. During past CLEF campaigns, the handling of compounds has received a fair amount of attention. Prior research has found that, for German, Dutch, or Finnish, breaking compounds into parts and searching on the parts was beneficial to both monolingual and crosslingual retrieval [13, 14]. Alternatively, some researchers have focused on character n-grams as indexing units for European languages (cf. [15]), limiting the reliance on compound identification. Indeed character n-grams may capture compound parts without explicitly identifying compounds.

Compounds are not Quite Like Phrases. At CLEF 2000, we investigated the impact of decompounding on monolingual retrieval for German. In those experiments, we found that decompounding was useful and that representing compounds using the #NPHR operator with partial credit was the most effective. The #NPHR operator corresponds to an unordered proximity of 3, and partial credit allows the children of the proximity operator to contribute to the final belief score, independently of the operator.

With this year's experiments, we revisited the operator and proposed a stricter proximity #NPHR0. In order to contribute to the document belief score, parts of the compound must appear in a compound, not in a "phrase" environment. Partial credit is still applied. In other words, we replaced the unordered proximity of 3 with a proximity of 0. This is made possible by our indexing scheme, where compounds and their parts are indexed.

Experimental Results and Discussion. Table 7 summarizes our experimental results with Finnish compounds. We observe a small improvement in both average precision and R-Precision, although the difference is not statistically significant.

Table 7. Experimental results using different operators in the representation of Finnish compounds. Differences are not statistically significant

Run	Avg. Prec.	R-Prec.	Prec. at 20 doc.
#NPHR	0.5418	0.4903	0.2722
#NPHR0	0.5562	0.5027	0.2744

Let us note that all documents that satisfy the #NPHR0 operator also satisfy the #NPHR operator, although their belief score may be different under each condition. For some queries, e.g. query 208, the #NPHR run ranks relevant documents higher in the list, suggesting that it finds useful proximities in addition to the exact compounds. On the other hand, for other queries, e.g. query 203, the additional proximities found in documents degrade the ranked list by pushing relevant documents further down the list. Future work is required to assess whether the difference in ranking is linked to the different *idf* values associated with the #NPHR and #NPHR0 operators.

4.2 Experiments with Stopword Lists

Two Sources to Identify Stopwords. At NTCIR-4, we built upon Savoy's work [4] and compared using collection and query log statistics to create stopword lists. We found little differences in retrieval effectiveness.

For our CLEF experiments, we merged both approaches. We selected the most frequent terms in the collection as stopwords. We subsequently enriched that list with terms extracted from query logs. No manual review of the list was performed.

For our runs, we selected the most frequent 100 and 200 stemmed terms in collections. To those collection-based lists, we added stemmed terms that occurred in over 20% of the query logs. For each language, a query log consisted of collected CLEF queries from previous campaigns.

Results and Discussion. In Table 8, we compare our base runs with no stopword removal (none) with removing stopwords extracted from collection statistics and query logs. Stopword lists are a useful tool to make search more effective in terms of average precision. We observe statistically significant differences in average precision for all runs.

Table 8. Summary of our monolingual runs, with an emphasis on using stopword lists. Finnish runs use the #NPHR0 operator. The ⋆⋆,⋆ sign indicates a statistical difference with the base run "none" with $\alpha = 0.01, 0.05$ using the Wilcoxon signed-rank test

Run	Avg. Prec.	R-Prec.	Above/equal/below Median
fi, none	0.5466	0.4947	–
fi, 100 (tlrfi1)	0.5551 ⋆	0.4994	23/8/13
fi, 200 (tlrfi2)	0.5562 ⋆	0.5027	23/9/12
pt, none	0.4250	0.3992	–
pt, 100 (tlrpt1)	0.4458 ⋆⋆	0.4017	16/15/14
pt, 200 (tlrpt2)	0.4469 ⋆⋆	0.4044	16/17/12
ru, none (tlrru2)	0.3176	0.2783	9/7/17
ru, 100 (tlrru1)	0.3702 ⋆⋆	0.3183	13/9/11
ru, 200	0.3820 ⋆⋆	0.3364	–

We conclude our discussion on stopword lists by outlining the need for human review. In the Finnish stopword list, we noticed cities such as Helsinki and Tampere, as well as terms like suomi (Finland, finnish language) and suomalainen (finnish). Similarly the Portuguese list contains Lisboa, Portugal, português, governo or ministro. While such terms are frequent in the collection, they are not truly stopwords and interfered with some queries (e.g. query 231).

5 Conclusion

Our bilingual experiments with IBM Model 3 are promising. Using a word by word translation, we were able to capture the translation of German compounds using translation and fertility probabilities. In the future, we will expand our work to select more than one translation per source term. In addition, we will investigate how to integrate a bias towards the search collection during translation. There may be value in looking at alternative scoring for the #NPHR operator, where partial credit is not allowed to dilute the contribution of other concepts. Finally, we will investigate whether there is added value in a more complex model in the context of word-by-word translation.

We find our monolingual runs satisfactory. Our reformulated compound handling in Finnish was beneficial when compared to our previous approach. Compound handling may also benefit from improved partial credit. We have observed similar findings with German and Korean. Our stopword experiments confirmed well-established results about stopword removal and retrieval effectiveness.

References

1. Brown, P., Della Pietra, V., Della Pietra, S., Mercer, R.: The mathematics of statistical machine translation: parameter estimation. Computational Linguistics **19** (1993)
2. Croft, W.B., Callan, J., Broglio, J.: The INQUERY retrieval system. In: Proceedings of the 3rd International Conference on Database and Expert Systems Applications, Spain (1992)
3. Turtle, H.: Natural language vs. boolean query evaluation: a comparison of retrieval performance. In: Proceedings of the 17th Annual International ACM SIGIR Conference on Research and Development in Information Retrieval, Dublin, Ireland (1994) 212–220
4. Savoy, J.: Report on CLEF-2001 experiments: Effective combined query-translation approach. In Evaluation of Cross-Language Information Retrieval Systems. CLEF 2001 revised papers, Springer LNCS 2406. (2001)
5. Sakai, T., Sparck-Jones, K.: Generic summaries for indexing in Information Retrieval. In: Proceedings of the 24th annual international ACM SIGIR conference on Research and development in information retrieval. (2001) 190–198
6. Haines, D., Croft, W.: Relevance feedback and inference networks. In: Proceedings of the Sixteenth Annual International ACM SIGIR Conference on Research and Development in Information Retrieval. (1993) 2–11
7. Kraaij, W., Nie, J.Y., Simard, M.: Web-based statistical translation models in cross-language information retrieval. Computational Linguistics **29** (2003) 381–419
8. Hull, D., Grefenstette, G.: Querying across languages: a dictionary-based approach to multilingual information retrieval. In: Proceedings of the 19th Annual International ACM SIGIR Conference on Research and Development in Information Retrieval. (1996) 49–57
9. Sheridan, P., Braschler, M., Schuble, P.: Cross-lingual information retrieval in a multilingual legal domain. In: Proceedings of the First European Conference on Research and Advanced Technology for Digital Libraries, Pisa, Italy (1997) 253–268
10. Pirkola, A.: The effects of query structure and dictionary setups in dictionary-based cross-language information retrieval. In: Proceedings of the 21th Annual International ACM SIGIR Conference on Research and Development in Information Retrieval, Melbourne, Australia (1998) 55–63
11. Och, F.J., Ney, H.: Improved statistical alignment models. In: The 38th Annual Meeting of the Association for Computational Linguistics, Hongkong, China (2000) 440–447
12. Koehn, P.: Europarl: A multilingual corpus for evaluation of machine translation. Draft (2002)
13. Hedlund, H., Keskustalo, H., Pirkola, A., Airio, E., Järvelin, K.: Utaclir at CLEF 2001 - effects of compound splitting and N-gram techniques. In Evaluation of Cross-Language Information Retrieval Systems. CLEF 2001 revised papers, Springer LNCS 2406. (2002) 118–136

14. Monz, C., de Rijke, M.: Shallow morphological analysis in monolingual information retrieval for dutch, german, and italian. In Evaluation of Cross-Language Information Retrieval Systems. CLEF 2001 revised papers, Springer LNCS 2406. (2002) 262–277
15. McNamee, P., Mayfield, J., Piatko, C.: A language-independent approach to european text retrieval. Cross-Language Information Retrieval and Evaluation. CLEF 2000 revised papers. Springer LNCS 2069. (2001) 129–139

Effective Translation, Tokenization and Combination for Cross-Lingual Retrieval

Jaap Kamps*, Sisay Fissaha Adafre, and Maarten de Rijke

Informatics Institute, University of Amsterdam,
Kruislaan 403, 1098 SJ Amsterdam, The Netherlands
{kamps, sfissaha, mdr}@science.uva.nl

Abstract. Our approach to cross-lingual document retrieval starts from the assumption that effective monolingual retrieval is at the core of any cross-language retrieval system. We devote particular attention to three crucial ingredients of our approach to cross-lingual retrieval. First, effective *tokenization* techniques are essential to cope with morphological variations common in many European languages. Second, effective *combination* methods allow us to combine the best of different strategies. Finally, effective *translation* methods for translating queries or documents turn a monolingual retrieval system into a cross-lingual retrieval system proper. The viability of our approach is shown by a series of experiments in monolingual, bilingual, and multilingual retrieval.

1 Introduction

The CLEF 2004 ad hoc track marked a departure from earlier evaluation campaigns, by its focus on a smaller set of languages, and on lesser known languages [1]. This new set-up prompted us to re-evaluate and extend our earlier approaches to cross-language document retrieval [2, 3, 4]. Our approach to cross-lingual information retrieval starts from the assumption that effective monolingual retrieval is the core of all cross-lingual retrieval tasks [5]. Effective monolingual retrieval requires particular attention to *tokenization*—what document representation is stored in the index? In the context of the CLEF 2004 campaign, we took part in monolingual retrieval for four non-English European languages: Finnish, French, Portuguese, and Russian. Portuguese was new for CLEF 2004. We experimented with a range of language-dependent tokenization techniques, in particular stemming algorithms for all European languages [6], and compound splitting for the compound rich Finnish language. We also experimented with various language-independent tokenization techniques, in particular the use of character n-grams, where we may also index leading and ending character sequences, and retain the original words. Finally, since different document representations have different merits, the use of *combination* methods can be crucial in order to try to get the best of all worlds [7].

* Currently at Archives and Information Studies, Faculty of Humanities, University of Amsterdam.

C. Peters et al. (Eds.): CLEF 2004, LNCS 3491, pp. 123–134, 2005.

On top of an effective monolingual retrieval system, one can build a bilingual system by the *translation* of either queries or documents. We performed two in-depth case studies of bilingual retrieval, one for the resource-poor Amharic language, and another for Portuguese. For Portuguese, we performed a comparative analysis of the effectiveness of a number of translation resources. We experimented with machine translation [8] versus a parallel corpus [9], and with query translation versus collection translation. For Amharic we investigated how far we could get by combining the scarcely available resources. Our overall goal in the bilingual experiments was to shed light on the robustness of our monolingual retrieval approaches for various degrees of imperfectly translated queries.

On top of a number of effective bilingual retrieval systems, one can build a multilingual system by *combining* the results in the different languages. We experimented with running English queries on the combined English, Finnish, French, and Russian collections. Here, we experimented with straightforward ways of query translation, using machine translation whenever available, and a translation dictionary otherwise. We also experimented with combination methods using runs made on varying types of indexes.

The rest of this paper is structured as follows. In Section 2 we describe the FlexIR retrieval system used as well as our approaches to tokenization and combination. Section 3 describes our monolingual experiments. Sections 4 (Amharic) and 5 (Portuguese) discuss in detail our bilingual experiments. Section 6 addresses our multilingual experiments. Finally, in Section 7, we offer some conclusions regarding our document retrieval efforts.

2 System Description

All retrieval runs used FlexIR, an information retrieval system developed at the University of Amsterdam. FlexIR supports many types of preprocessing, scoring, indexing, and retrieval models. It also supports several retrieval models, including the standard vector space model, and language models. Our default retrieval model is a vector space model using the Lnu.ltc weighting scheme [10] to compute the similarity between a query and a document. For the experiments on which we report in this paper, we fixed *slope* at 0.2; the pivot was set to the average number of unique words per document. We also experimented with language models [11]. Here, we used a uniform query term importance weight of 0.15.

Blind feedback was applied to expand the original query with related terms. We experimented with different schemes and settings, depending on the various indexing methods and retrieval models used. For our Lnu.ltc runs term weights were recomputed by using the standard Rocchio method [12], where we considered the top 10 documents to be relevant and the bottom 500 documents to be non-relevant. We allowed at most 20 terms to be added to the original query.

To determine whether the observed differences between two retrieval approaches are statistically significant, we used the bootstrap method, a non-parametric inference test [13, 14]. We take 100,000 samples with replacement of the topics with their original scores on the two retrieval approaches. We analyze the distribution of improvements over resamples, and look for significant improvements (one-tailed) at significance levels of 0.95 (*); 0.99 (**); and 0.999 (***).

2.1 Tokenization

We carried out extensive experiments with tokenization for monolingual retrieval [5]. These include the following:

Text normalization. We do some limited text normalization by removing punctuation, applying case-folding, and mapping diacritics to the unmarked characters. The Cyrillic characters used in Russian can appear in a variety of font encodings. The collection and topics are encoded using the UTF-8 or Unicode character encoding. We converted the UTF-8 encoding into KOI8 (*Kod Obmena Informatsii*), a 1-byte per character encoding. We did all our processing, such as lower-casing, stopping, stemming, and n-gramming, on documents and queries in this KOI8 encoding. Finally, to ensure proper indexing of the documents using our standard architecture, we converted the resulting documents into the Latin alphabet using the Volapuk transliteration. We processed the Russian queries similar to the documents.

Stop word removal. Both topics and documents were stopped using the stopword lists from the Snowball stemming algorithms [6]; for Finnish we used the Neuchâtel stopword list [15]. Additionally, we removed topic specific phrases such as 'Find documents that discuss ...' from the queries. We did not use a "stop stem" or "stop n-gram" list, but we first used a stop *word* list, and then stemmed/n-grammed the topics and documents.

Stemming. For all languages we used a stemming algorithm to map word forms to their underlying stems. We used the family of Snowball stemming algorithms, available for all the languages of the CLEF 2004 collections. Snowball is a small string processing language designed for creating stemming algorithms for use in information retrieval [6].

Decompounding. For Finnish, a compound-rich language, we apply a decompounding algorithm. We treat all words occurring in the Finnish collection as potential base words for decompounding, and use the associated collection frequencies. We ignore words of length less than 4 as potential compound parts, thus a compound must have at least length 8. As a safeguard against oversplitting, we only consider compound parts with a higher collection frequency than the compound itself. We retain the original compound words, and add their parts to the documents; queries are processed similarly.

n-Gramming. For all languages, we used character n-gramming to index all character-sequences of a given length that occur in a word. Unlike stemming, n-gramming is a language-independent approach to morphological normalization. We used three different ways of forming n-grams of length 4. First, we index pure 4-grams. For example, the word `Information` will be indexed as 4-grams `info nfor form orma rmat mati atio tion`. Second, we index 4-grams with leading and ending 3-grams. For the example this will give `_inf info nfor form orma rmat mati atio tion ion_`. Third, we index 4-grams plus original words. For the example this gives `info nfor form orma rmat mati atio tion information`.

2.2 Run Combination

Combination methods have two distinct purposes. For a number of indexes of the same collection, they can be used to mix evidence from different document representations. For a distributed collection, combination methods can be used to integrate the results for each of the individual subcollections. We combined various 'base' runs using either a weighted or unweighted combination methods. The weighted interpolation was produced as follows. First, we normalized the retrieval status values (RSVs), since different runs may have radically different RSVs. For each run we re-ranked these values in $[0, 1]$ using $RSV_i' = (RSV_i - min_i)/(max_i - min_i)$; this is the Min_Max_Norm considered in [16]. Next, we assigned new weights to the documents using a linear interpolation factor λ representing the relative weight of a run: $RSV_{new} = \lambda \cdot RSV_1 + (1 - \lambda) \cdot RSV_2$. The interpolation factors λ were loosely based on experiments on earlier CLEF data sets [7]. When we combine more than two runs, we give all runs the same relative weight, effectively resulting in the familiar combSUM [17].

3 Monolingual Finnish, French, Portuguese and Russian

In this section we discuss our monolingual retrieval experiments. As explained in the introduction, we view monolingual retrieval as the core of a cross-lingual retrieval system. All other cross-language tasks are performed on top of an a (set of) monolingual indexes. Hence, building an effective monolingual retrieval system is a crucial, first step toward effective bilingual or multilingual retrieval.

3.1 Experiments

All our monolingual runs used the title and description fields of the topics. We constructed five different indexes for each of the languages using *Words*, *Stems*, *4-Grams*, *4-Grams+start/end*, and *4-Grams+Words*:

- *Words*: no morphological normalization is applied, although for Finnish *Split* indicates that words are decompounded.
- *Stems*: topic and document words are stemmed using the morphological tools described in Section 2. For Finnish, *Split+stem* indicates that compounds are split, where we stem the words and compound parts.
- *n-Grams*: both topic and document words are n-grammed, using the settings discussed in Section 2. We have three different indexes: *4-Grams*; *4-Grams+words* where also the words are retained; and *4-Grams+start/end* with beginning and ending 3-grams.

On all these indexes we created runs using the Lnu.ltc retrieval model; on the *Words* and on the *Stems* index we also created runs with a language model, resulting in 7 base runs for French, Portuguese, and Russian.

3.2 Results

Table 1 contains the mean average precision (MAP) scores for all the monolingual 'base' runs described in the previous section. The language model experiments clearly indicate the effectiveness of the stemming algorithm. For the vector space model, there is a small loss for Portuguese, but also a gain in performance for the other three languages. The outcome for the n-gram runs is less clear: there is a substantial gain in effectiveness for Finnish, but no or only a moderate gain for the other three languages. When comparing 4-gram with 4-gram+start/end, we see that including leading and ending 3-grams is always effective. Similarly, including words is effective for three of the four languages.

Table 1. Overview of MAP scores for monolingual base runs. Best scores are in boldface, stars indicate a significant improvement over the word-based run

	Finnish	*French*	*Portuguese*	*Russian*
Words (baseline)	0.3776	0.4084	0.4032	0.3186
Stems	0.4549*	0.4312*	0.4023	0.3611
4-Grams	0.4949*	0.3673	0.3439	0.2783
4-Grams+start/end	**0.5264*** **	0.3794*	0.3653	0.3212
4-Grams+words	0.4930**	0.4133	0.3723	0.3357
Words LM	0.3825	0.4059	0.4040	0.2958
Stems LM	0.4530*	**0.4463**	**0.4269**	**0.3847**

For Finnish we also applied a decompounding algorithm [5], on words and on stems, from which we produced base runs with both the Lnu.ltc retrieval model and a language model, leading to a total of 11 base runs for Finnish. Table 2 contains the MAP scores for the Finnish decompounding experiments. Decompounding leads to improvements for both retrieval models; decompounding and stemming only leads to improvements for the language model run. All Finnish n-gram runs in Table 1 outperform all decompounded runs.

Finally, we experimented with combinations of the base runs just described. For each of the four languages we constructed two combinations of stemmed and n-grammed base runs, as well as a "grand" combination of all base runs. Table 3 lists the MAP scores for our run combinations. For these, the grand combination of all base runs always outperforms the combination of a single (non)stemmed run and a single n-grammed run. When comparing with the best scoring base runs in Tables 1, we see that there is only a substantial improvement for Russian.

Table 2. Overview of MAP scores for Finnish decompounding runs. Best scores are in boldface, stars indicate a significant improvement over the word-based run

	Words	*Split*	*Stems*	*Split+Stem*
Lnu.ltc	0.3776	0.4329**	0.4549*	0.4414
LM	0.3825	0.4021	0.4530*	**0.4617***

Table 3. Overview of MAP scores for our run combinations. Best scores are in boldface, stars indicate a significant improvement over the word-based run

	Finnish	*French*	*Portuguese*	*Russian*
4-Grams+words;(Split+)stem	0.4787**	0.4410	0.4110	0.4227**
4-Grams+start/end;(Split+)words	0.5007***	0.4092	0.4180	0.4058**
All base runs	**0.5203*****	**0.4499***	**0.4326**	**0.4412****

There is a moderate improvement for French and Portuguese. The best Finnish n-gram run even outperforms the grand combination.

4 Bilingual Retrieval: Amharic to English

In Amharic, which belongs to the Semitic family of languages, word formation involves affixation, reduplication, Semitic stem interdigitation, among others. The most characteristic feature of Amharic morphology is root-pattern phenomena. This is especially true of Amharic verbs, which rely heavily on the arrangement of consonants and vowels in order to code different morphosyntactic properties (such as perfect, imperfect, etc.). Consonants, which mostly carry the semantic core of the word, form the root of the verb. Consonants and vowel patterns together constitute the stems, and stems take different types of affixes (prefixes and suffixes) to form the fully inflected words; see [18].

For our bilingual Amharic to English runs, we attempted to show how the scarce resources for Amharic can be used in (Amharic-English) bilingual information retrieval settings. Since English is used on the document side, it is interesting to see how the existing retrieval techniques can be optimized in order to make the best use of the output of the error-prone translation component.

Our Amharic to English query translation is based mainly on dictionary look up. We used an Amharic-English bilingual dictionary which consists of 15,000 fully inflected words. Due to the morphological complexity of the language, we expected the dictionary to have limited coverage. In order to improve on the coverage, two further dictionaries, root-based and stem-based, were derived from the original dictionary. We also tried to augment the dictionary with a bilingual lexicon extracted from aligned Amharic-English Bible text. However, most of the words are old English words and are also found in the dictionary. The word dictionary also contains commonly used Amharic collocations. Multiword collocations were identified and marked in the topics. For this purpose, we used a list of multiword collocations extracted from an Amharic text corpus. The dictionaries were searched for a translation of Amharic words in the following order: word-dictionary, stem dictionary, root dictionary.

Leaving aside the ungrammaticality of the output of the above translation, there are a number of problems. One is the problem of unknown words. The words may be Amharic words not included in the dictionary or foreign words. Some foreign words and their transliteration have the same spelling or are nearly

Table 4. Coverage of the respective techniques over the words occurring in the Amharic topics

Total no. of words	Word dictionary	Root dictionary	English spell checker
1,893	813	178	57

Table 5. Overview of MAP scores for Amharic to English runs. Best scores are in boldface, stars indicate a significant improvement over the word-based run

	Amharic to English
Words (baseline)	0.2071
Stems	0.1961
4-Grams	0.1224**
4-Grams+start/end	0.1300*
4-Grams+words	0.1467***
Words LM	0.1694
Stems LM	0.1703
4-Grams+words;Stems	0.1915
All base runs	**0.2138**

identical. To take advantage of this fact, Amharic words not in the dictionary are checked using an English spellchecker (Aspell). We process the English words suggested by the spellchecker one by one, and if the suggestion is similar enough to the Amharic word, it will be taken as a translation. Specifically, we look for similarity in length (i.e., a difference in length < 4), and for string similarity (i.e., a longest common substring ration of > 0.7). In this way, we address the typographical variations between the English word and its transliteration. Other unknown words are simply passed over to the English translation. Another problem relates to the selection of the appropriate translation from among the possible translations found in the dictionary. In the absence of frequency information, the most frequently used English word is selected as a translation of the corresponding Amharic word. This is achieved by querying the web. The coverage of the translation is 55%. The number of correct translations is still lower. Table 4 gives some idea of the coverage of the translation strategy.

4.1 Experiments

In our experiments we focus on the translation of the Amharic topics to English as detailed above. We used a similar set of indexes as for the monolingual runs described earlier (*Words*, *Stems*, *4-Grams*, *4-Grams+start/end*, *4-Grams+words*). For all of these, Lnu.ltc runs were produced, and for the *Word* and *Stems* indexes we also produced a language model run, leading to 7 base runs for the Amharic to English task. Additionally, we created two run combinations: a combination of the stemmed and an n-grammed run, and a combination of all base runs.

4.2 Results

Table 5 shows the mean average precision scores for our base runs. For the resource-poor Amharic to English task, we expected a fairly low performance, somewhere in the 0.12–0.20 range. However, the vector space model run on the *Words* index is surprisingly effective. Furthermore, n-gramming leads to a significant loss of performance. Table 5 also lists results on run combinations. The combination of a stemmed and a n-grammed run does not lead to improvement. The combination of all base runs leads to the best performance for Amharic to English, but the score is not significantly better than for the word-based run.

5 Bilingual Retrieval: English to Portuguese

Having discussed experiments with the resource-poor language of Amharic in the previous section, we now focus on bilingual retrieval for Portuguese. We evaluate the relative effectiveness of various translation methods for English to Portuguese retrieval. All our runs used the title and description fields of the topics. For our bilingual runs, we experimented with the WorldLingo machine translation [8] for translations into Portuguese, with a parallel corpus for translations into Portuguese.

Machine Translation. We used the WorldLingo machine translation [8] for translating the English topics into Portuguese. The translation is actually in Brazilian Portuguese, but for retrieval purposes the linguistic differences between Portuguese and Brazilian are fairly limited.

Parallel Corpus. We used the sentence-aligned parallel corpus [9], based on the Official Journal of the European Union [19]. We built a Portuguese to English translation dictionary, based on a word alignment in the parallel corpus. Since the word order in English and Portuguese are not very different, we only considered potential alignments with words in the same position, or one or two positions off. We ranked potential translations with a score based on:

- *Cognate matching* Reward similarity in word forms, by looking at the number of leading characters that agree in both languages.
- *Length matching* Reward similarity in word lengths in both languages.
- *Frequency matching* Reward similarity in word frequency in both languages.

To further aid the alignment, we constructed a list of 100 most frequent Portuguese words in the corpus, and manually translated these to English. The alignments of these highly frequent words were resolved before the word alignment phase. We built a Portuguese to English translation dictionary by choosing the most likely translation, where we only include words that score above a threshold. The length of the translation dictionary is 19,554 words. We use the translation dictionary resulting from the parallel corpus for two different purposes. Firstly, we translate the English topics into Portuguese. Secondly, we translate the Portuguese collection into English.

Table 6. Overview of MAP scores for all English to Portuguese runs. Best scores are in boldface, stars indicate a significant improvement over the word-based run

	query EU	*query Wordlingo*	*collection EU*
Words (baseline)	0.2641	0.3220	0.3830
Stems	0.3201**	0.3281	0.3901
4-Grams	0.2134	0.2856	0.3704
4-Grams+start/end	0.2296	0.2856	0.3826
4-Grams+words	0.2355	0.3203	0.3678
Words LM	0.2511	0.3167	0.3471
Stems LM	0.2993	0.3257	0.3835
4-Grams+words;Stems	0.2755	0.3207	0.3850
All base runs		**0.4366**	

5.1 Experiments

For Portuguese we used a similar set of indexes as described earlier (*Words*, *Stems*, *4-Grams*, *4-Grams+start/end*, *4-Grams+words*). We produce runs with the Lnu.ltc retrieval model, and for the *Word* and *Stems* indexes we also produced a language model run. Additionally, for the English to Portuguese task we used three types of translation: query translation using machine translation (WorldLingo), query translation using a parallel corpus (query EU), and collection translation using a parallel corpus (collection EU). This gave rise to a total of 21 base runs for the English to Portuguese task. Finally, for each of the three translation methods, we look at the combination of the stemmed and a n-grammed run, and we also look at the combination of all 21 base runs.

5.2 Results

Table 6 shows the mean average precision scores for our base runs. Comparing the different translation methods for the plain *Words* index, we see that, for query translation, the machine translation is more effective than the parallel corpus. This is no surprise, since a word by word translation dictionary was derived from the parallel corpus. However, if the parallel corpus is used to translate the collection, we obtain a higher score for the *Words* index than both query translation methods. Applying a stemming algorithm is helpful for the MAP score for all three ways of translation. The use of n-gramming is not effective for any of the translation methods. Table 6 also lists results for run combinations. The combination of a stemmed and a n-grammed run only leads to improvement for the collection translation method. The combination of all base runs leads to the best performance for English to Portuguese. The resulting score for English to Portuguese is impressive, outperforming our best monolingual score.

6 Multilingual Retrieval

Based on the experience of monolingual and bilingual experiments discussed above, we now turn to the "grand" task in the ad hoc track: multilingual re-

Table 7. Overview of MAP scores for all multilingual runs (bottom half) and of the mono- and bilingual runs used to produce them (top half). Best scores are in boldface, stars indicate a significant improvement over the word-based run

	English	*Finnish*	*French*	*Russian*
Words (baseline)	0.4488	0.2057	0.3351	0.2012
Stems	0.4885*	**0.2719***	0.3677*	0.1478
4-Grams	0.3986*	0.2376	0.3585	0.2140
4-Grams+start/end	0.4369	0.2578	**0.3810**	**0.2623**
4-Grams+words	0.4387	0.2270	0.3596	0.2595
Words LM	0.4909	0.1913	0.3489	0.1935
Stems LM	**0.5156***	0.2303	0.3676	0.1978
4-Grams+words	0.2333			
Words LM;Stems LM	0.3040			
Words;Stems;4-Grams+start/end	0.3258			
All	**0.3427**			

trieval. In CLEF 2004, the target collection was the combined English, Finnish, French, and Russian collections. We experimented with a fairly straightforward approach to query translation, using machine translation if available and otherwise resorting to a translation dictionary.

6.1 Experiments

We submitted a total of 4 multilingual runs, all using the title and description fields of the English topic set. The multilingual runs were based on the following mono- and bilingual runs:

- *English to English* – This is just a monolingual run, similarly processed as the other monolingual runs discussed above.
- *English to Finnish* — We translated the English topics into Finnish using the Mediascape on-line dictionary [20]. For words present in the dictionary, we included all possible translations available. For words not present in the dictionary, we simply retained the original English words.
- *English to French* — We translated the English topics into French using the WorldLingo machine translation [8].
- *English to Russian* — Again, we translated the English topics into Russian using the WorldLingo machine translation [8].

We applied a straightforward combination method to the results of the mono- and bilingual runs just described. We use an unweighted combSUM of the following sets of runs: The single *4-Grams+words* run for each of the four languages; both a *Words LM* and a *Stems LM* run for each of the four languages; three runs (*Words*, *Stems*, and *4-Grams+start/end*) for each of the four languages; all seven runs for each of the four languages.

6.2 Results

Table 7 shows our mean average precision scores for all base runs used in the multilingual task. We did not apply decompounding to the Finnish topics. As an aside, we see that for monolingual English, the language model is particularly effective. The results for Finnish, French, and Russian are generally in line with the monolingual results discussed above, be it that the n-gramming approaches are generally more effective on the translated topics. Table 7 also includes the run combinations that result in the multilingual runs. Recall that all these combinations are unweighted. On the whole, the performance increases with the number of runs included in the combination.

7 Discussion and Conclusions

In this paper, we reported on a range of cross-lingual retrieval experiments. Our approach is rooted on building effective monolingual retrieval systems. We performed a comparative analysis of a range of tokenization techniques for monolingual retrieval in Finnish, French, Portuguese, and Russian, shedding light on the relative effectiveness of each of the methods. Since different document representations have different merits, combination methods can be extremely useful to combine the different sources of evidence.

With the translation of either queries or documents, a create a bilingual retrieval system. We investigated the robustness of our approach by focusing the resource-poor Amharic language. Making use of the scarcely available resources results in an error-prone translation. Much to our surprise, the retrieval results are fair. We also investigated one of the world's major languages, Portuguese, and examined the relative effectiveness of different translation resources, and of query versus collection translation. Our results indicate interesting differences between the bilingual approaches. The effectiveness of combining different translation methods was highlighted by the fact that the best bilingual score outperformed the best monolingual score.

Combination methods are also crucial in retrieving from a distributed multilingual collection. For multilingual retrieval from the combined English, Finnish, French, and Russian collections, we experimented with straightforward query translations for the translation of the English queries into Finnish, French, and Russian. Using only straightforward unweighted run combination methods, we constructed multilingual runs. Our results indicate that including a range of different document representations per language is generally beneficial.

Acknowledgments. We want to thank Valentin Jijkoun, Gustavo Lacerda de Melo, and Willem Robert van Hage. Sisay Fissaha Adafre was supported by the Netherlands Organization for Scientific Research (NWO) under project number 220-80-001. Jaap Kamps was supported by a grant from NWO under project number 612.066.302. Maarten de Rijke was supported by grants from NWO, under project numbers 365-20-005, 612.069.006, 612.000.106, 220-80-001, 612.000.207, 612.066.302, 264-70-050, and 017.001.190.

References

[1] Peters, C., Braschler, M., Di Nunzio, G., Ferro, N.: CLEF 2004: Ad hoc track overview and results analysis. In: Fifth Workshop of the Cross-Language Evaluation Forum (CLEF 2004), Springer (2005)
[2] Monz, C., de Rijke, M.: Shallow morphological analysis in monolingual information retrieval for Dutch, German and Italian. In: Evaluation of Cross-Language Information Retrieval Systems, CLEF 2001, Springer (2002) 262–277
[3] Kamps, J., Monz, C., de Rijke, M.: Combining evidence for cross-language information retrieval. In: Evaluation of Cross-Language Information Retrieval Systems, CLEF 2002, Springer (2003) 111–126
[4] Kamps, J., Monz, C., de Rijke, M., Sigurbjörnsson, B.: Language-dependent and language-independent approaches to cross-lingual text retrieval. In: Comparative Evaluation of Multilingual Information Access Systems, CLEF 2003, Springer (2004)
[5] Hollink, V., Kamps, J., Monz, C., de Rijke, M.: Monolingual document retrieval for European languages. Information Retrieval **7** (2004) 33–52
[6] Snowball: Stemming algorithms for use in information retrieval (2004) `http://www.snowball.tartarus.org/`.
[7] Kamps, J., de Rijke, M.: The effectiveness of combining information retrieval strategies for European languages. In: Proceedings of the 2004 ACM Symposium on Applied Computing, ACM Press (2004) 1073–1077
[8] Worldlingo: Online translator (2004) `http://www.worldlingo.com/`.
[9] Koehn, P.: European parliament proceedings parallel corpus 1996-2003 (2004) `http://people.csail.mit.edu/people/koehn/publications/europarl/`.
[10] Buckley, C., Singhal, A., Mitra, M.: New retrieval approaches using SMART: TREC 4. In: The Fourth Text REtrieval Conference (TREC-4), National Institute for Standards and Technology. NIST Special Publication 500-236 (1996) 25–48
[11] Hiemstra, D.: Using Language Models for Information Retrieval. PhD thesis, Center for Telematics and Information Technology, University of Twente (2001)
[12] Rocchio, Jr., J.: Relevance feedback in information retrieval. In: The SMART Retrieval System. Prentice-Hall, Englewood Cliffs NJ (1971) 313–323
[13] Efron, B.: Bootstrap methods: Another look at the jackknife. Annals of Statistics **7** (1979) 1–26
[14] Efron, B., Tibshirani, R.J.: An Introduction to the Bootstrap. Chapman and Hall, New York (1993)
[15] CLEF-Neuchâtel: CLEF resources at the University of Neuchâtel (2004) `http://www.unine.ch/info/clef`.
[16] Lee, J.: Combining multiple evidence from different properties of weighting schemes. In: Proceedings of the 18th Annual International ACM SIGIR Conference on Research and Development in Information Retrieval, ACM Press, New York NY, USA (1995) 180–188
[17] Fox, E., Shaw, J.: Combination of multiple searches. In: The Second Text REtrieval Conference (TREC-2), National Institute for Standards and Technology. NIST Special Publication 500-215 (1994) 243–252
[18] Nega, A.: Development of Stemming Algorithm for Amharic Text Retrieval. PhD thesis, University of Sheffield (1999)
[19] European Union: Official Journal of the European Union (2004) `http://europa.eu.int/eur-lex/`.
[20] Mediascape: English-Finnish-English on-line dictionary (2004) `http://efe.scape.net/`.

Two-Stage Refinement of Transitive Query Translation with English Disambiguation for Cross-Language Information Retrieval: An Experiment at CLEF 2004

Kazuaki Kishida[1], Noriko Kando[2], and Kuang-Hua Chen[3]

[1] Surugadai University, 698 Azu, Hanno, Saitama 357-8555, Japan
kishida@surugadai.ac.jp
[2] National Institute of Informatics (NII), Tokyo 101-8430, Japan
kando@nii.ac.jp
[3] National Taiwan University, Taipei 10617, Taiwan
khchen@ntu.edu.tw

Abstract. This paper reports experimental results of cross-language information retrieval (CLIR) from German to French. The authors focus on CLIR in cases where available language resources are very limited. Thus transitive translation of queries using English as a pivot language was used to search French document collections for German queries without any direct bilingual dictionary or MT system for these two languages. The two-stage refinement of query translations that we proposed at the previous CLEF 2003 campaign is again used for enhancing performance of the pivot language approach. In particular, disambiguation of English terms in the middle stage of transitive translation was attempted as a new experiment. Our results show that the two-stage refinement method is able to significantly improve search performance of bilingual IR using a pivot language, but unfortunately, the English disambiguation has almost no effect.

1 Introduction

This paper describes our experiment for cross-language IR (CLIR) from German to French in CLEF 2004. In CLEF 2003, the authors proposed the "two-stage refinement technique" for enhancing search performance of the pivot language approach in situations when only limited language resources are available. In those experiments, German to Italian search runs were executed using only three resources: (1) a German to English dictionary, (2) an English to Italian dictionary, and (3) a target document collection [1]. The target document collection was employed as a language resource for both translation disambiguation and query expansion by applying a kind of pseudo-relevance feedback (PRF) [1].

In CLEF 2004, we attempt to add an English document collection as a language resource for executing German to French search runs via English as a pivot. Thus, unlike CLEF 2003, a disambiguation procedure using a document collection is applied to the English term set in the middle position of transitive query translation. This is expected to reduce irrelevant French words by removing inappropriate English translations.

C. Peters et al. (Eds.): CLEF 2004, LNCS 3491, pp. 135 – 142, 2005.

This paper is organized as follows. In Section 2, the two-stage refinement technique and the English disambiguation method are introduced. Section 3 describes the system we used in the CLEF 2004 experiment. In Section 4, the results are reported.

2 Two-Stage Refinement of Query Translation

2.1 Basic Procedure

One purpose of the two-stage refinement technique is to modify the results of query translation in order to improve CLIR performance. The modification consists in two steps: (1) disambiguation and (2) expansion. In our approach, "disambiguation" means selecting a single translation for each search term in the source language, and "expansion" means executing a standard PRF technique using the set of translations selected in the disambiguation stage as an initial query. Although many researchers have performed the two processes together for CLIR, in our method, both processes are based on a PRF technique using the target document collection, i.e., under the assumption that only limited language resources are available, we use the target collection as a language resource for disambiguation.

We define the following mathematical notations:

s_j: term in the source query ($j = 1,2,...,m$),

T_j': a set of translations in the target language for term s_j, and

$T = T_1' \cup T_2' \cup ... \cup T_m'$.

First, the target document collection is searched for the set of terms T. Second, the most frequently appearing term in the top-ranked documents is selected from each set of T_j' ($j = 1,2,...,m$) respectively. That is, we choose a term $\tilde{t}_j$ for each T_j' such that

$$\tilde{t}_j = \arg\max r_t \quad (t \in T_j'), \tag{1}$$

where r_t is the number of top-ranked documents including the term t. Finally, a set of m translations through the disambiguation process is obtained, i.e.,

$$\tilde{T} = \{\tilde{t}_1, \tilde{t}_2, ..., \tilde{t}_m\}. \tag{2}$$

The disambiguation technique is clearly based on PRF, where some top-ranked documents are assumed to be relevant. The most frequently appearing term in the relevant document set is considered as a correct translation in the context of a given query. While standard disambiguation techniques based on term co-occurrence use statistics on the whole collection (see [2]), our method tries to extract information for disambiguation from a part of the collection that is relevant to the given query. We expect this disambiguation approach to find a correct combination of search terms within the context of the query (the combination is not always important in general, i.e., in the whole document set).

In the next stage, according to Ballesteros and Croft [2], a standard post-translation query expansion by the PRF technique is executed using $\tilde{T}$ in (2) as a query. In this study, we use a standard formula based on the probabilistic model for estimating term weights as follows:

$$w_t = r_t \times \log \frac{(r_t + 0.5)(N - R - n_t + r_t + 0.5)}{(N - n_t + 0.5)(R - r_t + 0.5)}, \tag{3}$$

where N is the total number of documents, R is the number of relevant documents, n_t is the number of documents including term t, and r_t is defined as before (see Equation (1)). The expanded term set is used as a final query for obtaining a list of ranked documents.

2.2 Disambiguation During Transitive Query Translation

The pivot language approach is adopted in this paper, i.e., a search term in the source language is translated into a set of English terms, and each English term is transitively translated into terms in the target language. As many researchers have pointed out, if the set of English terms includes erroneous translations, they will yield many more irrelevant terms in the target language.

One solution is to apply a disambiguation technique to the set of English translations (see Figure 1). If an English document collection is available, we can easily execute our disambiguation method described in the previous section.

3 System Description

3.1 Text Processing

Both German and French texts (in documents and queries) were basically processed by the following steps: (1) identifying tokens, (2) removing stopwords, (3) lemmatization, and (4) stemming. In addition, for German text, decomposition of compound words was attempted based on an algorithm of longest matching with headwords included in the German to English dictionary in machine-readable form. For example, a German word, "Briefbombe," is broken down into two headwords listed in the German to English dictionary, "Brief" and "Bombe," according to a rule that only the longest headwords included in the original compound word are extracted from it. If a substring of "Brief" or "Bombe" is also listed in the dictionary, the substring is not used as a separate word.

We downloaded free dictionaries (German to English and English to French) from the Internet[1]. Also, stemmers and stopword lists for German and French were obtained through the Snowball project[2]. Stemming for English was conducted by the original Porter's algorithm [3].

---

[1] http://www.freelang.net/

[2] http://snowball.tartarus.org/

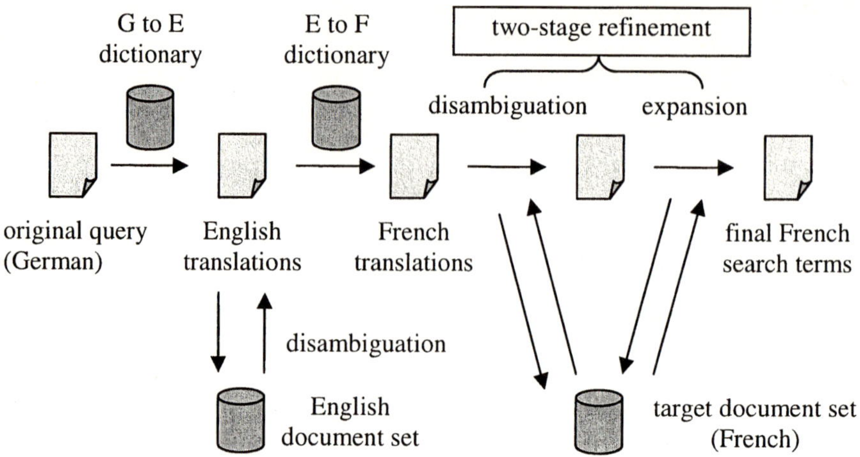

Fig. 1. Two-stage refinement of translation with English disambiguation

3.2 Transitive Translation Procedure

Before executing transitive translation by two bilingual dictionaries, all terms included in the dictionaries were normalized through stemming and lemmatization processes with the same procedure applied to texts of documents and queries. The actual translation process is a simple replacement, i.e., each normalized German term (to which the decomposition process was applied) in a query was replaced with a set of corresponding normalized English words, and similarly, each English word was replaced with the corresponding French words. As a result, for each query, a set of normalized French words was obtained. If no corresponding headword was included in the dictionaries (German–English or English–French), the unknown word was directly sent to the next step without any change. During the transitive translation process, we attempted to apply our disambiguation technique to the set of English words (see Section 2.2).

Next, the translations were refined by our two-stage technique described in the previous section. The number of top-ranked documents was set to 100 in both stages, and in the query expansion stage, the top 30 terms were selected from the ranked list in decreasing order of term weights (Equation (3)).

3.3 Search Algorithm

The standard Okapi BM25 [4] was used for all search runs, and we employed the term weighting formula (3) for all PRF procedures. Let y_t be the frequency of a given term in the query. If the top-ranked term was already included in the set of search terms, the term frequency in the query was changed into $1.5 \times y_t$. If not, the term frequency was set to 0.5 (i.e., $y_t = 0.5$).

3.4 Type of Search Runs

As for dictionary-based transitive query translation via a pivot language, we executed three types of run as follows:

- (a) Two-stage refinement of translation with English disambiguation
- (b) Two-stage refinement of translation without English disambiguation (as in CLEF 2003)
- (c) No refinement

In order to comparatively evaluate the performance of our two-stage refinement method, we decided to use commercial MT software produced by a Japanese company[3]. In this case, first the original German query was entered into the software. The software we used executes German to English translation automatically and then English to French translation (i.e., a kind of transitive translation). The resulting French text from the software was processed according to the procedure described in Section 3.1, and finally, a set of normalized French words was obtained for each query. In the case of MT translation, only post-translation query expansion was executed with the same procedure and parameters as in the case of dictionary-based translation.

Similarly, for comparison, we tried to execute French monolingual runs with post-translation query expansion.

We executed five runs in which <TITLE> and <DESCRIPTION> fields in each query were used, and submitted the results to the organizers of CLEF 2004. All runs were executed on the information retrieval system, ADOMAS (Advanced Document Management System) developed at Surugadai University in Japan.

4 Experimental Results

4.1 Basic Statistics

The target French collections include 90,261 documents in total. The average document length is 227.14 words. We also use the Glasgow Herald 1995 as a document set for English disambiguation. The English collection includes 56,742 documents and the average document length is 231.56. Other experimental settings are described in the overview [5].

4.2 Results

Scores of average precision and R-precision are shown in Table 1, and the recall-precision curves of each run are presented in Figure 2. Note that each value in Table 1 and Figure 2 is calculated for 49 topics.

As shown in Table 1, MT significantly outperforms dictionary-based translations, and its mean average precision (MAP) is .3368, which is 85.4% of that given by the monolingual run (.3944). Although the performance of the dictionary-based approach using free dictionaries downloaded from the Internet is lower than that of the MT approach, Table 1 shows that two-stage refinements improve the effectiveness of the

[3] http://www.crosslanguage.co.jp/english/

Table 1. Average precision and R-precision (49 topics)

Run	ID	Average Precision	R-Precision
French Monolingual	NiiFF01	.3944	.3783
MT	NiiMt02	.3368	.3125
Dictionary 1: Two-stage refinement with English disambiguation	NiiDic03	.2690	.2549
Dictionary 2: Two-stage refinement without English disambiguation	NiiDic04	.2746	.2542
Dictionary 3: No refinement	NiiDic05	.1015	.1014

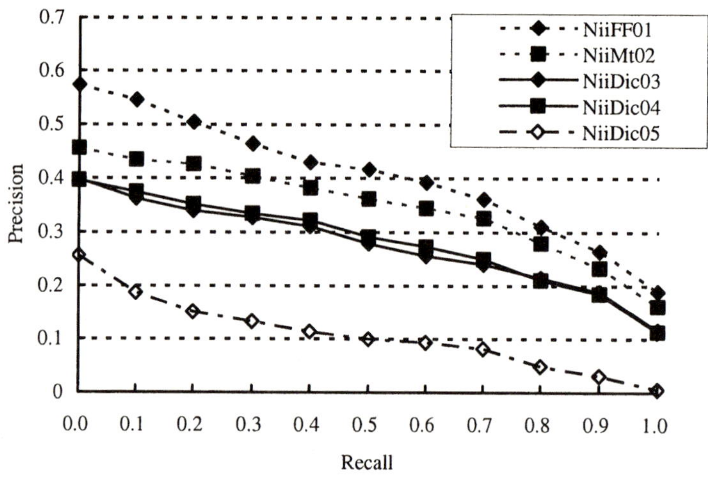

Fig. 2. Recall-precision curves

dictionary-based translation method, similar to our CLEF 2003 experiment. That is, the MAP score of NiiDic05 with no refinement is .1015, and NiiDic03 (with English disambiguation) and NiiDic04 (with no English disambiguation) significantly outperform NiiDic05.

However, English disambiguation appears to have almost no effect. The MAP score of NiiDic03 is .2690, which is slightly inferior to that of NiiDic04 (.2746), and clearly there is no statistically significant difference between them. Figure 3 shows average precision scores of NiiDic03 and NiiDic04 for each topic with some topic numbers. The x-axis represents the average precision score of NiiDic03, and the y-axis indicates that of NiiDic04. Therefore, each dot shows a pair of scores of NiiDic03 and NiiDic04 for a topic. For most topics, the scores of NiiDic03 are almost the same as those of NiiDic04. However, for topics 213, 245, 203, 229 and 206, NiiDic04 outperforms NiiDic03 significantly. On the other hand, scores of NiiDic03 are higher than those of NiiDic04 for topics 231, 233 and 242.

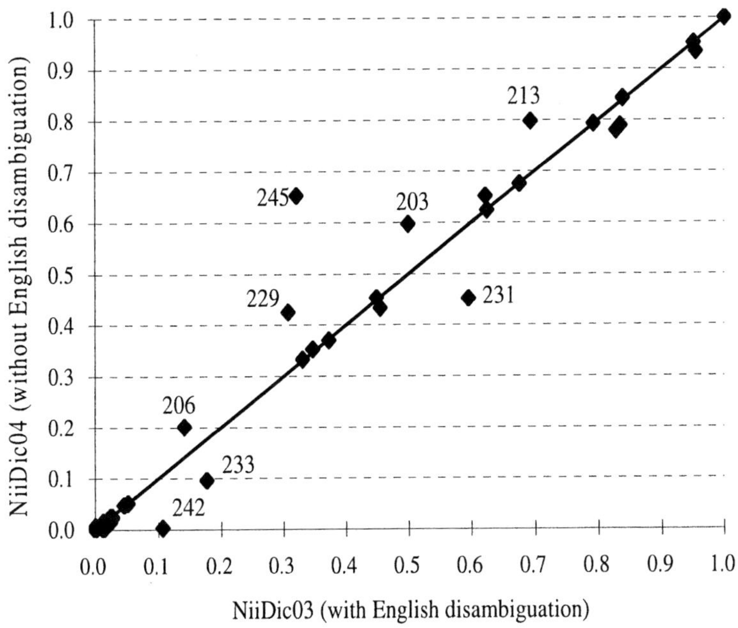

Fig. 3. Topic-by-topic analysis (average precision score)

Table 2 is a list of French translations in NiiDic03 and NiiDic04 for topic 245, in which the difference of average precision scores between NiiDic03 and NiiDic04 is the largest among the 49 topics. The <TITLE> field of topic 245 is "Christopher Reeve," and the text in the <DESC> field is "Finde Dokumente über die Karriere des Schauspielers Christopher Reeve und den Unfall der zu seiner Lähmung führte." It

Table 2. Example of French translations – topic 245

German Terms	NiiDic03 (with English disambiguation)	NiiDic04 (without English disambiguation)
christoph	christoph	christoph
fuhrt	fuhrt	fuhrt
karri	carri	carri
lahm	boiteux	boiteux
lahmung	lahmung	lahmung
reev	reev	reev
rist	instep	instep
schauspiel	jou	jou
uber	uber	uber
unfall	<u>casualt</u>	<u>mésaventur</u>
ung	contrecoeur	contrecoeur

turns out that both methods provide us with the same set of French translations except for "casualt" and "mésaventur." In topic 245, the shift of just one term has a large effect on the retrieval performance. However, on average, the English disambiguation process did not yield a drastic change in the resulting final set of terms. In view of the fact that disambiguating English translations increases the processing time, we conclude that English disambiguation in the pivot language approach has no advantage for improving information retrieval systems.

5 Conclusions

This paper reported the results of our experiment on CLIR from German to French, in which English was used as a pivot language. Two-stage refinement of query translation was employed to remove irrelevant terms in the target language produced by transitive translation using two bilingual dictionaries successively and to expand the set of translations. In particular, in CLEF 2004, disambiguation of English terms in the intermediate process of transitive translation was attempted. The results showed that:

- our two-stage refinement method significantly improves retrieval performance of bilingual IR using a pivot language, and
- English disambiguation has almost no effect.

Intuitively, English disambiguation is promising because theoretically, removing erroneous English terms should effectively prevent irrelevant terms from spreading in the final set of search terms in the target language. However, our experimental results indicate that English disambiguation is useless. Further research is needed.

References

1. Kishida, K., Kando, N.: Two stages refinement of query translation for pivot language approach to cross lingual information retrieval: a trial at CLEF 2003. In Working Notes for the CLEF 2003 Workshop (2003) 129-136
2. Ballesteros, L., Croft, W.B.: Resolving ambiguity for cross-language retrieval. In Proceedings of the 21st ACM SIGIR conference on Research and Development in Information Retrieval (1988) 64-71
3. Porter, M.F.: An algorithm for suffix stripping. Program. 14 (1980) 130-137
4. Robertson, S.E., Walker, S., Jones, S., Hancock-Beaulieu, M.M., Gatford, M.: Okapi at TREC-3. In Proceedings of TREC-3. National Institute of Standards and Technology, Gaithersburg (1995) http://trec.nist.gov/pubs/
5. Peters, C., Braschler, M., Di Nunzio, G., Ferro, N.: CLEF 2004: Ad hoc track overview and results analysis. In Peters, C., Clough, P., Gonzalo, J., Jones, G., Kluck, M., Magnini, B., Proceedings of Fifth Workshop of the Cross-Language Evaluation Forum (CLEF 2004), Lecture Notes in Computer Science (LNCS), Springer, Heidelberg, Germany. This volume.

Dictionary-Based Amharic – English Information Retrieval

Atelach Alemu Argaw[1], Lars Asker[1], Rickard Cöster[2], and Jussi Karlgren[2]

[1] Department of Computer and Systems Sciences,
Stockholm University/Royal Institute of Technology, Stockholm
[2] Swedish Institute of Computer Science, Stockholm

Abstract. We present two approaches to the Amharic - English bilingual track in CLEF 2004. Both experiments use a dictionary based approach to translate the Amharic queries into English Bags-of-words, but while one approach removes non-content bearing words from the Amharic queries based on their IDF value, the other uses a list of English stop words to perform the same task. The resulting translated (English) terms are then submitted to a retrieval engine that supports the Boolean and vector-space models. In our experiments, the second approach (based on a list of English stop words) performs slightly better than the one based on IDF values for the Amharic terms.

1 Background

Amharic is an Afro-Asiatic language belonging to the Southwest Semitic group. It uses its own unique alphabet (see Figure 1) and is spoken mainly in Ethiopia but also to a limited extent in Egypt and Israel [1]. Amharic is the official government language of Ethiopia and is spoken by a substantial segment of the population. In the 1998 census, 17.4 million people claimed Amharic as their first language and 5.1 as their second language. Ethiopia is a multi lingual country with over 80 distinct languages [2], and with a population of more than 59.9 million as authorities estimated on the basis of the 1998 census. Owing to political and social conditions and the multiplicity of the languages, Amharic has gained ground throughout the country. Amharic is used in business, government, and education. Newspapers are printed in Amharic as are numerous books on all subjects [3].

2 Introduction

In this paper we describe our experiments at the CLEF 2004 Amharic - English bilingual track. It consists of two approaches that are variants of the same basic dictionary based approach. At a general level the two approaches both consist of a first step that transforms the Amharic topics into English queries, followed by a second step that takes the English queries as input to a retrieval system. In

C. Peters et al. (Eds.): CLEF 2004, LNCS 3491, pp. 143–149, 2005.

ሀ hä	ለ lä	ሐ ḥä	መ mä	ሠ śä	ረ rä	ሰ sä	ሸ šä	ቀ qä	ቈ quä
ሁ hu	ሉ lu	ሑ ḥu	ሙ mu	ሡ śu	ሩ ru	ሱ su	ሹ šu	ቁ qu	
ሂ hi	ሊ li	ሒ ḥi	ሚ mi	ሢ śi	ሪ ri	ሲ si	ሺ ši	ቂ qi	ቊ qui
ሃ ha	ላ la	ሓ ḥa	ማ ma	ሣ śa	ራ ra	ሳ sa	ሻ ša	ቃ qa	ቋ qua
ሄ he	ሌ le	ሔ ḥe	ሜ me	ሤ śe	ሬ re	ሴ se	ሼ še	ቄ qe	ቌ que
ህ hə/ø	ል lə/ø	ሕ ḥə/ø	ም mə/ø	ሥ śə/ø	ር rə/ø	ስ sə/ø	ሽ šə/ø	ቅ qə/ø	ቍ quə
ሆ ho	ሎ lo	ሖ ḥo	ሞ mo	ሦ śo	ሮ ro	ሶ so	ሾ šo	ቆ qo	

በ bä	ተ tä	ቸ čä	ኀ ḫä	ኈ ḫuä	ነ nä	ኘ ñä	አ 'ä	ከ kä	ኰ kuä
ቡ bu	ቱ tu	ቹ ču	ኁ ḫu		ኑ nu	ኙ ñu	ኡ 'u	ኩ ku	
ቢ bi	ቲ ti	ቺ či	ኂ ḫi	ኊ ḫui	ኒ ni	ኚ ñi	ኢ 'i	ኪ ki	ኲ kui
ባ ba	ታ ta	ቻ ča	ኃ ḫa	ኋ ḫua	ና na	ኛ ña	ኣ 'a	ካ ka	ኳ kua
ቤ be	ቴ te	ቼ če	ኄ ḫe	ኌ ḫue	ኔ ne	ኜ ñe	ኤ 'e	ኬ ke	ኴ kue
ብ bə/ø	ት tə/ø	ች čə/ø	ኅ ḫə/ø	ኍ ḫuə	ን nə/ø	ኝ ñə/ø	እ 'ə/ø	ክ kə/ø	ኵ kuə
ቦ bo	ቶ to	ቾ čo	ኆ ḫo		ኖ no	ኞ ño	ኦ 'o	ኮ ko	

ኸ hä	ወ wä	ዐ 'ä	ዘ zä	ዠ žä	የ yä	ደ dä	ጀ ǧä	ገ gä	ጐ guä
ኹ hu	ዉ wu	ዑ 'u	ዙ zu	ዡ žu	ዩ yu	ዱ du	ጁ ǧu	ጉ gu	
ኺ hi	ዊ wi	ዒ 'i	ዚ zi	ዢ ži	ዪ yi	ዲ di	ጂ ǧi	ጊ gi	ጒ gui
ኻ ha	ዋ wa	ዓ 'a	ዛ za	ዣ ža	ያ ya	ዳ da	ጃ ǧa	ጋ ga	ጓ gua
ኼ he	ዌ we	ዔ 'e	ዜ ze	ዤ že	ዬ ye	ዴ de	ጄ ǧe	ጌ ge	ጔ gue
ኽ hə/ø	ው wə/ø	ዕ 'ə/ø	ዝ zə/ø	ዥ žə/ø	ይ yə/ø	ድ də/ø	ጅ ǧə/ø	ግ gə/ø	ጕ guə
ኾ ho	ዎ wo	ዖ 'o	ዞ zo	ዦ žo	ዮ yo	ዶ do	ጆ ǧo	ጎ go	

ጠ ṭä	ጨ çä	ጰ ṗä	ጸ ṣä	ፀ ẓä	ፈ fä	ፐ pä
ጡ ṭu	ጩ çu	ጱ ṗu	ጹ ṣu	ፁ ẓu	ፉ fu	ፑ pu
ጢ ṭi	ጪ çi	ጲ ṗi	ጺ ṣi	ፂ ẓi	ፊ fi	ፒ pi
ጣ ṭa	ጫ ça	ጳ ṗa	ጻ ṣa	ፃ ẓa	ፋ fa	ፓ pa
ጤ ṭe	ጬ çe	ጴ ṗe	ጼ ṣe	ፄ ẓe	ፌ fe	ፔ pe
ጥ ṭə/ø	ጭ çə/ø	ጵ ṗə/ø	ጽ ṣə/ø	ፅ ẓə/ø	ፍ fə/ø	ፕ pə/ø
ጦ ṭo	ጮ ço	ጶ ṗo	ጾ ṣo	ፆ ẓo	ፎ fo	ፖ po

Fig. 1. The Amharic alphabeth (Fidel) from http://www.omniglot.com/

both approaches the translation was done through a simple dictionary lookup that takes each stemmed Amharic word in the topic set and tries to get a match and the corresponding translation from a machine readable dictionary (MRD)[1] [4]. The first approach (AmEnI) reduces the number of Amharic words by removing those that have an IDF value below a certain threshold level (in this case we used 3.000 as the threshold value) and then looks up the remaining words in the

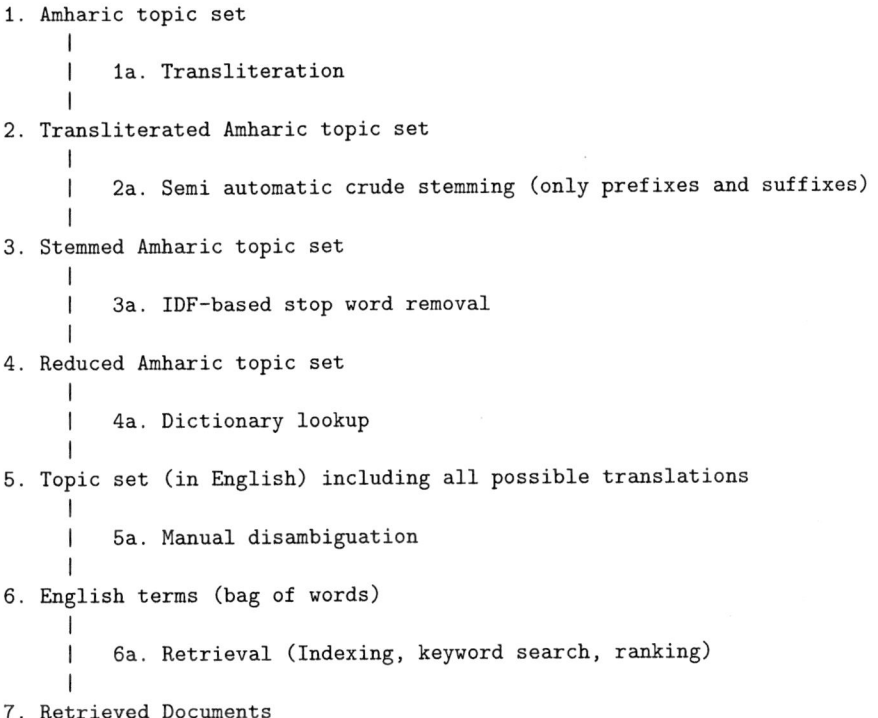

```
1. Amharic topic set
      |
      |    1a. Transliteration
      |
2. Transliterated Amharic topic set
      |
      |    2a. Semi automatic crude stemming (only prefixes and suffixes)
      |
3. Stemmed Amharic topic set
      |
      |    3a. IDF-based stop word removal
      |
4. Reduced Amharic topic set
      |
      |    4a. Dictionary lookup
      |
5. Topic set (in English) including all possible translations
      |
      |    5a. Manual disambiguation
      |
6. English terms (bag of words)
      |
      |    6a. Retrieval (Indexing, keyword search, ranking)
      |
7. Retrieved Documents
```

Fig. 2. Flow chart for AmEnI

MRD. An overview of this approach is presented in Figure 2 below. The second approach (AmEnA) uses the MRD to translate all Amharic words into English, and then reduces the number of English words by removing those that occur in a list of English stop words. An overview of this approach is given in Figure 3 below. The results from the two approaches differ somewhat, with AmEnA performing slightly better, but they both perform reasonably well, considering the simplicity of the approaches.

[1] The electronic version of the MRD is made available through the courtesy of Dr. Daniel Yacob of the Ge'ez Frontier Foundation.

```
1. Amharic topic set
        |
        |   1a. Transliteration
        |
2. Transliterated Amharic topic set
        |
        |   2a. Semi automatic crude stemming (only prefixes and suffixes)
        |
3. Stemmed Amharic topic set
        |
        |   3a. Dictionary lookup
        |
4. Topic set (in English) including all possible translations
        |
        |   4a. Manual disambiguation
        |
5. Translated English terms and phrases
        |
        |   5a. Stop word removal
        |
6. English terms (bag of words)
        |
        |   6a. Retrieval (Indexing, keyword search, ranking)
        |
7. Retrieved Documents
```

Fig. 3. Flow chart for AmEnA

3 Method

3.1 Translation and Transliteration

The English topic sets were translated into Amharic by human translators. Amharic uses its own and unique alphabet (Fidel) and there exist a number of fonts for this, but to date there is no standard for the language. The Amharic topics were originally represented using a Unicode compliant Ethiopic font called Visual Geez. For ease of use and compatibility reasons we transliterated it into an ASCII representation using SERA[2].

The title and description fields of the original 50 Amharic topics contained 781 terms (493 unique) distributed over 808 words (because a few Amharic terms consisted of more than one word). Out of these 493 unique terms 397 were found in the original Amharic - English Machine Readable Dictionary. This dictionary consists of a little more than 14,600 entries. The remaining 96 terms were included in a manually constructed dictionary consisting of these terms and their translation of the relevant sense. Almost all of the 96 terms in this dictionary were proper names.

[2] SERA stands for System for Ethiopic Representation in ASCII, http://www.abyssiniacybergateway.net/fidel/sera-faq.html

3.2 Stemming

Amharic is a Semitic language which is morphologically complex [2]. Words are inflected with prefixes, suffixes and infixes. Once the topic set was transliterated, a semi automatic crude stemming that stripped off the prefixes and suffixes from each word was performed. The MRD used in the experiments is one that consisted of an entry for words and their derivational variants. The infixed words were represented separately in the dictionary.

3.3 Dictionary Lookup and Disambiguation

A machine readable dictionary consisting of about 14,600 words was used in the experiments to perform the lexical lookup in translating the Amharic queries to English. The dictionary consisted of entries for words and their derivational variants.

The stemmed words in the Amharic query were automatically looked up for possible translations in the MRD. In cases where there was a match and there was only one sense of the word, then the corresponding English word/phrase in the dictionary was taken as the possible translation. When there was more than one sense to the term, then all possible translations were picked out and a manual disambiguation was performed. For most of the proper names there was no entry in the MRD. Hence the terms were added manually.

The Amharic query set contained 493 unique terms. Of these, 285 occurred in the dictionary with only one possible translation, 112 occurred in the dictionary with more than one sense (average number of senses for this group was 2.55), and 96 terms (mostly proper names) did not occur at all. The 96 terms that did not occur in the MRD were manually added in a separate dictionary.

In the MRD some of the translations were phrasal, and when the phrases are taken, it introduced more words in the query. Some of the Amharic entries were also phrasal (22 total/14 unique), which in turn reduced the number of words in the query.

3.4 Stop Word Removal

The main difference between the two approaches is in the way words that are likely to be less informative are identified and removed from the queries. For the first approach (AmEnI) the number of Amharic words was reduced by removing those that have an Inverted Document Frequency (IDF) value below a threshold value of 3.00. The IDF values were calculated from an Amharic news corpus consisting of approximately 2 million words of text. With a threshold value of 3.00, 123 of the 493 unique Amharic words were removed (25%). The second approach (AmEnA) removed those words from the translated queries that occurred in a list of 517 English stop words. With this approach, 118 unique terms were removed and the total number of remaining words in the resulting English query set was 559 compared to 547 for the AmEnI approach. Thus the two approaches left approximately the same number of words.

3.5 Retrieval Engine

The underlying retrieval engine is an experimental system developed at SICS. For retrieval, we use Pivoted Unique Normalization [5], where the score for a document d given a query with m query terms is defined as

$$\frac{\sum_{i=1}^{m} \frac{1+\log(tf_{i,d})}{1+\log(average\_tf_d)}}{(1 - slope) \times pivot + slope \times \# \, of \; unique \; terms}$$

where $tf_{i,d}$ is the term frequency of query term i in document d, and $average\_tf_d$ is the average term frequency in document d. The slope was set to 0.3, and the pivot to the average number of unique terms in a document, as suggested in [5].

4 Results

We participated in the cross language Amharic to English run. Two runs were performed on the data set using two sets of queries. In the first run stop word removal using IDF weights was done before the translation of terms, in the second one, the stop word removal was done only after the terms were translated into English. Table 1 lists the precision at various levels of recall for the two runs.

A summary of the results obtained in both runs is reported in Table 2. The number of relevant documents, the retrieved relevant documents, the non-interpolated average precision as well as the precision after R (=num_rel) documents retrieved (R-Precision) are summarized in the table.

Table 1. Recall-Precision tables for AmEnI and AmEnA

Recall	AmEnI	AmEnA
0.00	0.4799	0.5150
0.10	0.4597	0.4961
0.20	0.4535	0.4896
0.30	0.4074	0.4392
0.40	0.3863	0.4181
0.50	0.3724	0.4043
0.60	0.3458	0.3964
0.70	0.3356	0.3732
0.80	0.3273	0.3664
0.90	0.3109	0.3460
1.00	0.2961	0.3276

Table 2. Summary of results from both runs

	Relevant-tot	*Relevant-retrieved*	*Avg Precision*	*R-Precision*
AmEnI	375	297	0.3615	0.3251
AmEnA	375	307	0.4009	0.3663

5 Conclusions

We have described our experiments at the CLEF 2004 Amharic-English cross language track. The approach we followed is a dictionary based one to translate the Amharic queries into English Bags-of-words. One of the experiments reported removes non-content bearing words from the Amharic queries based on their IDF value, while the other uses a list of English stop words to perform the same task. The resulting translated (English) terms are then submitted to the retrieval engine.

As can be seen from the results, the second approach (based on a list of English stop words) has an average precision of 0.4009 while the first approach (based on IDF values for the Amharic terms) reports 0.3615. This could be attributed to the fact that although non content bearing words were removed from the Amharic queries in the first approach, a lot of stop words were introduced while performing the dictionary lookup, hence introducing noise. A combination of the two approaches may result in a better performance in terms of precision, while means of query expansion in order to increase the recall remains open for investigation.

In future experiments we plan to investigate the possibility to automatize some of the tasks that have been done manually in these experiments (sense disambiguation, addition of proper names in the MRD) using various techniques such as e.g. statistical co occurrence for disambiguation, cognate matching for proper names. Experimenting with different retrieval techniques, comparing the performance of the algorithms, and the effects of various levels of stemming (root, stem, word) etc are also issues that we plan to address.

References

1. URL: http://www.ethnologue.org/ (2004)
2. Bender, M.L., Head, S.W., Cowley, R.: The ethiopian writing system. In Bender, e.a., ed.: Language in Ethiopia. Oxford University Press, London (1976)
3. Leslau, W.: Amharic Textbook. Berkeley University, Berkeley, California (1968)
4. Aklilu, A.: Amharic - English Dictionary. Kuraz Printing Enterprise (1987)
5. Singhal, A., Buckley, C., Mitra, M.: Pivoted document length normalization. In: Proceedings of the 19th International Conference on Research and Development in Information Retrieval, Zürich, Switzerland, ACM SIGIR (1996)

Dynamic Lexica for Query Translation

Jussi Karlgren[1], Magnus Sahlgren[1], Timo Järvinen[2], and Rickard Cöster[1]

[1] Swedish Institute of Computer Science, Stockholm
[2] Connexor, Helsinki

Abstract. This experiment tests a simple, scalable, and effective approach to building a domain-specific translation lexicon using distributional statistics over parallellized bilingual corpora. A bilingual lexicon is extracted from aligned Swedish-French data, used to translate CLEF topics from Swedish to French, which resulting French queries are then in turn used to retrieve documents from the French language CLEF collection. The results give 34 of fifty queries on or above median for the "precision at 1000 documents" recall oriented score; with many of the errors possible to handle by the use of string-matching and cognate search. We conclude that the approach presented here is a simple and efficient component in an automatic query translation system.

1 Lexical Resources Should Be Dynamic

Multilingual information access applications, which are driven by modeling lexical correspondences between different human languages, are obviously reliant on lexical resources to a high degree — the quality of the lexicon is the main bottleneck for quality of performance and coverage of service. While automatic text and speech translation have been the main multilingual tasks for most of the history of computational linguistics, today the recent awareness within the information access field of the multilingual reality of information sources has made the availability of lexica an all the more critical system component.

Machine readable lexica in general, and machine readable multilingual lexica in particular, are difficult to come across. Manual approaches to lexicon construction vouch for high quality results, but are time- and labour-consuming to build, costly and complex to maintain, and inherently static as to their nature: tuning an existing lexicon to a new domain is a complex task that risks compromising existing information and corrupting usefulness for previous application areas. As a specific case, human-readable dictionaries, even if digitized and made available to automatic processing, are not vectored towards automatic processing. Dictionaries originally designed for human perusal leave much information unsaid, and belabor fine points that may not be of immediate use for the computational task at hand.

Automatic lexicon acquisition techniques promise to provide fast, cheap and dynamic alternatives to manual approaches, but have yet to prove their viability. In addition to this, they typically require sizeable computational resources.

C. Peters et al. (Eds.): CLEF 2004, LNCS 3491, pp. 150–155, 2005.

This experiment utilises a simple and effective approach to using distributional statistics over parallellized bilingual corpora — text collections of material translated from one language to another — for automatic multilingual lexicon acquisition and query translation. The approach is efficient, fast and scalable, and is easily adapted to new domains and to new languages. We evaluate the proposed methodology by first extracting a bilingual lexicon from aligned Swedish-French data, translating CLEF topics from Swedish to French, and then retrieving documents using the resulting French queries and a mono-lingual retrieval system from the French section of the CLEF document database. The results clearly demonstrate the viability of the approach.

2 Cooccurrence-Based Bilingual Lexicon Acquisition

Cooccurrence-based bilingual lexicon acquisition models typically assume something along the lines:

> "... If we disregard the unassuming little grammatical words, we will, for the vast majority of sentences, find precisely one word representing any one given word in the parallel text. Counterterms do not necessarily constitute the same part of speech or even belong to the same word class; remarkably often, corresponding terms can be identified even where the syntactical structure is not isomorphic".[1]

or alternatively formulated

> "... words that are translations of each other are more likely to appear in corresponding bitext regions than other pairs of words". [2]

These models, first implemented by Brown and colleagues [3] use aligned parallel corpora, and define a translational relation between terms that are observed to occur with similar distributions in corresponding text segments.

Our approach, the *Random Indexing* approach, by contrast with most other approaches to distributionally based algorithms for bilingual lexicon acquisition, takes the context — an utterance, a window of adjacency, or when necessary, an entire document — as the primary unit. Rather than building a huge vector space of contexts by lexical item types, we build a vector space which is large enough to accommodate the occurrence information of tens of thousands of lexical item types in millions of contexts, yet compact enough to be tractable; constant in size in face of ever-growing data sizes; and designed to model association between distributionally similar lexical items without compilation or explicit dimensionality reduction.

2.1 Random Indexing for Bilingual Lexicon Acquisition

Random Indexing [4, 5] is a technique for producing *context vectors* for words based on cooccurrence statistics. Random Indexing differs from other related vector space methods, such as Latent Semantic Indexing/Analysis ([6, 7]), by not requiring an explicit dimension reduction phase in order to construct the vector space. Instead of collecting the data in a word-by-word or word-by-document cooccurrence matrix that needs to be reduced using computationally expensive matrix operations, Random Indexing incrementally collects the data in a *context* matrix with fixed dimensionality k, such that $k \ll D < V$, where D is the size of the document collection, and V is the size of the vocabulary. The fact that no dimension reduction of the resulting matrix is needed makes Random Indexing very efficient and scalable. Furthermore, it can be used for both word-based and document-based cooccurrences.

The Random Indexing procedure is a two-step operation:

1. A unique k-dimensional *index vector* consisting of a small number of randomly selected non-zero elements is assigned to each context in the data.
2. Context vectors for the words are produced by scanning through the data, and each time a word occurs, the context's k-dimensional index vector is added to the row for the word in the context matrix. When the entire text has been scanned, words are represented in the context matrix by k-dimensional context vectors that are effectively the sum of the words' contexts.

In order to apply this methodology to the problem of automatic bilingual lexicon acquisition, we use aligned parallel data, and define a context as an aligned text segment (in this case documents, since the data used in these experiments are aligned at document level). Each such aligned text segment is then assigned a unique random index vector, which are used to accumulate context vectors for the words in both languages by the procedure described above: every time a word occurs in a particular text segment, the index vector of the text segment is added to the context vector for the word in question. The result is a bilingual vector space, which effectively constitutes a bilingual lexicon in the sense that translations (hopefully!) will occur close to each other in the vector space.

Thus, in order to extract a translation to a given word, we simply compute the similarity (using the cosine of the angles between the vectors) between the context vector for the word in question and the context vectors for all words in the other language. The word in the other language whose context vector is most similar to the context vector for the given word is then selected as translation.

The approach is described in more detail in [8, 9].

3 Experiment

We use the document-aligned Europarl corpus [10] which consists of parallel texts from the proceedings of the European Parliament, and is available in 11 European languages, freely downloadable. In this experiment, we used the Swedish-French section which we lemmatized and normalized using the commercially available FDG tools from Connexor Oy. The resulting data consist of 46,979 document-level aligned text segments.

The data was then used to extract a bilingual Swedish-French lexicon by applying Random Indexing as described in the previous section. As parameters for the Random Indexing procedure, we used default values — 1,000 dimensions with 10 non-zero elements in the index vectors. Compare this to the original dimensionality of the data, which is 46,979 dimensions — i.e. almost 47 times as much! It should be noted that the results are not optimized with regards to the Random Indexing parameters in any way, and that optimization would most likely enhance the results [8, 9].

The topic texts were lemmatized and normalized using the same morphological analysis tools from Connexor as were used for the Swedish corpus. We then translated the queries word-by-word from Swedish to French using the extracted lexicon.

The text retrieval engine used for our experiments is based on a standard retrieval system being developed at SICS. The system is described in more detail in our CLEF paper from 2002 [11]. The French target collection was indexed by the system and the translated French queries were used to retrieve texts from the French collection without manual intervention.

4 Results

The results were reasonably good with 34 of fifty queries on or above median, whereof 26 queries at top score for the "precision at 1000 documents" recall oriented score. For the other established two scoring schemes ("average precision" and "precision at 100 documents") the results were slightly lower, but the majority of queries in each case on, above or near median submitted scores. A more precision oriented evaluation scheme where average precision is calculated at 5 retrieved documents gives a satisfying score of 30 per cent.

5 Analysis

Three main factors affect our results:

Out-Of-Vocabulary (OOV) errors. The majority of the errors in the translation process are OOV errors, where some crucial word is not present in the bilingual vector space. For example, "könsbytesoperation" (eng. "sex-change operation") does not occur in the Swedish Europarl data, and is consequently not present in the bilingual vector space. A large number of the OOV errors are compound terms, where the individual constituents might occur in the parallel data. Thus, it would be possible to handle some of the OOV errors by performing decompounding, and by matching the individual constituents to counterparts in the other — in this case non-compounding — language.

Proper names. Since we do not use any typologization of individual query terms, we simply try to translate all terms that are present in a query. This includes proper names, such as "Tour de France," which tend to be identical across languages. Attempting to translate proper names generally distorts the query, since they often do not occur in the parallel data, and will thus be treated as an OOV term. A simple remedy to this problem would of course be to not translate proper names (under the assumption that they could be reliably identified), or to use simple string-matching in order to decide when to leave a particular query term as it is.

Polysemy. Polysemous terms are notoriously difficult to deal with in a vector space environment, since each term is represented by one vector only. This generally leads to one of two situations: either the polysems occur equally many times in the data, and thus contribute equally much to the context vector, in which case they will equally distort each other's representation (i.e. the resulting context vector will be an average of the two separate cooccurrence profiles); or one of the meanings will occur more frequently, in which case it will dominate the resulting context vector. The last situation tends to be more common in vector space models. One example is topic C229, where the Swedish word "damm" means both "dust" (a meaning that is not relevant to the query) and "dam" (which is the intended meaning), and is translated with "poussière," which is irrelevant in meaning.

Despite these problems — some of which could be remedied quite easily by the use of string-matching and cognate search — the approach is clearly viable as a cheap and efficient way to perform query translation. It should be noted that the quality of the parallel data is decisive for the performance of the method.

We conclude that the approach presented here is a simple and efficient alternative for automatic query translation.

Acknowledgements

The work reported here is partially funded by the European Commission under contract IST-2000-29452 (DUMAS) which is hereby gratefully acknowledged.

References

1. Karlgren, H.: Term-tuning, a method for the computer-aided revision of multilingual texts. International Forum for Information and Documentation **13** (1988) 7–13
2. Melamed, D.: Models of translational equivalence among words. Computational Linguistics **26** (2000) 221–249
3. Brown, P., Cocke, S., Della Pietra, V., Della Pietra, F., Jelinek, F., Mercer, R., Roossin, P.: A statistical approach to language translation. In: Proceedings of the 12th Annual Conference on Computational Linguistics (COLING 88), International Committee on Computational Linguistics (1988)
4. Kanerva, P., Kristofersson, J., Holst, A.: Random indexing of text samples for latent semantic analysis. In: Proceedings of the 22nd Annual Conference of the Cognitive Science Society, Erlbaum (2000) 1036
5. Karlgren, J., Sahlgren, M.: From words to understanding. In Uesaka, Y., Kanerva, P., Asoh, H., eds.: Foundations of Real-World Intelligence. CSLI Publications (2001) 294–308
6. Deerwester, S., Dumais, S., Furnas, G., Landauer, T., Harshman, R.: Indexing by latent semantic analysis. Journal of the Society for Information Science **41** (1990) 391–407

7. Landauer, T., Dumais, S.: A solution to plato's problem: The latent semantic analysis theory of acquisition, induction and representation of knowledge. Psychological Review **104** (1997) 211–240
8. Sahlgren, M.: Automatic bilingual lexicon acquisition using random indexing of aligned bilingual data. In: Proceedings of the fourth international conference on Language Resources and Evaluation, LREC 2004. (2004)
9. Sahlgren, M., Karlgren, J.: Automatic bilingual lexicon acquisition using random indexing of parallel corpora. Natural Language Engineering (forthcoming)
10. Koehn, P.: Europarl: A multilingual corpus for evaluation of machine translation. URL: http://people.csail.mit.edu/people/koehn/publications/europarl/ (2002)
11. Sahlgren, M., Karlgren, J., Cöster, R., Järvinen, T.: Automatic query expansion using random indexing. In: Proceedings of CLEF 2002. (2002)

SINAI at CLEF 2004: Using Machine Translation Resources with a Mixed 2-Step RSV Merging Algorithm

Fernando Martínez-Santiago, Miguel A. García-Cumbreras, Manuel C. Díaz-Galiano, and L. Alfonso Ureña

Department of Computer Science. University of Jaén, Jaén, Spain
{dofer, magc, mcdiaz, laurena}@ujaen.es

Abstract. In CLEF 2004, the SINAI group participated in the multilingual task. Our main interest was to test Machine Translation (MT) with a mixed 2-step RSV merging algorithm. Since 2-step RSV requires grouping the document frequency for each term with the translations for that term, and MT translates whole phrases better than working word for word, it is not directly feasible to use MT with a 2-step RSV merging algorithm. To solve this problem, we have tested an algorithm which aligns the original query and its translation(s) at term level.

1 Introduction

The aim of CLIR (Cross-Language Information Retrieval) systems is to retrieve a set of documents written in different languages as an answer to a query in a given language. There are several approaches to this task, such as translating the whole document collection into an intermediate language or translating the question into every language found in the collection. Two architectures are known for query translation: centralized and distributed architectures [1]. We use a distributed architecture, where documents in different languages are indexed and retrieved separately. Later on, all ranked lists are merged into a single multilingual ranked list. We have focused on a solution for the merging problem. Our merging strategy consists of calculating a new RSV (Retrieval Status Value) for each document in the ranked monolingual lists. The new RSV, called two-step RSV, is calculated by reindexing the retrieved documents according to a vocabulary generated from query translations, where words are aligned by meaning, i.e. each word is aligned with its translations [2]. The query is translated using an approach based on Machine Translation (MT), when available. Note that since MT translates the whole phrase better than working word for word, the 2-step RSV merging algorithm is not directly feasible with MT.

The rest of the paper has been organized into three main sections. Section 2 provides a brief revision of merging strategies and the 2-step RSV approach and gives a description of the proposed word-level alignment algorithm based on MT. Section 3 describes our experiments and the results and Section 4 proposes

C. Peters et al. (Eds.): CLEF 2004, LNCS 3491, pp. 156–164, 2005.

a new way to apply blind relevance feedback (BRF). The final section draws some conclusions and also suggests lines for future research.

2 Mixed 2-Step RSV Merging Algorithm and Machine Translation

The basic idea underlying 2-step RSV is straightforward: given a query term and the translation of this term into the languages of the document collections, the document frequencies are grouped together[2]. Therefore, the method requires recalculating the document score by changing the document frequency of each query term. Given a query term, the new document frequency will be calculated by means of the sum of the monolingual retrieved document frequency of the term and its translations. In the first step the query is translated and searched in each monolingual document collection. This phase produces a T_0 vocabulary made up of "concepts". A concept consists of each term together with its corresponding translation. We obtain a single multilingual collection D_0 of preselected documents as a result of the union of the first 1000 retrieved documents for each language. The second step consists of re-indexing the multilingual collection D_0, but considering solely the T_0 vocabulary. Finally, a new query formed by concepts in T_0 is generated and this query is executed against the new index.

2.1 Aligning a Phrase and Its Translation at Term Level Using Machine Translation

Since 2-step RSV requires grouping the document frequency for each term with the translations for that term, and MT translates the whole of the phrase better than word for word, it is not feasible to think of using the 2-step RSV merging algorithm directly with MT. This is because translations in all the document languages must be known for each term in the query. Thus, in this paper, we propose a straightforward, effective algorithm in order to align the original query and its translation at term level. We perceive machine translation as a black box which receives English phrases and generates translations of these phrases for other languages. Briefly, for each translation the algorithm works as follows (a more detailed description is available in [3]):

1. Let the original phrase be in English. The phrase is translated to the target language using an MT resource.
2. Extract word unigrams and bigrams from the English phrase. Both are translated with the same MT resource as used in 1.
3. Remove stopwords. Non-stopwords are stemmed.
4. Test the alignment of terms by matching terms into the translated phrase with the translation based on unigrams (Note that the translation based on unigrams is fully aligned. Thus, if a word in the translated phrase is translated in the same way as in a word for word translation method, we know the translation of the word in the translated phrase. Thus, this word is aligned).

5. After the alignment based on the translation of unigrams is finished, if any term in the translated phrase is not aligned, use the bigrams with exactly one term aligned in order to align the other term of the bigram.

This algorithm fails if there are bigrams without any aligned term after step 3. In addition, in order to improve the matching process, words are stemmed by removing at least gender and number indication. Finally, agglutinative languages, such as German, usually translate (adjetive, noun) bigrams by using a compound word. For example, "baby food" is translated by "säuglingsnahrung" instead of "säugling nahrung" (Babelfish translation). We decompound compound words if possible with the algorithm described in [4].

We have tested the proposed algorithm with previous CLEF query sets (Title+Description). It aligns about 85-90% of non-empty words (Table 1).

Table 1. Percent of aligned non-empty words (CLEF2001+CLEF2002+CLEF2003 query set, Title+Description fields, Babelfish machine translation)

Spanish	German	French	Italian
91%	87%	86%	88%

This year we used MT resources to translate the original English query into French and Russian. However, we did not find good quality, free Finnish MT, so we used a Machine Readable Dictionary (MRD) approach (see section 3.1 for more details about translation strategies). The percentage of aligned words is shown in Table 2.

Table 2. Percentage of aligned non-empty words (CLEF2004 query set, Title+Description fields, MT for French and Russian. MDR for Finnish)

Finnish	French	Russian
100%	85%	80%

2.2 Mixed 2-Step RSV

Although the algorithm proposed to align phrases and translations at term level works well, it does not obtain fully aligned queries. In order to improve system performance when some terms of the query are not aligned, we make two subqueries. The first is made up by the aligned terms only and the other one is formed with the non-aligned terms. Thus, for each query, every retrieved document obtains two scores. The first score is obtained using the 2-step RSV merging algorithm over the first subquery, whereas the second subquery is used in a traditional monolingual system with the respective monolingual list of documents. Therefore, we have two scores for each query, one is global for all languages and the other is local for each language. We then have to integrate both values. As a way to deal with partially aligned queries (i.e. queries with some terms not aligned), last year we proposed several approaches mixing evidence from aligned and non-aligned terms [4]. This year we have used raw mixed 2-step RSV and logistic regression:

- Raw mixed 2-step RSV method:

$$RSV_i' = \alpha \cdot RSV_i^{align} + (1-\alpha) \cdot RSV_i^{nonalign} \quad (1)$$

  where RSV_i^{align} is the score calculated by means of aligned terms, as the original 2-step RSV method shows, while $RSV_i^{nonalign}$ is calculated locally. α is a constant (usually fixed to $\alpha = 0.75$).
- Logistic regression: [5, 6] propose a merging approach based on logistic regression. Logistic regression is a statistical method for predicting the probability of a binary outcome variable according to a set of independent explanatory variables. The probability of relevance to the corresponding document D_i will be estimated according to both the original score and the logarithm of the ranking. Based on these estimated probabilities of relevance, the monolingual list of documents will be interleaved forming a single list:

$$Prob[D_i \ is \ rel|rank_i, rsv_i] = \frac{e^{\alpha+\beta_1 \cdot \ln(rank_i)+\beta_2 \cdot rsv_i}}{1+e^{\alpha+\beta_1 \cdot \ln(rank_i)+\beta_2 \cdot rsv_i}} \quad (2)$$

  The coefficients α, β_1 and β_2 are unknown parameters of the model. The methods usually adopted when fitting the model are the maximum likelihood or iteratively re-weighted least squares methods. Because this approach requires fitting the underlying model, the training set (topics and their relevance assessments) must be available for each monolingual collection. In the same way that the score and $\ln(rank)$ evidence was integrated by using logistic regression (Formula 2), we are able to integrate RSV^{align} and $RSV^{nonalign}$ values:

$$Prob[D_i \ is \ rel|\Theta] = \frac{e^{\alpha+\beta_1 \cdot \ln(rank_i)+\beta_2 \cdot rsv_i^{align}+\beta_3 \cdot rsv_i^{nonalign}}}{1+e^{\alpha+\beta_1 \cdot rsv_i^{align}+\beta_2 \cdot rsv_i^{nonalign}}} \quad (3)$$

  where $\Theta = rank_i, rsv_i^{align}, rsv_i^{nonalign}$ and RSV_i^{align} and $RSV_i^{nonalign}$ are calculated as in formula 1. Again, training data must be available in order to fit the model. This is a serious drawback, but this approach allows integrating not only aligned and non-aligned scores but also the original rank of the document:

$$Prob[D_i \ is \ rel|\Theta] = \frac{e^{\alpha+\beta_1 \cdot \ln(rank_i)+\beta_2 \cdot rsv_i^{align}+\beta_3 \cdot rsv_i^{nonalign}+\beta_4 \cdot rsv_i^{local}}}{1+e^{\alpha+\beta_1 \cdot \ln(rank_i)+\beta_2 \cdot rsv_i^{align}+\beta_3 \cdot rsv_i^{nonalign}+\beta_4 \cdot rsv_i^{local}}} \quad (4)$$

  where rsv_i^{local} is the local rank reached by D_i at the end of the first step, and $\Theta = rsv_i^{local}, rank_i, rsv_i^{align}, rsv_i^{nonalign}, rsv_i^{local}$.

3 Experiments and Results

Our multilingual information retrieval system uses English as the selected topic language, and the goal is to retrieve relevant documents for all languages in the collection, listing the results in a single, ranked list. The list must indicate the set of documents written in different languages retrieved in answer to a query in a given language, English in our case. There are several approaches to this task, such as translating the whole document collection to an intermediate language or translating the query into every language found in the collection. Our approach is the latter: we translate the query into each language present in the multilingual collection. Thus, every monolingual collection must be preprocessed and indexed separately. The preprocessing and indexing tasks are described below.

Table 3. Language preprocessing and translation approaches

	English	Finnish	French	Russian
Preprocessing	stop words removed and stemming			
Additional preprocessing		decompounding		Cyrillic → ASCII
Translation approach		FinnPlace MDR	Reverso MT	Prompt MT

3.1 Language-Dependent Features

In CLEF 2004 the multilingual task was on four languages: English, Finnish, French and Russian. These languages are very heterogeneous: the agglutinative character of Finnish, the Cyrillic alphabet of Russian and the morphologic complexity of French mean that it is difficult to apply a homogeneous strategy for the preprocessing and translation tasks:

- English has been preprocessed as usual in other years. Stop-words have been eliminated and we have used the Porter algorithm [7] as it is implemented in the ZPrise system.
- Finnish is an agglutinative language. Thus, we have used the same decompounding algorithm as last year [4]. The stopword list and stemmer algorithm have been obtained from the snowball site [1]. Since we have not found any good free machine translation for Finnish, we use *FinnPlace* online dictionary [2].
- The resources for French have been updated by using the stop-word list and French stemmer from http://www.unine.ch/info/clef. The translation from English has been carried out by using Reverso[3] software.

---

[1] Snowball is a small string-handling language in which stemming algorithms can be easily represented. Its name was chosen as a tribute to SNOBOL. Available at http://www.snowball.tartarus.org

[2] FinnPlace is available on-line at http://www.tracetech.net/db.htm

[3] Reverso is available on-line at translation2.paralink.com

– For Russian, the stop-word list and stemmer algorithm have been obtained from the snowball site. The Cyrillic alphabet has been transliterated with ASCII characters, following the standard Library of Congress transliteration scheme. We have used Prompt MT [4] in order to translate the queries from English into Russian

3.2 Language-Independent Features

Once collections have been pre-processed, they are indexed with the ZPrise IR system[5], using the Okapi probabilistic model (fixed at $b = 0.75$ and $k1 = 1.2$) [8]. The Okapi model has also been used for the on-line re-indexing process required by the calculation of 2-step RSV. This year, we have not used blind feedback because we found the improvement is very poor for these collections; the precision is even worse for some languages (English and Russian).

3.3 Results

Table 4 shows the results obtained by several merging approaches. Experiments UJAMLRSV2, UJAMLRL2P and UJAMLRL3P are based on mixed 2-step RSV which requires the combination of two scores per retrieved query (see section 2.2 for details).

Table 4. Results using several merging approaches

Merging strategy	Experiment	AvgPrec
Round robin	unofficial	0.220
Raw scoring	unofficial	0.280
Formula 2 (logistic regression)	UJAMLRL	0.277
Formula 1 (raw mixed 2-step RSV)	**UJAMLRSV2**	**0.334**
Formula 3 (logistic regression and 2-step RSV)	UJAMLRL2P	0.333
Formula 4 (logistic regression and 2-step RSV)	UJAMLRL3P	0.301

Perhaps the most surprising result is the poor performance achieved by logistic regression. The reason for this result could be that this merging approach requires relevance assessments for each collection in order to fit the underlying model. Nevertheless, we have no relevance assessment for 1995 *Le Monde* document collection (this collection was made available for the first time this year). Thus, we have trained the model with the rest of the French collections. For this reason, we think that the model has been trained poorly. This explains why the best result is obtained using the most straightforward mixed 2-step RSV approach (UJAMLRSV2), since the rest of approaches are based on the combination of logistic regression with 2-step RSV.

[4] Prompt is available on-line at http://www.online-translator.com/text.asp?lang=en

[5] ZPrise, developed by Darrin Dimmick (NIST). Available on demand at http://www.itl.nist.gov/iad/894.02/works/papers/zp2/zp2.html

Table 5. Bilingual results (source language: English. Okapi, no blind feedback)

Target Language	Translation strategy	AvgPrec
Finnish	MDR (FinnPlace)	0.270
French	MT (Reverso)	0.375
Russian	MT (Prompt)	0.302

An interesting result is the excellent result of the 2-step RSV merging algorithm taking into account the results achieved by our bilingual runs (Table 5). There are several groups with better bilingual results. In spite of such results, we obtain a very similar or even better results for the multilingual task.

4 Global Blind Relevance Feedback

This year we did not use blind feedback because the improvement obtained is poor. We have tested a new way to apply blind feedback *globally* which is better than *locally*. *Local blind relevance feedback* is the expansion of the query applied by every monolingual IR system. *Global relevance blind feedback* is the expansion of the query applied by the multilingual IR system. In this way, we analyze the top-N documents ranked into the multilingual list of documents. This idea is applied to the 2-step RSV merging algorithm as follows:

1. Merge the document rankings using 2-step RSV.
2. Apply blind relevance feedback to the top-N documents ranked into the multilingual list of documents.
3. Add the top-N more meaningful terms to the query. Since there are documents written in very different languages, the list of selected terms will be multilingual.
4. Expand the concept query[6] with the selected terms.
5. Apply 2-step RSV again over the ranked lists of documents, but using the expanded query instead of the original query.

Note that blind relevance feedback (we have used Okapi BM25 in this experiment) usually selects terms that are in the initial query. Thus, such terms will probably be aligned. The rest of the selected terms are integrated using mixed 2-step RSV.

Table 6 shows that there is no improvement with the application of global relevance blind feedback. We think that there are several possible reasons for this result:

1. Usually, blind relevance feedback is poorly suited to CLEF document collections.

[6] The concept query is the query used by 2-step RSV with aligned terms. A concept represents a term independently of the language

Table 6. Results using global blind relevance feedback (top 10 documents, best 10 terms, Okapi BM25)

Merging strategy	AvgPrec	
	without global BRF	with global BRF
Formula 1 (raw mixed 2-step RSV)	0.334	0.331
Formula 3 (logistic regression and 2-step RSV)	0.333	0.332
Formula 4 (logistic regression and 2-step RSV)+global BRF	0.301	0.309

2. We use the expanded query to apply 2-step RSV re-weighting the documents retrieved for each language, but the list of retrieved documents does not change (it only changes the score of such documents). We can also test the improvement of the results by sending the expanded query to each monolingual collection. Thus, the monolingual lists of documents will be modified. We could then apply 2-step RSV with the expanded query by recalculating the score of these modified monolingual lists of documents instead of the lists retrieved by means of the non-expanded query. In this way, new documents will be retrieved and evaluated.

5 Conclusions and Future Work

In past years, we used a merging approach called 2-step RSV with translations based on MRDs. This year we used the method described in this paper with several machine translation resources. The multilingual task requires working with very different languages (very different alphabets and morphological structures). In other years we tested the performance of 2-step RSV with MRDs, blind feedback and other languages and collections. In every experiment, the proposed merging algorithm works well. It outperforms traditional merging approaches by about 20-40%. Thus, 2-step RSV is a very stable and scalable merging strategy. Another aim for this year is the integration of learning-based algorithms such as logistic regression with 2-step RSV. The results obtained have been not so good. We think that the idea is good but the model has been trained poorly because we had no relevance assessments for one document collection (*Le Monde* 1995). A study in progress is evaluating this approach, filtering 2004 CLEF relevance assessment by eliminating relevant documents of *Le Monde* 1995. Thus, the whole of the multilingual collection would be covered by the relevance assessments used for training.

In spite of the bad results we think that the idea of global blind relevance feedback should improve the performance of our CLIR model, so we will continue working on this point.

Finally, we are interested in the application of other learning algorithms instead of logistic regression, such as Support Vector Machines (SVM)[9, 10] and Perceptron Learning Algorithm with Uneven Margins (PLAUM)[11].

Acknowledgments

This work has been supported by Spanish Government (CICYT) with grant TIC2003-07158-C04-04.

References

1. Chen, A.: Cross-language retrieval experiments at CLEF-2002. In Peters, C., Braschler, M., Gonzalo, J., Kluck, M., eds.: Advances in Cross-Language Information Retrieval, Third Workshop of the Cross-Language Evaluation Forum, CLEF 2002. Rome, Italy, September 19-20, 2002. Revised Papers. Volume 2785 of Lecture Notes in Computer Science., Springer Verlag (2003) 26–48
2. Martínez-Santiago, F., Martín, M., Ureña, L.: SINAI at CLEF 2002: Experiments with merging strategies. In Peters, C., Braschler, M., Gonzalo, J., Kluck, M., eds.: Advances in Cross-Language Information Retrieval, Third Workshop of the Cross-Language Evaluation Forum, CLEF 2002. Rome, Italy, September 19-20, 2002. Revised Papers. Volume 2785 of Lecture Notes in Computer Science. (2003) 103–110
3. Martínez-Santiago, F., Martín, M., Ureña, L.: A merging strategy proposal: the 2-step retrieval status value method. Technical Report. Department of Computer Science of University of Jaén (2004)
4. Martínez-Santiago, F., Montejo-Ráez, A., Ureña, L., Diaz, M.: SINAI at CLEF 2003: Merging and decompounding. Advances in Cross-Language Information Retrieval. Lecture Notes in Computer Science. Springer Verlag (2004) 192–200
5. Calvé, A., Savoy, J.: Database merging strategy based on logistic regression. Information Processing & Management **36** (2000) 341–359
6. Savoy, J.: Cross-Language information retrieval: experiments based on CLEF 2000 corpora. Information Processing & Management **39** (2003) 75–115
7. Porter, M.: An algorithm for suffix stripping. In: Program 14. (1980) 130–137
8. Robertson, S.E., Walker., S., Beaulieu, M.: Experimentation as a way of life: Okapi at TREC. Information Processing and Management **1** (2000) 95–108
9. Vapnik, V.: The Nature of Statistical Learning Theory. Springer, New York (1995)
10. Cortes, C., Vapnik, V.: Support-vector networks. Machine Learning **20** (1995) 273–297
11. Li, Y., Zaragoza, H., Herbrich, R., Shawe-Taylor, J., Kandola, J.: The perceptron algorithm with uneven margins. In: Proceedings of the International Conference of Machine Learning.(ICML'2002). (2002)

Mono- and Crosslingual Retrieval Experiments at the University of Hildesheim

René Hackl, Thomas Mandl, and Christa Womser-Hacker

University of Hildesheim, Information Science,
Marienburger Platz 22, D-31141 Hildesheim, Germany
mandl@uni-hildesheim.de

Abstract. In this year's participation we continued to evaluate open source information retrieval software. We used mainly the Lucene system and experimented with some of the most effective optimization strategies applied in the past CLEF campaigns. The effectiveness of open source and other free tools can be greatly enhanced by employing these optimization strategies. For most languages, blind relevance feedback led to considerable improvement. On the other hand, indexing strategies with n-grams did not lead to any improvements in our experiments.

1 Introduction

In the CLEF 2004 campaign, we tested an adaptive fusion system based on the MIMOR model with several mono- and multi-lingual core retrieval tasks. The MIMOR approach applies weighted fusion based on relevance feedback [1, 2, 3]. MIMOR has previously been applied to CLEF experiments [4, 5]. As a basic retrieval system we employed the open source API Lucene[1], which proved to be very effective and efficient in CLEF as well as in other projects [e.g. 6]. Lucene is becoming increasingly popular in many different contexts.

In this year's participation, our main interests focused on how different indexing methods contribute to retrieval success. It had been shown in previous work that n-gram techniques can contribute greatly to the retrieval performance, especially when language specific refinements are not available or easy to incorporate [7]. Therefore, we extended the Lucene source code to create n-gram based indices. Furthermore, we exploited some of the most promising optimization techniques applied at CLEF in order to observe the potential for improvement of standard IR systems like Lucene. This work contributes to the practical application of results from CLEF.

With respect to stemming we relied on Java™-based snowball[2] language analyzers. In this package, elaborate stemming algorithms for most of the major Western European languages and for Russian can be found. The performance of blind relevance feedback got a considerable boost because of changes in the Lucene indexing format between versions 1.3 and 1.4-final. In the current version, blind

[1] http://jakarta.apache.org/lucene/docs/index.html
[2] Snowball: http://jakarta.apache.org/lucene/docs/lucene-sandbox/snowball/

C. Peters et al. (Eds.): CLEF 2004, LNCS 3491, pp. 165–169, 2005.

relevance feedback can be much more easily applied than in previous releases. Last year we had also evaluated the MySQL's full text indexing and search module, but due to their poor performance they were excluded this year.

We took part in the monolingual tracks for Russian and Finnish, the bilingual track English to Russian and the multilingual track.

2 Preliminary Mono-lingual Retrieval Experiments

First, we ran some monolingual experiments on the collections from 2003 without using any query expansion (Table 1).

Table 1. Test runs with data from 2003, English and French collections from 1995 only

Language	Indexing	Recall	Average Precision
English	4-gram	516 / 1006	0.1256
English	5-gram	516 / 1006	0.1083
English	6-gram	507 / 1006	0.1034
English	snowball stemmer	497 / 1006	0.1608
English	lucene stemmer	499 / 1006	0.1690
Finnish	4-gram	391 / 483	0.2237
Finnish	5-gram	403 / 483	0.2261
Finnish	6-gram	391 / 483	0.2036
Finnish	snowball stemmer	450 / 483	0.4853
Finnish	lucene stemmer	N/A	N/A
Finnish	Fusion of all	452 / 483	0.3218
French	4-gram	548 / 946	0.1242
French	5-gram	549 / 946	0.1077
French	6-gram	560 / 946	0.1050
French	snowball stemmer	563 / 946	0.1498
French	lucene stemmer	525 / 946	0.1504
Russian	4-gram	98 / 151	0.0652
Russian	5-gram	98 / 151	0.0620
Russian	6-gram	96 / 151	0.0642
Russian	snowball stemmer	71 / 151	0.0810
Russian	lucene stemmer	88 / 151	0.1336

We excluded the LA Times 1994 and the 1994 material in the French collection, as they were not needed for this year. Secondly, we tested every combination of indexing methods for each language to find out which potential of the fusion could be found in the answer sets. This can be seen in the table for Finnish ("Fusion of all"), where all result lists from the different indices were merged into a single one. All the indices were given equal weights in the merging process and we only looked at unnormalized raw document scores.

Unfortunately, we experienced resource-consuming problems with automatic query construction for the n-gram indices and Russian character handling. As it can be derived from Table 1, the first matter could be solved with satisfying results. The second issue, however, continued to cause aggravation. Before CLEF 2004, our system had been used for ISO-8859-1 languages only. The introduction of Cyrillic as such didn't prove much of a problem: Java, the systems programming language, represents strings internally as Unicode characters. But for Russian, we couldn't get stopwords eliminated, which caused very low performance.

For evaluation of the test runs we used our beta stage Java clone of the official trec_eval program.

3 Submitted Retrieval Experiments

For the submitted runs we used the title and descriptor topic fields, which were mandatory. We applied pseudo-relevance feedback for all tasks. As algorithms to extract meaningful terms the Robertson-Selection-Value (RSV) or the divergence measure following Kullback and Leibler (KL) were adopted [8]. We used the Lucene stemmer for Russian, a fusion of both stemmers for English and French, and the snowball stemmer for Finnish. The results can be seen in Table 2.

Table 2. Results for runs in CLEF 2004

Runs	Optimization	Recall	Average Precision
UHImlt1	BRF 5 10 RSV	1031 / 1826	0.1974
UHImlt2	BRF 5 10 KL	973 / 1826	0.1849
UHIenru1	BRF 5 10 RSV	77 / 123	0.1353
UHIenru2	BRF 5 10 KL	73 / 123	0.1274
UHIenru3	no BRF	53 / 123	0.0484
UHIru1	BRF 5 10 RSV	88 / 123	0.1553
UHIru2	BRF 5 10 KL	82 / 123	0.1420
UHIru3	no BRF	56 / 123	0.0459
UHIfi1	BRF 5 10 KL	349 / 413	0.4699
UHIfi2	BRF 5 10 RSV	367 / 413	0.5042

For runs involving Russian, we also created one run without BRF. To translate the queries we used the internet service FreeTranslation.com[3] which provided some surprisingly good translations from English to Russian. In consequence of the aforementioned encoding problems our results are very bad. BRF still worked well under these circumstances. Moreover, the test runs had indicated that the Russian stemmer that comes with Lucene is very capable and it held up to that expectation.

For Finnish, the performance is quite high. The snowball stemmer works very well. We only have limited insight into the usefulness of InterTran[4] as a translation tool for Finnish. In most cases, we were glad to recognize the proper names in the Finnish translations.

The multilingual runs suffered severely from the obstacles that led to the bad results for Russian.

---

[3] http://www.freetranslation.com

[4] http://intertran.tranexp.de/

4 Conclusion

This year's Russian tracks posed some challenges we could not easily overcome. Despite working with Java only and Unicode-based character sets, the Russian stopwords could not be eliminated. N-Gram query construction was hardly optimal so we dropped this approach for the official submissions. We did not have the resources to work on a more sophisticated approach.

Our system has about 30 weighting parameters which are not yet well adapted to the task. This year, we could only experiment with a few ones. First post-submission experiments have indicated that the system got slightly better, e.g. for "Finnish – Fusion of All" four small adjustments produced two more relevant documents while improving the average precision by 3%.

5 Outlook

In future years we intend to exploit the observed relation between the number of named entities in topics and retrieval performance [9]. We also plan to work on a more reliable and high-performance n-gram query construction.

Acknowledgements

We would like to thank the Jakarta and Apache projects' teams for sharing Lucene with a wide community as well as the providers of Snowball. Furthermore, we acknowledge the work of several students from the University of Hildesheim who implemented MIMOR as part of their course work.

References

1. Womser-Hacker, C.: Das MIMOR-Modell. Mehrfachindexierung zur dynamischen Methoden-Objekt-Relationierung im Information Retrieval. Habilitationsschrift. Universität Regensburg, Informationswissenschaft. 1997.
2. Mandl, T.; Womser-Hacker, C.: A Framework for long-term Learning of Topical User Preferences in Information Retrieval. In: New Library World. vol. 105 (5/6). 2004. pp. 184-195.
3. Mandl, T.; Womser-Hacker, C.: Fusion Approaches for Mappings Between Heterogeneous Ontologies. In: Research and Advanced Technology for Digital Libraries: 5th European Conference (ECDL 2001) Darmstadt Sept. 4.-8. 2001, Springer LNCS 2163, pp. 83-94.
4. Hackl, R.; Kölle, R.; Mandl, T.; Ploedt, A.; Scheufen, J.-H.; Womser-Hacker, C.: Multilingual Retrieval Experiments with MIMOR at the University of Hildesheim. In: Peters, C.; Gonzalo, J.; Braschler, M.; Kluck, M. (eds.): Comparative Evaluation of Multilingual Information Access Systems. CLEF 2003 Workshop. Revised papers. Springer LNCS 2327. 2004.
5. Hackl, R.: Multilinguales Information Retrieval im Rahmen von CLEF 2003. Master Thesis, University of Hildesheim, Information Science. 2004.

6. Hackl, R.; Mandl, T.; Schwantner, M.: Evaluierung und Einsatz des open source Volltext-Retrievalsystems Lucene am FIZ Karlsruhe. In: Ockenfeld, Marlies (ed.): Information Professional 2011: Strategien – Allianzen – Netzwerke. Proceedings 26. DGI Online-Tagung. Frankfurt a.M. 15.-17. June 2004. pp. 147-153.
7. McNamee, P.; Mayfield, J.: Character N-Gram Tokenization for European Language Text Retrieval. In: Information Retrieval 7 (1/2) 2004. pp. 73-98.
8. Carpineto, C.; de Mori, R.; Romano, G.; Bigi, B.: An Information-Theoretic Approach to Automatic Query Expansion. In: ACM Transactions on Information Systems. 19 (1). 2001. pp. 1-27.
9. Mandl, T.; Womser-Hacker, C.: Analysis of Topic Features in Cross-Language Information Retrieval Evaluation. In: 4th International Conference on Language Resources and Evaluation (LREC) Lisbon, Portugal, May 24-30. Workshop Lessons Learned from Evaluation: Towards Transparency and Integration in Cross-Lingual Information Retrieval (LECLIQ). pp. 17-19.

University of Chicago at CLEF2004: Cross-Language Text and Spoken Document Retrieval

Gina-Anne Levow and Irina Matveeva

University of Chicago, Chicago, IL 60637, USA
{levow, matveeva}@cs.uchicago.edu,
http://people.cs.uchicago.edu/~levow

Abstract. The University of Chicago participated in the Cross-Language Evaluation Forum 2004 (CLEF2004) cross-language multilingual, bilingual, and spoken language tracks. Cross-language experiments focused on meeting the challenges of new languages with freely available resources. We found that modest effectiveness could be achieved with the additional application of pseudo-relevance feedback to overcome some gaps in impoverished lexical resources. Experiments with a new dimensionality reduction approach for re-ranking of retrieved results yielded no improvement, however. Finally, spoken document retrieval experiments aimed to meet the challenges of unknown story boundary conditions and noisy retrieval through query-based merger of fine-grained overlapping windows and pseudo-feedback query expansion to enhance retrieval.

1 Introduction

The University of Chicago participated in cross-language Multilingual, Bilingual, and Spoken Document Retrieval tasks. Cross-language experiments focused on meeting the challenges of new languages with freely available resources. We found that modest effectiveness could be achieved with the additional application of pseudo-relevance feedback to overcome some gaps in impoverished lexical resources. Experiments with a new dimensionality reduction approach for re-ranking of retrieved results yielded no improvement, however. Finally, spoken document retrieval experiments aimed to meet the challenges of unknown story boundary conditions and noisy retrieval through query-based merger of fine-grained overlapping windows and pseudo-relevance feedback query expansion to enhance retrieval.

2 Cross-Language Multilingual and Bilingual Retrieval

The University of Chicago participated in the CLEF2004 cross-language multilingual and bilingual retrieval tasks. The group submitted four official English $\rightarrow$ English, French, Finnish, Russian multilingual runs, three using only the title-based topic specification and one using both the title and description components

C. Peters et al. (Eds.): CLEF 2004, LNCS 3491, pp. 170–179, 2005.

of the topic specification. The group also submitted one official English → Russian bilingual run in the title only condition. Additional unofficial contrastive runs discussed below highlight the effects of different processing.

2.1 Linguistic Resources

All processing employed only freely available linguistic resources. Two main classes of linguistic resources were utilized: bilingual term lists to bridge the gap between the information need as expressed in one language and the document concepts expressed in another and stemmers to perform simple morphological analysis to improve matching by reducing surface variation between information need and document concept forms. We downloaded bilingual term lists from http://www.freedict.com and Porter-style rule-based stemmers from http://snowball.tartarus.org. The overall size and coverage statistics for the bilingual term lists appear in Table 1. The English-French and English-Russian bilingual term lists provide an average of 1.5 translations for each English language term, while the English-Finnish lexicon averages approximately 1.2 translations. Although the French and Russian term lists are of comparable size, Finnish term list, in contrast, is relatively impoverished, being only one-tenth the size of the other term lists, providing translations for approximately 2500 English terms.

Table 1. Bilingual Term List Statistics

Lexicon	English Terms	Total Translations
English-French	21041	34949
English-Finnish	2546	3177
English-Russian	22722	31771

2.2 Document and Query Processing

We adopted a dictionary-based query translation architecture for all our runs to facilitate relatively rapid experimentation in a range of conditions. We applied comparable basic processing to all languages and conditions. Where specialized language specific processing was required, it is introduced in the detailed discussion below.

Document Processing. Our goal in document processing was to reduce surface variation to enable matching with translated query forms or base queries in the case of English. All document languages undergo some morphological processing, although that of English is arguably simplest. Thus we applied the appropriate language-specific Snowball stemmer to each of the French, Finnish, and Russian document collections. Finally, all remaining accents were stripped. For English we relied on the INQUERY[1] retrieval system's built-in *kstem* stemmer.

For Russian and Finnish, some additional processing was required. For Russian, differences in coding formats required first conversion from the original document encoding to that correctly interpreted by the stemmer. Subsequently, to produce the 8-bit clean coding required by the retrieval engine, we produced an acceptable transliterated form. All Russian coding conversions employed the freely available *rucnv* (http://litwr.boom.ru) program.

Since Finnish is a highly agglutinative language, we also aimed to further reduce surface variation and identify suitable units for matching by decompounding. Specifically, we applied a greedy dictionary-based decompounder originally developed for previous experiments with German to split longer terms into word units attested by the translation resource.[2]

Query Processing. Our query processing involves two phases: the first, from term extraction through translation, involves matching terms in the query with terms in the translation resource, while the second, following translation, involves matching with the target language documents and thus conforming to the earlier document processing.

First, based on left-to-right, greedy longest match, we identify multi-word units in the query that are translatable given the bilingual term list. Next we apply pre-translation pseudo-relevance feedback query expansion to enrich the short query with additional topically relevant and, we hope, translatable terms. For pre-translation expansion, we use the English document collection itself as a source of relevant documents and enriching terms. Starting with the original query formulation, with a default stopword list and stemming but no additional stop structure, we use the INQUERY API to identify the top ten presumed relevant documents from the collection and to identify terms more likely to appear in relevant documents than non-relevant documents. These terms are concatenated to the original query.

Next we perform dictionary-based term-for-term translation using the appropriate bilingual term list. We apply a stemming backoff procedure where we first attempt to match the surface form from the query with surface forms in the term list. Only if there is no match, do we back off to matching stemmed forms of query terms with stemmed forms of term list entries. We integrate evidence from all translation alternatives using structured query formulation as proposed by [3].

Now to support matching with the target language documents, we perform analogous processing on the translated queries to that performed on the documents. Specifically, we stem as described above, and perform language specific coding conversion for Russian and decompounding for Finnish. Finally, to further enrich the query and compensate for variation in choice of expression by document authors, we also perform post-translation pseudo-relevance query expansion. We apply a comparable mechanism to that for pre-translation expansion. However, here we use the corresponding target language document collection as a source of both relevant documents and enriching terms.

2.3 Indexing and Retrieval

For baseline indexing and retrieval, we utilize the INQUERY information retrieval system version 3.1p1 licensed from the University of Massachusetts[1]. For each target document collection, we return the top 1000 ranked retrieved documents.

Locality Preserving Projection-Based Re-scoring. We applied a dimensionality reduction technique, the locality preserving projection (LPP) as described below, to perform a local re-scoring of the most highly ranked document in the ranked list.

LPP Algorithm. In many cases, including text and images, the data can be assumed to be intrinsically low-dimensional although the traditional representation puts it in a very high-dimensional space. There has been a considerable amount of theoretical research and empirical investigation of representing data as points on the underlying manifold [4, 5, 6]. One hopes to obtain better similarity information by using the distance on the manifold instead of the distance in the ambient space.

The Locality Preserving Projection (LPP) algorithm [7] computes a linear projection of the data that preserves the intrinsic geometric structure of the manifold. The input is n data points as vectors in R^N $X = (x_1, ..., x_n)$ that belong to a k-dimensional manifold M embedded in R^N. The goal to find a lower-dimensional representation for these points $y_1, ..., y_n \in R^k$, where $k < N$. First, a neighborhood graph of the data $G = (V, E)$ is constructed. W is the adjacency matrix of the graph. The entry W_{ij} is non-zero if the data points i and j are connected by an edge $e \in E$. The entries of W contain the information about the local similarities between the data points. The next step is to compute the diagonal matrix C of node's degrees, where $C_{ii} = \sum_{j=1}^{n} W_{ij}$, and the Laplacian of the graph $L = C - W$.

LPP finds a lower-dimensional representation $y_1, ..., y_n \in R^k$, where $k < N$ so as to minimize under certain constraints

$$\sum_{ij} ||y_i - y_j||^2 W_{ij}$$

where W_{ij} is the penalty on the distance between the points y_i and y_j. W_{ij} is large if the original points x_i and x_j corresponding to y_i and y_j are close. Thus, if data points are similar to each other in the input space, there will be a penalty for mapping them far apart and they will remain close to each other in the new representation.

It can be shown [7], that the solution is given by the generalized eigenvectors of the following generalized eigenvalue problem $XLX^Ta = \lambda XCX^Ta$.

A constraint is necessary to prevent the algorithm from collapsing all input vectors to just one point. Here we used the constraint $a^Ta = 1$ and thus we had to solve the eigenvalue problem $XLX^Ta = \lambda a$ to find the solution.

With any constraint, k (generalized) eigenvectors corresponding to the k smallest (generalized) eigenvalues form the projection matrix A_k. The new representation of the data is computed as $Y = A_k^T X$.

LPP Re-ranking of the Candidates List. We made the assumption that the baseline system performed well, specifically that the top thousand documents in the ranked list that this system returned contained the relevant documents. Thus, we could apply LPP locally, only to these documents, avoiding the computational intractability of this technique for larger document and term spaces which did not permit us to apply the technique to the collection as a whole.

Preprocessing. We used the following preprocessing steps. All documents from the Russian[1] part of the collection were used to compute the vocabulary as well as the term and document frequencies for the vocabulary terms. After that the top documents and queries were indexed and weighted using $tfidf$. We use the Rainbow document classification package [8] to perform the indexing.

LPP Projection. Using these top documents from the ranked list returned by the baseline system, we computed the LPP model:

- Using the Euclidean distance compute the nearest neighbor graph of the data
- Compute the graph Laplacian
- Compute the LPP projection vectors
- Using the LPP projection vectors, fold in the documents and the queries to obtain their low dimensional representation

The inner product between the new document and query vectors was used as the measure of their similarity. Using this similarity score, a new ranked list was computed.

LPP Perspective. We had the following motivation for using the LPP re-ranking. LPP is a dimensionality reduction algorithm and performs a certain kind of denoising. In the LPP space documents that are similar to each other in the original representation remain close. Thus, if some of the top documents in the ranked list returned by the baseline system were actually relevant to the query, LPP would map other documents that are placed at lower ranks close to the top ones. This can increase the rank of the other relevant documents.

Multilingual Merging. Finally, since we perform query translation into multiple document languages for the retrieval in the multilingual task, it is necessary to merge the ranked lists from the individual per-language retrieval runs to produce a single ranked list. Based on a previous side experiment, we determined

[1] Due to time limitations, the LPP re-scoring was applied only to the Russian bilingual and Russian portion of the multilingual retrieval task.

Table 2. Multilingual Runs

Query	Baseline	+Decompounding	+LPP Re-scoring
Title	0.1464	0.1545	0.1307

Table 3. Effects of Finnish Decompounding

Query	Baseline	+Decompounding
Title	0.1979	0.2207
Title+Description	0.2383	0.2308

that there was a clear relation between number of untranslated terms in the final query formulation and the retrieval effectiveness of the query. Previous experience had indicated that fully enriched CLIR techniques could achieve retrieval effectiveness comparable to or even better than monolingual retrieval effectiveness due to implicit and explicit enrichment processes.

We assumed a rank-based, round robin merge strategy across the per-language runs, up to a total of 1000 documents in the final ranked list. Based on the potential high effectiveness of CLIR where translation was highly successful, we assumed a uniform merge strategy when full or almost full translation was achieved. On a per-query basis, we reduced the contribution of each per-language ranked list based on observed decreases in translation success. Based on the side experiments, we identified thresholds for full, partial, and poor translation success, as indicated by the residual presence of untranslated terms in the final query formulation. Each reduction in translation success level resulted in a reduction of one-third in the contribution of that language's ranked list to the final ranked list.

Merging was not necessary for the monolingual or bilingual runs.

2.4 Results and Discussion

We present the results for the merged multilingual runs. We also present contrastive bilingual results for specialized processing that was applied only to one document language or that had different effects across languages that might not yield significant effects at the merged multilingual level. We apply the Wilcoxon signed ranks test to assess statistical significance of differences between two sets of retrieval results.

Multilingual Runs. We find that, relative to the baseline runs, decompounding for Finnish appears to enhance retrieval and the LPP re-ranking in Russian appears to decrease effectiveness (Table 2). These contrasts do not reach significance. Since these modifications affect only two of the target languages, it is not surprising that the changes do not lead to significant overall changes in effectiveness.

Table 4. Effect of LPP Re-scoring

Query	Baseline	LPP
Title	0.1199	0.0029
Title+Description	0.1611	0.0021

Table 5. Effects of query expansion

Query	No Expansion	Post-expansion	Pre- and Post-expansion
FR Title	0.1300	0.1710	0.1656
FR Title+Description	0.1538	0.1843	0.1866
FI Title	0.1427	0.1505	0.2279
FI Title+Description	0.1610	0.1616	0.2308
RU Title	0.1051	0.0963	0.1199
RU Title+Description	0.1270	0.1201	0.1611

Bilingual Contrasts: Finnish Decompounding. We find that relative to baseline effectiveness, changes due to Finnish decompounding did not reach significance.

Bilingual Contrasts: LPP-Based Re-scoring. We find that relative to baseline effectiveness, LPP-based re-scoring fares significantly more poorly (Table 4). One possible contribution to LPP's failure to improve over baseline is the relatively small number of on-topic documents in the Russian collection, resulting in large effects for changes in a few document positions. Another possible explanation for LPP's failure to improve the retrieval performance is that the LPP projection was computed using the similarity between the documents themselves, not their similarity to the query. However, documents that are relevant to the same query are not necessarily similar to each other. It has even been observed that every query defines a new similarity notion between the documents. In the future we will consider applying a pseudo-relevance approach in which we explicitly presume the highest ranked documents to be relevant and adapt the connectivity graph as appropriate.

Bilingual Contrasts: Pre- and Post-translation Expansion. We find an apparent trend to increases in effectiveness for pseudo-relevance feedback query expansion relative to retrieval without expansion(Table 5). However, we find that only for the Finnish case do these differences reach significance ($p < 0.01$). In particular, for Finnish, pre-translation expansion yields significant improvements over both no expansion and post-translation expansion alone. This large contrast can be best understood in the context of the highly impoverished - $\approx$2500 headword - bilingual term list available for Finnish. For comparison, the French and Russian term lists have almost ten times as many headwords. Thus pre-translation expansion plays a key role in enabling translation and matching of query concepts. This behavior is consistent with [9]'s prior findings on artificially impoverished translation resources.

3 Spoken Document Retrieval

The University of Chicago also participated in the CLEF2004 cross-language spoken document retrieval task. Runs were submitted in both the baseline English monolingual task and the French-English cross-language task, using only the resources provided by CLEF.

3.1 Query Processing

Query processing aimed to enhance retrieval of the potentially errorful ASR transcriptions through pseudo-relevance feedback expansion. The baseline conditions required the use of only the CLEF provided resources. This restriction limited our source of relevance feedback to the ASR transcriptions, segmented as described below. For both the monolingual English and the English translations of the original French queries, we performed the same enrichment process. We employed the INQUERY API to identify enriching terms based on the top 10 ranked retrieved segments and integrated these terms with the original query forms. Our hope was that this enrichment process would capture both additional on-topic terminology as well as ASR-specific transcriptions.

For the French-English cross-language condition, we performed dictionary-based term-by-term translation, as described in [2]. We employed a freely available bilingual term list (www.freedict.com). After identifying translatable multi-word units based on greedy longest match in the term list, we used a stemming backoff translation approach with statistically derived stemming rules[10], matching surface forms first and backing off to stemmed forms if no surface match was found. All translation alternatives were integrated through structured query formulation[3].

3.2 Spoken Document Processing

This year the SDR track focused on the processing of news broadcasts with unknown story boundaries. This formulation required that sites perform some automatic segmentation of the full broadcasts into smaller units suitable for retrieval. Using an approach inspired by [11], we performed story segmentation as follows. First we created 30 second segments based on the word recognition time stamps using a 10 second step to create overlapping segment windows. These units were then indexed using the INQUERY retrieval system version 3.1p1 with both stemming and standard stopword removal.

3.3 Retrieval Segment Construction

To produce suitable retrieval segments, we merged the fine-grained segments returned by the base retrieval process on a per-query basis. For each query,

Table 6. Spoken Document Retrieval

Query	Monolingual	French No-Exp	French Expanded
Description	0.2820	0.0885	0.0965

we retrieved 5000 fine-grained segment windows. We then stepped through the ranked retrieval list merging overlapping segments, assigning the rank of the higher ranked segment to the newly merged segment. We cycled through the ranked list until convergence. The top ranked 1000 documents formed the final ranked retrieval results submitted for evaluation.

3.4 Results and Discussion

In Table 6, we present the results for both the monolingual baseline and the cross-language English $\rightarrow$ French spoken document retrieval runs in the unknown story boundary condition. There is a substantial drop-off in retrieval effectiveness for the cross-language relative to the monolingual runs. Post-hoc examination of the translated queries strongly suggests the need for addition stopword and stop structure removal for the French topics. There is also an apparent, but not significant, 10% relative improvement for the expanded French query over the unexpanded case. The effectiveness of the monolingual runs suggests the potential of spoken document retrieval in the unknown story boundary condition, even with a simple window merging approach to segmentation.

4 Conclusion

In the CLEF2004 multilingual and bilingual experiments, we demonstrated the flexibility of a dictionary-based query translation architecture by extension to two new languages, Finnish and Russian, with freely available translation and stemming resources. We further found significant utility in pre-translation query expansion for a language with only a rudimentary translation resource, enabling translation of key concepts. Experiments with a locality preserving dimensionality reduction technique suggest future work in which the likely relevance of the highest ranked documents is used explicitly for result re-scoring. Finally the spoken document retrieval results suggest that even a simple window-based approach to segmentation can yield modest retrieval effectiveness. However, future research will explore augmenting the window-based segmentation approach with a richer topical, possibly query-independent, segmentation.

References

1. Callan, J.P., Croft, W.B., Harding, S.M.: The INQUERY retrieval system. In: Proceedings of the Third International Conference on Database and Expert Systems Applications, Springer-Verlag (1992) 78–83

2. Levow, G.A., Oard, D.W., Resnik, P.: Dictionary-based techniques for cross-language information retrieval. Information Processing and Management (to appear)
3. Pirkola, A.: The effects of query structure and dictionary setups in dictionary-based cross-language information retrieval. In: Proceedings of the 21st Annual International ACM SIGIR Conference on Research and Development in Information Retrieval. (1998) 55–63
4. Belkin, M., Niyogi, P.: Laplacian eigenmaps for dimensionality +reduction and data representation. Neural Computation **15** (2003) 1373–1396
5. Roweis, S.T., Saul, L.K.: Nonlinear dimensionality reduction by locally linear embedding. Science **290** (2000) 2323–2326
6. Tenenbaum, J., de Silva, V., Langford, J.C.: A global geometric framework for nonlinear dimensionality reduction. Science **290** (2000) 2319–2323
7. He, X., Niyogi, P.: Locality preserving projections. In: Proceeding of NIPS 2003. (2003)
8. McCallum, A.K.: Bow: A toolkit for statistical language modeling, text retrieval, classification and clustering. http://www.cs.cmu.edu/ mccallum/bow (1996)
9. McNamee, P., Mayfield, J.: Comparing cross-language query expansion techniques by degrading translation resources. In: Proceedings of the 25th Annual International ACM SIGIR Conference on Research and Development in Information Retrieval. (2002) 159–166
10. Oard, D.W., Levow, G.A., Cabezas, C.: CLEF experiments at the University of Maryland: Statistical stemming and backoff translation strategies. In: Cross-Language Information Retrieval and Evaluation, Workshop of the Cross-Language Evaluation Forum, CLEF 2000, Lisbon, Portugal, September 2000, Revised Papers. Volume LNCS 2069 of Lecture Notes in Computer Science., Heidelberg, Springer-Verlag (2001) 176–187
11. Abberley, D., Renals, S., Cook, G., Robinson, T.: Retrieval of broadcast news documents with the thisl system. In Voorhees, E., Harman, D., eds.: Proceedings of the Seventh Text REtrieval Conference (TREC-7). (1999) 181–190 NIST Special Publication 500-242.

UB at CLEF2004: Cross Language Information Retrieval Using Statistical Language Models

Miguel E. Ruiz[1] and Munirathnam Srikanth[2]

[1] State University of New York at Buffalo,
School of Informatics, Dept of Library and Information Studies,
534 Baldy Hall, Buffalo, NY 14260-1020 USA
meruiz@buffalo.edu,
http://www.informatics.buffalo.edu/faculty/ruiz

[2] Language Computer Corporation Richardson, TX, 75080, USA
srikanth@languagecomputer.com

Abstract. This paper presents the results of the State University of New York at Buffalo (UB) in the Mono-lingual and Multi-lingual tasks at CLEF 2004. For these tasks we used an approach based on statistical language modeling. Our Adhoc retrieval work used the TAPIR toolkit developed in house by M Srikanth. Our approach focused on the validation and adaptation of the language model system to work in a multilingual environment and in exploring ways to merge results from multiple collections into a single list of results. We explored the use of a measure of query ambiguity, also known as *clarity score*, for merging results of the individual collections into a single list of retrieved documents. Our results indicate that the use of clarity scores normalized across queries gives statistically significant improvements over using a fixed merging order.

1 Introduction

For CLEF 2004 we participated in the Adhoc mono and multilingual retrieval as well as in the medical image retrieval. The goal of our participation in the Adhoc retrieval task is to explore statistical language models for retrieval from non-English collections. For this task we used the TAPIR (Text Analysis and Processing for Information Retrieval) toolkit which was originally developed for English and later modified to support ISO-Latin-1 encoding and Porter stemmers for European languages.

Section 2 presents the details of the statistical language models and the results merging method based on clarity scores. Section 3 presents the experimental results for the monolingual and multilingual tasks and includes the analysis of results. The last section presents our conclusions and future work.

2 Multilingual Task

The two step process of mono-lingual retrieval followed by result combination was used in our multilingual submissions. The language modeling approach to in-

C. Peters et al. (Eds.): CLEF 2004, LNCS 3491, pp. 180–187, 2005.

formation retrieval using smoothed unigram models was experimented with both mono-lingual and multi-lingual experiments. For multilingual retrieval, the topics were translated using Intertran translation system [1] from English to the other three languages (French, Finnish and Russian) defined in the task. The translated queries are used against a search index for the corresponding language. Our experiments concentrated on techniques to combine the mono-lingual retrieval results for the multilingual task. Monolingual retrieval was done using statistical language modeling approaches discussed briefly in the next section.

2.1 Monolingual Retrieval Using Statistical Language Models

Statistical language models have been shown to be very effective for document retrieval. Experiments in English document collections have shown significant improvements over traditional vector space and probabilistic models. A language model is a probability distribution defined on strings of an alphabet. A language model is associated with a document in the document collection to indicate or capture its unique properties. Given a query, Q, the documents are ranked based on the likelihood of their language model generating the query,$P(Q|M_d)$ [2]. The query-likelihood probability is estimated using smoothed unigram language models.

$$P(Q|M_d) = \prod_i P(q_i|M_d) \tag{1}$$

The query term probability is estimated from document and corpus counts of the query term smoothed using Dirichlet priors. In Bayesian smoothing using Dirichlet priors, the language model is assumed to be multinomial with the conjugate prior for Bayesian analysis as the Dirichlet distribution $\{\mu P_C(w_i)\}$. The Dirichlet prior smoothed term probability is given by

$$P(w|M_D) = \frac{n(w,d) + \mu p_C(w)}{\sum_v n(v,d) + \mu} \tag{2}$$

where μ is the Dirichlet prior parameter, $n(w,d)$ is the count of occurrence of term w in document d, and $p_C(w)$ is the corpus probability of term w. A fixed value of $\mu = 1000$ was used in the experiments.

2.2 Results Merging

Different weighting schemes and merging methods have been experimented for multilingual retrieval. Documents are reweighted for multilingual retrieval and ranked based on the reweighted relevance value. We explored in our CLEF 2004 experiments the use of *query ambiguity* or *clarity score* for reweighting documents for multilingual retrieval. Clarity score, proposed by Cronen-Townsend and Croft [3], is defined for a query as a measure of lack of ambiguity in the given query with respect to a document collection. A query language model is generated for a given query based on the word usage in documents relevant to

[1] www.intertran.com

the given query. The simplest query model is a unigram language model based on word counts in documents deemed highly-relevant to the given query. The clarity score is computed as the relative entropy between the query model and the overall collection language model. Using Lavrenko and Croft's Method 1 [1], the query language model is given by

$$P(w|Q) = \sum_{D \in R} P(w|D)P(D|Q) \tag{3}$$

where the summation is over documents deemed highly-relevant to the given query. The top 100 documents returned using the smoothed unigram language model were used as the relevant set in our experiments. The query-likelihood probability, $P(Q|D)$ is estimated using smoothed unigram language model given by (1) and (2). The clarity score is given by the Kullback-Leibler divergence between the query language model and the collection language model,

$$\text{clarity}(Q) = \sum_{w \in V} P(w|Q) log_2 \frac{P(w|Q)}{P_C(w)} \tag{4}$$

The clarity score, $cl(Q, L)$ is computed for each query-language pair. For multilingual experiments, the source language query in English is translated to other languages, the monolingual retrieval using smoothed unigram language models is performed and the clarity scores for each query-language pair is computed. Result merging uses the clarity score to reweight the relevance status value of the documents from the monolingual results.

The clarity scores can be used "as-is" as weights assigned to different languages for a given query and relevance weight of a document for a given query can be adjusted as

$$RSV_{ASIS}(D, Q, L) = RSV_{mono}(D, Q, L) \times cl(Q, L) \tag{5}$$

However, the clarity scores are not comparable across the document collections in different languages. The range of values taken by clarity score depends on the characteristics of the document collection in a particular language and the retrieval performance using such a weighting scheme is expected to match a merging method that uses a fixed multiplier values for a language across queries.

Instead of using the absolute values of the clarity scores for different query-language pairs, we experimented with different normalization methods. The clarity score can be compared and normalized across languages as they correspond to the same query.

$$RSV_{BYLANG}(D, Q, L) = RSV_{mono}(D, Q, L) \times \frac{cl(Q, L)}{\sum_l cl(Q, l)} \tag{6}$$

Normalization can also be performed across queries as the clarity scores were computed for different queries with respect to a document collection in one language.

$$RSV_{BYQUERY}(D,Q,L) = RSV_{mono}(D,Q,L) \times \frac{cl(Q,L)}{\sum_q cl(q,L)} \quad (7)$$

We also experimented with normalizing the clarity scores, first across queries and then across languages (BYQUERYLANG) and also the reverse – normalize first across languages, then across queries (BYLANGQUERY). In all the above reweighting formulas, the relevance status value of a document for a given query is normalized across the documents deemed relevant to the query. This makes the comparison of relevance status values of documents across language for a given query meaningful.

Merging retrieval results using interleaving of documents with same rank has been experimented before for multilingual retrieval. While interleaving the results a fixed order of the languages is selected and documents with the same rank are listed based on the pre-selected order of their respective languages. The language order is usually fixed at random. We experimented with different normalized and unnormalized clarity scores to check whether they provide any clues for the order in which documents with same rank can be interleaved.

3 Experimental Results

The document collections for different languages were indexed separately using the TAPIR (Text Analysis and Processing for Information Retrieval) toolkit – an in-house information retrieval system that supports different retrieval models (VSM, language models) and languages. Document and collection statistics along with position information is collected and stored in the indexing system. The TAPIR toolkit was used to perform monolingual retrieval using the original and translated queries using the smoothed unigram retrieval model.

The mono-lingual retrieval results are given in Table 3. Figures 1 2 and 3 plot the difference between our submitted results and the median average precision values for French, Finnish and Russian. Our submission seems to have been the only submission for monolingual retrieval in English and hence is not included in the figures.

Our retrieval results performed well above average or the median systems in the French corpus. In the Finnish corpus our systems performs below average. We believe that this is due to the the fact that we are using Porter's stemmer,which is a suffix stripping algorithm. A better choice would be to use a morfologic stemmer but at the time we develop the system we did not have access to it. Russian performance seems to be around the median values. However, when we examined the query by query comparison we found that our system has a quite different behaviour across topics. We are not sure of the reason of such effect but suspect that there can be a combination of two factors. On one hand, our stemmer works with KOI8 encoding while the collection and topics were encoded in CP-1251. We had to convert from CP-1251 to KOI8 and this could have been a source of error. These performances correspond to the simple statistical retrieval model with no special linguistic processing other than stemming and stopword

Table 1. Monolingual retrieval performance using smoothed unigram language models

	AvgP.	Recall	R-Prec.	InitPr
English	0.5167	361/375	0.4608	0.3048
French	0.4629	863/915	0.4239	0.6418
Finnish	0.4599	318/413	0.4545	0.3067
Russian	0.2978	78/123	0.2807	0.1059

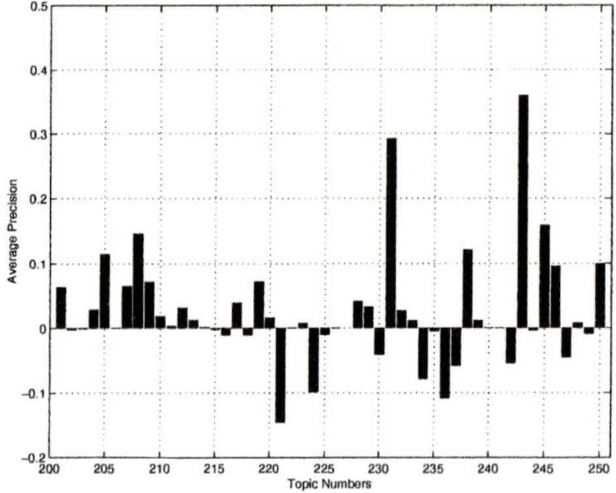

Fig. 1. Difference in Average Precision comparing our official submission and median average precision values for French

removal. We believe that using a more sofisticated linguistic processing as well as retrieval feedback could improve the system performance significantly.

Two runs were submitted as official runs for CLEF2004 multilingual retrieval task[2]. These correspond to merging documents by weighting their relevance status value using the clarity score (ASIS) and score reweighting using normalized relevance score, where the normalization is first performed across languages and then across queries (BYLANGQUERY). Table 2 includes performance metrics for the two official submitted runs (ASIS and BYLANGQUERY) and other experimental runs using different normalization conditions for clarity scores.

Normalizing across languages seems to give a significant improvement to the average precision values. However, normaling the clarity scores both across query and language gives the best performance. It is noted that the monolingual retrieval runs that are combined to obtain these results are based on smoothed unigram language models. The merging strategy is independent of the underlying retrieval model used for mono-lingual retrieval. Improvements using better query representation and relevance feedback for monolingual retrieval is expected

[2] We submitted a third run (UBmulti03) that was mistakenly labeled as automatic but was actually a run that combined the manual translations and will not be considered in the analysis.

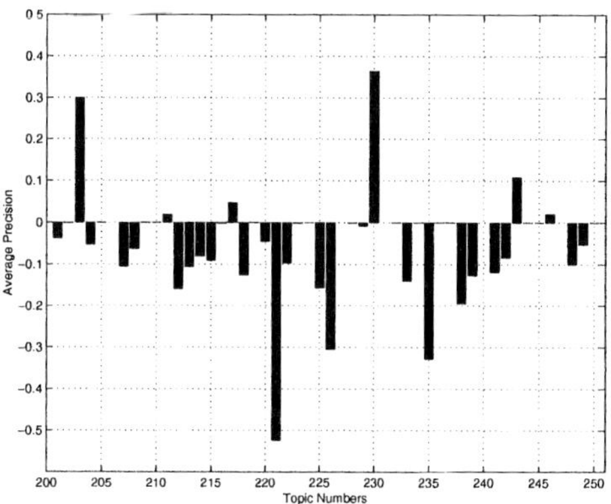

Fig. 2. Difference in Average Precision comparing our official submission and median average precision values for Finnish

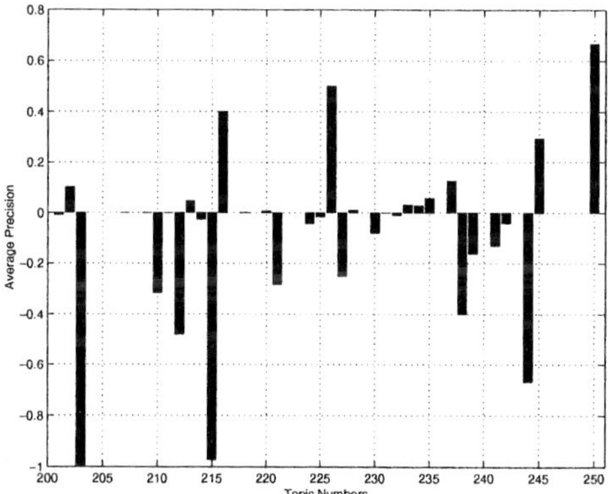

Fig. 3. Difference in Average Precision comparing our official submission and median average precision values for Russian

Table 2. Multilingual retrieval performance

	AvgP.	Recall	R-Prec.	P@10
ASIS	0.1453	1135/1826	0.1884	0.2400
BYLANGQUERY	0.1709	1092/1826	0.2003	0.2360
BYLANG	0.1711	1092/1826	0.2003	0.2360
BYQUERY	0.1163	857/1826	0.1501	0.2560
BYQUERYLANG	**0.1769**	1094/1826	0.2043	0.2400

to reflect positively on multilingual retrieval results. The clarity scores provides some clues on weighting the monolingual results. Appropriate methods need to be devised to incorporate such clues in the re-weighting document scores. We intend to explore such methods in future.

Table 3. Multilingual retrieval performance - merging results using interleaving of ranked documents

	AvgP.	Recall	R-Prec.	P@10
IL-ASIS	0.1381	1156/1826	0.1785	0.2220
IL-RANDOM	0.1443	1156/1826	0.1771	0.2420
IL-BYLANG	0.1489	1156/1826	0.1787	0.2420
IL-BYQUERY	**0.1553**	1156/1826	0.1794	0.2420
IL-BYLANGQUERY	0.1489	1156/1826	0.1787	0.2420
IL-BYQUERYLANG	0.1508	1156/1826	0.1787	0.2400

Table 4. Bilingual retrieval performance

	AvgP. (% of monoligual)	Recall	R-Prec.	P@10
English→French	0.2790 (60%)	720/915	0.2633	0.2408
English→Finnish	0.2029 (44%)	218/413	0.1776	0.1333
English→Russian	0.0723 (24%)	50/123	0.0397	0.0324

We experimented with merging using interleaving of documents with same rank. Table 3 gives the performance of different interleaving options. The different runs correspond to the selection of the order in which documents from different monolingual retrieval with same rank are selected. In IL-ASIS a fixed order of languages is used and results are interleaved. In IL-RANDOM, the order is randomly selected for each query. Random selection looks better that IL-ASIS based on the metrics in the table. However, it corresponds to one particular run and one can expect the performance measures to take values around the IL-ASIS performance values. There is not justification for either of these selection methods. The last four entries correspond to the language order selection based on normalized clarity scores. For a given query, the clarity scores are normalized either across languages or across queries or both. The language order is decided based on the ranking of the normalized clarity scores for a given query. Normalizing the clarity scores across queries and use them to decide the language order for interleaving seems to provide best performance for CLEF2004 topics.

While the performance of interleaving using clarity scores to select the language order does not perform as well as using the clarity scores directly as multipliers for the document weights for multilingual retrieval, it can be used as a metric for the results merging process. The improvement in average precision of interleaving using clarity scores normalized across queries is statistically significant than using a fixed language order.

We also examined the bilingual performance of each translation pair with English as the source language. The results of these bilingual performance is presented in Table 4. This table shows a significant drop in performance for monolingual performance for Finnish and Russian. This indicates that the Russian translation is a major problem for InterTran and we would need to find a better alternative to improve CLIR performance. This also explains the difference in performance between the merging method using RSV and rank interleaving methods. Clarity actually helps to rank higher the results obtained from the French and English collections while Russian and Finish results are ranked lower.

4 Conclusion and Future Work

In an effort to build the baseline multilingual retrieval systems, we extended an IR system developed to work with English document collections to handle non-English document collections and performed monolingual retrieval on English, French, Finnish and Russian using a smoothed unigram language model. For multilingual task we experimented with clarity scores of the queries in their document collections for merging the results of monolingual retrieval. Clarity score was used as a multiplier for the document weight as well as a mechanism to determine language order in the case of merging using interleaving of documents at the same rank. Using clarity scores as multipliers to reweight the document scores improves retrieval performance. Appropriate methods to incorporate the clues provided by clarity scores towards improving retrieval need to be investigated, and this is one of the areas of our future work.

References

1. Lavrenko, V. and Croft, W. B.: Relevance-based Language Models. In *Proceedings of SIGIR'01*, pages 120–127. ACM, New York, 2001.
2. Ponte, J. M. and Croft, W. B.: A language modeling approach to information retrieval. In *Proceedings of SIGIR'98*, pages 275–281. ACM, New York, 1998.
3. Cronen-Townsend, S. and Croft, W. B.: Quantifying Query Ambiguity. In *Proceedings of HLT'02*, 2002

MIRACLE's Hybrid Approach to Bilingual and Monolingual Information Retrieval

José M. Goñi-Menoyo[1], José C. González[1,3], J.L. Martínez-Fernández[2,3], and J. Villena[2,3]

[1] Universidad Politécnica de Madrid
[2] Universidad Carlos III de Madrid
[3] DAEDALUS - Data, Decisions and Language, S.A.
josemiguel.goni@upm.es, jgonzalez@dit.upm.es, joseluis.martinez@uc3m.es, julio.villena@uc3m.es

Abstract. The main goal of the bilingual and monolingual participation of the MIRACLE team in CLEF 2004 was to test the effect of combination approaches on information retrieval. The starting point was a set of basic components: stemming, transformation, filtering, generation of n-grams, weighting and relevance feedback. Some of these basic components were used in different combinations and order of application for document indexing and for query processing. A second order combination was also tested, mainly by averaging or selective combination of the documents retrieved by different approaches for a particular query.

1 Introduction

The MIRACLE team is made up of three university research groups located in Madrid (UPM, UC3M and UAM) along with DAEDALUS, a company founded in 1998 as a spin-off of two of these groups. DAEDALUS is a leading company in linguistic technologies in Spain[1], and is the coordinator of the MIRACLE team. This is the second participation in CLEF, following that of 2003 [3], [6]. In addition to the bi- and monolingual tasks, the team participated in the ImageCLEF and Q&A tracks.

The main purpose of the bi- and monolingual participation was to test the effect of combination approaches on information retrieval. The starting point was a set of basic components: stemming, transformation (transliteration, elimination of diacritics and conversion to lowercase), filtering (elimination of stop and frequent words), generation of n-grams, weighting (giving more importance to titles) and relevance feedback.

[1] DAEDALUS clients include leading companies in different sectors: media (EL PAÍS), publishing (Grupo SM), telecommunication (Grupo Telefónica), digital rights management (SGAE), photography (StockPhotos) and the reference institution for the Spanish language, Instituto Cervantes. Its portfolio of solutions includes STILUS® (professional spell, grammar and style checking of texts in Spanish), K-Site® (information retrieval, fuzzy search and knowledge management), LUCAS (universal locator of audiovisual contents, an Internet spider), etc.

C. Peters et al. (Eds.): CLEF 2004, LNCS 3491, pp. 188 – 199, 2005.

Some of these basic components are used in different combinations and order of application for document indexing and for query processing. A second order combination was also tested, mainly by averaging or by selective combination of the documents retrieved by different approaches for a particular query. When evidence is found of better precision of one system at one extreme of the recall level (i.e. 1,0), complemented by the better precision of another system at the other recall end (i.e. 0,0), then both are combined to benefit from their complementary results.

In addition, during the last year our group has been developing an indexing system based on the *trie* data structure [2]. Tries [1] are successfully used by the MIRACLE team for an efficient storage and retrieval of huge lexical resources, combined with a continuation-based approach to morphological treatment. However, the adaptation of these structures to manage efficiently document indexing and retrieval for commercial applications has been a hard task. The currently available prototype shows a great improvement in performance. (Both indexing and retrieval times are considerably reduced.) However, this system was not fully operational in this CLEF campaign. So, the Xapian [10] indexing system, robust, efficient, and well suited for our purposes, was used as in the last campaign.

For the 2004 campaign, runs were submitted for the following tracks:

a) Monolingual Russian.
b) Monolingual French.
c) Bilingual Dutch to French.
d) Bilingual German to French.

2 Description of the Tools in MIRACLE's Tool Box

The Xapian system was the basic indexing and retrieval tool for the bilingual and monolingual experiments by the MIRACLE group. Before indexing, document collections were pre-processed using different combinations of scripts, each one oriented to a particular experiment. For each of these, topic queries were also processed using the same combination of scripts. (Although some variants have been used, as will be described later).

The baseline approach to document and topic query processing is made up of the following sequence of steps:

1. **Extraction:** Ad-hoc scripts are run on the files that contain particular documents or topic query collections, to extract the textual data enclosed in XML tags. All those permitted for automatic runs were used. (Depending on the collection, all of the existing TEXT, TITLE, LEAD1, TX, LD, TI, or ST for document collections, and the contents of the TITLE and DESC fields for topic queries; NARR field contents were systematically ignored). The contents of these fields were concatenated to feed the following processing steps. However, in some experiments only the titles were extracted (including, in the run identifier, the strings *titnormal, titnostem* or *titngrams*), and in some *normal* experiments (see below) in monolingual Russian, the terms appearing within the TITLE fields were given more importance by repeating them several times (these experiments include the strings *nomaltitl, nor-*

maltit2 or *normaltit3* in the identifiers, when the titles terms are included one, two or three more times).

2. **Parsing:** A simple parsing process is followed to eliminate punctuation marks and detect basic indexing chunks (usually words, but some basic entities can also be detected, such as compounds, proper nouns, and so on). It is clear that the quality of this step is of paramount importance for precise document processing. A high-quality entity recognition (proper nouns or acronyms for people, companies, countries, locations, and so on) could improve the precision and recall figures of the overall retrieval, as well as a correct recognition and normalization of dates, times, numbers, etc.
3. **Lowercase words:** All document words are normalized by converting all uppercase letters to lowercase.
4. **Stopwords filter:** All words recognised as stopwords are eliminated from the document. Stopwords in the target languages were initially obtained from [9], but were extended using several other sources and our own knowledge and resources.
5. **Stemming:** This is applied to each of the words in the document. The stemmer used is the one referenced in [7].
6. **Remove accents:** All document words are normalized by eliminating accents in stemmed words. Note that this process can be done before stemming, but the resulting *lexemes* are different. Despite this, in some experiments, this step was performed before stemming.
7. **Final use:**

a. **Indexing:** When all the documents processed through the former steps are ready for indexing, they are fed into a Xapian ad-hoc front-end to build the Xapian document database.

b. **Retrieval:** When all the documents processed by the former steps are topic queries, they are fed to a Xapian ad-hoc front-end to search the previously built Xapian index. In the 2004 experiments, only OR combinations of the search terms were used.

In the case of the Russian language, the basic processing steps described above are slightly changed, due to the different encodings of the Russian files and the resources used for Russian: while document collection and topics files were encoded in UTF8, as well as stopword resources, the stemming resources worked in KOI8, so some recoding steps were added at appropriate processing points. In addition to this, some other tools did not work properly with the UTF8 encoding, so others had to be added: (a) The parsing process was simplified even more, using a *sed* script to achieve basic punctuation processing, and (b) a transliteration of the files to the ASCII charset was needed to get the XAPIAN indexing system to work. The transliteration script used was the one available in reference [9].

In addition to the baseline (or *normal*) experiments (identified with the suffix *normal* in the run identifiers), other experiments were also defined as variations: If the stemming step was not carried out, the resulting experiments were labeled with the suffix *nostem,* where the actual word forms appearing in the documents are used for indexing and retrieval. A variant of the *nostem* experiments was also tested, where a set of *n-grams* was generated from each of the actual word forms in the documents. These experiments were labeled with identifiers of the form *ngramsXY*, where X is the length of the n-grams and Y the number of characters that overlap between two consecutive n-grams. (For example, in an experiment referred to by an identifier with the suffix *ngrams54*, from *president* we would obtain the n-grams: *"_pres"*, *"presi"*, *"resid"*, *"eside"*, *"siden"*, *"ident"*, and *"dent_"*. The symbol "_" is introduced to denote word boundaries. Note that four characters overlap between two consecutive n-grams).

In the case of the topic queries, an additional variation is introduced: the FW (*Frequent Words*) filter is applied by filtering out the 20 most frequent words, or stems, that appear in the corpora from the queries, as well as some typical query terms. These variants were identified by using the *FW* string in the run identifier.

The Xapian engine allows us to use relevance feedback, so we use this technique in several experiments. When the terms of the first documents retrieved in the first retrieval step are fed back to a second retrieval step, we used the strings *R1*, *R2*, *R3*, *R4* or *R5*, in the run identifier depending on the actual number of documents used. Note that using relevance feedback does not affect the indexing processes, and can be applied in any of the variants used for processing the document collections or the topic queries.

For translation purposes, the SYSTRAN [10] system was used. Our tests carried out on the collections and topics of CLEF 2003, showed that SYSTRAN outperformed other on-line translators in the selected pairs of languages (Dutch to French and German to French) when used to find documents in the French collections from queries in Dutch or German. As other pairs such as Finnish and Swedish to French were not available on-line in SYSTRAN, other translators were tested with very poor results. So, no runs were prepared for them.

3 Description of the Baseline Experiments

Not all the possible combinations of the variants described in the previous section were tried in the experiments due to evident limitations of computing resources and time. The experiments were tried in a rather intuitive, non-systematic way, trying to test a wider and richer set of trials.

To compare these approaches, we used these techniques following the instructions given for CLEF 2003 (corpora and topic queries) and using the appropriate *qrels* available at the beginning of this campaign. The experiments that provided the best precision results in the CLEF 2003 scenario were selected for submission to CLEF 2004.

The appendix shows the baseline experiments, and the precision values obtained. It also shows those that were selected for submission to CLEF 2004, as well as the results obtained using the CLEF 2003 data.

In Figure 1, the results obtained using the best baseline experiments submitted to CLEF 2004 are compared with the results obtained by exactly the same system when applied to the 2003 tasks. The comparison shows qualitative differences between the 2003 and 2004 topics. No figure is presented for French, as all the submitted runs were, in this case, obtained through combination (see the next section).

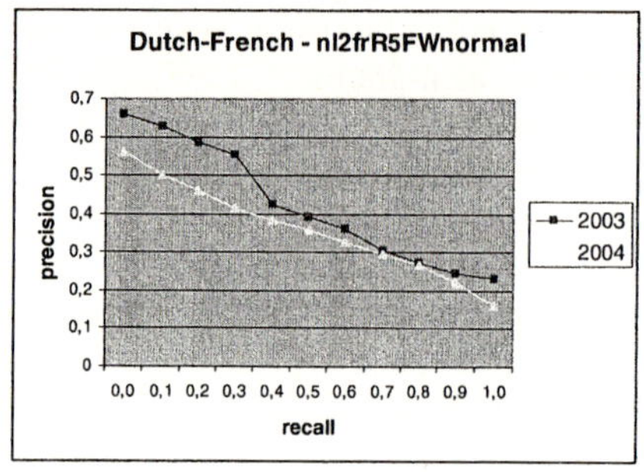

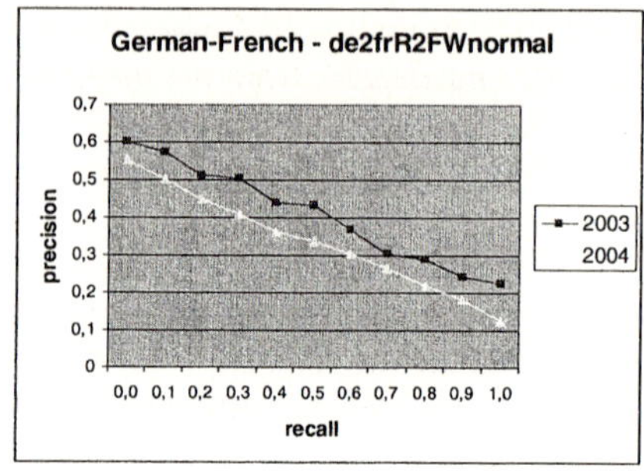

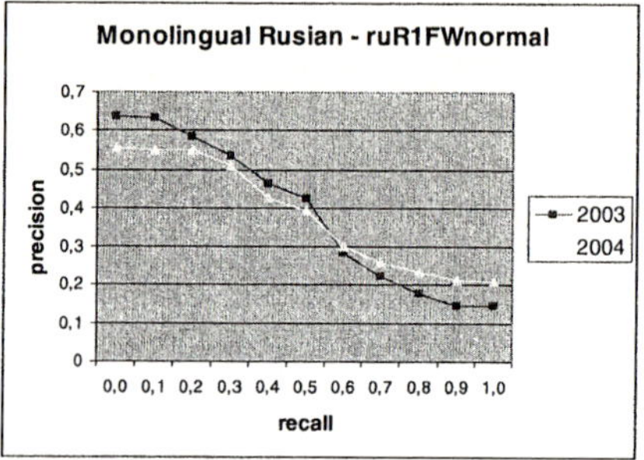

Fig. 1. Precision-recall curves for selected baseline experiments in CLEF 2003 and CLEF 2004

4 Description of Combined Experiments

In this campaign, some tests were carried out trying to combine the results from the basic experiments in different ways. The underlying hypothesis is that, to some extent, the documents with a good score in almost all experiments are more likely to be relevant than other documents that have a good score in one experiment but a bad one in others. Two strategies were followed for combining experiments:

- **Average:** The relevance figures obtained using the Xapian probabilistic retrieval in all the experiments to be combined for a particular document in a given query are added. This approach combines the relevance figures of the experiments without highlighting a particular experiment.
- **Asymmetric DWX combination:** In this particular type of combination, two experiments are combined in the following way: The relevance of the first D documents for each query of the first experiment is preserved for the resulting combined relevance, whereas the relevance for the remaining documents in both experiments are combined using weights W and X. We have only run experiments labeled "101" and "201", that is, the ones that get the one (or two) more relevant documents from the first basic experiment and all the remaining documents retrieved from the second basic experiment, re-sorting all the results using the original relevance.

Average combinations get better figures in average precision or in precisions at 0 or 1 points of recall than the original basic experiments. The reason could be that relevant documents that appear with a high score in the combined experiments are strengthened. Average combinations seem to improve results slightly, whereas asymmetric combinations do not. The particular experiments that were combined and the type of combination are shown in the appendix, for each one of the four tracks.

In Figure 2, the results obtained from the best combined experiments submitted to CLEF 2004 are compared with the results obtained using exactly the same systems when applied to the 2003 tasks. The comparison shows again the qualitative differences between the 2003 and 2004 topics.

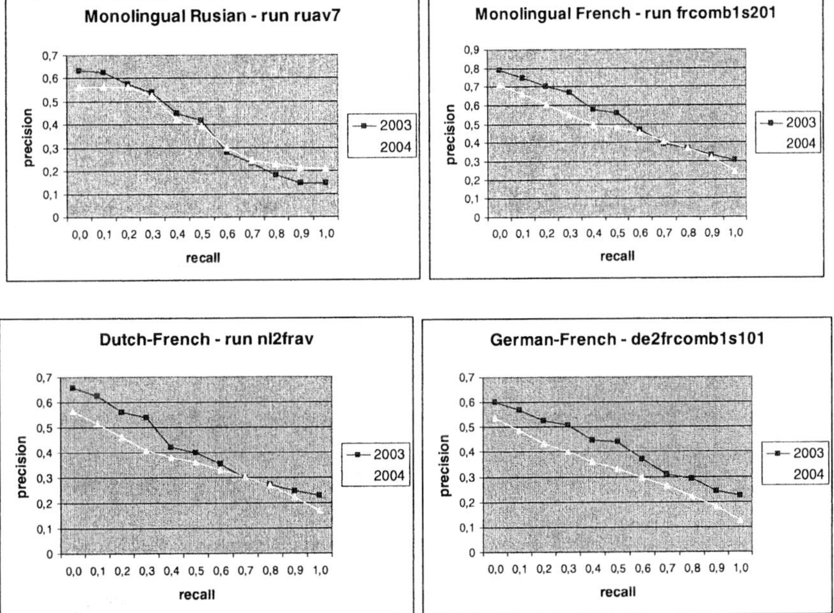

Fig. 2. Precision-recall curves for selected combined experiments in CLEF 2003 and CLEF 2004

5 Conclusions

The combination approach seems to improve the precision results slightly for IR retrieval tasks, although an in-depth analysis of the reasons for this is still needed. The differences shown between the 2003 and 2004 experiments seem to be highly idiosyncratic, depending to a great extent on the different topics selected each year. This is particularly true in the case of Russian, due to the low number of documents relevant for the topic set. Regarding the basic experiments, the general conclusions were known in advance: retrieval performance can be improved by using stemming, filtering of frequent words, appropriate weighting and relevance feedback with a few documents. On the other hand, n-grams performed worse than expected.

Future work of the MIRACLE team in these tasks will be directed to several lines of research: (a) Getting better performance in the indexing and retrieval phases in order to be able to carry out experiments in a more efficient way (indexing times for the huge document collection is now excessive for a flexible scheduling of experiments). This will be achieved using our own trie-based libraries for the indexing and retrieval phases. (b) Improving the first parsing step; in our opinion, this is one of the most critical processing steps and can improve the overall results of the IR process. A good entity recognition and normalization is still missing in our processing scheme for these tasks.

Acknowledgements

This work has been partially supported by the OmniPaper project (European Union, 5th Framework Programme for Research and Technological Development, IST-2001-32174).

The participation of the MIRACLE team in CLEF 2004 was also partially funded by the Regional Government of Madrid through the research project *"MIRACLE: Multilingual Information Retrieval System and its Evaluation under the CLEF European Initiative"* (07T/0055/2003) and through its Entrepreneurship Innovation Programme (Madrid Innova, project PIE/594/2003).

Special mention must be done to our colleagues at other members of the MIRACLE group: Ana M. García-Serrano, Paloma Martínez-Fernández, César de Pablo-Sánchez, and Javier Alonso-Sánchez.

References

1. Aoe, Jun-Ichi, Morimoto, Katsushi, Sato, Takashi: An Efficient Implementation of Trie Structures. Software Practice and Experience 22(9) (1992) 695-721.
2. Goñi-Menoyo, José Miguel, González-Cristóbal, José Carlos, Fombella-Mourelle, Jorge: An optimised trie index for natural language processing lexicons. MIRACLE Technical Report. Universidad Politécnica de Madrid (2004).
3. Martínez, J.L., Villena-Román, J., Fombella, J., García-Serrano, A., Ruiz, A., Martínez, P., Goñi, J.M., González, J.C.: Evaluation of MIRACLE approach results for CLEF 2003. Working Notes for the CLEF 2003 Workshop, 21-22 August, Trondheim, Norway (2003).
4. Peters, C.: What happened in CLEF 2004. In: Peters, C., Clough, P., Gonzalo, J., Jones, G., Kluck M., Magnini, B. (eds.): Fifth Workshop of the Cross-Language Evaluation Forum (CLEF 2004). Lecture Notes in Computer Science (LNCS), Springer, Heidelberg, Germany (in print) (2005).
5. Peters, C., Braschler, M., Di Nunzio, G., Ferro, N.: CLEF 2004: Ad Hoc Track Overview and Results Analysis. In: Peters, C., Clough, P., Gonzalo, J., Jones, G., Kluck M., Magnini, B. (eds.): Fifth Workshop of the Cross-Language Evaluation Forum (CLEF 2004). Lecture Notes in Computer Science (LNCS), Springer, Heidelberg, Germany (in print) (2005).
6. Villena-Román, J., Martínez, J.L., Fombella, J., García-Serrano, A., Ruiz, A., Martínez, P., Goñi, J.M., González, J.C.: MIRACLE results for ImageCLEF 2003. Working Notes for the CLEF 2003 Workshop, 21-22 August, Trondheim, Norway (2003).
7. Snowball stemmers and resources. On line http://www.snowball.tartarus.org. [Visited 27/11/2004]

8. SYSTRAN Language Translation Technlogies. On line http://www.systran.org/. [Visited 27/10/2004]
9. University of Neuchatel page of resources for CLEF (Stopwords, transliteration, stemmers ...). On line http://www.unine.ch/info/clef/. [Visited 27/10/2004]
10. Xapian: an Open Source Probabilistic Information Retrieval library. On line http://www.xapian.org. [Visited 27/10/2004]

Appendix

The appendix includes all the data that show the results obtained in the experiments. Tables 1, 3, 5, and 7 show the precisions at recall points 0 and 1, the average precision, the percentage of the latter with respect to the best average precision experiment (the first one in each table) for each experiment. The best value is marked with the symbol "*". The *comb* column in each table indicates whether the experiment is a combined experiment (cf. section 4), and the *sel* column shows which experiments were selected for CLEF 2004, usually the ones with a better result in precision (regarding CLEF 2003 experiments).

The results for the same experiments for the CLEF 2004 campaign are also included in Tables 2, 4, 6, and 8 (the experiments submitted are indicated by the cross in the *sub* column), once the *qrels* for this campaign were made available.

Finally, Tables 9-11 show what the combined experiments consist of, as well as the type of combination used. Note that Tables 1-8 mark these with the *comb* column.

Table 1. CLEF 2004 results for Monolingual Russian

at0	at1	avgp	%	run id	comb	sub
0.5707	0.2184*	0.3754*	0.00%	ruav5	X	
0.5742*	0.2143	0.3697	-1.52%	runormaltit3		
0.5638	0.2100	0.3695	-1.57%	ruav7	X	X
0.5706	0.2108	0.3685	-1.84%	runormaltit2		
0.5717	0.2080	0.3676	-2.08%	runormaltit1		
0.5553	0.2092	0.3672	-2.18%	ruR1FWnormal		X
0.5683	0.2014	0.3660	-2.50%	runormal		
0.5693	0.2094	0.3648	-2.82%	rucomb1s101	X	X
0.5574	0.2050	0.3641	-3.01%	ruav8	X	X
0.5597	0.2094	0.3608	-3.89%	rucomb1s201	X	
0.5558	0.1940	0.3584	-4.53%	ruFWnormal		
0.5225	0.1762	0.3309	-11.85%	ruR2FWnormal		
0.5102	0.1883	0.3195	-14.89%	rungrams54		
0.4906	0.1790	0.3125	-16.76%	rungrams43		
0.4885	0.1771	0.3012	-19.77%	ruFWnostem		
0.4731	0.1827	0.2907	-22.56%	rungrams76		
0.4757	0.1642	0.2884	-23.18%	runostem		
0.1715	0.0128	0.0764	-79.65%	rutitngrams43		
0.1538	0.0109	0.0723	-80.74%	rutitngrams54		
0.1166	0.0049	0.0433	-88.47%	rutitFWnormal		
0.1119	0.0003	0.0383	-89.80%	rutitnormal		

Table 2. CLEF 2003 results for Monolingual Russian

at0	at1	avgp	%	run id	comb	sel
0.6384*	0.1459	0.3799*	-0.00%	ruav8	X	X
0.6379	0.1465	0.3750	-1.29%	ruR1FWnormal		X
0.6323	0.1471	0.3706	-2.45%	ruav7	X	X
0.6344	0.1463	0.3697	-2.68%	ruav5	X	
0.6234	0.1593*	0.3695	-2.74%	rucomb1s101	X	X
0.6276	0.1575	0.3695	-2.74%	rucomb1s201	X	
0.6230	0.1563	0.3695	-2.74%	runormaltit1		
0.6234	0.1593*	0.3695	-2.74%	runormaltit3		
0.6228	0.1585	0.3694	-2.76%	runormaltit2		
0.6254	0.1430	0.3653	-3.84%	ruFWnormal		
0.6194	0.1423	0.3645	-4.05%	runormal		
0.6044	0.1482	0.3605	-5.11%	ruR2FWnormal		
0.5789	0.1318	0.3418	-10.03%	rungrams54		
0.5579	0.1438	0.3323	-12.53%	rungrams43		
0.5609	0.1052	0.3046	-19.82%	ruFWnostem		
0.5609	0.1052	0.3046	-19.82%	runostem		
0.5172	0.1058	0.2753	-27.53%	rungrams76		
0.2922	0.0584	0.1382	-63.62%	ruFWtitnormal		
0.2910	0.0584	0.1381	-63.65%	rutitnormal		
0.2716	0.0661	0.1377	-63.75%	rutitngrams43		
0.2378	0.0462	0.1125	-70.39%	rutitngrams54		

Table 3. CLEF 2004 results for Monolingual French

at0	at1	avgp	%	run id	comb	sub
0.7070	0.2444	0.4677*	0.00%	frav5	X	
0.7111	0.2459	0.4673	-0.09%	frcomb1s201	X	X
0.7107	0.2438	0.4670	-0.15%	frav3	X	
0.7100	0.2477*	0.4670	-0.15%	frcomb2s201	X	X
0.7032	0.2477*	0.4654	-0.49%	frR2FWnormal		
0.7242*	0.2349	0.4654	-0.49%	frFWnormal		
0.6986	0.2459	0.4653	-0.51%	frR1FWnormal		
0.6986	0.2459	0.4653	-0.51%	frcomb1s101	X	
0.6998	0.2477*	0.4639	-0.81%	frcomb2s101	X	
0.7170	0.2425	0.4635	-0.90%	frav9	X	
0.7186	0.2338	0.4628	-1.05%	frnormalinv		
0.7169	0.2378	0.4624	-1.13%	frav7	X	X
0.7172	0.2352	0.4596	-1.73%	frnormal		
0.7113	0.2371	0.4589	-1.88%	frav8	X	X
0.6634	0.2060	0.4206	-10.07%	frngrams54		
0.6797	0.2036	0.4187	-10.48%	frnostem		
0.6685	0.2014	0.4177	-10.69%	frFWnostem		
0.6393	0.0719	0.3263	-30.23%	frtitnormalinv		
0.6278	0.0719	0.3254	-30.43%	frtitnormal		
0.6066	0.0619	0.2999	-35.88%	frtitngrams54		
0.5932	0.0650	0.2985	-36.18%	frtitnostem		

Table 4. CLEF 2003 results for Monolingual French

at0	at1	avgp	%	run id	comb	sel
0.8053	0.3271*	0.5312*	0.00%	frav7	X	X
0.7993	0.2987	0.5288	-0.45%	frcomb2s201	X	X
0.8091*	0.3202	0.5287	-0.47%	frav8	X	X
0.7902	0.3049	0.5220	-1.73%	frcomb1s201	X	X
0.7707	0.2987	0.5207	-1.98%	frcomb2s101	X	
0.7707	0.2987	0.5207	-1.98%	frR2FWnormal		
0.7951	0.3029	0.5200	-2.11%	frav5	X	
0.7927	0.3017	0.5191	-2.28%	frav3	X	
0.7731	0.3049	0.5162	-2.82%	frcomb1s101	X	
0.7731	0.3049	0.5162	-2.82%	frR1FWnormal		
0.7954	0.2980	0.5124	-3.54%	frFWnormal		
0.7855	0.2987	0.5083	-4.31%	frnormal		
0.7717	0.2749	0.4913	-7.51%	frav9	X	
0.7281	0.2958	0.4875	-8.23%	frnormalinv		
0.7313	0.2778	0.4722	-11.11%	frngrams54		
0.6896	0.2753	0.4579	-13.80%	frFWnostem		
0.6806	0.2618	0.4452	-16.19%	frnostem		
0.6241	0.1725	0.3315	-37.59%	frtitnormal		
0.5850	0.1516	0.3117	-41.32%	frtitngrams54		
0.4939	0.1213	0.2288	-56.93%	frtitnostem		

Table 5. CLEF 2004 results for Bilingual Dutch to French

at0	at1	avgp	%	run id	comb	sub
0.5591	0.1716	0.3519*	0.00%	nl2frR2FWnormal		
0.5628	0.1668	0.3505	-0.40%	nl2frav	X	X
0.5558	0.1637	0.3486	-0.94%	nl2frR3FWnormal		
0.5458	0.1739	0.3483	-1.02%	nl2frR1FWnormal		
0.5598	0.1593	0.3483	-1.02%	nl2frR5FWnormal		X
0.5583	0.1595	0.3472	-1.34%	nl2frR4FWnormal		X
0.5653*	0.1717	0.3469	-1.42%	nl2frnormal		
0.5430	0.1750*	0.3451	-1.93%	nl2frFWnormal		
0.5515	0.1595	0.3449	-1.99%	nl2frcomb1s101	X	X

Table 6. CLEF 2003 results for Bilingual Dutch to French

at0	at1	avgp	%	run id	comb	sel
0.6766*	0.2323*	0.4159*	-0.00%	nl2frR4FWnormal		X
0.6564	0.2296	0.4112	-1.13%	nl2frR5FWnormal		X
0.6528	0.2323*	0.4087	-1.73%	nl2frcomb1s101	X	X
0.6583	0.2285	0.4069	-2.16%	nl2frav	X	X
0.6518	0.2286	0.4043	-2.79%	nl2frR3FWnormal		
0.6684	0.2230	0.4016	-3.44%	nl2frFWnormal		
0.6423	0.2321	0.3997	-3.90%	nl2frR2FWnormal		
0.6533	0.2225	0.3986	-4.16%	nl2frR1FWnormal		
0.6478	0.2159	0.3862	-7.14%	nl2frnormal		

Table 7. CLEF 2004 results for Bilingual German to French

at0	at1	avgp	%	run id	comb	sub
0.5419	0.1195	0.3217*	0.00%	de2frR5FWnormal		
0.5289	0.1209	0.3208	-0.28%	de2frR4FWnormal		
0.5485	0.1263	0.3201	-0.50%	de2frR2FWnormal		X
0.5340	0.1241	0.3199	-0.56%	de2frR3FWnormal		X
0.5349	0.1244	0.3178	-1.21%	de2frav	X	
0.5439	0.1250	0.3174	-1.34%	de2frR1FWnormal		
0.5381	0.1241	0.3166	-1.59%	de2frcomb1s101	X	X
0.5447	0.1265*	0.3134	-2.58%	de2frFWnormal		
0.5265	0.1265*	0.3116	-3.14%	de2frcomb2s201	X	X
0.5505*	0.1221	0.3100	-3.64%	de2frnormal		

Table 8. CLEF 2003 results for Bilingual German to French

at0	at1	avgp	%	run id	comb	sel
0.6064	0.2255	0.3999*	-0.00%	de2frR3FWnormal		X
0.6007	0.2255	0.3975	-0.60%	de2frcomb1s101	X	X
0.6017	0.2246	0.3942	-1.43%	de2frR2FWnormal		X
0.5931	0.2244	0.3938	-1.53%	de2frav	X	
0.5912	0.2273	0.3931	-1.70%	de2frR5FWnormal		
0.5867	0.2178	0.3899	-2.50%	de2frR1FWnormal		
0.5795	0.2288*	0.3890	-2.73%	de2frR4FWnormal		
0.6082*	0.2093	0.3837	-4.05%	de2frcomb2s201	X	X
0.5962	0.2093	0.3816	-4.58%	de2frFWnormal		
0.5857	0.2030	0.3770	-5.73%	de2frnormal		

Table 9. Combined experiments for Monolingual French

Experiment	Combination	Basic experiments				
fr1s101	asym101	frFWnormal,	frR1FWnormal			
fr1s201	asym201	frFWnormal,	frR1FWnormal			
fr2s101	asym101	frFWnormal,	frR2FWnormal			
fr2s201	asym201	frFWnormal,	frR2FWnormal			
frav3	average	frR2FWnormal	frFWnormal	frnormal		
frav5	average	frR2FWnormal	frFWnormal	frnormal	frR1FWnormal	frnormalinv
frav7	average	frR2FWnormal	frFWnormal	frnormal	frR1FWnormal	frnormalinv
		frFWnostem	frngrams54			
frav8	average	frR2FWnormal	frFWnormal	frnormal	frR1FWnormal	frnormalinv
		frFWnostem	frngrams54	frnostem		
frav9	average	frR2FWnormal	frFWnormal	frnormal	frR1FWnormal	frnormalinv
		frFWnostem	frngrams54	frnostem	frtitnormal	

Table 10. Combined experiments for Monolingual Russian

Experiment	Combination	Basic experiments				
rucomb1s101	asym101	runormaltit3	ruR1FWnormal			
rucomb1s201	asym201	runormaltit3	ruR1FWnormal			
ruav5	average	runormaltit3	ruR1FWnormal	ruFWnormal	runormal	rungrams54
ruav7	average	runormaltit3	ruR1FWnormal	ruFWnormal	runormal	rungrams54
		runormaltit1	ruR2FWnormal			
ruav8	average	runormaltit3	ruR1FWnormal	ruFWnormal	runormal	rungrams54
		runormaltit1	ruR2FWnormal	runostem		

Table 11. Combined experiments for Bilingual Dutch to French and German to French

Experiment	Combination	Basic experiments		
nl2frcomb1s101	asym101	nl2frFWnormal	nl2frR4FWnormal	
nl2frav	average	nl2frR1FWnormal	nl2frR2FWnormal	nl2frR3FWnormal
		nl2frR4FWnormal	nl2frR5FWnormal	nl2frFWnormal
de2frcomb1s101	asym101	de2frFWnormal	de2frR3FWnormal	
de2frcomb2s201	asym201	de2frR3FWnormal	de2frFWnormal	
de2frav	average	de2frR1FWnormal	de2frR2FWnormal	de2frR3FWnormal
		de2frR4FWnormal	de2frR5FWnormal	de2frFWnormal

Searching a Russian Document Collection Using English, Chinese and Japanese Queries

Fredric C. Gey

UC Data Archive & Technical Assistance,
University of California, Berkeley, CA 94720 USA
gey@berkeley.edu

Abstract. This UC Berkeley project experimented with English and German topics for bilingual retrieval from the CLEF Russian news collection with comparison to Russian→Russian monolingual retrieval. In CLEF 2004 we also experimented with Chinese and Japanese as topic languages, using English as the 'pivot' language. For bilingual retrieval our approaches were query translation (for English as a topic language) and 'fast' document translation from Russian to English (for Chinese and Japanese translated to English as the topic language). Chinese and Japanese topic retrieval significantly under-performed English → Russian retrieval because of the 'double translation' loss of effectiveness.

1 Introduction

CLEF 2004 was the second time a Russian language document collection was available in CLEF. We had worked previously with Russian topics in both the GIRT task and the CLEF main tasks and in CLEF 2003, we extended our techniques to Russian documents. In CLEF 2004 we again utilized fast document translation as an alternative methodology to query translation. Encoding remained an issue and we again used the KOI-8 encoding scheme for both Russian documents and topics.

2 Document Ranking

Berkeley's monolingual document ranking algorithm uses statistical clues found in documents and queries to predict a dichotomous variable (relevance) based upon logistic regression fitting of prior relevance judgments. The exact formula is:

$$\log O(R \mid D,Q) = \log \frac{P(R \mid D,Q)}{1 - P(R \mid D,Q)}$$

$$= \log \frac{P(R \mid D,Q)}{P(\overline{R} \mid D,Q)}$$

$$= -3.51 + 37.4 * x_1 + 0.330 * x_2$$

$$- 0.1937 * x_3 + 0.0929 * x_4$$

C. Peters et al. (Eds.): CLEF 2004, LNCS 3491, pp. 200–206, 2005.

where $O(R \mid D,Q)$, $P(R \mid D,Q)$ mean, respectively, *odds* and *probability* of relevance of a document with respect to a query, and

$$x_1 = \frac{1}{\sqrt{n}+1}\sum_{i=1}^{n}\frac{qtf_i}{ql+35}$$

$$x_2 = \frac{1}{\sqrt{n}+1}\sum_{i=1}^{n}\log\frac{dtf_i}{dl+80}$$

$$x_3 = \frac{1}{\sqrt{n}+1}\sum_{i=1}^{n}\log\frac{ctf_i}{cl}$$

$$x_4 = n$$

where n is the number of matching terms between a document and a query, and

ql : query length
dl: document length
cl: collection length
qtf_i: the within-query frequency of the ith matching term
dtf_i: the within-document frequency of the ith matching term
ctf_i: the occurrence frequency of the ith matching term in the collection.

This formula has been used since the second TREC conference and for all NTCIR and CLEF cross-language evaluations [1].

3 Russian Retrieval for the CLEF Main Task

CLEF 2004 marked the second time a document collection was available and evaluated for Russian language document retrieval effectiveness. The CLEF Russian collection consists of 16,716 articles from *Izvestia* newspaper for 1995. This is a small number of documents by most CLEF measures (the smallest other collection of CLEF 2003, Finnish, has 55,344 documents; the Spanish collection has 454,045 documents). We used the Russian and English indexes generated for CLEF 2003 for all our CLEF 2004 Russian runs. The collection is also rich in metadata, including specification of geography for news articles; this can be exploited for mapping and geotemporal querying of documents relating to place and time [2].

3.1 Encoding Issues

The Russian document collection was supplied in the UTF-8 unicode encoding, as were the Russian version of the topics. However, since the stemmer we employ is in KOI8 format, the entire collection was converted into KOI8 encoding, as with CLEF 2003 [3]. In indexing the collection, we converted upper-case letters to lower-case and applied Snowball's Russian stemmer (http://snowball.tartarus.org/russian

stemmer.html) together with Russian stopword list created by merging the Snowball list with a translation of the English stopword list. In addition the PROMT translation system would also only work on KOI8 encoding which meant that our translations from English also would come in that encoding.

3.2 Russian Monolingual Retrieval

We submitted two Russian monolingual runs, the results of which are summarized below. As in CLEF 2003, both runs utilized blind feedback, choosing the top 30 terms from the top ranked 20 documents of an initial retrieval run -- this methodology is described in detail in reference [3]. For BKRUMLRR1 and BKRUMLRR2 runs we used TITLE and DESCRIPTION document fields for indexing. The results of our retrieval are summarized in Table 1. Results were reported by the CLEF organizers for 34 topics which had one or more relevant Russian documents.

Table 1. Berkeley Monolingual Russian runs for CLEF 2004

Run Name	BKRUMLRR1	BKRUMLRR2
Index	Koi	Koi
Topic fields	TD	TDN
Retrieved	34000	34000
Relevant	123	123
Rel Ret	105	108
Precision		
at 0.00	0.5734	0.5856
at 0.10	0.5636	0.5688
at 0.20	0.5506	0.5394
at 0.30	0.4969	0.4871
at 0.40	0.4670	0.4465
at 0.50	0.4526	0.4459
at 0.60	0.3628	0.3619
at 0.70	0.2989	0.3175
at 0.80	0.2839	0.3175
at 0.90	0.2555	0.2573
at 1.00	0.2548	0.2555
Avg. Precision	0.4024	0. 4005

Adding the Narrative section to the query did not significantly improve results because the Narrative section did not contribute additional content terms beyond those found in the Title and Description fields of the topics.

3.3 Bilingual Retrieval from English to Russian

We submitted eight bilingual runs against the Russian document collection, four with English as topic language and two each with Chinese and Japanese as topic languages. These runs used an index in which only the TITLE and TEXT fields of each Russian document was indexed, so are directly comparable to the monolingual runs BKMLRURR1 and BKMLRURR2 above. The four English→Russian runs utilized query translation from English topics into Russian. We compared two web-available translation systems, SYSTRAN at http://babelfish.altavista.com/ for the first two runs (BKRUBLER1, BKRUBLER2) and the PROMT system (runs BKRUBLER3, BKRUBLER4) developed in Russia and found at http://www.translate.ru.

Table 2. Bilingual English → Russian runs

Run Name Translation Topic fields	BKRUBLER1 Babelfish TD	BKRUBLER2 Babelfish TDN	BKRUBLER3 PROMT TD	BKRUBLER4 PROMT TDN
Retrieved	34000	34000	34000	34000
Relevant	123	123	123	123
Rel Ret	69	85	98	93
Precision				
at 0.00	0.2444	0.2965	0.5158	0.4575
at 0.10	0.2430	0.2965	0.5147	0.4575
at 0.20	0.2423	0.2806	0.4951	0.4493
at 0.30	0.1809	0.2269	0.4328	0.4281
at 0.40	0.1563	0.2205	0.3617	0.3239
at 0.50	0.1445	0.1976	0.3470	0.2932
at 0.60	0.0896	0.0940	0.2648	0.1990
at 0.70	0.0796	0.0813	0.2268	0.1907
at 0.80	0.0771	0.0806	0.2145	0.1782
at 0.90	0.0764	0.0802	0.1997	0.1629
At 1.00	0.0764	0.0797	0.1997	0.1629
Avg. Prec.	0.1361	0.1638	0.3291	0.2850

The results demonstrate clearly the superiority of the PROMT system for this topic set.

3.4 Bilingual Retrieval from Chinese and Japanese to Russian

Because Chinese and Japanese were available as topic languages, we experimented with these languages by translating the topics to English (i.e. used English as a pivot language). Our approach to translation from Chinese or Japanese topics to English was to utilize a widely available software package, the SYSTRAN CJK Personal system available for less than $US100. from www.systransoft.com. However, instead of query translation a second time, we utilized a technique (also used for Russian in CLEF 2003) developed by Aitao Chen, called 'Fast Document Translation' [4]. Instead of doing complete document translation using MT software, the MT system is used to translate the entire vocabulary of the document collection on a word-by-word basis without the contextualization of position in sentence with respect to other words. Monolingual retrieval was performed by matching the English versions of the Chinese or Japanese topics against the translated English document collection. More details can be found in our CLEF-2003 final paper [3].

Table 3. Bilingual Chinese/Japanese → Russian runs

Run Name	BKRUBLER 3	BKRUBLER 4	BKRUMLZE 1	BKRUMLZE 2	BKRUMLJR 1	BKRUMLJR 2
Language	English	English	Chinese	Chinese	Japanese	Japanese
Translation	PROMT	PROMT	Systran CJK	Systran CJK	Systran CJK	Systran CJK
Topic fields	TD	TDN	TD	TDN	TD	TDN
Retrieved	34000	34000	34000	34000	34000	34000
Relevant	123	123	123	123	123	123
Rel Ret	98	93	57	68	64	67
Precision						
at 0.00	0.5158	0.4575	0.1659	0.1924	0.2036	0.1709
at 0.10	0.5147	0.4575	0.1659	0.1924	0.2036	0.1709
at 0.20	0.4951	0.4493	0.1559	0.1822	0.1888	0.1699
at 0.30	0.4328	0.4281	0.1167	0.1417	0.1689	0.1249
at 0.40	0.3617	0.3239	0.1137	0.1414	0.1607	0.1185
at 0.50	0.3470	0.2932	0.1051	0.1215	0.1288	0.1130
at 0.60	0.2648	0.1990	0.0844	0.1077	0.0858	0.0898
at 0.70	0.2268	0.1907	0.0704	0.0921	0.0808	0.0846
at 0.80	0.2145	0.1782	0.0551	0.0782	0.0653	0.0726
at 0.90	0.1997	0.1629	0.0540	0.0776	0.0611	0.0701
at 1.00	0.1997	0.1629	0.0540	0.0776	0.0611	0.0701
Avg. Prec.	0.3291	0.2850	0.0956	0.1197	0.1166	0.1050

The results, displayed in Table 3, show that there is considerable loss of performance when using English as a pivot language for these Asian language (we have re-displayed the best English→Russian runs for comparison). It may be that this performance was hampered by the reduced utility of the English documents translated from Russian, as was the case for our CLEF 2003 bilingual performance which used this method. We did not try merging of runs from the two methods to see if it would improvement performance.

3.5 Additional Experiments on Stemming and Blind Feedback Effects

Following the workshop we performed additional Russian monolingual experiments in order to determine the effect of combinations of methodologies on the retrieval results. The components tested were stemming / no stemming, blind feedback (BF) / no blind feedback for the various document and topic fields which were indexed. As mentioned above, we utilized the SNOWBALL Russian rule-based stemmer found at http://snowball.tartarus.org. When we indexed the Izvestia collection without using the Russian stemmer, our corpus dictionary (list of unique terms found in the collection) contained 253,202 terms. After using the stemmer to pre-process the collection, the dictionary size falls to 87,597 terms, a significant decrease. The results of these additional experiments are summarized in Table 4 below (numbers in parentheses are percent improvement over no stemming). For CLEF 2003, we found, in general the more techniques applied, the higher the overall average precision. However, for CLEF 2004 we found that primary cause for improved performance came from the application of rule-based stemming to the collection.

Table 4. Russian Monolingual Runs for Combination of Methodologies

Post CLEF 2004 Workshop Monolingual Russian Experiments		
Document fields indexed	Title, Text	Title, Text
Topic fields used	TD	TDN
No stemming j No blind feedback	0.2821	0.2683
No stemming Blind feedback on 20 docs and 30 terms	0.2946	0.2770
Stemming / No blind feedback	0.3933 (+39.4%)	0.3858 (+43.8%)
Official Runs (Stemming plus blind feedback on 20 docs and 30 terms)	0.4024 (+36.6%)	0.3655 (+32.0%)

3.6 Analysis of Retrieval Performance

Our monolingual Russian performance was acceptable but certainly not outstanding. For many topics, Title-Description runs out-performed Title-Description-Narrative runs, because the Narrative section added no new information and might sometimes add noise terms.

For all our runs our bilingual retrieval results were worse than monolingual (Russian-Russian) retrieval in terms of overall precision. However the translation of English to Russian by the PROMT system achieved 82% of monolingual for the TD runs. One puzzling and interesting topic was number 202 ("Nick Leeson's Arrest") where our bilingual retrieval out-performed our monolingual runs – it seems that the PROMT translation and transliteration "Арест Ника Лизона" came up with a better spelling of the last name than the Russian topic creator who used "Арест Ника Леесон", which did not seem to match any relevant documents. According to the summary results for Russian monolingual, the Hummingbird system achieved 1.00 precision for this topic using fuzzy matching techniques on variations of the first name 'Ника' as well as blind feedback to improve the match to the three relevant documents for this topic [5].

A cautionary note must be made about the CLEF-2004 Russian topic set. The total number of relevant documents was only 123 for the entire topic set, with a mean of 3.6 relevant documents per topic. Because of the nature of the retrieval results by query from the Russian collection (22 of the 34 topics have 2 or fewer relevant documents) one has to be careful about drawing conclusions from any submitted results.

Summary and Acknowledgments

For CLEF 2004, we experimented with the CLEF Russian document collection with both monolingual Russian and bilingual to Russian from English, Chinese and Japanese topics English was used as an intermediate 'pivot' language for Chinese to Russian and Japanese to Russian -- topics from those languages were translated to English (using the SYSTRAN CJK Personal package) and then to Russian in a second translation step. In addition to query translation methodology for bilingual retrieval, we tried a fast document translation method to convert the Russian document collection to English and then performed English-English monolingual retrieval with the translated topics from Chinese into English and Japanese into English. Chinese→Russian and Japanese→Russian bilingual performance results were significantly worse than English → Russian. For English to Russian cross-language search, the PROMT translation system outperformed the SYSTRAN on-line translation system, Babelfish.

We would like to thank Aitao Chen for writing the logistic regression ranking software and for performing the fast document translation from Russian to English.

References

1. Chen, A, Cooper, W. and Gey, F.: Full text retrieval based on probabilistic equations with coefficients fitted by logistic regression. In: D.K. Harman (Ed.), The Second Text Retrieval Conference (TREC-2), March 1994, pp 57-66,
2. Gey, F. and Carl, K.: Geotemporal Querying of Multilingual Documents. Proceedings of the SIGIR 2004 Workshop on Geographic Information Retrieval, Sheffield,England, July 29, 2004, available at http://www.geo.unizh.ch/~rsp/gir/abstracts/gey.pdf.
3. Petras, V., Perelman, N. and Gey, F.: UC Berkeley at CLEF-2003 – Russian Language Experiments and Domain-Specific Retrieval. In: Proceedings of the CLEF 2003 Workshop, LNCS 3237, Springer 2004. pp 401-411..
4. Chen, A. and Gey, F.: Multilingual Information Retrieval Using Machine Translation, Relevance Feedback, and Decompounding, Information Retrieval Journal: Special Issue on CLEF, Vol.7 No 1-2, pp 149-182, Jan-Apr 2004
5. Tomlinson, S.: Finnish, Portuguese and Russian Retrieval with Hummingbird SearchServer™ at CLEF 2004, in this volume.

Dublin City University at CLEF 2004: Experiments in Monolingual, Bilingual and Multilingual Retrieval

Gareth J.F. Jones, Michael Burke, John Judge, Anna Khasin, Adenike Lam-Adesina, and Joachim Wagner

School of Computing, Dublin City University, Dublin 9, Ireland
{gjones, mburke, jjudge, akhasin, adenike, jwagner}@computing.dcu.ie

Abstract. The Dublin City University group participated in the monolingual, bilingual and multilingual retrieval tasks. The main focus of our investigation for CLEF 2004 was extending our information retrieval system to document languages other than English, and completing the multilingual task comprising four languages: English, French, Russian and Finnish. Our retrieval system is based on the City University Okapi BM25 system with document preprocessing using the Snowball stemming software and stopword lists. Our French monolingual experiments compare retrieval using French documents and topics, and documents and topics translated into English. Our results indicate that working directly in French is more effective for retrieval than adopting document and topic translation. A breakdown of our multilingual retrieval results by the individual languages shows that similar overall average precision can be achieved when there is significant underlying variation in performance for individual languages.

1 Introduction

Dublin City University's (DCU) participation in the CLEF 2004 monolingual, bilingual and multilingual track builds on our existing work at the University of Exeter [1]. This previous work was limited to English language retrieval. For non-English retrieval, documents and topics were translated into English using machine translation. Thus English was used as a "pivot" language for all tasks. Retrieval was based on the City University distribution of the Okapi system augmented with a summary-based pseudo-relevance feedback system. Our work for CLEF 2004 concentrated on extending our retrieval system to work directly in the document language with topic translation when needed. Our strategy is to extend our existing Okapi based retrieval system to make use of the Snowball stemmers and stop word lists [2]. Using these tools we completed runs for monolingual French, Russian and Finnish documents, official bilingual runs for French and Russian, and the multilingual task consisting of English, French, Russian and Finnish, together with the additional monolingual and bilingual runs needed for the multilingual task.

C. Peters et al. (Eds.): CLEF 2004, LNCS 3491, pp. 207–220, 2005.

This paper is organised as follows: Section 2 outlines the details of our retrieval system and describes its extension to non-English retrieval, Section 3 reports our experimental results, and finally Section 4 concludes the paper.

2 Retrieval System

2.1 Summary of Okapi System

The basis of our experimental retrieval system is the City University research distribution version of the Okapi system, as used in our previous CLEF participation [1]. The standard Okapi environment includes tools for English language preprocessing. These preprocessing tools, including stopword removal and stemming, are coded directly into the software and cannot be readily modified or replaced in the distributed software. A further limitation is that it can only handle ASCII English characters and punctuation symbols. In order to extend the system to other languages we moved the preprocessing outside Okapi itself and encode the text using English language characters, as described in the next section, prior to entering the data into Okapi. Search terms are weighted using the standard BM25 weighting scheme and we use our summary-based pseudo relevance feedback (PRF) method [4].

For English language runs we continued to use the standard Okapi system system. The documents and search topics are processed to remove stopwords from a list of about 260 words; suffix stripped using the Okapi implementation of Porter stemming [3], and terms are further indexed using a small set of synonyms.

2.2 Language Independent Use of the Okapi System

By carrying out data preprocessing and then encoding the text into English language ASCII characters prior to entering the data into the Okapi system, it can be used as a language independent retrieval system. This section describes the preprocessing method we used for non-English documents for our CLEF 2004 experiments.

The documents and topics are prepared using a pipeline of pre-processing components. Firstly, the data is tokenised to isolate the text body from the SGML/XML markup tags. Then, all punctuation characters are deleted from the text body, with the following exceptions: full stops, commas, semi-colons, colons, exclamation marks and question marks. Whitespace is inserted to separate these punctuation characters from word tokens. The characters are then converted to lower case. Distinct mappings must be used for the character set of each language. The Russian characters were converted to KOI-8 character encoding as required by the Snowball tools, while the Finnish and French documents use ISO Latin 1. Conversion of the Russian data loses some data, for example the degree sign prevalent in weather forecasts is lost, further some corruption of the original data to “boxdrawing” symbols was observed. We made two different conversions: one that just replaces every character outside the KOI-8 set with whitespace, and one in which we tried to do optimal/most frequently correct substitutions.

At the next stage stop words are removed. The stop word lists provided by Snowball are used for French, Russian and Finnish. The Russian stopword list used here consists only of the simple first part of the Snowball list. The words are then passed to the Snowball stemmer. The only alteration to the default stemmer functionality is the conversion of the Russian character encoding from ISO to KOI-8. Finally, the whitespace preceding the maintained punctuation characters is removed[1].

Since the Okapi system does not accept the special characters outside English used in French, Russian and Finnish, all character strings in these languages were encoded using the 26 lowercase letters *a* to *z*. The encoding guarantees that different input words are discriminably represented and that the reverse operation (decoding) can be performed easily if required. The encoded form is not readable by humans and string similarities do not stay intact. However, neither of these is a problem, since no one will be reading the encoded documents, and fuzzy matching is not used in our query-document matching. For example, the three French words "pécheur", "pêcheur" and "pêcheurs" are encoded as *gropmdpbtfui*, *cbppmdpbtfui* and *klcgrwruwanejd*. Encoded strings are then passed into the Okapi system for indexing. When used in the this manner no stopword removal, stemming or other processing is performed within the Okapi system itself.

Topic statements are similarly processed to remove stopwords, apply stemming, and apply the character encoding, prior to being applied to the Okapi retrieval system.

3 Experimental Results

This section presents results and analysis of our experimental runs. Full details of the retrieval tasks are given in the track overview paper [5]. All runs use the Title and Description CLEF topic fields. For our experiments, we report precision at ranks 5,10, 15 and 20, average precision and total number of relevant documents retrieved.

System parameters were selected using CLEF 2003 test collections. In all cases Okapi parameters were set as follows: $k_1 = 1.0$ and $b = 0.75$. The summary generation method combines Luhn's keyword cluster method, a title terms frequency method, a location/header method and a query-bias method to form an overall significance score for each sentence. For PRF we explored four sentence selection criteria for document summary generation as follows: L = Luhn method, T = title method, Q = query-bias method, and A = linear sum of all methods. The L, T and Q methods in each case use only this single measure of sentence significance. The 20 top ranked PRF expansion terms were selected from the summaries of the top 5 ranked documents, with the top 20 ranked documents used to rank potential expansion terms for selection, unless otherwise specified for individual tasks. The original topic terms were upweighted by a fac-

[1] The punctuation symbols must be maintained in the document to facilitate summarization for PRF.

tor of 3.5 relative to terms introduced by PRF. Full details of the summary-based PRF method are given in [4].

3.1 Monolingual Retrieval

This section presents results for our monolingual retrieval experiments. Official runs were carried out for French, Russian and Finnish document collections. Monolingual English document results are also included here for use in comparative analysis of the multilingual retrieval results later in this section.

French Runs. Table 1 shows results for French monolingual retrieval. Separate results are shown for documents and topics in French, and documents and topics translated into English using Systran MT. For French language retrieval experiments, the PRF summary length was set to 4 sentences, and for translated documents and topics to 6 sentences. It can be seen that working in French produces superior retrieval performance with respect to both precision and recall metrics. This document and topic translation approach was used in our previous work [1]. The result here indicates that extending our retrieval system to the document language is immediately beneficial.

Russian Runs. Table 2 shows results for Russian monolingual retrieval. The PRF summary length is 6 sentences here. This is a small document collection and the lack of variation in recall for the different summary methods is perhaps not surprising. The Snowball preprocessing of Russian is rather limited, and further development of our Russian language preprocessing is planned, but these results are generally encouraging.

Finnish Runs. Table 3 shows results for Finnish monolingual retrieval. Summary length is 4 sentences with 30 documents this time used for expansion term selection. Our preprocessing of Finnish here again employs the Snowball stemming. This does not fully address the complex structure of Finnish word compounds, and again further work is planned to extend word decompounding. While average precision appears reasonable here, recall is poor in some cases, probably resulting from the failure to properly address the decompounding issues.

English Runs. Table 4 shows English monolingual results. Our retrieval system appears to be performing fairly well on this dataset.

3.2 Bilingual Runs

This section gives results for our bilingual retrieval experiments. Results are shown for our official runs for German and Dutch topics to French documents, and English topics to Russian documents, together with additional unofficial results for English topics to French and Finnish document sets also reported for later comparison with multilingual retrieval results.

German to French Runs. Table 5 shows results for German to French bilingual retrieval. PRF summary length is 4 sentences. Topics were translated directly from German to French using Systran via the Babelfish (`http://www.babelfish.`

Table 1. Monolingual French retrieval results. (Relevant: 915)

Documents		Original French				Translated to English			
		L	T	Q	A	L	T	Q	A
Prec.	5 docs	0.445	0.429	0.437	0.429	0.400	0.396	0.404	0.400
	10 docs	0.369	0.361	0.365	0.363	0.349	0.349	0.341	0.347
	15 docs	0.333	0.327	0.339	0.335	0.320	0.317	0.316	0.317
	20 docs	0.307	0.298	0.305	0.295	0.287	0.288	0.290	0.286
Av. Precision		0.420	0.410	0.414	0.424	0.394	0.400	0.397	0.393
Rel. Ret.		839	844	849	843	781	774	772	774

Table 2. Monolingual Russian retrieval results. (Relevant: 123)

		L	T	Q	A
Prec.	5 docs	0.177	0.200	0.200	0.177
	10 docs	0.136	0.129	0.138	0.132
	15 docs	0.104	0.102	0.106	0.102
	20 docs	0.084	0.088	0.087	0.085
Av Precision		0.363	0.379	0.372	0.350
Rel. Ret.		101	101	101	101

Table 3. Monolingual Finnish retrieval results. (Relevant: 413)

		L	T	Q	A
Prec.	5 docs	0.382	0.382	0.391	0.369
	10 docs	0.311	0.309	0.307	0.298
	15 docs	0.253	0.258	0.250	0.242
	20 docs	0.206	0.211	0.212	0.199
Av Precision		0.432	0.448	0.449	0.425
Rel. Ret.		311	333	327	304

Table 4. Monolingual English retrieval results. (Relevant: 375)

		L	T	Q	A
Prec.	5 docs	0.362	0.367	0.366	0.367
	10 docs	0.281	0.286	0.281	0.286
	15 docs	0.238	0.237	0.230	0.233
	20 docs	0.202	0.204	0.201	0.201
Av Precision		0.482	0.498	0.487	0.491
Rel. Ret.		356	348	343	359

`altavista.com`) website. Comparing these results to the monolingual French retrieval results in Table 1, we observe about a 30% reduction in average precision, accompanied by an average reduction in relevant documents retrieved of around 120.

Table 5. Bilingual retrieval results German topics to retrieve French documents. Topics translated into French using Systran MT. (Relevant: 915)

		L	T	Q	A
Prec.	5 docs	0.314	0.318	0.310	0.327
	10 docs	0.263	0.263	0.265	0.265
	15 docs	0.248	0.241	0.241	0.250
	20 docs	0.227	0.219	0.222	0.235
Av Precision		0.296	0.295	0.296	0.299
% mono.		70.5%	72.0%	71.5%	70.5%
Rel. Ret.		710	727	713	704
chg. Rel. Ret.		-129	-117	-136	-139

Table 6. Bilingual retrieval results Dutch topics to retrieve French documents. Topics translated into French using Systran MT. (Relevant: 915)

		L	T	Q	A
Prec.	5 docs	0.342	0.339	0.355	0.347
	10 docs	0.302	0.286	0.296	0.296
	15 docs	0.274	0.267	0.269	0.268
	20 docs	0.251	0.245	0.248	0.251
Av Precision		0.339	0.331	0.333	0.334
% mono.		80.7 %	80.7%	80.4%	78.8%
Rel. Ret.		768	777	770	778
chg. Rel. Ret.		-76	-67	-79	-65

Table 7. Bilingual retrieval results English topics to retrieve Russian documents. Topics translated into Russian using PROMT and a Merged combination of MT systems. (Relevant: 123)

		PROMT				Merged			
		L	T	Q	A	L	T	Q	A
Prec.	5 docs	0.177	0.182	0.177	0.182	0.177	0.171	0.159	0.177
	10 docs	0.109	0.106	0.109	0.106	0.118	0.106	0.100	0.109
	15 docs	0.077	0.080	0.078	0.077	0.086	0.078	0.075	0.078
	20 docs	0.063	0.068	0.065	0.063	0.074	0.068	0.0068	0.068
Av Precision		0.296	0.321	0.305	0.320	0.317	0.310	0.281	0.313
% mono.		81.5%	84.7%	82.0%	91.4%	87.3%	81.8%	75.5%	89.4%
Rel. Ret.		95	96	95	96	94	95	95	95
chg. Rel. Ret.		-6	-5	-6	-5	-7	-6	-6	-6

Dutch to French Runs. Table 6 shows results for Dutch to French bilingual retrieval. PRF parameters are the same as German to French retrieval, topics again being translated directly using Babelfish. In this case, we see that average precision is reduced by only 20% relative to the monolingual results in Table 1,

Table 8. Bilingual retrieval results English topics to retrieve French documents. Topics translated into French and documents translated into English using Systran. (Relevant: 915)

Documents		Original French				Translated to English			
		L	T	Q	A	L	T	Q	A
Prec.	5 docs	0.314	0.322	0.310	0.310	0.331	0.331	0.343	0.318
	10 docs	0.274	0.282	0.276	0.278	0.280	0.274	0.267	0.276
	15 docs	0.246	0.261	0.260	0.259	0.259	0.254	0.250	0.252
	20 docs	0.231	0.239	0.236	0.237	0.236	0.232	0.225	0.228
Av Precision		0.322	0.335	0.328	0.323	0.318	0.321	0.302	0.298
% mono.		76.7%	81.7%	79.2%	76.2%	80.7%	80.3%	76.1%	75.8%
Rel. Ret.		745	757	754	745	727	716	715	715
chg. Rel. Ret.		-94	-87	-95	-89	-51	-58	-57	-59

Table 9. Bilingual retrieval results English topics to retrieve Finnish documents. Topics translated into Finnish using InterTrans. (Relevant: 413)

		L	T	Q	A
Prec.	5 docs	0.191	0.182	0.187	0.187
	10 docs	0.171	0.160	0.167	0.167
	15 docs	0.147	0.141	0.150	0.145
	20 docs	0.124	0.124	0.126	0.120
Av Precision		0.200	0.200	0.202	0.203
% mono.		46.3%	44.6%	45.0%	47.8%
Rel. Ret.		212	201	218	192
chg. Rel. Ret.		-99	-121	-109	-112

with a smaller decrease in relevant retrieved relative to monolingual retrieval averaging around 70.

English to Russian Runs. Table 7 shows results for English to Russian bilingual retrieval. PRF summary length is 6 sentences with only 6 documents used for expansion term selection. Topics were translated using three online MT systems: Systran (`http://www.systranbox.com/systran/box`), PROMT (`http://www.online-translator.com/default.asp?lang=en`) and LogoMedia (`http://www.logomedia.net/`). Results are shown for PROMT topic translation, and a union merge of the three translations. The merged results show a marginal relative reduction in performance metrics, this is perhaps a little surprising with respect to the number of relevant retrieved, where the greater range of terms in the merged translated topics might be expected to locate more relevant documents. The bilingual average precision varies between 75% and 90% of the monolingual performance shown in Table 2, with only a small number of relevant documents not retrieved. However, the very small number of relevant documents available means that these results must be treated with caution.

English to French Runs. Table 8 shows unofficial results for English topic to French documents. Results are shown for both topic and document translation, using the same retrieval and PRF parameters used for the monolingual results in Table 1. Using topic translation average precision is between 75% and 80% of monolingual performance, with an average reduction in relevant documents retrieved of around 90. Using document translation there is a similar percentage reduction in average precision, but the reduction in relevant documents retrieved averages only 55 in this cases. Overall topic translation still outperforms document translation, as observed in Table 1, but the difference is smaller for bilingual than monolingual retrieval.

English to Finnish Runs. Table 9 shows unofficial runs for English topic to Finnish documents. Topic translation was carried out using InterTrans[2]. Results here compared to the monolingual results in Table 3 are relatively poor. Average precision is only about 45% of monolingual, with a reduction of around 100 in the number of relevant documents retrieved. This latter figure represents a reduction of more than 30% in the number of relevant documents retrieved relative to the monolingual results. The impact of this comparatively low performance on the multilingual retrieval task is examined in the next section.

3.3 Multilingual Runs

This section gives out multilingual retrieval results. These experiments investigate a number of different scenarios of document and topic translation, and merging to form a multilingual output list. Use of these alternative scenarios is intended both to better understand the behaviour of list merging under different circumstances for multilingual IR, and to simulate alternative operational conditions.

Results are reported for existing data fusion methods. The initial results show overall multilingual performance. These are then broken down by language to examine the retrieval behaviour for each separate language within the multilingual output and to compare the effect of the different merging strategies.

The data fusion methods used were designated s and u in our submission to CLEF 2003 [1]. For s data fusion each document is scored as follows,

$$sms_x(j) = \frac{ms_x(j)}{gms}$$

where $sms_x(j)$ is the revised matching score for document j in list x, $ms_x(j)$ is the original matching score of j in x, and gms is the global maximum matching score across the lists to be merged. For u data fusion each document is scored as follows,

$$ums_x(j) = \frac{ms_x(j)}{gms} \times rank_x$$

[2] Translations kindly provided by Jacques Savoy.

Table 10. Multilingual retrieval results with fused lists as described in the text using s data fusion. (Relevant: 1826)

		1	2	3	4	5
Prec.	5 docs	0.388	0.360	0.372	0.380	0.364
	10 docs	0.354	0.330	0.350	0.352	0.356
	15 docs	0.316	0.311	0.328	0.327	0.331
	20 docs	0.302	0.292	0.316	0.306	0.315
Av Precision		0.263	0.248	0.272	0.273	0.274
Rel. Ret.		1244	1119	1232	1244	1216

Table 11. Breakdown of multilingual retrieval results by language for the various merging schemes using s data fusion

Merging Scheme			English	French	Finnish	Russian
	Relevant		375	915	413	123
1	Prec.	5 docs	0.119	0.225	0.062	0.018
		10 docs	0.117	0.204	0.047	0.021
		15 docs	0.103	0.189	0.037	0.016
		20 docs	0.102	0.184	0.031	0.012
	Av Precision		0.166	0.232	0.058	0.057
	Rel. Ret.		310	714	145	75
2	Prec.	5 docs	0.176	0.118	0.076	0.041
		10 docs	0.164	0.118	0.058	0.035
		15 docs	0.148	0.125	0.049	0.029
		20 docs	0.133	0.126	0.046	0.023
	Av Precision		0.228	0.134	0.077	0.075
	Rel. Ret.		330	557	154	78
3	Prec.	5 docs	0.181	0.131	0.071	0.041
		10 docs	0.159	0.137	0.062	0.038
		15 docs	0.143	0.140	0.056	0.029
		20 docs	0.134	0.141	0.054	0.024
	Av Precision		0.230	0.165	0.077	0.108
	Rel. Ret.		319	680	155	78
4	Prec.	5 docs	0.195	0.122	0.071	0.047
		10 docs	0.171	0.127	0.067	0.035
		15 docs	0.149	0.129	0.061	0.029
		20 docs	0.135	0.128	0.057	0.024
	Av Precision		0.240	0.159	0.082	0.110
	Rel. Ret.		323	692	154	75
5	Prec.	5 docs	0.181	0.114	0.076	0.047
		10 docs	0.181	0.131	0.060	0.032
		15 docs	0.156	0.136	0.053	0.028
		20 docs	0.142	0.138	0.050	0.024
	Av Precision		0.228	0.153	0.074	0.106
	Rel. Ret.		328	663	151	74

Table 12. Results for merged English and translated French collections, and for separate English and translated French collections with PRF from merged collection

		English	French	English	French
Prec.	5 docs	0.233	0.196	0.381	0.351
	10 docs	0.214	0.196	0.288	0.289
	15 docs	0.182	0.197	0.241	0.283
	20 docs	0.162	0.191	0.212	0.254
Av Precision		0.267	0.206	0.492	0.321
Rel. Ret.		342	703	352	754

Table 13. Results for merged English and translated French collections combined with UK Times 1995, and for separate English and translated French collections with PRF from merged collection

		English	French	English	French
Prec.	5 docs	0.233	0.196	0.348	0.363
	10 docs	0.219	0.188	0.288	0.300
	15 docs	0.194	0.189	0.227	0.275
	20 docs	0.174	0.187	0.202	0.250
Av Precision		0.297	0.209	0.482	0.335
Rel. Ret.		344	713	351	774

where $ums_x(j)$ is the revised score of j in x, $ms_x(j)$ and gms have the same definitions as before, and $rank_x$ is the anticipated likelihood of finding a relevant document in list x. This merging scheme is related to the Collection Size-Based Interleaving method proposed in [6]. In this case retrieved documents were interleaved into a merged list based only on collection size. This strategy was based on the observation that CLEF topics often have a distribution of relevant documents across the different languages in proportion to collection size. In our case we combine this concept with the matching score. The principle of linear list weighting using $rank_x$ can be used more generally to take account of the variable effectiveness of retrieval for different collections. Notably for our experiments, based on our training results and those observed for the test topics in Table 9, we would anticipate performance for Finnish retrieval in the multilingual task to be weaker than that for the other languages, and hence we can choose to allocate it a low value of $rank_x$.

Multilingual with s Data Fusion. Table 10 shows results for our official multilingual retrieval experiments created using s merging. The topic language used in all cases is English. All runs were carried out using PRF with A type summaries. A number of different sets of document lists were formed as follows:

1. data fusion of monolingual English results and separate bilingual French, Russian and Finnish runs reported in Tables 4,7,8,9. For Russian the PROMT translated topics were used;

Table 14. Multilingual retrieval results with fused lists as described in the text using u data fusion. (Relevant: 1826)

		1	2	3	4	5
Prec.	5 docs	0.392	0.368	0.372	0.400	0.404
	10 docs	0.350	0.352	0.379	0.354	0.396
	15 docs	0.324	0.319	0.345	0.331	0.357
	20 docs	0.310	0.294	0.311	0.301	0.330
Av Precision		0.268	0.250	0.275	0.275	0.278
Rel. Ret.		1236	1106	1219	1221	1212

Table 15. Breakdown of multilingual retrieval results by language for the various merging schemes using u data fusion

Merging Scheme			English	French	Finnish	Russian
	Rel. Avail.		375	915	413	123
1	Prec.	5 docs	0.191	0.225	0.009	0.006
		10 docs	0.167	0.202	0.007	0.009
		15 docs	0.151	0.185	0.007	0.014
		20 docs	0.137	0.184	0.007	0.013
	Av Precision		0.238	0.230	0.022	0.046
	Rel. Ret.		338	716	115	67
2	Prec.	5 docs	0.286	0.110	0.013	0.012
		10 docs	0.224	0.139	0.013	0.024
		15 docs	0.184	0.140	0.009	0.024
		20 docs	0.163	0.138	0.008	0.022
	Av Precision		0.309	0.144	0.028	0.055
	Rel. Ret.		354	555	129	68
3	Prec.	5 docs	0.276	0.098	0.027	0.029
		10 docs	0.219	0.153	0.022	0.029
		15 docs	0.197	0.151	0.016	0.026
		20 docs	0.167	0.146	0.014	0.022
	Av Precision		0.363	0.158	0.033	0.104
	Rel. Ret.		336	682	128	73
4	Prec.	5 docs	0.291	0.106	0.031	0.035
		10 docs	0.226	0.118	0.024	0.038
		15 docs	0.191	0.133	0.022	0.029
		20 docs	0.166	0.132	0.0519	0.024
	Av Precision		0.366	0.159	0.035	0.102
	Rel. Ret.		337	689	125	70
5	Prec.	5 docs	0.224	0.184	0.013	0.035
		10 docs	0.202	0.194	0.018	0.029
		15 docs	0.178	0.182	0.015	0.024
		20 docs	0.154	0.179	0.012	0.022
	Av Precision		0.261	0.195	0.019	0.104
	Rel. Ret.		335	684	122	71

2. English and translated French documents merged into a single collection, retrieval run output fused with Russian and Finnish bilingual runs as in 1;
3. as 2, but a collection of *The Times* UK 1995 was combined with the merged English and translated French collection;
4. separate monolingual English and translated French document runs were data fused with the bilingual Russian and Finnish runs;
5. as 4, except that the English monolingual and translated French document retrieval runs used PRF expansion terms taken from merged collection used in 2.

From the results in Table 10, average precision is best for methods 3, 4 and 5, with best recall for methods 1 and 4. Overall method 4 is the most effective for this experiment.

Table 11 shows results for merging schemes 1 to 5 broken down by the individual languages in the merged lists. It can be seen that the overall dramatic reduction in performance between schemes 1 and 2 shown in Table 10 results entirely from loss in performance for the French documents. There is a significant reduction in all precision measures, and an average loss of more than 3 relevant documents per topic. Interestingly the combination with the *The Times* UK data in scheme 3 appears to overcome this problem to a significant extent with regard to recall, with a small improvement in the precision measures also being observed. By contrast while the precision for French is reduced in schemes 2 and 3 compared to scheme 1, it is much improved for English while the recall remains largely unchanged. There is also an improvement in the precision measures for Finnish and Russian in schemes 2 and 3 compared to scheme 1. The overall effect of improved precision for English, Finnish and Russian, with reasonable performance for French, mean that the multilingual result for scheme 3 is the overall best of these schemes with respect to precision, although the difference in recall between schemes 1 and 3 is marginal. Merging four separate lists in schemes 4 and 5 produces better average precision results than scheme 1. Looking again at Table 11, it can be seen that retrieval for English, Finnish and Russian is more effective for schemes 4 and 5, whereas French retrieval is more effective with the untranslated documents in scheme 1. The average French matching scores appear to introduce bias in scheme 1. The errors introduced by document translation may help to reduce this effect when merging four lists in schemes 4 and 5, but this issue needs to be investigated further.

Combined English and French Collections. Columns 1 and 2 of Table 12 show separate English and French retrieval within the combined collection used for merging scheme 2 in Table 10 prior to fusion with Russian and Finnish document lists. Comparing these results with those for scheme 2 in Table 11, it can be seen that loss in effectiveness in the multilingual retrieval results is caused mainly by the behaviour of the French documents. There is a large loss in average precision and the number of relevant documents retrieved, presumably because of low matching scores arising from document translation errors causing these documents to be dropped from the bottom of the merged list in Table 12.

By contrast Table 13 shows corresponding results for the English and translated French collections merged with *The Times* UK 1995 as used with merging scheme 3 in Table 10. This shows an improvement for English document retrieval, which is also reflected in the results in Table 12. While there is not a significant difference between the French results in Tables 12 and 13 prior to multilingual fusion, scheme 3 shows a good improvement over scheme 2 in Table 11. The additional information from *The Times* collection may produce more robust matching scores for the translated French documents based on selection of expansion terms or term weights.

Columns 3 and 4 of Tables 12 and 13 show results for the English and translated French documents with PRF using the respective merged collections. Column 3 can be compared with column A in Table 4, and column 4 with translated documents column A in Table 8. While there is little change to the effectiveness of English document retrieval from using merged collection PRF, there is an observable improvement in both precision and recall for the translated French documents. It is then a little surprising to see in Table 11 that the French retrieval performance is actually lower for scheme 5 than for scheme 4.

Multilingual with u Data Fusion. Table 14 shows multilingual IR results using the u data fusion scheme with $rank_x$ values set as follows: English: 1.5, French: 1.3, Russian: 1.2 and Finnish: 0.8. For the merged English and translated French documents the $rank_x$ value was set to 1.5. These values were set intuitively based on collection size and anticipated likelihood of retrieving relevant documents. The results in Table 14 show similar trends to those already observed in Table 10, although there is a general trend to slightly higher precision values and a very small reduction in relevant documents retrieved.

Table 15 again shows the breakdown in retrieval performance for the different languages. Comparing these results with those in Table 11, it can be seen that the $rank_x$ bias improves both the precision and recall for English in all conditions. Interestingly it makes no difference for French merging in scheme 1, suggesting that there is already a considerable bias towards French documents in this case.

The smaller $rank_x$ for Finnish and Russian leads to a reduction in both precision and recall for both of these languages. There are relatively few relevant documents available for Russian (123) compared to English (375), and, as noted earlier, bilingual performance for Finnish using our simple retrieval scheme is poor, with only about 30% of the available 413 relevant documents appearing in the data fused list. This compares to relevant document retrieved proportions in the data fused list of more than 80% for English, 70% for French and 60% for Russian. Hence biasing against Russian and Finnish has little impact on the overall multilingual result.

Thus, while these simple merging schemes can be biased towards larger collections containing more relevant documents to improve overall average precision multilingual, this is likely to be at the cost of retrieval effectiveness for the collections suspected of containing small numbers of relevant documents or for which the retrieval effectiveness is expected to be poor.

4 Conclusions and Further Work

Our work for CLEF 2004 has produced a retrieval framework based on BM25 that can be easily adapted to new document languages. While our experiments have demonstrated that this approach can be effective, further work is needed to improve preprocessing for specific languages. Our multilingual experiments reveal interesting behaviour for individual language components of merged retrieval lists. While these results help us understand the merged multilingual retrieval results, they do not solve the problem of achieving truly effective reliable merging.

References

[1] A. M. Lam-Adesina and G. J. F. Jones. Exeter at CLEF 2003: Experiments with Machine Translation for Monolingual, Bilingual and Multilingual Retrieval. In *Proceedings of Fourth Workshop of the Cross-Language Evaluation Forum (CLEF 2003)*, C. Peters, J. Gonzalo, M. Braschler and M. Kluck (Eds.), Lecture Notes in Computer Science, Springer, Heidelberg, Germany, pages 271-285, 2004.

[2] *Snowball* toolkit `http://snowball.tartarus.org/`

[3] Porter, M. F.: An algorithm for suffix stripping. *Program* 14:10-137, 1980.

[4] Lam-Adesina, A. M. and Jones, G. J. F.: Applying Summarization Techniques for Term Selection in Relevance Feedback. In *Proceedings of the 24th Annual International ACM SIGIR Conference*, pages 1-9, New Orleans, ACM, 2001.

[5] Peters, C., Braschler, M., Di Nunzio, G., and Ferro, N.: CLEF 2004: Ah Hoc Track Overview and Results Analysis. In *Proceedings of Fifth Workshop of the Cross-Language Evaluation Forum (CLEF 2004)*, Peters, C., Clough, P, Gonzalo, J., Jones, G., Kluck, M., and Magnini, B. (Eds.), Lecture Notes in Computer Science, Springer, Heidelberg, Germany (in print), 2005.

[6] Braschler, M., Göhring, A., and Schäuble, P.: Eurospider at CLEF 2002. In *Proceedings of Third Workshop of the Cross-Language Evaluation Forum (CLEF 2002)*, Peters, C., Braschler, M., Gonzalo, J., and Kluck, M. (Eds.), Lecture Notes in Computer Science (LNCS 2785), Springer, Heidelberg, Germany, pages 164-174, 2003.

Finnish, Portuguese and Russian Retrieval with Hummingbird SearchServer^{TM} at CLEF 2004

Stephen Tomlinson

Hummingbird, Ottawa, Ontario, Canada
stephen.tomlinson@hummingbird.com
http://www.hummingbird.com/

Abstract. Hummingbird participated in the Finnish, Portuguese, Russian and French monolingual information retrieval tasks of the Cross-Language Evaluation Forum (CLEF) 2004. SearchServer's experimental lexical stemmers significantly increased mean average precision for each of the 4 languages. For Finnish, mean average precision was significantly higher with SearchServer's experimental decompounding option enabled. Using the stemming interpretations which led to the highest score in each document instead of using the same interpretations for all documents was of significant benefit for Russian.

1 Introduction

Hummingbird SearchServer[1] is a toolkit for developing enterprise search and retrieval applications. The SearchServer kernel is also embedded in other Hummingbird products for the enterprise.

SearchServer works in Unicode internally [3] and supports most of the world's major character sets and languages. The major conferences in text retrieval experimentation (CLEF [1], NTCIR [4] and TREC [9]) have provided opportunities to objectively evaluate SearchServer's support for more than a dozen languages.

This paper describes experimental work with SearchServer for the task of finding relevant documents for natural language queries in 4 European languages (Finnish, Portuguese, Russian and French) using the CLEF 2004 test collections. Portuguese is new to CLEF this year, and the experimental SearchServer version has some enhancements which substantially affect Finnish and Russian, so we focus on these 3 languages.

2 Methodology

2.1 Data

The CLEF 2004 document sets consisted of tagged (SGML-formatted) news articles (mostly from 1995) in 4 different languages: Finnish, Portuguese, Russian and French. Table 1 gives the sizes.

[1] SearchServer^{TM}, SearchSQL^{TM}and Intuitive Searching^{TM} are trademarks of Hummingbird Ltd. All other copyrights, trademarks and tradenames are the property of their respective owners.

C. Peters et al. (Eds.): CLEF 2004, LNCS 3491, pp. 221–232, 2005.

Table 1. Sizes of CLEF 2004 Test Collections

Language	Text Size (uncompressed)	Documents	Topics	Rel/Topic
French	255,334,872 bytes (244 MB)	90,261	49	19
Portuguese	185,739,565 bytes (177 MB)	55,070	46	15
Finnish	143,902,109 bytes (137 MB)	55,344	45	9
Russian	68,802,653 bytes (66 MB)	16,716	34	4

The CLEF organizers created 50 natural language "topics" (numbered 201-250) and translated them into many languages. Some topics were discarded for some languages because no relevant documents existed for them. Table 1 gives the final number of topics for each language and their average number of relevant documents. For more information on the CLEF test collections, see the track overview paper [5] in this volume.

2.2 Indexing

The indexing approach was the mostly the same as last year [11]. Accents were not indexed except for the combining breve in Russian. The apostrophe was treated as a word separator for the 4 investigated languages. The custom text reader, cTREC, was updated to maintain support for the CLEF guidelines of only indexing specifically tagged fields (the new Portuguese collection necessitated a minor update).

Some stop words were excluded from indexing (e.g. "the", "by" and "of" in English). For these experiments, the stop word lists for Portuguese and Russian were based on the Porter lists [6], and this year we based the Finnish list on Savoy's [8]. We used our own list for French.

By default, the SearchServer index supports both exact matching (after some Unicode-based normalizations, such as decompositions and conversion to upper-case) and morphological matching (e.g. inflections, derivations and compounds, depending on the linguistic component used).

For many languages (including the 4 European languages investigated in CLEF 2004), SearchServer includes the option of finding inflections based on lexical stemming (i.e. stemming based on a dictionary or lexicon for the language). For example, in English, "baby", "babied", "babies", "baby's" and "babying" all have "baby" as a stem. Specifying an inflected search for any of these terms will match all of the others. The lexical stemming of the post-5.x experimental development version of SearchServer used for the experiments in this paper was based on internal stemming component 3.6.3.4 for the submitted runs and 3.7.0.15 for the diagnostic runs. We treat each linguistic component as a black box in this paper.

SearchServer typically does "inflectional" stemming which generally retains the part of speech (e.g. a plural of a noun is typically stemmed to the singular form). It typically does not do "derivational" stemming which would often change the part of speech or the meaning more substantially (e.g. "performer" is not stemmed to "perform").

SearchServer's lexical stemming includes compound-splitting (decompounding) for compound words in Finnish (and also some other languages not investigated this year, such as German, Dutch and Swedish). For example, in German, "babykost" (baby food) has "baby" and "kost" as stems.

Lexical stemmers can produce more than one stem, even for non-compound words. For example, in English, "axes" has both "axe" and "axis" as stems (different meanings), and in French, "important" has both "important" (adjective) and "importer" (verb) as stems (different parts of speech). SearchServer records all the stem mappings at index-time to support maximum recall and does so in a way to allow searching to weight some inflections higher than others.

2.3 Searching

Unlike previous years, this year we experimented with SearchServer's CONTAINS predicate (instead of the IS_ABOUT predicate) though it should not make a difference to the ranking. Our test application specified SearchSQL to perform a boolean-OR of the query words. For example, for Russian topic 250 whose Title was "Бешенство у людей" (Rabies inHumans), a corresponding SearchSQL query would be:

```
SELECT RELEVANCE('2:3') AS REL, DOCNO
FROM CLEF04RU
WHERE FT_TEXT CONTAINS 'Бешенство'|'у'|'людей'
ORDER BY REL DESC;
```

(Note that "y" is a stopword for Russian so its inclusion in the query won't actually add any matches.)

Most aspects of SearchServer's relevance value calculation are the same as described last year [11]. Briefly, SearchServer dampens the term frequency and adjusts for document length in a manner similar to Okapi [7] and dampens the inverse document frequency using an approximation of the logarithm. These calculations are based on the stems of the terms (roughly speaking) when doing morphological searching (i.e. when SET TERM_GENERATOR 'word!ftelp/inflect' was previously specified). SearchServer's RELEVANCE_METHOD setting was set to '2:3' and RELEVANCE_DLEN_IMP was set to 750 for all experiments in this paper.

An experimental new default is that SearchServer only includes morphological matches from compound words if all of its stems (from a particular stemming interpretation) are in the same or consecutive words. For example, in German, a morphological search for the compound "babykost" (baby food) will no longer match "baby" or "kost" by themselves, but it will match "babykost" and "baby kost" (and if SET PHRASE_DISTANCE 1 is specified, it will also match the hyphenated "baby-kost"). Words (and compounds) still match inside compounds (and larger compounds), e.g. a search for "kost" still matches "babykost". To restore the old behaviour of matching if just one stem is in common, one can specify the /decompound option (e.g. SET TERM_GENERATOR

Table 2. Scores of Finnish Diagnostic Title-only runs

Run	AvgP	Robust@1	Robust@5	Robust@10
FI-lex	0.561	32/45 (71%)	36/45 (80%)	38/45 (84%)
FI-chain	0.553	30/45 (67%)	36/45 (80%)	39/45 (87%)
FI-single	0.550	32/45 (71%)	35/45 (78%)	37/45 (82%)
FI-compound	0.469	28/45 (62%)	30/45 (67%)	33/45 (73%)
FI-alg	0.424	26/45 (58%)	30/45 (67%)	34/45 (76%)
FI-none	0.328	19/45 (42%)	26/45 (58%)	27/45 (60%)

'word!ftelp/inflect/decompound'). See Section 3.3 for several more decompounding examples.

This year's experimental SearchServer version contains an enhancement for handling multiple stemming interpretations. For each document, only the interpretation that produces the highest score for the document is used in the relevance calculation (but all interpretations are still used for matching and search term highlighting). Sometimes this enhancement causes the original query form of the word to get more weight than some of its inflections (and it never gets less weight). This approach overcomes the previous issue of terms with multiple stemming interpretations being over-weighted; it used to be better for CLEF experiments to workaround by using the /single or /noalt options, but Section 3.5 verifies that this is no longer the case.

2.4 Diagnostic Runs

For the diagnostic runs listed in Tables 2 and 3, the run names consist of a language code ("FI" for Finnish, "FR" for French, "PT" for Portuguese and "RU" for Russian) followed by one of the following labels:

- "lex": The run used SearchServer's lexical stemming with decompounding enabled, i.e. SET TERM_GENERATOR 'word!ftelp/inflect/decompound'. (Of the investigated languages, decompounding only makes a difference for Finnish.)
- "compound" (Finnish only): Same as "lex" except that /decompound was not specified.
- "single": Same as "lex" except that /single was additionally specified (so that just one stemming interpretation was used).
- "alg": The run used a different index based on the coarser algorithmic Porter "Snowball" stemmer [6] for the language. Decompounding is not available with this stemmer and the /single option is redundant.
- "chain": The run used a different index based on applying the SearchServer stemmer (as "lex") and then the algorithmic stemmer.
- "none": The run disabled morphological searching.

Note that all diagnostic runs just used the Title field of the topic.

The primary evaluation measure in this paper is "mean average precision" based on the first 1000 retrieved documents for each topic (denoted "AvgP" in

Table 3. Scores of Other Diagnostic Title-only runs

Run	AvgP	Robust@1	Robust@5	Robust@10
RU-lex	0.430	19/34 (56%)	27/34 (79%)	27/34 (79%)
RU-chain	0.405	18/34 (53%)	26/34 (76%)	26/34 (76%)
RU-single	0.396	17/34 (50%)	26/34 (76%)	27/34 (79%)
RU-alg	0.410	18/34 (53%)	26/34 (76%)	26/34 (76%)
RU-none	0.220	9/34 (26%)	20/34 (59%)	22/34 (65%)
PT-lex	0.405	24/46 (52%)	33/46 (72%)	35/46 (76%)
PT-chain	0.411	24/46 (52%)	34/46 (74%)	35/46 (76%)
PT-single	0.388	22/46 (48%)	31/46 (67%)	36/46 (78%)
PT-alg	0.387	25/46 (54%)	33/46 (72%)	34/46 (74%)
PT-none	0.327	18/46 (39%)	26/46 (57%)	31/46 (67%)
FR-lex	0.422	25/49 (51%)	39/49 (80%)	44/49 (90%)
FR-chain	0.418	26/49 (53%)	38/49 (78%)	42/49 (86%)
FR-single	0.423	26/49 (53%)	39/49 (80%)	44/49 (90%)
FR-alg	0.417	26/49 (53%)	38/49 (78%)	43/49 (88%)
FR-none	0.361	22/49 (45%)	39/49 (80%)	42/49 (86%)

Tables 2, 3 and 9). "Average precision" for a topic is the average of the precision after each relevant document is retrieved (using zero as the precision for relevant documents which are not retrieved). A more experimental measure is "robustness at 10 documents" (denoted "Robust@10") which is the percentage of topics for which at least one relevant document was returned in the first 10 rows (a measure investigated in the TREC Robust Retrieval track last year [12]).

2.5 Statistical Significance Tables

For tables comparing 2 diagnostic runs (such as Table 4), the columns are as follows:

- "Expt" specifies the experiment. The language code is given, followed by the labels of the 2 runs being compared. The difference is the first run minus the second run. For example, "FI lex-none" specifies the difference of subtracting the scores of the Finnish 'none' run from the Finnish 'lex' run (of Table 2).
- "AvgDiff" is the difference of the mean average precision scores of the two runs being compared.
- "95% Conf" is an approximate 95% confidence interval for the difference calculated using Efron's bootstrap percentile method[2] [2] (using 100,000 iterations). If zero is not in the interval, the result is "statistically significant" (at the 5% level), i.e. the feature is unlikely to be of neutral impact (on average), though if the average difference is small (e.g. <0.020) it may still be too minor to be considered "significant" in the magnitude sense.

[2] See [10] for some comparisons of confidence intervals from the bootstrap percentile, Wilcoxon signed rank and standard error methods for both average precision and Precision@10.

- "vs." is the number of topics on which the first run scored higher, lower and tied (respectively) compared to the second run. These numbers should always add to the number of topics (45 for Finnish, 49 for French, 46 for Portuguese, 34 for Russian).
- "3 Extreme Diffs (Topic)" lists 3 of the individual topic differences, each followed by the topic number in brackets (the topic numbers range from 201 to 250). The first difference is the largest one of any topic (based on the absolute value). The third difference is the largest difference in the other direction (so the first and third differences give the range of differences observed in this experiment). The middle difference is the largest of the remaining differences (based on the absolute value).

3 Results of Morphological Experiments

3.1 Impact of Lexical Stemming

Table 4 isolates the impact of SearchServer's lexical stemming on the average precision measure (e.g. "FI lex-none" is the difference of the "FI-lex" and "FI-none" runs of Table 2). For each of the 4 languages, the increase in mean average precision was statistically significant (i.e. zero was not in the approximate 95% confidence interval). Note that for some queries, it is still better to only match the original query form (not inflections); SearchServer allows this option to be controlled for each query term at search-time.

3.2 Comparison with Algorithmic Stemming

Table 5 contains the results of a diagnostic experiment comparing average precision when the only difference is the stemmer used: the experimental SearchServer lexical stemmer or Porter's algorithmic stemmer. Positive differences indicate that the SearchServer stemmer led to a higher score and negative differences indicate that the algorithmic stemmer led to a higher score. Using SearchServer's stemmer scored higher on average for each language and this increase was statistically significant for Finnish.

In this section, we look at the Portuguese and Russian topics with the largest differences. Finnish is examined in more detail in the subsequent decompounding section. French was investigated in last year's paper [11].

Table 4. Impact of Lexical Stemming on Average Precision

Expt	AvgDiff	95% Conf	vs.	3 Extreme Diffs (Topic)
FI lex-none	0.233	(0.146, 0.326)	31-9-5	1.00 (224), 0.96 (210), −0.24 (208)
RU lex-none	0.209	(0.108, 0.325)	22-1-11	1.00 (250), 1.00 (203), −0.04 (228)
PT lex-none	0.078	(0.037, 0.125)	25-8-13	0.61 (213), 0.53 (229), −0.08 (248)
FR lex-none	0.061	(0.030, 0.096)	23-20-6	0.42 (229), 0.40 (235), −0.07 (216)

Table 5. Lexical vs. Algorithmic Stemming on Average Precision

Expt	AvgDiff	95% Conf	vs.	3 Extreme Diffs (Topic)
FI lex-alg	0.137	(0.064, 0.219)	26-12-7	0.98 (210), 0.86 (226), −0.15 (219)
RU lex-alg	0.019	(−0.003, 0.050)	7-8-19	0.40 (227), 0.20 (202), −0.07 (224)
PT lex-alg	0.018	(−0.014, 0.055)	16-14-16	0.53 (229), 0.32 (217), −0.27 (204)
FR lex-alg	0.005	(−0.003, 0.013)	18-14-17	−0.09 (203), 0.06 (209), 0.08 (231)

Portuguese Stemming. Topic PT-229: Table 5 shows that the largest difference between the stemming approaches for Portuguese was on topic 229 (Construção de Barragens (Dam Building)) in which average precision was 53 points higher with SearchServer's stemmer. The main reason was that, unlike the algorithmic stemmer, the SearchServer stemmer matched "Barragem", an inflection used in many relevant documents. SearchServer additionally matched "construções" which may also have been helpful.

Topic PT-217: The next largest difference for Portuguese was on topic 217 (Sida em África (AIDS in Africa)) for which Table 5 shows that average precision was 32 points higher with SearchServer's stemmer. The main reason was that, unlike SearchServer, the algorithmic stemmer matched "sido", a common word unrelated to AIDS, which decreased precision substantially. SearchServer additionally matched "africanos" which may also have been helpful.

Topic PT-204: The largest negative difference was on topic 204 (Vítimas de Avalanches (Victims of Avalanches)) for which using the algorithmic stemmer scored 27 points higher. Both stemmers matched "Avalanche" but the algorithmic stemmer additionally matched "avalancha" which was the only variant used in 3 of the relevant documents. We are investigating this case further.

Russian Stemming. Topic RU-227: Table 5 shows that the largest difference between the stemming approaches for Russian was on topic 227 (Алтайская амазонка (Altai Ice Maiden)) for which average precision was 40 points higher with SearchServer's stemmer. For "Алтайская" (Altai), SearchServer internally produced 2 stems: itself and "Алтайскай". The words which had "Алтайская" as a stem (such as "Алтайской", "Алтайские", "Алтайскую" and "алтайских") were less common in the documents than the words which shared the "Алтайскай" stem ("Алтайского", "Алтайском" and "Алтайскому" plus the same words as before), so SearchServer's experimental new scoring scheme for alternative stems gives the former group a higher weight from inverse document frequency than the latter group. In this case, it turned out just 1 relevant document was matched by either stemmer and it just used the original word "Алтайская". The algorithmic stemmer produced just one stem for these words, so its weighting did not have a preference for the query form and some documents with the second group of terms ended up ranking higher. The algorithmic stemmer additionally matched "Алтайске" which was not helpful in this case. This topic illustrates a benefit from SearchServer's experimental new handling of multiple stemming interpretations.

Topic RU-202: The next largest difference was on topic 202 (Арест Ника Леесон (Nick Leeson's Arrest)) for which the score was 20 points higher with

SearchServer's stemmer. The 3 relevant documents used different spellings for "Leeson" ("Лисон", "Лизона", "Лизон" and "Лисона") which did not match the query form of "Леесон" with either stemmer. And inflections of "Арест" (Arrest) did not appear in the relevant documents. So the matches just came from variants of "Nick". Both stemmers matched the forms used in the relevant documents ("Ника" and "Ник"). But the algorithmic stemmer additionally matched other terms such as "Никому" and "никого" which lowered precision substantially in this case.

3.3 Impact of Decompounding (Finnish)

The first row of Table 6 ("FI lex-cmpd") isolates the impact of SearchServer's experimental new "/decompound" option for Finnish (decompounding is not new to SearchServer for Finnish, but an option to control its impact separately from inflectional stemming at search-time is). This option allows words to match if they share any stem of query compound words. Without the /decompound option, the (experimental new) default is to require all the stems of a compound word to be in the same or consecutive words to be considered a match. Table 6 shows that mean average precision was 9 points higher with /decompound set, and this difference was statistically significant.

The second row of Table 6 ("FI cmpd-none") shows that even without the /decompound option, use of SearchServer's stemming for Finnish scored 14 points higher than not using stemming. (Note that the first two rows of Table 6 add up to the 23 point gain from lexical stemming shown in Table 4.)

The third row of Table 6 ("FI cmpd-alg") compares SearchServer's stemming without the /decompound option to algorithmic stemming (which does not even decompound at index-time) and shows that using SearchServer's stemmer scored 4.5 points higher, though this difference did not quite pass the statistical significance test. (SearchServer's stemming with the /decompound option is compared to algorithmic stemming in Table 5 in which the difference is the sum of the differences of rows 1 and 3 of Table 6.)

Finnish Decompounding. Topic FI-210: Table 6 shows that the largest impact of Finnish decompounding was on topic 210 (Nobel rauhanpalkintoehdokkaat (Nobel Peace Prize Candidates)) for which using SearchServer's stemmer with the /decompound option scored 98 points higher than not using /decompound (and also 98 points higher than using the algorithmic stemmer according to Table 5). This topic had just 1 relevant document, and the only match for the non-decompounding approaches was the word "Nobel" which occurred in lots of documents, so the relevant document did not stand out among them. With Search-

Table 6. Decompounding Experiments (Finnish) on Average Precision

Expt	AvgDiff	95% Conf	vs.	3 Extreme Diffs (Topic)
FI lex-cmpd	0.092	(0.034, 0.162)	17-9-19	0.98 (210), 0.72 (226), −0.18 (219)
FI cmpd-none	0.141	(0.075, 0.214)	27-10-8	1.00 (224), 0.81 (204), −0.22 (208)
FI cmpd-alg	0.045	(−0.001, 0.094)	19-14-12	0.57 (204), 0.50 (216), −0.40 (205)

Server's decompounding, many more words in the relevant document matched such as "rauhan", "rauhanpalkituksi", "rauhanpalkinnon", "rauhanvälittäjänä", "ehdokasta" and "ehdokkaina" because these words shared at least one (but not all) the stems of the query compound "rauhanpalkintoehdokkaat", and the relevant document was ranked first.

Topic FI-226: Table 6 shows that the next largest impact of Finnish decompounding was on topic 226 (Sukupuolenvaihdosleikkaukset (Sex-change Operations)) for which using SearchServer's stemmer with the /decompound option scored 72 points higher than not using /decompound (and also 86 points higher than using the algorithmic stemmer according to Table 5). The algorithmic stemmer just found the one of the 13 relevant documents which contained the query word "Sukupuolenvaihdosleikkaukset". SearchServer without /decompound matched that document plus 3 other relevants, two which contained "sukupuolen vaihdosleikkaukseen" (an example of a consecutive-word match) and one which contained "Sukupuolenvaihdosleikkausta". SearchServer with /decompound matched all 13 relevant documents; key additional matches appeared to be "Sukupuolen-vaihdos", "sukupuolenvaihtoleikkaukset", "Sukupuolenvaihdoshan", "sukupuolenvaihdot", "sukupuolenkorjausleikkausten" and "sukupuolenvahvistusleikkaus", though other matching words may also have been helpful such as "leikkaussali", "sukupuoli" and "vaihdos".

Topic FI-219: Table 6 shows that the largest negative impact of Finnish decompounding was on topic 219 (EU:n komissaariehdokkaat (EU Commissioner Candidates)) for which using SearchServer's stemmer with the /decompound option scored 18 points lower than not using /decompound (and also 15 points lower than using the algorithmic stemmer according to Table 5). Without the /decompound option, SearchServer found a lot of precise matches in relevant documents such as "komissaariehdokasta", "komissaariehdokkaalle", "komissaariehdokkaista", "komissaariehdokkaalta", "komissaariehdokkaiden" and "komissaariehdokkaan". Furthermore, in some relevant documents SearchServer found matches in larger compounds, e.g. "tanskalaiseltakomissaariehdokkaalta" and "naiskomissaariehdokasta", which the algorithmic stemmer could not. With /decompound set, SearchServer would also find all these matches, but precision was substantially hurt in this case by additionally matching terms in non-relevant documents such as "jäsenehdokkaiden", "jäsenehdokkaita", "ykkösehdokkaista", "tutkimuskomissaari" and "henkilöstökomissaari". This topic shows why a user may prefer to have /decompound not set; in cases where the user does not need the component words to occur together, the user can either manually separate the terms or set the /decompound option. But for automatic ad hoc searches for topics, it is better on average to use the /decompound option.

3.4 Applying Algorithmic Stemming to Lexical Stems

Table 7 shows the impact of applying the algorithmic stemmer to the result of SearchServer's stemmer (this is possible because SearchServer's stemmer returns

Table 7. Impact of Applying Algorithmic Stemming to Lexical Stems

Expt	AvgDiff	95% Conf	vs.	3 Extreme Diffs (Topic)
FI chn-lex	−0.008	(−0.037, 0.019)	13-16-16	−0.38 (203), −0.30 (215), 0.31 (205)
RU chn-lex	−0.025	(−0.062, 0.000)	5-8-21	−0.50 (226), −0.20 (202), 0.02 (232)
PT chn-lex	0.006	(−0.007, 0.023)	9-14-23	0.27 (204), 0.08 (205), −0.15 (232)
FR chn-lex	−0.004	(−0.010, 0.003)	8-18-23	0.09 (203), −0.06 (220), −0.06 (209)

Table 8. Impact of Using All Lexical Stems on Average Precision

Expt	AvgDiff	95% Conf	vs.	3 Extreme Diffs (Topic)
FI lex-sing	0.010	(−0.002, 0.032)	7-10-28	0.44 (215), 0.05 (236), −0.02 (233)
RU lex-sing	0.033	(0.002, 0.082)	9-3-22	0.67 (203), 0.31 (210), −0.01 (233)
PT lex-sing	0.017	(−0.004, 0.049)	6-11-29	0.60 (213), 0.16 (236), −0.12 (248)
FR lex-sing	−0.001	(−0.004, 0.003)	2-9-38	0.06 (235), −0.03 (248), −0.03 (215)

real words; the other order would not work because the algorithmic stemmer often truncates to a non-word). This approach would still produce all the matches of SearchServer's stemming and may sometimes produce additional matches from algorithmic stemming. However, there was a decrease in mean average precision for Russian which was borderline significant. The other differences were not statistically significant. While algorithmic stemming may occasionally add a helpful match, it can also add poor matches that hurt precision. In a future experiment, perhaps it would be better to treat algorithmic stems as alternative stemming interpretations (instead of replacing the lexical stem) so that lexical inflections are likely to get higher weight when the algorithmic stem is too common.

3.5 Impact of Using All Lexical Stems

Table 8 shows the impact of using all stemming interpretations from SearchServer's lexical stemming instead of arbitrarily just using the first one. The increase in mean average precision was statistically significant for Russian. On the individual topics, there were some large increases, but (reassuringly) no correspondingly large decreases. In past years, mean average precision was typically lower when including all the stems because of over-weighting issues, so this result suggests that the enhancement for handling multiple stemming interpretations has succeeded at addressing this issue.

Topic RU-203: In Russian topic 203 (Партизанская война в Восточном Тиморе (East Timor Guerrillas)), the score was 67 points higher when using all stemming interpretations. The query word "Восточном" (Eastern) had 2 stems, "Восточнома" and "восточный". The inflections in the relevant document (namely "Восточного", "Восточный", "восточных" and "восточной") only shared the latter stem.

Table 9. Scores of Submitted Runs

Run	AvgP	Robust@1	Robust@5	Robust@10
humFI04t	0.556	34/45 (76%)	35/45 (78%)	37/45 (82%)
humFI04td	0.593	31/45 (69%)	37/45 (82%)	38/45 (84%)
humFI04tde	0.637	32/45 (71%)	40/45 (89%)	42/45 (93%)
humRU04t	0.430	19/34 (56%)	27/34 (79%)	27/34 (79%)
humRU04td	0.409	17/34 (50%)	26/34 (76%)	27/34 (79%)
humRU04tde	0.443	17/34 (50%)	26/34 (76%)	27/34 (79%)
humPT04t	0.405	24/46 (52%)	33/46 (72%)	35/46 (76%)
humPT04td	0.453	23/46 (50%)	32/46 (70%)	34/46 (74%)
humPT04tde	0.475	23/46 (50%)	32/46 (70%)	35/46 (76%)
humFR04t	0.421	25/49 (51%)	39/49 (80%)	44/49 (90%)
humFR04td	0.458	26/49 (53%)	43/49 (88%)	44/49 (90%)
humFR04tde	0.493	26/49 (53%)	43/49 (88%)	43/49 (88%)

4 Submitted Runs

For the runs submitted for assessment in May 2004 (e.g. "humFI04tde"), "t" and "d" indicate that the Title and Description field of the topic were used (respectively). "e" indicates that query expansion from blind feedback on the first 2 rows was used (see last year's paper [11] for more details). The submitted runs all used inflections from SearchServer's lexical stemming (including decompounding where applicable). From the Description fields, instruction words such as "find", "relevant" and "document" were automatically removed (based on looking at some older topic lists, not this year's topics). The scores of the submitted runs are listed in Table 9.

The submitted Title-only runs (e.g. "humFI04t" of Table 9) correspond to the "lex" diagnostic runs (e.g. "FI-lex" of Table 2) except that the submitted runs used an older experimental version of SearchServer (including an older version of the lexical stemming component) so the scores are not exactly the same.

References

1. Cross-Language Evaluation Forum web site. http://www.clef-campaign.org/
2. Bradley Efron and Robert J. Tibshirani. An Introduction to the Bootstrap. 1993. Chapman & Hall/CRC.
3. Andrew Hodgson. Converting the Fulcrum Search Engine to Unicode. *Sixteenth International Unicode Conference*, 2000.
4. NTCIR (NII-NACSIS Test Collection for IR Systems) Home Page. http://research.nii.ac.jp/~ntcadm/index-en.html
5. C. Peters, M. Braschler, G. Di Nunzio and N. Ferro. CLEF 2004: Ad Hoc Track Overview and Results Analysis. This volume.

6. M.F. Porter. Snowball: A language for stemming algorithms. October 2001. http://snowball.tartarus.org/texts/introduction.html
7. S.E. Robertson, S. Walker, S. Jones, M.M. Hancock-Beaulieu and M. Gatford. Okapi at TREC-3. *Proceedings of TREC-3*, 1995.
8. Jacques Savoy. CLEF and Multilingual information retrieval resource page. http://www.unine.ch/info/clef/
9. Text REtrieval Conference (TREC) Home Page. http://trec.nist.gov/
10. Stephen Tomlinson. Experiments in 8 European Languages with Hummingbird SearchServer™ at CLEF 2002. *Proceedings of CLEF 2002*, 2003.
11. Stephen Tomlinson. Lexical and Algorithmic Stemming Compared for 9 European Languages with Hummingbird SearchServer™ at CLEF 2003. *Working Notes for the CLEF 2003 Workshop*, 2003.
12. Ellen M. Voorhees. Overview of the TREC 2003 Robust Retrieval Track. *Proceedings of TREC 2003*, 2004.

Data Fusion for Effective European Monolingual Information Retrieval

Jacques Savoy

Institut interfacultaire d'informatique, Université de Neuchâtel,
Pierre-à-Mazel 7, 2001 Neuchâtel, Switzerland
Jacques.Savoy@unine.ch

Abstract. For our fourth participation in the CLEF evaluation campaigns, our first objective was to propose an effective and general stopword list and a light stemming procedure for the Portuguese language. Our second objective was to obtain a better picture of the relative merit of various search engines when processing documents in the Finnish and Russian languages. Finally, based on the Z-score method we suggested a data fusion strategy intended to improve monolingual searches in various European languages.

1 Introduction

Making use of experiments we carried out in previous years [1], [2], we are now participating in the French, Finnish, Russian and Portuguese monolingual tasks without relying on dictionaries. Moreover, the IR approaches suggested are fully automatic and used freely available resources. This paper describes the information retrieval models we used in the monolingual tracks and is organized as follows: Section 2 describes our general approach to building stopword lists and stemmers for use with languages other than English. Section 3 evaluates two probabilistic models and five vector-space schemes using five different languages. Section 4 describes and evaluates various data fusion operators that will hopefully improve retrieval effectiveness. Finally, Section 5 depicts our official runs and presents a broad failure analysis.

2 Stopword Lists and Stemming Procedures

In order to define general stopword lists, we first created a list of the top 200 most frequent words found in the various languages, from which some words were removed (e.g., Roma, police, minister, Chirac). From this list of very frequent words, we added articles, pronouns, prepositions, conjunctions or very frequently occurring verb forms (e.g., to be, is, has, etc.). We created a new one for the Portuguese language, adding it to last year's stopword lists [2] (these lists are available at www.unine.ch/info/clef/). For English we used the list provided by the SMART system (571 words), while for the other European languages, our

C. Peters et al. (Eds.): CLEF 2004, LNCS 3491, pp. 233–244, 2005.

stopword list contained 463 words for the French language, 747 for Finnish, 420 for Russian and 392 for Portuguese.

Once high-frequency words were removed, an indexing procedure generally applied a stemming algorithm, in an attempt to conflate word variants into the same stem or root. In developing this procedure for the various European languages [3], we first wanted to remove only inflectional suffixes such as singular and plural word forms, and also feminine and masculine forms, such that they conflate to the same root. Our suggested stemmers also tried to remove various case markings (e.g., accusative or genitive) used in the Finnish and Russian languages. The Finnish language however involved additional morphological difficulties, given that this language frequently uses more than 12 cases. However, one of the real stemming problems with Finnish is the fact that the stem is often modified when suffixes are added. For example, "matto" (carpet in nominative singular form) becomes "maton" (in genitive singular form, with "-n" as suffix) or "mattoja" (in partitive plural form, with "-a" as suffix). Once we removed the corresponding suffixes, we were left with three distinct stems, namely "matto", "mato", and "matoj". Of course such irregularities also occur in other languages, usually introduced to make the spoken language flow better, such as "submit" and "submission". In Finnish however, these irregularities are more common, thus rendering the conflation of various word forms into the same stem more problematic. Thus, in order to index Finnish documents, some authors suggest using a morphological analyzer (based on a dictionary) [4].

More sophisticated schemes have already been proposed for the removal of derivational suffixes (e.g., "-ize", "-ably", "-ship" in the English language), as for example the stemmer developed by Lovins [5] (based on a list of over 260 suffixes), or that of Porter [6] (which looks for about 60 suffixes). For the French language only, we developed a stemming approach to remove some derivational suffixes (e.g., "communicateur" → "communiquer", "faiblesse" → "faible"). Our various stemming procedures can be found at `www.unine.ch/info/clef/`. Currently, it is not clear whether a stemming procedure removing only inflections from nouns and adjectives would result in better retrieval effectiveness, when compared to other stemming approaches that also consider verbs or remove both inflectional and derivational suffixes (e.g., the Snowball stemmers).

Diacritic characters are usually not present in English collections (with certain exceptions, such as "cliché"). For the Finnish, Portuguese and Russian languages, these characters were replaced by their corresponding non-accentuated letter. For the Russian language, we converted and normalized the Cyrillic Unicode characters into the Latin alphabet.

Finally, most European languages manifest other morphological characteristics, with compound word constructions being just one example (e.g., handgun, worldwide). In Finnish, we encounter similar constructions as such as "rakkauskirje" ("rakkaus" + "kirje" for love & letter) or "työviikko" ("työ" + "viikko" for work & week). Recently, Braschler & Ripplinger [7] showed that decompounding German words would significantly improve retrieval performance. In our experiments with the Finnish language, we used our decompounding algorithm [2] (see also [8]), where both the compound words and their components were left in documents and queries.

3 Indexing and Searching Strategies

In order to obtain a broader view of the relative merit of various retrieval models, we represented each document (or request) by a set of weighted keywords. In order to define such weights, we would account for the term occurrence frequency (denoted tf_{ij} for indexing term t_j in document D_i), or we might also account for their frequency in the collection (or more precisely the inverse document frequency, denoted idf_j). However, we found that cosine normalization could prove beneficial, and in this case, each indexing weight could vary within the range of 0 to 1 (retrieval model notation: "doc=ntc, query=ntc" or "ntc-ntc"). Other variants might also be created. For example, the tf component could be computed as $0.5 + 0.5 \cdot [tf \ / \ \max tf$ in a document$]$ (retrieval model denoted "doc=atn"). We might also consider that a term's presence in a shorter document provides stronger evidence than it does in a longer document, leading to more complex IR models; for example, the IR model denoted by "doc=Lnu" [9], "doc=dtu" [10]. In Table 1, w_{ij} represents the indexing weight assigned to term t_j in document D_i, n indicates the number of documents in the collection, and nt_i the number of distinct indexing terms included in the representation of D_i.

Table 1. Weighting schemes

ntc	$w_{ij} = \frac{tf_{ij} \cdot idf_j}{\sqrt{\sum_{k=1}^{t}(tf_{ik} \cdot idf_k)^2}}$	atn	$w_{ij} = idf_j \cdot \left[\frac{0.5 + 0.5 \cdot tf_{ij}}{max\ tf_{i.}}\right]$
ltn	$w_{ij} = [ln(tf_{ij}) + 1] \cdot idf_j$	dtn	$w_{ij} = [ln(ln(tf_{ij}) + 1) + 1] \cdot idf_j$
Okapi	$w_{ij} = \frac{(k_1+1) \cdot tf_{ij}}{K + tf_{ij}}$ with $K = k_1 \cdot \left[(1-b) + b \cdot \frac{l_i}{avdl}\right]$		
dtu	$w_{ij} = \frac{[ln(ln(tf_{ij})+1)+1] \cdot idf_j}{(1-slope) \cdot pivot + (slope \cdot nt_i)}$		
Lnu	$w_{ij} = \frac{\frac{ln(tf_{ij})+1}{ln\left(\frac{l_i}{nt_i}\right)+1}}{(1-slope) \cdot pivot + (slope \cdot nt_i)}$		

In addition to the previous models based on the vector-space approach, we also considered probabilistic models. In this vein, we used the Okapi probabilistic model [11]. As a second probabilistic approach, we implemented the Prosit (or deviation from randomness) approach [12], [13] which is based on combining two information measures, formulated as follows:

$$\begin{aligned} w_{ij} &= Inf^1_{ij} \cdot Inf^2_{ij} = (1 - Prob^1_{ij}) \cdot -log_2\left[Prob^2_{ij}\right] \\ Prob^1_{ij} &= tfn_{ij} \ / \ (tfn_{ij} + 1) \ \text{ with} \\ tfn_{ij} &= tf_{ij} \cdot \log_2\left[1 + ((C \cdot mean\ dl)/l_i)\right] \end{aligned}$$

$$Prob^2_{ij} = [1/(1+\lambda_j)] \cdot [\lambda_j/(1+\lambda_j)]^{tfn_{ij}} \text{ with } \lambda_j = tc_j/n$$

where l_i indicates the number of indexing terms included in the representation of D_i, tc_j represents the number of occurrences of term t_j in the collection and n the number of documents in the corpus.

To measure the retrieval performance, we adopted the non-interpolated mean average precision (computed on the basis of 1,000 retrieved items per request by the TREC-EVAL program). To determine whether or not a given search strategy is better than another, a decision rule was required. To obtain this, we might apply statistical inference methods such as Wilcoxon's signed rank test, the Sign test [14] or the hypothesis testing based on bootstrap methodology [15]. In this paper, we based our statistical validation on the bootstrap approach because this methodology does not require that the underlying distribution of the observed data follow the normal distribution. Thus, in the tables found in this paper we have underlined statistically significant differences based on a two-sided non-parametric bootstrap test, based on those means having a significance level fixed at 5%.

Table 2. Mean average precision of various single searching strategies (English, French & Portuguese language)

	Mean average precision					
Language Query Model	English T 42 queries	English TD 42 queries	French T 49 queries	French TD 49 queries	Portug. T 46 queries	Portug. TD 46 queries
Prosit	0.4638	0.5313	<u>0.4111</u>	<u>0.4568</u>	0.3824	0.4695
Okapi	**0.4763**	**0.5422**	**0.4263**	**0.4685**	**0.3997**	**0.4835**
Lnu-ltc	0.4435	0.4979	<u>0.3952</u>	<u>0.4349</u>	0.3633	0.4579
dtu-dtn	0.4444	0.5319	<u>0.3873</u>	<u>0.4143</u>	0.3620	0.4600
atn-ntc	<u>0.4203</u>	<u>0.4764</u>	<u>0.3768</u>	<u>0.4210</u>	<u>0.3559</u>	<u>0.4454</u>
ltn-ntc	<u>0.3876</u>	<u>0.4602</u>	<u>0.3718</u>	<u>0.4035</u>	0.3737	0.4319
ntc-ntc	<u>0.3109</u>	<u>0.3706</u>	<u>0.3056</u>	<u>0.3309</u>	<u>0.2981</u>	<u>0.3708</u>

We indexed the English, French, and Portuguese collections using words as indexing units. The evaluations of our two probabilistic models and five vector-space schemes are listed in Table 2 in which the best performance is listed in bold type. This best performance is used as a baseline for our statistical testing. The underlined results therefore indicate that the difference in mean average precision compared to the best system can be viewed as being statistically significant. As depicted in Table 2, the Okapi model presents the best IR model for all collections. For the Portuguese corpus five IR models produce statistically similar performance (Okapi, Prosit, "Lnu-ltc", "dtu-dtn", and "ltn-ntc"), and a similar conclusion can be drawn from the English collection. Moreover, the data in Table 2 shows that when the number of search terms increases (from T to TD), the retrieval effectiveness usually does also. When considering the five best retrieval schemes (namely, Prosit, Okapi, "Lnu-ltc", "dtu-dtn" and "atn-ntc"), the improvement is around 24.4% when comparing title-only (or T) with TD queries for the Portuguese collection, 14.7% when comparing the English corpus or 10% for the French collection.

In order to represent Finnish and Russian documents and queries, we considered the n-gram, and word-based indexing schemes. The resulting mean average precision for these various indexing approaches is shown in Table 3 (Finnish word-based indexing with decompounding).

Table 3. Mean average precision of various single searching strategies (Finnish and Russian collection)

	Mean average precision				
Language	Finnish	Finnish	Finnish	Russian	Russian
Index	word	5-gram	4-gram	word	4-gram
Query	TD	TD	TD	TD	TD
Model	45 queries	45 queries	45 queries	34 queries	34 queries
Prosit	0.4620	0.4707	0.5357	<u>0.3448</u>	0.2879
Okapi	**0.4773**	0.4805	0.5385	**0.3800**	**0.2890**
Lnu-ltc	0.4643	0.4767	0.5022	0.3794	0.2852
dtu-dtn	0.4746	0.4629	0.5200	0.3768	0.2705
atn-ntc	0.4629	0.4735	**0.5428**	0.3422	0.2543
ltn-ntc	0.4580	**0.4824**	0.4880	0.3579	<u>0.2137</u>
ntc-ntc	<u>0.3862</u>	<u>0.4472</u>	<u>0.4466</u>	<u>0.2716</u>	<u>0.1916</u>

When looking at results for the Finnish language (Table 3), we can see that 4-gram indexing scheme usually performs better than both 5-gram indexing (e.g., with the TD queries, 4-gram: mean MAP of the five best IR models is 0.5278 vs. 0.4729 with 5-gram indexing approach, a performance difference of 11.6% in favor of the 4-gram model) or better than the word-based indexing model (mean of 5 best IR models of 0.4692, with a performance difference of 12.5% in favor of the 4-gram indexing approach). There are of course exceptions to this rule (e.g., for the "ntc-ntc" model, the 5-gram indexing scheme results in slightly better performance than the 4-gram strategy, or 0.4472 vs. 0.4466). Moreover, our statistical testing does not usually show any significant differences in mean average precision when comparing the best 6 IR models.

As illustrated in Table 3, the word-based indexing scheme used for the Russian language provides better retrieval performance than does the 4-gram schemes (based on the five best search models, the mean MAP of these five schemes is 0.3646 vs. 0.2774 for the 4-gram indexing scheme, a difference of 31.4%). Based on our statistical testing, we usually were not able to find any significant differences between 5 IR models.

It was observed that pseudo-relevance feedback (or blind-query expansion) seemed to be a useful technique for enhancing retrieval effectiveness. In this study, we adopted Rocchio's approach [9] with $\alpha = 0.75$, $\beta = 0.75$, and $\gamma = 0$, whereby the system was allowed to add m terms extracted from the k best ranked documents from the original query. To evaluate this proposition, we used the Okapi probabilistic models and enlarged the query by the 10 to 30 terms provided by the 3 or 10 best-retrieved articles.

The results depicted in Table 4 (depicting our best results for the Okapi model) indicate that the optimal parameter setting seemed to be collection-dependant. Moreover, performance improvement also seemed to be collection dependant (or language dependant), with the Portuguese corpus showing an increase of 6% (from a mean average precision of 0.4835 to 0.5127), 5.2% for the English collection (from 0.5422 to 0.5704), 3.8% for the Russian collection (from 0.3800 to 0.3945), and 3.5% for the French corpus (from 0.4685 to 0.4851). For the Finnish corpus and the 4-gram indexing scheme, the query expansion approach did not improve the mean average precision. In Table 4, the baseline upon which we based our statistical testing is the mean average precision before automatically expanding the query. In this case, it is interesting to note that our statistical testing usually cannot detect a significant difference in mean average precision before and after blind query expansion.

Table 4. Mean average precision using blind-query expansion (Okapi model)

	Mean average precision				
TD queries Index Model	English word 42 queries	French word 49 queries	Finnish 4-gram 45 queries	Russian word 34 queries	Portug. word 46 queries
Okapi	0.5422	0.4685	**0.5385**	0.3800	0.4835
k doc.	3/10 0.5582	3/10 **0.4851**	3/10 0.5308	3/15 0.3925	3/10 0.5005
$/m$ terms	3/15 0.5581	3/15 0.4748	3/15 0.5296	3/30 0.3678	3/15 **0.5127**
	5/10 **0.5704**	5/10 0.4738	5/10 0.5278	5/15 0.3896	3/20 0.5098
	5/15 0.5587	5/15 0.4628	5/15 0.5213	5/30 **0.3945**	5/10 0.4465
	10/10 0.5596	10/10 0.4671	10/10 0.5291	5/40 0.3796	5/15 0.5077
	10/15 0.5596	10/15 0.4547	10/15 0.5297	10/30 0.3912	10/15 0.4806

Using the same query expansion technique (Rocchio in this case), various IR models have resulted in varying degrees of evolution when increasing the number of terms to be included in the expanded query. Figure 1 illustrates this phenomenon showing the evolution of the mean average precision of four different IR models (French corpus, and using the 3 best ranked documents). When we increased the number of terms to be included in the expanded query, the "dtu-dtn" model showed a small but constant improvement. With this IR model, each parameter setting produced a retrieval performance not that far from the best one. A similar evolution could also be seen with the "Lnu-ltc" model, yet with even greater improvement. When compared to the Okapi or Prosit models however, performance levels achieved were lower. For the Prosit model as well as for the Okapi scheme, the mean average precision increased, reaching a maximum point and then subsequently slowly decreasing (however with the Prosit model

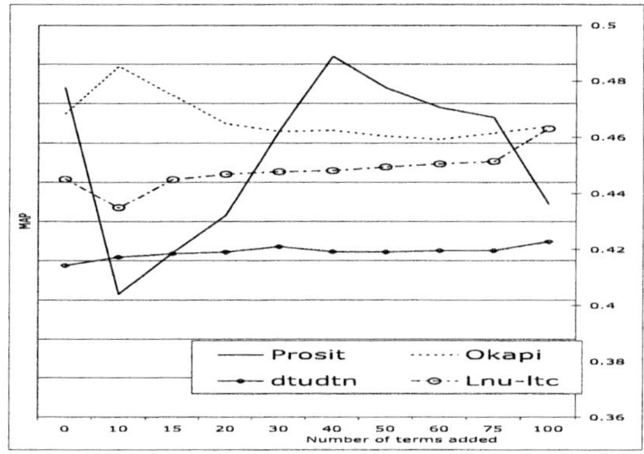

Fig. 1. Mean average precision using blind-query expansion within different retrieval models (French corpus, terms extracted from the 3 best ranked documents

showing greater variability). When a few terms were added to the original query however, the Prosit model usually performed at lower levels than did the Okapi.

4 Data Fusion

For each language studied, we may assume that different indexing and search models would retrieve different pertinent and non-relevant items, and that combining different search models would improve retrieval effectiveness. More precisely, when combining different indexing schemes we would expect to improve recall, due to the fact that different document representations might retrieve different pertinent items [16]. On the other hand, when combining different search schemes, we could suppose that these various IR strategies are more likely to rank the same relevant items higher on the list than they would the same non-relevant documents (viewed as outliers). Thus, combining them could improve retrieval effectiveness by ranking pertinent documents higher and ranking non-relevant items lower. In this study, we hope to enhance retrieval performance by making use of this second characteristic, while for the Finnish language our assumption would be that word-based and n-gram indexing schemes are distinct and independent sources of evidence regarding the content of documents. For this language only, we expect to improve recall due to the first effect described above.

In this current study we limited the number of IR schemes to be combined to two. To achieve this, we evaluated various fusion operators, and their precise descriptions are listed in Table 5. For example, the Sum RSV operator indicates that the combined document score (or the final retrieval status value) is simply the sum of the retrieval status value (RSV_k) of the corresponding document D_k computed by each single indexing scheme [17]. We can thus see from Table 5 that both the Norm Max and Norm RSV apply a normalization procedure when combining document scores. When combining the retrieval status value (RSV_k) for various indexing schemes, we may multiply the document score by a constant α_i (usually equal to 1) in order to favor the ith more efficient retrieval scheme.

Table 5. Data fusion combination operators used in this study

Sum RSV	$\alpha_i \cdot RSV_k$
Norm Max	$\alpha_i \cdot (RSV_k / Max^i)$
Norm RSV	$\alpha_i \cdot [(RSV_k - Min^i)/(Max^i - Min^i)]$
Z-Score	$\alpha_i \cdot [((RSV_k - \mu^i)/\sigma^i) + \delta^i]$, with $\delta^i = [(\mu^i - Min^i)/\sigma^i]$

In addition to using these data fusion operators, we also considered the round-robin approach, wherein we take one document in turn from all individual lists and remove any duplicates, keeping the most highly ranked instance. Finally we suggested merging the retrieved documents according to the Z-score, computed for each result list. Within this scheme, for the ith result list, we needed to compute the average of the RSV_k (denoted μ^i) and the standard deviation (denoted σ^i). Based on these values, we would then normalize the retrieval status value for each document D_k provided by the ith result list by computing the deviation of RSV_k with respect to the mean (μ^i). In Table 5, Min^i (Max^i) denotes the minimal (maximal) RSV value in the ith result list.

Table 6 depicts the evaluation of various data fusion operators, comparing them to the single approach using the Okapi and the Prosit probabilistic models. From this data, we could see that combining two IR models might improve retrieval effectiveness. When combining two retrieval models, the Z-score scheme tended to produce the best performance. In Table 6, under the heading "Z-scoreW", we attached a weight of 1.5 to the best performing model (depicted in bold in the first two lines), and 1 to the other. Using the best single IR as a

Table 6. Mean average precision using different combination operators (with blind-query expansion)

	Mean average precision				
Query TD Index Model	English word 42 queries	French word 49 queries	Finnish 4-gram 45 queries	Russian word 34 queries	Portug. word 46 queries
Okapi-PRF	5/10 0.5704	3/10 **0.4851**	0/0 0.5385	5/30 **0.3945**	3/15 0.5127
Prosit-PRF	3/30 **0.5742**	10/20 0.4643	3/40 **0.5684**	10/15 0.3736	5/75 **0.5230**
Round-robin	0.5790	0.4824	0.5643	0.3900	0.5251
Sum RSV	0.5837	0.4792	0.5500	0.4041	0.5153
Norm Max	0.5789	0.4851	0.5696	0.4081	0.5396
Norm RSV	0.5752	0.4864	0.5692	0.4130	0.5348
Z-Score	0.5818	0.4906	0.5718	**0.4160**	**0.5399**
Z-ScoreW	**0.5854**	**0.4933**	**0.5754**	0.4145	0.5359

baseline, our statistical testing was not able to detect a significant enhancement when combining two IR models.

5 Official Results and Analysis

Finally, in Table 7 we show the exact specifications of our 12 official monolingual runs. These experiments were based on different data fusion operators (mainly the Z-score and the round-robin schemes). Although we expected that combining the Okapi and the Prosit probabilistic models would provide good retrieval effectiveness, for some languages (e.g., French or Russian), we also considered other IR models (e.g., "dtu-dtn" or "Lnu-ltc"). We also sent some runs with longer queries formulations (TDN) in order to increase the number of relevant documents found for each language. In the "UniNEfi1" run, we filter all documents appearing in the year 1994 out before returning the final list (in order to search all newspaper articles that described events occurring in the year 1995. However, 66 (over 413) relevant items had been published in year 1994). This was not a good strategy. If we keep the articles appearing in the year 1994, we may achieve a MAP of 0.5340 (instead of 0.4967 obtained by the "UniNEfi1" run).

For both the Portuguese and French languages and compared to other experiments done during this CLEF evaluation campaign, it is our opinion that the IR approach we used produces very good results. Even though our statistical tests did not detect significant enhancement, we would still suggest automatically expanding the query and following this step, combining both the Okapi and Prosit probabilistic models.

For the Finnish language, it seems that a deeper morphological analysis will improve the retrieval effectiveness. Moreover, a better decompounding algorithm will clearly enhance the mean average precision. For example, Tomlinson [18] indicates that we may enhance the mean average precision from 0.469 to 0.561 (+ 19.6% for the Finnish collection, Title-only queries) when including a good decompounding approach. Moulinier & Williams [19] used a commercial morphological analyzer for Finnish and also obtained good overall retrieval performance levels with this language. On the other hand, an analysis of our IR system shows that we failed to decompound important search terms due to the fact that our decompounding strategy was too conservative.

For the Russian language, we were not able to draw any definitive conclusions due to the small size of the corpus (composed of 16,716 documents) and also due to the fact that for numerous queries the number of relevant items was rather small. For example, for ten queries out of a total of 34, we found only one relevant document in the corpus (and seven other queries found only two pertinent items in the collection). This fact may therefore only favor a given IR system by chance, and this to the detriment of another. For example, if a given system retrieves the single pertinent item in the first rank, it will obtain a precision of 1.0 for this query, and if this pertinent item is only retrieved in the 2nd position, it will only obtain a precision of 0.5. If we repeat this swapping between the first and second extracted document for the ten requests having only one relevant item,

Table 7. Description and mean average precision (MAP) of our official runs

Run name	Lan.	Query	Index	Model	Query exp.	Combined	MAP
UniNEfr1	FR	TD	word	dtu-dtn	5 d. / 40 t.		
		TD	word	Prosit	10 d. /30 t.	RR	0.4437
UniNEfr2	FR	TD	word	Prosit	10 d. / 30 t.		
		TD	word	Okapi	3 d. / 10 t.	Z-Score	**0.4849**
UniNEfr3	FR	TDN	word	Prosit	5 d. / 20 t.		
		TDN	word	dtu-dtn	10 d. / 30 t.	Z-ScoreW	0.4785
UniNEfi1	FI	TD	4-gram	Prosit	3 d. / 40 t.		
		TD	word	Prosit	3 d. / 20 t.	Z-ScoreW	0.4967
UniNEfi2	FI	TD	4-gram	Prosit	3 d. / 40 t.		
		TD	word	Prosit	3 d. / 20 t.		
		TD	4-gram	Okapi	3 d. / 20 t.	Sum RSV	**0.5453**
UniNEfi3	FI	TDN	4-gram	Prosit	3 d. / 30 t.		
		TDN	word	Prosit	3 d. / 20 t.	Z-ScoreW	0.5454
UniNEru1	RU	TD	word	Prosit			
		TD	word	Lnu-ltc	3 d. / 20 t.	RR	**0.3546**
UniNEru2	RU	TD	word	Prosit			
		TD	word	Okapi		Z-score	0.3545
UniNEru3	RU	TDN	word	Prosit	10 d. / 15 t.		
		TDN	word	Okapi	5 d. / 15 t.	RR	0.4070
UniNEpt1	PT	TD	word	Okapi	5 d. / 15 t.		
		TD	word	Prosit	10 d. / 10 t.	Norm RSV	0.5004
UniNEpt2	PT	TD	word	Prosit	5 d. / 30 t.		
		TD	word	Lnu-ltc	10 d. / 15 t.	Z-score	0.5105
UniNEpt3	PT	TD	word	Okapi	10 d. / 20 t.		
		TD	word	Prosit	10 d. / 50 t.	Norm RSV	**0.5188**

the mean average precision over 34 queries between these two systems will be 0.147 (or (0.5 · 10) / 34).

6 Conclusion

In this fifth CLEF evaluation campaign, we proposed a general stopword list and a light stemming procedure (removing only inflections attached to nouns and adjectives) for the Portuguese language. In order to enhance the retrieval performance, we suggest using a data fusion approach based on the Z-score in order to combine two probabilistic IR models. The results of this evaluation campaign seem to indicate that such an approach is effective for the French and Portuguese languages.

However, we also found that pseudo-relevance feedback based on Rocchio's model usually does not statistically improve mean average precision, even though mean precision following query expansion usually the shows a better value. Similarly, combining two retrieval models based on the same indexing strategy usually does not statistically enhance retrieval performance.

Acknowledgments. The author would like to also thank the CLEF-2004 task organizers for their efforts in developing various European language test-collections. The author would also like to thank C. Buckley from SabIR for giving us the opportunity to use the SMART system. This research was supported by the Swiss National Science Foundation under Grant #21-66 742.01.

References

1. Savoy, J.: Combining Multiple Strategies for Effective Monolingual and Cross-Lingual Retrieval. IR Journal, **7** (2004) 121–148
2. Savoy, J.: Report on CLEF-2003 Monolingual Tracks: Fusion of Probabilistic Models for Effective Monolingual Retrieval. In: Peters, C., Braschler, M., Gonzalo, J., Kluck, M. (Eds.): Advances in Cross-Language Information Retrieval. Lecture Notes in Computer Science. Springer, Heidelberg (2004), to appear
3. Sproat, R.: Morphology and Computation. The MIT Press, Cambridge (1992)
4. Hedlund, T., Airio, E., Keskustalo, H., Lehtokangas, R., Pirkola, A., Järvelin, K.: Dictionary-Based Cross-Language Information Retrieval: Learning Experiences from CLEF 2000-2002. IR Journal, **7** (2004) 99–119
5. Lovins, J.B.: Development of a Stemming Algorithm. Mechanical Translation and Computational Linguistics **11** (1968) 22–31
6. Porter, M.F.: An Algorithm for Suffix Stripping. Program **14** (1980) 130–137
7. Braschler, M., Ripplinger, B.: How Effective is Stemming and Decompounding for German Text Retrieval? IR Journal, **7** (2004) 291–316
8. Chen, A.: Cross-Language Retrieval Experiments at CLEF 2002. In: Peters, C., Braschler, M., Gonzalo, J., Kluck, M. (Eds.): Advances in Cross-Language Information Retrieval. Lecture Notes in Computer Science: Vol. 2785. Springer, Heidelberg (2003), 28–48
9. Buckley, C., Singhal, A., Mitra, M., Salton, G.: New Retrieval Approaches Using SMART. In Proceedings TREC-4. NIST Publication #500-236, Gaithersburg (1996) 25–48
10. Singhal, A., Choi, J., Hindle, D., Lewis, D.D., Pereira, F.: AT&T at TREC-7. In Proceedings TREC-7. NIST, Publication #500-242, Gaithersburg (1999) 239–251
11. Robertson, S.E., Walker, S., Beaulieu, M.: Experimentation as a Way of Life: Okapi at TREC. Information Processing & Management, **36** (2000) 95–108
12. Amati, G., Carpineto, C., Romano, G.: Italian Monolingual Information Retrieval with PROSIT. In: Peters, C., Braschler, M., Gonzalo, J., Kluck, M. (Eds.): Advances in Cross-Language Information Retrieval. Lecture Notes in Computer Science: Vol. 2785. Springer, Heidelberg (2003), 257–264
13. Amati, G., van Rijsbergen, C.J.: Probabilistic Models of Information Retrieval Based on Measuring the Divergence from Randomness. ACM Transactions on Information Systems, **20** (2002) 357–389
14. Hull, D.: Using Statistical Testing in the Evaluation of Retrieval Experiments. In Proceedings of the ACM-SIGIR'93. The ACM Press, New York (1993) 329–338
15. Savoy, J.: Statistical Inference in Retrieval Effectiveness Evaluation. Information Processing & Management, **33** (1997) 495–512
16. Vogt, C.C., Cottrell, G.W.: Fusion via a Linear Combination of Scores. IR Journal, **1** (1999) 151–173
17. Fox, E.A., Shaw, J.A.: Combination of Multiple Searches. In Proceedings TREC-2. NIST Publication #500-215, Gaithersburg (1994) 243–249

18. Tomlinson, S.: Finnish, Portuguese and Russian Retrieval with Hummingbird SearchServer^{TM}at CLEF 2004. In: Peters, C., Clough, P., Gonzalo, J., Jones, G., Kluck, M., Magnini, B. (Eds.): Advances in Cross-Language Information Retrieval. Lecture Notes in Computer Science. Springer, Heidelberg (in print)
19. Moulinier, I., Williams, K.: Report on Thomson Legal and Regulatory Experiments at CLEF 2004. In: Peters, C., Clough, P., Gonzalo, J., Jones, G., Kluck, M., Magnini, B. (Eds.): Advances in Cross-Language Information Retrieval. Lecture Notes in Computer Science. Springer, Heidelberg (in print)

The XLDB Group at CLEF 2004

Nuno Cardoso, Mário J. Silva, and Miguel Costa

Grupo XLDB - Departamento de Informática,
Faculdade de Ciências da Universidade de Lisboa
{ncardoso, mjs, mcosta} at xldb.di.fc.ul.pt

Abstract. This paper describes the participation of the XLDB Group in the CLEF monolingual ad hoc task for Portuguese. We present tumba!, a Portuguese search engine and describe its architecture and the underlying assumptions. We discuss the way we used tumba! in CLEF, providing details on our runs and our experiments with ranking algorithms.

1 Introduction

In 2004, for the first time, CLEF included Portuguese document collections for monolingual & bilingual ad hoc retrieval and question answering tasks. This collection [14] was based on news of several categories taken from Publico [13], a Portuguese newspaper, and compiled by Linguateca [7]. This year, the XLDB Group, from the University of Lisbon, made its debut in CLEF.

This paper is organized as follows: in Section 2, we introduce the XLDB Group. In Section 3, we describe tumba!, our IR system, and the modifications we made to it to handle the CLEF 2004 data set. Section 4 describes our official runs with the algorithms implemented for CLEF 2004, and Section 5 presents our results. Section 6 summarizes the conclusions we drew from this first participation in CLEF.

2 The XLDB Group

The XLDB Group is a research unit of LaSIGE (Large Scale Information Systems Laboratory) at FCUL - Faculdade de Ciências da Universidade de Lisboa. We study data management systems for data analysis, information integration and user access to large quantities of complex data from heterogeneous platforms. Current research lines span Web search, mobile data access, temporal web data management and bioinformatics.

The XLDB Group is involved in several projects and activities. One of our main projects is tumba! [8, 15], a Portuguese Web search engine. tumba! is described in Section 3.

Since January 2004, the XLDB Group hosts a node of Linguateca, a distributed language resource center for Portuguese [6].

The participation of the XLDB Group in the monolingual task for Portuguese with the tumba! search engine was motivated by two main reasons:

C. Peters et al. (Eds.): CLEF 2004, LNCS 3491, pp. 245–252, 2005.

1. Although we had previous experiences in evaluation contests, namely in the bio-text task of the KDD Cup 02 [4] and in the BioCreative workshop [5], this was our first opportunity to evaluate tumba! jointly with other IR systems, with the advantage of the evaluation being conducted on a Portuguese collection.
2. Although we were aware that our system was out of its natural environment, the Web, we could take the opportunity to tune the indexing and ranking engines of tumba!, by submitting our results using different ranking configurations and then analyzing the results.

3 tumba! in the Monolingual Task

3.1 Overview of tumba!

The tumba! search engine has been specifically designed to archive and provide search services to a Web community formed by those interested in subjects related to Portugal and the Portuguese people [8]. tumba! has been offered as a public service since November 2002.

tumba is mainly written in Java and built on open-source software: the Linux operating system. It has an index of over 3.5 million Web documents and a daily traffic of up to 20,000 queries per day. Its response time is less than 0.5 seconds for 95% of the requests. It is also a platform for PhD and MSc research projects at our university.

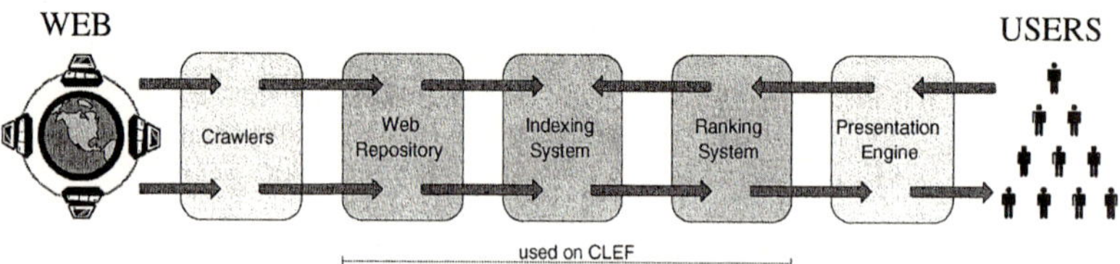

Fig. 1. tumba's architecture

The architecture of tumba! is similar to that of global search engines and adopts many of the algorithms used by them [1]. However, its configuration data is much richer in its domain of specialisation. tumba! has a better knowledge of the location and organization of Portuguese Web sites (both in qualitative and quantitative terms) [15].

The data flows from the Web to the user through a pipeline of the following tumba! sub-systems (See Figure 1):

Crawlers: collect documents from the Web, given an initial URL list. They parse and extract URLs from each document, and use these to collect new documents. These steps are performed recursively until a stop condition is met [10].

Web Repository: The Web data collected by the crawlers is stored in Versus, a repository of Web documents and associated meta-data [9].

Indexing system: the indexing system Sidra creates indexes over the documents in the Web Repository [3], so that when a query is received, Sidra uses the indexes built to find the documents that match that query.

Ranking system: computes, for each document *d* returned by the indexing system, a similarity value between *d* and the submitted query using a set of heuristics. It then sorts the documents by these similarities.

Presentation Engine: formats the result sets received from the ranking engine for the user's access platforms such as Web browsers, PDA devices or WAP phones.

3.2 The Portuguese Monolingual Task

The previous editions of CLEF showed that the top performing groups for the monolingual ad hoc tasks were systems that performed robust stemming, well-known weighting schemes (BM25, Lnu.ltn or Berkeley ranking) and blind feedback or query expansion [12]. tumba's system does not have a stemmer and a blind feedback or query expansion system, and the term weighting scheme is tuned for Web searches. However, we decided not to make any changes to the architecture of tumba! for this evaluation. We wanted to evaluate tumba!'s performance with its current components, so that we could have a baseline for comparison on future CLEF tasks. Nonetheless, we felt that our participation in CLEF would provide us with valuable ideas to optimize our search engine results, and resources to evaluate our system performance.

One of the difficulties we encountered in the CLEF monolingual task was related to the SGML-format used on the collection of Portuguese documents. The documents have tags for associated metadata like author, category and date of publication. The contents are in plain text, with no additional tags. tumba! was not conceived to work with document collections organized like this. Its ranking system was developed to profit from annotations extracted from the Web documents, such as:

- Information obtained from the Web graph, like links and anchor text, which are a valuable resource to find related pages that might interest the user;
- Documents' structural elements like titles and headings, which provide valuable information on the subject of the document.

We used the same alghorithms as those designed for the Web in CLEF, despite the different search context. The lack of this kind of "light semantic" annotation in the collection was a major handicap for the tumba! system, since the only semantic information we managed to extract from the documents was the title of the news. Our heuristic for extracting document titles consisted in finding paragraphs in the collection with a maximum of 15 terms and ending with no punctuation.

We disabled the query-independent ranking calculations and most of the emphasis ranking augmenters of the Indexing and Ranking system, since there was no information of this type on the collection.

tumba's Crawlers and Presentation Engine were not used for the CLEF Portuguese monolingual ad hoc task. We loaded the document collection directly into the Web Repository, bypassing the system's crawlers. The collection was then indexed by the Sidra Indexing system. Queries were sent directly to Sidra, bypassing the Presentation Engine, and the matching documents were then ranked according to some heuristics to compute document relevance.

4 Runs

In the monolingual ad hoc task, the number of runs that could be submitted was limited to 4.

4.1 Manual Run (XLDBTumba01)

Since this was the first time that CLEF used Portuguese collections in an evaluation campaign, this task didn't have previous relevant judgements and training collections. In order to have a prior evaluation of tumba!, we created our own baseline against which we could compare our runs to measure how much we were improving our system.

For each one of the 50 given topics, we created several different queries related to the topic and we used them to retrieve documents matching the query terms. Then, the returned results were manually examined by two doctoral students, with some IR system usage experience but unfamiliar with the tumba! system, and classified the documents as relevant or irrelevant according to the topic criteria. This was time-consuming work, which consumed most of the time for this task.

After that, we compiled a list of the relevant documents and submitted it to CLEF as our run XLDBTumba01, to measure the offset of our baseline compared with the CLEF solutions.

When the relevant judgements were released by CLEF, we observed that we had many errors in our manual experiment; from incorrect topic interpretation to bad query formulation. In the end, this was the run that had the worst performance. Yet, this run clearly showed us how difficult it is to formulate queries that correctly match an information need.

4.2 Flat Ranking Run (XLDBTumba02)

For subsequent runs, we chose among the different queries used to create the XLDB-Tumba01 run to select which 50 queries would be used on the remaining runs. Note that we didn't use more than one query per topic, neither did we do any kind of query expansion.

This run was produced by submitting the 50 queries directly to the Sidra Indexing and Ranking system, configured to perform an exact matching (flat-ranking algorithm), returning only the documents that match all the query terms.

We see this run as our automatic baseline run, and we were anticipating that the other runs would improve precision and recall compared to this run. Yet, this run outperformed all the other runs.

4.3 Distances Run (XLDBTumba05)

This run was generated using the following ranking algorithm:

- *distMinTerms(d,q)* - uses the minimum distances between any pair of query terms *q* in documents *d*, *minDist*, to increase the ranking of documents whose query terms are closer in the document. For distances above 10, the function gives similarity 0 to the document. If all query terms are adjacent on a document, their *minDist* value equals 1.

$$distMinTerms(d,q) = \begin{cases} 1 & minDist = 1 \\ 1 - \frac{minDist-1}{9} & 1 < minDist < 10 \\ 0 & minDist \geq 10 \end{cases}$$

This function indeed improved the results accordingly to our own evaluation, as the queries with more than one term we used for the topic tend to be adjacent.

4.4 Distances + Titles Run (XLDBTumba04)

This run was generated by using two ranking algorithms in Sidra:

- *distMinTerms(d,q)*
- *termsInTitle(d,q)* - this is a similarity function between the terms in the title of each document *d*, denoted *T*, and the query terms in a query *q*, denoted *Q*.

$$termsInTitle(d,q) = \frac{|T \cap Q|}{max(|T|,|Q|)}$$

This run evaluated the importance of the title in the document ranking, and turned out as the one with the worst performance in our self-evaluation. This was probably caused by the heuristic used to extract titles from the documents, which was a very naive approach and may have mislead the ranking engine. The tumba! search engine gives great importance to title texts, as many people search named entities on search engines and these are usually clearly stated in the titles.

5 Results

For a prior evaluation of our automatic runs, we compared the results with the manual run XLDBTumba01. We used precision@1, precision@3, precision@10, recall and F-Measure ($\beta = 1$) metrics in our self-evaluation. The results are summarized in Table 1.

The results obtained in CLEF are presented on Table 2 and Figure 2. The average precision (non-interpolated) for all relevant documents and the R-Precision (precision after R documents retrieved) are the measures presented by the trec_eval program. [2, 11]

Table 1. Automatic Submitted Runs, compared to the Manual Run XLDBTumba01

Run	Description	Precision@			Recall	F-Measure
		1	3	10		
XLDBTumba02	flat ranking	53.2%	47.2%	40.6%	89.6%	44.4%
XLDBTumba05	Distances	46.8%	53.5%	44.9%	89.6%	44.4%
XLDBTumba04	Distances & Titles	48.9%	45.0%	41.1%	89.6%	44.4%

Table 2. XLDB official runs evaluated by CLEF

Run	Manual Run (XLDBTumba01)	Flat ranking XLDBTumba02	Distances XLDBTumba05	Distances + titles XLDBTumba04
Nr. Docs Retrieved	209	2350	2350	2350
Nr. Relevant Docs	678	678	678	678
Relevant Docs Retrieved	79	168	168	168
Overall Precision	37,8%	7,1%	7,1%	7,1%
Overall Recall	11,6%	24,8%	24,8%	24,8%
Average Precision	21,84%	28,10%	25,13%	27,75%
R-Precision	22,41%	26,28%	26,73%	27,26%

The XLDBTumba02, XLDBTumba05 and XLDBTumba04 runs have the same overall precision and recall values, because we used the same queries which retrieved the same documents, differing only in the order in which the documents were submitted for each topic.

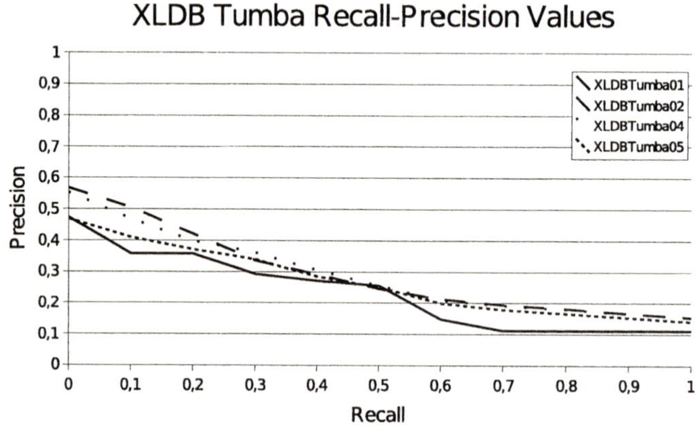

Fig. 2. Recall-Precision Values for our runs, according to CLEF results

6 Conclusion

We used the Web search engine tumba! in the CLEF 2004 monolingual task for Portuguese. Our main objective was to test, compare, and improve the quality of tumba's results, and gather ideas on how to do it. However, the enviroment that we work on, the Web, is different from the flat and small collection of document texts that we used in the CLEF task.

As we didn't have a baseline of relevant judgements, we manually annotated relevant and non relevant documents for the 50 topics. We found that this task is not easy. It is time consuming and requires experienced human annotators to review hundreds of documents, compare the results and eliminate erroneous judgements. The other runs submitted used combinations of two algorithms used on the tumba! ranking engine. We did our own evaluation with several metrics based on our own relevance judgements, and submitted 4 runs for CLEF evaluation. We presented both evaluations in this paper.

tumba! does not perform stemming or query expansion and relies heavily on detecting the presence of query terms in document titles and URLs. As these were not available for this evaluation, the performance of tumba! was below average when compared to other systems.

During the creation of the XLDBTumba01 run and while analysing our results together with the CLEF relevant judgements, we realized that in many cases, a simple query could not retrieve all the relevant documents. Take for instance, topic #204, looking for documents concerning avalanche victims. In the Portuguese monolingual task, this topic had 7 relevant judgements, which contained the relevant words of the 'avalanche' noun and the 'morrer' verb (*to die*) / 'morte' (*death*) family shown in Table 3.

Table 3. Relevant words in the relevant documents of the topic 204

Word	Rel #1	Rel #2	Rel #3	Rel #4	Rel #5	Rel #6	Rel #7
avalanche	x	x	x				
avalanches	x		x				x
avalancha				x	x	x	
mortos	x		x	x	x		
mortas							x
morte	x		x		x	x	x
morreu						x	
morreram		x	x				
morrido		x					
mata		x					

We can see that it would be impossible on a system like tumba! to achieve a good recall value with a query containing 'avalanche' 'morte' terms only. This is a situation that is not uncommon and systems must be able to deal with it. We intend to extend our Web search system to provide much better results in situations where the documents are not rich in HTML features, such as hyperlinks and meta-tags. tumba! is effective in named-page finding tasks, in particular when these have appropriate titles and have multiple links, but needs to become more effective in supporting other queries as well.

Acknowledgements

We should like to thank to Bruno Martins and Daniel Gomes for making changes to tumba! components for the CLEF task and their valuable comments, Marcírio Chaves and Lauro Nakayama for their manual retrieval and judgement of the documents for the XLDBTumba01 run, and Diana Santos and Luís Costa for their valuable suggestions and comments.

This work was financed by the Portuguese Fundação para a Ciência e Tecnologia through grant POSI / PLP / 43931 / 2001 (Linguateca) and by grant POSI / SRI / 40193 / 2001 (XMLBase Project).

References

1. Arvind Arasu, Junghoo Cho, Hector Garcia-Molina, Andreas Paepcke, and Sriram Raghavan. Searching the Web. *j-TOIT*, 1(1):2–43, August 2001. http://www.acm.org/pubs/contents/journals/toit.
2. Martin Braschler and Carol Peters. CLEF 2002 Methodology and Metrics, Advances in Cross-Language Information Retrieval: Results of the CLEF 2002 Evaluation Campaign. *Lecture Notes in Computer Science*, 2758, Spring 2003.
3. Miguel Costa and Mário J. Silva. Sidra: a Flexible Distributed Indexing and Ranking Architecture for Web Search. In *Proceedings of the VIII Conference on Software Engineering and Databases JISBD 2003*, Alicante, Spain, November 2003.
4. Francisco Couto, Bruno Martins, Mário J. Silva, and P. Coutinho. Classifying Biomedical Articles using Web Resources: application to KDD Cup 02. DI/FCUL TR 03–24, Department of Informatics, University of Lisbon, July 2003.
5. Francisco Couto, Mário Silva, and P. Coutinho. Finding Genomic Ontology Terms in Text using Information Content. In *Critical Assessment of Information Extraction systems in Biology (BioCreative)*, Granada, Spain, March 2004. BMC Bioinformatics Journal (accepted for publication).
6. Pólo XLDB da Linguateca. http://xldb.di.fc.ul.pt/linguateca/.
7. Linguateca Distributed Resource Center for the Portuguese Language. http://www.linguateca.pt.
8. Tumba! Portuguese Web Search Engine. http://www.tumba.pt.
9. Daniel Gomes, João P. Campos, and Mário J. Silva. Versus: a Web Repository. In *WDAS - Workshop on Distributed Data and Structures 2002*, Paris, France, March 2002.
10. Daniel Gomes and Mário J. Silva. Tarântula - Sistema de Recolha de Documentos da Web. In *CRC'01 - 4ª Conferência de Redes de Computadores*, November 2001. (in Portuguese).
11. Notes on TREC Eval. http://ir.iit.edu/~dagr/cs529/files/project_files/trec_eval_desc.htm.
12. Carol Peters and Martin Braschler. Cross-Language Evaluation Forum: Objectives, Results, Achievements. *Information Retrieval*, 7(1/2):7–31, January/April 2004.
13. Público. http://www.publico.pt.
14. Diana Santos and Paulo Rocha. CHAVE: Topics and Questions on the Portuguese Participation in CLEF. This volume, 2004.
15. Mário J. Silva. The Case for a Portuguese Web Search Engine. In *Proceedings of the IADIS International Conference WWW/Internet 2003, ICWI 2003*, pages 411–418, Algarve, Portugal, 5-8 Novembro 2003. IADIS.

The University of Glasgow at CLEF 2004: French Monolingual Information Retrieval with Terrier

Christina Lioma, Ben He, Vassilis Plachouras, and Iadh Ounis

Department of Computing Science,
University of Glasgow,
Glasgow G12 8QQ,
United Kingdom
{xristina, ben, vassilis, ounis}@dcs.gla.ac.uk

Abstract. This paper describes our participation in the CLEF 2004 French monolingual task. We used our Information Retrieval platform, Terrier, and experimented with query expansion and query length normalisation.

1 Introduction

Terrier (http://ir.dcs.gla.ac.uk/terrier) is a platform for the rapid development of large-scale Information Retrieval (IR) applications. It is based on a framework for deriving non-parametric probabilistic models for IR. The framework deploys more than 50 Divergence from Randomness (DFR) models for document weighting [1]. The document weighting models are derived by measuring the divergence of the actual term distribution from that obtained under a random process. Terrier was demonstrated to be highly effective at retrieving Web documents at the recent TREC-11 and TREC-12, and is currently available as the search engine of the Web site of the Department of Computing Science at the University of Glasgow (http://www.dcs.gla.ac.uk/search).

In this paper, we report on our participation in the French Monolingual task. Our main aim was to test to which extent our existing English monolingual Terrier retrieval system could perform French retrieval, simply by changing the stemmer and stopword list from English into French. We chose French in order to test our system on new unfamiliar grounds. We opted for minimal language-specific normalisation changes, namely the use of a French stemmer and stopword list, and chose to exclude other performance enhancing options, such as POS-taggers and morphological analysers. Our secondary aim was to continue and complement our earlier work (TREC-11, TREC-12) on studying the effect of length normalisation on the retrieval performance, through the investigation of its impact on French IR. The outcome of this experimentation has been put to practical use, as we have merged our existing English and French monolingual retrieval systems into one. Some unofficial results on our bilingual runs are briefly presented here.

This paper is organised as follows. Section 2 presents a brief overview of the retrieval approaches adopted for our participation in CLEF 2004. Section 3 presents our official retrieval runs for the French monolingual task and our English-French

C. Peters et al. (Eds.): CLEF 2004, LNCS 3491, pp. 253–259, 2005.

unofficial runs. Section 4 analyses the obtained results, along with a further series of unofficial runs for the said tasks. Section 5 concludes with a brief summary of our participation in CLEF 2004 and the direction of our future research work.

2 System Setup

The following preprocessing steps were applied both to documents and queries. All input was tokenized. Punctuation marks and numbers of more than 4 digits were omitted. Proper nouns, abbreviations, acronyms, multi word units and compounds were not extracted or processed. Accents were preserved. We used the standard French stopword list, which is available with the Snowball stemming algorithm for French [5]. We did not eliminate topic-specific phrases such as "Les documents pertinents devront mentionner/parler de/donner des details sur..." from the queries. We did not use a stop stem list, as we used the stopword list before the stemming stage. We used the French stemmer from the Snowball family of stemmers, developed by Martin Porter [5]. The stemmer stripped affixes from the index words in a specific order and applied repair strategies, where applicable, in order to reduce the input into clusters of words sharing the same stem.

We experimented with the PL2 weighting model, one of Terrier's DFR-based document weighting models. Using the PL2 model, the relevance score of a document d for a query q is given by:

$$\sum_{t \in q} qtf \cdot w(t,d)$$

where

- qtf is the frequency of term t in the query q,
- $w(t,d)$ is the relevance score of a document d for the query term t, given by:

$$w(t,d) = (tfn \cdot \log_2 \frac{tfn}{\lambda} + \left(\lambda + \frac{1}{12 \cdot tfn} - tfn\right) \cdot \log_2 e + 0.5 \cdot \log_2(2\pi \cdot tfn)) \cdot \frac{1}{tfn+1}$$

where

- λ is the mean and variance of a Poisson distribution. λ is given by $\frac{F}{N}$, $(F \ll N)$, where F is the term frequency of the term t in the whole collection and N is the number of documents in the collection.

- tfn is the normalised within-document frequency of the term t in the document d. It is given by the normalisation 2 [1, 3]:

$$tfn = tf \cdot \log_2(1 + c \cdot \frac{avg\_l}{l}), (c > 0)$$

where

- c is a parameter.
- tf is the within-document frequency of the term t in the document d.
- l is the document length and avg_l is the average document length in the whole collection.

We estimated the parameter c of the normalisation 2 by measuring the normalisation effect on the term frequency distribution with respect to the document length distribution [4]. More specifically, our tuning approach automatically adjusted the parameter c to a value dependent on the topic fields used. For the runs submitted to CLEF 2004, we obtained the following values: c=4.83 for short queries (only Title field was used), c=1.56 for long queries (all three fields were used), c=3.1 for queries using the Title and Description fields, and c=2.6 for queries using the Title and Narrative fields.

We have also used a query expansion mechanism, which follows the idea of measuring divergence from randomness. The approach can be seen as a generalisation of the approach used by Carpineto and Romano in which they applied the Kullback-Leibler (KL) divergence to the un-expanded version of BM25 [2, 3]. In our experiments, we applied the KL model for query expansion. It is one of the Terrier DFR-based term weighting models. Using the KL model, the weight of a term t in the *#documents* top-ranked documents is given by:

$$w(t) = P_x \cdot \log_2 \frac{P_x}{P_c}$$

In the above formula,

$$P_x = \frac{tf_x}{l_x}$$

and

$$P_c = \frac{F}{token_c},$$

where tf_x is the frequency of the query term in the top-ranked documents. l_x is the sum of the length of the *#documents* top-ranked documents, and *#documents* is a parameter of the query expansion methodology. F is the term frequency of the query term in the whole collection. $token_c$ is the total number of tokens in the whole collection.

For short queries, we extracted the 10 most informative terms from the top 3 retrieved documents as the expanded terms. For long queries, we extracted the 100 most informative terms from the top 25 retrieved documents as the expanded terms. For queries using the Title and Description fields we extracted the 10 most informative terms from the top 15 retrieved documents, and for queries using the Title and Narrative fields we extracted the top 15 informative terms from the top 3 retrieved documents. We added these terms to the query and repeated the retrieval stage.

3 Runs

This section presents our French monolingual retrieval runs submitted to CLEF 2004, and additional French monolingual and English-French bilingual runs. We realised our runs on the CLEF 2004 document collection for the French monolingual ad-hoc task, which consists of 90,261 newswire and newspaper articles published in 1995

(42,615 SDA and 47,646 Le Monde). There were 50 test topics. We submitted a total of 4 runs for the French monolingual task (Table 1), namely UOGLQ, UOGSQ, UOGLQQE, and UOGSQQE. The second column gives information on the topic fields selected for each run, namely T[itle], D[escription] and N[arrative]. The last column clarifies which runs used query expansion and which did not.

Table 1. Runs submitted to the CLEF 2004 French Monolingual task

Run id	*Topic fields*	*Query Expansion*
UOGLQ	TDN	No
UOGSQ	T	No
UOGLQQE	TDN	Yes
UOGSQQE	T	Yes

In addition to the above runs, we also undertook further experiments, in order to test additional query length and query expansion settings. Specifically, we varied the number of expanded terms and the number of top retrieved documents used, both on French monolingual and on English-French bilingual retrieval. In the case of English-French bilingual runs, we manually translated the French queries into English, since we did not have the corresponding CLEF English queries available at the time. We then used the freely available Babelfish machine translation technology [6] to convert our English queries to French, and repeated the procedure described above in order to retrieve relevant documents from the French collection only.

4 Results

This section summarises and discusses the results of our CLEF 2004 participation and of our additional runs. Table 2 reports the main settings and scores of our collective runs. The submitted runs are in boldface. The second column presents the topic fields

Table 2. Overview of our collective runs for CLEF 2004. Submitted runs are in boldface

Run id	*Topic Fields*	*c*	*MAP French*	*MAP English-French*
UOGSQ	**T**	**4.83**	**0.4237**	0.3456
UOGSQQE	**T**	**4.83**	**0.3400**	0.2754
UOGTD	TD	3.1	0.4485	0.3770
UOGTDQE	TD	3.1	0.4222	0.3425
UOGTN	TN	2.6	0.4431	0.3698
UOGTNQE	TN	2.6	0.3711	0.3024
UOGLQ	**TDN**	**1.56**	**0.4244**	0.3867
UOGLQQE	**TDN**	**1.56**	**0.4186**	0.3339

used for each run. The last two columns present the Mean Average Precision (*MAP*) figures achieved for French and for English-French retrieval accordingly.

The best French monolingual run was the one combining the topic fields of Title and Description (UOGTD), which slightly exceeded our best submitted run (UOGLQ). The best English-French bilingual run was the one combining the fields of Title, Description and Narrative. Overall, query length had little impact on the performance of the runs (*MAP* varied from 0.4237 to 0.4485 for French, and from 0.3456 to 0.3867 for English-French). It should be noted that the English-French retrieval performance of our system is highly correlated with the French monolingual retrieval performance. The rank correlation coefficient of the two lists of *MAP* values is R = 0.9286, with a p-value of 0.002232. This shows that Terrier has performed consistently.

Table 3. Query expansion deteriorated the retrieval performance independently of the query length

Run id	*c*	*#terms/ #documents*	*MAP French*
UOGSQQE	**4.83**	**10/3**	**0.3400**
UOGTDQE	3.1	10/15	0.4222
UOGTNQE	2.6	15/3	0.3711
UOGLQQE	**1.56**	**100/25**	**0.4186**

Table 4. Overview of our collective runs varying expanded terms (*#terms*)/top retrieved documents (*#docs*). Submitted runs are in boldface

Official Runs				*Unofficial Runs*			
Run id	*c*	*#terms/ #docs*	*MAP*	*Run id*	*c*	*#terms/ #docs*	*MAP*
UOGSQQE	4.83	10/2	0.2876	UOGTDQE	3.1	50/3	0.3574
UOGSQQE	**4.83**	**10/3**	**0.3400**	UOGTDQE	3.1	20/3	0.4021
UOGSQQE	4.83	10/5	0.2998	UOGTDQE	3.1	10/3	0.4098
UOGSQQE	4.83	10/10	0.3113	UOGTDQE	3.1	10/10	0.4106
UOGSQQE	4.83	10/15	0.2981	UOGTDQE	3.1	15/10	0.3993
UOGSQQE	4.83	15/10	0.2780	UOGTDQE	3.1	10/13	0.4114
UOGSQQE	4.83	20/10	0.2882	UOGTDQE	3.1	10/15	0.3971
UOGLQQE	1.56	100/10	0.3745	UOGTNQE	2.6	10/2	0.3475
UOGLQQE	1.56	100/15	0.3889	UOGTNQE	2.6	10/3	0.3661
UOGLQQE	1.56	100/20	0.4088	UOGTNQE	2.6	10/10	0.3514
UOGLQQE	**1.56**	**100/25**	**0.4186**	UOGTNQE	2.6	15/3	0.3711
UOGLQQE	1.56	90/25	0.3550	UOGTNQE	2.6	20/3	0.3698
UOGLQQE	1.56	80/25	0.3401	UOGTNQE	2.6	50/3	0.3291
UOGLQQE	1.56	70/25	0.3228	UOGTNQE	2.6	100/25	0.2983

In general, query expansion decreased the mean average precision of all the runs (see Table 2). Table 3 shows that query expansion does not work, independently of the length of the query.

In order to analyse the low performance of query expansion, we ran additional experiments with query expansion varying the number of expanded terms (*#terms*) and the number of top retrieved documents used (*#documents*) compared to the setting mentioned in Section 2. Table 4 shows the effect of that parameter tuning on the performance of the system. Overall, query expansion deteriorated performance, independently of the parameters used. The parameter settings in the official submitted runs were actually the optimal ones.

Finally, subsequent experiments revealed that the parameter *c* of the normalisation, which was estimated by our tuning approach automatically (see Section 2), was indeed optimal (see Table 5). This shows that the parameter tuning approach for term frequency normalisation [4] which we adopted is robust and efficient, performing as well on both French and English document collections [4].

Table 5. Overview of our collective runs varying the *c* value. Submitted runs are in boldface

Official Runs			*Unofficial Runs*		
Run id	*c*	*MAP*	*Run id*	*c*	*MAP*
UOGSQ	4.0	0.4222	UOGTD	2.5	0.4454
UOGSQ	4.50	0.4232	UOGTD	3.0	0.4442
UOGSQ	**4.83**	**0.4237**	UOGTD	3.1	0.4485
UOGSQ	5.0	0.4231	UOGTD	3.5	0.4481
UOGSQ	5.5	0.4199	UOGTD	4.0	0.4480
UOGLQ	1.0	0.4173	UOGTN	2.0	0.4425
UOGLQ	1.25	0.4227	UOGTN	2.5	0.4427
UOGLQ	**1.56**	**0.4244**	UOGTN	2.6	0.4431
UOGLQ	2.0	0.4240	UOGTN	3.0	0.4430
UOGLQ	2.5	0.4239	UOGTN	3.5	0.4422

5 Conclusions and Future Work

This paper presented a French monolingual IR system and an English-French bilingual IR system, both of which were developed at the University of Glasgow. The French monolingual IR system was evaluated in the French monolingual ad-hoc track of CLEF 2004.

The experiments on which we briefly reported indicated the following. Our existing Terrier retrieval platform was shown to be truly modular, as it was extended to perform French monolingual IR successfully, simply by changing the stemming and stopword components from English into French, therefore with a very low overhead. Moreover, we found that query expansion performed poorly, which is in agreement with a number of other retrieval systems participating at CLEF 2004, thus indicating that the specific data collection may be partly responsible for the bad performance of query expansion. We have now merged our French and English monolingual retrieval systems into a single bilingual retrieval platform. We are currently working towards improving and enhancing this bilingual platform, the performance of which will be tested in the CLEF 2005 multilingual track.

Acknowledgments

This project is funded by a UK Engineering and Physical Sciences Research Council (EPSRC) grant, number GR/R90543/01. The project funds the development of the Terrier Information Retrieval framework (http://www.ir.dcs.gla.ac.uk/terrier).

References

[1] G. Amati and C. J. van Rijsbergen. Probabilistic models of information retrieval based on measuring the divergence from randomness. ACM Transactions on Information Systems (TOIS), volume 20(4), pages 357-389, October 2002.
[2] C. Carpineto, R. de Mori, G. Romano, and B. Bigi. An information-theoretic approach to automatic query expansion. ACM Transactions on Information Systems (TOIS), 19(1), pages 1-27, January 2001.
[3] G. Amati. Probability Models for Information Retrieval based on Divergence from Randomness. Thesis of the degree of Doctor of Philosophy, Department of Computing Science, University of Glasgow, June 2003.
[4] B. He and I. Ounis. A study of parameter tuning for term frequency normalization. Proceedings of the Twelfth ACM CIKM International Conference on Information and Knowledge Management (CIKM), pages 10-16, New Orleans, LA, November 2003.
[5] http://www.snowball.tartarus.org/
[6] http://www.babelfish.altavista.com/

The Domain-Specific Track in CLEF 2004: Overview of the Results and Remarks on the Assessment Process

Michael Kluck

Informationszentrum Sozialwissenschaften (IZ) Bonn/Berlin,
Research and Development, Schiffbauerdamm 19, 10117 Berlin, Germany
kluck@bonn.iz-soz.de

Abstract. An overview of the research teams participating in the domain-specific track in CLEF 2004 and their runs is given together with a summary of approaches and results. The assessment procedure is also described and the problem of diverging judgments between the assessors is discussed. Some considerations for future research are made.

1 The Domain-Specific Track with GIRT in the CLEF 2004 Campaign

The track was called "Mono- and Cross-Language Information Retrieval on Structured Scientific Data (GIRT)". The underlying rationale was to study cross language information retrieval (CLIR) in a domain-specific context[1] using the GIRT4 German/English social science database. GIRT4 data is offered as pseudo-parallel German and English corpora. In addition multilingual controlled vocabularies (German-English, German-Russian) were made available. Monolingual and cross-language tasks were offered, and topics were available in English, German and Russian.[2]

1.1 A Short Overview of the "History" of the GIRT Corpora

The GIRT corpora have been changed over time, as shown in Table 1. The main changes refer to the size, the scope of the content, and the mixture or division of the text languages[3]. In the beginning the documents only contained German text, later English portions were added to many of the documents. Finally we separated German and English elements, reconstructed the original documents in German, and created (nearly) identical documents in English.

Thus, although the source GIRT data is German, the titles, abstracts or content descriptions and descriptors of most of the recent documents have been translated into English, making international access easier. The GIRT corpus is formed by an integrated database consisting of extracts of whole documents (which have additional

[1] See [1] for the rationale and for a description of the GIRT3 data.

[2] See the CLEF homepage at http://www.clef-campaign.org under CLEF 2004.

[3] The full chronicle is given in [2] including detailed descriptions of each GIRT version and all evaluation campaigns where GIRT data has been used. A more extensive version in German is presented in [3].

C. Peters et al. (Eds.): CLEF 2004, LNCS 3491, pp. 260 – 270, 2005.

information elements) derived from the SOLIS (social science literature) and FORIS (current research in the field of social sciences) databases that are built by IZ[4].

Table 1. German Indexing and Retrieval Testdatabase (GIRT) containing German social science data

Year	*Corpus Name*	*Number of Documents Language*	*Campaign*
1997	GIRT1	13.000 documents DE	internal tests
1998-1999	GIRT2	38.000 documents DE/EN	TREC
2000-2002	GIRT3	76.000 documents DE/EN	CLEF
2003-2005	GIRT4	151.319 documents DE + 151.319 documents EN	CLEF

The presentation of the pseudo-parallel corpora of GIRT aimed at extending the possibilities of multilingual retrieval on the domain-specific data.

1.2 The Main Characteristics of the Pseudo-Parallel GIRT-4 Corpora

All GIRT corpora contain well-structured social science data. All different versions of GIRT include the following attributes extracted from the original documents: author, title, document language, publication year. Additionally, for all documents, intellectually assigned descriptors (indexing terms) from the Thesaurus for the Social Sciences plus classifiers (classifying texts) from a social science classification scheme are provided. Detailed information on the specific variants of the GIRT corpus is given in a technical report of IZ [3].

GIRT4 has been divided into two language-distinct corpora: German (GIRT4-DE) and English (GIRT4-EN). The number of documents in each collection is 151,319 records; these are identical with respect to their contents. Each document included in the GIRT4 data has a corresponding title in German and English: this was the criterion for inclusion. The resulting GIRT4 corpus consists of 151,319 single documents in 2 languages:

- Original documents in German,
- Translations of these documents into English.

Translations have mostly been done by human translators from the social science domain, who are native English speakers. Some abstracts have been machine-translated with Systran.

The GIRT4 collections are called pseudo-parallel, because the English variant is mainly the result of translations, there are no English source documents, and the English part comprises essentially less text, as not all documents have a translation of German language abstracts. Occasionally, the English text is longer than the German one. Due to the lack of translations in some cases the distribution of text elements differs between the German and the English parts. The difference is mainly caused by

[4] IZ = Informationszentrum Sozialwissenschaften (Social Science Information Centre), Bonn / Berlin www.gesis.org/en/iz/index.html

the lack of translated abstracts (short texts, summaries). Only 15 % of the English documents have an abstract. However, there is an equal distribution in both parts of the title fields, the controlled indexing terms, and the classification texts. All documents have a title, about ten indexing terms, and approximately two classification texts per document.

To sum up: the English part of GIRT4 has less text, which in some cases makes it more difficult to retrieve relevant documents form the English side.

1.3 The GIRT Task and Sub-tasks in the CLEF 2004 Campaign

There were several GIRT sub-tasks in CLEF 2004. These reflected the fact that we had two language-distinct corpora and a related German thesaurus with translations in English and Russian. Thus, we offered German, English and Russian as topic languages, and German and English as target collections. The tasks were:

- Monolingual Task
  - German topics against German target data
  - English topics against English target data
- Bilingual Task
  - English or Russian topics against German target data
  - German or Russian topics against English target data

For all GIRT experiments we provided additional instruments, derived from our Thesaurus for the Social Sciences [4]. The machine-readable German-English thesaurus that was provided for GIRT in CLEF contains the following elements: German descriptors with broader and narrower terms and related terms, German non-descriptors (i.e. synonyms of descriptors that are not allowed to be used for indexing) and the respective English translations for all descriptors and most of the non-descriptors. The machine-readable German-Russian term list is taken from the respective German-English-Russian thesaurus [5] and provides the Russian equivalents for German descriptors, but no information on the thesaurus structure. To map the Cyrillic character set, this term list has been encoded in UTF-8.

2 Participating Research Groups and Their Runs

Over the years, the GIRT task has never shown a high participation, ranging from a low of one group in 2001 to a high of five participants in 2002. However, the number of officially submitted runs and of executed subtasks has generally increased and the participating groups have also performed additional unofficial runs, not only in order to re-run faulty runs, but also to perform further experiments or variants of experiments.

Four research groups participated in CLEF 2004, three from academia, and one from industry:

- Berkeley, University of California (USA)
- University of Hagen (Germany)
- IRIT, University of Toulouse (France)
- Ricoh (Japan)

Table 2. Number of Participants and Runs in GIRT Tasks

Year	*Campaign*	*Participants*	*Runs*	
				from these: ***Bilingual Runs***
1998/1999	TREC	2		
2000	CLEF	3	7	5
2001	CLEF	1	4	3
2002	CLEF	5	17	8
2003	CLEF	4	22	5
2004	CLEF	4	31	16

The GIRT4 data gave various possibilities of combining topic and target languages. These combinations have been used in different ways in CLEF 2003 and 2004. Russian was not used as topic language in 2004. The total number of runs, especially of bilingual runs, increased from 2003 to 2004.

Table 3. GIRT Sub-tasks and Runs in CLEF 2004 and 2003

Data	**Topic language**	**Judged Runs 2004**		**Judged Runs 2003**	
		monolingual	***bilingual***	***monolingual***	***bilingual***
GIRT4 DE	DE	8		13	
GIRT4 EN	EN	7		4	
GIRT4 DE	EN		6		1
GIRT4 DE	RU		0		2
GIRT4 EN	DE		10		1
GIRT4 EN	RU		0		1
Sum		15	16	17	5
		31		22	

3 Main Approaches and Some Results of GIRT Participants in CLEF 2004

The preliminary results of the CLEF 2004 campaign and its related workshop held in Bath in September are reported at the CLEF homepage [3], which also includes the first reports of the GIRT sub-task. This volume contains the revised papers reporting the results of the GIRT 2004 experiments in more detail.

The University of Hagen (Germany) applied natural language processing methods to process queries and documents [6]. The queries were transformed into a meaningful knowledge-rich representation called multilayered extended semantic network (MultiNet). MultiNet creates concepts and semantic relations and functions between them. A syntactic-semantic parser was used to pre-process queries and to parse the documents. The queries were transformed into an intermediate representation named database independent query representation (DIQR), which is the result of a rule-based transformation of the semantic network representation. Three different methods were employed to index the GIRT-DE collection: 1. indexing full word forms, 2. indexing concepts, 3. indexing semantic networks. For the bilingual German-English experiments, a combination of a concept translation lexicon and a translation wordlist was used to find semantically related words in the target language for a given concept in the source language. Different resources such as EuroWordNet and several online dictionaries were deployed. Five runs were submitted for both monolingual GIRT-DE and bilingual GIRT EN-DE.

IRIT/University of Toulouse (France) applied their retrieval system to the social science domain [7]. This system is based on a connectionist approach and modelled by a tree-layered network (with query layer, term layer, document layer). The query processing was based on WordNet and made use of two methods: 1. concept detection and weighting from queries, 2. disambiguation-expansion by expanding a query with its closest synset from WordNet. Five runs were submitted for the monolingual GIRT-EN corpus.

Ricoh's software research and development group (Japan) applied a probabilistic retrieval model with query expansion using pseudo-relevance feedback [8]. They used a morphological analyser for word decompounding and parallel corpora for cross-lingual information retrieval. Two official runs were submitted: monolingual German and bilingual English-German.

The University of California at Berkeley (USA) applied their well-known technique of logistic regression to the retrieval [9]. This year they tested their Entry Vocabulary Module and thesaurus matching method. The Entry Vocabulary Module is conceived as intermediary between natural language queries and the metadata "language" of a document repository supporting the search with the "correct" (most adequate) controlled vocabulary terms (in this case from the GIRT Thesaurus for the Social Sciences). Thesaurus matching is a translation technique where the query is split into words and phrases; these are then looked up in the thesaurus, and finally substituted with the target language terms from the thesaurus. For the monolingual task five runs were submitted: 3 German, 2 English, for the bilingual task 10 runs: 5 each for English-German and German-English.

A comparison of some of the results is shown below in Figure 1: the results of the top performing groups for German topics against German target data (GIRT to DE; Recall-Precision Graph) and for English topics against English target data (GIRT to EN; Recall-Precision Graph) are given.[5]

4 Relevance Assessment

The CLEF 2004 campaign offered 25 topics for the GIRT task. The topics were developed in German, and then translated into English and Russian. The pool of retrieved documents for 25 topics was 18,292, this are on average 732 documents per topic[6]. For GIRT4 as a whole (German and English) there was no topic without any

[5] From Appendix A – Run Statistics, p. 12 see www.clef-campaign.org under CLEF 2004 – Working Notes - Volume II Appendices - Results for CLEF 2004 Campaign.

[6] In CLEF 2003 we had 17,031 documents in the pool. Thus, again in 2004 we had an increase in documents to be assessed (+ 7%).

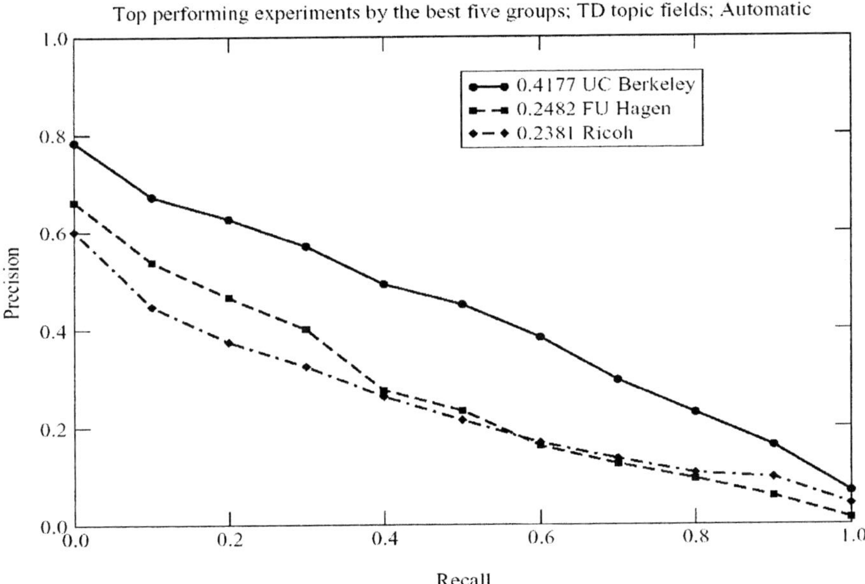

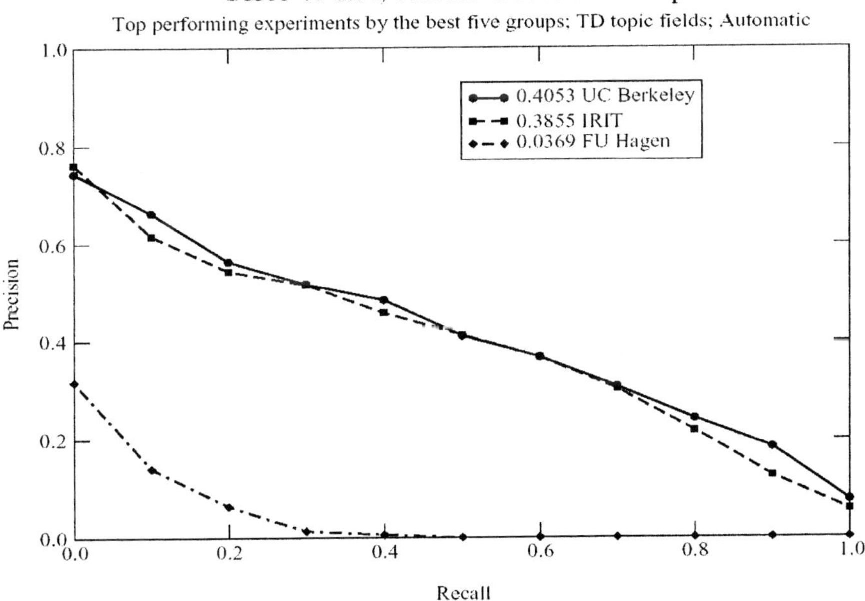

Fig. 1. Recall-Precision Graphs for best performing groups: DE topics to GIRT-DE (top graph) and EN topics to GIRT-EN (bottom graph)

retrieved document. The mean ratio of hits judged as relevant was 15.84 % (n = 116), with a minimum at 0.60 % (n = 3) and a maximum of 56.77 % (n = 232).

4.1 Relevance Assessment for the Pseudo-Parallel GIRT-Corpus

Looking at the different parts of GIRT-4, we discovered that 53 % of the retrieved documents were in GIRT4-DE and 47 % in GIRT4-EN. The search results in the different language parts were not congruent: Only for two topics (number 102, 118) was there an equal number of returned documents in both language parts, in all other cases the numbers were different, although theoretically they should have been the same. But even in the cases of equal numbers of retrieved documents, these documents were not identical.

At this stage we will have to explain our underlying reasoning in more detail: Supposed a system is doing the following runs: monolingual DE-DE, bilingual EN-DE, monolingual EN-EN, bilingual DE-EN, we would treat the monolingual runs as baselines and expect the bilingual runs for the same target language to be less effective (because of the bilinguality and the translations problems). But we also would expect that the monolingual runs DE and (!) EN would be nearly of the same quality. These runs should not only retrieve the same ratio of relevant documents, but also the identical ones (!), which indeed is a higher degree of quality. For the bilingual runs the systems should also deliver the identical documents (even if they later are judged relevant or irrelevant), although their number might be less than for the respective monolingual run. In our case of a parallel corpus with identical source documents we are able to make the respective comparisons.

As we did not get in all cases the identical documents as resulting retrieved documents, the fraction of identical pairs of documents was drastically lower than the optimum. In the whole pool of retrieved documents only 10 % of them show pairs of corresponding relevant documents German / English, and only 16 % of the retrieved documents show pairs of non-relevant documents German / English. That means the overall overlap of German / English retrieved documents (relevant and non-relevant) is 26 %. One reason might be that we had nearly the same number of monolingual runs (15) as bilingual ones (16), and this fact caused a different distribution of retrieved documents in the German and English part of the pooled GIRT4 results. But on the other hand we had nearly the same number of monolingual German runs (8) as monolingual English runs (7), and this fact should level out the skewness between the mono- and bilingual results.

The assessment was done by two assessors, one for the German part and the other for the English part of GIRT4. When in doubt about the contents or meaning of a certain topic they discussed the interpretation of the narrative attached to the respective topic. During assessment new aspects or facets of a certain query may evolve and influence the final relevance decision, thus, it sometimes becomes necessary to rediscuss the topic meaning.

For the German part we achieved an average of 17.08 % of retrieved documents judged as actually relevant (average n = 67) with a minimum at 0.79 % (n = 3) and a maximum of 64.27 % (n = 232). For the English part these figures were lower: an average 14.43 % (average n = 49) with a minimum of zero and a maximum of

55.14 % (n = 193). Unfortunately in no case was the theoretical optimum of equal numbers of relevant retrieved documents achieved for a single topic.

In the first run of the assessment the assessors also reported their impression of the clarity or vagueness of the topic with respect to the assessment. A clear topic will have distinct phrases and terminology on which to base the relevance decision. Vague topics contain imprecise or ambiguous terminology or many possible combinations with other areas of meaning, which are not related to the actual topic.

4.2 Re-assessment of Diverging Relevance Decisions

Our experience in the last year's campaign was that sometimes judgments differed for the same document in the different language parts, even when the assessment was done by the very same assessor [10]. In the CLEF 2003 campaign 171 out of 17,025 documents were reassessed which was 1% of all assessed documents.[7] We decided for the CLEF 2004 campaign to compare the assessments of the two language parts and then, in the case of diverging judgments, we reassessed the documents. At the same time we noted the probable reasons for the divergence of the assessments.

Unlike 2003 these re-assessed documents were included in the official statistics that were delivered to the participants as results.[8]

In 1.86 % cases (n = 340) we discovered diverging judgments for corresponding German and English documents. The re-assessment of these documents showed 35 %

Table 4. Problematic Cases in Reassessment

Case	Case description	Decision	N	%
TE	Very short English text, insufficient information within the title, but hints given by controlled terms	DE=EN=yes, change of EN into yes	52	15.29
TEX	Very short English text and insufficient information within the title, controlled terms not sufficient, but some significant words showed up within the German abstract	DE=yes, EN=no, no change, leave different judgments as they are	12	3.53
TDX	Very short German text and insufficient information within the title, controlled terms not sufficient, but some significant words showed up within the English abstract	DE=no, EN=yes, no change, leave different judgments as they are	7	2.06
DE	Wrong prior judgment, because significant terms are present either as controlled terms or within the German abstract	DE=yes, change of DE into yes	62	18.24
EN	Wrong prior judgment, because significant terms are present either as controlled terms or within the English abstract	EN=yes, change of EN into yes	58	17.06
DEA	Wrong prior judgment, because of different or changed interpretation of the contents	DE=yes, change of DE into yes	104	30.59
ENA	Wrong prior judgment, because of different or changed interpretation of the contents	EN=yes, change of EN into yes	45	13.24
		sum	340	100.00

[7] This article [10] reports on the re-assessments of the CLEF 2003 campaign (which there was wrongly indicated as 2004)

[8] In the CLEF 2003 campaign we also carried out the re-assessment, but we were not able to deliver these re-assessments in time for inclusion into the official figures.

real mistakes (n = 120; DE + EN), 44 % new interpretation of relevance (n = 201; DEA + ENA + TE), 21 % too short text for equal judgment (n = 19; TEX + TDX).

The reassessment became necessary for 340 documents, which means for 1.86 % of all documents. We have analyzed these problematic cases in depth and categorized them in the following way.

Table 5. Changes per Topic

Topic number	N retrieved documents	X changes	X / N in %	Impression during judgment
101	662	1	0.002	Clear topic
102	558	8	0.014	Clear topic
103	920	15	0.016	Vague topic
104	701	28	0.040	Clear topic
105	711	27	0.038	Clear topic
106	684	5	0.007	Clear topic
107	985	10	0.010	Vague topic
108	506	41	0.081	Clear topic
109	867	18	0.021	Clear topic
110	659	15	0.023	Clear topic
111	667	11	0.016	Vague topic
112	748	0	0.000	Clear topic
113	652	20	0.030	Vague topic
114	919	16	0.017	Clear topic
115	581	1	0.002	Clear topic
116	952	2	0.002	Clear topic
117	666	2	0.003	Clear topic
118	756	31	0.041	Vague topic
119	685	2	0.003	Clear topic
120	775	18	0.023	Vague topic
121	889	36	0.040	Clear topic
122	826	12	0.015	Clear topic
123	1,006	2	0.002	Vague topic
124	438	10	0.023	Clear topic
125	479	9	0.019	Vague topic
sum	18,292	340		
average	732	13.60	0.019	

The changes resulted for 211 cases in reassessing the document as relevant (yes), and for 117 cases in reassessing them as irrelevant (no). But 12 cases remained unchanged with different judgments of retrieved documents in the different language parts because the documents themselves really did not allow making congruent judgments. Finally, there is no evidence for a correlation of the "impression during judgment" with the actual amount of changes.

If you look at the topic 108, which has the most frequent changes of judgments, you can go into depth and you see 41 reassessments caused by the following reasons:

Table 6. Re-assessment Reasons for Topic 108

N	Reason
7	DE
13	DEA
14	EN
4	ENA
3	TE
0	TEX
0	TDX

For this topic in 17 cases there was a new interpretation of relevance after discussion among the assessors (DEA, ENA). In 3 cases there could have been a better (positive) decision in the English part, as the descriptors gave sufficient hints (TE). In 21 cases there was a wrong interpretation of relevance (DE, EN). No cases occurred where the English (or German) text was very short and not sufficient, even when the controlled terms gave insufficient information for a positive decision on relevance, additional information was given in the abstract, thus the systems could have derived a positive decision from that (TEX, TDX).

One remaining problem (which occurred more often for other topics) was that the reduced extent of text in the English part made judgments more difficult or vague (because of the lack of extended information which is mainly carried by the abstracts).

5 Further Research Questions

We have kept the concordance of document numbers of identical documents in GIRT4-DE and GIRT4-EN, this is available for further in-depth research on specific topics and certain retrieval strategies. The concordance allows a post-experiment analysis of results in both language parts. We would like to work together with the participants to analyze the following aspects:

- failure in delivering the corresponding document pairs DE/EN for bilingual runs
- failure in delivering known relevant documents for monolingual runs.

Acknowledgments

Marco Winter (graduate student of Humboldt-University at Berlin) gave much support to the hard work of assessment and to the calculation of data on the assessment and the re-assessment.

References

1. Kluck, M., Gey, F.C.: The Domain-Specific Task of CLEF – Specific Evaluation Strategies in Cross-Language Information Retrieval. In: Carol Peters (ed.): Cross-Language Information Retrieval and Evaluation. Workshop of Cross-Language Evaluation Forum, CLEF 2000, Lisbon, Portugal, September 21-22, 2000, Revised Papers. Berlin: Springer, 48-56, (2001)

2. Kluck, M.: The GIRT Data in the Evaluation of CLIR Systems – from 1997 until 2003. In: Peters, C., Gonzalo, J., Braschler, M., Kluck, M. (eds.): Comparative Evaluation of Multilingual Information Access Systems. 4th Workshop of the Cross-Language Evaluation Forum, CLEF 2003, Trondheim, Norway, August 21-22, 2003, Revised Selected Papers. Lecture Notes in Computer Science, Vol. 3237. Springer-Verlag Berlin Heidelberg New York, 379-393, (2004)
3. Kluck, M.: Die Evaluation von Cross-Language-Retrieval-Systemen mit Hilfe der GIRT-Daten des IZ. Ein Bericht über die Entwicklung im Zeitraum von 1997 bis 2003. Informationszentrum Sozialwissenschaften, Bonn (2003)
4. Schott, H. (Ed.): Thesaurus Sozialwissenschaften – Thesaurus for the Social Sciences [Aus-gabe – Edition] 1999. [Bd. 1:] Deutsch-Englisch – German-English, [Bd. 2] Englisch-Deutsch – English-German. Bonn: Informationszentrum Sozialwissenschaften (1999)
5. Basarnova, S., Magaj, H., Mdivani, R., Schott, H., Sucker, D. (eds.): Thesaurus Sozialwissenschaften Bd.1: Deutsch-Englisch-Russisch, Bd. 2: Russisch-Deutsch-Englisch, Bd. 3: Register. Bonn/Moskau: Informationszentrum Sozialwissenschaften / Institut für wissenschaftliche Information in den Gesellschaftswissenschaften (INION RadW) (1997)
6. Leveling, J.; Hartrumpf, S.: University of Hagen at CLEF 2004: Indexing and Translating Concepts for the GIRT Task. (this volume) (2005)
7. Baziz, M.; Boughanem, M.; Aussenac-Gilles, N.: IRIT at CLEF 2004: The English GIRT Task. (this volume) (2005)
8. Kojima, Y.: Ricoh at CLEF 2004. (this volume) (2005)
9. Petras, V.: GIRT and the Use of Subject Metadata for Retrieval. (this volume) (2005)
10. Kluck, M.: Evaluation of Cross-Language Information Retrieval Using the Domain-Specific GIRT Data as Parallel Corpus. In: Proceedings of the Fourth International Conference on Language Resources and Evaluation, LREC 2004, Lisbon – Portugal, 26 May - 28 May 2004. Paris: ELRA – European Language Resources Association, Vol. IV, 1343-1346 (2004)

University of Hagen at CLEF 2004: Indexing and Translating Concepts for the GIRT Task

Johannes Leveling and Sven Hartrumpf

Intelligent Information and Communication Systems,
University of Hagen (FernUniversität in Hagen),
58084 Hagen, Germany
{Johannes.Leveling, Sven.Hartrumpf}@fernuni-hagen.de

Abstract. This paper describes the second participation of the University of Hagen in the German Indexing and Retrieval Test (GIRT) task of the CLEF 2004 evaluation campaign with both monolingual and bilingual information retrieval experiments. For monolingual experiments with the German document collection, the focus is on applying and comparing three indexing methods targeting word forms, disambiguated concepts, and extended semantic networks. The bilingual experiments for retrieving English documents for German topics rely on translating and expanding query terms based on ranking semantically related English terms for a German concept. English translations are compiled from heterogeneous resources, including multilingual lexicons such as EuroWordNet and dictionaries available online.

1 Introduction

This paper investigates the performance of different indexing methods and automated retrieval strategies for the participation of the University of Hagen in the evaluation campaign of the Cross Language Evaluation Forum (CLEF) 2004. In 2003, retrieval strategies based on generating query variants for a natural language (NL) query were compared [1]. The result of our best experiment in 2003 with respect to mean average precision (MAP) was 0.2064 for a run using both topic title and description.

Before presenting the approaches and results for monolingual and bilingual retrieval experiments with the GIRT documents (German Indexing and Retrieval Test database, see [2]) in separate sections, a short overview of the analysis and transformation of natural language queries and documents is given. Natural language processing (NLP) as described in the following subsections is part of query processing for the NLI-Z39.50[1] [3], a natural language interface for databases

[1] The NLI-Z39.50 is being developed as part of the project "Natürlichsprachliches Interface für die internationale Standardschnittstelle Z39.50" and funded by the DFG (Deutsche Forschungsgemeinschaft) within the support program for libraries "Modernisierung und Rationalisierung in wissenschaftlichen Bibliotheken".

C. Peters et al. (Eds.): CLEF 2004, LNCS 3491, pp. 271–282, 2005.

supporting the Internet protocol Z39.50. The major part of our experimental infrastructure was developed for and is applied in this NLP system.

1.1 The MultiNet Paradigm

In the NLI-Z39.50, natural language queries (corresponding to a topic's title, description, or narrative) are transformed into a knowledge and meaning representation, Multilayered Extended Semantic Networks (abbreviated as MultiNet, see [4, 5]). The core of a MultiNet consists of concepts (nodes) and semantic relations and functions between them (edges). Figure 1 shows the relational structure of the MultiNet representation for the description of GIRT topic 116. The MultiNet paradigm defines a fixed set of 93 semantic relations (plus a set of functions) to describe the meaning connections between concepts, including synonymy (SYNO), subordination, i.e. hyponymy and hypernymy (SUB), meronymy and holonymy (PARS), antonymy (ANTO), and relations for change of sorts between lexemes. For example, the relation CHPA indicates a change from a property (such as *'deep'*) into an abstract object (such as *'depth'*). The relations shown in Fig. 1 are association (ASSOC), attachment of object to object (ATTCH), property relationship (PROP), predicative concept specifying a plurality (PRED), experiencer (EXP), an informational process or object (MCONT), carrier of a state (SCAR), state specifier (SSPE), conceptual subordination for objects (SUB), conceptual subordination for situations (SUBS), neutral object (OBJ), temporal restriction for a situation (TEMP), and a function for the introduction of alternatives (*ALTN1).

1.2 The WOCADI Parser

A syntactico-semantic parser is applied when preprocessing NL queries and for parsing all documents in the concept indexing approach and the network matching approach described in Sect. 2.1. This parser, WOCADI (WOrd ClAss based DIsambiguating parser; see for example [6, 7]), is based on the principles of Word Class Functional Analysis (WCFA). It generates for a given German sentence its semantic representation as a semantic network of the MultiNet formalism.

The NL analysis is supported by HaGenLex [8], a domain-independent computer lexicon linked to and supplemented by external sources of lexical and morphological information, in particular CELEX [9] and GermaNet [10]. HaGenLex includes a lexicon with full morpho-syntactic and semantic information of more than 22,000 lexemes, a shallow lexicon with morpho-syntactic information only on about 50,000 entries, and several lexicons with more than 200,000 proper nouns (names of cities, companies, countries, products, etc.).

MultiNet (and therefore also HaGenLex) differentiates between homographs, polysemes, and meaning molecules[2]. The WOCADI parser provides powerful

[2] A meaning molecule is a regular polyseme with different meaning facets which can occur in the same sentence. For instance, two facets of *'bank'* (building and legal person) are referred to in the sentence *'The bank across the street charges a nominal fee for account management.'*

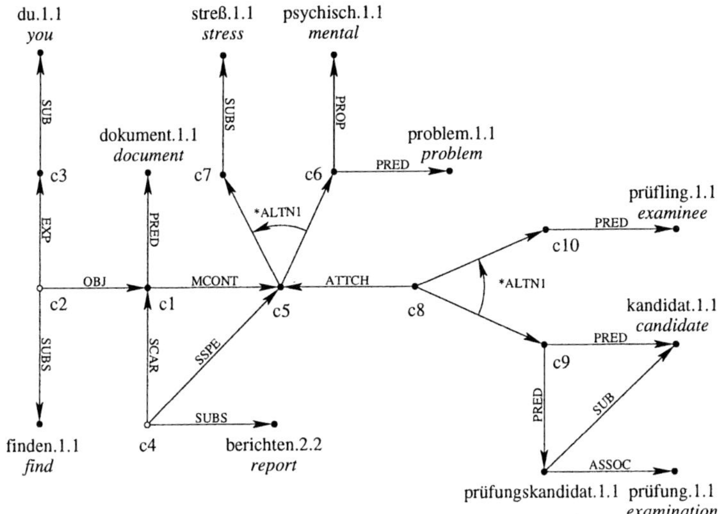

Fig. 1. The core MultiNet representation for the description of GIRT topic 116: *"Finde Dokumente, die über psychische Probleme oder Stress von Prüfungskandidaten oder Prüflingen berichten."/'Find documents reporting on mental problems or stress of examination candidates or examinees.'* Numerical suffixes for reading distinction of English concepts are omitted

disambiguation modules. Each module applies rules and statistics with syntactic and semantic information to disambiguate lexemes or structures.

The semantic network in Fig. 1 illustrates several features of the parser: the disambiguation of a verb (the correct reading represented by the concept *berichten.2.2*[3]), the representation of a nominal compound *prüfungskandidat.1.1*[4] not contained in the lexicons together with its constituents *prüfung.1.1* and *kandidat.1.1*, correct attachment of prepositional phrases, and correct coordination of noun phrases. These features are important for our approach to translate queries: linguistic challenges for translation such as lexical, syntactic, or semantic ambiguities are already resolved by the WOCADI parser.

1.3 The Database Independent Query Representation

To support access to a wide range of different target databases with different retrieval protocols and formal retrieval languages, the semantic network representation of a user query is transformed into an intermediate representation, a Database Independent Query Representation (DIQR). A DIQR expression comprises features typical for queries to library databases:

[3] A lemma followed by a numerical suffix consisting of a homograph identifier and a polyseme identifier forms a so-called concept identifier in HaGenLex. A concept in MultiNet corresponds to one reading or lexeme in HaGenLex.

[4] Compounds are written as one word in German.

- Attributes (so-called semantic access points), such as *author*, *publisher*, *title*, or *date-of-publication*.
- Term relations specifying how to search and match query terms. For example, the term relation '<' indicates that a matching document must contain a term with a value less than the given search term.
- Term types indicating a data type for a search term. Typical examples for term types are number, date, name, word, or phrase.
- Search terms identifying what terms a document representation should contain. Search terms include concepts (for example, *prüfung.1.1*/*'exam'*) and word forms (for example, *"Prüfungen"*/*'exams'*).
- Boolean operators in prefix notation for the combination of attributes, term relations, term types, search terms, or expressions to construct more complex DIQR expressions, for example 'AND' (conjunction) and 'OR' (disjunction). By convention, the operator 'AND' can be omitted because it is assumed as a default.
- Optional numeric weights associated with search terms. These weights are used in information retrieval (IR) tasks to indicate how important a search term is considered in a query.

The DIQR is the result of a rule-based transformation of the semantic network representation using a Rete-based compiler and interpreter (the implementation is described in more detail in [3]). It is mapped to a query in a formal language the database management system supports (such as a query for the Z39.50 protocol, an SQL query, or a SOAP request), which is then submitted to the target system. For example, the semantic network in Fig. 1 is transformed into the DIQR

```
((OR title abstract) = (AND (OR (phrase "psychologisch.1.1" "problem.1.1")
                                (word "stress.1.1"))
                            (OR (word "prüfungskandidat.1.1")
                                (wordlist "prüfung.1.1" "kandidat.1.1")
                                (word "prüfling.1.1"))  ))
```

After expanding query terms with a disjunction of semantically related terms, the DIQR is normalized into a disjunctive normal form (DNF). Its components, written as conjunctions, are interpreted as query variants. The DIQR example above results in twelve query variants after normalization.

2 Monolingual GIRT Experiments (German – German)

2.1 Investigated Approaches

In the CLEF 2004 experiments, our focus is on comparing different indexing and matching techniques on different levels of abstraction for a document representation. Three different methods for indexing the GIRT documents are employed.

Indexing word forms. One database containing the German document collection (database GIRT4DE) and one containing the English document collection (database GIRT4EN) are created by indexing word forms from the documents. No document preprocessing takes place, i.e., no stemming, decomposition of compounds, or removal of stopwords.

Indexing concepts. The WOCADI parser produces semantic networks for the sentences in the title and abstract fields of the documents. From these semantic networks, concepts are extracted and indexed (database GIRT4RDG). For compounds we add the concepts of their constituents (as determined by the compound module of the parser) to the index, e.g., we index *prüfungskandidat.1.1* in addition to *prüfung.1.1* and *kandidat.1.1.* To compensate for possible disambiguation errors, all word form readings determined by the morpho-lexical stage of the parser are chosen as index terms as well, but with a lower indexing weight. If the parser cannot construct a semantic network for a sentence, the latter terms are the only index terms to be added.

Indexing semantic networks. The parser returns the semantic network representations for a document's title and all sentences from its abstract (database InSicht). To reduce time and space requirements of this approach, each MultiNet (in its linearized or textual form) is simplified by omitting some semantic details less relevant for this application, and instance variables are replaced by artificial instance constants. Finally, to speed up matching even more by allowing optimized subset tests, every MultiNet is normalized by ensuring a canonical order of MultiNet terms. The resulting nets are indexed on the contained concepts to reduce the actual time for matching the simplified networks of the documents and the query. For the bilingual experiments, only the first method can be applied because currently WOCADI is restricted to analyzing texts in German.

2.2 Experimental Setup

Morpho-lexical functions of the WOCADI parser and background knowledge represented as a single, large MultiNet allow to look up search terms semantically related to a given search term. Search term variants include morphologic variants (like *"Stadt"/'city'* and *"Städte"/'cities'*), orthographic variants (such as *"Schiffahrt"* and *"Schifffahrt"*), and lexical variants (such as the synonyms *ansehen.2.3/'lookup upon as'* and *betrachten.1.2/'regard as'*). The semantic similarity *sim* between two terms x and y is determined by their MultiNet relation. For example, the semantic similarity $sim(x, y)$ is 0.95 if x and y are synonyms, 0.7 if x is a hyponym (a narrower term) of y, 0.6 if x and y are morphologically derived, and 0.5 if x is a hypernym (a broader term) of y. For concepts connected via a path of relations, the semantic similarity is calculated as the product of similarities along the path of relations connecting them.

Using the DIQR for the original query (OQ) as a starting point, the following steps are carried out as an automated retrieval strategy:

1. For each search term in OQ, the set of linguistically related concepts is obtained and OQ is expanded with the disjunction of search term variants (optionally weighted by semantic similarity). For a query translation, the translations of all term variants (concepts and words) are combined to produce semantically related translations which serve to expand a query term in OQ (as described in Sect. 3). In this case, semantic similarities are replaced by translation scores to weight query terms.

2. The expanded OQ is normalized into DNF and its components, written as conjunctions, are interpreted as query variants. The query variants are ranked by their score (the semantic similarity between a query variant and OQ), which is computed as the product of the semantic similarities of their search terms, normalized by query length.
3. To construct a single database query, all search terms in the top ranked 250 query variants are collected in a word list to build an extended query. The documents are retrieved until the result set exceeds a fixed size (here: 1000 documents). To perform multiple queries, the 250 top ranked query variants are separately used for retrieval. Documents scoring higher than the minimum score are retrieved and inserted into the result set.
4. Document scores s for a document d also depend on the query variant q. They are computed as the weighted sum of the score returned by the database ($s_{\mathrm{db}}(d,q)$, a standard *tf-idf* score as determined by the database ranking schema) and a query variant score ($s_{\mathrm{qv}}(q)$) (the semantic similarity between a query variant q and OQ) for the current query variant:
$$s(d,q) = s_{\mathrm{db}}(d,q) \cdot w_{\mathrm{db}} + s_{\mathrm{qv}}(q) \cdot w_{\mathrm{qv}}$$
If one document is retrieved for different query variants, the maximum of its scores is taken.

2.3 Results

We submitted five experimental runs for the monolingual GIRT task in 2004. The experiments vary in the following parameter settings: i) a single query is created from all query variants (Q-S), or multiple queries (the query variants) are processed separately and their results are merged successively (Q-M); ii) search terms and index terms are word forms (I-W), HaGenLex concepts (I-C), or concepts and relations from semantic networks (I-N); iii) an exact search for search terms is performed (no truncation) (R-E), or a search for words beginning with the specified search term is performed (R-T) i.e., we use a so-called right truncation or prefix match; iv) the document score ($s(d,q)$) is calculated as a weighted sum of database document score and query score with $w_{\mathrm{db}} = 0.7$ and $w_{\mathrm{qv}} = 0.3$. The query score is not normalized (D-1) or it is normalized by the query length (dividing w_{qv} by the number of query terms) (D-2). A third variant uses $w_{\mathrm{db}} = 0$ and $w_{\mathrm{qv}} = 1$ (D-3) to compute $s(d,q)$. Table 1 gives an overview of the experiments performed for the German document collection with their results.

2.4 Brief Success and Failure Analysis

The following observations can be made from the retrieval results:

- The methods under investigation perform best in the order of word form indexing (FUHds1, FUHdw1, FUHdw2), concept indexing (FUHdrw), and semantic network matching (FUHdm) with respect to MAP. There is a general low performance of the experiments using disambiguated concepts (FUHdrw) and indexing and matching semantic networks (FUHdm).

Table 1. Overview of parameter settings and results for monolingual GIRT experiments with the German document collection. The results displayed are the total number of documents retrieved (#docs) and the mean average precision (MAP)

Run	Setup					Results	
	Database	Q	I	R	D	#docs	MAP
FUHds1	GIRT4DE	S	W	T	1	25000	0.2446
FUHdw1	GIRT4DE	M	W	T	1	25000	0.2482
FUHdw2	GIRT4DE	M	W	T	2	25000	0.2276
FUHdrw	GIRT4RDG	M	C	E	1	25000	0.1162
FUHdm	InSicht	M	N	E	3	1309	0.1126

- Experiments with multiple queries and with a single query show a similar performance (FUHds1 vs. FUHdw1). (There is not as much difference as in the experiments in 2003.)
- Normalizing of the query score degraded performance (FUHdw2 vs. FUHdw1). (We expected an improved performance in the experiment using normalization.)

Experiments with indexing concepts and matching semantic networks (FUHdrw and FUHdm) were expected to show a higher precision due to disambiguation of concepts in queries and documents. A plausible explanation for the observed results is that these experiments rely on WOCADI for analysis of queries and documents. We have observed that documents in the GIRT collection (German titles and abstracts) are difficult to parse or to represent as semantic networks because their abstracts often contain grammatically incorrect, malformed language (for instance, the table of contents of a book) or spelling errors. For example, of 60,702 words occurring in the GIRT documents with a frequency of one, we judged 11,589 as spelling errors. The remaining words are word forms corresponding to domain-specific lexemes missing in HaGenLex, foreign words, proper nouns not in the name lexicons, unknown abbreviations, etc. Due to time constraints, we did not investigate words with a higher frequency.

WOCADI produced full semantic networks for 34.3% of the 1,111,121 sentences (with 23,088,562 words) in the GIRT documents, partial semantic networks[5] for 23.9% of the sentences, and no semantic networks for the remaining 41.8% of the sentences. These results are significantly worse than for other corpora (for example see [11] for WOCADI's parse statistics on the QA@CLEF 2004 newspaper corpora). One promising extension would be to include the available partial semantic networks in a modified matching procedure.

The MultiNet indexing experiment is based upon matching the semantic network for a query with semantic networks for a document on a per-sentence basis,

[5] WOCADI tries to produce such networks in a special chunk mode (or shallow parsing mode) when a full parse has failed.

i.e., one semantic network per sentence in a query or document is matched. However, relevant documents can contain search terms not co-occurring in the same sentence, which currently will not be found. But semantic networks are not restricted to represent the meaning of one sentence and the WOCADI parser is capable of analyzing a text consisting of multiple sentences (including coreference resolution) and returning a single semantic network. So, there are several directions for improving the MultiNet matching approach.

To summarize, indexing concepts or indexing and matching semantic networks showed a lower precision than the traditional IR approaches. It remains to be seen if this behavior is specific to the GIRT document corpus. Indexing full text, such as newspaper articles, may provide a better basis for experiments with matching and indexing semantic networks. One cannot conclude that our semantic retrieval approaches will not perform better in the near future or that they are not suited for IR. They still have potential for improvements.

3 Bilingual GIRT Experiments (German – English)

For the bilingual retrieval experiments with the GIRT document collection, we apply a dictionary-based translation of the concepts in the DIQR. Currently there is no English version of HaGenLex, but there is an incomplete mapping between HaGenLex concepts and GermaNet concepts [12]. GermaNet is the German part of EuroWordNet [13]. This translation lexicon contains about 10,000 translations of HaGenLex concepts into EuroWordNet concepts.[6] The high quality concept translation lexicon was combined with a translation word list with about 110,000 entries compiled from several resources for translating German word forms into English (from LEO: http://dict.leo.org; DICT resources: http://dict.tu-chemnitz.de). With these resources, a concept translation lexicon and a translation word list, there are two ways to translate a HaGenLex lexeme:

1. Remove the numerical suffix from the HaGenLex lexeme and try to find a word translation. For example, among the translations for the noun *"arbeit"* are the English words *'work'*, *'job'*, *'occupation'*, and *'exam'*.
2. Look up the EuroWordNet concept correspondences for the HaGenLex lexeme. The translation for the concept *arbeit.1.1*, for instance, includes the mapping to the correct EuroWordNet concepts for *'work'* and *'labor'*.

We combine both methods and create a tree representation to find a set of semantically related words in the target language for a given concept in the source language. The root of the tree denotes the concept for which semantically related translations are to be found. All immediate successors of the root node

[6] With this mapping between HaGenLex and EuroWordNet concepts, disambiguation information in the target language is still available. If standard machine translation software were used, readings would not be differentiated or the differentiation would differ from the concepts and meanings used in HaGenLex.

represent concepts and base forms (concepts without the numerical suffix) that are semantically related to the root concept. For words the semantic similarity is estimated to be half the semantic similarity between the original concept and the concept corresponding to the word. The corresponding arcs are associated with a numeric value subject to a probabilistic or frequentistic interpretation (i.e., the semantic similarity normalized to the interval [0, 1]). Leaves represent the translations found by applying one of the two methods mentioned above. Their arcs are marked with either a normalized frequency or an estimate of the translation quality depending on the source of the translation. Leaf nodes are marked with the product of numerical values on the edges from the root to the leaf node.

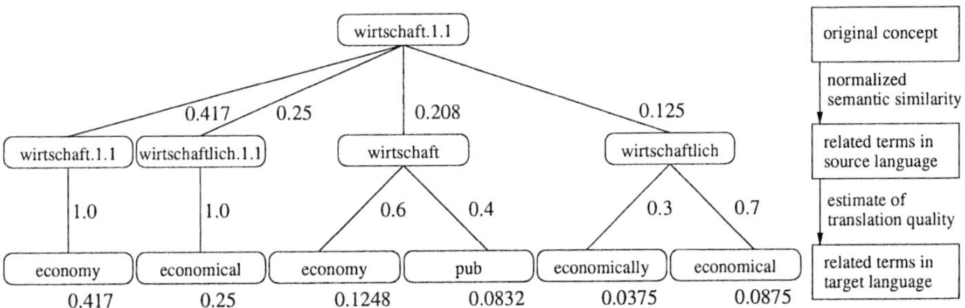

Fig. 2. Tree representation for translating the concept *wirtschaft.1.1*. Translation scores for concepts are computed as the sum of products of edge markings on the path to the leaf nodes containing this concept. The resulting order of possible translations is *'economy'* (score: $0.417 \cdot 1.0 + 0.208 \cdot 0.6 = 0.5418$), *'economical'* (0.3375), *'pub'* (0.0832), and *'economically'* (0.0375). Cross-part-of-speech translations are included, but disambiguation information may be partly lost. For instance, the English word *'pub'* is actually a translation of the HaGenLex concept *wirtschaft.1.2*. Some subbranches have been pruned from this example tree for readability

A ranking of all semantically related translations is obtained by collecting all leaf concepts and their translation score is calculated as the sum of all leaf values.[7] For example, the ranking of translations for the concept *wirtschaft.1.1* by their translation scores is *'economy'*, *'economical'*, *'pub'*, and *'economically'* (see Fig. 2). Extending this approach, leaf nodes in the target language might be expanded by semantically related concepts as well (e.g., a leaf can be expanded by concepts in its EuroWordNet synset). For the bilingual experiments, translation scores replace semantic similarities in the retrieval strategy described in Sect. 2.2.

[7] Assuming conditional independence between the nodes, the tree can be interpreted as a decision tree, in which case computing the translation score is equivalent to applying Bayes' theorem for computing probabilities.

3.1 Experimental Setup

Our first participation in the Bilingual GIRT task (matching German topics against the English data) consists of trying various parameter settings for translating German query concepts into English. The English GIRT document collection was indexed as is, i.e., English word forms were indexed (I-W). Document scores are calculated as in the monolingual experiments (D-2) and truncation is applied to the search terms (R-T).

The experimental parameters varied are: i) a single query is created by combining all query variants (Q-S), or multiple query variants (Q-M) are processed; ii) all terms semantically related to a search term are used as query term variants (G-A), or the top five semantically related terms (ranked by semantic similarity) are used (G-5); iii) all translations found are used as query term translations in a query (E-A), or the best five translations are used (E-5); iv) the translation scores are used to weight query search terms (W-T), or query terms are not weighted (W-U).

3.2 Results

After fixing a corrupted database index for the database GIRT4EN (only 15,955 documents out of 151,319 were indexed for the official runs), we started re-runs of our official experiments for the bilingual GIRT task (German – English) to obtain meaningful results. Parameter settings and results for the re-runs are shown in Table 2.

Table 2. Overview of parameter settings and results for bilingual GIRT experiments with German queries and the English document collection

Run	Setup					Results	
	Database	G	E	W	Q	#docs	MAP
FUHe1 re-run	GIRT4EN	5	5	U	M	23805	0.1117
FUHe2 re-run	GIRT4EN	A	5	T	M	23805	0.1135
FUHe3 re-run	GIRT4EN	5	A	T	M	23805	0.1288
FUHe4 re-run	GIRT4EN	5	5	T	M	23805	0.1275
FUHe5 re-run	GIRT4EN	5	5	T	S	23805	0.1104

3.3 Brief Failure Analysis

This brief failure analysis refers to our unofficial re-runs for the bilingual task.

- There is a lower performance for the bilingual experiments compared to the monolingual experiments.
- Queries that could not be processed successfully in German, could not be processed in English as well (for example, topic 115).

– For one query, no relevant documents were found in all experiments (topic 112). For several queries, less than 1000 documents were retrieved.

The bilingual experiments employ a dictionary based per-word or per-concept translation. The same number of documents was retrieved in all bilingual experiments because the translation process failed for the same topics due to missing translations. Less than 1000 or no documents were retrieved for these topics in all experiments. The missing translations are one major reason why the performance in comparison with the monolingual experiments is lower. The experiments should be repeated when the translation of concepts into EuroWordNet concepts has been completed with respect to HaGenLex coverage.

Translation ambiguities lead to noise in the results, which could be reduced if certain syntactic or semantic structures are treated differently for a translation. In particular, German compound nouns and adjective-noun phrases were translated by translating their constituents, but should be treated depending on their semantic context. Consider for example the compounds and their (correct) translations *"Klimaänderung"/'climate change'*, *"Klimaanlage"/'air conditioning (system)'*, *"Klimakammer"/'climatic chamber'*, *'environmental chamber'*. In these compounds, the common German constituent is translated differently, although its meaning should be represented by the same concept. Simply adding all translation alternatives for a compound constituent to expand a query adds too much noise to the results. In a similar form, this problem arises for adjective-noun phrases.

4 Conclusion

In comparison with the results for the monolingual GIRT task in 2003, performance with respect to the best MAP has improved (0.2482 in 2004 vs. 0.2064 in 2003 for a similar run). Monolingual experiments using word-based retrieval (i.e., retrieval based on indexed word forms) have a higher MAP than both the experiment with concept indexing and indexing of semantic networks. However, a comparison with other corpora suggests that the low performance of indexing semantic networks might be specific to the GIRT document collection. In contrast to the traditional approach we tested, the semantic network approach aims at representing the meaning of a document. For this approach, there are obvious improvements for further experiments, including matching across several sentences (with coreference resolution for multiple sentences) and matching partial semantic networks.

The re-runs of the official bilingual experiments showed encouraging results. After completing the mapping of HaGenLex concepts to readings of EuroWordNet, other languages will be available for cross-language IR experiments with the NLI-Z39.50. Additional lexeme translations and improved methods to translate multi-word expressions and compounds will be integrated to increase performance for bilingual IR.

References

1. Leveling, J.: University of Hagen at CLEF 2003: Natural language access to the GIRT4 data. In Peters, C., Gonzalo, J., Braschler, M., Kluck, M., eds.: Comparative Evaluation of Multilingual Information Access Systems, 4th Workshop of the Cross-Language Evaluation Forum, CLEF 2003, Revised Selected Papers. Volume 3237 of Lecture Notes in Computer Science (LNCS). Berlin, Springer (2005)
2. Kluck, M., Gey, F.C.: The domain-specific task of CLEF — specific evaluation strategies in cross-language information retrieval. In Peters, C., ed.: Cross-Language Information Retrieval and Evaluation. Volume 2069 of LNCS. Berlin, Springer (2001) 48–56
3. Leveling, J., Helbig, H.: A robust natural language interface for access to bibliographic databases. In Callaos, N., Margenstern, M., Sanchez, B., eds.: Proceedings of the SCI 2002. Volume XI. Orlando, Florida, International Institute of Informatics and Systemics (IIIS) (2002) 133–138
4. Helbig, H.: Die semantische Struktur natürlicher Sprache: Wissensrepräsentation mit MultiNet. Springer, Berlin (2001)
5. Helbig, H., Gnörlich, C.: Multilayered extended semantic networks as a language for meaning representation in NLP systems. In Gelbukh, A., ed.: Computational Linguistics and Intelligent Text Processing (CICLing 2002). Volume 2276 of LNCS. Berlin, Springer (2002) 69–85
6. Helbig, H., Hartrumpf, S.: Word class functions for syntactic-semantic analysis. In: Proceedings of the 2nd International Conference on Recent Advances in Natural Language Processing (RANLP'97), Tzigov Chark, Bulgaria (1997) 312–317
7. Hartrumpf, S.: Hybrid Disambiguation in Natural Language Analysis. Der Andere Verlag, Osnabrück, Germany (2003)
8. Hartrumpf, S., Helbig, H., Osswald, R.: The semantically based computer lexicon HaGenLex – Structure and technological environment. Traitement automatique des langues 44(2) (2003) 81–105
9. Baayen, R.H., Piepenbrock, R., Gulikers, L.: The CELEX Lexical Database. Release 2 (CD-ROM). Linguistic Data Consortium, University of Pennsylvania, Philadelphia, Pennsylvania (1995)
10. Kunze, C., Wagner, A.: Anwendungsperspektiven des GermaNet, eines lexikalisch-semantischen Netzes für das Deutsche. In Lemberg, I., Schröder, B., Storrer, A., eds.: Chancen und Perspektiven computergestützter Lexikographie. Volume 107 of Lexicographica Series Maior. Niemeyer, Tübingen, Germany (2001) 229–246
11. Hartrumpf, S.: Question answering using sentence parsing and semantic network matching. This volume
12. Osswald, R.: Die Verwendung von GermaNet zur Pflege und Erweiterung des Computerlexikons HaGenLex. LDV Forum 19(1/2) (2004) 43–51
13. Vossen, P., ed.: EuroWordNet: A Multilingual Database with Lexical Semantic Networks. Kluwer, Dordrecht, The Netherlands (1998)

IRIT at CLEF 2004: The English GIRT Task

Mustapha Baziz[1], Mohand Boughanem[1], and Nathalie Aussenac-Gilles[2]

[1] IRIT-UPS
Campus Univ. Toulouse III, 118 Route de Narbonne
F-31062 Toulouse Cedex 4
[2] IRIT-CNRS
Campus Univ. Toulouse III, 118 Route de Narbonne
F-31062 Toulouse Cedex 4

Abstract. This paper describes our participation to the monolingual English GIRT task. The main objectives of our experiments were to evaluate the use of Mercure IRS (designed at IRIT/SIG) on domain specific corpus. Two other techniques of automatic query reformulation using WordNet are evaluated.

1 Introduction

The objective of IRIT/SIG participation in 2004 was to evaluate the use of Mercure IRS on domain specific data. In addition to evaluate the Mercure system, two other techniques are experimented using WordNet. The first technique consists on detecting mono and multiword concepts from queries and then to weight them according to a proposed CF.IDF formula, a kind of TF.IDF. The second concerns disambiguation-expansion method consisting of selecting the closest synset (concept) to the initial query, from WordNet, to use for expanding the query.

This paper is organized as follows. In section 2, the used Mercure IRS model is described. In section 3, the additional tests are formally described: the concepts detection and weighting method from queries in 3.1, and the disambiguation-expansion method in 3.2. Section 4 presents the official evaluation results compared with the median average obtained by all participating systems. Finally, section 5 gives some conclusions and prospects.

2 Mercure Model

Mercure is an information retrieval system based on a connectionist approach and modelled by three-layered network (as shown in Figure1). The network is composed of a query layer (set of query terms), a term layer representing the indexing terms and a document layer [2].

Mercure includes the implementation of a retrieval process based on spreading activation forward and backward through weighted links. Queries and documents can be either inputs of the network. The links between two layers are symmetric and their weights are based on the TF.IDF measure inspired by the OKAPI [5] term weighting formula.

C. Peters et al. (Eds.): CLEF 2004, LNCS 3491, pp. 283 – 291, 2005.

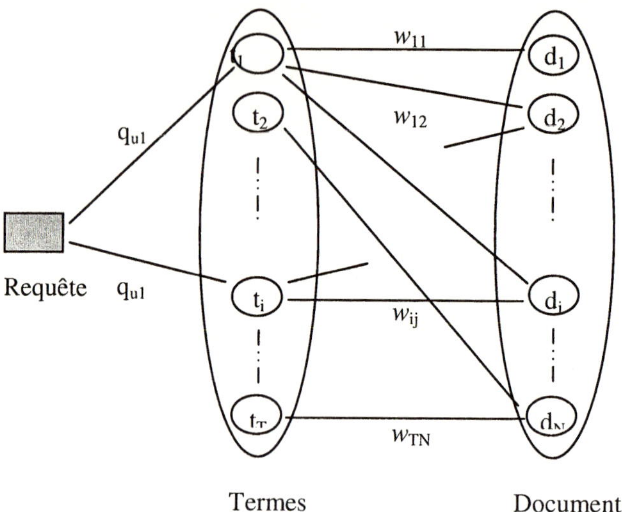

Fig. 1. Mercure Model

The term-document link weights are expressed by:

$$d_{ij} = \frac{tf_{ij} * (h_1 + h_2 * \log(\frac{N}{n_i}))}{h_3 + h_4 * \frac{dl_j}{\Delta d} + h_5 * tf_{ij}} \tag{1}$$

The query-term links (at stage s) are weighted as follows:

$$q_{ui}^{(s)} = \begin{cases} \frac{nq_u * qtf_{ui}}{nq_u - qtf_{ui}} if\,(nq_u > qtf_{ui}) \\ qtf_{ui}\, otherwise \end{cases} \tag{2}$$

The query weights are based on spreading activation. Each neural node computes an input and spreads an output signal:

The query k is the input of the network. $Input_k$=1. Then, each neuron from the term layer computes an input value from this initial query:

$$In(N_{ti}) = Input_k * q_{ki}^s \tag{3}$$

The output value is computed as follows:

$$Out(N_{ti}) = g(In(N_{ti})) \tag{4}$$

where g is the identity function.

These signals are propagated forward through the network from the term layer to the document layer. Each neuron computes an input and output value:

$$In(N_{dj}) = \sum_{i=1}^{T} Out(N_{ti}) * w_{ij} \tag{5}$$

and,

$$Out(N_{dj}) = g(In(N_{dj})) \tag{6}$$

The system output is:

$$Output_k(Out(N_{D1}), Out(N_{D2}),.., Out(N_{DN}))$$

Notations:

T:	the total number of indexing terms,
N:	The total number of documents,
q_{ui}:	The weight of the term t_i in the query u,
t_i:	The term t_i,
d_j:	The document d_j
w_{ij}	The weight of the link between the term t_i and the document d_j,
dl_j	Document length in words (without stop words),
Δd	Average document length,
tf_{ij}	The frequency of the term t_i in the document d_j,
n_i	The number of documents containing term t_i,
nq_u	The query length (number of unique terms)
qtf_{ui}	Query term frequency

3 Overview of the Additional Tests

In this section, we describe two methods used for query processing based on WordNet. The first consists of concept detection and weighting from queries. The second method, disambiguation-expansion, tends to expand a query with its closest synset from WordNet [4].

3.1 Concepts Detection and Weighting

Concept detection consists of extracting mono and multiword concepts from queries that correspond to nodes (synsets) in WordNet. Formally, let consider:

$$Q= \{w_1, w_2, \ldots, w_n\} \tag{7}$$

the initial query composed of n single words. The result of the concept detection process will be a query Q_c. It corresponds to:

$$Qc= \{c1, c2, \ldots, cm, w'1, w'2,\ldots,w'm'\} \tag{8}$$

Where c_1, c_2, , c_m are concepts recognized as entries in WordNet. These concepts could be mono or multiword. It can also happen that single words w'_1, $w'_{2,\ldots,}w'_{m'}$ of the initial query do not belong to ontology vocabulary. They will be used for disambiguating the query. They will then be added to the final expanded query.

For detecting concepts in the query, we use an ad hoc technique that relies solely on concatenation of adjacent words to identify compound (multiword) concepts of WordNet. In this technique, two alternative ways can be distinguished. The first one consists of projecting WordNet on the query by extracting all multiword concepts from WordNet and then identifying those occurring in the query. This method has the advantage of creating a reusable resource. Its drawback is the possibility to omit concepts which appear in the query and in WordNet with different forms. For example if WordNet recognizes a multiword concept *"solar battery"*, a simple comparison does not recognizes in the query the same concept appearing in its plural form *"solar batteries"*. The second way, which we adopt in this paper, consists in the opposite step, projecting the query on WordNet: for each multiword candidate concept derived by combining adjacent words in the query, we first question WordNet using these words just as they are, and then we use their base forms if necessary to resolve the problem of word forms.

Concerning word combination, the principle consists in selecting the longest successive terms for which a concept is detected.

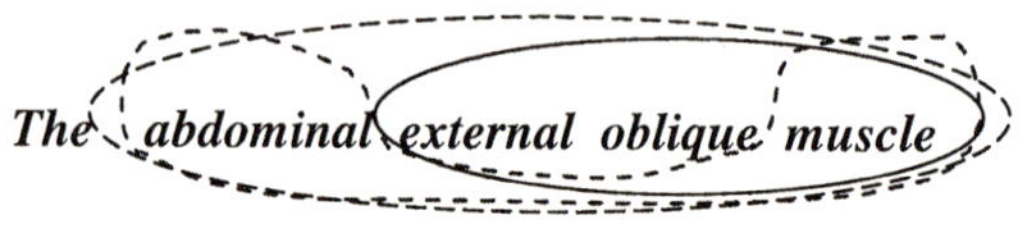

Fig. 2. Example of text with different concepts

If we consider the example shown in Figure 2, the sentence contains three (3) different concepts which are: *external oblique muscle, abdominal muscle* and *abdominal external oblique muscle*. The definition of the first concept according to WordNet is:

The noun abdominal muscle has 1 sense
1. abdominal, abdominal muscle, ab -- (the muscles of the abdomen).

This concept is not retained in our approach, because its words are not adjacent. The second *"external oblique muscle"* and the third *"abdominal external oblique muscle"* are synonyms, their definition is:

The noun external oblique muscle has 1 sense
1. external oblique muscle, musculus obliquus externus abdominis, abdominal external oblique muscle, oblique -- (a diagonally arranged abdominal muscle on either side of the torso).

The selected concept is associated to the longest multiword « *abdominal external oblique muscle* » which corresponds to the correct sense of the sentence. Remind that in words combination, the order must be respected (left to right) otherwise we could be confronted to the syntactic variation problem (*science library* is different from *library science*).

3.2 Why Using Multiword Concepts?

The extraction of multiword concepts in plain text is important to reduce ambiguity. These concepts generally are monosemous even though the words they contain can be individually ambiguous. For example, when taking each word separately in the concept *ear_nose_and_throat_doctor,* we have to disambiguate (according to WordNet) between 5 senses for the word *ear*, 13 senses (7 for the noun *nose* and 6 for the verb *nose*) for the word *nose*, 3 senses for *throat* (*and* is not used because it is a stop-word) and 7 senses (4 for the noun and 3 for the verb) for the word *doctor*. So, we would have a number of 5x13x3x7= 1365 possible combinations of candidate senses. But when considering all the words forming a single multiword concept (of course, the multiword concept must be recognized by WordNet), we only will have one sense.

In the case of this example, the full concept (WordNet synset) and its definition (gloss in WordNet) are as follows:

The noun ear-nose-and-throat doctor has 1 sense
1. ENT man, ear-nose-and-throat doctor, otolaryngologist, otorhinolaryngologist, rhinolaryngologist -- (a specialist in the disorders of the ear or nose or throat.)

Statistics we done on WordNet2.0 as shown in Table1, show that from a total of 63,218 multiword concepts (composed of 2-9 words), 56,286 (89%) of them are monosemous. 6,238 have 2 senses (9.867%) and only 694 (0.506%) multiword concepts have more than 2 senses. Thus, the more there are multiword concepts in a document to be analyzed, the easier is their disambiguation.

Table 1. Polysemy repartition on multiword concepts in WordNet 2.0

Number of senses	Number of multiword concepts (2-9 words)	%
1	56286	89,035%
2	6238	9,867%
3	375	0,593%
>=4	319	0,506%
Total	63218	100%

Example of Multiword Concepts Extracted from the Official Topics

All the concepts recognized by WordNet are identified. They should be mono or multiword. Below, examples of multiword concepts extracted from the official topics:

103 live_in
105 on_the_job
106 multiple_sclerosis
124 telephone_interview
125 infant_mortality
109 animal_husbandry
114 federal_republic_of_germany
117 carbon_dioxide
125 european_country

The extracted concepts are then weighted according to a kind of TF.IDF, we name CF.IDF. For a concept c_i composed of n words, its frequency in a query equals to the number of occurrences of a concept itself, and the one of all its sub-concepts.

Formally:

$$cf(c_i) = count(c_i) + \sum_{sc \in sub(c_i)} \frac{length(sc)}{length(c_i)} count(sc) \tag{9}$$

Where $length(c_i)$ represents the number of words that form c_i and $sub(c_i)$ is the set of all possible sub-concepts which can be derived from c_i: concepts of n-1 words from c_i, concepts of n-2, and all single words of c_i.

Example of Concept Weighting

If we consider a concept *"elastic potential energy"* in a given topic, composed of 3 words, its frequency is computed as follows:

> *cf("elastic potential energy") = count("elastic potential energy") + 2/3 count("potential energy") + 1/3 count("elastic") + 1/3 count("potential") + 1/3 count("energy").*

Knowing that *potential energy* is itself also a multiword concept and here, it is a question of adding the number of occurrences of *potential energy* and not its frequency.

3.3 Disambiguation-Expansion Using WordNet Synsets

Once mono and multiwords concepts of initial queries are extracted and weighed, an expansion process with WordNet synsets is carried out. And as each recognized concept c_k (formula 8) could have several senses (a set R_{Syns} of synsets containing C_k):

$$R_{Syns}(C_k) = \{C_k^1, C_k^2, \ldots, C_k^j, \ldots, C_k^t\} \tag{10}$$

They are disambiguated using an adapted Lesk [3] algorithm [6] which consists of overlapping each synset with the initial query. A concept-sense (synset) having the best overlapping (the greater number of common words) with the initial query is retained. Formally:

$$Best(R_{Syns}(C_k)) = \underset{k,j}{ArgMax} \left\| \{C_k^1, C_k^2, \ldots, C_k^j, \ldots, C_k^t\} \cap Q \right\| \tag{11}$$

Example of Disambiguation

Let us consider a query:

Q=[ecological farming animal husbandry].

It contains 4 single-word concepts which are:

C_1= "ecological", C_2 = "farming", C_3 = "animal", C_4 = "husbandry".

The first concept "ecological" has two synsets ($R_{Syns}(C_1)$={[1], [2]}) which appear in lines noticed [1] and [2] of Figure 3, the second "farming" has three synsets

Disambiguation-expansion with WordNet Synsets
Example: query *"ecological farming animal husbandry"*

Synsets of "**ecological**"

[1] ecological ecologic -- characterized by the interdependence of living organisms in an environment an ecological disaster
[2] ecological ecologic bionomical bionomic -- of or relating to the science of ecology ecological research

Synsets of "**farming**"

[3] farming agriculture husbandry -- the practice of cultivating the land or raising stock
[4] farming land1 -- working the land as an occupation or way of life farming is a strenuous life there s no work on the land any more
[5] agrarian agricultural farming -- relating to rural matters an agrarian or agricultural society farming communities

Synsets of "animal"

[6] animal animate being beast brute creature fauna -- a living organism characterized by voluntary movement
[7] animal carnal fleshly sensual -- of the appetites and passions of the body animal instincts carnal knowledge fleshly desire a sensual delight in eating music is the only sensual pleasure without vice
[8] animal -- of the nature of or characteristic of or derived from an animal or animals the animal kingdom animal instincts animal fats

Synsets of "husbandry"

[9] farming agriculture husbandry -- the practice of cultivating the land or raising stock

Similarities list: 1 1 2 1 1 1 1 1 2
Best Concept : -- farming agriculture husbandry --
Nbre of similarities : 2 (line : [3])

Fig. 3. Example of disambiguation-expansion using WordNet synsets

($R_{Syns}(C_2)$ ={[3], [4], [5]}), the third "animal" has three ({[6], [7], [8]}) and the last concept "husbandry" has only one synset (at line [9]).

As only one synset could be used for expanding the whole query in our "careful query expansion" approach, the best concept $Best(R_{syns}(C_k))$ which disambiguates the query Q is the synset of line [3] (or [9] which is identical to [3] in this example): farming agriculture husbandry -- the practice of cultivating the land or raising stock . In our "careful expansion" method, synset without its glossary was used to expand the query, so farming agriculture husbandry. As the first and the last words already belong to the initial query, the final query will be expanded only with the word agriculture.

4 Evaluation

We submitted five official runs to the monolingual English GIRT task ("GIRT_EN"): Run1T, Run2TD, Run3TDfc, Run4TWN and Run4TDWN. They are described in Table1.

The results obtained by the different runs are summarized in Table 2. These results are compared in the third column (Increment) of Table 2 with the median average precision (0.2990) obtained by all the systems that participated in the CLEF2004 English GIRT task.

Table 2. Description of the official runs

Run	Description
Run1T	Title part of the topics are used.
Run2TD	Title and Description parts of the topics are used.
Run3TDfc	Concept detection and weighting methods are used (Title and Description)
Run4TWN	Disambiguation-expansion method with WordNet Synsets is used (Title only)
Run4TDWN	Disambiguation-expansion method with WordNet Synsets is used (Title and Description)

Table 3. Results obtained for the five official runs compared to the median average

	Average Precision	Increment (%)
Run1T	0.3740	+25.08%
Run2TD	0.3855	+28.92%
Run3TDfc	0.3764	+25.88%
Run4TDWN	0.3640	+21.73%
Run5TWN	0.3764	+25.88%

Roughly the obtained results are about +25% better than the median average obtained by all participating systems. These results show also that using WordNet in disambiguation-expansion and concepts frequencies do not enhance significantly the average precision even though the precision for the first retrieved documents (not reported here) are better in the case of Run5TWN. Detecting and weighting concepts method, to bring better results, should be enhanced and then applied to queries as well as to documents.

5 Conclusion and Future Work

We have evaluated the performances of our IRS (Mercure) in domain specific corpus, and a method for query reformulation based on concepts detection and weighting using WordNet synsets. In this method, multiword concepts are removed into single words in the final queries in order to be conforming to the used IRS indexing process.

What is presented in this report is a part of a complete method achieved after our participation to 2004 CLEF campaign which is applied for queries and documents as well. This method is described in [1]. Next year, we intend to participate to CLEF with the new method.

References

1. Baziz M., Boughanem M., Aussenac-Gilles N.: "The Use of Ontology for Semantic Representation of Documents". In Proceeding of Semantic Web and Information Retrieval Workshop (SWIR) held in conjunction with the 27th ACM SIGIR Conference'04, July 25–29, 2004, Sheffield, United Kingdom.
2. Boughanem M., Dkaki T., Mothe J. and Soulé-Dupuy C. "Mercure at TREC-7" Proceeding of Trec-7, (1998).
3. Lesk, M. Automatic sense disambiguation using machine readable dictionaries: How to tell a pine cone from a ice cream cone. In Proceedings of SIGDOC '86, 1986.
4. Miller G., Wordnet: A lexical database. Communication of the ACM, 38(11):39-41, (1995).
5. Okapi at TREC-6, Proceeding of the 6th International Conference on Text Retrieval TREC, Harman D.K. (Ed.), NIST SP 500-236, pages: 125-136, (1997).
6. Patwardhan S., Banerjee S.,and Pedersen T. Using measures of semantic relatedness for word sense disambiguation. In Proceedings of the Fourth International Conference on Intelligent Text Processing and Computational Linguistics CICLING, Mexico City, 2003.

Ricoh at CLEF 2004

Yuichi Kojima

Software R&D Group, RICOH CO., Ltd.,
1-1-17 Koishikawa, Bunkyo-ku, Tokyo 112-0002, Japan
ykoji@src.ricoh.co.jp

Abstract. This paper describes Ricoh's participation is monolingual and bi-lingual information retrieval tasks done on the German Indexing and Retrieval Testdatabase (GIRT) at the Cross-Language Evaluation Forum (CLEF) 2004. We used a commercial morphological analyzer to decompound words and parallel corpora to retrieve bi-lingual information. While monolingual information retrieval was improved by using the analyzer, bi-lingual information retrieval still has room for improvement.

1 Introduction

We are enhancing our system of retrieving information in some languages [1, 2]. Our approach is to use the same basic system and modify language dependent modules. Our system performed reasonably with some European languages and revealed the importance of decompounding words in compound-rich languages such as German in the CLEF 2003 tasks [2].

This is the second time we have participated in CLEF tasks. We used a commercial morphological analyzer to decompound words and also participated in GIRT tasks. Our focus this year was:

1. To evaluate the effectiveness of word decompounding
2. To discover problems in applying our approach to bi-lingual information retrieval

Section 2 of this paper outlines our system, Section 3 describes the modifications we made to the experiments, Section 4 presents the results, and Section 5 is the conclusion.

2 System Description

The basic system is the same as last year's. Before describing our new modifications to the system for European languages, we will outline the background information for it. It uses a document ranking method based on the probabilistic model [3] with query expansion using pseudo-relevance feedback [4] and we found it was effective in TREC and NTCIR experiments.

We will now explain the processing flow for the system [5, 6].

C. Peters et al. (Eds.): CLEF 2004, LNCS 3491, pp. 292 – 297, 2005.

2.1 Query Term Extraction

We used "title" and "description" fields for each topic. An input topic string is transformed into a sequence of stemmed tokens using a tokenizer and stemmer. Stop words are eliminated using a stopword dictionary. Two kinds of terms are extracted from stemmed tokens for the initial retrieval: a "single term" is each stemmed token and a "phrasal term" consists of two adjacent tokens in a stemmed query string.

2.2 Initial Retrieval

Each query term is assigned weight w_t, and documents are ranked according to score $s_{q,d}$ as follows:

$$w_t = \log\left(k_4' \bullet \frac{N}{n_t} + 1\right), \tag{1}$$

$$s_{q,d} = \sum_{t \in q} \frac{f_{t,d}}{K + f_{t,d}} \bullet \frac{w_t}{k_4' \bullet N + 1}, \text{ and} \tag{2}$$

$$K = k_1 \bullet \left((1-b) + b \bullet \frac{l_d}{l_{ave}}\right), \tag{3}$$

where N is the number of documents in the collection, n_t is the document frequency of the term t, and $f_{t,d}$ is the in-document frequency of the term. Here, l_d is the document length, l_{ave} is the average document length, and k'_4, k_1, and b are parameters.

The weights for phrasal terms are set lower than those for single terms.

2.3 Query Expansion

As a result of the initial retrieval, the top 10 documents were assumed to be relevant (pseudo-relevance) to the query and selected as a "seed" for query expansion. Candidates for expansion terms were extracted from the seed documents in the same way as for the query term extraction previously explained. Phrasal terms were not used for query expansion. The candidates were ranked on Robertson's Selection Value [7], or RSV_t, and the top ranked terms were selected as expansion terms. The weight was recalculated as $w2_t$ using the Robertson/Sparck-Jones formula [8].

$$RSV_t = w2_t \bullet \left(\frac{r_t}{R} - \frac{n_t}{N}\right) \text{ and} \tag{4}$$

$$w2_t = \alpha \bullet w_t + (1-\alpha) \bullet \log \frac{\dfrac{r_t + 0.5}{R - r_t + 0.5}}{\dfrac{n_t - r_t + 0.5}{N - n_t - R + r_t + 0.5}}, \tag{5}$$

where R is the number of relevant documents, r_t is the number of relevant documents containing term t, and α is a parameter.

The weight of the initial query term was re-calculated using the same formula as above, but with a different α value and an additional adjustment to make the weight higher than the expansion terms.

2.4 Final Retrieval

Using the initial query and expansion terms, the ranking module does a second retrieval to produce the final results.

2.5 Bi-lingual Retrieval

We did English-to-German retrieval using a well known strategy based on English-German parallel corpora [9]. The bi-lingual retrieval process involved the following: 1) an English query was used for retrieval from the English database, 2) top-n documents were used to extract German query terms, 3) German query terms were extracted from counterparts of documents in the German database using the same mechanism for query expansion as in pseudo-relevance feedback regarding the counterparts as seed documents, and 4) the terms were used for retrieval from the German database.

3 Experiments

There were five items in the system that needed adjustment depending on the language, 1) the tokenizer, 2) the stemmer, 3) the stopword dictionary, 4) the training data, and 5) the parallel corpora.

We mainly used the same modules as last year and a commercial morphological analyzer that could tokenize a sentence, decompose a compound word, and stem a word.

Details on the items in the system are given in the following.

3.1 Stemming and Tokenizing

We had a selection of possible combinations of stemmers and tokenizers. The system could utilize the Snowball stemmer [10] and simple tokenizer that we used for last year's CLEF experiments. The system could also utilize the morphological analyzer that we imported into the system this year.

The possible combinations were limited by the behavior of the analyzer. It decomposed a compound word into single words and stemmed each single word with the same procedure. In other words, word decompounding was not selected without stemming in the analyzer.

After various experiments, we selected a combination of 1) word decompounding and 2) two-step stemming, which consisted on the first stemming step for decompounding and the second stemming using the Snowball stemmer.

Table 1 lists the results of the preliminary experiments in CLEF 2003 tasks.

Table 1. Results of preliminary experiments

Word decompounding	Stemming	Average precision*
No	German Snowball stemmer	0.3149
Yes	Stemmer A**	0.2944
Yes	Stemmer A** + German Snowball stemmer	0.3470

* Average precision using GIRT German monolingual task for CLEF 2003 after training
** German stemmer in the analyzer

3.2 Stopword Dictionary

This year, we used stopword dictionaries at the Snowball site.

3.3 Parallel Corpora

We prepared two additional document databases using the English and German GIRT corpus. We first prepared a database from the English corpus by extracting each tagged entity (TITLE, AUTHOR and ABSTRACT) as a document and used these for making lists of seed documents. We prepared the second database from German corpus with the same procedure used for making the German query terms from the lists of seed documents.

Each document was tokenized and stemmed depending on its language with the above mentioned methods.

We used all, half and a quarter of the parallel corpora to evaluate the performance.

3.4 Training

We searched the system parameters with the hill-climbing method, using average precision values of search results with query expansion for the monolingual and bilingual retrieval tasks.

Table 2 lists the average precision values after training.

Table 2. Average precision values after training

Language	Average precision	Years for documents used to prepare German query terms
DE->DE	0.3470	-
EN->DE	0.2644	1990-2000 (45-Mbyte English documents)
EN->DE	0.2449	1997-2000 (28 Mbytes)
EN->DE	0.1819	1999-2000 (16 Mbytes)

4 Results

Table 3 lists the summary of our results for CLEF 2004.

Our submitted results, rdedetde04 and rendetde04, had bugs during processing, so we prepared unofficial1 and unofficial4 instead of these. We also achieved results with other settings to observe the behavior of the system. The unofficial3 setting was the same as last year's. The unofficial5 and unofficial6 settings were to check what influence the document data capacity had.

The results for the monolingual task were improved with decompounding. Comparing unofficial1, unofficial2 and unofficial3, decompounding contributed to an improvement of about 17%. The results for the bi-lingual task were worse than those for training. The performance decreased by about 25% for bi-lingual retrieval while it only decreased by 2% for monolingual retrieval. The decreased performance from full-document to half-document size was smaller than that from half-document to quarter-document size. The former was 4% and the latter was 25%.

Table 3. Results for CLEF 2004

Language	Run-id	Relevant	Rel.Ret.	Average Prec.	R-Precision
DE->DE	Unofficial1	1663	1082	0.3393	0.3711
DE->DE	Unofficial2	1663	1072	0.2890	0.3203
DE->DE	Unofficial3	1663	1068	0.2828	0.3211
EN->DE	Unofficial4	1663	1030	0.1972	0.2392
EN->DE	Unofficial5	1663	961	0.1893	0.2198
EN->DE	Unofficial6	1663	917	0.1419	0.1827
DE->DE	Rdedetde04	1663	922	0.2381	0.2759
EN->DE	Rendetde04	1663	684	0.1261	0.1678

Unofficial1: Results using commercial morphological analyzer and Snowball stemmer
Unofficial2: Results using commercial morphological analyzer and Snowball stemmer without decompounding
Unofficial3: Results using Snowball stemmer and simple tokenizer
Unofficial4: Results using documents in 1990-2000 and unofficial1 setting
Unofficial5: Results using documents in 1997-2000 and unofficial1 setting
Unofficial6: Results using documents in 1999-2000 and unofficial1 setting
Rdedetde04: Results using commercial morphological analyzer and Snowball stemmer
Rendetde04: Results using documents in 1990-2000 and unofficial1 setting

5 Conclusion

We tested our new module for decompounding words and investigated problems we encountered in applying our approach to bi-lingual retrieval. The word decompounding that we used effectively improved performance by 17% according to our experiment. However, the results for bi-lingual information retrieval showed decreased performance from training to the experiment by about 25%, meaning there is room to improvement. The decreased performance from full to quarter documents indicates we require a reasonable document data capacity.

We intend to improve bi-lingual information retrieval and enhance target bi-lingual sets in future work.

References

1. Kojima, Y., Itoh, H., Mano, H., Ogawa, Y.: Ricoh at CLEF 2003. In: C. Peters, J. Gonzalo, M. Braschler, M. Kluck (eds.): Comparative Evaluation of Multilingual Information Access Systems: 4th Workshop of the Cross-Language Evaluation Forum, CLEF 2003, Trondheim, Norway, August 21-22, 2003, Revised Selected Papers. Lecture Notes in Computer Science, 3237: Berlin/Heidelberg/New York: Springer (2004) 367-372 online at http://www. springerlink.com/openurl.asp?genre=article&issn=0302-9743&volume=3237 &spage=367
2. Kojima, Y., Itoh, H.: Ricoh in the NTCIR-4 CLIR Tasks. At http://research.nii.ac.jp/ntcir-ws4/NTCIR4-WN/CLIR/NTCIR4WN-CLIR-KojimaY.pdf
3. Robertson, S. E., Walker, S.: On relevance weights with little relevance information. In: Proceedings of the 20th Annual International ACM SIGIR Conference (SIGIR '97), 16-24, 1997.
4. Ogawa, Y., Mano, H.: RICOH at NTCIR-2. In Proceedings of the Second NTCIR Workshop Meeting, pp. 121-123, 2001.
5. Itoh, H., Mano, H., Ogawa, Y.: RICOH at TREC-10. In: The Tenth Text Retrieval Conference (TREC-2001), pp.457-464, 2001.
6. Toyoda, M., Kitsuregawa, M., Mano, H., Itoh, H., Ogawa, Y.: University of Tokyo / RICOH at NTCIR-3 Web Retrieval Task. At http://research.nii.ac.jp/ntcir/workshop/ Online Proceeding3/NTCIR3/NTCIR3-WEB-ToyodaM.pdf
7. Robertson, S. E.: On term selection for query expansion. Journal of Documentation, 46 (4): 359-364, 1990
8. Robertson, S. E., Sparck-Jones, K.: Relevance weighting of search terms. Journal of ASIS, 27: 129-146, 1976.
9. Itoh, H.: NTCIR-4 Patent Retrieval Experiments at RICOH. At http://research.nii.ac.jp/ ntcir-ws4/NTCIR4-WN/PATENT/NTCIR4WN-PATENT-ItohH.pdf
10. Snowball web site. At http://snowball.tartarus.org/ visited 7th November 2002.

GIRT and the Use of Subject Metadata for Retrieval

Vivien Petras

School of Information Management and Systems,
University of California, Berkeley, CA 94720 USA
vivienp@sims.berkeley.edu

Abstract. The use of domain-specific metadata (subject keywords) is tested for monolingual and bilingual retrieval on the GIRT social science collection. A new technique, Entry Vocabulary Modules, which adds subject keywords selected from the controlled vocabulary to the query, has been tested. As in previous years, we compare our techniques of thesaurus matching and Entry Vocabulary Modules to simple machine translation techniques in bilingual retrieval. A combination of machine translation and thesaurus matching achieves better results, whereas the introduction of Entry Vocabulary Modules has negligent impact on the retrieval results. Retrieval results for the German and English GIRT collection for monolingual as well as bilingual retrieval (with English and German as query languages) will be represented.

1 Introduction

For several years now, the Berkeley group has been interested in how the use of subject metadata (additional to the full text of title and abstract of documents) can improve information retrieval and provide more precise results. For this year's CLEF evaluation, we once again focused on the GIRT collection with its thesaurus-enhanced records, giving us an experimental playing field. We believe that leveraging the high-quality keywords provided by a controlled vocabulary could help in disambiguating the fuzziness of the searcher language and aid searchers in formulating effective queries in order to match relevant documents better.

We are experimenting with a technique called Entry Vocabulary Modules, which suggests subject keywords from the thesaurus when given a natural language query. Like blind feedback terms, these subject keywords are added to the query with the goal of matching the controlled vocabulary terms added to the documents. Using the bilingual feature of the GIRT thesaurus, we substitute suggested thesaurus terms from the Entry Vocabulary Module in the query language with those in the target document language, thereby providing a crude translation mechanism for bilingual retrieval. The improvements over baseline retrieval were minimal, however. A description of the technique is provided in the next section.

Once again, we also tested thesaurus matching for bilingual retrieval against machine translation (described in section 1.2). We report positive results for a combination of thesaurus matching and machine translation.

C. Peters et al. (Eds.): CLEF 2004, LNCS 3491, pp. 298–309, 2005.

We have used both the German and English GIRT document collection for monolingual and bilingual retrieval. English and German were used as query languages. All runs are TD (title, description) runs only.

For all retrieval experiments, the Berkeley group is using the technique of logistic regression as described in [1].

1.1 Entry Vocabulary Modules

The concept of Entry Vocabulary Modules is based on the idea that searching the controlled vocabulary terms (i.e. thesaurus terms in the GIRT case) in the documents together with the free text natural language query terms will yield better and more complete results than using the randomly chosen query terms alone. The use of a thesaurus for document enhancement ensures that a certain document topic is unambiguously represented by a selected descriptor making sure that documents are retrieved even if only synonyms or related terms are found in the document's text. In an ideal case, the use of thesaurus terms in the query will retrieve a more precise result set, containing documents indexed in the searched subject area.

Entry Vocabulary Modules (EVMs) act as intermediaries between natural language queries and the topical metadata of a document repository. For a given query, they act as "interpreter" between the searcher and the system, proposing query terms from the controlled vocabulary. If using an EVM, the searcher is presented with a list of ranked controlled vocabulary terms that the EVM deems appropriate for the query. The searcher can then choose to add or substitute these terms in the query.

An Entry Vocabulary Module is created by building a dictionary of associations between terms in titles, author names, and / or abstracts and controlled vocabulary terms in documents. A likelihood ratio statistic is used to measure the association between any natural language term and a controlled vocabulary term and then to predict which metadata terms best mirror the topic represented by the searcher's search vocabulary. The methodology of constructing Entry Vocabulary Indexes has been described in detail by [2] and [3].

As the basic technique, a lexical collocation process between document words and controlled vocabulary terms is used. If words co-occur with a higher than random frequency, there exists a likelihood that they are strongly associated. The idea is that the stronger an association between the occurrence of two or more words (document word and controlled vocabulary term), the more likely it is that the collocation is meaningful. If an Entry Vocabulary Module is used to predict metadata vocabulary terms for a document, the association weights for document term and metadata term pairs are combined by adding them. By choosing the highest value of the added weights, the probability of relevance for metadata terms for a whole document can be determined.

For the GIRT experiments, we created an EVM for each of the English and German collections using the titles and abstracts and the GIRT thesaurus terms. We then automatically added the top ranked thesaurus descriptors to the query in the same way we would add blind feedback terms to a query. This leaves out the manual selection process where a searcher selects appropriate terms counting on the prediction that an EVM will rank the "best" or most effective controlled vocabulary terms first.

Using EVMs to add query terms automatically carries the risk of distorting the query and misrepresenting the content by putting too much weight on more ineffective query terms. Below is an example of the top 10 suggested controlled vocabulary terms from the German EVM for GIRT query number 2. We input the title and description of the query.

<num> 102 </num>
<DE-title> Deregulierung des Strommarktes </DE-title>
<DE-desc> Finde Dokumente, die über die Deregulierung in der Elektrizitätswirtschaft berichten. </DE-desc>

<cv> Deregulierung </cv>
<cv> Flexibilität </cv>
<cv> Elektrizitätswirtschaft </cv>
<cv> Arbeitsmarkt </cv>
<cv> Telekommunikation </cv>
<cv> Wettbewerb </cv>
<cv> Ordnungspolitik </cv>
<cv> Privatisierung </cv>
<cv> Wirtschaftspolitik </cv>
<cv> Elektrizität </cv>

Although some controlled vocabulary terms are wrongly suggested (e.g. Arbeitsmarkt), these terms could be specific enough to add more information to the query and not distort the original sense of the query. Following however is an example from the English EVM for GIRT where the EVM doesn't necessarily suggest "wrong" controlled vocabulary terms but also doesn't seem to add much valuable content to the query.

<num> 114 </num>
<EN-title> Illegal Employment in Germany </EN-title>
<EN-desc> Find documents reporting on illicit work in the Federal Republic of Germany. </EN-desc>

<cv>labor market </cv>
<cv>federal republic of germany </cv>
<cv>labor market policy </cv>
<cv>unemployment </cv>
<cv>employment policy </cv>
<cv>new bundeslaender </cv>
<cv>employment trend </cv>
<cv>employment </cv>
<cv>effect on employment </cv>
<cv>old bundeslaender </cv>

The controlled vocabulary term "Federal Republic of Germany" occurs over 60,000 times in the collection and "Labor Market" and "Unemployment" over 4,000 times respectively. Adding these words is not discriminating for the search at all and might unduly emphasize these very frequent terms.

More analysis is necessary to find a more selective way of adding controlled vocabulary terms, maybe based on distribution measures within the document collection and appropriate fit with the query (see section 1.3 for more data on thesaurus term distribution). It might be possible that EVMs cannot be used in a completely automatic manner (adding terms without manual pre-selection).

1.2 Thesaurus Matching

We have been experimenting with thesaurus matching for three years and yielded astonishingly good results. Thesaurus matching is a translation technique where the query is first split into words and phrases (the longest possible phrase is chosen). Secondly, these words and phrases are looked up in the thesaurus that is provided with the GIRT collection and, if found, substituted with the target language terms from the thesaurus. Words and phrases that cannot be translated (not found in the thesaurus) are kept in the original language. For a more detailed description of the technique, see [4] and for a discussion of efficiency and advantages and disadvantages, see our paper from last year [5].

Thesaurus matching is in essence leveraging the high-quality translations of controlled vocabulary terms in multilingual thesauri. The GIRT thesaurus provides a controlled vocabulary in English, German and Russian. We experimented with thesaurus matching from German to English and from English to German and achieved comparable results to machine translation.

Although thesaurus matching relies only on the exact terms and phrases as they appear in the query, enough seem to be found to achieve a reasonable representation of the query content in controlled vocabulary terms. Even though Entry Vocabulary Modules also represent the query content in controlled vocabulary terms, adding them to the query instead of substituting query terms with them doesn't yield as noticeable results in bilingual retrieval. This might have several reasons, among them the number of added terms, the preciseness and distinctiveness of the chosen terms and the size of the controlled vocabulary (how many records contain the same controlled vocabulary term and how effective is adding a controlled vocabulary term).

2 The GIRT Collection

The GIRT collection (German Indexing and Retrieval Test database) consists of 151,319 documents containing titles, abstracts and controlled vocabulary terms in the social science domain. The GIRT controlled vocabulary terms are based on the Thesaurus for the Social Sciences [6] and are provided in German, English and Russian.

In 2003, two parallel GIRT corpora were made available: (1) German GIRT 4 contains document fields with German text, and (2) English GIRT 4 contains the translations of these fields into English. Although these corpora are described as parallel, they are not identical.

Both collections contain 151,319 records, but the English collection contains only 26,058 abstracts (ca. one out of six records) whereas the German collection contains 145,941 - providing an abstract for almost all documents. Consequently, the German collection contains more terms per record to search on. The English corpus has 1,535,445 controlled vocabulary terms (7064 unique phrases) and 301,257 classification codes (159 unique phrases) assigned. The German corpus has 1,535,582 controlled vocabulary terms (7154 unique phrases) and 300,115 classification codes (158 unique phrases) assigned. On average, 10 controlled vocabulary terms and 2 classification codes have been assigned to each document.

Controlled vocabulary terms and classification codes are not uniformly distributed. Whereas the distribution of controlled vocabulary terms has no impact on the thesaurus matching technique, it influences the performance of the statistical association technique for Entry Vocabulary Modules, i.e. skews towards more often assigned terms. Fig. 1 shows the frequency distribution for thesaurus terms in the German GIRT collection. The English GIRT collection is similar.

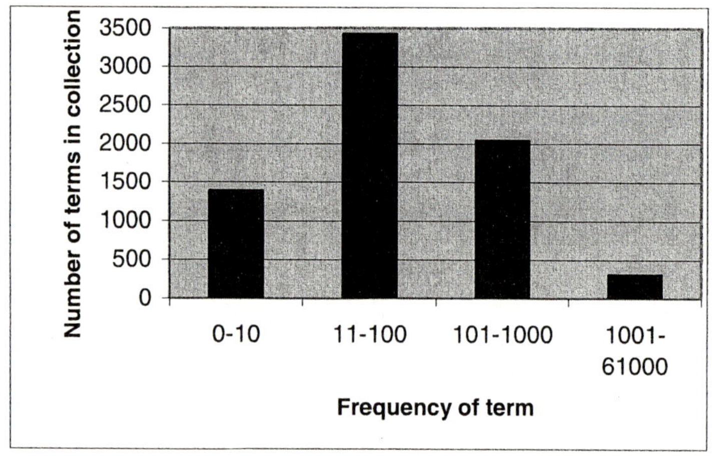

Fig. 1. Frequency distribution of thesaurus terms in the German GIRT collection

Most thesaurus terms occur less than a 100 times, but the most frequent one "Bundesrepublik Deutschland" occurs 60,955 times and occurs therefore in more than a third of the documents. Using this term in search will have no discerning effect but because it occurs so often, it is associated with a lot of natural language terms resulting in a high probability of relevance for the EVM. Of the 7154 unique thesaurus terms assigned, 307 occur more than 1,000 times – highly unlikely to have a discriminating effect in retrieval. For this year's submissions, we haven't made efforts to normalize the data to ensure optimal training of the EVMs, but analyzing the effect of those highly frequent terms will be a future task.

3 GIRT Retrieval Experiments

3.1 GIRT Monolingual

For GIRT monolingual retrieval, six runs for each language are presented, five of those twelve were official runs. We compared two ways of using controlled vocabulary terms provided by the EVMs and submitted one official run for each.

We submitted the required run against a GIRT document index without the added thesaurus terms. For both languages, this was the run with the lowest average precision. However, the English run is much worse than the German (both in the first column of tables 1 and 2), demonstrating the effect of added keywords to documents when a lot of the abstracts are missing (see section 1.3 for a small analysis of the GIRT collections).

As a baseline, a run against the full document collection (including thesaurus and classification terms) without additional query keywords was used (second column of both tables 1 and 2). This baseline run was only minimally surpassed by the EVM-enhanced runs, yielding an average precision of 0.4150 for German and 0.3834 for English respectively.

The first method of adding controlled vocabulary terms to the query was used in official runs BKGRMLGG2 and BKGRMLEE2 for German and English respectively. The top three ranked suggested thesaurus terms from the Entry Vocabulary Modules (one for German and one for English) were added to the title and description of the query. The added terms were then down weighted by half as compared to title and description terms in retrieval. In columns 3-5 of tables 1 and 2, retrieval runs adding one, three and five controlled vocabulary terms suggested by an EVM are compared.

The second method of utilizing EVMs was used in official runs BKGRMLGG1 and BKGRMLEE1. Whereas the terms from the title and description of the query were run against a full document index, the added thesaurus terms were run against a special index consisting of the controlled vocabulary terms added to the documents only. The results of these two runs were then merged by comparing values of the probability rank provided by our logistic regression retrieval algorithm. For both German and English, this merging yielded worse results than the baseline run indicating that the run against the index with thesaurus terms only distorted results. The thesaurus terms alone might not have enough distinctive power to discriminate against irrelevant documents.

3.1.1 German Monolingual

For all runs against the German GIRT collection, we used our decompounding procedure to split German compound words into individual terms in both the documents and the queries. The procedure is described in [7]. We also used a German stopword list and a stemmer in retrieval.

Additionally, we used our blind feedback algorithm for all runs except BKGRMLGG1 to improve performance. The blind feedback algorithm assumes the top 20 documents as relevant and selects 30 terms from these documents to add to the query. Using the decompounding procedure and our blind feedback algorithm usually increases the performance anywhere between 10 and 30%.

Table 1 summarizes the results for the German monolingual runs. The best run was adding 5 EVM-suggested thesaurus terms and then down weighting them in retrieval.

Table 1. Average precision for GIRT German Monolingual Runs

BKGRMLGG0			BKGRMLGG2		BKGRMLGG1
document index w/o thesaurus terms	baseline run	TD terms are weighted double	TD terms are weighted double	TD terms are weighted double	CV terms against separate CV index
	TD only	TD + 1 CV term	TD + 3 CV terms	TD + 5 CV terms	TD & 3 CV terms
0.3706	0.4150	0.4079	0.4177	***0.4280***	0.4102

Although the average precision over all queries for the baseline run without EVM input and the best EVM is almost the same, in a query-by-query comparison one can find distinctive differences. Table 2 compares the average precisions for the baseline run (TD only) and one EVM run for the most distinctive cases.

Table 2. Difference in average precision for selected queries

Query number	TD only	TD + 5 CV terms	Percent difference
101	0.0098	0.3372	+3341%
103	0.1450	0.0279	-81%
104	0.3798	0.2526	-33%
107	0.0809	0.3431	+324%
108	0.3836	0.6664	+74%
112	0.1012	0.3176	+214%
116	0.3443	0.0007	-99%

An additional run with an attempt to remove the most undiscriminating descriptors from the EVM suggestions (all descriptors that were assigned with a frequency higher than 1,000 were deleted and the next lowest ranked descriptor selected) did not improve the retrieval results (average precision over all queries 0.4203), however some questions improved their results. As one can see from the example in table 3, those questions did not only improve the EVM run but could also exceed the baseline results (or were similar).

It remains to be seen whether a manual selection could successfully pick those descriptors from a suggested list that will improve the retrieval results. If the controlled vocabulary terms are too broad, even a human will not be able to further specify the query with the help of the thesaurus.

Table 3. Difference in average precision for selected queries

Query number	TD + 5 CV terms	TD + 5 CV terms (frequent terms removed)	TD only
102	0.3372	0.7962	0.0098
103	0.0279	0.1442	0.1450
104	0.2526	0.3808	0.3798

3.1.2 English Monolingual

For all runs against the English GIRT collection, an English stopword list and stemmer were used. We also used our blind feedback algorithm for all runs except BKGRMLEE1.

The best run in this series was adding one EVM-suggested thesaurus term and down weighting it in retrieval. It is still unclear how many added thesaurus terms might be best, especially since this seems to differ between the German and English collection.

Table 4. Average Precision for GIRT English Monolingual runs

			BKGRMLEE2		BKGRMLEE1
document index w/o thesaurus terms	baseline run	TD terms are weighted double	TD terms are weighted double	TD terms are weighted double	CV terms against separate CV index
	TD only	TD + 1 CV term	TD + 3 CV terms	TD + 5 CV terms	TD & 3 CV terms
0.2131	0.3834	***0.3985***	0.3908	0.3445	0.3732

A comparison query-by-query between the best EVM run and the baseline run shows differences as well, although not as large as for the German monolingual runs.

Table 5. Difference in average precision for selected queries

Query number	TD only	TD + 1 CV term	Percent difference
102	0.7799	0.8212	+5%
107	0.6531	0.5994	-8%
108	0.7151	0.6177	-14%
109	0.1530	0.2193	43%
114	0.4078	0.5369	32%
120	0.2987	0.4095	37%
122	0.1198	0.1843	54%

3.2 GIRT Bilingual

For GIRT bilingual retrieval, 18 runs for each language are presented, 10 of which were official runs (5 for each language). For bilingual retrieval, we compared the behavior of machine translation, thesaurus matching, EVMs and any combination of these.

The best bilingual runs rival the monolingual runs in average precision with one German → English run (BKGRBLGE1) marginally outperforming all English monolingual runs.

Last year, we compared the Systran and L & H Power Translator against each other with L & H alone performing better on both English → German and German → English translations than Systran or the combination of both. All translations of the query title and description were therefore undertaken with the L & H Power Translator only.

Both machine translation (L & H Power Translator) and thesaurus matching performed equally well. However, the combination of machine translation and thesaurus matching (coupling the translated title and description from machine translation and thesaurus matching and then down weighting terms that are duplicates) achieved even better results. All three runs can be compared in the first 3 columns of tables 6 and 8. The combination runs were official runs (BKGRBLEG1 and BKGRBLGE1). The combined run outperforms all other runs in the German → English series and is second best in the English → German series.

Table 6. Average Precision for GIRT English → German Bilingual Runs

		BKGR BLEG1	BKGR BLEG5	BKGR BLEG2	BKGR BLEG4		BKGR BLEG3
MT	Thes. Match	MT + Thes. Match	MT + 3 CV terms	MT + 5 CV terms	Thes. Match + 5 CV terms	MT + Thes. Match + 3 CV terms	MT + Thes. Match + 5 CV terms
0.3146	0.3287	0.3868	0.3224	0.3176	0.2964	***0.3871***	0.3641

EVMs were used to suggest controlled vocabulary terms and substituting them with their target language equivalent. In a first experiment where we just took the foreign-language substitutes of five EVM-suggested thesaurus terms per query, the similar technique of thesaurus matching outperformed this run. This is not surprising since 5 terms or phrases seem not enough for effective retrieval whereas thesaurus matching tries to use all query terms in matching. It remains to be seen whether a higher number of suggested terms could achieve comparable results or deteriorate because of increasing impreciseness of query words.

Official runs BKGRBLEG2, BKGRBLEG5, BKGRBLGE2 and BKGRBLGE5 combined machine translation provided by L & H and 5 or 3 EVM-suggested thesaurus terms respectively.

Runs BKGRBLEG4 and BKGRBLGE4 combined thesaurus matching and 5 EVM-suggested thesaurus terms.

The last 2 columns of tables 6 and 8 show combination runs of machine translation, thesaurus matching and EVM-suggested thesaurus terms, BKGRBLEG3 and BKGRBLGE3 were official runs.

3.2.1 Bilingual English → German

For English to German bilingual retrieval, the combination of machine translation and suggested EVM terms marginally outperforms machine translation alone but not the combination of machine translation and thesaurus matching. The combination of thesaurus matching and EVM-suggested terms performs worse than thesaurus terms alone suggesting a deteriorating effect of the added terms. The combination of all three methods doesn't achieve better results than the combination of thesaurus matching and machine translation alone.

Table 7. Comparing machine translation, EVMs combined with machine translation and thesaurus matching

Query number	MT	MT + 3 CV terms	Percent difference to MT	Thes. Match	Percent difference to MT
102	0.7974	0.4657	-42%	0.7609	-5%
104	0.2699	0.3420	+27%	0.0283	-90%
108	0.3888	0.4257	+9%	0.6949	+79%
114	0.3306	0.0939	-72%	0.5083	+54%
117	0.0441	0.1933	+338%	0.0484	+10%
120	0.0279	0.5643	+1923%	0.2785	+898%
122	0.3148	0.3791	+20%	0.2519	-20%
124	0.5505	0.7321	+33%	0.7953	+44%

Table 8. Average Precision for GIRT German → English Bilingual Runs

		BKGR BLGE1	BKGR BLGE5	BKGR BLGE2	BKGR BLGE4		BKGR BLGE3
MT	Thes. Match	MT + Thes. Match	MT + 3 CV terms	MT + 5 CV terms	Thes. Match + 5 CV terms	MT + Thes. Match + 3 CV terms	MT + Thes. Match + 5 CV terms
0.3431	0.3370	***0.4053***	0.3370	0.3054	0.3340	0.3748	0.3668

Once again, it makes sense to look at a query-by-query comparison comparing machine translation and machine translation + EVM-suggested thesaurus terms and thesaurus matching results. As can be seen in table 8, although similar EVMs and thesaurus matching can achieve different results on the same query – sometimes even diametrical. If one could only find a way to distinguish between "good" and "bad" query additions (i.e. picking the most-yielding method per query), precision could be significantly increased.

3.2.2 Bilingual German → English

For German to English bilingual retrieval, the addition of EVM suggested thesaurus terms generally seems to deteriorate results probably by adding "noise" words to the query instead of relevant discriminative terms. Looking at the suggested EVM terms, however, doesn't confirm this hypothesis. Most EVM suggestions seem quite sensible, however they might simply be too broad. It should be interesting to find out how much a manual selection of terms could improve results and how much "wrongly" suggested thesaurus terms worsen it.

A query-by-query comparison once again does not give the combination of thesaurus matching and machine translation an unequivocal advantage over EVM suggestions and machine translations, the trend seems almost arbitrary. It will be task for next year to find a way to decide between these methods.

4 Conclusion

This research shows that the topical metadata provided by a document collection can be successfully used to improve automated methods of translation and retrieval.

Although the newly introduced technique of adding thesaurus terms suggested by an Entry Vocabulary Module only achieves negligent improvement over our baseline run in general, we have nevertheless shown that this technique can improve precision substantially in individual cases both for monolingual and as translation technique for bilingual retrieval in English and German.

More research is needed to ascertain whether individual methods of query enhancement and query translation can be chosen according to a fixed set of criteria for any individual query. A human intermediary might be necessary to make a first choice.

References

1. Chen, A.; Cooper, W.; Gey, F.: Full text retrieval based on probabilistic equations with coefficients fitted by logistic regression. In: D.K. Harman (Ed.), The Second Text Retrieval Conference (TREC-2), March 1994, (1994), 57-66
2. Plaunt, C.; Norgard, B. A.: An Association-Based Method for Automatic Indexing with Controlled Vocabulary. Journal of the American Society for Information Science 49, (10) (1998), 888-902
3. Gey, F. et al.: Advanced Search Technology for Unfamiliar Metadata. In: Proceedings of the Third IEEE Metadata Conference, April 1999, Bethesda, Maryland (1999)

4. Petras, V.; Perelman, N.: Gey, F.: Using Thesauri in Cross-Language Retrieval of German and French Indexed Collections. In: Peters, C.; Braschler, M.; Gonzalo, J.; Kluck, M. (eds.): Evaluation of Cross-Language Information Retrieval Systems: Second Workshop of the Cross-Language Evaluation Forum, CLEF 2001, Darmstadt, Germany, September 3-4, 2001; Revised Papers. Lecture Notes in Computer Science, Vol. 2406. Springer-Verlag, Berlin Heidelberg New York (2002), 349-362
5. Petras, V.; Perelman, N.; Gey, F.: UC Berkeley at CLEF-2003 – Russian Language Experiments and Domain-Specific Retrieval. In: Peters, C.; Gonzales, J.; Braschler, M.; Kluck, M. (eds.): Advances in Cross-Language Information Retrieval: third Workshop of the Cross-Language Evaluation Forum, CLEF 2002, Rome, Italy, September 19 - 20, 2002 ; revised papers. Lecture Notes in Computer Science, Vol. 2785, Springer-Verlag, Berlin Heidelberg New York (2003), 401-411
6. Schott, H.: Thesaurus for the Social Sciences. [Vol. 1:] German-English. [Vol. 2:] English-German. Informations-Zentrum Sozialwissenschaften, Bonn (2000)
7. Chen, A.; Gey, F.: Multilingual Information Retrieval Using Machine Translation, Relevance Feedback and Decompounding In: Information Retrieval, Volume 7, Issue 1-2, Jan. – Apr. (2004). 149-182

iCLEF 2004 Track Overview: Pilot Experiments in Interactive Cross-Language Question Answering

Julio Gonzalo[1] and Douglas W. Oard[2]

[1] Departamento de Lenguajes y Sistemas Informáticos,
Escuela Técnica Superior de Ingeniería Informática de la UNED,
c/ Juan del Rosal, 16, 28040 Madrid, Spain
julio@lsi.uned.es
http://nlp.uned.es/~julio

[2] Human Computer Interaction Laboratory,
College of Information Studies and
Institute for Advanced Computer Studies,
University of Maryland, College Park, MD 20742, USA
oard@glue.umd.edu.edu
http://www.glue.umd.edu/~oard

Abstract. For the 2004 Cross-Language Evaluation Forum (CLEF) interactive track (iCLEF), five participating teams used a common evaluation design to assess the ability of interactive systems of their own design to support the task of finding specific answers to narrowly focused questions in a collection of documents written in a language different from the language in which the questions were expressed. This task is an interactive counterpart to the fully automatic cross-language question answering task at CLEF 2003 and 2004. This paper describes the iCLEF 2004 evaluation design, outlines the experiments conducted by the participating teams, and presents some initial results from analyses of official evaluation measures that were reported to each participating team.

1 Introduction

The design of systems to support information access depends on three fundamental factors: (1) the user's task, (2) the way in which the system will be used to achieve that task, and (3) the nature of the information being searched. In the Cross-Language Evaluation Forum, it is assumed that the information being searched is expressed in a different natural language (e.g., Spanish) than that chosen by the user to express their information needs to the system (e.g. English). In the CLEF interactive track (iCLEF), it is further assumed that the user will engage in an iterative search process using a system that is designed to support human-system interaction. In 2001, 2002, and 2003, iCLEF modeled the user's task as finding documents that were topically relevant to a written

C. Peters et al. (Eds.): CLEF 2004, LNCS 3491, pp. 310–322, 2005.

statement of the information need. In 2004 iCLEF adopted a new task; to find specific answers to narrowly focused questions.

The iCLEF evaluations have two fundamental goals: (1) to explore evaluation design, and (2) to permit contrastive evaluation of alternative system designs. These goals are somewhat in tension; the first inspires us to try new tasks, while the second would benefit from stability and continuity in the task design. Over the first three years of iCLEF, our focus was on progressive refinement of the evaluation design for a consistent task (finding topically relevant documents), and substantial progress resulted. Individual teams can continue to use the evaluation designs that were developed at iCLEF over those three years, and evaluation resources that were produced over that period (e.g., official and interactive topical relevance judgments) can be of continuing value to both CLEF participants and to teams that subsequently begin to work on cross-language information retrieval.

When selecting a new task for iCLEF this year, we considered two options: (1) cross-language question answering, and (2) cross-language image retrieval. Ultimately, we selected cross-language question answering because there was a broader base of prior work on the evaluation of fully automated question answering systems to which we could compare our results. The Image CLEF track did, however, also explore the design of an interactive image retrieval task this year. We therefore achieved the best of both worlds, with the opportunity to learn about evaluation design for both tasks. Readers interested in interactive image retrieval should consult the Image CLEF track overview in this volume. In this paper, we focus on interactive Cross-Language Question Answering (CL-QA). The next section describes the iCLEF 2004 CL-QA experiment design. It is followed by sections describing the experiments and providing an overview of the results obtained by the participating teams. The paper concludes with some thoughts about future directions for iCLEF.

2 Experiment Design

Participating teams performed an experiment by constructing two conditions (identified as "reference" and "contrastive"), formulating a hypothesis that they wished to test, and using a common evaluation design to test that hypothesis. Human subjects were in groups of eight (i.e., experiments could be run with 8, 16, 24, or 32 subjects). Each subject conducted 16 *search sessions*. A search session is uniquely identified by three parameters: the human subject performing the search, the search condition tested by that subject (reference or contrastive), and the question to be answered. Each team used different subjects, but the questions, the assignment of questions to searcher-condition pairs, and the presentation order were common to all experiments. A latin-square matrix design was adopted to establish a set of presentation orders for each subject that would minimize the effect of user-specific, question-specific and order-related factors on the quantitative task effectiveness measures that were used. The remainder of this section explains the details of this experiment design.

2.1 Question Set

Question selection proved to be challenging. We adopted the following guidelines to guide our choice of questions:

- We selected only questions from the **CLEF 2004 QA question set** in order to facilitate insightful comparisons between automatic and interactive experiments that were evaluated under similar conditions.
- The largest **number of questions** that could be accommodated in three hours was needed in order to maximize the reliability of the quantitative measures of task effectiveness. Our experience in previous years suggests that three hours is about the longest we can expect subjects to participate in a single day, and extending an experiment across multiple days would adversely affect the practicality of recruiting an adequate number of subjects. We chose to allow up to five minutes for each search. Once training time was accounted for, this left time for 16 questions during the experiment itself.
- **Answers should not be known in advance** by the human subjects. This restriction proved to be particularly challenging in view of the breadth of cultural backgrounds that we expected among the participating teams in this international evaluation, resulting in elimination of a large fraction of the CLEF 2004 QA set (e.g., "What is the frequency unit?," "Who is Simon Peres?" and "What are Japanese suicide pilots called?"). Two types of questions were found to be more often compatible with this restriction: temporal questions (e.g., "When was the Convention on the Rights of the Child adopted?") and measure questions (e.g., "How many illiterates are there in the world?" or "How much does the world population increase each year?").
- Given that the question set had to be necessarily small, we wanted to **avoid NIL questions** (i.e., questions with no answer. Ideally, it should be possible to find an answer to every question in any collection that a participating team might elect to search. Ultimately, we found that we had to limit this restriction to presence in both the Spanish and English collections in order to get a sufficiently large number of questions from which to choose. Together, these cover four of the five experiments that were run (the fifth used the French collection).
- A small set of questions cannot have a representative number of questions for each question type. To avoid averaging over tiny sets of different types of questions, we decided to focus on **four question types**. The CLEF QA set includes eight question types: LOCATION (e.g., "In what city is St Peter's Cathedral?"), MANNER (e.g., "How did Jimi Hendrix die?"), MEASURE (e.g., "How much does the world population increase each year?"), OBJECT (e.g., "What is the Antarctic continent covered with?"), ORGANIZATION (e.g., "What is the Mossad?"), PERSON (e.g., "Who is Michael Jackson married to?"), TIME (e.g., "When was the Cyrillic alphabet introduced?"), and OTHER (e.g., "What is a basic ingredient of Japanese cuisine?"). We selected two question types that called for named entities as answers (PERSON and ORGANIZATION) and two question types that called for temporal or

Table 1. The iCLEF 2004 question set

#	QA#	type	Question
1	001	TIME	What year was Thomas Mann awarded the Nobel Prize?
2	109	MEAS	How many human genes are there?
3	314	PERS	Who is the German Minister for Economic Affairs?
4	514	ORG	Who committed the terrorist attack in the Tokyo underground?
5	122	MEAS	How much did the Channel Tunnel cost?
6	113	TIME	When did Latvia gain independence?
7	217	MEAS	How many people were declared missing in the Philippines after the typhoon "Angela"?
8	242	PERS	Who is the managing director of the International Monetary Fund?
9	511	TIME	When did Lenin die?
10	219	MEAS	How many people died of asphyxia in the Baku underground?
11	534	PERS	Who is the president of Burundi?
12	543	ORG	What is Charles Millon's political party?
13	646	ORG	Of what team is Bobby Robson coach?
14	506	TIME	When did the attack at the Saint-Michel underground station in Paris occur?
15	318	MEAS	How many people live in Bombay?
16	287	PERS	Who won the Nobel Prize for Literature in 1994?
17	002	PERS	Who is the managing director of FIAT? *(training)*
18	195	MEAS	How many pandas are there in the wild in China? *(training)*
19	505	PERS	Who is the Russian Minister of Finance? *(training)*
20	512	TIME	When did the Iranian Islamic revolution take place? *(training)*

quantitative measures (TIME and MEASURE) and sought to balance those four types of questions in the final set. Some iCLEF 2004 question types call for definitions rather than succinct facts (e.g., "What is the INCB?"). We decided to omit definition questions because we felt that evaluation might be difficult in an interactive setting (e.g., a user might combine information found in documents with their own background knowledge and then create answers in their own writing style that could not be judged using the same criteria as automatic QA systems).

The final set of sixteen questions, plus four additional questions for user training, are shown in Table 1.

2.2 Latin-Square Design

One factor that makes reliable evaluation of interactive systems challenging is that once a user has searched for the answer to a question in one condition, the same question cannot be used with the other condition (formally, the learning effect would likely mask the system effect). We adopt a within-subjects study design, in which the condition seen for each user-topic pair varies systematically in a balanced manner using a latin square, to accommodate this. This same approach has been used in the Text Retrieval Conference (TREC) interactive

Table 2. iCLEF 2004 Condition and Topic Presentation Order

user	**search order** (condition: $A\|B$, question: $1\ldots16$)															
1	A1	A4	A3	A2	A9	A12	A11	A10	B13	B16	B15	B14	B5	B8	B7	B6
2	B2	B3	B4	B1	B10	B11	B12	B9	A14	A15	A16	A13	A6	A7	A8	A5
3	B1	B4	B3	B2	B9	B12	B11	B10	A13	A16	A15	A14	A5	A8	A7	A6
4	A2	A3	A4	A1	A10	A11	A12	A9	B14	B15	B16	B13	B6	B7	B8	B5
5	A15	A14	A9	A12	A7	A6	A1	A4	B3	B2	B5	B8	B11	B10	B13	B16
6	B16	B13	B10	B11	B8	B5	B2	B3	A4	A1	A6	A7	A12	A9	A14	A15
7	B15	B14	B9	B12	B7	B6	B1	B4	A3	A2	A5	A8	A11	A10	A13	A16
8	A16	A13	A10	A11	A8	A5	A2	A3	B4	B1	B6	B7	B12	B9	B14	B15

tracks [1] and in past iCLEF evaluations [2]. Table 2 shows the presentation order used for each experiment.

2.3 Evaluation Measures

In order to establish some degree of comparability, we chose to follow the design of the automatic CL-QA task in CLEF-2004 as closely as possible. Thus, we used the same assessment rules, the same assessors and the same evaluation measures as the CLEF QA task:

- Human subjects were asked to designate a supporting document for each answer. Automatic CL-QA systems were required to designate exactly one such document, but for iCLEF we also allowed the designation of zero or two supporting documents:
  - We anticipated the possibility that people might construct an answer from information found in more than one document. Users were therefore allowed to mark either one or two supporting documents for an answer. When two documents were designated, assessors were instructed to determine whether both documents together supported the answer.
  - Upon expiration of the search time, users might wish to record an answer even though time would no longer be available to identify a supporting document. In such cases, we allowed users to write an answer with no supporting document. Assessors were instructed to judge such an answer to be correct if and only if that answer had been found by some automatic CLEF CL-QA system.

  Users were not encouraged to use either option, and in practice there were very few cases in which they were used.
- Users were allowed to record their answers in whatever language was appropriate to the study design in which they were participating. For example, users with no knowledge of the document language would generally be expected to record answers in the question language. Participating teams were asked to hand-translate answers into the document language after completion of the experiment in such cases in order to facilitate assessment.
- Answers were assessed by the same assessors that assessed the automatic CL-QA results for CLEF 2004. The same answer categories were used in

iCLEF as in the automatic CL-QA track: *correct* (valid, supported answer), *unsupported* (valid but not supported by the designated document(s)), *non-exact* or *incorrect*. The CLEF CL-QA track guidelines at http://clef-qa.itc.it/2004/guidelines.html provide additional details on the definition of these categories. Assessment in CLEF is distributed geographically on the basis of the document language, so some variation in the degree of strictness of the assessment across languages is natural. For iCLEF 2004, assessors reported that they sometimes held machines to a higher standard than they applied in the case of fully automated systems. For example, "July 25" was accepted as an answer to "When did the attack at the Saint-Michel underground station in Paris occur?" for fully automatic systems (because the year was not stated in the supporting document), but it was scored as inexact for iCLEF because the assessor believed that the user should have been able to infer the correct year from the date of the article.

– We reported the same official effectiveness measures as the CLEF-2004 CL-QA track. Strict accuracy (the fraction of correct answers) and lenient accuracy (the fraction of correct plus unsupported answers) were reported for each condition. Complete results were reported to each participating team by user, question and condition to allow more detailed analyses to be conducted locally.

2.4 Suggested User Session

We set a maximum search time of five minutes per question, but allowed our human subjects to move on to the next question after recording an answer and designating supporting document(s) even if the full five minutes had not expired. We established the following typical schedule for each 3-hour session:

Orientation	10 minutes
Initial questionnaire	5 minutes
Training on both systems	30 minutes
Break	10 minutes
Searching in the first condition (8 topics)	40-60 minutes
System questionnaire	5 minutes
Break	10 minutes
Searching in the second condition (8 topics)	40-60 minutes
System questionnaire	5 minutes
Final questionnaire	10 minutes

Half of the users saw condition A (the reference condition) first, the other half saw condition B first. Participating teams were permitted to alter this schedule as appropriate to their goals. For example, teams that chose to run each subject separately to permit close qualitative assessment by a trained observer might choose to substitute a semi-structured exit interview for the final questionnaire. Questionnaire design was not prescribed, but sample questionnaires were made available to participating teams on the iCLEF Web site (http://nlp.uned.es/iCLEF/).

3 Experiments

Five groups submitted results: The Swedish Institute of Computer Science (SICS) from Sweden, the University of Alicante, the University of Salamanca and UNED from Spain, and the University of Maryland from the USA. Four of the five groups had previously participated in iCLEF (the University of Salamanca joined the track this year). Remarkably, all of the participants used interactive CLIR systems of fairly conventional designs; none adapted existing QA systems to support this task. In the remainder of this section, we briefly describe the experiment run at each site.

Alicante. The experiment compared two passage retrieval systems. In both systems, the query was formulated in Spanish, automatically translated into English before passage retrieval, and then passages were shown to the users in English (untranslated). The reference system also showed ontological concepts for the query and the passage, ranking passages with the same concepts as the query higher. The contrastive system showed syntactic-semantic patterns (SSP) for the query and for each verb in the passage. The hypothesis being tested was that for users with low English skills, it would be more useful to find the answer through SSPs than through the whole passage.

Maryland. Two types of summaries were compared. The first was an indicative summary consisting of three sentence snippets sampled from the beginning, the middle, and the end of a document that each contain at least one query term. That type of summary aims to provide users with a concise overview of the document in order to permit rapid judgments of relevance. The second was an informative summary with one longer passage automatically selected by the system. Both systems used variants of the UMD MIRACLE interactive CLIR system, and the hypothesis being tested was that informative summaries would be more useful than indicative summaries for this task. Maryland was also interested in studying search behavior (query formulation, query refinement, user-assisted query translation, relevance judgment, and stopping criteria) for interactive CL-QA . The experiment involved eight native English speakers searching Spanish documents to answer questions written in English.

UNED. The UNED hypothesis was that a passage retrieval system that filtered out paragraphs which did not contain expressions of an appropriate type (named entities, dates or quantities, depending on the question) could outperform a baseline consisting of a standard information retrieval system (Inquery) that indexed and displayed Systran translations of the documents (i.e. performing monolingual searches over the translated collection). A second research goal was to establish a strong baseline for interactive CL-QA to be compared with automatic CL-QA in the context of CLEF.

Salamanca. The Salamanca team experimented with a passage retrieval system in which machine translation was used to translate the query. They tested whether the possibility of on-demand access to full documents would be more useful for CL-QA than display of a passage alone. Both systems included suggestions of query expansion terms; another goal of the experiment was to determine whether users would take advantage of that possibility in a question answering task.

SICS. SICS explored the effect of interactive query expansion using paired users (working on different questions) that could communicate within the pair (e.g., to discuss system operation or vocabulary selection). Additional research goals were to explore the nature of communication within pairs and the effect of a "bookmark" capability on user confidence in the reported result. The SICS experiment was monolingual, with French questions and French documents; the human subjects were all native speakers of Swedish with moderate skills in French.

4 Results and Discussion

In this section, we present the official results, draw comparisons with comparable results from the CLEF-2004 CL-QA track, and describe some issues that arose with the assessment of submitted answers.

Table 3. Official iCLEF 2004 results (bold: higher scoring condition)

Group	Users	Docs	Experiment Condition	Accuracy	
				Strict	Lenient
Maryland	EN	ES	indicative summaries	0.61	0.66
Maryland	EN	ES	informative summaries	**0.63**	0.66
UNED	ES	EN	doc. retrieval + Systran	**0.69**	**0.73**
UNED	ES	EN	passage ret. + entity filter	0.66	0.72
SICS	FR	FR	baseline	**0.27**	**0.41**
SICS	FR	FR	contrastive	0.19	0.28
Alicante	ES	EN	ontological concepts	0.38	0.50
Alicante	ES	EN	syntactic/semantic patterns	**0.45**	**0.56**
Salamanca	ES	EN	only passages	0.49	0.55
Salamanca	ES	EN	passages + full documents	**0.55**	**0.70**

4.1 Official Results

Table 3 shows the official results for each of the five experiments. The following points stand out from our initial inspection of these results:

- Three of the five experiments yielded differences in strict accuracy of approximately 1 answer out of 16 (0.0625% absolute), suggesting that the magnitude of detectable differences with this experiment design is likely appropriate

for the types of hypotheses being tested. Conformation of this result must, however, await the results of statistical significance tests (e.g., analysis of variance) at each site.
- Five of the ten tested conditions yielded strict accuracy above 0.50, indicating that the interactive CL-QA task is certainly feasible. There may still be room for improvement, however: even in the best condition, more than 30% of the answers were either incorrect, inexact, or unsupported. Inter-assessor agreement studies would be needed, however, before we can quantify the magnitude of the further improvement that could be reliably measured with this experiment design.
- Remarkably, the system used in the condition that yielded the highest strict accuracy (0.69) was one of the simplest baselines: a standard document retrieval system performing monolingual searches over machine translation results. This suggests that when user interaction is possible, relatively simple systems designs may suffice for CL-QA tasks.
- No evidence is yet available regarding the utility of more sophisticated question answering techniques (e.g., question reformulation or finding candidate answers in side collections) for interactive CL-QA because all iCLEF 2004 experiments employed fairly standard cross-language information retrieval techniques.

Readers are referred to the papers submitted by the participating teams for analyses of results from specific experiments.

4.2 Comparison with CLEF QA Results

English was the only document language for which multiple iCLEF experiment results were submitted, so we have chosen to focus our comparison with the CLEF 2004 CL-QA track on cases in which English documents were used. Results from 13 automatic systems were submitted to the CLEF-2004 CL-QA track for English documents. We compared the results of the six iCLEF 2004 conditions in which English documents were used (two conditions from each of three experiments) with the results from those 13 automatic runs.

Participating teams in the CLEF-2004 CL-QA track automatically found answers to 200 questions, of which 14 were common to iCLEF. Table 4 compares the results of the automatic systems on these 14 questions with the results of the interactive conditions on all 16 topics.[1]

Most of the interactive conditions yielded strict accuracy results that were markedly better than the fully automatic systems on these questions. These large differences cannot be explained by the omission of two questions in the case of the automatic systems; correct answers to those two questions would increase the strict accuracy of the best automatic system from 0.36 to 0.44, which is nowhere near the strict accuracy of 0.69 achieved by the best interactive condition. Nor

[1] Removal of two topics from the interactive results would unbalance some conditions, so the interactive results include the effect of two questions that were not assessed for the automatic systems.

Table 4. Automatic vs. interactive experiments X → EN

Group	question	docs	Run	Accuracy strict	lenient
Automatic Systems (14 questions)					
IRST	IT	EN	irst042iten	0.36	0.36
IRST	IT	EN	irst041iten	0.29	0.29
DFKI	DE	EN	dfki041deen	0.14	0.21
BGAS	BG	EN	bgas041bgen	0.07	0.07
LIRE	FR	EN	lire042fren	0.07	0.07
DLTG	FR	EN	dltg041fren	0.07	0.07
EDIN	DE	EN	edin041deen	0.07	0.07
EDIN	FR	EN	edin042fren	0.07	0.07
LIRE	FR	EN	lire041fren	0	0
DLTG	FR	EN	dltg042fren	0	0
EDIN	DE	EN	edin042deen	0	0
EDIN	FR	EN	edin041fren	0	0
HELS	FI	EN	hels041fien	0	0
Average				**0.09**	**0.10**
Interactive Experiments (16 questions)					
UNED	ES	EN	doc retr + Systran	0.69	0.73
UNED	ES	EN	passage retr + entity filter	0.66	0.72
Salamanca	ES	EN	passage ret. + access full docs.	0.55	0.70
Salamanca	ES	EN	passage ret. - access full docs.	0.49	0.55
Alicante	ES	EN	syntactic/semantic patterns	0.45	0.56
Alicante	ES	EN	ontological concepts	0.38	0.50
Average				**0.53**	**0.62**

could language differences alone be used to explain the large observed differences between the best interactive and automatic systems since the same trend is present over the five question languages that were tried with the automatic systems.

This observed difference is particularly striking in view of our expectation that the question types that we chose for the interactive evaluation would be particularly well suited to the application ofautomated techniques because the answers could be found literally in most cases. It seems reasonable to expect that the gap would be proportionally larger for more question types that required a greater degree of inference.

It is also notable that human subjects received a larger relative benefit from lenient rather than strict scoring. The automatic results in Table 4 cannot accurately reveal differences smaller than 1 answer out of 14 (0.07). But half of the six interactive experiments exhibited differences at least that large, while only one of the eight (non-zero) automatic systems showed such a difference. We interpret this as an indication that lenient accuracy reflects characteristics of an answer than may be more prevalent in human question answering than in automatic question answering.

4.3 The Assessment Process

Richard Sutcliffe and Alessandro Vallin, who coordinated the iCLEF assessment process for English, offered the following observations about the process:

- Users made more elaborate inferences than machines. For example:
  `Q: When did Latvia gain independence? answer: 1991`
  was judged correct even though the document said "*(..)breakup of the Soviet Union (..) in 1991*". In this case, the user inferred that Latvia was part of the Soviet Union. Another example of this effect is:
  `Q: When did Lenin die? answer: January 20 1924`
  The document states that "Friday is the 70th anniversary of Lenin's death." As it is dated on Saturday, 22 January 1994, the user could could have inferred the date. Of course, the user might also make mistakes that a machine would not; in this case, the date calculated by the user was off by one day, leading the answer to be scored as wrong.
- Sometimes inexact answers were provided when a more complete answer could be inferred. For example,
  `Q: When did the attack at the Saint-Michel underground station in Paris occur? answer: July 25`
  In this case, the user gave an incomplete answer "July 25," but the date of the document could have been used to accurately infer the year in which the event occurred. This could reflect a system limitation (the date of the document may not have been displayed to the user), or it may simply reflect a misunderstanding of the desired degree of completeness in the answer.
- The option to designate more than one supporting document was used only 9 times out of the 384 answers provided in the three experiments for which EN was the target language. In none of those 9 cases was it used correctly (i.e., no inference using combined information from both documents was appropriate). This suggests that this option may add an unhelpful degree of complexity to the evaluation process.
- People were more creative than machines regarding what constitutes a valid answer. For example, they might select "hundreds" as an answer, while automatic systems may fail to recognize such an imprecise expression as a possible answer.
- Manual translation of the answers into the document language after completion of the experiment introduced errors in a few cases. For example, a Spanish user correctly answered "15 mil millones de dolares," but it was translated with a typo "$15 billions" and therefore judged as inexact. When detected, these mistakes were corrected prior to generation of the official results (since it was not our objective to assess the manual answer translation process).

5 Conclusion and Future Plans

The iCLEF 2004 evaluation contributed a new evaluation design and results from five experiments in three language pairs with a total of 640 search sessions. The only similar evaluation of interactive question answering that we are aware of was the TREC-9 interactive track [1]. The iCLEF 2004 evaluation differs from the TREC-9 interactive track in two key ways: (1) iCLEF 2004 is focused on a cross-language task, while the TREC-9 interactive track focused on a monolingual task; and (2) iCLEF 2004 used questions and measures that facilitate comparison with an evaluation of automatic QA systems while the TREC-9 interactive track used more complex question types and document-oriented evaluation measures.

The iCLEF 2004 evaluations have already made a number of specific contributions, including:

- Developing a methodology to study user-inclusive aspects of CL-QA,
- Demonstrating that the accuracy of automatic QA systems is presently far below the accuracy that a typical user can obtain using a cross-language information retrieval system of fairly conventional design, and
- Establishing an initial baseline for the interactive CL-QA task, with a median across 8 tested conditions of about 50% strict accuracy for five-minute searches.

Much remains to be done, of course. Further analysis will be required before we are able to apportion the judged errors between the search and translation technologies embedded in the present systems. Moreover, we are now operating in a region where inter-assessor agreement studies will soon be needed if we are to avoid pursuing putative improvements that extend beyond our ability to measure their effect. Finally, there is a large design space that remains to be explored; no participating team has yet tried advanced techniques of the type normally used in fully automatic CL-QA systems in interactive systems.

Perhaps the most important legacy of iCLEF 2004 will be the discussions that it sparks about new directions for information retrieval research. How can we craft an evaluation venue that will attract participants with interests in both interactive and automatic CL-QA? What can we learn from the CLEF-2004 CL-QA evaluation that would help us design interactive CL-QA evaluations that reflect real application scenarios with greater fidelity? Given the accuracy achieved by interactive systems with a limited investment of the user's time, what applications do we see for fully automated CL-QA systems? With iCLEF 2004, we feel that we have gained a glimpse of these questions about our future.

Acknowledgments

The authors would like to thank Alessandro Vallin and Richard Sutcliffe for serving as our liaison to the CLEF 2004 CL-QA track, for their help with assessments, and for sharing with us their insights into the assessment process. We are also grateful to Christelle Ayache and Jesús Herrera for help with the

French and Spanish assessments, to Victor Peinado for file processing, to Fernando López and Javier Artiles for creating the iCLEF 2004 Web pages, and to Jianqiang Wang for creating the Systran translations that were made available to the iCLEF teams.

References

1. William Hersh and Paul Over. TREC-9 interactive track report. In *The Ninth Text Retrieval Conference (TREC-9)*, November 2000. http://trec.nist.gov.
2. Douglas W. Oard and Julio Gonzalo. The CLEF 2003 interactive track. In Carol Peters, editor, *Proceedings of the Fourth Cross-Language Evaluation Forum.* 2003.

Interactive Cross-Language Question Answering: Searching Passages Versus Searching Documents

Fernando López-Ostenero, Julio Gonzalo, Víctor Peinado, and Felisa Verdejo

Departamento de Lenguajes y Sistemas Informáticos,
Universidad Nacional de Educación a Distancia (UNED),
c/ Juan del Rosal, 16, Ciudad Universitaria, 28040 Madrid, Spain
{flopez, julio, victor, felisa}@lsi.uned.es

Abstract. iCLEF 2004 is the first comparative evaluation of interactive Cross-Language Question Answering systems. The UNED group has participated in this task comparing two strategies to help users in the answer finding task: the baseline system is just a standard document retrieval engine searching machine-translated versions of the documents; the contrastive system is identical, but searches passages which contain expressions of the appropriate answer type. Although the users prefer the passage system because searching is faster and simpler, it leads to slightly worse results, because the document context (which is not available in the passage retrieval system) turns out to be useful to verify the correctness of candidate answers; this makes an interesting difference with automatic Q&A systems. In addition, our experiment sets a strong baseline of 69% strict accuracy, showing that Cross-Language Question Answering can be efficiently accomplished by users without using dedicated Q&A technology.

1 Introduction

In spite of its long name, "Interactive Cross-Language Question Answering" is not an exotic task, but rather a quite natural problem in the context of web searches, for example. We want to know the answer to a question, and if the answer is out there in some web document, we want to find it as fast and easily as possible, and we do not want to miss the possibility of finding the answer just because it is written in a foreign language.

For our participation in the interactive CLEF track [1], which is for the first time focused on studying Cross-Language Question Answering (CL-QA) from a user inclusive perspective, we have designed an experiment aiming at:

- Establishing a reasonable baseline giving initial quantitative and qualitative data about the nature and difficulty of the task.
- Finding out whether passages are more adequate than full documents for interactive answer finding.
- Experimenting with interactive features specifically aimed at improving answer finding processes.

C. Peters et al. (Eds.): CLEF 2004, LNCS 3491, pp. 323–333, 2005.

To achieve these goals, we have designed and compared two CL-QA assistants:

- A reference search system which uses a document retrieval engine (Inquery [2]) to retrieve machine-translated versions (into the user's native language) of the target language documents. Our hypothesis is that standard Document Retrieval and Machine Translation technologies, coupled together, can be efficient tools to help users in the answer location task.
- A contrastive search system which is identical to the reference system, except for two aspects:
  1. It retrieves machine-translated passages rather than documents. The possibility of examining the context of a passage is intentionally excluded.
  2. At the beginning of the search, the user is asked to specify the type of answer (named entity, date, quantity), and only passages containing possible answers are retrieved and shown to the user.

In order to compare both systems, we recruited eight Spanish native speakers with low English skills, who searched the CLEF English collection to find answers for 16 questions extracted from the CLEF QA 2004 question set. Answers were collected in Spanish, manually translated into English, and sent to CLEF QA assessors for evaluation (see [3] for details on the evaluation criteria).

Section 2 describes our experimental design, Section 3 discusses the results, and finally we draw some conclusions in Section 4.

2 Experiment Design

Our experiment follows the iCLEF 2004 experiment design [4], which prescribes how to conduct searches with eight subjects, 16 fixed questions, fixed document collections for each available target language, and the two search systems being compared.

2.1 Test Data

We have used the Spanish version of the question set, and the English text collection, which comprises news data from 1994 and 1995 taken from the Los Angeles Times and the Glasgow Herald. Documents were translated with Systran Professional 3.0 (as provided by the iCLEF organisation).

2.2 User Profiles

Our eight users were between 20 and 43 years old, had low or medium-low English skills, all were very familiar with graphical interfaces and search engines, and on average they had little familiarity with Machine Translation systems.

2.3 Reference and Contrastive Systems

Our **Reference system** is a straightforward document retrieval system (see Figure 1). Users type in queries in Spanish, and the system performs monolingual

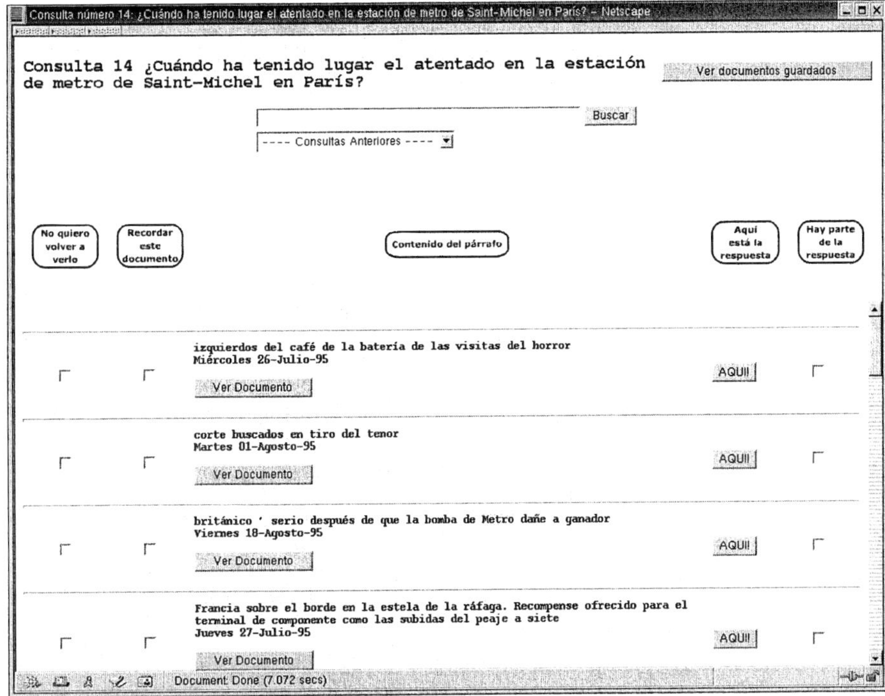

Fig. 1. Document system: Main interface

retrieval (using the Inquery API) against Systran translations of the original English news. The ranked list of results displays the document title, and the user can click to access the document contents. The interface has additional buttons to store a document, to view stored documents, and to end the search marking a document when an answer has been found.

The **Contrastive system** (Figure 2) begins by asking the user to select, from a radio button menu, which type of answer is appropriate for the question (a named entity, a date or a quantity). The search interface is similar to the other system but

1. It retrieves machine-translated passages rather than documents. The possibility of examining the context of a passage is intentionally excluded, to test whether context is necessary or not to find and validate answers.
2. only passages containing the type of possible answers are retrieved and shown to the user.

The filter that discards inappropriate passages is straightforward and does not involve using any NLP tool:

- A passage (sentences in our case) contains a named entity if there are expressions in uppercase where uppercase is not prescribed by punctuation rules.

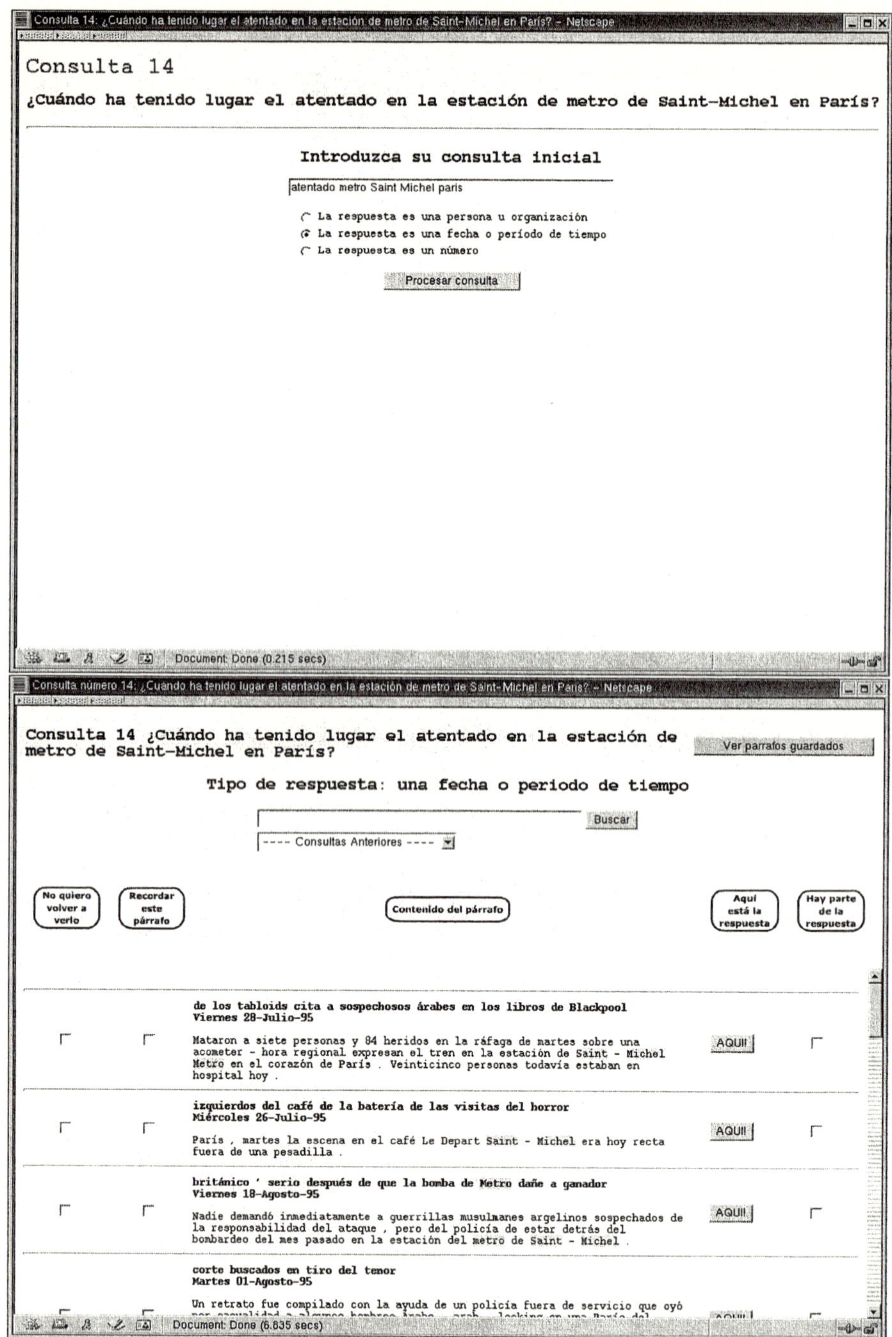

Fig. 2. Passage system: Initial query and main interface

Table 1. iCLEF 2004 Latin-Square Experiment Design

user	search order (system: $A\|B$, question: 1...16)
1	A1, A4, A3, A2, A9, A12, A11, A10, B13, B16, B15, B14, B5, B8, B7, B6
2	B2, B3, B4, B1, B10, B11, B12, B9, A14, A15, A16, A13, A6, A7, A8, A5
3	B1, B4, B3, B2, B9, B12, B11, B10, A13, A16, A15, A14, A5, A8, A7, A6
4	A2, A3, A4, A1, A10, A11, A12, A9, B14, B15, B16, B13, B6, B7, B8, B5
5	A15, A14, A9, A12, A7, A6, A1, A4, B3, B2, B5, B8, B11, B10, B13, B16
6	B16, B13, B10, B11, B8, B5, B2, B3, A4, A1, A6, A7, A12, A9, A14, A15
7	B15, B14, B9, B12, B7, B6, B1, B4, A3, A2, A5, A8, A11, A10, A13, A16
8	A16, A13, A10, A11, A8, A5, A2, A3, B4, B1, B6, B7, B12, B9, B14, B15

Locations are looked up in a gazetteer and filtered out, because "location" questions are excluded from the iCLEF question set.
- A passage contains a temporal reference if there is a match with a list of words denoting dates or a number between 1900 and 1999 (this temporal restriction is ad-hoc for CLEF data).
- Similarly, a passage contains a quantity if there is a number or a word from a given list.

Note that the task of the filter is to decide whether there are named entities, quantities or dates; not finding them makes the task much easier. Note also that recall is much more important than precision, because we do not want to miss any potential answer. That makes our simple filter effective for our purposes, and its potential mistakes relatively harmless.

Overall, the filter identifies named entities in 75% of the sentences, which is too permissive to be useful. A real Named Entity Recogniser, able to distinguish between people, organisations, locations, etc., would be a useful substitute for our naive filter. In the other two categories, however, the filter is useful: only 21% of the sentences contain dates, and 43% contain quantities.

2.4 Search Sessions

Every subject searches all 16 questions, eight with each system, according to the latin-square matrix design prescribed by the iCLEF guidelines (see Table 1). They filled in a pre-search questionnaire, two post-system questionnaires, and a final post-search questionnaire. The maximum search time per question was five minutes. Once time expired, the system stops the search, and the user has a last chance to write an answer.

3 Results and Discussion

3.1 Comparison Between Systems

The main differences (in search results and search behaviour) between systems can be seen in Table 2. The average (strict) accuracy is 8% higher for the baseline system, and the search behaviour (average searching time, confidence in the

Table 2. Comparison of results for both systems

System	Accuracy		Time	Confidence		# Refinements
	strict	lenient	(av.)	High	Low	(av.)
Documents	.69	.73	209.05	44	20	1.6
Passages	.66	.72	195.20	41	23	1.7

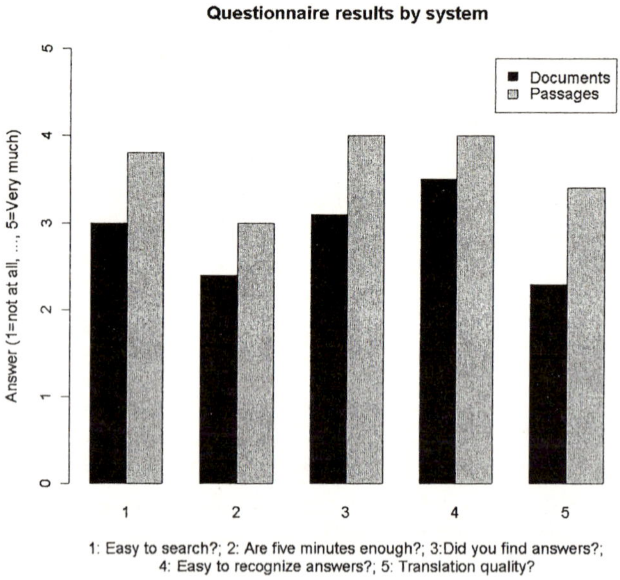

Questionnaire results by system

Answer (1=not at all, ..., 5=Very much)

Documents
Passages

1: Easy to search?; 2: Are five minutes enough?; 3:Did you find answers?; 4: Easy to recognize answers?; 5: Translation quality?

Fig. 3. Post-system questionnaires

answers, average number of refinements) is very similar for both systems. The absolute performance (between .64 and .69 strict accuracy) is remarkably high: there is room for improvement, but it is fair to say that users can find answers efficiently without QA-specific machinery. This accuracy is obtained in an average time of only 3.5 minutes, and with only 1.6 average refinements per question.

Why does our contrastive system, which has some QA-specific features, perform worse than the baseline system? Our observational studies, together with the questionnaires filled by our users, give some hints:

- The results of post-system questionnaires (where users evaluated each system separately) can be seen in Figure 3. For all individual questions, the passage-retrieval system had better results: according to users, it was easier to search with, faster, it was easier to recognise answers, and even the translation quality (which is the same) was perceived as better. We can conclude that users felt more comfortable when searching with the contrastive system. Therefore, this factor does not explain why users perform slightly better with the reference system.

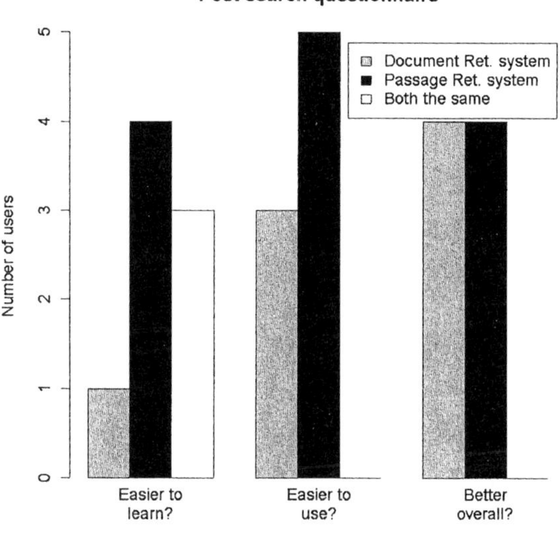

Fig. 4. Post-search questionnaire comparing systems

- The results of the post-search questionnaire (where users were explicitly instructed to compare systems) can be seen in Figure 4. In this explicit comparison, again the passage-retrieval system is perceived as "easier to learn" and "easier to use". But when asked for the better system overall, both systems receive fifty per cent of the votes. Why?
- The written comments made by our subjects, together with our observational study, give a clear answer: most subjects wrote that the passage retrieval system was easier and faster to use, but only the document retrieval system permitted looking at the full content of documents containing potential answers; and the context was perceived as a key factor to ensure that a potential answer was correct. In addition, the document context was also used to refine the query and/or search for similar documents that might verify a potential answer. This is a factor related not only to document content, but also to the translation quality, which often creates doubts about the correctness of an apparent answer.

From the comments made by our subjects, and from their search behaviour, it seemed clear that the preferred search facility would do passage retrieval, but provide the possibility of accessing the context of a passage when desired.

3.2 Failure Analysis

Out of 128 answers, there were 33 judged as "W" (wrong), 7 as "inexact" and 1 as "unsupported". 21 wrong answers were simply time outs: the user was not able to find an answer in five minutes. In the remaining $12 + 7 + 1 = 20$ cases, users gave an answer that was not correct. The sources of error are:

Misleading translations. In most cases, an incorrect or misleading translation is the reason for an incorrect answer. In some cases, users were doubtful about an answer, and looked for additional evidence supporting the answer. When the time expired, they preferred to give an answer with a low level of confidence, rather than no answer at all.

Human errors. In a few cases, the user just made a mistake when writing the answer. For instance, a user stated that the Channel Tunnel costed "15,000 millions", without specifying the currency. On another occasion, a cut-and-paste error repeated the answer given for a former question.

Responsiveness criteria. Occasionally, the user and the assessor had different opinions about the responsiveness or focus of an answer. For instance, when asking for the number of missing people caused by the typhoon Angela, a user said "more than 500 killed and 280 still missing", which was judged as inexact.

It is worth noticing that, while automatic Q&A systems may avoid translating documents (by translating only selected query terms), in an interactive system it is unavoidable to translate documents if the user does not have target-language skills. Thus, accurate targeted translation is a specific requirement of interactive CL-QA systems.

It is also worth noticing that, on some occasions, users were able to jump over significant translation problems. For instance, *When did Latvia gain independence?* was quite hard to answer, because Systran did not have "Latvia" in its bilingual vocabulary; thus, it remained untranslated in all documents. Users were looking for "Letonia" (Spanish translation of Latvia), but nothing was found. Some documents, however, spoke about "Latvia, Estonia y Lituania", and users were able to "disambiguate" Latvia from the context.

It is also worth mentioning that users were able to make more inferences than current Q&A systems. An interesting example is *When did Lenin die?* Some users found a document talking about the beginning of the celebrations of the 70th anniversary of Lenin's death. Subtracting from the date of the document (Sunday 22 January, 1994), users correctly deduced 1924. A couple of users, however, answered "20 January, 1924" (because the document asserts that "celebrations started last Friday") which was incorrect, because the celebrations started on January 20th but the real anniversary was on January 21st.

3.3 User Effects

The accuracy by user, and its correlation with average search time, can be seen in Figure 5. Both accuracy and average search time are rather homogeneous across users; more than in our previous experiences in interactive CL Document Retrieval. Our impression is that users find the Q&A task simpler to understand, easier and more amusing than document retrieval; thus, fatigue effects are less relevant. In some cases, a priori knowledge of the question domain permitted a better selection of query terms, but the effect on average accuracy is small.

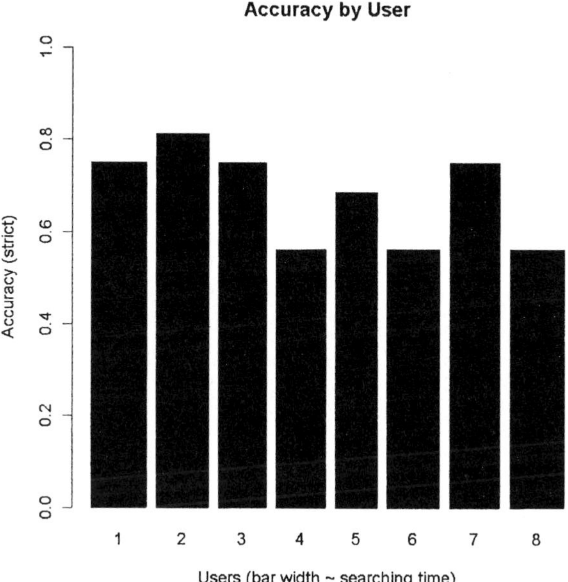

Fig. 5. Results by user

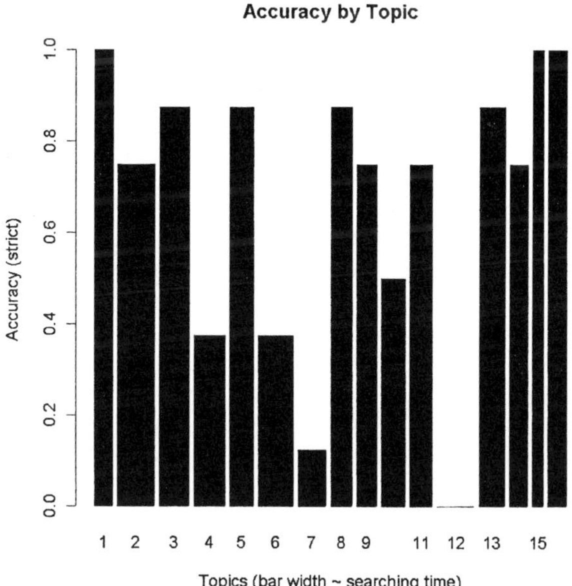

Fig. 6. Results by topic

3.4 Topic Effects

The accuracy by topic, and its correlation with average search time, can be seen in Figure 6. Obviously, the effect of topic difficulty is the predominant factor on accuracy. The most difficult topics are:

- *What is Charles Millon's political party?* (accuracy 0). No reference to Charles Millon was found by any user, probably due to mistranslation by Systran.
- *How many people were declared missing in the Philippines after the Typhoon "Angela"?* (accuracy 1/8). The source of difficulty here is not in translation quality. Some users answered with preliminary, vague information; others mixed dead and dissapeared people.
- *When did Latvia gain independence?* (accuracy 3/8). As commented above, the source of difficulty is that Systran left "Latvia", which is the key term in this question, untranslated.
- *Who committed the terrorist attack in the Tokyo underground?* (accuracy 3/8). Apparently the source of difficulty was cross-linguality: it was hard to find good query terms, specially because "Tokyo" was misspelled in the Spanish question (it used the English spelling, Tokyo, instead of the Spanish spelling, Tokio) and Systran mixed both spellings.

4 Conclusions

Our first experiment in interactive Cross-Language Question Answering has produced some interesting results:

- First, we have set a strong baseline (69% strict accuracy) for the task, using standard Document Retrieval and Machine Translation technologies. Can automatic CL-QA systems be adapted to interactive settings to achieve significantly higher user performance? This is an interesting research question for upcoming iCLEF events.
- The main source of difficulty is the cross-language nature of the search, rather than the idiosyncrasy of the QA task. Task-specific term suggestion and machine translation techniques might be useful for interactive CL-QA.
- Users prefer passage retrieval to document retrieval for the CL-QA task, partly because full Machine Translated documents are noisy and discouraging. But once a potential answer is found, the context is sometimes helpful to validate it.
- Interactivity can effectively be used to add Q&A specific restrictions to focus a passage search. In our contrastive system, users were asked to specify which type of answer was required for the question at hand. When, for instance, the answer had to be a date, only 21% of the sentences in the collection had to be searched.

Acknowledgements

This research has been partially supported by a grant from the Spanish Government, project R2D2 (TIC2003-07158-C04-01) and a grant by the UNED (Universidad Nacional de Educación a Distancia).

References

1. Gonzalo, J., Oard, D.: iCLEF 2004 Track Overview: Pilot Experiments in Interactive Cross-Language Question Answering. In: This volume. (2004)
2. Callan, J., Croft, B., Harding, S.: The INQUERY retrieval system. In: Proceedings of the 3rd Int. Conference on Database and Expert Systems applications. (1992)
3. Magnini, B., Vallin, A., Ayache, C., Rijke, M., Erbach, G., Peñas, A., Santos, D., Simov, K., Sutcliffe, R.: Overview of the CLEF 2004 Multilingual Question Answering Track. In: This volume. (2004)
4. : iCLEF website. (http://nlp.uned.es/iCLEF)

Improving Interaction with the User in Cross-Language Question Answering Through Relevant Domains and Syntactic Semantic Patterns

Borja Navarro, Lorenza Moreno, Sonia Vázquez, Fernando Llopis, Andrés Montoyo, and Miguel Ángel Varó

Departamento de Lenguajes y Sistemas Informáticos,
University of Alicante, Alicante, Spain
{borja, loren, svazquez, llopis, montoyo, mvaro}@dlsi.ua.es

Abstract. The iCLEF 2004 experiment at the University of Alicante has focused on how to assist users when searching the correct answer in passages written in a language different from the one of the query. The language of the users is Spanish and the language of the documents/passages English. In order to help users, a first system shows, together with the passage in English, the relevant domains of the passage and the relevant domains of the query. These relevant domains were extracted automatically from WordNet Domains. A second system shows, together with the passage in English, the syntactic-semantic patterns (SSP) of each passage and the SSP of the query. The SSP are formed by the verb and the main nouns of a sentence (that is, the head nouns of the main complements). For users with low English skills, our hypothesis is that knowing the relevant domain and/or the SSP will be useful to find the correct answer in the passage. The results show that the SSP are a little bit better in the interaction with the users. However, some users say that it is easier to find the answer knowing the relevant domains than through the SSP.

1 Introduction

The iCLEF 2004 experiment at the University of Alicante has focused on how to assist users in the task of searching correct answers in passages written in a language different from the one of the query. To achieve this objective, we have focused on two important issues:

1. What information must be shown to the user: It must be enough for the efficient localization of the correct answer. The user does not know the correct answer previously. He must infer the correctness of the answer from the context in which it appears. So it is important to show, not only the correct answer, but also enough context to attest that a possible answer is the correct one (or not).

C. Peters et al. (Eds.): CLEF 2004, LNCS 3491, pp. 334–342, 2005.

2. How the information is shown to the user: specifically, in what language the information is shown to the user. If users do not master the language of the passage, they must be helped to identify the correct answer.

In this experiment we have focused on how to assist the user when they do not have enough linguistic competence in the language of the passages. This is the most common case for Spanish people with English language. Most of them know English, but they can not formulate a correct query or understand correctly a possible answer. On other hand, we are looking for alternative methods to deal with large multilingual collection of documents avoiding the use of Machine Translations systems (due to the computational cost of machine translations of the complete collection) [1] [2].

2 Description of the Experiment

As we said before, the objective of the experiment is how to assist users in the location of the correct answer. For this purpose, the experiment has followed the following steps:

1. **Query formulation and translation.**
   We have taken the queries in Spanish, and they have been translated with a machine translation system to English.
2. **Extraction of relevant passages.**
   For the location of the relevant passages in the collection of English documents, we have used an Information Retrieval system: IR-n system [3]. This system extracts the passages with a possible answer and ranks them according to probability measures. The size of the passage consists of five sentences, which we think is an optimum size to locate the answer quickly and to infer whether it is correct or not.
3. **Interaction with the users and location of the answer.**
   The queries (in Spanish) and the passages (in English) are shown to the users through a web page. The users check the passages of each query until they find a passage with a (possibly) correct answer. Then they select the answer (the string of characters) and the passage where it appears, and then check the next query.

   The problem is the language: as we said before, the users do not have a deep knowledge of English. They need assistance for the correct location of the passage and the answer. Ruling out machine translation, two interaction methods have been compared for this task. The first one is based on relevant domains [4]: the system shows the users the passage in English, its relevant domains, and the relevant domains of the query. Our hypothesis is that with the relevant domains, the user can decide previously whether or not a correct answer is contained in any passage. The second method is based on syntactic semantic patterns (SSP): the system shows the users the passage in English and the SSP of each passage, which are formed by the main verbs and the main nouns (that is, the verbs and their subcategorization frame).

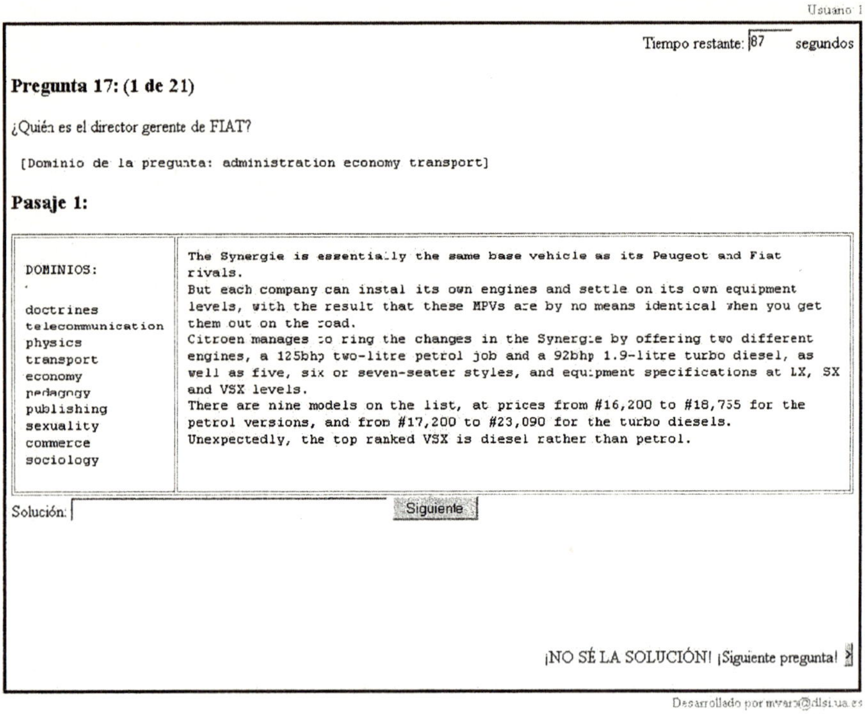

Usuario 1

Tiempo restante: 87 segundos

Pregunta 17: (1 de 21)

¿Quién es el director gerente de FIAT?

[Dominio de la pregunta: administration economy transport]

Pasaje 1:

DOMINIOS:	
doctrines telecommunication physics transport economy pedagogy publishing sexuality commerce sociology	The Synergie is essentially the same base vehicle as its Peugeot and Fiat rivals. But each company can instal its own engines and settle on its own equipment levels, with the result that these MPVs are by no means identical when you get them out on the road. Citroen manages to ring the changes in the Synergie by offering two different engines, a 125bhp two-litre petrol job and a 92bhp 1.9-litre turbo diesel, as well as five, six or seven-seater styles, and equipment specifications at LX, SX and VSX levels. There are nine models on the list, at prices from #16,200 to #18,755 for the petrol versions, and from #17,200 to #23,090 for the turbo diesels. Unexpectedly, the top ranked VSX is diesel rather than petrol.

Solución: Siguiente

¡NO SÉ LA SOLUCIÓN! ¡Siguiente pregunta!

Desarrollado por mvaro@dlsi.ua.es

Fig. 1. Interactive web page with relevant domains

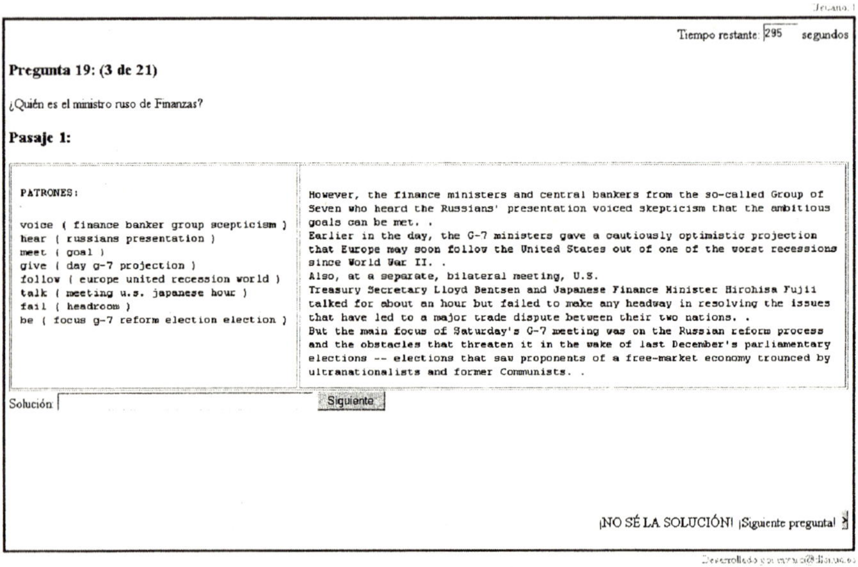

Usuario 1

Tiempo restante: 295 segundos

Pregunta 19: (3 de 21)

¿Quién es el ministro ruso de Finanzas?

Pasaje 1:

PATRONES:	
voice (finance banker group scepticism) hear (russians presentation) meet (goal) give (day g-7 projection) follow (europe united recession world) talk (meeting u.s. japanese hour) fail (headroom) be (focus g-7 reform election election)	However, the finance ministers and central bankers from the so-called Group of Seven who heard the Russians' presentation voiced skepticism that the ambitious goals can be met. . Earlier in the day, the G-7 ministers gave a cautiously optimistic projection that Europe may soon follow the United States out of one of the worst recessions since World War II. . Also, at a separate, bilateral meeting, U.S. Treasury Secretary Lloyd Bentsen and Japanese Finance Minister Hirohisa Fujii talked for about an hour but failed to make any headway in resolving the issues that have led to a major trade dispute between their two nations. . But the main focus of Saturday's G-7 meeting was on the Russian reform process and the obstacles that threaten it in the wake of last December's parliamentary elections -- elections that saw proponents of a free-market economy trounced by ultranationalists and former Communists. .

Solución: Siguiente

¡NO SÉ LA SOLUCIÓN! ¡Siguiente pregunta!

Desarrollado por mvaro@dlsi.ua.es

Fig. 2. Interactive web page with SSP

Our hypothesis is that knowing the SSP, the user can decide whether the passage contains the correct answer. In the next sections, both methods will be explained in depth.

Figure 1 and Figure 2 are the web pages used in the experiment. They show the query, the passage and the relevant domains of the query and the passage (Figure 1); or the query, the passage and the SSP of the passage (Figure 2). If the answer is in this passage, the user selects it, and the system stores the answer, the passage and the time spent. If the answer is not in this passage, the user checks the next passage up to the last one: 50 passages have been extracted from each query.

3 Interaction Method I: Relevant Domains

The fist method uses relevant domains to assist the location of the correct answer. The relevant domains of a word are the more relevant and representative ontological domains of this word. They are extracted from WordNet Domains (WND) [5]. Our hypothesis is that knowing the relevant domains will help user to decide whether the answer is or is not contained in the passage.

As we said before, this interaction method shows the user the passage in English, its relevant domains, and the relevant domains of the query. Theoretically, the relevant domains of both must agree: the passage with the correct answer must contain the same relevant domains (or very similar relevant domains) as the query. So if users previously know the relevant domains, they can decide whether the answer will or will not be contained in the passage.

WordNet Domains [5] is an extension of WordNet 1.6, where each synset is annotated with one or more domain labels selected from a set of about 250 labels hierarchically organized. To obtain relevant domains, WND glosses are used to collect the more relevant and representative domain labels for each word. Then, the domains associated to the analysed gloss is assigned. All glosses in WN undergo the same process.

We extract the relevant domains of the query and the relevant domains of each passage. This is done through a vector context which represents the relevant domains of the words of the query/passage. From this, we take only the common relevant domains to specify the relevant domains of the whole query/passage.

Furthermore, the passages ranking has been recalculated according to the similarity between the relevant domains of the query and the relevant domains of the passage. Therefore, the system shows first the passage with the highest similarity between its relevant domains and the relevant domains of the query.

4 Interaction Method II: Syntactic Semantic Patterns

The second method is based on syntactic semantic patterns. As we said before, with this method the system shows the user the passages in English and the SSP of each passage, formed by the main verbs and the main nouns (that is, the verbs ant their subcategorization frame). Our hypothesis is that knowing this information, the user can decide whether the passage contains the correct answer and locate it. The intuitive idea is that, when the user is looking for an answer in a text, he focuses on the main nouns and verbs, trying to locate the same or similar nouns/verbs as in the query. With the SSP, the main nouns and verbs have been previously extracted, so they might facilitate the task.

From a theoretical point of view, a syntactic semantic pattern is a linguistic pattern formed by three fundamental components [6]:

1. A verb with its sense or senses.
2. The subcategorization frame of the sense.
3. The selectional preferences of each argument.

However, this theoretical SSP is not easy to process automatically: it is difficult to extract patterns like these and to use them in iCL-QA. From this SSP model, we have developed a new one, easier to deal with from a computational point of view. In this new model, the verb is represented by the word and its sense (or senses) contained in EuroWordNet; the subcategorization frame is represented by the head noun of each argument[1]; and finally the selectional preferences of each argument are represented by the sense or senses of the head nouns.

With these syntactic semantic patterns, only the most important information of each sentence is shown to the user: the most important words of each sentence –the verb and the subcategorised nouns– and the syntactic and semantic relation between them. As users do not have a deep knowledge of the foreign language (English in our experiment), we think it is better not to process the sentences completely when we are looking for a possible answer. In order to decide whether a passage contains a correct answer, simply knowing the most important words of the document (that is, the syntactic semantic patterns) will facilitate this task. With these patters, it is difficult to understand completely a text written in a foreign language. However, this is not our goal. Our objective is to find a specific answer for a specific question: first, to decide if the answer is contained in the passage, and then to look for it and find it.

5 Results

5.1 General Accuracy

Figure 3 represents the average accuracy obtained by users with each interaction method. This table shows that users achieve similar results with both interaction methods, but the one based on SSP is slightly better. From a general point of view, the improvement of the SSP method over the relevant domains method is only 0.015.

[1] If the argument is a clause, the head will be a verb, not a noun. These verbs are, at the same time, a new SSP.

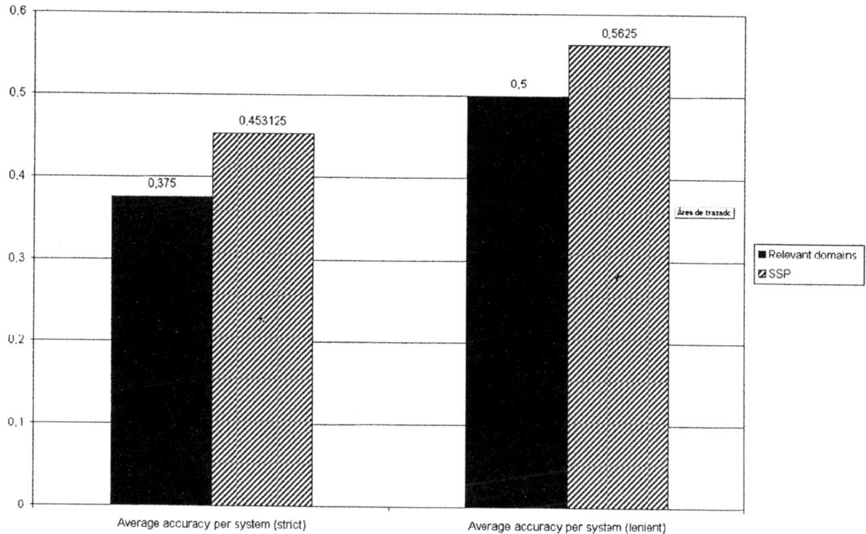

Fig. 3. General average

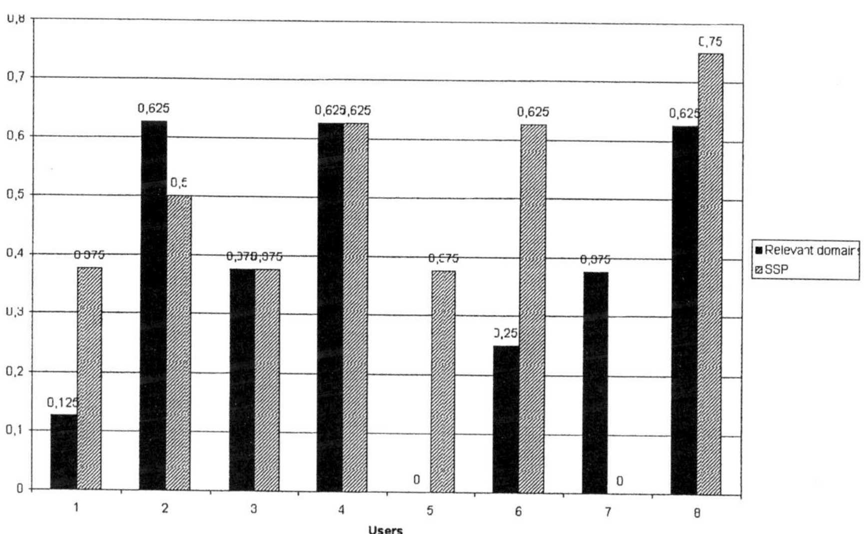

Fig. 4. Strict average by user

5.2 Accuracy by Each User

Figure 4 and 5 represent the accuracy achieved by each user. The first one (Figure 4) contains the correct answers located by each user in a passage that really contains the answer ("strict"). In this table, four users locate the correct answer with the correct passage with the SSP method, two users achieve the

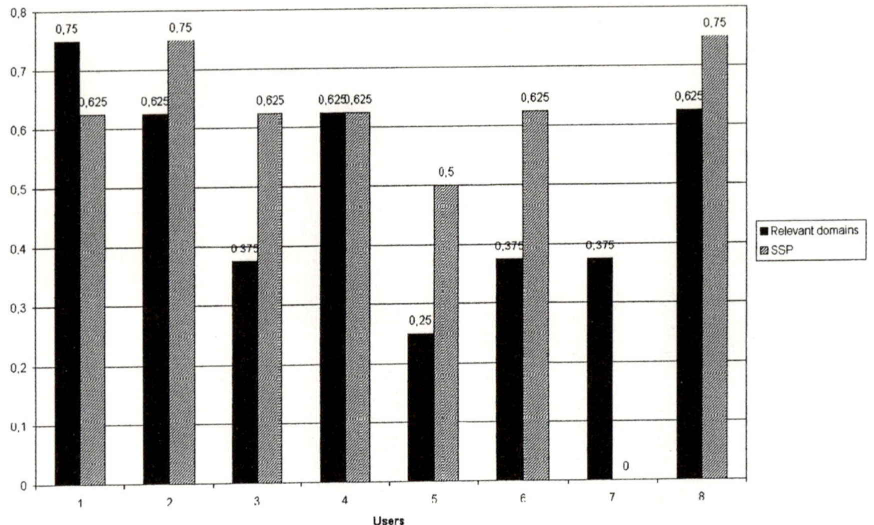

Fig. 5. Lenient average by user

same results with both methods, and two users achieve better results with the method based on relevant domain.

The second table (Figure 5) shows the correct answers located by each user, independently of the correctness of the passage ("lenient"). In these cases, five users have obtained better results with the interaction method based on SSP, one the same results with both methods, and two users have obtained better results with the relevant domain method.

5.3 Results of the Questionnaires

The results of the questionnaire (that users completed during the experiment) do not indicate preferences for any method: five users said that there were no differences between both interaction methods; two users preferred the SSP method, and one the relevant domain method.

About the actual help provided by each method (according to the personal opinion of the users), most of them had no preferences. One user clearly preferred the relevant domains method and an other one clearly preferred the SSP method. However, some users said that the actual help of the system in location the correct answer is rather low in both systems.

5.4 Search Time

Finally, Figure 6 shows the time consumed by each user. The time consumed with both interactive methods is similar. Two users spent more time with the SSP method, and the other six with the relevant domains method.

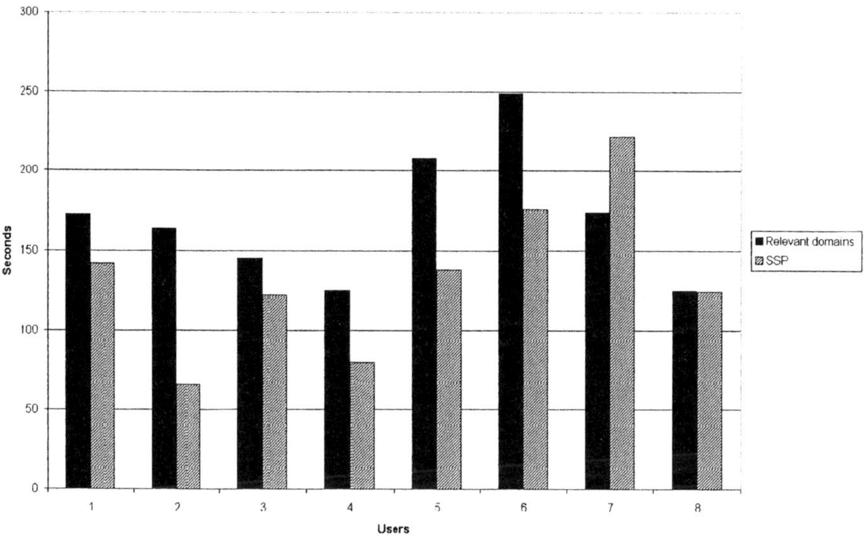

Fig. 6. Search time by each user

6 Conclusions and Future Works

From these data, we obtain the following general conclusions:

- The results are low, maybe because we have not used any kind of translation. In this sense, it is necessary some kind of translation (at least, superficial translation) to really help locating the answer.
- The order in which the passages are shown to the user in the SSP method (the output order of the IR-n system) seems to be correct.
- The order in which the passages are shown to the user in the relevant domains method (based on the similarity of relevant domains) does not seem optimal.
- According to the results and the personal opinion of the users, relevant domains method really helps the location of the answer. However, an error in the extraction of the relevant domains may confuse users. For these cases, it is necessary to improve the extraction of relevant domains.
- The SSP method achieves better results, but according to the users it is difficult to use, because it is not easy to interpret the patterns (only nouns and verb, without any linguistic connection). Because of this, it is necessary to spend much time reading the patterns. It is necessary to look for an other method to show the patters: for example, to translate the patterns into the language of the user.
- It is necessary to improve the extraction of SSP in order to ensure that the patterns will contain the possible answers: if the answer does not appear in a SSP, the user will not be able to locate it.

Future work is focused on two points:

- The syntactic semantic patterns: we are working now in a method to translate the patterns from one language to another which is based on verb alignment.
- The relevant domains: we are improving their automatic extraction. The idea is to improve the Information Retrieval system with the help of the information on the relevant domains of the passages.

Acknowledgements

We want to thank all users for their work and opinions in the development of this experiment.

This work has been partially financed by the Spanish Government (CICYT) with grant TIC2003-07158-C04-01.

References

1. Navarro, B.; Llopis, F. and Varó, MA.: Comparing syntactic semantic patterns and passages in Interactive Cross Language Information Access (iCLEF at University of Alicante). Workshop of Cross-Language Evaluation Forum (CLEF 2003) **Lecture Notes in Computer Science, Springer-Verlang** (2003)
2. López-Ostenero, F.; Gonzalo, J. and Verdejo, F.: UNED at iCLEF 2003: Searching Cross-Language Summaries. Workshop of Cross-Language Evaluation Forum (CLEF 2003) **Lecture Notes in Computer Science, Springer-Verlang** (2003)
3. Llopis, F.: IR-n: Un sistema de recuperación de información basado en pasajes. PhD thesis, University of Alicante (2003)
4. Vázquez S., Montoyo A., Rigau G.: Using Relevant Domains Resource for Word Sense Disambiguation. In: IC-AI'04. International Conference on Artificial Intelligence, Las Vegas (USA) (2004)
5. Magnini, B., Cavaglia, G.: Integrating Subject Field Codes into WordNet. In Gavrilidou, M., Crayannis, G., Markantonatu, S., Piperidis, S., Stainhaouer, G., eds.: Proceedings of LREC-2000, Second International Conference on Language Resources and Evaluation, Athens, Greece (2000) 1413–1418
6. Navarro, B.; Palomar, M. and Martínez-Barco, P.: A General Proposal to Multilingual Information Access based on Syntactic Semantic Patterns. In Anje Düsterhöft and Bernhard Thalheim, ed.: Natural Language Processing and Information Systems - NLDB 2003. Lecture Notes in Informatics, GI-Edition, Bonn (2003) 186–199

Cooperation, Bookmarking, and Thesaurus in Interactive Bilingual Question Answering

Preben Hansen, Jussi Karlgren, and Magnus Sahlgren

Swedish Institute of Computer Science, Stockholm

1 Three Simultaneous Experiments

The study presented involves several different contextual aspects and is the latest in a continuing series of exploratory experiments on information access behaviour in a multi-lingual context[1, 2]. This year's interactive cross-lingual information access experiment was designed to measure three parameters we expected would affect the performance of users in cross-lingual tasks in languages in which the users are less than fluent. Firstly, introducing new technology, we measure the effect of topic-tailored term expansion on query formulation. Secondly, introducing a new component in the interactive interface, we investigate - without measuring by using a control group - the effect of a bookmark panel on user confidence in the reported result. Thirdly, we ran subjects pair-wise and allowed them to communicate verbally, to investigate how people may cooperate and collaborate with a partner during a search session performing a similar but non-identical search task.

1.1 Thesaurus and Term Expansion

The term expansion experiment was the most important experiment made in this set of user tests. Subjects were first given eight queries without term expansion capabilities and then eight with an added window where a French word could be entered to retrieve up to five suggestions of related terms. The thesaurus used for expansion was generated automatically from parallel corpora of EU legislation by GSDM methodology (for details of the technology cf. Karlgren et al [3], in this volume) which relates terms by their distributional characteristics.

1.2 Bookmark Panel

Another feature introduced into this year's system by us was a bookmark panel (cf. the design of the CLARITY cross-lingual information retrieval system [4]). All users were given this feature in all queries. Users could mark an arbitrary selection from a displayed document and bookmark it to be used for answer extraction at the end of the task, as described below.

1.3 Cooperation

Finally, we introduced a novel and rather unexplored component of information access system evaluation dealing with how people may cooperate and collaborate

C. Peters et al. (Eds.): CLEF 2004, LNCS 3491, pp. 343–347, 2005.

when performing search tasks (for background, cf. previous studies by Hansen and Järvelin, e.g. [5] or [6]). In this case we gave support for the subjects to perform their information access tasks in partial collaboration with other subjects – exploring collaboration in an experimental setting. All 8 subjects performed the experiments in pairs. We selected the subjects to compose subject pairs who were social acquaintances in order to lower social thresholds to interaction and cooperation. The sequences of queries were kept different within pairs according to the iCLEF experimental matrix: the subjects never worked on the same query simultaneously. Subject communication was logged by encoding communication in one of a limited set of categories such as "vocabulary question" "system operation question". The research question we investigated was what types of characteristics we are able to extract from observing the collaborative activities, and what topics do people talk to each other about while searching.

2 Study Setting and Design

2.1 Data and Users

The target language was French. No translation service was provided. All sixteen queries were formulated in French, all documents were displayed in French, all answers were given in French. All subjects were primarily Swedish speakers and moderately competent in the target language: typically they had taken French as their second foreign language requirement in high school. No fluent French readers were accepted. The 8 participants were paired together two-and-two. 75 per cent of the users were female and the average age of all users was 34. None of the users had any experience performing a similar experiment. The average experience with online searching was 7,5 years.

2.2 System

The text retrieval engine used for our experiments is based on a standard retrieval system being developed at SICS. The base system is described in more detail in our CLEF paper from last year [7]. The interface built for this experiment allows users to enter French words into a search window and then displays search results in a standard *ranked list*. By clicking on a document title in the ranked list, the document itself is displayed in a *document display window* next to the ranked list.

A displayed document can be marked to be saved by clicking on a "Save Bookmark" button. Its title is then displayed in the *bookmark list*, a third window to the right of the document display window. Items from this list can be clicked and are then again displayed in the document display window for review. If a portion of text in the displayed document is selected, it is retained and displayed in the bookmark list.

Any number of documents can be bookmarked for display in the bookmark panel. Bookmarked items can be *checked* (and un-checked again) whereby the highlighted text snippet is copied to the *answer window* and the document title is automatically copied to the *reference window*. This enables users to easily click themselves through the question generation process. By clicking "Final Answer" the bookmarked answer which is displayed in the answer window is logged to a file. There also is an "Uncertain Answer" button to afford users the option of finishing a task with a more tentative answer. The first bookmarked selection is copied into the answer display field by default and the user has the option of manually editing or entering an answer into the answer display field.

The system also has a *thesaurus* component. A French word can be typed into a thesaurus query window and the thesaurus delivered all possible expansions for it into an expansion window. This component was made visible to users for half the topics.

3 Experiment Setting

As indicated above, the 8 participants were paired together in sessions. The two participants were sitting at a table, opposite to each other, so that they could see each others face-to-face. Each of them had a search terminal with network access and the search system installed. The table had enough space to write notes. Each individual participant was given 16 queries as per the iCLEF test matrix. This meant that the two subjects never performed the same search task simultaneously.

Each participant also received a topic protocol including a set of questionnaires individually designed as to the matrix. The questionnaires contained three sets of questions: one initial questionnaire, a questionnaire suited to each of the two systems tested (with and without query expansion) and a final questionnaire.

For the data collection, we observed the subjects when performing their search tasks. The observer had a copy of the set of queries the subjects were assigned and used a notebook to collect data for each specific query performed according to a set of pre-defined variables such as dialogues and conversations made for each query pair.

For the analysis of the data, all the written notes from each session were coded and analysed by content.

4 Results and Conclusions

4.1 Thesaurus and Term Expansion

The thesaurus was not useful due to its limited coverage, in spite of it having improved retrieval results in a wholly automatic setting. As it turned out, subjects were frustrated by its inherent unpredictability and its patchy coverage. Most subjects tested it once or twice and did not use it thereafter.

4.2 Bookmark Panel

Users were happy about the bookmark panel and commented on it favourably.

4.3 Cooperation

We found that users did cooperate and collaborate. We were able to distinguish and group the discussions into 5 different categories.

- Topic
- Search strategies
- Vocabularies
- Translation
- System functionalities

The data set from four sets of participants is too meager to draw any more fine-grained conclusions, but provisionally we were able to note that the more participants communicated, the more similar their results and answer turned out to be. We definitely are able to state that the experiment shows that people actually do communicate and collaborate when given opportunites to do so and that the reasons for this in the present experiment were related to: a) the topic; b) the language; and c) to the system functionalities.

One of the lasting results will be the continued development of evaluation methodology. We need a more robust framework for studying collaboration in information access – a task which is naturally cooperative rather than individual. This study points at one possible route to take: free form communication, interactional turns categorized by an experiment conductor, tasks similar but separate.

The results from all three studies need to be studied further but can even in this tentative guise confirm and add to knowledge that will have ramifications for the design of next generations of information access systems.

Acknowledgements

The work reported here is partially funded by the European Commission under contracts IST-2000-29452 (DUMAS) which is hereby gratefully acknowledged.

References

1. Karlgren, J., Hansen, P.: Continued experiments on cross-language relevance assessment. In Peters, C., Braschler, M., Gonzalo, J., Kluck, M., eds.: Fourth Workshop of the Cross–Language Evaluation Forum (CLEF 2003), Lecture Notes in Computer Science (LNCS), Springer, Heidelberg, Germany (2004)
2. Karlgren, J., Hansen, P.: Cross-language relevance assessment and task context. In Peters, C., ed.: Third Workshop of the Cross–Language Evaluation Forum (CLEF 2002), Lecture Notes in Computer Science (LNCS), Springer, Heidelberg, Germany (2003)
3. Karlgren, J., Sahlgren, M., Järvinen, T., Cöster, R.: Dynamic lexica for query translation. In Peters, C., Clough, P., Gonzalo, J., Jones, G., Kluck, M., Magnini, B., eds.: Fifth Workshop of the Cross–Language Evaluation Forum (CLEF 2004), Lecture Notes in Computer Science (LNCS), Springer, Heidelberg, Germany (in print) (2005)

4. Hansen, P., Petrelli, D., Karlgren, J., Beaulieu, M., Sanderson, M.: User-centered interface design for cross-language information retrieval. In: Proceedings of the 23th International Conference on Research and Development in Information Retrieval, Tampere, Finland, ACM SIGIR (2000) 383–384
5. Hansen, P., Järvelin, K.: The information seeking and retrieval process at the swedish patent- and registration office. moving from lab-based to real life work-task environment. In: Proceedings of the ACM-SIGIR 2000 Workshop on Patent Retrieval, Athens, Greece (2000) 43–53
6. Hansen, P., Järvelin, K.: Collaborative information searching in an information-intensive work domain: Preliminary results. Journal of Digital Information Management - JDIM **2 (1)** (2004) 26–30
7. Sahlgren, M., Karlgren, J., Cöster, R., Järvinen, T.: Automatic query expansion using random indexing. In: Proceedings of CLEF 2002. (2002)

Summarization Design for Interactive Cross-Language Question Answering

Daqing He[1,*], Jianqiang Wang[2], Jun Luo[2], and Douglas W. Oard[1,2]

[1] Institute for Advanced Computer Studies,
University of Maryland, College Park, MD 20742 USA
daqingd@umiacs.umd.edu

[2] College of Information Studies, University of Maryland,
College Park, MD 20742 USA
{wangjq, jun, oard}@glue.umd.edu

Abstract. This paper describes an experimental investigation of interactive techniques for cross-language information access. The task was to answer factual questions from a large collection of documents written in a language in which the user has little proficiency. An interactive cross-language retrieval system that included optional user-assisted query translation, display of translated summaries for individual document ranked in order of decreasing degree of match to the user's query, and optional full-text examination of individual documents was provided. Two alternative types of extractive summaries were tried using a systematically varied presentation order, one drawn from a single segment of the translated document and the other drawn from three (usually) shorter segments of the translated document. On average, users were able to correctly answer just 62% of the sixteen assigned questions in an average of 176 seconds per question. Little difference was found between the two summary types for this task in an experiment using eight human subjects. Time on task and the number of query iterations were found to exhibit a positive correlation with question difficulty.

1 Introduction

Question Answering (QA) is a type of information access task. It differs from the more traditional task of finding topically relevant documents in that the information need is modeled as a requirement for a specific factual answer (expressed as a short snippet of text), rather than relevant documents. Cross-Language Question Answering (CLQA) is a special case of the QA task in which the questions and the documents that contain the answers are expressed in different languages. Most QA research has focused on the design and evaluation of fully automatic QA systems. For the Cross-Language Evaluation Forum (CLEF) 2004 interactive

* Current address: School of Information Sciences, University of Pittsburgh, Pittsburgh, PA 15260 USA.

C. Peters et al. (Eds.): CLEF 2004, LNCS 3491, pp. 348–362, 2005.

track (iCLEF), we explored an interactive variant of CLQA in which the user and the system worked together to rapidly find answers to factual questions.

The usual approach to QA is to first identify a set of candidate documents using information retrieval techniques (e.g., term matching after question rewriting), and then to apply more sophisticated natural language processing (e.g., question type classification, named entity tagging, and logical inference) to identify the location and text span of the most likely answers in those candidate documents. We are not aware of any case in which fully automatic QA technology is yet deployed in an operational setting, but people routinely use information retrieval system of more traditional designs to find answers to factual questions. Therefore, we chose to assess the degree to which a Cross-Language Information Retrieval (CLIR) system could support the interactive CLQA task.

The QA task is a variant of the more traditional passage retrieval task. In the case of QA, however, an exact answer must be found. Our intuition suggested that searchers would be able to correctly recognize the exact answer if shown a longer passage that provided adequate context, so we elected to try two variants on passage retrieval. We rely on the searcher to reformulate the question appropriately for use in a term-based passage retrieval system, thus avoiding the complexity typically associated with the question rewriting component of present QA systems. While this decision places some burden on the searcher, it results in a simpler and less opaque system design, thus (hopefully) leveraging the searcher's ability to iterate towards an appropriate query formulation when their first attempt proves to be unsuitable.

We therefore chose to focus on two research questions:

- What are the effects of different types of summaries on the effectiveness of people finding answers in CLQA tasks?
- What types of search behavior do users of interactive CLQA systems exhibit, and in what ways does that behavior differ from that observed when CLIR systems are used to find entire documents that are relevant to a topic?

Passage selection is a form of extractive summarization. In iCLEF 2003, we explored the utility of alternative summarization techniques as a basis for making relevance judgment in interactive CLIR [1]. We are, however, not aware of any research on the application of summarization techniques for CLQA; our iCLEF 2004 experiments help to fill the gap.

Our interest in search behavior includes query formulation, query reformulation, translation disambiguation, relevance judgment, and search termination. Little is known about these topics for monolingual QA, and CLQA introduces additional complexity. In particular, we are interested in the effect of translation quality on the users ability to accurately recognize correct answers. We know from prior studies that present machine translation systems can often adequately support relevance judgment, even when it would not be adequate to convey a complete understanding of meaning [7].

We begin by describing the interactive CLIR system used in the experiment, including the two types of summaries that we tried, in Section 2. The design of the experiment is then explained in Section 3, and the analysis of results is in Section 4. The paper concludes in Section 5.

2 The MIRACLE System

We used the Maryland Interactive Retrieval Advanced Cross-Language Engine (MIRACLE) for the interactive CLQA experiments reported in this paper. MIRACLE is the result of an extensive revision of the interactive CLIR system that we used for iCLEF 2003. We made modifications to both the basic architecture of the system and the layout of the user interface (see Figure 1). The system includes an optional user-assisted query translation capability.

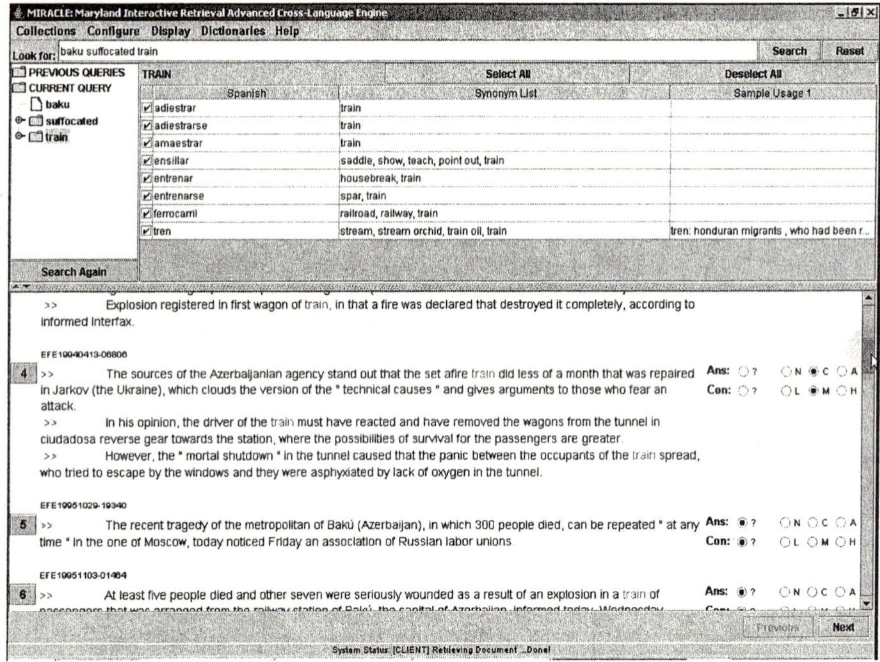

Fig. 1. The MIRACLE user interface for iCLEF 2004, showing KWIC summaries

MIRACLE uses the InQuery text retrieval system (version 3.1p1) from the University of Massachusetts to implement Pirkola's structured query technique (which has been shown to be relatively robust in the presence of unresolved translation ambiguity) [6]. All known translations are initially selected, and the user is offered the opportunity to deselect inappropriate translations. Three cues are provided to facilitate this task: (1) The translation itself (which may be recognizable as a loan word), (2) possible synonyms that may help to illustrate the meaning of a translation (obtained through back-translation using the same term list), and (3) examples of usage (extracted from either parallel text or the combination of the bilingual term list with a large English collection). A backoff translation strategy is used when the term to be translated is not known; first the term is stemmed, if translation still fails then a stemmed version of the term list is also used. This serves to maximize the coverage of the bilingual term list [5]. A fuller description of the MIRACLE system can be found in [4].

Users recorded answers by hand on the same form as the post-search questionnaire (which also asked for information about prior familiarity with the topic of the question and for an assessment of the subjective difficulty of the question). We modified the logging functions in MIRACLE to accommodate the requirement to designate supporting documents. The user could designate a document as supporting the answer based on either the summaries or on the full document by clicking the numbered button at the left side of the summary. Choices included "“N" (not containing an answer), *“C”* (cannot tell), or *“A”* (containing an answer). He/She also could also optionally mark their confidence in that judgment as *“L”* (low confidence), *“M”* (medium confidence), or *H”* (high confidence). Users were not instructed to designate only one single supporting document when possible, and they were not told about the option of designating exactly two documents, each of which provided only partial support. When users designated more than one supporting document, we therefore chose one arbitrarily to submit for official scoring. Because this may not be the same document that the user would have chosen had we instructed them properly, our results may show a somewhat higher rate of unsupported (but otherwise correct) answers than would have been the case with proper user instruction.

2.1 Two Types of Summaries

To help users to identify potentially relevant documents in a ranked list, MIRACLE normally provides a Keyword-In-Context (KWIC) summary of the document. Each KWIC summary consists of up to three sentences that each contain at least one query term. In order to reflect the topical coverage of the document as accurately as possible in a limited space, we sample these three sentences from the beginning, the middle, and the end of the document respectively. This type of summary aims to provide a concise overview of the topical content of the document in order to support the task of relevance judgment. KWIC can therefore be viewed as a type of indicative summary. Figure 2 shows an example of a KWIC summary.

To support our iCLEF 2004 experiment, we added longer single-passage summaries to MIRACLE in an effort to provide the user with more context than

>> The chief of a main directorate of the International Monetary Fund (the IMF), Michel Camdessus, today started up in Peru the first plan of " social stabilization " to eradicate the poverty in the Andean country.

>> The elaboration of the plan was approved in the Agreement of Extended Facility signed by Peru and the IMF in August of 1993, by means of which the bases of the Peruvian program of economic stabilization for period 1993-1995 also settled down.

>> The IMF will maintain its aid to Peru for the fight against the poverty and the execution of the plan of social stabilization, added.

EFE19940825-12696

Fig. 2. KWIC summary

the single-sentence KWIC summaries can provide. Our goal in this case was to help the user find answers directly using the single-passage summary; these summaries were therefore intended to be informative rather than indicative. We adapted a passage retrieval module that we had developed for the High Accuracy Retrieval from Documents (HARD) track of the 2003 Text Retrieval Conference (TREC) [3]. The module first uses the density of unique query terms to identify the possible locations of relevant passages, then extends those passages to the nearby paragraph boundaries. When no clear annotation of paragraph boundaries can be found, the module extends the passage to a preset window size, and then further extends the passage to the next sentence boundary in each direction. If two passages are found that are adjacent or overlapping, they are then merged. Passages constructed in this way typically contain several sentences. When a document contains several passages, they are ranked based on a linear combination of the density of unique query terms in the passage and the score assigned by InQuery to the document hat contains the passage. In the passage retrieval condition, we rank passages rather than documents; multiple passages from the same document can appear in the ranked list. Figure 3 shows a one-sentence passage summary (many passage summaries are longer than this).

Lima, 25 ago (EFE). - The chief of a main directorate of the International Monetary Fund (the IMF), Michel Camdessus, today started up in Peru the first plan of " social stabilization " to eradicate the poverty in the Andean country.
EFE19940825-12696::(0:252)::(1483:142)::(767:511)

Fig. 3. Passage summary

Results from the TREC 2003 HARD track indicated that our passage retrieval module typically identified the locations of relevant passages about as accurately as we were able to identify relevant documents, but that the passages we generated were typically far shorter (averaging 207 characters) than the ground truth passages specified by the HARD assessors (which averaged 5,945 characters). This probably is not a problem in the iCLEF 2004 setting, since we would expect that identifying short answers to factual questions would not require very long passages

We provided two variants of MIRACLE system to help the user to perform CLQA task. With all other components of the MIRACLE system remaining the same, one variant used the KWIC summaries as the surrogates of returned documents, which we call *KWIC condition*, and the other variant used the passage summaries, which we refer as *Passage condition.*

We can think of possible advantages for each condition in an interactive CLQA task. For example, KWIC summaries might help the user quickly identify documents that could contain the answer, and their inherent diversity may make them more robust in the presence of machine translation errors. Passage summaries, by contrast, may be more coherent and they might more often tell the user the answer directly. We are not aware of any systematic study on this question for interactive CLQA; our work in iCLEF 2004 was intended to fill that gap. In particular, we were interested in the following questions:

1. Is there a measurable difference in task performance between using informative and indicative summaries for a CLQA task?
2. Is there a subjective preference for informative summaries over indicative summaries, or vice versa?
3. Is there a difference in users' search behavior (e.g., the frequency of consulting the full document) when the users are given informative summaries rather than indicative summaries?

3 Experiment Design

We followed the standard protocol for iCLEF 2004 experiments. Searchers were sequentially given 16 questions (stated in English), eight using the KWIC condition, and the other eight using the Passage condition. Eight searchers (umd01-umd08) performed the experiment using the eight-subject design specified in the track guidelines.[1] Presentation order for questions and systems was varied systematically across searchers using the required Latin Square design. After an initial training session, each searcher was given a maximum of 5 minutes for each search to find the answer, print it on a piece of that we provided, and (using the radio buttons) identify which documents supported that answer. The searchers were asked make sure that they actually found the correct answers.

We asked each searcher to fill out brief questionnaires before the first question (for demographic data), after each question, and after using each system. Each searcher completed the experiment at a different time, so we were able to observe each individually and make extensive observational notes. In addition, we used Camtasia Studio (www.techsmith.com) to record each searcher's screen activities and we asked searchers to think aloud. We also conducted a semi-structured interview (in which we tailored our questions based on our observations) after all questions were completed.

3.1 Resources

We chose English as the query language and Spanish as the document language. The Spanish document collection contained 454,045 news stores from EFE News Agency that were written in 1994 and 1995. We used the standard Spanish-to-English translations provided by the iCLEF organizers (which had been run using Systran Professional 3.0 at the University of Maryland) as a basis for construction of document summaries and for display of the full document translations.

We obtained a Spanish-English bilingual term list containing 24,278 terms that was constructed from multiple sources from earlier experiments that were run in our lab [2]. We used InQuery's built-in Spanish stemmer to stem both the collection and the Spanish translations of the English queries. The examples of usage shown in MIRACLE to support user-assisted query translation require

[1] http://nlp.uned.es/iCLEF/

a parallel Spanish/English text collection and a large monolingual English collection. We obtained the parallel text from the Foreign Broadcast Information Service (FBIS) TIDES data disk (release 2) and the large collection of English text from the English part of the TDT-4 collection (which is available from the Linguistic Data Consortium, http://www.ldc.upenn.edu).

3.2 Measures

We computed two types of measures to gain insight into search behavior and search results:

- Objective measures of the performance, such as the accuracy of identified answers;
- Objective measures of the search effort, such as the average time in seconds to find answers, the total number of query iterations for each search, and the fraction of answers found using a summary alone without examining the full document.

4 Results

Our analysis is not yet complete (notably, we have not yet looked at the data we collected on examination of full documents), but in this section we present the results that were available at the time this paper was due.

4.1 Searchers

We had relatively homogeneous searchers, who were:

Educated. All eight searchers either had already earned a Bachelors degree or were undergraduate students.

Mature. The average age was 26, with the youngest being 19 and the oldest 35.

Experienced searchers. The searchers reported an average of about 10 years of on-line searching experience, with a minimum of 7 years and maximum of 15 years. All searchers reported extensive experience with Web search services, and all reported at least some experience searching computerized library catalogs (ranging from "some" to "a great deal"). All eight reported that they search at least once or twice a day.

Inexperienced with machine translation. All eight searchers reported never having, or having only some, experience with any machine translation software or Web translation services.

Not previous study participants. None of the eight subjects had previously participated in a TREC or iCLEF study.

Native English speakers. All eight searchers were native speakers of English.

Not skilled in Spanish. Seven of the eight searchers reported no reading skills in Spanish at all. The remaining one reported poor reading skills in Spanish.

4.2 Quantitative Analysis

Searchers achieved over 60% accuracy in both conditions (0.625 for the Passage and 0.609 for the KWIC). The difference was not statistically significant (at p¡0.05) using a Wilcoxon signed-rank test (see Figure 4).

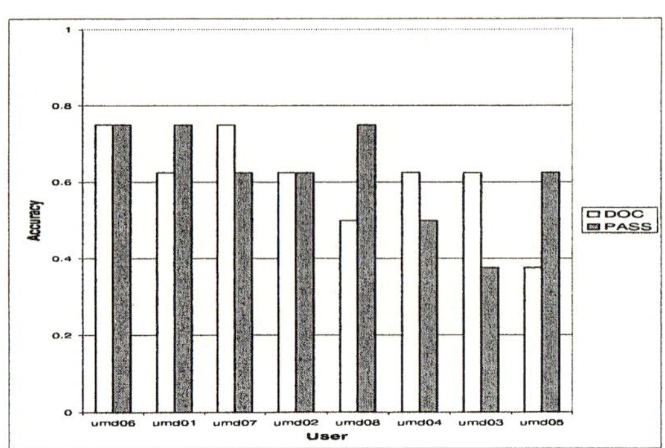

Fig. 4. Accuracy of answers identified under passage condition (i.e. PASS) and KWIC condition (i.e., DOC)

We observed that the questions roughly fall into three categories of difficulty according to the proportion of the correct answers to all answers: easy (Questions 8, 11, 13, 4, 16, 6), moderate (Questions 14, 7, 2, 10, 15, 12), and difficult (Questions 1, 3, 9, 5) (see Figure 5). Table 1 shows the questions themselves in order of increasing difficulty.

One possible factor contributing to question difficulty is the type of information that a question asks for. As Table 1 shows, questions asking for names (person's name, team's name) are generally easier than questions asking for quantities (e.g., number of people, amount of money). When seeking a person's

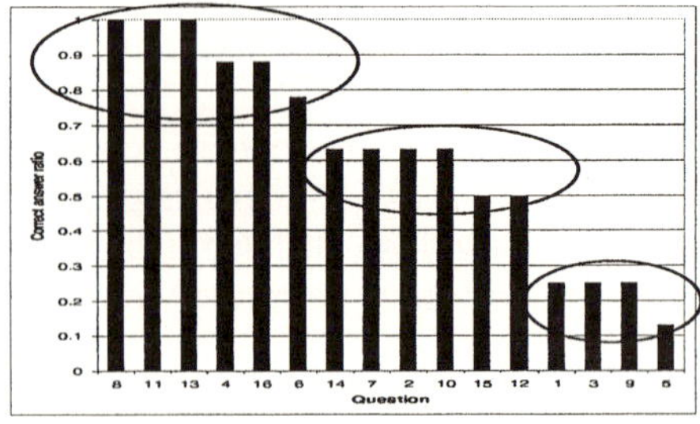

Fig. 5. Questions ranked in order of increasing difficulty (decreasing accuracy), clustered in three groups

Table 1. The 16 questions, sorted in order of increasing difficulty (decreasing accuracy)

Question 8	Who is the managing director of the International Monetary Fund?
Question 11	Who is the president of Burundi?
Question 13	Of what team is Bobby Robson coach?
Question 4	Who committed the terrorist attack in the Tokyo underground?
Question 16	Who won the Nobel Prize for Literature in 1994?
Question 6	When did Latvia gain independence?
Question 14	When did the attack at the Saint-Michel underground station in Paris occur?
Question 7	How many people were declared missing in the Philippines after the typhoon "Angela"?
Question 2	How many human genes are there?
Question 10	How many people died of asphyxia in the Baku underground?
Question 15	How many people live in Bombay?
Question 12	What is Charles Millon's political party?
Question 1	What year was Thomas Mann awarded the Nobel Prize?
Question 3	Who is the German Minister for Economic Affairs?
Question 9	When did Lenin die?
Question 5	How much did the Channel Tunnel cost?

name, queries consisting of terms describing the person's role (e.g., president, director, or winner) and terms naming a related organization (e.g., International Monetary Fund, Burundi, or Nobel Prize) were generally effective; such terms are typically highly selective. On the other hand, for questions about figures, good query terms may be harder to find (as was the case for "when did Lenin die?"), or it may be difficult to determine which of several possible answers is correct (particularly for events that evolve with time such as "How many people were declared missing in the Philippines after the typhoon 'Angela'?").

Searchers spent less time finding the answer to a question under the passage condition than under the KWIC condition (167 seconds vs. 185 seconds). Six of the eight searchers spent less time answering questions under the passage condition (see Figure 7), and Figure 6 shows a clear relationship between increasing question difficulty and increasing search time.

When people encounter a question whose answer is difficult to find, one of the strategies they often apply is to modify their query, a process that we call iterative query refinement. The average number of query iterations per question, shown in Figure 8, can be used as an alternative to search time as an indicator of effort. A general trend towards an increasing number of iterations with increasing question difficulty is evident, although there are several clear counterexamples. Five of the eight searchers performed fewer query iterations in the Passage condition (see Figure 9).

Figures 4, 7 and 9 reveal substantial differences among the eight users participating in the experiment. Accuracy varied between 0.5 and 0.75 for both systems, and average search time spanned an even larger range. For example, on average umd03 spent 108 seconds to find the answer to a question, while umd01

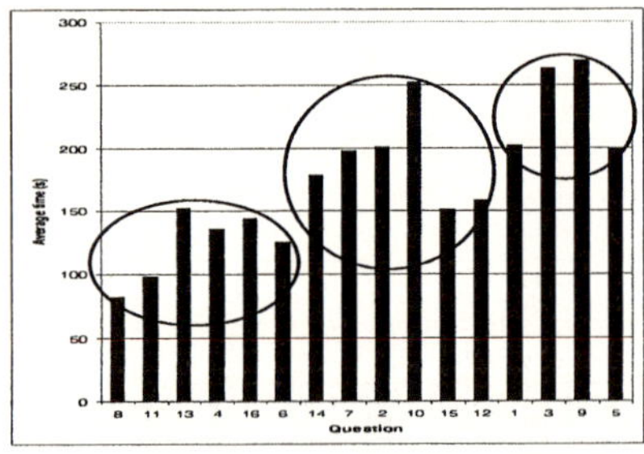

Fig. 6. Average search time, in order of question difficulty (grouped as in Figure 5

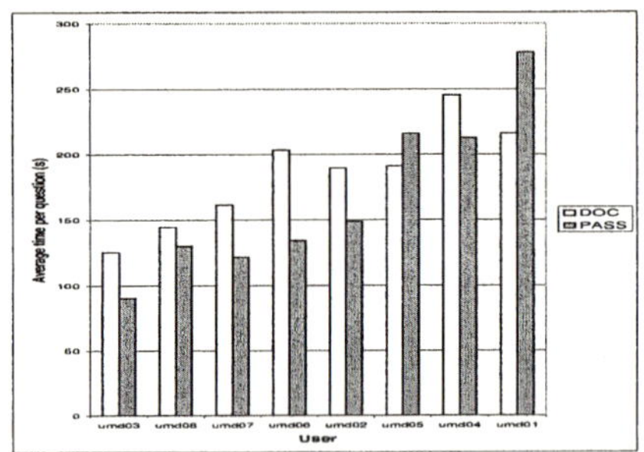

Fig. 7. Average search time per question under passage condition (PASS) and KWIC condition (DOC)

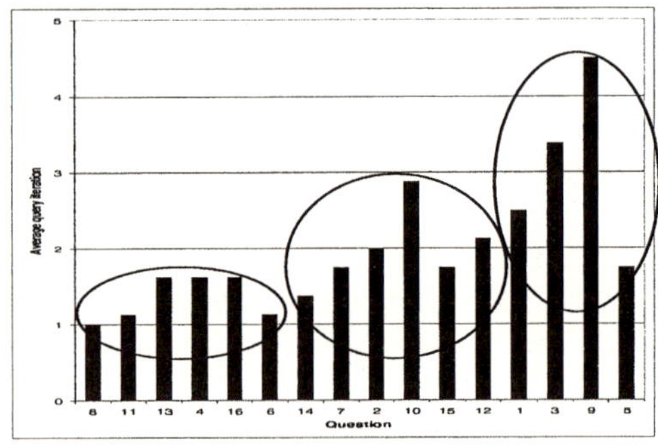

Fig. 8. Average query iterations, in order of question difficulty grouped as in Figure 5

doubled that time for the same task. No correlation between time and accuracy was evident; spending more time doesn't necessarily lead to high accuracy. For example, umd07 achieved 32% better accuracy over umd05 while spending 44% less time. The average number of query iterations exhibited even larger varia-

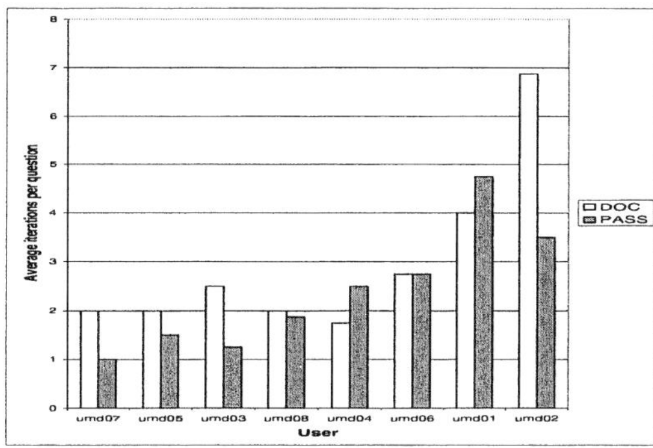

Fig. 9. Average query iterations per question under passage condition (PASS) and KWIC condition (DOC)

tion, raging from 1.5 iterations per question to 5.2 iterations per question. Again, however, no correlation between the number of iterations and accuracy, nor between the number of iterations and the average time per question is evident. In other words, performing more query iterations does not necessarily lead to higher accuracy, nor does it necessarily take more time.

4.3 Search Behavior

We observed some clear differences between the search behavior exhibited in this CLQA task and the search behavior that we have previously observed when using a CLIR system to search for relevant documents. The most striking difference was that the searches were all precision oriented in the CLQA case. Searchers usually stopped their search after they became convinced that they had found the answer. This usually involved one document providing the answer, and then one or two additional documents providing confirming evidence. Searchers found confirmation in the text surrounding the answer string, either in the summary or in the full document, or in the text of other documents. In some cases, these other documents were found in the same ranked list; in others the searchers reformulated the query to generate a more focused ranked list of documents. One tactic that was observed repeatedly was to include the answer as part of query. For example, one reformulated query for the initial query "charles millon political party" was "charles millon udf" ("udf" was the party abbreviation), which was the answer. This is very similar to the strategy used in the answer verification stage of many automatic QA systems; this coincidence suggests that observing search strategies in interactive CLQA may offer insights that could be useful in the design of fully automated systems.

One commonly search tactic observed in our previous experiments on finding topically relevant documents was that the searchers first identify the key concepts of a search topic and then formulate the query as a set of keywords that are synonyms or morphological variants expressing those key concepts, with the hope of bringing back as many relevant documents as possible. This is akin to

the "*building blocks*" technique that professional searchers are taught for use with systems that support Boolean query logic. Obviously, this tactic is recall oriented. However, although our searchers performing a CLQA task mentioned that they did pay attention to key concepts, they almost always used the exact words from the question in their initial queries. For example the common initial queries for the question "how many pandas are there in the wild in China" were "pandas china" and "pandas wild China." Only when no good search term was present in a question for a key concept did searchers introduce a new search term in their initial query. For example, the word "population" was included in the initial query "Bombay population" for the question "how many people live in Bombay." Synonyms or morphological variants were used in subsequent queries only when the initial query failed to return the answer. This is more similar to the professional searcher's "pearl growing" technique.

4.4 Other Factors

We did observe numerous interactions between the accuracy of the answers, the time used for search, the number of relevant documents in the collection, and the way that the answer are stated in those documents. For example, "who is the director of international monetary fund" was a question for which none of our searchers had previous knowledge, but it turned out to be an easy question (all 8 searchers marked this question as easy) because many returned documents directly stated the exact string "the director of international monetary fund" with the answer "Michel Camdessus." All eight searchers found the correct answer, in an average of 83 seconds, about half the 176 seconds average time for all 16 topics. However, although five searchers stated that the question "when did Lenin die?" sounded familiar, six searchers marked it as a difficult question, and only two searchers found the correct answer. This was probably because the only relevant document they could find was one that indirectly implied the answer with "after 70 anniversary of Lenin's death" in an article from 1994. The average time that the searchers spent on that question was 267 seconds; six of them used all 5 minutes without finding the answer. Interestingly, these two questions suggest that a searcher's *pre-search familiarity* with a question does not always play an important role in finding the answer rapidly, or even correctly.

The suboptimal quality of machine translation was another factor that we observed could affect the accuracy of answers, but only for the more difficult or vague questions. For example, the searchers did not have any problem finding the answer for "who is the director of international monetary fund," but they did have trouble finding a correct answer for "who is the German Minister of Economic Affairs" because many machine-translated documents contained phrases such as "German Minister of Outer Subjects" and "German Minister of Economic Cooperation." Because the searchers knew that machine translation may not be perfect, they could mistakenly assume that the person associated with "German Minister of Outer Subjects" or "German Minister of Economic Cooperation" (and especially the latter) was the correct answer. As a result, only two searchers correctly found the answer to that question, whereas three other searchers gave an incorrect answer. That question also had the second longest average search time (264 seconds). Another example of the quality of machine translation affecting the searchers' judgments was that there were many returned documents mentioning "bogging bear." It took a while for the searchers to become convinced that "bogging bear" was a bad translation of "panda."

Summarization quality was also observed to affect the results, but only for the more difficult questions. Because of time pressure, the searchers made extensive use of summaries to find documents that potentially contained an answer. When the answer strings were present in the summaries, they could find them with ease, but they would miss the relevant documents if the answer strings were not in the summary. For example, although the question about Lenin's death was a difficult, two searchers just happened to use the a query that resulted in inclusion of the answer string "70 years anniversary of Lenin's death" in the displayed summary. Therefore, those two searchers found the answer fairly easily.

The clarity in expressing a question could also affect the results. Two questions asked about times; one was "When did the attack at the Saint-Michel underground station in Paris occur," and the other was "When did Latvia gain independence." The answer to the first one was "July 25, 1995," while the answer to the second one was less precise: "September 1991." Some searchers wondered whether the exact date of Latvia's independence was required. A more problematic question was "How many people were declared missing in the Philippines after the typhoon 'Angela'?" Of course, the immediate aftermath of a disaster (which can be expected to dominate the reporting) is typically somewhat chaotic, so data appearing in the media might initially be inaccurate. This naturally led to different interpretations by different searchers. Problems of that sort could be minimized by including clearer criteria in the question (e.g., by specifying a time frame "after four days," or a source "in the final government statistics.")

4.5 Subjective Evaluation

Overall, all the searchers thought that finding answers under both conditions was easy and that both types of summaries were effective in supporting their tasks. The searchers liked the display of additional text around the answers because it allowed them to judge the correctness of the answer. Five of the eight searchers preferred the passage summaries because the summaries typically offered more context information than the KWIC ones. The other three searchers preferred the KWIC summaries because the summaries allowed them to gets a sense of the content of the full documents and because took less time to read. They also felt that the passage summaries did not always give the information they needed, and sometimes the passage summaries were too long. Highlighting query terms in both summaries and full documents was appreciated because it helped the searchers to zoom in to the right text, a very useful feature in longer texts.

5 Conclusion and Future Work

In this experiment, we compared the effectiveness of an interactive cross-language information retrieval system enhanced with two alternative types of document summaries for supporting the task of finding answers in Spanish documents to questions expressed in English. We found that our MIRACLE system was moderately effective, with correct answers found in 62% of the 128 searches that were performed. Users achieved comparable accuracy with either type of summary, but they achieved that accuracy somewhat more rapidly (167 vs. 185 seconds), on average, when using single-passage summaries. Our experiment results revealed substantial differences among the eight users participating in our study, both in terms of the number of questions they answered correctly (accuracy) and the average time they spent answering a question. We also investigated question difficulty, finding that both the amount of time needed to answer a question and the number of queries that were posed increased as the questions became harder (i.e., as accuracy decreased).

Question answering is an attractive task for evaluation of interactive cross-language information retrieval systems because it is grounded in something that real users really do. Our initial results from these first experiments with interactive question answering are indeed promising, but there are many interesting questions that remain to be explored. The first and most obvious is how our systems might be tailored to better support this task. In our iCLEF 2004 experiments, we tried alternative types of summaries, but we used the same summary for every question type. Can we tailor the summary to the question type, either automatically or under the user's control? Are there other system functions (e.g., term highlighting) that might also be adapted based on the question type? Thinking more broadly, are there other important question types that would yield new insights? What functions might we provide to support inference across documents? Can we design experiments to model the more realistic case in which the user has partial knowledge of the answer that they seek?

Over the past six years, CLEF has become increasingly grounded in real tasks. In its first two years, CLEF focused on building ranked lists. The 2001 iCLEF evaluation introduced a focus on interactive selection of documents from those ranked lists. In 2002 and 2003, we expanded this focus to include iterative refinement of the queries from which those ranked lists were produced. And now, in 2004, we focus on a complete task that end users sometimes actually perform, seeking answers to factual questions. As we move closer to real tasks, we have learned more about the kind of system support that are needed. CLEF plays a unique and important role in the CLIR community by uniting this focus on the task with the challenge of building systems to support that task. We look forward to continuing this exploration, and to working with the CLEF community to identify the next directions for this important effort.

Acknowledgments

The authors would like to thank Julio Gonzalo for coordinating iCLEF and Nizar Habash for providing the Spanish-English bilingual term list. This work has been supported in part by DARPA cooperative agreements N660010028910.

References

1. Bonnie J. Dorr, Daqing He, Jun Luo, Douglas W. Oard, Richard Schwartz, Jianqiang Wang, and David Zajic. iCLEF 2003 at Maryland: Translation Selection and Document Selection. In *Proceeding of CLEF 2003*, 2003.
2. Nizar Y. Habash. *Generation-heavy Hybrid Machine Translation.* PhD thesis, Department of Computer Science, University of Maryland at College Park, 2003.
3. Daqing He and Dina Demner-Fushman. HARD Experiment at Maryland: from Need Negotiation to Automated HARD Process. In *Proceeding of TREC 2003*, 2003.
4. Daqing He, Douglas W. Oard, Jianqiang Wang, Jun Luo, Dina Demner-Fushman, Kareem Darwish, Philip Resnik, Sanjeev Khudanpur, Michael Nossal, Michael Subotin, and Anton Leuski. Making MIRACLEs: Interactive Translingual Search for Cebuano and Hindi. *ACM Transaction of Asian Language and Information Processing*, 2003.
5. Douglas W. Oard, Gina-Anne Levow, and Clara I. Cabezas. CLEF Experiments at Maryland: Statistical Stemming and backoff translation. In C. Peters, editor, *Cross-Language Information Retrieval and Evaluation: Workshop of Cross-Language Evaluation Forum, CLEF 2000*, pages 176–187, Lisbon, Portugal, 2000.
6. Ari Pirkola. The Effects of Query Structure and Dictionary Setups in Dictionary-Based Cross-Language Information Retrieval. In *Proceedings of the 21st Annual International ACM SIGIR Conference on Research and Development in Information Retrieval*, Melbourne, Australia, 1998. ACM.
7. Jianqiang Wang and Douglas W. Oard. iCLEF 2001 at Maryland: Comparing Word-for-Word Gloss and MT. In C. Peters, M. Braschler, J. Gonzalo, and Kluck M, editors, *Evaluation of Cross-Language Information Retrieval Systems: Second Workshop of the Cross-Language Evaluation Forum, CLEF 2001*, pages 336–354, Darmstadt, Germany, 2001.

Interactive and Bilingual Question Answering Using Term Suggestion and Passage Retrieval

Carlos G. Figuerola, Angel F. Zazo, José L. Alonso Berrocal, and Emilio Rodríguez Vázquez de Aldana

University of Salamanca, REINA Research Group
{figue, afzazo, berrocal, aldana}@usal.es
http://reina.usal.es

Abstract. The Question Answering Task requires user interaction. Users can help the system by reformulating the questions, adding information to them or selecting the documents on which the system should work to obtain the answers. Our group has researched the effects on user interaction of suggesting terms to be added to the question, and the differences between using fragments or complete documents. This article describes the experiments we carried out and discusses the results we obtained.

1 Introduction

Several tasks in Information Retrieval require user interaction. In the case of the task known as Question Answering, the objective is to provide specific answers to specific information needs. Some approaches to this problem are based on the retrieval of passages or fragments of text [1, 2], assuming that the answer is to be found in these passages. The answer can then be extracted either through an automatic process or through user interaction. If the system is not able to provide a valid answer immediately, some kind of feedback process should be provided so that the user can further express his/her information needs.

Moreover, the task proposed in CLEF 2004 in the *i-track* was multilingual. Thus user interaction must work on a translation of the questions, and not on the target documents [3]. The questions are in one language and the documents (or passages from them) are in at least one other language. Thus, the questions must be translated to the same language as the documents. An alternative approach is to translate the documents to the language of the questions [4], but this is more expensive in terms of processing capability.

This year, the activity of our group has focused on exploring the effects of two kinds of user interaction: on the one hand, making the system suggest a set of terms translated into the language of the documents to the user, on the other hand, allowing the system to work not only on passages but, at the user's request, also on complete documents. In both cases the goal was to evaluate not only the number of correct answers, but also the subjective evaluation that the user makes of this type of help.

C. Peters et al. (Eds.): CLEF 2004, LNCS 3491, pp. 363–370, 2005.

This article is organised as follows: first a description of the task to be performed is provided; then the system used for the exercise is described together with the experimental design; finally the results are discussed.

2 Experimental Design

2.1 Task Proposed

This year's task was Cross Language Question Answering. The initial scenario was the following: a collection of documents in English and questions in Spanish. The users' native language was Spanish and they had a passive knowledge of English, which allowed them to understand the content, albeit only partially, and to interact using some simple terms in that language.

All the users selected for the experiments (8 in all) were students of information science, accustomed to working with point-and-click interfaces, as well as to making searches in computerised library catalogues and using the search services of the WWW. Their experience with machine translation programs, however, was scarce (see Table 1).

2.2 Retrieval System

Since we did not have a true Question Answering system available, we used a conventional retrieval system based on the vectorial model, but with some adaptations. The process was the following:

- translate the question using a machine translation software
- carry out a conventional retrieval based on the translated question
- let a user read the retrieved documents and deduce the answer to the question

Our base system for retrieval was the same as the one we used in some prior editions of CLEF [5], with a classic scheme for calculating the weights of the terms based on $tf \times idf$ [6]. We made some additions and changes to this base system:

Table 1. Pre-experiments Questionnaire Averages

Age	24.13
Experience in using a point-and-click interface	4.38
Exp. in computerized OPACs	4.26
Experience in searching commercial systems	3.25
Searching on www search services	4.5
Using Machine Translation software	2.38
How often conduct a search	4.25
Enjoy carriyng out information searches	3.75
Reading skills in document language (english)	3.13

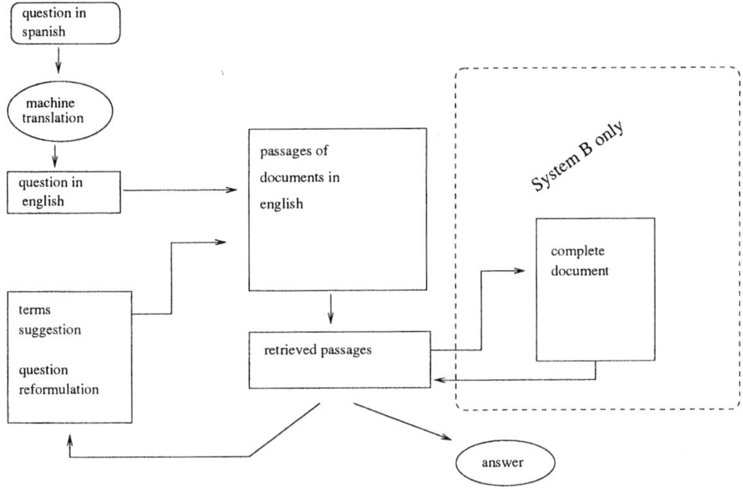

Fig. 1. Layout of the Retrieval System

- The machine translation programme used was Reverso [7]. The version we used is freely available to the public through the web page of a well-known newspaper (`http://www.elmundo.es/traductor`); The quality of its translations is slightly superior to that offered by other similar software, but one of its features is that it offers several alternative translations of the same term. In this version there are no specialised dictionaries nor, obviously, any type of training.
- the basic indexing unit is not the document but rather passages or fragments of it. The documents were divided into windows of 100 words each (including stop words). Only the `TEXT` field of the documents was used. The list of stop words was the standard list of `SMART` [8], to which the words appearing in more than 15 % of the documents were added. The final average of words per passage was less than 100, owing to the end fragments of the documents; note that the documents of the CLEF collections used are relatively short since they are news items (see Table 2).
- the capability of suggesting terms to the user was added to the system so that the user could add these terms to the question translated. These suggested terms were in English (the language of the documents); the idea was

Table 2. Documents Collection and Passage Division

Collection	LA94 & GH95	Passage Division
Documents	169,477	915,283
Total index terms	302,241	302,241
Averaged doc length (words)	229.94	42.71
Averaged doc length (unique index terms)	163.77	38.01

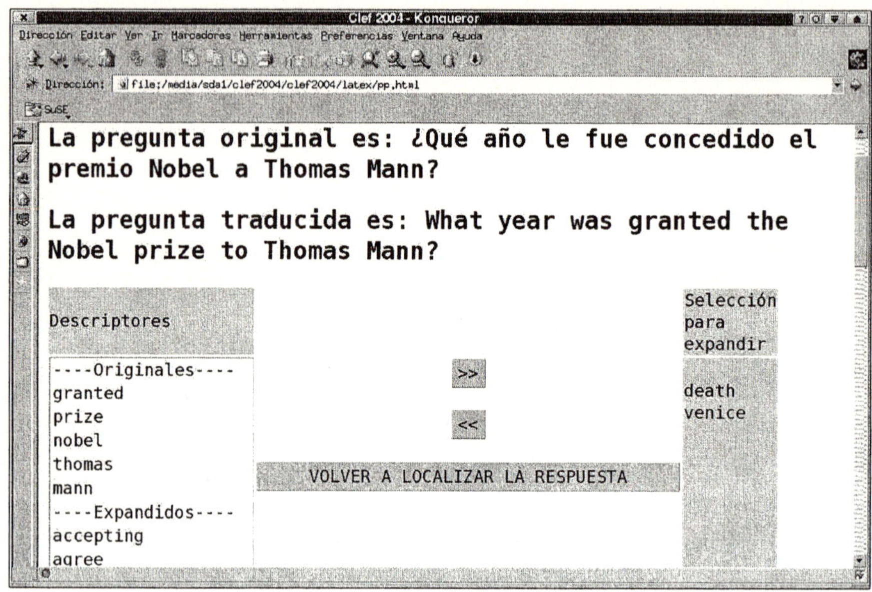

Fig. 2. Screen of Suggesting Terms

that these terms could improve the translation of the questions obtained automatically. It was expected that, since the users had a passive knowledge of the language of the documents, they would be capable of understanding and including some of the terms suggested. The terms suggested for each question were obtained by means of query expansion techniques. Our group has a lot of experience in query expansions applied to classic tasks of information retrieval [5, 9, 10]. Thus, we chose the expansion technique offering the best results, i.e. the use of local association thesauri. The cooccurrence relations of the terms in the first documents retrieved were used to construct the thesaurus. Hence, the terms best related to all the terms of the original question are selected. For each question the 30 best related terms are obtained, and are shown to the user so that they can incorporate them in the original question if they wish. Term suggestion mechanisms are used frequently in interactive experiments[11].

- Both the access to and the interaction with the system were carried out through a web server and several forms. The most important features of the system are the possibility to make several iterations (reformulating the translated question, examining the passages retrieved etc.) and the possibility to obtain and read the complete document for the passage retrieved.

2.3 The Experiment

All the users were given prior training. For the experiment the retrieval system was prepared in two different ways (`system A` and `system B`): System B permitted access to complete documents, while while system A did not.

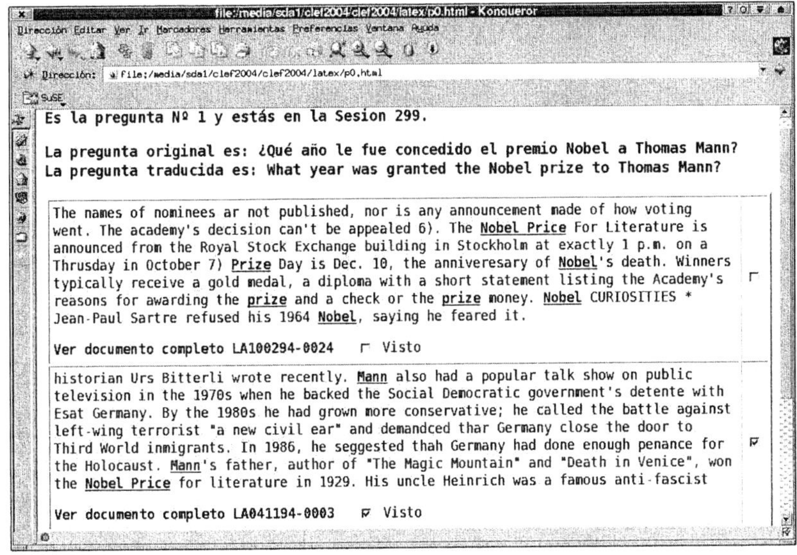

Fig. 3. Retrieved Passages from Question 1

Table 3. Averaged Time per Question in seconds (excluding more than 5 minutes)

	Time per Question
System A	146.6
System B	115.8
Total	198.9

Table 4. Terms Added per Question (excluding question during more than 5 minutes)

System A	
	0 terms added 33
	2 terms added 11
System B	
	0 terms added 51
	2 terms added 8

All the users were asked to submit 16 questions, half using system A and the other half using system B. However, the questions and systems were ordered in such a way that half the users began with system A and the other half with system B. Each user worked with a different sequence of questions.

All the user operations were logged by the system. Each question was allowed a maximum of 5 minutes to be processed; those that took longer, were considered invalid (19.5 %). The duration of each session seemed to be related to the number of iterations (question reformulation) and each iteration, in turn, to the number

Table 5. Reformulation or Iterations por Question (excluding questions during more than 5 minutes)

System A	
0 iterations	33
2 iterations	11
System B	
0 iterations	51
2 iterations	8

Table 6. Terms added per Question

Fails	
0 terms added	20
2 terms added	26
6 terms added	2
Hits	
0 terms added	71
2 terms added	9

of terms added to the original question. In all cases system B (which allows the user to see the complete documents) required fewer resources.

3 Results

The evaluation of the *i-track* can be carried out in two ways: strict and lenient. The latter is more favourable, and also more realistic. For example, the answer to question 12 can take diverse forms, all of them correct: UDF, French Democratic Union, UDF party, etc. Since the users were not instructed as to a specific way of expressing the answer, it seemed more appropriate to take into consideration the lenient evaluation.

In any case, the superiority of system B is quite clear; this means that the possibility of accessing the complete document based on the passages retrieved is more successful (an improvement of 28.75 %), which was expected, but not to that degree. But there are more interesting data: we can see that the possibility of adding the terms suggested by the system to the question, was was not greatly employed by the users. When they did do so, few terms were added. 91 of the 128 questions(16 × 8 users) had no term added to them, and only 2 terms were added in 35. Of the 80 questions answered correctly (with both systems), terms were only added in 9. However, keywords were added to more than half of the incorrect questions.

At first glance this seems to indicate that the suggestion of terms is not effective to obtaining correct answers. However, of the 48 failed questions, 28 were not answered at all or took up all 5 minutes of the time. Of these 28, 17 had 2 terms added, and in 2 of them up to 6 terms each were added. This leads us to think that the users did not value the utility of adding suggested terms and that they only applied this possibility when they had difficulty finding the answers. The iterations are related to the addition of terms, since the only way to reformulate a question is to change terms.

The results, however, should be interpreted taking into account the nature of the documents and also that of the questions. The documents, being news items from the press, tended to be short and have a single theme; their fragmentation into passages, therefore, was probably of little interest. The questions were also short; furthermore, they contained proper names or other terms that either did not need translation or the translation was obvious, even for a machine translation system. In fact, a manual revision of the machine translation showed that in general they were fairly correct. Thus, adding or removing terms was not of interest since they started from correct translations.

4 Conclusions

We have explored user interaction by finding terms related to those of the questions and suggesting them to the user. We also worked with passages but allowed the user to obtain complete documents as well. The possibility of adding related terms was not highly rated by the users, who considered it of little use. However, the possibility to obtain and see the complete documents, based on the passages retrieved, improved the number of correct answers, as well as the time required to obtain a correct answer. Nevertheless, the results should be viewed taking into account the small number of documents as well as the conciseness of the questions.

References

1. Vicedo, J.L.: Recuperación de información de alta precisión: los sistemas de búsqueda de respuestas. Sociedad Española para el Procesamiento del Lenguaje Natural (SEPLN), Alicante (2003)
2. Woods, W.A., Green, S., Martin, P., Houston, A.: Halfway to question answering. In: The Ninth Text REtrieval Conference (TREC 9), Gaithersburg, Maryland (USA), NIST Special Publication 500-249 (2000) 489–500
3. Dorr, B.J., He, D., Luo, J., Oard, D.W., Schwartz, R., Wang, J., Zajic, D.: iCLEF 2003 at Maryland: Translation selection and document selection. In Peters, C., ed.: Results of the CLEF 2003 Cross-Language System Evaluation Campaign. Working Notes for the CLEF 2003 Workshop, Trondheim, Norway (2003)
4. López-Ostenero, F., Gonzalo, J., Verdejo, F.: UNED at CLEF 2003: Searching cross-language summaries. In Peters, C., ed.: Results of the CLEF 2003 Cross-Language System Evaluation Campaign. Working Notes for the CLEF 2003 Workshop, Trondheim, Norway (2003)

5. Zazo, Á.F., Figuerola, C.G., Berrocal, J.L.A., Rodríguez, E., Gómez, R.: Experiments in term expansion using thesauri in Spanish. In: Advances in Cross-Language Information Retrieval. Third Workshop of the Cross-Languge Evaluation Forum, CLEF 2002, Rome, Italy. September, 2002 Revised Papers, Springer-Verlag (LNCS num. 2785) (2003) 301–310
6. Salton, G., Yang, C.S.: On the specification of term values in automatic indexing. Journal of Documentation **29** (1973) 351–372
7. Softissimo. (in http://www.softissimo.com)
8. Salton, G.: The SMART Retrieval System. Experiments in Automatic Document Processing. Prentice Hall, Englewoods Cliffs, N. J. (1971)
9. Zazo, Á.F.: Técnicas de expansión en los sistemas de recuperación de información. PhD thesis, Departamento de Informática y Automática. Universidad de Salamanca (2003)
10. Zazo, Á.F., Figuerola, C.G., Berrocal, J.L.A., Rodríguez, E.: Reformulation of queries using similarity thesauri. Information Procession & Management (2004) In Press
11. Belkin, N.J., Cool, C., Kelly, D., Lin, S.J., Park, S.Y., Pérez-Carballo, J., Sikora, C.: Iterative exploration, design and evaluation of support for query reformulations in interactive information retrieval. Information Processing & Management **37** (2001) 403–434

Overview of the CLEF 2004 Multilingual Question Answering Track

Bernardo Magnini[1], Alessandro Vallin[1], Christelle Ayache[2], Gregor Erbach[3], Anselmo Peñas[4], Maarten de Rijke[5], Paulo Rocha[6], Kiril Simov[7], and Richard Sutcliffe[8]

[1] ITC-Irst, Trento, Italy
{magnini, vallin}@itc.it
[2] ELDA/ELRA, Paris, France
ayache@elda.fr
[3] DFKI, Saarbrücken, Germany
erbach@dfki.de
[4] Departamento de Lenguajes y Sistemas Informáticos, UNED, Madrid, Spain
anselmo@lsi.uned.es
[5] Informatics Institute, University of Amsterdam, The Netherlands
mdr@science.uva.nl
[6] Linguateca, Braga Node, Universidade do Minho, Potugal
Paulo.Rocha@alfa.di.uminho.pt
[7] IPP, Bulgarian Academy of Sciences, Sofia, Bulgaria
kivs@bultreebank.org
[8] DLTG, University of Limerick, Ireland
richard.sutcliffe@ul.ie

Abstract. Following the pilot Question Answering Track at CLEF 2003, a new evaluation exercise for multilingual QA systems took place in 2004. This paper reports on the novelties introduced in the new campaign and on participants' results. Almost all the cross-language combinations between nine source languages and seven target languages were exploited to set up more than fifty different tasks, both monolingual and bilingual. New types of questions (How-questions and definition questions) were given as input to the participating systems, while just one exact answer per question was allowed as output. The evaluation exercise has highlighted some difficulties in assessing definition questions and can be improved in the future, but the overall analysis of submissions shows encouraging results.

1 Introduction

Question Answering (QA) systems have been evaluated for the last six years at the TREC campaigns. The TREC QA tracks have evolved over the years, so that increasingly difficult tasks have been proposed, addressing not only factoid but also list and definition questions, and requiring exact answers instead of longer text snippets as output [8]. Nevertheless, multilinguality has never been investigated at TREC's QA track, thus leaving room for challenging tasks in languages other than English or even across different languages, which is actually in the focus of the CLEF campaigns.

C. Peters et al. (Eds.): CLEF 2004, LNCS 3491, pp. 371 – 391, 2005.

The first multilingual QA track at CLEF took place in 2003. Eight groups from Europe, the U.S. and Canada participated in nine tasks, submitting a total of seventeen runs. Three languages were addressed in the monolingual tasks (Dutch, Italian and Spanish), while in the bilingual tasks questions were formulated in five source languages (Dutch, French, German, Italian and Spanish) and answers were searched in an English document collection. It was a pilot evaluation exercise and 200 simple, fact-based questions were given as input in all tasks, and participants were allowed to return up to three responses per question, either exact or 50 bytes-long answer-strings [6].

In 2004 the QA@CLEF track[1] attracted considerable attention within the CLEF framework. It involved two different tasks and another track: the main QA task, a Spanish pilot task and iCLEF, the interactive track. The main track included more European languages than CLEF 2003 and all the cross-language combinations between them were exploited to set up a number of different tasks. As a result, the CLEF QA community has grown and eighteen groups tested their systems, submitting forty-eight runs.

This paper provides an overview of the main QA track. The following sections report on the languages considered in the experiments, on the procedure that was adopted to build the test sets, and on the participants' results. Each target language will be treated separately, as a different subtask.

2 Tasks

Though Chinese has the highest number of speakers in the world, English has become a sort of lingua franca, as the fact that most web pages world wide are in English testifies. Nevertheless, a lot of information is available in other European languages, among which Spanish, German, French, Italian and Portuguese are the most prominent. This motivates the study of multilingual information access.

In a multilingual QA task two main variables need to be considered: the source language, i.e. the language in which the questions are formulated, and the target language, i.e. the language of the document collection. A cross-language QA system should enable users to search documents that are written in a language they do not know, which is a promising application in a multilingual society. Answer-strings, which are usually retrieved from the corpus without any changes, could be translated into the source language, but this further cross-lingual step was not required in the track.

2.1 Languages

In 2004 nine source languages (Bulgarian, Dutch, English, Finnish, French, German, Italian, Portuguese and Spanish) and seven target languages (Dutch, English, French, German, Italian, Portuguese and Spanish) were considered at the CLEF QA track. Almost all combinations between source and target have been exploited in order to propose as many tasks as possible: since no document collections were available, Bulgarian and Finnish were considered as source languages only, while the

---

[1] URL: http://clef-qa.itc.it/2004/

monolingual English task was discarded because it has been "traditionally" in the focus of the TREC campaigns. A total of 56 tasks were set up, divided into 6 monolingual (Dutch, French, German, Italian, Portuguese and Spanish) and 50 bilingual.

2.2 The Evaluation Exercise

Since QA systems process natural language questions rather than keywords and retrieve precise answers rather than entire documents, 200 questions were provided as input in all the tasks, and exact answer-strings were required as output.

The target corpora in all the languages were collections of newspapers and news agency articles. The texts were SGML tagged, and each document had a unique identifier (docid) that systems had to return with the answer, in order to support it. The corpora were large, unstructured, open-domain text collections.

The 200 questions given as input in the tasks were fact-based, but about 10% of each test set was made up of definition questions such as *What is UNICEF?* or *Who is Tony Blair?*, which were not included in 2003. In addition, another 10% did not have any answer in the corpora, and the right response to those questions was the string "NIL".

Each target language had its own 200 questions and, despite the efforts of the co-ordinators, there was just a little overlap between the test sets of different target languages: just two questions recurred in all the test sets and, on average, each test set shared 10 questions with the others.

As far as the answers are concerned, the requirements were stricter than in 2003, when participants were allowed to submit either exact or 50 bytes-long answers. Due to the potential number of participants attracted by so many tasks, the evaluation efforts needed to be minimised, so in 2004 the output was reduced to a single, exact answer-string.

Generally speaking, on the one hand the QA track at CLEF 2004 tried to attract as many participants as possible in a non-competitive setting, while on the other hand the co-ordinators aimed at reflecting the development that the TREC tracks have been undergoing over the years. For this reason, the guidelines reflected to a large extent those of the TREC 2002 QA track, adopting similar requirements and evaluation measures.

3 Test Set Preparation

Multilingual QA entails a number of subtasks, such as the development of tools (PoS-taggers, parsers and Named Entity recognisers) for languages other than English and the translation of questions and answers into other languages [1]. The construction of a reusable, multilingual collection of questions with the related [answer-strings, docid] pairs represents a useful resource, and the CLEF QA evaluation exercise offers the opportunity to create such a benchmark. As in the 2003 campaign, when two multilingual Gold Standard collections of questions and answers were built [5 and 6], in 2004 the generation of the test sets was closely monitored and exploited in order to build similar test sets for all the tasks, and to translate all the questions proposed into the track in all the source languages. Because of the number of languages involved, there was no attempt to have exactly the same test set in all the tasks, as we managed to do in 2003.

Eight groups were involved in the generation, translation and manual verification of the questions: the IPP group at the Bulgarian Academy of Sciences translated the entire collection of questions and answers in Bulgarian, DFKI created the German test set, ELRA/ELDA took over the work on the French questions, ITC-Irst was in charge of the Italian and English test sets, Linguateca provided the Portuguese part of the benchmark, UNED prepared the Spanish part, the University of Amsterdam worked on Dutch and the University of Helsinki joined the activity translating 200 English questions into Finnish, in order to set up the Finnish-English task.

3.1 Question Generation

The questions in the test sets addressed large (on average 230 Mb), open domain corpora. The document collections for all the target languages were comparable because they were made up of newspapers and news agencies articles that referred to the same time-span: *NRC Handelsblad* (years 1994 and 1995) and *Algemeen Dagblad* (1994 and 1995) for Dutch; *Los Angeles Times* (1994) and *Glasgow Herald* (1995) for English; *Le Monde* (1994) and *SDA French* (1994 and 1995) for French; *Frankfurter Rundschau* (1994), *Der Spiegel* (1994 and 1995) and *SDA German* (1994 and 1995) for German; *La Stampa* (1994) and *SDA Italian* (1994 and 1995) for Italian; *PÚBLICO* (1994 and 1995) for Portuguese and *EFE* (1994 and 1995) for Spanish.

As a first step in the test sets preparation, each co-ordinating group generated 100 questions in its own target language, searched manually for at least one answer per question supported by a document and then translated into English, used as the interlingua between all the groups, for both questions and answers. The questions had to be compliant with specific, previously established criteria: list questions (e.g. *What are the three most important export products of Italy?*), embedded questions (e.g. *When did the king who succeeded Queen Victoria die?*), yes/no questions (e.g. *Did Shakespeare have any sisters?*) and Why- questions (e.g. *Why did Nixon resign?*) were not considered in the track [2].

On the other hand, the test set included two question types that were avoided in 2003: How- questions and definition questions. These two categories, which can have longer answer-strings than the factoid questions, were approached basically in the same way, although assessors were less demanding in terms of exactness.

How- questions (e.g. *How did Hitler die?*), may have several different responses (e.g. *He committed suicide*, or *in mysterious circumstances* or *hit by a bullet*, or even *alone*) that provide different kinds of information.

Similarly, definition questions (e.g. *What is the atom?* or *Who are the Martians?*) are considered very difficult because though their target is clear, they are posed in isolation, and different questioners might expect different answers depending on their previous assumptions. They were first introduced at TREC 2001 and then proposed again in 2003, when organisers tried to define a potential user of the QA system, who would be "an adult, a native speaker of English, and an 'average' reader of US newspapers" [8]. TREC assessors created a list of "information nuggets" (i.e. significant facts that were likely to appear in the desired response), some of which were necessary, and judged the content of each answer checking how many nuggets it contained. This way of assessing the definition questions was quite complex and far from being exhaustive, so the CLEF approach in this sense has been simplified: first of all only definition questions that referred to either a person or an organisation were chosen, in order to avoid more abstract "concept definition" questions such as *What is religion?*, which would be too complex to be judged. The restriction to persons (*Who is Kofi Annan?*) and organisations (*What is Amnesty International?*) aimed at generating simple definition questions, whose answer could be a single, well defined text snippet such as *British spies listened in to UN Secretary General Kofi Annan's office* or *Amnesty International campaigns for human rights*, without any previous expectations regarding the most relevant information that a system should return. Secondly, as they were introduced as a stepping stone in 2004, the most general answers were judged as correct, assuming that potential users did not know anything about the addressed person or organisation.

The track co-ordinators attempted to balance the test sets according to the different answer types of the questions. Eight answer types were considered: TIME (e.g. *What year was Thomas Mann awarded the Nobel Prize?*), MEASURE (e.g. *How many years of imprisonment did Nelson Mandela serve?*), PERSON (e.g. *Who was Lisa Marie Presley's father?*), ORGANISATION (e.g. *What is the name of the Kurdish separatist party?*), LOCATION (*What is the capital of Japan?*), OBJECT (e.g. *Name an odourless and tasteless liquid.*), MANNER (e.g. *How did Pasolini die?*) and OTHER (e.g. *What animal coos?*). It is not easy to determine the intrinsic difficulty of a question, but the distribution of several answer types in the test sets could differentiate the task and offer some insights into the systems' performance with regard to particular categories of questions, as we will show in the results section below.

Each organising group (except IPP and the University of Helsinki) collected 100 questions that had at least one answer in their own target corpus. Those questions would be shared with the other groups, so they were translated into English and saved in a simple XML format. For instance, during this work phase ELRA/ELDA generated the factoid question *Où se trouve Halifax ?*, that had a LOCATION as answer type, translating it into *Where is Halifax located?*.

3.2 Translation

Seven hundred questions were formulated in an original source language, manually verified against a document collection, translated into English and collected in a common XML format. In order to share them in a multilingual scenario, a second translation in all the nine source languages of the track was necessary. Native speakers of each source language with a good command of English were recruited, and they were asked to translate the questions trying to adhere as much as possible to the English version. In case of any discrepancies between the original and the English form, they were expected to follow the former, and to communicate the changes that the latter presented. Nevertheless, cultural differences made some cross-lingual obstacles unavoidable: so, for example, the English question *What does a luthier make?* became tautological in German (*Was macht ein Geigen- und Gitarrenbauer?*), while some other concepts, such as *CEO*, were ambiguous and were translated in different ways (*chairman, managing director* or *president*). Moreover, translators encountered difficulties in the transliteration of proper names: for instance, *Vladimir Zhirinovsky* is written *Wladimir Schirinowski* in German, *Vladimir Zhirinovskij* in Italian and *Vladimir Jirinovski* in French. Translators usually chose the most frequent form in which proper names appeared in their target corpus.

Finally, in carrying out the assessments it became clear that translation has a discernible effect on the integrity of the judgement process. For example is a *Finance Minister* the same as a *Minister for Economic Affairs*? These might be (and in fact are) different roles but they could equally be the same one translated differently. Similarly, when is a *General Manager* the same as a *Secretary General*? In English a General Manager is quite a junior managerial position so the answer is probably "never". However in another language they might be quite equivalent. It is hard therefore to know what to conclude from judgements relating to questions describing translated versions of ranks, titles and so on.

In order to reduce inconsistencies, questions were translated into the form in which a native speaker would *naturally* ask it. The fact that manual translation captured some of the cross-cultural as well as cross-language problems is good since QA systems are designed to work in the real world.

3.3 Gold Standard

Once all the 700 questions were translated into eight languages (Finnish was added only shortly before the beginning of the experiments, and just for 200 questions), 100 additional questions for each target language were selected from the collection, in order to collect 200 questions per test set.

Around twenty of them did not have any answer in the document collections, and the right response to them was the string "NIL". The organisers decided not to include any NIL question among the definitions. The usual procedure to choose them was to select those containing proper nouns that did not occur in the document collection. Though it was easy to implement, this strategy probably made it too easy for participating systems to identify NIL questions, and should be reconsidered for future campaigns. Being aware of this drawback, some groups randomly selected the required NIL questions from those that seemed to have no answer in the document collections, and double checked them.

Additional questions were manually verified and new answers were added to those that were just the translation of the original one. Figure 1 below shows a sample from the multilingual collection of questions and answers built by the organising groups, called *Multieight-04 corpus*. From this XML file the plain text test sets used for the evaluation exercise were extracted. Each question is described according to its category (either factoid or definition) and to its answer type. The information concerning the category was kept also in test sets released to participants, where the character *F* designated a factoid, and *D* a definition. Questions appear in eight languages, and in one or more of them at least one [answer-string, docid] pair is given. The Boolean attribute "original" keeps track of the language in which each question was first generated and verified.

```
<q cnt="0504" category="F" answer_type="LOCATION">
  <language val="BG" original="FALSE">
    <question group="BTB">Къде се намира Халифакс?</question>
    <answer n="1" docid="">TRANSLATION[Канада]</answer>
  </language>
  <language val="DE" original="FALSE">
    <question group="DFKI">Wo liegt Halifax?</question>
    <answer n="1" docid="">TRANSLATION[Kanada]</answer>
  </language>
  <language val="EN" original="FALSE">
    <question group="ELDA">Where is Halifax located?</question>
    <answer n="1" docid="">TRANSLATION[Canada]</answer>
    <answer n="2" docid="LA112094-0062">Canada</answer>
  </language>
  <language val="ES" original="FALSE">
    <question group="UNED">¿Dónde se encuentra Halifax?</question>
    <answer n="1" docid="">TRANSLATION[Canadá]</answer>
    <answer n="2" docid="EFE19940927-15402">Canadá</answer>
  </language>
  <language val="FR" original="TRUE">
    <question group="ELDA">Où se trouve Halifax ?</question>
    <answer n="1" docid="ATS.950616.0005">Canada</answer>
  </language>
  <language val="IT" original="FALSE">
    <question group="IRST">Dove si trova Halifax?</question>
    <answer n="1" docid="">TRANSLATION[Canada]</answer>
  </language>
  <language val="NL" original="FALSE">
    <question group="UoA">Waar is Halifax?</question>
    <answer n="1" docid="">TRANSLATION[Canada]</answer>
  </language>
  <language val="PT" original="FALSE">
    <question group="LING">Onde fica Halifax?</question>
    <answer n="1" docid="">TRANSLATION[Canadá]</answer>
    <answer n="2" docid="LING-940526-150">West Yorkshire</answer>
    <answer n="3" docid="LING-941009-021">Nova Escócia, no Canadá</answer>
    <answer n="4" docid="LING-941201-050">Canadá</answer>
  </language>
</q>
```


Fig. 1. Sample of the *Multieight-04* collection of questions and answers

The entire collection is made up of 608 factoid and 92 definition questions, and the eight answer types are rather balanced: 173 PERSON, 118 LOCATION, 98 ORGANISATION, 88 OTHER, 84 MEASURE, 82 TIME, 31 OBJECT and 26 MANNER. Each question has at least one answer in one or more target document collections, but due to the variety of languages, just a few were manually verified in all the languages and consequently appeared in all the test sets.

Similar to the *DISEQuA* and the *Multisix* collections built for the CLEF 2003 QA track, *Multieight-04* is a valuable and reusable benchmark resource that can be further enlarged and distributed. Unfortunately it does not contain all the responses to each question, but just those that were manually found for the test sets preparation. It could be enriched with automatically retrieved pattern sets of correct answers in all the languages.

4 Participants

The encouraging results of the 2003 campaign, which led to the consolidation of the CLEF QA community, and probably the variety of the proposed tasks, gave rise to an increase in the number of participating teams. At the CLEF 2003 QA track 8 groups (3 from the U.S. and 5 from Europe) submitted a total of 17 runs in 9 tasks, while in 2004 18 teams (all of them from Europe except one from Mexico) returned 48 runs distributed over 19 monolingual and bilingual tasks. These figures are similar to those of the TREC-8 pilot QA evaluation exercise, where 20 groups submitted 46 runs, and represent a promising starting point for future campaigns, in which participants from other parts of the world should be involved.

Table 1. The tasks and the corresponding number of submitted runs at the CLEF 2004 QA track

Target Languages

Source Languages	DE	EN	ES	FR	IT	NL	PT
BG		1		2			
DE	2	3		2			
EN				2		1	
ES			8	2			
FI		1					
FR		6		2			
IT		2		2	3		
NL				2		2	
PT				2			3

As Table 1 shows, many of the 56 tasks that were set up did not attract any participants, but in all the six monolingual tasks, highlighted in the table with grey cells, two or more runs were returned. Black cells indicate the tasks that were not enacted.

The bilingual tasks with English (EN) as target were chosen by six different groups. On the contrary, English as source language did not receive much attention. French (FR) as target registered the highest number of submissions, but they were returned by a single participating team. Five Spanish groups participated in the monolingual Spanish (ES) task, while in 2003 only the University of Alicante managed to run its system. New Dutch (NL) and Italian (IT) research groups registered in 2004 (only one Dutch group actually participated) in the corresponding monolingual tasks, which testifies the growing interest in QA for languages other than English. German (DE), which in 2003 was source language only, was chosen by two groups as target, like Portuguese (PT), at its first time at CLEF.

5 Results

Participants were allowed to submit just one response per question and up to two runs per task. Submissions were manually judged by human assessors, who considered both the correctness and the exactness of each answer.

A response was judged as correct when its form was clear and its content was responsive, while exactness is more related to the quantity than to the quality of the information retrieved by the systems. In the track guidelines [2], articles and prepositions were tentatively indicated as acceptable parts of speech that would not penalise the exactness of an answer. Adjectives, verbs and adverbs could instead add irrelevant or unnecessary information, as in the answer *Ex IMF Secretary General Dies* (that was returned in response to the question *Of what organisation was Pierre-Paul Schweitzer general manager?*), where only *IMF* would have been the exact and required string. At any rate, exactness was never precisely defined, so a certain degree of subjectivity in the judgements could not be eliminated.

In 2003, in order to facilitate participation, both exact and 50 bytes-long answer-strings were accepted (though assessed separately), but most participants chose to return exact responses. So, in 2004 only exact answers were allowed, which made the tasks more difficult. Responses were judged either as right, wrong, inexact or unsupported (when the answer-string contained a correct answer but the returned docid did not support it).

Factoid questions with the answer type MANNER (i.e. How- questions) and definition questions, that were included in the test sets in 2004 for the first time, needed more heuristically oriented evaluation criteria because their answers could also be long circumlocutions or even entire sentences. In particular, answers to definition questions were judged considering their usefulness for a potential user who was assumed to know nothing of the person or the organisation addressed by the question. For instance, a correct answer returned in response to the question *Who is Jorge Amado?* was the following sentence: *American authors such as Stephen King and Sidney Sheldon are perennial best sellers in Latin American countries, while Brazilian Jorge Amado, Colombian Gabriel Garcia Marquez and Mexican Carlos Fuentes are renowned in U.S. literary circles.* In fact, it is clear from the sentence that Jorge Amado is a Brazilian writer and, moreover, it would have been difficult to extract a shorter and responsive string from this snippet.

The assessors were basically less demanding in terms of exactness when they judged these types of questions. However, accepting such long answers might be seen as equivalent to considering passage extraction rather than QA, so some judges disagreed on this subject. Because of the unnecessary information included in the answer-string above, some assessors would judge the response as inexact. No specific assessment training was offered to all the groups, which should be taken into account in the future.

The organising group that had generated the questions in a particular language was in charge of the assessment of the runs with the same target language (except for the judgement of the English runs, which was taken over by the University of Limerick). As a common procedure, each run, containing 200 answers, was judged by more than one assessor. The DLTG group used a different approach, as described in section 5.2.

The main measure was *accuracy*, that is the fraction of right answers. Answers had to be unranked (i.e. in the same order as in the test set), but a confidence value could be given for each response. Though it was not mandatory, this absolute value which could range between 0 and 1 was considered to calculate an additional *Confidence-weighted Score* (CWS), borrowed from the TREC-2002 track [7]. Both accuracy and CWS reward systems for recognising correct answers, and both penalise them for mistaking wrong responses for correct ones. However, only CWS rewards systems that can predict their own performance.

The restriction to a single exact answer per question made the task harder than that proposed in 2003, when three ranked responses were accepted and the *Mean Reciprocal Rank* was computed. At CLEF 2003 the average performance was 41% of correct answers in the monolingual tasks and 25% in the cross-language ones, but if we consider just the first response to each question, the results drop to 29% and 17% respectively. In 2004 the average accuracy over the 20 runs submitted in the monolingual tasks was 23.7%, and 14.7% over the 28 bilingual runs. So, the average results of the two evaluation exercises are not so different, and the slight downgrade registered in 2004 is probably due to the introduction of the definition questions.

In the following seven sections the results of the runs for each target language are thoroughly discussed. For each target language two kinds of results are given in two separate tables. In the first one the systems' performance is described considering the number of right (R), wrong (W), inexact (X) and unsupported (U) answers that were returned, the overall accuracy, the partial accuracy on factoid and definition questions, the accuracy in recognising NIL questions (both Precision and Recall are given) and the Confidence-weighted Score of all the submitted runs. In the second table systems' accuracy is analysed with respect to the answer types of the questions in the test set. Answer types are designated by the following abbreviations: *loc* ≡ LOCATION, *mea* ≡ MEASURE, *org* ≡ ORGANISATION, *per* ≡ PERSON, *man* ≡ MANNER, *obj* ≡ OBJECT, *oth* ≡ OTHER and *tim* ≡ TIME. Below each answer type, the number of questions posed of that type is shown in square brackets. The last row of the second table shows a virtual run, called *combination*, in which an answer is classified as right if any of the participating systems found it. This virtual run aims at showing the potential achievement if one merged all answers and considered the set of right answers, provided at least one answer per question were right.

5.1 Dutch as Target

Two research groups registered for tasks with Dutch as the target language, but only one team submitted runs: the University of Amsterdam, who had also participated in 2003. They submitted two monolingual runs, and one bilingual run (English to Dutch).

Table 2. Results of the monolingual and bilingual Dutch runs

Run Name	R (#)	W (#)	X (#)	U (#)	Overall Accuracy (%)	Accuracy over F (%)	Accuracy over D (%)	NIL Accuracy		CWS
								P	R	
uams041nlnl	88	98	10	4	44.00	42.37	56.52	0.00	0.00	-
uams042nlnl	91	97	10	2	45.50	45.20	47.83	0.56	0.25	-
uams041ennl	70	122	7	1	35.00	31.07	65.22	0.00	0.00	-

The Dutch test set contains 200 questions. Table 2 below details the results of the three submitted runs. Interestingly, on definition questions the bilingual English to Dutch run performed better than either of the two monolingual runs.

Table 3. Results of the Dutch runs, according to answer types of questions

Run Name	Given correct answers											
	Definition (#)		Factoid (#)								Total	
	org [11]	per [12]	loc [32]	man [15]	mea [15]	obj [10]	org [22]	oth [17]	per [49]	tim [17]	# [200]	%
uams041nlnl	6	7	14	3	6	1	10	5	26	10	88	44.00
uams042nlnl	4	7	15	3	4	1	11	5	30	11	91	45.50
uams041ennl	6	9	11	0	4	1	8	1	21	9	70	35.00
combination	7	10	20	3	8	2	13	5	36	16	120	60.00

The aim of the virtual run called *combination* is to provide an upper bound on the possible performance of a system that would merge the existing runs and somehow select the right answers from the combined pool of candidate answers. As an aside, this is actually how the University of Amsterdam's QA system works: separate streams each generate result files, and these are combined into a joint pool of candidate answers from which the final answers are selected.

5.2 English as Target

The work of assessing questions with English answers was assigned to the Documents and Linguistic Technology Group at Limerick. The five tasks enacted involved questions in Bulgarian, Finnish, French, German, Italian with English answers being

Table 4. Results of the runs with English as target language

Run Name	R (#)	W (#)	X (#)	U (#)	Overall Accuracy (%)	Accuracy over F (%)	Accuracy over D (%)	NIL Accuracy		CWS
								P	R	
bgas041bgen	26	168	5	1	13.00	11.67	25.00	0.13	0.40	0.056
dfki041deen	47	151	0	2	23.50	23.89	20.00	0.10	0.75	0.177
dltg041fren	38	155	7	0	19.00	17.78	30.00	0.17	0.55	-
dltg042fren	29	164	7	0	14.50	12.78	30.00	0.14	0.45	-
edin041deen	28	166	5	1	14.00	13.33	20.00	0.14	0.35	0.049
edin041fren	33	161	6	0	16.50	17.78	5.00	0.15	0.55	0.056
edin042deen	34	159	7	0	17.00	16.11	25.00	0.14	0.35	0.052
edin042fren	40	153	7	0	20.00	20.56	15.00	0.15	0.55	0.058
hels041fien	21	171	1	0	10.88	11.56	5.00	0.10	0.85	0.046
irst041iten	45	146	6	3	22.50	22.22	25.00	0.24	0.30	0.121
irst042iten	35	158	5	2	17.50	16.67	25.00	0.24	0.30	0.075
lire041fren	22	172	6	0	11.00	10.00	20.00	0.05	0.05	0.032
lire042fren	39	155	6	0	19.50	20.00	15.00	0.00	0.00	0.075

returned from the *LA Times* (American English) *and Glasgow Herald* (Scottish English) collections. The starting point in carrying out the assessment comprised the TREC Evaluation Software written by Ellen Voorhees and the *Multieight-04* collection of manually retrieved answers.

Having studied the TREC software it was decided that it should be used on a question-by-question basis rather than on a run-by-run basis. This means that a single assessor reviews and evaluates all candidate answers to a given question. before moving to the next question. Originally we had envisaged that a given evaluator would assess all answers to different questions comprising a complete run before moving on to the next run.

The method used in carrying out the assessment was as follows. There were four primary assessors plus one secondary assessor. Each primary assessor - a native speaker of English - was assigned a set of questions, 1-50, 51-100, 101-150 and 151-200 respectively. The assessors, provided with a set of guidelines, then carried out their work, noting any doubtful cases. A series of meetings then took place at which these cases were considered in turn by all five assessors and a joint decision was made. To ensure consistency, the consequences of each decision were then cross-checked by each assessor against judgements of comparable cases. It should be noted therefore that while all responses to a particular question were judged by the same person, we did not use double-blind assessment where each judgement is made independently by two assessors.

Table 5. Results of the bilingual English runs, according to answer types of questions

Run Name	Given correct answers											
	Definition (#)		Factoid (#)								Total	
	org [11]	per [9]	loc [28]	man [15]	mea [20]	obj [12]	org [20]	oth [27]	per [28]	tim [30]	# [200]	%
bgas041bgen	2	3	5	2	1	2	1	2	4	4	26	13.00
dfki041deen	4	0	10	2	2	1	5	5	6	12	47	23.50
dltg041fren	3	3	8	5	2	1	1	2	4	9	38	19.00
Dltg042fren	3	3	4	3	1	1	1	2	3	8	29	14.50
edin041deen	1	3	6	2	0	0	2	2	4	8	28	14.00
edin041fren	0	1	7	3	1	1	2	4	3	11	33	16.50
edin042deen	1	4	6	4	1	2	2	5	3	6	34	17.00
edin042fren	0	3	7	4	3	1	2	4	4	12	40	20.00
hels041fien[2]	0	0	3	0	2	0	5	4	5	2	21	10.88
irst041iten	0	5	11	0	1	0	6	3	8	11	45	22.50
irst042iten	0	5	5	0	1	0	2	5	6	11	35	17.50
lire041fren	3	1	9	0	1	0	3	0	1	4	22	11.00
lire042fren	2	1	13	0	1	0	4	1	6	11	39	19.50
combination	7	5	26	6	7	5	18	10	22	24	130	65.00

[2] Since some typos were found in the FI=>EN test set, seven questions were not taken into consideration in the evaluation. None of them had received a right answer, so their exclusion did not affect the data in Table 5.

We should point out that our reasoning and judgements were made with respect to the English versions of the questions. However, all the systems in this task group were using the 'same' questions in languages other than English. It is possible therefore that a question inadvertently asked something different in a particular language due to differences of translation. This could affect the results though perhaps not to a major degree.

In Table 5 the results are sorted by category of questions. Some answer types (i.e. manner, measure and object) turned out to be difficult for systems, while the performance on location, factoid-person and time is quite good.

In making judgements concerning definitions we decided to err on the side of generosity and made no correction for the length of submissions although in practice these tended to be short. A response was considered correct if it provided salient information concerning the topic. Generally the task specification for such questions was considered somewhat vague and so the results while being interesting are not necessarily that informative. What seems to be necessary is a means of punishing answers which contain both relevant and irrelevant information. This has been attempted in TREC with mixed results. While the level of participation in the English target task group was very encouraging, the number participating was still very small in statistical terms and also varied from language pair to language pair. Therefore we should be careful not to conclude too much from the results in terms for example of the relative difficulty of different language pairs.

5.3 French as Target

A single research group took part in evaluation tasks with French as a target language: Neuchatel University. It took part in both monolingual and bilingual tasks. This participating team submitted 16 runs, two runs per source language, taken from the 8 available source languages: Bulgarian, German, English, Spanish, French, Italian, Dutch and Portuguese. In particular, two runs were submitted for the monolingual task.

Table 6 shows the assessment of the sixteen submitted runs. The monolingual runs appear in italics.

The best results were obtained for one of the monolingual runs (gine042frfr). This proves once again that it is *a priori* easier for the systems to answer correctly when the source language is the same as the target language. However, it is noticeable that the 2nd and 3rd best results are obtained by the two German-French runs (better than the other monolingual French run).

It is important to notice that the number of unsupported answers is 0 for all runs. This is expectable as all 16 runs are versions of the same system, and indicates that this system always supports the answers it gives.The correct answers given for all the runs are presented in Table 7, clustered by answer type of questions.

Neuchatel system's weaknesses obviously lie in definition-organisation (recall 0%) and in factoid-manner (max. recall 21%) questions, whereas it gives its better results for definition-person (max. recall 50%), measure (32%) and location (34.5%) questions.

Table 6. Results of the monolingual and bilingual French runs

Run Name	R (#)	W (#)	X (#)	U (#)	Overall Accuracy (%)	Accuracy over F (%)	Accuracy over D (%)	NIL Accuracy		CWS
								P	R	
gine041bgfr	13	182	5	0	6.50	6.67	5.00	0.10	0.50	0.051
gine041defr	29	161	10	0	14.50	14.44	15.00	0.15	0.20	0.079
gine041enfr	18	170	12	0	9.00	8.89	10.00	0.05	0.10	0.033
gine041esfr	27	165	8	0	13.50	14.44	5.00	0.12	0.15	0.056
gine041frfr	*27*	*160*	*13*	*0*	*13.50*	*13.89*	*10.00*	*0.00*	*0.00*	*0.048*
gine041itfr	25	165	10	0	12.50	13.33	5.00	0.15	0.30	0.049
gine041nlfr	20	169	11	0	10.00	10.00	10.00	0.12	0.20	0.044
gine041ptfr	25	169	6	0	12.50	12.22	15.00	0.11	0.15	0.044
gine042bgfr	13	180	7	0	6.50	6.11	10.00	0.10	0.35	0.038
gine042defr	34	154	12	0	17.00	15.56	30.00	0.23	0.20	0.097
gine042enfr	27	164	9	0	13.50	12.22	25.00	0.06	0.10	0.051
gine042esfr	34	162	4	0	17.00	17.22	15.00	0.11	0.10	0.075
gine042frfr	*49*	*145*	*6*	*0*	*24.50*	*23.89*	*30.00*	*0.09*	*0.05*	*0.114*
gine042itfr	29	164	7	0	14.50	15.56	5.00	0.14	0.30	0.054
gine042nlfr	29	156	15	0	14.50	13.33	25.00	0.14	0.20	0.065
gine042ptfr	29	164	7	0	14.50	13.33	25.00	0.10	0.15	0.056

Table 7. Results of the monolingual and bilingual French runs, according to answer types of questions

Run Name	Given correct answers											
	Definition (#)		Factoid (#)								Total	
	org [8]	per [12]	loc [29]	man [14]	mea [28]	obj [15]	org [20]	oth [21]	per [32]	tim [21]	# [200]	%
gine041bgfr	0	1	1	3	2	2	1	1	2	0	13	6.50
gine041defr	0	3	6	0	5	3	4	2	4	2	29	14.50
gine041enfr	0	2	5	0	4	1	0	1	3	2	18	9.00
gine041esfr	0	1	7	0	4	3	3	2	4	3	27	13.50
gine041frfr	*0*	*2*	*8*	*0*	*8*	*0*	*1*	*3*	*2*	*3*	*27*	*13.50*
gine041itfr	0	1	3	1	5	3	4	2	3	3	25	12.50
gine041nlfr	0	2	6	1	5	1	1	2	1	1	20	10.00
gine041ptfr	0	3	5	0	5	2	1	2	3	4	25	12.50
gine042bgfr	0	2	2	1	2	2	0	2	2	0	13	6.50
gine042defr	0	6	7	0	5	3	3	2	6	2	34	17.00
gine042enfr	0	5	7	0	5	1	2	1	4	2	27	13.50
gine042esfr	0	3	8	0	4	2	5	3	4	5	34	17.00
gine042frfr	*0*	*6*	*10*	*0*	*9*	*1*	*6*	*6*	*4*	*7*	*49*	*24.50*
gine042itfr	0	1	5	1	4	3	4	3	4	4	29	14.50
gine042nlfr	0	5	5	0	7	2	2	4	3	1	29	14.50
gine042ptfr	0	5	5	0	5	2	2	3	3	4	29	14.50
combination	0	7	19	3	17	5	8	8	11	9	97	48.50

The virtual run in the last row, called combination, aims at getting an idea of what could be the expected potential performance of a system giving all the correct answers. The best run (gine042frfr) is able to supply only 50.51% of the correct answers of "combination". This ratio could be enhanced if results for definition-organisation and factoid-manner, in particular, were improved.

5.4 German as Target

Two research groups took part in tasks with German as target language, and only in the monolingual German task: DFKI, which had participated at CLEF-2003, and Fernuniversität Hagen, at its first participation, submitted one run each.

The German test set contained 200 questions. However, three questions contained spelling errors and were subsequently excluded from the evaluation, so that only 197 questions were taken into consideration.

Table 8. Results of the monolingual German runs

Run Name	R (#)	W (#)	X (#)	U (#)	Overall Accuracy (%)	Accuracy over F (%)	Accuracy over D (%)	NIL Accuracy		CWS
								P	R	
fuha041dede	67	128	2	0	34.01	31.64	55.00	0.14	1.00	0.333
dfki041dede	50	143	1	3	25.38	28.25	0.00	0.14	0.85	-

Table 8 shows the assessment of the two runs which were submitted. DFKI did not handle any definition questions. Both groups produced short and exact answers; no answer was longer than 6 words or 48 characters.

Table 9. Results of the monolingual German runs, according to answer types of questions

Run Name	Given correct answers											
	Definition (#)		Factoid (#)								Total	
	org [11]	per [9]	loc [22]	man [20]	mea [21]	obj [23]	org [23]	oth [22]	per [23]	tim [23]	# [197]	%
fuha041dede	6	5	12	4	4	4	5	7	10	10	67	34.01
dfki041dede	0	0	8	2	4	2	8	4	9	13	50	25.38
combination	6	5	14	4	5	4	11	8	13	16	86	43.65

The combination run in the last row shows that the best performing system (fuha041dede) is able to respond correctly to 78% of the questions that have been correctly answered by both teams in conjunction.

The DFKI group conducted an experiment to compare the QA system performance against human QA performance under time constraints [3]. Three subjects answered all 200 questions of the monolingual German test set with the help of a search engine. The time between the presentation of each question and the submission of the document ID was measured, and the answers were assessed. Only answers that were found within a given time limit were considered. The accuracy a human could achieve was then calculated. It was found that a human who is allowed a maximum of 42 seconds per question achieves the same level of accuracy as the German "combination" run (DFKI run ≈ 30s, FUHA run ≈ 34s). In addition, the experiment revealed the difficulty of different answer types for humans, e.g., the average definition questions required 39 seconds and the average factoid questions 81 seconds.

5.5 Italian as Target

Two research groups took part in tasks with Italian as target language, and only in the monolingual Italian task: ITC-Irst, that had participated also in CLEF-2003, and the Institute for Computational Linguistics in Pisa[3], at its first participation.

In 2003 ITC-Irst submitted two runs, and the system answered correctly at the first rank to 37.5% and 41.5% of the questions respectively. The lower results achieved in 2004 with the same system demonstrate that the task was harder. Nevertheless, as Table 10 shows, the overall accuracy of the runs ILCP and irst041 is above the average performance of the participants in the monolingual tasks.

Table 10. Results of the monolingual Italian runs

Run Name	R (#)	W (#)	X (#)	U (#)	Overall Accuracy (%)	Accuracy over F (%)	Accuracy over D (%)	NIL Accuracy		CWS
								P	R	
ilcp041itit	51	117	29	3	25.50	22.78	50.00	0.62	0.50	-
irst041itit	56	131	11	2	28.00	26.67	40.00	0.27	0.30	0.155
irst042itit	44	147	9	0	22.00	20.00	40.00	0.66	0.20	0.107

Table 11. Results of the monolingual Italian runs, according to answer types of questions

Run Name	Given correct answers											
	Definition (#)		Factoid (#)								Total	
	org [11]	per [9]	loc [25]	man [12]	mea [30]	obj [10]	org [17]	oth [33]	per [28]	tim [25]	# [200]	%
ilcp041itit	5	5	9	4	3	2	2	4	5	12	51	25.50
irst041itit	5	3	8	1	6	3	5	3	8	14	56	28.00
irst042itit	5	3	7	0	3	2	2	2	8	12	44	22.00
combination	8	7	12	4	8	4	7	6	13	19	88	44.00

The analysis of the results in Table 11 shows that *location*, *person* and *time* were the easiest answer types for the participating systems. How-questions constituted a problem for the Irst system, while ILCP answered four of them correctly, retrieving long text snippets that were judged as responsive. The accuracy over definition

[3] Joint work with the Department of Information and Communication Technology of the University of Pisa.

questions in all three submitted runs is relatively high. While the Irst system returned very short answers, trying to select the most relevant portion of text, the ILCP system often gave long answer-strings, and many of them (14.5%) were judged as inexact, although they often contained the required information.

The runs ilcp and irst042 were the most precise in the whole track in identifying the questions with no response, though their recall is not very high.

5.6 Portuguese as Target

Two research groups took part in tasks with Portuguese as target language, both in the monolingual task; one of them submitted two runs. None provided a confidence score.

Since there was a duplicated question, (*Who was the first President of the United States?*), only 199 questions were taken into account in the summary statistics.

Table 12. Results of the monolingual Portuguese runs

Run Name	R (#)	W (#)	X (#)	U (#)	Overall Accuracy (%)	Accuracy over F (%)	Accuracy over D (%)	NIL Accuracy		CWS
								P	R	
ptue041ptpt	57	125	18	0	28.64	29.17	25.81	0.14	0.90	-
sfnx041ptpt	22	166	8	4	11.06	11.90	6.45	0.13	0.75	-
sfnx042ptpt	30	155	10	5	15.08	16.07	9.68	0.16	0.55	-

The table above shows the assessment of the three submitted runs. While the answers of the SFNX system were generally rather short, the PTUE system occasionally submitted longer answers (in one case, reaching 35 words).

Table 13. Results of the monolingual Portuguese runs, according to answer types of questions

Run Name	Given correct answers											
	Definition (#)		Factoid (#)								Total	
	org [14]	per [17]	loc [43]	man [4]	mea [23]	obj [6]	org [12]	oth [21]	per [44]	tim [15]	# [199]	%
ptue041ptpt	3	5	19	1	5	1	4	3	14	2	57	28.64
sfnx041ptpt	0	2	4	0	3	1	2	3	7	0	22	11.06
sfnx042ptpt	1	2	8	0	4	2	2	4	7	0	30	15.08
combination	3	6	25	1	5	3	4	6	19	2	74	37.18

5.7 Spanish as Target

Five groups submitted eight runs having Spanish both as target and source language. The test set contained 200 questions with the type distribution shown in Table 15.

Since, as Table 15 shows, some systems performed better for certain types of questions, the following question arises: why do we not reward specialisation? This issue has been explored in the Pilot Question Answering Task [4], in which the confidence score has been taken into account in the evaluation measure in order to reward systems' self-knowledge and answer validation when responding to different types of questions.

As the virtual *combination* run in the last row of Table 15 shows, the best performing system (aliv042eses) is able to respond correctly to only 57.5% of the questions that would have been correctly answered by all teams in conjunction. Systems show better behaviour when answering about locations, organisations, dates and persons. It is interesting to remark that, whereas individual systems show important differences with respect to the number of correct answers depending on the type of question, the combination of systems shows a quite uniform distribution.

Table 14. Results of the monolingual Spanish runs

Run Name	R (#)	W (#)	X (#)	U (#)	Overall Accuracy (%)	Accuracy over F (%)	Accuracy over D (%)	NIL Accuracy		CWS
								P	R	
aliv041eses	63	130	5	2	31.50	30.56	40.00	0.17	0.35	0.121
aliv042eses	65	129	4	2	32.50	31.11	45.00	0.17	0.35	0.144
cole041eses	22	178	0	0	11.00	11.67	5.00	0.10	1.00	-
inao041eses	45	145	5	5	22.50	19.44	50.00	0.19	0.50	-
inao042eses	37	152	6	5	18.50	17.78	25.00	0.21	0.50	-
mira041eses	18	174	7	1	9.00	10.00	0.00	0.14	0.55	-
talp041eses	48	150	1	1	24.00	18.89	70.00	0.19	0.50	0.087
talp042eses	52	143	3	2	26.00	21.11	70.00	0.20	0.55	0.102

Table 15. Results of the monolingual Spanish runs, according to answer types of questions

Run Name	Given correct answers											
	Definition (#)		Factoid (#)								Total	
	org [10]	per [10]	loc [22]	man [22]	mea [23]	obj [22]	org [23]	oth [22]	per [23]	tim [23]	# [200]	%
aliv042eses	7	2	6	4	6	4	12	6	7	11	65	32.50
aliv041eses	7	1	5	4	7	4	12	6	6	11	63	31.50
talp042eses	7	7	10	3	3	6	3	1	9	3	52	26.00
talp041eses	7	7	9	4	1	5	3	0	5	7	48	24.00
inao041eses	4	6	9	3	2	2	5	3	3	8	45	22.50
inao042eses	4	1	9	3	2	2	5	2	2	8	37	18.50
cole041eses	1	0	2	2	2	2	3	3	3	4	22	11.00
mira041eses	0	0	3	2	4	2	2	1	2	2	18	9.00
combination	7	9	16	7	10	9	15	11	14	15	113	56.50

Though different questions and different text collections were used, the overall results obtained for monolingual Spanish in 2004 are better than those in the 2003 track. The best result obtained in the last edition was 40% of questions with a correct answer. However, three answers per question were allowed in 2003: if we consider only the percentage of correct answers found at the first rank, which was 24.5% for the best system, this is outperformed by the run aliv042eses, submitted by the University of Alicante, which reached an accuracy of 32.5% in 2004.

6 Remarks on Evaluation

The four judgements adopted by the assessors (right, wrong, inexact and unsupported) have been used at TREC for many years and seem to cover most of the possible answers of a real QA system. Even so, the evaluation of the runs submitted at CLEF shows that sometimes they are somehow simplistic, and that they do not enable assessors to grasp the responsiveness of all the answers.

In particular, as the disagreement between assessors has shown, exactness is really difficult to judge, considering also that it has never been defined with objective criteria. The tentative rules we tried to draft concerning the acceptable and the unacceptable parts of speech did not always match the sensibility of the human assessors. Furthermore, some types of questions, such as How- questions and definitions, have relatively long strings as answers, and for the time being it would be too demanding to require essential and not redundant responses. Maybe we should consider going back to the retrieval of short, meaningful passages (similar to the optional *justifications* that could be attached to the answers at TREC 2002), possibly rewarding those systems that are able to return just the minimal piece of information. Alternatively, the judgement *inexact* could be kept, but differentiated so as to distinguish between an incomplete answer and one that is too long.

In addition, the judgement *unsupported* could be considered independently from *right* and *wrong* because assessors came across wrong answers that were completely unrelated to the document indicated in the docid.

Finally, an additional heuristic judgement that quantifies the *usefulness* of a response could be introduced; in fact an answer can be either wrong or inexact, but at the same time a potential user could draw some partial information from it.

As far as the NIL questions are concerned, they were usually generated using proper names or keywords that did not appear in the document collection. This procedure needs to be reconsidered, because a simple IR system could trivially identify them, though in 2004 the NIL accuracy was not very high. If NIL questions addressed entities that actually appear in the corpus, the task would be more challenging and significant.

The confidence-weighted score, that was used at TREC 2002 [7], could not be calculated for all the runs because the confidence value was not mandatory. When computed, it seemed to reflect the overall accuracy, and it does not provide further insight into the systems' performance.

7 Conclusions

Thanks to the high number of proposed tasks and to a growing interest in Question Answering by the European research community, the QA@CLEF-2004 attracted more participants than the previous edition. In addition, the benchmark resources built within the framework of these evaluation exercises contribute to the development and tuning of systems, and can be reused as training resources.

The results of the 2004 track are not fully comparable to those achieved in 2003, in fact the two tasks were designed differently: nonetheless, the accuracy in answering specific questions, such as those that had *location* and *time* as answer types, was encouragingly high in all the seven target languages. The introduction of definition and How- questions made the task harder, and the assessors encountered some difficulties in defining and judging objectively the responsiveness and exactness of the responses. It seems that in assessing these particular questions, it would be reasonable to accept short text passages instead of exact answer-strings. Furthermore, the evaluation process as it was designed, i.e. split over different sites with multiple assessors, lacked uniformity and would need stricter, common guidelines that cover as many as possible real output cases. This aspect should be reconsidered for future campaigns.

The evaluation measures adopted in 2004 followed closely the TREC-2002 QA track, but since the assessors sometimes found the four judgements (right, wrong, inexact and unsupported) inadequate, some changes might be introduced in the next exercises, aimed for instance at rewarding the usefulness of responses for a potential user. However, coming up with a user model that is useful, satisfactory, and realistic is certainly non-trivial.

Acknowledgements

The authors would like to thank Donna Harman for her valuable feedback and suggestions in designing the track, and Ellen Voorhees for providing the NIST software for the assessment of the submitted runs.

Gregor Erbach wishes to thank the German Federal Ministry of Education and Research (BMBF) through the project COLLATE II (01 IN C02), for supporting the work.

Bernardo Magnini and Alessandro Vallin have been partially supported by the WEBFAQ project funded by the Autonomous Province of Trento.

Anselmo Peñas has been partially supported by the Spanish Government under projects TIC-2002-10597-E and R2D2-Syembra TIC-2003-07158-C04-02.

Maarten de Rijke was supported by the Netherlands Organization for Scientific Research (NWO) under project numbers 612-13-001, 365-20-005, 612.069.006, 612.000.106, 220-80-001, 612.000.207, 612.066.302, and 264-70-050.

Paulo Rocha was supported by the Portuguese Fundação para a Ciência e Tecnologia, through grant POSI/PLP/43931/2001.

References

1. Burger, J., Cardie, C., Chaudhri, V., Gaizauskas, R., Harabagiu, S., Israel, D., Jacquemin, C., Lin, C.-Y., Maiorano, S., Miller, G., Moldovan, D., Ogden, B., Prager, J., Riloff, E., Singhal, A., Shrihari, R., Strzalkowski, T., Voorhees and E., Weishedel, R.: Issues, Tasks and Program Structures to Roadmap Research in Question & Answering (2001).
2. URL: http://www-nlpir.nist.gov/projects/duc/papers/qa.Roadmap-paper_v2.doc

3. CLEF 2004 Question Answering Track Guidelines (2004)
4. URL: http://clef-qa.itc.it/2004/guidelines.html
5. Erbach, G.: Evaluating Human Question Answering Performance under Time Constraints, (2004). URL: http://purl.org/net/gregor/pub/human-qa/
6. Herrera, J., Peñas, A. and Verdejo, F.: Question Answering Pilot Task at CLEF 2004. In this volume
7. Magnini, B., Romagnoli, S., Vallin, A., Herrera, J., Peñas, A., Peinado, V., Verdejo, F. and de Rijke, M.: The Multiple Language Question Answering Track at CLEF 2003. In: Peters, C., Braschler, M., Gonzalo, J. and Kluck, M., (eds), Results of the CLEF 2003 Evaluation Campaign. Lecture Notes in Computer Science, Vol. 3237. Springer-Verlag, Berlin Heidelberg New York (2004)
8. Magnini, B., Romagnoli, S., Vallin, A., Herrera, J., Peñas, A., Peinado, V., Verdejo, F. and de Rijke, M.: Creating the DISEQuA Corpus: a Test Set for Multilingual Question Answering. In: Peters, C., Braschler, M., Gonzalo, J. and Kluck, M., (eds), Results of the CLEF 2003 Evaluation Campaign. Lecture Notes in Computer Science, Vol. 3237. Springer-Verlag, Berlin Heidelberg New York (2004)
9. Voorhees, E. M.: Overview of the TREC 2002 Question Answering Track. In: Voorhees, E. M. and Buckland, L. P., (eds), Proceedings of the Eleventh Text Retrieval Conference (TREC 2002). NIST Special Publication 500-251, Washington DC (2002) 115-123
10. Voorhees, E. M.: Overview of the TREC 2003 Question Answering Track. In: Voorhees, E. M. and Buckland, L. P., (eds), Proceedings of the Twelfth Text Retrieval Conference (TREC 2003). NIST Special Publication 500-255, Washington DC (2003) 54-68

A Question Answering System for French

Laura Perret

Institut interfacultaire d'informatique,
University of Neuchâtel, Pierre-à-Mazel 7, 2000 Neuchâtel, Switzerland
Laura.Perret@unine.ch

Abstract. This paper describes our first participation in the QA@CLEF monolingual and bilingual task, where our objective was to propose a question answering system designed to respond to French queries searching French documents. We wanted to combine a classic information retrieval model (based on the Okapi probabilistic model) with a linguistic approach based mainly on syntactic analysis. In order to utilize our monolingual system in the bilingual task, we automatically translated into French queries written in seven other source languages, namely Dutch, German, Italian, Portuguese, Spanish, English and Bulgarian.

1 Introduction

For the first time QA@CLEF-2004 has proposed a question-answering track that allows various European languages to be used either as a source or target language. Our aim in this study was to develop a question answering system for the French language and to evaluate its performance. In Section 2, we describe how we developed our question answering system to carry out the monolingual French task. As a first step in this process, we applied a classical information retrieval model (based on the Okapi probabilistic model) to extract a small number of responding paragraphs for each query. We then analyzed the queries and sentences included in retrieved paragraphs using a syntactic analyzer (FIPS) developed at the Laboratoire d'analyse et de Technologie du Langage (LATL) at the University of Geneva. Finally, we suggested a matching strategy that would extract responses from the best-ranked sentences. In Section 3, we describe methods used to overcome language barriers by accessing various translation resources to translate various queries into French and then, with French as target language, utilize our question answering system to carry out this bilingual task. In Section 4, we discuss the results obtained from this technique and in the last section we draw conclusions on what improvements we might envisage for our system.

2 Monolingual Question Answering

The monolingual task was designed for six different languages, namely Dutch, French, German, Italian, Portuguese, and Spanish. Given that our question answering system is language dependant, we only addressed the French monolingual task.

C. Peters et al. (Eds.): CLEF 2004, LNCS 3491, pp. 392–403, 2005.

2.1 Overview of the Test-Collection

Given that we did not have previous experience in building a QA system, we developed a test set consisting of 57 homemade factual queries from corpora consisting of the newspapers *Le Monde* (1994, 157 MB) and *SDA French* (1994, 86 MB). Table 1 shows some examples of these queries.

Table 1. Examples of factoid test queries

Query	Answer string	Supporting document
Où se trouve le siège de l'OCDE ?	Paris	LEMONDE94-000001-19941201
Qui est le premier ministre canadien ?	Jean Chrétien	LEMONDE94-000034-19941201
Combien de collaborateurs emploie ABB ?	206 000	ATS.941214.0105

2.2 Information Retrieval Scheme

Firstly, we split the test collection into paragraphs using the <TEXT> tag as delimiter for *Le Monde* documents and the <TX> tag as delimiter for the *SDA French* documents.

For each paragraph, we then removed the most frequent words, using the French stopword list available at www.unine.ch/info/clef/. From this stopword list we removed numeral adjectives such as « premier » (first), « dix-huit » (eighteen), « soixante » (sixty), assuming that answers to factoid questions may contain numerical data. The final stopword list contained 421 entries.

After removing high frequency words, we also used an indexing procedure with a stemming algorithm (also available at www.unine.ch/info/clef/ [1]). We assumed that looking for exact answers requires a lighter stemmer, one that would not affect the part-of-speech categorization for terms. Our stemmer thus only removed inflectional suffixes so that singular and plural, and also feminine and masculine forms, would conflate to the same root. Figure 1 describes our stemming algorithm.

```
if word length greater than 5
    if word ends with « aux » then replace « aux » by « al »    chevaux -> cheval
    else
        if word ends with 's' then remove 's'                   chatons -> chaton
        if word ends with 'r' then remove 'r'                   chanter -> chante
        if word ends with 'e' then remove 'e'                   chatte -> chatt
        if word ends with 'é' then remove 'é'                   chanté -> chant
        if word ends with a double letter then remove the last letter   chatt -> chat
```

Fig. 1. Stemming algorithm

For our indexing and search system, we used a classical SMART information retrieval system [3] to retrieve the ten best paragraphs for each query from the underlying collection. In our experiment, we chose the Okapi probabilistic model (BM25), setting our constants to the following values: b=0.8, k_l=2 and $avdl$=400.

2.3 French Syntactic Analysis

In a second step, we used the French Interactive Parsing System (FIPS), a robust French syntactic analyzer developed at the LATL in Geneva [4], [5]. This tool is based on the Chomsky's Theory of Principles and Parameters [6] and the Government and Binding model [7]. It takes a text as input, splits it into sentences, and then for each sentence computes a syntactic structure.

We took advantage of this tool to analyze the queries as well as the paragraphs retrieved by our classical IR system. Table 2 shows the analysis obtained for the Query #1 « Quel est le directeur général de FIAT ? » (Who is the managing director of FIAT?)

The last row in Table 2 shows a syntactic analysis of the complete sentence while the other rows show items of information on each word in the sentence. For each word, the first column contains the original term, the second column the part-of-speech and the third the concept number. The forth column lists the named entities, the fifth the lexeme number while the last column shows the lemma used as the dictionary entry.

The original tool was adapted in order to provide two sorts of named entities recognition: numeral named entities (Table 3) and noun named entities (Table 4).

From a collection of all available information from FIPS, we built a tree structure to represent the syntactic analysis of each query and sentence that would then be used for the rest of the process.

Table 2. Example of FIPS analysis

Term	POS	Concept number	Named entities	Lexeme number	Lemma
quel	PRO-INT-SIN-MAS	211049516		0	quel
est	VER-IND-PRE-SIN	211000095 211021507 211048855 211049530		4	être
le	DET-SIN-MAS	211045001		8	le
directeur	NOM-SIN-MAS	211014688	{0, 13, 24}	11	directeur
général	ADJ-SIN-MAS	211014010		21	général
de	PRE	211047305		29	de
FIAT	NOM-SIN-ING	0	{16}	32	FIAT
?	PONC-interrogation	0		37	?
[CP[DP quel]i[C [TP[DP ei][T est [VP [DP le [NP directeur [AP[DP ej][A général [PP de [DP FIAT]]]]]j]]]] ?]]					

Table 3. Examples of numeral named entities recognized by FIPS

Named entity	Example
Numeral	premier (first)
Percent	23%
Ordinal	1er
special number	751.04.09
Cardinal	1291
Digit	12, douze (twelve)

Table 4. Examples of noun named entities recognized by FIPS

Named entity	Example	
Human	homme	(man)
animate	chat	(cat)
quantity	kilo	(kilo)
time	heure	(hour)
day	lundi	(Monday)
month	mai	(Mai)
weight	gramme	(gram)
length	mètre	(meter)
location	bureau	(office)

2.4 Matching Strategy

Once we had the queries and the best responding paragraphs analyzed by FIPS, we developed a matching scheme, one that allowed our system to find the best answer snippet.

Query Analysis
We analyzed the queries in order to determine their relevant terms, targets and expected answer types. To facilitate the retrieval of a response, we selected the relevant terms from a query. A term was considered relevant if its *idf* was greater than 3.5 (*idf* = ln (*n* / *df*), where *n* denotes the number of documents in the collection and *df* the number of documents that contain the term). This threshold was chosen empirically according to our collection size (730,098 paragraphs) and corresponds to a *df* of about 20,000.

We then looked within the query for an interrogative word. As our syntactic analyzer was able to supply the lemma for any known term (last column of Table 2), our interrogative words set was reduced to the following list {quel, qui, que, quoi, où, quand, combien, pourquoi, comment}. Most queries contain an interrogative word from this list except queries such as « Donnez le nom d'un liquide inodore et insipide. » (Name an odourless and tasteless liquid.).

We defined the query target by choosing the first term after the interrogative word, whose part-of-speech tag was labelled by FIPS as NOM-* (noun). If the query did not contain an interrogative word, the target was searched from the beginning of the query. Some particular words were however excluded from the allowed targets since they did not represent relevant information. The list of excluded targets was:

nombre, quantité, grandeur, dimension, date, jour, mois, année, an, époque, période, nom, surnom, titre, lieu

As illustrated in Table 5, using the query interrogative word and target, we categorized queries under six classes.

Once we classified the queries into their corresponding classes, we identified the expected answer type for each class. Their order has no influence on the system. Table 6 shows the details of these classes.

Table 5. Query classes

Class	Interrogative words	Specific target	Example
Class 1	quel, quoi, comment, pourquoi, que, qu'est-ce que		Comment appelle-t-on l'intérieur d'un bâteau ? Qu'a inventé le baron Marcel Bich ?
Class 2	où		Où se trouve le siège de l'OCDE ?
Class 3	combien quel + num. target none + num. target	numeral target: pourcentage, nombre, quantité, distance, poids, longueur, hau-teur, largeur, âge, grandeur, dimension, super-ficie	Combien de membres compte l'OCDE ? A quel âge est mort Massimo Troisi ?
Class 4	quand, quel + time target none + time target	time target date, jour, mois, année, an, époque, période	Quand est né Albert Einstein ? En quelle année est né Alberto Giacometti ?
Class 5	qui, quel + func. target none + func. target	function target président, directeur, ministre, juge, sénateur, acteur, chanteur, artiste, présentateur, réalisateur	Qui est Jacques Chirac ? Quel est le président du parti socialiste suisse ?
Class 6	other		Donnez le nom d'un liquide inodore et insipide.

Table 6. Expected answer type per query class

Class	Expected answer type
Class 1	all noun named entities
Class 2	location, country, town, river, mountain, proper name
Class 3	quantity, weight, length and all numeral named entities
Class 4	time, day, month, numeral, ordinal, special number, cardinal, digit
Class 5	human, animate, collective, people, corporation, title, function, proper name
Class 6	all noun named entities

Sentence Ranking

Given that the analyzer split the paragraphs into sentences, we ranked the sentences according to the score computed by the Formula 1 where *sentenceRelevant* is the number of relevant query terms in the sentence, *sentenceLen* is the number of terms in the sentence and *queryRelevant* is the number of relevant terms in the query (without stopwords):

$$score = sentenceRelevant * sentenceLen \,/\, (sentenceLen - queryRelevant) \qquad (1)$$

We then chose the ten sentences having the highest score. Table 7 shows the four best selected sentences for Query #19 « Où se trouve la mosquée Al Aqsa ? » (Where is the Al Aqsa Mosque?).

Table 7. Best sentences selected for Query #19

Rank	Score	Document and sentence
1	2.148	[ATS.950417.0033] : la police interdit aux juifs de prier sur l' esplanade où se trouve la mosquée al-Aqsa , troisième lieu saint de l' islam après la Mecque et Médine .
2	2.102	[ATS.940304.0093] : la police a expliqué qu' elle bouclait le site le plus sacré du judaïsme jusqu' à la fin de la prière du vendredi à la mosquée Al -- Aqsa , laquelle se trouve sur l' Esplanade du Temple qui domine le Mur des Lamentations .
3	1.4	[ATS.940405.0112] : la mosquée al Aqsa rouverte aux touristes .
4	1.117	[ATS.940606.0081] : cette phrase laisse ouverte la possibilité pour M. Arafat d' aller prier à la mosquée al-Aqsa à Jérusalem .

Snippet Extraction

For each selected sentence, we searched the identified query target. If the target was never found, we selected the first sentence for the rest of the process. We then listed the terms of the expected answer types in a window containing the 4 terms before and after the target term. *Confidence* in this sentence was computed according to Formula 2 where score was the initial score of the sentence and *maxScore* the score of the best-ranked sentence for the current query. If the *maxScore* was equal to zero, the confidence was also set to zero.

$$confidence = score \,/\, maxScore \quad (2)$$

For each expected type term found, we extracted the closest DP (determiner-phrase) or NP (noun-phrase) group node from the sentence analysis tree. Thus, each sentence may produce one or more nodes (as shown in Table 8, 2nd and 3rd row). From the list obtained in the previous step, we then eliminated all nodes contained in other nodes whose difference level was less than 7. The level represents the node depth in the syntactic analysis tree.We then pruned the remaining nodes by extracting the part of the node that did not contain query term. Finally, following the pruning process, we eliminated any snippets that did not contain expected answer terms. For Query #19 where the correct answer is "Jérusalem", Table 8 lists the remaining nodes.

Table 8. Remaining nodes for Query #19

Document	Confidence	Answer candidate
ATS.940304.0093	0.978	Al -- Aqsa
ATS.940606.0081	0.520	M. Arafat
ATS.940606.0081	0.520	Jérusalem
LEMONDE94-001632-19940514	0.509	Jérusalem
ATS.941107.0105	0.507	Jérusalem
ATS.940304.0093	0.496	Ville
ATS.940304.0093	0.496	Al-Aqsa l'un des lieux saints de l' islam
LEMONDE94-001740-19940820	0.494	le Saint-Sépulcre
ATS.940405.0112	0.494	le Waqf
ATS.951223.0020	0.492	à Jérusalem
ATS.951223.0020	0.492	Bethléem

Voting Procedure

We supposed that an answer having a lower confidence than the best candidate could nevertheless be a good answer if it was supported by more documents. Therefore, the last step of the process was to choose which remaining snippet should be returned as the response by implementing it with the voting procedure.

First we split each snippet into words and computed its length (*snippetLen*) as the number of words of the snippet. Then we counted the occurrences of each non-stopword in other snippets (*occurrencesCount*). Finally, we ranked the snippets according to their scores computed using Formula 3 where *len* was equals to the *snippetLen* for factoid queries or *1* for definition queries. Indeed, as definition responses may be longer than factoid responses, we did not want to penalize long definition responses.

$$score = occurrencesCount \,/\, len \quad (3)$$

If the occurrencesCount was equal to zero, we chose the first snippet but decreased its confidence. Else, we chose the snippet with the higher score as answer. Table 9 shows the snipped chosen for Query #19.

Table 9. Snippet chosen for Query #19

Document	Confidence	Answer candidate
ATS.940606.0081	0.520	Jérusalem

3 Bilingual Question Answering

Given that our question answering system was developed for the French language, we only addressed bilingual tasks in which French was the target language. We therefore submitted results for Dutch, German, Italian, Portuguese, Spanish, English and Bulgarian as source languages, with French as the target language.

3.1 Automatic Query Translation

Since our QA system was designed to respond to French queries concerning French documents, we needed to translate original the queries formulated in other languages into French. In order to overcome language barriers, we based our approach on free and readily available translation resources that would automatically translate queries into the desired target language, namely French [2]. These resources were:

1. Reverso (www.reverso.fr)
2. TranslationExperts.com (intertran.tranexp.com)
3. Free2Professional Translation (www.freetranslation.com)
4. AltaVista (babelfish.altavista.com)
5. Systran (www.systranlinks.com)
6. Google.com (www.google.com/language_tools)
7. WorldLingo (www.worldlingo.com)

Table 10 shows the languages supported by each translation resource when the target language is French, with the chosen resource for each language being marked with a star (*). Since the Bulgarian language uses the Cyrillic alphabet, we added a specific step to transliterate non-translated words using the table available at www.world-gazetteer.com/pronun.htm#cyr.

Table 10. Available translation resources with French as target

	Source language						
Translation resource	bg	de	en	es	it	nl	pt
Reverso		√ *	√ *	√ *			
TranslationExperts.com	√ *	√	√	√	√	√	√
Free2Professional Translation			√				
AltaVista		√	√	√	√	√	√
Systran		√	√	√	√	√	√
Google.com		√	√				
WorldLingo		√	√	√	√ *	√ *	√ *

3.2 Translation Examples

Table 11 shows the translations obtained for the original French Query #1 « Quel est le directeur général de FIAT ? » (Who is the managing director of FIAT?).

Table 11. Exemples of French translations for Query #1

Source language	Original query	Translated query
Bulgarian	Кой е управителният директор на ФИАТ?	Qui å upravitelniiat direktor na FIAT?
German	Wer ist der Geschäftsführer von FIAT?	Qui est le directeur de FIAT ?

4 Results

Each answer was assessed and marked as correct, inexact, unsupported or wrong, as illustrated in the following examples. An answer was judged correct by a human assessor when the answer string consisted exactly of the correct expected answer and this answer was supported by the returned document. For example, the pair ["Cesare Romiti", ATS.940531.0063] was judged correct for the Query #1 « Quel est le directeur général de FIAT ? » (Who is the managing director of FIAT?), since the supporting document contained the string « directeur général de Fiat Cesare Romiti ». Secondly, an answer was judged inexact when the answer string contained more or less than just the correct answer and the answer was supported by the returned document. For example, the pair ["premier ministre irlandais", ATS.940918.0057] was judged inexact for the Query #177 « Quelle est la fonction d'Albert Reynolds en Irlande ? » (What office does Albert Reynolds hold in Ireland?), since the adjective « irlandais » was redundant. Thirdly, an answer was judged unsupported when the returned document didn't support the answer string. Since our system only searched within collection documents provided, none of our answers was judged unsupported. Finally, an answer was judged wrong when the answer-string was not a correct answer. For example, the pair ["Underground", ATS.950528.0053] was judged wrong

Table 12. Results

	Mono-lingual	**Bilingual**						
Source language	fr	de	es	nl	it	pt	en	bg
Right	49	34	34	29	29	29	27	13
Inexact	6	12	4	15	7	7	9	7
Unsupported	0	0	0	0	0	0	0	0
Wrong	145	154	162	156	164	164	164	180
Accuracy	24.5%	17.0%	17.0%	14.5%	14.5%	14.5%	13.5%	6.5%
Nil correct	9.1%	23.5%	11.8%	14.8%	14.3%	10.0%	6.7%	10.1%
Translation cost		-30.6%	-30.6%	-40.8%	-40.8%	-40.8%	-44.9%	-73.5%

for the Query #118 « Qui a remporté la palme d'or à Cannes en 1995 ? » (Who won the Cannes Film Festival in 1995?), since « Underground » is the movie title whereas « Emir Kusturica » is the movie director and was the expected answer. Table 12 shows the results obtained for each source language. Given that the target language was French, logically the best score was obtained in the monolingual task where no translation was needed.

We can see that the translation process resulted in an important drop in the performance compared to the monolingual French experiment (up to 73.5% for Bulgarian). It was surprising to note that the English translation was listed as having the next to worst performance, just before the Bulgarian Cyrillic alphabet language. However, a deeper analysis showed that in 7.5% (15/200) of the cases, a majority of the various source languages translations (> 4) provided a correct answer whereas in 2.5% (5/200) of cases, they agreed on inexact answers. This might suggest that the translation did not have much affect on the system's ability to find a correct or inexact answer for about 10% of the queries. Looking at the answers marked as wrong in more detail, we detected some possible causes in addition to the translation problem. First of all, for some queries, we could not retrieve any corresponding document from the collection. Sometimes, we chose the wrong target and/or expected answer type. Thirdly, we were not able to account for the time reference, as in Query #22 « Combien a coûté la construction du Tunnel sous la Manche ? » (How much did the Channel Tunnel cost?) for which we provided the answer ["28,4 milliards de francs", LEMONDE94-002679-19940621] supported by the sentence "à l'origine, la construction du tunnel devait coûter 28,4 milliards de francs". In this case, our answer gave the initial estimate but not the final cost.

5 Conclusion

For our first participation in the QA@CLEF track, we proposed a question answering system designed to search French documents in response to French queries. To do so we used a French syntactic analyzer and a named entities recognition technique in order to assist in identifying the expected answers. We then proposed a matching strategy based on the node extraction from the analysis tree, followed by a ranking process.

In our bilingual task we used automatic translation resources to translate the original queries from Dutch, German, Italian, Portuguese, Spanish, English and Bulgarian into French. The remainder of this process was the same as that used in the monolingual task. The results showed performance levels of 24.5% for the monolingual task and up to 17% (German) for the bilingual task. There are several reasons for these results, among them being the selection process for the target and expected answer types. In the bilingual task, we verified that, as expected, the translation step was a significant factor in performance level losses, given that for German the performance level had decreased by about 30%.

Our system could be improved by using more in-depth syntactic analyses for both queries and paragraphs. Also, the target identification and queries taxonomy could be extended in order to obtain a more precise expected answer type.

Acknowledgments. The author would like to thank Eric Wehrli, Luka Nerima and Violeta Seretan from LATL (University of Geneva) for supplying the FIPS French syntactic analyzer as well as the task CLEF-2004 organizers for their efforts in developing various European languages test-collections. The author would also like to thank C. Buckley from SabIR for giving us the opportunity to use the SMART system. Furthermore, the author would like to thank J. Savoy for his advice on the preliminary version of this article as well as Pierre-Yves Berger for his contributions in the area of automatic translation. This research was supported in part by the SNSF (Swiss National Science Foundation) under grant 21-66 742.01.

References

1. Savoy, J.: A Stemming Procedure and Stopword List for General French Corpora. Journal of the American Society for Information Science, **50** (1999) 944-952
2. Savoy, J.: Combining Multiple Strategies for Effective Cross-Language Retrieval. Information Retrieval, **7** (2004) 121-148
3. Salton, G.: The Smart Retrieval System Experiments in Automatic Document Processing. Prentice-Hall, Englewood Cliffs (1971)
4. Laenzlinger, C., Wehrli, E.: FIPS : Un Analyseur Interctif pour le Français. TA Informations, **32** (1991) 35-49
5. Wehrli, E.: Un Modèle Multilingue d'Analyse Syntaxique. In: A. Auchlin, M. Burer, L. Filliettaz, A. Grobet, J. Moeschler, L. Perrin, C. Rossari et L. de Saussure (ed.), Structures et Discours - Mélanges Offerts à Eddy Roulet, Québec, Editions, Nota Bene (2004) 311-329
6. Chomsky, N., Lasnik, H.: The Theory of Principles and Parameters. In: Chomsky N. (Ed.), The Minimalist Program. MIT Press, Cambridge (1995) 13-127
7. Haegeman, L.: Introduction to Government and Binding Theory. Basil Blackwell, Oxford (1994)
8. Magnini, B., Romagnoli, S., Vallin, A., Herrera, J., Peñas, A., Peinado, V., Verdejo, F., de Rijke, M.: The Multiple Language Question Answering Track at CLEF 2003. In: Proceedings of CLEF 2003 (2003) 299-310
9. Negri, M., Tanev, H., Magnini, B.: Bridging Languages for Question Answering: DIOGENE at CLEF 2003. In: Proceedings of CLEF 2003 (2003) 321-329
10. Echihabi, A., Oard, D., Marcu, D., Hermjakob, U.: Cross-Language Question Answering at the USC Information Sciences Institute. In: Proceedings of CLEF 2003 (2003) 331-337
11. Jijkoun, V., Mishne, G., de Rijke, M.: The University of Amsterdam at QA@CLEF2003. In: Proceedings of CLEF 2003 (2003) 339-342
12. Plamondon, L., Foster, G.: Quantum, a French/English Cross-Language Question Answering System. In: Proceedings of CLEF 2003 (2003) 355-362
13. Neumann, G., Sacaleanu, B.: A Cross-Language Question/Answering-System for German and English. In: Proceedings of CLEF 2003 (2003) 363-372
14. Sutcliffe, R., Gabbay, I., O'Gorman, A.: Cross-Language French-English Question Answering Using the DLT System at CLEF 2003. In: Proceedings of CLEF 2003 (2003) 373-378
15. Voorhees, E. M.: Overview of the TREC 2003 Question Answering Track. In: Voorhees E.M., Buckland L.P. (Eds.): Proceedings of the Twelfth Text REtrieval Conference (TREC 2003) (2004) 54-68

16. Harabagiu, S., Moldovan, D., Clark, C., Bowden, M., Williams, J., Bensley, J.: Answer Mining by Combining Extraction Techniques with Abductive Reasoning. In: Voorhees E.M., Buckland L.P. (Eds.): Proceedings of the Twelfth Text REtrieval Conference (TREC 2003) (2004) 375-382
17. Soubbotin, M., Soubbotin, S.: Use of Patterns for Detection of Likely Answer Strings: A Systematic Approach, In: Voorhees E.M., Buckland L.P. (Eds.): Proceedings of the Eleventh Text REtrieval Conference (TREC 2002) (2003) 325-331

Cross-Language French-English Question Answering Using the DLT System at CLEF 2004

Richard F.E. Sutcliffe, Igal Gabbay, Michael Mulcahy, and Aoife O'Gorman

Documents and Linguistic Technology Group, Department of Computer Science and Information Systems, University of Limerick, Limerick, Ireland
{Richard.Sutcliffe, Igal.Gabbay, Michael.Mulcahy, Aoife.OGorman}@ul.ie

Abstract. We describe the system built by the Documents and Linguistic Technology (DLT) Group at University of Limerick for participation in the French-English Question Answering Task of the Cross Language Evaluation Forum (CLEF). The starting point was the system we used for the same task last year. Besides incremental improvements to the query type identification and named entity recognition components, the query analysis and translation stage was much more sophisticated than last year. This resulted in improved performance.

1 Introduction

This article outlines the participation of the Documents and Linguistic Technology (DLT) Group in the Cross Language French-English Question Answering Task of the Cross Language Evaluation Forum (CLEF). Following our experiences last year [1], our aim was to improve the system particularly in the early stages of processing, and to make further refinements to other components.

2 Architecture of the CLEF 2004 DLT System

2.1 Outline

The basic architecture of our system is standard in nature and comprises query type identification, query analysis and translation, retrieval query formulation, document retrieval, text file parsing, named entity recognition and answer entity selection.

2.2 Query Type Identification

As last year, simple keyword combinations and patterns were used to classify the query. This was accomplished by using the CLEF 03 queries and translated TREC queries from RALI [2] as a model.

C. Peters et al. (Eds.): CLEF 2004, LNCS 3491, pp. 404–410, 2005.

Table 1. Some of the Question Types used in the DLT system. The second column shows a sample question for each type. Translations based on submission to WorldLingo are listed in the third column

Question Type	Example Question	Google Translation
what_capital	130 Quelle est la capitale du Vénézuela?	What is the capital of Venezuela?
company	149 Qui fabrique Invirase?	Who manufactures Invirase?
what_country	37 Dans quel pays européen est située la ville de Galway?	In which European country is the town of Galway located?
mountain	162 Quelle est la plus haute montagne du monde?	What is the highest mountain of the world?
where	166 Où se trouve Halifax?	Where is Halifax?
how_did_die	47 Comment est mort River Phoenix?	How did River Phoenix die?
who	40 Qui a réalisé "Braveheart"?	Who directed "Braveheart"?
when	30 Quand est-ce que le prince Charles et Diana se sont mariés?	When did prince Charles and Diana get married?
unknown	36 Citez une unité de radioactivité.	Name a unit of radioactivity.

2.3 Query Analysis and Translation

This stage differed greatly from last year. We started off by tagging the Query for part-of-speech using XeLDA [3]. We then carried out shallow parsing looking for various types of phrase. Each phrase was then translated using three different methods. Two translation engines and one dictionary were used. The engines were Reverso [4] and WorldLingo [5] which were chosen because we had found them to give the best overall performance in various experiments. The dictionary used was the Grand Dictionnaire Terminologique (GDT) [6] which is a very comprehensive terminological database for Canadian French with detailed data for a large number of different domains. The three candidate translations were then combined – if a GDT translation was found then the Reverso and WorldLingo translations were ignored. The reason for this is that if a phrase is in GDT the translation for it is nearly always correct. It is an excellent resource. For example 'equipe de football' becomes 'football team' and not 'team of football', 'salle d'opera' (Canadian dialect for 'opera') becomes 'opera house' not 'room of opera' and so on. In the case where words or phrases are not in GDT, then the Reverso and WorldLingo translations were simply combined.

The types of phrase recognised were determined after a study of the constructions used in French queries together with their English counterparts. The aim was to group words together into sufficiently large sequences to be independently meaningful but to avoid the problems of structural translation, split particles etc which tend to occur in the syntax of a question, and which the engines often analyse incorrectly.

The structures used are listed here, each followed by an example from the Clef03 Fr-En queries: number (Q96: '8'), quote (Q100: '"Operation Unity"'), cap_nou_prep_det_seq (Q80: 'Corée du Sud?'), all_cap_wd (Q146: 'GIA'), cap_adj_cap_nou (Q42: 'Première Dame'), cap_adj_low_nou (Q4: 'Premier ministre'), cap_nou_cap_adj (Q83: 'Nations Unis'), cap_nou_low_adj (Q156: 'Ligue nationale'), low_nou_low_adj (Q5: 'tours jumelles'), low_nou_prep_low_nou (Q170: 'pièces d'artillerie'), low_adj_low_nou (Q56: 'autre nom'), nou_seq (Q187: 'acteur' – multiple nouns are allowed) and wd (Q40: 'né').

Table 2. Results by query type for correctly classified questions. The columns C and NC show the numbers of queries of a particular type which were classified correctly and not correctly. Those classified correctly are then broken down into Right, ineXact, Unsupported and Wrong for each of the two runs Run 1 and Run 2

Query Type	Classif.		Correct Classification							
			Run 1				Run 2			
	C	NC	R	X	U	W	R	X	U	W
animal	1	0	0	0	0	1	0	0	0	1
colour	1	0	0	0	0	1	0	0	0	1
company	3	0	1	0	0	2	1	0	0	2
def_org	9	0	2	1	0	6	2	1	0	6
def_person	10	1	3	2	0	5	3	2	0	5
distance	1	0	1	0	0	0	1	0	0	0
how_did_die	3	0	3	0	0	0	3	0	0	0
how_many3	11	2	1	0	0	10	0	0	0	11
how_old	1	0	0	0	0	1	0	0	0	1
name_part	1	0	0	0	0	1	0	0	0	1
nationality	1	0	0	0	0	1	0	0	0	1
pol_party	3	0	0	0	0	3	0	1	0	2
population	2	0	0	0	0	2	0	0	0	2
team	2	0	0	0	0	2	0	0	0	2
what_capital	1	0	0	0	0	1	0	0	0	1
what_country	4	0	1	0	0	3	0	0	0	4
what_mountain	1	0	0	0	0	1	0	0	0	1
what_river	1	0	0	0	0	1	0	0	0	1
when	17	0	8	0	0	9	7	0	0	10
when_wk_day	2	0	0	0	0	2	0	0	0	2
when_year	10	0	1	0	0	9	1	0	0	9
where	17	2	7	0	0	10	4	0	0	13
who	21	2	4	0	0	17	3	0	0	18
unknown	47	23	3	1	0	43	3	1	0	43
Totals	**170**	**30**	**35**	**4**	**0**	**131**	**28**	**5**	**0**	**137**

These constructs were chosen based on our observations that (1) Proper names usually only start with a capital letter with subsequent words uncapitalised, unlike English; (2) Adjective-Noun combinations either capitalised or not can have the status of compounds in French and hence need special treatment; (3) Certain noun-preposition-noun phrases are also of significance.

As part of the translation and analysis process, weights were assigned to each phrase in an attempt to establish which parts were more important in the event of query simplification being necessary.

2.4 Retrieval Query Formulation

The starting point for this stage was a set of possible translations for each of the phrases recognised above. For each phrase, a boolean query was created comprising the various alternatives as disjunctions. In addition, alternation was added at this stage to take account of morphological inflections (e.g 'go'<->'went', 'company'<->'companies' etc) and European English vs. American English spelling ('neighbour'<->'neighbor', 'labelled'<->'labeled' etc). The reason for this last step was the addition for this year of the Glasgow Herald collection to the existing LA

Table 3. Results by query type for incorrectly classified questions. Once again, results are broken down into Right, ineXact, Unsupported and Wrong for each of the two runs Run 1 and Run 2

Query Type	**Incorrect Classification**							
	Ru n 1				**Run 1**			
	R	**X**	**U**	**W**	**R**	**X**	**U**	**W**
animal	0	0	0	0	0	0	0	0
colour	0	0	0	0	0	0	0	0
company	0	0	0	0	0	0	0	0
def_org	0	0	0	0	0	0	0	0
def_person	0	0	0	1	0	0	0	1
distance	0	0	0	0	0	0	0	0
how_did_die	0	0	0	0	0	0	0	0
how_many3	0	0	0	2	0	0	0	2
how_old	0	0	0	0	0	0	0	0
name_part	0	0	0	0	0	0	0	0
nationality	0	0	0	0	0	0	0	0
pol_party	0	0	0	0	0	0	0	0
population	0	0	0	0	0	0	0	0
team	0	0	0	0	0	0	0	0
what_capital	0	0	0	0	0	0	0	0
what_country	0	0	0	0	0	0	0	0
what_mountain	0	0	0	0	0	0	0	0
what_river	0	0	0	0	0	0	0	0
when	0	0	0	0	0	0	0	0
when_wk_day	0	0	0	0	0	0	0	0
when_year	0	0	0	0	0	0	0	0
where	1	0	0	1	1	0	0	1
who	0	0	0	2	0	0	0	2
unknown	1	3	0	19	1	2	0	20
Totals	**2**	**3**	**0**	**25**	**2**	**2**	**0**	**26**

Times. The list of the above components was then ordered by the weight assigned during the previous stage and the ordered components were then connected with AND operators to make the complete boolean query.

2.5 Document Retrieval

During document retrieval, the boolean query was submitted to the DTSearch search engine [7] which had previously been indexed on the LA Times and Glasgow Herald collections, with each sentence in the collection being considered as a separate document for indexing purposes. This followed our observation that in most cases the search keywords and the correct answer appear in the same sentence.

In the event that no documents were found, the conjunction in the query (corresponding to one phrase recognised in the query) with the lowest weight was eliminated and the search was repeated. Some attempts were made this year to avoid the situation in which the query is inadvertently simplified to something insufficiently selective and highly frequent in the corpus (e.g. United States).

2.6 Text File Parsing

This stage is straightforward and simply involves retrieving the matching 'documents' (i.e. sentences) from the corpus and extracting the text from the markup.

2.7 Named Entity Recognition

Named Entity recognition was carried out in the standard way using a mixture of grammars and lists. The number of types was increased to 75 by studying previous CLEF and TREC question sets. These types were incorporated into the query categoriser also.

2.8 Answer Entity Selection

We used the highest-scoring method of answer selection. In this, the named-entity instance is selected which occurs in the vicinity of the maximum number of keywords taken from the translated query, across all document passages. We also experimented with Google re-ordering using a Magnini-type method [8].

3 Results

3.1 Results

We submitted two runs which differed slightly in their term translation strategy. Results are summarised by query type in Tables 2 and 3. Concerning query classification it shows for each query type the number of queries assigned to that type which were correctly categorised along with the number incorrectly categorised. The overall rate of success was 85% which is identical to the one achieved in TREC last year [9]. The number of queries classified as unknown was 70.

The performance of question answering in Run 1 can be summarised as follows. Out of the 170 queries classified correctly, 35 were answered correctly. Out of the remaining 30 queries classified incorrectly a further three were answered correctly. Overall performance was thus 38 / 200 i.e. 19%. Results for Run 2 were similar. 28 of the 170 queries were answered correctly along with two of the 30 queries giving a total of 30 / 200 i.e. 15%. In both runs 63 questions were answered NIL.

3.2 Platform

We used a Dell PC running Windows NT4 and having 256 Mb RAM. The whole system was ported this year to SICStus Prolog 3.11.1 [10] which is much faster than Quintus.

4 Conclusions

The overall performance this year was 19% compared to the 11.5% we achieved last year. We can attribute this improvement mostly to a superior translation strategy although much further work on this is required.

If we exclude query types of which there was only one example, the best performance (100%) was on how_did_die queries. However, there were only three queries of this type. On the more common types the best performance was achieved when answering 'when' and 'where' queries (47% and 41%, respectively). The performance on the relatively common types how_many and when_year was poor (9%, 10%, respectively). A better answer selection strategy may improve performance on these. It is hard to assess performance on many of the other query types due the small number of each.

Query categorisation for this year stood at 85% compared to 79.5% last year. The reduction in the number of correctly classified unknown queries from 58 last year to 47 in the current run may reflect an improvement in the coverage of categorisation. However, among the unknown queries several categories emerged which may be added in future systems. These include queries which are similar in nature to list questions but ask for a single item of a specific entity or a hypernym (e.g. Q17: 'Citez le nom d'un cétacée.' – 'Name a cetacean.'), queries about materials (e.g. Q70: 'De quoi sont composées les fibres optiques ?' – 'What are fibre-optic cables made of?'), queries of the type 'What does company X sell/produce?', and queries about diseases (treatment, way of transmission), newspaper names, wars, and musical bands. This year the test set included 'how' and 'why' queries (e.g. Q8: 'Comment va le Pape ?' – 'How is the pope?', Q87: 'Citez l'une des raisons de suicides chez les jeunes.' – 'Tell me a reason for teenage suicide.', Q107: 'En quoi consiste l'acupuncture ?' – 'How does acupuncture work?') which our system cannot answer.

A significant proportion of the queries are likely to remain unknown in increasingly difficult evaluations. The poor performance on unknown queries highlights the need to develop an alternative to our current strategy of answering such queries (i.e., finding a sequence of capitalised words). Less than a quarter of the correctly classified unknown queries could be answered by this rather simple-minded approach.

Simple heuristics may improve performance on exiting categories. For example, year numbers could often be eliminated from answers to how_many queries.

Our boolean search query formulation strategy was a big improvement on last year but was not without its problems. In particular the combination for each phrase of translation alternatives, inflection alternatives and spelling alternatives could result on occasion in highly complex queries which were a problem for our relatively lightly engineered search engine.

References

1. Sutcliffe, R.F.E., Gabbay, I., O'Gorman, A.: Cross-Language French-English Question Answering using the DLT System at CLEF 2003. In: Proceedings of the Cross Language Evaluation Forum, CLEF 2003, , August 21-22, 2003, Trondheim, Norway (2003) 373-378
2. RALI: http://www-rali.iro.umontreal.ca/LUB/qabilingue.en.html (Accessed 2004)
3. XeLDA: http://www.temis-group.com/temis/XeLDA.htm (Accessed 2004)
4. Reverso: http://grammaire.reverso.net/textonly/default.asp (Accessed 2003)
5. WorldLingo: http://www.worldlingo.com/products_services/worldlingo_translator.html (Acc -essed 2004)
6. GDT: http://w3.granddictionnaire.com/btml/fra/r_motclef/index1024_1.asp (Accessed 2004)
7. DTSearch: www.dtsearch.com (Accessed 2000)
8. Magnini, B., Negri, M., Prevete, R., Tanev H.: Is it the Right Answer? Exploiting Web Redundancy for Answer Validation. In: Proceedings of the 40th Annual Meeting of the Association for Computational Linguistics, July 6-12, 2002, Philadelphia, PA (2002) 425-432
9. Sutcliffe, R.F.E., Gabbay, I., Mulcahy, M., White, K.: Question Answering using the DLT System at TREC 2003. In: Voorhees, E.M., Buckland, L.P. (eds.) Proceedings of the Twelfth Text REtrieval Conference (TREC 2003), Gaithersburg, Maryland, November 18-21, 2003. NIST Special Publication 500-255. Department of Commerce, National Institute of Standards and Technology, Gaithersburg, MD (2004) 686-692
10. SICStus: http://www.sics.se/isl/sicstuswww/site/index.html (Accessed 2004)

Experiments on Robust NL Question Interpretation and Multi-layered Document Annotation for a Cross–Language Question/Answering System*

Günter Neumann and Bogdan Sacaleanu

LT–Lab, DFKI, Saarbrücken, Germany
{neumann, bogdan}@dfki.de
http://www.dfki.de/~neumann|bogdan

Abstract. This report describes the work done by the QA group of the Language Technology Lab at DFKI, for the 2004 edition of the Cross-Language Evaluation Forum (CLEF). Based on the experience we obtained through our participation at QA@Clef-2003 with our initial cross-lingual QA prototype system BiQue (cf. [1]), the focus of the system extension for this year's task was a) on robust NL question interpretation using advanced linguistic-based components, b) flexible interface strategies to IR-search engines, and c) on strategies for off-line annotation of the data collection, which support query-specific indexing and answer selection.

The overall architecture of the extended system, as well as the results obtained in the CLEF–2004 Monolingual German and Bilingual German/English QA tracks will be presented and discussed throughout the paper.

1 Introduction

The basic functionality of an open–domain cross–language question/answering (QA) system is simple: given a Natural Language query in one language (say German) find answers for that query in textual documents written in another language (say English). In contrast to a standard cross-language IR system, the NL queries are usually well-formed NL–query clauses (instead of a set of keywords), and the identified answers should be the *exact* answer string (instead of complete documents containing the answer). Thus, for a question like "Welches Pseudonym nahm Norma Jean Baker an?" (*Which pseudonym did Norma Jean Baker use?*) the answer should be "Marilyn Monroe" rather than an English document containing this name. In contrast to QA@Clef-2003, this year the

* The work presented in this paper has been funded by the BMBF project Quetal, FKZ 01 IW C02. Many thanks to Jumamurat Bayjanov and Olga Goldmann for their implementation support.

C. Peters et al. (Eds.): CLEF 2004, LNCS 3491, pp. 411–422, 2005.

task was made further difficult by demanding that only *one* exact answer should be returned instead of a ranked list of (say three) answer candidates.

Last year our group participated for the very first time at Clef. We learned a lot and found several sources of potential improvements for our initial system. Especially two aspects have drawn our attention.

Firstly, the use of a statistical based chunk-parser turned out to be a major bottleneck for the complete NL question processor. In our Clef–2003 system, we implemented a two-stage question process: first we performed a shallow chunk analysis using a statistical based chunker (trained for German as well as English) on which output we applied a manually written specialized question grammar. The rules of this grammar represented direct relationships between relevant chunks and their interpretation wrt. question and expected answer type. However it turned out that the error rate of the first stage actually caused to much noisy input for the second stage, so that in many cases we were not able to determine the expected answer type correctly. This was further effected by the low coverage of the manually specified question grammars, so that the whole question processor actually performed quite poor. However, it is known that a high number of errors in question answering can be attributed to errors in question analysis (cf. [2]). Furthermore, since the Clef-2004 QA task required that only one exact answer should be returned, we were convinced that it would be at least a good strategy to prefer a more deeper linguistic–based question analysis strategy.

Secondly, in the Clef-2003 system we applied a very simple strategy for determining relevant paragraphs which are then used as starting points for determining possible answer candidates, simply by directly using the SGML paragraph tags from the original corpus. Furthermore, the IR-query language of the full–text IR–engine MG (cf. [3]) actually turned out to be too inflexible so that we could not take advantage of a preprocessing of the corpus wrt. different dimensions. Hence, we could only perform a very basic word/stem–level oriented paragraph indexing.

Based on these experiments, we decided to extent the Clef–2003 system to the following directions:

- development of a robust NL question interpretation using sophisticated deeper linguistic-based strategies,
- development of adaptive interface strategies to IR-search engines, and
- development of strategies for off-line annotation of the data collection, which support query-specific indexing and answer selection.

We now start with an overview of the whole Clef–2004 system, and highlight some technical aspects. Finally, we present and discuss the results we have obtained for the task.

2 System Overview

Figure 1 displays the architecture of our Clef–2004 QA–system. Basically, the same system is used for the monolingual as well as the bilingual QA task with only very few additional task–specific parameterizations. The core architecture consists of five major components:

1. the linguistic core engine
2. the multi-dimensional index of the document collection
3. the robust NL query processor
4. the information search component
5. the answer processor

The linguistic core engine consists of two major sub-components (see section 3 for details): a) LingPipe, which performs NE and sentence boundary recognition, as well as NE co-reference resolution, and b) SMES, a robust wide-coverage unification–based parser for German. This parser is used for both, German NL question and document analysis.

For each corpus of the individual task (German and English), a multi–dimensional index structure is computed off–line. This is done by first preprocessing the whole corpus with the LingPipe component of the linguistic core engine, which basically adds named entities, sentence boundary, NE–co-references to each document in form of XML–tags. Additionally, abbreviations are determined by a specialized component into the same XML–format. For each specific dimension

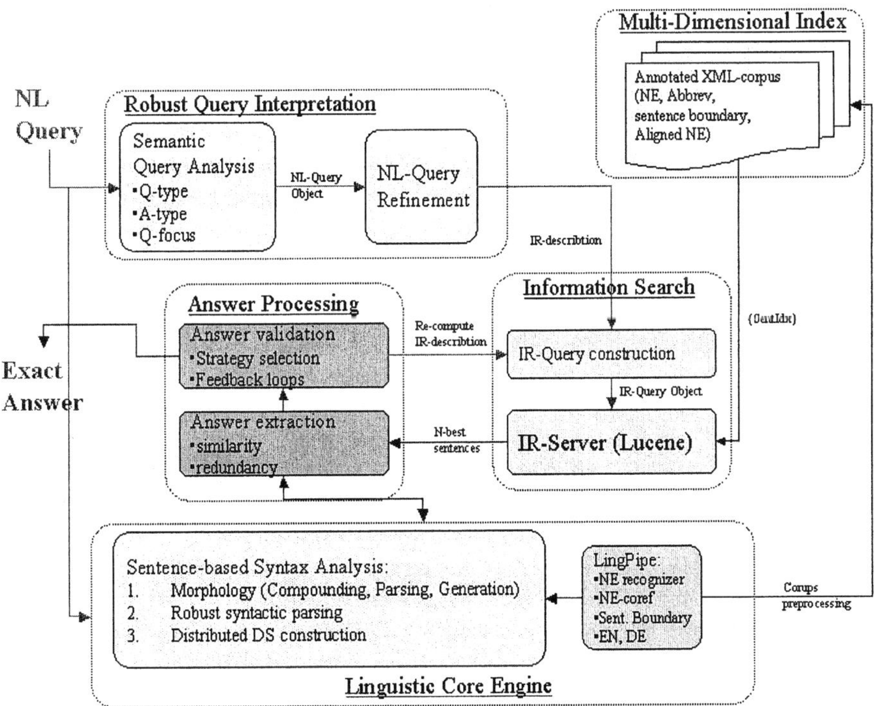

Fig. 1. The architecture of DFKI's Clef–2004 QA-system

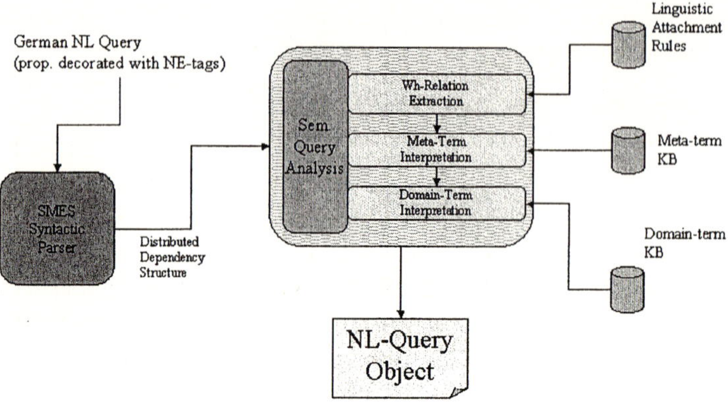

Fig. 2. The architecture of the query analysis component

a separate index is computed which can be accessed via the IR server (we are using the Jakarta Lucene full–text search engine, see also sec. 4.1).[1]

The major control flow for both QA tasks can now briefly be described as follows:

Robust NL Question Analysis. The main purpose of the NL question analysis in the context of a QA-system is to determine the expected answer type, the set of relevant keywords, and the set of recognized NE–instances in order to guide information search and answer processing. Consider, for example, the NL–query result presented in figure 4, where the value of tag A-TYPE represents the expected answer type, S-CTR's value represents the answer control strategy, and the value of SCOPE represents additional constraints for the search space (for more details, see sec. 4.2).

NL Question Refinement. Refinement of the result of the NL–query covers the translation of the NL–query and its expansion. The cross-language aspect of the system has been approached by using machine translation engines for query translation (along the line of the approach described in [1]). We have selected a number of 8 translation services (7 online + 1 offline) in order to account for a better lexical coverage for the translated queries. The results of translation have been linguistically processed, annotated with named entities and merged into a translation object consisting of named entity instances and keywords (open class words which were not parts of named entities). The question analysis has yielded a similar structure for the original question plus additional information about expected answer type and scope. By using a dictionary-based alignment technique this additional information has been transferred to the translation object. The same happened with the named entities of types PERSON, DATE (year instances) and NUMBER, which should remain unchanged through translation.

[1] cf. http://jakarta.apache.org/lucene/docs/index.html

As for the remaining types of named entities (LOCATION, ORGANIZATION and DATE without year instances), which might have different lexical representations in source and target language, the following heuristic applied: if the original string and its translation were different (e.g., "Europäische Gemeinschaft" vs. "European Union") they were regarded as unreliable, added as keywords and discarded from named entities. The distinction made between named entities and keywords along the question analysis process will be used later on in constructing the IR-query and defining search strategies.

In contrast to our previous system, we wanted to implement and test question expansion methods based on *natural language generation* (NLG), instead of using WordNet (cf. [1]). The main reason for doing this is the fact, that the NL–query analysis actually normalizes all words to their corresponding lemmas. On the other side, the morphological component of our German parsing system SMES (cf. section 3.2) is *reversible*, i.e., can also be used for the generation of word forms. Of course, one could directly use the word forms of the input query (accessible via indices). However, generating all plausible word forms directly from the input query actually would perform a controlled morpho-syntactic query expansion. Thus, in the case of the monolingual German task, for all relevant lemmas of the NL–query analysis (these are basically belonging to the open-class words), we generate all word forms which are *consistent* with the feature description of the syntax analysis of the parsing result. This means that the parsing output directly controls the generation input. For example, for the lemma *geben* (`to give`) and the feature `verb` we are generating the word forms *gaben, gab, gegeben, gibt.*[2]

Information Search. In order to perform the information search, the (possibly refined) NL–query has to be mapped to a concrete IR-query. Most today's information search engines come with powerful IR-query interfaces, which support a flexible user-driven filtering of the index space. In order to take advantage of this rich parameterization and to support the use of multiple IR-engines in the future, we actually perform the mapping from a NL-query to a IR-query in two steps (cf. also figure 3):

1. construction of a IR-query schema
2. construction of a IR-query

An IR-query schema is actually an under-specified representation of an IR-query. It is constructed directly from the NL–query result. Although it contains all relevant information from the NL–query, this information is under-specified, because it still lacks the use of IR-specific syntax (e.g., the '+'–prefix for necessary terms) and a specification of logical connectives. The main task of the IR–query construction component is to create a concrete IR–query from this

[2] Note that our method also allows to specify additional constraints for the generation process, e.g., that only word forms of a certain tempus should (not) be generated. In this way, a more sensitive morpho-syntactic-based control of query expansion is possible.

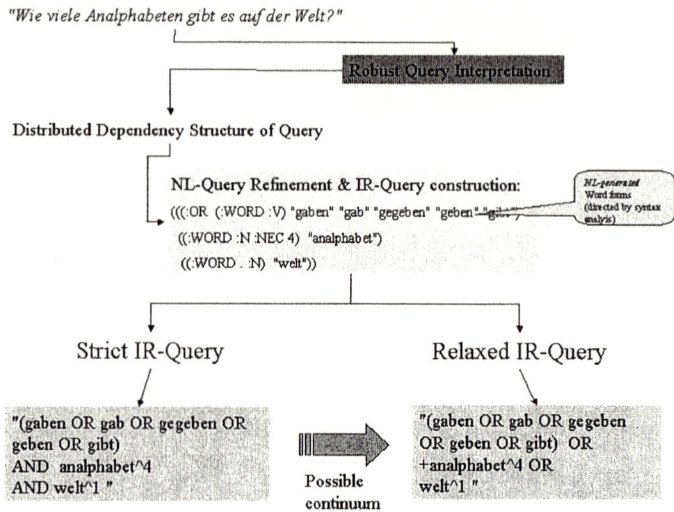

Fig. 3. Example of query refinement and IR-Query construction

schematic description, which directly can be feed into a IR–engine (in our current QA system, we are using the Jakarta Lucene text search engine. However, it would also be possible to create, say a Google-specific expression from it using a different script). Which mapping to perform is expressed in form of search strategies which are activated on basis of concrete values of the question type of NL–query. Furthermore, based on input from the answer validation component (through feedback loops), the component might use different sorts of logical connectives resulting in different IR–queries, e.g., in figure 3 two alternatives are displayed: a strict IR–query (using only logical AND), and a relaxed IR–query (using only OR).

Performing the IR–query construction process in the way just described allows us to selectively make use of different indexing structures.

Answer Processing. The result of the information search is a set of N hits (currently N=10), where each hit is a pointer to a single sentence of an annotated document. Each sentence is tagged with all NE–instances recognized by LingPipe during the document preprocessing phase. Note that, because we do indexing on a sentence level (and not on a paragraph level as done in our Clef–2003 system), we actually can take advantage of cross–document sentence–level answer redundancies.

Next, all NE–instances which are type compatible with the expected answer type of the question are selected as possible answer candidate. All identified exact answer candidates are stored in a global list together with its frequency counts (determined on basis of the selected N–sentences). During that step a similarity function is applied on the NE–instances in order to identify variants of the same name. Note that this means that the quality of the answer extraction step currently depends directly on the quality of the used NE–recognition system.

By default, we do the information search with a strict IR–query. If in this case, no sentence can be retrieved or no answer can be extracted, we perform a new information search using a relaxed IR–query and re-call the answer processing component.

3 Linguistic Core Engine

Our linguistic core engines consists of two major components which we describe briefly in the next two subsections.

3.1 LingPipe

LingPipe, which is a software package from Alias–i, consists of several language processing modules: a statistical named entity recognizer, a heuristic sentence splitter, and a heuristic within-document co-reference resolution system.[3]

LingPipe comes with a English language model. The types of NE covered by LingPipe are locations, persons and organizations. We have re–trained LingPipe so as to cover more named entities types: DATE for English, and both DATE and NUMBER for German. We extended the co-reference resolution algorithm to count for German pronouns as well. A large Gazetteer of named entity instances has been used for both languages and for English a PERSON Gazetteer with gender attributes has been integrated for a better co-reference resolution.

3.2 SMES

SMES is a robust wide-coverage unification-based system for the parsing of German texts (cf. [4, 5]).[4] It produces a partial analysis of natural language texts by combining shallow processing techniques (i.e., finite state regular expression recognizers) with generic linguistic resources (e.g., subcategorisation, morphology, online compound analysis). In contrast to the common approach of deep grammatical processing, where the goal is to find all possible readings of a syntactic expression, we provide a complete but underspecified representation, by only computing a general coarse-grained syntactic structure which can be thought of as domain independent. This rough syntactic analysis can be then made more precise by taking into account domain-specific knowledge. Our parser recognizes basic syntactic units and grammatical relations (e.g., subject/object) robustly by using relatively underspecified feature structures, by postponing attachment decisions and by introducing a small number of heuristics.

Originally, SMES was developed as an Information Extraction core system, however we now extended SMES substantially for its use as a core-engine in

[3] LingPipe is available at http://www.alias-i.com/lingpipe/

[4] SMES is available at http://www.dfki.de/~neumann/pd-smes/pd-smes.html.

textual question answering systems. Major extensions of SMES concern the development of the robust interpretation of NL questions (see sec. 4) and the development of a distributed representation for the dependency structures, which we will describe now in more detail.

Distributed representation In the original SMES system, the analysis of a sentence is represented in form of a possibly recursive dependency tree where each node and edge is decorated with rich feature information. During the development of our Clef–2004 system it turned out that the nested parse trees (which can be very huge for very long sentences) are unsuited as a generic interface, because they do not support a flexible and efficient access to relevant linguistic information. Furthermore, a nested representation cannot easily be enriched with additional linguistic structure, e.g., additional grammatical functions or deeper attachment, scopus etc. The same is true for a selective, local integration of domain–specific information (e.g., to perform a sort of concept–spotting on basis of domain-independent syntactic normalization of relevant text fragments).

For that reason, we re–represent dependency trees in form of a distributed representation, adapting the approach of [6]. A distributed representation provides the robustness of a bag–of–object approach with the ability to use higher level relational information where this can provide a more accurate analysis. Thus distributed representations are more flexible wrt. the integration of shallow and deep linguistic analysis, and the integrating domain knowledge. In our distributed representation, we explicitly separate the representation of linguistic entities like words/chunks/named entities (the "bag–of–objects" or *BaseObjects*) from their structural relationship like head/modifier/topology/grammatical functions (the "bag–of–links" or *LinkObjects*). Both layers are connected through indices which allow a simple bidirectional traversal between the different object types. Linguistic and application specific extension can then be described as operations (typing, re-organization of attachment) applied on LinkObjects. Actually, this is how the strategies of the semantic NL–query interpretation are implemented for determining the expected answer type and question scope (cf. sec. 4.2). It is also basis for the specification of a flexible similarity function applied on two distributed dependency trees.

4 Some More Details

4.1 Multi-layered Document Annotation

The current annotation performed on the document collection consists in sentence boundary identification, named entities annotation and co-reference resolution of named entities and personal pronouns. A heuristic syntax–based algorithm for identifying abbreviations and their possible extensions enriches the annotation with an NE–similar format, e.g., <ENAMEX TYPE="PERSON">BILL CLINTON</ENAMEX> and <ENAMEX TYPE="ORGANIZATION" ABBREV="UNO"> UNITED NATIONS ORGANISATION</ENAMEX>.

```
<IOOBJ msg='quest' s-ctr='C-DESCRIPTION' q-weight='1.0'>
 <A-TYPE>NUMBER</A-TYPE>
 <SCOPE>analphabet</SCOPE>
 <BRELS>
  <BREL rel='GOV' level='0'>
   <ARG1 pos='V'>geb</ARG1>
   <ARG2 pos='N'>analphabet</ARG2>
  </BREL>
  <BREL rel='GOV' level='0'>
   <ARG1 pos='V'>geb</ARG1>
   <ARG2 pos='N'>es</ARG2>
  </BREL>
  <BREL rel='GOV' level='0'>
   <ARG1 pos='V'>geb</ARG1>
   <ARG2 pos='P'>auf</ARG2>
  </BREL>
  <BREL rel='GOV' level='1'>
   <ARG1 pos='P'>auf</ARG1>
   <ARG2 pos='N'>welt</ARG2>
  </BREL>
  <BREL rel='GOV' level='0'>
   <ARG1 pos='N'>analphabet</ARG1>
   <ARG2 pos='WP'>wieviel</ARG2>
  </BREL>
 </BRELS>
 <PRELS>
  <PREL rel='GOV' level='1'>
   <ARG1 pos='N'>welt</ARG1>
   <ARG2 pos='QUANT'>d-det</ARG2>
  </PREL>
 </PRELS>
 <KWS>
  <KW type='UNIQUE'>
   <TK pos='V'>geb</TK>
  </KW>
  <KW type='UNIQUE'>
   <TK pos='N'>analphabet</TK>
  </KW>
  <KW type='UNIQUE'>
   <TK pos='N'>welt</TK>
  </KW>
 </KWS>
 <NEL/>
 <NETS/>
</IOOBJ>
```

Fig. 4. The result of the robust NL question interpretation for the example *Wie viele Analphabeten gibt es auf der Welt?* (How many illiterates are there on the world?)

Throughout the document processing part of the system we have insisted on a systematic analysis of named entities and a reduction of the amount of information necessary to answer a question. Based on experiments and results with the question set of the previous competition, we have confined the information amount to sentence level and added named entity and abbreviation types, along words, as basic units of information in the indexing process. By doing this, we could query the IR component not only by keywords extracted from the questions, but also by NE types corresponding to their expected answer types. An example would make this clear: for the question *Where did John Lennon die?* beside creating an IR–query containing the keywords: {`+''John Lennon''`, `+die`}, we could supply also the expected answer type `LOCATION` querying an additional field neTypes: {`+text:''John Lennon''`, `+text:die +neTypes:LOCATION`}. This will not only narrow the amount of data being analyzed for answer extraction, but will also guarantee existence of an answer candidate.

4.2 Robust NL Question Analysis

In context of a QA system or information search in general, we interpret the result of a NL question analysis as *declarative description of search strategy and control information.* Consider, for example, the NL question result presented in figure 3, where the value of tag A-TYPE represents the expected answer type, S-CTR the answer control strategy, and SCOPE additional constraints for the search space. Parts of the information can already be determined on simple local lexico-syntactic criteria (e.g., for the Wh-phrase *where* we known that the expected answer type is `location`), however in most cases we have to consider larger syntactic units in combination with information extracted from external knowledge sources. For example for a definition question like *What is a battery?*, we have to combine syntactic and type information from the verb and the relevant NP (e.g., consider definite/indefinite NPs together with certain auxiliary verb forms) in order to distinguish it from a description question like *What is the name of the German Chancellor?*

In our system, we are doing this by following a two-step parsing schema, where in a first step a full syntactic analysis is performed (cf. sec. 3.2), and in a second step a question–specific semantic analysis. During the second step, the values for the question tags A-TYPE, SCOPE and S-CTR are determined on the basis of syntactic constraints applied on relevant NP and VP phrases, and by taking into account information from two small knowledge bases, see also figure 2. They basically perform a mapping from linguistic entities to values of the questions tags, e.g., trigger phrases like *name_of*, *type_of*, *abbreviation_of* or lexical elements to expected answer types, like *town*, *person*, *president*. For German, we perform a sort of fuzzy match to the knowledge bases taking into account on–line compound analysis and string–similarity tests. For example, assuming the lexical mapping *Stadt*$\Longrightarrow$*LOCATION* for the lexeme `town`, then automatically we will also map the nominal compounds *Hauptstadt* (`capital`), *Großstadt* (`large city`) to the A-TYPE *LOCATION*.

5 Results and Discussion

We have submitted two runs. One for the monolingual German task, and one for the bilingual German/English task. The results are as follows:

Track	#Answ	#T	#F	#Inexact	#Unsup.	Overall Acc	Fact. Acc.	Def. Acc.	NIL prec.
DE-DE	197	50	143	1	3	25.3%	28.25%	0	13.6%
DE-EN	200	47	151	0	2	23.5%	23.8%	20%	10.79%

Compared to our results obtained at QA@Clef2003 this is a good improvement because the tasks were more difficult and because we could use nearly the same system for both, the bilingual track as well as the monolingual track. We will now discuss the results for the two individual tasks, comparing them where possible.

In both cases, we only considered answers which directly where recognized as NE instances, i.e., for all questions which would refer to more general noun phrases or to NE types and instances LingPipe did not recognize, we did not identify any answer candidates. Note that although in both tasks we were able to properly analyze all definition questions as such, in our current system we only determine possible answer candidates for abbreviation based questions (by the way: not such questions were found in the German test set, which explains, why we did not recognize any definition question). The fact, that we did not answer definition question (modulo abbreviation) correlates with our restrictions to only consider NE instances as answer candidates.

As previously mentioned, both the monolingual and bilingual tasks have shared the same QA-framework, which was presented above. Nevertheless, there were task specific system configurations, resulting in different retrieval and answer extraction methods, which will shortly be mentioned in the following lines.

Monolingual Task. For the German monolingual task we were able to have the system recognize named entity instances of type *NUMBER*, as result of training LingPipe on a German corpus with a larger coverage of named entity types than its English counterpart. Even though the indexing method was similar for both tasks, the monolingual task did not make any use of the named entity type field (neType) during information search.

Bilingual Task. No questions with a *MEASURE* expected answer type were considered, because the bilingual settings were not able to identify named entity instances of type *NUMBER*. The system used a similarity function, which compared to the monolingual task, resembles a co–reference algorithm by identifying answers mentioning the same NE instance in the answer candidate set (e.g., "Bill Clinton" and "Clinton" will count as two references to the same person).

References

1. Neumann, G., Sacaleanu, B.: A cross-language question/answering-system for german and english. In: proceedings of the CLEF 2003 working notes of the QA@CLEF, Trondheim, August. (2003).

2. Moldovan, D., Pasca, M., Harabagiu, S., Surdeanu, M.: Performance issues and error analysis in an open-domain question answering system. In: Proceedings of the ACL-2002, Philadelphia (2002) 33–40.
3. Witten, I.H., Moffat, A., Bell, T.C.: Managing Gigabytes: Compressing and Indexing Documents and Images. Morgan Kaufmann Publishers, San Francisco, CA (1999).
4. Neumann, G., Backofen, R., Baur, J., Becker, M., Braun, C.: An information extraction core system for real world german text processing. In: ANLP 97, Washington, USA (1997) 208–215.
5. Neumann, G., Piskorksi, J.: A shallow text processing core engine. Journal of Computational Intelligence **18** (2002) 451–476.
6. Milward, D.: Distributed representation for robust interpretation of dialogue utterances. In: Proceedings of the ACL-2000, Hong Kong (2000) 133–141.

Making Stone Soup: Evaluating a Recall-Oriented Multi-stream Question Answering System for Dutch

David Ahn, Valentin Jijkoun, Karin Müller,
Maarten de Rijke, Stefan Schlobach*, and Gilad Mishne

Informatics Institute, University of Amsterdam,
Kruislaan 403, 1098 SJ Amsterdam, The Netherlands
{ahn, jijkoun, kmueller, mdr, schlobac, gilad}@science.uva.nl

Abstract. We describe the participation of the University of Amsterdam in the Question Answering track at CLEF 2004. We took part in the monolingual Dutch task and, for the first time, also in the bilingual English to Dutch task. This year's system is a further elaboration and refinement of the multi-stream architecture we introduced last year, extended with improved candidate answer re-ranking and filtering, and with additional answer finding strategies. We report the evaluation results for the whole system and its various components. The results indicate the recall-oriented approach to QA is an effective one.

1 Introduction

To address the question answering (QA) task, one has to address a challenging *recall* problem. As with many language processing tasks, we face a vocabulary gap—the phenomenon that the question and its answer(s) may be phrased in different words. For QA, the vocabulary gap can be especially challenging as systems have to return highly relevant and focused text snippets as output, given very short questions as input. To address the vocabulary gap problem, we advocate a *multi-stream* architecture which offers multiple ways of identifying candidate answers. Each stream serves as an essential ingredient to the whole system, and in this way it is reminiscent of *stone soup* (`http://en.wikipedia.org/wiki/Stone_soup`). This kind of approach needs an elaborate filtering and ranking mechanism to weed out incorrect candidate answers. In 2003, we completed a first version of this architecture, of which we made good use for the QA tracks both at CLEF [10] and at TREC [11]. For the 2004 edition of the QA@CLEF task, we fine-tuned and extended the architecture.

At CLEF 2004, we took part in the monolingual Dutch QA task and the bilingual English-to-Dutch QA task. For the monolingual task, the questions—factoid and definition questions—were given in Dutch and for the bilingual task, the questions were given in English. For both tasks, the answers had to be identified in the Dutch CLEF collection. Our main aim with our monolingual work was to extend and improve our QA system following an error analysis after the 2003 edition of the task. The bilingual English-to-Dutch task was new for us. We translated the questions into Dutch and

* Currently at the Division of Mathematics and Computer Science, Free University Amsterdam.

C. Peters et al. (Eds.): CLEF 2004, LNCS 3491, pp. 423–434, 2005.

we then proceeded as in the monolingual task. Our main aim here was to evaluate the applicability of our system in a cross-language setting and to see whether correct results obtained by the bilingual run are a subset of the monolingual one—or whether something can be gained by combining them.

The paper is organized as follows. In Section 2, we describe the architecture of our QA system. Section 3 describes our official runs. In Section 4, we discuss the results obtained and give an analysis of the performance of different components of the system. We summarize and conclude in Section 5.

2 System Description

Many QA systems share the following pipeline architecture. A question is first associated with a *question type* such as DATE-OF-BIRTH or CURRENCY, chosen from a predefined set. A query is then formulated on the basis of the question, and an information retrieval engine is used to identify a list of documents that are likely to contain the answer. Those documents are sent to an *answer extraction* module, which identifies candidate answers, ranks them, and selects the final answer. On top of this basic architecture, numerous add-ons have been devised, ranging from logic-based methods [12] to ones that rely heavily on the redundancy of information available on the World Wide Web [5].

In essence, our system implements multiple copies of the standard architecture, each of which is a complete standalone QA system. The general overview of the system is given in Figure 1. Each copy shares (at least) two modules: the question classification and the answer identification module. The question classifier is based on manually developed patterns that take different types of information into account: the question word, certain classes of verbs, etc. This year, we improved our question classifier by incorporating Dutch WordNet to deal with questions such as *Which X… ?*, where the semantic type of *X* is now used for classification.

Each of the streams produces a ranked list of candidate answers, but not necessarily for all types of questions. The overall system's answer is then selected from the combined pool of candidates through a combination of merging and filtering techniques. We add to the answer selection procedure a type checking module which checks whether the answer is of the correct type given the expected answer type identified during question analysis. For a reasonably detailed discussion of our QA system architecture, we refer to [10, 11].

This year's system contains 8 streams organized in four groups, depending on the main data source from which they try to answer questions. The streams either consult the Dutch CLEF corpus, the English CLEF corpus, or the Web. We added one new stream to our system which consults information sources like Wikipedia. We now provide a brief description of these four groups.

2.1 Streams That Consult the Dutch CLEF Corpus

Four streams generate candidate answers from the Dutch CLEF corpus in parallel: *Lookup*, *Pattern Match*, *Ngrams*, and *Tequesta*.

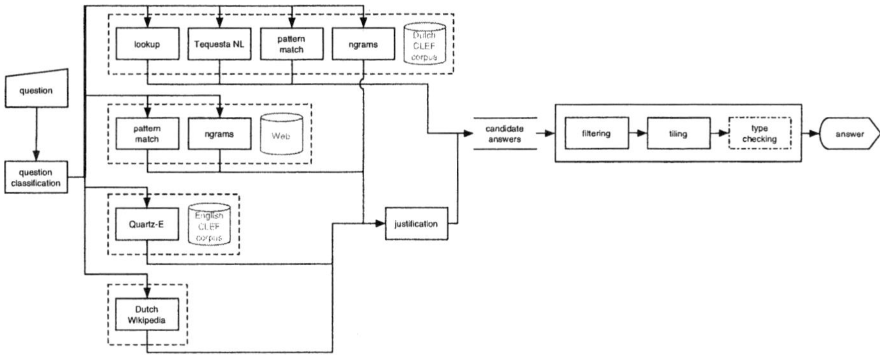

Fig. 1. Quartz-N: the University of Amsterdam's Dutch Question Answering System

The *Table Lookup* stream uses specialized knowledge bases constructed by preprocessing the collection, exploiting the fact that certain types of information (such as country capitals, abbreviations, and names of political leaders) tend to occur in a small number of more or less fixed patterns. When a question type indicates that the question might potentially have an answer in these tables, a lookup is performed in the appropriate knowledge base and answers which are found there are assigned high confidence. For a detailed overview of this stream, see [9]. In addition to the knowledge bases used in CLEF 2003, we built new ones (such as AWARDS and MEASUREMENTS, storing facts about winners of various prizes and information about dimensions of objects, respectively). Furthermore, we enriched our previous knowledge bases, which were extracted using surface patterns, with information extracted with syntactic patterns from the Dutch CLEF collection parsed by the Alpino parser, a wide coverage dependency parser for Dutch [2]. Earlier experiments on the AQUAINT corpus had suggested that offline extraction using syntactic extraction patterns can substantially improve recall [8].

The *Dutch Tequesta* stream is a linguistically informed QA system for Dutch that implements the traditional architecture outlined above. Among others, it uses a Part-of-Speech tagger (a TnT-based tagger [3] trained on the *Corpus Gesproken Nederlands* [15]), our own named entity tagger for Dutch [6], as well as proximity-based candidate answer selection [13].

In the *Pattern Match* stream, zero or more regular expressions are generated for a question according to its type and structure. These patterns match strings which have a high probability of containing the answer with high probability and are used to extract such strings from the entire document collection.

The *Ngram* stream, similar in spirit to [4], constructs a weighted list of queries for each question using a shallow reformulation process, similar to the *Pattern Match* stream. These queries are fed to a retrieval engine (we used our own FlexIR[14], with the `Lnu.ltc` weighting scheme), and the top retrieved documents are used for harvesting word ngrams. The ngrams are ranked according to the weight of the query that generated them, their frequency, NE type, proximity to the query keywords and other parameters; the top-ranking ngrams are taken as candidate answers. The output of this stream is piped to the *Justification* module (see below).

As mentioned earlier, we aim at higher recall at the earlier stages, relying on various filtering mechanisms to "clean" the results later, and achieve high precision as well. Therefore, for both the *Ngram* and the *Pattern Match* streams, we extended the generated regular expressions and queries, compared to our system at CLEF 2003—sometimes creating ungrammatical ones under the assumption that possibly incorrectly extracted candidate answers would be filtered out later.

2.2 Streams That Consult the English CLEF Corpus

One of the streams used by Quartz-N is the English language version of our QA system, which consults the English CLEF corpus instead of the Dutch version (but which is otherwise similar to the Dutch version). The answers found by Quartz-E are also piped to the *Justification* module.

2.3 Streams That Consult the Web

Quartz-N also has two streams that attempt to locate answers on the web: *Ngram* and *Pattern Match*. We retrieve documents using Google: ngrams are harvested from the Google snippets, while pattern matching is done against the *full* documents retrieved. In all other respects, those two streams work the same way as the corresponding streams that consult the Dutch CLEF corpus.

2.4 Streams That Use Other Resources

A new stream this year was the Wikipedia stream. Like the streams that consult the Web or the English document collection, this stream also uses an external corpus—the Dutch Wikipedia (`http://nl.wikipedia.org`), the Dutch version of an open-content encyclopedia. Since this corpus is much "cleaner" than newspaper text, the stream operates in a different manner. First, the *focus* of the question is identified—this is usually the main named entity in the question—and looked up in the encyclopedia. Then, the focus's encyclopedia entry is looked up; since Wikipedia is standardized to a large extent, the entry has a template-like form. Thus, using knowledge about the templates employed in Wikipedia, information such as DATE-OF-DEATH and FIRST-NAME can easily be extracted.

2.5 Answer Selection Procedures

While each of the above streams is a "small" QA system in itself, many components are shared between the streams, including an Answer Justification module, a Type Checking module, and a Filtering and Tiling module, all of which we will now describe.

Answer justification. As some of our streams obtain candidate answers *outside* the Dutch CLEF corpus, and as answers need to be supported, or *justified*, by a document in the Dutch CLEF corpus, we need to find justification for candidate answers found externally. To this end, we construct a query with keywords from a given question and candidate answer, and take the top-ranking document for this query to be the justification. We use an Okapi-based retrieval model as this tends to do well on early high precision in our experience. Additionally, we use some retrieval heuristics, such as marking the answer words as boolean terms in the query (requiring them to appear in retrieved documents).

Type Checking. To compensate for named entity errors made during answer extraction, our type checking module (see [16] for details) uses WordNet and several geographical knowledge bases to remove candidates of incorrect type for location questions. Since the resources used by the type checker are English, some adaptation for the Dutch language was needed. The question target of a Dutch question is extracted and automatically translated into English. Candidate answers are also translated, and then the method described in [16] is applied to check whether the candidates match the expected answer type.

Filtering and Tiling. A detailed error analysis carried out after the 2003 edition of QA@CLEF revealed that the two most important sources of errors were answer selection and named entity recognition [10]. For this year's task, we used a new final answer selection module (similar to that described in [7]) with heuristic candidate answer filtering and merging and with stream voting, both to improve answer selection and to filter out NE errors.

3 Runs

We submitted two runs for the monolingual Dutch QA task—`uams041nlnl` and `uams-042nlnl`—, and one run for the bilingual English to Dutch task—`uams041ennl`. All runs return exact answers, and combine answers from all streams. The `uams042nlnl` run is identical to `uams041nlnl`, except that it executes additional filtering and sanity checks on the candidate answers before final answer selection. These checks included zero-count filters (assuming that answers which do not appear as a phrase on the web are incorrect and that questions for which the focus does not appear in the local collection have no answer), and type-checking for location questions [16] (see Section 2.5). Our bilingual run included a simple translation of the questions from English to Dutch using a publicly-available interface of Systran (`http://www.systranet.com`), and then using Quartz-N for the translated questions.

4 Results and Further Analysis

Table 1 shows the evaluation results of our CLEF 2004 submissions. In addition to the number of right, wrong, inexact, and unsupported answers for all 200 questions, we

Table 1. Official results of our three submitted runs; the total number of test questions was 200. "Overall accuracy" is the percentage of questions answered correctly, "Accuracy over F (D)" is the percentage of factoid (definition) questions answered correctly, and "NIL accuracy" concerns the performance on questions with no known answer in the corpus

Run	*Right*	*Wrong*	*Inexact*	*Unsupp.*	*Overall accuracy*	*Accuracy over F*	*Accuracy over D*	*NIL accuracy precision*	*recall*
uams041nlnl	88	98	10	4	44.00%	42.37%	56.52%	0.00	0.00
uams042nlnl	91	97	10	2	45.50%	45.20%	47.83%	0.56	0.25
uams041ennl	70	122	7	1	35.00%	31.07%	65.22%	0.00	0.00

also report accuracy figures (the percent of correct answers) for factoid and definition questions separately.

The run uams042nlnl scored slightly better than uams041nlnl. Interestingly, the gain is only in the factoids: uams042nlnl scored worse than uams041nlnl on definitions. Had we combined the answers to factoid questions produced by uams042nlnl with the answers to definition questions produced by uams041nlnl, we would have obtained on overall accuracy of 46.5%. This suggests that factoids benefit from additional checks and filters (which work well on short candidate answers), while definition questions benefit from a more lenient approach.

Additionally, our filters prove useful for detecting questions with no answers: 5 out of the 9 NIL answers returned (as part of the run uams042nlnl) were correctly identified using the filters, while none were identified without them.

When we compare the results of our Dutch QA system with the results of our participation in the QA track at TREC 2004 [1], we find that our Dutch QA system performs much better than our English QA system. It seems that the type of questions that are asked in the CLEF task are much easier for our Dutch QA system than the ones asked in the TREC task. One difference is that the questions at QA@CLEF are much shorter and additionally are back-generated from the CLEF corpus. In contrast, for the QA track at TREC the test questions are mainly compiled from log-files. Another probable explanation is that we spent more tuning our Dutch QA system than our English version.

4.1 Ranking Candidate Answers

Our system produces a ranked list of candidate answers, and then the highest ranked candidate is considered to be *the* answer to the question. Table 2 gives an evaluation over the ranking scheme: the number of correct answers at different cut-off levels and the Mean Reciprocal Rank (MRR). Our ranking method seems to be quite robust: only 12% of the questions are answered at ranks worse than 3, while for 65% one of the top-3 answers is correct. For 155 questions (77.5%) the system did extract a correct answer candidate (with an average of 26 candidates per question), and for 62% of these questions the correct answer was ranked highest.

Table 2. Evaluation of our ranking mechanism for the mono- and bilingual runs: the number of questions answered correctly and the mean reciprocal rank (MRR)

Top n-answers	`uams041nlnl`	`uams042nlnl`	`uams041ennl`
top 1	96 (48%)	94 (47%)	70 (35%)
top 2	122 (61%)	117 (58%)	85 (42%)
top 3	131 (65%)	123 (61%)	96 (48%)
top 10	142 (71%)	133 (66%)	117 (58%)
top 20	152 (76%)	139 (69%)	122 (61%)
any rank	155 (77%)	141 (70%)	125 (62%)
MRR	0.57	0.55	0.43

Note that the evaluation results presented differ somewhat from the official results in Table 1, because in our automatic evaluation, unsupported and inexact answers were also taken into account.

4.2 Contributions of the Streams

To analyze the contribution of different answer streams to the performance of the whole system, we carried out a number of experiments, disabling each stream individually and evaluating the resulting sub-systems using the assessors' judgements available for our official runs. The *Lookup* stream proved to be the most essential (the system answered 19 fewer questions when the *Lookup* was switched off), followed by the *Web Ngrams* stream (13 questions), *Collection Pattern Match* stream (4 questions) and *Collection Ngrams* (3 questions).

We also evaluated performance of each stream separately. Again, the *Lookup* stream had the best results, answering 57 questions (28.5%) on its own, while the precision-oriented *Pattern Match* streams answered the smallest number of questions (20 and 18, from the collection and Web, respectively).

As in our previous experiments, every stream does find a number of answers, but some streams seem more orthogonal to the rest of the system, answering questions that no other stream is capable of answering. Other streams are more redundant—for example, the *Quartz-E* stream itself found 20% of the answers, but the system had the same performance even without this stream. We should note that our final answer selection module makes use of the essential redundancy of the multi-stream architecture: 70% of the correct answers come from two or more answer streams!

We also compared two variants of the *Lookup* stream: an older version, which consults the databases extracted using only surface text patterns, and a new one, incorporating the results of the syntactic pattern extraction module on the dependency-parsed collection (similar to [8]). Although the tables from the syntactic module are much bigger, they also contain a significant amount of noise, which can potentially hurt the performance of the *Lookup* stream and the whole system. The version of the stream with the syntactic extraction module answered 8 questions more than the surface-based one. Evaluation of the two streams within the whole system showed that the syntactic extraction method helped Quartz to answer 2 more questions. This also supports the validity of our recall-based approach to QA: all possible ways to find answers should be exploited, and then the candidates should be carefully checked and cleaned.

4.3 Comparing the Mono- and Bilingual Runs

Since the questions for the bilingual task are translations of those in the monolingual task, it is interesting to compare the performance of the two types of runs. The overall accuracy of the bilingual run `uams041ennl` is lower than that of the monolingual runs, as was to be expected. The drop in accuracy can largely be attributed to the imperfect machine translation. Surprisingly, the correct answers in this run are not a subset of the correct answers found by the monolingual runs; while 44 questions (22%) were answered correctly by `uams041nlnl` and not by `uams041ennl`, there are 25 questions (12.5%) that were answered correctly by the bilingual run and not the monolingual one. Does translation make some questions easier to answer?

Table 3. A closer look at question translations

monolingual:	*Q3. Met hoeveel groeit de wereldbevolking elk jaar?*
	(With how much does the world's population grow each year?)
bilingual:	*Q3. Hoeveel verhoogt de wereldbevolking elk jaar?*
original question	(How much does the world population increase each year?)
monolingual:	*Q35. Waar is de Al Aqsa moskee?*
	(Where is the Al Aqsa moskee?)
bilingual:	*Q35. Waar is Al Moskee Aqsa?*
original question	(Where is the Al Aqsa Mosque?)
monolingual:	*Q25. Hoeveel jaar heeft Nelson Mandela in de gevangenis doorgebracht?*
	(How many years did Nelson Mandela spend in prison?)
bilingual:	*Q25. Hoeveel jaren van opsluiting diende Nelson Mandela?*
original question	(How many years of imprisonment did Nelson Mandela serve?)
monolingual:	*Q116. Hoe heet de premier van Rwanda?*
	(How is the premier of Rwanda called?)
bilingual:	*Q116. Wie is de Rwandese Eerste Minister?*
original question	(Who is the Rwandese Prime Minister?)

We carefully analyzed the differences between bilingual and monolingual runs. There were five questions which were only answered by `uams041ennl` but not by the monolingual run. In all other cases, `uams041nlnl` did find the correct answer candidate, but it was not ranked highest. One reason why correct answers were found only in the bilingual run was that the questions were slightly reformulated and synonymous words were used (e.g., "verhoogt" instead of "groeit"—"grows," in question *Q3*; see Table 3) or the word order was changed by the translation module (e.g., "Al Moskee Aqsa" instead of "Al Aqsa moskee" in question *Q35*). A different type of reformulation is illustrated by questions *Q25* and *Q116* in Table 3, where the sentences were changed more dramatically. An interesting point is that the reformulation (actually, double translation) does not necessarily result in grammatically correct sentences, but can

Table 4. Accuracy vs. question classification for `uams041ennl`

`uams041ennl`	answer correct	answer wrong	
question type correct	86	87	173
question type wrong	10	17	27
	96	104	200

still lead to a useful paraphrasing. Apart from reformulation, we found that 6 questions in the bilingual run were identical to the ones of the monolingual run. However, in those cases, the answers of the bilingual run were ranked differently than in the monolingual run, leading to 6 correctly answered questions of the bilingual run.

4.4 Error Analysis

In this section we take a closer look at the errors made by our system, more specifically, at the errors made by our question classifier. For the run labeled `uams041nlnl` our system could not assign a question type to 9 questions (4.5%). In the bilingual run, `uams041ennl`, the number of questions without a question type increases to 24 (12%), which shows that our classifier is sensitive to lexical and grammatical features coded in the patterns; see Table 4. The evaluation of the question classifier based on the `uams041nlnl` run shows that in total, 27 questions were incorrectly classified (this includes the questions with no type assigned) and 10 of them were nonetheless correctly answered by the system. Out of the 87 incorrectly answered questions, 17 were misclassified which means that misclassification could have led to wrong answers in as many as 17 cases. The subsequent table displays the results of the evaluation of the question classifier.

The classifier could not assign a type to difficult questions like *Q167* and *Q168*:

Q167.	*Wat verkoopt Oracle?*
	(What does Oracle sell?)
Question type	none
Candidate 1	Microsoft
Q168.	*Wat bouwt Frank Gehry in Bilbao?*
	(What is Frank Gehry building in Bilbao?)
Question type	none
Candidate 1	Guggenheim Museum

Although our system did not assign a question type to question *Q168*, it did find the correct answer: the candidate co-occurring with the question terms happened to be the correct one. For a similarly difficult question Q167, is was not the case: as a competitor of Microsoft, Oracle often appears close to the word "Microsoft," but the answer is of the wrong type. In most cases, where the question did not receive a question type, the type could only be derived from from the semantics of the verb and the question word.

Many instances of misclassification are either due to classification patterns that are mainly based on the question word, or to the fact that the arguments of the question are not correctly taken into account. The question type "manner" is assigned to question *Q44* as only the question word "hoe" is considered. In question *Q73*, "welk" and "president" lead to the question class "agent" whereas the correct class is "organization." Lexical ambiguities are also a source of errors, like the word "positie (position)" which can occur in the context of a geographic location or in the context of a category of employment.

Q44.	*Hoe wordt de snelheid van een chip gemeten?* (How does one measure the speed of a chip?)
Question type	manner
Candidate 1	gemiddelde snelheid (average speed)
Q73.	*Van welk bedrijf is Christian Blanc president?* (Christian Blanc is president of which company?)
Question type	agent
Candidate 1	Morgen raad Hans (tomorrow committee Hans)
Q172.	*Welke positie had Redha Malek in 1994?* (Which position did Redha Malek have in 1994?)
Question type:	location
Candidate 1	Algerije (Algeria)

Our error analysis suggests that deeper features of the questions often need to be used by the classifier: verb semantics and intersections with question words, predicate-argument structure, etc. Moreover, a different expected answer type extraction strategy might be needed for bilingual QA, where translated questions are often not well-formed sentences.

5 Discussion and Future Work

We presented our multi-stream question answering system as well as the official runs it produced for CLEF 2004. Running in parallel several subsystems that approach the QA task from different angles proved successful, as some approaches seem better suited to answering certain types of questions than others. Although this year's task was made more complex through the inclusion of definition questions, we were able to slightly increase the performance of our system. It seems that the combination of improving modules and incorporating additional information sources (such as the Dutch Wikipedia) led to the reported improvements. We found that some of the correct answers found by the bilingual run were not amongst the correct answers of the monolingual run. This suggests that the translation procedure produces paraphrased questions—grammatical or not—which in turn yield different answers. Thus, a combination of the two tasks will likely increase the recall of our system, and, with a careful answer selection procedure, this might lead to higher overall accuracy scores.

We also found that our system performs much better on Dutch at QA@CLEF than on English questions at the QA track at TREC 2004. One obvious reason was that the Dutch version of our QA system can deal much better with back-generated questions that are based on the corpus from against which the questions have to be answered. Another reason might be that the patterns used in our Dutch QA system were written by native speakers and are more advanced than the ones for English. Finally, we simply spent more time fine-tuning and debugging our Dutch QA system than our English language version.

Our ongoing work on the system is focused on additional filtering and type checking mechanisms, and on exploiting high-quality external resources such as the CIA world fact book, Wikipedia, and WordNet. Our comparison of the monolingual and bilingual runs suggests that question paraphrasing through translation can be a useful method for improving recall. We are also working on refining and improving the closely related modules for question classification, named entity extraction and type checking, to address a frequent source of errors: the mismatch between the expected answer type and the answers found.

Acknowledgments

We are grateful to Gertjan van Noord for supplying us with a dependency parsed version of the Dutch CLEF corpus. This research was supported by the Netherlands Organization for Scientific Research (NWO) under project number 220-80-001. In addition, Maarten de Rijke was also supported by grants from NWO, under project numbers 365-20-005, 612.069.006, 612.000.106, 612.000.207, 612.066.302, and 264-70-050.

References

[1] D. Ahn, V. Jijkoun, J. Kamps, G. Mishne, K. Müller, M. de Rijke, and S. Schlobach. The University of Amsterdam at TREC 2004. In *TREC 2004 Conference Notebook*, Gaithersburg, Maryland USA, 2004.

[2] G. Bouma, G. Van Noord, and R. Malouf. Alpino: Wide-coverage computational analysis of Dutch. In *Computational Linguistics in The Netherlands 2000*. 2001.

[3] T. Brants. TnT – a statistical part-of-speech tagger. In *Proceedings of the 6th Applied NLP Conference, ANLP-2000*, 2000.

[4] S. Dumais, M. Banko, E. Brill, J. Lin, and A. Ng. Web question answering: Is more always better? In P. Bennett, S. Dumais, and E. Horvitz, editors, *Proceedings of SIGIR'02*, pages 291–298, 2002.

[5] M. Banko et al. AskMSR: Question answering using the Worldwide Web. In *Proceedings EMNLP 2002*, 2002.

[6] C. Foeldesi, K. Müller, and M. de Rijke. Using the Corpus Gesproken Nederlands to Build a Named Entity Recognizer. In *14th Meeting of Computational Linguistics in the Netherlands (CLIN-2003)*, 2003.

[7] V. Jijkoun and M. de Rijke. Answer selection in a multi-stream open domain question answering system. In S. McDonald and J. Tait, editors, *Proceedings 26th European Conference on Information Retrieval (ECIR'04),*, volume 2997 of *LNCS*, pages 99–111. Springer, 2004.

[8] V. Jijkoun, M. de Rijke, and J. Mur. Information extraction for question answering: Improving recall through syntactic patterns. In *Proceedings of the 20th International Conference on Computational Linguistics (COLING 2004)*, 2004.

[9] V. Jijkoun, G. Mishne, and M. de Rijke. Preprocessing Documents to Answer Dutch Questions. In *Proceedings of the 15th Belgian-Dutch Conference on Artificial Intelligence (BNAIC'03)*, 2003.

[10] V. Jijkoun, G. Mishne, and M. de Rijke. How frogs built the Berlin Wall. In *Proceedings CLEF 2003*, LNCS. Springer, 2004.

[11] V. Jijkoun, G. Mishne, C. Monz, M. de Rijke, S. Schlobach, and O. Tsur. The University of Amsterdam at the TREC 2003 Question Answering Track. In *Proceedings TREC 2003*, pages 586–593, 2004.

[12] D. Moldovan, S. Harabagiu, R. Girju, P. Morarescu, F. Lacatusu, A. Novischi, A. Badulescu, and O. Bolohan. LCC Tools for Question Answering. In E.M. Voorhees and D.K. Harman, editors, *The Tenth Text REtrieval Conference (TREC 2002)*. National Institute for Standards and Technology. NIST Special Publication 500-251, 2003.

[13] C. Monz and M. de Rijke. Tequesta: The University of Amsterdam's textual question answering system. In E.M. Voorhees and D.K. Harman, editors, *The Tenth Text REtrieval Conference (TREC 2001)*, pages 519–528. National Institute for Standards and Technology. NIST Special Publication 500-250, 2002.

[14] C. Monz and M. de Rijke. Shallow morphological analysis in monolingual information retrieval for Dutch, German and Italian. In *Proceedings CLEF 2001*, LNCS. Springer, 2002.

[15] N. Oostdijk. The Spoken Dutch Corpus: Overview and first evaluation. In *Proceedings LREC 2000*, pages 887–894, 2000.

[16] S. Schlobach, M. Olsthoorn, and M. de Rijke. Type checking in open-domain question answering. In *Proceedings of the 16th European Conference on Artificial Intelligence (ECAI 2004)*, 2004.

The DIOGENE Question Answering System at CLEF-2004

Hristo Tanev, Matteo Negri, Bernardo Magnini, and Milen Kouylekov

ITC-irst, Centro per la Ricerca Scientifica e Tecnologica
Via Sommarive, 38050 Povo (TN), Italy
{tanev, negri, magnini, kouylekov@itc.it}

Abstract. This paper presents the ITC-irst Multilingual Question Answering system DIOGENE. The system was used successfully on the CLEF-2003, TREC-2003, TREC-2002 and TREC-2001 QA tracks. DIOGENE relies on a classical three-layer architecture: question processing, document retrieval, answer extraction and validation. DIOGENE uses MultiWordNet [8] (http://multiwordnet.itc.it) which facilitates the transfer of knowledge between languages. For answer validation we used the Web. This year we also used a set of linguistic templates for answering specific questions like definition questions, location questions, and a subset of who-is and what-is questions. DIOGENE participated in both the monolingual Italian-Italian task and in the cross-language Italian-English task. We also collaborated with the Bulgarian Academy of Sciences in the cross-language Bulgarian-English QA task.

1 Introduction

Research in Question Answering (QA) has received a strong boost in recent years form the QA track organized within the TREC conferences [11], which aims at assessing the capability of systems to return exact answers to open-domain English questions. However, the TREC conferences are concentrated exclusively on the English language. In contrast, the CLEF conferences provide a multilingual forum for evaluation of NLP systems in languages other than English. Multilinguality has been recognized as an important issue for the future of QA [1]. In CLEF-2003 a multilingual QA task was introduced for the first time. Our system showed promising results in CLEF-2003 in the monolingual Italian and cross-language Italian-English tasks. This encouraged us to participate also in the Bulgarian-English cross-language task, promoted this year.

The multilingual version of DIOGENE was built upon the same well-tested three-layer architecture of the English version [2]. Figure 1 shows the main constituents of this common backbone: these are the *question processing* component, the *document retrieval* component, and the *answer extraction and validation* component. In all its monolingual and cross-language modalities, DIOGENE relies on the knowledge in the multilingual ontology MultiWordNet [8], manually created rules for named entity recognition and question type identification, a set of handcrafted answer extraction templates and statistical information collected from the Web and off-line multilingual corpora. The DIOGENE CLEF-2004 architecture was similar to the CLEF-2003

C. Peters et al. (Eds.): CLEF 2004, LNCS 3491, pp. 435 – 445, 2005.

version [7]. A novel feature for the CLEF-2004 version is the answer extraction and validation via linguistic templates. Linguistic templates were particularly important for the definition questions.

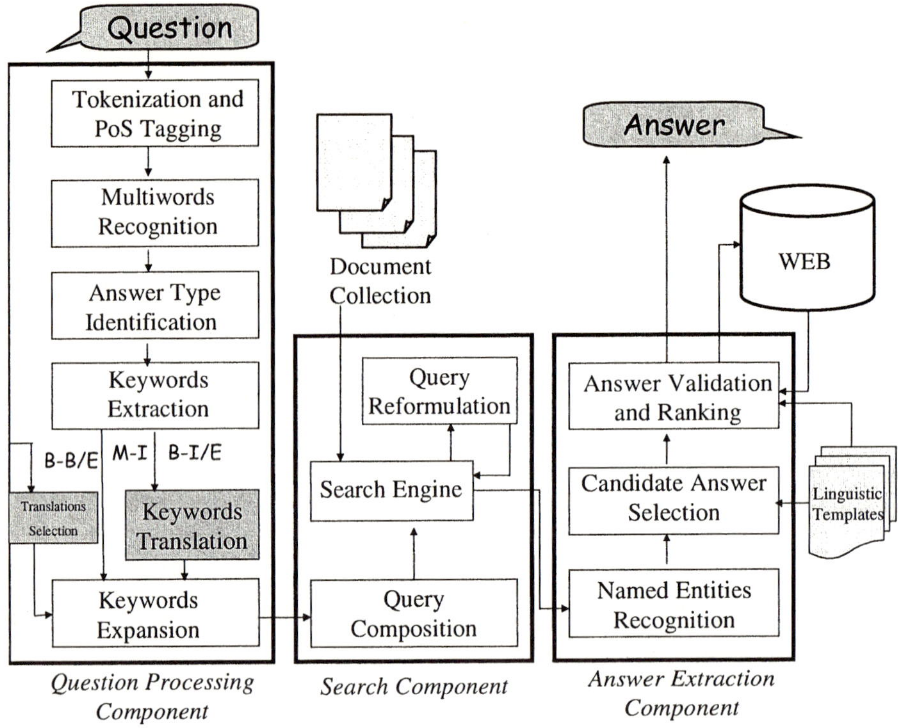

Fig. 1. The architecture of the DIOGENE system

The following sections will provide a general overview of our participation in the *monolingual Italian* (M-I), *bilingual Italian/English* (B-I/E) and *bilingual Bulgarian/English* (B-B/E) tasks of the multiple-language QA track at CLEF-2004. In all the three tasks 200 questions were posed to the QA systems. For the M-I task, questions were posed in Italian and the answer had to be searched in an Italian text collection (the 193Mb corpus of the *La Stampa* 1994 newspaper and the 172Mb corpus of the *SDA* 1994 and 1995 press agency),. For the bilingual B-I/E and B-B/E tasks, questions were posed in Italian or Bulgarian, respectively, and the answer had to be retrieved from English corpus (the 425Mb corpus of the *Los Angeles Times* 1994 and 157Mb corpus of the *Glasgow Herald* 1995). The rest of the paper is structured as follows: Section 2 provides a high-level description of the basic components of the DIOGENE architecture. Section 3 discusses the use of linguistic templates for answer extraction. Section 4 describes the Web validation approach which we used this year. Section 5 discusses the results in all the tasks where we participated. Finally, we describe future directions for our system development.

2 System Architecture Overview

The overall system architecture was the same as the architecture with which we participated in CLEF-2003 [7], apart from the linguistic templates which we plugged into the system and the new Web validation procedure which we used. DIOGENE is capable of processing questions in Italian and English and searching the answers in text collections in Italian and English. The system has a multilingual architecture – the same modules work both for English and Italian, using language-specific rules and resources when necessary. In the bilingual Bulgarian-English task (B-B/E) the questions were processed in the Bulgarian Academy of Sciences. For each question in Bulgarian, DIOGENE obtained a *question type* (what the question is about – person, location, etc.) list of keywords with all the possible translations in English. Next, DIOGENE chose the right keyword translations using a statistical approach described earlier in [7]. In both cross-language tasks after the question processing, all the other modules work in the same manner as the monolingual English version of DIOGENE (see [2] and [7] for more details).

2.1 Question Processing

The Question processing module has five basic stages: question pre-processing (part-of-speech tagging, multiword recognition); *answer type identification* which defines what the question is about: person, location, date, definition, etc.; *keyword extraction* from the question; *keyword translation* for cross-language tasks; *keyword expansion* with synonyms and morphological derivations. All these components were described earlier in our CLEF-2003 system report (see [7]). Here we will just sketch the most interesting stages of the question processing.

Answer type identification. For Italian we used hand-crafted, language specific rules for answer type identification similar to those used for English. These rules operate on part-of-speech tagged questions. Semantic predicates defined over the synsets of the MultiWordNet hierarchy are used in the answer type identification. For instance, the rule described in (1) matches any question starting with "quale" ("*what*"), whose first noun, if any, is a person.

(1) **RULENAME: QUALE-CHI**
TEST: ["quale" [¬NOUN]* [NOUN:person-p]$_J$ +]
OUTPUT: ["PERSON" J]

For example, this rule matches the question *"Quale presidente americano è stato renitente alla leva?"* (*"Which American President failed to report for military service?"*), since the predicate *person-p* returns *true* for *"presidente"*. However, the rule will not be activated for the question. *"Qual è il partito di Charles Millon?"* (*"What is the party of Charles Milton?"*), since *"partito"*(*"party"*) in MultiWordNet is not a hyponym of the concept *"person"* . Rule (1) gives as output the type of entity for which the question is asking (*"person"* in this case).

Since in MultiWordNet both English and Italian synsets are aligned, the predicates in the answer-identification rules like *person-p* can be used for both languages.

Keyword translation. Both B-I/E and B-B/E require translation of the question into the target language (English). Since state-of-the-art translation systems are not optimized for the translation of short pieces of text such as the questions, we have developed a methodology specifically designed for keyword translation. First, for each keyword from the question, all the possible English translations are found using bilingual dictionaries and MultiWordNet (for Bulgarian this has been done at the Bulgarian Academy of Sciences). Next, the most plausible combination of keyword translations is chosen. We chose the combination of keyword translations $(k_1, k_2,...,k_n)$ with the highest frequency of co-occurrence in an English corpus (we used the AQUAINT and TIPSTER collections). The main assumption is that the more frequently a keyword translation combination appears with the translations close to each other (in one and the same paragraph), the more plausible this combination.

2.2 Search Component

In the QA tasks at CLEF-2004 DIOGENE relied on the same search component as that developed for the English version of DIOGENE, as described in [2]. This component first combines the question keywords and their lexical expansions in a Boolean query; then performs document retrieval accessing the target document collections.

The search is performed by Managing Gigabytes (MG) [12], an open-source indexing and retrieval system for text, images, and textual images covered by a GNU public license and available from *http://www.cs.mu.oz.au/mg/*. MG allows for a fast and customizable indexing. We opted to index the document collection at the paragraph level, using the paragraph markers provided in the SGML format of the document collection. This way, although no proximity operator is implemented in MG, the paragraph index makes the "AND" Boolean operator perform proximity search. In order to divide very long paragraphs into short passages, we set 20 text lines as the limit for paragraph length.

The document retrieval module uses the Boolean query mode of MG. At the first step of the search phase all the basic keywords are connected in a complex "AND" clause, where the term variants (morphological derivations and synonyms) are combined in an "OR" clause. As an example, given the question "*Quando morì Lenin?*" ("*When did Lenin die?*"), the basic keywords resulting from the translation process (i.e. "*die*" and "*Lenin*") are expanded and combined into:

[**Lenin** AND (**die** OR **dies** OR **died** OR **dying** OR **death** OR **deaths**)]

However, Boolean queries often tend to return too many or too few documents. To cope with this problem, we implemented a feedback loop which starts with a query containing all the relevant keywords and gradually simplifies it by ignoring some of them. Several heuristics are used by the algorithm. For example, a word is removed if the resulting query does not produce more than a fixed number of hits. Other heuristics consider the capitalization of the query terms, their part of speech, their position in the question, WORDNET class, etc. [2].

A post-processing procedure finally orders the paragraphs on the basis of the number and proximity of the keywords and their synonyms which are present.

2.3 Answer Extraction Component

Two types of questions were present in the questions set this year: *factoid questions*, which usually ask for a named entity: person, location, organization, etc., and *definition questions* (e.g. "*Who is Valentina Tereshkova?*") which ask for person or concept definitions. For the factoid questions, the answer extraction component first performs a selection of the answer candidates through named entities recognition and linguistic templates; then, a Web-based procedure for answer validation is applied over the selected named entities to choose the best one. As for definition questions, DIOGENE extracts the answers using linguistic templates and then chooses the most plausible definition using semantic and syntactic clues.

Named Entities Recognition (NER). The named entities recognition module is responsible for identifying, within the relevant passages returned by the search engine, all the entities that match the answer type category (e.g. person, organization, location, measure, etc.). The Italian version of the NER module tested on a 77Kb text corpus[1] revealed a performance comparable to the English NER [4], with an overall F-Measure score of 83%.

Linguistic templates. In order to increase system precision we have applied linguistic templates to several question types: definition questions (both for English and Italian), dove-è (where-is) questions (only for Italian) and quale/chi-è (what/who-is) questions (only for Italian). The templates were the only source of information for answer extraction with definition questions. The other two types of templates were applied for the respective question types and if an answer was extracted it was validated on the Web through answer validation templates; if no candidate was captured by the patterns, the classical DIOGENE answer extraction and validation was applied.

Answer validation. In CLEF-2003 we used AltaVista for answer validation. Since this year AltaVista has changed its access interface and has not provided any further support for the proximity search on which we base our statistical approach, we opted for an alternative method based on the analysis of the snippets returned by AllTheWeb. Each named entity returned as a candidate answer to a factoid question was tested for close co-occurrence with the question keywords. This provides DIOGENE with clues as to the plausibility of the candidate answer.

3 Linguistic Templates for Answer Extraction and Validation

The adoption of linguistic templates has proved to be an appropriate technique for certain question types such as definition and location questions. For our CLEF-2004 participation we plugged into DIOGENE linguistic templates which perform answer extraction and validation for: (i) definition questions, (ii) location questions of the type "Where is <LOCATION>?", and (iii) what-is or who-is questions of the type "(What | Who) is <NOUN PHRASE>?" (e.g. "What is the Iraq currency?"). For

[1] Reference transcripts of two broadcast news shows, including a total of about 7,000 words and 322 tagged named entities, were manually produced for evaluation purposes and have been kindly provided by Marcello Federico and Vanessa Sandrini.

definition questions we created bilingual templates which work both for English and Italian. For the other two classes of questions, we manually created templates for Italian.

3.1 Definition Questions

In the CLEF-2004 QA track 10% of the questions (20) were definition questions (e.g. *"What is UNICEF?" "What is yakuza?" "Who is Jorge Amado?"*). While definition questions are among the most natural and frequent kinds of queries posed by humans, they raise specific issues in the development of QA systems. First, the answer of a definition question is not a named entity. Next, while for most of the questions we have many content words whose co-occurrence may indicate the position of the answer, for definition questions we only have one content word or multiword (i.e. the *focus* of the question, the entity for which the question seeks a definition).

The CLEF-2004 QA track organizers stated in the guidelines that questions will be about persons and organizations. This makes the definition extraction more feasible, since capturing information about organizations and persons is usually easier than finding definitions for random concepts.

We adopted the approach described in [10]. Our approach relies on linguistically regular expressions, much more expressive than the string templates introduced by [9]. Since the syntactic structure of the definitions in Italian and English is fairly similar, we aligned the templates for English and Italian, obtaining multilingual templates. For example, the following bilingual template (2) was used for capturing canonical definitions in English and Italian:

(2) **[~ Prep] <FOCUS> [~ Noun](1) [eng: lemma:be | ita: lemma:essere] [~ Prep Verb Conj](3) Noun**

This pattern captures the following sequence of words: a word which is not a preposition ([~ Prep]); followed by the focus (<FOCUS>) of the question; possibly followed by one word which is not a noun ([~ Noun](1)); followed by the auxiliary verb "be" appearing in one of the languages; followed by at most 3 words ([~ Prep Verb Conj](3)), none of which is a preposition, a finite verb form or a conjunction; followed by a noun (Noun). This patter captures a broad range of canonical definitions of the type *"yakuza is the Japanese mafia"* (English), or *"yakuza è la mafia giapponese"* (Italian). Correctly, it will not capture *"The members of yakudza are..."*, since no preposition is allowed before the focus.

Different templates have different levels of reliability, therefore each extracted definition obtains a syntactic score depending on the template with which it was extracted. Currently, we have defined the reliability score for the definition extraction templates manually; however, we consider learning it automatically.

Our experiments revealed that the syntactic score does not provide reliable ranking. Therefore, we applied a complementary scoring strategy based on MultiWordNet (this multilingual ontology allowed us to work on both Italian and English):

If the question is about a person we search the extracted definition for a concept which is a hyponym of the concept "person" in MultiWordNet.

If the question is not about a person, it will be about an organization, so we search for hyponyms of the concept "organization".

If the focus of the definition question is present in MultiWordNet, an additional score is given if terms from the gloss of the focus or its hypernyms appear in the candidate definition.

When the focus of the definition question was not present in MultiWordNet, we searched in the Wickipedia database and assigned an additional score if a term with hyperlink from the Wickipedia article (usually these hyperlinks mean that the term is important) appeared in the candidate definition.

For the definition questions we obtained 40% accuracy in the monolingual Italian task and 25% on the cross-language Italian-English task. Although there is a lot of space for improvement, the definition question accuracy was higher than that for the answers of the factoid questions, especially in the monolingual Italian task.

3.2 Location Questions

We have only developed templates for location questions for Italian. We noted that in many cases the answer of questions such as: *"Dove si trova la Valle dei Re?" ("Where is the Valley of the Kings?") or "Dove si tiene il Motorshow?" ("Where does the Motorshow take place?")* is expressed through phrases like "*La Valle dei Re in Egitto*" (*"Valley of the Kings in Egypt"*) or "*Motorshow a Bologna*" (*"Motorshow in Bologna"*). Such answers are captured easily through superficial patterns like:

(3) **<FOCUS> (in|nel|nella) <LOCATION>**
<FOCUS> a <LOCATION>
<FOCUS> si trova in <LOCATION>
<FOCUS> ed in tutt(a|o|i) (il| l'| la | gli | i)? <LOCATION>

The extraction of the focus was carried out through specific question processing patterns. For each answer we also count how many times it appears in a location template; if it appears too infrequently or if many candidates are extracted, we further validate the answers by querying the Web:

"<FOCUS> in <LOCATION>" OR "<FOCUS> nel <LOCATION>" OR "<FOCUS> nella <LOCATION>"

For example: "Motorshow in Bologna" OR "Motorshow nel Bologna" OR "Motorshow nella Bologna" OR "Motorshow a Bologna"

The number of documents returned by the search engine as a response to this query together with repetition of the answer within templates in the local corpus are clues to the reliability of the answer.

3.3 Questions of the Type "(What|Who) Is <NOUN PHRASE>"

We only implemented templates for these questions for Italian where these questions begin with *"Chi è"* or *"Qual è"* . Questions of this class do not contain any other verb apart from the auxiliary. Examples of such questions from the CLEF-2004 monolingual Italian test set are:

Qual è la unita di frequenza? ("What is the frequency unit?")
Chi è il ministro delle finanze russo?("Who is the Russian minister of finances?")

These questions are somehow opposite to the definition questions. In effect, such questions represent short definitions and the answers are entities which can be described via these definitions. We call this kind of question *inverted definition questions* since, if you ask a definition question about their answer, the focus of the inverted definition question will represent the correct definition. For example

Question: *Chi è il ministro delle finanze russo?("Who is the Russian minister of finances?")*
Answer: Boris Fiodorov

Definition question: *Chi è Boris Fiodorov? ("Who is Boris Fiodorov?")*
Answer: *il ministro delle finanze russo ("the Russian minister of finances")*

Taking this into account, we applied patterns that were similar to the definition question patterns described in Section 3.1. For this question type we used also Web validation via patterns when necessary.

4 Using the Web to Validate Answers

When the named entity recognizer returns a list of candidate answers, those which are closest to the question keywords (and therefore considered more reliable) are passed to the answer validation algorithm which chooses the best candidate (if this exists).

The basic idea behind our approach to answer validation is to identify semantic relations between the question and each candidate answer by searching for their co-occurrences in a large document collection. In this framework, we consider the Web as the largest open domain text corpus containing information about almost all the different areas of the human knowledge.

In our previous participation in CLEF-2003 we used a Web validation method based on a co-occurrence statistical formula (see [5] and [7] for details). The frequency information used in this formula was taken from AltaVista. We used AltaVista's proximity operator "NEAR" which allowed identification of the number of pages in which certain words co-occur close to each other. However, AltaVista changed its interface, providing no further support for proximity searches, neither were we able to find a publicly available search engine which offers the same feature. Therefore, we opted for the *content-based answer validation*, whose main idea we described earlier in [3], and we used the AllTheWeb search engine (www.alltheweb.com). Our Web validation algorithm performs the following basic steps:

1. It queries the Web with the question keywords *QK* and the answer *a*. For example, for the question *"Quanti anni di prigionia ha subito Nelson Mandela?"* (*"How many years did Nelson Mandel spend in the prison?"*) and the (correct) candidate answer "27", we have: *QK={anni, prigionia, subito, Nelson, Mandela}; a=27*

2. The top 100 hits returned by AllTheWeb are explored and for each text fragment where the answer *a* co-occurs with some of the *QK* words we calculate a score on the

basis of the distance between a and the number of keywords present in QK which also appear in the snippet, according to the following formula:

$$score(snippet) = \prod_{k \in snippet \cap QK} 2^{1+|ak|^{-1}},$$

where $|ak|$ is the distance in tokens between the candidate answer a and a question keyword k which appears in the snippet.

For example for the text fragment: "*Nelson Mandela viene liberato dopo 27 anni di dura prigionia e di torture*" this formula assigns a score of 55,08, while for the text "*Nelson Mandela, che a Robben Island, l'isola-prigione a largo di Citta' del Capo dove ha trascorso 18 dei suoi 27 anni di prigionia*", we assign 43,14, since the distance between *27* and both keywords *Nelson* and *Mandela* is greater.

3. The score gained from different fragments are summed for each candidate answer.

4. The candidate answer which gains the highest score is chosen.

DIOGENE returns as answer the candidate for which the answer validation returns the highest score. If the answer validation module returns zero for all the candidate answers, DIOGENE returns NIL as answer. After some normalization the answer validation score is returned as a confidence score, as required this year by the CLEF QA track guidelines.

5 Results and Discussion

DIOGENE was evaluated in five runs: two in the monolingual Italian QA task, two in the Italian-English task, and one in the Bulgarian-English task. In each task the system had to answer 200 questions, returning one answer per question. For some questions NIL was allowed, which is interpreted as "no answer exists to the question". The following table shows the results in all these tasks.

Table 1. Results of DIOGENE at the CLEF-2004 QA track

Run	R	W	U	X	Factoid	DEF	NIL	**Overall Accuracy**	**Conf. Score**
irst041itit	56	131	2	11	26.7%	40%	27.0%	28.00%	0.156
irst042itit	44	147	0	9	20.0%	40%	66.7%	22.00%	0.107
irst041iten	45	146	3	6	22.2%	25%	24.0%	22.50%	0.122
irst042iten	35	158	2	5	16.7%	25%	24.0%	17.50%	0.075
bgas041bgen	26	168	1	5	11.7%	25%	13.6%	13.00%	0.056

The first two rows of Table 1 show our results in the monolingual Italian task, the second two show the results in the cross-language Italian-English task, and the last row shows the results from our joint participation in the Bulgarian-English task. The first runs in both tasks (irst041itit and irst041iten) use the Web validation to calculate the final score of the answer candidates. The second runs (irst042itit and irst042iten) combine the results from the Web validation with the keyword density in the paragraph of the local text collection where the answer was found. The first column in Table 1 is the run tag, the second column (R) shows the number of correct answers, the third column (W) contains the number of the wrong answers, the fourth column (U) indicates the number of unsupported answers (these are correct answers but extracted from document which do not support them), the fifth column (X) contains the number of inexact answers, the sixth column (Factoid) shows the precision of answering the factoid questions, the seventh column (DEF) contains the precision for the definition questions, the eighth column (NIL) contains the precision of the returned NIL answers, the ninth column (Overall Accuracy) shows the main evaluation criteria - the percent of the correctly answered questions - and the last column (Conf. Score) shows the value of the confidence weighted measure calculated by the CLEF judges.

The table shows that our results for this year QA tracks are lower than our CLEF-2003 results. We can explain this with the increased difficulty of this year's questions. The main obstacle in front of DIOGENE was the factoid questions which do not require a named entity as an answer (e.g. "*Quale animale tuba?*" ("*What animal coos?*")) .

The templates which we used for factoid questions in the monolingual Italian task found answers to 13 out of 180 factoid questions, 8 of them were correct, 2 were judged inexact, and 3 answers were wrong. These numbers show that the template answer extractor contributed 4% to the overall accuracy and its precision was 61.5%.

The difference in the accuracy for monolingual Italian and Italian-English tasks is not large, which means that our translation mechanism works satisfactory.

6 Conclusion and Future Work

We have described the architecture of our multilingual system DIOGENE, focusing on the improvements for CLEF-2004. The system combines the multilingual knowledge in MultiWordNet, a set of linguistic templates and information mined on the fly from the Web.

There is still a lot of space for improvement in the performance of our QA system. In the future development we intend to strengthen the linguistic infrastructure for the Italian language by trying to make use of the syntactic information in the question and in the answer context; in this way answer extraction and validation will become linguistically more motivated. We intend also to use MultiWordNet more extensively. We would like DIOGENE to also answer questions which do not have named entities as answers.

Finally, we would like to extend the applicability of our QA system to the multilingual dimension by considering other languages.

References

1. Burger, J., Cardie, C., Chaudhri, V., Gaizauskas, R., Harabagiu, S., Israel, D., Jacquemin, C., Lin, C.-Y., Maiorano, S., Miller, G., Moldovan, D., Ogden, B., Prager, J., Riloff, E., Singhal, A., Shrihari, R., Strzalkowski, T., Voorhees, E., Weishedel, R.: Issues, Tasks and Program Structures to Roadmap Research in Question & Answering (Q&A) (2001). URL: *http://www-nlpir.nist.gov/projects/duc/papers/qa.Roadmap-paper_v2.doc.*

2. Magnini, B., Negri, M., Prevete, R., Tanev, H.: Mining Knowledge from Repeated Co-occurrences: DIOGENE at TREC-2002 Proceedings of the Eleventh Text Retrieval Conference (TREC-2002), Gaithersburg, MD, (2002).
3. Magnini, B., Negri, M., Prevete, R., Tanev, H.: Comparing Statistical and Content-Based Techniques for Answer Validation on the Web. Proceedings of the VIII Convegno AI*IA, Siena, Italy, (2002).
4. Magnini, B., Negri, M., Prevete, R., Tanev, H.: A WORDNET-Based Approach to Named Entities Recognition. Proceedings of SemaNet02, COLING Workshop on Building and Using Semantic Networks, Taipei, Taiwan, (2002).
5. Magnini, B., Negri, M., Prevete, R., Tanev, H.: Is It the Right Answer? Exploiting Web Redundancy for Answer Validation. Proceedings of the 40th Annual Meeting of the Association for Computational Linguistics (ACL-2002), Philadelphia, PA, (2002).
6. Manning, C., Shutze, H.: Foundations of Statistical Natural Language Processing. MIT Press, (1999).
7. Negri M., Tanev H., and Magnini B.: Bridging Languages for Question Answering: DIOGENE at CLEF-2003 Proceedings of CLEF-2003, Trondheim, Norway, August (2003).
8. Pianta, E., Bentivogli, L., Girardi, C.: MULTIWORDNET: Developing an Aligned Multilingual Database. Proceedings of the 1st International Global WordNet Conference, Mysore, India, 2002.
9. Ravichandran D., Hovy, E.: Learning Surface Text Patterns for a Question Answering System. In Proceedings of the 40th ACL Conference. University of Pennsylvania, Philadelphia, 2002
10. Tanev H., Kouylekov M., Negri M., Coppola B., Magnini B. :Multilingual Pattern Libraries for Question Answering: a Case Study for Definition Questions, Fourth International Conference on Language Resources and Evaluation (LREC-2004) Proceedings, Lisbon, Portugal, May 26-28, 2004.
11. Voorhees, E.: Overview of the TREC 2003 Question Answering Track. In Proceedings of the Sixth Retrieval Conference (TREC-2003) , Gaithersburg, MD., 2004.
12. Witten, I. H., Moffat, A., Bell T.: Managing Gigabytes: Compressing and Indexing Documents and Images (second ed.), Morgan Kaufmann Publishers, New York, 1999.

Cross-Lingual Question Answering Using Off-the-Shelf Machine Translation

Kisuh Ahn, Beatrice Alex, Johan Bos, Tiphaine Dalmas, Jochen L. Leidner, and Matthew B. Smillie

University of Edinburgh, Scotland, UK
treq-qa@inf.ed.ac.uk

Abstract. We show how to adapt an existing monolingual open-domain QA system to perform in a cross-lingual environment, using off-the-shelf machine translation software. In our experiments we use French and German as source language, and English as target language. For answering factoid questions, our system performs with an accuracy of 16% (German to English) and 20% (French to English), respectively. The loss of correctly answered questions caused by the MT component is estimated at 10% for French, and 15% for German. The accuracy of our system on correctly translated questions is 28% for German and 29% for French.

1 Introduction

In this paper we investigate the use of off-the-shelf machine translation (MT) software to adapt monolingual automatic question answering (QA) to perform in a cross-lingual situation. We will describe QED, a question answering system developed at the University of Edinburgh [1], and its performance on two cross-lingual QA tasks organised by the Cross Language Evaluation Forum (CLEF-2004).

QED was originally developed for monolingual (English) QA tasks, and our aim was to turn it into a cross-lingual system with a minimum of required changes. The obvious way to do this is by adding an MT component to the front-end of the system, with English as target language. We concentrated on the languages French and German for the cross-language QA task, resulting in a QA system that responds to German or French questions with English answers. So we only required an MT component to translate the questions.

The CLEF evaluation exercise for QA is based on that of TREC [2]. In short, the task is to give answers as exact as possible for factoid and definition questions, and back these up with a document that supports the answer. Questions for which no answer can be found in the document collection have to be answered with the string "NIL". Each answer needs to be associated with a confidence value (a number between 0 and 1), in order to reward systems that are able to model their own performance.

We have organised this paper as follows. First, we describe the general architecture of the cross-lingual QED question answering system as well as its

C. Peters et al. (Eds.): CLEF 2004, LNCS 3491, pp. 446–457, 2005.

individual components (Section 2). In Section 3, we present our results obtained in the CLEF-2004 evaluation, give a detailed error analysis of the MT component, and compare the performance of the cross-lingual with the monolingual task. We summarise our work and conclude in Section 4.

2 The QED System

2.1 Architecture

QED is a system originally designed for monolingual (English) QA tasks [1]. It has a traditional sequential QA architecture. From a bird's eye view, it consists of question analysis, document retrieval, and answer selection. Most of the QED system as used in this paper is similar to that described in our earlier work [1], minus the more elaborate question-typing, the use of Lemur instead of MG for Information Retrieval (IR), several minor enhancements in the various components, and, of course, the MT component. We used the 200 French and German questions from CLEF-2003 [3] as development data.

Figure 1 gives a detailed overview of QED's architecture. After the questions are translated from the source language (German and French) into the target language (English), they are tokenized and possibly reformulated to increase the precision of parsing. After stemming and part-of-speech (POS) tagging, the question is parsed. A semantic representation is generated from the grammatical relations, which is used to construct a query for the document retrieval module to obtain documents.

A passage segmenting and ranking tool is used to prune the search space and find document regions likely to contain answers. Its output is parsed and a semantic representation for answer candidates is created likewise. An answer extraction module attempts to match and score representations of question and answer candidates. Finally, evidence from the Web in the form of co-occurrence counts is used to check answer candidates for validity and the best answer is output.

This is QED's architecture in a nutshell. We will consider some of these components in more detail in the following sections. We will illustrate our approach to machine translation, passage selection, question typing, linguistic analysis, semantic interpretation, and finally answer selection.

2.2 Machine Translation

Our translation component is built around Babelfish[1], an online MT engine based on Systran. This is a rule-based MT engine, which makes use of both bilingual dictionaries and linguistic rules designed empirically for specific language pairs. In order to assess the quality of a pure off-the-shelf component, we ran an experiment by translating 200 CLEF-2003 questions from German to English and judge the results for acceptability. Perhaps unsurprisingly, we ini-

[1] `http://babelfish.altavista.com/`

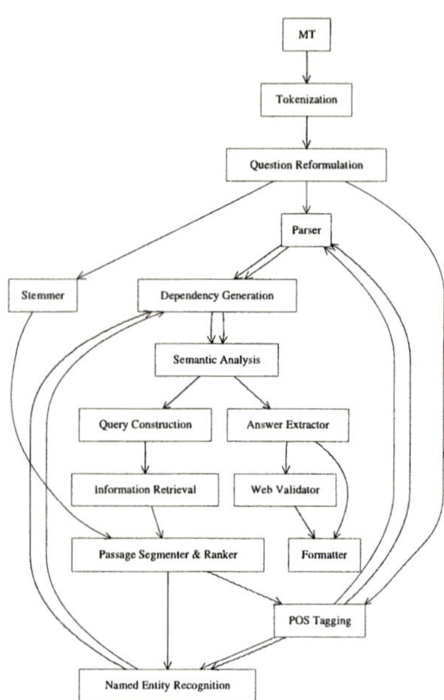

Fig. 1. The QED system architecture for CLEF-2004 (dataflow graph). Normal arrows represent processing of the question, bold arrows represents processing of answers

tially observed several translation mistakes. Only 29% of the translations were judged acceptable. Many of the errors were caused by foreign words and literally translated named entities.

However, we also noticed that the majority of the errors were systematic, and we decided to develop pre- and post-processing rules to improve the quality of the MT output. As the English MT output serves as input into the QA system, our aim was to produce MT output as correct as possible. We therefore invested some time in examining the types of errors that occurred in the Systran output for both language pairs (German to English, and French to English) and devised language-pair specific reformulation rules. We found that the best results were achieved by employing a set of meaning preserving reformulation rules before MT, as well as applying a set of rules after MT. We refer to these sets of rules as pre-MT and post-MT rules, respectively. Both sets of rules were implemented using Perl's regular expression matching techniques.

The pre-MT rules mostly reformulate certain types of questions not covered by the MT component into simpler constructions which it can actually deal with. For example, we reformulated French questions starting with *À quel moment* into questions beginning with *Quand*. In total, we created 24 pre-MT rules for French, and 9 for German.

The post-MT rules deal with systematic errors encountered in the MT output. A case in point are French questions distinguished by the inversion of subject pronoun and verb, such as *Où X travaille-t-il?*. The English MT output for this type of question is *Where X does it work?* instead of *Where does X work?*.

Another case in point are German questions such as *Wie heißt X?*, which are literally translated into *How is X called?* rather than *What is X called?*. The surface pattern-oriented pre-MT and post-MT rules enabled us to correct such errors automatically. We implemented 24 post-MT rules for French, and 25 for German.

These pre-MT and post-MT rules improved the MT component considerably, although the results were far from perfect. However, we expected them to be good enough for the cross-lingual QA challenge.

2.3 Document Retrieval, Passage Extraction and Ranking

We used the Lemur toolkit[2] to realise document retrieval based on a Vector-Space Model. The question was analysed syntactically and semantically and a weighted set of phrases was constructed from the Discourse Representation Structures (see Section 2.6), which were converted into structured queries for Lemur. The most relevant 300 documents were retrieved for subsequent processing.

Our passage segmentation and ranking component takes a query and a set of retrieved documents and extracts n-sentence passages (called "tiles"), and assigns a score to them. This is done by sliding an n-sentence window over the document stream (where we set $n=3$, as this gave the best results in training), retaining all window tiles that contain *at least one* of the words in the query and also always must contain *all* upper-case query words. The score is based on heuristic rules based on the following features:

- the number of non-stopword query word tokens (as opposed to types) present in the tile;
- a comparison of the capitalization of query occurrence and tile occurrence of a term;
- the occurrence of bigrams and trigrams in both question and tile.

Each tile's score is multiplied with a slightly asymmetric triangular window function to weight sentences in the centre of a window higher than in the periphery and to break ties. The output of the tiler is the top-scoring 100 tiles (eliminating duplicates). More information on this component can be found in our earlier work [1].

2.4 Question Typing

We used a hierarchical taxonomy of eleven basic question types (Fig. 2), based on the strategies used for finding suitable answers within the large variety of question patterns. This division is based on answers in the form of the linguistically motivated categories S (sentence), ADJ (adjective) and NP (noun phrase). Some of the question-types are further divided into subtypes, where C is a concept, R a relation, and U a unit of measurement. Note that although there are only

[2] `http://www-2.cs.cmu.edu/~lemur/`

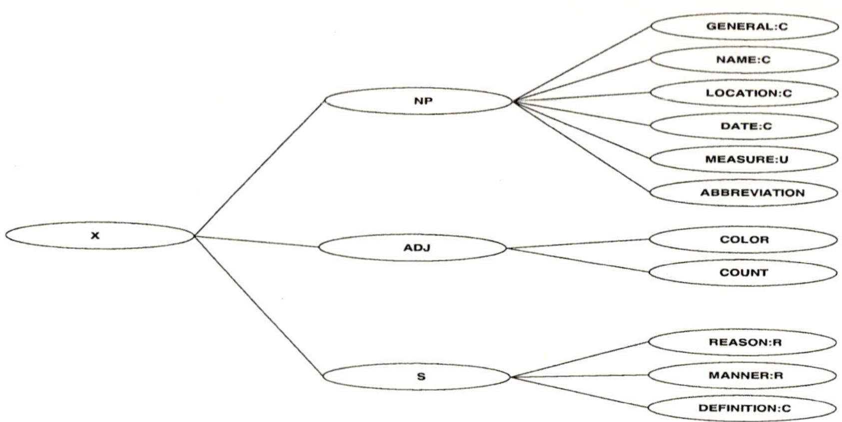

Fig. 2. The Question Type Taxonomy used in QED

eleven basic types, the values of the subtype parameters allow us to generate an infinite number of question types.

The question types are determined after the semantic analysis of the question using a rule-based system. For instance, *How hot is the sun?* is assigned the question type MEASURE:TEMPERATURE, and *Who is Janis Joplin?* the question type DEFINITION:PERSON. The question types are used by the answer selection component to constrain the set of potential answers.

2.5 Linguistic Analysis

The C&C maximum entropy POS tagger [4] is used to tag the question words and the text segments returned by the tiler. The C&C named entity tagger [5] is also applied to the question and text segments, identifying named entities from the standard MUC-7 data set (locations, organisations, persons, dates, times and monetary amounts). The POS tags and named entity tags are used to assist semantic interpretation (see Section 2.6).

We used the Radisp system [6] to parse the question and the text segments returned by the tiler. The Radisp parser returns syntactic dependencies represented by grammatical relations such as NCSUBJ (non-clausal subject), DOBJ, (direct object), NCMOD (non-clausal modifier), and so on. The set of dependencies for a sentence are annotated with POS and named entity information and converted into a graph in Prolog format.

The parser's performance on questions is not fantastic, probably because it is trained on newspaper texts. To increase the quality of the parser's output for questions, we reformulated questions in imperative form (e.g. *Name countries in Europe*) into interrogative form (*What are countries in Europe?*), and applied this reformulation technique to other question types not handled well by the parser. The Radisp parser was much better at returning the correct dependencies for these reformulated questions.

The output of the parser, a graph describing a set of dependency relations between syntactic categories, is used to build a semantic representation—both for the question under consideration and for the text passages that might contain an answer to the question. Categories contain the following information: the surface word-form, the lemmatized word-form, the word position in the sentence, the sentence position in the text, named-entity information, and a POS tag defining the category.

2.6 Semantic Interpretation

Our semantic formalism is based on Discourse Representation Theory [7], but we use an enriched form of Discourse Representation Structure (DRS), combining semantic information with syntactic and sortal information. DRSs are constructed from the dependency relations in a recursive way, starting with an empty DRS at the top node of the dependency graph, and adding semantic information to the DRS as we follow the dependency relations in the graph, using the POS information to decide on the nature of the semantic contribution of a category.

Following Discourse Representation Theory, a DRS is defined as an ordered pair of a set of discourse referents and a set of DRS-conditions. We consider the following types of DRS-conditions: `pred(x,S)`, `named(x,S)`, `card(x,S)`, `event(e,S)`, and `argN(e,x)`, `rel(x,y,S)`, `mod(x,S)`, where `e`, `x`, `y` are discourse referents, `S` a constant, and `N` a number between 1 and 3, designating an abstract semantic role. Questions introduce a special DRS-condition of the form `answer(x,T)` for a question type `T`, called the the *answer literal*. Answer literals play an important role in answer selection (see Section 2.7).

Implemented in Prolog, we reached a recall of around 80%. (By *recall* we mean the percentage of categories that contributed to semantic information in the DRS.) Note that each passage or question is translated into one single DRS, hence DRSs can span several sentences. Some basic techniques for pronoun resolution are implemented as well. However, to avoid complicating the answer extraction task too much, we only considered non-recursive DRSs in our implementation, i.e. DRSs without complex conditions introducing nested DRSs for dealing with negation, disjunction, or universal quantification.

Finally, a set of DRS normalisation rules are applied in a post-processing step, thereby dealing with active-passive alternations, question typing, inferred semantic information, and the disambiguating of noun-noun compounds. The resulting DRS is enriched with information about the original surface word-forms and POS tags, by co-indexing the words, POS tags, the discourse referents, and DRS-conditions.

2.7 Answer Selection

The answer extraction component takes as input a DRS for the question, and a set of DRSs for selected passages. The task of this component is to extract answer candidates from the passages. This is realised by performing a match between the question-DRS and a passage-DRS, by using a relaxed unification method and a scoring mechanism indicating how well two DRSs match each other.

Taking advantage of Prolog unification, we use Prolog variables for all discourse referents in the question-DRSs, and Prolog atoms in passage-DRSs. We then attempt to unify all terms of the question DRSs with terms in a passage-DRS, using an A* search algorithm. Each potential answer is associated with a score, which we call the DRS-score. High scores are obtained for perfect matches (i.e., standard unification) between terms of the question and passage, low scores for less perfect matches (i.e., obtained by "relaxed" unification). Less perfect matches are granted for different semantic types, predicates with different argument order, or terms with symbols that are semantically familiar according to WordNet [8].

After a successful match the answer literal is identified with a particular discourse referent in the passage-DRS. Recall that the DRS-conditions and discourse referents are co-indexed with the surface word-forms of the source passage text. This information is used to generate an answer string, simply by collecting the words that belong to DRS-conditions with discourse referents denoting the answer. Finally, all answer candidates are output in an ordered list. Duplicate answers are eliminated, but answer frequency information is added to each answer in this final list.

3 Evaluation and Results

3.1 Results at the CLEF-2004 Campaign

We submitted two runs for each language pair, differing in the way reranking of answers was executed. We considered two reranking parameters: S, the normalised DRS-score, and F, the normalised frequency. The answers of the first runs for each language pair (`edin041deen` and `edin041fren`) were ranked using the formula $Rank = 0.2{*}S{+}0.8{*}F$, the answers of the second runs (`edin042deen` and `edin042fren`) were ranked using the formula $Rank = 0.8 * S + 0.2 * F$ for location and measure question types, and on $Rank = 1.0 * S$ for all other question types. The weights were estimated on the basis of running QED on TREC-2003 data.

For both languages, the second runs performed the best (as expected), with an overall accuracy of 17.00% for German and 20.00% for French. The results for the factoid and definition questions are listed in Table 1 and Table 2.

Table 1. CLEF-2004 Performance of QED on Factoid Questions

Run	Right	Inexact	Unsupported	Accuracy
`edin041deen`	24	4	1	13.33%
`edin042deen`	29	5	0	16.11%
`edin041fren`	32	4	0	17.78%
`edin042fren`	37	6	0	20.56%

Table 2. CLEF-2004 Performance of QED on Definition Questions

Run	Right	Inexact	Unsupported	Accuracy
edin041deen	4	1	0	20.00%
edin042deen	5	2	0	25.00%
edin041fren	1	2	0	5.78%
edin042fren	3	1	0	15.00%

For the German edin041deen and edin042deen runs, the answer-string "NIL" was returned 47 times, and correctly returned 7 times (14.89%). For the French edin041fren and edin042fren, the answer-string "NIL" was returned 70 times, and correctly returned 11 times (15.71%). The confidence-weighted score for the four runs varied between 0.04922 and 0.05889, which is low compared to other systems, and indicates that tbere is a lot of room for improvement on self-assessment in QED.

3.2 Measuring Impact of MT

After the CLEF-2004 campaign we ran several more experiments to assess the impact of the errors introduced by the MT component. Both the French and German questions were translated from the same set of source English questions. Running the QED system on these English questions, surpassing the MT component, would give us concrete information in terms of performance loss when using off-the-shelf MT in cross-lingual QA.

Obviously, there are some problems with evaluating the results compared to the evaluation at the CLEF campaign. It is difficult to get objective judgements for exactness, and to a certain extent this also holds for the documents that support the answers. To overcome these difficulties, we compared the results of answers comprising all correct, inexact, and unsupported answers. Also, we didn't consider NIL answers in the comparison, because the relatively high number of correct NIL answers for the French run would bias the comparison considerably. We used the list of all correct answers generated by all entries of CLEF-2004 for our judgements.

The results of this experiment were interesting. For the English to English configuration, the total of correctly answered questions was 40. For French to English, the number of correct answers was 36, indicating a loss of only 10%. For German to English, the number of correct answers was 34, corresponding to a drop of 15%. Therefore, the loss of answers introduced by the MT component was reasonably low.

3.3 Error Analysis of Question Translation

In order to gain a better understanding as to where MT errors occur and how to improve the system, we performed an error analysis of the translated CLEF-2004 questions. The types of errors in the output of the MT component can be classed into nine separate categories. We will present these categories and give examples of each (some of them are hilarious, but they illustrate the difficulties in MT).

1. **Content Word**
   DE: Nenne einen Grund für Selbstmord bei Teenagern.
   EN: Name a reason for suicide with dte rodents.
2. **Word Order**
   FR: En quelle année les jeux Olympiques ont eu lieu à Barcelone?
   EN: In which year the Olympic Games did take place in Barcelona?
3. **Untranslated Word**
   FR: Quel animal roucoule?
   EN: Which animal roucoule?
4. **Translated Named Entity**
   DE: Was verkauft Faust dem Teufel?
   EN: What sells fist to the devil?
5. **Untranslated Named Entity**
   DE: Wo ist die Eremitage?
   EN: Where is the Eremitage?
6. **Mistranslated Named Entity**
   FR: Qui a écrit le Petit Prince?
   EN: Who wrote the Small Prince?
7. **Verb Form, Tense or Number**
   DE: Wer sind die Simpsons?
   EN: Who is the Simpsons?
8. **Missing Verb**
   FR: Qu'est-ce que l'UEFA?
   EN: What the UEFA?
9. **Minor**
   DE: Nenne eine Ölgesellschaft.
   EN: Name a oil company.

We classified all incorrectly translated question into one of these nine categories. In some cases more than one type of error occurred, in which case we picked the category which made the translation most incomprehensible. Table 3 lists the types of errors and their frequency in the English MT output that was obtained from the original 200 German and French questions. The table shows that the types of errors that occur are relatively language-specific, since the distribution of errors is very different for the two language pairs.

The main source of error for both systems (DE→EN: 27%; FR→EN: 35.5%) are wrong and awkwardly phrased translations of content words. For instance, in the above example, the noun "Teenagern" was mistakenly treated as the German compound "Tee+nagern". Moreover, the output quality of the French to English system also suffers from wrong word order for 11.5% of the questions which only happened 6.5% of the time when translating from German to English. The German to English system, however, produces considerably more errors when dealing with unknown words and named entities that should not be translated (see

Table 3. Source of MT errors and their frequency distributed over different categories, plus the number of correctly answered questions in each category

Type of Error	DE → EN		Correct	FR → EN		Correct
Content Word	54	27.0%	7	71	35.5%	13
Word Order	13	6.5%	1	23	11.5%	3
Untranslated Word	11	5.5%	0	7	3.5%	0
Translated Named Entity	8	4.0%	0	1	0.5%	0
Untranslated Named Entity	5	2.5%	0	4	2.0%	0
Mistranslated Named Entity	4	2.0%	0	5	2.5%	0
Verb Form, Tense or Number	8	4.0%	1	5	2.5%	0
Missing verb	0	0.0%	0	8	4.0%	0
Minor errors	22	11.0%	4	17	8.5%	3
Total incorrectly translated	125	62.5%	13	141	70.5%	19
Total correctly translated	75	37.5%	21	59	29.5%	17
Total	200	100.0%	34	200	100.0%	36

Table 3). The German to English system also makes more mistakes in choosing the correct verb form, tense and number. The French to English system on the other hand never translates the verb in questions beginning with "Qu-est-ce que" (What is). This is an error specific to the French-English language pair that never occurs for other language pair scenarios. The category "Minor errors" contains correct translations but with missing or wrong articles or wrong case which will not necessarily affect the performance of the QA system. Overall, the German to English MT system produces 8% more correct output than the French to English system.

Table 3 also lists the number of incorrectly translated questions for which our QA system nevertheless produced correct answers. Here, we refer to correct, inexact and unsupported answers as in the previous section. For German, 38.2% of correctly answered questions (13 out of 34) contain translation mistakes, including 4 questions with minor errors. For French, this percentage is considerably higher at 52.8% (19 out of 36) and includes 3 questions with minor errors.

Even though the output of the French to English MT system is of significant lower quality, it yields better QA scores than in the German to English scenario. One of the reasons for this seeming inconsistency is the fact that translation errors vary in severity. It appears that QED is still able to produce correct answers for some questions with incorrectly or awkwardly translated content words. Despite these errors, such questions still provide sufficient information and are therefore easier to answer than questions with wrong named entities, an error which was made more frequently by the German to English MT system.

Interestingly, the ratio of correctly answered to correctly translated questions is approximately the same for both languages (28.0% for German, and 28.8% for French). However, the ratio of correctly answered to incorrectly translated questions is only around 10% for the German to English system and 13% for the French to English system. This clearly shows that by further improving the quality of the MT output, the performance of the QA system can still be increased.

For future work, we suggest using several competing MT systems in a parallel architecture. Automatic MT evaluation scores like Bleu [9] could also be considered to select the best translation from a set of candidate translations if multiple engines are available. Questions translated by multiple MT systems could be used together as query expansions. Another proposed extension is recognition (and alignment) of Named Entities in source and target questions to avoid literal translations of proper nouns (for instance, *Spielberg→play mountain* and *Neufeld→new field*).

4 Conclusion

We have presented extensions to a mono-lingual QA system to enable it for a cross-lingual task. Our approach consisted of composing existing software (with minor enhancements) for machine translation and question answering in a sequential pipeline. The translation was enhanced using pattern replacements to correct systematic mistakes. We obtained an accuracy of 16% (German to English) and 20% (French to English), respectively, for answering factoid questions. For definition questions, we obtained an accuracy of 25% (German to English) and 15% (French to English), respectively. Definition questions constituted a minor portion of the test set.

We showed that it is feasible to use out-of-the-box machine translation software to transform a monolingual QA system into a multilingual one. Despite the large number of translation mistakes, the majority do not affect the overall result of question answering, and some simple pre- and postprocessing rules can successfully deal with systematic errors. For the questions at the CLEF-2004 campaign, the loss of correct answers for French to English was only 10%, and for German to English 15%, compared to English to English processing. Only considering correctly translated questions, the accuracy of the system was 28% for German and 29% for French on factoid and definition questions.

Acknowledgements

We are grateful to Steve Clark, James Curran, Malvina Nissim, and Bonnie Webber for assistance and helpful discussions, and would like to thank the system administrators Bill Hewitt and Andrew Woods for their computing support. Special thanks go to John Carroll for his help with the Radisp parser, and in general to all developers of all external programs that we used in QED. We also would like to thank Bernardo Magnini, Carol Peters, Maarten de Rijke (in particular for supplying us with a crucial password at a crucial time), and Alessandro Vallin for all organisational CLEF issues they dealt with so adequately.

Alex is supported by Scottish Enterprise Edinburgh-Stanford Link (R36759), the Economic and Social Research Council, UK and the School of Informatics, University of Edinburgh. Dalmas is supported by the School of Informatics, University of Edinburgh. Leidner is supported by the German Academic Exchange Service (DAAD) under scholarship D/02/01831 and by Linguit GmbH (research contract UK-2002/2).

References

1. Leidner, J.L., Bos, J., Dalmas, T., Curran, J.R., Clark, S., Bannard, C.J., Steedman, M., Webber, B.: The QED open-domain answer retrieval system for TREC 2003. In: Proceedings of the Twelfth Text Retrieval Conference (TREC 2003). NIST Special Publication 500-255, Gaithersburg, MD (2004) 595–599.
2. Voorhees, E.M.: Overview of TREC 2003. In: Proceedings of the Twelfth Text Retrieval Conference (TREC 2003). NIST Special Publication 500-255, Gaithersburg, MD (2004) 1–13.
3. Magnini, B., Romagnoli, S., Vallin, A., Herrera, J., Peñas, A., Peinado, V., Verdejo, F., de Rijke, M.: Creating the DISEQuA corpus: a test set for multilingual question answering. In Peters, C., ed.: Working Notes for the CLEF 2003 Workshop, Trondheim, Norway (2003).
4. Curran, J.R., Clark, S.: Investigating GIS and smoothing for maximum entropy taggers. In: Proceedings of the 11th Annual Meeting of the European Chapter of the Association for Computational Linguistics (EACL'03), Budapest, Hungary (2003) 91–98.
5. Curran, J.R., Clark, S.: Language independent NER using a maximum entropy tagger. In: Proceedings of the Seventh Conference on Natural Language Learning (CoNLL-03), Edmonton, Canada (2003) 164–167.
6. Briscoe, T., Carroll, J.: Robust accurate statistical annotation of general text. In: Proceedings of the 3rd International Conference on Language Resources and Evaluation, Las Palmas, Gran Canaria (2002) 1499–1504.
7. Kamp, H., Reyle, U.: From Discourse to Logic; An Introduction to Modeltheoretic Semantics of Natural Language, Formal Logic and DRT. Kluwer, Dordrecht (1993).
8. Fellbaum, C., ed.: WordNet. An Electronic Lexical Database. The MIT Press (1998).
9. Papineni, K., Roukos, S., Ward, T., Zhu, W.J.: Bleu: a method for automatic evaluation of machine translation. Technical Report RC22176 (W0109-022), IBM Thomas J. Watson Research Center (2001).

Bulgarian-English Question Answering: Adaptation of Language Resources

Petya Osenova[1], Alexander Simov[1], Kiril Simov[1], Hristo Tanev[2], and Milen Kouylekov[2]

[1] Laboratory for Linguistic Modelling,
Bulgarian Academy of Sciences, Bulgaria
{petya, alex, kivs}@bultreebank.org
[2] ITC-irst, Trento, Italy
{tanev, kouylekov}@itc.it

Abstract. This paper describes the Bulgarian part of a Bulgarian–English question answering system. The Bulgarian modules are implemented as a question analysis procedure within a Bulgarian question answering system — **BulQA**. The paper presents the available language resources and corresponding technology which is used for the analysis of the questions in Bulgarian and their translation into English format, which is necessary for answer extraction. CLaRK System is used as an implementation platform.

1 Introduction

This paper describes the first steps in the development of a question answering system for Bulgarian — **BulQA**. The system is planned to have three main modules: *Question analysis module*, *Interface module*, *Answer extraction module*. The *Question analysis module* deals with the syntactic and semantic interpretation of the question. The result of this module is independent from task and domain representation of the syntactic and semantic information in the question. The *Interface module* bridges the interpretation received from the first module to the input necessary for the third module. The *Answer extraction module* is responsible for the actual detection of the answer in the corresponding corpus. This architecture allows reusing some of these modules in other tasks, such as Bulgarian as source language in a multilingual question answering, or Bulgarian as a target language. In general, only *the Interface module* has to be re-implemented in order to tune the connection between Bulgarian modules and the modules for the other languages.

Here we describe the current question analysis module and the *Interface module* in a Bulgarian to English question answering system. In this system the *Answer searching module* is based on the Diogene system implemented at the ITC-Irst, Trento, Italy.

The structure of the paper is as follows: first we describe the language resources and tools developed within the BulTreeBank Project; then in section

C. Peters et al. (Eds.): CLEF 2004, LNCS 3491, pp. 458–469, 2005.

3 we discuss their adaptation for the analysis of Bulgarian questions; section 4 describes briefly the DIOGENE system for document retrieval and answer extraction; in section 5 we discuss the interface between the system BulQA for the analysis of Bulgarian questions and DIOGENE System; section 6 gives a general overview of the CLaRK System in which the modules of BulQA are implemented; the last section reports on the results of the question answering track and concludes the paper.

2 The BulTreeBank Language Resources and Tools

In this section we describe the available language resources and tools which we have adapted in order to implement *the Question analysis module* for Bulgarian. Generally, a language technology is supposed to include the following modules: tokenization and named entities recognition, morphological analyzer and disambiguator, syntactic and semantic analyzer. Most of them have already been implemented during the creation of the syntactic treebank for Bulgarian — [12].

2.1 BulTreeBank Language Technology

Here we list the tools that we had at our disposal before the implementation of our system:

Tokenizers. There is a hierarchy of tokenizers within the CLaRK system (see below), which tokenizes the texts in an appropriate way. Additionally, one can decide what the category of the token is and assign it.

The Morphosyntactic Analyzer. It assigns all possible analyses to the word tokens. The lexicon is too large to be loaded as one grammar in CLaRK and this is why we have divided it into several grammars which are applied in a group. The separation of the lexicon is on the basis of the frequencies of the word forms. In this way the application has been speeded up. As it was mentioned above, together with the morphosyntactic analyzer we use the gazetteers, which are also implemented within the CLaRK system. Where competing analyses arise between a common word and a name or an abbreviation, we try to use the token classification strategy and the prompts of the context. The token classification strategy is a procedure for analyzing tokens into common words, names or abbreviations — [7].

MorphoSyntactic Disambiguator. We have already implemented a preliminary version of a rule-based morpho-syntactic disambiguator, encoded as a set of constraints within the CLaRK system. This rule-based disambiguator exploits context information like *agreement between an adjective and a noun in a noun phrase*, specific positions like *a noun after a preposition*, but it also deals with some fixed phrases. The disambiguator does not try to solve unsure cases, but leaves them for further processing. Its coverage is about 80 %. For automatic disambiguation we have developed a neural-network-based disambiguator — [11]. It achieves accuracy of 95.25% for part-of-speech and 93.17% for complete morphosyntactic disambiguation.

Partial Grammars. We have constructed grammars for:

1. **Sentence splitting.** At the moment it is fully automated and reliable only for basic and clear cases. For solving complex and ambiguous cases this grammar is combined with supporting modules for abbreviation detection.
2. **Named-entity recognition.** Identifying numerical expressions, names, abbreviations, special symbols — [2], [6]. They are designed to work in cooperation with the morphosyntactic analyzer. If necessary, the grammars can overwrite the analysis of the morphosyntactic analyzer.
3. **Chunking.** Two basic modules have been developed: an NP chunker — [5], [6] — and a VP chunker — [16]. Generally speaking, the chunking process conforms to the following requirements: it deals with non-recursive constituents; relies on a clear-indicator strategy; delays the attachment decisions; ignores the semantic information; aims at accuracy, not coverage. Additionally, there are chunk grammars for APs, AdvPs, PPs and some non-problematic clauses.

2.2 BulTreeBank Language Data

Among the language resources the most important for the task are the lexicons:

The Morphological Dictionary. The dictionary is an electronic version of [9] extended with new words from the corpus. It covers the grammatical information of about 100 000 lexemes (1 600 000 word forms) and serves as a basis for the morphological analyzer.

The Gazetteers. Three basic lists with items, missing in the morphological dictionary, have been compiled with respect to their frequency:

1. Gazetteers of names. These consist of 15 000 items and include Bulgarian as well as foreign person names, international and national locations, organizations. The most frequent names are additionally classified according to three criteria: (1) grammatical (gender and number); (2) semantic - with respect to an extended SIMPLE core ontology (names for different types of locations, organizations, artifacts, persons' social roles etc.) and (3) ontological - some person names were connected with specific individuals in the world and thus some encyclopedic information was provided in addition to the semantic classification. All this information was ready to be used for practical applications like Information Extraction, Question Answering etc. Special attention was paid to the names of mountains and artifacts (books, films, broadcasts), because their internal agreement does not always coincide with the external one, which is an important fact for the sentence analysis.
2. Gazetteers of abbreviations. They consist of 1500 acronyms and graphical abbreviations. The acronyms' extensions were mapped against the names (mostly organizations) and therefore, assigned the same semantic and grammatical label. In cases of idiosyncratic grammatical behaviour, the relevant patterns have been added as well.

3. Gazetteers of the most frequent introductory expressions and parentheticals. This is considered to be a step towards a basic list of collocations. They were classified according to their morphological type or behavior: verbal, adverbial, linking (for conjunctions), nominal (vocatives), idiomatic etc. We used them as an extended supplementary lexicon during the phase of the syntactic annotation.

The Valence Dictionary. It consists of 1000 most frequent verbs and their valence frames and it is based on a paper dictionary — [1]. Each frame defines the number and the kind of the arguments and imposes morphosyntactic and semantic restrictions on them. The semantic restrictions on the arguments are extracted and matched against the SIMPLE core ontology. The frames of the most frequent verbs are compared to the corpus data and repaired if necessary (new frames are added, some of the existing frames are deleted or fine-grained). We envisage to enlarge the coverage of the dictionary with the help of some derivational means, such as the verb prefixes.

The Semantic Dictionary. Semantic information plays a crucial role in the process of named entity recognition. Thus, in order to support the selectional restrictions imposed by the valence dictionary and to facilitate its usage, we decided to compile a semantic dictionary along the guidelines of SIMPLE project. It is worth mentioning that we follow an extended variant of the SIMPLE core ontology. At the moment we are classifying the most frequent nouns with respect to the ontological hierarchy without specifying the synonymic relations between them. Up to now we have classified about 3 000 nouns. Recall that the named entities also have been classified with respect to the same ontology.

3 Adaptation to Question Answering Task

Although the above listed language processing tools were extensively tested during the compilation of our treebank, they needed some additional tuning to the task of question analysis. The main difference is that most of them were implemented in such a way that in unsure cases the ambiguity remained unresolved or the analysis was not produced. This tools' application was required when an annotator had to inspect the result of the processing.

With respect to the Question Answering task some ambiguities were resolved in the following way: (1) in ambiguities between 2nd and 3rd person or 1st and 3rd person, always the 3rd person was selected; (2) in ambiguities between present and past verb tense, the past tense was selected, etc. The first ambiguity was resolved because the questions given in CLEF are never in 1 or 2 person. Resolving between the different tenses in the question with respect to validation of the found answers is not currently supported by the Answer extraction module. Some other ambiguities we resolved on a frequency basis only — for each ambiguity class the most frequent option was selected.

The major addition with respect to the available tools was the construction of a lemmatizer for Bulgarian. We defined the lemma to be functionally determined by the wordform and its morphosyntactic characteristics. The cases of ambiguous lemmas were not resolved and all possible lemmas were assigned to the corresponding wordform. Lemmas are also used later to access the semantic information from the semantic dictionary and the English equivalents in the Bulgarian–English dictionary.

Here is an example of the analysis of the question "Prez koya godina Tomas Man poluchi Nobelova nagrada?" (in English: *Which year did Thomas Mann receive the Nobel Prize?*):

```
<analysis group="BTB">
    <PP>
        <Prep><w ana="R" bf="prez">Prez</w></Prep>
        <NPA>
            <Pron><w ana="Pie-os-f" bf="koya">koya</w></Pron>
            <N><w ana="Ncfsi" bf="godina">godina</w></N>
        </NPA>
    </PP>
    <NPA sort="NE-Pers">
        <N><name ana="Npmsi" sort="PersNE">Tomas</name></N>
        <H><name ana="Hmsi" sort="PersNE">Man</name></H>
    </NPA>
    <V><w ana="Vpptf-o3s" bf="polucha">poluchi</w></V>
    <NPA>
        <A><w ana="Hfsi" bf="nobelov">Nobelova</w></A>
        <N><w ana="Ncfsi" bf="nagrada">nagrada</w></N>
    </NPA>
    <pt>?</pt>
</analysis>
```

Here each common word is annotated within the following XML element ⟨*w ana="MSD" bf="LemmaList"*⟩*wordform*⟨*/w*⟩, where the value of attribute *ana* is the correct morpho-syntactic tag for the wordform in the given context. The value of the attribute *bf* is a list of the lemmas assigned to the wordform. Names are annotated within the following XML element ⟨*name ana="MSD" sort="Sort"*⟩*Name*⟨*/name*⟩, where the value of the attribute *ana* is the same as above. The value of the attribute *sort* determines whether this is a name of a person, a location, an organization or some other entity.

The next level of analysis is the result of the chunk grammars. In the example there are three *NPA* elements (NPA stands for a noun phrase of head-adjunct type) and one *PP* element. Also, one of the noun phrases is annotated as a name with a sort attribute with value: *NE-Pers.*

The result of this analysis had to be translated into the format which the answer extraction module uses as an input.

4 DIOGENE System in Brief

In this section we briefly describe DIOGENE System which was used for document retrieval and answer extraction. DIOGENE — [4] — relies on the knowledge in multilingual ontology MultiWordNet — [8], manually created rules for named entity recognition and question type identification, a set of handcrafted answer extraction templates and statistical information collected from the Web and off-line multilingual corpora.

In its cross-language mode the DIOGENE system works as follows:

1. The question is processed and all the possible translations of the keywords from the source language into English are found (for the Bulgarian-English task this is performed in the BulQA system).
2. Finding correct combination of translations: We always chose the combination of keyword translations (k_1, k_2,. . .,k_n) which had the highest frequency of co-occurrence in an English corpus (we used AQUAINT and TIPSTER collections). The main assumption is: the more often a keyword translation combination appears with the translations close to each other (in one and the same paragraph), the more plausible this combination is.
3. From keywords and their synonyms DIOGENE forms a Boolean query which is passed to Managing Gigabytes (MG) search engine. Some keywords can be deleted from the query if it generates no hit or just a few hits. In this way several feedback loops can be performed. The output of this processing stage is a list of paragraphs where question keywords and their synonyms appear together.
4. Named entity recognition and answer extraction templates are applied to extract candidate answers. In the cross-language mode DIOGENE applies answer extraction templates just for the definition questions. Candidate answers of the factoid questions are captured using named entity recognition and proximity to the question keywords.
5. Finally, the candidate-answers of the factoid questions are evaluated using Web based answer validation technique described in [3]. On the other hand, we evaluate the answers of the definition questions using different syntactic and semantic clues,such as the presence of hyponym of the "person" or "organization" concept, the presence of definite lexical templates, etc.

The format which had to be supplied to DIOGENE System was as follows:

- **Head of the question**. The head of each question depends on the interrogative word in the question and helps to determine the kind of the answer. Some examples of question heads are: *what*, *who*, *what-who* etc.
- **Type of the question**. It determines the semantic category of the possible answers.
- **Head word of the question**. It is the word in the question which provides the type of question. It can be a non-functional word or the interrogative word.
- **Sense of the head word**. This is the sense derived from WordNet for the head word. If such a sense cannot be determined, then the value is *NIL*.

- **Part of speech of the head word.** This is the POS tag of the head word with respect to the Pentreebank tagset.
- **Position of the head word.** A digit which determines where in the question the head word is.
- **List of key words.** A list of the non-functional words in the question. Each keyword is also annotated with its part of speech.

5 Interface Module

Here we describe the implemented interface module which translates the result of the question analysis module into the template necessary for DIOGENE System, which extracts the answers of the questions. The process includes the following steps:

- Determining the head of the question.
  The determination of the question head was performed by searching for the chunk which contains the interrogative pronoun. There were cases in which the question was expressed with the help of imperative forms of verbs: *nazovete* (name-plural!), *kazhete* (point out-plural!; say-plural!), *izbrojte* (list-plural!; enumerate-plural!). After the chunk selection we classify the interrogative pronoun within a hierarchy of question's heads. In this hierarchy some other elements of the chunks — mainly prepositions — play an important role as well.
- Determining the head word of the question and its semantic type.
  The chunk determined in the previous step also is used for determining the head word of the question. There are five cases. First, the chunk is an NP chunk in which the interrogative pronoun is a modifier. In this case the head noun is the head word of the question. For example, in the question: **What nation** *is the main weapons supplier to Third World countries?* the noun 'nation' is the head word of the question. In the second case the chunk is a PP chunk in which there is an NP chunk similar to the NP chunk from the previous case. Thus, again the head noun is a head word for the question. For example, in the question: **In what music genre** *does Michael Jackson excel?* the noun 'genre' is the head word of the question. Third, the interrogative pronoun is a complement of a copula verb and there is a subject NP. In this case the head word of the question is the head noun of the subject NP chunk of the copula. For example, in the question: **What** *is a basic ingredient of Japanese cuisine?* 'ingredient' is the head of the question. The fourth case covers the questions with imperative verbs. Then again the head of the question is the head noun of the complement NP chunk. For example, in the question: *Give a symptom of the Ebola virus.* the noun 'symptom' is the head of the question. The last case covers all the remaining questions. Then the head word of the question is the interrogative phrase (or word) itself. For example, in the question: **When** *was the Convention on the Rights of the Child adopted?* the head of the question is the interrogative word 'when'. The semantic type of the head word is determined by the

annotation of the words with semantic classes from the semantic dictionary. When there are more than one semantic classes we add all of them. The type of the interrogative pronoun is used later for disambiguation. If no semantic class is available in the dictionary, then the class 'other' is assigned.

- Determining the type of the question.
  The type of the question is determined straightforwardly by the semantic type of the head word.
- Determining the keywords of the question and their part of speech.
  The keywords are determined by the non-functional words in the question. Their part of speech is determined by a function from the Bulgarian tagset into the tagset used by DIOGENE System. Sometimes it is possible to construct multi-token keywords, such as names (Thomas Mann), terms or collocations (Nobel prize). This is done after the translation into English.
- Translation of the question head word and the keywords into English.
  We have two Bulgarian–English dictionaries: one for the common vocabulary and one for the names. The dictionary of names contains the transliterations of most frequent names that we found in both Bulgarian and English corpora. This dictionary is necessary because a vast amount of foreign names do not follow the same transliteration principles for Bulgarian. For instance, Washington as a name of the president George Washington, the state Washington and the capital of the USA is written as *Vashington*, which follows the literal traditional transliteration, i.e. letter by letter. However, in all other cases this name is written as *Uoshingtyn*, which follows the new principles of transliteration, i.e. closer to the original pronunciation of the word. For the names which are not in the dictionary we apply the transliteration from Bulgarian into Latin as it is defined by the Bulgarian Post Services. Note that the last solution is far form perfect and it has to be improved afterwards. The main problem is that this transliteration does not take into account the sound representation of the names in the original language. For instance, the name Thomas (*Tomas* in Bulgarian) will be transliterated as Tomas without 'h'. This problem will require much more work in future. Some names of famous people and places are kept as one complex expression in the dictionary. For example, 'Thomas Mann' is a multi-token name in the dictionary. This helps us during the translation phase: for example, if we take the two names separately, we can receive, wrongly, also Thomas Man as a potential translation, where 'Man' is transliterated with one 'n'. For the words which have more than one translation we give all possibilities.
  Another very useful resource at this stage is the collocation dictionary for English. For example, the chunk *Nobelova nagrada* (Nobel prize) is a collocation in English, but we also translate it into Bulgarian as 'Nobel award'. If we have a collocation dictionary we could use it in order to recognize such multi-token expressions. In future work we also will try to use the Internet to judge statistically between the different possibilities. For the above examples, 'Nobel prize' is much more frequent than 'Nobel award'.

Here we give the result of the analysis for the first mentioned question:

```
<analysis group="BTB">
  <QHead qhead="what" qtype="time">
    <PP>
      <Prep><w>Prez</w></Prep>
      <NPA>
        <Pron><w>koya</w></Pron>
        <N><w sort="time" eng="year">godina</w></N>
      </NPA>
    </PP>
  </QHead>
  <NPA sort="NE-Pers">
    <N><name sort="Pers" eng="Thomas">Tomas</name></N>
    <H><name sort="Pers" eng="Mann;Man">Man</name></H>
  </NPA>
  <V><w eng="get,receive;obtain">poluchi</w></V>
  <NPA>
    <A><w eng="Nobel">Nobelova</w></A>
    <N><w sort="other" eng="prize;award">nagrada</w></N>
  </NPA>
 <pt>?</pt>
</analysis>
```

Here the new element is *QHead* which determines the chunk head of the question. It has two attributes: *qhead* which has the question head — *what* as a value in the example; and *qtype* which has as a value the type of the question — *time* here. Some of the words received additional attributes: *sort* for the semantic class of the word, and *eng* for the possible translations into English.

– Filling in the template.
  This step means the conversion of the information that has already been explicated into the form necessary for the DIOGENE System. Here also we tried to produce multi-token keywords. In the example above, such a keyword is Thomas Mann — a name that we had in the dictionary.

All the steps during the analysis of the questions and their transformation into the DIOGENE format were implemented in the CLaRK system, which is shortly described in the next section.

6 CLaRK System

In this section we describe the basic technologies of the CLaRK System — [10] (`http://www.bultreebank.org/clark`). CLaRK is an XML-based software system for corpora development. It incorporates several technologies: *XML technology*; *Unicode*; *Regular Grammars*; and *Constraints overon XML Documents.*

XML Technology. The XML technology is at the heart of the CLaRK System. It is implemented as a set of utilities for data structuring, manipulation and management. We have chosen the XML technology because of its popularity, its ease of understanding and its already wide use in description of linguistic information. In addition to the XML language — [17] — processor itself, we have implemented an XPath language — [18] — engine for navigation in documents and an XSLT engine — [19] — for transformation of XML documents. We started with basic facilities for creation, editing, storing and querying XML documents and developed this inventory further into a powerful system for processing not only single XML documents but an integrated set of documents and constraints over them. The main goal of this development is to allow the user to add the desirable semantics to the XML documents. The XPath language is used extensively to direct the processing of the document pointing where to apply a certain tool. It is also used to check whether some conditions are present in a set of documents.

Tokenization. The CLaRK System supports a user-defined hierarchy of tokenizers. At the very basic level the user can define a tokenizer in terms of a set of token types. In this basic tokenizer each token type is defined by a set of UNICODE symbols. Above this basic level tokenizers the user can define other tokenizers for which the token types are defined as regular expressions over the tokens of some other tokenizer, the so called parent tokenizer. For each tokenizer an alphabetical order over the token types is defined. This order is used for operations like the comparison between two tokens, sorting and similar operations.

Regular Grammars. The regular grammars in CLaRK System — [13] — work on token and element values generated from the content of an XML document and they incorporate their results back in the document as XML mark-up. The tokens are determined by the corresponding tokenizer. The element values are defined with the help of XPath expressions, which determine the important information for each element. In the grammars, the token and element values are described by token and element descriptions. These descriptions could contain wildcard symbols and variables. The variables are shared among the token descriptions within a regular expression and can be used for the treatment of phenomena like agreement. The grammars are applied in cascaded manner. The evaluation of the regular expressions, which define the rules, can be guided by the user. We allow the following strategies for evaluation: 'longest match', 'shortest match' and several backtracking strategies.

Constraints on XML Documents. The constraints that we have implemented in the CLaRK System are generally based on the XPath language — [14]. We use XPath expressions to determine some data within one or several XML documents and thus we evaluate some predicates over the data. Generally, there are two modes of using a constraint. In the first mode the constraint is used for validity check, similarly to the validity check based on a DTD or an XML schema. In the second mode, the constraint is used to support the change of the document to satisfy the constraint. The constraints in the CLaRK System are defined in the following way: (`Selector, Condition, Event, Action`), where the selector defines to which node(s) in the document the constraint is applicable. The condition defines the state of the document when the constraint is applied. The condition is stated as an XPath expression, which is evaluated with respect to each node, selected by the selector. If the result from the evaluation is improved, then the constraint is applied. The event defines when this constraint is checked for application. Such events can be: selection of a menu item, pressing of key shortcut, an editing command. The action defines the way of the actual constraint application.

Cascaded Processing. The central idea behind the CLaRK System is that every XML document can be seen as a "blackboard" on which different tools write some information, reorder it or delete it. The user can arrange the applications of the different tools to achieve the required processing. For more on application construction abilities of CLaRK System — [15].

7 Results and Outlook

The result from the Bulgarian–English QA track are: 26 out of the 200 extracted answers were correct, 168 were wrong, 5 inexact and 1 unsupported. The distribution of the correct answers among the question categories is as follows: 5 definition questions: 2 for organizations and 3 for persons; 21 factoid questions: 5 for locations, 2 for manner, 1 for measure, 2 for objects, 1 for organizations, 2 for other categories, 4 for persons, and 4 for time. The main problem that caused wrong answer extraction was the degree of the ambiguity in the translation from Bulgarian to English. Interestingly, the percentage of the ambiguities for nouns had bigger impact on the results than the ambiguity of verbs. Another problem is that our semantic dictionary does not have a mapping to the English WordNet synsets. Such a connection is necessary for the better performance of the answer extraction in DIOGENE System.

Our plans for future work are in two directions. Firstly, we plan to implement a complete question answering system for Bulgarian. Secondly, with respect to the Bulgarian–English task we envisage extending the dictionaries, to map our semantic dictionary (at least the top part) to the WordNet synsets and to implement an efficient translation disambiguation module.

References

1. Balabanova, E., Ivanova, K.: Creating a Machine-Readable Version of Bulgarian Valence Dictionary: (A case study of CLaRK system application). Proceedings of The TLT Workshop. Sozopol, Bulgaria. (2002) 1–12
2. Ivanova, K., Doikoff, D.: Cascaded Regular Grammars and Constraints over Morphologically Annotated Data for Ambiguity Resolution. Proceedings of The TLT Workshop. Sozopol, Bulgaria. (2002) 96–113

3. Magnini, B., Negri, M., Prevete, R., Tanev, H.: Comparing Statistical and Content-Based Techniques for Answer Validation on the Web. Proceedings of the VIII Convegno AI*IA, Siena, Italy. (2002)
4. Negri M., Tanev H., and Magnini B.: Bridging Languages for Question Answering: DIOGENE at CLEF-2003. Proceedings of CLEF-2003, Trondheim, Norway. (2003) 321–330
5. Osenova, P.: Bulgarian Nominal Chunks and Mapping Strategies for Deeper Syntactic Analyses. Proceedings of The TLT Workshop. Sozopol, Bulgaria. (2002) 150–166
6. Osenova, P., Kolkovska, S.: Combining the named-entity recognition task and NP chunking strategy for robust pre-processing. Proceedings of The TLT Workshop. Sozopol, Bulgaria. (2002) 167–182
7. Osenova P., Simov, K.: Learning a token classification from a large corpus. (A case study in abbreviations). Proceedings of the ESSLLI Workshop on Machine Learning Approaches in Computational Linguistics, Trento, Italy. (2002) 16–28
8. Pianta, E., Bentivogli, L., Girardi, C.: MULTIWORDNET: Developing an Aligned Multilingual Database. Proceedings of the 1st International Global WordNet Conference, Mysore, India. (2002)
9. Popov, D., Simov, K., Vidinska, S.: A Dictionary of Writing, Pronunciation and Punctuation of Bulgarian Language. Atlantis LK, Sofia, Bulgaria. (1998)
10. Simov, K., Peev, Z., Kouylekov, M., Simov, A., Dimitrov, M., Kiryakov, A.: CLaRK — an XML-based System for Corpora Development. Proceedings of the Corpus Linguistics 2001 Conference. (2001) 558–560
11. Simov, K., Osenova, P.: A Hybrid System for MorphoSyntactic Disambiguation in Bulgarian. Proceedings of the RANLP 2001, Tzigov chark, Bulgaria. (2001) 288–290
12. Simov, K., Popova, G., Osenova, P.: HPSG-based syntactic treebank of Bulgarian (BulTreeBank). A Rainbow of Corpora: Corpus Linguistics and the Languages of the World, edited by Andrew Wilson, Paul Rayson, and Tony McEnery; Lincom-Europa, Munich. (2002) 135–142
13. Simov, K., Kouylekov, M., Simov, A.: Cascaded Regular Grammars over XML Documents. Proceedings of the 2nd Workshop on NLP and XML (NLPXML-2002), Taipei, Taiwan. (2002)
14. Simov, K., Simov, A., Kouylekov, M.: Constraints for Corpora Development and Validation. Proceedings of the Corpus Linguistics 2003 Conference. (2003) 698–705
15. Simov, K., Simov, A., Osenova, P.: An XML Architecture for Shallow and Deep Processing. Proceedings of the ESSLLI 2004 Workshop on Combining Shallow and Deep Processing for NLP. Nancy, France. (2004) 51–60
16. Slavcheva, M.: Segmentation Layers in the Group of the Predicate: a Case Study of Bulgarian within the BulTreeBank Framework. Proceedings of The TLT Workshop. Sozopol, Bulgaria. (2002) 199–210
17. XML: Extensible Markup Language (XML) 1.0 (Second Edition). W3C Recommendation. http://www.w3.org/TR/REC-xml. (2000)
18. XPath: XML Path Language (XPath) version 1.0. W3C Recommendation. http://www.w3.org/TR/xpath. (1999)
19. XSLT: XSL Transformations (XSLT). version 1.0. W3C Recommendation. http://www.w3.org/TR/xslt. (1999)

Answering French Questions in English by Exploiting Results from Several Sources of Information

Brigitte Grau[1], Gabriel Illouz[1], Laura Monceaux[2], Isabelle Robba[1], Anne Vilnat[1] Guillaume Bourdil[1], Faïza Elkateb-Gara[1], Olivier Ferret[3], and Benoît Mathieu[3]

[1] LIR group, LIMSI-CNRS, BP 133, 91403 Orsay Cedex
firstName.name@limsi.fr
[2] LINA, 2 rue de la Houssinière, BP 92208, 44332 Nantes Cedex 3
firstName.name@lina.univ-nantes.fr
[3] LIC2M, CEA-LIST, BP 6, 92265 Fontenay-aux-Roses
firstName.name@cea.fr

Abstract. Our bilingual QA system MUSCLEF, is based on QALC, the monolingual system with which we have participated in the previous TREC[1], where our best results were obtained when we combined the results of several searches. First, QALC searched a reliable document collection for answers, and second the WEB. We kept this strategy for CLEF, returning two runs. In the first one, we modified QALC so as to handle multilinguality by translating the terms identified in the question. In the second run, we combined the results of the first run with those obtained by first translating the question, then applying the full QALC strategy i.e. searching both the collection and the WEB. The final evaluation confirms the fact that the best results are obtained by combining different sources of information.

1 Introduction

Open-domain Question-Answering (QA) is a growing area of research whose aim is to find precise answers to questions in natural language, unlike search engines that return whole documents. When these engines also return snippets, as Google[2], they aim at providing justifications of documents rather than just giving an answer. One challenge in this field consists in finding only one answer in which we are sufficiently confident. The approach we developed in QALC, our monolingual English question answering system, consists in estimating the reliability of an answer by scoring it according to the kind of knowledge or the kind of process used for its elaboration. However, we found that providing just an endogenous estimation with respect to the collection was not sufficient. Thus,

[1] TREC evaluations are campaigns organised by the NIST: http://trec.nist.gov
[2] http://www.google.com

C. Peters et al. (Eds.): CLEF 2004, LNCS 3491, pp. 470–481, 2005.

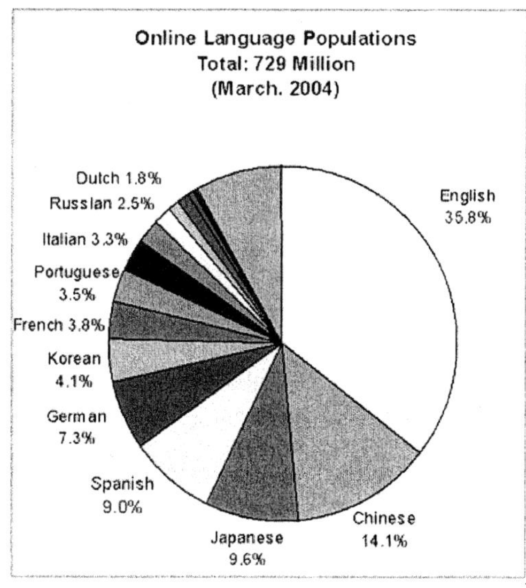

Fig. 1. The languages on the Web

we decided to apply our system on another source of knowledge in order to confront the results provided by both sources. We chose then to favour propositions common to both sources over unique ones, even if the latter had a high score. Because such reasoning applies better if the sources of knowledge are different enough, we chose the Web as second source. Moreover, the diversity and redundancy of the Web lead to find a lot of answers, as we can see in [9], [10], [5] and [3].

In CLEF evaluation, the problem is to adapt this strategy in a multilingual context. Moreover, we must take into account the fact that the interest in using the Web (i.e. its redundancy), is only effective in English, as proved[3] by Figure 1. Thus, searching the French Web would not give as significant results as searching the English Web. For CLEF evaluation, we developed MUSCLEF (Multilingual System for CLEF) which uses two strategies. The first one consists in analyzing the French question, translating "interesting parts", and then using these translated terms to search the reference collection. MUSQAT, which is our multilingual module, follows this strategy. The second strategy consists in translating the question in English using a professional version of Systran (which was possible thanks to CEA), then, applying QALC, our existing monolingual system, including the Web search. The first strategy corresponds to our first run, while we did the second run with the combination of the multilingual and the two monolingual results (browsing both the collection and the Web).

[3] This figure is extracted from the Centre for Public Policy of the University of Melbourne: www.public-policy.unimelb.edu.au/egovernance/papers/33_Skidmore.pdf

After introducing our approach to multilingualism, we present the global architecture of MUSCLEF (MUSQAT and QALC), and then detail MUSQAT, the multilingual module.

2 Multilingualism: Different Approaches

In Question Answering, several solutions exist for dealing with multilingualism. The first one consists in using machine translation for the question. In this first case, the advantage for us is that our monolingual system may then be applied without any modification. The major problem is that automatic translation does not deal correctly with disambiguation problems in open-domain question-answering systems. Machine translation is the solution we adopted as a basic line for the CLEF 04 campaign. The second solution consists in translating the complete collection of documents. In this second case, the translation may be guided by the context, and the system does not have to be changed. A major drawback is that the collection size is n times its initial length for n languages! Another difficult problem is posed by the impossibility to translate the whole Web! The last solution is to proceed to the analysis of the question in the source language (French in our case), and then to translate only the information produced by the analysis. In this solution, we do not try to obtain a complete translation: only the terms that are considered important by the analysis are translated. It is the solution we adopted for our multilingual module, which we detail in the following paragraphs, after presenting an overview of the MUSCLEF system.

3 Overview of MUSCLEF

The global architecture of MUSCLEF is illustrated in Figure 2. First, its question analysis module aims at deducing characteristics which may help to find possible answers in selected passages and to reformulate questions in a declarative form dedicated to the Web search engine (Google). These characteristics are the question focus, the main verb and syntactic relations for modifiers. We focused our translation efforts on these elements, as explained in the next section. For CLEF 04 campaign, we developed a new version of this module for questions in French. The analysis is based on the results of the French version of XIP, the robust syntactic parser of Xerox [2]. For the analysis of the translated question, we use IFSP, another robust syntactic parser of Xerox[1]. We made an evaluation of the French question analysis module for questions whose answer type is a named entity. For these 119 questions, recall is 95% and precision is 97%.

Queries are not the same for the Web search and for the CLEF collection search. In the last case, we use MG[4] for retrieving passages. For querying the Web, we choose to send a nearly exact formulation of the answer assuming that the Web redundancy would always provide documents.

[4] MG for Managing Gigabytes http://www.cs.mu.oz.au/mg/

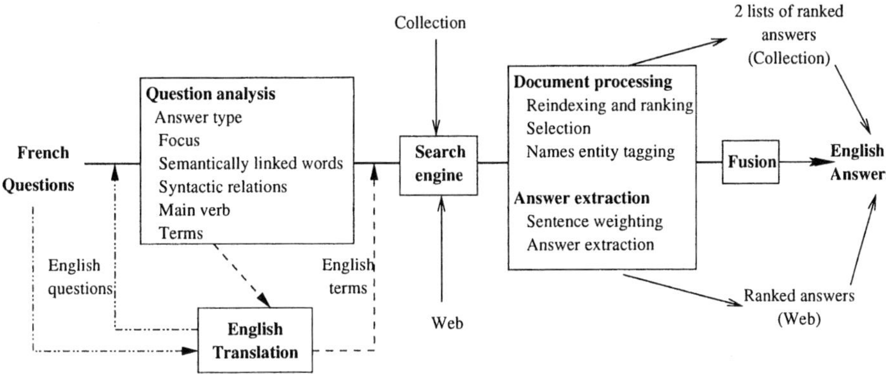

Fig. 2. MUSCLEF architecture

Retrieved documents are then processed. They are re-indexed by the question terms and their linguistic variants, reordered according to the number and the kind of terms found in them, so as to select a subset of them. Named entity recognition processes are then applied. The answer extraction process relies on a weighting scheme of the sentences, followed by the answer extraction itself. We apply different processes according to the kind of expected answer, each of them leading to propose weighted answers. For our second run, the final step consists in comparing, for the translated questions, (a)the results issued from the collection, (b)the results issued from the Web and, for the translated terms, (c) the results issued from the multilingual system, and computing a final score. Its principle was to boost an answer if all the chains ranked it in the top 5 propositions, even with relatively low scores.

4 Question Processing

As mentioned in section 1, two solutions were tested for building a representation of questions that can be matched with documents. The first one makes use of an automatic translator for translating questions from French to English and then, performs the analysis of the translated questions. The second solution consists in analyzing questions in the source language, which is French in our case, and translating in the target language, which is English, those terms that are considered as the most important ones.

4.1 Automatic Translation of Questions

Thus, the first solution we tested for solving the language mismatch between questions and documents relies on the automatic translation of questions. In our case, this automatic translation was performed by the SYSTRANLinks online interface provided by Systran[5]. No additional dictionary was used. As most of the

[5] We would like to thank Systran for the access they give to us to this service in the context of the ALMA project.

questions of the CLEF evaluation are not very complex from a syntactical point of view and address general subjects, their translations can often be considered as reliable, as illustrated by Figure 3.

0009 - Quand est apparu pour la première fois le virus Ebola ?
0009 - When did the Ebola virus appear for the first time?

0166 - Où se trouve Halifax ?
0166 - Where is Halifax?

Fig. 3. Examples of correct question translation

However, translation mistakes may also occur for simple questions, as we can see it in Figure 4. These mistakes may concern syntax: in question 175 for instance, "Quel est" should be translated as "Who is" and not as "Which is" and in question 165, the phrase "Qu'est-ce que", that is specific to questions, is only partially translated[6]. But these mistakes also may concern semantics: in question 175 again, "réalisateur" is translated as "realizer" while an answer is more likely to be found if it is translated as "director" or "film director". Finally, question 165 also illustrates the problem of the uncompleteness of dictionaries, which is impossible to circumvent fully in an open-domain system, especially for acronyms: "OMC" (Organisation Mondiale du Commerce) should be translated as "WTO" (World Trade Organization), just as "OTAN" is translated as "NATO" in question 143.

0175 - Quel est le réalisateur de "Nikita" ?
0175 - Which is the realizer of "Nikita"?
0165 - Qu'est-ce que l'OMC ?
0165 - What OMC?
0143 - En quelle année a été créée l'OTAN ?
0143 - In which year was creates NATO?

Fig. 4. Examples of mistakes in question translation

4.2 Term Translation

Different methods can be used to achieve term translation. Results may be obtained by a translation based on bilingual ontologies; but as mentioned in the previous section, the required tools do not really exist in open-domain. Among the other translation possibilities, we considered the easiest one, which consists in using a bilingual dictionary to translate the terms from the source language to

[6] By the way, this observation shows that as for part-of-speech taggers or syntactic analyzers, questions should be specifically taken into account by machine translation systems while they are generally not.

the target language. This simple method presents two drawbacks: it is impossible to directly disambiguate the various meanings of the words to be translated, and the two languages must be of equivalent lexical richness. Since this last constraint is verified for the couple English/French, we used this method. To give an idea of the ambiguities we may encounter in a QA context, we studied the corpus of 1893 questions in English of TREC. After analysis, we kept 9000 of the 15624 words used in this corpus. The average of the number of meanings was 7.35 in WordNet. The extrema were 1 (example: *neurological*) and 59 (example: *break*). Around the average value, we found common words such as *prize, blood, organization*. Hence, we could not consider a dictionary giving only one meaning for a word, moreover we needed to define a measure of the value of a translation in our QA context.

With these constraints, we studied the different dictionaries we could use: the online dictionaries (such as Reverso[7], Systran[8], Google[9], Dictionnaire Terminologique[10] or FreeTranslation [11]), and the dictionaries under GPL licences (such as Magic-Dic[12] or Unidic). The online dictionaries are generally complete. But they resolve the ambiguity and they only give one translation per word. Another limitation was the fact that we could not modify these dictionaries, and that we had to deal with some technical constraints such as the limited number of requests we may adress and the access time. Concerning the GPL dictionaries, they are obviously less complete, but they can be modified, they are very fast and for most of all, they give several translations for a request, as classical bilingual dictionaries. Among the GPL dictionaries, we chose Magic-dic, because of its evolutivity: terms can be added by any user, but they are verified before being integrated, which is not the case for Unidic. For example the query for the French word *porte* gives the following results (we only give an excerpt):

– porte bagages - luggagerack, luggage rack
– porte cigarette - cigarette holder
– porte clefs - key-ring
– porte plume - fountain pen
– porte parole, locuteur - spokesman
– porte - door, gate

To prevent its uncompleteness, and because it has been proved that the use of several dictionaries gives better results than a unique one, we intend to enrich it with the Google dictionary.

[7] http://translation2.paralink.com
[8] http://babel.altavista/translate.dyn
[9] http://www.google.com/language_tools
[10] http://granddictionnaire.com
[11] http://www.freetranslation.com
[12] http://magic-dic.homeunix.net/

4.3 The Multilingual Module

We will illutrate the strategy defined in MUSQAT on the following example: *"Quel est le nom de la principale compagnie aérienne allemande?"*, which is translated in English *"What is the name of the main German airline company?"*.

The first step is the parsing of the French question that provides a list of the uni-terms and all the bi-terms (such as *adjective/common noun*) which were in the question, and eliminates the stop words. The biterms are useful, because they (indirectly) disambiguate by giving a (small) context to a word. In our example, the biterms (in their lemmatized form) are: *principal compagnie, compagnie aérien, aérien allemand*; and the uniterms: *nom, principal, compagnie, aérien, allemand.*

With the help of the Magic-dic dictionnary, we attempted to translate the biterms (when they exist), and the uniterms. All the proposed translations were taken into account. All the terms were grammatically tagged. If a bi-term could not be directly translated, it was recomposed from the uniterms, following the English syntax. For our example, we obtained for the biterms: *principal compagny/main compagny, air compagny, air german*; and for the uniterms: *name/appellation, principal/main, compagny, german.* When a word does not exist in the dictionnary, we keep it as it whithout any diacritic.

These terms plus their categories (given by the Tree Tagger) instead of the original words were then given as input to the other modules of MUSQAT, instead of the original words. The translation module did not try to solve the ambiguity between the different translations: the MG request is made from the union of all the translations and the disambiguisation takes place during document selection. If the different terms are synonyms, pertinent documents are then retrieved with these synonyms, thanks to a larger search. If the word is incoherent within the context, we suppose its influence is not sufficient to generate noise.

We made an evaluation of the translation given by MUSQUAT. The 200 questions in French contained 731 words, corresponding to 1091 English words, and 932 terms (uni-terms + bi-terms) corresponding to 1464 terms in English. Studying this translation, we observed that:

- 59% of the translated terms were correct, (but for 12,63% of terms the translation may be enhanced)
- 8% of the translated terms were correct, but identical to the terms in the source language
- 33% of the translated terms were incorrect

It is obvious that the dictionary was not complete enough for this campaign. We would obtain a greater cover by completing manually the missing translations (no translation of the French verb *jouer* in its meaning *to play*, for example). We are also adding translations by requests to the Google translation module.

Another evaluation concerns the biterms, that we presented as very important to disambiguate ambiguous uniterms. To accomplish this goal, we determined the document frequency of each translation of the different biterms in the CLEF corpus. If the frequency is high, then the biterm may be an adequate translation. According to this study, 47.5% of the biterms were found in the corpus. An interesting approach could be to validate the translations, by scoring them following their frequency both in a bilingual corpus, and in a monolingual corpus (target language).

We also noticed that an important work had to be done on proper nouns, especially geographic names, organization names and acronyms. We then need to develop bilingual lists for the most frequent nouns.

5 Fusion of Several Sources of Information

As it was said in section 3 (overview of MUSCLEF), our second run is obtained by comparing three sets of results: the first is given by MUSQAT, the second by QALC searching on the Web and the third by QALC searching on the CLEF collection. The Web provides our system with a knowledge source obviously much larger than the CLEF collection. Using such source gives to our system a relevant way to confirm some of its answers and to reinforce its confidence score. However, among the answers provided by the Web search, some are not found in any CLEF document. So, it is to be noticed that Web answers must be present in CLEF collection.

Each of the three results sets contains for each question a set of answers which are ordered according to a confidence score. This score is updated all along the different steps of the answer extraction. Before describing the algorithm we wrote for the final selection, we will describe the way the confidence score is attributed to each candidate answer.

5.1 Answer Weighting

All the sentences provided by the document processing were examined in order to give them a weight reflecting both the possibility that the sentence contains the answer, and the possibility that the system can locate the answer within the sentence. The criteria that we used were closely linked with basic information extracted from the question. The resulting sentence ranking should not miss obvious answers. Our aim should be that the subsequent modules of answer extraction and final answer selection are able to raise a lower weighted answer to an upper rank according to added specific criteria. The criteria that we retained are based on the following features within the candidate sentences:

- question lemmas, weighted by their specificity degree[13],
- variants of question lemmas,
- exact words of the question (only in the "all english" version),
- mutual closeness of the question words,
- presence of the expected named entity type.

[13] The specificity degree of a lemma depends on the inverse of its relative frequency computed on a large corpus.

First we compute a basic weight of the sentence based on the presence of question lemmas or variants of these lemmas (the two first criteria). The basic weight is relative. We subsequently add an additional weight to this basic weight for each additional criteria that is satisfied. Each additional criteria weight cannot be higher than about 10% of the basic weight.

During answer extraction this weight is further refined. If the expected answer type is a named entity, then selected answers are the words of the sentence that correspond to the expected type. To order the answers, MUSCLEF computes additional weights taking into account:

- the precise or generic named entity type of the answer,
- the location of the potential answer with regard to the question words within the sentence,
- the redundancy of the answer in the top ten sentences.

When the expected answer type is not a named entity, we use extraction patterns. Each candidate sentence provided by the sentence selection module is analysed using the extraction pattern associated with the question type that has been determined by the question analysis. Extraction patterns are composed of regular expressions with the focus noun as pivot. More detail can be found in [7].

After the extraction and weighting procedure, the five best weighted answers are retained for the final selection module.

5.2 Final Selection Algorithm

The underlying idea is to compare results obtained from diverse sources of knowledge. Our comparison allows us to reinforce the score of answers belonging to the different result sets, thus allowing a significant number of correct answers to be assigned the first rank. Table 1 contains an example of these sets corresponding to the question: *"En quelle année Thomas Mann a-t-il obtenu le Prix Nobel ?"*, translated in English *"In what year did Thomas Mann win the Nobel Prize?"*.

The three sets of results are compared two by two using an algorithm written for TREC. This algorithm examines each couple ($answer_i$, $answer_j$), i and j being the answer positions in their own set. When both answers are equal or included one in the other, the algorithm attributes a bonus to the best score of the couple. This bonus is calculated according to both positions i and j:

Table 1. Answer set example

QALC + Web		MUSQAT		QALC + Collection	
Answer	Score	Answer	Score	Answer	Score
0) **in 1929**	**1082**	0) *in 1976*	721	0) October 11 , 1994	878
1) 1875-1955	1005	1) *in 1976*	721	1) **in 1929**	**853**
2) 08th March 1879	903	2) *in 1929*	664	2) *in 1976*	798
3) in 1903	877	3) 2	640	3) October 12 , 1994	703
4) *in 1929*	849	4) 1964	561	4) in 1979	696

$(10 - (i + j)) * 100$. The additional bonus was chosen in order to place the confirmed answers before the unconfirmed ones. Thus the algorithm builds a set of answer couples ordered according to their new score. Since in CLEF we had to compare three sets of results, we applied the algorithm on each couple of answer sets (three times), the answer finally returned belongs to the couple which obtains the best score.

Looking at Table 1, we see that two dates appear in the three sets: *in 1929* and *in 1976*. The couple which appears in bold font in Table 1 receives 900 as a bonus. So the answer *in 1929* obtains the best final score (1082 + 900) and is then returned.

This algorithm which compares answer sets two by two is thus easy to apply on more than two sets. Nevertheless, we observed that a comparison made directly between the three answer sets would give different results. Indeed making the comparisons two by two, we do not take into account in the same way the answers appearing in the three sets.

6 Results

Table 2 presents a comparative evaluation between MUSQAT and QALC. The evaluation was made by an automatic process that looks for the answer patterns in the system answers, applying regular expressions. These results were computed with 178 answer patterns that we built for the 200 questions of CLEF.

The first line indicates the number of correct answers found in the 5 first sentences given by MUSQAT (using term translation) and both applications of QALC (collection and Web search). The second line, "NE answers", gives the number of correct answers on questions that had a Named Entity as answer, the third line, "non NE answers", concerns the other questions. Results are presented when the system just gives one answer and when it gives 5 answers. The last column indicates the best official result of our system on the 200 questions. The official score of MUSQAT was 22 (11%), thus we can observe that merging answers obtained by different strategies enables a gain of 17 answers (77%).

At TREC 2002, the systems had to provide a unique answer for each question. On 500 questions, QALC alone found 128 right answers (25%). When making

Table 2. Comparative evaluation of the different strategies

		MUSQAT	QALC + Collection	QALC + Web	Fusion (Official results)
Sentences	5 first ranks	56	65	61	
NE answers	Rank 1	17	26	24	
	5 first ranks	33	37	43	
Non NE answers	Rank 1	7	3	0	
	5 first ranks	12	8	0	
Total	Rank 1	24 (12%)	29 (14.5%)	24(12%)	39 (19,5%)
	5 first ranks	44	45	43	

the fusion between Web answers and TREC collection answers, QALC found 148 answers (29,68%). These results have to be compared with the numbers on the last line (Table 2) for correct answers at rank 1: the multilingual problem entails a reduction of performance of 10%.

We can also notice that the three strategies are equivalent, and that a weak point of our system remains the extraction of answers from selected sentences for non Named Entity questions[14].

7 Conclusion

Even if its first results are encouraging, MUSCLEF, our first multilingual system, can yet be enhanced. However, its architecture, organized into several independent modules, was chosen to be able to easily make these enhancements. Moreover, we observed that both strategies that we adopted (term translation and question translation) were relevant and should be maintained together in further experiences.

Obviously, better multilingual resources will be necessary, but since complete resources are not available, it could be interesting to search the Web to control the obtained translations.

References

1. Aït-Mokhtar, S., Chanod, J.-P.: Incremental finite-state parsing. Proceedings of the 5th Conference on Applied Natural Language Processing (ANLP-97), Washington, DC, USA (1997)
2. Aït-Mokhtar, S., Chanod, J.-P., Roux, C.: Robustness beyond shallowness: incremental deep parsing. Natural Language Engineering Vol. 8 (2/3), (2002)121–144
3. Brill, E., Lin, J., Banko, M., Dumais, S., Ng, A.: Data-Intensive Question Answering. TREC 10 Notebook, Gaithersburg (2001)
4. Chu-Carroll, J., Prager, J., Welty, C., Czuba, K., Ferruci, D.: A Multi-Strategy and multi-source Approach to Question Answering. TREC 11 Notebook, Gaithersburg, USA (2002)124–133
5. Clarke,C.L., Cormack, G.V., Lynam, T.R., Li, C.M., McLearn,G.L.: Web Reinforced Question Answering (MultiText Experiments for Trec 2001), TREC 10 Notebook, Gaithersburg, USA (2001)
6. Fellbaum, C.: WordNet: An Electronic Lexical Database. Cambridge, MA: MIT Press (1998)
7. Ferret, O., Grau, B., Hurault-Plantet, M., Illouz, G., Jacquemin, C., Monceaux, L., Robba, I., Vilnat, A.: How NLP Can Improve Question Answering Knowledge Organization, Vol. 29, N3-4 (2002)135–155
8. Hermjakob, U., Echihabi, A., Marcu, D.: Natural Language Based Reformulation Resource and Web Exploitation for Question Answering, TREC 11 Notebook, Gaithersburg, USA (2002)

[14] Even if we discovered, but too late, a bug on the Web run.

9. Magnini, B., Negri, M., Prevete, R., Tanev, H.: Is It the Right Answer? Exploiting Web redundancy for Answer Validation, Proceedings of the 40 th ACL (2002)425–432
10. Magnini, B., Negri, M., Prevete, R., Tanev, H.: Mining Knowledge from Repeated Co-occurrences: DIOGENE at TREC-2002, TREC 11 Notebook, Gaithersburg, USA (2002)
11. Moldovan, D., Harabagiu, S., Girju, R., Morarescu, P., Lacatusu, F., Novischi, A., Badalescu, A., Bolohan, O.: LCC Tools for Question Answering, TREC 11 Notebook, Gaithersburg, USA (2002)

Finnish as Source Language in Bilingual Question Answering

Lili Aunimo, Reeta Kuuskoski, and Juha Makkonen

Department of Computer Science, University of Helsinki,
P.O. Box 68, FIN-00014 University of Helsinki, Finland
{aunimo, jamakkon, rkuuskos}@cs.helsinki.fi

Abstract. This paper presents a bilingual question answering system that has Finnish as its source language and English as its target language. The system was evaluated in the QA@CLEF 2004 evaluation campaign. It is the only officially evaluated QA system that takes Finnish as input. The system is based on question classification and analysis, translation of important query terms, document retrieval, answer pattern instantiation and answer selection. The system achieves an accuracy of 10,88%.

1 Introduction

This paper presents a bilingual question answering (QA) system that has Finnish as its source language and English as its target language. The system was evaluated in the QA@CLEF 2004 [1, 2] evaluation campaign. It is the only QA system that has been officially evaluated and that takes Finnish as input. Previously, our system had been unofficially evaluated with QA@CLEF 2003 data[3].

The name of our QA system is *Tikka*[1]. It has three modules: *Question Processor*, *Document Retrieval* and *Answer Extractor*. The system architecture is shown in Fig. 1. The *Question Processor* and *Answer Extractor* are the modules which are especially developed for QA. The *Document Retrieval* module is a standard information retrieval (IR) engine. The *Question Processor* first produces a syntactic parse of the question, then it classifies the question and finally it translates the relevant terms of the question. Question processing includes also the special processing required by the Finnish language. These requirements are mostly due to the morphology and vocabulary of Finnish. They are described in detail in Aunimo et al. [3]. The *Answer Extractor* first instantiates the answer extraction pattern prototypes with the translated words of the question. Then it applies the patterns to the documents retrieved by the *Document Retrieval* module and finally it selects the best answer among the candidates and gives it a confidence value.

At QA@CLEF 2004, *Tikka*'s document database consisted of 579 megabytes (169 477 documents) of newspaper text (The Glasgow Herald from 1995 and Los

[1] Tikka means Woodpecker in English.

C. Peters et al. (Eds.): CLEF 2004, LNCS 3491, pp. 482–493, 2005.

Angeles Times from 1994)[2]. Other external knowledge sources that the system used were the *MOT* dictionary software from *Kielikone Ltd.* [2], the functional dependency grammar parser from *Connexor Ltd.* [3] and a *Country and Capital Translation Database* extracted from the web site of *Statistics Finland* [4].

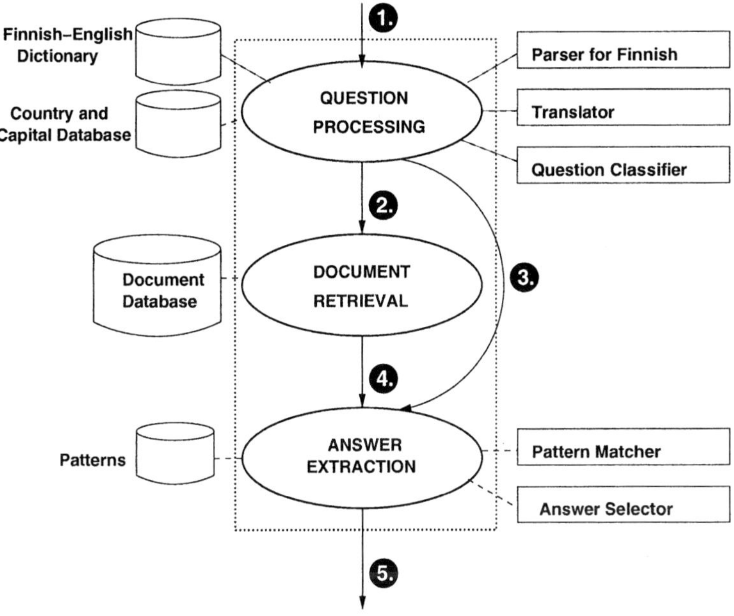

Fig. 1. System architecture of Tikka

In the following chapters each of the main components of the system are described in detail. Section 2 describes the different phases of question processing. In Section 3, the document retrieval component of our system is detailed. The answer extraction component is described in Section 4. Section 5 is about evaluation and it presents our official results at QA@CLEF 2004. It also discusses the inter-translator agreement rate of the test set questions and the complexity of the translation task. Finally, Section 6 concludes.

2 Question Processing

2.1 Question Classification

The question classifier classifies the questions into the following classes: *location*, *manner*, *measure*, *object*, *organization*, *other*, *person* and *time*. The time-related

[2] http://www.kielikone.fi/en/
[3] http://www.connexor.com/
[4] http://www.tilastokeskus.fi/index_en.html

questions in the test corpus typically fall into one of three categories: a general 'when'[5], a specific interval, e.g., 'what year|month|time'[6] and a duration, 'how long'[7]. The first two are *time*-questions and the last a *measure*-question.

Likewise, many *measure*-questions are somewhat straight-forward to recognize. The question is scanned for occurrence of quantity-related question words[8]. Then there are 'what-is'-questions, such as 'What is the population of Finland?'[9] Question classification relies on identifying the complement (population) as a *measure*-related word. The same technique is used with *person*, *location*, and *organization* related question: the type is determined by classifying the object or the complement. Sometimes verbs are helpful indicators of the question type.

A question is classified as *other*-type, when the complement is a verb or if the complement or the object does not relate to person, location or organization. The *manner*-questions typically start with either 'how'[10] or 'in what manner|way'[11]. It has been difficult to identify *object*-questions as they vary considerably. Hence, we regard them as *other*-type.

2.2 Translator

Once the question has been classified, it is passed on to the *Translator*. It decides which of the words are translated, how to deal with proper names, homographs and polysemous words and with words that have no translation in the dictionary. The *Translator* also decides which words are used in the query that is given to the document retrieval module, and which words are used in answer extraction pattern prototype instantiation. For these decisions, it uses the syntactic parse tree of the question.

Once a question and its type is received by the *Translator*, it checks for country and capital names in the *Country and Capital Translation Database*. It contains 244 country and capital names in Finnish and their translations into English. The country and capital inventory updated as a new database is fetched from the web pages of *Statistics Finland* every once in a while. The version that we used in the QA@CLEF 2004 evaluation exercise dates from 16.4.2004. This caused some problems, because the World has changed since 1994 and 1995 from where the CLEF newspaper text database dates. For example, two questions were about Yugoslavia, which our *Country and Capital Translation Database* naturally did not contain.

If the question contains a name that is in the database, it is translated and removed from the list of words that will be passed on to the dictionary software. It is crucial that the proper names have been transformed into their base forms before their existence in the database is checked because the database naturally

[5] milloin, koska

[6] *minä vuonna?, missä kuussa?, mihin aikaan?*

[7] *kuinka kauan, kauanko, miten kauan, kuinka pitkän aikaa*

[8] e.g., kuinka|miten moni|kauan|paljon, montako|moniko|paljonko|kauanko

[9] Mikä on Suomen väkiluku?

[10] miten|kuinka

[11] millä tavoin|tavalla|keinoin

does not contain any inflected proper names. For example, among the 34 country and capital names occurring in this year's questions, only 2 were uninflected.

After the *Country and Capital Translation Database* checking routine the translator determines which words are passed on to the dictionary software. All nouns are translated. If no translation is found, and the noun is a compound word, it is split into two parts both of which are used in the search from the dictionary. If there are more than two parts in the compound, then the last part forms the first search word and the remaining parts form the second search word. This is sensible, because quite often the preceding parts together are a modifier of the last part. For example (compound boundaries are marked with #): In *kori#pallo#joukkue* (basketball team) *kori#pallo* (basketball) modifies *joukkue* (team). This very coarse heuristic also has many counter-examples. One of them is *kulttuuri#pää#kaupunki* (Capital of Culture) where *kulttuuri* (culture) modifies *pää#kaupunki* (capital). In those cases where the noun is a compound word containing at least three parts and where the first part begins with a capital and ends with a hyphen, we split the word into dictionary search words from the hyphen, because the first part is most probably a proper noun and an uninflected modifier of the latter part and the latter part is the main part of the compound and it is inflected. For example in *Andrew-#pyörre#myrsky* (Hurricane Andrew) *Andrew* is a modifier for *pyörre#myrsky* (Hurricane). The proper noun could also contain several parts, for example *La# Scala -#ooppera#talo* (La Scala opera house), where *La# Scala* modifies *ooppera#talo* (opera house).

In addition to nouns, the system translates all the adjectives that are attributes to nouns that are heads of a noun phrase. For example, in *How many Japanese students were there in the United States in 1990?*, *Japanese* is translated because it is a modifier of *students.*

If a word has no translation in the dictionary, and it looks like a proper name (beginning with a capital letter and being not the first word of the question), its case is checked. If it is not nominative, but one of the other fourteen cases in which a noun can appear, the base form is passed on. Otherwise, the original word in the question is processed. This is because in the nominative case, no inflection is added to the proper name, while in the other cases, a suffix is added to the end of the word. In order to be able to use an inflected proper name as an English query term, we have to find its base form.

The main reason for only translating nouns and adjective attributes of those nouns that are heads of noun phrases is that the verbs used in the questions tend to be highly polysemous and they tend to have one or more homonyms. For example, in the case of this year's question number 40: *Who directed "Braveheart"?*, in Finnish *Kuka ohjasi elokuvan "Braveheart - Taipumaton"?* the verb *ohjata (to direct)* has 22 different senses in English, and only the seventh is the correct sense. However, the problem of polysemous words and homonyms also exists for nouns [3]. Sometimes there are several translations with the same sense for a word. In this case, we take all of them, pass them to the document retrieval module, and use them in the extraction pattern instantiation phase. Each of the translations, which are usually synonyms, get their own instantiated patterns. For example, the word *vocalist* is translated as *laulaja*, *laulusolisti* and *vokalisti.*

Finding the correct translation or translations for a word in a given question is a question that we should investigate further. At the moment, we take at most the two first senses - which might mean more than two words - and hope that the correct one is among these. Usually it is, because in general, the dictionary software lists the translation alternatives in the order of their frequency. This was a practical solution to a very hard problem. As mentioned in subsection 5.2, ambiguity is a problem for human translators also.

3 Document Retrieval

We used Managing Gigabytes (MG) [12] [4] for document retrieval task. MG is an open source text indexing and retrieval engine developed as a joint venture of multiple Australian universities. It is capable of indexing large document collections using only a small amount of time and space.

The document corpus was first split so that each document was in its own file. The more fine-grained segmentation was not applied, since we anticipated it would be possible that some of the answers and their evidence would not occur within one sentence, or even one paragraph. This assumption was due to our experiments with the training data, the questions and answers used in QA@CLEF year 2003. The resulting files were then fed to MG for indexing. The contents of the documents were not otherwise preprocessed, although it might have been wise to do that.

MG has two query modes, boolean and ranked. The maximum number of retrieved documents was limited to one hundred. By default, MG was run in boolean query mode.

The boolean mode proved to work better than the ranked query especially with questions that included proper names. In the boolean mode , the presence of all terms was enforced, because only the 'AND' operator was used, whereas in the ranked mode the result set may include documents that lack some query terms completely. Therefore the ranked query could sometimes give lots of irrelevant results. Sometimes the boolean query conditions were too strict, however, and when the result set was empty the system switched mode.

Phrase and proximity constraints could have been done with MG using regular expressions. In MG, phrase search is done as postprocessing of the search results, which is sensitive to line feeds. There are also other difficulties in phrase search in bilingual information retrieval. In Finnish, we have quite many compound words whose counterparts in English are phrases. For instance, in question 159 there is *Capital of Culture* is in Finnish *kulttuuripääkaupunki.* This term did not appear in the dictionary, so *Tikka* split it to parts, *kulttuuri* and *pääkaupunki.* The first translations found in the dictionary for these terms were *culture* and *civilization* for *kulttuuri* and *principal town* and *capital, capital city*

[12] http://www.mds.rmit.edu.au/mg

for *pääkaupunki*. Executing a phrase search with these translations might not produce any correct results. The usefulness of phrase search in *Tikka*'s document retrieval is to be investigated more thoroughly.

One useful feature that is not present in MG is the possibility to weight the query terms. This would have made the search more accurate by defining which query terms are obligatory, and which are less important. The most important terms in the query are the proper nouns [5]. Our experiments seemed to prove that after the proper nouns come the common nouns, and next to them are the verbs. The importance of the adjectives is hard to determine, since it depends on the syntactic role of the adjective in the sentence. It seems that the adjectives are important when they appear as attributes of a noun that serves as the head in a noun phrase. This is the case for example in question 79 of the training set: *What is the highest active volcano in Europe?* where *highest* and *active* are of this kind. In other contexts, the adjectives seem to be less important.

A minor discomfort with MG was the fact that in the boolean mode search of MG, no special characters (dots, hyphens, dollar signs etc.) can be used, although they might have been of use in some situations. This could have been solved by preprocessing the corpus.

Once the query had been executed, the search results were passed onward to the next module for the extraction of the answer.

4 Answer Extraction

4.1 Answer Extraction Patterns

Answer extraction pattern instantiation is the first step in answer extraction. This is done by creating instances of pattern prototypes. Each question type has a set of pattern prototypes that have been induced from the 1994 L.A. Times and the 1995 Glasgow Herald using the Multisix Corpus [6]. The pattern prototypes have slots where translated words from the question are inserted in order to form pattern instances.

Tikka contains pattern prototypes for six question types. They are: *definition*, *location*, *measure*, *person*, *other* and *time*. Based on the question types in the Multisix Corpus [6], we could have developed pattern prototypes also for the classes *object* and *organization*. However, we picked the most common categories for pattern prototype development. *Other* is a class where we classify all those questions that do not belong to the other five classes. In addition, the QA@CLEF 2004 contained the class *manner*, but we did not develop pattern prototypes for these since we had no training data.

The answer pattern prototypes consist of regular expressions and of slots for proper names and other words that have been picked from the question. The answer pattern prototypes do not contain any syntactic or morphological information at the moment. Table 2 lists all the pattern classes and the number of prototype patterns that each class contains. Examples of pattern instances that are derived from the same location pattern prototype:

```
the city of ([^ ,\.\?\!0-9]+), Mike Kelley[^\.\?\!0-9]*
the town of ([^ ,\.\?\!0-9]+), Mike Kelley[^\.\?\!0-9]*
```

In the above example, the word *kaupunki* has two translations, *city* and *town*, and the pattern prototype is expanded with both.

Another example:

```
PROPER NAME[^,\.\?\!0-9]* TITLE,? [^A-Z]*(([A-Z][a-z]+[ -])*[A-Z][a-z]+)
```

In the above person pattern prototype the slots for *PROPER NAME* and *TITLE* are filled with words from the question. For example, in the question 2 from 2003, *Kuka on YK:n pääsihteeri?, Who is the head of the United Nations?*, the slot for *PROPER NAME* is filled by *UN*, *United Nations* and *UN (United Nations)*. The slot for *TITLE* is filled by *Secretary General* and *secretary-general.* When all these instantiations are combined, we end up with 6 different pattern instances. The different variations for the slots except for the combination *UN (United Nations)* are retrieved from the dictionary. For all acronyms that have the longer form listed in the dictionary, the system performs the same type of expansion as for *UN*.

4.2 Answer Selection and Scoring

Answer selection is based on frequency. If there are several answer candidates with the same frequency, the one appearing first in the results retrieved by MG, is selected. This is a reasonable approach, because when MG is set to the ranked query mode, it sorts the search results by relevance. If MG is run in the boolean mode, the number of retrieved documents is much more constrained and thus usually substantially smaller.

Confidence measure generation is a function of both the total number of candidates retrieved and of the frequency of the selected candidate. This function is illustrated as an area plot in Figure 2. The confidence score is 1, if the number of different candidates is a number between 1 and 5, or if the number of different candidates is a number between 6 and 14 and the frequency of the candidate is greater than 1 (the area marked with tiles in figure 2). The confidence score is 0.5 if the number of different candidates is between 6 and 10 and the frequency is 1 (the area marked with diagonal lines in figure 2). The confidence score is 0.25 if the number of different candidates is between 11 and 14 and the frequency is 1, or if the number of different candidates is over 14 (the area marked blank in figure 2). All those answers that we detected as not having an answer in the text database (answers of type *NIL*) had a confidence score of 0.

Table 1 lists the number of occurrences of each confidence measure and the number of correct answers in these classes. In addition to the official QA@CLEFF 2004 results, also *Tikka*'s unofficial results obtained using the data from QA@CLEF 2003 are presented.

As can be seen in Table 1, the confidence function should have been more strict, i.e. the score 1 should have been given to fewer answers. However, the confidence function depends heavily on the data and questions at hand and on

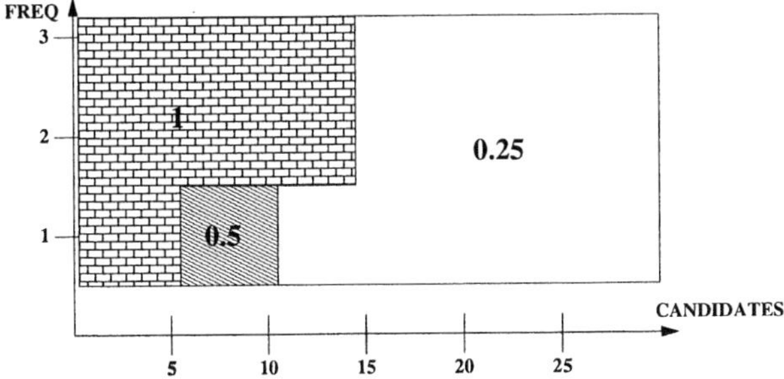

Fig. 2. Area plot of the confidence score of *Tikka* as a function of candidate frequency and total number of different candidates

Table 1. Number of occurrences of different confidence measures and number of correct answers. No figures are given for the NIL-answers

Confidence	CLEF 2004 (official)		CLEF 2003 (unofficial)	
	Occurrences	Correct	Occurrences	Correct
1	27	5 (one inexact)	51	29
0.5	2	0	3	0
0.25	5	0	14	4
0	0	0	0	0

how well the answer extraction patterns match to that data. We trained *Tikka* with questions and answers from QA@CLEF from 2003, and it seems that the answer extraction pattern prototypes were too specific to those answers. With the 2003 questions we got 132 NIL answers, but with this years material, the number of NIL answers was 159.

5 Evaluation

5.1 Results

The detailed results of the QA@CLEF 2004 evaluation are presented in the overview paper of the CLEF 2004 QA Track [1]. The evaluation metrics used in the QA@CLEF 2004 campaign are described in the *Evaluation measure* section of the campaign guidelines[13]. The main evaluation measure is accuracy, i.e. the proportion of correct answers. The second evaluation measure is the confidence-weighted score. It gives a score between 0 and 1, inclusive, with 1 being a perfect score. The confidence-weighted score rewards systems that can evaluate their own performance. In order to obtain a system's confidence weighted score, the answers are first sorted according to their confidence score. Then the confidence-weighted score is calculated based on either equation 1 or equation 2. The official

[13] http://clef-qa.itc.it/2004/guidelines.html

confidence-weighted score of QA@CLEF 2004 was calculated according to equation 1, which defines $score_{cw}(run)$, the confidence-weighted score of a run, as follows:

$$score_{cw}(run) = \frac{1}{N}\sum_{i=1}^{N} correct(i) \times \frac{number\ correct\ up\ to\ question\ i}{i}, \quad (1)$$

where N is the number of questions in the test set and where the function $correct(i)$ is defined as:

$$correct(i) = \begin{cases} 1 \text{ if answer to question } i \text{ is correct} \\ 0 \text{ otherwise} \end{cases}$$

In the TREC[14] QA campaign, a similar, but slightly different confidence-weighted score has been used. It was introduced at TREC 2002 [7]. It defines $score_{cw}(run)$, as follows:

$$score_{cw}(run) = \frac{1}{N}\sum_{i=1}^{N} \frac{number\ correct\ up\ to\ question\ i}{i} \quad (2)$$

The confidence-weighted score calculated by equation 2 is an analog to document retrieval's uninterpolated average precision. Unlike the scoring calculated by equation 1, it can have a value that is higher than the run's accuracy. In both of the confidence-weighted scores, the order in which the equal confidence scores are sorted has significance, because the denominator runs from 1 to N. For example, for answers with confidence 1.0, having the correct answers before the incorrect ones results in higher score than in reverse order. We sorted the judgments having the same confidence by the question id.

Table 2 shows the correct answers per question type as well as the number of prototype patterns in use. It also shows the overall accuracy of our system and the confidence-weighted accuracy according to the measures of equation 1 and of equation 2. As can be seen, the number of pattern prototypes correlates with the number of correct answers. An exception is the class $Organization(Factoid)$ where the number of pattern prototypes is 0 and the number of correct answers is 5. Either these questions have been classified wrongly as $Person(Factoid)$ questions[15], or the default patterns that are used for unclassified questions and for those classes that don't have their own patterns, have been successful.

5.2 Inter-translator Agreement

The questions for Finnish-English QA were translated from English. The assessor of the evaluation campaign compared the English questions against the results given by *Tikka*. However, the translation process introduces some problems into the problem that the QA system has to solve. For example, not all questions

[14] http://trec.nist.gov/

[15] Some *organization*-questions look a lot like *person*-questions, for example: Question 16 *Who was the embargo against Iraq imposed by?*

Table 2. Our results at CLEF 2004. Question type classes, number of questions belonging to each class in QA@CLEF 2004, number of prototype patterns in each class, number of correct answers in each class and percentage of correct answers in each class

Question		**Patterns**	**Correct**	
Type	#	#	#	%
Definition(Person and Organization)	20	3	0	0
Location (Factoid)	28	18	3	10,7
Manner (Factoid)	14	0	0	0
Measure (Factoid)	19	22	2	10.5
Object (Factoid)	12	0	0	0
Organization (Factoid)	20	0	5	25
Other (Factoid)	26	5	4	15,4
Person (Factoid)	26	16	5	19,2
Time (Factoid)	28	3	2	7,1
Total	193	64	21	10.88
equation 1				0.046
equation 2				0.091

are sensible when translated. This is the case with question number 86 from the QA@CLEF 2004 test set, *What does a luthier make?*, became pointless in Finnish, because the Finnish word for luthier[16] tells what a luthier does. Another example of the influence of translation on the questions is question 85 *What did the artist Christo wrap up?. to wrap up* is an ambiguous verb in English and in this context, it can be translated in two ways which have a completely different meaning. It can be translated as denoting concrete wrapping up, which was the correct meaning according to the answer[17]. The other meaning of *to wrap up* is an abstract one, and it means finishing something. We did three more translations of the English questions. Out of these translations, three translated *to wrap up* with its concrete sense[18], but one translation has the abstract sense[19]. Ambiguity is a problem for human translators as well as for our translator component.

The three additional translations of the questions were done by translators who had not seen the official translation. The parallel translations of the same questions are useful in order to measure the difficulty of the translation task that the QA system has to face. The amount of inter-translator agreement is illustrated in Figure 3. The fourth translation is the official translation where errors have been corrected [20].

Because the same question can be formed in several ways, the QA system has to be able to analyze the different variants and to extract the semantic skeleton

[16] Luthier can be translated as *soitinrakentaja* or *viulunrakentaja* in Finnish.
[17] The correct answer to the question 85 is *The artist Christo wrapped up the Reichstag in silver fabric tied with blue rope.*
[18] paketoida
[19] saattaa päätökseen
[20] http://clef-qa.itc.it/2004/down/clef04-test-FI-EN-correct.txt

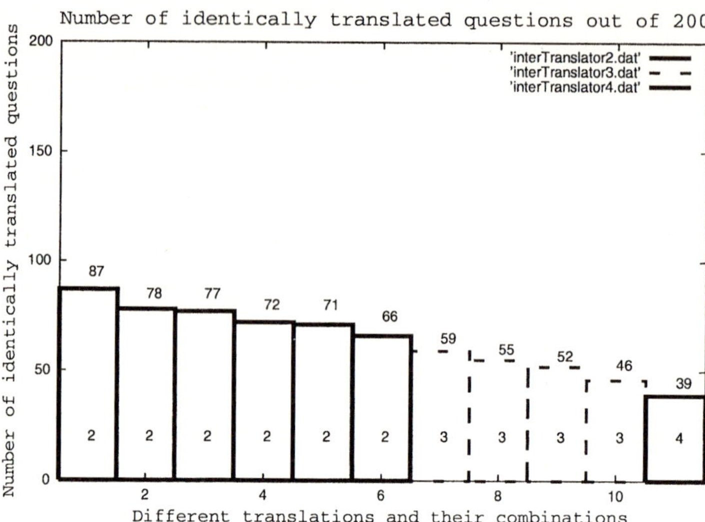

Fig. 3. A histogram showing the number of identically translated questions out of 200. The columns 1, 2, 3, 4, 5 and 6 show the number of similar questions between two translations. The columns 7, 8, 9 and 10 show the number of similar questions in sets containing three translations. The column 11 shows the number of similar questions in a set of four translations

from them. One way of dealing with the problem would be to preprocess the questions and to transform the questions judged complicated into their more simple variants. A similar approach has been taken when preprocessing questions before passing them on to machine translation [8]. We calculated the results of *Tikka* with all four different translations, but there were no significant differences in performance.

6 Conclusions

To the best of our knowledge, our QA system is the only QA system that can handle Finnish as a source language and that has been officially evaluated. Altogether, there has been very little work on any type of QA for Finnish. Keeping this in mind, it was interesting to get the system up and running and to observe that it could answer 10,88 % of the questions presented to it correctly.

Due to the very different nature of Finnish in comparison to any of the other languages participating in the QA@CLEF, special attention has been paid to question translation and to the effects of the translation phase to the overall performance of the system.

Another interesting subfield is that of answer extraction patterns. We plan to study carefully which patterns matched well and which didn't and to find out the reasons for this. We are also planning to investigate the use of POS tags and possibly surface syntactic tags in the answer extraction patterns. The results obtained in this evaluation showed that by developing further the question and answer processing modules, as well as by tuning the document retrieval module more carefully, the performance of our system is very likely to improve.

References

1. Magnini, B., Vallin, A., C.Ayache, Erbach, G., Penas, A., de Rijke, M., Rocha, P., Simov, K., Sutcliffe, R.: Overview of the CLEF 2004 Multilingual Question Answering Track. In Peters, C., Borri, F., eds.: Proceedins of the CLEF 2004 Workshop, Bath, United Kingdom (2004)
2. Peters, C.: What happened in CLEF 2004? In Peters, C., Borri, F., eds.: Proceedins of the CLEF 2004 Workshop, Bath, United Kingdom (2004)
3. Aunimo, L., Makkonen, J., Kuuskoski, R.: Cross-language Question Answering for Finnish. In Hyvönen, E., Kauppinen, T., Salminen, M., Viljanen, K., Ala-Siuru, P., eds.: Proceedings of the 11th Finnish Artificial Intelligence Conference STeP 2004, September 1-3, Vantaa, Finland. Volume 2 of Conference Series – No 20., Finnish Artificial Intelligence Society (2004) 35–49
4. Witten, I.H., Moffat, A., Bell, T.C.: Managing Gigabytes: Compressing and Indexing Documents and Images. second edn. Morgan Kaufmann Publishers (1999)
5. Pirkola, A., Järvelin, K.: Employing the resolution power of search keys. Journal of the American Society for Information Science and Technology **52** (2001) 575–583
6. Magnini, B., Romagnoli, S., Vallin, A., Herrera, J., Penas, A., Peinado, V., Verdejo, F., de Rijke, M.: The Multiple Language Question Answering Track at CLEF 2003. In Peters, C., ed.: Working Notes for the CLEF 2003 Workshop, Trondheim, Norway (2003)
7. Voorhees, E.M.: Overwiew of the TREC-2002 Question Answering Track. In Voorhees, E.M., Buckland, L.P., eds.: Proceedings of TREC-2002, Gaithersburg, Maryland, Department of Commerce, National Institute of Standards and Technology (2002)
8. Ahn, K., Alex, B., Bos, J., Dalmas, T., Leidner, J., Smillie, M.: Cross-lingual question answering with QED. In: Working Notes for the CLEF 2004 Workshop, Bath, United Kingdom (2004) 335 – 342

miraQA: Experiments with Learning Answer Context Patterns from the Web

César de Pablo-Sánchez[1], José Luis Martínez-Fernández[1], Paloma Martínez[1], and Julio Villena[2]

[1] Advanced Databases Group, Computer Science Department,
Universidad Carlos III de Madrid,
Avda. Universidad 30, 28911 Leganés , Madrid, Spain
{cdepablo, jlmferna, pmf}@inf.uc3m.es
[2] DAEDALUS – Data, Decisions and Language S.A.
Centro de Empresas "La Arboleda", Ctra N-III km 7,300 Madrid 28031, Spain
jvillena@daedalus.es

Abstract. We present the miraQA system which is MIRACLE's first experience in Question Answering for monolingual Spanish. The general architecture of the system developed for QA@CLEF 2004 is presented as well as evaluation results. miraQA characterizes by learning the rules for answer extraction from the Web using a Hidden Markov Model of the context in which answers appear. We used a supervised approach that uses questions and answers from last years evaluation set for training.

1 Introduction

Question Answering has received a lot of attention during the last years due to the advances in IR and NLP. As in other applications in these areas, the bulk of the research has been mainly in English while perhaps one of the most interesting applications of QA systems could be in cross and multilingual scenarios. Access to concrete quality information in a language that is not spoken or just poorly understood could be advantageous to current IR systems in many situations. QA@CLEF [8] has encouraged the development of QA systems in other languages than English and in crosslingual scenarios.

QA systems are usually complex because of the number of different modules that they use, and the need for a good integration among them. Even if questions are expecting a simple fact or a short definition as an answer, the requirement of more precise information has entailed the use of language and domain specific modules. On the other hand, some other approaches relying on data-intensive [4], machine learning and statistical techniques [10] have achieved wide spread and relative success. Moreover, the interest of these approaches for multilingual QA systems lies on the possibility of adapting them quickly to other target languages.

In this paper we present our first approach to the QA task. As we have not taken part before in any of the QA evaluation forums, most of the work has been done integrating different available resources. So far, the system we present is targeted only

C. Peters et al. (Eds.): CLEF 2004, LNCS 3491, pp. 494 – 501, 2005.

to the monolingual Spanish task. The system explores the use of Hidden Markov Models [9] for Answer Extraction and uses Google[1] to collect training data. The results prove that further improvements and tuning are needed, both in the system and the answer extraction method. We expect to continue working on this system to enhance their results and inspect the suitability of the approach for different languages.

2 Description

miraQA, the system that MIRACLE group has developed for QA@CLEF 2004, represents our first attempt to face the Question Answering task. The system has been developed for the monolingual Spanish subtask as we are familiar with available tools for Spanish. Despite we only address this task, we believe that our approach for Answer Extraction could be easily adapted to other target languages, as it uses resources available for most of the languages like POS (Part-Of-Speech) taggers and partial parsers.

The architecture of the system follows the usual structure of a QA with three modules as shown in Figure 1: Question Analysis, Document Retrieval and Answer Extraction.

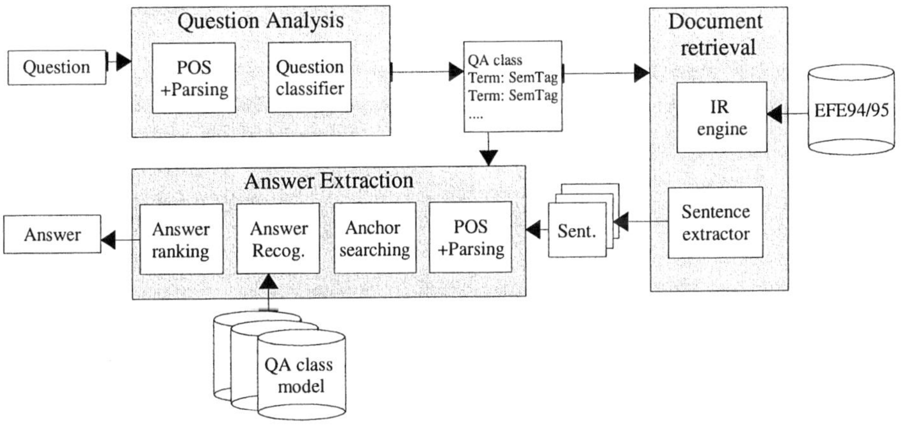

Fig. 1. miraQA architecture

Besides these modules that we use in the question-answering phase, our approach requires a system to train the models that we use for answer recognition. The system uses pairs of questions and answers to query Google and select relevant snippets that contain the answer and other questions terms. In order to build the model we have used QA@CLEF 2003 [7] evaluation set with questions and the answers identified by the judges.

---

[1] Google: http://www.google.com

2.1 Question Analysis

This module classifies questions and selects the terms that are relevant for later processing stages. We have used a taxonomy of 17 different classes in our system that is presented in Table 1. The criteria for the election of the classes has considered the type of the answer, the question form and the relation of the question terms with the answer. Therefore, we refer to classes in this taxonomy as question-answers (QA) classes. General QA classes were split into more specific classes depending on the number of examples in last year evaluation set. As we were planning to use a statistical approach for answer extraction, we were also required to have enough examples in every QA class which determines when to stop subdividing.

Table 1. Question answer (QA) classes used in miraQA

Name	Time	Location	Cause
Person	Year	Country	Manner
Group	Month	City_0	Definition
Count	Day	City_ 1	Quantity
Rest			

In this module, questions are analyzed using ms-tools [1], a package for language processing that contains a POS tagger (MACO) and a partial parser (TACAT) as well as other tools like a Name Entity Recognition and Classification (NERC) module. MACO is able to recognize basic proper names (np) but the NERC module is needed to classify them. As this module is built using an statistical approach using a corpus of a different genre, its accuracy was not good enough for questions and we decided not

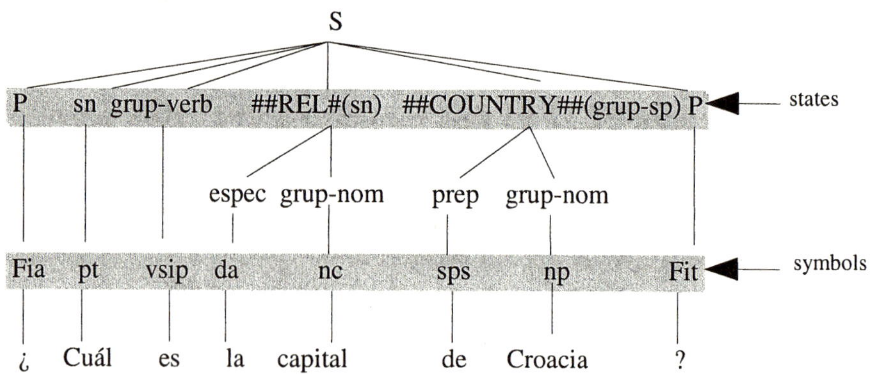

Fig. 2. Analysis of question #1 in QA@CLEF 2003 evaluation set

to use it. We also modified TACAT to prevent prepositional attachment as it was more appropriate to our interests. Once the questions are tagged and parsed, a set of manually developed rules are used to classify questions. This set of rules is also used to assign a semantic tag to some of the chunks according to the class they belong. These tags are a crude attempt to represent the main relations between the answer and the units appearing in the question. A simple example for the question: *"¿Cual es la capital de Croacia?" ("What is the capital city of Croatia?")* is shown in Figure 2 together with the rule that is applied.

An example of the rule that classifies question as city_1 QA class and assigns (M/) the ##CAPITAL## and ##COUNTRY## semantic tags. (C/ means that the word is a token, S/ means that the word is a lemma).

```
{13,city_1,S_[¿_Fia sn_[C/cuál] grup-verb_[S/ser]
sn_[ C/capital;M/##REL##] M/##COUNTRY## ?_Fit ]}
```

2.2 Document Retrieval

The IR module retrieves the top most relevant documents for a query and extracts those sentences that contain any of the words that were used in the query. Words that were assigned a semantic tag during question analysis are used to build the query. For robustness reasons, the content is scanned again to remove stopwords. Our system uses Xapian[2] probabilistic engine to index and search for the most relevant documents. The last step of the retrieval module tokenizes the document using DAEDALUS Tokenizer[3] and extracts the sentences that contain relevant terms. The system assigns two scores to every sentence, the relevance measure provided by Xapian to the document and another figure proportional to the number of terms that were found in the sentence.

2.3 Answer Extraction

The answer extraction module uses a statistical approach to answer pinpointing that is based on a syntactic-semantic context model of the answer built for any of the classes that the system uses. The following operations are performed:

1. **Parsing and Anchor Searching.** Sentences selected in the previous step are tagged and parsed using ms-tools. Chunks that contain any of the terms are retagged with their semantic tags and will be used as anchors. Finally, the system select pieces in a window of words around anchor terms that will go to the next phase.
2. **Answer Recognition.** For every QA class we have previously trained a HMM that models the context of answers found in Google snippets as explained later. A variant of N-best recognition strategy is used to identify the most probable sequence of states (syntactic and semantic tags) that originated the POS sequence. A special semantic tag that identifies the answer (##ANSWER##) represents the

[2] Xapian: http://www.xapian.org
[3] DAEDALUS: http://www.daedalus.es

state where words that form the answer are generated. The recognition algorithm is guided to visit states marked as anchors in order to find a path that passes through the answer state. The algorithm assigns a score to every computed path and candidate answer based on the log probabilities of the HMM.

3. **Ranking.** Candidate answers are normalized (stopwords are removed) and ranked attending to a weighted score that takes into account their length, the score of original documents and sentences and the paths followed during recognition.

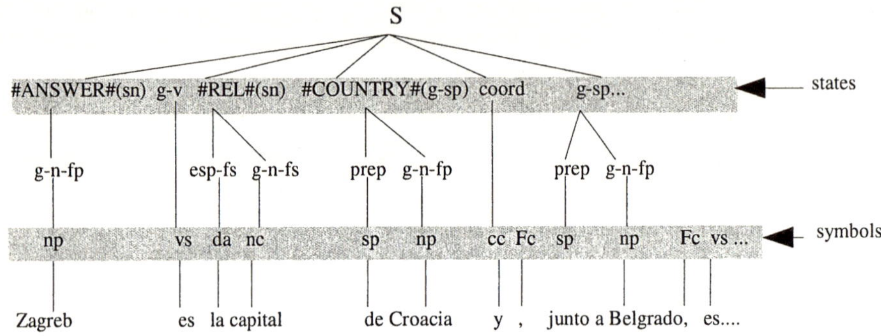

Fig. 3. Answer extraction for *"Zagreb is the capital city of Croatia and, together with Belgrade, is...."* The model suggest the most probable sequence of states for the sequence of POS tags and assigns ##ANSWER## to the first np (proper noun), giving *"Zagreb"* as candidate answer

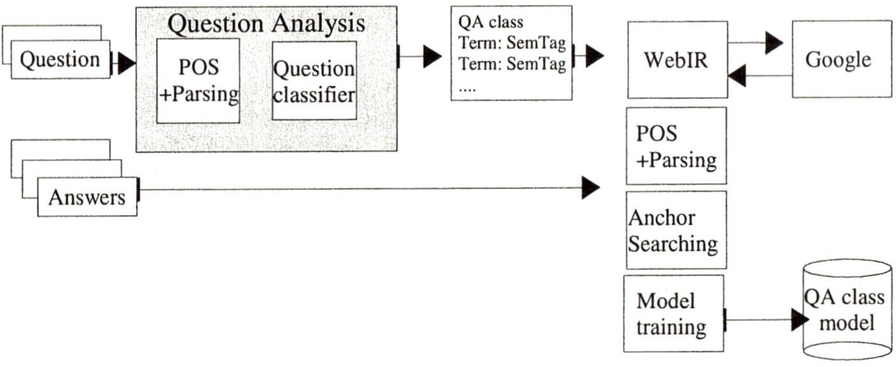

Fig. 4. Architecture for the training of models for extraction

2.4 Training for Answer Recognition

Models that are used in the answer extraction phase are trained before from examples. For training the models we have used questions and answers from CLEF 2003. Questions are analyzed as in the main QA system. Question terms and answers strings are combined and sent to Google using the Google API[4]. Snippets for the top 100 results are retrieved and stored to build the model. They are split into sentences, then they are analyzed and finally, terms that appeared in the question are tagged. The tag is either the semantic class assigned to that term in the question or the answer tag (##ANSWER##). Only sentences containing the answer and at least one of the other semantic tags are selected to train the model.

In order to extract answers we train a HMM in which states are syntactic-semantic tags assigned to the chunks and symbols are POS tags. To estimate the transition and emission probabilities of the automata, we have counted the frequencies of the bigrams for POS-POS and POS-CHUNKS. Besides, a simple add-one smoothing technique is used. For every QA class we train a model that will be used to estimate the score of a given sequence and to identify the answer as explained above.

3 Results

We submitted one run for the monolingual Spanish task (mira041eses) that provides one exact answer to every question. Our system is unable to compute the confidence measure so we have limited us to assign the default value of 0. There are two main kinds of questions, factoid and definition and we have tried the same approach for both of them. Besides, the question set contains some questions whose answer could not be found in the document corpus and the valid answer in that case is the NIL string.

Table 2. Results form mira041eses

Question type	Right	Wrong	IneXact	Unsupported
Factoid	18	154	4	1
Definition	0	17	3	0
Total	18	174	7	1

The results we have obtained are fairly low if we compare them with other systems. We attribute these bad results to the fact that the system is in a very early stage of development and tuning. We have obtained several conclusions from the analysis of correct and wrong answers that will guide our future work. The extraction algorithm is working better for factoid questions than definitional. Among factoid questions results are also better for certain QA classes (DATE, NAME...) which are found with higher frequency in our training set. For other QA classes (MANNER, DEFINITION) there were not enough to efficiently build a model. Another noteworthy fact is that our HMM algorithm is somewhat greedy when trying to identify answer and in that case shows some preference for words appearing near anchor terms. Finally, the algorithm is actually doing two jobs at once as it identifies

[4] Google API: http://www.google.com/apis/

answers and, in some way, recognises answer types or entities according to patterns that were present in training answers of the same kind.

Another source of errors in our system is induced by the document retrieval process and the way we posed questions and score documents. Terms that we select from queries have the same relevance when it is clear that proper names would benefit the retrieval of probably more precise documents. Besides, the simple scoring schema that we used for sentences (one term-one point) contributes to mask some of the useful fragments.

Finally, some errors are also generated during the question classification step as it is unable to handle some of the new surface forms introduced in this year question set. For that reason a catch all classification was also defined and used as a ragbag, but results were not expected to be good for that class. Moreover, POS tagging with MACO fails more frequently for questions and these errors are propagated to the partial parsing. Our limited set of rules was not able to cope with some of these inaccurate parses.

The evaluation also provides results for the percentage of NIL answers that we have returned. In our case we returned 74 NIL answers and only 11 of them were correct (14.86%). NIL values were returned when the process did not provided any answer and their high value is due to the chaining of the other problems mentioned above.

4 Future Work

Several lines for further research are open along with the deficiencies that we have detected in the different modules of our system. One of the straightest improvements is the recognition of Named Entities and other specific types that should entail changes and improvements in the different modules. We believe that these improvements could enhance precision in answer recognition and also retrieval.

With regard to the Question Analysis module we are planning to improve the QA taxonomy as well as coverage and precision of the rules. We are considering manual and automatic methods for the acquisition of classification rules.

Besides the use of NE in the Document Retrieval module, we need to improve the interface with the other two main subsystems. We are planning to develop better strategies for transforming questions into queries and effective scoring mechanism.

Results show that the answer extraction mechanism could work properly with appropriate training. We are interested in determining the amount of training data that would be needed in order to improve recognition results. We would likely need to acquire or generate larger question-answer corpus. In the same line, we expect to experiment with different finite state approaches and learning techniques.

In a cross-cutting line our interest lies in the development of multilingual and crosslingual QA. Some attempts started already for this campaign in order to face more target languages but revealed that the question classification needs a more robust approach to accept the output of current machine translation systems, at least for questions. Finally we would like to explore if our statistical approach for answer recognition is practical for other languages.

Acknowledgements

The work has been partially supported by the projects OmniPaper (European Union, 5th Framework Programme for Research and Technological Development, IST-2001-32174) and MIRACLE (Regional Government of Madrid, Regional Plan for Research, 07T/0055/2003)

Special mention to our colleagues at other members of the MIRACLE group should be done: Ana García-Serrano, José Carlos González, José Miguel Goñi and Javier Alonso.

References

1. S. Abney, M. Collins, and A. Singhal. Answer extraction. In Proceedings of Applied Natural Language Processing (ANLP-2000), (2000).
2. Atserias J., J. Carmona, I. Castellón, S. Cervell, M. Civit, L. Màrquez, M.A. Martí, L. Padró, R. Placer, H. Rodríguez, M. Taulé and J. Turmo Morphosyntactic Analysis and Parsing of Unrestricted Spanish Text. Proceedings of the 1st International Conference on Language Resources and Evaluation (LREC'98). Granada, Spain, 1998.
3. Baeza-Yates R. Ribeiro-Neto B. (Ed.) Modern Information Retrieval. Addison Wesley, New York (1999).
4. Brill E. Lin J. Banco M, Dumais S, Ng A. Data-Intensive Question Answering. In Proceedings of TREC 2001 (2001)
5. Jurafsky D. Martin J.H. Speech and Language Processing. Prentice Hall, Upper Saddle River, New Jersey. (2000)
6. Manning C, Schütze H. Foundations of Statistical Natural Language Processing.. MIT Press (1999)
7. Magnini B., Romagnoli S., Vallin A., Herrera J.,Peñas A., Peinado V, Verdejo F and de Rijke M. The Multiple Language Question Answering Track at CLEF 2003. (2003) Available at http://clef.isti.cnr.it/2003/WN_web/36.pdf
8. Magnini, B., Vallin, A., Ayache, C., Erbach, G., Peñas A., de Rijke, M., Rocha, P., Simov, K. and Sutcliffe R.: Overview of the CLEF 2004 Multilingual Question Answering Track. In : Peters, C., and Clough, P., and Gonzalo, J., and Jones, G., and Kluck, M. and Magnini, B.: Fifth Workshop of the Cross--Language Evaluation Forum (CLEF 2004),Lecture Notes in Computer Science (LNCS), Springer, Heidelberg, Germany (2005)
9. Mérialdo, B.: Tagging English Text with a Probabilistic Model. In Computational Linguistics, Vol 20 (1994) 155-171.
10. Ravichandran, D. and E.H. Hovy. : Learning Surface Text Patterns for a Question Answering System. In Proceedings of the 40th ACL conference. Philadelphia, PA (2002)
11. Vicedo J.L. Recuperando información de alta precisión. Los sistemas de Búsqueda de Respuestas. Phd Thesis. Universidad de Alicante. (2003).

Question Answering for Spanish Supported by Lexical Context Annotation

M. Pérez-Coutiño, T. Solorio, M. Montes-y-Gómez[§], A. López-López, and L. Villaseñor-Pineda

Instituto Nacional de Astrofísica, Óptica y Electrónica (INAOE), Luis Enrique Erro No. 1, Sta Ma Tonantzintla, 72840, Puebla, Pue, México
{mapco, thamy, mmontesg, allopez, villasen}@inaoep.mx

Abstract. This paper describes the prototype developed by the Language Technologies Laboratory at INAOE for Spanish monolingual QA evaluation task at CLEF 2004. Our approach is centered on the use of context at a lexical level in order to identify possible answers to factoid questions. This method is supported by an alternative one based on pattern recognition in order to identify candidate answers to definition questions. We describe the methods applied at different stages of the system and our prototype architecture for question answering. The paper shows and discusses the results we achieved with this approach.

1 Introduction

Question Answering (QA) systems has become an alternative to traditional information retrieval systems because of its capability to provide concise answers to questions asked by the user in natural language. This fact, along with the inclusion of QA evaluation as part of the Text Retrieval Conference (TREC)[1] in 1999, and recently [7] in Multilingual Question Answering as part of the Cross Language Evaluation Forum (CLEF)[2], have arisen a promising and increasing research field.

The Multilingual Question Answering evaluation track at CLEF 2004 is similar to last year edition. For each subtask, participants are provided with 200 questions requiring short answers. Some questions may not have any known answer, and systems should be able to recognize them. However there are some important differences, this year answers included fact based instances or definitions, and systems must return exactly one response per question, and up to two runs.

Our laboratory has developed a prototype system for Spanish monolingual QA task. Two important things should be considered: a) this is our first QA prototype and has been developed from scratch, and b) this the first time that our laboratory participates in an evaluation forum.

---

§ This work was done while visiting the Dept. of Information Systems and Computation Polytechnic University of Valencia, Spain.

1 http://trec.nist.gov/

2 http://clef-qa.itc.it/

C. Peters et al. (Eds.): CLEF 2004, LNCS 3491, pp. 502–511, 2005.

The prototype described in this document relies on the fact that several approaches of QA systems like [4, 6, 9, 11, 14] use named entities recognition at different stages of the system in order to find a candidate answer. Generally speaking, the use of named entities is performed at the final stages of the system, i.e., either in the passage selection or as a discriminator in order to select a candidate answer at the final stage. Another interesting approach is the use of *Predictive Annotation* which was first presented at TREC-8 by Prager et al. [9]. One meaningful characteristic of this approach is the indexing of anticipated semantic types, identifying the semantic type of the answer sought by the question, and extracting the best matching entity in candidate answer passages. In their approach, the authors used nothing but simple pattern matching to get the entities. Our prototype was developed to process both, questions and source documents in Spanish. Our system is based on the methods mentioned above, but differs in the following: i) Semantic class identification relies on the preprocessing of the whole document collection by a POS tagger that simultaneously works as named entity recognizer and classifier. ii) The indexing stage takes as item the lexical context associated to each single named entity contained in every document of the collection. iii) The searching stage selects as candidate answers those named entities whose lexical contexts match better the context of the question. iv) At the final stage, candidate answers are compared against a second set of candidates gathered from the Internet. v) Final answers are selected considering a set of relevance measures which encompass all the information collected in the searching process.

The rest of this paper is organized as follows; section two describes the architecture and functionality of the system; section three details the process of question processing; section four details the process of indexing; section five shows the process of searching; section six describe the process of answer selection; section seven discusses the results achieved by the system; and finally section eight exposes our conclusions and discusses further work.

2 System Overview

The system adjusts to a typical QA system architecture [15]. Figure 1 shows the main blocks of the system. The system could be divided into the following stages: *question processing*, which involves the extraction of named entities and lexical context in the question, as well as question classification to define the semantic class of the answer expected to respond the question; *indexing*, where the document collection is preprocessed, building the representation of each document that become the searching space to find candidate answers to the question; *searching*, where a set of candidate answers is obtained from the index and the Internet (here candidate answers are classified by a machine learning algorithm, and provides information to perform different weighting schemes); and finally *answer selection* where candidate answers are ranked and the final answer recommendation of the system is returned. Next sections describe each of these stages.

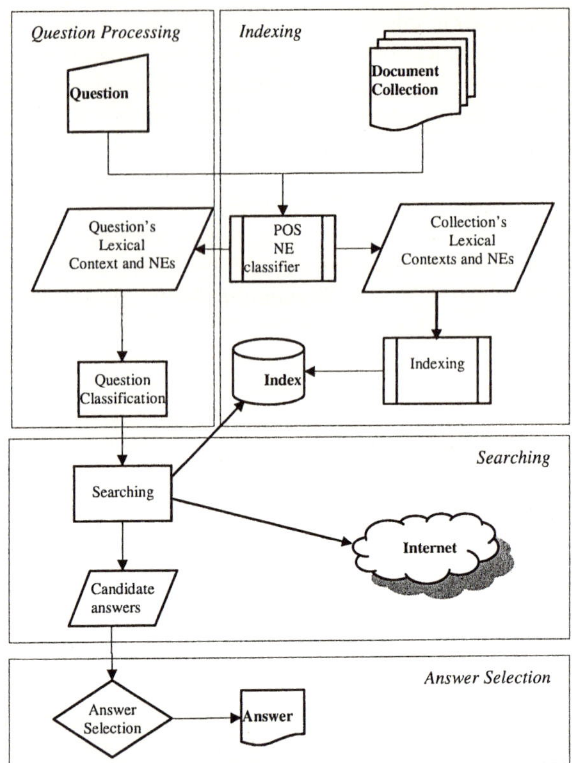

Fig. 1. Block diagram of the system. There are four stages: question processing, indexing, searching and answer selection

3 Question Processing

MACO [3] is a POS tagger and lemmatizer capable of recognizing and classifying named entities (NEs). The possible categories for NEs are the following: person, organization, geographic place, date, quantity and miscellaneous. In order to reduce the possible candidate answers provided by our system we perform a question classification process. The purpose of this classification is to match each question with one of the six named entities provided by MACO.

We use a straightforward approach, where the attributes for the learning task are the prefixes of the words in the question and additional information acquired by an Internet search engine.

In order to gather this information from Internet we first use a set of heuristics and extract from the question the first noun word or words w. We then employ a search engine, in this case Google, submitting queries using the word w in combination with the five possible semantic classes. For instance, for the question *Who is the President of the French Republic?* the word President is extracted as the noun in the question using our heuristics, and 5 queries, one for each possible class, are run in the search engine. The queries take the following forms:

- "President is a person"
- "President is a place"
- "President is a date"
- "President is a measure"
- "President is an organization"

For each query *(q_i)* the heuristic takes the number of results *(Cr_i)* returned by Google and normalizes them according to equation 1. This means that for each question, the summatory of their five performed queries is 1. Normalized values *($Iw(q_i)$)* are taken as attributes values for the learning algorithm. As can be seen it is a very direct approach, but experimental evaluations showed that this information gathered from Internet is quite useful [12].

$$Iw(q_i) = Cr_i \Big/ \sum_{i=0}^{n} Cr_i \qquad \text{Equation [1]}$$

The machine learning technique used was Support Vector Machines [13] implemented in WEKA [16]. The question classification process is discussed in Section 7.

4 Indexing

Each document in the collection is modeled by the system as a factual text object whose content refers to several named entities even when it is focused on a central topic. As mentioned, named entities could be one of these objects: persons, organizations, locations, dates, quantities and miscellaneous. The model assumes that the named entities are strongly related to their lexical context, especially to nouns (subjects) and verbs (actions). Thus, a document can be seen as a set of entities and their contexts. For details about the document model see [8]. In order to obtain the representation of the documents, the system begins preprocessing each document with MACO, where this process is performed off-line. Once the document collection has been tagged, the system extracts the lexical contexts associated to named entities. The context considered for this experiment consists of four verbs or nouns that appear both at the left and right of its corresponding NE (table 1 shows a sample). The final step in the indexing stage is the storage of the extracted contexts, populating a relational database[3] which preserves several relations between each named entity, its semantic class, associated contexts, and the documents where they appeared. In other

Table 1. Context associated to named entity "CFC". Verbs and common nouns in cursive are gathered from a preprocessing with a POS tagger

<DOCNO>EFE19941219-11009</DOCNO> ... Los CFC son usados en los productos anticongelantes, de insuflación y como *refrigerantes*, que *tienen* al *cloro* como un *ingrediente* común. "Los CFC *son* los *responsables* del *agujero* de la *capa* de ozono",...

[3] Due to performance constraints, the index has been distributed over a cluster of 5 CPUs.

words, the index is an adaptation of the well known inverted file structure used in several information retrieval systems.

5 Searching

The search engine developed for the system and the searching process differ in several aspects from traditional search engines. This process relies on two information sources: first the information gathered from question processing, i.e., the expected semantic class of the answer to the question, and the named entities and lexical context of the question; and second, the index of named entities, contexts and documents created during indexing.

5.1 Searching Algorithm

Considering the document representation, all the named entities (NE) mentioned in a given document can be known beforehand. Thus, the named entities from the question become key elements in order to define the document set more likely to provide the answer. For instance, in the question *"¿Dónde se entregan los Oscar?"*, the named entity "Oscar" narrows the set of documents to only those containing such name entity. At the same time, another assumption is that the context in the neighborhood of the answer has to be similar to the lexical context of the question. Once more, from the question of the example, the fragment *"...reciben esta noche, en la sexagésimasexta edición de los Oscar, el homenaje de Hollywood..."* contains a lexical context close to the answer which is similar to that of the question.

Following is the algorithm in detail:

1. Identify the set of relevant documents according to the named entities in the question.
2. Retrieve all contexts in each relevant document.
3. Compute the similarity between question context and those obtained in step 2.
   3.1. Preserve only those contexts whose associated named entity corresponds to the semantic class of the question.
   3.2. Compute a similarity function based on frequencies to perform further ranking and answer selection. This function is based on the number of question's named entities found in each pair *(NE,Context)* retrieved and the number of similar terms in both contexts.
4. Rank the candidate named entities in decreasing order of similarity.
5. Store similarity and named entity classification information (step 3.2) for next stage.

6 Answer Selection

Analyzing the output from the local index we find out that we had a lot of possible answers with the same values for similarity and named entity classification information. Thus, we develop a method for selecting the final possible answer based on answers retrieved from Internet and automated classification of answers using a bagged ensemble of J48 [16].

The final answer presented by our system was selected by calculating the intersection among words between the local index candidate answers and the answers provided by the Internet search. We consider the candidate answer with highest intersection value to be more likely to be the correct answer. However, in some cases all the candidate answers have the same intersection values. In this case we selected from the candidates the first one classified by the learning algorithm as belonging to the positive class. When no positive answer was found among the candidates for a question, then we selected the first candidate answer with the highest value from the local index.

The following sections briefly describe the Internet search and the answer classification processes.

6.1 Internet Searching

As we mention above, at the final stage the system uses information from the Internet in order to get more evidence of the possible accuracy of each candidate answer. From the perspective of the overall system, Internet search and local search occurs simultaneously. This subsection reviews the process involved in such task.

The module used at this step was originally developed at our laboratory to research the effectiveness of a statistical approach to web question answering in Spanish [5]. Such approach lies on the concept of redundancy in the web, i.e, the module applies several transformations in order to convert the question into a typical query and then this query along with some query reformulations are sent to a search engine assuming that the answer would be contained –several times– in the snippets retrieved by the search engine[4]. Candidate answers are selected from the Internet computing all the n-grams, from unigrams to pentagrams, as possible answers to the given question. Then, using some statistical criteria the n-grams are ranked by decreasing confidence score. The top ten are used to validate the candidates gathered from the local searching process.

6.2 Answer Classification

Discriminating among possible answers was posed as a learning problem. Our goal was to train a learning algorithm capable of selecting from a set of possible candidates the answer that most likely satisfies the question. We selected as features the values computed by the local indexing. We used five attributes: 1) the number of times the possible answer was labeled as the entity class of the question; 2) the number of times the possible entity appeared labeled as a different entity class; 3) number of words in common in the context of the possible answer and the context of the question, excluding named entities; 4) the number of entities that matched the entities in the question, and 5) the frequency of the possible answer along the whole collection of documents. With these attributes, we then trained a bagged ensemble of classifiers using as base learning algorithm the rule induction algorithm J48 [10].

---

[4] The search engine used by this module is Google (http://www.google.com)

In this work we build the ensemble using the bagging technique which consists of manipulating the training set [1].

Given that we had available only one small set of questions, we evaluated the classification process in two parts. We divided the set of questions into two subgroups of the same size and performed two runs. In each run, a half of the questions was used for training and a half for testing.

6.3 Answering Definitions

Due to the length and elements in a definition answer, we treated these questions in a different way. In order to reach accurate definition answers, we have implemented a set of heuristics able to find patterns like those described in [11]. Table 2 shows some samples of applying such heuristics.

The heuristics are based on punctuation and some stopwords (articles, pronouns and prepositions) which provide evidence for identification of pairs *<Answer><Name>*. Thus could be easily gathered by regular expressions.

Table 2. Examples of definition questions and their answers

Question	Text fragment containing the answer
¿Quién es Arabella Kiesbauer?	...otra carta-bomba dirigida, al parecer, a una conocida periodista austriaca de raza negra, *Arabella Kiesbauer*, y que fue enviada desde Austria...
¿Qué es UNICEF?	Naciones Unidas, 3 ene (EFE).- El Fondo de las Naciones Unidas para la Infancia (*UNICEF*), formuló hoy, lunes, una petición...
¿Quién es Andrew Lack?	...Tanto es así, que el presidente del departamento de noticias de la cadena NBC, *Andrew Lack*, confesó en una entrevista...

7 Evaluation

We participate in the evaluation exercise with two runs. The first one *inao041eses* was gathered applying all components of the system, while our second run *inao042eses* didn't make use of heuristics for definition answers. Table 3 shows prototype results.

It is important to remark that the average accuracy of the monolingual tasks was 23.7% and 21.88% in the monolingual Spanish task. Nevertheless we note that our results –with respect to evaluation questions– show a drop in the overall system performance of over 60% compared to training results. A preliminary analysis of our approach has let us note some considerations in order to improve its performance. For instance, to experiment with different elements included in the context as well as context length (which couldn't be fixed before questions' release due to time constraints). Question classification is also an issue. Figure 2 shows the accuracy of the classifier, from a total of 200 questions, the classifier only can assign an accurate semantic class to 157 questions, which represents a precision of 78.5%. Besides, searching and candidate answers selection were also very low, only 29.41% of questions right classified as person were answered, 63.63 % of organizations, 39.10% of locations, 37.50% of dates, 28.57% of quantities and 18.18% of miscellaneous were answered.

Table 3. Results of submitted runs

Run	*inao041eses*	*inao042eses*
Right	45	37
Wrong	145	152
ineXact	5	6
Unsupported	5	5
Overall Accuracy	22.50%	18.50%
Factoid Questions	19.44%	17.78%
Definition Questions	50%	25%
"NIL" Accuracy	19.61%	21.74%

We have begun a detailed analysis looking for inconsistencies in the overall approach, as well as programming bugs. The initial step is to get an improved configuration of the POS tagger and NE classifier (MACO) in order to label the corpus and rebuild our indexes (databases) with a non restricted version of document model, i.e.

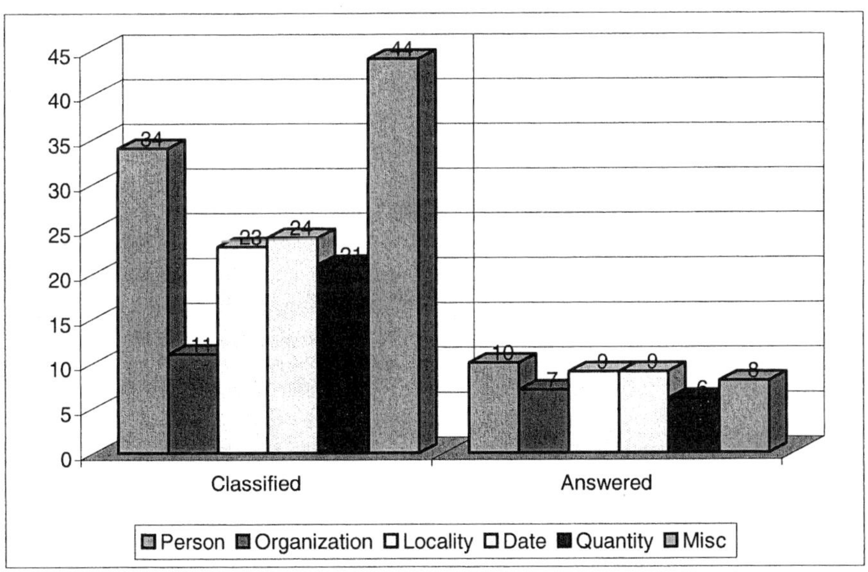

Fig. 2. Question classifier accuracy. Numbers in data labels refers to total number of the questions that were correctly classified or answered

without pre-established elements and length in the context. Thus we will evaluate precision and recall at different stages and repeat some experiments with a refined method for candidates answer ranking, and finally for answer selection.

8 Conclusions

In this paper we presented a lexical context approach for QA in Spanish. The strength of this work lies on the model we used for the source documents. The identification and annotation during the preprocessing phase of named entities and their associated contexts serves as key information in order to select possible answers to a given factoid question. On the other hand, the discrimination of candidate answers is a complex task that requires more research and experimentation of different methods. In this work we have experimented the merging of evidence coming from three main sources: a ranked list of candidate answers gathered by a similarity measure, answer classification by a bagged ensemble of classifiers, and a set of candidate answers collected from the Internet.

Definition questions require more study and a better document model in order to reuse the information extracted during the indexing stage. Further work includes exploring the inclusion of more information as part of the context refining of the semantic classes for questions and named entities, and improving answer selection methodology.

Acknowledgements. This work was done under partial support of CONACYT (Project Grant 43990 and U39957-Y), SNI-Mexico, and the Human Language Technologies Laboratory of INAOE. We also like to thanks to the CLEF as well as EFE agency for the resources provided.

References

1. Breiman L. *Bagging predictors. Machine Learning*, 24(2):123-140, 1996.
2. Burger, J. et al. *Issues, Tasks and Program Structures to Roadmap Research in Question & Answering (Q&A).* NIST 2001.
3. Carreras, X. and Padró, L. *A Flexible Distributed Architecture for Natural Language Analyzers.* In Proceedings of the LREC'02, Las Palmas de Gran Canaria, Spain, 2002.
4. Cowie J., et al., *Automatic Question Answering*, Proceedings of the International Conference on Multimedia Information Retrieval (RIAO 2000)., 2000.
5. Del Castillo-Escobedo A., Montes-y-Gómez M. and Villaseñor-Pineda L. *QA on the Web: A Preliminary Study for Spanish Language.* In Proceedings of Fifth Mexican International Conference on Computer Science, Eds. Baeza-Yates et al., IEEE Computer Society, Mexico 2004.
6. Hirshman L. and Gaizauskas R. *Natural Language Question Answering: The View from Here*, Natural Language Engineering 7, 2001.
7. Magnini B., Romagnoli S., Vallin A., Herrera J., Peñas A., Peinado V., Verdejo F. and Rijke M. *The Multiple Language Question Answering Track at CLEF 2003.* CLEF 2003 Workshop, Springer-Verlag.

8. Pérez-Coutiño M., Solorio T., Montes-y-Gómez M., López-López A. and Villaseñor-Pineda L., *Toward a Document Model for Question Answering Systems.* In Advances in Web Intelligence. LNAI3034 Springer-Verlag 2004.
9. Prager J., Radev D., Brown E., Coden A. and Samn V. *The Use of Predictive Annotation for Question Answering in TREC8.* NIST 1999.
10. Quinlan J. R. *C4.5: Programs for machine learning.* 1993. San Mateo, CA: Morgan Kaufmann.
11. Ravichandran D. and Hovy E. *Learning Surface Text Patterns for a Question Answering System.* In ACL Conference, 2002.
12. Solorio T., Pérez-Coutiño M., Montes-y-Gómez M., Villaseñor-Pineda L., and López-López A. 2004. *A language independent method for question classification.* In COLING-04. 2004. Switzerland.
13. Vapnik, V. *The Nature of Statistical Learning Theory*, Springer, 1995.
14. Vicedo, J.L., Izquierdo R., Llopis F. and Muñoz R., *Question Answering in Spanish.* CLEF 2003 Workshop, Springer-Verlag.
15. Vicedo, J.L., Rodríguez, H., Peñas, A. and Massot, M. *Los sistemas de Búsqueda de Respuestas desde una perspectiva actual.* Revista de la Sociedad Española para el Procesamiento del Lenguaje Natural, n.31, 2003.
16. Witten H. and Frank E. 1999. *Data Mining, Practical Machine Learning Tools and Techniques with Java Implementations.* The Morgan Kaufmann Series in Data Management Systems. Morgan Kaufmann.

Question Answering Using Sentence Parsing and Semantic Network Matching

Sven Hartrumpf

Intelligent Information and Communication Systems (IICS),
University of Hagen (FernUniversität in Hagen), 58084 Hagen, Germany
Sven.Hartrumpf@fernuni-hagen.de

Abstract. The paper describes a question answering system for German called InSicht. All documents in the system are analyzed by a syntactico-semantic parser in order to represent each document sentence by a semantic network. A question sent to InSicht is parsed yielding its semantic network representation and its sentence type. The semantic network is expanded by applying equivalence rules, implicational rules, and concept variations based on semantic relations in computer lexicons and other knowledge sources. During the search stage, every semantic network generated for the question is matched with semantic networks for document sentences. If a match succeeds, an answer is generated from the matching semantic network for the supporting document. InSicht is evaluated on the QA@CLEF 2004 test set. A hierarchy of problem classes is proposed and a sample of suboptimally answered questions is annotated with these problem classes. Finally, some conclusions are drawn, main problems are identified, and directions for future work as suggested by these problems are indicated.

1 Introduction

This paper presents the InSicht question answering (QA) system implemented for German. Its key characteristics are:

- Deep syntactico-semantic analysis with a parser for questions and documents.
- Independence from other document collections. No other documents, e.g. from the web (World Wide Web), are accessed, which helps to avoid unsupported answers. QA that works on web documents is sometimes called web-based QA in contrast to textual QA, see for example [1].
- Generation of the answer from the semantic representation of the documents that support the answer. Answers are not directly extracted from documents.

There are few QA systems for German. The system described by [1] differs mainly in its general approach: it relies on shallow, but robust methods, while InSicht is built on deep sentence parsing. In this respect, InSicht resembles the (English) QA system presented by [2]. In contrast to InSicht, this system applies a theorem prover and a large knowledge base to validate candidate answers.

C. Peters et al. (Eds.): CLEF 2004, LNCS 3491, pp. 512–521, 2005.

Sections 2–7 present InSicht's main components. In Sect. 8, the system is evaluated on the QA@CLEF 2004 questions. Furthermore, problem classes are defined and attributed to individual questions. The final Sect. 9 draws conclusions and describes perspectives for future work.

2 Document Processing

The corpus files distributed for QA@CLEF 2004 are split in a first preprocessing step into article files using an SGML parser (*nsgmls*) and a shell script. Then, each article is tokenized, split into sentences, and stored in a separate SGML file conforming to the Corpus Encoding Standard [3]. The tags for words (w) and sentences (s) are annotated, but it is not attempted to determine paragraph borders because of the mixed encoding quality of the original files.

Duplicate articles are eliminated. Especially in the subcorpus of the *Frankfurter Rundschau* (FR), the percentage of articles with one or more articles showing the same word sequence (ignoring white space and control characters) is astonishingly high (12.3%); for details, see Table 1. Duplicate elimination has several advantages: selecting among candidate answers (see Sect. 7) becomes more accurate, and debugging during further development of the QA system becomes clearer and faster.

After document preprocessing, the WOCADI (WOrd ClAss based DIsambiguating) parser [4, 5] parses article by article. For each sentence in an article, this syntactico-semantic (deep) parser tries to generate a correct representation as a semantic network of the MultiNet formalism [6, 7]. To speed up this parsing step, which takes 5–6 months on one standard PC for the whole document collection, parser instances were run in parallel in a Linux cluster of 4–6 PCs. Each PC was equipped with one AMD Athlon XP 2000+ or similar CPU. The documents must be parsed only once; questions never require any reprocessing of documents. The subcorpus from the *Schweizerische Depeschenagentur* (SDA), which is written in Swiss German, is parsed with a special WOCADI option that reconstructs sharp *S* (*ß*) from *ss* where appropriate, because WOCADI is not primarily developed for Swiss German.

Table 1. Statistics from Document Preprocessing (FR: *Frankfurter Rundschau*, SDA: *Schweizerische Depeschenagentur*, SP: *Der Spiegel*)

subcorpus	articles without duplicates	sentences	words	average sentence length	duplicates: byte-for-byte identical	duplicates: word-for-word identical
FR	122541	2472353	45332424	18.3	22	17152
SDA	140214	1930126	35119427	18.2	333	568
SP	13826	495414	9591113	19.4	0	153
all	276581	4897893	90042964	18.4	355	17873

Table 2. Statistics from Document Parsing

subcorpus	parse results	full parse (%)	chunk parse (%)	no parse (%)
FR	2469689	44.3	21.7	34.0
SDA	1930111	55.8	19.0	25.2
SP	485079	42.7	19.3	38.0
all	4884879	48.7	20.4	30.9

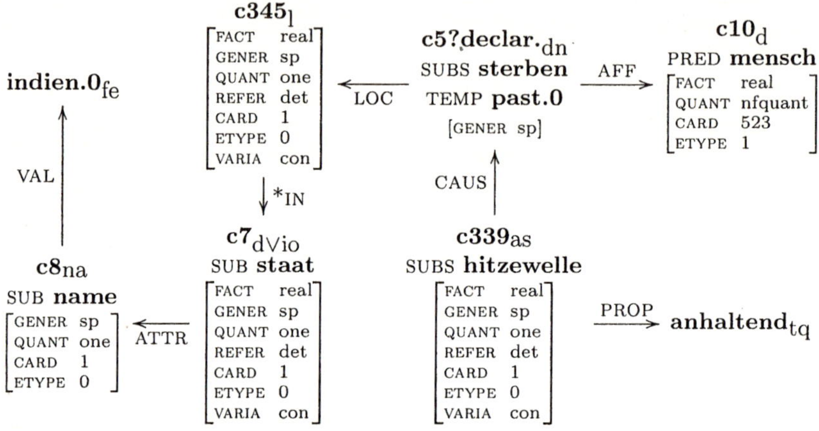

Fig. 1. Graphical form of the MultiNet generated by the WOCADI parser for (simplified) document sentence SDA.950618.0048.377: *In Indien starben [...] 523 Menschen infolge der [...] anhaltenden Hitzewelle.* (*'523 people died in India due to the continuing heat wave.'*)

The parser produced complete semantic networks for 48.7% of all sentences and only partial semantic networks (corresponding to a WOCADI parse in chunk mode) for 20.4%. The percentages for the three subcorpora differ considerably (see Table 2). This reflects the differences in encoding quality of the original SGML files and in language complexity. For example, the SDA subcorpus is parsed best because newswire sentences are typically simpler in structure than newspaper sentences and the original SGML files show fewer encoding errors than the ones for FR and *Der Spiegel* (SP). The numbers in the second column of Table 2 are slightly smaller than the corresponding numbers in the third column of Table 1 because for efficiency reasons the analysis of a text will be stopped if a certain maximal number of semantic network nodes is produced during parsing the sentences of the text. This criterion causes WOCADI to stop parsing a text after around 250 sentences.

A semantic network for a simplified document sentence is shown in Fig. 1. Edges labeled with the relations PRED, SUB, SUBS, and TEMP are *folded* (printed below the name of the start node) if the network topology allows this, e.g. SUB *name* below node name *c8*. As a last document processing step, semantic

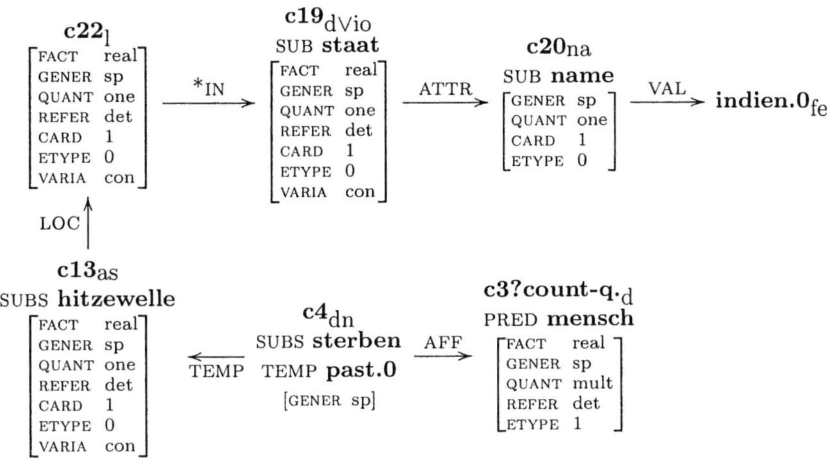

Fig. 2. Graphical form of the MultiNet generated by the WOCADI parser for question 164: *Wie viele Menschen starben während der Hitzewelle in Indien?* (*'How many people died during the heat wave in India?'*)

networks are simplified and normalized as described in Sect. 5 to allow more efficient answer search.

3 Question Processing

A question posed by a user (online) or drawn from a test collection (offline, e.g. the 200 questions for QA@CLEF 2004), is parsed by the WOCADI parser, which also produced the semantic networks for the documents. The parser relies only on the question string; it ignores the question type (F for factoid and D for definition) provided at QA@CLEF 2004. The parsing result is a semantic network of the MultiNet formalism plus additional information relevant for the QA system: the (question) focus (marked in graphical semantic networks by a question mark) and the sentence type (written directly behind the focus mark in graphical semantic networks). The MultiNet for question 164 from QA@CLEF 2004 is shown in graphical form in Fig. 2.

For the questions of QA@CLEF 2004, the sentence type is determined with 100% correctness. Only 3 out of 10 values for the sentence type attribute occur for these questions, namely *wh-question*, *count-question*, and *definition-question*.

4 Query Expansion

During query expansion, equivalent and similar semantic networks are produced for the question representation in order to find answers that are not explicitly contained in a document but only implied by it. Equivalent networks are generated by applying *equivalence rules* (or paraphrase rules) for MultiNet. In contrast to such semantic rules, some QA systems (e.g. the one described by [8]) use reformulation rules working on strings. The freer the word order, the more problematic surface string operations. As the word order in German is less constrained than in English, such operations may be more problematic and less effective for German.

For maintenance reasons, many rules are abstracted by *rule schemas*. For example, three rule schemas connect a state with its inhabitant and the respective adjective, e.g. *Spanien* (*'Spain'*), *Spanier* (*'Spaniard'*), and *spanisch* (*'Spanish'*). These three rule schemas lead to around 600 rules. In addition, the female and male nouns for the inhabitant are connected in the computer lexicon HaGenLex (*Ha*gen *Ge*rma*n* *Lex*icon; see [9]) by a certain MultiNet relation. Similar rule schemas exist for regions.

```
((rule
  (
    (subs ?n1 "ermorden.1.1")
    (aff ?n1 ?n2)
  →
    (subs ?n3 "sterben.1.1")
    (aff ?n3 ?n2)))
  (ktype categ)
  (name "ermorden.1.1_entailment"))
```

Fig. 3. Entailment rule for *ermorden* (*'to kill'*) and *sterben* (*'to die'*)

In addition to equivalence rules, *implicational rules* for lexemes are used in backward chaining, e.g. the logical entailment between *ermorden.1.1.* (*'to kill'*) and *sterben.1.1* (*'to die'*); see Fig. 3. A lemma followed by a numerical homograph identifier and a numerical polyseme identifier forms a so-called concept identifier (or concept ID) in HaGenLex, e.g. *ermorden.1.1*; the numerical suffix of concept IDs is sometimes omitted to improve readability. All rules are applied to find answers that are not explicitly contained in a document but only implied by it. Fig. 4 shows one of the 109 semantic networks[1] generated for question 164 from Fig. 2 during query expansion. This semantic network was derived by applying two default rules for MultiNet relations (in backward chaining). The first rule transfers the LOC edge from the abstract situation (subordinated to *hitzewelle*) to the situation node (subordinated to *sterben*). The second rule expresses as a default that a causal relation (CAUS) implies (under certain conditions) a temporal overlap (TEMP). Reconsidering the semantic network in Fig. 1 for a document sentence, the similarity to the question variant from Fig. 4 becomes obvious. This similarity allows a match and the generation of a correct answer (namely just *523*) in the remaining stages of InSicht.

[1] This number does not include any concept variations (described in the next paragraph).

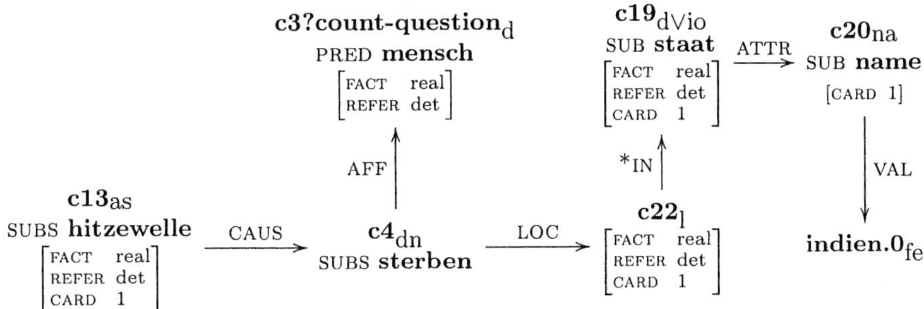

Fig. 4. One result from query expansion for question 164 from Fig. 2

Besides rules, InSicht applies other means to generate equivalent (or similar) semantic networks. Each concept in a semantic network can be replaced by concepts that are synonyms, hyponyms, etc. Such *concept variations* are based on lexico-semantic relations in HaGenLex. As HaGenLex contains a mapping from lexemes to GermaNet concept IDs [10], synonymy and subordination relations from GermaNet were used in a separate experiment in addition to the lexico-semantic relations from HaGenLex. For the questions from the test set, this extension led to no changes in the answers given. On average, query expansion using rules led to 6.5 additional semantic networks for a question from QA@CLEF 2004. If one counts the combination with concept variations, around 215 semantic networks are used per question.

Using inference rules during query expansion is just a pragmatic decision. In an ideal system without memory constraints, rules could come into play later: the semantic representation of all documents would be loaded as a huge knowledge base (where one had to cope with inconsistencies) and rules would be used by a theorem prover to test whether the question (or some derived form) can be deduced from the knowledge base. The main reasons to avoid such a system are the huge amount of facts from the documents and the problem of inconsistencies.

5 Search for Matching Semantic Networks

The main idea for answer searching in InSicht is to find a document sentence containing an answer by semantic network matching. Before this matching, the semantic network for the question is split in two parts: the *queried network* (roughly corresponding to the representation of the phrase headed by the interrogative pronoun or determiner) and the *match network* (the semantic network without the queried network). The implemented matcher module calls a concept index server for all concepts in the match network to speed up the search. Efficient matching is achieved by simplifying networks as described in the next paragraph (for question networks and document networks in the same way) so that a subset test with a large set of query expansions (generated as described

```
(*in "c1*in" "c1staat.1.1")                  (loc "c1sterben.1.1" "c1*in")
(aff "c1sterben.1.1" "c1mensch.1.1")         (prop "c1hitzewelle.1.1" "anhaltend.1.1")
(attr "c1staat.1.1" "c1name.1.1")            (temp "c1sterben.1.1" "past.0")
(caus "c1hitzewelle.1.1" "c1sterben.1.1")    (val "c1name.1.1" "indien.0")
```

Fig. 5. Simplified and normalized semantic network for the MultiNet of Fig. 1. For better readability, features of nodes are omitted

in Sect. 4) can be employed. Average answer time is several seconds on a standard PC. A variant of this matching approach has been tried in the monolingual GIRT task (see one of the five runs reported by [11]), currently with retrieval results that are not sufficient yet.

Semantic networks are simplified and normalized to achieve acceptable answer times. The following simplifications are applied: First, inner nodes of a semantic network that correspond to instances (for example *c4* and all nodes named *cN* in Fig. 4) are combined (collapsed) with their concept nodes (typically connected by a SUB, SUBS, PRED, or PREDS relation) to allow a canonical order of network edges. Sometimes this operation necessitates additional query expansions. (These semantic networks are basically variations of possible instance node names.) Second, semantic details from some layers in MultiNet are omitted, e.g. the feature ETYPE (extension type) of nodes and the knowledge types of edges [6]. After such simplifications, a lexicographically sorted list of MultiNet edges can be seen as a canonical form, which allows efficient matching. The simplified and normalized semantic network corresponding to the MultiNet in Fig. 1 is shown in Fig. 5.

6 Answer Generation

Generation rules take the semantic network of the question (the queried network part), the sentence type of the question, and the matching semantic network from the document as input and generate a German phrase (typically a noun phrase) as a candidate answer. The generation rules are kept simple because the integration of a separately developed generation module is planned so that InSicht's current answer generation is only a temporary solution. Despite the limitations of the current answer generation, it proved advantageous to work with small coverage rules because they filter what a good answer can be. For example, no rule generates a pronoun; so uninformative pronouns cannot occur in the answer because answer generation will fail for pronouns. If the expected answers become more complex, this filtering advantage will shrink.

An answer extraction strategy working on surface strings in documents is avoided because in languages showing more inflectional variation than English, simple extraction from surface strings can lead to an answer that describes the correct entity, but in an incorrect syntactic case. Such an answer should be judged as inexact or even wrong; e.g. a semantically correct answer for question 096 is contained in sentence SDA.951003.0054.96 in accusative case, but given the question context the answer should be in nominative case. Only after using the generation module, InSicht delivers an answer in the expected syntactic case.

7 Answer Selection

The preceding steps typically result in several pairs of generated answer string and supporting document ID[2] for a given question. In order to select the best answer, length and frequency are jointly considered so that longer and more frequent answers are preferred. Answer length is measured by the number of characters and words. In case of several supporting documents, the document whose ID comes alphabetically first is picked. This strategy is simple and open to improvements but has worked surprisingly well so far.

To automatically detect cases where question processing (or some later stage) made a mistake that led to a very general matching and finally to far too many competing candidate answers, a maximum for different answer strings is defined (depending on question type). If it is exceeded, the system will retreat to an empty answer (*NIL*) with a reduced confidence score.

8 Evaluation on the QA@CLEF 2004 Test Set

By annotating each question leading to a suboptimal answer[3] with a *problem class*, the system components which need improvements most urgently can be identified. After fixing a general programming error, InSicht achieved 80 correct answers and 7 inexact answers[4] for 200 questions in an unofficial re-run. This leaves 113 questions (where the system gave an incorrect empty answer) to be annotated. The hierarchy of problem classes shown in Table 3 was defined before annotation started. Three questions have been excluded from the evaluation by the coordinators of the German QA task after my report of spelling errors; they are counted for the problem class *q.ungrammatical* in Table 3. 15 questions were parsed incorrectly (problem class *q.incorrect_parse*). As the annotation of the remaining 95 questions consumes much time, only a sample of 59 questions has been classified so far. Therefore the percentages for subclasses of *d.error* and *q-d.error* are estimates from the sample.

For a question, a problem subclass (preferably a most specific subclass) for *q.error*, *d.error*, and *q-d.error* could be annotated in theory. But the chosen approach is more pragmatic: If a problem is found in an early processing stage,

---

[2] As each answer is generated from a semantic network corresponding to one document sentence, the system also knows the ID (the byte offset) of the supporting sentence in this document.

[3] A suboptimal answer is one not marked as correct (R) by the assessors.

[4] In the submitted run, both numbers are somewhat lower: 67 correct answers and 2 inexact answers.

Table 3. Hierarchy of problem classes and problem class frequencies for QA@CLEF 2004

name	description	%
problem		
q.error	error on question side	
q.parse_error	question parse is not complete and correct	
q.no_parse	parse fails	0.0
q.chunk_parse	only chunk parse result	0.0
q.incorrect_parse	parser generates full parse result, but it contains errors	13.3
q.ungrammatical	question is ungrammatical	2.7
d.error	error on document side	
d.parse_error	document sentence parse is not complete and correct	
d.no_parse	parse fails	22.8
d.chunk_parse	only chunk parse result	5.7
d.incorrect_parse	parser generates full parse result, but it contains errors	7.1
d.ungrammatical	document sentence is ungrammatical	2.8
q-d.error	error in connecting question and document	
q-d.failed_generation	no answer string can be generated for a found answer	1.4
q-d.matching_error	match between semantic networks is incorrect	5.7
q-d.missing_cotext	answer is spread across several sentences	5.7
q-d.missing_inferences	inferential knowledge is missing	32.8

one should stop looking at later stages, no matter whether one could investigate them despite the early problem, or speculate about them, or just guess.

Seeing the high numbers for the problem class *d.parse_error* and its subclasses one could suspect that a parse error for the relevant document sentence[5] excludes a correct answer in general. Fortunately this is not the case. Several questions from QA@CLEF 2004 were answered correctly although the semantic network for the supporting sentence contained some errors; but the semantic network part relevant for the answer was correct.

9 Conclusions and Perspectives

The InSicht QA system achieves high precision: non-empty answers (i.e. non-*NIL* answers) are rarely wrong (for the QA@CLEF 2004 questions not a single one; in the submitted run only one). Furthermore, the deep level of representation based on semantic networks opens the way for intelligent processes like paraphrasing on the semantic level and inferences.

The experience with the current system revealed the following five problem areas[6] (after naming the area, a solution for future work is suggested):

---

[5] If several document sentences are relevant, InSicht (as other QA systems) can often profit from this redundancy.

[6] The first two correspond to the two most frequent problem classes in Table 3.

- Inferential knowledge: encoding and semi-automatically acquiring entailments etc.
- Parser coverage: extending the lexicons and improving the robustness and grammatical knowledge of the parser.
- Partial semantic networks (produced by the parser in chunk mode): devising methods to utilize partial semantic networks for finding answers.
- Answers spread across several sentences of a document are not found: applying the parser in text mode (involving intersentential coreference resolution, see [12]).
- Processing time for documents: optimizing the parser and developing a strategy for on-demand processing.

References

1. Neumann, G., Xu, F.: Mining answers in German web pages. In: Proceedings of the International Conference on Web Intelligence (WI-2003), Halifax, Canada (2003)
2. Harabagiu, S., Moldovan, D., Paşca, M., Mihalcea, R., Surdeanu, M., Bunescu, R., Gîrju, R., Rus, V., Morărescu, P.: The role of lexico-semantic feedback in open-domain textual question-answering. In: Proceedings of the 39th Annual Meeting of the Association for Computational Linguistics (ACL-2001), Toulouse, France (2001) 274–281
3. Ide, N., Priest-Dorman, G., Véronis, J.: Corpus Encoding Standard. (1996)
4. Helbig, H., Hartrumpf, S.: Word class functions for syntactic-semantic analysis. In: Proceedings of the 2nd International Conference on Recent Advances in Natural Language Processing (RANLP'97), Tzigov Chark, Bulgaria (1997) 312–317
5. Hartrumpf, S.: Hybrid Disambiguation in Natural Language Analysis. Der Andere Verlag, Osnabrück, Germany (2003)
6. Helbig, H.: Die semantische Struktur natürlicher Sprache: Wissensrepräsentation mit MultiNet. Springer, Berlin (2001)
7. Helbig, H., Gnörlich, C.: Multilayered extended semantic networks as a language for meaning representation in NLP systems. In Gelbukh, A., ed.: Computational Linguistics and Intelligent Text Processing (CICLing 2002). Volume 2276 of LNCS., Berlin, Springer (2002) 69–85
8. Echihabi, A., Oard, D.W., Marcu, D., Hermjakob, U.: Cross-language question answering at the USC Information Sciences Institute. In Peters, C., ed.: Results of the CLEF 2003 Cross-Language System Evaluation Campaign, Working Notes for the CLEF 2003 Workshop, Trondheim, Norway (2003) 331–337
9. Hartrumpf, S., Helbig, H., Osswald, R.: The semantically based computer lexicon HaGenLex – Structure and technological environment. Traitement automatique des langues 44(2) (2003) 81–105
10. Osswald, R.: Die Verwendung von GermaNet zur Pflege und Erweiterung des Computerlexikons HaGenLex. LDV Forum 19(1/2) (2004) 43–51
11. Leveling, J., Hartrumpf, S.: University of Hagen at CLEF 2004: Indexing and translating concepts for the GIRT task. This volume
12. Hartrumpf, S.: Coreference resolution with syntactico-semantic rules and corpus statistics. In: Proceedings of the Fifth Computational Natural Language Learning Workshop (CoNLL-2001), Toulouse, France (2001) 137–144

First Evaluation of Esfinge – A Question Answering System for Portuguese

Luís Costa

Linguateca at SINTEF ICT,
Pb 124 Blindern, 0314 Oslo, Norway
Luis.Costa@sintef.no

Abstract. This paper starts by describing Esfinge, a general domain Portuguese question answering system that uses the redundancy available in the Web as an important resource to find its answers. The paper also presents the strategies employed to participate in CLEF-2004 and discusses the results obtained. Three different strategies were tested: searching the answers only in the CLEF document collection, searching the answers in the Web and using the CLEF document collection to confirm these answers and finally searching the answers only in the Web. The intriguing question of why the system performed better when joining the two information sources, even though it was designed for the Web is discussed; in this connection, different language varieties and some problems of Google are mentioned. The paper concludes describing some of the work planned for the near future.

1 What Is Esfinge?

For a given question a question answering system returns answers with the help of an information repository. This task requires the processing of the question and of the information repository. Existing systems use various linguistic resources like taggers, named entities extractors, semantic relations, dictionaries, thesauri, etc. to do this.

Esfinge (http://acdc.linguateca.pt/Esfinge/) is based on the architecture proposed by Eric Brill [1]. Brill tried to check the results that could be obtained by investing less in the resources to process the question and the information repository and more in the volume of the information repository itself. The Web, being the biggest free information repository that we know, is the best candidate for these experiments. Brill's approach was never tried for Portuguese and this language is quite used in the Web [2]. The motivation to start developing Esfinge was to check the results that could be obtained by applying Brill's approach to Portuguese.

Brill's architecture has four modules:

1. Question reformulation
2. N-grams harvesting
3. N-grams filtering
4. N-Grams composition

C. Peters et al. (Eds.): CLEF 2004, LNCS 3491, pp. 522–533, 2005.

1.1 Question Reformulation

In this module, patterns of plausible answers to a given question are obtained. These patterns are based on the words in the question. For example, a plausible pattern for the question *In which year did Vasco da Gama arrived in India?* would be *Vasco da Gama arrived in India in.*

It is too optimistic to expect the existence of pages with answers in "friendly" formats for all the questions (with the exact format as the result of the question reformulation module). Therefore, patterns of plausible answers with less ambitious strings, like for example the simple conjunction of the question words are also considered. Each one of these patterns is scored according to how good it can help to find correct answers. The patterns were initially scored according to my intuition with scores ranging from 1 to 20.

The linguistic information of this module is encapsulated in a text file using the regular expression syntax of the Perl programming language. Each triple (question pattern, answer pattern, score) is defined in a line separated by a slash (/). Follows a sample of the referred text file (simplified for clarity's sake).

O que ([^\s?]*) ([^?]*)\??/"$2 $1"/10

The rule states that, for a question starting with *O que X Y?* (*What X Y?*), answers with the pattern *"Y X"* should be granted a score of 10 (since Y and X are enclosed in double quotes, it means this is a phrase pattern – Y must appear just before X). For the question *O que é a MTV?* (*What is MTV?*), this rule generates the pattern *"a MTV é"* with the score 10.

1.2 N-Grams Harvesting

In this module, the resulting patterns of the Question Reformulation module are queried against an information repository. For that purpose they are submitted to a web search engine (Google[1] for the moment).

The next step is to extract and measure the frequency of word N-grams from the resulting snippets (considering the first 100 snippets), using the Ngram Statistics Package (NSP) [3] for that purpose.

For example, from the query *"a antiga capital da Polónia"* (*the former capital of Poland*), one gets the following N-gram distribution (16 most frequent N-grams):

da: 185
a: 99
antiga: 96
capital: 91
de: 78
e: 73
Polônia: 54
capital<>da: 47
do: 46
da<>Polônia: 38

[1] http://www.google.com/help/index.html

em: 30
antiga<>capital: 30
o: 28
que: 28
com: 26
é: 25

The correct answer is expected to be among the extracted N-grams. Next, these N-grams of different lengths will be scored accordingly to their frequency, length and the scorings of the patterns that originated them, using the following equation:

N-gram score = $\sum (F * S * L)$, through the first 100 snippets resulting from the web search where:

F = N-gram frequency
S = Score of the search pattern which recovered the document
L = N-gram length

1.3 N-Grams Filtering

This module re-evaluates the scorings obtained in the N-grams harvesting module, analysing the N-grams' particular features.

For some questions, even if we do not know the answer, we can predict the type of expected answer. For example:

- A When-question implies an answer of type "date". It can be more or less precise, for instance a year (like *1973*) or an extended date (like *11/10/1973*), but such answers as *Lisboa* or *George W. Bush* do not make any sense in this context.
- A "How many?" question implies an answer of type "number". Strings like *Oslo* or *5/8/2004* are not acceptable answers.

In analysing the N-grams as regards the presence of digits, capitalization and typical patterns may allow to reclassify those N-grams or even discarding them. Also, the PoS information provided by a morphologic analyser or tagger may be used to enhance the scorings of N-grams with interesting sequences of PoS categories.

1.4 N-Grams Composition

This module tries to cope with questions with a set of answers, like *Who were the musicians in Queen?*. The complete answer to this question demands the composition of the word N-grams *Freddy Mercury*, *Brian May*, *Roger Taylor* and *John Deacon*, that can be expected among the top scored word N-grams obtained from the three previous modules.

The first task in this module is to determine whether the type of answer is singular (ex: *Who was the first king of Norway?*), plural with a known number of items (ex: *Which are the three largest cities in Portugal?*) or plural with an unknown number of items (ex: *What are the colours of Japan's flag*?).

For the first type this module will return the best scored word N-gram resulting from the previous modules. For the second type it will return the required number of best scored word N-grams (three, in the example above).

For the third type, it will need to decide which word N-grams will be part of the answer. This can be done using a threshold that will define which word N-grams will be part of the answer according to their scoring. The proximity of the scoring values can also be used as a decisive factor.

2 Strategies for CLEF 2004

Although Esfinge is still in its early stages of development, participating in the CLEF-2004 QA track seemed a good way of evaluating the work done so far, experimenting some of the difficulties in this field and getting in touch with the state-of-the-art of actual QA systems and their approaches.

For the QA-CLEF monolingual track, one had to supply, along with each answer, the ID of one document in the document collection that supported it. As said above, Esfinge originally used Google's search results and was mainly statistical (tried to use the redundancy existing in the Web), so I knew I would need to add some extra functionalities.

I tested three different strategies. In the first one, the system searched the answers in the CLEF document collection (Run 1). In the second one, it searched the answers in the Web and used the CLEF document collection to confirm these answers (Run 2). Finally, in the third strategy Esfinge searched the answers only in the Web (this one was not submitted to the organization).

2.1 Run 1

The first thing I needed was some way of searching in the document collection. I have some experience in encoding corpora using IMS Corpus Workbench [4] as well as using its query capabilities. So, it seemed a good idea to use it to encode the CLEF document collection and to use its query capabilities to search for desired patterns.

Another important decision concerned the size of the text unit to be searched for patterns, i.e. whether to consider the entire text of each document or only a passage. I had not a definitive answer for this question, so I chose to do some experiments.

Since the document length seemed too big for a unit, I tried the three following strategies:

1. Considering the text unit as 50 contiguous words. This is done dynamically: it is possible to query corpora encoded using IMS Workbench for the context (in terms of words) in which the required patterns co-occur.
2. Dividing each document into sentences. Those sentences were considered as the text unit. To segment the document collection into sentences, I used the Perl Module Lingua::PT::PLNbase freely available at CPAN. The collection had in average 28 words per sentence.
3. Dividing each document into sets of three sentences. Those sets of three sentences were considered as the text unit.

For each question in the QA track, Esfinge proceeded by the following steps:

Question reformulation. Submitting the question to the question reformulation module. The result was a set of pairs (answer pattern, score).

Passage extraction. Searching each of these patterns in the document collection and extracting the text units (50 contiguous words, one sentence or three sentences) where the pattern was found. The system discards stop-words without context. For example in the query *"a" "antiga" "capital" "da" Polónia"*, the words *"a"* and *"da"* are discarded while in the query *"a antiga capital da Polónia"* (phrase pattern) they are not discarded. Currently I discard the 22 most frequent words in the CETEMPúblico corpus [5]. At this stage the system retrieved a set of document passages {P1, P2 ... Pn}.

N-grams harvesting. Computing the distribution of word N-grams (from length 1 to length 3) of the document excerpts. Ordering the list of word N-grams according to a score based on the frequency, length and scorings of the patterns that originated the document excerpts where the N-grams were found, computed using the formula above. At this stage, the system has an ordered set of possible answers {A1, A2 ... An}.

N-grams filtering. Discarding some of these possible answers using a set of filters, namely:

- First, a filter to discard answers that are contained in the questions. Ex: for the question *Qual é a capital da Rússia* (*What is the capital of Russia?*), the answer *capital da Rússia* (*capital of Russia*) is not desired and should be discarded.
- Then, a filter that used the morphologic analyser *jspell* [6] to check the PoS of the various words in each answer. The analyser returns a set of possible PoS tags for each word. This filter considered some PoS as "interesting": adjectives (adj), common nouns (nc), numbers (card) and proper nouns (np). All answers whose first and final word did not belong to one of these "interesting" PoS were discarded. Example: before this filter, the highest scored answers for the question *Quem é Andy Warhol?* (*Who is Andy Warhol?*) were:

  que: prel
  um: art
  de Andy: prep np
  por: prep
  como: con
  pela primeira vez: cp nord nc
  sua: ppos
  mais: pind
  ou: con
  artista: nc
  que Andy: prel np
  com esta dimensão: prep pdem nc

segundo andar chamado: nord nc v
cola em garrafa: nc prep nc

After applying the filter, the set of highest scored answers are:

artista: nc
cola em garrafa: nc prep nc

For the CLEF runs, I erroneously assumed that the order in which the PoS tags were returned was related to their frequency. With that in mind, I used only the first PoS for each word. Recently, I found out that this assumption was wrong. It is fair to say that most probably my misinterpretation of the analyser's results led to a poor performance of this filter.

The final answer was the candidate answer with the highest score in the set of candidate answers which were not discarded by any of the filters above. If all the answers were discarded by the filters, then the final answer was NIL (meaning the system is not able to find an answer in the document collection).

From the three previous experiments, I selected to send to the organization the one considering sets of three sentences as the text unit, because it seemed the one with (slightly) best results.

2.2 Run 2

Since it was possible to send two sets of results to the organization, I did some experiments using also the Web as source since that is the line of work where I expect to get better results.

The next experiment used the strategy described in another paper by Brill [7]. First, it looked for answers in the Web, and then tried to find documents in the document collection supporting those answers. It submitted the patterns obtained in the question reformulation module to Google. Then, the document snippets $\{S_1, S_2 \ldots S_n\}$ were extracted from Google's results pages. These snippets are usually composed by fragments of the different sentences in the recovered documents that contain the query words and have approximately 25 words.

The next step was to compute the distribution of word N-grams (from length 1 to length 3) existing in this document snippets. From this point the algorithm followed the one described in run 1, with an extra filter in the N-grams filtering module: a filter that searched the document collection for documents supporting the answer – containing both the candidate answer and a pattern obtained from the question reformulation module.

2.3 Brazilian Portuguese. A Problem?

Using texts in Brazilian web pages definitely enlarges the corpus that the system uses to find answers, but may also bring problems. The system may return an answer in the Brazilian variety which is not possible to support in the document collection, which was built with newspaper texts written in European Portuguese.

For example, for the question *Qual é a capital da Rússia?* (*What is the capital of Russia?*), the system returned the answer *Moscou* (in the Brazilian variant). Since we were checking in a European Portuguese collection, it would be much easier to support the answer *Moscovo* (same word in the European variant).

Another problem may occur when the scoring gets diluted by the two variants (like *Moscou* and *Moscovo* in the example), thus allowing other answers to get better scores. Searching only in pages published in Portugal can obviate this problem, but will diminish the corpus to search into.

Yet another example can be illustrated by the query: "a antiga capital da Polónia" presented above. Even though using the word *Polónia* (Portuguese variant) in the query, this word is not on the top 10 of harvested N-grams. On the other hand, *Polônia* (in the Brazilian variant) is third placed on the N-gram ranking. The reason for this is that Google does not differentiate between accentuated and non-accentuated characters, so the characters *ó*, *ô* and *o* are considered exactly the same thing by this search engine. This can be a serious problem when one is processing a language with the variety and heavy use of accentuation as Portuguese. One way to solve this problem is to develop a post-Google filter to discard non-interesting documents, thus overcoming Google's limitations regarding Portuguese.

2.4 Web-Only Experiment

For the present paper, I did an extra run using the Web as document collection and without crosschecking the answers in CLEF's document collection. I thought this experiment could give some insight on whether there are advantages in combining two different information sources (Web and CLEF's document collection) or whether one can get better results using only one of these information sources.

3 Results

Table 1 shows that the results in Run 2 (the one which used the Web crosschecking the results in the document collection) are slightly better. However, we can also see that the type of question is not irrelevant to the results. For example, Run 1 had better results for questions of type "Qual" (Which). There are also some relatively frequent question types without any right answer in either run (like "Como", "Quando", "De que"). This probably means that there is something in these types of questions which Esfinge does not deal properly within the answer-finding procedure.

Both Run 1 and Run 2 were evaluated by the organization. The Web-only experience is in some aspects a different task from the one proposed in CLEF. For example, CLEF's guidelines [8] stated that some questions might have no answer in the document collection (NIL answer), but it is much more difficult to say such thing when using the Web as the document collection. For this reason, I considered not answered questions as wrong when evaluating this experience. Since Esfinge was not recording the addresses of the documents it used to get the answers in the Web, it was not possible to check whether the answers were supported or not.

Table 1. Results by type of question

	#questions	#right (Run 1)	#right (Run 2)	#right (Web-only)
Quem (Who)	53	8	9	3
Qual (Which)	34	8	6	2
Onde (Where)	24	1	5	3
O que (What)	18	0	2	1
Em que (In which)	15	0	2	0
Quanto(a)s (How many)	13	2	3	1
Como (How)	9	0	0	0
Que (What, Which)	9	2	2	1
Quando (When)	9	0	0	0
De que (Of what, which)	7	0	0	0
A que (To which, what)	3	0	0	0
Mencione, Nomeie, Indique (Name)	4	1	1	0
X ... em que (... in which)	1	0	0	0
Total	199	22	30	11

Table 2. Results by question length

# words in question	# questions	#right (Run 1)	#right (Run 2)
3 words	8	1	3
4 words	27	3	2
5 words	37	1	6
6 words	37	4	6
7 words	26	4	3
8 words	32	4	3
9 words	15	1	2
10 words	8	1	2
11 words	2	1	1
12 words	2	1	1
13 words	4	1	1
16 words	1	0	0
Total	199	22	30

Globally, we can see that the best results were obtained combining the use of the document collection and the Web. The worst results are the ones obtained using solely the Web. It is somehow surprising that the results using solely the document collection are better than the ones using solely the Web, since the approach I am testing was designed to take advantage of the redundancy in larger corpora. Possible explanations for this are:

- Esfinge is not extracting efficiently text from the Web. Possibly it is getting control symbols and documents in other languages - according to Nuno Cardoso (p.c.), it is common for search engines to mistake UTF for iso8859-1 character encoding.
- Some documents in the Web, rather than helping to find answers, do the exact opposite (jokes, blogs, ...). Discarding some kinds of pages could be of help [9].
- The text size unit of 3 sentences ≈ 90 words gives a larger context, while many Google snippets do not even include all the words in the query.

Table 2 displays the influence of the question length in the results of Run 1 and Run 2.

In order to determine the length of the questions, I used the Perl Module Lingua::PT::PLNbase to tokenize the questions.

In Run 1 the most significant results are obtained in questions from length 6 to 8, while in Run 2 the system gets better results in questions from length 5 to 6. This slight difference can be explained by the different length of the passages recovered from the Web and from the document collection. These passages contain the question patterns and hopefully the answers. Being the passages recovered from the Web shorter, they may be more suitable for shorter questions, while passages retrieved from the document collection are usually longer, therefore more suitable to answer longer questions, as the following examples show:

- It is more likely to find the question pattern and an answer to the question *What is the name of the widow of Samora Machel, the deceased Mozambican president?* in a three sentence context than in a Google snippet.
- Conversely, extracting N-grams related to the question *Who is Christo?* in a three sentence context can provide too many N-grams, making the task of finding the right answer very difficult.

Table 3. Causes for wrong answers

Problem in...	#wrong Answers (Run 2)	%wrong (Run 2)
Document recovery	86	43 %
Filter "discard answers contained in questions"	8	4 %
Filter "interesting PoS"	20	10 %
Filter "documents supporting answer"	23	12 %
Answer scoring algorithm	75	37 %
Answer length >3	21	11 %

It would be interesting to do a similar study regarding the answer length, since the question and answer lengths are not directly related. One can have a long question with a short answer and vice versa. Classifying the answers is, however, more problematic, since a question may have a short and a long answer and both can be considered correct. For CLEF, Esfinge extracted only up to trigrams, so the system was unable to answer correctly questions which required an answer longer than 3 words. Such limitation was due to efficiency constraints: longer N-grams require longer processing time and I assumed that for most of the questions, a three word answer would suffice.

A log file was used to find out why the system produces wrong answers. In this file was possible to check an ordered list (best scored first) of all the word N-grams analyzed for each question. The reasons why they were discarded or not is also registered in this file. In any case, this evaluation takes some time, so I started with the run with best results (Run 2). For some questions I counted more than one reason for failure.

Table 3 provides a detailed error analysis. This sort of evaluation can give some insight into the system modules that are causing more errors and therefore should be looked into more in detail.

4 Future Work

The results gathered in table 3 (Causes for wrong answers) show that the main problems in Esfinge at the moment are in the document recovery and in the answer scoring algorithm stages. Now, if the first component (document recovery) is not working properly, it is very difficult to evaluate the other components of the system.

With that in mind, work in Esfinge will mainly address the two following areas in the near future:

1. Checking the questions with wrong answers due to "Document recovery", grouping then by their type (ex: Quem/Who, Qual/Which, Onde/Where). Understanding why the patterns used for the document recovery are not recovering the right documents. Changing the patterns, and testing the new patterns with the questions of a particular type (usually a pattern is closely related to a particular type of question).
2. Using the log file, I will compute a frequency list of all the solutions provided by Esfinge to the CLEF QA track questions (not only the best answer, but all the answers that managed to go through all system's filters). With this frequency list and some common sense, I plan to build a list of 'undesired answers' that will be used in an extra filter. The words in this list will be frequent words that do not really answer questions in isolation (like anos/years, mesmo /same, dia/day, maior /bigger, tempo/time).

4.1 Other Improvements

Question Reformulation. In this module the linguistic information is encapsulated in a text file using Perl's regular expression syntax. This syntax is quite powerful, however it is much more suited to the thought processes of computer-scientists than to linguists' ones. In case we intend to include professionals in that area to improve the question reformulation patterns at a more advanced stage of development, it would be better to use a friendlier syntax. As an example, the patterns could be automatically generated from real examples of questions and answers.

N-grams Harvesting. I plan to experiment extracting word N-grams not from the snippets returned by the search engine, but from the actual pages. Other planned experiences are related to the type of web pages to be considered: only European Portuguese pages, pages written in other languages, only news sites…

Machine Learning Techniques. An interesting experiment/refinement is to use a set of questions associated with their answers as a training set for the system.

The results of the system on the training set questions can be compared with the correct answers. The scorings of the patterns and/or the word N-grams can then be changed and the system executed again against the training set, the new results compared with the right answers and the results checked again to understand if the system is improving.

4.2 Further Evaluation of Esfinge

I plan to use a multitude of sources to further evaluate Esfinge:

- The questions and answers created by QA@CLEF;
- A set of real questions and answers found on the web, created by humans, using several distinct methods for collecting them;
- A set of questions posed by real users (from Esfinge's logs);
- A set of questions with answers, created and validated by myself.

Acknowledgements

I thank my colleague Diana Santos for all the valuable suggestions and for helping me to write this paper in a more understandable way. I also thank Nuno Cardoso for revisions on previous versions of this paper and Alberto Simões for the hints on using the Perl Modules "jspell" [6] and "Lingua::PT::PLNbase". This work is financed by the Portuguese Fundação para a Ciência e Tecnologia through grant POSI/PLP/ 43931/2001, co-financed by POSI.

References

1. Brill, E.: Processing Natural Language without Natural Language Processing. In: Gelbukh, A. (ed.): CICLing 2003. LNCS 2588. Springer-Verlag Berlin Heidelberg (2003) 360-9
2. Aires, R. & Santos, D.: Measuring the Web in Portuguese. In: Euroweb 2002 conference (Oxford, UK, 17-18 December 2002) 198-199
3. Banerjee, S. & Pedersen, T.: The Design, Implementation, and Use of the {N}gram {S}tatistic {P}ackage. In: Proceedings of the Fourth International Conference on Intelligent Text Processing and Computational Linguistics (Mexico City, February 2003) 370-381
4. Christ, O., Schulze, B.M., Hofmann, A. & Koenig, E.: The IMS Corpus Workbench: Corpus Query Processor (CQP): User's Manual. University of Stuttgart, March 8, 1999 (CQP V2.2)

5. Santos, D. & Rocha, P.: "Evaluating CETEMPúblico, a free resource for Portuguese". In: Proceedings of the 39th Annual Meeting of the Association for Computational Linguistics (Toulouse, 9-11 July 2001) 442-449
6. Simões, A. M. & Almeida, J.J.: Jspell.pm - um módulo de análise morfológica para uso em Processamento de Linguagem Natural. In: Gonçalves, A. & Correia, C.N. (eds.): Actas do XVII Encontro da Associação Portuguesa de Linguística (APL 2001) (Lisboa, 2-4 Outubro 2001). APL Lisboa (2002) 485-495
7. Brill, E., Lin, J., Banko, M., Dumais, S. & Ng, A.: Data-Intensive Question Answering. In: Voorhees, E.M. & Harman, D.K. (eds.): Information Technology: The Tenth Text Retrieval Conference, TREC 2001. NIST Special Publication 500-250. 393-400
8. Magnini et al.: "Overview of the CLEF 2004 Multilingual Question answering track". This volume.
9. Aires, R., Manfrin, A., Aluísio, S.M. & Santos, D.: What Is My Style? Stylistic features in Portuguese web pages according to IR users' needs. In: Lino, M.T., Xavier, M.F., Ferreira, F., Costa, R. & Silva, R. (eds.): Proceedings of LREC 2004 (Lisboa, Portugal, 26-28 May 2004) 1943-1946

University of Évora in QA@CLEF-2004

Paulo Quaresma, Luís Quintano, Irene Rodrigues,
José Saias, and Pedro Salgueiro

Departamento de Informática, Universidade de Évora, Portugal
{pq, ljcq, ipr, jsaias, pds}@di.uevora.pt

Abstract. The approach followed by the University of Évora team when building a system for participation in the CLEF 2004 question answering task for Portuguese is described. The system is based on two steps: for each question, a first search selects a set of potentially relevant documents; each of these documents is then analysed to obtain a semantic representation and the answer to the initial query. This approach was applied to the QA@CLEF test set for Portuguese with interesting results that have allowed us to identify the strong and weak features of our system.

1 Introduction

Question answering systems are an important topic of research in the natural language processing field and much research has been done in this field in recent years. Several international conferences have tracks dedicated to this topic, namely, TREC – Text REtrieval Conference (http://trec.nist.gov) and CLEF – Cross Language Evaluation Forum (http://www.clef-campaign.org).

In the QA track in the 2004 campaign, CLEF added Portuguese as a possible language for both the queries and the target documents.

In the last few years, the Informatics Department of the University of Évora has been working in the natural language processing field, namely trying to develop specialised tools for Portuguese.

This paper describes the approach adopted by the University of Évora for the question answering task for Portuguese in CLEF 2004. The collection of target documents is the set of news published by the Portuguese newspaper "Público" during 1994 and 1995. Questions (200) can be factoids or definitions and some of them may have no answer in the target set of documents.

Our system operates in two steps:

- For each question, a first search selects a set of potentially relevant documents.
- Next, each of the documents is analysed in a preparatory phase to extract the facts they convey, and the user query is then interpreted on each selected text knowledge base. When an answer to the query is obtained, the process stops and the system outputs the answer and identifies the document from where the answer was obtained.

C. Peters et al. (Eds.): CLEF 2004, LNCS 3491, pp. 534–543, 2005.

Our question answering system needs the preliminary information retrieval search, in which a smaller set of potentially relevant documents is identified, in order to limit problems of computational complexity. The main component of the system then analyses this set of documents to obtain a partial semantin representation of their content. Next, each query is transformed into its semantic form and an inference process tries to obtain the answer to the query. However, this approach showed many scalability problems due to the large number of documents and associated data and it was necessary to strongly reduce its cardinality.

Section 2 describes the preparatory phase in which the set of documents are preprocessed in order to build the IR indexes and the knowledge base for each text.

Section 3 describes the proposed architecture for the question answering system and section 4 describes each of the architectural modules. A preliminary evaluation is presented in section 5 and some conclusions and future work is discussed in section 6.

2 Pre-processing the Set of Target Documents

The first step is an important pre-processing phase of the target collection of documents in order to obtain the input data for our question answering system.

There are two main tasks in this phase:

- *Semantic/Pragmatic Interpretation* – creates a set of knowledge bases, *Text facts collection*, where each knowledge base contains the facts conveyed by each text.

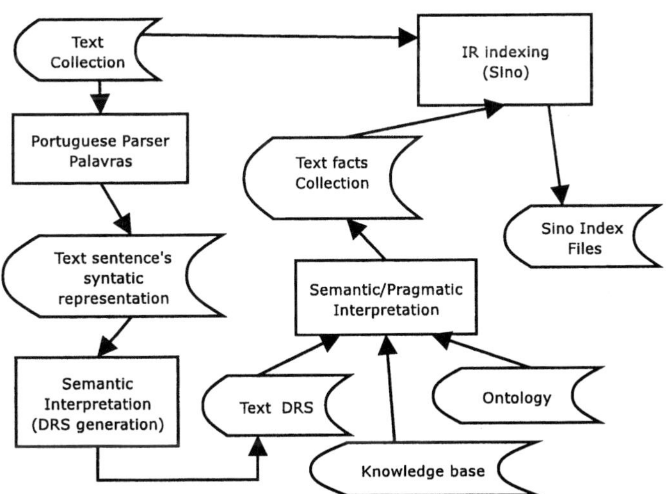

Fig. 1. Texts preprocessing

- *Information retrieval indexing* – creates the files that index the full set of documents with references to the knowledge base associated with each document, *Sino Index Files.*

The other tasks of this phase are:

- Portuguese Parser - each text of the collection is analysed by the Portuguese parser PALAVRAS [1] developed in the context of the VISL[1] project at the *Institute of Language and Communication* of the *University of Southern Denmark*. The output of the parser is a file with the syntactic analysis of each text.
  We have chosen to keep the first syntactic analysis for each sentence; however, this option is one of the sources of our problems.
- Semantic Interpretation – each syntactic structure is rewritten into a First-Order Logic expression. The technique used for this analysis is based on DRS (Discourse Representation Structures)[2].
  This technique identifies triggering syntactic configurations on the global sentence structure, which activate the rewriting rules. We always rewrite the pp's by the relation $rel(prep, A, B)$ postponing its interpretation to the semantic pragmatic module.
  The semantic representation of a sentence is a DRS built with two lists, one with the newly rewritten sentence and the other with the sentence discourse referents.

One of the most important requirements of the proposed QA system is to have a knowledge base of facts inferred from the analysis of the set of target documents and an ontology containing the concepts identified in the documents.

- Ontology – From the output generated by the DRS and from an existing top ontology of concepts, a new ontology containing the concepts referred identified in the documents was created [3, 4].
  This step was found to be very problematic, due to the large number of concepts identified in the documents and to the complexity and difficulty of finding correct relations between them.
  The ontology obtained was created in the OWL (Ontology Web Language) format and in a logic programming framework, ISCO [5, 6], which allows the integration of Prolog-like inference mechanisms with classes and inheritance, and constraint solving algorithms.
- Knowledge base – From this ontology and from the semantic representation of each sentence we can obtain an interpretation of each text sentence which will produce a set of facts to add to our knowledge base [7].
  However, this task was found to be extremely resource demanding in terms of computational time and space and the knowledge base obtained was very large and created many problems for the inference processes.

[1] Visual Interactive Syntax Learning.

It was thus decided to first decrease the set of relevant documents for each query (via IR techniques) and, then, to create a smaller knowledge base. The knowledge base shown in Figure 1 was built with a set of facts extracted from the target text collection and with rules and facts that we import from other applications.

2.1 Semantic/Pragmatic Interpretation of Text Sentences

In order to infer the set of facts associated with each text sentence, we must use the ontology to be able to extract the meaning of each sentence.

The semantic/pragmatic module receives the sentence rewritten in a First Order Logic form and tries to interpret it in the context of the document database information (ontology). The system tries to find the best explanations for the sentence logic form to be true in the context of its knowledge base. This strategy for interpretation is known as "interpretation as abduction" [8].

The knowledge base used for the semantic/pragmatic interpretation is built from the ontology. The inference in this knowledge base uses abduction and restrictions (GNU Prolog Finite Domain (FD) constraint solver). The knowledge base rules contain the information for the interpretation of each term in the sentence logic form as a prolog term.

For example, the sentence:

"O gato do João comeu o rato do Manuel/John's cat ate Manuel's mouse."

is transformed into a DRS-like term showing the 4 referents and their relations:

```
drs([def-A-m-s, def-B-m-s,
     def-C-m-s, def-D-m-s],
    [cat(A), rel(of,A,B),
     name(B,'João'), comer(A,C),
     mouse(C), rel(of,C,D),
     name(D,'Manuel')]).
```

The semantic interpretation module using the ontology will rewrite this DRS into:

```
drs([def-A-m-s, def-B-m-s,
     def-C-m-s, def-D-m-s],
    [cat(A), owns(B,A), person(B),
     name(B,'João'), eats(A,C),
     mouse(C), owns(D,C), person(D),
     name(D,'Manuel')]).
```

The interpretation of *rel(of,A,B)* as owns(A,B) is possible due to the existence of the relation *owns* that relates persons and animals.

Another important step in this task is to create new individuals (new identifiers) for discourse referents when they are not instantiated during the interpretation. This step is a source of problems for our QA system since it is possible to have different identifiers for the same individual if this task fails to identify the sentences entities. The opposite can also happen: this task may unify individuals that are different.

The option of building a knowledge base with the facts extracted from each document helps us to deal with the problem of scalability: there are fewer entities.

A problem that remains to be solved is how to choose the best meaning for a sentence.

2.2 Information Retrieval Indexing

SINO [9, 10], originally obtained from the Australasian Legal Information Institute, was used to index the full set of documents. It creates inverted index files and, in the new version, uses Portuguese-specific information, i.e. stop words and lemmatization. In fact, SINO was extended to use a set of Portuguese stop words (such as articles, pronouns, prepositions) and transforming each word into its lemma (using the Portuguese lexicon POLARIS).

Documents are indexed by a specialized search engine for the Portuguese language – SINO [9, 10] – and an information retrieval system for this collection is built. As will be described in more detail in the next section, the information retrieval system is used for each query to decrease the cardinality of the target set of documents.

3 Architecture

The architecture is composed by several independent modules. Figure 2 gives a graphical view of their relations.

In the following sub-sections a brief description of each module is presented.

3.1 Query Processing

Each query is processed using the same natural language tools used to analyse the full set of documents, i.e. the Portuguese syntactic Parser Palavras and the DRS generator. After obtaining the query DRS, two tasks are performed concurrently:

- Semantic/Pragmatic Interpretation of the query. The semantic representation of the query is obtained using the ontology of concepts and a knowledge base with some general world knowledge.
- Query preprocessing and Search.
  Once obtained, the query DRS is transformed into a search term for the IR engine – SINO. This step is necessary because it was computationally impossible to handle inferences over the complete knowledge base created in the pre-processing phase of the documents. We thus use an information retrieval system to obtain a set of relevant documents and make inferences only over the knowledge base created with the information conveyed by these documents.

The queries to be sent to the IR system are created from the semantic representation, DRS, of each query. Their structure will be described in the next section. Using the queries, the search engine obtains an ordered set of relevant documents. This set is used to create a smaller DRS knowledge base containing only the information conveyed by these relevant documents. In this way it is possible to strongly decrease the complexity of the knowledge base and it is possible to handle inferences over it.

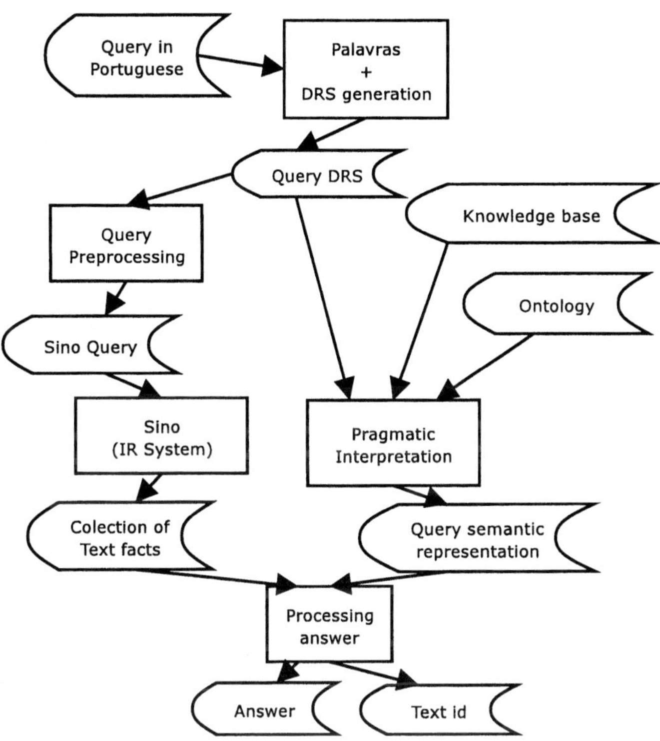

Fig. 2. QA System's architecture

Finally the *Process answer* task receives the set of relevant knowledge bases in which the query semantic/pragmatic representation should be evaluated and tries to infer the answer to the query.

The inference process is based in a logic programming framework, ISCO [5, 6], which allows the integration of Prolog-like inference mechanisms with classes and inheritance, and constraint solving algorithms.

4 Modules

This section gives a more detailed description of the main system modules.

4.1 Natural Language Query Processing

This tasks executed by this module, Palavras+Drs generation and pragmatic interpretation, follow an approach similar to that of the semantic/pragmatic interpretation of the documents and use the same natural language tools: the PALAVRAS parser, the DRS generator and semantic/pragmatic interpreter.

After the DRS generation we ca/ identify the referents which are the focus of each query and the kind of query performed.

For instance, the query: "Quem comeu o rato do Manuel/Who ate Manuel's rat?" is transformed into the DRS-like term:

```
drs([who-A-X-Y, def-B-m-s, def-C-m-s],
     [eat(A,B),
      mouse(B), rel(de,B,C),
      name(C,'Manuel')]).
```

After obtaining the query DRS, the semantic-pragmatic interpretation using the ontology of concepts created in the pre-processing phase gives the final query representation:

For the above example this will be:

```
drs([who-A-X-Y, def-B-m-s, def-C-m-s],
     [eat(A,B),
      mouse(B), owns(C,B),person(C),
      name(C,'Manuel')]).
```

This final query representation will be evaluated in each knowledge base selected by the last SINO query.

4.2 Query Preprocessing

The query DRS is transformed into a search term for the IR engine – SINO.

The approach followed was to create three query terms for each natural language query and to order the set of documents retrieved. The overall idea is to create a very restrictive query, a very general one, and one in the middle. The queries created are boolean and they are obtained from the DRS of each query:

```
''Em que cidade se encontra a
  prisão de San Vittore?''

cidade AND encontrar AND prisão
AND (San  AND Vittore)

cidade AND (encontrar OR
prisão OR (San  AND Vittore))
```

```
cidade OR encontrar OR prisão
OR (San  AND Vittore)
```

The first query is the most specific and is created with the boolean AND of each term; the second query is created with the boolean AND for the head of the query and OR for the other terms; the third most general query uses OR for each term.

4.3 SINO - DRS Extraction of Relevant Documents

This module receives the three queries and retrieves the corresponding relevant documents. As has been already described, the IR engine used was an extension of the SINO engine from the AustLII institute.

SINO retrieves the relevant documents (using the boolean operators) and orders them using a ranking function. This ranking function gives higher priority to documents with more word hits or with hits in the title. It should be noted that documents are first ordered according to the kind of query: first the documents retrieved by the most specific query and last the documents retrieved by the most general one. Each set of retrieved documents is ordered using the SINO ranking function.

From an ordered list of relevant documents, the first 50 are selected as the basis to create a knowledge base of facts relevant to the query. The reason why the first 50 were chosen is related with the goal of reducing the computational complexity and assuming a good performance of the SINO engine.

4.4 Answer Inference Process

This module is responsible for finding the correct, exact answer to each query. It receives the semantic/pragmatic interpretation of each query (in a DRS-like format) and a logic-programming based knowledge base built from the set of the most relevant 50 documents of each query.

The inference process uses the Prolog resolution algorithm, which tries to unify the referent in the query with facts extracted from the documents. This unification takes into account the information associated with the referents, such as genre and number. Moreover, the inference process uses wh-questions, such as where/when/who, to identify the feature addressed by the query. For instance, if the query is about a place of a specific entity, e.g. "Em que cidade se encontra a prisão de San Vittore?", the system tries to find a location as a feature of that entity.

As can be seen from this description, our system relies on the quality of the inferred ontology and on a good semantic/pragmatic interpretation of sentences and queries.

As a consequence of our approach, the system always returns 1 as a confidence value for each answer: if it finds an answer, then it is sure about it!

5 Evaluation

The system described was run on the set of 200 questions (in fact they were 199, because one question was not considered by the judges). It obtained 47 correct answers, 18 inexact and 134 wrong with an overall accuracy of correct answers of 23.62% and a confidence-weighted score of 0.21619. If the accuracy is calculated over the correct and the inexact answers, then it is 32.66%.

We believe these are quite interesting results, that show the potential of the proposed approach. However, they also show the main problem of the system: it gave 127 "nil" answers and only 9 of them were correct.

The most important question now is: what happened in the 118 questions that were not answered by the system? A preliminary evaluation showed that there were two main causes of problems:

- the information retrieval system
- the ontology

The information retrieval system used to decrease the complexity of the knowledge base was quite often able to find the relevant documents. In fact, this problem can be clearly seen in the results of the Ad-Hoc task of CLEF 2004, in which SINO showed very low recall values. This problem can be overcome by improving the queries sent to SINO or by solving the complexity problems that made the construction of a large, single knowledge base impossible. We intend to explore both possibilities.

The second problem was the quality of the ontology. The inference process relies heavily on the ontology. For instance, it is important to know what are places, persons, dates, synonyms. In the example presented previously, if the ontology does not have information that relates "cidade" with the class of "places", then the system would not be able to answer the query. We will also continue to develop new strategies for constructing and merging ontologies.

6 Conclusions and Future Work

This proposal represents a first approach for a question answering system for the Portuguese language. Our system uses natural language processing techniques to create a knowledge base from the information conveyed by the target documents. Queries are analysed by NLP tools and inferences are made over the knowledge base trying to find a correct answer. The inference process is done using a logic programming framework and Prolog resolution.

The initial idea of creating a single, large knowledge base with the facts extracted from all the documents was not feasible due to computational complexity problems. These problems led to the creation of an IR pre-analysis of the queries to decrease the complexity of the knowledge base. However, the IR engine showed some recall problems and lead to the QA system being unable to answer many queries.

The ontology used was also a major problem and was the origin of many other wrong answers. As the QA@CLEF task uses general domain documents, this is a very complex problem: how to obtain a good general purpose ontology?

As future work, we intend to try to develop new strategies to (partially) overcome these problems. Working with new implementation strategies, it may be possible to have a unique knowledge base and using existing ontologies and Wordnets may improve the quality of the final ontology.

Finally, we also intend to explore the problem of inter-sentence anaphoric references and to be able to identify the correct referents in the documents.

References

1. Bick, E.: The Parsing System "Palavras". Automatic Grammatical Analysis of Portuguese in a Constraint Grammar Framework. Aarhus University Press (2000)
2. Kamp, H., Reyle, U.: From Discourse to Logic:An Introduction to Modeltheoretic Semantics of Natural Language, Formal Logic and Discourse Representation Theory. Dordrecht: D. Reidel (1993)
3. Saias, J., Quaresma, P.: Using nlp techniques to create legal ontologies in a logic programming based web information retrieval system. In: Workshop on Legal Ontologies and Web based legal information management of the 9th International Conference on Artificial Intelligence and Law, Edinburgh, Scotland (2003)
4. Saias, J.: Uma metodologia para a construção automática de ontologias e a sua aplicação em sistemas de recuperação de informação – a methodology for the automatic creation of ontologies and its application in information retrieval systems. Master's thesis, University of Évora, Portugal (2003) In Portuguese.
5. Abreu, S.: Isco: A practical language for heterogeneous information system construction. In: Proceedings of INAP'01, Tokyo, Japan, INAP (2001)
6. Abreu, S., Quaresma, P., Quintano, L., Rodrigues, I.: A dialogue manager for accessing databases. In: 13th European-Japanese Conference on Information Modelling and Knowledge Bases, Kitakyushu, Japan, Kyushu Institute of Technology (2003) 213–224 To be published by IOS Press.
7. Quaresma, P., Rodrigues, I.P.: A natural language interface for information retrieval on semantic web documents. In Menasalvas, E., Segovia, J., Szczepaniak, P., eds.: AWIC'2003 - Atlantic Web Intelligence Conference. Lecture Notes in Artificial Intelligence LNCS/LNAI 2663, Madrid, Spain, Springer-Verlag (2003) 142–154
8. Hobbs, J., Stickel, M., Appelt, D., Martin, P.: Interpretation as abduction. Technical Report SRI Technical Note 499, 333 Ravenswood Ave., Menlo Park, CA 94025 (1990)
9. Quaresma, P., Rodrigues, I.P.: PGR: Portuguese attorney general's office decisions on the web. In Bartenstein, Geske, Hannebauer, Yoshie, eds.: Web-Knowledge Management and Decision Support. Lecture Notes in Artificial Intelligence LNCS/LNAI 2543, Springer-Verlag (2003) 51–61
10. Greenleaf, G., Mowbray, A., King, G.: Law on the net via austlii - 14 m hypertext links can't be right? In: In Information Online and On Disk'97 Conference, Sydney. (1997)

COLE Experiments at QA@CLEF 2004 Spanish Monolingual Track

Enrique Méndez Díaz, Jesús Vilares Ferro, and David Cabrero Souto

Departamento de Computación, Universidade da Coruña,
Campus de Elviña s/n, 15071 La Coruña, Spain
{jvilares, cabrero}@udc.es
http://www.grupocole.org

Abstract. This paper is a report on our third participation in CLEF. More precisely, this year we have participated in the Spanish Monolingual Question Answering Track for the first time. As a result we have developed a prototype of a QA system. Our prototype continues to apply the Natural Language Processing techniques we had already developed for single word conflation. In addition, the question analysis is based on complex pattern matching either over forms, part-of-speech tags or lemmas of the words involved. Regarding the search for relevant parts of documents containing the required answer, we use conventional IR techniques, whilst the extraction of the answer from the relevant parts of documents is again based on pattern matching.

1 Introduction

In this paper we report our experience at CLEF. This is our first participation in the Question Answering Track, and our third participation in CLEF in general. Our preceding participations took place at the Spanish monolingual Information Retrieval (IR) track [1, 2], applying Natural Language Processing (NLP) techniques in order to conflate the documents to be indexed. As a result of this year's participation, we have developed a prototype that continues our effort in the field of IR.

In past editions our main premise has been simplicity, motivated by the lack of freely available linguistic resources for Spanish such as large tagged corpora, treebanks or advanced lexicons. This year, in our first participation in the Spanish monolingual Question Answering (QA) track, our premise remains the same in order to get a valid prototype which can then be improved by continuous refinements. As usual, in our QA system we can identify three tasks: analysis of the question, retrieval of the passages of the documents related to the question and identification of the exact fragment of the document that constitutes the answer. Thus, this paper should be read as a progress report. Our research in QA is at an early stage and much work still has to be done.

This article is outlined as follows. Section 2 introduces the NLP techniques we have used in our prototype. After that, section 3 describes the overall design

C. Peters et al. (Eds.): CLEF 2004, LNCS 3491, pp. 544–551, 2005.

of the prototype, followed by the different modules of the system, which are described in subsequent sections: the analysis of questions, the information retrieval module and the answer delimitation process are detailed in subsections 3.1, 3.2 and 3.3 respectively. Finally, our conclusions and future work are presented in sections 4 and 5.

2 NLP Processing

In this section we introduce the NLP techniques used as the basis for our QA prototype, focused on dealing with inflectional variation. Both in Information Retrieval and Question Answering systems, one of the major limitations we have to deal with is the *linguistic variation* of natural languages [3]. When managing this type of phenomena, the employment of Natural Language Processing techniques becomes feasible. This has been our working hypothesis since our research group started its work on Spanish Information Retrieval some time ago, and it remains our working hypothesis now we have started working on Spanish Question Answering.

Continuing with our previous work in IR, we have chosen the use of lemmatization instead of classical approaches such as stemming. The effectiveness of *stemming* is dependent on the morphology of the language, so, when processing languages with complex morphology and a high number of irregularities, the performance of stemmers becomes irregular [3,4]. In the case of Spanish, inflectional modifications exist at multiple levels (gender and number for nouns and adjectives, and person, mood, time and tense for verbs), with many irregularities [5]: for nouns and adjectives, more than 20 variation groups for gender inflection and more than 10 variation groups for number inflection have been identified; for verbs, 3 regular groups and almost 40 irregular groups have been identified, each group containing more than 100 inflected forms. This level of complexity cannot be managed through stemming alone. Moreover, stemming can also create problems for NLP systems by causing the loss of information needed in further processing [6], as in the case of Question Answering.

Lemmatization therefore appears to be an advisable alternative to stemming, since it can properly manage these complex phenomena of Spanish morphology with no loss of information. The encouraging results obtained in the Spanish monolingual IR track [1,2] support this choice.

The lemmatization process is performed in two steps: a first phase of linguistic preprocessing and a second phase of part-of-speech tagging and lemmatization, properly speaking.

2.1 Linguistic Preprocessing

One of the most important prior tasks in NLP is *text segmentation*, the task of dividing a text into linguistically meaningful units —words (*tokenization*) and sentences (*sentence segmentation*)—, since the words and sentences identified at this stage are the fundamental units passed to further processing stages, such as part-of-speech taggers, Information Retrieval systems, Question Answering systems, etc [7]. Nevertheless, this stage is often obviated in many current applications, which assume that input texts are already correctly segmented in *tokens* or high level information units. This working hypothesis is unrealistic due to the heterogeneous nature of the application texts and their sources, and gives rise to erroneous behaviors during further processing.

Preprocessing is therefore an indispensable task in practice, and it can involve processes which are much more complex than the simple identification of the different sentences in the text and each of their individual components. For this reason, we have developed a linguistically-motivated preprocessor module for Spanish [8, 9] in order to perform tasks such as format conversion, tokenization, sentence segmentation, morphological pretagging, contraction splitting, separation of enclitic pronouns from verbal stems, expression identification, numeral identification and proper noun recognition.

2.2 Tagging and Lemmatization

Once the text has been preprocessed, the output generated by our preprocessor —the words and sentences which form the text— is then taken as input by our tagger-lemmatizer, `MrTagoo` [10], although any similar high-performance tool could be used instead. `MrTagoo` is based on a second order Hidden Markov Model (HMM), whose elements and procedures of estimation of parameters are based on Brant's work [11], and also incorporates certain capabilities which led to its use in our system. Such capabilities include a very efficient structure for storage and search —based on finite-state automata [12]—, management of unknown words, the possibility of integrating external dictionaries in the probabilistic frame defined by the HMM [13], and the possibility of managing ambiguous segmentations [14].

Nevertheless, these kind of tools are very sensitive to spelling errors, as, for example, in the case of sentences written completely in uppercase —e.g., news headlines and subsection headings—, which cannot be correctly managed by the preprocessor and tagger modules. For this reason, when documents are processed in order to be indexed, the initial output of the tagger is processed by an *uppercase-to-lowercase* module [1] in order to process uppercase sentences, converting them to lowercase and restoring the diacritical marks when necessary.

3 Architecture

The overall architecture of our prototype is composed of three main modules: question processing, related passage retrieval and answer extraction. The first module analyzes the query, obtaining a list of keywords, which the next module then takes and uses to perform a mostly conventional information retrieval process, thereby obtaining a list of paragraphs expected to contain the answer. Finally, the last module takes these paragraphs and extracts the answer from them. In the first stages of the prototype we focus on question processing and information retrieval for several reasons:

- Simplicity is a premise.
- Once the system is capable of returning to the user a paragraph containing the right answer, the average user will find the system satisfactory.
- If you cannot find the paragraph containing the answer, you cannot extract it.

3.1 Question Processing

For question processing we are using a kind of simplified shallow parsing [15]. This parsing is made at two levels: lemmatization and pattern matching. The result of the pattern matching phase is a list of keywords to be used in order to search relevant documents.

Therefore the first step of the process consists in tagging and lemmatizing the question using our *preprocessor* and our tagger-lemmatizer, Mr Tagoo, as has previously been described in section 2. Once the question has been tagged and lemmatized, the keyword selection process is performed by means of pattern matching. In a previous study we have identified different categories of questions, such as:

```
¿ Quién ser ... ? / Who (be) ... ?
¿ Quién ... ?     / Who ... ?
¿ Dónde ... ?     / Where ... ?
```

Each category has been associated with a list of patterns composed of tags and/or words. For each tagged question, the system goes through this list of patterns till one of them matches and the keywords matched are extracted.

Our first prototype uses all the keywords extracted from the query. This approach showed a poor performance, since only in 25% of the cases did it lead to the retrieval of paragraphs containing the answer. To overcome this problem, our next prototype will reduce the specificity of the queries by removing useless elements from the list of keywords.

3.2 Passage Retrieval

At this stage of the process, the system performs a mostly conventional IR task on the set of available documents in order to retrieve the portions of documents supposed to contain the answer. As usual this requires the documents to be indexed before the system becomes operative.

In order to identify the candidate documents which are relevant to a given question and in which we will look for the answer, a *Passage Retrieval* (PR) approach has been used [16, 17] to delimit not only the relevant document but also the relevant portion of text. This way, documents are split into passages made up of three sentences, with an overlap factor of two sentences[1].We found that using passage retrieval instead of document retrieval overcomes two main disadvantages:

[1] That is, the first passage contains sentence 1 to 3, the second passage contains from sentence 2 to 4, and so on.

- The search engine would find as relevant those documents that containts most of the keywords of our query, even when those keywords are scarce in the document. That situation probably means that the document does not contain the answer. On the other hand, when keywords are close enough the answer will eventually be found in the same part of the document.
- It is more difficult to extract the answer from a document than from a small part of it.

As in our previous contributions to CLEF Adhoc Spanish Monolingual Track [1, 2], text is conflated through lemmatization in order to solve the problems derived from inflection in Spanish. Thus, once text has been tagged and lemmatized, the lemmas of the *content words* [18] —nouns, verbs and adjectives— are extracted to be indexed, since they contain the main semantics of the text [18, 19]. Before indexing, the terms obtained are converted to lowercase and their spelling signs are eliminated in order to reduce typographical errors.

The resulting conflated text is indexed using the probabilistic engine ZPrise [20], employing the Okapi BM25 weight scheme [21] with the constants defined in [22] for Spanish ($b = 0.5$, $k_1 = 2$). The stopword list used was obtained by lemmatizing the content words of the Spanish stopword list provided with the well-known indexing engine SMART [23].

3.3 Answer Extraction

The answer extraction module takes the list of paragrahs retrieved by the previous module and attempts to extract the answer to the question formulated by the user. Currently, this module is quite naive and simply tries to find a coherent answer near the keywords extracted from the question. Work is in progress in order to improve this module. In order to achieve this goal we intend to develop several methods of extracting the answer. Each method will select some answer candidates and a vote system will be used to choose the best one. The methods currently scheduled are:

- A module determine the answer type and use that information to select the probable answer.
- Use of word distances. A suitable implementation [24] is in progress.

4 Results and Conclusions

As we stated at the outset, the results of our first prototype are not outstanding. The specific data are as follows. Given the 200 questions of the test, our protoype obtained 200 answers:

- 22 Right (21 Factoid + 1 Definition)
- 178 Wrong
- 0 Inexact
- 0 Unsupported

That means an overall accurary of 11.00%. Also, the system answered NIL 195 times. Although these figures show low performance, further analysis showed more encouraging results. After looking at the trace of the process of our prototype, we realized that over half of the times it answered NIL, it had actually found the passages of the documents containing the right answer, but was not able to extract the latter. Therefore we expect that by improving the answer extraction module, we will boost the performance of the overall system.

5 Future Directions

We have built a small prototype using the tools created for IR tasks and new ones specifically developed for QA tasks. As expected for an early prototype, it is far from optimal, showing an irregular performance. However, we find the design architecture is good enough. Regarding the modules, further experimentation with the question processing module has shown that our approach works well, but new improvements are desirable. More precisely the list of patterns we use is by no means complete and we need a better solution for non-expected question patterns.

Regarding the passage retrieval module, NLP techniques once again proved quite usefull. Finally, the answer extraction module needs futher research and new approaches in order to get satisfactory results. A new approach, based on the employment of a locality-based retrieval model [24], is also being considered in order to locate the relevant portion of the document with a higher degree of precision.

Acknowledgements

The research reported in this article has been partially supported by Ministerio de Ciencia y Tecnología (HF2002-81), FPU grants of Secretaría de Estado de Educación y Universidades (AP2001-2545), Xunta de Galicia (PGIDIT02PXIB30501PR and PGIDIT02SIN01E) and Universidade da Coruña.

References

1. Vilares, J., Alonso, M.A., Ribadas, F.J., Vilares, M.: COLE experiments at CLEF 2002 Spanish monolingual track. In: Advances in Cross-Language Information Retrieval. Volume 2785 of Lecture Notes in Computer Science. Springer-Verlag, Berlin-Heidelberg-New York (2003) 265–278
2. Vilares, J., Alonso, M.A., Ribadas, F.J.: COLE experiments at CLEF 2003 Spanish monolingual track. In Peters, C., Braschler, M., Gonzalo, J., Kluck, M., eds.: Advances in Cross-Language Information Retrieval. Lecture Notes in Computer Science. Springer-Verlag, Berlin-Heidelberg-New York (2004)
3. Arampatzis, A., van der Weide, T.P., van Bommel, P., Koster, C.: Linguistically-motivated information retrieval. In: Encyclopedia of Library and Information Science. Volume 69. Marcel Dekker, Inc, New York-Basel (2000) 201–222

4. Figuerola, C.G., Gómez, R., Zazo Rodríguez, A.F., Alonso Berrocal, J.L.: Stemming in Spanish: A first approach to its impact on information retrieval. In Peters, C., ed.: Results of the CLEF 2001 Cross-Language System Evaluation Campaign, Working Notes for the CLEF 2001 Workshop, 3 September, Darmstadt, Germany. (2001)
5. Vilares, M., Graña, J., Alvariño, P.: Finite-state morphology and formal verification. Journal of Natural Language Engineering, special issue on Extended Finite State Models of Language **3** (1997) 303–304
6. Kowalski, G.: Information Retrieval Systems: Theory and Implementation. The Kluwer international series on Information Retrieval. Kluwer Academic Publishers, Boston-Dordrecht-London (1997)
7. Palmer., D.D.: Tokenisation and Sentence Segmentation. In: Handbook of Natural Language Processing. Marcel Dekker, Inc., New York & Basel (2000)
8. Graña, J., Barcala, F.M., Vilares, J.: Formal methods of tokenization for part-of-speech tagging. In Gelbukh, A., ed.: Computational Linguistics and Intelligent Text Processing. Volume 2276 of Lecture Notes in Computer Science. Springer-Verlag, Berlin-Heidelberg-New York (2002) 240–249
9. Barcala, F.M., Vilares, J., Alonso, M.A., Graña, J., Vilares, M.: Tokenization and proper noun recognition for information retrieval. In: 3rd International Workshop on Natural Language and Information Systems (NLIS 2002), September 2-3, 2002. Aix-en-Provence, France, Los Alamitos, California, USA, IEEE Computer Society Press (2002)
10. Graña, J.: Técnicas de Análisis Sintáctico Robusto para la Etiquetación del Lenguaje Natural. PhD thesis, Departamento de Computación, Universidade da Coruña, A Coruña, Spain (2000)
11. Brants, T.: TnT - a statistical part-of-speech tagger. In: Proceedings of the Sixth Applied Natural Language Processing Conference (ANLP'2000), Seattle, WA. (2000)
12. Graña, J., Barcala, F.M., Alonso, M.: Compilation methods of minimal acyclic automata for large dictionaries. In Watson, B.W., Wood, D., eds.: Proc. of the 6th Conference on Implementations and Applications of Automata (CIAA 2001), Pretoria, South Africa (2001) 116–129
13. Graña, J., Chappelier, J.C., Vilares, M.: Integrating external dictionaries into stochastic part-of-speech taggers. In Angelova, G., Bontcheva, K., Mitkov, R., Nocolov, N., Nikolov, N., eds.: EuroConference Recent Advances in Natural Language Processing. Proceedings, Tzigov Chark, Bulgaria (2001) 122–128
14. Graña Gil, J., Alonso Pardo, M.A., Vilares Ferro, M.: A common solution for tokenization and part-of-speech tagging: One-pass Viterbi algorithm vs. iterative approaches. In Sojka, P., Kopeček, I., Pala, K., eds.: Text, Speech and Dialogue. Volume 2448 of Lecture Notes in Computer Science. Springer-Verlag, Berlin-Heidelberg-New York (2002) 3–10
15. Abney, S.: Partial parsing via finite-state cascades. Natural Language Engineering **2** (1997) 337–344
16. Kaszkiel, M., Zobel, J.: Effective ranking with arbitrary passages. Journal of the American Society of Information Science **52** (2001) 344–364
17. Llopis, F., Vicedo, J.L., Ferrández, A.: IR-n system at CLEF-2002. In Peters, C., Braschler, M., Gonzalo, J., Kluck, M., eds.: Advances in Cross-Language Information Retrieval. Volume 2785 of Lecture Notes in Computer Science. Springer-Verlag, Berlin-Heidelberg-New York (2003) 291–300

18. Jacquemin, C., Tzoukermann, E.: NLP for term variant extraction: synergy between morphology, lexicon and syntax. In Strzalkowski, T., ed.: Natural Language Information Retrieval. Volume 7 of Text, Speech and Language Technology. Kluwer Academic Publishers, Dordrecht/Boston/London (1999) 25–74
19. Koster, C.H.A.: Head/modifier frames for information retrieval. In Gelbukh, A., ed.: Computational Linguistics and Intelligent Text Processing. Volume 2945 of Lecture Notes in Computer Science. Springer-Verlag, Berlin-Heidelberg-New York (2004) 420–432
20. `http://www.itl.nist.gov/iaui/894.02/works/papers/zp2/zp2.html` (site visited August 2004).
21. Robertson, S.E., Walker, S.: Okapi/Keenbow at TREC-8. In Voorhees, E.M., Harman, D.K., eds.: NIST Special Publication 500-246: The Eighth Text REtrieval Conference (TREC 8), Gaithersburg, MD, USA, Department of Commerce, National Institute of Standards and Technology (2000) 151–162
22. Savoy, J.: Report on CLEF-2002 Experiments: Combining Multiple Sources of Evidence. In Peters, C., ed.: Results of the CLEF 2002 Cross-Language System Evaluation Campaign, Working Notes for the CLEF 2002 Workshop, 19-20 September, Rome, Italy. (2002) 31–46
23. `ftp://ftp.cs.cornell.edu/pub/smart` (site visited August 2004).
24. Vilares, J., Alonso, M.A.: Dealing with syntatic variation through a locality-based approach. In: To be published. Volume 3246 of Lecture Notes in Computer Science. Springer-Verlag, Berlin-Heidelberg-New York (2004) 255–266

Does English Help Question Answering in Spanish?

José L. Vicedo, Maximiliano Saiz, Rubén Izquierdo, and Fernando Llopis

Departamento de Lenguajes y Sistemas Informáticos,
University of Alicante, Spain
{vicedo, max, rib1, llopis}@dlsi.ua.es

Abstract. This paper describes the architecture, operation and results obtained with the Question Answering prototype for Spanish developed in the Department of Language Processing and Information Systems at the University of Alicante for the CLEF-2004 Spanish monolingual QA evaluation task. Our system is based on the prototype developed for the CLEF-2003 Spanish monolingual task [3]. This system has been enhanced with capabilities regarding the use of documents in different languages to obtain evidence for supporting and complementing the CLEF Spanish corpora. In particular, the experiments described are intended to study how to use English Web documents to support monolingual Spanish QA.

1 Introduction

The Cross-Language Evaluation Forum Campaigns[1] (CLEF) aim at fostering investigation in multilingual information access systems from the perspective of European language integration. In particular, last year, CLEF organized the *first Multiple Language Question Answering task (QA@CLEF-2003)* directed at the evaluation of QA systems in several languages. This evaluation was very important since it stimulated the creation of a series of resources for the development and testing of QA systems from a multilingual perspective.

The QA@CLEF-2004 campaign proposed new difficulties and therefore, the features of the evaluation changed significantly. Participants were provided with document collections and question sets in seven European languages: Spanish, Portuguese, Italian, Dutch, German, French and English.

Participants had to choose the language both of the question and of the target document collection. This way, the exercise could consist either in a monolingual task (where question and document languages were the same) or in different combinations of bilingual QA (where selected languages were different) or in both.

For each language, the organisation provided 200 questions requiring factual or definition answers whose answer was not guaranteed to occur in the document collection. Systems had to return only one response per question.

[1] http://clef-qa.itc.it/

C. Peters et al. (Eds.): CLEF 2004, LNCS 3491, pp. 552–556, 2005.

Our participation was restricted to the Spanish monolingual task. The novelty in our experiments was the use of documents in languages different from Spanish in order to obtain evidence to support answers obtained from CLEF Spanish corpora. In particular, we performed the monolingual task from two different perspectives: (1) using Web Spanish documents and (2) using English Web documents to support monolingual Spanish QA. In this way we were able to investigate using English (or by extent, other language) documents to support monolingual Spanish QA.

This paper is organised as follows: Section 2 describes the main characteristics of our QA system. We then present and analyse the results obtained at the QA@CLEF-2004 Spanish monolingual task. Finally, we draw some conclusions and discuss directions for future work.

2 System Description

Our system is based on the QA system described in [3] where two main enhancements have been added: (1) the inclusion of a dictionary-based NE tagger and (2) the possibility of using Web documents in other languages to support monolingual Spanish QA.

As this system is described in detail in [3] we only present here the main characteristics and describe the new modules. Our system is organized in the following main modules:

1. Question analysis.
2. Passage retrieval.
3. Answer extraction.

Question analysis processes questions fed to the system in order to detect and extract the useful information contained. The *passage retrieval* module retrieves relevant passages from the Spanish EFE document collection and also from the Internet in the selected language (Spanish or English). Finally, the *answer selection* module processes relevant passages in order to locate and extract the final answer. Figure 1 shows the system architecture.

2.1 Question Analysis

The question analysis module carries out two processes: *answer type classification* and *keyword selection*. The former detects the type of information that the question expects as answer (a date, a quantity, etc) and the latter selects those question terms (*keywords*) that will make it possible to locate the documents that are likely to contain the answer. These processes are performed by using a manually developed set of lexical patterns. The answer types have been increased and now the system currently deals with seven possible answer types: NUMBER, DATE, LOCATION, PERSON, ORGANIZATION, DEFINITION and OTHER.

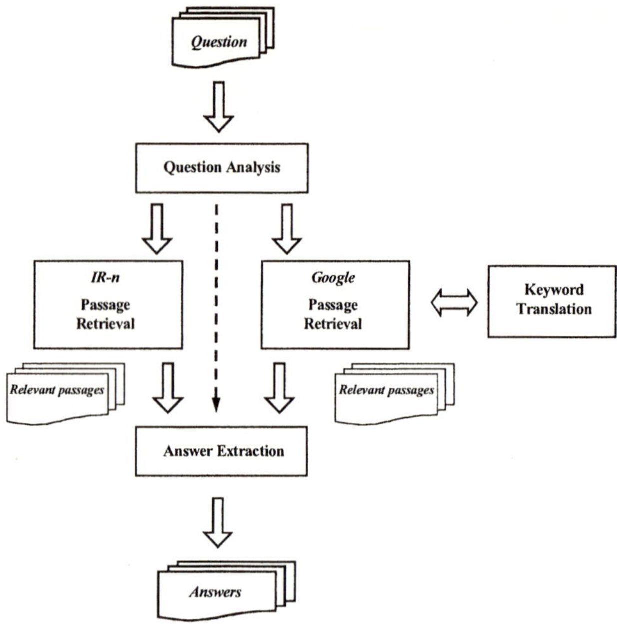

Fig. 1. System architecture

2.2 Passage Retrieval

The passage retrieval stage is accomplished in parallel using two different search engines: IR-n [2] and Google[2]. The IR-n system performs passage retrieval over the entire Spanish EFE document collection. In this case, keywords detected at the question analysis stage are processed using the MACO Spanish lemmatiser [1] and their corresponding lemmas are used to retrieve the 50 most relevant passages from the EFE document database.

In parallel, the same keyword list (without being lemmatised) is translated to the language the system is required to use for searching the Web (in this case Spanish or English) and submitted to the Google Internet search engine. The system selects the 50 best short summaries returned by the Google main retrieval pages. Keywords have been translated using the SysTran[3] online translation service.

2.3 Answer Extraction

This module processes in parallel both sets of passages selected at passage retrieval stage (IR-n and Google) in order to detect and extract the most probable answer to the query. This process involves: (1) selecting and scoring candidate

[2] http://www.google.com/

[3] http://www.systransoft.com/

answers from the CLEF Spanish document collection, (2) selecting candidate answers from Web retrieved documents and (3) adding Web evidence to candidate lists obtained from the Spanish collection. This process is explained in detail in [3].

3 Results

We submitted two runs. The first run (*aliv041eses*) was obtained applying the system described above and using the Spanish Web retrieved documents while the second run performed the QA process by activating English Web retrieval (*aliv042eses*). Table 1 shows the results obtained for each run.

Table 1. Spanish monolingual task results

Run	**Accuracy (%)**		
	Factoid	**Definition**	**Overall**
aliv041eses	30.56	40.00	31.50
aliv042eses	31.11	45.00	32.50

Our result analysis shows that evidence obtained through English Internet documents (*aliv042eses*) performs better than using Spanish Web documents for this purpose (*aliv041eses*). Nevertheless, performance differences are almost insignificant (32.5% – 31.5%). These results contradicted our initial hypotheses since we thought that English web documents would probably help Spanish monolingual QA more significantly. After a shallow error analysis we detected several translation problems that seriously affected the English Web document processing:

- *Keyword translation.* The lack of context when translating question keywords produces non-adequate translations. This implies sometimes retrieving English documents that have no semantic relation with the original Spanish question.
- *Proper noun translation.* Proper noun translation is an unresolved problem. Usually, proper nouns referring to people or companies have no translation (eg. Bill Clinton). On the other hand, names of countries (*España vs.* Spain) and many cities (*Londres vs.* London) differ depending on the language.
- *Abbreviation translation.* Abbreviations usually refer to language-dependent expressions. Thus, if we want to correctly translate abbreviations and acronyms we need to know the whole expression or terms they refer to in the original language.
- *Title translation.* Literal translation is usually useless when translating titles (names of books, films, etc.) as generally, books and films are given completely different titles in different languages. The basic problem here resides in detecting these expressions and applying the correct translation technique.

All these translation problems affect passage retrieval and answer extraction stages. First, an incorrect translation of content words in questions leads to the retrieval of useless documents that do not support the original question. And second, it makes it impossible to take advantage of evidence in other languages to support candidate answer selection if proper nouns, abbreviations and titles are not correctly translated.

4 Future Work

This study is a first attempt to perform monolingual QA in Spanish by using evidence obtained form corpora in different languages, in this case, English.

We have seen that using corpora in other languages to support monolingual QA is possible and worthwhile if we are able to solve correctly the translation problems described above. Consequently, a main line of future work will be directed toward adopting translation techniques that minimize the currently detected errors.

Moreover, we argue that surely this problem is the main bottleneck towards the long-term objective of developing a whole system capable of performing multilingual question answering.

Acknowledgements

This work has been partially supported by the Spanish Government (CICYT) with grant TIC2003-07158-C04-01.

References

1. Atserias, J., Carmona, J., Castellón, I., Cervell, S., Civit, M., Màrquez, L., Martí, M.A., Padró, L., Placer, R., Rodríguez, H., Taulé, M. and Turmo J.: Morphosyntactic Analysis and Parsing of Unrestricted Spanish Text. In: Proceedings of First International Conference on Language Resources and Evaluation. LREC'98, pages 1267-1272, Granada, Spain. 1998.
2. Llopis, F., Vicedo, J.L. and Ferandez, A.: IR-n system, a passage retrieval systema at CLEF 2001. In: CLEF, editor, Proceedings CLEF-2001 Lecture Notes in Computer Science, Darmstadt, Germany, 2001.
3. Vicedo, J.L., Izquierdo, R., Llopis, F. and Muñoz, R.: Question answering in Spanish. In: CLEF, editor, Proceedings CLEF-2003 Lecture Notes in Computer Science, Tronheim, Norwey, August 2003.

The TALP-QA System for Spanish at CLEF 2004: Structural and Hierarchical Relaxing of Semantic Constraints

Daniel Ferrés, Samir Kanaan, Alicia Ageno, Edgar González, Horacio Rodríguez, Mihai Surdeanu, and Jordi Turmo

TALP Research Center, Universitat Politècnica de Catalunya,
Jordi Girona 1-3, 08043 Barcelona, Spain
{dferres, skanaan, ageno, egonzalez, horacio, surdeanu, turmo}@lsi.upc.es
http://www.lsi.upc.es/~nlp

Abstract. This paper describes TALP-QA, a multilingual open-domain Question Answering (QA) system that processes both factoid and definition questions. The system is described and evaluated in the context of our participation in the CLEF 2004 Spanish Monolingual QA task. Our approach to factoid questions is to build a semantic representation of the questions and the sentences in the passages retrieved for each question. A set of Semantic Constraints (SC) are extracted for each question. An answer extraction algorithm extracts and ranks sentences that satisfy the SCs of the question. If matches are not possible the algorithm relaxes the SCs structurally (removing constraints) and/or hierarchically (abstracting the constraints using a taxonomy).

Answers to definition questions are generated by selecting the text fragment with more density of those terms more frequently related to the question's target (the Named Entity (NE) that appears in the question) throughout the corpus.

1 Introduction

This paper describes TALP-QA, a multilingual open-domain Question Answering (QA) system under development at UPC for the past 2 years. The paper focuses on our participation in the CLEF 2004 evaluation. Our aim in developing TALP-QA has been to build a system as far as possible language independent, where language dependent modules could be substituted to allow the system to be applied to different languages. A first preliminary version of TALP-QA for English was used to participate in the TREC 2003 QA track (see [7]). From this initial version, a new version for Spanish was built and was used in CLEF 2004. An improved version, again for English, was used in TREC 2004.

In this paper we present the overall architecture of TALP-QA and describe briefly its main components, focusing on those components that have been most changed since our initial prototype, and on those components that process Spanish. We also present an evaluation of the system used in the CLEF 2004 evaluation for both factoid and definition questions.

C. Peters et al. (Eds.): CLEF 2004, LNCS 3491, pp. 557–568, 2005.

2 System Description

2.1 Overview

The system architecture follows the most commonly used schema, splitting the process into three phases that are performed sequentially. The QA components may contain iterative algorithms (e.g. Passage Retrieval) but no feedback is propagated to the previous modules. There are three main subsystems (as shown in Figure 1), one corresponding to each phase: Question Processing (QP), Passage Retrieval (PR) and Answer Extraction (AE).

These subsystems are described below, but first we will describe some pre-processing tasks that were carried out on the document collection (the EFE corpus in this case). As mentioned, our aim is to develop a language independent system. Language dependent components are only included in the Question Pre-processing and Passage Pre-processing components, and can be substituted by components for other languages.

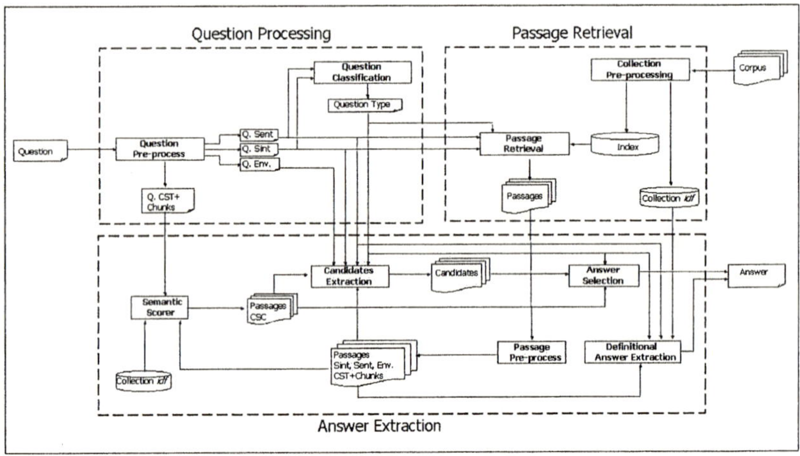

Fig. 1. Architecture of TALP-QA system

2.2 Collection Pre-processing

We have used the *Lucene*[1] Information Retrieval (IR) engine to perform the PR task. Before CLEF 2004 we indexed the entire EFE collection: EFE 1994 and EFE 1995 (i.e. 454,045 documents). We pre-processed the whole collection with linguistic tools (described in the next sub-section) to mark the part-of-speech (POS) tags, lemmas and Named Entities (NE). This information was used to built an index with the following parts:

[1] http://jakarta.apache.org/lucene

- Lemmatized and NE recognized text: this part is built using the lemmas of the words and the results of the Named Entity Recognition (NER) module. This text is then indexed and used in the PR module.
- Original text with NE recognition: the original text that is retrieved when a query succeeds on the lemmatized text.

As an additional knowledge source that will be used in the AE task, an *idf* weight is computed at document level for the whole collection.

2.3 Question Processing

The main goal of this subsystem is to detect the expected answer type and to generate the information needed for the other subsystems. For PR, the information needed is basically lexical (POS and lemmas) and syntactic, and for AE, lexical, syntactic and semantic. We use a language-independent formalism to represent this information. We use the same semantic primitives and relations for both languages (English and Spanish) processed by our system.

For CLEF 2004 (for Spanish) we used a set of general purpose tools produced by the UPC NLP group (see [3] and [1]). The same tools are used for the linguistic processing of both the questions and the passages. These tools are:

- **FreeLing**, which performs tokenization, morphological analysis (including identification of quantities, dates, multiword terms, etc.), POS tagging and lemmatization. See [3].
- **Tacat**, a partial parser that recognises shallow nominal, prepositional and verbal phrases. See [1].
- **ABIONET**, a Named Entity Recognizer and Classifier that classifies NEs in basic categories (person, place, organization and other). See [2].
- **EuroWordNet (EWN)**, used to obtain the following semantic information: a list of synsets (with no attempt at Word Sense Disambiguation), a list of hypernyms of each synset (up to the top of each hypernymy chain), the EWN's Top Concept Ontology (TCO) class [10], and Magnini's Domain Codes (DC) [5].
- **Gazetteers**, with the following information: acronyms, obtained using a Decision Tree approach [4], location-nationality relations (e.g. España-español, Spain-Spanish) and actor-action relations (e.g. escribir-escritor, write-writer).

The application of these language dependent linguistic resources and tools to the text of the question is represented in two structures, see the example in Figure 2:

- **Sent**, which provides lexical information for each word: form, lemma, POS tag (an Eagles compliant rich tagset was used), semantic class of NE, list of EWN synsets and, finally, whenever possible the verbs associated with the actor and the relations between locations and their nationality.

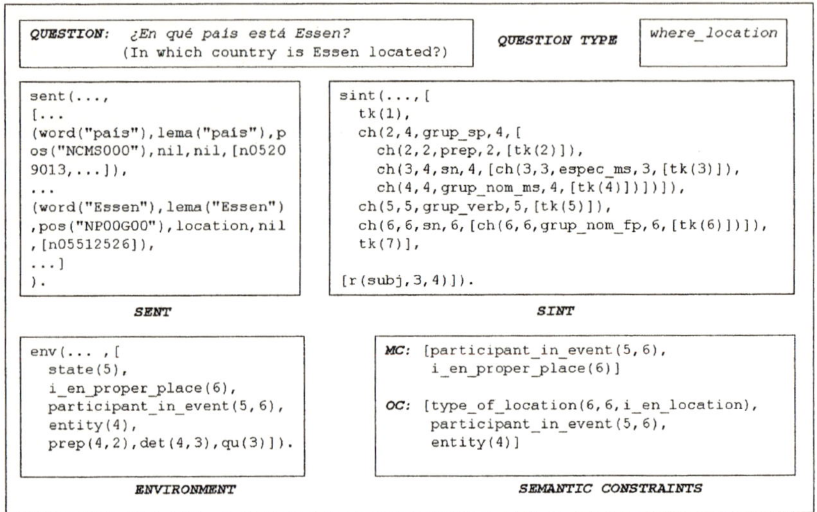

Fig. 2. Results of question pre-processing

- **Sint**, composed by two lists, one recording the syntactic constituent structure of the question (basically nominal, prepositional and verbal phrases) and the other collecting the information of dependencies and other relations between these components.

Once this information is obtained we can find the information relevant to the following tasks:

- **Question type**. The most important information we need to extract from the question text is the Question Type (QT), which is needed by the system when searching the answer. Failure to identify the QT practically disables the correct extraction of the answer. Currently we are working with about 25 QTs. The QT focuses the type of expected answer and provides additional constraints. For instance, when the expected type of the answer is a person, two types of questions are considered, *Who_action*, which indicates that we are looking for a person who performs a certain action and *Who_person_quality*, that indicates that we are looking for a person having the desired quality. The action and the quality are the parameters of the corresponding QT. The following are examples of questions correctly classified respectively as *Who_person_quality* and *Who_action* type:

  - *¿Quién fue jefe del XII Gobierno de Israel? (Who was the head of the XII Israel government?)*
  - *¿Quién ganó el Premio Nobel de Literatura en 1994? (Who won the Nobel Prize for Literature in 1994?)*

  In order to determine the QT our system uses an Inductive Logic Programming (ILP) learner that learns a set of weighted rules from a set of positive

and negative examples. We used as learner the FOIL system [9]. A binary classifier (i.e. a set of rules) was learned for each QT. As training set we used the set of questions from TREC 8 and 9 (~900 questions) manually tagged and as test set the 500 questions from TREC 11. All these questions were previously manually translated into Spanish. For each classifier we used as negative examples the questions belonging to the other classes. For the classification task, the following features were used: word form, word position in the question, lemma, POS, semantic class of NE, synsets together with all their hypernyms, TCO, DC and subject and object relations.
The set of rules for each class was manually revised and completed by a set of manually built rules (with lower weights) in order to ensure a greater coverage. See below a couple of such rules:

- A learned rule:
```
regla(non_human_actor_of_action,A,weight_1000,[],TT) :-
  sent(A,_,TT), TT=[_,W2|_],
  has_tco(W2,cObject),has_domain(W2,dTransport).
```
- A manual rule:
```
regla(non_human_actor_of_action,A,weight_994,[T1,T3],T) :-
  sent(A,_,[T1|T]), the_lema(T1,lema("qué")),
  has_chunk_with_hypernym(_,T,[T2|TT],
    [sArtifact,sObject,sAnimal],T3),
  the_pos(T2,pos("SP")),not(has_term_with_pos(TT,pos("AQ"),_)).
```

– **Environment.** The semantic process starts with the extraction of the semantic relations that hold between the different components identified in the question text. These relations are organized into an ontology of about 100 semantic classes and 25 relations (mostly binary) between them. Both classes and relations are related by taxonomic links. The ontology tries to reflect what is needed for an appropriate representation of the semantic environment of the question (and the expected answer). For instance, *Action* is a class and *Human_action* is another class related to *Action* by means of an *is_a* relation. In the same way, *Human* is a subclass of *Entity*. *Actor_of_action* is a binary relation (between a *Human_action* and a *Human*). When a question is classified as *Who_action* an instance of the class *Human_action* has to be located in the question text and its referent is stored. Later, in the AE phase, an instance of *Human_action* co-referring with the one previously stored has to be located in the selected passages and an instance of *Human* related to it by means of the *Actor_of_action* relation must be extracted as a candidate to be the answer.
The environment of the question is obtained from *Sint* and from information included in *Sent*. A set of about 150 rules was built to perform this task. The environment extracted from a question is presented in Figure 2.
– **Semantic Constraints.** The environment tries to represent the whole semantic content of the question. However, not all the items belonging to the

```
get_semantic_constraints(Question,MC,OC,Environment,where_location,1) :-
  ...
  state(C,Question,Environment),
  get_related_tokens_in_environment(C,Environment,ListRelatedTokens),
  filter_tuple_tokens(ListRelatedTokens,MC,_,OC,
          [theme_of_event,time_of_event,location_of_event,which_entity],
          []),
  ...
  filter_related_tokens(ListRelatedTokens,
          [
                [human_participant_in_event(C,_X)],
                [participant_in_event(C,_X), i_en_proper_person(_X)],
                [participant_in_event(C,_X), i_en_proper_organization(_X)],
                [participant_in_event(C,_X), i_en_proper_named_entity(_X)]
          ],
          MCRelations),
  ...
  extend_mandatory(ListRelatedTokens,MCRelations,MC,OC,Question,Environment).
```

Fig. 3. A rule to obtain the Semantic constraints of a question

environment are useful to extract the answer. So, depending on the QT, a subset of the environment has to be extracted. Sometimes additional relations, not present in the environment, are used and sometimes the relations extracted from the environment are extended, refined or modified. We define in this way the set of relations (the semantic constraints) that are supposed to be found in the answer. These relations are classified as mandatory, Mandatory Constraints (MC), (i.e. they have to be satisfied in the passage) or optional, Optional Constraints (OC), (if satisfied the score of the answer is higher). In order to build the semantic constraints for each question a set of rules (typically 1 or 2 for each type of question) has been manually built. A fragment of the rule applied in the example is presented in Figure 3. The rule can be paraphrased as follows: If the relation *state(C)* holds in the environment, then get recursively all the predicates related to C, and then filter out the appropriate ones to be included in MC and OC and finally extend these sets for the sake of completeness. The application of the rule results in the constraints shown in Figure 3.

2.4 Passage Retrieval

The main function of the passage retrieval component is to extract small text passages that are likely to contain the correct answer. Document retrieval is performed using the *Lucene* Information Retrieval system. For practical purposes we currently limit the number of documents retrieved for each query to 1000. The passage retrieval algorithm uses a data-driven query relaxation technique: if too few passages are retrieved, the query is relaxed first by increasing the accepted keyword proximity and then by discarding the keywords with the lowest priority. The reverse happens when too many passages are extracted. Each keyword is assigned a priority using a series of heuristics fairly similar to [8]. For example, a proper noun is assigned a higher priority than a common noun, the question focus word (e.g. "state" in the question "What state has the most Indians?") is assigned the lowest priority, and stop words are removed.

2.5 Factoid Answer Extraction

After PR, for factoid AE, two tasks are performed in sequence: Candidate Extraction (CE) and Answer Selection (AS). In the first component, all the candidate answers are extracted from the highest scoring sentences of the selected passages. In the second component the best answer is chosen.

- **Candidate Extraction**. This process is carried out on the set of passages obtained from the previous subsystem. These passages are segmented into sentences and each sentence is scored according to its semantic content using the $tf * idf$ weighting of the terms from the question and taxonomically related terms occurring in the sentence (see [7]).
  The linguistic process of extraction is similar to the process carried out on questions and leads to the construction of the environment of each candidate sentence. The rest is a mapping between the semantic relations contained in this environment and the semantic constraints extracted from the question. The mandatory restrictions must be satisfied for the sentence to be taken into consideration; the satisfaction of the optional constraints simply increases the score of the candidate. The final extraction process is carried out on the sentences satisfying this filter.
  The knowledge source used for this process is a set of extraction rules with a credibility score. Each QT has its own subset of extraction rules that leads to the selection of the answer. An example of an extraction rule is presented in Figure 4. The rule can be paraphrased as follows: Look in MC for predicates *state(C)* and *location(X)* satisfied in the environment. Then look in the environment for the predicates related to C, *location_of_event* and *location*. Make sure that the two locations are different and adjust the corresponding score.
  The application of the rules follows an iterative approach. In the first iteration all the semantic constraints have to be satisfied by at least one of the candidate sentences. If no sentence satisfies the constraints, the set of semantic constraints is relaxed by means of structural or semantic relaxation rules, using the semantic ontology. Two kinds of relaxation are considered: i) moving some constraint from MC to OC and ii) relaxing some constraint in MC substituting it for another more general constraint in the taxonomy. If no candidate sentence occurs when all possible relaxations have been performed the question is assumed to have no answer.
- **Answer selection**. In order to select the answer from the set of candidates, the following scores are computed for each candidate sentence:
  - The rule score, which uses factors such as the confidence of the rule used, the relevance of the OC satisfied in the matching, and the similarity between NEs occurring in the candidate sentence and the question.
  - The passage score, which uses the relevance of the passage containing the candidate.
  - The semantic score, defined previously.
  - The relaxation score, which takes into account the level of rule relaxation in which the candidate has been extracted.

```
extract_contextual_answer_from_tokens(DS,SS,_,_,Env, where_location,1, MT,A1,Sc2,_):-
  satisfy_MT_esp_obl([state(C),location(X)],MT,_),Sc=10,
  satisfy_strict([location_of_event(C,A,DS,Env),location(A,DS,Env)]),
  X\==A,
  nth(A,SS,A1),
  nth(X,SS,A2),
  smooth_scr(SS,X,A,Sc,Sc1),
if(
satisfy_MT_esp_obl([type_of_location(_,_,TL)],MT,_),
(check_type_of_location(A1,TL,A2,Sc3),Sc3 > 0.4, Sc2 is (Sc1 + Sc3 * 10)/ 2),
Sc2 is Sc1).
```

Fig. 4. One of the extraction rules used in the example

For each candidate the values of these scores are normalized and accumulated in a global score. The answer to the question is the candidate with the best global score.

2.6 Answer Extraction for Definitions

The approach taken to extract definitions can be viewed as a three-step process:

1. **Question analysis and target extraction**. The question is analyzed with the same module as for factoid questions. This module outputs the question's target (the NE that appears in the question) and its type (human/organization). The type of the target makes it possible to apply more specific heuristics to each question.
2. **Relative word significance computation**. The Relative Significance of a word stem is a measure of how the word stem is related to the question target; this relative significance is computed as follows. For each occurrence of the target in the corpus, a window with its 15 previous and following words is extracted. From each window extracted, adjectives and nouns (proper and common nouns) are selected and stemmed (in order to reduce the high morphological variability of Spanish). This window is expected to capture the context of the target. Our observations determine +/-15 word as an adequate distance, at least for Spanish.
The number of occurrences of each stem in the context windows is computed, and then multiplied by the *idf* of the stem as computed from the whole corpus, in order to obtain its relative significance to the target. Moreover, there are two lists of stems (one for persons and one for organizations) that contain stems likely to appear in definitions of either persons (as professions, awards, etc.) or organizations (words like "partido", "organización"). The significance of stems appearing on the corresponding list (depending on the question target type) is multiplied by a factor determined experimentally (3.2) in order to boost its importance.
3. **Selection of the most informative fragment**. The definition has to be selected from the corpus. Definitions are usually found in fragments that follow some high-level patterns, as "<def> (<target>)" or "<target> , <def>". To obtain the definition, for each occurrence of one of these patterns in the text, we calculated its information density, that is, the sum of

the relative significance of its words divided by the number of nouns and adjectives it contains. The definition is expected to contain between 4 and 15 non-stop words, so the length of each definition is the one that maximizes its information density. The text fragment produced as final output is the definition with highest information density.

3 Results

This section evaluates the behaviour of our system at CLEF 2004. We evaluated the three main components of our system and the global results:

- **Question Processing**. This subsystem has been manually evaluated for factoid questions (see Table 1) and the following components: basic NLP tools (POS, NER and NE Classification (NEC)), semantic pre-processing (Environment, MC and OC construction) and finally, Question Classification. These results are accumulatives.
- **Passage Retrieval**. The evaluation of this subsystem was performed using the set of correct answers given by the CLEF organization (see Table 2). We submitted two runs. In both runs we retrieved only the 1000 top documents (no passages) for definition questions. These runs differ only in the parameters of the passage retrieval module for factoid questions:
  - Windows proximity: in run1 the proximity of the different windows that can compose a passage was lower than run2's (from 60 lemmas to 80).
  - Threshold for minimum passages: the PR algorithm relaxes the query to obtain more passages if the number of extracted passages is lower than this threshold. These values are: 4 (run1) and 1 (run2) passages.
  - Number of passages retrieved: we have chosen a maximum of 3000 passages in run1 and 50 passages in run2.

  In this part we computed two measures: the first one (called *answer*) is the accuracy taking into account the questions that have a correct answer in its set of passages. The second one (called *answer+docID*) is the accuracy taking into account the questions that have a minimum of one passage with a correct answer and a correct document identifier in its set of passages.

Table 1. Results of Question Processing evaluation

Subsystem	Total units	Correct	Incorrect	Accuracy	Error
POS-tagging	1667	1629	38	97.72%	2.28%
NE Recognition	183	175	8	95.63%	4.37%
NE Classification	183	137	46	74.86%	25.14%
Environment	180	81	99	45.00%	55.00%
MC	180	77	103	42.78%	57.22%
OC	180	131	49	72.78%	27.22%
Q. Classification	180	105	75	58.33%	41.67%

Table 2. Passage Retrieval results

Question type	Measure	run1	run2
FACTOID	Accuracy (*answer*)	64.37% (103/160)	59.37% (95/160)
	Accuracy (*answer+docID*)	48.12% (77/160)	43.12% (69/160)
DEFINITION	Accuracy (*answer*)	85.00% (17/20)	85.00% (17/20)
	Accuracy (*answer+docID*)	55.00% (11/20)	55.00% (11/20)

Table 3. Factoid Answer Extraction results

Subsystem	Measure	run1	run2
Candidate Extraction	Accuracy (*answer*)	33.00% (34/103)	35.78% (34/95)
Answer Selection	Accuracy (*answer*)	70.58% (24/34)	79.41% (27/34)
Answer Extraction	Accuracy (*answer*)	23.30% (24/103)	28.42% (27/95)

Table 4. Results of TALP-QA system at CLEF 2004

Measure	run1	run2
Total Num. Answers	200	200
Right/Wrong	48/150	52/143
IneXact/Unsupported	1/1	3/2
Overall accuracy	24.00% (48/200)	26.00% (52/200)
Accuracy over Factoid	18.89% (34/180)	21.11% (38/180)
Accuracy over Definition	70.00% (14/20)	70.00% (14/20)
Answer-string "NIL" returned correcty	19.23% (10/52)	20.37% (11/54)
Confidence-weighted Score	0.08780 (17.560/200)	0.10287 (20.574/200)

- **Answer Extraction**. The evaluation of this subsystem for factoid questions has been done in three parts: evaluation of the Candidate Extraction (CE) module, evaluation of the Answer Selection (AS) module and finally evaluation of the AE subsystem's global accuracy for factoid questions in which the answer appears in our selected passages.
- **Global Results**. The overall results of our participation in CLEF 2004 are listed in Table 4.

4 Evaluation and Conclusions

This paper summarizes our participation in the CLEF 2004 Spanish monolingual QA task. Out of 200 questions, our system provided the correct answer to 48 questions in run1 and 52 in run2. Hence, the global accuracy of our system was 24% and 26% for run1 and run2 respectively. We conclude with a summary of the system behaviour for the two question classes:

- **Factoid questions**. The accuracy over factoid questions is 18.89% (run1) and 21.11% (run2). Although no direct comparison can be done with other evaluations in another language, we think that we have improved substantially our factoid QA system with respect to the results of the TREC 2003 QA evaluation (5.3%) in English. In comparison with the other participants of the CLEF 2004 Spanish QA track (see [6]), our system has obtained the best results in the following type of questions: location, person and objects. On the other hand, our system has a poor performance in the classes: manner, measure, organization, other and time.

- **Question Processing**. The Question Classification subsystem has an accuracy of 58%, a similar accuracy as the *environment*, MC and OC constraints. These values are influenced by the previous errors in the POS, NER and NEC subsystems.
- **Passage Retrieval**. In the PR we evaluated that 64.37% (run1) and 59.37% (run2) of questions have a correct answer in their passages. Taking into account the document identifiers the evaluation shows that 48.12% (run1) and 43.12% (run2) of the questions are really supported.
- **Answer Extraction**. The accuracy of the AE module for factoid questions for which the answer occurred in our selected passages was of 23.32% (run1) and 28.42% (run2). This means that we achieved a significant improvement of our AE module, since the results for this part in TREC 2003 were 8.9%.

– **Definition questions**. The definition answer extraction module has obtained rather satisfactory results, 14 right definitions out of 20 proposed (70%), indeed the highest score for definition questions in the Spanish language track. The errors are due to the shortage of passages retrieved for the target, which caused the module to fail to determine the right set of significant words.

Acknowledgments

This work has been partially supported by the European Comission (CHIL, IST-2004-506909) and the Spanish Research Dept. (ALIADO, TIC2002-04447-C02). TALP Research Center is recognized as a Quality Research Group (2001 SGR 00254) by DURSI, the Research Department of the Catalan Government.

References

1. Atserias, J., Carmona, J., Castellón, I., Cervell, S., Civit, M., Márquez, L., Martí, M.A., Padró ,L., Placer, R., Rodríguez, H., Taulé, M., Turmo, J.: Morphosyntactic Analisys and Parsing of Unrestricted Spanish Text. Proceedings of LREC-98. Granada, Spain.
2. Carreras, X., Márquez, L. and Padró, L.: Named Entity Extraction Using Adaboost. Proceedings of the CoNLL-2002. Shared Task Contribution. Taipei, Taiwan. September 2002.
3. Carreras, X., Chao, I., Padró, L., Padró, M.: FreeLing: An Open-Source Suite of Language Analyzers. Proceedings of LREC-2004. Lisbon, Portugal, 2004

4. Ferrés, D., Massot, M., Padró, M., Rodríguez, H., Turmo, J.: Automatic Building Gazetteers of Co-referring Named Entities. Proceedings of LREC-2004. Lisboa, Portugal, 2004.
5. Magnini, B., Cavagliá, G.: Integrating Subject Field Codes into WordNet. Proceedings LREC-2000. Athens, Greece, 2000.
6. Magnini, B., Vallin, A., Ayache, C., Erbach, G., Peñas, A., de Rijke, M., Rocha, P., Simov, K., Sutcliffe, R.: Overview of the CLEF 2004 Multilingual Question Answering Track. Fifth Workshop of the Cross–Language Evaluation Forum (CLEF 2004). Lecture Notes in Computer Science (LNCS), Springer, Heidelberg, Germany. 2005.
7. Massot, M., Ferrés, D., Rodríguez, H.: QA UdG-UPC System at TREC-12. Proceedings of the TREC-2003. Gaithersburg, Maryland, United States, 2003.
8. Moldovan, D., Harabagiu, S., Pasca, M., Mihalcea, R., Goodrum, R., Gîrju, R., Rus, V.: LASSO: A Tool for Surfing the Answer Net. Proceedings of the Text Retrieval Conference (TREC-8). Gaithersburg, Maryland, United States, 1999.
9. Quinlan, J.R.: FOIL: A midterm report. Proc. of the sixth European Conf. on Machine Learning. Springer-Verlag, 1993.
10. Rodríguez, H., Climent, S., Vossen, P., Bloksma, L., Peters, W., Alonge, A., Bertanga, F., Roventini, A.: The Top-Down Strategy for Bulding EuroWordNet: Vocabulary Coverage, Base Conceps and Top Ontology. Computer and Humanities 32. 1998, Kluwer Academic Publishers.

ILC-UniPI Italian QA*

Francesca Bertagna[1], Luminita Chiran[2], and Maria Simi[3]

[1] Istituto di Linguistica Computazionale (Consiglio Nazionale delle Ricerche), Via Moruzzi 1, 56100 Pisa, Italy
francesca.bertagna@ilc.cnr.it,
[2] Universita' "A. I. Cuza", Str. General Berthelot 16, 700483, Iasi, Romania
luminitachiran@yahoo.com
[3] Dipartimento di Informatica (Università di Pisa), Via Buonarroti 2, 56100 Pisa, Italy
simi@di.unipi.it

Abstract. This paper introduces the general architecture of a prototype for monolingual Italian QA. The adopted strategies, the tools and resources for the linguistic processing are presented, together with the system results.

1 Introduction

This is the first time the Istituto di Linguistica Computazionale of the Italian National Council of Research and the Department of Computer Science at the University of Pisa has taken part in the QA track at CLEF. The participation in CLEF was an important opportunity to finalize a first version of a prototype for Italian QA and to individuate the most important problems, to discuss and study possible solutions and also to share our first results in a collaborative and experimental environment. The aim of this paper is thus twofold: on the one hand we want to describe the QA prototype and its modules of analysis, on the other we would like to present the most important problems which emerged and discuss possible ways to overcome them.

2 General Architecture

The system described in Fig 1 is heavily inspired by the FALCON [1], [2] and by the PIQASso [3] applications and it is organized following the classic three-module architecture consisting of question analysis, search engine and answer extraction modules.

Some important, even crucial, external modules are missing (a Named Entity Recognizer and modules for WSD and multiword recognition). We will consider this first version of the prototype as a starting point and a trial assembly of different modules and resources, in the hope of being able to add what is missing in the near future. In what follows we will describe each of these steps in detail, focusing on the adopted solutions and on the analysis of the problems we encountered.

* We would like to thank Simone Pecunia and Giuseppe Attardi for their indispensable help and Nicoletta Calzolari and Irina Prodanof for their comments and suggestions. We also thank Roberto Bartolini, Alessandro Lenci, Simonetta Montemagni and Vito Pirrelli for the kind concession of text analysis tools.

C. Peters et al. (Eds.): CLEF 2004, LNCS 3491, pp. 569 – 580, 2005.

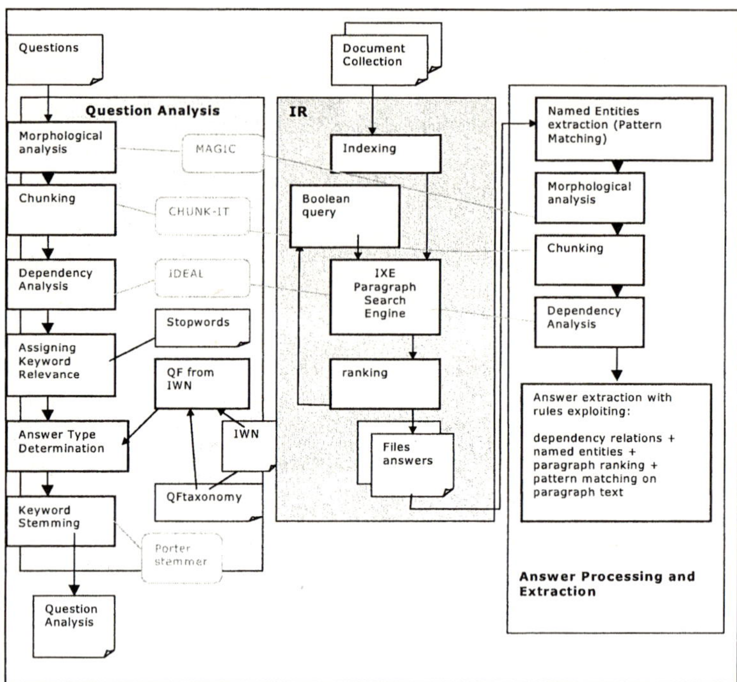

Fig. 1. Prototype General Architecture

3 Question Analysis Module

In this module the system performs a multi-layered analysis of the question:

- first of all, a sequence of steps leads to the linguistic representation of the question: each word of the question is isolated, morphologically analysed and associated to one or more lemmas. Then a two-stage (chunking and dependency) syntactic analysis is performed, allowing the system to: i) segment the question into syntactically organized text units, ii) perform POS-tagging of the words in the question, iii) identify grammatical functions;
- the system applies a set of rules in order to assign to each word in the question a specific weight in term of its relevance as a keyword of the query;
- the system extracts from the question the Question Stem (the interrogative element usually introducing the sentence) and, where needed, the Answer Type Term [2];
- the Question Focus (i.e. the expected answer type) is individuated, by merely relying on the Question Stem type or by recurring, via the Answer Type Term and via the Question Focus Taxonomy, to the information stored in the ItalWordNet database;
- a stemmer is used on some of the keywords of the query.

  The next paragraphs will describe more in detail each of these steps.

3.1 Linguistic Analysis

First of all, the question goes through a chain of tools for the analysis of Italian language developed at ILC-CNR by [4]. The analysis chain includes: i) morphological analyser, ii) chunker, iii) dependency analyser.

The morphological analysis is performed by Magic [5]. Magic produces, for each word form of the question, all its possible lemmas together with their morpho-syntactic features. Magic also recognizes the capitalization of the word, a small set of basic multi-word expressions (such as *al di là*[1] but also some proper names like *San Vittore* in question#3) and analyses verbs containing clitic pronouns.

The chunker, CHUNK-IT [6], first performs the morpho-syntactic disambiguation of the question and then segments it into an unstructured sequence of syntactically organized text units (the *chunks*). We will see how even this initial, flat and *linguistically poor* syntactic representation can be exploited to extract crucial information for the task of question classification on the basis of the type of expected answer (i.e. what the user is looking for with his/her question). This information is the Question Stem (QS) and the Answer Type Term (ATT).

The chunked file is the input of IDEAL (Italian DEpendency AnaLyzer) that builds a representation of the sentence using binary, asymmetric relations (modifier, object, subject, complement etc.) between a head and a dependent based on the FAME annotation schema [7]. The success of a QA application highly depends on the quality of the parser output and it is very important to efficiently parse interrogative forms and extracting the syntactic relations that allows the system to recognize information such as direct object, subject etc. that have such an importance in the semantic interpretation of the sentence. In order to reach this goal, a specific set of rules has been written, starting with an analysis of a corpus of Italian interrogative forms. Also the paragraphs returned by the Search Engine and candidate to be identified as answers will be subjected to these same linguistic analysis and tools.

3.2 Determining the Question Focus

The Question Stem is the interrogative element (adjective, pronoun, adverb) that we find in the first chunk of the sentence (*Cosa*, *Chi*, *Quando*, etc.. [2]), while the Answer Type Term is the element modified by the QS (*Quale animale tuba?*[3] or *Quale casa automobilistica produce il "Maggiolone"?*[4]). The convergence between these two pieces of information allows us to get closer to the expected answer type and to the text portion that is likely to contain the answer. Some QSs, for example *Quando* (*When*) and *Dove* (*Where*), reveal which kind of answer we can expect to receive and a set of simple rules was encoded in order to enable the system to establish univocal correspondences between them and specific QFs. Other QSs are, on the contrary, completely ambiguous: *Che* and *Quale*, being interrogative adjectives, do not provide

---

[1] *Beyond.*

[2] *What, Who, When* etc..

[3] *What animal coos?*

[4] *What car company produces "the Beetle"?*

any clues about the semantic category of the expected answer. In these cases, to obtain the expected answer type (to individuate what we call the Question Focus) the system has to analyse the noun modified by *Che* and *Quale* and resort to its representation in the source of lexical-semantic knowledge, ItalWordNet.

ItalWordNet (IWN) [8] is the extension of the Italian component of the EuroWordNet database [9]. IWN follows the linguistic design of EuroWordNet (with which it shares the Interlingual Index and the Top Ontology as well as the large set of semantic relations[5]) and consists now of about 70,000 word senses organized in 50,000 *synsets*. In order to better exploit the information available in ItalWordNet, a Question Focus Taxonomy has been created and connected to ItalWordNet, allowing the system to go from the Answer Type Term to the Question Focus via the ItalWordNet hyperonymical links.

3.2.1 Question Focus Taxonomy

The Question Focus Taxonomy has been defined by analysing about 500 questions obtained by translating into Italian the English question collection of the QA track of the tenth Text Retrieval Conference and downloading Italian factoid questions from web sites dedicated to on-line quizzes. Two disjointed types of expected answer can be identified: the first type consists of the answers referring to single factual information (a person's name, a specific location, a length expressed in meters etc.); the second type refers to more complex answers, describing a series of events, explanation, reasons etc. The highest nodes, FACT and DESCR refer respectively to these two most general categories.

Many nodes in the QFTaxonomy have been projected on the branches of the ItalWordNet taxonomies[6] but often the QF has to be addressed on scattered portions of the semantic net. For example, the node Location of the Question Focus taxonomy can be mapped on the synset {luogo 1 – parte dello spazio occupata o occupabile materialmente o idealmente[7]}, that has 52 first level hyponyms and that we can further organize with other (at least) 10 sub-nodes, such as:

- country (mappable on {paese 2, nazione 2, stato 4}),
- river, {fiume 1},
- region, {zona 1, terra 7, regione 1, territorio 1},
- etc..

Most of these taxonomies is led by the same synset {luogo 1}, which circumscribes a large taxonomical portion that can be exploited in the QF identification. We also added four other sub-hierarchies to this area:

- {corso d'acqua 1, corso 4- l'insieme delle acque in movimento},
- {mondo 3, globo 2, corpo_celeste 1, astro 1},
- {acqua 2 – raccolta di acqua},
- {edificazione 2, fabbricato 1, edificio 1 – costruzione architettonica}.

[5] For a complete list of the available semantic relations cf. (Roventini et al., 2003).

[6] The ItalWordNet tool developed at ILC-CNR was used to encode both the QFTaxonomy and the links to IWN.

[7] *place 1- part of the space that can be ideally or physically took up.*

Fig. 2 gives an idea of this situation: the circumscribed taxonomical portion includes the nodes directly mapped on the QFs, all their hyponyms (of all levels) and all the synsets linked to the hierarchy by means of the BELONGS_TO_CLASS/HAS_INSTANCE relation[8].

This allows a specific module of the system to retrieve the Question Focus of many questions of the type *Quale* and *Che*. For example, the system identifies the Question Focus (CITY) of question#3 (*In quale citta' si trova il carcere di San Vittore?*[9]).

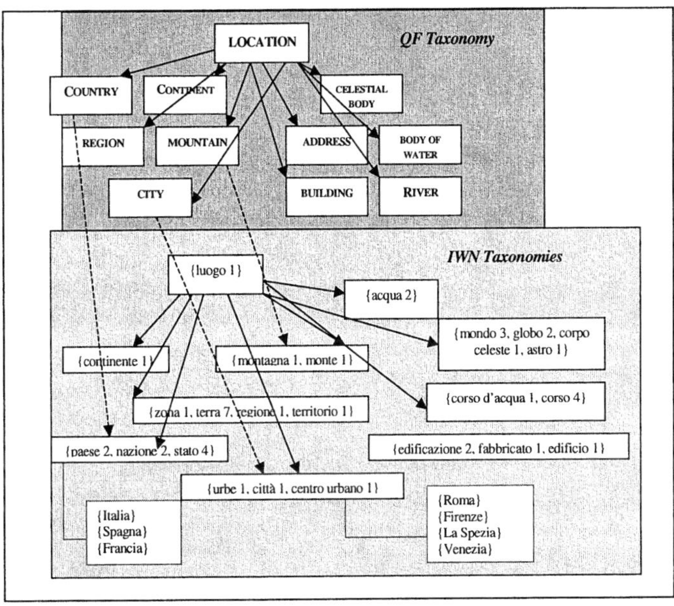

Fig. 2. Mapping the node Location of the QfTaxonomy on the lexical nodes of IWN

At the moment, no module performing Word Sense Disambiguation is available in this phase. As a consequence, the sub-module retrieves not only the relevant sense but also all the others: for example, for question#155 (*Di quale squadra di calcio francese era presidente Bernard Tapie?*[10]) beyond the correct HUMAN GROUP the system identifies an incorrect QF INSTRUMENT, determined by the fact that the ATT *squadra* has, among the other senses, the sense of *square*. This is not a strong limit for this specific task: the Information Retrieval phase works as a kind of *implicit* Word Sense Disambiguator since, in general, the co-occurrence of more than one keyword submitted to the Search Engine determines the extraction of pertinent para-

[8] While in WordNet the synsets of type instance are linked to their superordinates by means of the normal HAS_HYPERONYM relation (not distinguishing, in this way, classes from instances), in ItalWordNet the HAS_INSTANCE/BELONGS_TO_CLASS relation is used in these cases.

[9] *In what city is the San Vittore prison?*

[10] *Of which French football team was president Bernard Tapie?*

graphs which exclude other readings (in this case, for example, no instruments can be found in the paragraph extracted: *Nuovi momenti difficili per l'industriale francese Bernard Tapie, ex ministro delle aree urbane, deputato e presidente della squadra di calcio di Marsiglia, l'Olympique...*[11]). On the contrary, the lack of a WSD module determined the impossibility to exploit the ItalWordNet synonyms to perform query expansion in this first version of the system.

3.3 Keyword Relevance

The selection of the keywords for the query is a very important but difficult task. For example, in the first question of the collection (*In quale anno venne conferito il premio Nobel a Thomas Mann?*[12]), we would like to submit a vector to the search engine containing at least the words: *premio*, *Nobel*, *Thomas*, *Mann*. It would be unlikely to find the word *anno* (year) in the expected paragraph (in its place we would more probably find the year we are looking for) while the word *conferito* can be easily substituted by a synonym (like *assegnato*, assigned) or by *vincere* (win) if in the answer *Thomas Mann* is indicated as the person who won the Nobel prize.

In order to deal with the majority of the cases, we adopted a general rule on the basis of the different Parts Of Speech and of the syntactic and semantic function of the word in the question. To each morphological word an attribute "relevance" is assigned which is set to the minimal value (0) if the word belongs to a list of stopwords and to the maximum value (10) if the word is a number, has a capital letter or is in inverted commas. The Part of Speech of the remaining words is analysed and an intermediate value (7) is assigned to the relevance of nouns while a smaller value (5) is assigned to verbs, adjectives and adverbs (the minimun value is assigned to auxiliary or modal verbs).

All the nouns that are "answer type terms" in questions introduced by the interrogative adjectives *Quale* and *Che* (*What*, *Which*) (for example the word *anno* in the question *In quale anno venne conferito il premio Nobel a Thomas Mann?*) received a low score (2) as did their modifiers. This choice is not always the best strategy to follow: in case of question#17 (*A quale partito apparteneva Hitler?*[13]), submitting the keyword *partito* to the Search Engine would have significantly cut the number of the retrieved paragraphs, allowing the easy individuation of the correct answer since in the pertinent paragraphs we always find the text "*..il partito nazista..*". In the same way, the choice to assign a higher score to the ATT in the case of questions introduced by *Quale* in pronominal function is very useful for questions like *Quale è la capitale della Russia?* but has some negative consequences in the case of question#31 (*Qual è la professione di James Bond?*) since it is highly unlikely to find the word *professione* in the retrieved paragraphs. Some initial observations seem to suggest that in the case of questions introduced by the pronoun *Quale*, the Answer Type Terms referring to concrete entities are more likely to appear in the paragraphs containing the

---

[11] *Bernard Tapie, former minister for urban areas etc...*

[12] *What year was Thomas Mann awarded the Nobel Prize?*

[13] *What party did Hitler belong to?*

answer but the usefulness of a module exploiting the difference between abstract and concrete entities has still to be evaluated.

Other rules handle more specific yet frequent cases, for example assigning the minimum value to the relevance of the verb *chiamare* in question#121 (*Come si chiama la moglie di Kurt Cobain?*[14]) or of the verb *trovarsi* in question#134 (*Dove si trova l'arcipelago delle Svalbard?*[15]).

Other more subtle distinctions may be introduced: for example, the first name is *more optional* than the surname in the retrieval of the paragraphs and this is the reason for the failure of retrieval for question#28 (*Qual è il titolo del film di Stephen Frears con Glenn Close, John Malkovich e Michelle Pfeiffer?*[16]) where all the names with capital letters are submitted together (connected by AND) to the Search Engine while in the answer only the surname of John Malkovich is present. At the moment we prefer not to introduce this distinction since we do not have yet a systematic and general strategy to handle proper names.

3.4 Stemming

The Porter stemmer for Italian[17] was used on all the keywords with relevance smaller than the maximum value (so in general only Proper Nouns and keywords in inverted commas were not stemmed). The use of a stemmer was preferred because it seemed more simple and straightforward than the automatic generation of morphological forms but it has some important drawbacks. For example, question#127 (*Quale animale tuba?*[18]) was badly treated because the only keyword sent to the Search Engine was *tub** (the Answer Type Term *animale* was correctly omitted in the query vector). For this reason, the Search Engine retrieved a lot of non pertinent paragraphs, such as paragraphs talking about ***tub**eri* (*tuber*) or ***tub**ercolosi* (*tubercolosis*).

This would be avoided by using the morphological expansion in place of the stemmer, even if this would obviously not avoid retrieving all the document talking about the musical instrument *tuba*.

3.5 Question XML Data Structure

In order to collect all the information derived from the various steps of question analysis, we recurred to an XML representation. Fig. 3 shows an example question represented in our XML data Structure. It would be very useful in the future to exploit fully the *ids* of the various layers of linguistic representation in order to better represent the links between morphological forms, chunks and the heads/dependents of the functional analysis. This would facilitate the identification of the text portion containing the answer in the answer extraction module.

---

[14] *What is the name of Kurt Cobain's wife?*

[15] *Where is the Svalbard archipelago?*

[16] *What's the title of the Stephen Frears' movie with Glenn Close, John...?*

[17] Freely available at http://snowball.tartarus.org/italian/stemmer.html

[18] *What animal coos?*

```
- <question clef_id="D IT IT 0008" q_id="q_8">
    Chi e' Shimon Peres?
  - <words>
    - <word cl="M1" relevance="0" value="chi" w_id="q_8w_70">
        <morph forma="chi" m_id="q_8w_70m_1" others="!,_,_,!,!,!,pos" pos="pron" value="chi" />
        <morph forma="chi" m_id="q_8w_70m_2" others="!,m,p,!,!,!,pos" pos="nn" value="cha" />
      </word>
    - <word relevance="0" value="e'" w_id="q_8w_71">
        <morph forma="e'" m_id="q_8w_71m_1" others="3,!,s,pres,ind,!,!" pos="v_fin" value="essere" />
      </word>
      <word cl="M1" relevance="10" value="shimon" w_id="q_8w_72" />
      <word cl="M1" relevance="10" value="peres" w_id="q_8w_73" />
      <word punc="Y" relevance="0" value="?" w_id="q_8w_74" />
    </words>
  - <chunks>
      <chunk AGR="@FP@FS@MP@MS" CC="N_C" POTGOV="CHI#P@FP@FS@MP@MS" c_id="q_8c_1" />
      <chunk AGR="@S3" CC="FV_C" POTGOV="ESSERE#V@S3IP" c_id="q_8c_2" />
      <chunk AGR="@MS@FS@MP@FP" CC="N_C" POTGOV="SHIMON#SP@NN" c_id="q_8c_3" />
      <chunk AGR="@MS@FS@MP@FP" CC="N_C" POTGOV="PERES#SP@NN" c_id="q_8c_4" />
      <chunk CC="PUNC_C" PUNCTYPE="?#@" c_id="q_8c_5" />
    </chunks>
  - <relations>
      <relation dep="CHI[1]" head="ESSERE[2]" plaus="100" r_id="q_8r_1" role="PERSON" type="SUBJ" />
      <relation dep="SHIMON[3]" head="ESSERE[2]" plaus="100" r_id="q_8r_2" type="PRED" />
      <relation dep="PERES[4]" head="SHIMON[3]" plaus="100" r_id="q_8r_3" role="APPOS" type="MODIF" />
    </relations>
    <stem value="chi" />
    <question_focus value="ROLE" />
  </question>
```


Fig. 3. The Question XML Data Structure

4 IR Module and Query Definition

The inner part of the ILC-UniPi-QA system consists of a passage retrieval application built on a search engine developed at the Computer Science Department at the University of Pisa. The search engine, the same used in the PiQASso [3] document indexing and retrieval subsystem, is based on IXE [10], a high-performance C++ class library for building full-text search engines.

The search engine stores the full documents in compressed form and retrieves single paragraphs. However full documents are indexed and sentence boundary information is added to the index, to enable a wider search to nearby paragraphs. In fact in many cases all the relevant terms do not appear within a paragraph, but some may be present in nearby sentences. If the option to search in a wider context is chosen, those terms may still contribute to the retrieval and ranking of the paragraph.

Whether this feature is effective with respect to a more standard strategy of paragraph indexing is still an open issue and deserves further investigation. The strategy followed to retrieve the candidate answers consists in the iteration of the boolean query on the basis of the score "relevance" of each keyword and of the number of retrieved documents. In the first loop we send to the Search Engine all the keywords with relevance higher than 2 connected with the AND operator. If no paragraph is retrieved then the system performs the second loop, creating a query connecting with AND all the keywords with relevance higher than 7 and with OR the keywords with relevance 5. If no paragraphs are retrieved or if at least all the keywords in AND and one in OR are not present in the returned paragraphs then the system performs the third loop. This consists in a query with all the keywords with relevance 10 in AND and the keywords with relevance 5 in OR. Again, if no paragraph is returned or if at least all the keywords in AND and one in OR are not present in the returned paragraphs then the fourth and last iteration is performed with only the keywords with relevance 10.

The system also foresees a mechanism to restrict the proximity in case of queries that contain a sequence of first names and surnames (so the keywords *Thomas* and *Mann* of question#1 are searched in the paragraphs without any other elements in between). This scheme has to be revised and inserted in the future in the more general strategy for handling poly-lexical units of the type name+surname, name+preposition+name (the *Mostro di Firenze* of question#48) etc.

A new version of the IXE Search Engine is under development at the Uni-Pi Computer Science Department: it will allow queries constrained with information about the expected answer type, so for example in the case of the question#11 (*Qual è la città sacra per gli Ebrei?*[19]) it will be possible to submit a query of the type "*città sacra ebrei location:**" and retrieve only paragraphs containing the name of a city.

5 Answer Processing

The Search Engine returns a file for each query. The file returned follows a specific DTD having the paragraph as sub-element and the information about the match and the source document as attributes. The attribute "best_ranking" is also created at root element level, equivalent to the number of keywords actually submitted to IXE for the current query. For each paragraph, the system also calculates the value of the "ranking" attribute, consisting in the number of keywords of the query actually found in each single paragraph.

After this step, a set of simple regular expressions are used to discover in the paragraphs the named entities that can be found by recurring to simple pattern matching; in this way, the element "Named_entity" is created for the pertinent paragraphs, having as attribute the value, the type[20] and the plausibility score of the NE identification.

The meta-information representing the *coordinates* of the journalistic article (i.e. who wrote the article, where and when and for which news agency) are eliminated from the text in order to provide a *clean* input to the text analysis tools and are saved in a specific sub-element of type "MetaInfo". The paragraphs are then submitted to the morphological and syntactic analysers and the results are saved in specific elements.

5.1 Answer Extraction

This module is the one that most needs a serious rethinking and integration of information sources. Only few rules have been implemented in the current system, partially exploiting:

---

[19] *What is the Jewish holy city ?*

[20] Year, Date, Day, Season, Time, Money, Length, Weight, Speed, HumanName and Company. Names referring to Human and Company are identified only if they are respectively preceded by abbreviations like Dott., Sig. or followed by Inc. etc..

1. Dependency relations
   Some types of question (determined by the QS and by the QF) can be handled by looking in the paragraphs for syntactic structures typically indicating the presence of a candidate answer. This is the case, for example, of questions: i) introduced by *Chi* (Who), that can be resolved by looking for relations of coordination and of modification of type adposition[21], ii) introduced by *Dove* (*Where*), that can be resolved by searching among the complements of the keyword[22] introduced by the preposition *di* (*of*) or *in* (*in*)[23], iii) asking about a quantity, that can be answered searching among the modifications of "card" type. An answer identified by recurring to expected patterns of syntactic relations is probably a right answer but syntactic regularities are quite rare and the rules depend too much on the quality of the parser output.
2. Named Entities
   When it is not possible to rely solely on syntactic clues to individuate the answer, it would be very useful to exploit the Named Entities corresponding to the Question Focus of the question. Since at the moment the system doesn't make use of any module of NERecognition, only NEs of the type Time, Year, Day were exploited in answer extraction rules.
3. Pattern matching on the text of the paragraph
   In case of *definition* questions asking about organizations, the system follows a very simple strategy consisting in the extraction of the text between brackets that follows the keyword. The system accuracy for definition questions is 50%.
4. Paragraph ranking
   When no other ways to individuate the answer can be found, the system provides the paragraph with the highest ranking score as the answer. The 14.5% of the answers judged inexact are due to this strategy.

6 Results and Future Work

The overall accuracy of the system is quite low, only 25.5% of exact answers (22.78% over Factoid questions and 50% over Definition questions). This is the first release of the prototype and many things have still to be fixed or even developed.

Between the question processing phase and the Search Engine, the system does not perform query expansion since we do not have at our disposal a WSD module to individuate the *right sense* to expand. This is the reason for the failure on question#44 (*Chi è l'inventore del televisore?*[24]), where the paragraph containing the answer is not retrieved since it doesn't contain *televisore* but its synonym *televisione*. In the future,

[21] See for example question#2 - *Chi è l'amministratore delegato della Fiat?* – and the candidate answer: *Nel corso dell'assemblea dell'Ugaf, a cui ha partecipato anche l'amministratore delegato della Fiat, Cesare Romiti,...*

[22] Question: "*Dove è Bassora?*", Candidate answer: " *..sono a Bassora nel sud dell'Irak*"

[23] In case of *Dove* questions, a last check consists in verifying in IWN that the proposed answer is of type Location or that at least its PoS is of type Proper Name.

[24] *Who is the inventor of the television?*

we will concentrate our efforts on the possibility of expanding the queries using the synonyms in ItalWordNet.

Moreover, it would be useful, during the question processing, to be able to individuate multiword expressions, such as *unità di misura* (*unit of measurement* - question#4), *casa discografica* (*record company* - question#43), *parte dell'organismo* (*body part* - question#96), *compagnia di bandiera* (*national airline* - question#113) etc. that would allow an easier individuation of the expected answer type.

As we already said, we think that performing morphological expansion instead of stemming may be a good strategy for QA on Italian language but at the moment we are not able to evaluate the exact cost and benefits of such a change in our strategy.

The Answer Extraction module is the one that most needs to be restructured and fixed. First of all, since for about 68% of the questions the expected answer is a Named Entity, the possibility of exploiting the results of a NE Recognizer to extract important items such as names of people, organization, location etc. would be of great help. With respect to this, the opportunity to use the new version of the Search Engine under development at the Uni-Pi Computer Science Department could determine an important improvement in the system performance.

Moreover, we expected to be able to improve the overall results of the system by starting to use at least the hyp(er)onyms and the synonyms of the ItalWordNet synsets in order to individuate the answer. For many questions, also without query expansion, the system was able to retrieve the "right" set of paragraphs and in some cases the use of IWN relations could have helped to pinpoint the answer. For example, exploiting the IWN IS-A relation between the word *membro* (*member*) and *uomo* (*men*) could have helped to individuate the answer to question#7 (*Quanti membri della scorta sono morti nell'attentato al giudice Falcone?*[25]) in the retrieved paragraph: "*..nella strage di Capaci... dove furono uccisi il giudice Giovanni Falcone ..e tre uomini della scorta..*"[26]. In the same way, the synonymy between *causare* (*to cause*) and *provocare* (*to provoke*) on one hand and *tumore* (*tumor*) and *cancro* (*cancer*) on the other could have helped to match question and answer in case of question#64 (*Cosa può causare il tumore ai polmoni?*[27]) and the candidate answer text: "*...alimentando l'ipotesi...che gli scarichi diesel provochino il cancro*"[28]. This is something different from performing query expansion since this strategy does not enlarge the set of paragraphs that are obtained using the keywords of the question but rather helps to restrict the number of possible candidates[29].

As final remark, we think that CLEF represented a very important occasion to highlight the problems and to look for new solutions and strategies for Italian QA. In the next future, we will work on a new release of the system in order to overcome its current limits and to improve its performance.

---

[25] *How many members of the escort died in the attack to Judge Falcone?*

[26] *in the Capaci massacre...where Judge Falcone..and three men of his escort died..*

[27] *What causes lungs tumor?*

[28] *it fosters the hypothesis that...diesel exhaust provokes cancer*

[29] In this case, the lack of a module for explicit WSD would not effect the identification of useful connections.

References

1. Harabagiu S., Moldovan D., Pasca M, Mihalcea R., Surdeanu M., Bunescu R., Girju R., Rus R. and Morarescu P.: FALCON: Boosting Knowledge for Answer Engines. Proceedings of the Text Retrieval Conference (TREC-9) (2000)
2. Paşca M.: Open-Domain Question Answering from Large Text Collections. CSLI Studies in Computational Linguistics, USA (2003)
3. Attardi G., Cisternino A., Formica F., Simi M., Tommasi A., Zavattari C.: PIQAsso: Pisa Question answering System. Proceeding of the 10th TREC Conference (2001)
4. Bartolini R., Lenci A., Montemagni S., Pirrelli V.: Grammar and Lexicon in the Robust Parsing of Italian: Towards a Non-Naïve Interplay. Proceedings of COLING 2002 Workshop on Grammar Engineering and Evaluation, Taipei, Taiwan (2002)
5. Battista M, Pirrelli V.: Una Piattaforma di Morfologia Computazionale per l'Analisi e la Generazione delle Parole Italiane. ILC-CNR Technical Report (1999)
6. Lenci A., Montemagni S., Pirrelli V.: CHUNK-IT. An Italian Shallow Parser for Robust Syntactic Annotation. In: Linguistica Computazionale, Istituti Editoriali e Poligrafici Internazionali, Pisa-Roma, ISSN 0392-6907 (2001)
7. Lenci A., Montemagni S., Pirrelli V., Soria C.: FAME: a Functional Annotated Meta-Schema for multi-modal and multilingual Parsine Evaluation. Proceeding of the LREC-2000 (2000)
8. Roventini A., Alonge A., Bertagna F., Calzolari N., Girardi C., Magnini B., Marinelli R., Speranza M., Zampolli A.: ItalWordNet: Building a Large Semantic Database for the Automatic Treatment of Italian. In: Zampolli A., Calzolari N., Cignoni L. (eds.), Computational Linguistics in Pisa, Special Issue of Linguistica Computazionale, Vol. XVIII-XIX, Istituto Editoriale e Poligrafico Internazionale, Pisa-Roma (2003)
9. Vossen, P. (ed.): EuroWordNet General Document (1999) http://www.hum.uva.nl/~ewn.
10. 10.Attardi G., Cisternino A.: Reflection support by means of template metaprogramming. Proceedings of Third International Conference on Generative and Component-Based Software Engineering, LNCS, Springer-Verlag, Berlin (2001)

Question Answering Pilot Task at CLEF 2004

Jesús Herrera, Anselmo Peñas, and Felisa Verdejo

Departamento de Lenguajes y Sistemas Informáticos,
Universidad Nacional de Educación a Distancia,
Juan del Rosal, 16, E-28040 Madrid, Spain
{jesus.herrera, anselmo, felisa}@lsi.uned.es

Abstract. A Pilot Question Answering Task has been activated in the Cross-Language Evaluation Forum 2004 with a twofold objective. In the first place, the evaluation of Question Answering systems when they have to answer conjunctive lists, disjunctive lists and questions with temporal restrictions. In the second place, the evaluation of systems' capability to give an accurate self-scoring about the confidence on their answers. In this way, two measures have been designed to be applied on all these different types of questions and to reward systems that give a confidence score with a high correlation with the human assessments. The forty eight runs submitted to the Question Answering Main Track have been taken as a case of study, confirming that some systems are able to give a very accurate score and showing how the measures proposed reward this fact.

1 Introduction

A Pilot Question Answering (QA) Task has been activated this year within the Main QA Track of the CLEF[1] 2004 campaign. The Pilot Task aims at investigating how QA systems are able to cope with types of questions different from the ones posed in the Main Track. To accomplish it, a set of questions has been prepared and new evaluation measures have been proposed.

Few questions were similar to those posed in the Main Track (factoid and definition questions) although they were selected with more than one correct and distinct answer. Questions whose answer is a list of items were also posed, following TREC[2] and NTCIR[3] previous experiences. Finally, more than half of the questions in the Pilot Task aim at dealing with temporal restrictions.

The evaluation measure proposed for this Pilot Task has been designed to take into consideration all these types of questions and, simultaneously, reward systems that, even focusing their attention on a few types of questions, are

[1] Cross-Language Evaluation Forum, http://www.clef-campaign.org

[2] Text REtrieval Conference, http://trec.nist.gov

[3] NII-NACSIS Test Collection for IR Systems, http://research.nii.ac.jp/ntcir/index-en.html

C. Peters et al. (Eds.): CLEF 2004, LNCS 3491, pp. 581–590, 2005.

able to obtain very accurate results, with a good answer validation and a good confidence score.

In the present edition, the Pilot Task has been activated only for Spanish and has been carried out simultaneously with the Main QA Track. Participants in the Pilot Task have made a special effort to accomplish the extra work.

Section 2 describes the task and the different types of questions, including those with temporal restrictions. Section 3 presents some criteria to design the evaluation measure and presents the K and $K1$ measures. The results for the Main QA Track at CLEF [3] are taken as a case of study to discuss and compare these measures with the previous ones used at TREC, NTCIR and CLEF. Section 4 presents the results obtained by the participants in the Pilot Task and, finally, Section 5 points out some conclusions and future work.

2 Task Definition

The QA Pilot Task followed the rules stated in the QA Main Track guidelines except for the source and the target languages, the type and number of questions, and the evaluation measure.

One hundred of questions were posed in Spanish and the corpus used was the EFE Spanish press agency collection of news from 1994 and 1995. The questions of this Pilot Task were distributed among the following types: factoid (18), definition (2), conjunctive list (20), temporally restricted by date (20), temporally restricted by period (20), and temporally restricted by event (20 nested questions). A little amount of questions had no answer in the document collection (2 NIL factoid questions). As usual, a question was assumed to have no answer when neither human assessors nor participating systems could find one.

Ideally, QA systems should tend to give only one answer for each question but, however, there exist some questions whose answer depends on the context or changes in time. In these cases, *disjunctive lists* are obtained, that is, lists of different and correct items representing a disjunction of concepts. The decision of which one of them is the most correct is strongly dependent on the user's information need, text errors, consistency between different texts (specially in the news domain), etcetera. Therefore, being able to obtain all the possible correct and distinct answers to a question seems to be a desirable feature for open domain QA systems.

For this reason, there was no limit to the number of answers at the Pilot Task, but at least one answer to each question had to be given. If systems believed that it was no response to a question in the corpus, they had to answer NIL.

In the *conjunctive list* type of questions, a determined or undetermined quantity of items is required to set up a single answer. For the Pilot Task, the goal was to obtain the largest amount of different items within each answer.

Three subtypes of *temporally restricted* questions have been proposed at the Pilot Task (by date, by period and by event), and three moments with regard to the restriction (before, during or after the temporal restriction):

- **Restriction by Date,** where a precise date contextualises the question, which can refer either to a particular moment, or to a time before or after it. A date could consist in a day, a month, a year, etcetera, depending on the question. Examples:
  - T ES ES 0011 `¿Qué sistema de gobierno tenía Andorra hasta mayo de 1993?` [4]
  - T ES ES 0014 `¿Quién visitó Toledo el 22 de febrero de 1994?` [5]
- **Restriction by Period.** In this case, questions are referred explicitly to a whole period or range of time. A period could be expressed by a pair of dates delimiting it, or by a name accepted as designation of some important periods as, for example, *Cuaresma*[6]. Examples:
  - T ES ES 0086 `¿Quién reinó en España durante el Siglo de Oro de su literatura?` [7]
  - T ES ES 0037 `¿Quién gobernó en Bolivia entre el 17 de julio de 1980 y el 4 de agosto de 1981?` [8]
- **Event restriction,** that implies an embedded or implicit extra question so that it is necessary to answer the nested question to determine the temporal restriction. Then, the temporal restriction refers to the moment in which the second event occurred. For example:
  - T ES ES 0098 `¿Quién fue el rey de Bélgica inmediatamente antes de la coronación de Alberto II?` [9]
  - T ES ES 0079 `¿Qué revolución estudiantil surgió en Francia al año siguiente de la Guerra de los Seis Días?` [10]

The degree of inference necessary to solve the temporal restrictions was not the same for all the questions. In some questions a reference to the temporal restriction could be found in the same document, while in other questions it was necessary to access other documents to temporally locate the question.

3 Evaluation Measure

The evaluation measure has been designed in order to reward systems that return as many different and correct answers as possible to each question but, at the same time, punishing at the same time the incorrect answers. Two reason motivate the penalization of incorrect answers: First, it is assumed that a user of a QA system would prefer a void answer rather than an incorrect one. Systems must validate their answers and must give an accurate confidence score. Second,

[4] What kind of government did Andorra have until May 1993?
[5] Who visited Toledo on 22nd February 1994?
[6] Cuaresma is the Spanish word for Lent.
[7] Who reigned in Spain during what is called in the literature "The Golden Age"?
[8] Who governed Bolivia between 17th July 1980 and 4th August 1981?
[9] Who was the king of Belgium just before the coronation of Albert II?
[10] What student revolution took place in France in the year after the Six-Day War?

since there was no limit in the number of answers, systems had to prevent the risk of giving too much incorrect ones. The effect was that no more than three answers per question were given.

In order to evaluate systems' self-scoring, a mandatory confidence score represented by a real number ranged between 0 and 1, was requested. 0 meant that the system had no evidence on the correctness of the answer, and 1 meant that the system was totally sure about its correctness.

The evaluation measure has been designed to reward systems that:

- answer as many questions as possible,
- give as many different right answers to each question as possible,
- give the smallest number of wrong answers to each question,
- assign higher values to right answers,
- assign lower values to wrong answers,
- give answer to questions that have less known answers.

3.1 The *K*-Measure

According to the criteria above, the evaluation measure is defined as follows:

$$K(sys) = \frac{1}{\#questions} \cdot \sum_{i \in questions} \frac{\sum_{r \in answers(sys,i)} score(r) \cdot eval(r)}{max\,\{R(i), answered(sys,i)\}} \tag{1}$$

$$K(sys) \in \mathbb{R} \;\wedge\; K(sys) \in [-1, 1]$$

where $R(i)$ is the total number of known answers to the question i that are correct and distinct; *answered(sys,i)* is the number of answers given by the system *sys* for the question i; $score\,(r)$ is the confidence score assigned by the system to the answer r; $eval\,(r)$ depends on the judgement given by a human assessor.

$$eval\,(r) = \begin{cases} 1 & \text{if } r \text{ is judged as correct} \\ 0 & \text{if } r \text{ is a repeated answer} \\ -1 & \text{if } r \text{ is judged as incorrect} \end{cases}$$

When $K\,(sys)$ equals 0 it matches with a system without knowledge that assigns 0 to the confidence score of all their answers. Therefore, $K\,(sys) = 0$ is established as a baseline and K-measure gives an idea about the system's knowledge.

The answer finding process, accomplished by human assessors, is strongly determined by the evaluation measure. In the case of K-measure the parameter $R(i)$ requires a knowledge of all the correct and distinct answers contained in the corpus for each question. This fact introduces a very high cost in the pre-assessment process because it is not easy to ensure that, even with a human search, all distinct answers for each question have been found in a very large corpus. One alternative is to make the pre-assessment process less strict and consider only the set of different answers found by humans or systems along the process. Another alternative is to request only one answer per question and ignore recall.

3.2 The *K1*-Measure

A second measure, derived from the K-measure, is proposed to evaluate exercises when just one answer per question is requested (number of questions equals number of answers) or when the achievement of all the possible answers by the system is not outstanding for the exercise. That measure has been called *K1*-measure (K-measure for systems giving 1 answer per question) and it is defined as follows:

$$K1(sys) = \frac{\sum\limits_{r \in answers(sys)} score(r) \cdot eval(r)}{\#questions} \qquad (2)$$

$$K1(sys) \in \mathbb{R} \ \wedge \ K1(sys) \in [-1, 1]$$

where $score\,(r)$ is the confidence score assigned by the system to the answer r and $eval\,(r)$ depends on the judgement given by a human assessor.

$$eval\,(r) = \begin{cases} 1 & \text{if } r \text{ is judged as correct} \\ -1 & \text{in other case} \end{cases}$$

Again, $K1\,(sys) = 0$ is established as a baseline.

3.3 Comparison with Precedent Measures

Comparing K and *K1* measures with other measures used in precedent QA evaluation exercises, the following differences and similarities are found:

- **Accuracy measure**, commonly used in all QA evaluations [1] [2] [4] [7] [8] [9] [10] [11], measures the precision in giving correct answers. But it does not take into account the confidence score, as in K and *K1* measures, nor the recall when more than one answer per question is given, as in F-measure or K-measure.
- **Mean F-measure**, used in the QA Track at TREC 2003 [11] and in the QA Challenge at NTCIR 2002 [1], gives a combination between precision and recall, generally the mean of both. As the K-measure, it is designed for systems that must give all the correct answers existing in the corpus for every question. The K-measure takes into account a combination of precision and recall by means of the $max\{R(i), answered(sys,i)\}$ denominator. In addition, K and *K1* measures include the confidence score into their calculations.
- **Mean Reciprocal Rank**, used in the QA Track at TREC [7] [8] [9] [10], in the QA Challenge at NTCIR 2002 [1] and in the QA Track at CLEF 2003 [2] [4]. It is designed for systems that give one or more answers per question, in a decreasing order of confidence. It rewards systems assigning a higher confidence to the correct answers. However, Mean Reciprocal Rank cannot evaluate systems that find several different and correct answers for the same question, and the incorrect answers are not considered as a worse case than the absence of answers.
- **Confident-Weighted Score** (CWS), used in the QA Track at TREC 2002 [10] and in the QA Track at CLEF 2004 [3] as a secondary measure. It is

designed for systems that give only one answer per question. Answers are in a decreasing order of confidence and CWS rewards systems that give correct answers at the top of the ranking. Hence, correct answers in the lower zone of the ranking make a very poor contribution to the global valuation, and this contribution is determined by the ranking position instead of the system's self-scoring.

3.4 Correlation Between Self-scoring and Correctness

Since the confidence score has been included in the K-measure, a high correlation between self-scoring and correctness is expected to produce higher values of K. However, it is interesting to know separately the quality of the scoring given by every system. Hence, it is proposed the use of the correlation coefficient (r) between self-scoring value (in range [0,1]) and the value associated to the human assessment: 1 for the correct answers and 0 otherwise. That is:

$$r(sys) = \frac{\sigma_{assess(sys)score(sys)}}{\sigma_{assess(sys)} \cdot \sigma_{score(sys)}} \tag{3}$$

$$r(sys) \in \mathbb{R} \wedge r(sys) \in [-1, 1]$$

where $assess(sys)$ and $score(sys)$ are the two multidimensional variables containing the values of the human assessment and the confidence score for the system sys, respectively; $\sigma_{assess(sys)}$, $\sigma_{score(sys)}$ are the typical deviations for $assess(sys)$ and $score(sys)$, respectively, and $\sigma_{assess(sys)score(sys)}$ is the covariance between the two variables.

When a system assigns a $score = 1$ to its correct answers and $score = 0$ to the rest, it obtains a correlation coefficient $r = 1$, meaning that such a system has a perfect knowledge about the correctness of its response. A correlation coefficient equal to 0 indicates that score and correctness have no correlation. A negative value indicates that there is a certain correlation but in the opposite direction.

3.5 A Case of Study

In the QA 2004 Main Track [3], the confidence score has been requested in order to calculate the CWS as a secondary evaluation measure. This confidence score, together with the human assessments of all the submitted runs, permitted to study the effect of the *K1*-measure in the ranking of systems, and to compare the official measures with this one. No conclusions should be stated about the quality of systems because they should not be compared across different target languages, and also because they did not develop any strategy in order to obtain good values of *K1*. However, evaluation measures are evaluated here, not systems.

Table 1 shows the number of given correct answers, CWS, *K1* and the correlation coefficient for all the systems participating in the QA at CLEF 2004 Main Track.

A higher correlation coefficient (higher score for the correct answers) brings associated better values of *K1* for the same or similar number of given correct answers. For example, *ptue041ptpt*, with the higher correlation coefficient ($r >$

Table 1. Values and rankings for accuracy, CWS, K1, and correlation coefficient r, for all runs submitted to the Main QA Track at CLEF 2004

	correct answers			CWS		*K1*		
run	#	%	ranking	value	ranking	value	ranking	r
uams042nlnl	91	45.50	1	0.3262	2	0.0078	2	0.1148
uams041nlnl	88	44	2	0.2841	3	0.0063	3	0.0987
uams041ennl	70	35	3	0.2222	4	0.0055	4	0.1105
fuha041dede	67	33.50	4	0.3284	1	-0.3271	28	0.0094
aliv042eses	65	32.50	5	0.1449	8	-0.0416	15	0.1711
aliv041eses	63	31.50	6	0.1218	9	-0.0500	16	0.1099
irst041itit	56	28	7	0.1556	7	-0.1853	19	0.2128
talp042eses	52	26	8	0.1029	13	-0.2252	20	-0.0366
dfki041dede	51	25.50	9..10	N/A †	N/A	0	5..14	N/A
ilcp041itit	51	25.50	9..10	N/A	N/A	0	5..14	N/A
gine042frfr	49	24.50	11	0.1140	11	-0.2748	23	-0.0339
talp041eses	48	24	12	0.0878	15	-0.2464	22	-0.0483
ptue041ptpt	47	23.62	13	0.2162	5	0.0201	1	0.5169
dfki041deen	47	23.50	14	0.1771	6	-0.5131	45	-0.0453
inao041eses	45	22.50	15..16	N/A	N/A	0	5..14	N/A
irst041iten	45	22.50	15..16	0.1215	10	-0.2310	21	0.1411
irst042itit	44	22	17	0.1075	12	-0.3248	27	-0.0188
edin042fren	40	20	18	0.0589	21	-0.4066	38	0.0004
lire042fren	39	19.50	19	0.0754	17	-0.1738	18	0.3707
dltg041fren	38	19	20	N/A	N/A	0	5..14	N/A
inao042eses	37	18.50	21	N/A	N/A	0	5..14	N/A
irst042iten	35	17.50	22	0.0751	18	-0.3300	29	0.0566
edin042deen	34	17	23..25	0.0527	27	-0.3556	31	0.1124
gine042defr	34	17	23..25	0.0970	14	-0.2812	24	-0.0371
gine042esfr	34	17	23..25	0.0750	19	-0.3442	30	-0.0282
edin041fren	33	16.50	26	0.0570	22	-0.5336	46	-0.0560
dltg042fren	29	14.50	27..31	N/A	N/A	0	5..14	N/A
gine041defr	29	14.50	27..31	0.0790	16	-0.3747	34	-0.0471
gine042itfr	29	14.50	27..31	0.0540	26	-0.3948	37	-0.0467
gine042nlfr	29	14.50	27..31	0.0650	20	-0.3682	33	-0.0507
gine042ptfr	29	14.50	27..31	0.0560	24..25	-0.3818	35	-0.0359
edin041deen	28	14	32	0.0492	30	-0.5515	47	-0.0077
gine041frfr	27	13.50	33..35	0.0480	32	-0.4425	41	0.0099
gine041esfr	27	13.50	33..35	0.0560	24..25	-0.4463	43	0.0991
gine042enfr	27	13.50	33..35	0.0510	29	-0.3184	25	-0.0336
bgas041bgen	26	13	36	0.0564	23	-0.3618	32	0.2023
gine041itfr	25	12.50	37..38	0.0490	31	-0.3926	36	-0.0368
gine041ptfr	25	12.50	37..38	0.0440	34..35	-0.4412	40	-0.0595
sfnx042ptpt	22	11.06	39..41	N/A	N/A	0	5..14	N/A
cole041eses	22	11	39..41	N/A	N/A	0	5..14	N/A
lire041fren	22	11	39..41	0.0330	38	-0.3200	26	0.2625
hels041fien	21	10.61	42	0.0443	33	-0.1136	17	0.0359
gine041nlfr	20	10	43	0.0440	34..35	-0.4438	42	-0.0369
mira041eses	18	9	44..45	N/A	N/A	0	5..14	N/A
gine041enfr	18	9	44..45	0.0333	37	-0.4389	39	-0.0349
sfnx041ptpt	14	7.04	46	N/A	N/A	0	5..14	N/A
gine041bgfr	13	6.50	47..48	0.0514	28	-0.5603	48	-0.0181
gine042bgfr	13	6.50	47..48	0.0380	36	-0.4945	44	0.0928

†**CWS** and **r** are Not Available because 0 was given as confident score for every answer.

0.5), has the 13th position in the ranking for accuracy but reaches the 1st position for *K1*.

On the contrary, there are some interesting examples, as *fuha041dede* or *dfki041deen*, that have a low or even negative correlation coefficient and experiment a huge drop in the ranking of *K1*.

However, these systems obtain a very good CWS value, showing that CWS does not reward a good correlation between self-scoring and correctness. Why do these systems obtain good values of CWS? The reason can be found looking at their answers in detail. When they have not enough confidence in the answer, they return NIL with a score 1, ensuring 20 correct answers (the 20 NIL questions) very high weighted in the CWS measure. All wrong NIL answers (up to 149, with score 1) affect negatively the correlation coefficient and also the *K1*-measure. Somehow, they tuned their score to obtain a better CWS and, obviously, not a better *K1*. Adopting a *K1* oriented strategy, they would obtain very good results. For example, if all NIL answers of *fuha041dede* had a score equal to 0 then the correlation coefficient would have been very high ($r = 0.7385$) and the system would have reached again the first place in the ranking with $K1 = 0.218$.

These systems are an example of how state-of-the-art systems can give a very accurate self-scoring.

Since *K1* depends on the number of correct given answers, a good correlation coefficient is not enough to obtain good results: the more correct answers are given, the more positive components conform the global calculation of *K1*. For example, to beat *fuha041dede* using the mentioned *K1*-oriented strategy ($K1 = 0.218$), a system with perfect scoring (r=1) would need to answer correctly more than 40 questions (20%).

4 Results of the Pilot Task

The data from the assessment process for the Pilot Task are shown in Table 2. Only one run from the University of Alicante (UA) [6] was submitted and, therefore, a comparison with other participants cannot be done. The UA system is based on the splitting of nested questions in order to answer questions with temporal restrictions. The UA team has evaluated its system over the TERQAS corpus [5], obtaining better results than in this Pilot Task at CLEF 2004.

The UA system has correctly answered 15% of the questions. The best result corresponds to factoid questions with 22.22% of questions with a correct answer. However, in the past edition of QA at CLEF, this team obtained better results

Table 2. Results of the assessment process for the Pilot Task at CLEF 2004. Data from the run of the University of Alicante

		# questions	# known distinct answers	# answers	questions with at least 1 correct answer	# correct answers	recall	precision	K	r
Definition		2	3	2	0 (0%)	0	0%	0	0	N/A †
Factoid		18	26	42	4 (22.22%)	5	19.23%	11.9%	-0.029	-0.089
List		20	191	55	4 (20%)	6	3.14%	10.9%	-0.070	0.284
Temporal	Date	20	20	30	2 (10%)	2	10%	6.67%	-0.019	N/A
	Event	20	20	42	2 (10%)	2	10%	4.76%	-0.024	0.255
	Period	20	20	29	3 (15%)	3	15%	10.3%	-0.003	0.648
Total		100	280	200	15 (15%)	18	6.43%	9%	-0.086	0.246

†r is Not Available because 0 was given for every component of any variable.

(up to 40% of questions with a correct answer) [2]. This results show that the questions posed in the Pilot Task were too difficult.

The UA system never gave more than three answers per question, independently of the type of formulated question. It seems an heuristically established limit for the system that has affected the achievement of good conjunctive and disjunctive list answers.

41 questions got NIL as an answer, with a confidence score of 0 for all them. Unfortunately, these 41 questions had at least one answer in the corpus. On the other hand, the UA system did not identify the 2 posed NIL questions.

Finally, it seems that the UA system did not manage the score value in the best way. The maximum value given for the confidence score was 0.5002 and several questions with only one correct answer in the corpus had associated several different answers with similar confidence score. The K-measure for the UA's exercise was $K = -0.086$ with a correlation coefficient of $r = 0.246$ between self-scoring and real assessment.

5 Conclusions

Questions whose answer is a conjunctive or a disjunctive list, and questions with temporal restrictions, still remain a challenge for most QA systems. However, these are only a few types of *difficult* questions that QA systems will have to manage in the near future. A specialization and further collaboration among teams could be expected in order to achieve QA systems with higher accuracy and coverage for different types of questions. In fact, the QA Main Track at CLEF [3] shows that different participant systems answer correctly different subsets of questions.

Two measures have been proposed in order to reward systems that give a confidence score with a high correlation with human assessments and, at the same time, return more correct answers and less incorrect ones. The case of study shows that systems are able to give very accurate self-scoring, and that the K and $K1$ measures reward it. However, systems do not need to respond all the questions to obtain good results, but to find a good balance between the number of correct answers and the accuracy of their confidence score.

On the one hand, this seems a good way to promote the development of more accurate systems with better answer validation. On the other hand, it is a good way of permitting some specialization, openingn the possibility of posing new types of questions, dealing with multilinguality and, at the same time, leaving the door open for new teams starting to develop their own systems.

Acknowledgements

We are grateful to Julio Gonzalo, from UNED-NLP Group, and Alessandro Vallin, from ITC-Irst (Italy), for their contributions to this work. In addition, we would like to thank the University of Alicante team for their effort in participating in the Pilot Task.

This work has been partially supported by the Spanish Ministry of Science and Technology within the following projects: TIC-2002-10597-E Organization of a Competitive Task for QA Systems; TIC-2003-07158-C04 Answer Retrieval from Digital Documents, R2D2; and TIC-2003-07158-C04-02 Multilingual Answer Retrieval Systems and Evaluation, SyEMBRA.

References

1. Fukumoto, J., Kato, T., Masui, F.: Question Answering Challenge (QAC-1). An Evaluation of Question Answering Task at NTCIR Workshop 3. In Keizo Oyama, Emi Ishida, Noriko Kando, editors: *Proceedings of the Third NTCIR Workshop on Research in Information Retrieval, Automatic Text Summarization and Question Answering*. National Institute of Informatics (2003)
2. Magnini, B., Romagnoli, S., Vallin, A., Herrera, J., Peñas, A., Peinado, V., Verdejo, F. , de Rijke, M.: The Multiple Language Question Answering Track at CLEF 2003. In C. Peters, J. Gonzalo, M. Braschler, M. Kluck, editors: *Comparative Evaluation of Multilingual Information Access Systems. Results of the CLEF 2003 Evaluation Campaign*. Lecture Notes in Computer Science **3237** Springer (2004) 479–495
3. Magnini, B., Vallin, A., Ayache, C., Erbach, G., Peñas, A., de Rijke, M., Rocha, P., Simov, K., Sutcliffe, R.: Overview of the CLEF 2004 Multilingual Question Answering Track. In C. Peters, F. Borri, editors: *Results of the CLEF 2004 Croos-Language System Evaluation Campaign. Working Notes for the CLEF 2004 Workshop*. Bath, United Kingdom (2004)
4. Peñas, A., Herrera, J., Verdejo, F.: Spanish Question Answering Evaluation. In A. Gelbukh editor: *Computational Linguistics and Intelligent Text Processing, CICLing 2004*. Lecture Notes in Computer Science **2945** Springer (2004) 472–483
5. Pustejovsky, J., Belanger, L., Casta, J., Gaizauskas, R., Hanks, P., Ingria, B., Katz, G., Radev, D., Rumshisky, A., Sanfilippo, A., Sauri, R., Sundheim, B., Verhagen, M.: TERQAS Final Report. Technical Report, MITRE, http://www.cs.brandeis.edu/˜jamesp/arda/time/readings.html (2002)
6. Saquete, E., Martínez-Barco, P., Muñoz, R., Vicedo, J.L.: Splitting Complex Temporal Questions for Question Answering Systems. Proceedings of the 42nd Meeting of the Association for Computational Linguistics (ACL'04), Main Volume (2004) 566–573
7. Voorhees, E. M.: The TREC-8 Question Answering Track Report. In E. M. Voorhees, D. K. Harman, editors: *Proceedings of the Eigthh Text REtrieval Conference (TREC 8)*. NIST Special Publication **500-246** (1999) 77–82
8. Voorhees, E. M.: Overview of the TREC-9 Question Answering Track. In E. M. Voorhees, D. K. Harman, editors: *Proceedings of the Ninth Text REtrieval Conference (TREC 9)*. NIST Special Publication **500-249** (2000) 71–79
9. Voorhees, E. M.: Overview of the TREC 2001 Question Answering Track. In E. M. Voorhees, D. K. Harman, editors: *Proceedings of the Tenth Text REtrieval Conference (TREC 2001)*. NIST Special Publication **500-250** (2001) 42–51
10. Voorhees, E. M.: Overview of the TREC 2002 Question Answering Track. In E. M. Voorhees, L. P. Buckland, editors: *Proceedings of the Eleventh Text REtrieval Conference (TREC 2002)*. NIST Special Publication **500-251** (2002)
11. Voorhees, E. M.: Overview of the TREC 2003 Question Answering Track. In: *Proceedings of the Twelfth Text REtrieval Conference (TREC 2003)*. NIST Special Publication **500-255** (2003) 54–68

Evaluation of Complex Temporal Questions in CLEF-QA*

E. Saquete, J.L. Vicedo, P. Martínez-Barco, R. Muñoz, and F. Llopis

Grupo de Investigación en Procesamiento
del Lenguaje y Sistemas de Información,
Departamento de Lenguajes y Sistemas Informáticos,
University of Alicante, Spain
{stela, vicedo, patricio, rafael, llopis}@dlsi.ua.es

Abstract. This paper presents the evaluation of a QA system for the treatment of complex temporal questions. The system was implemented in a multilayered architecture where complex temporal questions are first decomposed into simple questions, according to the temporal relations expressed in the original question. These simple questions are then processed independently by our standard Question Answering engine and their respective answers are filtered to satisfy the temporal restrictions of each simple question. The answers to the simple decomposed questions are then combined, according to the temporal relations extracted from the original complex question, to give the final answer. This evaluation was performed as a pilot task in the Spanish QA Track of the Cross Language Evaluation Forum 2004.

1 Introduction

Although current operational Question Answering systems deal with simple factual questions, there is growing awareness that systems dealing with complex questions are needed in order to extract more complex information. One of these kinds of questions are temporal questions, i.e., questions requiring a date as answer ("When did Bob Marley die?") or questions that use temporal expressions in their formulation ("Who won the U.S. Open in 1999?"). This kind of question is usually processed by identifying explicit temporal expressions in questions and relevant documents in order to also detect the temporal expressions that are necessary to answer the queries. We can point to the system described in [1] as the only one that also uses implicit temporal expression recognition for Question Answering purposes by applying the temporal tagger developed by Mani and Wilson [2]. In general, questions referring to the temporal properties of the entities being questioned and the relative ordering of events mentioned in the questions are beyond the scope of current Question Answering systems:

* This paper has been supported by the Spanish government, project TIC-2003-07158-C04-01.

C. Peters et al. (Eds.): CLEF 2004, LNCS 3491, pp. 591–596, 2005.

- "Is Bill Clinton *currently* the President of the United States?"
- "Who was spokesman of the Soviet Embassy in Baghdad *during* the invasion of Kuwait?"
- "Were there any meetings between the terrorist hijackers and Iraq *before* the WTC event?"

This paper describes the participation of the University of Alicante in the Spanish CLEF 2004 Pilot Task. The aim of this task was to investigate how Question Answering systems answer complex questions with temporal restrictions, either with more than one correct answer, or with an answer which is a list of items. Our participation was focused on processing these complex temporal questions. Our approach was based on the decomposition of complex questions into simple questions, which were then solved by a conventional Question Answering system as describe above.

2 Answering Temporal Questions

The study of two corpora [3] [7] containing information and questions related to time produced a classification of temporal questions according to the way in which the questions could be solved [4] [5]. We can distinguish between simple questions, that can be solved directly, and complex questions that must be processed by means of a temporal expression analyzer.

The temporal analyzer that we used in this task is based on the TERSEO temporal resolution system [6]. The analyzer processes the temporal expressions in the question, and then a question decomposition module is used in order to split the complex question into simple questions. Finally, the answers to these simple questions have to be combined to answer the complex question.

In order to perform these tasks, the system classifies the following question types:

- **No temporal Questions:** *Type 0*
- **Simple Temporal Questions**
  - *Type 1: Single event temporal questions without temporal expression.* Solved by a Question Answering System directly without pre or post-processing of the question. *When did Jordan close the port of Aqaba to Kuwait?*
  - *Type 2: Single event temporal questions with temporal expression.* Questions containing one or more temporal expressions that need to be recognized, solved and annotated. *Who won the 1988 New Hampshire republican primary?.*
- **Complex Temporal Questions**
  - *Type 3: Multiple events temporal questions with temporal expression.* Questions containing two or more events, related by a temporal signal. The temporal expressions need to be recognized, solved and annotated. *What did George Bush do after the U.N. Security Council ordered a global embargo on trade with Iraq in August 90?*

- *Type 4: Multiple events temporal questions without temporal expression.* Questions consist of two or more events, related by a temporal signal. *What happened to world oil prices after the Iraqi "annexation" of Kuwait?*.

The processing of these questions will be explained in detail in the following sections.

3 System Description

Our Temporal Question-Answering system is based on a multilayered architecture extending the functionality of a current Question-Answering system to solve any type of temporal question. This architecture superimposes additional processing layers, one for each type of complex question, on the General Purpose Question Answering system.

Our system is focused on the Temporal QA processing module, however other kinds of question could be solved according to this architecture (script questions, template questions, ...).

3.1 Temporal Question Answering Module

Figure 1 shows the different modules of the architecture of our Temporal Question Answering System and their interaction. The main components of this system are:

- Question Decomposition Unit,
- General purpose Question-Answering system, and
- Answer Recomposition Unit.

These components work together to produce a final answer. The Question Decomposition Unit and the Answer Recomposition Unit are the units that make up the Temporal Question-Answering layer, and process the temporal questions, before and after using the General Purpose Question Answering system.

- *The Question Decomposition Unit* is a preprocessing unit which has three main tasks. First of all, because we are dealing with questions related to temporality, any temporal expressions in the question must be recognized and solved. As shown before in the taxonomy of questions, there are different types of questions and each type has to be treated differently. For this reason, type identification is necessary. The complex questions are then split into simple ones. These simple questions are input to the General Purpose Question-Answering system.
- *General Purpose Question-Answering system.* Any generic Question-Answering system could be used here. In this case, we use the QA System for Spanish developed at the University of Alicante [8].
- *The Answer Recomposition Unit* is the last module in the process. This unit combines the different answers, using temporal information obtained from the question, such as temporal signals (explained in Section 4) or temporal expressions, and returns the correct answer to the original question.

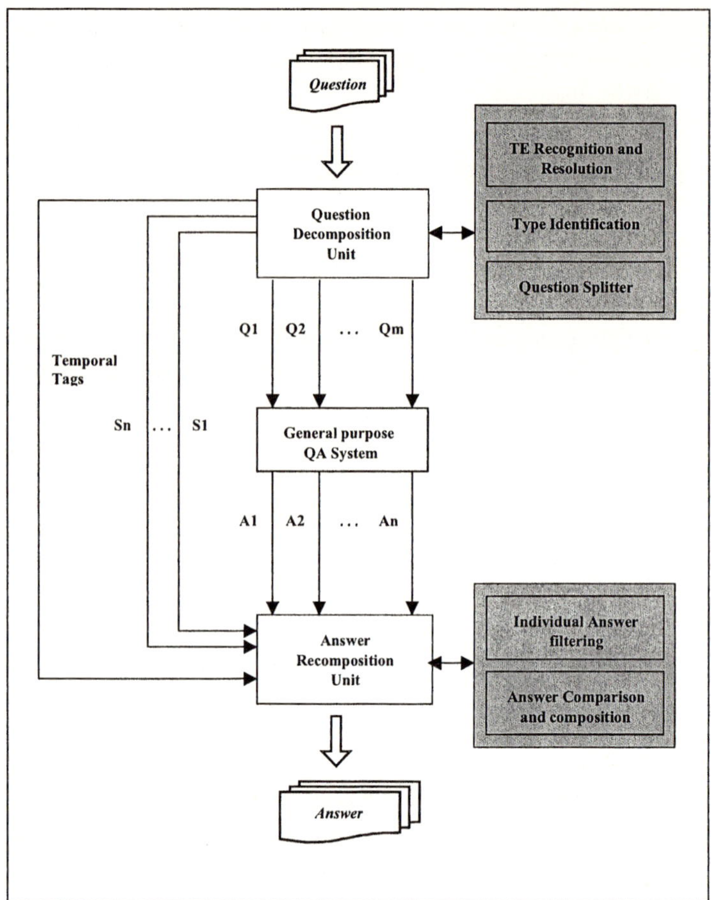

Fig. 1. Graphic representation of the Temporal Question Answering System

4 CLEF Evaluation

Participants in the CLEF Spanish QA Pilot Task had to answer 100 questions, which were equally distributed over the following types:

- Factoid questions with temporal restriction
  - Date restriction: A precise date contextualises the focus of the question, which can refer either to that particular moment, or before or after that date. "¿Quién gobernaba en Francia en 1988?". "¿Qué país visitó Berlusconi antes de junio de 1994?". This kind of question is recognized by our system as a type 2 question.
  - Period restriction: In this case, questions refer explicitly to a whole period. "¿Quién gobernaba en Irak entre 1985 y 1987?". "¿Cuántos coches se vendieron en España en la década de los ochenta?". These questions

Table 1. Results for the Pilot Task at CLEF 2004

question type	# questions	# given answers	# question with correct answer
Definition	2	2	0 (0%)
Factoid	18	42	4 (22.22%)
List	20	55	4 (20%)
Date restriction	20	30	2 (10%)
Event restriction	20	42	2 (10%)
Period restriction	20	29	3 (15%)
TOTAL	100	200	15 (15%)

also correspond to type 2, although TERSEO solves this temporal expression as a period of time instead of a concrete date.

- Event restriction (embedded question): Temporal restriction refers here to the moment in which a second event occurred. "¿Quién gobernaba en Argentina durante la guerra de las Malvinas?". "¿Qué le ocurrió al precio del crudo tras la invasión iraquí de Kuwait?". These questions are recognized by our system as types 3 and 4.

– Lists: Participating groups are given questions whose answer is a list of items, persons, organisations, etc. "Enumere los países que pertenecen a la UE". "¿Quién ha presidido el gobierno español desde 1992?". As our system is focused on temporal questions, it cannot solve most questions of this type. However, with the multilayered architecture described above, a layer specialized in lists could be integrated in the system to address this challenge.

The results reported by the Alicante University Team at CLEF 2004 are shown in Table 1.

5 Conclusions

This paper presents the participation of the University of Alicante in the Spanish CLEF QA Pilot Task. We present a new method for answering complex temporal questions using current factual-based Question Answering systems. The method is based on a multilayered architecture extending the functionality of actual Question-Answering systems to solve any type of temporal questions. The architecture superimposes an additional processing layer on the General Purpose Question Answering system.

The complex temporal QA layer is based on a new proposal for the decomposition of temporal questions where complex questions are divided into simpler ones through the detection of temporal signals. The TERSEO system, a temporal information extraction system applied to event ordering, has been used to detect and solve temporal expressions in questions and answers in the following steps:

- decomposition of the question into simple events to generate simple questions (sub-questions),
- ordering of the sub-questions,
- filtering of the sub-answers,
- and finally, the comparison between sub-answers to build the final complex answer.

Moreover, as TERSEO is a multilingual system, the layer used for complex temporal questions in Spanish could be easily extended to other languages, obtaining a multilingual Temporal QA system.

Although our participation has been focussed on solving complex temporal questions, the same approach can be applied to other kinds of complex questions that allow question decomposition such as script questions, or template-like questions.

References

1. Breck, E., Burger, J., Ferro, L., Greiff, W., Light, M., Mani I. and Rennie, J.: Another sys called quanda. In: Ninth Text REtrieval Conference, volume 500-249 of NIST Special Publication, pages 369–378, Gaithersburg, USA, nov 2000. National Institute of Standards and Technology.
2. Mani, I. and Wilson, G.: Robust temporal processing of news. In: ACL, editor, Proceedings of the 38th Meeting of the Association of Computational Linguistics (ACL 2000), Hong Kong, October 2000.
3. Radev, D. and Sundheim, B.: Using timeml in question answering. http://www.cs.brandeis.edu/ ~jamesp/ arda/ time/ documentation/ TimeML-use-in-qa-v1.0.pdf, 2002.
4. Saquete, E., Martínez-Barco, P., Muñoz, R. and Vicedo, J.L.: Splitting complex temporal questions for question answering systems. In: ACL, editor, Proceedings of the 42nd Meeting of the Association of Computational Linguistics (ACL 2004), pages 567–574, Barcelona, July 2004.
5. Saquete, E., Martínez-Barco, P., Muñoz, R. and Vicedo, J.L.: Multilayered question answering system applied to temporality evaluation. Procesamiento del Lenguaje Natural, (33):25–34, September 2004.
6. Saquete, E., Muñoz, R. and Martínez-Barco, P.: Terseo: Temporal expression resolution system applied to event ordering. In: TSD, editor, Proceedings of the 6th International Conference ,TSD 2003, Text, Speech and Dialogue, pages 220–228, Ceske Budejovice,Czech Republic, September 2003.
7. Eighth Text REtrieval Conference, volume 500-246 of NIST Special Publication, Gaithersburg, USA, nov 1999. National Institute of Standards and Technology.
8. Vicedo, J.L., Izquierdo, R., Llopis, F. and Muñoz, R.: Question answering in Spanish. In: CLEF, editor, Proceedings CLEF-2003 Lecture Notes in Computer Science, Tronheim, Norwey, August 2003.

The CLEF 2004 Cross-Language Image Retrieval Track

Paul Clough†, Henning Müller‡, and Mark Sanderson†

† University of Sheffield, Western Bank, Sheffield, S10 2TN, UK
‡ University and University Hospitals of Geneva, Service of Medical Informatics, rue Micheli–du–Crest 24,1211 Geneva 14, Switzerland
{p.d.clough, m.sanderson}@sheffield.ac.uk
henning.mueller@sim.hcuge.ch

Abstract. The purpose of this paper is to outline efforts from the 2004 CLEF cross–language image retrieval campaign (ImageCLEF). The aim of this CLEF track is to explore the use of both text and content–based retrieval methods for cross–language image retrieval. Three tasks were offered in the ImageCLEF track: a TREC–style ad-hoc retrieval task, retrieval from a medical collection, and a user–centered (interactive) evaluation task. Eighteen research groups from a variety of backgrounds and nationalities participated in ImageCLEF. In this paper we describe the ImageCLEF tasks, submissions from participating groups and summarise the main findings.

1 Introduction

A great deal of research is currently underway in the field of Cross–Language Information Retrieval (CLIR) [1]. Campaigns such as CLEF and TREC have proven invaluable in providing standardised resources for comparative evaluation for a range of retrieval tasks. However, one area of CLIR which has received less attention is image retrieval. In many collections (e.g. historic or stock–photographic archives, medical databases and art/history collections), images are often accompanied by some kind of text (e.g. metadata or captions) semantically related to the image. Retrieval can then be performed using primitive features based on pixels which form an image's content (Content–Based Image Retrieval or CBIR [2]), using abstracted textual features assigned to the image, or a combination of both. The language used to express the associated texts or metadata should not affect the success of retrieval, i.e. an image with English captions should be searchable in languages other than English. Practically, this would enable organisations who manage image collections such as Corbis[1] or Getty Images[2] to be able to offer the same collection to a wider and more diverse range of users with different language backgrounds. It is this area of CLIR

[1] See http://www.corbis.com/
[2] See http://www.gettyimages.com/

C. Peters et al. (Eds.): CLEF 2004, LNCS 3491, pp. 597–613, 2005.

which we address in ImageCLEF[3], the CLEF cross–language image retrieval campaign.

In 2003, we organised a pilot experiment with the following aim: given a multilingual statement describing a user need, find as many relevant images as possible [3]. A collection of historic photographs from St. Andrews University Library was used as the dataset and 50 representative search topics created to simulate the situation in which a user expresses their need in text in a language different from the collection and requires a visual document to fulfil their search request (e.g. searching an on–line art gallery or stock–photographic collection). Four groups from industry and academia participated using purely text–based retrieval methods and a variety of translation and query expansion methods.

To widen the scope of tasks offered by ImageCLEF and offer greater diversity to participants, in 2004 we offered both a medical retrieval and a user–centered evaluation task, along with a bilingual ad hoc retrieval task based on the St. Andrews photographic collection. To encourage participants to use content–based retrieval methods in combination with text–based methods, we did the following: (1) provided participants with access to a default CBIR system[4], and (2) created a medical retrieval task where initial retrieval is visual. These ideas payed off as many groups used visual retrieval only [4, 5, 6], and the supplied visual system was also used several times [7, 8]. A number of groups combined visual and textual approaches [9, 10]. Also, to promote ImageCLEF as the CLEF entry–level CLIR task, we offered topics in 12 languages rather than the 6 offered in 2003. In the following sections of this paper we describe the test collections, the search tasks, participating research groups, results from ImageCLEF 2004 and a summary of the main findings.

2 The ImageCLEF 2004 Tasks

Evaluation of a retrieval system is either system–focused (e.g. comparative performance between systems) or user–centered, e.g. a task–based user study. ImageCLEF offers the necessary resources and framework for comparative and user–centered evaluation. Two image collections were provided: (1) the St. Andrews collection of historic photographic images, and (2) the CasImage radiological medical database. In addition, example search topics and relevance assessments or ground truths (called *qrels*) based on submitted entries were also provided.

Two tasks were offered which used the St. Andrews collection: (1) a bilingual ad hoc retrieval task: given an initial topic find as many relevant images as

[3] See `http://ir.shef.ac.uk/imageclef2004/` for further information about the ImageCLEF 2004 campaign.

[4] We offered access to the VIPER system (`http://viper.unige.ch/`) through: (1) PHP, (2) a list of the top N images from a visual search using given exemplar images, and (3) via local download and installation of GIFT `http://www.gnu.org/software/gift/`.

Table 1. Participating Groups in ImageCLEF 2004

Group	ID	Country	Medical (#Runs)	Ad-hoc (#Runs)	Interactive
National Taiwan University	ntu	Taiwan		⋆ (5)	
I-Shou University	KIDS	Taiwan	⋆ (3)	⋆ (4)	⋆
University of Sheffield	sheffield	UK		⋆ (5)	
Imperial College	imperial	UK	⋆ (1)		
Dublin City University	dcu	Ireland		⋆ (79)	
University of Montreal	montreal	Canada		⋆ (11)	
Oregon Health and Science U.	OSHU	USA	⋆ (1)		
State University of New York	Buffalo	USA	⋆ (3)		
Michigan State University	msu	USA		⋆ (4)	⋆
University of Alicante	alicante	Spain		⋆ (27)	
Daedalus	daedalus	Spain	⋆ (4)	⋆ (40)	
UNED	uned	Spain		⋆ (5)	
University Hospitals Geneva	geneva	Switzerland	⋆ (14)	⋆ (2)	
Dept. Medical Informatics, Aachen	aachen–inf	Germany	⋆ (2)		
Dept. Computer Science, Aachen	aachen–med	Germany	⋆ (8)	⋆ (4)	
University of Tilburg	tilburg	Netherlands	⋆ (1)		
CWI	cwi	Netherlands	⋆ (4)		
Commissariat Energie Automique	cea	France	⋆ (2)	⋆ (4)	
			11 (43)	12 (190)	2

possible, and (2) a known–item interactive task: given a target image, users must find it again. For the CasImage collection, a query–by–example search task was offered: given an initial medical image find as many relevant images as possible. It is, of course, difficult to create evaluation resources which test all kinds of retrieval systems, but the tasks offered do pose different challenges and will appeal to researchers from a variety of backgrounds.

Short title: Rev William Swan.
Long title: Rev William Swan.
Location: Fife, Scotland
Description: Seated, 3/ 4 face studio portrait of a man.
Date: ca.1850
Photographer: Thomas Rodger
Categories: `[ ministers ][ identified male ][ dress - clerical ]`
Notes: ALB6-85-2 jf/ pcBIOG: Rev William Swan ( ) ADD: Former owners of album: A Govan then J J? Lowson. Individuals and other subjects indicative of St Andrews provenance. By T. R. as identified by Karen A. Johnstone " Thomas Rodger 1832-1883. A biography and catalogue of selected works".

Fig. 1. An example image and caption from the St. Andrews collection

2.1 Participating Groups

In total 18 groups participated in ImageCLEF 2004 (Table 1): 11 in the medical task, 12 in the bilingual ad hoc task and 2 in the interactive task. This evaluation attracted research groups from 10 countries with various retrieval backgrounds including text, visual and medical. In total 43 submissions (*runs*) were submitted to the medical task, 190 to the ad-hoc task and 2 to the interactive task.

2.2 Ad Hoc Retrieval from the St. Andrews Collection

Similar to the TREC ad hoc retrieval task, we test retrieval when a system is expected to match a user's one-time query against a more or less static collection (i.e. the set of documents to be searched is known prior to retrieval, but the search requests are not). Multilingual text queries are used to retrieve as many relevant images as possible from the St. Andrews image collection. Queries for images based on abstract concepts rather than visual features are predominant in this task. This limits the effectiveness of using visual retrieval methods alone as either these concepts cannot be extracted using visual features and require extra external semantic knowledge (e.g. the name of the photographer), or images with different visual properties may be relevant to a search request (e.g. different views of Rome).

The St. Andrews collection consists of 28,133 images, all of which have associated textual captions written in British English (the target language). The captions consist of 8 fields including title, photographer, location, date and one or more pre–defined categories (all manually assigned by domain experts). Examples can be found in [11] and the St. Andrews University Library[5].

A new set of 25 topics was generated by the authors familiar with the St. Andrews collection. We first decided on general topic areas and then refined them to create representative search requests to test the capabilities of both cross-language and image retrieval systems. General categories were obtained from an analysis of log files from on–line access to the St Andrews' collection, a discussion with staff from St. Andrews University Library - the proprietors of the collection, and categories identified by Armitage and Enser [12] for users of picture archives. The type of information that people typically search for in the St. Andrews collection include the following:

- Social history, e.g. old towns and villages, children at play and work.
- Environmental concerns, e.g. landscapes and wild plants.
- History of photography, e.g. particular photographers.
- Architecture, e.g. specific or general places or buildings.
- Golf, e.g. individual golfers or tournaments.
- Events, e.g. historic, war related.
- Transport, e.g. general or specific roads, bridges etc.
- Ships and shipping, e.g. particular vessels or fishermen.

Given these general categories (and others), topics were created by refinement based on attributes such as name of photographer, date and location. A list of topic titles can be found in [13]. These are typical of retrieval requests from picture archives where semantic knowledge is required in addition to the image itself to perform retrieval. Topics consist of title (a short sentence or phrase describing the search request in a few words) and a narrative (a description of what constitutes a relevant or non-relevant image for that search request). We also provided an example relevant image which we envisaged could be used for relevance

[5] `http://www-library.st-andrews.ac.uk/`

feedback (both manual and automatic) and query–by–example searches. Topic titles were translated into French, German, Spanish[6], Dutch, Italian, Chinese, Japanese, Finnish, Swedish, Danish, Russian and Arabic by native speakers. An example topic is shown in Figure 2.

```
<top>
<num> Number: 1 </num>

<title> Portrait pictures of church ministers by
Thomas Rodger </title>

<narr> Relevant images are portrait photographs
of ministers or church leaders by the photographer
Thomas Rodger. Images from any era are relevant,
but must show one person only taken within a studio,
i.e. posing for the picture. Pictures of groups are
not relevant. </narr>

</top>
```

Fig. 2. An example ad hoc topic in English

Participants were asked to classify their runs according to four main query dimensions: query language, manual vs. automatic (automatic runs involve no user interaction; whereby manual runs are those in which a human has been involved in query construction), with or without query expansion[7] (QE), and use of title vs. title and narrative (narratives were translated by participants for French topics). As training data, 5 topics from 2003 were provided together with relevance assessments (197 relevant images). The main challenges of this task include: (1) captions and queries which are typically short in length (limited context), (2) images of varying content and quality (mostly black and white which limits the effectiveness of using colour as a visual feature), (3) captions containing text not directly associated with the visual content of an image (e.g. expressing something in the background). (4) use of colloquial and domain-specific language in the caption, and (5) filtering out images which contain query terms but are not judged relevant (e.g. the image is too dark or the subject of the query is not clearly visible).

Table 2 shows the 190 submitted experiments/runs for the ad hoc task listed by the query/topic language where predominant languages are Spanish and French. All groups were asked to submit an English monolingual run for comparison with cross–language retrieval (although not all groups did). Table 3 shows the proportion of submitted runs based on the query dimension. Almost all runs were automatic (99%) and pleasing to us were the large proportion of text+visual submissions (41%).

---

[6] UNED found errors in the original Spanish queries and released a revised topic set which was used by participants for the Spanish submission.

[7] Query expansion refers to adding further terms to a text query (e.g. through PRF or thesaurus lookup) or more images to a visual query.

Table 2. Ad hoc experiments listed by query/topic language

Language	#Participants	#Runs
Spanish	6	41
English (mono)	9	29
French	6	23
German	5	20
Italian	5	20
Dutch	3	20
Chinese	5	18
Japanese	2	4
Russian	2	4
Swedish	2	2
Finnish	2	2
Danish	1	1
Visual only	2	*6*

Table 3. Ad hoc experiments listed by query dimension

Query Dimension	#Runs
Manual	1 (1%)
Automatic	189 (99%)
With QE	135 (71%)
Visual only	6 (3%)
Text Only	106 (56%)
Text +Visual	78 (41%)
Title + Narrative	5 (3%)

2.3 Medical Retrieval from CasImage

The use of Content–Based Image Retrieval (CBIR) systems is becoming an important factor in medical imaging research making this a suitable domain for a second ImageCLEF task. The goal being to find similar images with respect to the following features: modality (e.g. CT, radiograph or MRI), anatomic region (e.g. lung, liver or head) and radiological protocol (e.g. contrast agent or T1/T2 weighting for MRI) where applicable. Identifying images referring to similar medical conditions is non–trivial and may require the use of visual content and additional semantic information not obtainable from the image itself. However, the first query step has to be visual and it is this which we test in ImageCLEF 2004. Participants were not expected to require a deep clinical knowledge to perform well in this task. Given the query image the simplest submission is to find visually similar images (e.g. based on texture and colour). However, more advanced retrieval methods can be tuned to features such as contrast and modality.

The dataset for the medical retrieval task is called CasImage[8] and consists of 8,725 anonymised medical images, e.g. scans, and X–rays from the University Hospitals of Geneva. The majority of images are associated with *case notes*, a written description of a previous diagnosis for an illness the image identifies. Case notes are written in XML and consist of several fields including: a diagnosis, free-text description, clinical presentation, keywords and title. The task is multilingual because case notes are mixed language written in either English or French (approx. 80%). An example case notes field for description and corresponding images is shown in Figure 3. Not all case notes have entries for each field and the text itself reflects real clinical data in that it contains mixed–case text, spelling errors, erroneous French accents and un–grammatical sentences as well as some entirely empty case notes. In the dataset there are 2,078 cases to be exploited during retrieval (e.g. for query expansion). Around 1,500 of the 8,725 images in the collection are not attached to case notes and 207 case notes are empty. The case notes may be used to refine images which are visually similar to ensure they match modality and anatomic region.

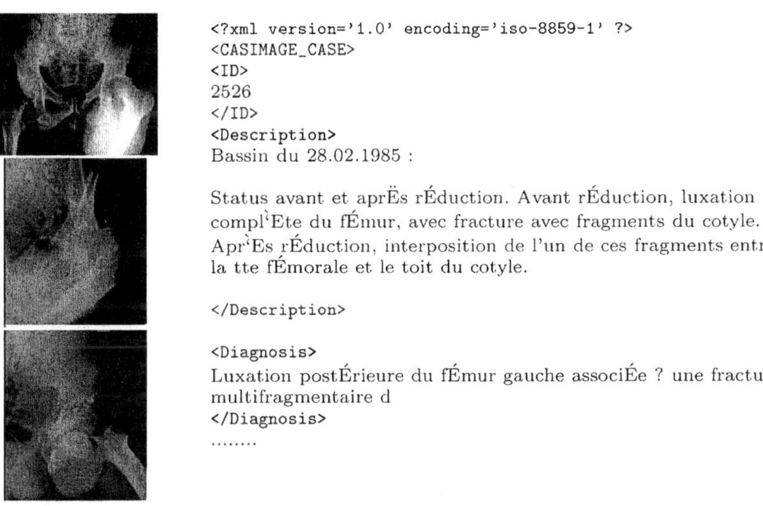

```
<?xml version='1.0' encoding='iso-8859-1' ?>
<CASIMAGE_CASE>
<ID>
2526
</ID>
<Description>
Bassin du 28.02.1985 :

Status avant et aprËs rÉduction. Avant rÉduction, luxation
compl`Ete du fÉmur, avec fracture avec fragments du cotyle.
Apr`Es rÉduction, interposition de l'un de ces fragments entre
la tte fÉmorale et le toit du cotyle.

</Description>

<Diagnosis>
Luxation postÉrieure du fÉmur gauche associÉe ? une fracture
multifragmentaire d
</Diagnosis>
........
```

Fig. 3. An example medical case note (in French) and associated images

For the selection of topics, a radiologist familiar with CasImage was asked to chose a number of topics (images only) that represented the database well. They corresponded to different modalities, different anatomic regions and several radiological protocols such as contrast agents or weightings for the MRI. This resulted in 30–35 images being chosen. One of the authors then used these images

[8] See [14] and http://www.casimage.com/ for more information about the CasImage collection.

Table 4. Medical experiments listed by query dimension

Query Dimension	# Runs
Manual	9 (21%)
Automatic	34 (79%)
With RF	13 (30%)
Visual only	29 (67%)
Text +Visual	14 (33%)

for query–by–example searches to find further images in the database resembling the query using feedback and the case notes and selected 26 of these for the final topic set (see [14],[13]). Similar to the ad hoc task, participants were free to use any method for retrieval, but were asked to identify their runs against three main query dimensions: with and without relevance feedback, visual vs. visual+text, and manual vs. automatic. Table 4 shows submissions to the medical task categorised according to these query dimensions.

2.4 User–Centered Search Task

The user–centered search task aims to allow participants to explore variations of their retrieval system within a given scenario, rather than compare systems in a competitive environment. There are at least four aspects of a cross–language image retrieval system to investigate including: (1) how the CLIR system supports user query formulation for images with English captions, particularly for users in their native language which may be non–English; (2) whether the CLIR system supports query re–formulation, e.g. the support of positive and negative feedback to improve the user's search experience; (3) browsing the image collection; and (4) how well the CLIR system presents the retrieval results to the user to enable selection of relevant images. The interactive task is based on the St. Andrews collection with a known–item search.

Given an image from the St Andrews collection, the goal for the searcher is to find the same image again using a cross–language image retrieval system. This aims to allow researchers to study how users describe images and their methods of searching the collection for particular images, e.g. browsing or by conducting specific searches. The scenario models the situation in which a user searches with a specific image in mind (perhaps they have seen it before) but without knowing key information thereby requiring them to describe the image instead, e.g. searches for a familiar painting whose title and painter are unknown. This task can be used to determine whether the retrieval system is being used in the manner intended by the system designers and determine how the interface helps users reformulate and refine their search requests.

Participants compared two interactive cross–language image retrieval systems (one intended as a baseline) that differ in the facilities provided for interactive query refinement. For example, the user is searching for a picture of an arched bridge and starts with the query "bridge". Through query modification (e.g. query expansion based on the captions), or perhaps browsing for similar images and using feedback based on visual features, the user refines the query until relevant images are found. As a cross–language image retrieval task, the initial query is in a language different from the collection (i.e. not English) and translated into English for retrieval. The simplest approach is to translate the query and display only images to the user (assuming relevance can be based on the image only, i.e. that images are language independent), maybe using relevance feedback on visual features only, enabling browsing, or categorising the images in some way and allowing users to narrow their search through selecting these categories. Any text displayed to the user must be translated into the user's source language. This might include captions, summaries, pre–defined image categories etc.

A minimum of 8 users (who can search with non–English queries) and 16 example images (topics) are required for this task (we supply the topics). The interactive ImageCLEF task is run similar to iCLEF 2003 using the same experimental procedure. However, because of the type of evaluation (i.e. whether known items are found or not), the experimental procedure for iCLEF 2004 (Q&A) is also very relevant and we made use of both iCLEF procedures. Given the 16 topics, participants get the 8 users to test each system with 8 topics. Users are given a maximum of 5 minutes only to find each image. Topics and systems are presented to the user in combinations following a latin–square design to ensure user/topic and system/topic interactions are minimised.

3 Evaluating Submissions

3.1 Methodology

In this section we describe the evaluation methodology for the ad hoc and medical retrieval tasks (which is similar to ImageCLEF 2003 [3]). Submissions were assessed in the following way: (1) the top N runs (for ad-hoc $N = 50$; for medical $N = 60$) were extracted from each submission (190 submissions for ad hoc; 43 for medical), (2) a document pool was created for each topic by computing the union overlap of submissions, (3) three sets of assessments for documents in each topic pool (images judged as relevant, partially relevant and not relevant) were obtained, (4) different sets of relevant images for each topic (called *qrels*) were computed, (5) each system run was compared against one of the sets of qrels and (6) uninterpolated mean average precision was computed[9] (MAP). To ensure maximum pool coverage, we used Interactive Search and Judging [15] for the ad hoc task and added a set of previously identified ground truths to the medical pools.

3.2 Relevance Assessments

Judging whether an image is relevant or not is highly subjective (e.g. due to knowledge of the topics or domain, different interpretations of the same image

[9] A version of `trec_eval` from U. Massachusetts and `ireval.pl` from the Lemur IR toolkit distribution - `http://www-2.cs.cmu.edu/~lemur/` were used for evaluation.

and searching experience). Therefore to minimise subjectivity we obtained three sets of relevance judgements per topic and task. For the ad hoc task, relevance assessments were performed by students and staff at the University of Sheffield (each assessor given 5 topics to judge); for the medical task three scientists familiar with the CasImage collection from the University Hospitals Geneva (one radiologist, a medical doctor and a medical computer scientist) each judged all 26 topics.

An on-line system built specifically for ImageCLEF was used by assessors to judge the relevance of documents in the topic pools. No time limit was specified for carrying out assessments and judges could alter their assessments before submitting final results. A ternary relevance scheme was used by assessors consisting of relevant, partially relevant and not relevant. The partially relevant judgement was used to pick up images where the judge thought it was in some way relevant, but could not be entirely confident (e.g. the required subject is in the background of the image in the case of ad hoc retrieval).

Given three sets of assessments per topic, we used a "voting" scheme to generate sets of relevant images (qrels) based on the overlap of relevant images between assessors, and whether partially relevant images were included. For each topic the assessments were used to vote for each image in the document pool. For the medical task, all assessors were given an equal vote of 1; in the ad hoc task the topic creator was given a count of 2 and other assessors a vote of 1. We created 6 basic relevance sets based on the voting score obtained for each image:

1. **isec–rel:** images judged as relevant by all three assessors.
2. **isec–total:** images judged as either relevant or partially relevant by all three assessors.
3. **pisec–rel:** images judged as relevant by the topic creator and 1 other assessor (ad hoc) or at least two assessors (medical).
4. **pisec–total:** images judged as either relevant or partially relevant by the topic creator and 1 other assessor (ad hoc) or at least two assessors (medical).
5. **union–rel:** images judged as relevant by at least 1 assessor.
6. **union–total:** images judged as either relevant or partially relevant by at least 1 assessor.

Any of these qrels sets can be used for evaluation, ranging from the strictest set of judgments (isec–rel) to the most relaxed (union-total). In ImageCLEF 2004 we used *pisec–total* as a compromise between the two extremes.

4 Results and Main Findings

4.1 Bilingual Ad Hoc Retrieval Task

Table 5 shows the top run for each query language (ordered by MAP) and parameters used. The %monolingual score is computed as a proportion of the highest English submission (0.5865). Excluding the English and visual results, 45% of the best runs used CBIR to complement text retrieval, and 64% used some kind of query expansion (either text-based or by adding "relevant" images to a visual query). In Table 5, 73% of runs used MT systems for translation, although statistical models trained on parallel corpora [10] and bilingual dictionaries were also used [16, 17]. Finnish is a particularly difficult language to process and results in the lowest MAP score. This was also observed in results from other CLEF tracks in 2004. Query translation proved to be the predominant translation approach, although Clough [18] combined query and document translation and found a combination of both approaches gave highest retrieval effectiveness.

Taking the top 5 runs for each language, the average MAP score for runs with QE is 0.4155. Without QE, average MAP=0.2805 (t = 3.255 p = 0.002) indicating that some kind of text or visual QE based on PRF is beneficial. For runs using text-based methods only, average MAP=0.3787; for text+visual runs average MAP=0.4508 ($t = -2.007$, $p = 0.052$). On average it appears that combining text and visual features for ad-hoc multilingual retrieval improves effectiveness, although the results are not significant (at $p < 0.05$). However, some groups did observe improvements for individual topics [17, 10] where visual features can distinguish relevant images.

Table 5. Systems with highest MAP for each language in the ad-hoc retrieval task

Language	Group	Run ID	MAP (%mono)	QE	Text	Visual	Title	Narr
English	daedalus	mirobaseen	0.5865		⋆		⋆	
German	dcu	delsmgimg	0.5327 (90.8)	⋆	⋆	⋆	⋆	
Spanish	UNED	unedesent	0.5171 (88.2)	⋆	⋆		⋆	
French	montreal	UMfrTFBTI	0.5125 (87.4)	⋆	⋆	⋆	⋆	
Italian	dcu	itlsstimg	0.4379 (74.7)	⋆	⋆		⋆	
Dutch	dcu	nllsstimg	0.4321 (73.7)	⋆	⋆		⋆	
Chinese	ntu	NTU-adhoc-CE-T-WE	0.4171 (71.1)		⋆	⋆	⋆	
Russian	daedalus	mirobaseru	0.3866 (65.9)		⋆		⋆	
Swedish	montreal	UMsvTFBTI	0.3400 (58.0)	⋆	⋆	⋆	⋆	
Danish	daedalus	mirobaseda	0.2799 (47.7)		⋆		⋆	
Japanese	daedalus	mirobaseja	0.2358 (40.2)		⋆		⋆	
Finnish	montreal	UMfiTFBTI	0.2347 (40.0)	⋆	⋆	⋆	⋆	
Visual	geneva	GE_andrew4	0.0919 (15.7)	⋆		⋆		

Two groups submitted runs using a purely visual search which performed poorly [5, 4]. We would expect this because for topics for the ad-hoc task, pure visual similarity plays a marginal role; whereas semantics and background knowledge are extremely important. A number of groups used methods to identify named entities such as photographer, date and location to try and improve retrieval by performing structured or constrained searches [8, 19, 16, 10]. Retrieval was performed by using the text or image (the exemplar image supplied by ImageCLEF) as initial query and then combining results. More often than not iterative searches would then include both text and visual retrieval methods. One of the main problems tackled by groups was how best to combine ranked lists from separate text and visual searches. Two groups experimented with using "bi-media" dictionaries where text is mapped to visual representatives showing promising further areas for research [10, 17].

4.2 User–Centered Retrieval Task

For the interactive task, we had 2 submissions: one from I–Shou University (KIDS) and another from Michigan State University (MSU). No formal evaluation was undertaken this year. KIDS [20] tested 2 retrieval systems: a baseline system allowing users to search and refine queries with text only (`T_ICLEF`), and an alternative system enabling users to refine queries using both text and based upon the colour of the target image (`VCT_ICLEF`). Both systems provided text retrieval in Chinese and they found that allowing users to refine queries using a colour palate did improve retrieval effectiveness (89% of searchers found the target image if permitted to select colours compared to 56.25% without; on average a 63% reduction in time spent looking for the target image and 82% reduction in the number of retrieval iterations).

MSU [21] focused on methods of term selection for query expansion. They compared two systems in their user study: a baseline system where users were able to search for images in Chinese, refining and modifying queries using their own terms (`Standard Interface`) and an alternative system where 10 additional terms were suggested automatically to the user allowing them to add to and remove from existing query terms (`URF`). Results showed that the `Standard Interface` performed significantly better than `URF`. The main cause was found to be due to the suggestion of terms by the system which were unfamiliar with the user and hence not useful, or suggested terms not useful in identifying the target image. The results for MSU highlight some of the issues involved in interactive cross-language image retrieval when the collection is specialised like the St. Andrews collection of photographs and unfamiliar to multilingual users.

4.3 Medical Retrieval Task

Table 7 shows the results for the medical task using manual runs only (the rank position is the rank position within all runs ordered by descending MAP score). The highest MAP score is obtained for systems using both visual and text features. Based on all submissions (manual and automatic) average MAP=0.2882. For visual only submissions, average MAP=0.2863; visual+text submissions average MAP=0.2922, although these differences are not statistically significant ($t = 0.140$, $p = 0.084$). The *kids_run3* run has low MAP due to a misconfiguration in their submission. Table 7 shows the top 10 results for the medical task using automatic runs only.

The State University of New York at Buffalo[22] achieved the highest result using both text and visual features; although University of Aachen [5] and Imperial [6] came close using visual features only (difference is not statistically significant). On average, we find that for runs using relevance feedback, average MAP=0.2675; without relevance feedback, average MAP=0.2972 ($t = 0.805$, $p = 0.337$). It would appear that some kind of relevance feedback helps (but the average difference is not statistically significant). Still, for single systems and techniques such as manual relevance feedback, automatic query expansions and mix of textual and visual features delivered significant improvements in retrieval

Table 6. All results for the medical manual experiment

Group	Run ID	MAP	Rank	With RF	Visual	Text
geneva	GE_rfvistex20	0.4764	1		⋆	⋆
geneva	GE_rfvistex10	0.4757	2		⋆	⋆
geneva	GE_rfvistex1	0.4330	3		⋆	⋆
geneva	GE_4d_4g_rf	0.4303	4		⋆	
aachen–inf	i6-rfb1	0.3938	5	⋆	⋆	
KIDS	kids_run2	0.3799	8		⋆	
geneva	GE_8d_16g_rf	0.3718	12		⋆	
geneva	GE_4d_16g_rf	0.3584	14		⋆	
KIDS	kids_run3	0.0843	43		⋆	

Table 7. Top 10 results for the medical automatic experiment

Group	Run ID	MAP	Rank	With RF	Visual	Text
Buffalo	UBMedImTxt01	0.3904	6		⋆	⋆
aachen–inf	i6-025501	0.3858	7		⋆	
imperial	ic_cl04_base	0.3784	9		⋆	
aachen–inf	i6-qe0255010	0.3741	10	⋆	⋆	
Buffalo	UBMedImTxt03	0.3722	11		⋆	⋆
Buffalo	UBMedImTxt02	0.3696	13		⋆	⋆
aachen–inf	i6qe02100010	0.3535	15	⋆	⋆	
geneva	GE_4g_4d_qe1	0.3500	16		⋆	
geneva	GE_4d_4g_vis	0.3499	17	⋆	⋆	
KIDS	kids_run1	0.3273	18		⋆	

quality. Best overall results were obtained combining visual and textual features in manual relevance feedback queries [23].

When analysing the manual submissions, we find that the three best runs combine both visual and textual features, whereas the third and fourth use only visual searching. Low level visual features such as Gabor filters and simple grey level distributions seem to perform best. It would appear that combined systems result in better performance when including text than without, but the contribution of text retrieval should be weighted fairly low (10

When comparing several features [6], individually, the Gabor filters perform best, which are used in four out of the five best automatic systems. Still, a mixture of several features performs better as the performance of features for the various topics varies strongly. Having a topic-dependent feature selection could help improve results. Two of the top five automatic systems are based on the same visual methods but different text search strategies. This implies that even with the same visual starting point, significant differences are possible depending upon the text-retrieval strategy chosen.

5 Conclusions

5.1 Comments from Participants

For ImageCLEF 2005 we will take into account comments received from participants at the 2004 workshop. In general, ImageCLEF was seen as a valuable effort: it is currently the only image retrieval evaluation event and the accessibility of datasets for image retrieval evaluation including ground truths was regarded as very important.

A negative comment was the lack of training data. This can be remedied in 2005 by the provision of topics and ground truths used in 2004. Another comment was with respect to the time from the release of the topics to the time that the results had to be sent in. Several groups remarked that a shorter time frame would be better to not allow research groups to optimize their system too much for perfect results. Participants also commented on the topics and data used in the ad hoc task. The St. Andrews collection, although realistic, proved very hard to use for CBIR and topics did not involve enough use of visual features.

5.2 ImageCLEF 2005

The bilingual ad hoc task will use more general topics to provide more suitable searches for CBIR systems. We will also provide more exemplar images to enable more effective use of CBIR systems (one image is not enough for effective retrieval). The task, however, will remain predominantly text-based involving multilingual topics (where the entire topic statement is translated).

The medical image retrieval task will be performed with a larger set of images and a new set of queries. The goal will be to obtain at least one or two radiology teaching files that can be added to the current casImage database. The retrieval task will again be single images, although tests will be run using using several images as a query for case-based retrieval or by adding short multilingual texts to an image that describes visual content.

A new automatic annotation task is planned for ImageCLEF 2005. This task will be similar to the medical image retrieval task based on a visual analysis of the images. It will be undertaken with help from the IRMA group[10] (Image Retrieval in Medical Applications) of the Technical University of Aachen. It will use a database of 10,000 images that are classified according to a four-code axis - the IRMA code. This code allows image annotation in several languages. Half of the database will be given out as training data, and then the other half given to participants for classification based on visual features in the images only. We hope this task will attract interest from the machine learning community.

5.3 Summary

In this paper we have described the ImageCLEF 2004 campaign for evaluating cross–language image retrieval. We were successful at attracting a range of

[10] http://www.irma-project.org/

groups from a variety of research backgrounds for two retrieval tasks in different domains. The ImageCLEF task was very successful this year and by encouraging the use of a CBIR system, we are able to compare systems based on a large–scale evaluation.

Participants applied a variety of methods to bridge the language and media barriers and the fact that many of the best performing systems all used a combination of visual and textual methods shows that there is a potential for improving retrieval effectiveness over any single method. Some tasks, such as the ad hoc retrieval task, are better suited to text-based image retrieval (assuming that metadata is associated with the images to be retrieved), but other tasks, such as the medical retrieval task, are naturally better suited to visual retrieval (although requiring extra information provided by associated texts to enable more advanced retrieval). Although several systems in ImageCLEF used visual and textual features together, we assume that there is still much potential for further research. Better results for one can help the other through automatic query expansion, for example. If the best visual and textual techniques are combined, we can expect optimal results.

The high participation at ImageCLEF 2004 has shown that there is a need for such an evaluation event, especially given the multilingual and multimedia environment in which current retrieval systems must operate. To create more dynamic research in the field of multi–modal visual/textual retrieval we need to attract visual and multilingual information retrieval groups for the future and promote combined submissions of different research groups.

The rather visual medical task and the rather textual ad hoc task should be complemented with tasks that are somewhere in between. This could be realised by using collections that are closer to existing CBIR evaluation collections containing colour images with a limited number of objects and themes, having more search requests which include an element of both textual and visual search, having more exemplar images and maybe also negative examples. For the medical collection we can well imagine having a short description of the image written by a medical doctor that can be used in addition to the image. Simple semantic retrieval tasks may also help attract further visual retrieval research groups. These could be based on the visual content of images, such as finding all images that contain sunsets or at least three faces. Another community to attract for the medical task would be the image analysis and classification community. This could be achieved through a simple classification task.

Acknowledgements

We thank everyone who participated in ImageCLEF 2004 for making this such an interesting and successful evaluation. In particular we thank St. Andrews University Library (esp. Norman Reid) for use of the St. Andrews collection and University Hospitals Geneva for use of CasImage images. What makes this evaluation possible are the relevance assessments and we want to thank Hideo Joho, Simon Tucker, Steve Whittaker, Wim Peters, Diego Uribe, Horacio Saggion,

Paul Fabry, and Tristan Zand. Our thanks also go out to those people involved in translating the captions including Jian–Yun Nie, Jesper Kallehauge, Assad Alberair, Hiedi Christensen, Xiao Mang Shou, Michael Bonn, Maarten de Rijke, Diego Uribe, Jussi Karlgren, Carol Peters, Eija Airio, Natalia Loukachevitch and Hideo Joho.

References

1. Grefenstette, G.: Cross Language Information Retrieval. Kluwer Academic Publishers, Norwell, MA, USA (1998)
2. Smeulders, A.W.M., Worring, M., Santini, S., Gupta, A., Jain, R.: Content–Based Image Retrieval at the end of the early years. T-PAMI **22 No 12** (2000) 1349–1380
3. Clough, P., Sanderson, M.: The CLEF Cross Language image retrieval track. In: Working Notes for the CLEF 2003 Workshop, 21-22 August, Trondheim, Norway. http://clef.isti.cnr.it/2003/WN_web/45.pdf. (2003)
4. Müller, H., Geissbuhler, A., Ruch, P.: Report on the ImageCLEF Experiment: How to Visually Retrieve Images from the St. Andrews Collection using GIFT. In: these proceedings. (2005)
5. Deselaers, T., Keysers, D., Ney, H.: FIRE - Flexible Image Retrieval Engine: ImageCLEF 2004 Evaluation. In: these proceedings. (2005)
6. Howarth, P., Yavlinsky, A., Heesch, D., Rüger, S.: Visual Features for Content-based Medical Image Retrieval. In: these proceedings. (2005)
7. Jones, G.J.F., Groves, D., Khasin, A., Lam-Adesina, A., Mellebeek, B., Way, A.: Dublin City University at CLEF 2004: Experiments with the ImageCLEF St Andrew's Collection. In: these proceedings. (2005)
8. Martínez-Fernández, J.L., Garcia Serrano, A., Villena, J., Méndez Sáenz, V.: MIRACLE approach to ImageCLEF 2004: merging textual and content-based image retrieval. In: these proceedings. (2005)
9. van Zaanen, M., de Croon, G.: FINT: Find Images aNd Text. In: these proceedings. (2005)
10. Alvarez, C., Oumohmed, A.I., Mignotte, M., Nie, J.Y.: Toward Cross-Language and Cross-Media Image Retrieval. In: these proceedings. (2005)
11. Clough, P., Sanderson, M., Müller, H.: A proposal for the CLEF Cross-Language Image Retrieval Track 2004. In: Poster at the Third International Conference for Image and Video Retrieval (CVIR 2004). (2004) 243–251
12. Armitage, L., Enser, P.: Analysis of User Need in Image Archives. Journal of Information Science (1997) 287–299
13. Clough, P., Müller, H., Sanderson, M.: The CLEF Cross Language Image Retrieval Track (ImageCLEF) 2004. In: Working Notes for the CLEF 2004 Workshop, 15-17 September, Bath, UK. http://clef.isti.cnr.it/2004/working_notes/CLEF2004WN-Contents.html. (2004)
14. Müller, H., Rosset, A., Geissbuhler, A., Terrier, F.: A reference data set for the evaluation of medical image retrieval systems. CMIG (2004 (to appear))
15. Chen, K., Chen, H., Kando, N., Kuriyama, K., Lee, S., Myaeng, S.: Overview of clir task. In: Third NTCIR Workshop, Japan. (2002)
16. Peinado, V., Artiles, J., López-Ostenero, F., Gonzalo, J., Verdejo, F.: UNED@ImageCLEF 2004: Using Image Captions Structure and Noun Phrase Based Query Expansion for Cross-Language Image Caption Retrieval. In: these proceedings. (2005)

17. Lin, W.C., Chang, Y.C., Chen, H.H.: From Text to Image: Generating Visual Query for Image Retrieval. In: these proceedings. (2005)
18. Clough, P.: Caption and Query Translation for Cross-Language Image Retrieval. In: these proceedings. (2005)
19. Saiz-Noeda, M., Vicedo, J.L., Izquierdo, R.: Pattern-based Image Retrieval with Constraints and Preferences on ImageCLEF 2004. In: these proceedings. (2005)
20. Cheng, P.C., Yeh, J.Y., Chien, B.C., Ke, H.R., Yang, W.P.: NCTU-ISU's Evaluation for the User-Centered Search Task at ImageCLEF 2004. In: these proceeedings. (2005)
21. Bansal, V., Zhang, C., Joyce, C.Y., Jin, R.: MSU at ImageCLEF: Cross Language and Interactive Image Retrieval. In: these proceeedings. (2005)
22. Ruiz, M.E., Srikanth, M.: UB at CLEF2004: Part 2 Cross Language Medical Image Retrieval. In: these proceedings. (2005)
23. Müller, H., Geissbuhler, A., Ruch, P.: Report on the CLEF Experiment: Combining Image and Multilingual Search for Medical Image Retrieval. In: these proceedings. (2005)

Caption and Query Translation for Cross-Language Image Retrieval

Paul Clough

University of Sheffield, Western Bank, Sheffield, S10 2TN, UK
p.d.clough@sheffield.ac.uk

Abstract. For many cross-language retrieval tasks, the predominant approach is to translate the query into the language of the document collection (target language). This often gives results as good as, if not better, than translating the document collection into the query language (source language). In this paper, we evaluate query versus document translation for the ImageCLEF 2004 bilingual ad hoc retrieval task. Image retrieval is achieved through matching textual queries to associated image captions for the following languages: French, German, Spanish and Italian using commercially and publicly available resources. On average, we find query translation to outperform document translation (77% of English MAP compared to 65% respectively) but this varies widely across language and query. Combining document and query translation we achieve an average MAP of 85% of English.

1 Introduction

Cross-Language Information Retrieval (or CLIR) deals with retrieval of documents written in one language by a query written in another (see, e.g. [1][2]). Retrieval is achieved by translating queries or documents (or both) into the same (or a common) language and then applying standard monolingual retrieval [3]. Translation methods include: (1) using bilingual dictionaries, (2) extracting word/phrase equivalents from parallel or comparable corpora, and (3) using a Machine Translation (MT) system. Each approach varies in the degree of knowledge and linguistic resources required for translation.

Dictionary-based methods dominate query translation, but these often require extensive language processing to deal with issues such as lexical ambiguity, morphological variation, orthography, tokenisation and compound word splitting (see, e.g. [1]). MT approaches have proven to be popular in recent years due to the availability of on-line MT systems which can be exploited for query translation [1]. The MT system can often be treated as a "black box" where a single translation is provided from the input query. This can be a disadvantage for query translation where short, ungrammatical queries can be mistranslated due

[1] See, for example, the large number of submissions in CLEF 2003 and 2004 which utilised on-line MT systems.

C. Peters et al. (Eds.): CLEF 2004, LNCS 3491, pp. 614–625, 2005.

to limited context. However, an advantage of MT methods is that little or no further linguistic processing or resources are necessary to produce usable CLIR systems (see, e.g. [4]).

One area of CLIR research which has received less attention is image retrieval. In collections such as historic or stock-photographic archives, medical case notes and art/history collections, images are accompanied by some kind of text (e.g. meta-data or captions) semantically related to the image. Images can then be retrieved using standard text-based IR methods. For those organisations managing image repositories in which text is associated with images (e.g. on-line art galleries), one way to exploit these is by enabling multilingual access to them.

Like other CLIR tasks, query translation often provides the user with adequate retrieval [5], however one area which has not been explored is caption (or document) translation. Researchers have successfully used document translation in the past, but the main drawback is the amount of time and resources required. However, given that image captions are typically much smaller than standard test-collection documents, it is feasible to perform document translation, even on large image collections. In this paper we compare query and document translation for the ImageCLEF ad hoc CLIR task. This paper divides into the following: section 2 describes some past work in document translation, section 3 describes our experimental setup, section 4 presents our results, section 5 compares these results with the official ImageCLEF results, and section 6 summaries our findings.

2 Background

In document translation, the entire collection is first translated prior to searching. Previous research by Oard [6] showed that for German–English TREC-6 data, MT-based query translation out-performed various dictionary-based methods, and document translation out-performed MT query translation, especially for longer queries. McCarley [7] showed that for French–English TREC-6 and TREC-7 data and using a statistical MT method, retrieval effectiveness was influenced by the direction of translation (French–English performed better than English–French for query and document translation). Fujii and Ishikawa [8] presented a two-stage method where initial retrieval was first performed using query translation, then the top 1000 documents translated into the query language using MT, finally documents re-ranked based on a translation score. This method was shown to outperform query translation alone and be well suited to large collections.

Advantages of document translation include: (1) no query translation is required at run-time, and (2) no further translation is required when presenting the results to the user. However, a major disadvantage is that translation of large collections is expensive both in time and resources. For example, Oard [6] spent ten machine-months translating the SDA/NZZ German collection (251,840 newswire articles).

3 Experimental Setup

3.1 The ImageCLEF Ad Hoc Test Collection

The ImageCLEF ad hoc test collection was used for evaluation. This consists of documents (images and captions), queries (or topics) and relevance assessments [9]. Topics and relevance judgements are provided for an ad hoc retrieval task which is this: given a multilingual statement describing a user need, find as many relevant images as possible from the document collection. This retrieval task simulates when a user is able to express his need in natural language, but requires a visual document to fulfil their search request.

The document collection consists of 28,133 images from the St Andrews Library photographic collection[2] and all images have an accompanying textual description consisting of 8 distinct fields written in British English. These fields can be used individually or collectively to facilitate image retrieval. The 28,133 captions consist of 44,085 terms and 1,348,474 word occurrences; the maximum caption length is 316 words, but on average 48 words in length.

The ImageCLEF 2004 collection provides 25 topics designed to simulate a range of realistic search requests to a cross-language image retrieval system. English versions of the topics consist of a title (a short sentence or phrase describing the search request in a few words), and a narrative (a description of what constitutes a relevant or non-relevant image for that search request). The *titles* of each topic have been translated into 12 languages: Spanish, Italian, German, French, Dutch, Danish, Swedish, Finnish, Chinese, Japanese, Russian and Arabic by native speakers. Evaluation is performed using the `pisec-total` set of relevance judgements.

3.2 The Lemur Retrieval System

In the `Lemur` implementation of language modelling for IR, documents and queries are viewed as observations from generative unigram language models (see, e.g. [10] for more information). Queries and documents are represented as estimated language models with word probabilities derived from the documents, queries and the collection as a whole. In these experiments, the KL-divergence language model is used with the absolute discounting method of smoothing ($\Delta = 0.7$). `Lemur` offers query expansion by supplementing the initial query with collection-specific terms obtained from a feedback model. In these experiments, a two-component mixture model is used to estimate word probabilities in the feedback model. Default parameter values are used for the feedback model: $\alpha = \beta = 0.5$, with 20 terms selected from the top 10 documents retrieved from the initial query (pseudo relevance feedback or PRF), with one feedback iteration.

3.3 Translation Resources

In these experiments, translation is performed using the `Systran` and `Babelfish` machine translation (MT) resources. The original English captions were trans-

[2] `http://specialcollections.st-and.ac.uk/photcol.htm`

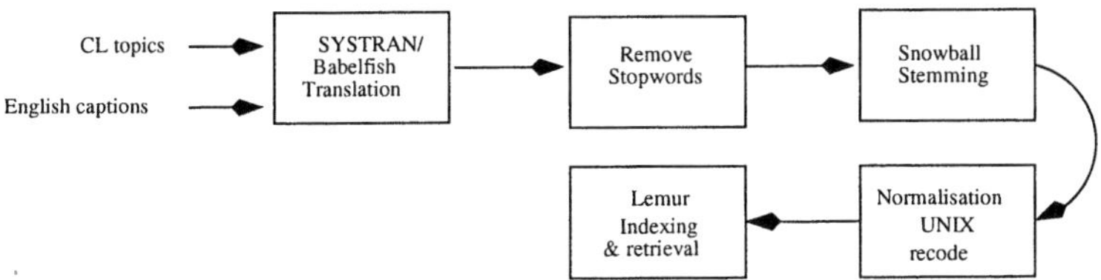

Fig. 1. The cross-language retrieval process

lated into German, French, Italian and Spanish using `Systran Professional Premium 3.0` which took about 2 hours for each language pair[3]. For query translation `Babelfish` from Alta Vista was used. This free on-line resource is powered by `Systran` thereby allowing comparison between query and document translation with the same resource.

Like any form of translation method, MT can result in erroneous queries because of difficulties encountered during translation including: short queries resulting in little if none syntactic structure to exploit, errors in the original cross-language text (e.g. spelling mistakes or incorrect use of diacritics), lack of coverage by the translation lexicon, incorrect translation of phrases, mistranslation of proper names, and incorrect translation of ambiguous words (e.g. selecting the wrong sense of a noun or verb). The effect of translation errors on retrieval performance for ImageCLEF 2003 topics is discussed in [11]. For more information on Systran, see e.g. [12].

3.4 Cross-Language Retrieval

Given multilingual captions and queries, we compare query versus document translation using the cross-language retrieval process shown in Figure 1. Given multilingual topics to translate into English, or English captions to translate into French, German, Italian or Spanish, we first translate the texts using the MT system. Next, stopwords are removed using stopword lists provided with the `Snowball` stemmer[4]. To improve recall, we then apply stemming using `Snowball` and remove diacritics using the UNIX `recode` tool. To perform this, we recode the character set from latin1 to HTML (e.g. German topic 7 "Außenansichten von Tempeln in Ägypten" is transformed into "Außenansichten von Tempeln in Ägypten", and then replace the HTML characters by their original ASCII characters (e.g. "Au*ss*enansichten von Tempeln in *A*gypten"). Finally, all characters are converted to lower case. So, for example, "Außenansichten von Tempeln in Ägypten" is reduced to "aussenansicht tempeln agypt". The resultant captions are indexed with `Lemur` and retrieved using the KL-divergence language model. All fields from the image caption are used during indexing.

We perform two retrieval experiments: query and document translation. For query translation (QT) the original multilingual queries are translated into En-

[3] Captions were translated by Jianqiang Wang and Doug Oard at Maryland University.

[4] `http://snowball.tartarus.org/`

glish using the MT system and retrieval performed on the English collection. For document translation (DT), the original multilingual queries are used to retrieve captions translated by the MT system into the query language. In both experiments we also perform retrieval with and without feedback and compare retrieval effectiveness for individual topics.

We use uninterpolated Mean Average Precision (MAP), Precision at rank 10 (P@10) and recall to measure retrieval effectiveness. We also compute the number of queries which return no relevant images within the top 100 (called *bad*[5]. topics).

4 Results

4.1 General Observations

Results for all 18 runs are shown in the following tables: Table 1 summarises retrieval effectiveness for document translation, and Table 2 for query translation. In general, results show that feedback reduces performance after initial retrieval[6]. The most likely reasons for this are: (1) non-optimal parameter settings for the feedback model, and (2) few relevant documents in the top 10 being used for relevance feedback.

Table 1. A summary of retrieval effectiveness for document translation (DT)

Language	PRF	MAP	%English	Recall	P@10	#bad
English		0.6185	-	0.9566	0.7000	0
	x	0.5829	-	0.9614	0.6920	1
German		0.3019	48.8%	0.7407	0.3080	2
	x	0.2769	44.8%	0.6791	0.3160	6
French		0.4328	70.0%	0.7817	0.4680	2
	x	0.4365	70.6%	0.8914	0.4680	2
Italian		0.3947	63.8%	0.7250	0.4320	1
	x	0.4355	70.4%	0.8552	0.4280	2
Spanish		0.4836	78.2%	0.9469	0.5600	1
	x	0.4365	70.6%	0.8372	0.6080	2
Avg		0.4033	65.2%	0.7986	0.4420	6
	x	0.3964	64.1%	0.8157	0.4550	13

On average, across all multilingual runs (excluding the feedback runs), query translation outperforms document translation. Based on MAP: 0.4788 (77% of highest English MAP) vs. 0.4034 (65% of highest English MAP) respectively.

[5] We explain and justify the use of this measure further in [13].

[6] Higher MAP scores after feedback are typically due to ranking effects and not the addition of further relevant documents - see, e.g. the recall figures.

Table 2. A summary of retrieval effectiveness for query translation (QT)

Language	PRF	MAP	%English	Recall	P@10	#bad
German		0.5047	81.6%	0.8408	0.5680	1
	x	0.4994	80.7%	0.8251	0.5920	2
French		0.4516	73.0%	0.7768	0.5000	3
	x	0.4567	73.8%	0.8613	0.5120	4
Italian		0.4934	79.8%	0.7648	0.4920	1
	x	0.4507	72.9%	0.7153	0.4800	2
Spanish		0.4654	75.2%	0.8842	0.4800	1
	x	0.4718	76.3%	0.7503	0.4880	3
Avg		0.4788	77.4%	0.8167	0.5100	6
	x	0.4697	75.9%	0.7880	0.5180	11

On average, the results for each query are highly correlated (0.9890 using Spearman's rho $p < 0.01$) indicating that similar results are obtained regardless of the method (document or query translation) used. However, this varies across language where document translation for Spanish (without feedback) is higher than results for query translation (a MAP of 0.4836 vs. 0.4654 respectively). Differences between results without feedback between document and query translation are statistically significant only for Italian and German (using Wilcoxon with $p < 0.05$).

Query translation is more successful because the translation pair X→English is typically better than English→X[7]. English→German performs worst and upon inspection we find that most errors are due to English words being incorrectly combined to form German compound terms. For example, the phrase "Falls of Cruachan Station above Loch Awe" is translated into "Fälle der StationCruachan über Lochawe". In this example, "Cruachan Station" and "Loch Awe" are combined rather than left as proper names. We also find determiners and conjuctions are wrongly combined, e.g. "below embankment" translates to "unterDamm" and "lining banks" to "dieBänke". Part of the problem is caused by captions texts being "dirty" and ungrammatical. This could be improved by cleaning up the English texts prior to translation. This is less problematic for query translation thereby resulting in higher retrieval effectiveness. Document translation is more successful for other languages other than German because they are less compound-rich making X→English translation better.

4.2 Variations Across Language and Query

Figures 2 to 5 show average precision results for individual queries for both document and query translation. Although in general query translation outperforms document translation for all languages (except Spanish), it is interesting to observe that this is not true for all queries. For retrieval in German, 9 queries perform better with document translation, 10 for French, 11 for Spanish and 6

[7] McCarley [7] also found this to be true for French–English.

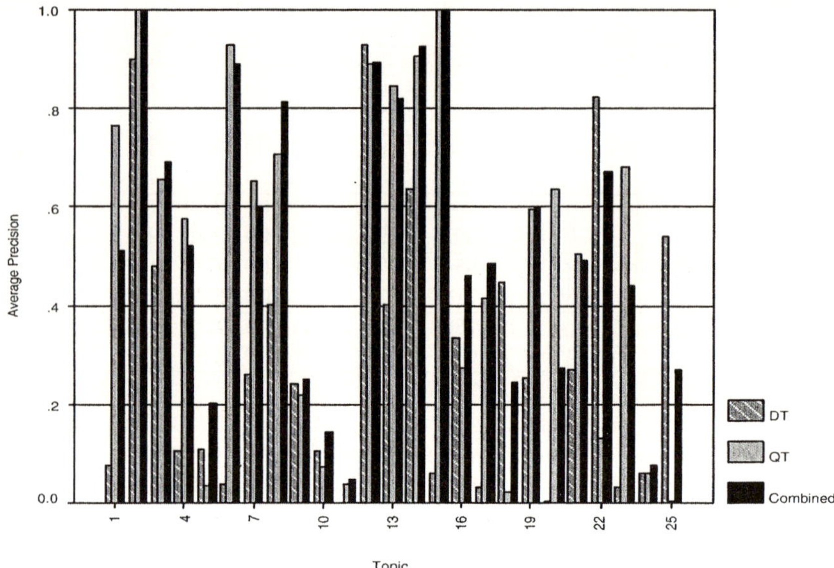

Fig. 2. Average Precision for German topics

for Italian. Because retrieval effectiveness depends upon translation, queries of 2-3 words cause poor retrieval performance even if translation of just one word is wrong. For example, topic 25 performs better across all languages with document translation. This is because the word for "canal" is mis-translated in all languages to "channel" in English, but correctly translated from English into the four target languages (e.g. "canal"→"kanale"→"channel"). This shows that translation for this word is not symmetric, i.e. that English→X $\neq$ X→English.

As well as mis-translation, query translation can also perform poorly due to words not being translated at all (e.g. "External views of Egyptian templi" rather than "Exterior views of Egyptian temples"), or the use of synonymous terms which are correct but do not match the caption terms (e.g. "images of English beacons" rather than "images of English lighthouses"). Of course, in some cases query translation is better than document translation. For example, German topic 20 ("river with a viaduct in the background") performs badly for document translation because crucial words are not translated, e.g. "viaduct", or words are mis-translated altogether.

We find the following correlations between average precision scores for query and document translation (using Spearman's rho with $p < 0.01^{**}$): German (0.123), Spanish (0.511**), French (0.736**) and Italian (0.725**). The last three languages show a significant correlation between average precision using either document or query translation (i.e. topics perform similarly using either approach). However, German is not correlated because of reasons given previously for query and document translation.

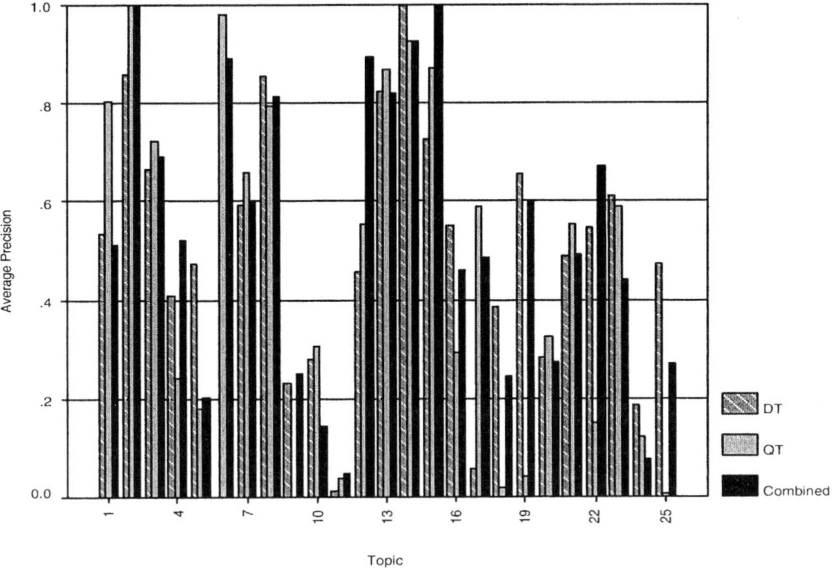

Fig. 3. Average Precision for Spanish topics

4.3 Combining Query and Document Translation

Given the varied success of query and document translation for each topic an obvious additional step is to combine the results of each approach. We tried merging the ranked lists using various data fusion methods, but experiments showed the result to be detrimental to using either QT or DT separately[8]. An alternative and much simpler approach we found achieved better results was to combine the English and MT versions of the captions to create a mixed-language index. In this case, each image is represented by a caption which contains the original English version followed by an MT version from each language.

Table 3 shows the results of three experiments against the mixed-language index: (1) document translation (DT) - using the original multilingual queries, (2) query translation (QT) - using MT English versions of the the original multilingual queries, and (3) combined (QT + DT) - the query consists of the original multilingual query and the MT English version. Compared with Tables 1 and 2 the effects of using a mixed-language index have greatest impact on document translation giving on average an increase in MAP of 19%. This is mainly due to having both English and multilingual terms in the index increasing the likelihood of terms matching despite translation errors (i.e. proper names in English which are not translated manually in the multilingual but are wrongly translated by the MT system are now able to match the English terms in the caption. How-

[8] We tried various rank fusion techniques such as weighted sum but these require the normalisation of scores and training data to learn optimal weights.

Table 3. A summary of retrieval effectiveness for QT and DT on a merged collection

Method	Measure	German	French	Italian	Spanish	Avg
DT	MAP	0.3992	0.5074	0.5075	0.5113	0.4814
	P@10	0.4120	0.5520	0.5760	0.5840	0.5310
	Recall	0.7901	0.8432	0.7720	0.9819	0.8468
	#bad	1	1	2	1	5
QT	MAP	0.5007	0.4641	0.4712	0.4468	0.4707
	P@10	0.5600	0.5000	0.4680	0.4920	0.5050
	Recall	0.8456	0.8022	0.7587	0.8951	0.8254
	#bad	0	3	2	1	6
QT+DT	MAP	0.5330	0.5037	0.5344	0.5242	0.5238
	P@10	0.5880	0.5400	0.5640	0.5560	0.5620
	Recall	0.8733	0.8866	0.7937	0.9855	0.8848
	#bad	0	0	2	1	3

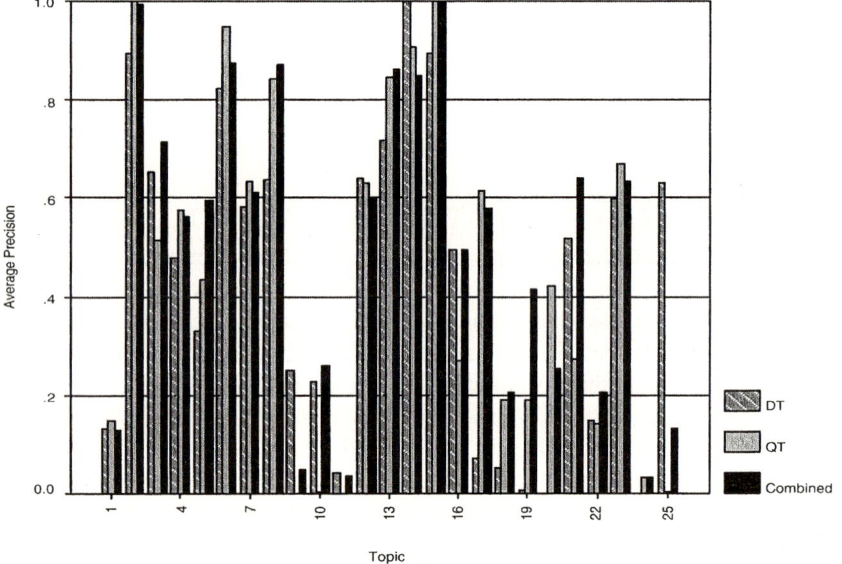

Fig. 4. Average Precision for French topics

ever, using a mixed-language index does reduce the MAP of query translation by 2%. Combining the original multilingual query and adding the MT English version gives an 8% increase over QT alone (from Table 2).

Perhaps most interesting, though, is the impact on individual queries. It appears, from Figures 2 to 5, that the effect of combined QT and DT against the mixed-language collection is to, in general, provide a compromise over using DT or QT alone resulting in fewer bad queries (3 vs. 6 for QT) and average precision scores which are more stable. Although some queries using the com-

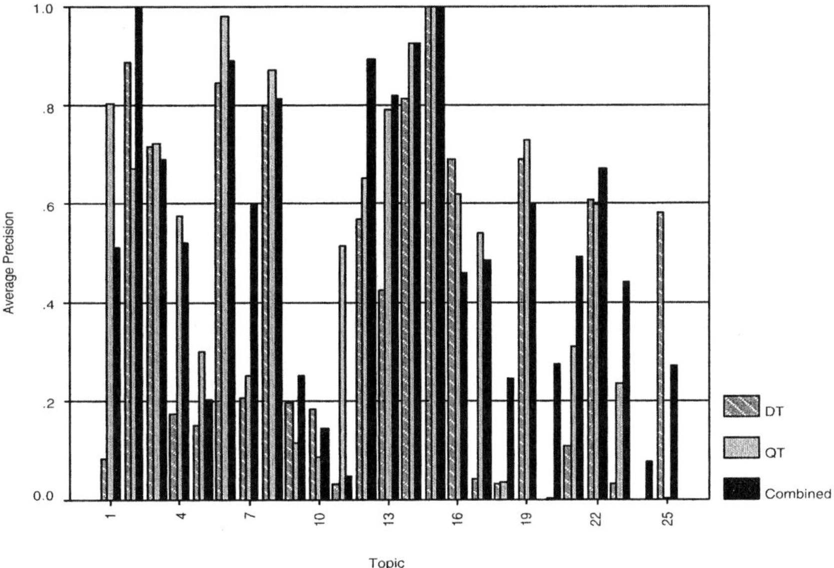

Fig. 5. Average Precision for Italian topics

bined approach do have a lower average precision than using DT or QT alone, many queries are more stable and even perform highest suggesting this to be an interesting approach for cross-language image retrieval.

5 Comparison with Other ImageCLEF Submissions

Table 4 summarises the results obtained compared with the official ImageCLEF results. We submitted results for document translation with relevance feedback only assuming these would be the highest results, but this did not prove to be true. The average rank position across all languages using the submitted results is 4.6; whereas using the highest results give an average rank position of 1.3 (for combined QT + DT). It is somewhat surprising that our approach which used very little language processing and knowledge of translation gives such high

Table 4. A comparison of the Sheffield results with other submissions

	Rank Position	
Language	With Submitted	With Highest Result
English	3	1
Italian	2	1
German	13	1
French	4	2
Spanish	1	1

results compared with submissions which combined text and visual features and used more language processing.

6 Conclusions and Future Work

In this paper we have presented experiments comparing document and query translation using the `Systran Professional` and `Babelfish` MT systems for the ImageCLEF 2004 ad hoc image retrieval task. On average query translation outperforms document translation for Spanish, Italian, French and German texts, but this varies across both language and topic. Various translation errors cause low retrieval effectiveness for both document and query translation methods. Given the effort involved in document translation and lower retrieval performance than query translation, it would appear that the latter approach is better for this retrieval task. Document translation can be applied after retrieval prior to presenting captions to the user rather than introducing errors into the retrieval process.

However, we observe some interesting effects across individual topics where document translation outperforms query translation. This is particularly true when queries are short and crucial query terms are mis-translated or not translated at all. Because caption translation is feasible for image collections due to typically short captions, we have shown that combining both document and query translation approaches by using multilingual queries and MT English versions and retrieving from a mixed-language collection (a concatenation of English and MT versions of the captions) gives an increase of around 8% over query translation alone. In particular the effect is to reduce the number of queries which retrieve no relevant images within the top 100, which is likely to be more satisfactory for the user.

In future work, we would like to explore improving the feedback model by training parameters for optimal values and methods to improve document translation, e.g. by cleaning texts prior to running the MT system.

Acknowledgements

We would like to thank Jianqiang Wang and Doug Oard from Maryland University for translating the ImageCLEF captions into Spanish, Italian, French and German. Also, thanks to Henning Müller for reviewing a draft version of the paper.

References

1. Grefenstette, G.: Cross Language Information Retrieval. Kluwer Academic Publishers, Norwell, MA, USA (1998)
2. Peters, C., Braschler, M.: Cross Language System Evaluation: The CLEF Campaigns. Journal of the American Society for Information Science and Technology **22** (2001) 1067–1072

3. Oard, D.: Serving Users in Many Languages. D-Lib magazine (1997)
4. Clough, P., Sanderson, M.: User Experiments with the Eurovision Cross-Langauge Image Retrieval System. In: Journal of the American Society for Information Science and Technology, to appear. (2005)
5. Flank, S.: Cross-Language Multimedia Information Retrieval . In: Proceedings of the sixth conference on Applied natural language processing, Morgan Kaufmann Publishers Inc. (2000) 13–20
6. Oard, D.: A comparative study of query and document translation for cross-language information retrieval. In: Proceedings of the 3rd Conference of the Association for Machine Translation in the Americas. (1998) 472–483
7. McCarley, S.: Should we translate the documents or the queries in cross language information retrieval? In: Proceedings of the 37th Annual Meeting of the Association for Computational Linguistics. (1999) 208–214
8. Fujii, A.and Ishikawa, T.: Applying machine translation to two-stage cross-language information retrieval. In: Proceedings of the 4th Conference of the Association for Machine Translation in the Americas (AMTA-2000). (2000) 13–24
9. Clough, P., Müller, H., Sanderson, M.: The CLEF Cross Language Image Retrieval Track (ImageCLEF) 2004. In Peters, C., Clough, P., Gonzalo, J., Jones, G., Kluck, M., Magnini, B., eds.: Fifth Workshop of the Cross–Language Evaluation Forum (CLEF 2004) , Lecture Notes in Computer Science (LNCS), Springer, Heidelberg, Germany (in print) (2005)
10. Zhai, C., Lafferty, J.: A study of smoothing methods for langauge models applied to ad hoc information retrieval. In: Proceedings of SIGIR'2001. (2001) 334–342
11. Clough, P., Sanderson, M.: Assessing translation quality for cross language image retrieval. In: Comparative Evaluation of Multilingual Information Access Systems: 4th Workshop of the Cross-Language Evaluation Forum (CLEF 2003), Lecture Notes in Computer Science (LNCS 3237), Springer, Heidelberg, Germany (2004) 594–607
12. Hutchins, W., Somers, H.: An Introduction to machine Translation. Academic Press, London, England (1986)
13. Clough, P., Sanderson, M.: The effects of relevance feedback in cross language image retrieval. In: Proceedings of the 26th European Conference on Information Retrieval (ECIR'04). (2004) 353–363

Pattern-Based Image Retrieval with Constraints and Preferences on ImageCLEF 2004*

Maximiliano Saiz-Noeda, José Luis Vicedo, and Rubén Izquierdo

Departamento de Lenguajes y Sistemas Informáticos,
University of Alicante, Spain
{max, vicedo, ruben}@dlsi.ua.es

Abstract. This paper presents the approach used by the University of Alicante in the ImageCLEF 2004 adhoc retrieval task. This task is performed through multilingual search requests (topics) against an historic photographic collection in which images are accompanied with English captions. This approach uses these captions to perform retrieval and is based on a set of constraints and preferences that allow the rejection or scoring of images for the retrieval task. The constraints are implemented through a set of co-occurrence patterns based on regular expressions and the approach is extended in one of the experiments with the use of WordNet synonyms.

1 Introduction

Bilingual ad hoc retrieval is one of the tasks defined within the ImageCLEF 2004 campaign [1] as part of the Cross Language Evaluation Forum (2004). The objective of this task, celebrated since last 2003 campaign [2], is to retrieve relevant photographic documents belonging to a historic photographic collection in which images are accompanied with English captions. These photographs integrate the *St Andrews photographic archive* consisting of 28,133 (approximately 10% of the total) photographs from *St Andrews University Library photographic collection* [3].

The method followed to retrieve relevant images is based on three experiments where a set of preferences and constraints are applied. The constraints, based on a set of co-occurrence patterns will reject potentially incompatible (non-relevant) images related to the query. Preferences will score the images in order to give a list according to their degree of relevance. Furthermore, a Wordnet-based query expansion is tested.

This is the first time that the University of Alicante has participated in this specific task and the main objective in the starting premise is to make a simple and low cost approach for this kind of search task.

* This work has been partially supported by the Spanish Government (CICYT) with grant TIC2003-07158-C04-01.

C. Peters et al. (Eds.): CLEF 2004, LNCS 3491, pp. 626–632, 2005.

The next sections describe specific characteristics of the dataset, relevant for the retrieval process, and the strategy used by the University of Alicante's team in order participate in the forum. Finally, some evaluation results will be discussed and some future improvements to the system will be presented.

2 Photographic Dataset

As mentioned, the photographic dataset used for the ImageCLEF 2004 ad hoc evaluation is a collection of 28,133 historical images from *St Andrews University Library photographic collection*. Photographs are primarily historic in nature from areas in and around Scotland; although pictures of other locations also exist.

All images have an accompanying textual description consisting of a set of fields. In this approach, we have used a file containing all image captions in a TREC-style format as detailed below:

```
<DOC>
 <DOCNO>stand03_2096/stand03_10695.txt</DOCNO>
 <HEADLINE>Departed glories - Falls of Cruachan Station above Loch
 Awe on the Oban line.</HEADLINE>
 <TEXT>
  <RECORD_ID>HMBR-.000273</RECORD_ID>
  <SHTITLE>Falls of Cruachan Station.</SHTITLE>
  <DESCRIPTION>Sheltie dog by single track railway below embankment,
  with wooden ticket office, and signals; gnarled trees lining
  banks.</DESCRIPTION>
  <DATE>ca.1990</DATE>
  <PHOTOGRAPHER>Hamish Macmillan Brown</PHOTOGRAPHER>
  <LOCATION>Argyllshire, Scotland</LOCATION>
  <NOTES>HMBR-273 pc/ADD: The photographer's pet Shetland collie
  dog, 'Storm'.</NOTES>
  <CATEGORIES>[tigers],[Fife all views],[gamekeepers],[identified
  male],[dress - national],[dogs]</CATEGORIES>
  <SMALL_IMG>stand03_2096/stand03_10695.jpg</SMALL_IMG>
  <LARGE_IMG>stand03_2096/stand03_10695_big.jpg</LARGE_IMG>
 </TEXT>
</DOC>
```

The 28,133 captions consist of 44,085 terms and 1,348,474 word occurrences; the maximum caption length is 316 words, but on average 48 words in length. All captions are written in British English, although the language also contains colloquial expressions. Approximately 81% of captions contain text in all fields, the rest generally without the description field. In most cases the image description is a grammatical sentence of around 15 words. The majority of images (82%) are in black and white, although colour images are also present in the collection.

The type of information that people typically look for in this collection include the following: Social history, e.g. old towns and villages, children at play and work. Environmental concerns, e.g. landscapes and wild plants. History of photography, e.g. particular photographers. Architecture, e.g. specific or general places or buildings. Golf, e.g. individual golfers or tournaments. Events, e.g. historic, war related. Transport, e.g. general or specific roads, bridges etc. Ships and shipping, e.g. particular vessels or fishermen.

Although all these fields can be used individually or collectively to facilitate image retrieval, in this approach only a few of them have been used. In particular, fields related to the photographer, location and date (apart from the headline) have been selected for the retrieval.

3 A Description of Our Technique

As it is the first time this group has participated in this task, we decided to make use of a naive approach with the smallest possible quantity of resources and implementation-time required. So, this technique does not use any kind of indexing, dictionary or entity recognition and makes use of a single POS tagging approach. Nevertheless, within the three experiments, improvements of the method includes the use of co-occurrence patterns and WordNet for query expansion.

Figure 1 shows the process followed by the system. This figure includes three steps related to the three experiments carried out for the evaluation that will be detailed below. To apply this basic strategy to retrieval, it is necessary to create files with questions and images. As mentioned, the file with the whole set of images in TREC format has been used for retrieval.

Constraints and preferences applied to the retrieval process make use of morphological information. Furthermore, the retrieval process is based on word lemmas. This means POS tagging of both the question and the image files is necessary. This POS tagging has been performed using the TreeTagger analyzer [4]. For the retrieval process itself, a file of stop words have been used in order to eliminate unhelpful words and improve speed of the system.

In order to cope with multilingual retrieval, we use a translation method to perform query translation. In concrete terms, the Babelfish [5] Machine Translation (MT) tool is used. This resource has allowed us to test the system with topics in German, Chinese, Spanish, French, Dutch, Italian, Japanese and Russian. Following translation into English, all languages are treated equally thereafter. According to the information required for retrieval, three different experiments have been carried out:

1. Preferences-based retrieval
2. Constraints and Preferences-based retrieval
3. Constraints and Preferences-based retrieval with question expansion

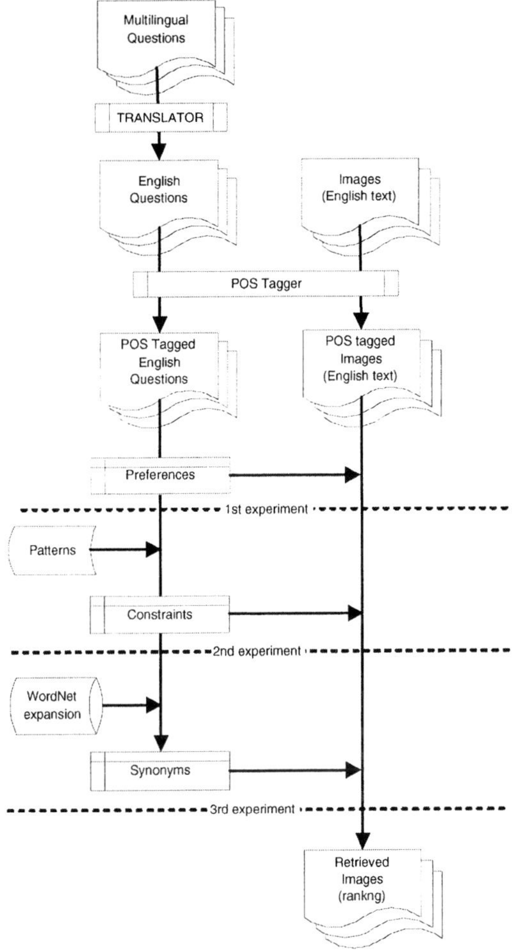

Fig. 1. Image retrieval process for different experiments

At the beginning of the process, all the images are suggested as a solution for each question[1]. From this scoring, some images will be added.

3.1 Experiment 1 - Preferences

For applying preferences, a single word matching between the question and the *HEADLINE* field of the image is used. This experiment is used as a baseline and its main function, as discussed later, is to determine the effects of additional information added in other experiments on the retrieval process.

[1] This condition is guided by the idea of giving 1000 images for each question, what constitutes a misunderstanding of the evaluation process and will be discussed bellow as an evaluation handicap.

For scoring in this experiment, we have assumed the relevance of proper nouns, nouns and verbs. So we have scored following this order when matching is related to these elements. Furthermore, if applicable, relations between nouns and verbs with the same lemma are also scored (if we are looking for "golfers swinging their clubs" probably we are interested in a "golfer's swing").

It seems almost obvious that good performance of this technique should be based on good entity recognition that ensures the correct detection of proper nouns in the question and in the image text. Probably, as it will be discussed later, using a better named-entity recognizer would improve the overall performance of this experiment.

3.2 Experiment 2 - Constraints and Preferences (The Patterns)

This experiment makes use of the previously described preferences and integrates constraints as a new selection criterion. The main aspect of the constraint is that it should be a rule strong enough to reject an image based on a compatibility guideline. This rule is built through the definition of a set of co-occurrence patterns that establish rejecting rules related to three of the fields contained in the image information: *DATE*, *PHOTOGRAPHER* and *LOCATION*.

These patterns are applied to the question (topic) and generate an XML-style file with information provided by the patterns. For example, topic:

```
1. Portrait pictures of church ministers by Thomas Rodger
```

is converted into the file:

```
<PREG>
 <PREGNO>1</PREGNO>
 <HEADLINE> Portrait pictures of church ministers by Thomas
  Rodger</HEADLINE>
 <DATE> </DATE>
 <PHOTOGRAPHER> by Thomas Rodger </PHOTOGRAPHER>
 <LOCATION> </LOCATION>
</PREG>
```

where labels $< DATE >$, $< PHOTOGRAPHER >$ and $< LOCATION >$ contain all information extracted about these information items.

The patterns are built over regular expressions that allow the extraction of a string contained in any of the mentioned labels. *DATE* constraints try to reject images by comparing not only question and image years, but applying extra information such as months or quantifiers. This way, if the topic asks for "Pictures of Edinburgh Castle taken before 1900", all the photos taken after 1900 will be discarded. *PHOTOGRAPHER* constraints are based in the whole name of the photographer. *LOCATION* constraints use not only the location itself but also, if applicable, possible relations with other locations (city, country, ...).

As can be seen, this technique is very general and, therefore, the possibility of error is also high. To reduce the possibility of errors, the strategy also uses statistical information from the image corpus. This way, matches that are incorrectly treated by the pattern as photographers or locations are considered as noise and rejected because of their low or null appearance frequency in the corresponding field in the image caption. In fact, we can use the same pattern for both location and photographer and then decide what to apply depending on the image. For example, according to the image captions, a capitalized word after a comma can be consider both a photographer or a location (as shown in topics "Men in military uniform, *George Middlemass Cowie*" and "College or university buildings, *Cambridge*"). After including the extracted string in both fields of the topic generated, the statistical information will determine what is a photographer and what is a location (unless there is a town called George Middlemass or a photographer called Cambridge).

Once the constraint features are determined and included in the topic through their corresponding labels, the system makes a matching task to reject non-compatible images. For example, if it determines that the photographer of the searched pictures is "Thomas Rodger", all the images that don't contain "Thomas Rodger" (or any of its parts) in the *PHOTOGRAPHER* label are rejected.

3.3 Experiment 3 - Query Expansion Using Wordnet

The last experiment has been designed to incorporate extra information regarding potential synonym relations between terms in the query and image. In this case, the system expands the topic with all noun and verb synonyms contained in WordNet [6].

Using this the scoring for each image is increased not only if a lemma of a word appears in the topic, but also if its synonyms from WordNet also appear in the image *HEADLINE* text. Due to there being no lexical disambiguation in the process, noun synonyms are best scored than verb synonyms assuming that the former tend to be less generic than the latter. If the synonym is found but with different POS tag, a smaller score is added.

4 Evaluation

Although we knew this to be a very general approach to this task, the results obtained after the evaluation of the system are not as successful as desired. At the moment of the writing of this paper we are trying to determine if there is any kind of computing processing mistake that has affected the final scoring. Anyway, there are some considerations extracted from the results.

For the evaluation results, the system was prepared to always provide 1000 images as output. This is an error because some images given by the system are not relevant at all (they have no specific nor score).

Another problematic issue is the way the system scores the images. This scoring is also very general and often generates the same score for a large number of images (in fact, all the images can be grouped in four or five different scores). All the images that are equally scored have, for the system, the same order in the final evaluation scored list. For the evaluation, comparing results we see that there are big differences depending on the order of the images.

Related to the results of the three experiments, one of the most "eye-catching" things is that, in general, the preferences-baseline experiment gives the best result or is improved in a very small degree by the rest of experiments. This situation can be put down to the lack of additional information regarding named-entity and recognition of proper nouns.

Another interesting observation from the evaluation is that although there are not large differences between the monolingual and the bilingual results, it is clear that automatic translation (such as the method used in these experiments) introduces errors and noise which ultimately decreases system performance. Furthermore, basic techniques of lexical disambiguation and restricted-domain ontologies could improve the use of WordNet.

In summary, although the results are not very good, the system itself presents many possibilities for improvement through the refinement of the scoring system, the addition of new techniques based on named-entity recognition, the use of better translation resources and dictionaries and the incorporation of new semantic and ontological information that enforces WordNet access.

5 Conclusions

In this paper we have described the system carried out by the University of Alicante in the ImageCLEF 2004 adhoc retrieval task. Information about the process itself, the strategies and experiments developed for the retrieval task have been given. The results of the evaluation have been justified and different solutions to improve these results have been outlined in order to define future improvements to obtain a better retrieval system.

References

1. www: Image CLEF in the Cross Language Evaluation Forum 2004. http://ir.shef.ac.uk/imageclef2004/index.html (2004) Last visited 2-Aug-2004.
2. Clough, P., Sanderson, M.: The CLEF 2003 cross language image retrieval task. In: Working Notes for the CLEF 2003 WorkShop, Trondheim, Norway (2003) 379–388
3. www: St Andrews University Library photographic collection. http://special collections.st-and.ac.uk/photcol.htm (2004) Last visited 2-Aug-2004.
4. Schmid, H.: Probabilistic Part-of-Speech Tagging Using Decision Trees. In: International Conference on New Methods in Language Processing, Manchester, UK (1994) 44–49
5. www: BabelFish translator. http://world.altavista.com/ (2004) Last visited 2-Aug-2004.
6. Miller, G.A., Beckwith, R., Fellbaum, C., Gross, D., Miller, K.J.: Five Papers on WordNet. Special Issue of the International Journal of Lexicography **3** (1993) 235–312

How to Visually Retrieve Images from the St. Andrews Collection Using GIFT

Henning Müller and Antoine Geissbühler

University and University Hospitals of Geneva, Service of Medical Informatics, 21 Rue Micheli-du-Crest, CH-1211 Geneva 4, Switzerland
henning.mueller@sim.hcuge.ch

Abstract. The ImageCLEF task of CLEF has a main goal in the retrieval of images from multi–lingual collections. The 2003 imageCLEF saw no group using the visual information of images, which is inherently language independent. The query topics of the St. Andrews collection are defined in a way that makes visual retrieval hard as visual similarity plays a marginal role whereas semantics and background knowledge are extremely important, which can only be obtained from text. This article describes the submission of an entirely visual result. It also proposes improvements for visual retrieval systems with the current data. Section 4 explains possible ways to make this query task more appealing to visual retrieval research groups, explaining problems of visual retrieval and what the task can do to overcome present problems. A benchmarking event is needed for visual information retrieval to remove barriers in performance. ImageCLEF can be this event and identify areas where visual retrieval might be better than textual and vice–versa. The combination of visual and textual features is an important field where research is needed.

1 Introduction

Visual retrieval of images has been an extremely active research area for more then ten years now [1, 2]. Still, there has not been neither a benchmarking event nor the use of standard datasets to compare the performance of several systems or techniques. Despite efforts such as the Benchathlon[1] [3] and several articles on evaluation [4–7], no common framework has been created, yet. This is different in textual information retrieval where several initiatives such as TREC[2] [8] (Text REtrieval conference) and CLEF[3] [9] (Cross Language Evaluation Forum) exist. In 2003, CLEF added a cross language image retrieval task [10] using a collection of historic photographs. The task in 2004 uses the same collection but adds an interactive and a medical task [11]. Figure 1 shows examples from the St. Andrews collection.

Images are annotated in English and query topics are formulated in another language containing a textual description of the query and an example image.

1 http://www.benchathlon.net/
2 http://trec.nist.gov/
3 http://www.clef-campaign.org/

C. Peters et al. (Eds.): CLEF 2004, LNCS 3491, pp. 633–642, 2005.

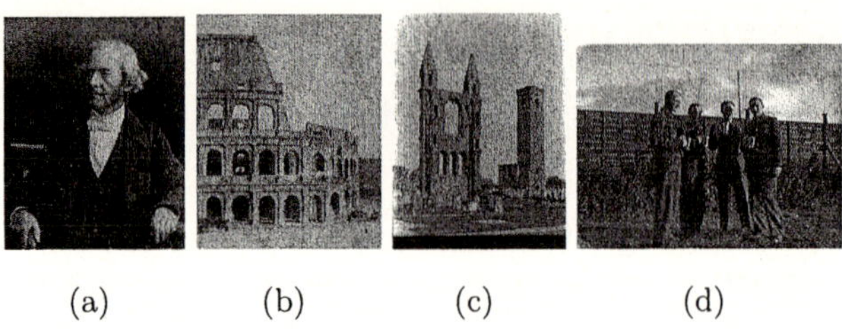

(a) (b) (c) (d)

Fig. 1. Example images of the St. Andrews database

English retrieval performance is taken as a baseline. Normally, only the title of the query was translated whereas the narrative was available as additional information in some languages. The topics for which results can be submitted look as follows (a French example for image 1(a)):

```
<title>
Portraits photographiques de pasteurs d'église par Thomas Rodger
</title>
<narr>
Les images pertinentes sont des portraits photographiques de
pasteurs ou de leaders d'église pris par Thomas Rodger. Les images
de nimporte quelle époque sont pertinentes, mais ne doivent montrer
qu'une personne dans un studio, c'est-à-dire posant pour la photo.
Des photos de groupes ne sont pas pertinentes.
</narr>
```

From this topic description we only took the image to start queries with our system, the textual information was discarded. No manual relevance feedback or automatic query expansion was used. This means that important information on the query task can not be obtained. With the visual information only, we do not know that we are searching for church ministers and we do not know who actually took the picture. Only a very good domain expert might be able to get this information from the image alone. Actually, all this information is only findable if the annotation is of a very high quality and is known to be complete. It has to be assured that all images with church ministers have these words in the text, otherwise we can not be sure whether the person is a church minister or might have a similar function. The producer (photographer) of the images also needs to be marked, otherwise a relevance judge would not be able to mark a result as relevant, although two images might be extremely similar in style. What about images where we do not have any name of the photographer but that look very similar to images from "Thomas Ridger"? What about collections with a mediocre text quality such as those that we often find in the real world, for example the Internet?

Some retrieval tasks led to subjectively good results with a visual retrieval system whereas others did not manage to show any relevant images within the top 20 results. Figure 2 shows one example result of a visual retrieval system.

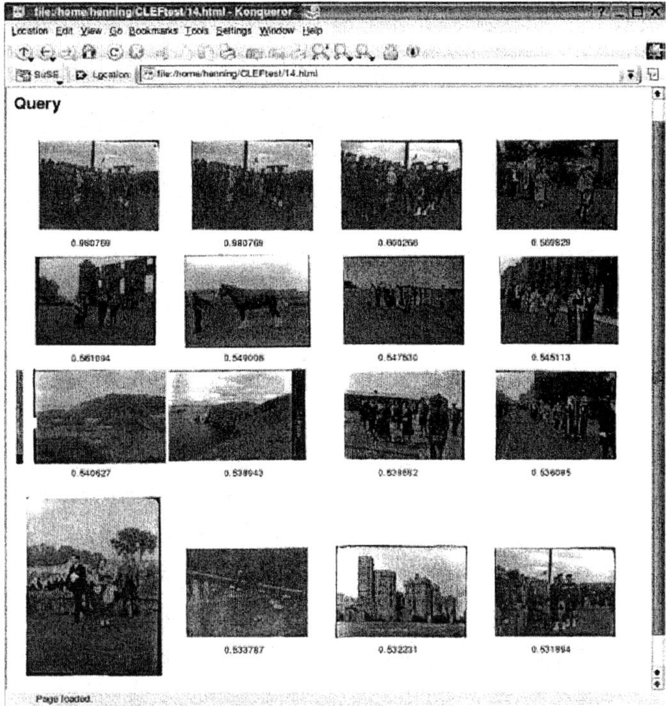

Fig. 2. Example for a "good" query result based on visual properties

The first image is the query image and we can see that the same image was found as well as a few other images with the queen that apparently show the same scene.

Although this might look like a reasonable retrieval results, we can definitely tell that the system had no idea that we were looking for a queen at a military parade. The images were basically retrieved because they have very similar properties with respect to the grey levels contained, and especially with respect to the frame around the image. These images were most likely taken with the same camera and digitised with the same scanner. These properties can be found with a visual retrieval system.

Combinations of visual and textual features for retrieval are only rarely researched and need much more attention [12].

2 Basic Technologies Used for the Task

The technology used for the content–based image retrieval is mainly taken from the *Viper*[4] project of the University of Geneva. Much information is available on the system [13]. Outcome of the Viper project is the GNU Image Finding Tool,

[4] `http://viper.unige.ch`

GIFT[5]. We used a version that slightly modifies the feature space and is called *medGIFT*[6] as it is mainly developed for the medical domain. These software tools are open source and can consequently also be used by other participants of ImageCLEF. Demonstration versions for participants were made available as well as not everybody can be expected to install an entire tool for such a benchmarking event, only. The feature sets that are used by *medGIFT* are:

- local colour features at different scales by partitioning the images successively four times into four subregions and taking the mode colour of each region as features;
- global colour features in the form of a colour histogram;
- local texture features by partitioning the image and applying Gabor filters in various scales and directions. Gabor responses are quantised into 10 strengths;
- global texture features represented as a simple histogram of the responses of the local Gabor filters in various directions and scales.

A peculiarity of GIFT is that it uses many techniques from text retrieval. Visual features are quantised/binarised, and open a feature space that is similar to the distribution of words in texts (similar to a Zipf distribution). A simple *tf/idf* weighting is used and the query weights are normalised by the results of the query itself. The histogram features are compared based on a simple histogram intersection. This allows us to apply a variety of techniques that are common in text retrieval to the retrieval of images. Experiments show that especially relevance feedback queries on images are much better using this feature space than with continuous feature whereas one–shot queries might perform better with other techniques.

3 Runs Submitted for Evaluation

Unfortunately, there was not enough time this year to submit a mixed visual and textual run for ImageCLEF but we are working on this for next year.

3.1 Only Visual Retrieval with One Query Image

For the visual queries, the *medGIFT* system was used. It allows easy changes of system parameters such as the configuration of the Gabor filters and the grey level/colour quantisations. Input for these queries were only the query images. No feedback or automatic query expansion was used. The following system parameters were submitted:

- 18 hues, 3 saturations, 3 values, 4 grey levels, 4 directions and 3 scales of the Gabor filters, the GIFT base configuration made available to all participants of ImageCLEF; *(GE_4g_4d_vis)*

[5] http://www.gnu.org/software/gift/
[6] http://www.sim.hcuge.ch/medgift/

– 9 hues, 2 saturations, 2 values, 16 grey levels, 4 directions and 5 scales of the Gabor filters. *(GE_16g_4d_vis)*

Some queries delivered surprisingly good results but this was not due to a recognition of image features with respect to the topic but rather due to the fact that images from a relevance set were taken at a similar time and have a very similar appearance. Content–based image retrieval can help to retrieve images that were taken with the same camera or scanned with the same scanner if they are similar with respect to their colour properties. Mixing text and visual features for retrieval will need a fair amount of work to optimise parameters and really receive good results. For this task we did not have the resources to do so.

The evaluation results show the very low performance of all visual only runs that were submitted. Mean average precision (MAP) is 0.0919 for the GIFT base system and 0.0625 for the modified version. It is actually surprising that the system with only four grey levels performed better than a system having a larger number. Most of the images are in grey and brown tones so we expected to obtain better results when giving more flexibility to this aspect. It needs to be analysed whether other techniques can obtain better results such as a normalisation of the images or even a change of the brown tones into grey tones to make images better comparable. The current brow tones only deliver limited information with respect to colours and are hard to compare automatically. Still, these results will be far away from the best systems that reach a MAP of 0.5865 such as the Daedalus system using text retrieval with only a fairly small visual component. Several participating systems include visual information into the retrieval and some of these systems are indeed ranked high, a actually the best runs use combinations of visual and textual features. All systems that relied on visual features, only, receive fairly bad results, in general the worst results in the competition.

3.2 Techniques to Improve Visual Retrieval Results

Some techniques might be of help to increase the performance of visual retrieval results. One such techniques is a pre–processing of images to bring all images to a standard grey level distribution and maybe removing colour completely. At least the brown levels should be changed to grey levels so images can be retrieved based on real content and not based on general appearance. Background removal can also removed part of the noise of the images.

Another possibility is the change of the colour space of the images. Several spaces have been analysed with respect to invariance regarding lighting conditions with good results [14]. For the tasks of ImageCLEF it might be useful to reduce the number of colours and slightly augment the number of grey levels for best retrieval. Some form of normalisation could also be used as some images used the entire grey spectrum whereas others only use an extremely limited number of grey levels. A proper evaluation will have to show what actually works.

Mixed visual/textual strategies can lead to a better result. If, in a first step, only the textual information is taken as a query and then the first N images are visually fed back to the system the results can be much better and can manage to find images that are without text or with a bad annotation and that would not have been found otherwise. More research is definitely needed on mixed textual/visual strategies for retrieval to find out which influence each one can have, depending on the query task. It might also be possible to have a small influence of the visually most similar images in a first query step as well but the text will need to be the dominating factor for best results as the query topics are semantics–based.

4 How to Make the Queries More Appealing to Visual Retrieval Research?

Although CLEF is on cross–language retrieval and thus mainly on text, image information should exploited in this context for the retrieval of visual data. Images are inherently language–independent and they can provide important additional information for cross–language retrieval tasks. To foster these developments it might even be the best to have an entirely visual task to attract the content–based retrieval community and later come back to a combination of visual/textual techniques. This can also help to develop partnerships between visual and textual retrieval groups to submit common runs. Techniques for visual information retrieval are currently not good enough to respond properly to semantic tasks [15]. Sometimes the results look indeed good but this is most often linked to secondary parameters and not really to the semantic concepts being searched for or the low–level features being used.

4.1 More Visual Information for the Current Topics

The easiest way to make the St. Andrews task more attractive to visual retrieval groups is simply to supply more visual information as task description. Having three to five example images instead of one helps visual retrieval significantly as systems can search for the really important information that these images have in common. A single image for retrieval is a little bit "a shot in the dark" but several images do supply important information. Besides positive examples, an important improvement is be to supply several negative examples to have an idea of what not to look for. Negative relevance feedback has shown to be extremely important in visual information retrieval [16] and feedback with negative examples substantially changes the result sets whereas positive examples only do a slight reordering of the highest–ranked results. Finding 3-5 negative examples per query task in addition to the positive examples is easy to perform.

4.2 Topics Based on the Visual "Appearance" of an Image

It is discussed a lot what visual image retrieval cannot do but there are quite a few things that visual image retrieval can indeed do. Although searching on semantics seems currently infeasible, similarity based on the appearance of the images can be obtained with a fairly good quality. Visual appearance is often described as a first impression of an image or preattentive similarity [17]. Tasks can also contain easy semantics that are modelled by their visual appearance. Possible topics can be:

- Sun sets – modelled by a yellow round object in the middle and mainly variations of red.
- Mountain views – upper part blue and in the middle part sharp changes, in grey/white tones, bottom sometimes green.
- Beach – Lower part yellow and the upper part in blue with a clear line between the two.
- City scenes – very symmetric structures with a large number of horizontal lines and right angles.

It will need to be analysed whether these queries do actually respond to what real users are looking for in retrieval systems, but they have the potential to attract a much larger number of visual information retrieval groups to participate and compare their techniques in such a benchmarking event.

4.3 Easy Semantic Topics

TRECVID[7] introduced several topics for video retrieval in 2003 that can also be used for visual image retrieval, maybe with slight variations. These are fairly easy semantic topics such as finding out whether there are people in images. Some examples for topics are:

- People: segment contains at least three humans.
- Building: segment contains a building. Buildings are walled structures with a roof.
- Road: segment contains part of a road - any size, paved or not.
- Vegetation: segment contains living vegetation in its natural environment.
- Animal: segment contains an animal other than a human .

ImageCLEF could define topics similar in style for the image collections being available (topics that actually correspond to images in the collection). Retrieval systems can then try to find as many of the images with respect to the topic as possible based on visual features, only, or based on visual and textual features. This can also help to find out the influence of text and visual information on fairly low–level semantic concepts. This can especially stimulate the creation of simple binary detectors for semantic concepts. These detectors can later be combined for the retrieval of higher–level semantic retrieval, so they do deliver important intermediary results.

4.4 An Easier Image Collection

The St. Andrews collection is definitely a hard collection for purely visual analysis. The images do not contain many clearly separated objects and the small amount of colour pictures and variances in sharpness/quality make automatic

[7] `http://www-nlpir.nist.gov/projects/trecvid/`

analysis extremely hard. Other collections such as the Corel Photo CDs are much easier for automatic analysis and query/retrieval [18]. This collection contains 100 images each for a large number of topics (tigers, planes, eagles, ...). Often the collections have a distinct object in each of the sets, sometimes the sets also correspond to regions (Paris, California, Egypt, ...). The only problem is to get a collection without strong copyright constraints. As the Corel Photo CDs are not sold anymore, this might be a possibility if Corel agrees to make the images in a lower resolution available to participants. The Corbis[8] image archive also offers a limited selection of around 15.000 images for research purposes that are annotated in a hierarchical code. Such a collection might be an easier topic for visual and combined visual/textual retrieval.

4.5 Interactive Tasks Evaluated by Users

A different idea is the evaluation of interactive systems based on real users performing queries. Normally, image retrieval is not extremely good in a first query step but with feedback, very good results can be obtained [16, 19]. Similar to the interactive task using text introduced in 2004 we can imagine a task with only a visual description with an example image. Users can subsequently perform queries until they are satisfied with the results. Evaluation could be done directly by the users, for example by counting how many relevant images they found with which system, and how many refinement steps were necessary to find a satisfactory result. It has to be stated that the user satisfaction can vary considerable with respect to his knowledge of the content of the database. When not knowing anything about the total number of relevant images, users tend to be satisfied fairly easily.

5 Conclusions

This article describes a submission to the ImageCLEF task using the St. Andrews historical image collection. The two submitted runs were based on visual features of the images only, without using the text supplied for the queries. No other techniques were used such as manual relevance feedback or automatic query expansion. The results show the problems of purely visual image retrieval: no semantics are currently included in the visual low–level features and as a consequence the performance is low.

Still, visual information retrieval based on low–level non–semantic features can be an important part in the general information retrieval picture. Visual information retrieval can be used to find images with a similar visual appearance or with simple semantic concepts if learning data for these concepts are available. Thus, it is important for evaluation events such as ImageCLEF to create topics that are more suitable to visual retrieval groups and that correspond to desires of real users as well. Visual and textual retrieval need to be brought together with overlapping retrieval tasks to find out where each one works best and where

[8] `http://www.corbis.com/`

the two can be combined for optimal results. Currently, there is no experience in this domain, hence the importance of benchmarking events such as ImageCLEF but also the creation of retrieval tasks suitable for visual retrieval. This article gives a few ideas on how to make the ImageCLEF task more appealing for visual retrieval groups. Hopefully, these changes will be able to attract more attention in the visual retrieval community so people start working on the same data sets and start comparing systems and techniques. To advance retrieval systems, a critical evaluation and comparison of existing systems is currently more needed than new retrieval techniques. ImageCLEF might be an important factor in advancing information retrieval and especially visual information retrieval.

References

1. Smeulders, A.W.M., Worring, M., Santini, S., Gupta, A., Jain, R.: Content–based image retrieval at the end of the early years. IEEE Transactions on Pattern Analysis and Machine Intelligence **22 No 12** (2000) 1349–1380
2. Goodrum, A.: Image information retrieval: An overview of current research. Journal of Information Science Research **3** (2000) –
3. Gunther, N.J., Beretta, G.: A benchmark for image retrieval using distributed systems over the internet: BIRDS–I. Technical report, HP Labs, Palo Alto, Technical Report HPL–2000–162, San Jose (2001)
4. Smith, J.R.: Image retrieval evaluation. In: IEEE Workshop on Content–based Access of Image and Video Libraries (CBAIVL'98), Santa Barbara, CA, USA (1998) 112–113
5. Müller, H., Müller, W., Squire, D.M., Marchand-Maillet, S., Pun, T.: Performance evaluation in content–based image retrieval: Overview and proposals. Pattern Recognition Letters **22** (2001) 593–601
6. Leung, C., Ip, H.: Benchmarking for content–based visual information search. In Laurini, R., ed.: Fourth International Conference On Visual Information Systems (VISUAL'2000). Number 1929 in Lecture Notes in Computer Science, Lyon, France, Springer–Verlag (2000) 442–456
7. Narasimhalu, A.D., Kankanhalli, M.S., Wu, J.: Benchmarking multimedia databases. Multimedia Tools and Applications **4** (1997) 333–356
8. Harman, D.: Overview of the first Text REtrieval Conference (TREC–1). In: Proceedings of the first Text REtrieval Conference (TREC–1), Washington DC, USA (1992) 1–20
9. Savoy, J.: Report on clef–2001 experiments. In: Report on the CLEF Conference 2001 (Cross Language Evaluation Forum), Darmstadt, Germany, Springer LNCS 2406 (2002) 27–43
10. Clough, P., Sanderson, M.: The clef 2003 cross language image retrieval task. In: Proceedings of the Cross Language Evaluation Forum (CLEF 2003). (2004)
11. Clough, P., Sanderson, M., Müller, H.: A proposal for the clef cross language image retrieval track (imageclef) 2004. In: The Challenge of Image and Video Retrieval (CIVR 2004), Dublin, Ireland, Springer LNCS (2004)
12. La Cascia, M., Sethi, S., Sclaroff, S.: Combining textual and visual cues for content–based image retrieval on the world wide web. In: IEEE Workshop on Content–based Access of Image and Video Libraries (CBAIVL'98), Santa Barbara, CA, USA (1998)

13. Squire, D.M., Müller, W., Müller, H., Pun, T.: Content–based query of image databases: inspirations from text retrieval. Pattern Recognition Letters (Selected Papers from The 11th Scandinavian Conference on Image Analysis SCIA '99) **21** (2000) 1193–1198 B.K. Ersboll, P. Johansen, Eds.
14. Gevers, T., Smeulders, A.W.M.: A comparative study of several color models for color image invariants retrieval. In: Proceedings of the First International Workshop ID-MMS'96, Amsterdam, The Netherlands (1996) 17–26
15. Forsyth, D.A.: Benchmarks for storage and retrieval in multimedia databases. In: Storage and Retrieval for Media Databases. Volume 4676 of SPIE Proceedings., San Jose, California, USA (2002) 240–247 (SPIE Photonics West Conference).
16. Müller, H., Müller, W., Squire, D.M., Marchand-Maillet, S., Pun, T.: Strategies for positive and negative relevance feedback in image retrieval. In Sanfeliu, A., Villanueva, J.J., Vanrell, M., Alcézar, R., Eklundh, J.O., Aloimonos, Y., eds.: Proceedings of the 15th International Conference on Pattern Recognition (ICPR 2000), Barcelona, Spain, IEEE (2000) 1043–1046
17. Santini, S., Jain, R.: Gabor space and the development of preattentive similarity. In: Proceedings of the 13th International Conference on Pattern Recognition (ICPR'96), Vienna, Austria, IEEE (1996) 40–44
18. Müller, H., Marchand-Maillet, S., Pun, T.: The truth about corel – evaluation in image retrieval. In: Proceedings of the International Conference on the Challenge of Image and Video Retrieval (CIVR 2002), London, England (2002)
19. Rui, Y., Huang, T.S., Ortega, M., Mehrotra, S.: Relevance feedback: A power tool for interactive content–based image retrieval. IEEE Transactions on Circuits and Systems for Video Technology **8** (1998) 644–655 (Special Issue on Segmentation, Description, and Retrieval of Video Content).

UNED at ImageCLEF 2004: Detecting Named Entities and Noun Phrases for Automatic Query Expansion and Structuring

Víctor Peinado, Javier Artiles, Fernando López-Ostenero, Julio Gonzalo, and Felisa Verdejo

Departamento de Lenguajes y Sistemas Informáticos,
Universidad Nacional de Educación a Distancia (UNED),
c/ Juan del Rosal, 16, Ciudad Universitaria, 28040 Madrid, Spain
victor@lsi.uned.es

Abstract. This paper describes UNED experiments at the Image CLEF bilingual ad hoc task. Two different strategies are attempted: i) automatic expansion and translation using noun phrases; ii) automatic detection of named entities in the query for structured search on image caption fields.

All our experiments obtain results above the average MAP for the bilingual task. Structured searches using named entities improve performance over a strong baseline (Pirkola's structured query approach), achieving one of the best results for the whole bilingual track. Expansion with noun phrases, however, degrades results, possibly due to the mismatch between train and test collections.

1 Introduction

For its first participation in the Image CLEF task, the UNED NLP & IR Group took part in the bilingual ad hoc retrieval task, using Spanish and English as source and target languages, respectively. As in the the classic TREC ad hoc task, the main goal was, given a set of topics in a source language, to retrieve as many relevant images as possible from a collection in the target language.

Participants were provided with a list of topic statements and a collection of images with semi-structured captions in English. Every topic consisted of a title (a short description of the required search in few words) and a narrative (a description of what constituted a relevant and a non-relevant image for the search). Narrative was not provided for Spanish, hence our experiments use only the title field. The collection comprises 28,133 photographs from one of the most important sets of historic photography in Scotland.[1] All images have an accompanying textual description consisting of 8 distinct fields (e.g. a unique ID, both short and long titles, the location, a description of the image, the date, the author and some categories in which the photograph may be included). This rich meta information was the basis to retrieve relevant images in our approach.

[1] See http://ir.shef.ac.uk/imageclef2004/stand.html for further details.

C. Peters et al. (Eds.): CLEF 2004, LNCS 3491, pp. 643–652, 2005.

We experimented with two different strategies:

1. Expand queries with noun phrases. Queries are expanded with related noun phrases, looking up a bilingual Spanish-English noun phrase list which was extracted from the CLEF news comparable corpus (LA Times 1994, Agencia EFE 1994).
2. Identify named entities and dates in queries, and perform structured queries against appropriate image caption fields:
   a) Proper names are searched in the "author" and/or "location" fields. If the search is non-nil, the retrieval mechanism favours images containing these entities in that fields.
   b) Temporal references are searched in the "date" field. If the search is non-nil, images matching the temporal reference in the date field are favoured.

Prior to experimenting with these strategies, we first built an improved English-Spanish translation resource, merging our in-site dictionaries with free web resources.

Reasons to try the above techniques include:

1. Expansion with Natural Language approaches is more benefitial with short queries [1] or short documents such as image captions [2]. Being in a Cross-Language search context, we decided to experiment with our query expansion technique based on aligned noun phrases, that gave excellent results in the CLEF interactive track [3, 4, 5].
2. Since the ImageCLEF collection contains structured image captions (including author, date, location and description fields) it seems interesting to explore the possibility of detecting different types of information in the query to perform more precise searches. Then, we experiment with a simple strategy that tries to match every named entity as a possible author name or location.

This paper is structured as follows: in Section 2, we first discuss the possibilities of using noun phrases in query expansion and interactive tasks, then we present the linguistic resources used (Section 2.1), our preliminary CLIR experiments on the CLEF collection (Section 2.2) and the settings of our Image CLEF experiments (Section 2.3). Then, we explain the structured searches approach (Section 3) and discuss the official results obtained in the track (section 4). Finally, in Section 5, we draw some conclusions.

2 Query Expansion with Noun Phrases

2.1 Linguistic Resources

We used two comparable corpora from the CLEF ad-hoc track: the Spanish newswire collection EFE 1994, and the Los Angeles Times 1994 news collection.

Table 1. Example aligned phrases using CLEF comparable corpora

English	Spanish
Orange County	Condado de Orange
abortion issue	tema del aborto
free trade agreement	acuerdo de libre comercio
World War II	Segunda Guerra Mundial

Out of these comparable corpora, we built a bilingual dictionary containing more than five million aligned noun phrases[2]. Noun phrases are automatically recognized and extracted using statistical data such as the frequency of sequences of two or three informative words (nouns and adjectives) in both languages [6]. We consider that two phrases are aligned if they have the same amount of informative words and there is a one-to-one correspondence using a bilingual dictionary (see Table 1 for examples).

Previous UNED participations in the iCLEF track[3] proved the utility of noun phrases for document selection [3], query translation and refinement ([4, 5]).

Finally, we built a new bilingual Spanish-English dictionary made up from heterogeneous lexicographic resources such as dictionaries and word lists (some of them freely available in the Web) and semantic networks such as WordNet [7] and EuroWordNet [8]. Every source went through a cleaning process before merging them in an XML-structured dictionary showing up all the information from each original source, almost without typos or inconsistencies. As a result of this merging, our final dictionary contains more than 57,000 entries in Spanish and 85,000 in English, with a total size of about 50 Mb[4].

2.2 Preliminary Experiments over the CLEF Collection

In order to check the usefulness of noun phrases for Cross-Language ad hoc retrieval, we have performed a number of experiments with 140 Spanish CLEF topics (corresponding to 2001-2003 campaigns) and the LA Times 1994 English CLEF collection. We start with the three following baselines based on word by word translation using bilingual dictionaries:

naive baseline. Word by word translation, building a bag of words with all the possible translations appearing in our dictionaries.

frequencies. We built a bag of words from only those possible translations appearing in more than one lexicographic source, assuming that they should be the most common and reliable.

[2] Roughly, there are more than 4.5 million phrases containing two informative words and 850,000 containing three.

[3] The Interactive track for the Cross-Language Evaluation Forum webpage is available at `http://nlp.uned.es/iCLEF`.

[4] Using this merged dictionary instead of the original VOX dictionary we used in previous approaches, there is an improvement in CLIR experiments with the CLEF collection of 36%

Following this strategy, we pursued two goals: on one hand, we used only those translations considered reliable. On the other hand, we rejected residuary translations from semantic networks in order to reduce the noise produced by the expansion.

strong baseline. We used Pirkola's proposal [9] to build structured translated queries, using the synonymy operators implemented in the INQUERY search engine [10] to wrap alternative translations for every word in the query.

systran The queries were translated using the Systran machine translation system.

These baselines are compared with three runs using the bilingual noun phrase list:

phrases + pirkola. We used our noun phrases dictionary to expand the query with related noun phrases and translate them using a bilingual dictionary. Our strategy was the following: firstly, we expanded each topic term with the ten most frequent noun phrases containing the term in the CLEF collection and then we translated the phrases using the aligned noun phrase list. Those query terms from which no phrases were identified were included in the translated query using Pirkola's approximation, i.e. using synonymy operators.

"multi-lemma" phrases + pirkola. In order to limit the noise produced by the phrase expansion of the previous experiment, we only use noun phrases containing at least two query terms.

phrases + pirkola + systran. Combined run using all three resources, i.e. noun phrases, structured translations using our dictionaires and the Systran machine translation system.

As shown in Table 2, our experimental proposals using noun phrases outperformed the baselines. The differences were statistically significant according to a non-parametric Wilcoxon sign test. The strong baseline obtained the same average precision than Systran's translations, showing that the combination of Pirkola's structured query approach with reliable lexicographic resources is an excellent CLIR baseline.

Table 2. Results of our preliminary experiments

run	Avg. precision
`naive baseline`	.19
`frequencies`	.25
`strong baseline`	.27
`systran`	.27
`phrases + pirkola`	.29
`phrases + pirkola + systran`	.30
`''multi-lemma'' phrases + pirkola`	**.31**

In summary, our results show that:

- Phrases do improve CLIR results, at least when the training corpus and the test corpus are similar. Even though the porcentual gain is not very high, in a setting with very small documents (e.g. image captions or topic titles) it would be reasonable to expect higher improvements.
- There is no need to use external machine translation systems, at least when translating small documents.
- The "multi-lemma" variant of noun phrase expansion performs slightly better for batch CLIR, although the difference is not statistically relevant according to a Wilcoxon sign test.
- The quality of a translation strongly depends on the resources used.

2.3 Settings for ImageCLEF Experiments

Extending the above results to the Image CLEF bilingual ad hoc task, we have used the corpus and the set of Spanish topics provided by the organization, our bilingual XML dictionary, the Systran machine translation system[5] and the set of aligned noun phrases between English and Spanish.

Topic titles were processed, stopwords and punctuation removed[6] and content words lemmatized before translation using the merged dictionary or the noun phrase bilingual list.

Since the image captions contain structured information, we decided to use it by identifying which query terms could be understood as authors, locations or dates.

3 Structured Search Using Image Caption Fields

3.1 Entities Recognizer

We used a set of simple rules to identify named entities, temporal references and numbers in the queries:

Named entities. Expressions in uppercase wherever uppercase is not prescribed by punctuation rules.

Temporal references. Those ones matching words such as names of weekdays, months or seasons.

Numbers. Those ones matching any numerical expression or words from a given list (e.g. *dos* (2), *cien* (100), *mil* (1,000) ...)

3.2 Structured Search over Image Caption Fields

For each entity located in the Spanish topic titles:

- If it is a named entity, we ask the search engine to find any document containing the entity in the "author" or "location" fields, first in Spanish and

[5] Systran web-based interface available at `http://www.systransoft.com`

[6] In order to adapt the stopword list to this specific task, we included as stopwords *fotografías*, *fotos* (photographs), *retrato* (portrait)...

Table 3. Named entities, temporal references and cardinal numbers located for each topic title

topic #	Entities
1	Retratos de ministros de la iglesia por [$_{NE}$ Thomas Rodger].
2	Fotos de [$_{NE}$ Roma] que fueron tomadas en [$_{DATE}$ Abril] de [$_{CARD}$ 1908].
3	Vistas de la catedral de [$_{NE}$ St. Andrews] por [$_{NE}$ John Fairweather].
4	Hombres vestidos militarmente, [$_{NE}$ George Middlemass Cowie].
5	Buques de pesca en [$_{NE}$ Irlanda] del [$_{NE}$ Norte].
6	Vistas panorámicas en [$_{NE}$ British Columbia], [$_{NE}$ Canadá].
7	Vistas exteriores de templos en [$_{NE}$ Egipto].
8	Edificios de la universidad o colegios universitarios, [$_{NE}$ Cambridge].
9	Fotos de faros ingleses.
10	Calles en plena actividad en [$_{NE}$ Londres].
11	Tarjetas [$_{NE}$ Postales] con múltiples vistas de [$_{NE}$ Bute], [$_{NE}$ Escocia].
12	Desastre ferroviario en el [$_{NE}$ Tay Bridge], [$_{CARD}$ 1879].
13	Torneo del [$_{NE}$ Campeonato Abierto] de golf, [$_{NE}$ St. Andrews] [$_{CARD}$ 1939].
14	Elizabeth la [$_{NE}$ Reina Madre], en su visita a [$_{NE}$ Crail Camp], [$_{CARD}$ 1954].
15	Daños provocados por bombas en la [$_{NE}$ Segunda Guerra Mundial].
16	Fotos de la catedral del [$_{NE}$ York].
17	Vistas de [$_{NE}$ North Street], [$_{NE}$ St. Andrews].
18	Fotos del castillo de [$_{NE}$ Edimburgo] antes de [$_{CARD}$ 1900]
19	Gente marchando o desfilando.
20	Río con un viaducto al fondo.
21	Monumentos a los caídos en la guerra en forma de cruz.
22	Fotos mostrando tradicionales bailarines escoceses.
23	Fotos de cisnes en un lago.
24	Golfistas golpeando con sus palos de golf.
25	Barcos en un canal.

then in English.[7] If the search is non-nil, we assume that the role of the entity is the field in which it was found.

- If it is a cardinal number, we ask the search engine to find any document containing the entity in the "date" field. If the search in non-nil, we assume that the cardinal number represents a date.
- If it is a temporal reference, we check if it is a date, in the same fashion.

3.3 Entities, Dates and Numbers Found in the Queries

In Table 3, we show the entities found for each Spanish topic title. Our recognizer located 31 entities (named entities, temporal references and cardinal numbers), although some of them are incorrect. For instance, on topic 5 *Irlanda* and *Norte* should have been identified as a unique named entity *Irlanda del Norte. Elisabeth,*

[7] We perform the search in both languages because there is no general rule for translating proper names. Entities were translated using Systran because of the lack of proper names in our dictionary.

on topic 14, was not identified as a possible entity. Besides, on topics 11 and 13, expressions such as *Postales* and *Campeonato Abierto* were misidentified as named entities.

Entities such as *Postales*, *Campeonato Abierto*, *Reina Madre* and *Segunda Guerra Mundial* did not represent any author, location or date. In any case, our strategy did not identify them as such either.

Regarding the other located entities, a manual analysis about their roles showed that:

authors. Every possible author (*Thomas Rodger*, *John Fairweather* and *George Middlemass Cowie*) was correctly identified using this strategy.

locations. *Roma*, *Irlanda*, *Norte*, *British Columbia*, *Canadá*, *Egipto*, *Londres*, *Bute*, *Escocia* and *York* were correctly identified. *St. Andrews*, *Cambridge*, *Tay Bridge*, *Crail Camp*, *North Street* and *Edimburgo* were not.

dates. *Abril*, *1908*, *1879*, *1939*, *1954*, *1900*. All dates were identified with this strategy.

Overall, the algorithm is reasonably precise, given the very simple heuristic rules used for detection. But there is still room for improvement using proper Named Entity Recognizers.

4 Results and Discussion

4.1 Submitted Runs

Given the preliminary results discussed in Section 2.2, we decided to use the following strategies in our ImageCLEF experiments:

- Naive baseline using a word by word translation (`UNEDESBASE`). For instance, topic 13 (*Torneo del Campeonato Abierto de Golf, St. Andrews 1939)* produces:
  topic 13: `turn tourney tournament tourney joust tilt championship title open frank open-minded opened overt unconcealed undone up extrovertish unfastened unlatched unlocked unsecured exposed hospitable forthright open-ended unresolved outgoing assailable undefendable undefended unhealed open undo dig head lead blossom unlock spread unfold brighten clear golf st andrews 1939`
- Strong baseline using a structured query, following Pirkola's approach (`UNEDES`). This is the core of the structured query for the next approaches, using INQUERY's synonymy operators:
  topic 13: `#syn (turn tourney) #syn(tournament tourney joust tilt) #syn(championship title) #syn(open frank open-minded opened overt unconcealed undone up extrovertish unfastened unlatched unlocked unsecured exposed hospitable forthright open-ended unresolved outgoing assailable undefendable undefended unhealed) #syn(open undo dig head lead blossom unlock spread unfold brighten clear) golf st andrews 1939`

- Structured query using INQUERY's operators and structured search over captions (UNEDESENT).
  If some entity is located and identified as a possible author name, location or date, we include the structured search over the caption fields. In this case, the search engine will favor those images in whose caption fields *1939* is tagged as a date. So, the following operator is added to the previous query:
  `#field( DDATE #sum( 1939 ) )`
- Structured query using INQUERY's operators and structured search over captions + noun phrases (UNEDESENTNOO and UNEDORENTNOO).
  We detected several errors in the original Spanish query set. These were fixed and sent to ImageCLEF organizers for distribution among other participants. However, for completeness, we submitted the most complex runs both with the original and the fixed query set (UNEDORENTNOO and UNEDESENTNOO, respectively).
  In order to expand the queries, we added the set of noun phrases extrated from the query terms using the "multi-lemma" phrases strategy. For topic 13 and UNEDESENTNOO, the phrases included are:

```
#phrase( golf course manager ) #phrase( world golf championship )
#phrase( world championship tournament ) #phrase( first golf tournament )
#phrase( day after a golf tournament ) #phrase( chiefs into the title )
#phrase( clear the tournament ) #phrase( champions tournament )
#phrase( conference tournament title ) #phrase( day golf tournament )
#phrase( golf tournament last ) #phrase( league golf tournament )
#phrase( tournament of champions ) #phrase( phoenix golf tournament )
#phrase( tennis tournament in st ) #phrase( championship golf course )
#phrase( ups for golf ) #phrase( championships golf tournament )
#phrase( gains after a bond ) #phrase( final of the tournament
of champions ) #phrase( tournament at st ) #phrase( bond gains )
#phrase( title of chief )
```

Summing up, the set of submitted runs and its features are shown in Table 4.

4.2 Results

All five runs obtained results above the average (average MAP for Spanish as query language is 0.30). Our best run, UNEDESENT, was the best Spanish → English submission, 88% of the best monolingual run and 97% of the best cross-language submission (DCU German → English). Our results are shown in Table 5.

Structured queries over image captions (UNEDESENT) obtained an improvement of around 8.3 % with respect to Pirkola's approach (UNEDES). Apparently, a very simple detection of entities can be useful to improve retrieval results using the rich structure of image metadata.

Expansion with noun phrases does not improve over the baseline. The main reason is that our set of aligned noun phrases had been previously extracted from a collection of very different genre (newswire). As shown on section 4.1, the expansion inserted too much noise to get better average results.

Table 4. UNED submitted runs

run	word translation	noun phrases	structured caption
UNEDESBASE	bag of words	X	X
UNEDES	Pirkola	X	X
UNEDESENT	Pirkola	X	√
UNEDESENTNOO	Pirkola	√	√
UNEDORENTNOO	Pirkola	√	√

Table 5. Results for UNED runs

run	MAP	% monolingual
Best monolingual	0.59	-
Best cross-language	0.53	90
Best ES - EN	0.52	88
UNEDESENT	0.52	88
UNEDES	0.48	82
UNEDESENTNOO	0.47	80
UNEDORENTNOO	0.42	72
UNEDESBASE	0.38	64
average	0.30	50.87

Finally, it is worth noticing that our weakest baseline (UNEDESBASE) is about 26% better than the average MAP for the Spanish participants, confirming that a good bilingual resource is at least as important as the CLIR technique being used.

5 Conclusions

In this paper, we have presented two different strategies applied to the ImageCLEF bilingual ad hoc task:

- Expand queries with noun phrases, translating and expanding the queries with noun phrases automatically extracted from a different corpus. This expansion degrades retrieval results in our experiments, indicating that techniques based on bilingual comparable corpora can be useless when the training and test domains are very different.
- Perform structured searches using named entities and dates automatically located in the query. This technique obtains an improvement of 8.3 % with respect to our baseline (Pirkola's approach) and can be easily extended to other searches over structured documents.

In addition, even our simplest baselines have performed above the average, showing that work on merging bilingual dictionaries can be as important as the retrieval strategy in CLIR tasks.

Acknowledgements

This work has been partially supported by a grant from the Spanish Government, project R2D2 (TIC2003-07158-C0401), and UNED Ph.D. grants to Víctor Peinado and Javier Artiles.

References

1. Mandala, R., Tokunaga, T., Tanaka, H.: Combining multiple evidence from different types of thesaurus for query expansion. In: SIGIR '99: Proceedings of the 22nd Annual International ACM SIGIR Conference on Research and Development in Information Retrieval, August 15-19, 1999, Berkeley, CA, USA, ACM (1999) 191–197
2. Smeaton, A.F., Quigley, I.: Experiments on using semantic distances between words in image caption retrieval. In Frei, H.P., Harman, D., Schäuble, P., Wilkinson, R., eds.: Proceedings of the 19th Annual International ACM SIGIR Conference on Research and Development in Information Retrieval, SIGIR'96, August 18-22, 1996, Zurich, Switzerland (Special Issue of the SIGIR Forum), ACM (1996) 174–180
3. López-Ostenero, F., Gonzalo, J., Peñas, A., Verdejo, F.: Noun phrase translations for Cross-Language Document Selection. In Peters, C., Braschler, M., Gonzalo, J., Kluck, M., eds.: Evaluation of Cross-Language Information Retrieval Systems, Second Workshop of the Cross-Language Evaluation Forum, CLEF 2001, Darmstadt, Germany, September 3-4, 2001, Revised Papers. Volume 2406 of Lecture Notes in Computer Science., Springer (2002) 320–331
4. López-Ostenero, F., Gonzalo, J., Peñas, A., Verdejo, F.: Interactive Cross-Language Searching: phrases are better than terms for query formulation and refinement. In Peters, C., Braschler, M., Gonzalo, J., Kluck, M., eds.: Advances in Cross-Language Information Retrieval, CLEF 2002. Volume 2785 of Lecture Notes in Computer Science., Springer (2003)
5. López-Ostenero, F., Gonzalo, J., Verdejo, F.: UNED at iCLEF 2003: Searching Cross-Language Summaries. In: Evaluation of Cross-Language Information Systems, CLEF 2003. Volume 3237 of Lecture Notes in Computer Science., Springer (2004)
6. López-Ostenero, F.: Un sistema interactivo para la búsqueda de información en idiomas desconocidos por el usuario. PhD thesis, Departamento de Lenguajes y Sistemas Informáticos, Universidad Nacional de Educación a Distancia (2002)
7. Miller, G., Beckwith, R., Fellbaum, C., Gross, D., Miller, K.J.: WordNet: An on-line lexical database. International Journal of Lexicography 3(4) (1990)
8. Vossen, P.: Introduction to EuroWordNet. Computers and the Humanities, Special Issue on EuroWordNet (1998)
9. Pirkola, A.: The Effects of Query Structure and Dictionary Setups in Dictionary-Based Cross-Language Information Retrieval. In: Proceedings of SIGIR'98, 21st ACM International Conference on Research and Development in Information Retrieval. (1998) 55–63
10. Callan, J.P., Croft, W.B., Harding, S.M.: The Inquery Retrieval System. In: Proceedings of the Third International Conference on Database and Expert Systems Applications, Springer-Verlag (1992) 78–83

Dublin City University at CLEF 2004: Experiments with the ImageCLEF St. Andrew's Collection

Gareth J.F. Jones, Declan Groves, Anna Khasin, Adenike Lam-Adesina, Bart Mellebeek, and Andy Way

School of Computing, Dublin City University, Dublin 9, Ireland
{gjones, dgroves, akhasin, adenike, bart.mellebeek, away}
@computing.dcu.ie

Abstract. For the CLEF 2004 ImageCLEF St Andrew's Collection task the Dublin City University group carried out three sets of experiments: standard cross-language information retrieval (CLIR) runs using topic translation via machine translation (MT), combination of this run with image matching results from the GIFT/Viper system, and a novel document rescoring approach based on automatic MT evaluation metrics. Our standard MT-based CLIR works well on this task. Encouragingly combination with image matching lists is also observed to produce small positive changes in the retrieval output. However, rescoring using the MT evaluation metrics in their current form significantly reduced retrieval effectiveness.

1 Introduction

Dublin City University's participation in the CLEF 2004 ImageCLEF St Andrew's collection task comprised three sets of experiments for Dutch, French, German, Italian and Spanish topic languages. First, we explored the application of our existing CLIR system used in previous CLEF workshops [1] with topic translation using three web-based translation resources. Second, the output from our standard CLIR system was combined with image matching results provided by the track organisers, generated using the GIFT/Viper system. Finally, we explored a novel approach to rescoring the potentially relevant documents retrieved using our standard system based on automatic machine translation (MT) evaluation metrics.

This paper is organised as follows: Section 2 briefly outlines the details of our standard retrieval system, Section 3 gives results for our experiments using standard MT-based CLIR and combination with the provided GIFT/Viper system image retrieval output, Section 4 reports our results using MT evaluation metrics, and finally Section 5 concludes the paper.

2 CLIR Retrieval System

The basis of our experimental retrieval system is the City University research distribution version of the Okapi system, as used in our previous CLEF partici-

C. Peters et al. (Eds.): CLEF 2004, LNCS 3491, pp. 653–663, 2005.

pation [1]. In this system documents and search topics are processed to remove stopwords from a list of about 260 words, suffix stripped using the Okapi implementation of Porter stemming, and terms are further indexed using a small set of synonyms.

Terms are weighted using the standard BM25 weighting scheme and all runs use our summary-based pseudo relevance feedback (PRF) method [2]. The summary generation method combines Luhn's keyword cluster method, a title terms frequency method, a location/header method and a query-bias method to form an overall significance score for each sentence. Sentences are ranked by significance score and the top ranked ones used to form a document summary. PRF expansion terms are selected from these summaries. Full details of this PRF method are given in [2].

3 Standard CLIR and Text-Image Combination Experimental Results

For all the experiments reported here the Okapi system parameters were selected using the training topics provided for the track. The parameter values were set as follows: $K1 = 1.0$ and $b = 0.5$ for baseline runs and $K1 = 1.5$ and $b = 0.6$ for PRF runs. The 20 top ranked PRF expansion terms from the summaries of the top 5 ranked documents were added to the baseline topic, with the top 20 ranked documents used to rank potential expansion terms for selection. The original topic terms were upweighted by a factor of 3.5 relative to terms introduced by PRF.

Topics were translated into English, the language of the documents, using the following web-based MT systems: Systran (`http://www.systransoft.com/`), SDL (`http://www.freetranslation.com/`) and InterTrans (`http://www.intertrans.com/`). Results are shown for precision at cutoffs of 5, 10, 15 and 20 documents, average precision and total number of relevant documents retrieved. The total number of relevant images available in the document collection for these topics is 829. Monolingual English results are shown for comparison for both baseline results without feedback and with the application of PRF. Baseline CLIR results are given for Systran topic translation, and for PRF and other conditions results are given for the three separate topic translations and a merged union of the translated topics.

3.1 Baseline Runs

Table 1 shows baseline retrieval runs for monolingual English and Systran topic translation without application of PRF. The reduction in average precision for CLIR compared to monolingual IR varies between -15% and -30% with a variation in loss of total relevant documents retrieved of between -76 and -168. There is no clear correlation between the loss in average precision and relevant documents retrieved.

Table 1. Baseline retrieval runs using Systran topic translation

		English	Dutch	French	German	Italian	Spanish
Prec.	5 docs	0.664	0.464	0.488	0.536	0.408	0.384
	10 docs	0.624	0.424	0.488	0.536	0.396	0.416
	15 docs	0.587	0.405	0.451	0.501	0.384	0.381
	20 docs	0.552	0.384	0.418	0.440	0.378	0.362
Av Precision		0.545	0.384	0.427	0.464	0.402	0.383
% chg.		—	-29.5%	-21.7%	-14.9%	-26.2%	-29.7%
Rel. Ret.		774	698	631	695	606	654
chg. Rel. Ret.		—	-76	-143	-79	-168	-120

Table 2. Monolingual runs with application of PRF

		Sentences		
		1S	2S	3S
Prec.	5 docs	0.608	0.600	0.608
	10 docs	0.640	0.620	0.644
	15 docs	0.608	0.592	0.619
	20 docs	0.554	0.550	0.560
Av Precision		0.524	0.546	0.545
Rel. Ret.		809	809	809

3.2 PRF Runs

The text annotations of the images are typically very short, comprising only a few sentences. In developing our PRF system for this retrieval task, we compared our summary-based approach, developed for use with newspaper document archives, with a standard PRF approach selecting terms from complete documents. For news document collections our summary-based PRF method consistently outperforms a document-based approach [2]. Since the documents in the St Andrew's collection are so short, we felt it unlikely that use of document summaries would be useful for PRF. We were a little surprised to find that selecting terms from summaries of even these short documents when using the CLIR training topics worked better than the whole document approach. The summary-based approach is used for all PRF runs reported in this paper.

Table 2 shows monolingual feedback results for document summaries of the top ranked 1, 2 and 3 sentences. It can be seen that there is little change in average precision compared to the baseline result in Table 1. There is an improvement in total relevant documents retrieved, but a reduction in precision at cutoff 5. This result suggests that for monolingual retrieval with short documents and topics, while recall can be improved and average precision maintained, retrieval accuracy problems may be introduced for documents retrieved at high ranks in the baseline run.

Table 3 shows feedback results for each topic language with the three MT systems and the merged translated topics. Spanish results shown in Table 3 are

Table 3. Text retrieval runs with application of PRF

			SDL	INT	ST		MG
Dutch (3S)	Prec.	5 docs	0.520	0.296	0.480		0.504
		10 docs	0.472	0.276	0.500		0.472
		15 docs	0.451	0.264	0.467		0.445
		20 docs	0.398	0.244	0.420		0.402
	Av Precision		0.398	0.273	0.432	(+12.5%)	0.421
	% chg. mono.		-27.0%	-49.9%	-20.7%		-22.8%
	Rel. Ret.		683	637	709	(+11)	791
	chg. Rel. Ret.		-126	-172	-100		-18
French (1S)	Prec.	5 docs	0.456	0.560	0.496		0.432
		10 docs	0.472	0.532	0.496		0.432
		15 docs	0.461	0.512	0.475		0.403
		20 docs	0.412	0.472	0.438		0.376
	Av Precision		0.409	0.466	0.431	(+0.9%)	0.399
	% chg. mono.		-21.9%	-11.1%	-17.7%		-23.9%
	Rel. Ret.		666	707	658	(+27)	695
	chg. Rel. Ret.		-143	-102	-151		-114
German (3S)	Prec.	5 docs	0.592	0.528	0.512		0.648
		10 docs	0.592	0.528	0.540		0.632
		15 docs	0.563	0.475	0.507		0.603
		20 docs	0.498	0.426	0.454		0.528
	Av Precision		0.501	0.468	0.474	(+2.6%)	0.531
	% chg. mono.		-8.1%	-14.1%	-13.0%		-2.6%
	Rel. Ret.		763	804	691	(-4)	804
	chg. Rel. Ret.		-46	-5	-118		-5
Italian (3S)	Prec.	5 docs	0.400	0.280	0.424		0.352
		10 docs	0.400	0.288	0.444		0.384
		15 docs	0.403	0.296	0.429		0.389
		20 docs	0.380	0.292	0.404		0.352
	Av Precision		0.366	0.288	0.438	(+9.0%)	0.351
	% chg. mono.		-30.2%	-47.2%	-19.6%		-35.6%
	Rel. Ret.		633	591	602	(-4)	639
	chg. Rel. Ret.		-176	-218	-207		-170
Spanish (2S)	Prec.	5 docs	0.472	0.312	0.440		0.432
		10 docs	0.484	0.316	0.460		0.448
		15 docs	0.475	0.312	0.445		0.432
		20 docs	0.430	0.290	0.400		0.388
	Av Precision		0.444	0.318	0.406	(+6.0%)	0.398
	% chg. mono.		-18.7%	-41.8%	-25.6%		-27.1%
	Rel. Ret.		767	666	649	(-5)	755
	chg. Rel. Ret.		-42	-143	-160		-54

for the original topic release. PRF results for the later released revised Spanish topics are shown in Table 4. Spanish results in later tables all relate to the original translated topics as used in Table 3. The number of sentences in the

Table 4. Text retrieval runs with application of PRF for revised Spanish topics

			SDL	INT	ST	MG
Spanish (revised) (2S)	Prec.	5 docs	0.520	0.320	0.488	0.440
		10 docs	0.532	0.320	0.492	0.488
		15 docs	0.499	0.312	0.451	0.477
		20 docs	0.464	0.302	0.414	0.422
	Av Precision		0.472	0.312	0.410	0.446
	% chg. mono.		-13.6%	-42.9%	-24.9%	-18.2%
	Rel. Ret.		775	657	647	774
	chg. Rel. Ret.		-34	-152	-162	-35

Table 5. Data fusion retrieval runs with PRF

		Dutch (3S)	French (1S)	German (3S)	Italian (3S)	Spanish (2S)
Prec.	5 docs	0.360	0.480	0.512	0.376	0.392
	10 docs	0.324	0.476	0.516	0.352	0.408
	15 docs	0.293	0.451	0.488	0.344	0.384
	20 docs	0.264	0.430	0.444	0.328	0.342
Av Precision		0.284	0.426	0.445	0.327	0.376
% chg.		-47.9%	-18.7%	-18.3%	-40.0%	-31.1%
Rel. Ret.		742	712	793	651	747
chg. Rel. Ret.		-67	-97	-16	-158	-62

summary for each topic language is shown in the left column (xS). This was selected for each language pair using the training topics. The percentage differences shown here are relative to the monolingual results for PRF using the same number of summary sentences. For Systran, the difference relative to the baseline result shown in Table 1 is shown adjacent to the average precision and total relevant documents retrieved results. Comparing the runs for the Systran translated topics, we can see that PRF produces an improvement in average precision for each language pair. There is no clear trend for relevant document recall, a small improvement is observed for Dutch and French, and a small decrease for the other languages. Comparing retrieval effectiveness for the alternative topic translations, it can be seen that different systems produce the best average precision for different language pairs, although in general InterTrans is the least effective. Results for the merged topics are rather mixed. It was hoped that the increased term coverage of the merged topics would improve recall and aid precision; this does happen in some cases, but in others it reduces effectiveness. Further investigation is needed into specific cases of success and failure to see if any general conclusions can be made.

The results in Table 3 show that the effect of merging the three separate topic translations is variable. An alternative method of combining multiple topic translations in a CLIR system is to combine the output of the three separate runs by merging the individual ranked lists in a process of data fusion. We

Table 6. Retrieval results using image matching output from the GIFT/Viper system

Prec.	5 docs	0.320
	10 docs	0.196
	15 docs	0.144
	20 docs	0.114
Av Precision		0.091
Rel. Ret.		142

have previously successfully used data fusion to combine the output of multiple topic translations in CLIR for news retrieval in CLEF 2001 [4]. Table 5 shows the results of merging the output from our three separate translation runs with PRF using a simple summation of the matching scores. It can be seen that these results are in all cases, except French, lower with respect to average precision than the merged translated topic results in Table 3. In most cases there is also a small reduction in the total number of relevant documents retrieved. However, the merged result for French in Table 3 is itself unusual, since the merged topic average precision is lower than that of any of the individual translations. Clearly simple list merging data fusion is not effective for this task. Determining the reason for this result requires further investigation.

3.3 Text and Image Combination Runs

The St Andrew's documents are composed of images and text annotations as described in [3]. The search topics are similarly composed of a search image and text description. The experiments in the previous sections are based only on text retrieval. It is interesting to consider whether retrieval effectiveness might be improved by making use of the image data. The track organizers provided a set of image matching retrieval results generated using the GIFT/Viper image retrieval system. For each sample topic image, the top ranked 500 images from the test collection were provided together with their matching scores. Table 6 shows retrieval results using only these GIFT/Viper results. These results are not particularly good, with only a small proportion of the relevant documents having been retrieved. However, the GIFT/Viper system does successfully retrieve a number of relevant images, and precision at high ranks is reasonable, indicating that where relevant images have been retrieved, this can be achieved with good precision. Probably the topic images match well with relevant images similar to themselves, but fail to locate other relevant documents with rather different images. The GIFT/Viper system was not tuned for this task, so these results form a lower bound on its potential effectiveness for this task.

We wanted to see if these image results could usefully be combined with out existing text results. Table 7 shows results for a simple sum data fusion combination of the matching score for the PRF runs shown in Table 3 and the GIFT/Viper runs provided by the track organizers. The merged score $merge\_score(j)$ of document j is formed as follows,

$$merge\_score(j) = 1.5 \times text\_score(j) + 1.3 \times GIFT/Viper\_score(j)$$

Table 7. Retrieval runs fusing PRF runs with standard GIFT/Viper image matching results

			SDL	INT	ST	MG
Dutch	Prec.	5 docs	0.504	0.272	0.480	0.488
		10 docs	0.480	0.276	0.508	0.464
		15 docs	0.448	0.264	0.469	0.445
		20 docs	0.396	0.242	0.422	0.398
	Av Precision		0.394	0.273	0.433	0.419
	Rel. Ret.		638	637	709	791
French	Prec.	5 docs	0.464	0.552	0.488	0.416
		10 docs	0.472	0.520	0.496	0.428
		15 docs	0.456	0.512	0.472	0.405
		20 docs	0.414	0.470	0.436	0.380
	Av Precision		0.407	0.466	0.428	0.399
	Rel. Ret.		666	707	658	695
German	Prec.	5 docs	0.600	0.528	0.528	0.664
		10 docs	0.604	0.524	0.548	0.636
		15 docs	0.557	0.472	0.504	0.594
		20 docs	0.502	0.428	0.460	0.530
	Av Precision		0.501	0.467	0.474	0.532
	Rel. Ret.		763	804	691	804
Italian	Prec.	5 docs	0.400	0.280	0.424	0.344
		10 docs	0.400	0.288	0.440	0.392
		15 docs	0.400	0.304	0.427	0.387
		20 docs	0.380	0.290	0.402	0.352
	Av Precision		0.369	0.289	0.437	0.351
	Rel. Ret.		633	591	602	639
Spanish	Prec.	5 docs	0.464	0.296	0.432	0.424
		10 docs	0.472	0.324	0.452	0.444
		15 docs	0.461	0.299	0.429	0.432
		20 docs	0.428	0.288	0.392	0.384
	Av Precision		0.441	0.316	0.405	0.397
	Rel. Ret.		767	666	649	755

The scalar constants used in this combination were again selected using the training topics. The results in Table 7 are only slightly different from the text-only PRF runs in Table 3. However, some potentially important positives can be taken from this. First, in image retrieval it is often found that adding image matching information does not improve over text caption-only retrieval. For our experiments in some cases the image matching score does help, albeit only marginally. Second, the GIFT/Viper system was not adjusted for the St Andrew's collection task, suggesting that a better image matching run should be possible with some task-specific training of the image matching process. Given the relatively small number of relevant documents retrieved by the GIFT/Viper system, it is encouraging that it does not exert a significant negative impact on the text retrieval results.

4 Machine Translation Quality Metric Runs

For our final set of experiments we explored the use of a novel strategy for IR evaluation using automatic translation metrics. In recent years, several automatic MT evaluation methods have been proposed as a supplement to, or, in certain cases, a replacement for costly human MT evaluations [5][6][7][8]. These automatic evaluation methods rely on the idea that the quality of an MT output can be measured by its similarity to that of a professional human translation. With each of the currently available automatic evaluation methods, this similarity is measured using a word-error metric between the sentences in the MT-produced text output and the sentences in one or more human reference translations. The success of automatic MT evaluation depends largely on the amount of available comparable material and on the number of human reference translations, with more reference translations resulting in a more accurate measure of system performance.

In order to be able to use these metrics to calculate the similarity between a topic and a document in an IR system, in a novel procedure we regard the original document and the MT-translated topic as translations of an unknown source text, as is shown in Figure 1.

In the first step, we extracted information from the headline and description sections of the original document text, as these sections contain the most relevant information pertaining to the documents. The same three sets of topic translations were used as in the previous experiments. The topic translations and documents were pre-processed to remove stopwords, capitalisation and punctuation, which allowed us to retain the most meaningful components of the text.

If we think of the topic translations as human reference translations, it is possible to measure the accuracy of the would-be "machine translations" (the documents) using automatic MT evaluation metrics. The best "machine translation" is the translation with the lowest word-error score with regard to the

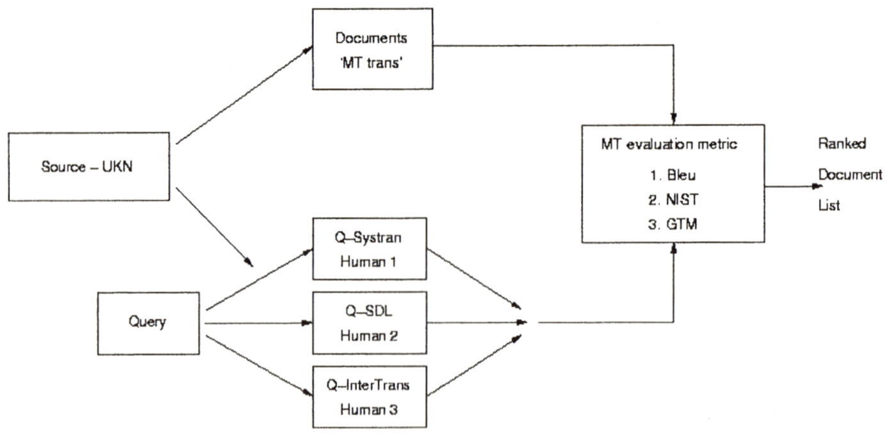

Fig. 1. Document scoring based on MT Evaluation metrics

reference translations. The goal of our experiment was to find out to what extent the best "machine translation" corresponded with a relevant document.

Experiments with the development topics showed that best results were obtained with a combination of two existing MT evaluation methods (NIST and GTM) and an adaptation of the BLEU evaluation metric. BLEU ranks different MT output texts based a combination of an N-gram similarity score and a sentence brevity penalty with respect to a corpus of human reference translations. The BLEU evaluation script was adapted in two ways. First, we eliminated the sentence brevity penalty. The original BLEU metric penalizes short sentences to avoid the possibility that very short segments such as "the" would receive a maximum score when compared to any sentence containing "the". This penalty is clearly not relevant for the retrieval task at hand. A second modification to the script consisted of allowing a non-zero BLEU score, regardless of the fact that for one or more of the N-gram categories (unigram to 4-gram), no positive matches were found between the MT output and human reference translations.

The NIST metric differs from BLEU with respect to both the co-occurrence score and the sentence brevity penalty. The NIST metric alters the co-occurrence score in favour of lower order N-grams (i.e. low trigrams or quadrigram matches play less of a role in the overall score) and more informative N-grams (i.e. N-grams that occur less frequently receive a higher weight). The sentence brevity penalty used by NIST is less severe than the one used by BLEU for sentences with small variations with respect to the reference translation.

GTM allows the calculation of standard precision and recall scores for automatically produced translations. It also calculates an f-measure score, which combines both the precision and recall scores for a given translation. It is this f-measure score, along with the NIST and adapted BLEU scores, that we used in our automatic ranking of the documents.

For our retrieval experiments the translated topics were ranked against the top 1000 documents retrieved for each topic using the text-only PRF approach described in the previous section. We used a summation of the NIST, f-measure and adapted BLEU scores to rescore the topic-document matches. We carried out two sets of experiments. In the first, we evaluated the retrieved document list against only one reference translation, as produced by each of the three online MT systems, giving us three resulting ranking lists of documents for each topic. In the second set of experiments we merged the translated topics, using the three different translations of the topic as three different reference translations.

Table 8 shows the results of document rescoring using MT evaluation metrics. Comparing these results to those using standard PRF methods in the earlier tables, it can be seen that the MT evaluation metrics are not effective for IR scoring in their present form for these languages. The main goal of our experiments was not to substantially improve the best available Image Retrieval methods, but to investigate a novel idea for IR of treating topic documents and translated user topics as comparable translations of an unknown source text. Clearly based on the results shown here we need to explore further whether this approach can be adapted successfully for IR applications. Nonetheless, if our best score via

Table 8. Retrieval runs with pseudo relevance feedback

			SDL	INT	ST	MG
Dutch	Prec.	5 docs	0.096	0.184	0.128	0.128
		10 docs	0.116	0.172	0.124	0.140
		15 docs	0.101	0.168	0.123	0.123
		20 docs	0.100	0.154	0.120	0.114
	Av Precision		0.105	0.127	0.141	0.121
	Rel. Ret.		638	637	709	791
French	Prec.	5 docs	0.104	0.128	0.096	0.088
		10 docs	0.128	0.120	0.128	0.112
		15 docs	0.133	0.115	0.125	0.101
		20 docs	0.130	0.106	0.122	0.100
	Av Precision		0.107	0.110	0.117	0.100
	Rel. Ret.		666	707	658	695
German	Prec.	5 docs	0.160	0.208	0.120	0.184
		10 docs	0.164	0.172	0.124	0.148
		15 docs	0.155	0.189	0.128	0.168
		20 docs	0.144	0.190	0.128	0.178
	Av Precision		0.146	0.169	0.132	0.148
	Rel. Ret.		763	804	691	804
Italian	Prec.	5 docs	0.168	0.128	0.160	0.136
		10 docs	0.132	0.132	0.140	0.112
		15 docs	0.133	0.139	0.128	0.109
		20 docs	0.126	0.128	0.120	0.104
	Av Precision		0.132	0.119	0.118	0.108
	Rel. Ret.		633	591	602	639
Spanish	Prec.	5 docs	0.128	0.120	0.128	0.128
		10 docs	0.140	0.140	0.140	0.132
		15 docs	0.157	0.128	0.149	0.133
		20 docs	0.160	0.128	0.156	0.131
	Av Precision		0.145	0.111	0.128	0.131
	Rel. Ret.		767	666	649	755

this method (0.190 German, Intertrans, cutoff 20 docs) is compared to the set of results for (say) Russian, where the second best score was 0.147 [3], this may indicate that over novel method is potentially of greater use for "less-widely used" languages, especially in a bootstrapping phase before more standard IR techniques are employed.

5 Conclusions and Further Work

Our experiments for the CLEF 2004 ImageCLEF have demonstrated that our standard CLIR method works effectively for the short text documents in the St Andrew's collection, and further that there is potential for improvement in retrieval effectiveness from the use of image matching in cross-language image retrieval. Experiments using MT evaluation metrics for scoring CLIR have so far not been successful, but we intend to explore alternative means of applying this idea to see whether it can be used usefully in CLIR, especially for less-widely used or studied language pairs.

References

[1] Lam-Adesina, A. M., and Jones, G. J. F.: Exeter at CLEF 2003: Experiments with Machine Translation for Monolingual, Bilingual and Multilingual Retrieval. In Proceedings of Fourth Workshop of the Cross-Language Evaluation Forum (CLEF 2003), Peters, C., Gonzalo, J., Braschler, M., and Kluck, M., (Eds.), Lecture Notes in Computer Science (LNCS 3237), Springer, Heidelberg, Germany, pages 271-285, 2004.

[2] Lam-Adesina, A. M., and Jones, G. J. F.: Applying Summarization Techniques for Term Selection in Relevance Feedback. In Proceedings of the 24th Annual International ACM SIGIR, pages 1-9, New Orleans, ACM, 2001.

[3] Clough, P., Müller, H., and Sanderson, M.: The CLEF Cross Language Image Retrieval Track (ImageCLEF) 2004. In Proceedings of the Fifth Workshop of the Cross-Language Evaluation Forum (CLEF 2004), Peters, Clough, P., Gonzalo, J., Jones, G., Kluck, M., and Magnini, B. (Eds), Lecture Notes in Computer Science (LNCS), Springer, Heidelberg, Germany (in print), 2005.

[4] Jones, G. J. F., and Lam-Adesina, A. M.: Exeter at CLEF 2001: Experiments with Machine Translation for Bilingual Retrieval. In Proceedings of the Second Workshop of the Cross-Language Information Evaluation (CLEF 2001), Peters, C., Braschler, M., Gonzalo, J., and Kluck, M. (Eds.), Lecture Notes in Computer Science (LNCS 2406), Springer, Heidelberg, Germany, pages 59-77, Darmstadt, Germany, 2001.

[5] K. Papineni, K., Roukos, S., Ward, T., and Zhu, W.-J.: Bleu: a method for automatic evaluation of machine translation. In Proceedings of the 40th Annual Meeting of the Association for Computational Linguistics, pages 311-318, Philadelphia, USA, 2002.

[6] Doddington, G.: Automatic Evaluation of Machine Translation Quality Using N-gram Co-Occurrence Statistics. Human Language Technology: Notebook Proceedings: 128-132. San Diego, 2002.

[7] General Text Matcher `http://nlp.cs.nyu.edu/GTM/`

[8] NIST's MT Evaluation Toolkit `http://www.nist.gov/speech/tests/mt/resources/scoring.htm`

From Text to Image: Generating Visual Query for Image Retrieval

Wen-Cheng Lin, Yih-Chen Chang, and Hsin-Hsi Chen

Department of Computer Science and Information Engineering,
National Taiwan University,
Taipei, Taiwan
{denislin, ycchang}@nlg.csie.ntu.edu.tw; hhchen@csie.ntu.edu.tw

Abstract. This paper explores the uses of visual features for cross-language access to an image collection. An approach which transforms textual queries into visual representations is proposed. The relationships between text and images are mined. We employ the mined relationships to construct visual queries from textual ones. The retrieval results using textual and visual queries are combined to generate the final ranked list. We conducted English monolingual and Chinese-English cross-language retrieval experiments. The performances are quite good. The average precision of English monolingual textual run is 0.6304. The performance of cross-lingual retrieval is about 70% of monolingual retrieval. Comparatively, the gain of the generated visual query is not significant. If only appropriate query terms are selected to generate visual query, retrieval performance could be increased.

1 Introduction

Multimedia data has an explosive growth nowadays. People need effective and efficient tools to help them find the required information from a huge amount of multimedia data. Text retrieval, image retrieval, video retrieval, spoken data retrieval, music retrieval, etc., have been widely studied in recent years. Several evaluation tasks are organized to enhance research in multimedia information retrieval technologies. TREC 2001 and 2002 proposed a video track to investigate technological developments like automatic segmentation, indexing, and content-based retrieval of digital video. Beginning in 2003, TRECVID[1] became an independent evaluation. In CLEF 2003, ImageCLEF[2] was organized to promote research in cross-language image retrieval.

Two types of approach, content-based and text-based approaches, are usually adopted in multimedia retrieval. Content-based approaches use low-level features to represent multimedia objects. In image retrieval, low-level visual features such as color, texture and shape are often used. Text-based approaches use collateral text to describe the objects. Text can describe the content of multimedia objects in detail. Several hybrid approaches [14, 15, 16] that integrate visual and textual information have been proposed. Experimental results showed that the optimal technique depends

[1] http://www.itl.nist.gov/iaui/894.02/projects/trecvid/
[2] http://ir.shef.ac.uk/imageclef2004/

C. Peters et al. (Eds.): CLEF 2004, LNCS 3491, pp. 664 – 675, 2005.

on the query. The combined approach could outperform text- and content-based approaches in some cases.

In ImageCLEF 2003, we adopted text-based approaches to deal with the Chinese-English cross-language image retrieval problem [10]. Textual image captions were used to represent images. Query translation was adopted to unify the languages in queries and image captions. Named entities, not included in dictionary, were translated using a similarity-based backward transliteration model. Experimental results showed that using similarity-based backward transliteration increased retrieval performances.

In this paper, we explore the uses of visual features for cross-language image retrieval. We propose an approach that transforms textual queries into visual representations. We mine the relationships between text and images. Visual queries are constructed from textual queries using the mined relationships. In addition to textual index, a visual index is built for retrieving images by visual query. The retrieval results using textual and visual queries are combined to generate the final ranked list. The rest of this paper is organized as follows. Section 2 discusses translingual transmedia information access. Section 3 models the relationships between text and images. The method of generating visual representation of textual query is introduced. Section 4 shows the query translation methods. Section 5 shows how to integrate textual and visual information. Section 6 discusses the experimental results. Finally, we conclude our work in Section 7.

2 Translingual Transmedia Information Retrieval

Multimedia data consist of different types of media. Some media are language dependent, e.g. text and speech, while the others are language independent, e.g. image and music. How to represent multimedia data is an important issue in multimedia retrieval. If queries and documents are in different types of media, media transformation is needed to unify the representations of queries and documents. If queries and documents are represented by text, but are in different languages, language translation is also needed. The combination of media transformation and language translation is shown in Figure 1.

A horizontal direction indicates language translation, and a vertical direction indicates media transformation. There are several alternatives to unify the media forms and languages of queries and documents. We can transform queries into the same representation as documents, transform documents into the same representation as queries, or transform both of them into an intermediate representation. Take spoken cross-language access to image collection via captions as an example [9]. The data that users request are images while the query is in terms of speech. Images are language independent, thus are in part E of Figure 1. Spoken queries are in part A. Images are represented by captions in a language different from that of query. In this way, the medium of the target document is transformed into text, i.e., from E to D. We can transform spoken queries in source language into text using a speech recognition system, then translate the textual queries into target language and retrieve documents in target language. The transformation path is from A to B, then from B to D.

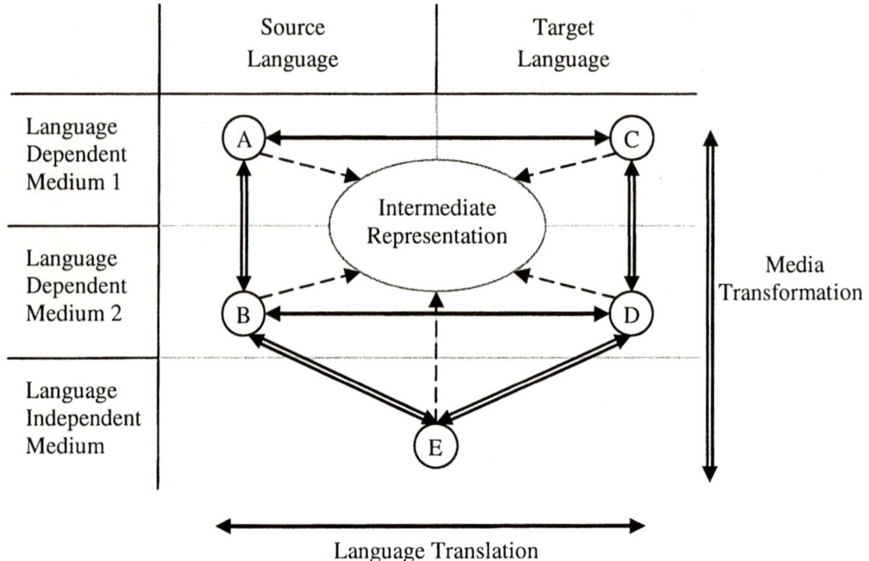

Fig. 1. Media transformation and language translation

To deal with text queries to image collections, using text descriptions to represent images is an approach to unify the representations of queries and images. Image captions that describe the content of images are good material to represent images. In this way, traditional information retrieval systems can be used to retrieve captions. Although using text descriptions to represent images is effective, manually assigned captions are not always available. Automatic annotation has been studied to generate text descriptions of images automatically [5, 6, 7, 11].

An alternative approach to unify representations is transforming textual queries into visual representations, i.e., from B to E in Figure 1. Content-based approaches can be used to retrieve images using the visual representations of queries. In cross-language information retrieval, translation ambiguity and target polysemy problems have to be tackled in the translation process. If a word is not translated correctly, we cannot capture the correct meaning of the word in its context. If the translation is polysemous, the undesired documents that contain the translation with other senses could be reported even if the translation is the correct one. Using visual queries could avoid these problems. Visual query shows images that user is looking for, and is used to retrieve images directly. In next section, we introduce how to generate visual query from textual query.

3 Visual Representation of Text

Given a set of images with text descriptions, we can learn the relationships between images and text. For an image, each word in its description may relate to a portion of this image. If we divide an image into several smaller parts, e.g. blocks or regions, we could link the words to the corresponding parts. This is analogous to word alignment in sentence aligned parallel corpus. If we treat the visual representation of the image as a language, the textual description and visual parts of an image is an aligned sentence. The correlations between the vocabularies of two languages can be learned from the aligned sentences. In automatic annotation task, several approaches are proposed to model the correlations of text and visual representation, and generate text descriptions from images. Mori, Takahashi and Oka [11] divided images into grids, and then the grids of all images are clustered. Co-occurrence information is used to estimate the probability of each word for each cluster. Duygulu, *et al.* [5] used blobs to represent images. First, images are segmented into regions using a segmentation algorithm like Normalized Cuts [13]. All regions are clustered and each cluster is assigned a unique label (blob token). The EM algorithm is used to construct a probability table that links blob tokens with word tokens. Jeon, Lavrenko, and Manmatha [6] proposed a cross-media relevance model (CMRM) to learn the joint distribution of blobs and words. They further proposed continuous-space relevance model (CRM) that learned the joint probability of words and regions, rather than blobs [7].

As in Duygulu, *et al.* [5], we use blobs as the visual representation of images. Blobworld [2] is used to segment an image into regions. The regions of all images are clustered into 2,000 clusters by the K-means clustering algorithm. The correlations between caption words and blobs are learned from a set of images with text descriptions. Mutual Information (MI) is adopted to measure the strength of correlation between an image blob and a word. Let x be a word and y be an image blob. The Mutual Information of x and y is defined as follow.

$$MI(x,y) = p(x,y) \times \log \frac{p(x,y)}{p(x)p(y)} \tag{1}$$

where $p(x)$ is the occurrence probability of word x in text descriptions,
$p(y)$ is the occurrence probability of blob y in image blobs, and
$p(x,y)$ is the probability that x and y occur in the same image.

Given a word w_i, we generate relative blobs according the learned MI. We can set a threshold to select blobs. The blobs whose MI values with w_i exceed the threshold are associated to w_i. The generated blobs can be regarded as the visual representation of w_i. In this way, a transmedia (word-blob) dictionary which is similar to bilingual dictionary is established.

4 Query Translation

In these experiments we used the Chinese query set as source queries. Chinese queries are translated into English to retrieve English captions of images. We adopted the translation approach used previously in ImageCLEF 2003 to translate Chinese queries [10]. First, the Chinese queries are segmented by a word recognition system and then tagged by a POS tagger. Named entities are identified [3] and for each Chinese query term, we find its translations using a Chinese-English bilingual dictionary. The bilingual dictionary is integrated from four resources, including the LDC Chinese-English dictionary, Denisowski's CEDICT[3], BDC Chinese-English dictionary v2.2[4] and a dictionary used in query translation in MTIR project [1]. The dictionary contains 200,037 words, where a word may have more than one translation. If a query term has more than one translation, we use the first-two-highest-frequency method to select translations. The first two translations with the highest frequency of occurrence in the English image captions are considered as the target language query terms.

For named entities that are not included in the dictionary, we use a similarity-based backward transliteration scheme to translate them. First, we adopt transformation rules [4] to identify the name and keyword parts of a name. The keyword parts are general nouns, e.g., "湖" (lake), "河" (river) and "橋" (bridge), and translated by dictionary lookup as described above. The name parts are transliterations of foreign names, and are transliterated into English in the following way.

(1) The personal names and the location names in the English image captions are extracted. We collect a list of English names that contains 50,979 personal names and 19,340 location names. If a term in the captions can be found in the name list, it is extracted. In total 3,599 names are extracted from the image captions.
(2) For each Chinese name, 300 candidates are selected from the 3,599 English names by using an IR-based candidate filter. The document set is the International Phonetic Alphabet (IPA) representations of the 3,599 English names. Each name is treated as one document. The query is the IPA representation of the Chinese name. The phonemes of the Chinese name are expanded with their most co-transliterated English phonemes. The co-transliterated Chinese-English phoneme pairs are trained from a Chinese-English personal name corpus, which has 51,114 pairs of Chinese transliterated names and the corresponding English original names. Mutual Information is adopted to measure the strength of co-transliteration of two phonemes. A Chinese phoneme x is expanded with the English phonemes that have positive MI values with x. The augmented phonemes are weighted by *MI(x, y)/the number of augmented terms*. After retrieving, top 300 English names are reported as candidates.
(3) The similarities of the Chinese name and the 300 candidates are computed at phoneme level. First, the Chinese name and candidate names are transformed into IPA. For each candidate word, the score of optimal alignment, i.e., the alignment with the highest score, between its IPA string and the IPA string of the Chinese name is computed as their similarity score. Given two strings S_1 and S_2, let Σ be the alphabet of S_1 and S_2, $\Sigma'=\{\Sigma, `\_'\}$, where '_' stands for space. Space could be inserted into S_1 and S_2 such that they are of equal length and denoted as S_1' and S_2'. S_1' and S_2' are aligned when every character in either string has a one-to-one mapping to a character or space in the other string. The similarity score of an alignment is measured by the following formula.

$$Score = \sum_{i=1}^{l} s(S_1'(i), S_2'(i)) \qquad (2)$$

where $s(a, b)$ is the similarity score between characters a and b in Σ',

[3] The dictionary is available at http://www.mandarintools.com/cedict.html
[4] The BDC dictionary is developed by the Behavior Design Corporation (http://www.bdc.com.tw)

$S'(i)$ is the ith character in the string S', and
l is the length of S_1' and S_2'.

The similarity score $s(a, b)$ is automatically learned from a bilingual name corpus [8]. After the similarities are computed, the top 6 candidates of the highest similarities are considered as the translations of the Chinese name.

5 Combining Textual and Visual Information

As described in Section 1, there are two types of approaches to retrieve images: content-based and text-based approaches,. Content-based approaches use low-level features to represent images, while text-based approaches use collateral texts to describe images. Given an image collection, we can build two kinds of index for image retrieval. One is textual index of captions; the other one is visual index of images. In our experiments, we use blobs as the visual representation of images. Images are segmented into regions at first, and then the regions of all images are clustered. Each cluster is assigned a unique label. Each image is represented by the blobs that its regions belong to. We can treat blobs as a language in which each blob token is a word. In this way, we can use text retrieval system to index and retrieve images using blobs language. In the experiments, both textual index and visual index are built by Okapi IR system [12].

Given a textual query, we can retrieve images using a textual index. In addition to textual information, we can generate a visual representation of the textual query to retrieve images using the visual index. The retrieval results of text-based and content-based approaches are merged to generate the final results. For each image, the similarity scores of textual and visual retrieval are normalized and combined using linear combination. In the ImageCLEF topic set, each topic also contains an example image. The example image can be used as a visual query to retrieve images. The example image is represented as blobs, then is submitted to IR system to retrieve images using the visual index. The retrieval result can be combined with the results of the textual query and generated visual query using linear combination.

6 Experimental Results

In the experiments, both the textual and visual indexes were built using the Okapi IR system. For the textual index, the caption text, <HEADLINE> and <CATEGORIES> sections of English captions were used for indexing. For visual index, the blob tokens of each image were indexed. The weighting function used was BM25. Chinese queries were used as source queries. Query translation was adopted to unify the languages used in queries and captions and visual queries were generated from Chinese queries. In order to learn the correlations between Chinese words and blob tokens, image captions were translated into Chinese by SYSTRAN[5] system.

We submitted four Chinese-English cross-lingual runs and one English monolingual run to ImageCLEF 2004. For the English monolingual run, only textual queries were used. In the four cross-lingual runs we compared using the supplied example image or

[5] http://www.systransoft.com/

not and using the generated visual query or not. The details of the cross-lingual runs are described as follows.

(1) **NTU-adhoc-CE-T-W**
This run used only textual queries to retrieve images. The translation method described in Section 4 was used to translate Chinese queries into English and retrieve images using textual index.

(2) **NTU-adhoc-CE-T-WI**
This run used both the textual and generated visual queries. We used nouns, verbs, and adjectives in the textual query to generate blobs, the generated visual query. Named entities were not used to generate blobs. For each term, the top 30 blobs with MI value exceed a threshold (0.01) were selected as its visual representation. The textual query used the textual index and the generated visual query used the visual index to retrieve images. For each image, the similarity scores of textual and visual retrieval were normalized and linearly combined using weights 0.9 and 0.1 for the textual and visual runs respectively. The top 1000 images with highest combined scores were taken as the final results.

(3) **NTU-adhoc-CE-T-WE**
This run used the textual query and example image. The example image was represented as blobs. The textual query used textual index and example image used visual index to retrieve images. For each image, the similarity scores of textual and visual retrieval were normalized and linearly combined using weights 0.7 and 0.3 for textual and example image runs respectively.

(4) **NTU-adhoc-CE-T-WEI**
This run used the textual query, generated visual query, and example image. Each topic had three retrieval runs. For each image, the similarity scores of the three runs were normalized and linearly combined using weights 0.7, 0.2, and 0.1 for textual query, example image, and generated visual query runs, respectively.

The performances of official runs are shown in Table 1. We found that we made a mistake when building the textual index. Long captions were truncated, thus some words were not indexed. After fixing the error, we ran the experiments again. The performance of the unofficial runs is shown in Table 2. From Table 2, the performance of monolingual retrieval is good. The average precision of the monolingual run is 0.6304. The cross-lingual runs also have good performances which are the top 4 Chinese-English runs. When using textual query only, the average precision of run NTU-CE-T-W-new is 0.4395, which is 69.72% of monolingual retrieval. Comparing to the results using ImageCLEF 2003 test set, the performance of this year is better. In ImageCLEF 2003 test set, the performance of Chinese-English cross-lingual textual run is 55.56% of English monolingual run when using intersection strict relevance set. One of the reasons is that several named entities are not translated into Chinese in Chinese query set of ImageCLEF 2004. These English names don't need to be translated when translating queries, thus there is no translation error. There are six topics, i.e., Topic 1, 3, 4, 11, 12, and 14, containing original English named entities. Total three of these topics, i.e., Topic 1, 12 and 14, have an average precision higher than 40%. The average precisions of each query are shown in Figure 2.

Combining textual query and example image, average precision is increased to 0.4589. When using example image only to retrieve images, the average precision is

0.0523 which is contributed mostly by example image itself. In the result list of example image run, the top one entry is the example image itself and is relevant to the topic except Topic 17 (the example image of Topic 17 is not in the *pisec-total* relevant set of Topic 17). This makes the example image have a high score after combining the results of the textual query and example image runs.

Table 1. Results of official runs

Run	Merging Weight			Average Precision
	Textual Query	Example Image	Generated Visual Query	
NTU-adhoc-CE-T-W	1.0	-	-	0.3977
NTU-adhoc-CE-T-WI	0.9	-	0.1	0.3969
NTU-adhoc-CE-T-WE	0.7	0.3	-	0.4171
NTU-adhoc-CE-T-WEI	0.7	0.2	0.1	0.4124
NTU-adhoc-EE-T-W				0.5463

Table 2. Performances of unofficial runs

Run	Merging Weight			Average Precision
	Textual Query	Example Image	Generated Visual Query	
NTU-CE-T-W-new	1.0	-	-	0.4395
NTU-CE-T-WI-new	0.9	-	0.1	0.4409
NTU-CE-T-WE-new	0.7	0.3	-	0.4589
NTU-CE-T-WEI-new	0.7	0.2	0.1	0.4545
NTU-EE-T-W-new				0.6304

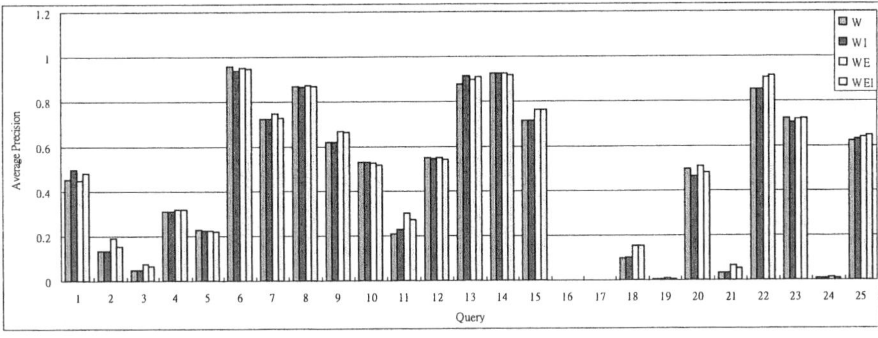

Fig. 2. Average precisions of each topic in unofficial cross-lingual runs

In runs NTU-CE-T-WI-new and NTU-CE-T-WEI-new, the contribution of the generated visual query is not clear. When using generated visual query only to retrieve images, the average precision is only 0.0103. The performance is average across 24 topics, since Topic 10 doesn't generate any blob. The poor performance of the generated visual query run does not help to increase final retrieval performance. Although the over all performance is not good, there are 8 topics gaining better performances after combining textual query and generated visual query runs. These topics have better performances than the others using the generated visual query.

The performance of the generated visual query run does not meet our expectations. There are several factors which affect the performance of visual query. First, the performance of image segmentation is not good enough. The objects in an image can't be segmented perfectly. Furthermore, the majority of images in the St. Andrews image collection are in black and white. This makes image segmentation more difficult. Second, the performance of clustering affects the performance of the blobs-based approach. If image regions that are not similar enough are clustered together, this cluster (blob) may have several different meanings. This is analogous to the polysemy problem.

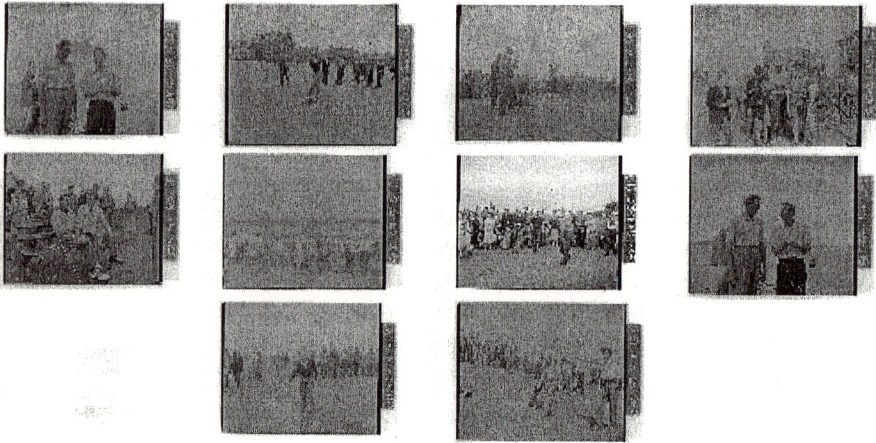

Fig. 3. The top 10 images of Topic 13 in generated visual query run using manually selected terms

The third factor is the quality of training data. The St. Andrews image collection has only English captions. In order to learn the correlations between Chinese words and blob tokens, image captions were translated into Chinese by SYSTRAN system. However, there are many translation errors that affect the correctness of learned correlations. We conducted a monolingual experiment using English captions to learn the correlations between text and images. Visual queries were generated from English queries. The results of English textual run and English generated visual query run were combined. The average precision is increased from 0.6304 to 0.6561. We can see that the generated visual query helps to increase retrieval performance when using good training data that has no translation error. Another problem is that we used all words in captions to learn correlations. Many words, e.g. stopwords, date expressions, and names of photographers, are not relative to the content of images. These words should be excluded in training stage.

The fourth problem is which word in a query should be used to generate a visual query. In the experiments, nouns, verbs, and adjectives in query were used to generate a visual query. While not all of these words are relative to the content of an image or discriminative, e.g. "照片" (picture). Thus, "照片 (picture) should not be used to generate a visual query. We conducted an experiment that manually selected query terms to generate visual query. For each query, we selected the most important terms, i.e. the focus, of the query. There are 7 topics that don't generate any blob. The average precision across 18 topics is 0.0146. After the result of manually selecting run merging with textual query run, the performance is slightly increased to 0.4427.

The performance of the manually selecting run is better than of the generated visual query run, but is still not good enough. We note that in some topics the retrieved images are not relevant to the topics, while they are relevant to the query terms that are used to generate visual query. Take Topic 13, i.e., 1939年聖安德魯斯高爾夫球公開賽 (The Open Championship golf tournament, St. Andrews 1939), as an example, "高爾夫球" (golf) and "公開賽" (Open Championship) are chosen to generate visual query. The top 10 images shown in Figure 3 are all about the Open Championship golf tournament, but are not the one held in 1939. It shows that using visual information only is not enough, integrating textual information is needed.

7 Conclusion

In this paper, we explored the help of visual features to cross-language image retrieval. We proposed an approach that transforms textual queries into visual representations. The relationships between text and images are mined. We use blobs as a visual representation of image and the textual description and visual representation of an image is treated as an aligned sentence. Correlations between words and blobs are learned from the aligned sentences. Visual queries are generated from textual queries using these relationships. In addition to the textual index, a visual index is built for retrieving images by visual query. The retrieval results using textual and visual queries are combined to generate the final ranked list.

We conducted English monolingual and Chinese-English cross-language retrieval experiments. The performances are quite good. The average precision of the English monolingual textual run is 0.6304. The performance of cross-lingual retrieval is about 70% of monolingual retrieval. Combining textual query run with generated visual query run, the performance is increased in the English monolingual experiment. However, the generated visual query has little impact in the cross-lingual experiments. One of the reasons is that using machine translation system to translate English captions into Chinese introduces many translation errors which affect the correctness of learned correlations. Although the help of the generated visual query is limited, using this could retrieve images relevant to the query terms that the visual query is generated from. Without the help of other query terms, the retrieved images are not relevant to the topics. How to select appropriate terms to generate visual query and how to integrate textual and visual information effectively will be further investigated.

Acknowledgments. Research of this paper was partially supported by National Science Council, Taiwan, under the contract NSC 93-2752-E-001-001-PAE.

References

1. Bian, G.W. and Chen, H.H.: Cross Language Information Access to Multilingual Collections on the Internet. Journal of American Society for Information Science, 51(3). (2000) 281-296.
2. Carson, C., Belongie, S., Greenspan, H. and Malik, J.: Blobworld: Image Segmentation Using Expectation-Maximization and Its Application to Image Querying. IEEE Transactions on Pattern Analysis and Machine Intelligence, 24(8). (2002) 1026-1038.
3. Chen, H.H., Ding, Y.W, Tsai, S.C. and Bian, G.W.: Description of the NTU System Used for MET2. In: Proceedings of Seventh Message Understanding Conference. (1998).
4. Chen, H.H., Yang, C. and Lin, Y.: Learning Formulation and Transformation Rules for Multilingual Named Entities. In: Proceedings of ACL 2003 Workshop on Multilingual and Mixed-language Named Entity Recognition: Combining Statistical and Symbolic Models. Association for Computational Linguistics (2003) 1-8.
5. Duygulu, P., Barnard, K., Freitas, N. and Forsyth, D.: Object Recognition as Machine Translation: Learning a Lexicon for a Fixed Image Vocabulary. In: Proceedings of Seventh European Conference on Computer Vision, Vol. 4. (2002) 97-112.
6. Jeon, J., Lavrenko, V. and Manmatha, R.: Automatic Image Annotation and Retrieval using Cross-Media Relevance Models. In: Proceedings of the 26th Annual International ACM SIGIR Conference on Research and Development in Information Retrieval (SIGIR 2003). ACM Press (2003) 119-126.
7. Lavrenko, V., Manmatha, R. and Jeon, J.: A Model for Learning the Semantics of Pictures. In: Proceedings of the Seventeenth Annual Conference on Neural Information Processing Systems. (2003).
8. Lin, W.H. and Chen, H.H.: Backward Machine Transliteration by Learning Phonetic Similarity. In: Proceedings of Sixth Conference on Natural Language Learning. Association for Computational Linguistics (2002) 139-145.
9. Lin, W.C., Lin, M.S. and Chen, H.H.: Cross-Language Image Retrieval via Spoken Query. In: Proceedings of RIAO 2004: Coupling Approaches, Coupling Media and Coupling Languages for Information Retrieval. Le Centre de Hautes Études Internationales d'Informatique Documentaire – C.I.D. (2004) 524-536.
10. Lin, W.C., Yang, C., and Chen, H.H.: Foreign Name Backward Transliteration in Chinese-English Cross-Language Image Retrieval. In: Comparative Evaluation of Multilingual Information Access Systems: Fourth Workshop of the Cross-Language Evaluation Forum, CLEF 2003. Lecture Notes in Computer Science, Vol. 3237. Springer (2004) 611-620.
11. Mori, Y., Takahashi, H. and Oka, R.: Image-to-Word Transformation Based on Dividing and Vector Quantizing Images with Words. In: Proceedings of the First International Workshop on Multimedia Intelligent Storage and Retrieval Management. (1999).
12. Robertson, S.E., Walker, S. and Beaulieu, M.: Okapi at TREC-7: Automatic Ad Hoc, Filtering, VLC and Interactive. In: Proceedings of the Seventh Text REtrieval Conference (TREC-7). National Institute of Standards and Technology (1998) 253-264.
13. Shi, J. and Malik, J.: Normalized Cuts and Image Segmentation. IEEE Transactions on Pattern Analysis and Machine Intelligence, 22(8). (2000) 888-905.

14. The Lowlands Team: Lazy Users and Automatic Video Retrieval Tools in (the) Lowlands. In: Proceedings of the Tenth Text REtrieval Conference (TREC 2001). National Institute of Standards and Technology (2002) 159-168.
15. Westerveld, T.: Image Retrieval: Content versus Context. In: Proceedings of RIAO 2000, Vol. 1. Le Centre de Hautes Études Internationales d'Informatique Documentaire – C.I.D. (2000) 276-284.
16. Westerveld, T.: Probabilistic Multimedia Retrieval. In: Proceedings of the 25th Annual International ACM SIGIR Conference on Research and Development in Information Retrieval (SIGIR 2002). ACM Press (2002) 437-438.

Toward Cross-Language and Cross-Media Image Retrieval*

Carmen Alvarez, Ahmed Id Oumohmed, Max Mignotte, and Jian-Yun Nie

DIRO, University of Montreal, CP. 6128, succursale Centre-ville, Montreal, Quebec, H3C 3J7 Canada
{bissettc, idoumoha, mignotte, nie}@iro.umontreal.ca

Abstract. This paper describes our approach used in ImageCLEF 2004. Our focus is on image retrieval using text, i.e. Cross-Media IR. To do this, we first determine the strong relationships between keywords and types of visual features such as texture or shape. Then, the subset of images retrieved by text retrieval are used as examples to match other images according to the most important types of features of the query words.

1 Introduction

There has been a large amount of research on Cross-Language Information Retrieval (CLIR), but much less for Cross-Media Information Retrieval (CMIR). By CMIR, we mean that a user issues a query in one medium (e.g. in natural language), but retrieves information in another medium (e.g. images). CMIR is similar to CLIR. The key problem is still (query) translation, but from one medium to another, instead of from one language to another. We call this problem media translation (in contrast to language translation). Media translation is more difficult than language translation. For language translation, there are a large number of resources and tools. In each language, for the purposes of IR, one can reasonably assume that text can be decomposed into words, and there is a finite number of words in each language. There is also a great similarity in the meanings that one can express in different languages, despite the fact that some languages can express meanings that cannot be expressed in others. This means that translation between languages is a feasible, although difficult, task.

For CMIR, the picture is different. There is no equivalent of words in languages for images. Indeed, we do not have a finite number of features that are semantically meaningful and which can be used to characterise the semantics of each image. Representing an image by a set of pixels does not help to understand what the image "means". In such a situation, it is impossible to build a system equivalent to Machine Translation (MT) between natural languages. It is impossible to even build a kind of "bi-media" dictionary that maps a word to

* This study has been partly supported by the Center of Interdisciplinary Research en Emerging Technologies (CITÉ) of the University of Montreal.

C. Peters et al. (Eds.): CLEF 2004, LNCS 3491, pp. 676–687, 2005.

one or several image components or characteristics. How can one build a CMIR system that automatically "translates" a text query into an image query? This is the key problem that we investigate in our study. Our approach is inspired by CLIR approaches based on parallel corpora. Using a parallel corpus, one can train a statistical translation model between two languages. We notice that it is relatively easy to obtain such a parallel corpus between text and images: any set of images annotated with words, or accompanied by text, can be regarded as such a parallel corpus between images and text. The problem is to have a reasonable approach to train a translation model.

Our initial goal in this research was to build a translation model as in natural languages. We intended to extract image characteristics that can play a similar role to words in text and then, train a statistical translation model between words and these characteristics. However, this task proved too ambitious. The approach used in our experiments for ImageCLEF 2004 was to use the parallel texts in a manner similar to that of Yang et al. [1]. The original query is used to retrieve a set of documents from the parallel corpus in the source language. Target words are extracted from parallel texts of these documents, and the target words are used as query translation. We also use a text query (one keyword) to retrieve the images that contain the keyword in annotation. Then, the common characteristics of these images (their centroid) are used as image query. The results of this approach seem promising: although the effectiveness of the CMIR approach alone is far lower than using text queries to match text annotations, we observe that the images retrieved for keywords with strong visual characteristics such as "garden" and "boat" are relevant even if not annotated with these words. Such a CMIR approach allows us to extend retrieval results to cover the relevant images without text annotation, which is the case for most images on the Web.

2 Existing Image Retrieval Approaches

Different approaches have been used for image retrieval. A user can submit a text query and the system can search for images using image captions. A user can submit an image query (using an example image - either selected from a database or drawn by the user). In this case, the system tries to determine the most similar images to the example by comparing various visual features such as shape, texture, or color. A third group of approaches tries to assign semantic meaning to images. This approach is often used to annotate images by concepts or keywords [2]. Once images have been associated with keywords, they can be retrieved by text. The approaches have their own advantages and weaknesses. The first approach is indeed text retrieval. There is no image processing. Coverage of the retrieval is limited to images with captions or annotation, which can be explicit or implicit (file name). The second approach does not require images to be associated with captions. However, the user is required to provide an example image and a visual feature or a combination of some features to be used for comparison. This is often difficult for a non-expert user and the retrieval effectiveness (for high-level queries) is lower than for text retrieval. The third approach, if successful, allows us to automatically recognise the semantics of images, and thus allow users to query images by keywords. Currently, only annotation of images by to typical components or features seems possible. For example, according to a texture analysis, one can recognise a region of images as corresponding to a tiger due to the texture of tigers [3]. The particular feature to be used is selected manually according to the objects to be annotated. It is still impossible to recognise all semantic meanings of images.

Recent studies [4] have tried to automatically create associations between visual features and keywords. The basic idea is to use a set of annotated images as a set of learning examples, and to extract associations between annotations and the visual features of images. In our study, we initially tried to use a similar approach in ImageCLEF. That is, we wanted to extract strong relationships between the keywords in the captions and the visual features of the images. If such relationships could be created, then it would be possible to use them to retrieve non-annotated images by a textual query. In this case, the relationships play a role of translation between media. However, we discovered that this approach is extremely difficult in the context of ImageCLEF for several reasons:

1. The annotations in the ImageCLEF corpus often contain keywords that are not strongly associated with particular visual features. They correspond to abstract concepts. Examples of such keywords are "Scotland", "north", and "tournament". If we use the approach systematically for every word, there will be noisy relationships.
2. Even if there are relationships between keywords and visual features, the relationships may be difficult to extract because there are a huge number of possible visual features. In fact, visual features are continuous. Even if we use some discretisation techniques, their number is still too high to be associated with keywords. For example, for a set of images associated with the keyword "water", one would expect to extract strong relationships between the keyword and the color and texture features. However, "water" in images may only take up a small region of the image. There may be other objects, making it difficult to automatically isolate the typical features for "water".

Due to this, we take a more flexible approach. We also use images with captions as a set of training examples, but we do not try to create relationships between keywords and particular visual features (such as a particular shade of blue for the word "water"). We only try to determine which type(s) of feature are the most important for a keyword. For example, "water" may be associated with "texture" and "color". Only strong relationships are retained. During the retrieval process, a text query is first matched with a set of images using captions. This is a text retrieval step. Then, the retrieved images are used as examples to retrieve other images, which are similar according to the determined types of features associated with the keywords. The process of our system is illustrated in Figure 1.

This approach, if successful, is very useful in practice. In many cases, image captions contain abstract keywords that cannot be strongly associated with visual features, and even if they can, it is impossible to associate a single vector to a keyword. Our approach does not require determining such a single feature

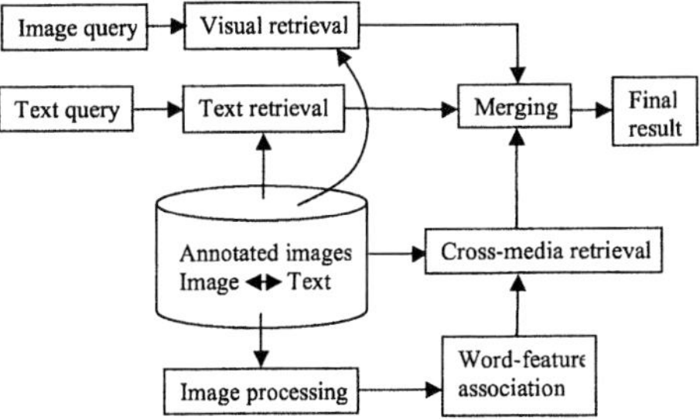

Fig. 1. Workflow of image retrieval

vector for a given keyword. It abandons the third approach mentioned earlier, but combines the first two approaches. The advantage of extracting keyword-feature associations is to avoid the burden of requiring the user to indicate the appropriate types of features to be used in image comparison.

3 Image Processing-Based Learning Procedure

Objective of the automatic image processing-based learning procedure is:

- to determine the most discriminant type(s) of high-level visual features for each annotated keyword. We have considered the three fundamental visual characteristics; namely, *texture* (including color information), *edge* and *shape*. For example, the keyword "animal" could belong to the *shape* class since the measure using *shape* information will be the most discriminant to identify images with animals (although "zebra" and "tiger" will probably belong to the *edge* and *texture* classes).
- to identify candidate images that are most representative for a keyword.

The type of high-level visual feature along with its discriminant measure and a set of representative images will be used to refine the image retrieval process.

3.1 Edge Class and Its Measure

Wavelet-based measures have often been used in content-based image retrieval system because of the appealing ability to describe local texture and the distribution of the edges of a given image at multiple scales. We use the Harr wavelet transform [5] for the luminance (grey-level) component of the image. This transform is chosen for its better localisation properties and it requires less computation compared to others (e.g., Daubechies' wavelet). The image decomposition into wavelets involves recursive numeric filtering. At each step in the recursion, we obtain four sub-bands, which we refer to as LL, LH, HL and HH according to their frequency characteristics (L: Low and H: High). The LL sub-band is then decomposed into four sub-bands at the next decomposition step. We use three steps in our case. For each sub-band, we compute the mean and the standard deviation of the energy distribution. This leads to a vector of 20 (i.e., $(2 \times 3 \times 3) + 2$) components considered as the descriptors (or signature) of the *edge* characteristics.

3.2 Texture Class and Its Measure

Tamura *et al.* [6] proposed to characterise image texture along the dimensions of contrast, directionality, coarseness, line-likeness, regularity and roughness. In this class of visual features, we use only the coarseness property which yields a histogram of six bins, for the following reasons:

- Contrast is not very discriminant for texture retrieval,
- Edge information is already treated in the wavelet and shape class,
- Line-likeness, regularity and roughness are correlated to coarseness, contrast and directionality.

Coarseness refers to the size of the *texton*; the smallest unit of a texture. This measure depends on the resolution of the texture. With this measure, we can compute a histogram with 6 bins (a 6-component attribute vector), which will be used as the descriptor of the *texture* of a given image.

3.3 Shape Class and Its Measure

Description and interpretation of shapes in an input image remains difficult. Several methods use a contour detection in the images (such as Canny or Sobel edge detectors) as a preliminary step. These methods remain dependent on parameters such as thresholds (on the magnitude of the image gradient). In image compression, a vector quantisation method is used [7] on the set of vectors of dimension K^2 of grey-levels corresponding to $K \times K$ blocks extracted from the image. By using a clustering procedure into K classes, we can obtain an image with separate regions (a set of connected pixels belonging to the same class) from which we extract the contours of regions. These edges are connected and obtained without parameter adjustment and noise is taken into consideration. We use this strategy of edge detection and as clustering procedure, we use the Generalised Lloyd [8] [9] method. In our implementation, we use the QccPack Library[1]. For each edge pixel, we define a direction (horizontal, vertical, first or second diagonal) depending on the disposition of its neighbouring edge pixels. For each direction we count the number of edge pixels associated with it, which yields a 4 bin histogram.

4 Relationships Between Words and Visual Features

4.1 The Learning Procedure

The learning procedure determines the type of high-level visual features that are most representative for each annotated keyword:

[1] `http://qccpack.sourceforge.net/`

Fig. 2. *Result of learning procedure applied to "garden". Below each image, we put the ID of the image and its similarity score. If the image is not annotated by the word "garden", its ID is put in a gray box.*

1. Let $\mathbf{I}_w$ be the set of all images I_w (each described by its three vectors or descriptors $[D_{I_w}^{texture}, D_{I_w}^{edge}, D_{I_w}^{Shape}]$) in the training database that are annotated with the keyword w and $|\mathbf{I}_w|$, the number of images in $\mathbf{I}_w$.
2. For each CLASS { *Texture, Edge, Shape* }
   (a) We use a K-mean clustering procedure [10] (euclidean distance as similarity measure) on the set of samples $D_{I_w}^{class}$.
   (b) This clustering allows us to approximate the distribution of the set of samples $D_{I_w}^{class}$ by K spherical distributions (with identical radius) and to give K prototype vectors $[D_{1,w}^{class}, ..., D_{k,w}^{class}]$ corresponding to the centers of these distributions. Several values of K are used to find the best clustering representation of $D_{I_w}^{class}$.
   (c) For each PROTOTYPE VECTOR $\{ D_{1,w}^{class}, ..., D_{k,w}^{class} \}$
      - We search in the training database for the closest descriptors (or images) of $D_{k,w}^{class}$, according to euclidean distance. Let $\mathbf{I}_{k,w}^{class}$ be this set of images.
      - We compute the number of the first top-level T samples of $\mathbf{I}_{k,w}^{class}$ also belonging to $\mathbf{I}_w$ (best results obtained with $T = 10$). Let $N_{k,w}^{class}$ be this number.
3. We retain the CLASS(ES) and $\mathbf{I}_{k,w}^{class}$ for which we have $N_{k,w}^{class}$ above a given threshold ξ. At this point, a keyword may be associated with some strong class(es) of features as well as a typical image cluster (i.e. $\mathbf{I}_{k,w}^{class}$).

4.2 Cross-Media Retrieval

The simplest case of CMIR is with only one keyword. For image retrieval with a keyword, the set of the associated image clusters $\mathbf{I}_{k,w}^{class}$ is used as example image to match the whole image database, according to the feature class(es). For a text query with several keywords, this process is repeated for each keyword. The lists of retrieved documents (images) are first normalized by relevance score (i.e. the relevance score is divided by the maximum score in the list) and then merged with equal importance (1/3 for each list). The final list is the result of CMIR.

We observe that this method works well for keywords with strong visual features such as "garden" and "boat". The first 24 images of the set of images associated to the word *garden* are shown in Figure 2. We can see that, even if most images are not annotated by the word *garden* (the word does not exist in any field of the text associated with the image), we can visually count about 9 images related to gardens from the 14 non-annotated images.

5 Cross-Language Text Retrieval

5.1 Translation Models

Two approaches are used for query translation, depending on the resources available for the different languages. For Spanish, Italian, German, Dutch, Swedish, and Finnish, FreeLang bilingual dictionaries [2] are used in a word-for-word translation approach. The foreign language words in the dictionaries are stemmed using Porter stemmers[3], and the English words are left in their original form. The queries are also stemmed, and stop words are removed with a stoplist in the language. The translated query consists of the set of all possible English word translations for each query term, each translated word having equal weight. For French, a translation model trained on a web-aligned corpus is used [11]. The model associates a list of English words and their corresponding probabilities with a French word. As with the bilingual dictionaries, the French words are stemmed, and the English words are not. Word-for-word translation is done. For a given French root, all possible English translations are added to the translated query. The translation probabilities determine the weight of the word in the translated query. The term weights are represented implicitly by repeating a given translated word a number of times according to its translation probability. For French as well as for the other languages, the words in the translated query are stemmed using the Porter stemming algorithm.

5.2 CLIR Process

For retrieval, the Okapi retrieval algorithm [12] is used, implemented by the Lemur Toolkit for Language Modeling and Information Retrieval. The BM 25 weighting function is used. We also use pseudo-relevance feedback. The parameters are trained on the TREC-6 AP89 document collection and 53 queries in English, French, Spanish, German, Italian, and Dutch. Since no training data was available for Finnish and Swedish, the average of the optimal values found

---

[2] `http://www.freelang.net`

[3] `http://snowball.tartarus.org`

for the other languages is used. While the training collection, consisting of news articles about 200-400 words in length, is quite different from the test collection of image captions, the volume of the training data (163'000 documents, 25 or 53 queries, depending on language, 9403 relevance assessments) is much greater than the training data provided by the image collection (5 queries, 167 relevance assessments). For our experiments, the above parameters are set as follows:

- Okapi parameters: k1=1.0-1.5, b=0.75-0.8 and k3=7-9;
- Feedback parameters: FeedbackDocCount=20, FeedbackTermCount=5 and qtf (weight of query terms added) =0.2-0.6.

Given a text query, we retrieve a list of images using the above parameters. We annotate this image relevance score based on textual retrieval as $R_{text}(i, q)$.

6 Combining Text and Images in Image Retrieval

6.1 The Image Relevance Score Based on Clustering

The image analysis based on clustering, described in section 4, provides a list of retrieved images i for a given word w, with a relevance score for each image, $R_{cluster}(i, w)$. The relevance score, based on clustering, is a weighted sum of the relevance scores for that image for each (non stopword) query term:

$$R_{cluster}(i, q) = \sum_{w \in q} \lambda_w R_{cluster}(i, w) \quad (1)$$

Each word has the same weight and the relevance score for the query is normalised with $\lambda_w = \frac{1}{|q|}$, where $|q|$ is the number of words in the query.

6.2 Image Retrieval Using Image Queries

In ImageCLEF, we are also provided with one example image for each topic. These images can be used for content-based image retrieval using visual features. We use the same visual features (i.e. edge, texture and shape) as described in 3 for the calculation of image similarity. Using the three classes of visual features, the following relevance scores are obtained: $R_{edge}(i, q)$, $R_{texture}(i, q)$ and $R_{shape}(i, q)$. They are merged into a visual similarity score as follows:

$$R_{visual}(i, q) = \lambda_{edge} R_{edge}(i, q) + \lambda_{texture} R_{texture}(i, q) + \lambda_{shape} R_{shape}(i, q) \quad (2)$$

In our experiments, we give equal importance to the three visual features.

6.3 Combining the Five Image Relevance Scores

We now have 5 lists of images, with the following three types of scores:

- $R_{text}(i, q)$: Text retrieval score;
- $R_{cluster}(i, q)$: Cross-media retrieval score;
- $R_{edge}(i, q)$, $R_{texture}(i, q)$, $R_{shape}(i, q)$: Visual similarity scores.

Each of these relevance scores contributes to the final relevance score as follows:

$$R(i,q) = \lambda_{text} R_{text}(i,q) + \lambda_{cluster} R_{cluster}(i,q) + \lambda_{visual} R_{visual}(i,q) \quad (3)$$

The coefficients chosen for the contribution of each approach are as follows: $\lambda_{text} = 0.8$, $\lambda_{cluster} = 0.1$, $\lambda_{visual} = 0.1$. These values have been determined empirically using the training data.

6.4 Filtering Images Based on Location, Photographer, and Date

A final filtering is applied to the list of images for a given query for location, photographer, and date, when these latter are specified in the query. These entities were extracted from the data associated with the images.

7 Experiments

7.1 Monolingual and Bilingual Text Retrieval

Our experiments only use topic titles. For query translation, English-French translation is performed with a statistical translation model trained on a set of parallel Web pages. For other languages, the translation is done with bilingual dictionaries. Table 1 shows the effectiveness obtained for monolingual text retrieval (E-E) and bilingual retrieval with French (F-E) and Spanish (S-E) queries.

Table 1. Effectiveness of text retrieval

	F-E	E-E	S-E
Title	0.4976	0.5530	0.4843

The above results were obtained with filtering by date, place and photographer when this is specified in the query. Without filtering, we observe a decrease for F-E and S-E experiments: 0.4838 for F-E and 0.4513 for S-E. For monolingual retrieval (E-E), without filtering, the effectiveness is slightly higher: 0.5729.

7.2 Cross-Media Retrieval

If we only use the CMIR method (or the method based o clustering) we developed, we obtain the effectiveness shown in table 2:

Notice that in these experiments, the queries are still written in different languages. So they have to be translated into English before the CMIR method is used. The effectiveness for F-E and S-E is indeed a combined effectiveness of CLIR and CMIR. We can observe that the effectiveness obtained is much lower than with text retrieval, although visual retrieval performs better than CMIR. This clearly shows that the CMIR method cannot be used alone for image retrieval.

Table 2. Effectiveness of CMIR

E-E	F-E	S-E
0.0536	0.0486	0.0321

Table 3. Effectiveness of combined approaches

T(0.8)+C(0.2)	T(0.8)+V(0.2)	T(0.8)+C(0.1)+V(0.1)		
E-E	E-E	E-E	F-E	S-E
0.5502	0.5699	0.5620	0.5125	0.4890

7.3 Visual Retrieval

If we use the example images provided with the queries to retrieve similar images, we obtain an average precision of 0.0586. If we use filtering by date, place and photographer, we have to use CLIR to some degree. Then, the effectiveness for E-E, F-E and S-E is respectively 0.0999, 0.0952 and 0.0972. The difference in language translation has almost no impact on the filtering process.

7.4 Combined Approaches

As both CMIR and visual retrieval have low effectiveness and cannot be used alone for image retrieval, we combine these methods with text retrieval in order to improve the latter. The following table shows the combinations and the effectiveness obtained (where T(X)+C(Y)+V(Z) means that text retrieval, CMIR and visual retrieval are signed an importance X, Y and Z):

We can see in the third column that when CMIR and visual retrieval are combined with text retrieval, the latter can be further improved. We tested with different importance values for the three types of retrieval. It turns out that text retrieval should be attributed with a high importance value (above 0.6) for the combined approach to be effective. The two other retrieval methods should be given low importance (about 0.1). These importance values are consistent with the effectiveness level of each retrieval method.

In order to see the impact of visual retrieval and CMIR, we combine these two methods separately with text retrieval (first two columns) for English queries. It turns out that when visual retrieval is combined with text retrieval to some extent, the effectiveness can be slightly improved (from 0.5530 to 0.5699). The combination of 0.8 for text retrieval and 0.2 for visual retrieval seems to be the best one. On the other hand, when CMIR is combined with text retrieval, the effectiveness seems to decrease (from 0.5530 to 0.5502). This result may suggest that our current way to do CMIR for querying is inappropriate. Indeed, for a query, we currently retrieve a list of images for each single word, then combine them with equal importance. It may be better to consider the relative importance of each word in the query. Our examination on some of the lists retrieved for keywords such as "garden" suggests that our CMIR method may work well for these words with strong relationships with visual features. On the other hand, more abstract words such as "tournament" are not connected with any particular visual features. It would be appropriate to use CMIR for the first group of words, but not for the second group. We will investigate the proper utilisation of our CMIR approach in the future.

8 Discussions

In this study, we propose a method to automatically extract relationships between keywords and visual features. The extraction approach is inspired by the CLIR approach based on parallel corpora. For image retrieval with words that are strongly related to visual features, this method seems to work well. However, when CMIR is used in a simplistic way for a query with several words in our ImageCLEF experiments, the method does not seem to bring any positive impact. We also tested the combination of image retrieval with both text and image queries. Such a combination brings improvements in comparison with text retrieval alone. The current implementation is still quite simple, and the idea of CMIR using annotated images as a parallel corpus is not yet fully tested. There are several possible improvements that we can do in the future:

- In our current experiments, we retrieve a list of documents (images) for each keyword in a text query, and we assign equal importance to all the keywords. In fact, it would be possible to attribute a higher importance to a keyword that is judged more important, or related more strongly to some particular visual features. In this way, we will be able to rely more on keywords such as "garden" and "water", and less on "golf" and "tournament".
- In our visual retrieval, we attributed the three classes of features an equal importance. It would be possible to assign different importance according to the keywords in the query. For example, if the keywords are more related to texture than to shape, then the texture similarity could be given higher importance in the merged result.
- In our experiments on CLIR with French queries, it turns out that using short queries (titles) are better than using long queries (titles and narratives). It is related to the number of translation words that we select for the translation. When we translate with a statistical translation model, the number of translation words to be selected is important. The higher effectiveness with titles suggests that the translation of query with a translation model indeed produce a desirable query expansion effect - the effect that has been mentioned in several previous studies on CLIR. As a consequence, statistical translation models could be particularly adapted to short queries.

In our future research, we will further investigate the CMIR approach in order to understand how words should be translated into visual features.

References

1. Yang, Y., Carbonell, J., Brown, R., Frederking, R.: Translingual information retrieval: learning from bilingual corpora. Artificial Intelligence **103** (1998) 323–345

2. Liu, W., Dumais, S., Sun, Y., Zhang, H., Czerwinski, M., Field, B.: Semi-automatic image annotation (2001)
3. Carson, C., Thomas, M., Belongie, S., Hellerstein, J.M., Malik, J.: Blobworld: A system for region-based image indexing and retrieval. In: Third International Conference on Visual Information Systems, Springer (1999)
4. Jeon, J., Lavrenko, V., Manmatha, R.: Automatic image annotation and retrieval using cross-media relevance models. In: ACM SIGIR. (2003)
5. Mallat, S.: A theory for multiresolution signal decomposition : The wavelet representation. IEEE Transactions on Pattern Analysis and Machine Intelligence **11** (1989) 674–693
6. Tamura, H., Mori, S., , Yamawaki, T.: Texture features corresponding to visual perception. IEEE Transactions on Systems, Man, and Cybernetics **8** (1978) 460–473
7. Goldberg, M., Boucher, P., Shlien, S.: Image compression using adaptative vector quantization. Communications, IEEE Transactions on [legacy, pre - 1988] **34** (1986) 180–187
8. Lloyd, S.: Last square quantization in pcm's. Bell Telephone Laboratories Paper (1957)
9. Linde, Y., Buzo, A., Gray, R.: An algorithm for vector quantizer design. IEEE Transactions on Communications **COM-28** (1980) 84–95
10. Banks, S.: Signal processing image processing and pattern recognition. Prentice Hall (1990)
11. Nie, J.Y., Simard, M.: Using statistical translation models for bilingual ir. In: Revised Papers from the Second Workshop of the Cross-Language Evaluation Forum on Evaluation of Cross-Language Information Retrieval Systems. (2001) 137–150
12. Robertson, S., Walker, S., Jones, S., Hancock-Beaulieu, M., Gatford, M.: Okapi at trec-3. In: Proc. of the Third Text REtrieval Conference (TREC-3), NIST Special Publication 500-225. (1995)

FIRE – Flexible Image Retrieval Engine: ImageCLEF 2004 Evaluation

Thomas Deselaers, Daniel Keysers, and Hermann Ney

Lehrstuhl für Informatik VI – Computer Science Department,
RWTH Aachen University – D-52056 Aachen, Germany
{deselaers, keysers, ney}@cs.rwth-aachen.de

Abstract. We describe *FIRE*, a content-based image retrieval system, and the methods we used within this system in the ImageCLEF 2004 evaluation. In *FIRE*, various features are available to represent images. The diversity of available features allows the user to adapt the system to the task at hand. A weighted combination of features admits flexible query formulations and helps with processing specific queries. For the ImageCLEF 2004 evaluation, we used the image content alone and obtained the best result in the category "only visual features, fully automatic retrieval" in the medical retrieval task. Additionally, the results compare favorably to other systems, even if they make use of the textual information in addition to the images.

1 Introduction

Content-based image retrieval is an area of active research in the field of pattern analysis and image processing. The need for content-based techniques becomes obvious when considering the enormous amounts of digital images produced day by day e.g. by digital cameras or digital imaging methods in medicine. The alternative of annotating large amounts of images manually is a very time consuming task. Furthermore, a very important aspect is that images can contain information that no words can convey [1]. Thus, even the most complete annotation is useless if it does not contain the details that might be of importance to the actual users in their context. The only way to solve these problems is to use fully automatic, content-based methods.

In this work we describe *FIRE*, a content-based image retrieval system and the methods we used within this system in the ImageCLEF 2004 evaluation. *FIRE* is easily extensible, offers a wide repertoire of features and distance functions. These varieties allow for assessing the performance of different features for different tasks. *FIRE* is freely available under the terms of the GNU General Public License[1].

[1] http://www-i6.informatik.rwth-aachen.de/~deselaers/fire.html

C. Peters et al. (Eds.): CLEF 2004, LNCS 3491, pp. 688–698, 2005.

2 Retrieval Techniques

In content-based image retrieval, images are searched by their appearance and not by textual annotations. Thus, the appearance of the images is encoded by features and these features are compared to search for images similar to a given query image. In *FIRE*, each image is represented by a set of features. To find images similar to a given query image, the features from the images in the database are compared to the features of the query image using an appropriate distance measure d.

Given a query image Q and the goal to find images from the database which are similar to the given query image, we calculate a score $S(Q, X)$ for each image $X \in \mathcal{B}$ from the database $\mathcal{B}$:

$$S(Q, X) = \exp\left(-\gamma \sum_{m=1}^{M} w_m \cdot d_m(Q_m, X_m)\right). \tag{1}$$

Here, Q_m and X_m are the mth features of the images Q and X, respectively, d_m is the corresponding distance measure, and w_m is a weighting coefficient, $\gamma = 1$. For each d_m, $\sum_{X \in \mathcal{B}} d_m(Q_m, X_m) = 1$ is enforced by re-normalization. The K database images with highest $S(Q, X)$ are returned. When *Relevance Feedback* [2] is used, that is, a user selects a set of relevant images Q^+ and a set of irrelevant images Q^- to refine a query, we calculate the scores for each of the

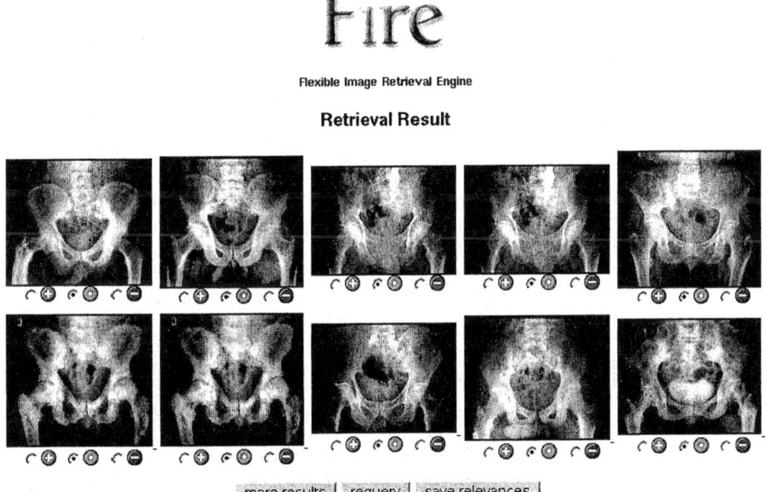

Fig. 1. Interface for relevance feedback. The user is presented the best matches from the database (top left is the query image) and can select for each image whether it is relevant, irrelevant, or neutral

images from the sets of relevant and irrelevant images and combine these into one score

$$S(Q^+, Q^-, X) = \sum_{q \in Q^+} S(q, X) + \sum_{q \in Q^-} (1 - S(q, X)). \tag{2}$$

Again, the set of the K images with the highest scores is returned. The interface used for relevance feedback is shown in Figure 1.

A frequent method for enhancing the query results is *query expansion*. In FIRE, query expansion is implemented as "automatic relevance feedback" [2]. The user specifies a number of images G that he expects to be relevant after the first query. Then a query is processed in two steps: First the query is evaluated and the first G images are returned. These G images are automatically used as the set of relevant images Q^+ to requery the database and the K best matches of this query are returned.

3 Features and Associated Distance Measures

This section gives a short description of each of the features used in the FIRE image retrieval system for the ImageCLEF 2004 evaluation. Table 1 gives an overview of the features and associated distance measures.

Table 1. Features extracted for the ImageCLEF 2004 evaluation and their associated distance measures

number	feature	associated distance measure
1	32 × 32 down scaled version of the image	Euclidean
2	32 × X down scaled version of the image	IDM
3	global texture descriptor	Euclidean
4	Tamura texture histogram	Jeffrey divergence
5	invariant feature histogram with monomial kernel	Jeffrey divergence
6	invariant feature histogram with relational kernel	Jeffrey divergence
7	binary feature: color/gray	equal/not equal

3.1 Color Histograms

Color histograms are widely used in image retrieval [3, 4, 1]. They are one of the most basic approaches and to show performance improvements, image retrieval systems are often compared to a system using only color histograms. The color space is partitioned and for each bin the pixels with a color within its range are counted, resulting in a representation of the relative frequencies of the occurring colors. In accordance with [5], we use the Jeffrey divergence to compare histograms.

3.2 Appearance-Based Image Features (1,2)

The most straight-forward approach is to directly use the pixel values of the images as features. For example, the images might be scaled to a common size and compared using the Euclidean distance. In optical character recognition and for medical data improved methods based on image features usually obtain excellent results [6, 7, 8].

Here, we use 32×32 and $32 \times X$(keeping the aspect ration) versions of the images. The 32×32 images are compared using Euclidean distance and the $32 \times X$ images are compared using image distortion model distance (IDM) [6].

3.3 Global Texture Descriptor (3)

In [3] a texture feature consisting of several parts is described: *Fractal dimension* measures the roughness or the crinkliness of a surface. Here, the fractal dimension is calculated using the reticular cell counting method [9]. *Coarseness* characterizes the grain size of an image. Here it is calculated depending on the variance of the image. *Entropy* is used as a measure of unorderedness in an image. The *Spatial gray-level difference statistics* (SGLD) describes the brightness relationship of pixels within neighborhoods. It is also known as co-occurrence matrix analysis [10]. The *Circular Moran autocorrelation function* measures the roughness of the texture [11].

3.4 Tamura Features (4)

In [12] the authors propose six texture features corresponding to human visual perception: *coarseness*, *contrast*, *directionality*, *line-likeness*, *regularity*, and *roughness*. From experiments that tested the significance of these features with respect to human perception, it was concluded that the first three features are very important. Thus in our experiments we use coarseness, contrast, and directionality to create a histogram describing the texture [3] and compare these histograms using the Jeffrey divergence [5]. In the QBIC system [4] histograms of these features are used as well.

3.5 Invariant Feature Histograms (5,6)

A feature is called invariant with respect to certain transformations if it does not change when these transformations are applied to the image. The transformations considered here are translation, rotation, and scaling. In this work, invariant feature histograms as presented by Siggelkow [13] are used. These features are based on the idea of constructing features invariant with respect to certain transformations by integration over all considered transformations. The resulting histograms are compared using the Jeffrey divergence [5]. Previous experiments have shown that the characteristics of invariant feature histograms and color histograms are very similar but that invariant feature histograms often outperform color histograms [14]. Thus, in this work color histograms are not used.

3.6 Color/Gray Binary Feature (7)

Since the databases contain both color images and gray value images, an obvious feature is whether the image is a color or gray valued image. This can be extracted easily by examining a reasonably large amount of pixels in the image. If all of these pixels are gray valued, the image is considered to be a gray valued image, otherwise it is considered to be a color image. This feature can easily be tested for equality.

4 Submissions to the ImageCLEF 2004 Evaluation

The ImageCLEF 2004 evaluation [15] covered 3 tasks: 1. *Bilingual ad-hoc task* using the St. Andrews database of historic photographs, 2. *Medical Retrieval Task* using the Casimage database of medical images, and 3. *Interactive Retrieval task* using the St. Andrews database.

We participated in the bilingual ad-hoc task and the medical retrieval task. For the experiments, a set of features was extracted from each of the images from both databases and the given query images. Table 1 gives an overview of the features extracted from the databases and the distance measures used to compare these features. The features extracted were chosen based on previous experiments with other databases [16, 14].

4.1 Medical Retrieval Task

In the *Medical Retrieval Task* [15] we submitted results in three different categories: 1. fully automatic visual retrieval, 2. query expansion using visual data only, 3. manual relevance feedback using only visual information. We would like to emphasize that no textual data was used at all during the experiments.

4.2 Fully Automatic Visual Retrieval

Fully Automatic Retrieval means that the system is given the query image and must return a list of the most similar images without any further user interaction.

To this task we submitted 3 runs differing in the feature weightings used. The precise feature weightings are given in Table 2 along with the obtained mean average precision and were chosen on the following basis:

- Use all available features equally weighted. This run can be seen as a baseline and is labelled with the run-tag `i6-111111`.
- Use the features in the combination that produces the best results on the IRMA database [17], labelled `i6-020500`.
- Use the features in a combination which was optimized towards the given task. See Section 4.5 on how we optimized the parameters towards this task. This run is labelled with the run-tag `i6-025501`.

Table 2 clearly shows that the parameters optimized for this task outperformed the other parameters and thus that optimizing the feature weightings in image retrieval for a given task improves the results. Two example queries are given in Figure 2.

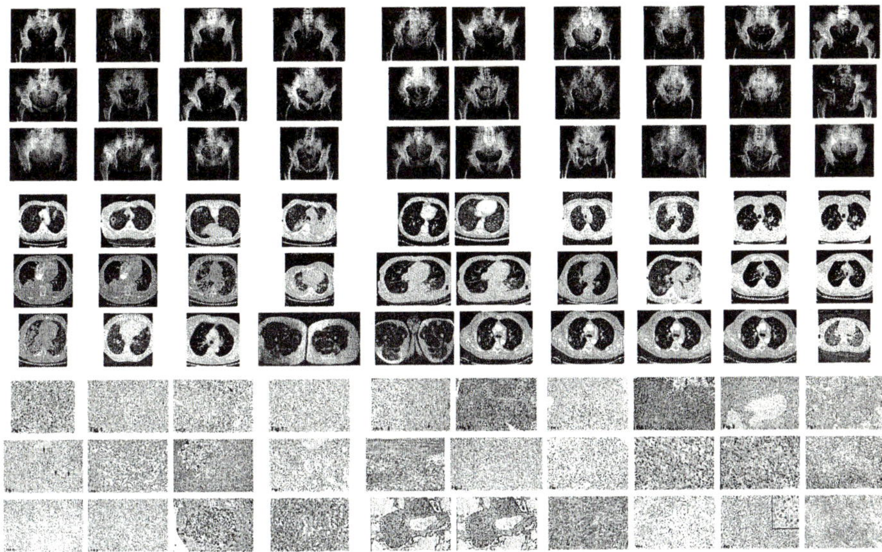

Fig. 2. Two example queries with results from the fully automatic medical retrieval task

Table 2. Different feature weightings and the mean average precision (MAP) from the ImageCLEF 2004 evaluation used for the medical retrieval task for the fully automatic runs with and without query expansion (QE) and for the run with relevance feedback (RF)

run-tag	weight for feature number							MAP		
	1	2	3	4	5	6	7	w/o QE	w/ QE	w/ RF
`i6-111111`	1	1	1	1	1	1	1	0.318	0.278	-
`i6-020500`	0	5	0	2	0	0	0	0.308	0.354	-
`i6-025501`	5	5	0	2	1	0	0	**0.386**	0.374	-
`i6-rfb1`	10	0	0	2	1	0	0	-	-	0.394

4.3 Fully Automatic Queries with Query Expansion

This task is similar to the *fully automatic task*. The system is given the query image only and can perform the query in two steps, but without any user interaction as described in Section 2:

1. normal query.
2. query expansion, i.e. use the query image and its first nearest neighbor to requery the database.

We decided to use this method after we observed that for most query images the best match was a relevant one. In our opinion, this method slightly enhanced the retrieval result visually, but the results are worse than the single-pass runs in two of three cases in the ImageCLEF 2004 evaluation. In Table 2 the results for these runs are given in comparison to the fully automatic runs without query expansion. For these experiments we used the same three settings as for the fully automatic runs with and without query expansion. The fact that the results deteriorate (against our expectation) can be explained by the missing medical relevance of the first query result. Another reason might be that we looked only at the first 30 results, but for the evaluation the first 1000 results were assessed.

4.4 Queries with Relevance Feedback

In the runs described in the following, *relevance feedback* was used. The system was queried with the given query image and a user was presented the 20 most similar images from the database. Then the user marked one or more of the images presented (including the query image) as relevant, irrelevant or neutral. The sets of relevant and irrelevant images were then used to requery the system as described in Section 2. Although in some scenarios several steps of relevance feedback might be useful, here only one step of query refinement was used.

As user interaction was involved, a fast system was desirable. To allow for faster retrieval, the image distortion model was not used for the comparison of images. The feature weighting used is given in Table 2.

The mean average precision of 0.394 reached here is slightly better than in the best of the fully automatic runs (0.386).

4.5 Manual Selection

To find a good set of parameters for this task, we manually compared some parameter combinations. Therefore, we manually created relevance estimates for some of the images. These experiments were carried out as follows:

1. Start with an initial feature weighting.
2. Query the database with all query images using this weighting.
3. Present the first 30 results for each query image to the user. The user marks **all** images as either relevant or irrelevant. The system calculates the number of relevant images in total.
4. Slightly change the weighting and go back to 2.

As starting point, we performed experiments to assess the quality of particular features, i.e. we used only one feature at a time (cf. Table 3(a)). With this information in mind we combined different features. First we tried to use all features with identical weight at the same time and the setting which proved best on the IRMA task. Then we modified these settings to improve the results. In this way we could approximately assess the quality of the results for different settings. We tried 11 different settings in total and manually chose the best one for submission. The complete results for these experiments are given in Table 3(b).

Table 3. a) The subjective performance of particular features on the medical retrieval task measured as precision of the first 30 results, b) Effect of various feature combinations on the precision for the medical retrieval task

a)

feature no	precision of the first 30 results
1	0.55
2	0.44
3	0.31
4	0.54
5	0.40
6	0.36
7	0.03

b)

weight for feature no							precision of the first 30 results
1	2	3	4	5	6	7	
1	1	1	1	1	1	1	0.60
0	5	0	2	0	0	0	0.65
0	5	0	2	2	0	0	0.61
0	10	0	2	2	0	0	0.63
0	5	0	2	0	2	0	0.59
10	0	0	2	2	0	0	0.65
0	10	0	2	0.5	0	0	0.63
5	0	0	2	0	0	0	0.65
0	10	0	2	1	0	0	0.65
5	5	0	2	1	0	0	0.67
10	0	0	2	0.5	0	0	0.65

Table 4. Different feature weightings used for the bilingual retrieval task for the fully automatic runs and the run with relevance feedback

run-tag	weight for feature number							MAP
	1	2	3	4	5	6	7	
`i6-111111`	1	1	1	1	1	1	0	0.086
`i6-010012`	0	0	0	1	2	1	0	0.077
`i6-010101`	0	1	0	1	1	0	0	0.086
`i6-rfb1`	0	0	0	1	1	0	0	0.084

4.6 Bilingual Retrieval Task

For the *Bilingual Retrieval Task* [15] we used only the 25 example images to query the database. That is, we used only the visual information provided and not the textual information at hand.

4.7 Fully Automatic Queries

Here, the example images given were used to query the database. Different feature weightings were used:

1. equal weight for each feature (run-tag `i6-111111`).
2. two weightings which had been proven to work well for general purpose photographs [3] (run-tags `i6-010012` and `i6-010101`).

The exact weightings are given in Table 4 along with the results from the ImageCLEF 2004 evaluation.

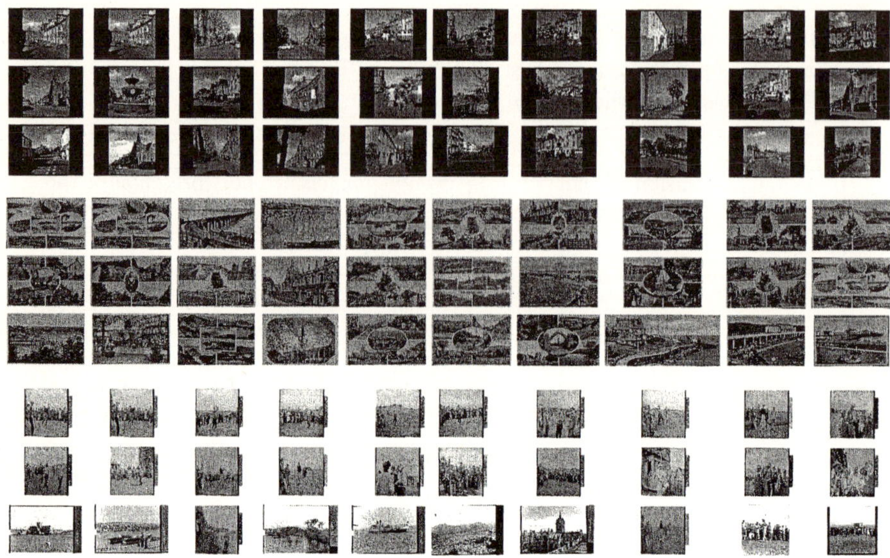

Fig. 3. Query results for the bilingual retrieval task for two different queries using only visual information

A look at the query topics clearly showed that pure content-based image retrieval would not be able to deliver satisfactory results because queries such as "Portrait pictures of church ministers by Thomas Rodger" are not processible by image content only (church ministers do not differ significantly in their appearance from any other person and it is usually not possible to see from an image who made it). The mean average precision values clearly show that visual information alone is not sufficient to obtain good results, although the results from queries are visually quite promising as shown in Figure 3. As this task was quite futile we did not focus on this task.

4.8 Queries with Relevance Feedback

Using the feature weighting given in Table 4, i.e. column `i6-rfb`, we submitted one run using relevance feedback for this task. No improvement can be observed: A mean average precision of 0.084 was measured. This is even worse than the best of the fully automatic runs.

5 Conclusion

In this section, the results are analyzed and compared to the results of other groups in the ImageCLEF 2004 evaluation.

Table 5 shows for each of the tasks the MAP of our best run compared to the best run in this task and to the average MAP in this task and to the best result for

Table 5. Comparison of our results to the results of other groups [15]

Task	best result from this work		# participants	MAP		
	MAP	rank		best result for this task	average	best result using text
Med: Auto (visual only)	0.386	1	23	0.386	0.273	0.390
Med: RF (visual only)	0.394	2	6	0.430	0.336	0.476
AdHoc: Visual	0.086	2	5	0.092	0.081	0.587
AdHoc: Vis,RF	0.084	1	1	0.084	0.084	0.587

the database used. It can clearly be seen that our system compares favorably well with the other systems, e.g. in the task of fully automatic retrieval using visual information only, we obtain the best result and this result is only slightly less precise than the best fully automatic result where textual information was used. The addition of manual feedback did not improve our results further in contrast to the results of other groups. It can clearly be seen that suitable selection and weighting of the features used improves the results strongly. The optimization here is not critical as only a few settings were compared. Comparing the results using only visual information to those using text and user feedback it can be seen that slight improvements are possible in the medical retrieval task and that textual information is indispensable for the ad-hoc retrieval task.

For the future, several things will be improved in the FIRE system. On the one hand, it can be seen that textual information strongly improves the results for some tasks. Thus we are planning to integrate a textual information retrieval component in our content-based image retrieval system. On the other hand, even using visual information only, the results can be strongly improved by using relevance feedback. As our results are only slightly improved using relevance feedback, we are planning to improve the relevance feedback techniques in our system.

References

1. Smeulders, A.W.M., Worring, M., Santini, S., Gupta, A., Jain, R.: Content-based image retrieval: The end of the early years. IEEE Trans. on Pattern Analysis and Machine Intelligence **22** (2000) 1349–1380
2. Müller, H., Müller, W., Marchand-Maillet, S., Squire, D.M.: Strategies for positive and negative relevance feedback in image retrieval. In: International Conference on Pattern Recognition. Volume 1 of Computer Vision and Image Analysis, Barcelona, Spain (2000) 1043–1046
3. Deselaers, T.: Features for image retrieval. Diploma thesis, Lehrstuhl für Informatik VI, RWTH Aachen University, Aachen, Germany (2003)
4. Faloutsos, C., Barber, R., Flickner, M., Hafner, J., Niblack, W., Petkovic, D., Equitz, W.: Efficient and effective querying by image content. Journal of Intelligent Information Systems **3** (1994) 231–262

5. Puzicha, J., Rubner, Y., Tomasi, C., Buhmann, J.: Empirical evaluation of dissimilarity measures for color and texture. In: International Conference on Computer Vision. Volume 2, Corfu, Greece (1999) 1165–1173
6. Keysers, D., Gollan, C., Ney, H.: Classification of medical images using non-linear distortion models. In: Bildverarbeitung für die Medizin, Berlin, Germany (2004) 366–370
7. Keysers, D., Gollan, C., Ney, H.: Local context in non-linear deformation models for handwritten character recognition. In: International Conference on Pattern Recognition. Volume 4, Cambridge, UK (2004) 511–514
8. Keysers, D., Macherey, W., Ney, H., Dahmen, J.: Adaptation in statistical pattern recognition using tangent vectors. IEEE Trans. on Pattern Analysis and Machine Intelligence **26** (2004) 269–274
9. Haberäcker, P.: Praxis der Digitalen Bildverarbeitung und Mustererkennung. Carl Hanser Verlag, München, Wien (1995)
10. Haralick, R.M., Shanmugam, B., Dinstein, I.: Texture features for image classification. IEEE Trans. on Systems, Man, and Cybernetics **3** (1973) 610–621
11. Gu, Z.Q., Duncan, C.N., Renshaw, E., Mugglestone, M.A., Cowan, C.F.N., Grant, P.M.: Comparison of techniques for measuring cloud texture in remotely sensed satellite meteorological image data. Radar and Signal Proc. **136** (1989) 236–248
12. Tamura, H., Mori, S., Yamawaki, T.: Textural features corresponding to visual perception. IEEE Trans. on Systems, Man, and Cybernetics **8** (1978) 460–472
13. Siggelkow, S.: Feature Histograms for Content-Based Image Retrieval. PhD thesis, University of Freiburg, Institute for Computer Science, Freiburg, Germany (2002)
14. Deselaers, T., Keysers, D., Ney, H.: Features for image retrieval – a quantitative comparison. In: DAGM 2004, Pattern Recognition, 26th DAGM Symposium. Number 3175 in LNCS, Tübingen, Germany (2004) 228–236
15. Clough, P., Müller, H., Sanderson, M.: The CLEF Cross Language Image Retrieval Track (ImageCLEF) 2004. In: Fifth Workshop of the Cross–Language Evaluation Forum (CLEF 2004). LNCS (2005) in press
16. Deselaers, T., Keysers, D., Ney, H.: Classification error rate for quantitative evaluation of content-based image retrieval systems. In: International Conference on Pattern Recognition. Volume 2, Cambridge, UK (2004) 505–508
17. Lehmann, T., Güld, M., Thies, C., Fischer, B., Spitzer, K., Keysers, D., Ney, H., Kohnen, M., Schubert, H., Wein, B.: The irma project – a state of the art report on content-based image retrieval in medical applications. In: Korea-Germany Joint Workshop on Advanced Medical Image Processing, Seoul, Korea (2003) 161–171

MIRACLE Approach to ImageCLEF 2004: Merging Textual and Content-Based Image Retrieval

J.L. Martínez-Fernández[1,4], A. García-Serrano[2], J. Villena[3,4], and V. Méndez-Sáenz[2]

[1] Advaced Databases Group, Computer Science Department,
Universidad Carlos III de Madrid,
Avda. Universidad 30, 28911 Leganés, Madrid, Spain
[2] Artificial Intelligence Department, Universidad Politécnica de Madrid,
Campus de Montegancedo s/n, Boadilla del Monte 28660, Spain
{agarcia, vmendez }@isys.dia.fi.upm.es
[3] Department of Telematic Engineering, Universidad Carlos III de Madrid,
Avda. Universidad 30, 28911 Leganés, Madrid, Spain
[4] DAEDALUS – Data, Decisiond and Language, S.A.
Centro de Empresas "La Arboleda", Ctra. N-III km. 7,300 Madrid 28031, Spain
{jmartinez, jvillena}@daedalus.es

Abstract. This paper presents the image retrieval techniques tested by the MIRACLE (Multilingual Information RetrievAl for the CLEf campaign) research group as part of the ImageCLEF 2004 initiative. Two main lines of research continuing the past year's experiments were considered: the application of linguistic techniques to improve retrieval performance and the combination of textual and content-based image retrieval.

1 Introduction

The Multilingual Information RetrievAl for the CLEf campaign (MIRACLE) research group participation in ImageCLEF 2004 centred on two main goals:

- The application of lexical linguistic knowledge in the image retrieval task (based on morphological, syntactic and semantic features of lexical entries).
- To make a first attempt at the use of content-based image retrieval techniques and the combination of these techniques with text-based ones.

The task defined for the ImageCLEF track is centred on the retrieval of images according to a user query based on two different sources of information: the textual descriptions of the pictures and the content of the image file.

Taking into account the textual source of data, linguistic knowledge is introduced using well-known tools for the English language such as the Brill tagger 2, WordNet 3, EuroWordNet 5 and previously developed modules for entity recognition. The availability of EuroWordNet for German, French, Spanish and Italian allowed the definition of experiments where semantic information for these languages is applied. The success of applying this lexical linguistic knowledge depends highly on the quality of the resources for the different languages under consideration. For these languages, EuroWordNet was used for translation and query expansion.

C. Peters et al. (Eds.): CLEF 2004, LNCS 3491, pp. 699–708, 2005.

Regarding the content-based analysis of images files, the tool GIFT/Viper 0.1.9 6, a public package devoted to image processing, was used. This software provides an implementation of an index and retrieval engine for images. An adapted client is also provided, which has been integrated with the retrieval system used by the MIRACLE team.

The organization of ImageCLEF 2004 proposed three different tasks:

1. an ad hoc bilingual retrieval task, where images are accompanied by English captions,
2. a medical retrieval task, where a set of scan, x-ray, pictures and short textual descriptions of the medical diagnosis are provided, and
3. a user-centred search task, where the main goal is to take user interaction into account in the retrieval process.

In 1 an in-depth description of the different tasks can be found. The MIRACLE team took part in the first two tasks, the first one paying more attention to textual descriptions and the second one to testing the aforementioned content-based image indexing and searching tool. As a result, 45 runs were submitted for both tasks, and a great human effort was made for this CLEF track. The following sections include a detailed description of the experiments, evaluation and analysis of the results.

2 Text-Based Image Retrieval

A flexible system was built to process the text captions provided for each image. The figure in the appendix shows a graphic representation of the different processes followed in the retrieval process according to the languages considered. As previously mentioned, different tools were used to process English queries. A *tagger*, based on Brill's work 2, can be used to attach a morphosyntactic tag to each word. A *proper-names* detection module can be applied at the output of the Brill tagger. A *shallow parser* which, in a final step, was in charge of dividing the text into sentences, whose constituent phrases could be recognized and extracted. Finally, a *semantic component* was used to implement query expansion based on semantic information contained in the WordNet database. Optionally, the linguistic category of a given word was used when the semantic expansion was carried out. For example, if a word acting as a name is going to be expanded, only synonyms of the given word that could act as a name are considered.

For languages other than English, EuroWordNet was used, where available. For languages not covered by EuroWordNet, web translation tools, like Systran[1] or Translation Experts[2] were applied. The main objectives of these experiments were to test EuroWordNet when used in translation tasks and as a synonym expansion tool. For translation purposes, the inter-lingual index (ILI) supplied with EuroWordNet was applied. Again, it was possible to consider the linguistic category of the word when asking for its translations. So, if a name was going to be translated, only words that could act as a name in the target language were taken into account.

[1] "*Altavista's Babel Fish Translation Service*", http://babelfish.altavista.com/

[2] "*Translation Experts*", http://www.transexp.com

2.1 Monolingual English Experiments

The monolingual English experiments were defined by applying different combinations of the modules described in the figure included in the appendix. This allows for the definition of experiments where the linguistic category of the word could be used to filter out possible synonyms. Detected proper names can be treated as special words and used to drive the retrieval process. All tested combinations of these modules are detailed in Table 1, where five different sets of experiments can be distinguished, depending on the kind of linguistic knowledge applied. Of course, image captions must also be indexed according to the process followed in the query. This means that, when proper names were used in the query, image captions were indexed using the same proper-names recognition module. The same applies when common nouns were recognized in the query.

Table 1. Run definitions for the ad hoc retrieval task

	Monolingual English Experiments	
	Query Process	**Run Name**
Baseline	Topic Words	**mirobaseen**
	Topic Words + Synonyms	**mirosbaseen**
Only Nouns	Nouns	**mironounen**
	Nouns + Synonyms without category	**mirosnounen**
	Nouns + Synonyms with category	**miroscnounen**
Baseline + Proper Names	Topic Words + Proper Names	**miroppbaseen**
	Topic Words +Synonyms + Proper Names	**mirosppbaseen**
Nouns + Proper Names	Nouns + Proper Names	**miroppnounen**
	Nouns + Synonyms without category + Proper Names	**mirosppnounen**
	Nouns + Synonyms with category + Proper Names	**miroscppnounen**
Shallow Parsing	Topic and Narration Words	**mirorppbaseen**
	Topic and Narration Words + Synonyms with category	**mirorscppbaseen**

In Table 1, 'Topic Words' means that all recognized words (excluding stopwords) were used to search for the corresponding index database. 'Synonyms' means that all synonyms for a word found in WordNet were used to expand the query, without any refinement, i.e., no disambiguation process is carried out to select the right synonym. 'Nouns' stands for the situation where the query text was tagged and only words acting as nouns were selected as part of the final query. 'Proper Names' is used to mark that only recognized proper names in the text were used as part of the query. 'Synonyms with category' is used to distinguish the process in which not all the synonyms of a word were taken into account, but only those synonyms that could act with the same category as the initial word were included in the query. Finally, in the last two experiments, the narrative of the query (only available for the English queries) was used as the input to the Shallow Parsing module. This module is used to parse the text and get a more precise category for the word.

Average precision results obtained for monolingual experiments are shown in Table 2. The position obtained for each defined run in the absolute ranking produced by ImageCLEF organizers is shown in the third column. This ranking is an ordered list of average precision numbers obtained for every experiment submitted. This simplifies the comparison between different experiments and systems.

Taking these results into account, it is important to highlight some points: first of all, the basic experiment (taken as the baseline) produced the best results. In Table 2, there are two jumps in average precision scores: after run 4 and 8. These differences in precision show that, when all words are used in the characterization of the textual captions, the results are better and the inclusion of more linguistic information (such as proper nouns or synonyms) does not lead to an improvement. On the other hand, if only common or proper nouns are used to represent the documents there is a loss of precision, perhaps due to the fewer number of words used for document characterization. These initial results must be analyzed by taking into account the

Table 2. Average precision results for monolingual English experiments

Run Name	Average Precision	Rank
mirobaseen	0.5865	1
mirosbaseen	0.5623	4
miroppbaseen	0.5609	6
mirosppbaseen	0.5388	8
miroppnounen	0.3384	87
mirosnounen	0.3383	88
mirorppbaseen	0.3366	90
mirosppnounen	0.3337	92
mirorscppbaseen	0.2703	112
miroscppnounen	0.2568	116
mironounen	0.2525	119
miroscnounen	0.2461	120

features of the image captions, i.e., titles are too short for linguistic tools to carry out good parsing. So, further experiments regarding the length of captions should be made.

2.2 Bilingual Experiments

For the bilingual experiments two different approaches, depending on available resources, were considered. These two approaches were:

- A EuroWordNet-based approach, where information contained in the ILI was used to translate the original query. This approach was used for Spanish, German, French and Italian languages.
- A translator-based approach, where online translation tools, in particular Systran and Translation Experts tools, were used to translate queries from the source (or query) language to the target language (English in Image CLEF tasks).

All bilingual experiments used a base indexing process, where all words (excluding stopwords) were included in the index. In Table 3, the last two letters of the run name shown in the first column indicate the query language for the corresponding experiment. Run names where a 'w' appears after the 'miro' part are those where EuroWordNet is used. In every experiment, the target language is English.

Table 3 shows average precision figures obtained for the multilingual experiments defined in the previous section.

Table 3. Average precision for multilingual ad hoc retrieval experiments

Run Name	MAP	%Monolingual	Rank
mirobaseru	0.3866	65.93	73
mirobasedu	0.3807	64.91	76
mirobasesw	0.3043	51.89	99
mirowbaseit	0.2857	48.72	106
mirobaseda	0.2799	47.72	107
mirowbasees	0.2687	45.82	113
mirowbaseesc	0.2615	44.59	114
mirowbasege	0.2455	41.87	122
mirobaseja	0.2358	40.21	124
mirowbasefr	0.2188	37.31	127
mirobasezh	0.1777	30.30	135
mirobasefi	0.1700	28.99	141

According to these results, one important fact worth mentioning is the loss of precision. Taking into account the best monolingual experiment (%Monolingual column), a decrease of 34% in precision is obtained, again highlighting the importance of the quality of the translators used in multilingual environments. Situations in which EuroWordNet have been used as a translation tool can be compared with the results obtained from CLEF 2003 4 and an important decrease in precision can be noticed. This fact could mean that EuroWordNet is not a good tool for translation purposes. Last year bilingual experiments with French, German, Italian and Spanish achieved around 40% average precision, while this year average precision for these languages is around 30%. It is also worth mentioning that other participants, according to official results, have obtained only a decrease of 10% in precision for some bilingual tasks (but not using EuroWordNet as a translation tool), so, in our situation, there is room for improvement.

3 Content-Based Image Retrieval

In 2004, ImageCLEF organizers defined a new task where the main focus is image content-based retrieval. For this purpose a set of medical images, including scans, x-ray images and photographs of different illnesses were made available to ImageCLEF participants. A more detailed description of the image collection used can be found in 1.

The CBIR system used was GIFT/Viper 0.1.9 6 developed under the GNU licence which enables query by example (using an image as the starting point for the search process) and implements relevance feedback methods. This software was developed by the Vision Group at the Computer Science Center of the University of Geneva. Although different search algorithms can be added, the provided *separate normalisation* algorithm has been used in these experiments.

The first step in the search process for this task must involve an image, but textual descriptions of the medical cases were used to try to improve the retrieval results. The search process can be divided into the following steps:

1. The initial query, made up of one image, is introduced into the CBIR system to obtain a set of images related to the query.
2. The CBIR system returns a list of images along with the corresponding relevance values. Relevance feedback is applied to try to improve results and the number of images used in this refinement process is a configuration parameter of the system.

The MIRACLE research group has not submitted runs where only image content is used in the retrieval process. Algorithms and methods to characterize images based on their content is not the main focus of this research group. Nevertheless, there was a great deal of interest in testing whether the analysis of the content of the image could improve text-based image retrieval. The next section is devoted to the description of the approach followed to mix both kinds of technique.

4 Merging Text-Based and Content-Based Image Retrieval

The first step of the MIRACLE team in content-based image retrieval led to the definition of experiments where content-based image retrieval was applied in combination with text retrieval. This was the case of the ad hoc retrieval task, where some runs mixing results obtained using textual search and CBIR search were submitted. The text retrieval subsystem was the one used in text-based experiments, although for the initial test and tuning of the overall system, last year's data and text search systems was used.

The process of mixing textual and image results begins by taking the first N elements of the list with the images returned by the text search subsystem and their relevance figures and building a query for the CBIR subsystem. The content search is carried out followed by a new search considering the 5 (RF_IMG in Fig. 1) first elements returned. Finally, results obtained with this last relevance feedback approach are combined with the original results list returned by the textual search subsystem. Fig. 1 shows the search process followed.

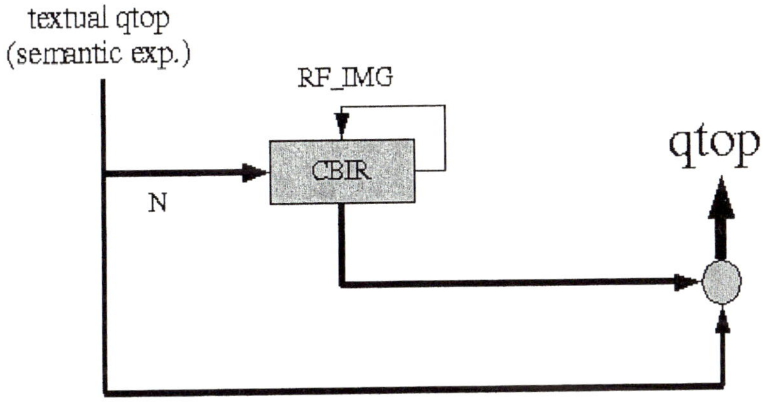

Fig. 1. Text and CBIR subsystem combination model

The combination of the partial results lists provided by each system to provide a unique results list with a global relevance value is:

$$\begin{cases} \sqrt[k]{REL\_VIS^{weight\_vis} \times REL\_TXT^{weight\_txt}}, & \text{for elements in both lists and } k = \text{weight\_vis} + \text{weight\_txt} \\ \text{factor\_vis}, & \text{for elements appearing only in the list obtained with the CBIR subsystem} \\ \text{factor\_txt}, & \text{for elements appearing only in the list obtained with the textual search subsystem} \end{cases}$$

In this expression, *REL_VIS* and *REL_TXT* are the relevance value returned by the CBIR subsystem and the text search subsystem respectively. *factor_vis*, *factor_txt*, *weight_vis* and *weight_txt* are parameters to be empirically established and can be used to adjust the overall system according to the results obtained, for example, giving more importance to textual results or CBIR results.

Several sets of experiments were carried out applying this system. One of them was built using the results of the textual runs described in Section 2. The goal was to evaluate the effect of the image content analysis subsystem on the retrieval process. Table 4 shows average precision obtained for these runs. In these experiments, the values for the parameters defined for the image and textual results combination expression were: N=10, *factor_vis* = 0.5, *factor_txt* = 0.75, *weight_vis* = 1 and *weight_txt* = 2.

Table 4. Average precision values for text and CBIR mixing experiments

Run Name	Average Precision	Rank	Initial Text search Experiment
enenrunexp1	0.5838	2	mirobaseen
enenrunexp7	0.5339	9	mirosppbaseen
enenrunexp4	0.3373	89	mirosnounen
enenrunexp10	0.2533	118	miroscppnounen

Compared to results in Table 2, these results are very close to (and always below) the ones where only a textual search was applied. This could be due to the selected values of the configuration parameters defined in the combination algorithms. These results show, at least, that textual retrieval performance is not compromised by the inclusion of the CBIR system, but more tests should be made to extract a more valid conclusion.

5 Conclusions

The basic objective to be fulfilled this year was to take another step forward in finding a right combination of linguistic and statistical methods to improve the Information Retrieval process. The MIRACLE group is also very interested in the field of multimedia retrieval so, the content-based image retrieval task defined this year, as part of the ImageCLEF track, was a great opportunity to take a first step in this direction. From our point of view, the results obtained for the ad hoc retrieval task were good enough as we explain in the following.

The average precision values for the monolingual English task were a little bit better than those obtained last year, highlighting that it is difficult to improve the results for this task. For monolingual experiments, it seems that the best performance figures that can be obtained with current technology have been reached, so new techniques and methods must be included in the retrieval process. On the other hand, bilingual tasks, in the way we have developed them, have to be improved until the same level of precision as that of monolingual environments is reached.

Some more refined ways of managing semantic information in the retrieval process could be investigated given that the improvement of the retrieval performance, when semantic lexical knowledge is applied, highly depends on the quality of the resources for the different languages to be considered. Besides, different semantic domains have different degrees of development of the lexical resources, so we also want to prove the influence of that aspect in the results obtained for the different tasks.

In the CLEF workshop held this year, participants had a great deal of interest in content-based image retrieval, but the results obtained were not as good as those of the textual task. This fact compels us to increase our efforts devoted to this kind of retrieval for the following campaigns.

Acknowledgements

This work has been partially supported by the projects OmniPaper (European Union, 5th Framework Programme for Research and Technological Development, IST-2001-32174) and MIRACLE (Regional Government of Madrid, Regional Plan for Research, 07T/0055/2003).

Special mention must be done to our colleagues at other members of the MIRACLE group: Santiago González Tortosa, Michelangelo Castagnone, José Carlos González, José Miguel Goñi, Javier Alonso, Paloma Martínez, César de Pablo y Francisco Bueno.

References

1. Clough, P., Müller, H. and Sanderson, M.: The CLEF Cross Language Image Retrieval Track (ImageCLEF) 2004, in Fifth Workshop of the Cross--Language Evaluation Forum (CLEF 2004), Lecture Notes in Computer Science (LNCS), Springer, Heidelberg, Germany (in print), 2005.
2. Brill E.: Some Advances in Transformation Based Part of Speech Tagging, Proceedings of the Twelfth National Conference on Artificial Intelligence, 1994
3. Miller, G.A.: WordNet: A lexical database for English. Communications of the ACM, 38(11):39—41, 1995
4. Villena J., Martinez-Fernandez J.L., Fombella J., García-Serrano A., Ruíz-Cristina A., Martínez P., Goñi J.M., González-Cristóbal J.C.: Image Retrieval: the MIRACLE Approach, 4th Workshop of the Cross-Language Evaluation Forum, CLEF 2003, Trondheim, Norway, August 21-22, 2003, Revised Selected Papers, Series : LNCS , Vol. 3237, Peters, C.; Gonzalo, J.; Braschler, M.; Kluck, M. (Eds.), 2005
5. Eurowordnet: Building a Multilingual Database with Wordnets for several European Languages", http://www.illc.uva.nl/EuroWordNet/, March, 1996
6. The GNU Image-Finding Tool GIFT 0.1.9, http://www.gnu.org/software/gift/, last accessed 12.08.2004

Appendix. Query Processing Applied for the Ad Hoc Retrieval Task

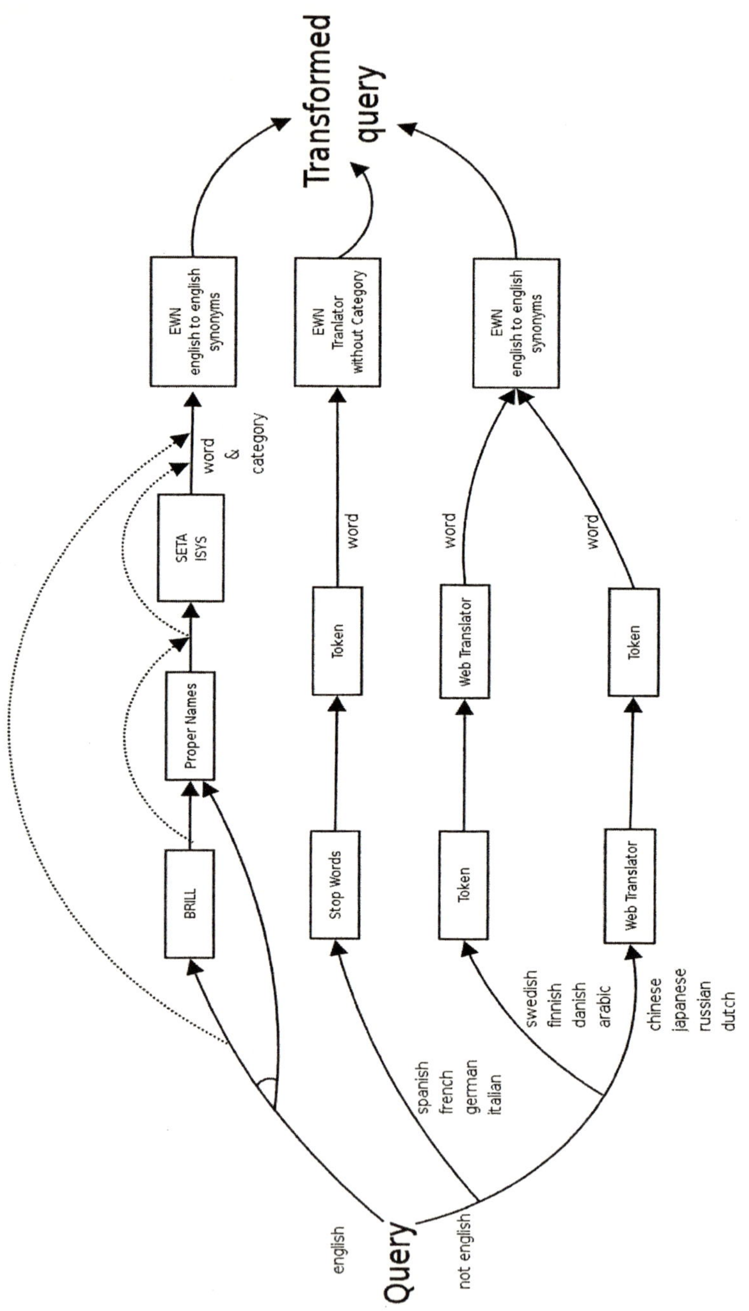

Cross-Media Feedback Strategies: Merging Text and Image Information to Improve Image Retrieval

Romaric Besançon, Patrick Hède, Pierre-Alain Moellic, and Christian Fluhr

CEA-LIST, LIC2M (Multilingual Multimedia Knowledge Engineering Laboratory),
B.P.6 - F92265 Fontenay-aux-Roses Cedex, France
{romaric.besancon, patrick.hede, pierre-alain.moellic, christian.fluhr}@cea.fr

Abstract. The CEA-LIST/LIC2M develops both cross-language information retrieval systems and content-based image retrieval systems. The ad hoc and medical tasks of the ImageCLEF campaign offered us the opportunity to perform some experiments on merging the results of the two systems. The results obtained show that the performance of each system highly depends on the corpus and the task: feedback strategies can improve the results, but the parameters used are to be tuned according to the confidence of each system on the task and corpus: for the ad hoc task, text retrieval performs good whereas results of image retrieval are poor. On the other hand, for the medical task, the image retrieval performs better, and text retrieval can improve overall results only with reinforcement strategies.

1 Introduction

In the framework of the ImageCLEF campaign, our goal was to perform some first experiments on merging strategies to integrate the information retrieved from both cross-language text retrieval systems and content-based image retrieval (CBIR) systems that are developed in our lab.

The goal of the ImageCLEF ad hoc task is to retrieve relevant images based on a text query. In this case, we tried to improve the results by merging the results of the cross-language text retrieval with content-based image retrieval, using the example image given with the topic.

The goal of the ImageCLEF medical task is to retrieve relevant images based on an image query. We tried, for this task, to improve the results of the CBIR system by using automatic feedback on the text description of the medical cases associated with the images retrieved.

In section 2, we present the retrieval systems for text and images. We then present the strategies used for the ad hoc task and the medical task and their results in sections 3 and 4 respectively.

C. Peters et al. (Eds.): CLEF 2004, LNCS 3491, pp. 709–717, 2005.

2 Retrieval Systems

2.1 Cross-Language Text Retrieval System

The cross-language text retrieval system used for these experiments is the same as the one used for the CLEF multilingual task, and a more detailed description can be found in the section of the proceedings corresponding to this task or in the proceedings of the CLEF 2003 campaign [1]. The system has not been specially adapted to work on the text of the ImageCLEF corpora, and has simply been used as is. This system is a weighted boolean search engine based on a linguistic analysis of the query and the documents. Its basic principle is briefly described here.

Document Processing. The documents are processed through a language-dependent linguistic analyzer, that performs in particular part-of-speech tagging, lemmatization, and extracts compounds and named entities from the text. All these elements are indexed using inverted files. For both the St. Andrews and CasImage corpora, no special treatment has been performed to take into account the structure of the documents (such as photographer's name, location, date for the captions and description, diagnosis, clinical presentation in the medical cases): all fields have been taken as a single text to be analyzed. For the medical task, the CasImage corpus contains French and English documents, so we first used a statistical language identification module to split the corpus and analyze each part independently using the corresponding analyzer.

Query Processing. The query is first processed through a similar analyzer (corresponding to the query language) to extract the informative elements from the text. These elements are used as query "*concepts*". Each concept is reformulated into a set of *search terms*, either using a monolingual expansion dictionary (that introduces synonyms and related words), or using a bilingual dictionary, depending on the index languages.

Search and Merging. Each search term is searched in the index, and documents containing the term are retrieved. All retrieved documents are then associated with a *concept profile*, indicating the presence of query concepts in the document. Documents sharing the same concept profile are clustered together, and a weight is associated with each cluster according to its concept profile and to the weight of the concepts (the weight of a concept depends on the weight of each of its reformulated term in the retrieved documents). The clusters are sorted according to their weights and the first 1000 documents in this sorted list are retrieved.

2.2 Content-Based Image Retrieval System

For image retrieval, we used a system developed at our lab, the CEA-LIST/LIC2M, called PIRIA (Program for the Indexing and Research of Images by Affinity)[2]. A user query is submitted to the system, which returns a list of images ranked by their similarity to the query image. The similarity is obtained by a metric distance that operates on every image signature. These indexed images are compared according to several classifiers : principally *Color*, *Texture* and *Form* if the segmentation of the images is relevant. The system takes into account geometric transformations and variations like rotation, symmetry, mirroring, etc. PIRIA is a global one-pass system, feedback or "relevant/non relevant" learning methods are not used.

Color Indexing. PIRIA uses a global normalized color histogram. The choice of the color space is very important for a good color division. The model based on *Hue, Saturation and Value* is used to obtain a strong semantic content. Global histogram is used for the global image or after the segmentation of the image in several blocks. Splitting the image by blocks enables computation of spatial relationship. A more complex color analysis can be used with a region based segmentation. Color information of each region are mixed with form analysis (Fourier descriptors). The distance uses for the color indexing is a classical L1 norm.

Texture Indexing. A global texture histogram is used for the texture analysis. The histogram is computed from the Local Edge Pattern descriptors [3]. These descriptors describe the local structure according to the edge image computed with a Sobel filtering.

Merge of Results. The merging of results from several indexers is computed with a boundary fusion based on the position of the result images.

3 Ad Hoc Task

For the ad hoc task, we experimented merging techniques using topics in English, French and Spanish. For English, we tried using all information available in the query (title and narrative), or using only the title; for French and Spanish, only the title was available. For each of the topic languages, we used as baseline the simple text retrieval, with no use of the image retrieval system. We then experimented simple merging strategies integrating the results of both text and image retrieval: in this case, the image used for the image retrieval was the example image provided with each topic. The first merging strategy tested is quite straightforward: each image x is given a score that is a weighted sum of the scores given by each retrieval system: $w(x) = \alpha \times w_t(x) + (1 - \alpha) \times w_i(x)$, where $w_t(x)$ and $w_i(x)$ are respectively the scores of the text and image retrieval systems, normalized so that they are comparable.

The results of the different tests are presented in Table 1 for various values of parameter α ($\alpha = 1$ correspond to the retrieval using only text information).

From these results, the merging strategy using both text and image shows little improvement with respect to the simple text search. More precisely, for $\alpha = 0.9$, the mean average precision is often increased, but the total number

Table 1. Results for the ad hoc task – simple merging: average precision (*avg_p*), number of relevant document retrieved (*relret*)

English topics					
	α=1	0.9	0.8	0.7	0.6
avg_p	0.428	**0.439**	0.424	0.29	0.176
relret	**766**	656	544	468	364
English topics (title only)					
	α=1	0.9	0.8	0.7	0.6
avg_p	0.409	**0.429**	0.424	0.376	0.317
relret	675	**679**	667	545	479
French topics					
	α=1	0.9	0.8	0.7	0.6
avg_p	**0.247**	0.245	0.238	0.202	0.156
relret	**549**	529	495	471	356
Spanish topics					
	α=1	0.9	0.8	0.7	0.6
avg_p	0.16	**0.175**	0.162	0.137	0.126
relret	**603**	555	509	334	310

of relevant documents retrieved actually decreases. The improvement of average precision is only due to the reordering of retrieved documents (increasing the score of documents retrieved by both systems). But the CBIR system also introduces a lot of new images that are not relevant.

This is mainly due to the fact that the image retrieval does not perform well on this corpus (indeed, the images need a complex local analysis - based on interest points). The image retrieval alone (using the example images from the queries) has an average precision of less than 7% and retrieves only 122 relevant images out of the 829 relevant images of the `partial-isec-total` assessments. Only 6 out of these 122 images were not found by the original text retrieval, based on English topics with all information (16 using only title, 41 for French topics, 42 for Spanish topics).

In order to exploit the reordering and decrease the number of non-relevant images introduced, we tested a more conservative merging strategy, using the image retrieval system only to reinforce the results found by the text retrieval system: the score of a document is increased only if the document has been found by the text retrieval system: a image x is given a score $w(x) = \alpha w_t(x) + (1-\alpha)w_i(x)$ if $w_t(x) \neq 0$, $w(x) = \alpha w_t(x)$ otherwise. Nevertheless, if the text retrieval system did not retrieve enough documents (less than 1000 in this case), we added at the end of the results the best remaining images retrieved by the CBIR system.

The results of this reinforcement merging are given in Table 2 for various values of parameter α.

These results show improvement for both average precision and number of relevant documents retrieved. In case of English topics, the number of relevant

Table 2. Results for the ad hoc task – reinforcement merging: average precision (*avg_p*), number of relevant document retrieved (*relret*)

	English topics				
	α=1	0.9	0.8	0.7	0.6
avg_p	0.428	0.444	0.452	**0.454**	0.421
relret	**766**	**766**	**766**	**766**	**766**
	English topics (title only)				
	α=1	0.9	0.8	0.7	0.6
avg_p	0.409	**0.43**	0.428	0.426	0.398
relret	675	**686**	**686**	**686**	**686**
	French topics				
	α=1	0.9	0.8	0.7	0.6
avg_p	**0.247**	0.239	0.237	0.221	0.206
relret	549	**572**	**572**	**572**	**572**
	Spanish topics				
	α=1	0.9	0.8	0.7	0.6
avg_p	0.16	0.171	**0.172**	0.169	0.171
relret	603	**613**	**613**	**613**	**613**

documents does not change (the 6 missing documents were not added since by using all information in query, text retrieval system did retrieve enough documents). For the other cases, the addition of image retrieval results allow to increase the number of relevant documents retrieved (between 1% and 4%). In all cases except for French topics, the reordering caused by reinforcement of text retrieval results by CBIR scores show improvement of average precision, for a value of α between 0.7 and 0.9 (around 5% of improvement).

Other tests are planned using only the text query as starting point, without using the image example for image retrieval system: the first images retrieved by the text system should be used as query for image retrieval, introducing an automated image feedback.

The image indexers will also be adapted to treat images such as the old photographs of the St. Andrews collection: this image base is particularly difficult for the kind of image indexers we used in this experiments since most of the images are in a kind of monochrome color (with not always the same tone), so that a color segmentation of the image cannot be performed to identify the interesting elements of the images.

4 Medical Task

For the medical task, we used as a baseline the image retrieval search using a CBIR system on the image query. We tried to improve this baseline using the text information contained in the cases associated with the retrieved images, and implementing an automated feedback on the basis of this information.

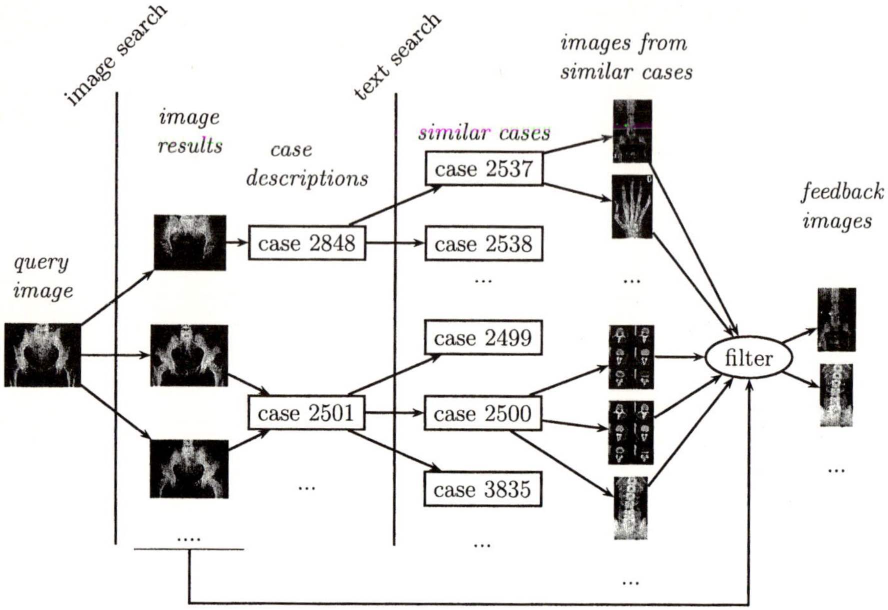

Fig. 1. Text feedback strategy for the medical task

The process of this feedback is the following (a schema presenting the outline of this feedback strategy is proposed in Figure 1):

1. we first take the set R_i of images retrieved by the CBIR system: these images are given a score by the CBIR system (we call it the *image score*, denoted $w_i(x)$ for an image x);
2. we collect the cases associated with the first images retrieved by the CBIR system: the case of an image x is denoted $case(x)$; the number N_i of images used for feedback is a parameter of the system;
3. we then use these cases as queries to the text retrieval system to retrieve similar cases, based on the textual description of the cases: we retrieve the set of the N_c most similar cases. This set is denoted $S_c(c)$ for a case c. Each case $c_s \in S_c(c)$ is given a score by the text retrieval system (*text score*, denoted $w_t(c_s, c)$);
4. we collect the images associated with the cases retrieved by the text retrieval system: these images are candidate images for feedback;
5. since the images retrieved must have the same modality as the query image, we introduced an optional phase of filtering: the similarity between each candidate image and the retrieved image that lead to this feedback image can be used to filter out noise images;
6. The set of feedback images is then used to modify the first set of retrieved images (step 1), each retrieved image x is given a score

$$w(x) = \alpha \times w_i(x) + (1-\alpha) \times \sum_{y \in R_i, case(y) \in S_c(case(x))} w_t(case(y), case(x))) . \quad (1)$$

Giving little importance to feedback images (large values of α) will increase scores of images retrieved by CBIR by reinforcing images that are also candidate for feedback, and cause a reordering of the results that will increase precision. On the other hand, giving more importance to feedback image (smaller values of α) will give a chance to introduce new images that were not found in first step, and increase the recall.

We ran the tests with N_i between 1 and 10 N_c between 5 and 100 and a value of α between 0.5 and 0.9. The best results, obtained for a small value of N_i, a large value of N_c and a large value of α, are presented in Table 3.

Table 3. Results for the medical task: average precision (*avg_p*) and number of relevant document retrieved (*relret*)

		avg_p						relret					
N_i	N_c	α=1	0.9	0.8	0.7	0.6	0.5	α=1	0.9	0.8	0.7	0.6	0.5
1	50	0.278	**0.293**	0.284	0.266	0.254	0.228	2135	2134	2134	2132	2135	**2141**
	100	0.278	**0.295**	0.286	0.272	0.261	0.245	2135	2134	2134	2130	2133	**2158**
2	50	0.278	**0.288**	0.273	0.261	0.245	0.224	**2135**	**2135**	**2135**	2127	2128	2126
	100	0.278	**0.289**	0.277	0.263	0.252	0.237	2135	2135	2135	2130	2130	**2144**
3	50	0.278	**0.29**	0.273	0.262	0.245	0.232	2135	2135	2133	2127	2127	**2137**
	100	0.278	**0.29**	0.27	0.258	0.243	0.232	2135	2135	2134	2133	2132	**2140**

The best result for mean average precision (6% improvement) is actually obtained when using only the first image retrieved by the CBIR system, with $\alpha = 0.9$ and $N_c = 100$ (large values of $\alpha = 0.9$ are compatible with larger values of $N_c = 100$ since the reinforcement strategy can gain from more candidates).

We also tried using a second CBIR phase (step 4) to filter out feedback images that are not relevant, applying a threshold on the similarity between the feedback image and the retrieved image that has generated this feedback image. The threshold values we tested are 0.9, 0.8 or 0.7 (the scores of the CBIR system are in [0,1]). We also tested the same threshold applied only on new images (feedback images not found by the first CBIR step), to avoid introducing noisy images. The results are presented in Table 4.

The results obtained tend to show that this filtering does not improve the results: the results for mean average precision are improved for $\alpha \leq 0.7$, but are still worse than results with larger values of α (for large values of α, the noise images are not given enough importance to be introduced and results are not changed drastically with the filtering step). However, for small values of α, the filtering phase allows to increase the number of relevant documents retrieved.

A deeper analysis of the feedback process shows that 16027 feedback images are produced (for N_i=1 and N_c=100), in which 805 images are relevant, and only 212 images from this relevant set were not found by the first CBIR step.

Table 4. Results for the ad hoc task using a filtering phase on feedback images: average precision (*avg_p*) and number of relevant document retrieved (*relret*)

	simple threshold									
	α=0.9		0.8		0.7		0.6		0.5	
threshold	avg_p	relret	avg_p	relret	avg_p	relret	avg_p	relret	avg_p	relret
none	**0.295**	2134	**0.286**	2134	0.272	2130	0.261	2133	0.245	2158
0.9	0.285	**2135**	0.28	**2135**	**0.275**	**2135**	**0.27**	2135	**0.268**	2134
0.8	0.288	**2135**	0.277	**2135**	0.266	**2135**	0.259	2136	0.254	2140
0.7	0.289	2134	0.278	2134	0.264	2134	0.255	**2139**	0.245	**2164**

	threshold on new images									
	α=0.9		0.8		0.7		0.6		0.5	
threshold	avg_p	relret	avg_p	relret	avg_p	relret	avg_p	relret	avg_p	relret
none	**0.295**	**2134**	**0.286**	**2134**	0.272	2130	0.261	2133	0.245	2158
0.7	**0.295**	**2134**	**0.286**	**2134**	**0.273**	**2134**	**0.289**	**2134**	**0.252**	**2165**

The conservative feedback strategy chosen (large values of α), does not change this configuration much: for the best run in average precision, the set of relevant images retrieved is the same as the one retrieved by the direct CBIR search. For a less restrained feedback, feedback images are given more importance, and more images are introduced: for the best run with respect to the number of relevant images retrieved, 832 new images are introduced, containing 43 new relevant images. On the other hand, 13 relevant images found by the CBIR system are no longer in the result. The gain of the trade-off is not sufficient to improve the results significantly. Further testing on merging strategies should be performed to improve this gain.

Since the task imposes that the retrieved images are of the same modality as the query images, a general similarity on the textual description of the cases is not sufficient: it can retrieve cases relative to the same kind of pathology but it is not obvious that the images associated with these cases will be similar to the original image. We tried to avoid this problem using a second step of image similarity, but a deeper analysis of the text would be needed so that informations on the image modality and anatomic region are extracted from the case description.

Another possible reason for the small improvement using text feedback on this task is that our text retrieval system is very general. A specialized corpus such as this medical corpus contains many technical words that are treated by the system as unknown words. A more adapted processing of the medical text, giving special importance to terms such as disease names, anatomic regions, medical acts should increase the relevance of the case similarity.

5 Conclusion

These first experiments on cross-media feedback strategies in the ImageCLEF campaign are very interesting: with the same two general purpose systems (no particular adaptation of the systems was made for the two tasks), the results lead to very different conclusions depending on the task and corpus.

The ad hoc task with the St. Andrews collection of old photographs is not well adapted to the kind of image indexers we used, that relies mostly on color for segmentation. On the other hand, this task is easier for text retrieval, since the descriptions of the images in the captions are small and precise and the elements in the queries are often found as is in the documents (even without treating the structure of the captions). In this case, a conservative feedback strategy that uses image retrieval to reinforce results obtained by text retrieval shows a small improvement of the results.

The medical task offers a better field for image retrieval, the images being "easier" to index (at least, to separate the images by their modality, quite different in nature and colors) but in that case, and given the particularity of the task and the specialization of the corpus, text retrieval is not as important and only a feedback strategy using text information to reinforce results obtained by CBIR improves the results.

The conclusions drawn from these first experiments are that cross-media feedback strategies improve results as long as they stay conservative and are used to reinforce the best single-media retrieval. The parameters of merging strategies are also conditioned by the task, the corpus and a knowledge of the expected performance of the each system for the task/corpus.

References

1. Besançon, R., de Chalendar, G., Ferret, O., Fluhr, C., Mesnard, O., Naets, H.: The LIC2M's CLEF 2003 system. In: Working Notes for the CLEF 2003 Workshop, Trondheim, Norway (2003)
2. Joint, M., Moëllic, P.A., Hède, P., Adam, P.: PIRIA : A General Tool for Indexing, Search and Retrieval of Multimedia Content. In: Proceedings of SPIE Electronic Imaging 2004, San Jose, California USA (2004)
3. Cheng, Y.C., Chen, S.Y.: Image Classification Using Color, Texture and Regions. Image and Vision Computing **21** (2003)

ImageCLEF 2004: Combining Image and Multi-lingual Search for Medical Image Retrieval

Henning Müller[1], Antoine Geissbühler[1], and Patrick Ruch[1,2]

[1] University and University Hospitals of Geneva, Service of Medical Informatics, 21 Rue Micheli-du-Crest, CH-1211 Geneva 4, Switzerland
{henning.mueller, antoine.geissbuhler, patrick.ruch}@sim.hcuge.ch
[2] Swiss Federal Institute of Technology, LITH
IN-Ecublens, CH-1015 Lausanne, Switzerland

Abstract. This article describes the technologies used for the various runs submitted by the University of Geneva in the context of the 2004 ImageCLEF competition. As our expertise is mainly in the field of medical image retrieval, most of our effort was concentrated on the medical image retrieval task. Described are the runs that were submitted including technical details for each of the single runs and a short explication of the obtained results compared with the results of submissions from other groups. We describe the problems encountered with respect to optimising the system and with respect to finding a balance between weighting textual and visual features for retrieval. A better balance seems possible when using training data for optimisation and with relevance judgements being available for a control of the retrieval quality.

The results show that relevance feedback is extremely important for optimal results. Query expansion with visual features only gives minimal changes in result quality. If textual features are added in the automatic query expansion, the results improve significantly. Visual and textual results combined deliver the best performance.

1 Introduction

The goals of ImageCLEF are in the field of cross–language information retrieval. From our point of view, this is of extremely high importance for a country such as Switzerland with four official languages and equally within the European Union with an even larger variety. CLEF has been held since 2000 as an independent workshop, always following the European conference on digital libraries (ECDL). 2003 saw the first ImageCLEF conference [1] and all submitted runs took into account the textual but not the visual data of the images supplied. The goal of the 2004 conference was clearly to create an image retrieval task with a realistic outline description that needs a visual component in addition to the textual multi–lingual part. The medical image retrieval task is such a (at least partly) realistic task where a medical doctor has produced one or several image(s) and likes to get evidence for or against a certain diagnosis. Ground truthing can, for now, not be on a diagnosis basis as the image dataset contains mainly one

C. Peters et al. (Eds.): CLEF 2004, LNCS 3491, pp. 718–727, 2005.

example per diagnosis. Still, a task is born with a visual query being a starting point [2]. Relevant documents were in this case images that show the same anatomic region, were taken with the same modality, from the same viewing direction and the same radiologic protocol if applicable (for example, contrast agent or not, T1 vs. T2 weighting when using the MRI). In [3], the main ideas for the 2004 task are described. The data for the task were taken from a medical case database called *casImage*[3] [4]. The database contains almost 9000 images from 2000 medical cases. Images are annotated in XML format but very rudimentary and not at all controlled with respect to quality or fields that have to be filled in. About 10% of the records do not contain any annotation. A majority of the documents are in French (70%), with around 20% in English.

In this paper we will mainly discuss the un–interpolated mean average precision of every run that we submitted as this measure was used for the official ranking of systems. Other measures might change the ranking of systems and might be more appropriate for certain tasks.

2 Basic Technologies Used

For our first ImageCLEF participation, we aim at combining content-based retrieval of images with cross–language retrieval applied on textual case reports. Considering that benchmarks are not available, investigating such a combination is challenging in itself. Once training data is available, systems can be optimised.

2.1 Image Retrieval

The technology used for the content–based retrieval of medical images is mainly taken from the *Viper*[4] project of the University of Geneva. Much information about this system is available [5]. Outcome of the *Viper* project is the GNU Image Finding Tool, *GIFT*[5]. This software tool is open source and can in consequence also be used by other participants of ImageCLEF. A ranked list of visually similar images for every query task was made available for participants and will serve as a baseline to measure the quality of submissions. Demonstration versions of gift were made available for participants to query visually as not everybody can be expected to install an entire Linux tool for such a benchmark. The feature sets that are used by GIFT are:

- Local colour features at different scales by partitioning the images successively into four equally sized regions (four times) and taking the mode colour of each region as a descriptor;
- global colour features in the form of a colour histogram, compared by a simple histogram intersection;

[3] `http://www.casimage.com/`

[4] `http://viper.unige.ch`

[5] `http://www.gnu.org/software/gift/`

- local texture features by partitioning the image and applying Gabor filters in various scales and directions. Gabor responses are quantised into 10 strength;
- global texture features represented as a simple histogram of responses of the local Gabor filters in various directions and scales.

A particularity of *GIFT* is that it uses many techniques from text retrieval. Visual features are quantised and the feature space is very similar to the distribution of words in texts, corresponding to a Zipf distribution. A simple *tf/idf* weighting is used and the query weights are normalised by the results of the query itself. The histogram features are compared based on a histogram intersection.

The medical version of the *GIFT* is called *medGIFT*[6] [6]. It is also accessible as open source and adaptations concern mainly visual features and the interface that shows the diagnosis on screen and is linked with a radiologic teaching file so the MD can not only browse images but also get the textual data and other images of the same case. Grey levels play a more important role for medical images and their numbers are raised, especially for relevance feedback (RF) queries. The number of the Gabor filter responses also has an impact on the performance and these are changed with respect to directions and scales.

2.2 Textual Case Report Search

The basic granularity of the casimage collection is the case. A case gathers a textual report, and a set of images. Because the original queries are images, textual case–based retrieval is used for feedback only.

Indexes. Textual experiments were conducted with the easyIR engine[7]. As a single report is able to contain both French and English written parts, it would have been necessary to detect the boundaries of each language segment. Ideally, French and English textual segments would be stored in different indexes. Each index could have been translated into the other language using a general translation method, or more appropriately using a domain-adapted method [7]. However, such a complex architecture would require to store different segments of the same document in separate indexes. Considering the lack of data to tune the system, we decided to index the casimage collection using a unique index: 1) using an English stemmer, 2) using a French stemmer. We use the Porters stemmer for English and a modified version of Savoy's conflation tool for French. Depending on the index, a list of stop words was used: 544 items for English, 792 for French. We also use a biomedical thesaurus, which has proven its effectiveness in the context of the TREC Genomics track [8]. For English, 120'000 string variants were extracted from UMLS, while the French thesaurus contains about 6'000 entries. Both resources were merged for the experiments. Our submitted runs were produced using the English index without specific translation.

Weighting Schema. Because queries were not provided, a generally good weighting schema of the term frequency - inverse document frequency family.

[6] `http://www.sim.hcuge.ch/medgift/`

[7] `http://lithwww.epfl.ch/~ruch/softs/softs.html`

Following weighting convention of the SMART engine, cf. Table 1, we used atc-ltn parameters, with $\alpha = \beta = 0.5$ in the augmented term frequency.

Table 1. Usual *tf-idf* weight; for the cosine normalisation factor, the formula is given for Euclidean space: $w_{i,j}$ is the document term weight, $w_{j,q}$ is the query term weight

Term Frequency	
First Letter	$f(tf)$
n (natural)	tf
l (logarithmic)	$1 + log(tf)$
a (augmented)	$\alpha + \beta \times (\frac{tf}{max(tf)})$, where $\alpha = 1 - \beta$ and $0 < \alpha < 1$
Inverse Document Frequency	
Second Letter	$f(\frac{1}{df})$
n(no)	1
t(full)	$log(\frac{N}{df})$
Normalisation	
Third Letter	$f(length)$
n(no)	1
c(cosine)	$\sqrt{\sum_{i=1}^{t} w_{i,j}^2} \times \sqrt{\sum_{j=1}^{t} w_{j,q}^2}$

2.3 Combining the Two

Combinations of visual and textual features are rather scarce in the literature [9], so many of the mechanism and fine tuning of the combinations will need more work. As the query is an image only, we had to use some automatic mechanism to expand the query to text. We use automatic query expansion (QE) to the first and the first three images retrieved visually. The text of the case report of these images was taken as free text for the query. XML tags of the casImage files were removed and unnecessary fields such as MD name or date of the entry were removed. All terms in the case reports were used. These free–text queries deliver a ranked list of cases and their similarity score. This score was normalised by the highest score available to have a result within [0; 1]. Afterwards, the similarity score is extended from the case to all the images that are part of the case. This includes a high number of visually very dissimilar images that just appear on the same case but are from a differing modality. Afterwards, visual and textual result list are merged. Such a list might not contain all images but at least images that have similarity in the visual and in the textual part will be ranked highly. Problem is to find a balance between the visual and the textual component. In our experience, the visual part needs to be ranked higher than the textual part as the task description is based on visually similar images but the textual part does improve the final results significantly. Manual RF is another tool that improves the results very strongly.

3 Runs Submitted for Evaluation

This section gives an introduction to the techniques and variations used for our submitted runs and their identifications.

3.1 Only Visual Retrieval with One Query Image

For the visual queries, the *medGIFT* system was used that allows an easy change of system parameters such as the configuration of Gabor filters and grey level/colour quantisations. Input for these queries were the query images. The following system parameters were submitted:

– 18 hues, 3 saturations, 3 values, 4 grey levels, 4 directions and 3 scales of the Gabor filters, the GIFT base configuration made available to all participants; *(GE_4g_4d_vis)*
– 9 hues, 2 saturations, 2 values, 16 grey levels, 8 directions and 5 scales of the Gabor filters; *(GE_16g_8d_vis)*
– 9 hues, 2 saturations, 2 values, 16 grey levels, 4 directions and 5 scales of the Gabor filters. *(GE_16g_4d_vis)*

It is hard to actually analyse visually and without ground truth, which of the runs performed best. The three runs were submitted as a trial and because previous results suggest that a small number of grey levels performs better, especially within the first few images retrieved. Studies show that a larger number of grey levels performs better for feedback with a larger number of input images [10]. The ImageCLEF results show that the best of the visual runs is the *GIFT* base system that uses only 4 grey levels, 3 scales and four directions of the Gabor filters (mean average precision (MAP) **0.3757**). Much worse is the system when using 16 grey levels and five scales (**0.2998**). We have to test whether the five scales have a strong influence on these results. When using five scales, 16 grey levels and 8 directions instead of four, the results get better (**0.3084**)

3.2 Visual Retrieval with Automatic Query Expansion

This section describes QE, automatically feeding back the query image and the 1 or 3 best images retrieved in a first step. Manual observations showed that the first few images seem to be very similar in most configurations. Only a few queries did not turn up visually relevant images as the first response. Thus, we attempted to feed back the first retrieved image as feedback with the initial query image. In a second try we submitted the first three retrieved images automatically which can contain more information but has also a higher risk of error as non-relevant images can be used. When wrong images are used in the expansion, the results risk becoming much worse. The submitted runs are a mixture of these containing one quantisation with 1 and 3 images fed back and two other quantisation with only 1 image fed back. The runs submitted were not analysed for performance beforehand thus the selection of the submitted runs was arbitrary.

– 8 directions, 16 grey levels, 1 image fed back *(GE_8d_16g_qe1.txt)*;
– 4 directions, 16 grey levels, 1 image fed back *(GE_4d_16g_qe1.txt)*;

- 4 directions 16 grey levels 3 images fed back *(GE_4d_16g_qe3.txt)*;
- normal gift system with 1 image being fed back *(GE_4d_4g_qe1.txt)*;

Results show that with automatic QE the best results are again obtained with the standard gift system (MAP **0.3727**). This is actually not as good as the results without QE. When using 16 grey levels the results do slightly improve over the first query step when feeding back 1 (MAP **0.3020**) but not with 3 (MAP **0.2977**) query images. Results are almost unchanged between expansion with 1 and 3 images. The system with 8 directions and 16 grey levels improves stronger than with only four directions (**0.3126**). This seems to underline the idea that a small number of grey levels is much better in the first query step but with expansion it is better to have more information on the images in form of grey levels and Gabor filter responses.

3.3 Visual Retrieval with Manual Feedback

This RF part was performed in a manual way with the same three quantisations as were used in the one–shot queries. Only difference is that a user was retrieving the first 20 images for every query and performed manual RF for 1 step. We would have liked to have an evolution over several steps to show how much RF can do and when a saturation is expected, but finally this was not attempted due to a lack of expert resources to perform the manual feedback. The person performing the RF does not have a medical education and some errors with respect to the feedback might be due to wrong images being be fed back.

- *(GE_4d_4g_rf)*;
- *(GE_4d_16g_rf)*;
- *(GE_8d_16g_rf)*.

The result images from the first query step were taken to query the system and observe the first 20 results for the run. Positive and negative images were marked for feedback to optimise the system response. A few images were marked as neutral when they were regarded as irrelevant but visually similar to the correct images or when the feedback person was not sure about the relevance of the image.

The results show that the performance difference between a small number of grey levels and a larger number is reduced when using RF. Still, the *GIFT* base systems stays the best in the test (**0.4469**). Worst RF system is the system with 16 grey levels and four directions (**0.3791**). Most improved system is the one with 16 grey levels but 8 directions (**0.3921**). RF shows its enormous potential and importance for visual information retrieval as the results improve significantly with its use. Taking a larger number of feedback images, an expert feedback person and several steps of feedback can further improve results.

3.4 Visual and Textual Multi-lingual Retrieval, Automatic Run

This combination uses the same automatic QE based on the images retrieved with the *medGIFT* system. The first 1 or 3 images added for visual QE are also used for the textual query. The text from these images was cleaned from the XML tags of the casimage case notes and unnecessary fields. ACR codes are equally deleted as they are currently not translated into their correct textual description which could be an important help for textual indexing and retrieval.

The remaining text was submitted to the *easyIR* system. The result list contains the most similar case notes with respect to the text and a weighting. This weighting was normalised based on the highest weighting in the list to get values in $[0;1]$. Afterwards, all images of the case receives the value of the case, thus containing visually similar and very dissimilar images. A total of 200 cases was retrieved, which results in a list of 800–1000 images containing a similarity value.

Merging of visual and textual results was done in various ways. As the unit for retrieval and similarity assessment is the image, the visual similarity plays an important role. Textual similarity might be better with respect to the semantics of the case but a case contains relevant and also many irrelevant images that are in the same case but of a different modality. Thus, visual similarity had to be weighted higher than textual similarity, so visually non-similar images were not weighted higher than visually similar but textually dissimilar ones. We were not sure to have correct cases in the first $N = 1..3$ images so care is be important to not expand the query into a wrong direction. Three runs were submitted using 75% visual and 25% textual retrieval:

- 4 directions, 16 grey levels, visual/textual with QE 1 image; *(GE_4d_16g_vt1)*
- 4 directions, 16 grey levels, visual/textual with QE 3 images; *(GE_4d_16g_vt3)*
- 4 directions, 4 grey levels, visual/textual with QE 1 image; *(GE_4d_4g_vt1)*

Another run was submitted with a ratio of 80% for the visual and 20% for the textual features:

- *(GE_4d_4g_vt2)*.

Another idea was based on the fact that most visually important images should be within the upper part of the visually similar images retrieved. This means that the goal should be to augment the value of those in the list of the visually similar that also appear in the list of the textually similar. For this run we multiplied the score of all those images that were within the first 200 cases retrieved textually and within the first 1000 images visually by a factor of 1.5. The resulting series has the tag:

- *(GE_4d_16g_vtx)*.

Evaluation results show that the use of textual information significantly improves the retrieval, also when using the text of a single image, for example with 16 grays and four directions (MAP **0.3361**). This is an improvement of 0.036 and thus more than 10% better than the visual QE with one image. When executing QE with 3 images, the results improve slightly less strong (MAP **0.3322**).

Better results were again obtained when using only 4 grey levels. When feeding back one image, the MAP is **0.3901** and thus better than all other submitted automatic runs in the competition. Best results in our test were obtained when changing the weighting between visual and textual features from 25% to 20% which delivered a MAP of **0.4020**. The selective weighting change for images that were visually similar and that appeared in the top retrieved by text also delivered very good results (MAP **0.3940**).

When analysing these results, we think that feeding back (maybe more) images with text using a 20% weighting can produce better results. We think that the optimal result with this technique can be in the range of a MAP of **0.45**.

3.5 Visual and Textual Multi-lingual Retrieval, Manual Feedback

As we do not yet have an integrated interface of visual and textual search engines, these results are based on manual RF queries based on the visual retrieval results, only. Based on images marked relevant after a first visual query step a query was constructed. For the textual query, only positive documents were taken whereas for the visual part positive and negative images were taken into account. The text was generated in the same way as before by adding case notes without names, dates, XML tags and ACR codes into one large file. If there were several images of the same case, the text was copied several times. These texts were submitted to the easyIR system. Again, the resulting list of case results and scores was normalised. The system we use employs 16 grey levels and 4 directions and thus the worst system in a first visual result as well as the worst in visual feedback, which we did not know at that point. Still, the textual component alone improves the results significantly. For the visual query, the results were equally normalised to a range between 0 and 1. For merging the results we used three different ratios between visual and textual characteristics:

- 25% textual, 75% visual; *GE_rfvistex1*
- 20% textual, 80% visual; *GE_rfvistex20*
- 10% textual, 90% visual; *GE_rfvistex10*

At this point we were sure that the text contains relevant information and not only automatically expanded case texts. Still, it is important to not have a too strong influence of the textual features as they are on a case and not an image basis whereas the gold standard is generated based on an image basis. The gradient of similarity within the textual results list is much higher than within the visual result list which explains part of the risk of too strongly weighing the textual features.

Results show that our RF results are by far the best results in the entire competition. Best results are obtained when combining the results by 10% textual and 90% visual (**0.4847**). When weighing the textual features high (25 %) the results drop significantly (**0.4520**). When weighting the textual features at 20%, the results drop in performance but only very slightly (**0.4827**). This suggests that the optimal weighting in our case should be around the 10%. Tests will have to confirm whether it is lower or higher than the 10Having the gift base system with 4 grey levels for this run would also improve retrieval quality as the query results seem to be much better in a first query step. Optimal results might be obtained with 4 grey in a first query steps and then several grey levels for the feedback.

4 Further Ideas That Are Currently not Explored

The ACR codes should be translated into text for better indexing and retrieval. They contain valuable information and are part of several case notes. We currently do not use ACR codes attached to cases at all.

Image normalisation should be applied to avoid that images which lye in a different grey spectrum are not properly retrieved. Currently, this can be the case quite often as there is no control on the level/window settings for a medical doctor when inserting images. Images are in JPEG and so information from the original DICOM images might have got lost. Other pretreatment steps such as background removal can also improve results.

Using a gradient of the similarity scores to define how many of the first N images might be relevant and could be sent back as automatic QE is another promising idea. This can allow a more reasonable way to choose images for automatic QE. Currently, the values used are fairly conservative as a wrong QE can delete the quality of retrieval completely.

Work is also needed with respect to quantisations of the feature space. Currently, a surprisingly small number of grey levels leads to best results but we need to analyse which queries were responsible for this and which other factors such as directions, scales and quantisations of Gabor filters might play a vital role.

5 Conclusions

We had a lack of manpower to do a proper adaptation and evaluation of the parameters that we could use within our system. Thus we could not use the software tools up to their full potential. Especially the use of RF over several steps is expected to lead to a much better performance. The use of ground truth data to optimise the system will also lead to much better results. For further ImageCLEF competitions it is expected to have training data accessible before the conference, and a different database during the conference. There was also a lack of experience with combining textual and visual features for retrieval. Many ideas can be performed for this combination to optimise retrieval results.

The most important conclusions for the evaluation of our system are surely:

- a surprisingly small number of grey levels led to best results in a first query step;
- QE for visual retrieval does not change the performance;
- a larger number of grey levels is better for RF;
- textual features improve performance with automatic QE as well as with manual RF;

– RF improves results enormously and remains a power tool for information retrieval;
– RF and visual/textual combinations led to the best overall results in the ImageCLEF competition;
– there is still a lot to be tried out!

This leaves us with several important outcomes and many ideas to prove now that the ground truth is available. Next year's ImageCLEF will for sure deliver much better systems and more optimised solutions based on training data.

References

1. Clough, P., Sanderson, M.: The clef 2003 cross language image retrieval task. In: Proceedings of the Cross Language Evaluation Forum (CLEF 2003). (2004)
2. Müller, H., Rosset, A., Geissbuhler, A., Terrier, F.: A reference data set for the evaluation of medical image retrieval systems. Computerized Medical Imaging and Graphics (2004 (to appear))
3. Clough, P., Sanderson, M., Müller, H.: A proposal for the clef cross language image retrieval track (imageclef) 2004. In: The Challenge of Image and Video Retrieval (CIVR 2004), Dublin, Ireland, Springer LNCS (2004)
4. Rosset, A., Müller, H., Martins, M., Dfouni, N., Vallée, J.P., Ratib, O.: Casimage project – a gidital teaching files authoring environment. Journal of Thoracic Imaging **19** (2004) 1–6
5. Squire, D.M., Müller, W., Müller, H., Pun, T.: Content–based query of image databases: inspirations from text retrieval. Pattern Recognition Letters (Selected Papers from The 11th Scandinavian Conference on Image Analysis SCIA '99) **21** (2000) 1193–1198 B.K. Ersboll, P. Johansen, Eds.
6. Müller, H., Rosset, A., Vallée, J.P., Geissbuhler, A.: Integrating content–based visual access methods into a medical case database. In: Proceedings of the Medical Informatics Europe Conference (MIE 2003), St. Malo, France (2003)
7. Ruch, P.: Query translation by text categorization. In: Proceedings of the conference on Computational Linguistics (COLING 2004), Geneva, Switzerland (2004)
8. Ruch, P., Chichester, C., Cohen, G., Coray, G., Ehrler, F., Ghorbel, H., Müller, H., Pallotta, V.: Report on the trec 2003 experiment: Genomic track. In: Proceedings of the 2003 Text REtrieval Conference (TREC), Gaithersburg, MD, USA (2004)
9. La Cascia, M., Sethi, S., Sclaroff, S.: Combining textual and visual cues for content–based image retrieval on the world wide web. In: IEEE Workshop on Content–based Access of Image and Video Libraries (CBAIVL'98), Santa Barbara, CA, USA (1998)
10. Müller, H., Rosset, A., Vallée, J.P., Geissbuhler, A.: Comparing feature sets for content–based medical information retrieval. In: Proceedings of the SPIE International Conference on Medical Imaging, SPIE Vol. 5371, San Diego, CA, USA (2004)

Multi-modal Information Retrieval Using FINT

Menno van Zaanen[1] and Guido de Croon[2]

[1] ILK*, Tilburg University, the Netherlands
mvzaanen@uvt.nl
[2] Department of Computer Science,
Universiteit Maastricht, the Netherlands
g.decroon@cs.unimaas.nl

Abstract. In this article, we describe the FINT system, which stands for Find Images aNd Text. This system is built in the context of the VindIT project, which focuses on handling large amounts of multi-media data. The system described here iteratively searches through a multi-media database by computing distances between the data entries (images and text). From each entry, a feature vector is computed. Distances between database entries are computed using a weighted version of their corresponding feature vector and entries similar to the initial search query are selected based on these distances. Here, we will describe the system and settings that were used in the medical retrieval task of the ImageCLEF 2004 competition.

1 Introduction

This article will describe the Find Images aNd Text (FINT) system. This system was developed within the context of the VindIT project[1], which is part of the ToKeN2000 research programme[2].

The ToKeN2000 research programme focuses "on fundamental problems of interaction between a human user and a knowledge and information system". This research programme contains several projects, of which VindIT is one. The VindIT project concentrates on handling large collections of multi-media data. At the moment, the project focuses on clustering, indexing, retrieving, and navigating of mainly textual and visual information. The project is a co-operation between researchers of the universities of Maastricht, Nijmegen and Tilburg, all in the Netherlands.

The FINT system is the first implementation of a flexible multi-modal system build within VindIT. It has several requirements, the most important being flexibility. Ideally, one should be able to use the system for many tasks, such

* The first author currently works at ICS, Macquarie University, Sydney, Australia.

[1] See http://www.niwi.knaw.nl/en/oi/nod/onderzoek/OND1297559/toon for more information.

[2] See http://www.ins.cwi.nl/projects/Token2000/index-en.html for more information.

C. Peters et al. (Eds.): CLEF 2004, LNCS 3491, pp. 728–739, 2005.

as searching the database, clustering and indexing entries, but also including interactive, user-driven tasks.

The ImageCLEF competition is taken to be an initial test case of the system. The main aim is not necessarily to get the best results in the competition, the current system is too simple for that, but to show the flexibility of the approach taken.

The original task for which FINT is developed is a search tool that should help searching large databases of pairs of images and corresponding text. Instances can be found, for example, in museums or other institutions that have pictures and descriptions of items.

The actual setup of the ImageCLEF task does not completely match the original idea behind FINT. However, participating in the competition will show the flexibility of the system. Additionally, it indicates problems of the current implementation and the outcomes may help to specify directions for future work.

In the rest of the article, we first give a brief description of the task of the ImageCLEF competition mainly focusing on how the task is different from the intended task of the FINT system (section 2). Section 3 describes the system in detail. Next, both the visual and textual features that are incorporated in the current system are described respectively in sections 3.1 and 3.2. The actual implementation is discussed in section 4 and is followed by the conclusions.

2 Task Description

The goal of the medical information retrieval task in the ImageCLEF competition is to find similar images in a given set of images starting from a search image. The underlying idea here is that a doctor who has, for example, an image of an X-ray, can find similar images belonging to known cases. Additionally, information from the case corresponding to the found images can give clues on how to treat the patient further.

As described in [1] in more detail, the dataset used for the competition is taken from the CasImage medical database and is developed by the University Hospitals Geneva. The dataset consists of medical cases. A case contains textual case information and is linked to one or more images. All images belong to a case and a case may have several images linked to it.

The 8,725 images contained in the database are mainly X-rays, scans and some photos. All images are encoded using the JPG format. The size of the images is not always the same, which introduces some problems as will be discussed below.

The database consists of 2,078 XML encoded cases. A case has several entries containing plain text. Not all fields contain information (and some cases are completely empty apart from a case number). We store all information of the cases in our own database, but we only use the following information per case:

File. This field contains the filename of the case;
Description. This field contains general information on the case;

Diagnosis. Here, the diagnosis of the case is given;

ClinicalPresentation. More information on the case is given in this field. It may be more general information on the case or on the patient;

Commentary. In this field, general comments can be given;

Chapter. This indicates a certain subset in the database. Related cases are stored in the same chapter;

The information contained in other fields in the database might provide additional information, but since they are often empty, we decided not to incorporate them in the current system.

There are several aspects of the competition that do not completely match with the original task set for the FINT system. Because of the flexibility of the system, it can be applied to the competition tasks, although some adjustments need to be made.

- The cases contain textual information in two languages, English and French. This aspect will be discussed in more detail in section 3.2.
- There is a many to one relationship between the images and the text. The fact that certain images are related because they belong to the same case may represent important information. However, at the moment this information is not used.
- The search query is an image only. Of course, this is not a problem, but it means that textual information can only be used when at least a two stage search is used. The first stage searches for similar images. These images have textual information attached to them, so the second stage can use this information as well.

3 System Overview

The FINT system is a generic multi-modal system. Here it is used for information retrieval, but it could be used for other tasks as well. It is completely feature-based, which allows for the integration of all types of data as long as features of the data can be extracted.

The advantages of using features are manifold. If a types of multi-modal data can be represented using features, it can be incorporated in the system. In practice, this is true for many types of data. A system based on features, therefore, remains relatively simple and flexible. Additionally, feature vectors can be applied to machine learning techniques.[3]

Figure 1 gives an overview of the FINT system. The upper row illustrates the initial step. First of all, the search information (in this case a search image)

[3] In this particular case, no annotated data was provided, so supervised machine learning techniques could not be used. We expected that unsupervised techniques would not provide adequate results. In section 5, we describe some parameter tuning, but this was only done after the competition.

is handed to the feature extractor. This outputs a feature vector representing the original data.

The lower row shows the iterative phase of the system. It matches the search feature vector against a database containing the feature vectors from the images and corresponding cases in the database provided for the competition. These feature vectors are generated similarly to the feature vector in the second step in the upper row.

The iterative phase, in general, starts with one or more feature vectors. The input feature vectors are compared to the feature vectors in the database and distances are computed. The feature vectors that have the smallest distances to the input feature vectors are returned and can be used as input feature vectors in another iteration.

In this particular competition, there is always only one input feature vector. The first iteration describes the search image, so the feature vector only contains visual features. The output of this iteration gives the image (according to the features), that best matches the input image. Since this image is in the database, textual features can now also be used, so the second iteration uses, next to visual features, textual information as well.

The final output of the system is a list of the best 1,000 images that correspond to the feature vectors that are the output of the second phase. To summarise, the first iteration searches for the image in the database that closely resembles the original search image. The second iteration uses visual and textual features of the output of the first iteration and this feature vector is used to generate the output of the system that is checked according to the trec evaluation method.

Of course, the performance of the system depends heavily on the features used. Additionally, feature weighting is implemented, which allows for certain features to have more influence in the distance computation.

Next, we will describe the features that have been implemented in the system. We will start with a discussion of the visual features, followed by the textual features.

3.1 Visual Features

The medical database offered by the University Hospitals of Geneva contains X-rays, scans, and normal pictures. Therefore, the content of the image-database is rather specific. Our image retrieval techniques are based on the specific properties of the database. We use three types of features for the image retrieval part of the system: *color features*, *principal components of the images*, and *intensity grid features.* All features are relatively simple, but are rather effective in this particular context. We discuss the three types of features in the following subsections.

Color. There are two reasons why color is rather irrelevant for the medical retrieval task. First, the amount of color images in the medical database is almost negligible. Most of the images in the database are gray-value images. In fact, most images represent X-rays or black-and-white scans. Second, the medical

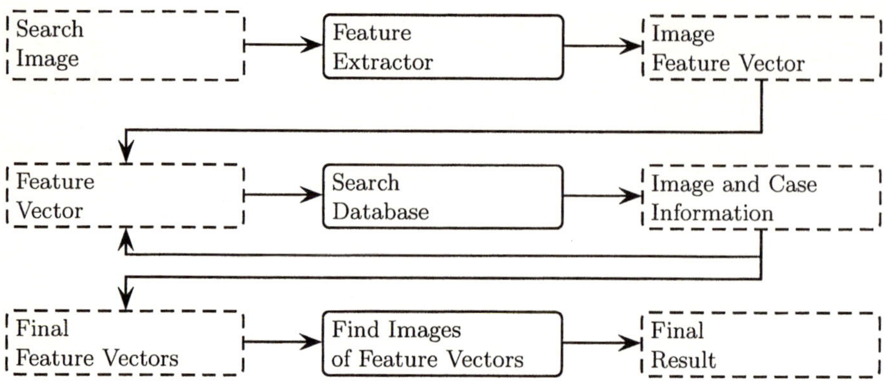

Fig. 1. Overview of the FINT system

image retrieval task demands some color-insensitivity. If the query to the image database consists of a color photo of a leg, we do not want to exclude black-and-white photos from the result set.

Because of the relatively low importance of color in the medical database, the simplest of color features adequately captures the necessary color information. We use three features to code the color information: the average red, green, and blue values of all pixels in an image. The average values are divided by 255, mapping them to the interval [0, 1]. As stated before, color plays only a complementary role in our image retrieval technique.

Principal Components. The shape of the "object" in the image is much more important to image retrieval in the medical database than color information. How can we measure the shape of an object? The gray-values of the image contain all shape-information, but it would be too cumbersome to use all gray-values as features for retrieving images from the database. Principal component analysis (PCA) is a technique that reduces data dimensionality, while retaining as much information as possible. PCA searches for orthogonal eigenvectors that capture as much variance of the data as possible. PCA is often used in image analysis, for example in facial expression recognition [2, 3].

PCA can only be applied to images of the same size. Therefore, the first step in PCA is to resize all images from the database to the same size, in our case to a 40×40 pixel format. Naturally, this results in some information-loss. In particular, the ratio of width and height of an object is neglected. After resizing, an image can be represented by a vector of 1600 gray-values. We constructed the data-matrix for PCA by combining such vectors of all images in the database. With the help of the data matrix, 20 principal components were obtained. Since the principal components are also vectors of size 1600, we can visualize them to illustrate the shape-information that they capture. Figure 2 shows the first 20 principal components. The principal components capture some "elementary" shapes occurring in the medical database. A clear example is the 14th principal component that seems to represent pictures of multiple X-rays on the same sheet.

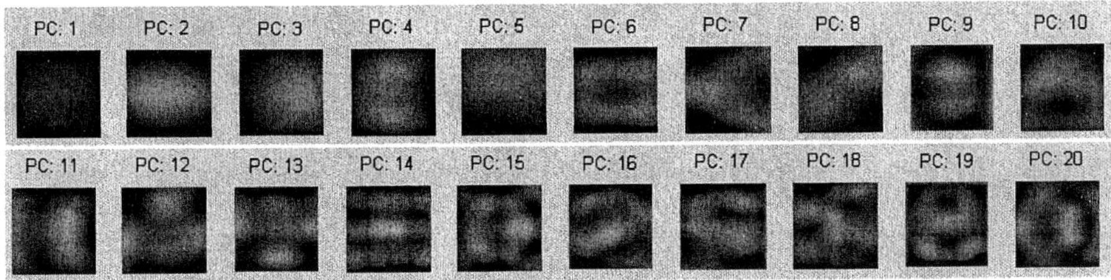

Fig. 2. Principle components

After PCA, every picture in the medical database can be represented by its projection on the principal components shown in figure 2. We normalize the resulting 20 feature values so that they are in [-1, 1]. The calculation of the projection on the 20 principal components comes down to a multiplication of the image vector with the matrix containing all principal components. Hence, projecting a query image on these components is computationally cheap.

Intensity Grid. The final type of visual features that we extract from the images also captures shape information. The shape of an object is partly determined by the overall intensity-distribution in the images. We measure the intensity-distribution by placing a grid over each image in the database and determining the average intensity per grid cell. This average value is divided by 255, so that the values will be in [0, 1]. In the implementation of the FINT system we have chosen for a grid of 5×5, as a trade-off between the number of features and the results that the method yields. In consequence, the number of features per image is 25. This is comparable to the 20 features resulting from the principal component analysis. The intensity grid is important, because it complements the principal-component approach to shape representation. Both types of features lead to different retrieved images.

3.2 Textual Features

Images are linked to cases that contain text describing the patient, diseases and treatments. To be able to treat the text in a similar way to the visual information, features need to be extracted from the texts. These features should represent the "important" aspects of the text as close as possible. However, selecting features that do this is not easy.

Before features can be extracted, the text should be as "clean" as possible. Unfortunately, the content of the cases showed some aspects that have to be addressed before. First of all, the original text is not proper UNICODE, so accented characters need to be converted into their proper codes. Fortunately, a straightforward mapping to UNICODE can be found.

Once the proper UNICODE encoding of the text was created, we tried to do more complex language handling. However, we noticed that the text contains many spelling errors, non-accented characters that should have been accented, unexpected punctuation marks, incorrect or incomplete abbreviations, ungrammatical and incomplete sentences. This made the linguistic tools we have available (such as stemmers, taggers, chunkers, etc.) almost unusable.

Additionally, the multi-lingual aspect of the competition, that will be discussed in the next section, makes the task even more difficult. Whereas the focus of the VindIT system is mainly to search in multi-modal information, multi-lingual information can be incorporated, but it is not an important aspect of our current research.

Languages. A case may contain English or French text. The "Language" field in the case should indicate what language is used in that particular case. Unfortunately, some cases even contain fields of both English and French. Additionally, deciding the language of a case, is quite difficult, because the "Language" field of a case is often incorrect or empty.

To figure out what language a field in a case is in, we have tried to run it through van Noord's implementation[4] of the TextCat Language Guesser [4]. Unfortunately, this does not work well, since most fields do not contain enough text to decide on which language it is. Also, the words are mainly medical terms, which look similar in English and French. The language models used by the guesser are build on "standard" English and French. However, even with specially built language models, the language guesser cannot be certain in which language certain fields are.[5]

Since the focus of the project is not really on solving multi-lingual retrieval, we have effectively given up on performing complex linguistic feature extraction methods. Firstly, we cannot easily find language of a piece of text. Secondly, the fact that (especially the French texts) contain a large number of errors, which make even an extremely simple word-for-word translation of the texts difficult. Thirdly, the actual text consists of mainly highly specific medical terms, for which we cannot find a good electronic dictionary. Based on these findings, we decided on taking a generic approach to try and incorporate English and French texts together in one cluster of features.

Infomap. The text contained in the cases needs to be encoded in the form of feature values. Of course, there are many different ways in which this can be accomplished. The FINT system can incorporate features (numeric and symbolic), so the actual decisions made here are not restricted by the FINT system. Here we describe relatively simple features, because the focus of the VindIT project is not directed towards multi-lingual information retrieval. We expect that selecting better textual features will improve the results of the system.

We extract plain text from the "Description", "Diagnosis", "ClinicalPresentation", "Commentary", and "Chapter" fields. These fields are often filled with a varying amount of text. Next, we remove the most obvious errors from the text. This included removing all punctuation, correcting some abbreviations, expand-

[4] Implementation can be found at `http://odur.let.rug.nl/~vannoord/TextCat/`.

[5] We have also tried to annotate language information semi-automatically, but often even humans could not decide in what language certain cases were.

ing all truncated words (such as converting "l' " to "le" in French and "doesn't" to "does not" in English). Also, dates, ranges, percentages, numbers, units and words containing numbers are grouped together in their respective class (e.g., denoted by "[DATE]"). We argue that, for example, specific numbers are not very important, but the fact that there is a number present is indeed important.

The cleaned-up plain text excerpts are used as input of the *infomap* system.[6] This system is developed by Schütze [5] and uses frequency of co-occurring words in the context. When words are often used in the same context, this indicates that they share a similar meaning. Clustering words together gives some sort of semantic clusters. This is generalized between the texts per case, showing how similar cases are conceptually.

Infomap has been applied in several systems. Interesting applications (and related to this research) is the use of infomap in multi-lingual information retrieval systems [6]. Multi-lingual, aligned corpora are used to find semantically similar clusters, that can be used to handle the texts or queries in the different languages.

Unfortunately, we do not have bi-lingual, aligned corpora here, so we simply treat all the data as similar. In effect this will probably result in a strong preference for texts that are in the same language as the query. Of course, this is not preferable, but at least texts within languages are grouped according to semantic content.

Applying the infomap system to the texts extracted from the cases, results in 33 numeric features ranging [-1, 1].

4 Implementation

The implementation of the FINT system is currently divided over several components, that run on different computers (although that is not necessary). The user interface is implemented using PHP to work over the web. This has several advantages. Firstly, it allows for easy access for the members of the project, who are working in different locations, using different operating systems. Secondly, it is easy to display the graphical content of the database. Thirdly, specific system settings and selections can be made using forms that can be linked to underlying software. Output can again easily be fed back to the user.

The FINT program starts after the user has made a selection of the test image, the distance function, the features, and the weights assigned to the features. This program extracts the correct feature vector from the test image and computes the distances of all the similar feature vectors in the database. The images of the best feature vectors are returned to the user. The textual case information attached to the images can be reached by clicking on the images. This allows for an easy way to get all the information related to an image.

---

[6] The implementation and documentation of the infomap system can be found at `http://infomap.stanford.edu/`.

Next, the user can continue with the new images and perform a next iteration of the system. Again, the settings can be adjusted. In the final iteration, the user can specify that TREC output is needed. This will generate a web-page with the TREC output of the current image ordering with their distances.

The database is implemented in MySQL [7]. It is extremely flexible in that the features themselves are encoded in the database as well. This means that using information taken from the database, select statements are created dynamically. This allows the entire system to be reused with a different dataset without any re-implementation. All parts that need to be changed can be found in the database itself.

The interface between the web interface and the database is a program that computes the distances between feature vectors and returns this information to the user. Effectively, the PHP page starts this program with the settings given by the user, the program connects to the database to retrieve the correct feature vectors and computes distances between them. These are then ordered and the images belonging to the best feature vectors are put in a new PHP page that is presented to the user again.

The computation of the results documented in the competition is done in two iterations. The first iteration is based on all visual features, with weight 10 for the red, green, and blue features, and 1 for the other visual features.[7] From the results of this iteration, we only select the best image. This corresponds to the image from the database that looks most similar to the original search image.

The second iteration uses the textual infomap features with weight 30 in addition to the visual features (with the same weights). Using these settings, the distances from all images in the database are computed. These results were submitted to the competition.

Several distance functions have been implemented. We have used a weighted numeric Euclidean distance here. This is computed between two vectors $V_1 = (i_1, i_2, \ldots, i_n)$ and $V_2 = (j_1, j_2, \ldots, j_n)$ and weight vector $W = (w_1, w_2, \ldots, w_n)$ as follows:

$$d(V_1, V_2, W) = \sqrt{\sum_{l=1}^{n} (w_l * i_l - w_l * j_l)^2} \tag{1}$$

There is an interesting problem with the distance computation. Even though the distance function works, using it to compute distances over multiple iterations does not work as expected. The problem is illustrated in figure 3. The first iteration finds the image that is most similar to the original search image. There is of course a distance between these feature vectors. In the image, this distance is called d. In the next iteration, the feature vector of this image is taken as the seed to find similar images. This means that the distances of the final images after two iterations are computed with respect to the best image of the first iteration.

[7] In the first iteration, textual features cannot be used, because the input image does not have textual information attached to it.

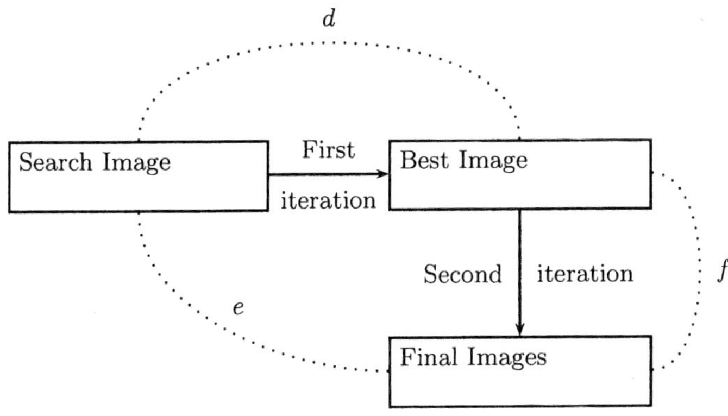

Fig. 3. Distance computation in multiple iterations

Of course, the result image of the first iteration is in the set of final images (because the distance is 0).[8] Since the distances of the other images of the final result are computed with respect to the image of the first iteration, this can be seen as e, whereas to correctly compare the distances of all the final images, distance f should have been computed. However, it is only possible to compute f with respect to visual features, because the search image does not have any case information associated with it.

5 Parameter Tuning

The FINT system does not perform spectacularly well in the competition, but this could be expected. It is an extremely simple system that does not use many features to get a good description of the data. However, we are especially interested in the influence of the second iteration with respect to the textual information.

To investigate the influence of the second iteration and hence the usefulness of the textual information (in its current form), we performed some parameter tuning based on the annotated data that was made available after the completion of the competition.

Table 1[9] gives an overview of the results. The best parameters are given together with the results obtained with these settings. Note that the distance computation in these results is slightly different. These results are denoted by "New". We used the absolute distances here, in contrast to the distances given in the competition, where the maximum distance minus the absolute distance

[8] As a temporary fix, we add the distances of the separate iterations. This means that the distance of the image of the first iteration still has distance d in the final result.

[9] PC denotes the principle components features and MIV denotes the mean intensity values features.

Table 1. Best parameters for first and second iteration

Distance Computation	Iteration	Visual					Textual	Result
		Red	Green	Blue	PC	MIV	Infomap	
New	1	12	12	12	4	2	n/a	0.2508
Original	1	12	12	12	4	2	n/a	0.2406
New	2	4	4	4	1	1	2	0.2752
Original	2	4	4	4	1	1	2	0.2752
ImageCLEF	2	See text						0.1519

is used.[10] Additionally, in the results of the second iteration, the distance of the image that is used as the seed is 0. The results with the same parameter setting according to the original system are denoted by "Original". Finally, the original results (with non-tuned parameters) of the ImageCLEF competition are given (denoted by ImageCLEF). These results were generated with the following weights: red, green, blue have 10, principle components and mean intensity values have values 1 in the first iteration, and the same values in the second iteration, but additionally, the infomap features are added with weight 30.

From the results it is clear that adding textual information improved the results of the system. We have tried many parameter settings, but the one including the textual infomap features performs best.

6 Conclusion and Future Work

The ImageCLEF competition allowed us to apply the FINT system to real data for the first time. It shows that the system is flexible and usable with different datasets. Multiple iterations allow for different visual and textual features to be used, even when these features cannot be found in the initial search data.

The main results of the system showed that with the ImageCLEF competition data, including textual information improved the results over the same system with visual features only. We expect that the results of FINT can be further improved by incorporating more (and perhaps more informative) features.

The application of the system also revealed problems and shortcomings of the system. The main problem is the incorrect distance calculations (as described above). This will need to be solved in future versions of the system. Additionally, certain implementation problems had to be solved. The speed of the current system could be improved by moving functionality to different parts of the system (such as moving the distance computation to the database itself).

In the future, we would also like to incorporate machine learning algorithms that automatically learn the best parameter settings. Of course, in order to do this, one needs training data (which was not available in the competition). Parameter tuning can of course vary weights for each feature (and each iteration),

[10] The competition required the distances to be descending instead of ascending.

but it may also tune the number of iterations, the distance metric, the amount of images that are retained after each iteration (which may be combined using several clustering techniques), etc. Adjusting these parameters may result in a wide range of results.

References

1. Clough, P., Müller, H., Sanderson, M.: The clef cross language image retrieval track (imageclef) 2004. In Peters, C., Clough, P., Gonzalo, J., Jones, G., Kluck, M., Magnini, B., eds.: Fifth Workshop of the Cross–Language Evaluation Forum (CLEF 2004). Lecture Notes in Computer Science, Berlin Heidelberg, Germany, Springer-Verlag (2005)
2. Calder, A.J., Burton, A.M., Miller, P., Young, A.W., Akamatsu, S.: A principal component analysis of facial expressions. Vision Research **41** (2001) 1179–1208
3. Dailey, M.N., Cottrell, G.W., Pradgett, C., Adolphs, R.: EMPATH: A neural network that categorizes facial expressions. Journal of Cognitive Neuroscience **14** (2002) 1158–1173
4. Cavnar, W.B., Trenkle, J.M.: N-gram-based text categorization. In: Proceedings of Third Annual Symposium on Document Analysis and Information Retrieval; Las Vegas:NV, USA, UNLV Publications/Reprographics (1994) 161–175
5. Schütze, H.: Ambiguity Resolution in Language Learning. Number 71 in Lecture Notes. Center for Study of Language and Information (CSLI) Publications, Stanford:CA, USA (1997)
6. Masuichi, H., Flournoy, R., Kaufmann, S., Peters, S.: Query translation method for cross language information retrieval. In: Proceedings of the Workshop on Machine Translation for Cross Language Information Retrieval, MT Summit VII; Singapore. (1999) 30–34
7. Widenius, M.M.: MySQL Reference Manual. O'Reilly, Sebastopol:CA, USA (2002)

Medical Image Retrieval Using Texture, Locality and Colour

Peter Howarth, Alexei Yavlinsky, Daniel Heesch, and Stefan Rüger

Multimedia Information Retrieval, Department of Computing,
South Kensington Campus, 180 Queen's Gate,
Imperial College London, SW7 2AZ, UK
{peter.howarth, alexei.yavlinsky, daniel.heesch, s.rueger}@imperial.ac.uk
http://km.doc.ic.ac.uk

Abstract. We describe our experiments for the Image CLEF medical retrieval task. Our efforts were focused on the initial visual search. A content-based approach was followed. We used texture, localisation and colour features that have been proven by previous experiments. The images in the collection had specific characteristics. Medical images have a formulaic composition for each modality and anatomic region. We were able to choose features that would perform well in this domain. Tiling a Gabor texture feature to add localisation information proved to be particularly effective. The distances from each feature were combined with equal weighting. This smoothed the performance across the queries. The retrieval results showed that this simple approach was successful, with our system coming third in the automatic retrieval task.

1 Introduction

Content based image retrieval (CBIR) aims to provide a way to search generic image collections. Traditionally, for highly constrained domains, such as medical images, CBIR has been viewed as being too imprecise. Our aim was to determine if the CBIR approach could be viable for an initial search or filtering step in a medical image collection. We focused on choosing high quality visual features that have good discriminatory power for the collection.

In this paper we first present a brief overview of our system. Section 3 explains the rationale for using specific visual features and details how they are computed. Results of our run are presented in Section 4, followed by a postmortem analysis. Some of our ideas for future work are presented in Section 5. We would like to have applied classification methods to the collection but the lack of training data precluded this. We also discuss the use of a browsing paradigm for this type of collection. Our conclusions round off the paper.

2 System Overview

The initial visual search task was very straightforward, with 26 single image queries, it is described in [1]. With no training data it was not possible to use

C. Peters et al. (Eds.): CLEF 2004, LNCS 3491, pp. 740–749, 2005.

any learning classifiers. We therefore used a simple system to tackle the retrieval task, using the features described in the next section. The following steps were carried out:

1. Features were generated for the test collection and query images;
2. For each feature the Manhattan distance between the query images and the test set was calculated;
3. The set of distances from each feature was normalised by dividing by their median. This ensured that each feature would have an equal weighting;
4. The distances for each query were summed over all features. This gave the overall distance from each query image to the test set. These were then sorted to produce a ranked list of retrieval results.

3 Features

The initial step in our work was to look at the collection and determine its characteristics. As a relatively specific domain it displayed a large degree of homogeneity. We realised this could be exploited by choosing features that would differentiate the image types.

The collection contained a large number of monochrome images, such as x-rays and CT scans, with very specific layout. The patients are positioned very precisely to show the area under investigation at the centre of the image. The layout can be used to indicate both modality and anatomic region. For this reason a localisation feature, thumbnail, was used to detect images with similar layouts. Within the modalities the images could be discriminated by structure and texture. We therefore chose to use a convolution feature to discriminate structure and two texture features, co-occurrence matrices and Gabor filters. The two texture features were applied to non-overlapping image tiles. This adds some locality discrimination to the feature. Finally, for the relatively small number of colour images we deployed a colour structure descriptor.

3.1 Thumbnail

This is perhaps the simplest feature in our feature set, yet it is highly effective in detecting images with a near identical layout. Each image is converted to grey scale and then scaled down to a thumbnail of fixed size. For these experiments we used 40×30 pixels. The pixel values of this new image then make up the feature vector.

3.2 Convolution

This feature is based on Tieu and Viola's method [2]. It relies on a large number of highly selective features that can determine structure within an image and capture information about texture and edges. A vast set of features are defined such that each feature will have a high value for only a small proportion of images. This enables an effective search by matching the features that are defined by the query. Due to the nature of the image collection we applied the feature to grey level images rather than RGB.

The feature generation process starts with a set of 25 primitive features (eg, edge detectors) that are applied to the grey level image. This generates 25 feature maps. Each of these is rectified and down-sampled before being filtered again by each of the 25 primitive filters. This gives 625 feature maps. The second stage of the process discovers arrangements of features in the previous levels. The values of each feature map are summed to give a single number. These are combined into a feature vector of 625 values.

3.3 Co-occurrence

Haralick [3] suggested the use of grey level co-occurrence matrices (GLCM) to extract second order statistics from an image. They have been used very successfully for texture classification. The GLCM of an image is defined as a matrix of frequencies at which two pixels, separated by a certain vector, occur in the image. The distribution in the matrix will depend on the angular and distance relationship between pixels. Varying the vector used allows the capturing of different texture characteristics. Once the GLCM has been created, various features can be computed from it. These have been classified into four groups: visual texture characteristics, statistics, information theory and information measures of correlation [3, 4].

Using the results of our recent evaluation [5] we chose the following configuration for creating the GLCM:

- The original image was split into 7×7 non-overlapping tiles and the feature run for each of these;
- The colour image was quantised into 64 grey levels;
- 16 GLCMs were created for each image tile using vectors of length 1, 2, 3, and 4 pixels and orientations 0, $\pi/4$, $\pi/2$ and $3\pi/4$;
- For each normalised co-occurrence matrix $P(i,j)$ we calculated a homogeneity feature H_p,

$$H_p = \sum_i \sum_j \frac{P(i,j)}{1 + |i - j|} \ . \tag{1}$$

  This feature was chosen as it had performed consistently well in previous evaluations.

3.4 Gabor

One of the most popular signal processing based approaches for texture feature extraction has been the use of Gabor filters. These enable filtering in the frequency and spatial domain. It has been proposed that Gabor filters can be used to model the responses of the human visual system. Turner [6] first implemented this by using a bank of Gabor filters to analyse texture. A range of filters at different scales and orientations allows multichannel filtering of an image to extract frequency and orientation information. This can then be used to decompose the image into texture features.

Our implementation is based on that of Manjunath et al [7]. The feature is built by filtering the image with a bank of orientation and scale sensitive filters and computing the mean and standard deviation of the output in the frequency domain.

Filtering an image $I(x, y)$ with Gabor filters g_{mn} designed according to [7] results in its Gabor wavelet transform W_{mn},

$$W_{mn}(x, y) = \int I(x_1, y_1) g^{*}_{mn}(x - x_1, y - y_1) dx_1 dy_1 \tag{2}$$

The mean and standard deviation of the magnitude $|W_{mn}|$ are used for the feature vector. The outputs of filters at different scales have different ranges. For this reason each element of the feature vector is normalised using the standard deviation of that element across the entire database.

From our evaluation [5] we found that a filter bank with 2 scales and 4 orientations gave the best retrieval performance. We used this configuration and applied it to 7×7 non-overlapping tiles created from the original image.

3.5 Colour Structure Descriptor HDS-S

For the colour images in the collection we used a feature that is good at capturing local colour image structure. It is defined in the HMMD (hue, min, max diff) colour space. This is used in the MPEG-7 standard and is derived from both RGB and HSV spaces. The hue component is taken from HSV and the min and max components are from the maximum and minimum values in the RGB space. The diff component is the difference between min and max. We follow the MPEG-7 standard and quantise this space non-uniformly into 184 bins in the 3 dimensional hue, diff and sum (HDS) colour space, see Manjunath and Ohm [8] for details of the quantisation.

To calculate the colour structure descriptor an 8×8 window is slid over the image. Each of the 184 bins of the HDS histogram contains the number of window positions for which there is at least one pixel falling into the bin under consideration. This feature, which we call HDS-S, is capable of discriminating between images with the same global colour distribution but differing local colour structures. For this reason it is suited to colour medical images which tend to have similar overall colour but differing structure depending on the detail of the photograph.

4 Results

Fig 1 shows the precision recall graph for our run. Our system achieved 37.8% mean average precision (m.a.p.) retrieval across all queries. This put us in third place for the automatic retrieval task. The best performance was achieved by Buffalo [9] with a m.a.p. of 39.0%. The median was 28.8%, with 34 runs submitted. All the runs primarily used visual features. In addition 11 used text and 12 query expansion. A summary of all the results is given in [1]. The performance of our system shows that our simple approach, using good quality visual features, produced results comparable with the top systems.

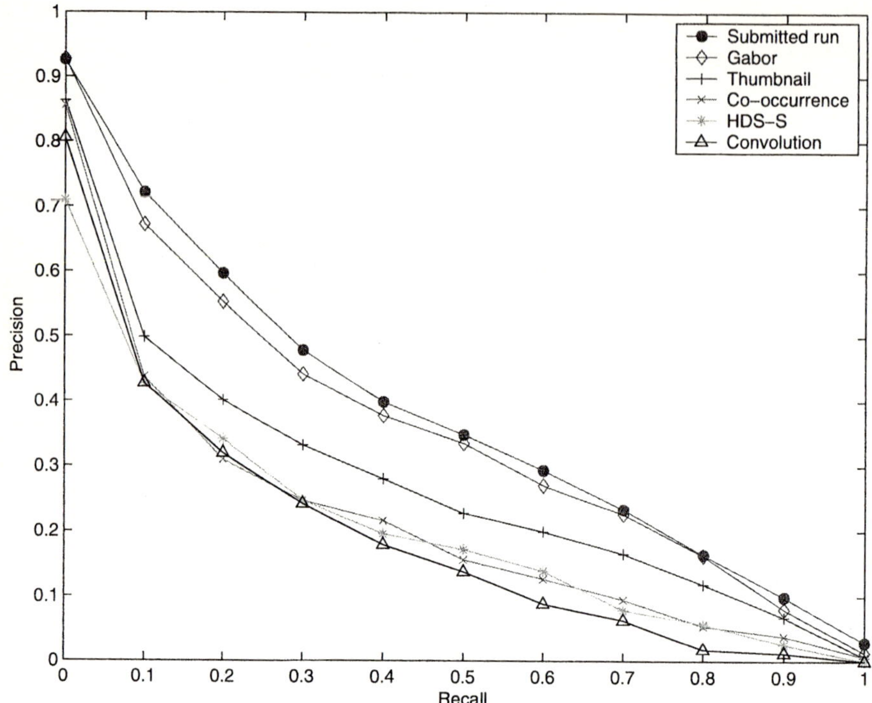

Fig. 1. Precision-recall graph for combined and individual features

Table 1. Mean average precision for combined and individual features

Feature	Mean average precision
Submitted run (combined)	37.8%
Gabor	35.3%
Thumbnail	26.3%
Co-occurrence	19.8%
HDS-S	19.5%
Convolution	18.1%

4.1 Analysis of Results

With the relevance judgements available it was possible to look at how individual features had performed. Fig. 1 shows the precision recall graph for the individual features together with that for the combined features of the submitted run. Table 1 shows the mean average precisions for the same features.

From these results it is clear that all features performed reasonably well. Considering individual features, Gabor performed best, with thumbnail a clear second and the remaining 3 closely grouped. Some additional feature combinations were tested, including adding the Gabor feature to each of the others in

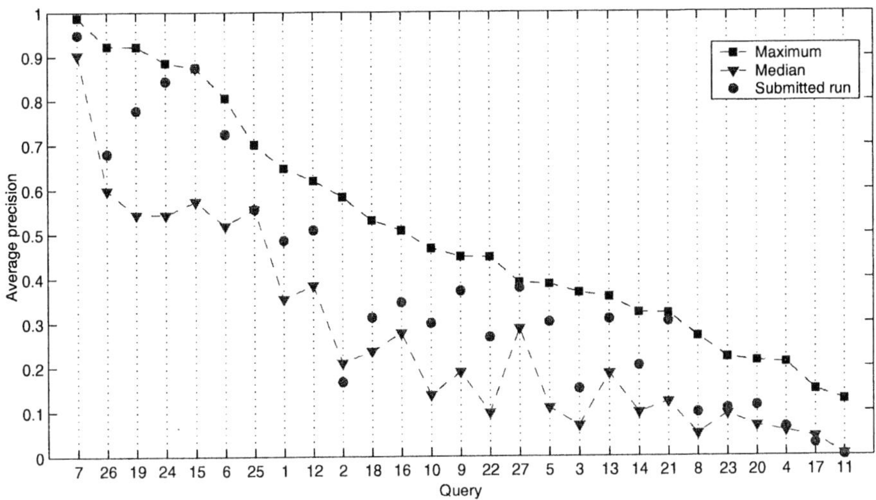

Fig. 2. Average precision by query

turn. However, none of these improved the mean average precision above that of the submitted run.

To get further insight into the results we looked at average precision by query. Fig. 2 shows the maximum and median average precision together with the results for our run. The queries are ordered by maximum precision to sort them by difficulty. It is clear from this graph that our system performed consistently well across all the queries. It was above median for 24 of the 26 queries and performed the best for one query.

To determine the reason for our consistency we looked at the performance of individual features by query. Fig 3 shows the average precision for each feature and the combination of features. We can pull several interesting facts from the figure:

- The submitted run outperformed all individual features for 16 of the 26 queries.
- In all cases the submitted rum was better than the mean and median of the individual features.
- The most consistent feature was Gabor. It was top for 14 queries.
- HDS-S (colour feature) showed the most variation. It was the worst for 13 queries and best for 4. Of these 4, half of the query images were colour.
- Thumbnail beat the maximum (of all submitted runs) for 3 queries.

It appears from these facts that the main reason for our consistency was the good performance by all the features used coupled with the effect of summing the features. Combining distances using equal weighting evens out the performance variation from each feature across the queries.

Individually, Gabor and thumbnail performed best. This was expected and is almost certainly due to the locality information within both the features.

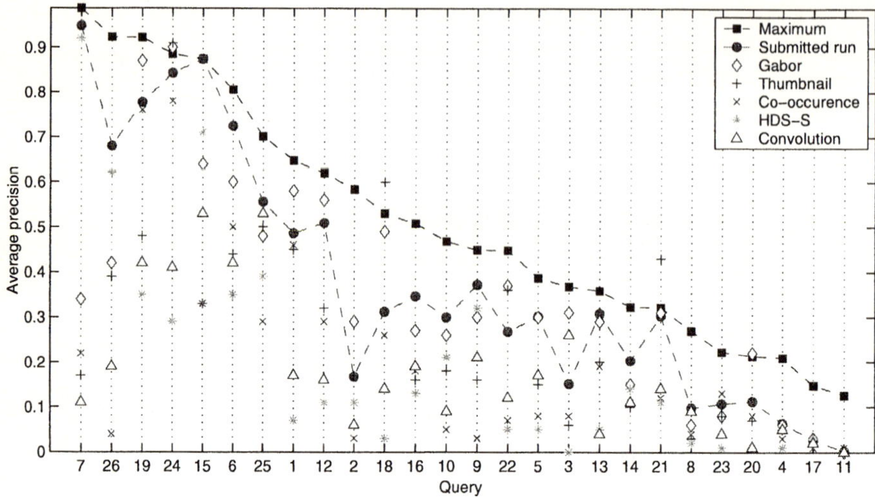

Fig. 3. Average precision by query for individual features

This is an effective discriminator due to the characteristic composition of images within the collection. HDS-S gave good discrimination for the colour queries but otherwise was poor. The feature is a histogram and contains no locality information.

The variation in average precision indicates that it would be possible to improve performance by weighting features differently depending on the query. However, this is not a trivial problem. Other than increasing the importance of the colour feature for colour images there are no obvious links between image types and feature performance. To tackle this problem we would need to apply learning methods.

4.2 Comparison with Other Systems

We also compared our approach to the methods used by the other top performing systems. The top seven systems were from Buffalo, Aachen and us.

Aachen [10] used a similar approach with visual features. They used a wide selection of features and optimised the weightings to the collection. They did this by creating their own relevance judgements and then evaluating different weightings to find the best. They also employed a simple query expansion method, using the query image and its nearest neighbour to query the collection.

Buffalo [9] used a different approach, combining visual and text retrieval. An initial visual query was used to rank the images. The text associated with the top images was then used to generate a text query. Finally the text and visual results were combined linearly.

Our approach was simpler than those above yet it gave similar performance. We believe that this was due to the quality of features used.

5 Future Work

In addition to the search task we also put the data set into a novel browsing network, NN^k, developed in our group [11]. Although we did not carry out a

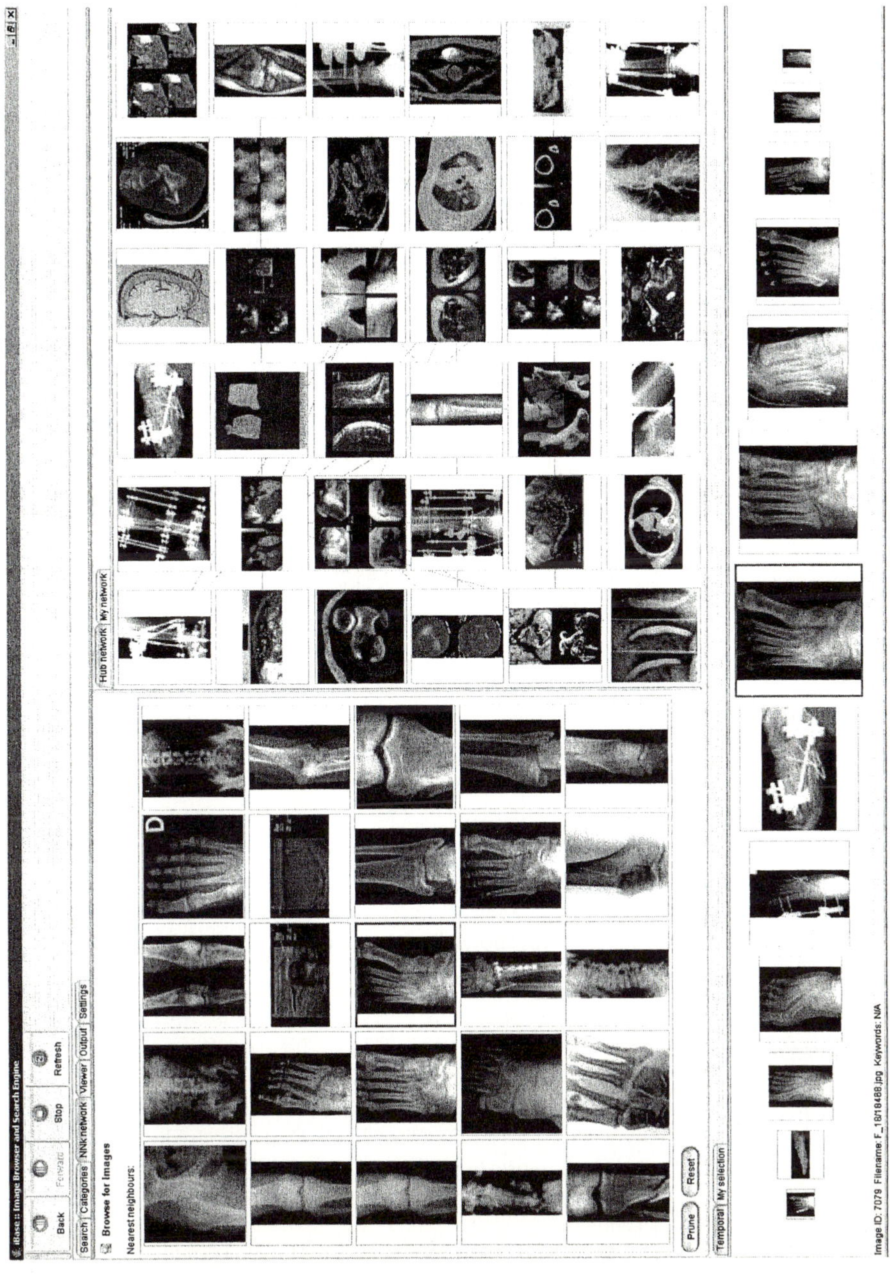

Fig. 4. iBase showing the NN^k browsing window

formal evaluation we found that through browsing it was possible to rapidly access similar images in the collection. A medical expert would be presented with a range of images to review and identify those that they were particularly interested in. It is clear that the browsing paradigm is an effective way of searching data collections of this size and complexity.

This system can be accessed at `http://km.doc.ic.ac.uk`, via the demo page. Open the iBase application and then select the CasImage collection on the settings tab. A screen shot of the application is shown in Fig 4.

The experiments carried out used very effective features. However, they were combined in a simple way, by summing the distances obtained from each feature. As shown shown in the postmortem analysis there was a wide variation in performance of features for different queries. This would indicate that when querying for certain modalities or anatomic regions different combinations of features may perform better. By varying the weights applied to features we can introduce a degree of plasticity into our system and then use machine learning techniques to improve retrieval performance.

Given training data we would like to train a support vector machine as a meta classifier. We have deployed this technique in other contexts, see Yavlinsky et al. [12]. We propose that it would be possible to learn the optimal weights for retrieving a specific modality, such as CT scan or x-ray.

6 Conclusion

Our experiments showed that it is possible to achieve good retrieval performance on a medical image collection using a CBIR approach. We used global features, which is in contrast to the highly specialised methods normally used for medical imaging. Given the constrained domain we were able to choose visual features that had good discriminatory power for the collection. We identified texture and locality as the key discriminators. Correspondingly, we predicted that a tiled Gabor feature would be an ideal feature for the dataset. The analysis of our results subsequently showed this to be the case.

Combining features using equal weighting was beneficial across the query set. It smoothed out the effect of individual features and gave the maximum retrieval performance. In addition, the analysis of individual features indicates that there is scope for applying learning methods to fuse features with optimised weights and further improve retrieval performance.

References

1. Clough, P., Müller, H., Sanderson, M.: The CLEF Cross Language Image Retrieval Track (ImageCLEF) 2004. In Peters, C., Clough, P., Gonzalo, J., Jones, G., Kluck, M., Magnini, B., eds.: Fifth Workshop of the Cross–Language Evaluation Forum (CLEF 2004), Lecture Notes in Computer Science (LNCS), Springer, Heidelberg, Germany (in print) (2005)
2. Tieu, K., Viola, P.: Boosting image retrieval. In: International Conference on Spoken Language Processing. (2000)

3. Haralick, R.: Statistical and structural approaches to texture. Proceedings of the IEEE **67** (1979) 786–804
4. Gotlieb, C.C., Kreyszig, H.E.: Texture descriptors based on co-occurrence matrices. Computer Vision, Graphics and Image Processing **51** (1990) 70–86
5. Howarth, P., Rüger, S.: Evaluation of texture features for content-based image retrieval. In: Proceedings of the International Conference on Image and Video Retrieval, Springer-Verlag (2004) 326–324
6. Turner, M.: Texture discrimination by Gabor functions. Biological Cybernetics **55** (1986) 71–82
7. Manjunath, B., Ma, W.: Texture features for browsing and retrieval of image data. IEEE Trans on Pattern Analysis and Machine Intelligence **18** (1996) 837–842
8. Manjunath, B.S., Ohm, J.R.: Color and texture descriptors. IEEE Transs on circuits and systems for video technology **11** (2001) 703–715
9. Ruiz, M., Srikanth, M.: UB at CLEF2004: Part 2 – cross language medical image retrieval. CLEF Workshop (2004)
10. Deselaers, T., Keysers, D., Ney, H.: FIRE - flexible image retrieval engine: ImageCLEF 2004 evaluation. CLEF Workshop (2004)
11. Heesch, D., Rüger, S.: NN^k networks for content-based image retrieval. In: 26th European Conference on Information Retrieval, Springer-Verlag (2004) 253–266
12. Yavlinsky, A., Pickering, M., Heesch, D., Rüger, S.: A comparative study of evidence combination strategies. In: IEEE International Conference on Acoustics, Speech, and Signal Processing. Volume III. (2004) 1040–1043

SMIRE: Similar Medical Image Retrieval Engine

Pei-Cheng Cheng[1], Been-Chian Chien[2], Hao-Ren Ke[3], and Wei-Pang Yang[1,4]

[1] Department of Computer & Information Science, National Chiao Tung University, 1001 Ta Hsueh Rd., Hsinchu, Taiwan 30050, R.O.C.
{cpc, wpyang}@cis.nctu.edu.tw

[2] Department of Computer Science and Information Engineering, National University of Tainan
33, Sec. 2, Su-Lin Street, Tainan, 700, Taiwan, R.O.C.
bcchien@mail.ntntc.edu.tw

[3] University Library, National Chiao Tung University, 1001 Ta Hsueh Rd., Hsinchu, Taiwan 30050, R.O.C.
claven@lib.nctu.edu.tw

[4] Department of Information Management, National Dong Hwa University
1, Sec. 2, Da Hsueh Rd., Shou-Feng, Hualien, Taiwan, R.O.C.

Abstract. This paper aims at finding images that are similar to a medical image example query. We propose several image features based on wavelet coefficients, including *color histogram, gray-spatial histogram*, *coherence moment*, and *gray correlogram*, to facilitate the retrieval of similar medical images. The initial retrieval results are obtained via visual feature analysis. An automatic feedback mechanism that clusters visually and textually similar images among these initial results was also proposed to help refine the query. In the Image-CLEF 2004 evaluation, the experimental results show that our system is excellence in mean average precision.

1 Introduction

The importance of digital image retrieval techniques increases in the emerging fields of medical image databases. The increasing reliance of modern medicine on diagnostic techniques such as radiology, histopathology, and computerized tomography has led to an explosion in number and importance of medical images stored by most hospitals. There is increasing interest in the use of CBIR (content-based image retrieval) techniques to aid diagnosis by identifying similar past cases.

In the past years, content-based image retrieval has been one of the hottest research areas in the field of computer vision. The commercial QBIC [1] system is definitely the most well known system. Another commercial system for image and video retrieval is Virage [2,3] that has well-known commercial customers such as CNN. In the academia, some systems including Candid [4], Photobook [5], and Netra [6] use simple color and texture characteristics to describe image content. The Blobword system [7,8] exploits higher-level information, such as segmented objects of images, for queries. A system that is available free of charge is the GNU Image Finding Tool (GIFT) [9]. Some systems are available as demonstration versions on the Web such as Viper,

C. Peters et al. (Eds.): CLEF 2004, LNCS 3491, pp. 750 – 760, 2005.

WIPE or Compass. There is a variety image retrieval systems designed for visual image queries but most of the available systems are hard to compare.

Imaging systems and image archives have often been described as an important economic and clinical factor in the hospital environment [10]. Several methods from computer vision and image processing have already been proposed for the use in medicine [11]. Medical images have often been used for retrieval systems, and the medical domain is often cited as one of the principal application domains for content-based access technologies [4,12,13] in terms of potential impact. Still, it is hard to evaluate the performance of systems.

One of the most significant problems in content-based image retrieval results from the lack of a common test-bed for researchers. Although many published articles report on content-based retrieval results using color photographs, there has been little effort in establishing a benchmark set of images and queries. It is very important that image databases are made available free of charge for the comparison and verification of algorithms. Only such reference databases allow comparing systems and to have a reference for the evaluation that is done based on the same images. ImageCLEF [14] offers numerous medical images for evaluation and has many benefits in advancing the technology and utilization of content-based image retrieval systems.

In the ImageCLEF 2004 evaluation, we participated in the medical retrieval task. In the following sections, we detail the approach taken for the medical retrieval task. We analyze the results of the various evaluations, and have a discussion about the relative performance of our system. In the first experiment, we use the visual features to retrieve similar images. In the continued experiment we analyze the results of visual example queries and exploit a refinement mechanism to improve the result. In the third experiment, the relevance examples are picked manually from previous results to reformulate the query. We find that user relevance feedback improves the result strongly. This paper is organized as follows. In Section 2, we describe the features we use to represent the images. The similarity metric is proposed in Section 3. In Section 4, we explain the automatic feedback mechanism. The experiment results are discussed in Section 5. Section 6 concludes this paper.

2 Feature Extraction

The medical image collection of the ImageCLEF 2004 evaluation contains gray and color images. In color images, users are usually attracted by the change of colors more than the positions of objects. Thus, we use a *color histogram* as the feature of color images to retrieve similar color images. A color histogram is suitable to compare images in many applications. A color histogram is computationally efficient, and generally insensitive to small changes in the camera position.

The color histogram has some drawbacks. It looses all spatial information; it merely describes which colors are present in an image, and in what quantities. Because gray images encompass few levels (usually 256 gray levels), directly using a color histogram on grayscale images will result in bad retrieval. For grayscale images, we must emphasize a spatial relationship analysis; furthermore, object and contrast analysis are important for medical images; therefore, three kinds of features that can indicate the spatial, coherence, and shape characteristics, *gray-spatial histogram*, *coherence moment*, and *gray correlogram*, are employed as the features of grayscale images.

In the following, we describe the four kinds of features, one for color images and three for grayscale images, used in this paper.

2.1 Color Image Features

The color histogram [15] is a basic method and has good performance for representing the image content. The color histogram method gathers statistics about the proportion of each color as the signature of an image. Let C be a set of colors, $(c_1, c_2 \ldots c_m) \in$ C, that can occur in an image. Let I be an image that consists of pixels p(x,y)[1]. The color histogram $H(I)$ of image I is a vector $(h_1, h_2, \ldots, h_i, \ldots, h_m)$, in which each bucket h_i counts the ratio of pixels of color c_i in I. Suppose that p is the color level of a pixel. Then the histogram of I for color c_i is defined in Eq. (1):

$$h_{c_i}(I) = \Pr_{p \in I}\{p \in c_i\} \ . \tag{1}$$

In other words, $h_{c_i}(I)$ corresponds to the probability of any pixel in I being of the color c_i. For comparing the similarity of two images I and I', the distance between the histograms of I and I' can be calculated using a standard method (such as the L_1 distance or L_2 distance). Then, the image in the image database most similar to a query image I is the one having the smallest histogram distance with I.

Any two colors have a degree of similarity. The color histogram cannot capture these similarities. In this paper, each pixel does not only assign a single color. We set an interval range δ to extend the color of each pixel. Then the histogram of image I is redefined as the Eq. (2):

$$h_{c_i}(I) = \frac{\sum_{j=1}^{m} \frac{[p_j - \frac{\delta}{2}, p_j + \frac{\delta}{2}] \cap c_i}{\delta}}{m} \ . \tag{2}$$

where p_j is a pixel of the image, and m is the total number of pixels.

The colors of an image are represented in the HSV (Hue, Saturation, Value) space, which is closer to human perception than spaces such as RGB (Red, Green, Blue) or CMY (Cyan, Magenta, Yellow). In our implementation, we quantize HSV space into 18 hues, 2 saturations and, 4 values, with four additional levels of gray values; as a result, there are a total of 148 bins.

Using the modified color histogram, the similarity of two color images q and d is defined in Eq. (3):

$$\text{SIMcolor(H(q), H(d))} = \frac{\text{H(q)} \cap \text{H(d)}}{|\text{H(q)}|} = \frac{\sum_{i=1}^{n} \min(h_i(q), h_i(d))}{\sum_{i=1}^{n} h_i(q)} \ . \tag{3}$$

---

[1] p(x, y) indicates the color of the corresponding pixel as well.

2.2 Grayscale Image Features

Grayscale images are different from color images in human perception. Grey level images have no colors but only a maximum of 256 different grey levels. Human's visual perception is influenced by the contrast of an image. The contrast of an image from the viewpoint of a human is relative rather than absolute. To emphasize the contrast of an image and handle images with less illuminative influence, we normalize the value of pixels before quantization. In this paper we propose a relative normalization method. First, we cluster the whole image into four clusters by the K-means cluster method [16]. We sort the four clusters ascending according to their mean values. We shift the mean of the first cluster to value 50 and the fourth cluster to 200; then, each pixel in a cluster is multiplied by a relative weight to normalize. Let m_{c1} be the mean value of cluster 1 and m_{c4} be the mean value of cluster 4. The normalization formula of pixel p(x,y) is defined in Eq. (4).

$$p(x,y)_{normal} = (p(x,y) - (m_{c1} - 50)) \times \frac{200}{(m_{c4} - m_{c1})} \quad (4)$$

After normalization, we resize each image into 128*128 pixels, and use a one level wavelet with a Haar Wavelet function [17] to generate the low frequency and high frequency sub-images. Processing an image using the low pass filter will obtain an image that is more consistent than the original one; on the contrary, processing an image using the high pass filter will obtain an image that has high variation. The high-frequency part keeps the contour of the image. Fig. 1 is an example of a wavelet

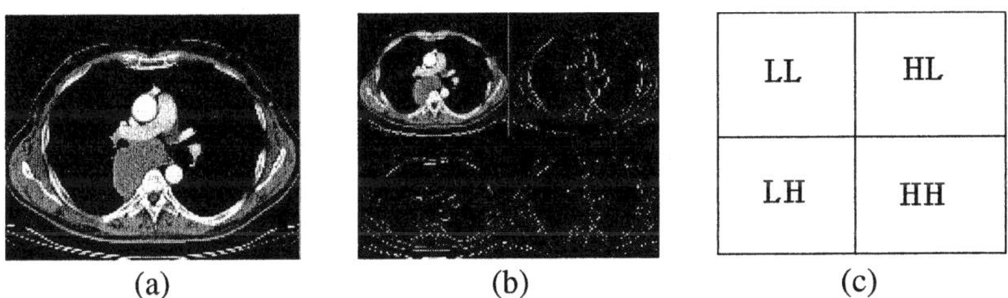

Fig. 1. (a) is the original image; (b) is a one-level wavelet transformed image;(c) there are four sub-bands denoted by Low_Low (LL), Low_High (LH), High_Low (HL), High_High (HH)

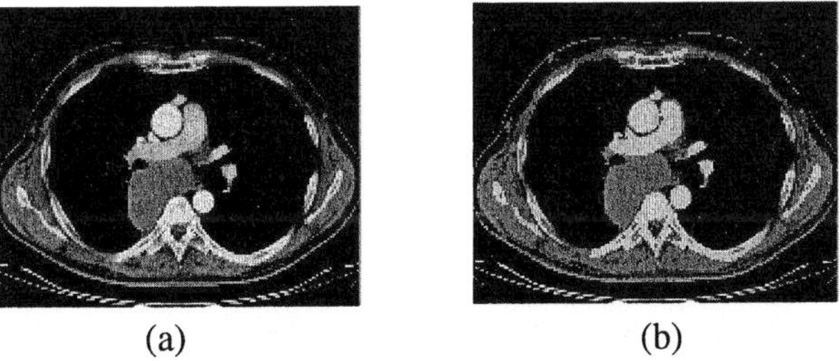

Fig. 2. (a) original image with 256 levels; (b) new image after clustering with only 4 levels

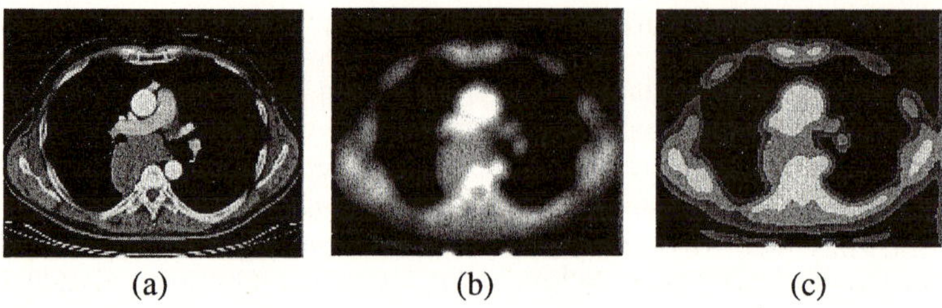

Fig. 3. (a) original image; (b) image after smoothing; (c) image after clustering into four classes

transformation. By performing the OR operation for LH, HL, and HH bands, we get the contour of a medical image.

Gray-Spatial Histogram. In a grayscale image the spatial relationship is very important especially in medical images. Medical images always contain particular anatomic regions (lung, liver, head, and so on); therefore, similar images have similar spatial structures. We add spatial information into the histogram so we call this representation a gray-spatial histogram in order to distinguish from color histograms. We use the LL band for the gray-spatial histogram and coherence analysis. To get the gray-spatial histogram, we divide the LL band image into nine areas. The gray values are quantized into 16 levels for computational efficiency.

The gray-spatial feature estimates the probability of each gray level that appears in a particular area. The probability equation is defined in Eq. (2), where δ is set to 10. Our gray-spatial histogram of an image has a total of 144 bins.

Coherence Moment. One of the problems to design an image representation is the semantic gap. The state-of-the-art technology still cannot reliably identify objects. The coherence moment feature attempts to describe the features from the human's viewpoint in order to reduce the semantic gap.

We cluster an image into four classes by the K-means algorithm. Fig. 2. is an example. Fig. 2. (a) is the original image and Fig. 2. (b) is the four-level grayscale image. We almost cannot visually find the difference between the two images. After clustering an image into four classes, we calculate the number of pixels (COH_{κ}), mean value of gray value (COH_{μ}) and standard variance of gray value (COH_{ρ}) in each class. For each class, we group connected pixels into eight directions as an object. If an object is bigger than 5% of the whole image, we denote it as a big object; otherwise it is a small object. We count how many big objects (COH_{o}) and small objects (COH_{v}) are in each class, and use COH_{o} and COH_{v} as parts of image features.

Since we intend to know the reciprocal effects among classes, so we smooth the original image. If two images are similar, they will also be similar after smoothing. If their spatial distributions are quite different, they may have a different result after smoothing. After smoothing, we cluster an image into four classes and calculate the number of big objects (COH_{τ}) and small objects (COH_{ω}). Fig. 3. is an example. Each pixel will be influenced by its neighboring pixels. Two close objects of the same class may be merged into one object. Then, we can analyze the variation between the two images before and after smoothing. The coherence moment of each class is a seven-feature vector, (COH_κ, COH_μ, COH_ρ, COH_o, COH_ν, COH_τ, COH_ω). The coherence moment of an image is a 28-feature vector that combines the coherence moments of the four classes.

Gray Correlogram. The contour of a medical image contains rich information. In this task we are going to find similar medical images, not to detect the affected part. A broken bone in the contour may be different from a healthy one. Thus we choose a representation that can estimate the partial similarity of two images and can be used to calculate their global similarity.

We analyze the high frequency part by our modified correlogram algorithm. The definition of the correlogram [18,19] is in Eq. (5). Let D denote a set of fixed distances $\{d_1, d_2, d_3,\ldots, d_n\}$. The correlogram of an image I is defined as the probability of a color pair (ci, cj) at a distance d.

$$\gamma^{d}_{c_i,c_j}(I) = \Pr_{p_1 \in c_i, p_2 \in I}\{p_2 \in c_j \| p_1 - p_2 | = d\} . \tag{5}$$

For computational efficiency, the autocorrelogram is defined in Eq. (6)

$$\lambda^{d}_{c_i}(I) = \Pr_{p_1 \in c_i, p_2 \in I}\{p_2 \in c_i \| p_1 - p_2 | = d\} . \tag{6}$$

The contrast of a gray image dominates human perception. If two images have different gray levels they still may be visually similar. Thus the correlogram method cannot be used directly.

Our modified correlogram algorithm works as follows. First, we sort the pixels of the high frequency part in descending order. Then, we order the results of the preceding sorting by ascendant distances of pixels to the center of the image. The distance of a pixel to the image center is measured by the L2 distance. After sorting by gray value and distance to the image center, we select the top 20 percent of pixels and the gray values higher than a threshold to estimate the autocorrelogram histogram. We set the threshold zero in this task. Any two pixels have a distance, and we estimate the probability that the distance falls within an interval. The distance intervals we set are {(0,2), (2,4), (4,6), (6,8), (8,12), (12,16), (16,26), (26,36), (36,46), (46,56), (56,76), (76,100)}. The high frequency part comprises 64*64 pixels, thus the maximum distance will be smaller than 100. The first n pixels will have n*(n+1)/2 numbers of distances. We calculate the probability of each interval to form the correlogram vector.

3 Similarity Metric

While an image has features to represent it, we need a metric to measure the similarity between two feature vectors (and consequently, the similarity between two images). The similarity metric of the color histogram is defined in Eq. (3) and that of gray-spatial histogram is defined in Eq. (7):

$$\mathrm{SIM}_{\mathrm{gray\_spatial}}(\mathrm{H(q), H(d)}) = \frac{\mathrm{H(q)} \cap \mathrm{H(d)}}{|\mathrm{H(q)}|} = \frac{\sum_{i=1}^{n}\min(h_i(q), h_i(d))}{\sum_{i=1}^{n} h_i(q)} . \tag{7}$$

The similarity metric of the coherence moment is defined in Eq. (8)

$$\begin{aligned} & DIS_{coh}(COH(q),COH(d)) = \\ & \sum_{i=1}^{4classes}(|COH_{\kappa}^{q_i} - COH_{\kappa}^{d_i}| + |COH_{\mu}^{q_i} - COH_{\mu}^{d_i}| \times |COH_{\rho}^{q_i} - COH_{\rho}^{d_i}| \\ & + |COH_{o}^{q_i} - COH_{o}^{d_i}| + |(COH_{v}^{q_i})^{1/2} - (COH_{v}^{d_i})^{1/2}| \\ & + |COH_{\tau}^{q_i} - COH_{\tau}^{d_i}| \times 2 + |(COH_{\omega}^{q_i})^{1/2} - (COH_{\omega}^{d_i})^{1/2}|) \; . \end{aligned} \tag{8}$$

The correlogram metric is defined in Eq. (9):

$$\mathrm{DIS}_{\mathrm{hf}}(\mathrm{H(q)},\ \mathrm{H(d)}) = \frac{\sum_{i=1}^{n} |h_i(q) - h_i(d)|}{\sum_{i=1}^{n} |h_i(q) + h_i(d)|} \; . \tag{9}$$

The similarity of two images Q and D is measured by Eq. (10):

$$\begin{aligned} \mathrm{SIM}_{\mathrm{image}}(\mathrm{Q, D}) = {} & W_1 \times \mathrm{SIM}_{\mathrm{color}}(\mathrm{H(Q),H(D)} + W_2 \times \mathrm{SIM}_{\mathrm{gray\text{-}spatial}}(\mathrm{H(Q),H(D)} \\ & + \\ & W_3 \times 1/(1+\mathrm{DIS}_{\mathrm{coh}}(\mathrm{COH(Q),COH(D)})) + W_4 \times \\ & 1/(1+\mathrm{DIS}_{\mathrm{hf}}(\mathrm{COH(Q),COH(D)})), \end{aligned} \tag{10}$$

where W_i is the weight of each feature. In this task the database contains color and grayscale images. When the user queries an image by example, we first determine whether the example is color or grayscale. We calculate the color histogram, if the four bins of gray values occupy more than 80% of the whole image, we decide that the query image is gray; otherwise it is color. If the input is a color image, then we set W_1=10, W_2=0.1, W_1=10, and W_1=10; Otherwise we set W_1=0.1, W_2=1, W_1=100, and W_1=100.

4 Feedback Mechanism

When the user inputs the visual query example, the system first employs visual features to retrieve relevant images from the database. After the initial retrieval, the system selects the top-n relevant images as candidate images. The similarity between the visual query example and each of the top-n images must also be greater than a threshold. In the next step, we cluster the top-n images into k classes. The system selects the class that is closest to original query example as positive examples.

In addition to images, the database of ImageCLEF 2004 contains a textual case description. However, a patient case contains a variety of images. The images of the same case are sometimes not visually similar. So, in this paper while doing the relevance feedback, the weight of text is lower.

We first translate the case description from French into English if possible. The vector space model [20] is used to create a vector representation of a diagnosis text. Each entry of the vector represents a term of the text and the value of the entry is the term frequency (tf) * inverse document frequency (idf) value. The similarity between two diagnoses is computed as the cosine between their vector representations, as shown in Eq. (11)

$$\cos(q,d) = \frac{\sum_{i=1}^{n} w_i^q \times w_i^d}{\sqrt{\sum_{i=1}^{n} (w_i^q)^2} \times \sqrt{\sum_{i=1}^{n} (w_i^d)^2}} . \quad (11)$$

where W_i^q is the weight of term i in text q, and n is the numbers of terms.

The similarity between two images consists of visual similarity and textual similarity. We set the weight of the textual part to 0.1 and the visual feature part to 0.9. In our implementation, we cluster the top-20 images into 6 classes by the minimum distance hierarchical cluster algorithm [16]. The class most similar to the query example in vision becomes the next query image class. We use the OR operation among exemplary images to measure the similarity of database images; in other words, we use the maximum similarity between positive query images and an image in the database to measure the similarity of the latter image to the query.

The definition of similar images is very subjective for humans. Thus, the relevance feedback method is very useful in image retrieval systems. In our system we also offer the user to manually select positive images as query examples for relevance feedback. The query reformulation equation is given in Eq. (12).

$$q_i = \sum_{j=1}^{n} \frac{q_j}{n} . \quad (12)$$

q_i is one of the query vectors. q_j is correspond feature vector of the positive image example. There are n positive images. We use the mean of the positive images as the next query example.

5 Experimental Results

We follow the ImageCLEF 2004 evaluation to evaluate the performance of our system. The process of evaluation and the format of results employ the trec_eval tool. There are 26 queries. The corresponding answer images of every query were judged as either relevant or partially relevant by at least 2 assessors.

In this task, we have three experiments. The first run uses the visual features of the query image to query the database. The second run is the result of the automatic feedback mechanism, which uses the images of the most similar class as the positive query examples to query the image database. The third run is the result where the user manually selects the relevant images as positive examples. The test result shows that the auto-feedback mechanism, KIDS-2, has better result than the first run. In the results summary, the mean average precision of the first run (KIDS-1) of our system is 0.3273. The mean average precision of run2 (KIDS-2) is 0.3799. The mean average precision of run3 (KIDS-3) is 0.4474. Fig. 4. shows the precision and recall graphs.

The results show that the image features we propose can represent the medical image content well. The medical image's background is very similar. Relevance feedback can extract the dominant features; thus it can improve the performance strongly.

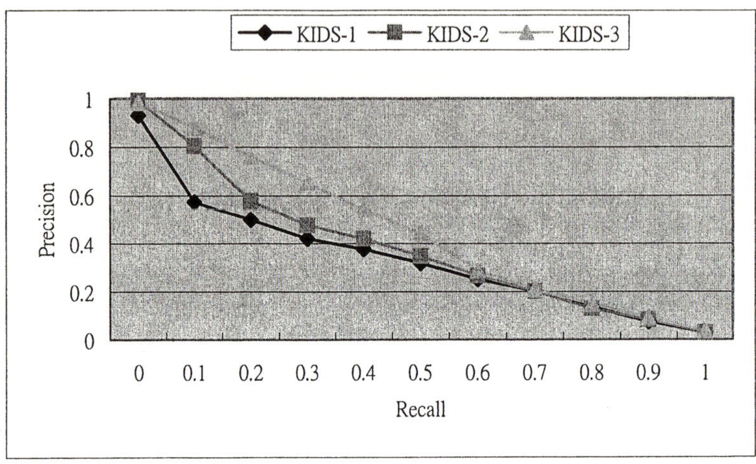

Fig. 4. Precision Vs. Recall graphs without and with feedback. KIDS-1 is the result without relevance feedback. KIDS-2 is auto-feedback results. KIDS-3 is the result with manual feedback

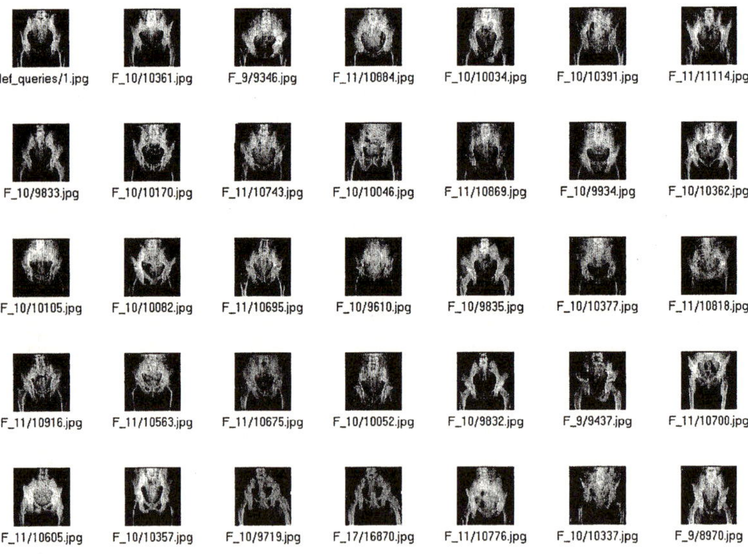

Fig. 5. Result of an example query

In this paper we consider that the contrast of a grayscale image dominates human perception. We use a relative normalization method to reduce the impact of illumination. Fig. 5. is the result of an example query returned by our system. It can be observed from Fig. 5. that 9719.jpg and 16870.jpg are darker than the query image (def_queries/1.jpg), but our system still can find them out.

The first run has an accuracy above 50% in the first 20 images. The really similar images may have similar features in some aspect. The misjudged images are always less consistent. So we try to refine the initial result by the automatic feed back mechanism. We cluster the first 20 images into six classes. If the class contains diverse images, the center of the class will become farther, and consequently more different, from the query image. Thus we can improve the result by our feedback method.

6 Conclusion

In this paper we propose several image features to represent medical images. Although the color histogram of content-based image retrieval methods has good performance in general-purpose color images, unlike general-purpose color images the X-ray images only contain gray level pixels. Thus, we concentrate on the contrast representation of images.

The image representations we propose have obtained good results in this task. Our representation is immune to defective illumination. A total of 322 features are used. It is very efficient in computation. The auto feedback mechanism also provides a good result in medical images.

An image represents thousands of words. An image can be viewed from various aspects; furthermore, different people may have different interpretations of the same image. This means that many parameters need to be tuned. In the future, we will try to learn the user behavior and tune those parameters by learning methods.

References

[1] Flickner, M., Sawhney, H., Niblack, W., Ashley, J., Huang, Q., Dom, B., Gorkani, M., Hafner, J., Lee, D., Petkovic, D., Steele, D., Yanker, P.: Query by Image and Video Content: The QBIC system. IEEE Computer Vol. 28 (9). (1995) 23-32

[2] Bach, J. R., Fuller, C., Gupta, A., Hampapur, A., Horowitz, B., Humphrey, R., Jain, R., Shu, C.-F: The Virage Image Search Engine: An Open Framework for Image Management. Proceedings of IS&T/SPIE: Storage & Retrieval for Image and Video Databases IV, Vol. 2670. (1996) 76-87

[3] Hampapur, A., Gupta, A., Horowitz, B., Shu, C.-F., Fuller, C., Bach, J., Gorkani, M., Jain, R.: Virage video engine. In: I. K. Sethi, R. C. Jain (eds.): Storage and Retrieval for Image and Video Databases of SPIE Proceedings, Vol. 3022. (1997) 352-360

[4] Ma., P., Cannon, M., Hush, D. R.: Query by Image Example: The CANDID Approach. In: W. Niblack, R. C. Jain (eds.): Storage and Retrieval for Image and Video Databases III, Vol. 2420 of SPIE Proceedings. (1995) 238-248

[5] Pentland, A., Picard, R. W., Sclaro, S.: Photobook: Tools for Content-Based Manipulation of Image Databases. International Journal of Computer Vision, Vol. 18 (3). (1996) 233-254

[6] Ma, W. Y., Deng, Y., Manjunath, B. S.: Tools for Texture- and Color-Based Search of Images. In: B. E. Rogowitz, T. N. Pappas (eds.): Human Vision and Electronic Imaging II, Vol. 3016 of SPIE Proceedings. San Jose, CA (1997) 496-507

[7] Belongie, S., Carson, C., Greenspan, H., Malik, J.: Color and Texture Based Image Segmentation Using EM and Its Application to Content-Based Image Retrieval. Proceedings of the International Conference on Computer Vision. Bombay, India, (1998) 675-682

[8] Carson, C., Thomas, M., Belongie, S., Hellerstein, J. M., Malik, J.: Blobworld: A System for Region-Based Image Indexing and Retrieval. In: D. P. Huijsmans, A. W. M. Smeulders (eds.), Third International Conference On Visual Information Systems (VISUAL' 99), Lecture Notes in Computer Science, Vol. 1614. Springer-Verlag, Amsterdam, The Netherlands (1999) 509-516

[9] Squire, D. M., Muller, W., Muller, H., Pun, T.: Content-Based Query of Image Databases: In: Spirations from Text Retrieval, Pattern Recognition Letters Vol. 21 (13-14), (2000) 1193-1198

[10] Greenes, R. A., Brinkley, J. F.: Imaging systems. In: Medical Informatics: Computer Applications in Healthcare (2nd edition). Springer, New York (2000) 485- 538

[11] Pun, T., Gerig, G., Ratib, O.: Image Analysis and Computer Vision in Medicine. Computerized Medical Imaging and Graphics, Vol.18 (2). (1994) 85-96

[12] Beretti, S., Bimbo, A. D., Pala, P.: Content- Based Retrieval of 3D Cellular Structures. Proceedings of the second International Conference on Multimedia and Exposition (ICME'2001), IEEE Computer Society. Tokyo, Japan, (2001) 1096-1099

[13] Orphanoudakis, S. C., Chronaki, C. E., Kostomanolakis, S.: I_2Cnet: A System for The Indexing, Storage and Retrieval of Medical Images by Content. Medical Informatics, Vol. 19 (2). (1994) 109-122

[14] Clough, P., Sanderson, M., Müller, H.: The CLEF Cross Language Image Retrieval Track. In: Working Notes of the CLEF 2004 Workshop. (2004)

[15] Swain M.J., and Ballard, D. H.: Color Indexing. International Journal of Computer Vision, Vol. 7. (1991) 11-32

[16] Han, J., Kamber, M.: Data Mining: Concepts and Techniques. Academic Press, San Diego, CA, USA (2001)

[17] Stollnitz, E. J., DeRose, T. D., and Salesin, D. H.: Wavelets for Computer Graphics – Theory and Applications. Morgan Kaufmann Publishers, San Francisco, CA (1996)

[18] Huang, J., Kumar, S. R., Mitra, M., Zhu, W. –J., Zabih, R.: Image Indexing Using Color Correlograms, Proceedings of IEEE Conference on Computer Vision and Pattern Recognition. San Juan, Puerto Rico (1997)

[19] Ojala, T., Rautiainen, M., Matinmikko, E., and M. Aittola: Semantic Image Retrieval with HSV Correlograms. Proceedings of 12th Scandinavian Conference on Image Analysis. Bergen, Norway (2001)

[20] Salton, G.: Automatic Text Processing. Addison-Wesley Publishing Company (1988)

A Probabilistic Approach to Medical Image Retrieval

Koen Lubbers[1], Arjen P. de Vries[2], Theo Huibers[1], and Paul van der Vet[1]

[1] University of Twente, Enschede, The Netherlands
{k.f.lubbers, t.w.c.huibers, p.e.vandervet}@ewi.utwente.nl
[2] Centrum voor Wiskunde en Informatica (CWI), Amsterdam, The Netherlands
arjen@acm.org

Abstract. We present a probabilistic approach to the medical retrieval task. We experimented with the Westerveld method [1] to obtain our results for ImageCLEF. In addition to these results we describe our findings of involving a medical expert in our research. The expert helped us identifying useful image retrieval applications and reflected upon the setup of ImageCLEF's medical task. Finally we describe the evaluation of an interactive implementation of the probabilistic approach.

1 Introduction

The amount of information available through all kinds of sources is growing larger and larger. The goal of information retrieval systems is to help a user in efficiently finding relevant information. Image retrieval is a sub domain of information retrieval. This relatively new research area is about gaining access to images that match a query. Apart from text, such a query can consist of a sketch or an actual image.

Several information retrieval techniques have been applied to the image retrieval field lately [2]. Although probabilistic methods are often used to determine the relevance of textual documents, they have hardly been applied to image retrieval tasks. The goal of our work is to explore the possibilities of the probabilistic Westerveld method [3, 1].

In recent years, much research has been done into specific medical image retrieval systems [4, 5, 6, 7, 8]. For comparison reasons, we have chosen to test the *generic* Westerveld method in a medical environment. A part of testing a method is to compare it to other (specific) systems. Until recently, a fair comparison of content-based image retrieval methods under similar circumstances was lacking [9]. The ImageCLEF medical retrieval task [10] is an evaluation that tries to change this. We have participated in CLEF to experiment with a medical image collection and to be able to compare our results with other systems.

Few studies are known in which medical experts have participated in the evaluation of medical retrieval systems [11]. Therefore, in addition to our participation in CLEF, we have involved a medical physicist from the Academic Medical Centre (AMC) in Amsterdam in our research. We have asked the expert

C. Peters et al. (Eds.): CLEF 2004, LNCS 3491, pp. 761–772, 2005.

to identify useful applications of image retrieval techniques within the medical domain, and to reflect upon the setup of ImageCLEF's medical search task.

1.1 Image Retrieval in a Medical Environment

Researchers from the University of Berkeley estimate that about 2 billion X-rays are produced in hospitals worldwide each year [12] (this corresponds to approximately 5.5 million new medical images every day!). A growing number of hospitals is switching to handling their image data in digital format. Current Picture Archiving and Communication Systems (PACS) offer the possibility to save images with additional relevant information, like a patient name or number, and additional information from a medical case. Subsequently, all this data will be available from the different workstations throughout the hospital.

To identify useful applications of image retrieval systems, we first looked at the present situation with the PACS in the AMC. When images are produced they will be stored automatically with information like patient name, number, body region, and modality as metadata. This metadata is available because of the electronic request a doctor has to submit before the image is produced. This means that searching by body part or modality with a content-based retrieval method will often not be useful, because most of the time the correct modality and body part are available in text.

However, an image retrieval system could serve as a control tool. People do make mistakes, and images could, for example, end up at the wrong patient or a doctor who produces an image of the left knee is actually supposed to deliver an image of the right knee. Furthermore, error rates with respect to automatically stored anatomical regions seem to be very high: about 15 to 20% [13]. This is where a retrieval system could be convenient: on a basis of already classified images it can determine how much the new image differs from the expected visual features.

An important finding in this study is that the PACS used at AMC does not associate images and pathology. When a medical doctor wants to look at images with the same or similar pathology, for example for comparison to the image shown on his screen, no suitable solution exists. The AMC medical experts therefore indicated three particularly useful fields for application of image retrieval tools: education, research and diagnosis.

For educational purposes, a medical doctor would like to find images in a corresponding field of pathology. These images could serve as cases for medical students. In the research area, image retrieval could be used to analyze the visual features of clusters of images with corresponding syndromes. This could result in a thesaurus of visual features connected to different kinds of images and syndromes. The third application is the diagnosis of problematic cases. When a medical doctor is not sure about a certain image, he would like to be able to use a retrieval method to find other images of the same kind. In this way, he will find useful information in the cases connected to the retrieved images.

Apart from identifying useful applications, image retrieval research in a medical environment shows medical experts a way in which technology can support their daily activities. Medical doctors do not always believe in the abilities of computer systems to offer added value to their work. By involving them in image retrieval research, the technological frontiers of the medical sector are explored.

2 Background

The Westerveld image retrieval approach [3, 1] has not been designed for specific images. It has been tested mainly on collections with a large variety in images. Westerveld, following Vasconcelos [14], models the visual features by using Gaussian Mixture Models (GMMs). The basic idea is that an image consists of a certain number of 'aspects', where each of these aspects can be described in one component of the GMM. Each sample that is taken from an image is assumed to have been generated by one of these components. A Gaussian Mixture Model (GMM) is a weighted sum of multivariate Gaussian distributions, where the weights are considered as prior probabilities of the different components. We will explain briefly what happens when the parameters for a GMM are estimated. For a more detailed explanation of the generative probabilistic retrieval model the reader is referred to [3, 1].

The steps of creating a probabilistic image model are shown in Figure 1. First, the RGB representation of the image is converted into YCbCr colour space. Next, each of the colour channels of the image is divided into samples of 8 by 8 pixels. Then, a discrete cosine transform (DCT) is performed on every sample. By default, the different samples are described by 14-dimensional vectors. Each vector consists of the first 10 DCT coefficients from the Y channel, the DC coefficient of both the Cb and the Cr channel, and the x and y position of the sample in the image.

The feature vectors of an image are fed to the EM algorithm to find the parameters of the mixture models. The algorithm starts with introducing a given number of components by grouping the samples randomly. This is the first expectation step. In the maximization step, the parameters of each component are calculated, based on the samples assigned to that component. A component represents the average colour and texture of the samples assigned to it. In the second expectation step, the samples are regrouped. For example: a sample of a blue sky will be assigned to the component that explains best the visual characteristics of the blue sky. The E-step and the M-step iterate until the algorithm converges.

A collection of images can be indexed by estimating the GMM for each of the images. Query images are represented as a collection of samples. The basis of the retrieval step is to estimate, for each model of the collection images, the probability that the query samples could be observed given that collection image model. In other words, the goal is to find the document that is most likely to have produced a certain query. The joint probability of a document producing this certain query is calculated by multiplying the probabilities for each individual sample of the query.

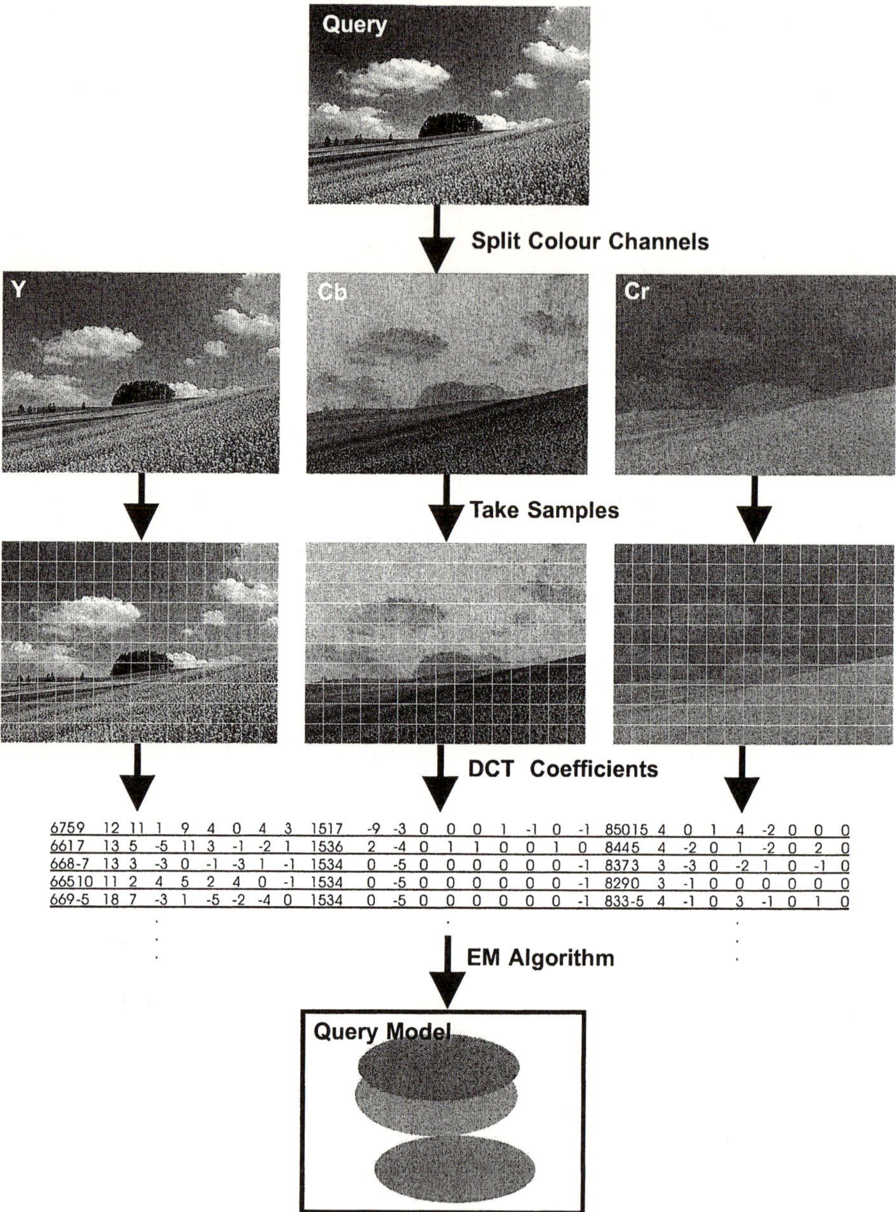

Fig. 1. Building a Gaussian Mixture Model from an image [15]

3 Experimental Setup

The main research question in our ImageCLEF experiments is how a generic image retrieval system would perform on a domain-specific retrieval problem. We decided to ignore the textual information in the medical cases, to provide a solid basis to judge the possible merits of content-based retrieval techniques for search in medical image archives. The combination with textual information is postponed to future research.

Table 1. Standard settings of the Westerveld image retrieval method

Parameter	Default	Description
blocksize	8	size of the samples in pixels
C	8	number of mixture components
convert	1	binary, convert image from RGB to YCbCr colour space
imagesize	240x352	size to which an image is scaled before samples are taken
ncoeffcbcr	1	number of DCT coefficients from Cb and Cr channel
ncoeffy	10	number of DCT coefficients from Y channel
overlap	0	samples will overlap or not
Scale	1	image is scaled before samples are taken or not
XYpos	1	x and y position of a sample are used in feature vector

The default values of the method (see Table 1) are the point of departure of testing with different parameters. During the process of testing with different parameter settings, we varied one parameter at a time. We have tested with both values for each of the binary parameters. The basic rule for adjusting the other values is that we will never reduce the information represented below the default settings.

First, we indexed a sub-collection of the medical CLEF collection to find out which parameters would qualify to be used to get the results for the submission. The selected settings from this experiment were used to build eight different indices of the whole medical collection. We then chose the four best indices by ranking all retrieval results with all queries, based on an 'educated guess' of the precision at a document cut-off level of 20 (doing manual assessments ourselves). We distinguished precision A and precision B. The first value is based on an image being relevant or not according to the CLEF task (image being relevant on both body part and modality) and the second one is only based on the modalities of the images. A modality describes the way in which medical images are produced: MRI, CT, etc.

After the submission of the runs, we have performed more experiments with the system. Several new experiments indicated that the conversion to YCbCr affected the performance of the system negatively. These new experiments were performed with a new sub-collection, which consisted of ten relevant images per query. The relevant images were manually selected from the medical CLEF collection with the help of the medical expert from the AMC.

Because we knew the number of relevant images for each query in de sub collection, we were able to follow Kraaij [16] and compare the retrieval results with R-recall. This means that recall is measured at a document cut-off level, which equals the number of relevant images for a certain query.

Because of the new findings with the second sub-collection, we indexed the whole collection with parameter convert=0 in order to create a new run. Furthermore, we used the setting without conversion as a new basic state and started varying the other parameters to find another way to improve retrieval results.

4 Analysis

The results of the experiment we used to select four out of eight runs for submission are shown in Table 2.

We submitted the first four runs. Since new experiments showed that results were far better when conversion was not applied, we did not expect very good results from the official medical evaluation. After indexing the medical CLEF collection without conversion, retrieval with the queries proved that results with the whole collection were indeed far better: the average precision A equals 0.47.

Table 2. Qualifying runs for submission

Rank	Parameter	Avg precision A	Avg precision B	Avg rank
1	ncoeffy=20	0.22	0.57	3.8
2	default	0.20	0.58	3.8
3	c=16	0.24	0.56	4.0
4	c=4	0.20	0.55	4.1
5	XYpos=0	0.18	0.55	4.9
6	ncoeffcbcr=2	0.18	0.54	5.0
7	imagesize=300x440	0.17	0.50	6.5
8	overlap=1	0.18	0.46	6.6

Further experiments with the second sub-collection showed that there were no parameter settings that improved the retrieval results of the new basic state with convert=0. We concluded that the best way to use the current version of the Westerveld method with the medical CLEF collection is with only one adjustment: disable the conversion to the YCbCr colour space.

We found that R-recall in the experiments with the second sub collection varied from 0.41 to 0.48. We got these results by testing with the fixed settings convert=0, while varying the other parameters one by one. After the release of the judgements from the CLEF medical task (the so-called qrels), we were able to calculate R-recall values for the results we found after retrieval with the total medical image collection. The average R-recall value over the 26 queries equals 0.29. This means that our sub-collection may have been a more ideal test environment than the whole CLEF collection, but it can also imply that we evaluated the results less strictly than the CLEF assessors did.

The official results are expressed in Mean Average Precision (MAP). The best result from the runs we submitted has a MAP of 0.1069. The use of the new parameter settings showed the improvement we expected: the Westerveld method performs about twice as good when the colour space is not converted. Using the RGB representation of the images, the systems scores a MAP of 0.2359, which is a satisfying initial retrieval result.

4.1 Conversion of Colour Spaces

Based on our experience with the retrieval model on other image retrieval tasks, we expected that indexing the collection without conversion to the YCbCr colour space would have given inferior results. The results after the submission of the runs however, showed that without conversion the retrieval method performed about twice as good. This finding proved to be reproducible.

Since earlier testing with the Westerveld method turned out that better results were obtained when working with YCbCr colour space, the following question remains: why does conversion perform less well with the medical collection? We have not yet found a perfect explanation for the degraded retrieval effectiveness after conversion to YCbCr colour space. We believe that the cause of the observed change in performance is to be found in the difference between the medical collection and the previously used testing collections: the medical collection consists almost completely of greyscale images.

In colour images, the three channels in RGB all contain information on both intensity and colour, so the different dimensions are correlated. The motivation for conversion is that in YCbCr colour space, the intensity channel (Y) is separated from the colour channels (Cb and Cr), and the information in each channel is independent from the information in the other channels. In a greyscale situation however, there is no colour information, and the three channels represent the same amount of intensity: R=G=B. Given a greyscale image, Y will be created as usual, but the Cb and the Cr channel both equal 128 in every possible greyscale situation.

Now, recall that the feature vectors to represent the image samples are computed from the DCT transformation over 8x8 pixel blocks. In the feature vectors for an RGB image, the first DCT coefficient (corresponding to the average intensity in the pixel block) is represented in three dimensions. In the YCbCr case, this information is only represented in one dimension. Theoretically, because we assume a diagonal covariance matrix, the complete correlation between the three dimensions in the RGB case (those corresponding to the first DCT coefficient of the three (identical) colour channels) should however affect retrieval negatively rather than improve its results. Yet, the experiments proof otherwise.

Our current intuition is that the duplicated information separates, in feature space, the intensity information more than the textural information (which is represented in the higher coefficients of the DCT transformation). This 'encourages' the EM algorithm model during training to prefer textural information over the intensity information in the image samples. For medical images, textural information seems more important than the intensity information, so this could explain the improved effectiveness of the model. This hypothesis is further supported by observations in earlier experiments (on TRECVID data) [17], where we demonstrated that the textural information in images was dominated by colour information (on YCbCr colour space). Further research is however needed to (in)validate this explanation of the experimental results.

5 Interactive Experiments

After identifying useful applications of medical image retrieval systems, we applied the probabilistic approach in an interactive retrieval system. This system tries to learn from the relevance feedback given by the user [18], attempting to reduce the semantic gap by inserting a human 'in-the-loop'. More information about this research activity can be found in [19]. In order to realise a suitable system, we had to shorten the retrieval time and make the method user-friendly. Again, since we want to learn the strengths of the content-based image retrieval method, we did not use the text in the medical case descriptions. Note that Smeulders describes two other ways to deal with semantics: interpretation and similarity between features [9].

After a medical doctor of the AMC uploads a query image, the system estimates the parameters of its GMM. It then compares the query model to the GMMs of the images in the CLEF collection and presents an initial retrieval result. For efficiency reasons, an approximation of the Kullback Leibler distance between the image models is used as an alternative to the likelihood of observing the query image samples. The results obtained are very similar to those of the original system. After this initial retrieval step, the medical doctor marks retrieved images as relevant or irrelevant; the next iteration takes the feedback into account to re-rank the remaining images.

The interactive system turned out to be very intuitive and easy to use, partially because the doctors in the AMC are already used to a web-based interface for accessing the PACS system. After a query has been uploaded the system is sufficiently fast in presenting the retrieval results. Within a minute, a medical doctor can go through about five iterations. Figure 2 shows a screenshot of the interactive retrieval system (it shows the results after uploading topic 24 of the medical CLEF collection). When a query has been posted the results are displayed within a second.

The interactive experiment pointed out two possible improvements for our retrieval system. First, although the medical CLEF collection is representative for the type of images encountered in the AMC, two main differences are observed in relation to the background and the greyscale representation of the images. When we save an AMC image as JPEG and make it anonymous, all greyscale images are represented as greyscale instead of RGB. Of course, only a minor modification fixes this. A more significant difference is that the AMC data consist for a large part of the image of black background only. The subjects within the images of the CLEF collection seem to have been cropped cleverly.

Finally, explaining the search task applied at the ImageCLEF medical retrieval task to the medical expert has raised some issues with the task evaluated at this first medical image CLEF evaluation, and also demonstrated clearly the existence of 'the semantic gap'. From the system point of view, the results did not look bad, and any mistakes could be easily explained from its inner workings. The system performs well at retrieving images with the same kind of visual features, which often means the same modality. However, medical doctors are interested in finding images with corresponding syndromes, or at least corre-

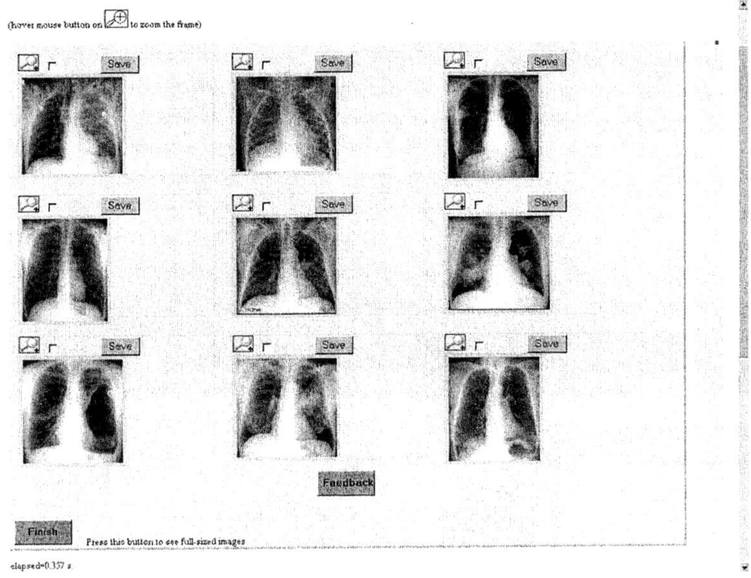

Fig. 2. Screenshot of the initial retrieval results after searching with query 24

sponding body parts. It is far more interesting to retrieve a CT of the brain with an MRI of the brain as a query, than to find an abdomen MRI with it. It may be more useful to measure the performance of retrieval systems using body part only (as opposed to the performance on modality and body part).

6 Conclusions and Future Work

The main goal of our research was to investigate if a generic image retrieval model could also be applied to a domain-specific task such as the retrieval of medical images. We have tested the probabilistic image retrieval model developed by Westerveld using the CLEF medical image test collection, which allows the objective comparison of different approaches to the retrieval problem. We also evaluated an interactive version of our system with a medical expert from the AMC.

The best performance of the Westerveld method has been obtained after adjusting one of the parameters in the representation of the image data. When the medical images are not converted from RGB to YCbCr colour space, the Mean Average Precision in our runs equals 0.2359. This is a satisfying result, especially when considering that we have not used the text of the medical cases in our system.

It is essential that medical doctors - the future users of image retrieval systems - are involved in image retrieval research. With the help from the AMC we identified a number of useful medical retrieval applications. Evaluating the

CLEF images with a medical expert showed that the collection seems to be a rather ideal representation of the images present in the hospital. Furthermore, an experiment with the probabilistic Westerveld method indicated the semantic gap. Retrieval results are most likely to be useful when a system can deal with this gap.

Since we neglected text in our approach, we tried to apply the retrieval method in an interactive system. This system proved to be easy to use and to work fast. However, it still needs to learn from the relevance feedback of experts. Improvements of the Westerveld method itself and allowing the interactive system to learn from medical doctors can lead to adequate support of the daily activities in medical practise.

The AMC image collection showed that an image retrieval method needs to be able to work with greyscale images. Furthermore, it seemed that images from this hospital contained a large black background. An experiment with the smoothing function of the Westerveld can show if the system can automatically neglect this background.

To obtain better retrieval results, we have to deal with the semantic gap. The interactive system will only improve when real users give relevance feedback to initial results. Further research should point out if the system is really able to learn from experience.

Another way to deal with semantics is to embrace a text retrieval method. The Westerveld method has already been tested in combination with a probabilistic text retrieval approach [3].

During a next medical retrieval task it may be possible to increase the performance of retrieval systems through interpretation and similarity between features. The clusters of relevant images per query offer the possibility to create a sort of medical thesaurus, which consists of visual features of certain modalities, body parts, or even syndromes.

Evaluation with the AMC showed that searching for images with identical modality and body part is not a useful task for image retrieval systems. Medical doctors will be interested in a certain pathology: they want to find images with corresponding syndromes. It would be useful if the next medical CLEF collection contained a number of sub-collections. A sub collection can, for example, contain images with corresponding body parts. A challenge for image retrieval systems is to distinguish the visual features of images that do contain a certain abnormality, and images that do not.

Finally, we would like to add another challenge for image retrieval research. The basis of an image retrieval method is a certain image collection that can be indexed. However, when a medical doctor wants to use an application to search for clues regarding the diagnosis of his query image, he might not find satisfying results in the image collection at his own hospital. Retrieval systems can really add value when experts from several hospitals can learn from each others experience. This implies the need for a standard way of indexing and searching. Such a standard can only be reached when different research groups meet to evaluate their results together. This shows the importance of evaluations like ImageCLEF in the future.

Acknowledgements

Without the help of Thijs Westerveld we would not have been able to participate and test with a probabilistic approach to image retrieval. We would also like to thank Lioudmila Boldareva for making it possible to combine the used method with the interactive relevance feedback system. Finally, we thank Jan Habraken, who helped us evaluating our image retrieval work from a medical point of view.

References

1. Westerveld, T.: Using generative probabilistic models for multimedia retrieval. PhD thesis, University of Twente, CTIT Ph.D.-thesis series, ISSN 1381-3617; No. 04-67, Enschede, The Netherlands (2004)
2. Squire, D.M., Müller, W., Müller, H., Pun, T.: Content-based query of image databases: inspirations from text retrieval. Pattern Recognition Letters **21** (2000) 1193–1198
3. Westerveld, T., de Vries, A., van Ballegooij, A., de Jong, F., Hiemstra, D.: A probabilistic multimedia retrieval model and its evaluation. EURASIP Journal on Applied Signal Processing **2003** (2003) 186–198
4. Korn, P., Sidiropoulos, N., Faloutsos, C., Siegel, E., Protopapas, Z.: Fast and effective retrieval of medical tumor shapes. IEEE Transactions on Knowledge and Data Engineering **10** (1998) 889–904
5. Lehmann, T., Guld, M., Thies, C., Fischer, B., Spitzer, K., Keysers, D., Ney, H., Kohnen, M., Schubert, H., Wein, B.: Content-based image retrieval in medical applications. Methods of Information in Medicine **43** (2004) 354–361 In press.
6. Mattiea, M., Staib, L., Stratmann, E., Tagare, H., Duncan, J., Miller, P.: Pathmaster: Content-based cell image retrieval using automated feature extraction. Journal of the American Medical Informatics Association **7** (2000) 404–415
7. Müller, H., Rosset, A., Vallée, J., Geissbuhler, A.: Comparing feature sets for content-based medical information retrieval. In: SPIE Medical Imaging, San Diego, CA, USA (2004)
8. Shyu, C., Brodley, C., Kak, A., Kosaka, A., Aisen, A., Broderick, L.: Assert – a physician-in-the-loop content-based retrieval system for hrct image databases. Computer Vision and Image Understanding **75** (1999) 111–132
9. Smeulders, A., Worring, M., Santini, S., Gupta, A., Jain, R.: Content-based image retrieval: the end of the early years. IEEE transactions on Pattern Analysis and Machine Intelligence **22** (2000) 1349–1380 invited review.
10. Clough, P., Müller, H., Sanderson, M.: The CLEF Cross Language Image Retrieval Track (ImageCLEF) 2004. In Peters, C., Clough, P., Gonzalo, J., Jones, G., Kluck, M., Magnini, B., eds.: Fifth Workshop of the Cross–Language Evaluation Forum (CLEF 2004), Lecture Notes in Computer Science (LNCS), Springer, Heidelberg, Germany (in print) (2005)
11. Müller, H., Michoux, N., Bandon, D., Geissbuhler, A.: A review of content-based image retrieval systems in medicine - clinical benefits and future directions. International Journal of Medical Informatics **73** (2004) 1–23
12. Lyman, P., Varian, H.R.: "how much information", 2003 (2003) Retrieved from http://www.sims.berkeley.edu/how-much-info-2003 on 1/11/2004.

13. Güld, M., Kohnen, M., Keysers, D., Schubert, H., Wein, B., Bredno, J., Lehmann, T.: Quality of dicom header information for image categorization. In: Proceedings SPIE. Volume 4685. (2002) 280–287
14. Vasconcelos, N.: Bayesian Models for Visual Information Retrieval. PhD thesis, Massachusetts Institut of Technology (2000)
15. Westerveld, T., de Vries, A.: Experimental evaluation of a generative probabilistic image retrieval model on 'easy' data. In: Proceedings of the Multimedia Information Retrieval Workshop 2003. (2003) in conjunction with the 26th annual ACM SIGIR conference on Information Retrieval.
16. Kraaij, W.: Variations on language modeling for information retrieval. PhD thesis, CTIT PhD thesis series No. 04-62, Neslia Paniculata (2004)
17. Westerveld, T., de Vries, A.: Experimental result analysis for a generative probabilistic image retrieval model. In: Proceedings of the 26th ACM SIGIR Conference on Research and Development in Information Retrieval (SIGIR'03). (2003) 135–142
18. Boldareva, L.: Improving objects similarities with relevance judgements from the searchers. In: 27th European Conference on Information Retrieval (ECIR '05), Santiago de Compostela, Spain (2005) To appear (poster).
19. Lubbers, K.: Image retrieval in de medische praktijk: mogelijkheden van een probabilistische aanpak. Master's thesis, University of Twente (2004) In Dutch.

UB at CLEF2004 Cross Language Medical Image Retrieval

Miguel E. Ruiz[1] and Munirathnam Srikanth[2]

[1] State University of New York at Buffalo,
School of Informatics, Dept. of Library and Information Studies,
534 Baldy Hall, Buffalo, NY 14260-1020 USA
meruiz@buffalo.edu
http://www.informatics.buffalo.edu/faculty/ruiz
[2] Language Computer Corporation Richardson, TX, 75080, USA
srikanth@languagecomputer.com

Abstract. This paper presents the results of the State University of New York at Buffalo in the cross-language medical image retrieval task at CLEF 2004. Our work in image retrieval explores the combination of image and text retrieval using automatic query expansion. The system uses pseudo relevance feedback on the case descriptions associated with the top 10 images to improve ranking of images retrieved by a CBIR system. The results show significant improvements with respect to a base line that uses only image retrieval.

1 Introduction

The cross language medical image retrieval task requires participants to retrieve information from a collection that includes medical images and physician's annotations, given an initial query that consists only of an image [1]. In this track our goal is to improve image retrieval by using retrieval feedback on the related case descriptions of the top n retrieved images to re-rank the final list of retrieved images. Because our statistical language model system (TAPIR) did not support retrieval feedback (which is a feature that was still under development by the time we worked on this task) we decided to use a version of the SMART retrieval system that we used in our participation in CLEF2003 [3].

Section 2 presents a description of our system for the medical image retrieval task. Section 3 discusses the details about document and image processing, indexing and query expansion. Section 4 presents our experimental results and analysis. The last section presents our conclusion and future work.

2 Combining Retrieval of Medical Images and Case Descriptions

Our goal in this task is to explore ways to expand the initial image retrieval with the multilingual text of the case descriptions associated to each image. For this

C. Peters et al. (Eds.): CLEF 2004, LNCS 3491, pp. 773–780, 2005.

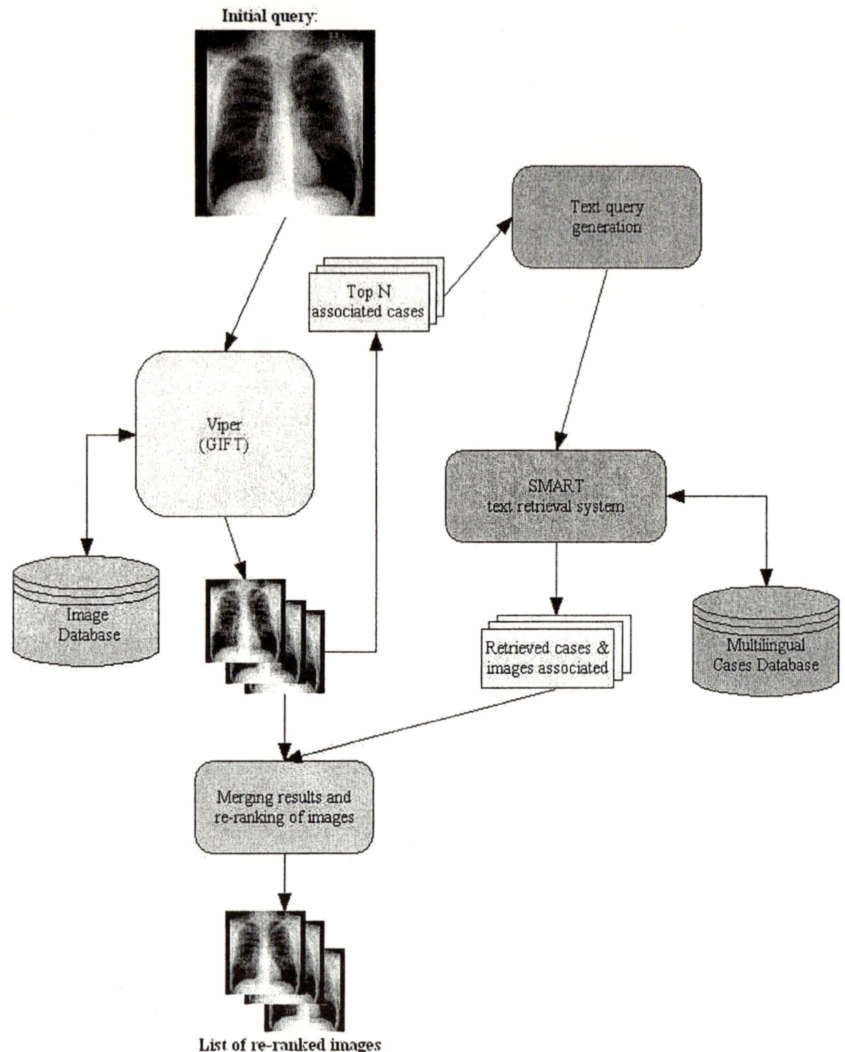

Fig. 1. Diagram of our text and image retrieval system

purpose we use a pseudo relevance feedback mechanism. The first step consists in performing retrieval using the database of images indexed. The top n images are used to locate the corresponding case descriptions. These case descriptions are used to build a query that is submitted to the text retrieval system to obtain other related case descriptions. Figure 1 presents an schematic design of this system.

Our system combines the Viper system [5], which is a publicly available image retrieval system developed at University of Geneva, and the well known SMART system [4], which is an information retrieval system deloped by G. Salton and his collaborators.

3 Collection Preparation and Indexing

The collection consists of 8,726 images and 2,081 cases descriptions that contain clinical information (details about the collection can be found in [1]. Our initial inspection of the data revealed that there were 209 cases that have images associated with them but no textual information. We discarded these cases from our experiments because they would not be suited for our evaluation. In consequence, our text collection consists of 1,872 cases.

We used the list of images retrieved by *Viper*, which was supplied by the organizers of this track. Details about the preparation of this list of images can be found in [1]. For this reason, our efforts in pre-processing concentrated on manipulating the text descriptions associated with these images.

We decided to use almost all tags included in the documents with the exception of dates, URLs, and personal information from the patients (i.e. birth date, age, etc). The tags were classified and grouped into 9 types:

- Textual description: this includes fields such as title, description, commentary, questions, and answers.
- Diagnosis: The actual diagnosis associated to each case.
- Keywords and codes: This type includes keywords assigned to the case and radiology classification codes (ACR).
- Authors and organizations: Author, reviewer, hospital, department.
- Language.
- Orthopedic information: This includes all tags related to orthopedic annotations.
- Images: We added the list of image ids associated with each case.

Each of these types of information has its own characteristics that merit a different treatment during text processing and indexing. Our initial design creates a separate index for each type. The final score for ranking the retrieved cases is a weighted linear combination of each index score. Ideally, the weight of the contribution of each type should be determined experimentally. However, because we did not have a reliable way to estimate the contribution of each type to the final score of the document we decided to use the same weight for all parts.

Most of the case descriptions have a language field that indicates the language used in them. However, some case descriptions have no language specified in this filed or text in both languages (French and English) and we were not sure how often this occurred in the collection. We use a simple algorithm to estimate whether the actual language used in the document corresponds with the language assigned to the case in the language field. This algorithm identifies stop words in English and French and computes a score for each language based on the proportion of English and French stopwords present in the document. Through this process we found that 1,693 cases were in French, 177 were in English and 16 cases have text in both languages (i.e. French description with English comments). Given the nature of these bilingual texts we decided to build a single retrieval index for all documents instead of separating them into two subcollections.

Our previous experience with medical documents has shown that using an aggressive stemming such as Porter's stemmer could reduce terms to roots that are actually quite different from their intended meaning. For example, "organization" is stemmed to "organ", which has a very different meaning from the original word. For this reason we use a simple stemming strategy that takes care only of plurals (in both English and French). We also used a stopword list that combined English and French stopwords and was manually reviewed to assure that it did not contain stop words that could have medical meaning (for example, the original stopword list from SMART includes "B" and "E" as a stop words, but if we discard this words it would be difficult for the system to distinguish between articles that talk about "vitamin B" and "vitamin E").

Indexing of the case descriptions was performed using a version of the SMART system adapted to handle the ISO-latin-1 encoding in our CLEF 2003 work [3]. The documents were indexed using *atc* weighting (augmented term frequency, idf, and cosine normalization) while the queries used *atn* weighting (augmented term frequency, idf, no normalization).

3.1 Query Expansion

Our retrieval approach follows a classical pseudo relevance feedback method. The initial image is send as a query to *Viper* and the top ten images retrieved are used to build a query for the textual database. Our initial text query consists of the image ids of the top ten images retrieved (Note that we have added the list of image ids related to each case). We perform an initial retrieval step using these queries and retrieve the top 1000 cases. The top n cases are marked as relevant while the bottom 100 cases are marked as non relevant. This information is used to obtain terms to expand the original query. The query expansion step uses Rocchio's formula to compute the weight of each of the terms as follows:

$$Q_{new} = \alpha \times Q_{orig} + \beta \times \frac{\sum_{D \in Rel} D}{R} + \gamma \times \frac{\sum_{D \ni Rel} D}{N - R} \tag{1}$$

Terms are ranked according to Rocchio's score and the top m terms are selected for expansion. We tried several values for the number of cases assumed to be relevant after the initial retrieval (n = 5, 10, 20) and for the number of terms used to build the expanded query (m = 20, 50, 100). Since we were not sure whether the usage of the original image ids would be important or not to the final retrieval we decided to use two different values for the coefficient α: 0 (don't take into account these original terms) and 1. The second coefficient (β) of the Rocchio's formula controls the contribution of the relevant documents. We set it to 64 because this is the most important information that will allow us to expand the query. The third coefficient γ controls the penalty assigned to terms that appear in the "non-relevant" documents (bottom 100 cases retrieved in the initial retrieval) and was set to 16. In summary, we tried two different sets of coefficients for the Rocchio expansion formula ($\alpha = 1$, $\beta = 64$ and $\gamma = 16$)

Table 1. Top 30 terms generated by the query expansion method for the first image query

Weight	Term	Weight	Term
0.28935	im10654	0.08574	iliite
0.27833	im10361	0.08092	pied
0.26395	im11040	0.07697	acr33.3320
0.26294	im11114	0.07697	acr44.3320
0.25794	im10945	0.07697	im10362
0.25652	im10170	0.07212	l'èvolution
0.25585	im9832	0.07180	dèmasquage
0.25585	im9833	0.06919	sènile
0.25585	im9835	0.06819	kindyni
0.23936	im10916	0.06573	psoriasi
0.13769	sacro	0.06572	patiente
0.11502	bassin	0.06379	toutefoi
0.09297	iliaque	0.06258	im11042
0.08798	acr44.562	0.06258	im11041
0.08798	im10655	0.06169	collection

and ($\alpha = 0$, $\beta = 64$ and $\gamma = 16$). An example of the expanded query is shown in Table 1.

The expanded query is then submitted to the text retrieval system and the score of each retrieved case is assigned to the images associated with it. A final score for each image was computed by combining the scores obtained from the image retrieval system and the text retrieval system. We use a linear combination of the scores to compute the final image score:

$$W_k = \lambda Iscore_k + \delta Tscore_k \tag{2}$$

where $Iscore_k$ and $Tscore_k$ are the scores assigned to the image k by the image retrieval system (Viper) and text retrieval system (SMART) respectively, λ and δ are coefficients that weight the contribution of each score. Usually the coefficients are estimated from experimental results. However, due to the lack of training data we decided tu use $\lambda = \delta = 1$ (observe that this simple addition of scores is possible due to the fact that both scores are scaled between 0 and 1).

4 Analysis of Results

We submitted three runs. The first run (UBMedImTxt01) used the top 10 documents to expand the query with the top 100 terms ranked by Rocchio's formula with coefficients $\alpha = 1$, $\beta = 64$ and $\gamma = 16$. This is a run that uses an aggressive expansion strategy and takes into account the image ids of the top ten images retrieved by *Viper* as actual terms. The second run (UBMedImTxt02) differs from the first run in the fact that the coefficient $\alpha = 0$ disregards the image ids as actual query terms. The third run (UBMedImTxt03) uses a more conservative strategy for expansion with only the top 5 cases and coefficients $\alpha = 1$, $\beta = 64$ and $\gamma = 16$.

Our official results are presented in Table 2. The performance of the system shows a positive impact in improving relevance of the images retrieved. The best run UBMedTxt01 performed above the median in all queries and obtained the best performance of all official runs in automatic query construction (note that the difference between the top 5 systems is very small and would not be statistically significant). Our second run (UBMedImTxt02) performs 5.3% below our best run and performs above the median in 20 queries. Observe that the only difference between these two runs is that we use the ids of the images as actual terms for query expansion. These image ids work as anchors that reinforce the notion that cases that those cases, which have images associated with the assumed top 10 retrieved images, are regarded as relevant in our initial retrieval. Our third run (UBMedImTxt03) performs 4.7% below the best run and performs above the median systems in 20 queries. This third run uses a more conservative query expansion assuming that only the top 5 retrieved cases are relevant and perform query expansion.

Table 2 also includes the performance for our baseline system that corresponds to the list of images retrieved by Viper. The performance of our baseline is 0.3502. Our best run performs 11.5% above the baseline and this difference is statistically significant.

Table 2. Performance of official runs in Medical Image Retrieval

	AvgP	diff with Baseline	number of queries > median	number of queries > baseline
UBMedImTxt01	0.3904	11.5% **	26	19
UBMedImTxt02	0.3696	5.5%	20	14
UBMedImTxt03	0.3722	6.2%	20	16
Baseline	0.3502	–	–	–

We have to note that improvements to the final performance of the expanded queries are highly dependent of the quality of the initial set of images retrieved by the CBIR system. Figure 2 shows that there is a strong correlation between the performance of the expanded queries and the original initial retrieval using only the image retrieval system. This figure also shows a line that represents the performance of the baseline system. The points above this line are queries that have improved performance after the pseudo-relevance feedback of image and text.

Observe that because we have indexed French and English documents as a single collection the expanded query actually includes terms in both languages. A different approach could be to perform query expansion in two separate collections and then merge the results in a single list. Another approach could identify the language of a terms and add the corresponding translation. However, this will require the use of a specialized bilingual lexicon.

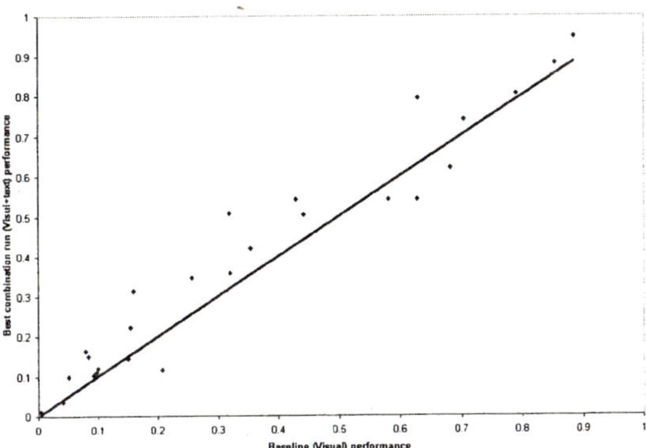

Fig. 2. Query by query comparison of best visual+text run vs visual baseline

We asked two physicians (an specialist in pneumonology and an urologist) to help us validate the results of the retrieved images (although we did not use this feedback to change the ranking of the images or the way the system processed the queries). We asked them to give general feedback to understand whether the results retrieved by the system would make sense to a medical professional. This helped us to realize that some of the aspects of how a medical professional could use this type of system in their daily work. They also emphasized that the actual diagnostic of a patient is usually a complex process that includes not only the review of images but also the analysis of the clinical data that in many cases is more indicative of a specific diagnosis than the image itself. This seems to be corroborated by the fact that adding the text description of the actual cases associated to the image makes a significant difference.

5 Conclusions and Future Work

We can conclude that our experiments confirm the hypothesis that pseudo-relevance feedback on the case descriptions associated with the medical images can be used to improve performance of a CBIR system.

Our method for preprocessing the actual structure of the cases have to be refined but it seems to work well for retrieval purposes.

We plan to add some extra query expansion using the UMLS Metathesaurus produced by NLM to add related medical phrases to the cases and verify whether this would actually improve performance.

Acknowledgement

We would like to thank Doctors Freddy and Adriana Karausch for their help in validating the results retrieved by the system and giving positive feedback that we will use for making general improvements to our system.

References

1. Clough, P. and Müller, H. and Sanderson, M.: The CLEF Cross Language Image Retrieval Track (ImageCLEF) 2004. In Peters, C. and Clough, P. and Gonzalo, J. and Jones, G. and Kluck, M. and Magnini, B. (Eds.) Fifth Workshop of the Cross Language Evaluation Forum (CLEF 2004) Lecture Notes in Computer Science (LNCS), Springer, Heidelberg, Germany (in print), 2005.
2. Rocchio, J. J.: Relevance feedback in information retrieval. In G. Salton (Ed.) The SMART Retrieval System: Experiments in Automatic Document Processing (pp.313.323). Englewood Cliff, NJ, Prentice Hall, 1971.
3. Ruiz, M. E.: Automatically generated phrases and relevance feedback for improving Cross-Language Information Retrieval. In Proceedings of the Cross Language Evaluation Forum (CLEF) 2003, August 21st . 22nd, Trondheim, Norway, 2003.
4. Salton, G. (Ed.): The SMART Retrieval System: Experiments in Automatic Document Processing. Englewood Cliff, NJ, Prentice Hall, 1971.
5. Viper Research Group URL: viper.unige.ch

Content-Based Queries on the CasImage Database Within the IRMA Framework

A Field Report

Christian Thies, Mark Oliver Güld, Benedikt Fischer, and Thomas M. Lehmann

Department of Medical Informatics, University of Technology Aachen, Pauwelsstrae 30, 52057 Aachen, Germany
cthies@mi.rwth-aachen.de

Abstract. Recent research has suggested that there is no general similarity measure, which can be applied on arbitrary databases without any parameterization. Hence, the optimal combination of similarity measures and parameters must be identified for each new image repository. This optimization loop is time consuming and depends on the experience of the designer as well as the knowledge of the medical expert. It would be useful if results that have been obtained for one data set can be transferred to another without extensive re-design. This transfer is vital if content-based image retrieval is integrated into complex environments such as picture archiving and communication systems. The image retrieval in medical applications (IRMA) project defines a framework that strictly separates data administration and application logic. This permits an efficient transfer of the data abstraction of one database on another without re-designing the software. In the ImageCLEF competition, the query performance was evaluated on the CasImage data set without optimization of the feature combination successfully applied to the IRMA corpus. IRMA only makes use of basic features obtained from grey-value representations of the images without additional textual annotations. The results indicate that transfer of parameterization is possible without time consuming parameter adaption and significant loss of retrieval quality.

1 Introduction

Classical architectures of content-based image retrieval (CBIR) systems consist of an image repository, along with visualization tools and query functionality. The principle of data storage and visualization does not vary notably among different databases whereas classes of retrieval approaches are differentiated by the query principle. In medical applications, this becomes a fundamental question since several requirements for data entry, retrieval time, and content representation must be considered [1, 2].

The first class of approaches associates and stores the secondary annotated content descriptions with each image. When textual information is used, the

C. Peters et al. (Eds.): CLEF 2004, LNCS 3491, pp. 781–792, 2005.

retrieval task becomes a text search in the descriptions. Since the information is added by a human observer, it can be subjective based on the annotator and reflects his semantical view on the image content. However, inter- and intra-individual variances in perception, knowledge and capability of expression lead to different descriptions for a single issue, as do homonyms and synonyms in standardized medical language. Due to the fact that each image has to be categorized manually, the effort at data entry time is high, which is infeasible in clinical applications. Furthermore, there is no means of objective verification for the added data.

The second class of retrieval approaches overcomes the data entry problem by making use of information that is exclusively contained in the image. Here, the retrieval task is the detection of the nearest neighbors to the query image in the image database. This is based on the similarity of abstract representations of images in a feature space. Consequently, CBIR depends on an appropriate selection of the similarity measure, which again depends on the considered image features. In general, explicit selection of feature computations and similarity measures cannot be done by a physician in clinical routine. Thus, an abstraction from the low-level feature handling is required [3].

Besides the data entry cost and the content representation a third problem arises from the state of the image database: In a clinical environment the set of available images is continuously growing. This must be considered since one aims at CBIR to make clinical routine data available as a source of knowledge for education and diagnostics. Consequently, the feature selection and similarity computation must be as flexible as possible [4].

The image retrieval in medical applications (IRMA) project integrates these three aspects of query design into a single framework [5]. In this paper, the application of the IRMA framework to the previously unknown CasImage database of the University Hospitals of Geneva [6] is described with respect to the ImageCLEF competition. This work has two main goals. It is verified if it is possible to transfer the IRMA query approach to another domain without significant loss of retrieval quality and if it is sufficient to focus on basic image features for content description in contrast to text or text/feature combinations.

2 Designing a Query in the IRMA Framework

2.1 Feature Computation

Numerous features are described in the literature. They are roughly categorized into shape [7], color [8] and texture [9]. Those features are extracted from an image and form a size-reduced representation of the content. The first task in query design is the definition of relevant features. With respect to the large variety it is useful to provide as many features as possible and to select an appropriate subset for a distinct task. In the IRMA system, each newly presented image is automatically transformed into all available feature representations. This causes computational time for initial database processing but ensures short update and querying cycles when presenting unknown single images as well as implementing new features since only the new information must be calculated. For this purpose, IRMA provides an automated storage concept that applies the implemented image-to-feature mappings at data entry time [10]. A new feature computation is integrated into an image processing chain by providing the transformation code. The actual database handling is hidden from this implementation by an interface providing an exclusive view on the image.

2.2 Feature Comparison

A query is modeled as a nearest neighbor classification. Consequently, it is designed by defining a similarity measure as a metric in the feature space. The corpus is represented as a sorted list, where the most similar images with the smallest distance to the query image form the head. The selection of actually correct matches must be made from this list. This is task specific and, therefore, a runtime parameter of the system that cannot be determined in advance. Furthermore, the selection depends on the actual number of relevant images in the database. Thus, a sufficient set of results must be presented to the user who has to make the final decision. For this purpose, the IRMA system offers a set of database processing sequences, which enable the sequential or parallel access to the stored image features via iteration or fan-in/fan-out processing over the corpus. Those sequences are combined on a binary execution level by abstract methods. Consequently, the data handling is also hidden from the application by specialized data flow interfaces [10].

2.3 Integration of New Image Data

The component-based software architecture provides a platform where new data is integrated without re-implementing the available features and distance measures. New images typically require the adoption of existing feature extractions and similarity computations. Yet when introducing a new image corpus there is no a-priori knowledge on the classes of images and their sizes. Therefore, finding the appropriate features and similarity measures equals the optimization task to find an unknown target function. However, brute force learning approaches for optimal query parameters can only be performed if the ground truth is known. Alternatively, a manual optimization of query methods to a distinct database is inapplicable for clinical routine solutions, since there is simply no time to supervise the learning process. Thus, the designer of an application combines a set of features and similarity methods in advance and then hands it over to the medical expert who has to verify the results. Once such a retrieval engine is integrated, for instance, into a picture archiving and communication system (PACS), it can hardly be modified or optimized, since the database continuously evolves. In contrast, the IRMA framework allows a hot swap of the feature extraction, similarity computation and database without affecting each other [10].

In case of the CasImage data set there was no ground truth given, so the results could only be generated by transfer of successfully applied query settings from other applications. This was performed for the ImageCLEF task. Main objective was the transfer of already implemented code and associated experience from recent experiments onto a new domain without parameter adaption.

3 Applied Features and Queries

The methods were taken from recent applications on the IRMA database consisting of 10,000 images from clinical routine, which were categorized by medical experts and used to train parameters [5]. Thus, the unmodified transfer of the methods is reasonable. Since the IRMA system processes only gray-scale images, RGB color conversion was done by using the standard color weighting [11]:

$$Y = \frac{6969 \cdot R + 23434 \cdot G + 2365 \cdot B}{32768} \tag{1}$$

Recent experiments indicated that spatial and intensity features must be considered equally to obtain reasonable results [12, 13].

3.1 Texture Features by TAMURA

TAMURA et al. use coarseness, contrast and directionality to capture an image's texture properties [14]. Those features are computed per pixel and reflect the texture affiliation. The value ranges for coarseness, contrast and directionality are quantized into 6, 8 and 8 equidistant intervals, respectively. They form the $6 \times 8 \times 8 = 384$ bins of a three-dimensional histogram, which serves as the global texture description. However, different image sizes result in different and therefore incomparable histogram counts. To obtain comparable features, each image is scaled to a size of 256×256 pixels, ignoring the aspect ratio.

To compare the TAMURA histograms of two images $H_T(Q)$ and $H_T(R)$ with $M = 384$ bins each, the Jensen-Shannon divergence is used [15], where Q and R denote the query and verified image, respectively:

$$\mathrm{D}_{\mathrm{JS}}(Q,R) = \frac{1}{2}\sum_{m=1}^{M}\left[H_T^m(Q)\log\frac{2H_T^m(Q)}{H_T^m(Q)+H_T^m(R)} + H_T^m(R)\log\frac{2H_T^m(R)}{H_T^m(Q)+H_T^m(R)}\right] \tag{2}$$

3.2 Aspect Ratio

Comparing the aspect ratio of images is an unspecific measure. Yet it is useful to consider the dimension of images. Since normalization for some texture features requires the deformation of the image dimensions into a square shape, the aspect ratio of an original image is a means of image comparison. Furthermore, the aspect ratio is characteristic for different classes of medical images. For instance, slices from magnetic resonance imaging (MRI) have identical edge dimensions while radiographs of limbs are rectangular elongated in direction of the principal bone. The aspect ratio is compared by:

$$\mathrm{D}_{\mathrm{AR}}(Q,R) = \left|\frac{X(Q)}{Y(Q)} - \frac{X(R)}{Y(R)}\right| \tag{3}$$

where $X(I)$ and $Y(I)$ denote the size of an image I: $(X,Y) :\rightarrow x \in \{0..X-1\}, y \in \{0..Y-1\}$.

3.3 Image Distortion Model

While histogram-based methods provide invariance against some transforms such as translation, scaled representations of the original images can preserve spatial properties, which are especially important to recognize medical images [16]. A drastic reduction in size also reduces noise and small image defects. The image distortion model (IDM) expands the naive pixel-by-pixel comparison of the scaled representations. It allows local displacements for each pair of pixels compared within the distance measure. This is especially useful for medical images due to individual anatomical properties in each image. The policy is to match each pixel of the sample image to one in the reference image. This ensures that all sample information is evaluated. To prevent a completely unordered vector field of pixel mappings between two images, it is useful to include the local context into the search process for a correspondence hypothesis. Denoting the coordinate offsets by x'' and y'', while x' and y' term the offsets within the search window for a corresponding pixel, the distance is computed by:

$$\mathrm{D}_{\mathrm{IDM}}(Q,R) = \sum_{x=1}^{X}\sum_{y=1}^{Y} \min_{|x'|,|y'|\leq W_1} \left\{ \sum_{|x''|,|y''|\leq W_2} ||R(x+x'+x'', y+y'+y'') - Q(x+x'', y+y'')||_2 \right\} \quad (4)$$

The results are improved if the image gradient is used instead of the intensity values. For our experiment, we used $W_1 = 2$ (5×5 pixel-sized search window for corresponding pixels) and $W_2 = 1$ (3×3 pixels of local context). The images were scaled to a fixed maximal height or width of 32 pixels keeping their original aspect ratio.

3.4 Classifier Combination

A parallel classifier combination is used. In order to avoid value domination of a single large addend, the results of each classifier are transformed to a common scale. This is done by dividing each result for a single classifier by the sum of all distances of the respective classifier. The weighting for each addend determines the combined vote for a distinct classifier. The described similarity measure is finally obtained from:

$$\rho(Q,R) = \alpha \cdot \mathrm{D}_{\mathrm{JS}}(Q,R) + \beta \cdot \mathrm{D}_{\mathrm{IDM}}(Q,R) + \gamma \cdot \mathrm{D}_{\mathrm{AR}}(Q,R) \quad (5)$$

As a matter of fact α, β and γ are parameters of the function ρ. Yet for the retrieval application described in this paper they are considered as constants that were empirically determined beforehand on the IRMA medical image corpus.

3.5 Determination of Relevance

The relevance of an image with respect to the query image Q is computed by sorting the database DB into a sequence:

$$\mathrm{S}_{\mathrm{REL}}(Q,B) = (R_1..R_n)|\rho(Q,R_1) \leq ... \leq \rho(Q,R_n), R_1..R_n \in B, n = |B| \quad (6)$$

$n = |B|$ denotes the number of images in the repository. Relevance determination applies the classifier to all elements of the database. Consequently, time consuming ρ-functions are computed for many irrelevant comparisons. For this purpose, a sieve is applied to reduce the number of potentially relevant references. It is computed by selecting a fixed number of elements from the beginning of a list, which has been sorted with respect to the applied similarity measure. In the IRMA framework, the sieve is applied to the IDM classifier by the following steps. First, a neighbor list is computed by using Euclidian distance on 16×16 representations of the query image and the database images. Afterwards, the IDM is applied to the closest k database images. Consequently, the computation time is reduced by the factor n/k. Based on this sieve function, the most relevant images are selected by the application of $\mathrm{S}_{\mathrm{REL}}(Q, \mathtt{sieve}(Q, B, k))$, where the IDM can only reorder the results.

```
images[] sieve(image QueryImage, image B[], int CutOff)
  Let image Q = scale (QueryImage, 16x16); //downscale query image
  Let int N=bound(B[]);                    //Size of the database B
  Define image P[N];                       //Buffer for B processing
  Define double delta[N];                  //for distance computation

  For (i = 0; i < N;  i++)                 //downscale each image in
   Bs[i] = scale (B[i], 16x16);            //the database and compute
   delta[i] = euclidian_distance (P[i],Q); //euclidian distance to query

  sort (P, delta);                         //sort database by distance
  sieve = P[0] .. P[min(CutOff,N)];        //truncate list at cutoff
```

4 Experiments

The experiments aim at verifying whether the query design that yielded good results on the IRMA database could be transferred into another image domain such as the CasImage database without parameterization. This approach was chosen since the ImageCLEF task was explicitly laid out to demonstrate the current state of CBIR research [6]. With respect to the competitive character of the workshop, it is instructive to learn to which degree sophisticated techniques for optimization on the given image domain is necessary to obtain useful results.

4.1 Reference Data

The CasImage database consists of 8,723 images and represents a mixture of diagnostic images from clinical routine and drawings for medical education. Furthermore, there are images with secondary added contents such as pseudo-colorings of segmentation or manual annotations for operation planning.

From this data set, $i = 26$ samples were arbitrarily selected as queries Q_i. The experimental task was to extract similar images to each of the samples and provide a list of retrievals for manual evaluation [6]. Thus, the ground truth for each

Table 1. The weights for the classifiers as used for the similarity functions in the experiments

Classifier	α	β	γ
D_{AR}	0.0	0.0	1.0
D_{JS}	1.0	0.0	0.0
D_{IDM}	0.0	1.0	0.0
C_1 & C'_1	0.225	0.675	0.1
C_2 & C'_2	0.25	0.75	0.0

query was a-priori unknown and optimization was only possible in an empirical and heuristic manner. In this work, no heuristic manipulation of the parameters for result optimization was performed. Hence, there is no specific quantization and threshold computation to cut off the list from $S_{REL}(Q_i, B)$ with respect to each Q_i. Since the actual amount of relevant images in the database is unknown for each Q_i, a fixed set of possible results is returned. In the IRMA concept a combined evaluation of precision, recall, and visual plausibility is used to evaluate and parameterize the system for different applications. Since automatically generated quality measures like precision and recall do not necessarily reflect the visual relevance of query results moreover it must be verified manually by an expert. This demands a trade-off between full database processing and interactively manageable results. For this purpose the cutoff value for the size of the result set is required. Its automated computation is applictation specific and not yet integrated in the IRMA concept. A fixed cutoff value of 100 images was found to be a suitable compromise with respect to common class sizes in the IRMA database. For comparable quantitative evaluation of the CasImage database, a ground truth is provided by three medical experts from the Geneva University Hospital [6].

4.2 Quality of Results

Similarity Function. The adjustment of $\rho(Q, R)$ as defined in (5), means the empirical adaptation of the weights α, β and γ, as explained in Section 3.4. Table 1 lists the settings that were tested for the combined classifier weights. Each of the distance measures D_{AR}, D_{JS}, and D_{IDM} is verified separately by setting the respective weight to 1 and all others to 0. Based on those experiments two weighted combinations C_1 and C_2 were acquired on the IRMA database [12], which were also applied to the CasImage database. The corresponding runs were submitted as mi_combine1 (C_1) and mi_combine2 (C_2). C_1 combines D_{AR}, D_{JS}, and D_{IDM} while C_2 combines D_{JS} and D_{IDM}. The sieve function $\texttt{sieve}(Q, B, k)$ must be evaluated separately, since the cutoff after k images eventually affects the retrieval results, causing two additional parameterizations C'_1 and C'_2.

Result Evaluation. For each query image Q_i, the first 100 images from the sequence $S_{REL}(Q_i, B)$ were compared to the ground truth by the usual measures of precision and recall:

$$\text{precision} := \frac{\#\text{ of relevant images}}{100} \tag{7}$$

$$\text{recall} := \frac{\#\text{ of relevant images}}{\#\text{ of relevant images in } B} \tag{8}$$

Ground truth was the pisec_total data set, which was provided by the medical experts from the Geneva University Hospital [6]. Due to the restriction to 100 replies, the recall will never reach 100% for queries with more than 100 relevant results in the database. Precision will as well be low for query images, which have significantly less than 100 images among the data set. This bias is accepeted with respect to the compromise between visual verification and automated quality measurement.

4.3 Runtime Behavior

Finally, the setup of the parameters has to be efficient for fast verification cycles. For this purpose, the IRMA framework supports the separate consideration of the feature extraction at the image entry time (Sec. 2.1) from the actual feature comparison (Sec. 2.2). Furthermore, runtime is optimized by preliminary application of the sieve function to reduce the number of necessary similarity computations. In the conducted experiments, the cutoff value was set to $k = 500$. For quality comparison the combinations C_1 and C_2 are applied to the result of $\texttt{sieve}(Q, B, 500)$, which extends the set of experiments by C_1' and C_2' (Tab. 1).

5 Results

5.1 Quality of Results

The precision for each of the classifier combinations is listed in Table 2. For the combined classifiers C_1 and C_2, the best precision was obtained for Q_{24} and the worst precision for image Q_{14}. While best recall for the combined measures was also for image Q_{14} the worst recall for C_1 and C_2 was for image Q_{23}. Overall, C_1 yielded the highest average precision. For query Q_7 only, D_{AR} returns no relevant image while the precision constantly increases with D_{JS}, and D_{IDM} and finally obtains the highest value of 0.36 with C_1. Only for Q_{11}, no useful result could be retrieved. The results for C_1' and C_2' on the reduced datasets are only slightly inferior with respect to average precision. Several single results are even better such as for query Q_5. For query images Q_1, Q_6, Q_{15}, Q_{24}, precision is perfect or near perfect, whereas several query images yielded unsatisfactory results. Especially, queries Q_4, Q_{11}, Q_{14}, Q_{17} and Q_{23} returned only 43, 9, 11, 31, and 74 relevant images, respectively.

5.2 Runtime Behavior

The computation of all required feature representations takes approximately 7.5 hours while the query computation for the combined measures for a single image requires about 5 minutes on a standard Pentium PC running at 2.4 GHz (Tab. 3). The sieve-based computation of the combined measures C_1' and C_2' yields a significantly faster runtime of 18.7 seconds for a single query.

Table 2. Precision for the experiments. The boxes indicate the best and least precise result

Q_i	D_{AR}	D_{JS}	D_{IDM}	C_1	C_2	C'_1	C'_2
1	0.10	0.63	0.97	0.97	0.97	0.97	0.97
2	0.01	0.70	0.66	0.81	0.82	0.71	0.72
3	0.08	0.23	0.25	0.35	0.29	0.27	0.27
4	0.09	0.02	0.02	0.04	0.03	0.02	0.02
5	0.03	0.03	0.36	0.40	0.39	0.43	0.42
6	0.20	0.81	0.94	0.97	0.99	0.96	0.95
7	0.00	0.24	0.24	0.36	0.31	0.35	0.33
8	0.09	0.06	0.11	0.23	0.20	0.11	0.11
9	0.01	0.16	0.15	0.25	0.29	0.26	0.26
10	0.04	0.17	0.41	0.42	0.38	0.37	0.42
11	0.00	0.01	0.00	0.03	0.03	0.00	0.00
12	0.23	0.47	0.69	0.67	0.72	0.72	0.71
13	0.02	0.10	0.36	0.42	0.38	0.37	0.35
14	0.01	0.03	0.01	[0.01]	0.04	0.02	0.01
15	0.14	0.96	0.87	0.97	0.98	0.88	0.89
16	0.02	0.57	0.34	0.58	0.51	0.34	0.34
17	0.00	0.04	0.07	0.10	0.11	0.11	0.11
18	0.20	0.10	0.43	0.36	0.38	0.38	0.39
19	0.01	0.81	0.50	0.73	0.78	0.67	0.68
20	0.06	0.06	0.10	0.10	0.09	0.09	0.08
21	0.02	0.11	0.52	0.40	0.39	0.35	0.33
22	0.10	0.36	0.68	0.59	0.64	0.59	0.60
23	0.03	0.06	0.10	0.15	0.08	0.15	0.09
24	0.15	0.80	1.00	[1.00]	1.00	0.99	1.00
25	0.38	0.41	0.36	0.46	0.41	0.42	0.40
26	0.13	0.21	0.02	0.30	0.20	0.32	0.21
avg	0.08	0.31	0.39	0.45	0.44	0.42	0.41

Table 3. Integral running times of the feature extraction for all 8,728 images, of the feature comparison for all 26 query images and of a single query on a standard PC running at 2.4 GHz

Classifier	feature extraction	Query 26 Images	Single Query
D_{AR}	0.5 h	< 1 s	$\ll 1$ s
D_{JS}	4 h	13 s	< 1 s
D_{IDM}	3 h	0.25 h	300 s
C_1	7.5 h	0.25 h	300 s
C_2	7 h	0.25 h	300 s
C'_1	7.5 h	0.15 h	18.7 s
C'_2	7 h	0.15 h	18.7 s

5.3 ImageCLEF Ranking

Within the ranking of all ImageCLEF submissions the mean average precision (MAP) was chosen as a measure for the quality of a result [6]. According to the overall evaluation the IRMA approach yielded a MAP of 0.2980 with C_1 and a MAP of 0.2809 for C_2, which corresponded to rank 24 and 31 from 44 runs submitted [6]. The MAPs were ranging from the best value of 0.48 to the worst of 0.1, where the mean of all MAPs was 0.29 with a standard deviation of 0.11. There were 19 submissions where no query expansion and additional textual information was used. In this more comparable ranking, the IRMA approach achieves the 9th and 11th position respectively. Here, the mean of all MAPs is 0.26 while the standard deviation remains 0.11.

6 Discussion

Since the MAPs lie within the standard deviation of the MAPs for all submitted runs in the ImageCLEF task, the outcome is encouraging,. Note that there was no effort taken in task specific optimization of the parameters. In the ImageCLEF task, the ranked retrieval results are a mixture of text-based, content-based, and hybrid approaches with eventual query expansion. However, the IRMA framework neither takes advantage of

- multichannel information such as color nor of
- textual annotations,

but still, the results are in the center field of the ranking.

By application of the query related sieve on the database, the number of costly IDM comparisons is significantly reduced with only slight loss of average precision and recall. This also encourages the use of sophistically implemented classifiers for online retrieval applications such as differential diagnosis support via queries to a PACS. In such routine applications the physician needs immediate response to compare a given image to possibly related cases with known findings.

7 Conclusion

The application of a parameterization and evaluation concept that was optimized for the IRMA domain yields useful retrieval results on the previously unknown CasImage domain. It was one of the two main goals of this work to show that it is possible to obtain good results with the IRMA system without parameter adoption. Even if the results are not optimal time consuming training cycles are avoided. This is important since optimization of powerful classifiers such as D_{IDM} is infeasible in online systems such as PACS due to running times of several hours. The second goal was to verify the need for sophisticated features and similarity measures. It can be stated that complex integration of multichannel and textual information yields better results in comparison to the basic IRMA approach.

However the trade-off between time input for parameter adjustment and flexible domain adoption must be considered.

By separating the application logic from the storage concept, the software architecture also supports the transfer of new features and classifiers as well as images without changes in the existing implementation. Furthermore, there is still the commonly observed gap between fast computable query designs and good retrieval results. Powerful classifiers as required for medical applications still need computation times, which are not applicable in fast reacting retrieval environments. This remains a field of ongoing research, where the IRMA system provides a supporting framework for efficient verification and also application.

References

1. Smeulders, A.W.M., Worring, M., Santini, S., Gupta, A., Jain, R.: Content-based image retrieval at the end of the early years. IEEE Transactions on Pattern Analysis and Machine Intelligence **22** (2000) 1349–1380
2. Müller, H., Michoux, N., Bandon, D., Geissbuhler, A.: A review of content-based image retrieval systems in medical applications. clinical benefits and future directions. International Journal of Medical Informatics **73** (2004) 1–23
3. Faloutsos, C., Barber, R., Flickner, M., Hafner, J., Niblack, W., Petkovic, D., Equitz, W.: Efficient and effective querying by image content. Journal of Intelligent Information Systems **3** (1994) 231–262
4. Tagare, H.D., Jaffe, C.C., Duncan, J.: Medical image databases: A content-based retrieval approach. Journal of the American Medical Informatics Association **4** (1997) 184–198
5. Lehmann, T.M., Güld, M.O., Thies, C., Fischer, B., Spitzer, K., Keysers, D., Ney, H., Kohnen, M., Schubert, H., Wein, B.: Content-based image retrieval in medical applications. Methods of Information in Medicine **43** (2004) 354–361
6. Clough, P., Müller, H., Sanderson, M.: The CLEF Cross-Language Image Retrieval Track (ImageCLEF)2004. In Peters, C., Clough, P., Gonzalo, J., Jones, G., Kluck, M., Magnini, B., eds.: Fifth Workshop of the Cross–Language Evaluation Forum (CLEF 2004), Lecture Notes in Computer Science (LNCS), Springer,Heidelberg, Germany (in this volume) (2005)
7. Zhou, X.S., Huang, T.S.: Edge-based structural features for content-based image retrieval. Pattern Recognition Letters **22** (2001) 457–468
8. Swain, M.J., Ballard, D.H.: Color indexing. International Journal of Computer Vision **7** (1991) 11–32
9. Castelli, V., Bergman, L.D., Kontoyiannis, I., Li, C.S., Robinson, J.T., Turek, J.J.: Progressive search and retrieval in large image archives. IBM Journal of Research and Development **42** (1998) 253–268
10. Güld, M.O., Thies, C., Fischer, B., Keysers, D., Wein, B.B., Lehmann, T.M.: A platform for distributed image processing and image retrieval. In: Procs SPIE. Volume 5150. (2003) 1109–1120
11. ITU: Basic parameter values for the hdtv standard for the studio and for international programme exchange. ITU-R Recommendation BT.709, [formerly CCIR Rec. 709] ITU, 1211 Geneva:Switzerland (1990)
12. Güld, M.O., Keysers, D., Deselaers, T., Leisten, M., Schubert, H., Ney, H., Lehmann, T.M.: Comparison of global features for categorization of medical images. In: Procs SPIE. Volume 5371. (2004) 211–222

13. Lehmann, T.M., Güld, M.O., Keysers, D., Schubert, H., Kohnen, M., Wein, B.B.: Determining the view position of chest radiographs. Journal of Digital Imaging **16** (2003) 280–291
14. Tamura, H., Mori, S., Yamawaki, T.: Textural features corresponding to visual perception. IEEE Transactions on Systems, Man, and Cybernetics **SMC-8** (1978) 460–472
15. Puzicha, J., Rubner, Y., Tomasi, C., Buhmann, J.: Empirical evaluation of dissimilarity measures for color and texture. In: Procs International Conference on Computer Vision. Volume 2. (1999) 1165–1173
16. Deselaers, T., Keysers, D., Ney, H.: Features for image retrieval: A quantitative comparison. In: DAGM 2004 Pattern Recognition, 26th DAGM Symposium Tübingen, Germany. Volume 3175., Lecture Notes in Computer Science (LNCS), Springer,Heidelberg, Germany (2005) 228–236

Comparison and Combination of Textual and Visual Features for Interactive Cross-Language Image Retrieval

Pei-Cheng Cheng[1], Jen-Yuan Yeh[1], Hao-Ren Ke[2], Been-Chian Chien[3], and Wei-Pang Yang[1,4]

[1] Department of Computer & Information Science, National Chiao Tung University, 1001 Ta Hsueh Rd., Hsinchu, Taiwan 30050, R.O.C.
{cpc, jyyeh, wpyang}@cis.nctu.edu.tw
[2] University Library, National Chiao Tung University, 1001 Ta Hsueh Rd., Hsinchu, Taiwan 30050, R.O.C.
claven@lib.nctu.edu.tw
[3] Department of Computer Science and Information Engineering, National University of Tainan, 33, Sec. 2, Su Line St., Tainan, Taiwan 70005, R.O.C.
bcchien@mail.nutn.edu.tw
[4] Department of Information Management, National Dong Hwa University, 1, Sec. 2, Da Hsueh Rd., Shou-Feng, Hualien, Taiwan 97401, R.O.C.
wpyang@mail.ndhu.edu.tw

Abstract. This paper concentrates on the user-centered search task at ImageCLEF 2004. In this work, we combine both textual and visual features for cross-language image retrieval, and propose two interactive retrieval systems – T_ICLEF and VCT_ICLEF. The first one incorporates a relevance feedback mechanism based on textual information while the second one combines textual and image information to help users find a target image. The experimental results show that VCT_ICLEF had a better performance in almost all cases. Overall, it helped users find the topic image within a fewer iterations with a maximum of 2 iterations saved. Our user survey also reported that a combination of textual and visual information is helpful to indicate to the system what a user really wanted in mind.

1 Introduction

The ImageCLEF campaign [2] under the CLEF[1] (Cross-Language Evaluation Forum) conducts a series of evaluations on systems which are built to accept a query in one language and to find images with relevant captions in different languages. In 2004, three tasks were proposed based on different domains, scenarios, and collections: (1) *the bilingual ad hoc retrieval task*, (2) *the medical retrieval task*, and (3) *the user-centered search task.*

This paper concentrates on the user-centered search task. The task follows the scenario that a user is searching with a specific image in mind, but without any key information about it. The goal is to determine whether the retrieval system is being used

[1] The official website is available at http://clef.iei.pi.cnr.it:2002/.

C. Peters et al. (Eds.): CLEF 2004, LNCS 3491, pp. 793 – 804, 2005.

in the manner intended by the designers as well as to determine how the interface helps users reformulate and refine their search topics. We proposed two systems: (1) *T_ICLEF*, and (2) *VCT_ICLEF* to address the task. T_ICLEF is a cross-language image retrieval system, which is simply enhanced with a relevance feedback mechanism; VCT_ICLEF is practically T_ICLEF but provides a color table that allows users to indicate color information about the target image. Our principal objective is to compare and to combine textual and visual features under an interactive cross language image searching situation.

In the following sections, the overview of the proposed interactive search process is described. Section 2 introduces previous work on query reformulation. Sections 3-4 illustrate the proposed methods for the interactive search task, and some preliminary results are presented in Section 5. Finally, we finish with a conclusion in Section 6.

1.1 Overview of the Proposed Interactive Search Process

Fig. 1 shows an overview of the proposed interactive search process. Given an initial query, $Q = (Q_T, Q_I)$, in which Q_T denotes a Chinese text query, and Q_I stands for a query image, the system performs cross-language image retrieval and returns a set of "relevant[2]" images to the user. The user then evaluates the relevance of the returned images, and gives a relevance value to each of them. This process is called relevance feedback. At the following stage, the system invokes the query reformulation process to derive a new query, $Q' = (Q'_T, Q'_I)$. The new query is believed to be closer to the user's information need. Finally, the system performs once again image retrieval according to Q'. The process iterates until the user finds the target image.

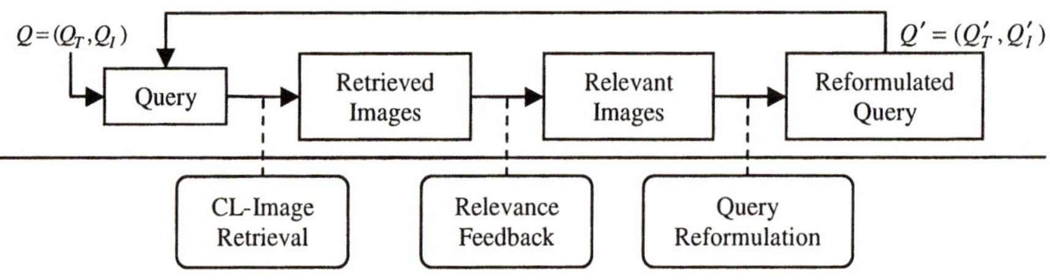

Fig. 1. Overview of the proposed user-centered search process

2 Previous Work

Previous work on image retrieval usually exploits low-level features, for example, *color*, *texture*, *shape*, etc., extracted from an image to measure its similarity to the query (e.g., [4]). However, the retrieval performance is always limited due to the gap between semantic concepts which are explained as humans' perceptions, and low-level image features used to represent an image. Recently, relevance feedback has

[2] The degree of relevance is judged by the similarity metric used in the retrieval system.

been successfully employed to alleviate the above-mentioned problem (e.g., [3] [8] [9] [12]).

Previous work (e.g., [7]) has shown that interactive search helps improve recall and precision in the retrieval task. Some work defined a new weighted query by associating more significant features with larger weights, and less important ones with smaller weights. The strategy is mostly used (e.g., [5], [12], [13]). For example, [13] proposed a low-level feature-based relevance feedback framework, in which for each feature *i*, an ideal query, q_i, is modeled as a weighted sum of all positive examples, which is shown in Eq. (1)

$$q_i = \frac{\pi^T Y_i}{\sum_{j=1}^{n} \pi_j} \tag{1}$$

where Y_i an $n \times K_i$ training matrix for feature *i*, which is obtained by stacking the first *n* positive examples, K_i the length of feature *i*. The *n*-dimension vector, $\pi = [\pi_1, \ldots, \pi_n]$, represents a relevance degree for the *n* positive images. Ciocca *et al.* (2002) [1] proposed a novel query reformulation method for relevance feedback. After the relevant images are selected, they contribute their features to a new query feature vector when their similarities to the average of all relevant images are significantly large. The new query feature vector is the average of the contributing features.

There are still other researches which address relevance feedback with probabilistic models. For example, Cox *et al.* (2000) [3], Vasconcelos and Lippman (1999) [16], Meilhac and Nastar (1999) [9], employed Bayesian estimation to update the probability distribution of all images. The main idea is to consider feedback examples as a sequence of independent queries and to try to minimize the retrieval errors by Bayes' rule.

3 Cross-Language Image Retrieval

In this section, we describe how to create the representation for an image or a query, and how to compute the similarity between an image and the query on the basis of their representations.

3.1 Image/Query Representations

We represent both an image and a query as a vector in the vector space model [14]. First of all, we explain the symbols used in the following definitions of representations. $P = (P_T, P_I)$ denotes an image where P_T and P_I stand for the captions of *P* and the image *P* respectively, and $Q = (Q_T, Q_I)$ represents a query, which is defined in Section 1.1. In our proposed approach, a textual vector representation, such as P_T and Q_T, is modeled in terms of three distinct features – *term*, *category*, and *temporal* information, whilst an image vector representation, for example, P_I and Q_I, is represented with a color histogram.

Textual Vector Representation

Let W (|W| = n) the set of significant keywords in the corpus, C (|C| = m) the set of categories defined in the corpus, and Y (|Y| = k) the set of publication years of all images. For an image P, its textual vector representation (i.e., P_T) is defined as Eq. (2),

$$P_T =< w_{t_1}(P_T),...,w_{t_n}(P_T), w_{c_1}(P_T),...,w_{c_m}(P_T), w_{y_1}(P_T),...,w_{y_k}(P_T) > \quad (2)$$

where the first n dimensions indicate the weighting of a keyword t_i in P_T, which is measured by TF-IDF [14], as computed in Eq. (3); the following n+1 to n+m dimensions indicate whether P belongs to a category c_i, which is shown as Eq. (4); the final n+m+1 to n+m+k dimensions express whether P was published in year y_i, which is defined as Eq. (5).

$$w_{t_i}(P_T) = \frac{tf_{t_i,P_T}}{\max tf} \times \log \frac{N}{n_{t_i}} \quad (3)$$

$$w_{c_i}(P_T) = \begin{cases} 1 & \text{if } P \text{ belongs to } c_i, \\ 0 & \text{otherwise} \end{cases} \quad (4)$$

$$w_{y_i}(P_T) = \begin{cases} 1 & \text{if } P \text{ was published in the year } y_i, \\ 0 & \text{otherwise} \end{cases} \quad (5)$$

In Eq. (3), $\frac{tf_{t_i,P_T}}{\max tf}$ stands for the normalized frequency of t_i in P_T, maxtf is the maximum number of occurrences of any keyword in P_T, N indicates the number of images in the corpus, and n_{t_i} denotes the number of images in whose caption t_i appears. Regarding Eq. (4) and Eq. (5), both of them compute the weighting of the category and the temporal feature as a Boolean value.

In the above, we introduce how to create a textual vector representation for P_T. As for a query Q, one problem is that since Q_T is given in Chinese, it is necessary to translate Q_T into English, which is the language used in the image collection. We first perform the word segmentation process to obtain a set of Chinese words. For each Chinese word, it is then translated into one or several corresponding English words by looking it up in a dictionary. The dictionary that we use is pyDict[3]. Up to now, it is still hard to determine the correct translation; therefore, we tend to keep all English translations in order not to lose the consideration of any correct word.

Another problem is the so-called short query problem. A short query usually cannot cover many useful search terms because of the lack of sufficient words. We address this problem by performing the query expansion process to add new terms to the original query. The additional search terms are taken from a thesaurus – WordNet [10]. For each English translation, we include its *synonyms*, *hypernyms*, and *hyponyms* into the query.

---

[3] An English/Chinese dictionary written by D. Gau, which is available at http://sourceforge.net/projects/pydict/.

It comes out as a new problem. Assume $AfterExpansion(Q_T) = \{e_1,...,e_h\}$ is the set of all English words obtained after query translation and query expansion, it is obvious that $AfterExpansion(Q_T)$ may contain a lot of words which are not correct translations or useful search terms. To resolve the translation ambiguity problem, we exploit *word co-occurrence relationships* to determine final query terms. The main idea is if the co-occurrence frequency of e_i and e_j in the corpus is greater than a predefined threshold, both e_i and e_j are regarded as useful search terms for monolingual image retrieval. So far, we have a set of search terms, $AfterDisambiguity(Q_T)$, which is presented as Eq. (6),

$$\begin{aligned} AfterDisambiguity(Q_T) = \{e_i, e_j \mid\ & e_i, e_j \in AfterExpansion(Q_T) \\ & \& \ e_i, e_j \text{ have a significant cooccurrence}\} \end{aligned} \tag{6}$$

After giving the definition of $AfterDisambiguity(Q_T)$, for a query Q, its textual vector representation (i.e., Q_T) is defined in Eq. (7),

$$Q_T = < w_{t_1}(Q_T),...,w_{t_n}(Q_T), w_{c_1}(Q_T),...,w_{c_m}(Q_T), w_{y_1}(Q_T),...,w_{y_k}(Q_T) > \tag{7}$$

where $w_{t_i}(Q_T)$ is the weighting of a keyword t_i in Q_T, which is measured as Eq. (8), $w_{c_i}(Q_T)$ indicates whether there exists an $e_j \in AfterDisambiguity(Q_T)$ and it also occurs in a category c_i, which is shown as Eq. (9), and $w_{y_i}(Q_T)$ presents whether there is an $e_j \in AfterDisambiguity(Q_T)$, e_j is a temporal term, and e_j satisfies a condition caused by a predefined temporal operator.

In Eq. (8), $\frac{tf_{t_i,Q_T}}{\max tf}$ stands for the normalized frequency of t_i in $AfterDisambiguity(Q_T)$, max*tf* is the maximum number of occurrences of any keyword in $AfterDisambiguity(Q_T)$, N indicates the number of images in the corpus, and n_{t_i} denotes the number of images in whose caption t_i appears. Eq. (9) and Eq. (10) compute the weighting of the category and the temporal feature as a Boolean value.

$$w_{t_i}(Q_T) = \left\{ \frac{tf_{t_i,Q_T}}{\max tf} \times \log \frac{N}{n_{t_i}} \right. \tag{8}$$

$$w_{c_i}(Q_T) = \begin{cases} 1 & \text{if } \exists j, e_j \in AfterDisambiguity(Q_T) \text{ and } e_j \text{ occurs in } c_i, \\ 0 & \text{otherwise} \end{cases} \tag{9}$$

$$w_{y_i}(Q_T) = \begin{cases} 1 & \text{if } Q_T \text{ contains "Y年以前," and } y_i \text{ is BEFORE Y}, \\ 1 & \text{if } Q_T \text{ contains "Y年之中," and } y_i \text{ is IN Y}, \\ 1 & \text{if } Q_T \text{ contains "Y年以後," and } y_i \text{ is AFTER Y}, \\ 0 & \text{otherwise} \end{cases} \tag{10}$$

To be mentioned, with regard to $w_{y_i}(Q_T)$, three operators – "BEFORE," "IN," and "AFTER" – are defined to take into account a query such as "1900年以前拍攝的愛丁堡城堡的照片 (Pictures of Edinburgh Castle taken before 1900)," which also concerns time. Take, for example, the above query that targets only images taken before 1900; a part of the textual vector of the above query about the temporal feature is given in Table 1, it gives an idea that P_I will be retrieved since its publication year was in 1899 while P_2 will not be retrieved because of its publication year, 1901. Note that in our current implementation, we only consider *years* for the temporal feature. Hence, for a query like "1908 年四月拍攝的羅馬照片 (Photos of Rome taken in April 1908)," "四月 (April)" is treated as a general term, which only contributes its effect to the term feature.

Table 1. An example which shows how the time operators work while considering the time dimension

Year	...	1897	1898	1899	1900	1901	1902	...
P_I	0	0	0	1	0	0	0	0
P_2	0	0	0	0	0	1	0	0
Q_T	1	1	1	1	0	0	0	0

Image Vector Representation

Color histogram [15] is a basic method and has good performance for representing the visual contents of an image. The color histogram method gathers statistics about the proportion of each color as the signature of an image. In our work, the colors of an image are represented in the HSV (Hue/Saturation/Value) space, which is believed to be closer to human perceptions than other models, such as RGB (Red/Green/Blue) or CMY (Cyan/Magenta/Yellow). We quantize the HSV space into 18 hues, 2 saturations, and 4 values, with additional 4 levels of gray values; as a result, there are a total of 148 (i.e., 18×2×4+4) bins. Let C ($|C| = m$) a set of colors (i.e., 148 bins), P_I (Q_I) is represented as Eq. (11), which models the color histogram $H(P_I)$ ($H(Q_I)$) as a vector, in which each bucket h_{c_i} counts the ratio of pixels of P_I (Q_I) in color c_i.

$$P_I = < h_{c_1}(P_I), \ldots, h_{c_m}(P_I) >, \quad Q_I = < h_{c_1}(Q_I), \ldots, h_{c_m}(Q_I) > \tag{11}$$

In many previous studies, each pixel is only assigned a single color. Consider the following situation: I_1, I_2 are two images, all pixels of I_1 and I_2 fall into c_i and c_{i+1} respectively; I_1 and I_2 are indeed similar to each other, but the similarity computed by the color histogram will regard them as different images. To address the problem, we set an interval range δ to extend the color of each pixel and introduce the idea of a partial pixel as shown in Eq. (12),

$$h_{c_i}(P_I) = \frac{\sum_{p \in P_I} \frac{|\alpha_p - \beta_p|}{\delta}}{|P_I|} \tag{12}$$

Fig. 2 gives an example to explain what we call a partial pixel. In the figure, c_{i-1}, c_i, and c_{i+1} stand for a color bin, a solid line indicates the boundary of c_i, p is the value of a pixel, $[p-\frac{\delta}{2}, p+\frac{\delta}{2}]$ denotes the interval range δ, the shadow part, $[\alpha_p, \beta_p]$, is the intersection of $[p-\frac{\delta}{2}, p+\frac{\delta}{2}]$ and c_i. The contributions of the pixel to c_i and c_{i-1} are computed as $\frac{|\alpha_p - \beta_p|}{\delta}$ and $\frac{|(p-\delta/2)-\alpha_p|}{\delta}$ respectively. It is clear that a pixel has its contributions not only to c_i but also to its neighboring bins.

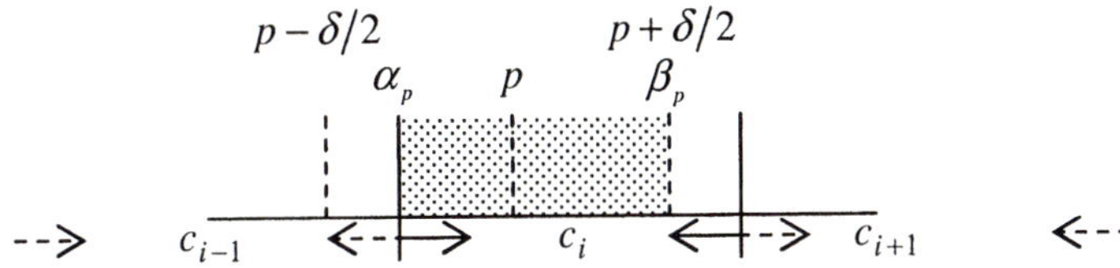

Fig. 2. An illustration of the partial pixel idea

3.2 Similarity Metric

While a query $Q=(Q_T, Q_I)$ and an image $P=(P_T, P_I)$ are represented in terms of a textual and an image vector representation, we propose two strategies to measure the similarity between the query and each image in the collection. In the following, we briefly describe the proposed strategies: Strategy 1, which is exploited in the system T_ICLEF, only takes into account the textual similarity while Strategy 2[4], which combines the textual and the image similarity, is employed in the system VCT_ICLEF.

Strategy 1 (T_ICLEF): Based on the textual similarity

$$Sim_1(P,Q) = \frac{\vec{P}_T \cdot \vec{Q}_T}{|\vec{P}_T||\vec{Q}_T|} \tag{13}$$

Strategy 2 (VCT_ICLEF): Based on both the textual and the image similarity

$$Sim_2(P,Q) = \alpha \cdot Sim_1(P,Q) + \beta \cdot Sim_3(P,Q)$$

where

$$Sim_3(P,Q) = \frac{H(P_I) \cap H(Q_I)}{|H(Q_I)|} = \frac{\sum_i \min(h_{c_i}(P_I), h_{c_i}(Q_I))}{\sum_i h_{c_i}(Q_I)} \tag{14}$$

[4] In our implementation, α is set to 0.7, and β is set to 0.3.

4 Interactive Search Mechanism

In this section a user interface for each proposed system is introduced. Then, the proposed query reformulation methods are described regarding textual and visual queries.

4.1 User Interface

Fig. 3 and Fig. 4 demonstrate the user interfaces designed for the user-centered search task at ImageCLEF 2004. Both systems have a search panel on the top, which allows users to type a Chinese query. In the display area, a pull-down menu below each image allows users to feedback the relevance of each image, which is provided as "*non-relevant*," "*neutral*," and "*relevant*." In our design, the system first returns 80 images for the initial search, but 40 images in later iterations. This is because in the initial search the system does not develop an idea about what the user wants exactly. A further set of images may induce the user to mark more relevant images and to assist the system to reformulate the query.

In fact, it is the color table shown in VCT_ICLEF that distinguishes the two systems. Users can provide color information to help the system determine the best query strategy. According to the experimental results, VCT_ICLEF has a better performance by exploiting color information for searching.

Fig. 3. The user interface of T_ICLEF

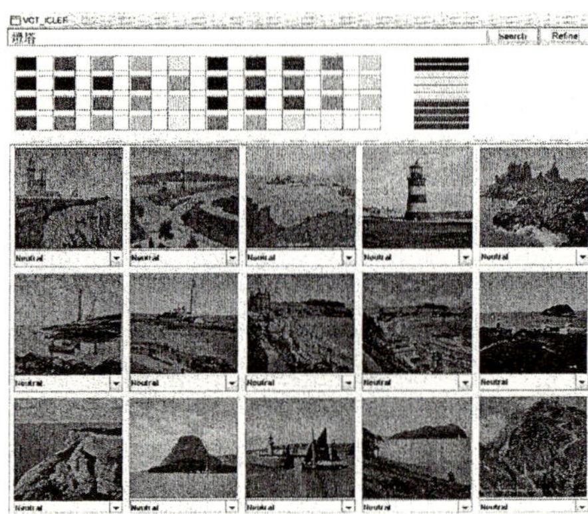

Fig. 4. The user interface of VCT_ICLEF

4.2 Query Reformulation

As mentioned before, in the relevance feedback process, the user evaluates the relevance of the returned images, and gives a relevance value (i.e., non-relevant, neutral, and relevant) to each of them. At the next stage, the system performs query reformulation to modify the original query on the basis of the user's relevance judgments, and invokes cross-language image retrieval again based on the new query.

Recall that we denote the original query as $Q=(Q_T,Q_I)$ and the new query $Q'=(Q'_T,Q'_I)$; regarding Q'_T, we exploit a practical method, as shown in Eq. (15), for query reformulation. This mechanism, which has been suggested by [11], is achieved with a weighted query by adding useful information extracted from relevant images as well as decreasing useless information derived from non-relevant images to the original query. Regarding Q_I', it is computed as the centroid of the relevant images, which is defined as their average. We do not take into account the irrelevant images for Q_I', since in our observation there is always a large difference among the non-relevant images. Empirically, adding the irrelevant information to Q_I' makes no helpful contribution.

$$Q_T' = \alpha \cdot Q_T + \frac{\beta}{|REL|} \sum_{P_{i_T} \in REL} P_{i_T} - \frac{\gamma}{|NREL|} \sum_{P_{j_T} \in NREL} P_{j_T} \tag{15}$$

$$Q_I' = \frac{1}{|REL|} \sum_{P_I \in REL} P_I \tag{16}$$

In Eq. (15) and Eq. (16), α, β, $\gamma \geq 0$ are parameters, *REL* and *NREL* stand for the sets of relevant ad irrelevant images marked by the user.

5 Evaluation Results

In this section we present our evaluation results for the user-centered search task at ImageCLEF 2004. The collection used for evaluation is the St. Andrews historic photographs. For detailed information about the St. Andrews Collection, the topic images, and the evaluation methodology, please refer to [2].

5.1 The Searchers' Backgrounds

There are 8 people involved in the task, including 5 male and 3 female searchers. Their average age is 23.5, with the youngest 22 and the oldest 26. Three of them major in computer science, two major in social science and the others are librarians. In particular, three searchers have experiences in participating in projects about image retrieval. All of them have an average of 3.75 years (with a minimum of 2 years and a maximum of 5 years) accessing online search services, specifically for Web search. On average, they search approximately 4 times a week, with a minimum of once and a maximum of 7 times. However, only a half of them have experiences in using image search services, such as Google images search.

5.2 Results

We are interested in which system helps searchers find a target image most effectively. We summarize the average number of iterations[5] and the average time spent by a searcher for each topic in Fig. 5. In the figure, it does not give information in the

[5] Please note that our system does not have an efficient performance; since for each iteration it spent about 1 minute to retrieve relevant images, approximately 5 iterations is performed within the time limit.

case that all searchers did not find the target image. (For instance, regarding topic 2, all searchers failed to complete the task by using T_ICLEF within the definite time.) The figure shows that overall VCT_ICLEF helps users find the image within a fewer iterations with a maximum of 2 iterations saved. For topics 2, 5, 7, 11, 15 and 16, no searcher can find the image by making use of T_ICLEF. With regard to topics 10 and 12, VCT_ICLEF has a worse performance. In our observation, the reason is that most images (82%) in the corpus are in black and white, once the user gives imprecise color information, VCT_ICLEF needs to take more iterations to find the image consequently.

Table 2 presents the number of searchers who failed to find the image for each topic. It is clear that VCT_ICLEF outperforms T_ICLEF in almost all cases. Considering topic 3, we believe that it is caused by the same reason we mentioned above for topics 10 and 12. Finally, we give a summary of our proposed systems in Table 3. The table illustrates that while considering those topics that at least one searcher completed the task, T_ICLEF cost additional 0.4 iterations and 76.47 seconds. By using VCT_ICLEF, on average 89% of searchers successfully found the image, while when using T_ICLEF, around 56.25% of searchers were successful.

To show the effects of color information used in VCT_ICLEF, we take Fig. 3 and Fig. 4 as examples. Regarding topic 6, the query used was "燈塔 (Lighthouse)." For T_ICLEF, it returned a set of images corresponding to the query; however, the target image could not be found in the top 80 images. Since topic 6 is a color image, while we searched the image with color information using VCT_ICLEF, the image was found in the first iteration. We conclude that color information can assist the user to tell the system what he is searching for. For an interactive image retrieval system, it is necessary to provide users not only an interface to issue a textual query but also an interface to indicate the system the visual information of the target.

Table 2. Number of searchers who did not find the target image for each topic

Topic	1	2	3	4	5	6	7	8	9	10	11	12	13	14	15	16
T_ICLEF	1	4	1	0	4	0	4	1	0	1	4	0	0	0	4	4
VCT_ICLEF	1	0	2	0	0	0	0	0	0	0	2	0	0	0	2	0

Table 3. Average steps to find the target image, and the average spent time

	Avg. Iterations (Not including not found)	Avg. Spent Time for each topic	Avg. percent of searchers who found the target image (#/4×100%)
T_ICLEF	2.24	208.67s	56.25%
VCT_ICLEF	1.84	132.20s	89.00%

5.3 Search Strategies

In our survey of search strategies exploited by searchers, we found that 5 searchers thought that additional color information about the target image was helpful to indicate to the system what they really wanted. Four searchers preferred to search the image with a text query first, even when using VCT_ICLEF. They then considered color information for the next iteration in the situation that the target image was in color but the system returned images all in black and white. When searching for a color image, 3 searchers preferred to use color information first. Moreover, 2 searchers hoped that in the future, users can provide a textual query to indicate color information, such as "黃色 (Yellow)." Finally to be mentioned, in our systems the user is allowed to provide a query consisting of temporal conditions. However, since it is hard to decide in which year the image was published, no one used a query which contains temporal conditions.

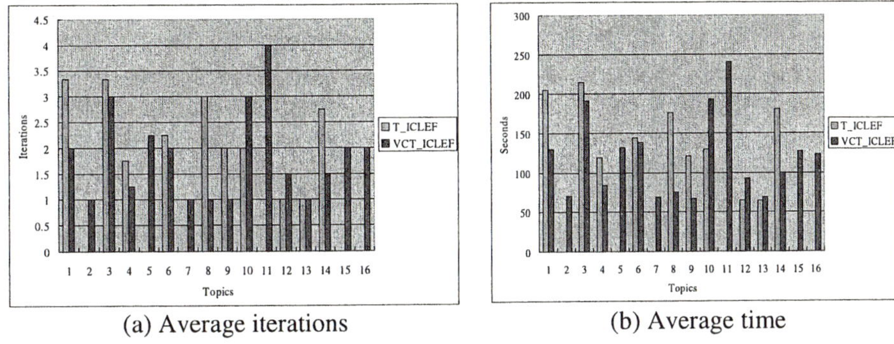

(a) Average iterations (b) Average time

Fig. 5. The average number of iterations and time spent searching for each topic

6 Conclusions

We participated in the user-centered search task at ImageCLEF 2004. In this paper, we proposed two interactive cross-language image retrieval systems – T_ICLEF and VCT_ICLEF. The first one is implemented with a practical relevance feedback approach based on textual information while the second one combines textual and image information to help users find a target image. The experimental results show that VCT_ICLEF has a better performance than T_ICLEF in almost all cases. Overall, VCT_ICLEF helps users find the image within a fewer iterations with a maximum of 2 iterations saved.

In the future, we plan to investigate user behaviors to understand in which cases users prefer a textual query as well as in which situations users prefer to provide visual information for searching. Besides, we also intend to implement a SOM (Self-Organizing Map) [6] on image clustering, which we believe that it can provide an effective browsing interface to help searchers find a target image.

Acknowledgements

This research was partially supported and sponsored by National Science Council, R.O.C. under NSC93-2213-E-009-044.

References

1. Ciocca G., Gagliardi I., Schettini R.: Quicklook2: An integrated multimedia system. International Journal of Visual Languages and Computing, Special Issue on Querying Multiple Data Sources, Vol. 12, No. 1 (2001), 81-103.
2. Clough P., Sanderson M., Müller H.: The CLEF Cross Language Image Retrieval Track (ImageCLEF) 2004. Proceedings of the CLEF 2004 Workshop, Bath, UK (2004), 459-473.
3. Cox I. J., Minka T. P., Papathomas T. V., Yianilos P. N.: The Bayesian image retrieval system, pichunter: Theory, implementation, and psychophysical experiments. IEEE Transactions on Image Processing, Special Issue on Digital Libraries, Vol. 9, No. 1 (2000), 20-37.
4. Flickner M., Sawhney H., Niblack W., Ashley J., Huang Q., Dom B., Gorkani M., Hafner J., Lee D., Petkovic D., Steele, D., Yanker P.: Query by Image and Video Content: The QBIC system. IEEE Computer, Vol. 28, No. 9 (1995), 23-32.
5. Ishikawa Y., Subramanya R., Faloutsos C.: Mindreader: Query databases through multiple examples. Proceedings of 24th VLDB Conference, New York, (1998), 218-227.
6. Kohonen T.: The Self-Organizing Map. Neurocomputing, Vol. 21, No. 1-3 (1998), 1-6.
7. Kushki A., Androutsos P., Plataniotis K. N., Venetsanopoulos A. N.: Query Feedback for Interactive Image Retrieval. IEEE Transactions on Circuits and Systems for Video Technology, Vol. 14, No. 5 (2004), 644-655.
8. Lu Y., Hu C., Zhu X., Zhang H., Yang Q.: A unified framework for semantics and feature based relevance feedback in image retrieval systems. Proceedings of 8th ACM Multimedia International Conference, Los Angeles, CA (2000), 31-37.
9. Meilhac C., Nastar C.: Relevance feedback and category search in image databases. IEEE Int. Conf. Multimedia Computing and Systems (1999), 512-517.
10. Miller G.: WordNet: A Lexical Database for English. Communications of the ACM (1995), 39-45.
11. Rocchio J. J.: Relevance feedback in information retrieval. In Salton G. (ed.): The SMART Retrieval System: Experiments in Automatic Document Processing, Englewood Cliffs, NJ: Prentice-Hall (1971), 313-323.
12. Rui Y., Huang T. S.: Relevance feedback: A power tool for interactive content-based image retrieval. IEEE Circuits Syst. Video Technol., Vol. 8, No. 5 (1999), 644-655.
13. Rui Y., Huang T. S.: A novel relevance feedback technique in image retrieval. Proceedings of the 7th ACM International Conference on Multimedia, Orlando, FL (1999), 67-70.
14. Salton G., McGill M. J. (eds.): Introduction to Modern Information Retrieval. McGraw-Hill (1983).
15. Swain M. J., Ballard D. H.: Color Indexing. International Journal of Computer Vision, Vol. 7 (1991), 11-32.
16. Vasconcelos N., Lippman A.: Learning from user feedback in image retrieval systems. Proc. NIPS'99, Denver, CO (1999).

MSU at ImageCLEF: Cross Language and Interactive Image Retrieval

Vineet Bansal, Chen Zhang, Joyce Y. Chai, and Rong Jin

Department of Computer Science and Engineering, Michigan State University, East Lansing, MI48824, U.S.A.
{bansalvi, zhangch6, jchai, rongjin}@cse.msu.edu

Abstract. In this report, we describe our studies with cross language and interactive image retrieval in ImageCLEF 2004. Typical cross language retrieval requires special linguistic resources, such as bilingual dictionaries. In this study, we focus on the issue of how to achieve good retrieval performance given only an online translation system. We compare two approaches, i.e., a translation-based approach and a model-based approach, and find that the later one performs substantially better than the former one. For interactive image retrieval, we investigated the potential use of user relevance feedback (URF), which was designed to address the mismatch problem between user queries and system descriptions. Our strategy is to let the system select important terms for user feedback before expanding queries. However, our preliminary results appear to indicate that the URF approach developed at the current stage is not working. We report our current investigation and discuss lessons learned from this experience.

1 Introduction

Empirical studies have shown that using image features to find similar images is usually insufficient [15]. First, it is difficult for users to specify visual queries with low-level visual features. Second, low level image features cannot precisely describe user information needs. There is a gap between low-level visual descriptions and user's semantic expectation [10]. Text queries, on the other hand, are more intuitive and natural for users to specify their information needs and expectations.

In this year's ImageCLEF, we investigated two challenging tasks related to text-based image retrieval:

1) Given image descriptions in one language and user query in another language, how to effectively retrieve images using cross language retrieval? In particular, given limited bilingual resources (e.g., the online bilingual translation system), how to improve the accuracy of cross lingual information retrieval?
2) Given a target image in user's mind, how to interactively help users to find such an image. In particular, we investigated the use of user relevance feedback in such a task.

In the following sections, we devote two sections to these two tasks respectively.

C. Peters et al. (Eds.): CLEF 2004, LNCS 3491, pp. 805 – 815, 2005.

2 Cross Language Retrieval Using Only an Online Translation System

Cross lingual retrieval has been one of the major research areas in information retrieval during last few years [1, 2, 5-7, 9]. Most cross lingual retrieval algorithms fall into two categories: the translation-based approaches, and the approaches based on statistical models.

A simple translation-based approach will translate a query into the language of documents, and relevant documents will be found by matching the translated queries with the documents[1]. Different algorithms can be applied to translate queries, ranging from the simplest one that is based on bilingual dictionaries to the sophisticated one that is based on a full-scale machine translation system. Compared to dictionary-based translation, using a full-scale machine translation system has the advantage in that the ambiguity of a query is reduced by a full-scale translation system and only the best translation of the query is used. However, on the other hand, a cross lingual approach based on the full-scale translation system can perform poorly if a query is truly ambiguous and multiple possible translations need to be considered. In those cases, dictionary-based translation approaches for cross lingual retrieval will have advantages because it include all possible translations of query words. Thus, a good cross lingual retrieval system should be able to, on one hand, reduce the uncertainty in translating queries when possible, and on the hand, maintain the uncertainty of query translation if the query is ambiguous.

A model-based approach usually utilizes the existing statistical machine translation models that were developed by the IBM group [16]. Given a translation model θ, the relevance of a document d to a given query q is computed as $p(q \mid d;\theta)$, which is the likelihood of translating document d into query q. Compared to the translation-based approaches, the model-based approaches have advantage in that by using the translation probabilities learned from a parallel corpus, we are able to reduce translation ambiguity and yet maintain the uncertainty in translation at the same time. This is done through the adjustment of translation probabilities: an unlikely translation will be assigned with a small probability; meanwhile equally likely translations of a query will be assigned with similar translation probabilities. However, in order to build a statistical translation model, a sufficiently large bilingual parallel corpus is required. Acquiring a large parallel corpus is usually expensive and time consuming, especially for minor languages.

In this report, we study an approach that first utilizes the online translation system to create a bilingual parallel corpus and then learns a statistical translation model based on the created bilingual corpus. Unlike the translation based approaches where only the best translation is used in information retrieval, this approach maintains the uncertainty in translation and therefore will be more robust to the translation errors. On the other hand, unlike the typical model-based approaches where a large bilingual parallel corpus is required, this approach automatically creates a bilingual parallel corpus by applying the online translation system to translate test documents into the language of queries. In the following subsections, we will first overview the statistical machine translation model, and then discuss the empirical results with the proposed approach.

2.1 A Statistical Translation Model for Cross Language Information Retrieval

For the convenience of discussion, let's assume that the language of queries is Chinese and the language of documents is English. Let the set of translation probabilities denoted by $\theta = \{t(w_i^e \mid w_j^c)\}$. Each $t(w_i^e \mid w_j^c)$ is the probability that translates a Chinese word w_j^c into an English word w_i^e. The key to statistical translation model for cross lingual information retrieval is to automatically learn the set of word translation probabilities from a parallel corpus. Let the bilingual parallel corpus for training a statistical translation model be denoted by $\Omega = \{(\mathbf{s}_i^c, \mathbf{s}_i^e)\}_{i=1}^{N}$. Each $(\mathbf{s}_i^c, \mathbf{s}_i^e)$ is a translation pair in which sentence $\mathbf{s}_i^c$ is the Chinese translation of sentence $\mathbf{s}_i^e$. N is the total number of translation pairs in the corpus Ω. According to the IBM translation model, $p(\mathbf{s}_i^e \mid \mathbf{s}_i^c; \theta)$, i.e., the probability of translation an English sentence $\mathbf{s}_i^e$ into a Chinese sentence $\mathbf{s}_i^c$, can be written as:

$$p(\mathbf{s}_i^e \mid \mathbf{s}_i^c; \theta) \propto \prod_{j=1}^{V_e} \left(\sum_{k=1}^{V_c} o(w_k^c, \mathbf{s}_i^c) t(w_j^e \mid w_k^c) \right)^{o(w_k^e, \mathbf{s}_i^e)}$$

where V_e and V_c stand for the size for Chinese vocabulary and English vocabulary, respectively. $o(w_k^c, \mathbf{s}_i^c)$ represents the occurrence of Chinese word w_k^c in Chinese sentence $\mathbf{s}_i^c$. So does $o(w_k^e, \mathbf{s}_i^e)$. Thus, in order to learn translation probabilities, we can maximize the log-likelihood of all translation pairs used for training, i.e.

$$\theta = \arg\max_{\theta \in \Theta} l(\Omega; \theta) = \arg\max_{\theta \in \Theta} \sum_{i=1}^{N} \log p(\mathbf{s}_i^e \mid \mathbf{s}_i^c; \theta)$$

A well-known Expectation Maximization algorithm can be used to efficiently learn the optimal translation probabilities. More details can be found in [3]. Finally, in order to estimate the relevancy of a document d to a query q, probability $p(q \mid d)$ is estimated using the following expression:

$$\log p(q^c \mid d^e; \theta) = \log \int dq^e p(q^c \mid q^e) p(q^e \mid d^e) \approx \sum_i p(w_i^e \mid q^c) \log p(w_i^e \mid d^e)$$

$$\approx \sum_i \left(\sum_j o(w_j^c, q^c) p(w_i^e \mid w_j^c) \right) \log p(w_i^e \mid d^e)$$

More details of applying statistical translation model to cross lingual information retrieval can be found in [16].

2.2 Our Approach: Training a Statistical Model Using an Online Translation System

Given the success of the statistical translation model for cross lingual information retrieval in the TREC evaluations [13, 14], we would like to apply it to the cross language image retrieval. However, the biggest problem is to acquire a bilingual parallel corpus that shares the similar content as the text collection used in the ImageCLEF evaluation. In order to acquire a bilingual corpus, we tried a simple strategy. We first applied an online translation system to translate the textual descriptions in ImageCLEF into Chinese sentences. To enhance the diversity of our translation pairs, the Chinese sentences that are generated by the online translation system are further translated back into English sentences. The final bilingual corpus is created by aggregating all the translation pairs together. The online translation system used in our experiment is Systran (http://www.systransoft.com/). With the acquired translation pairs, we now can apply the statistical translation model to automatically learn translation probabilities between Chinese words and English words. Examples of learned translation probabilities are listed in Table 1. Note that all English words are stemmed using the Porter algorithm.

Table 1. Examples of translation probabilities learned from the bilingual parallel corpus that is generated by the online translation model. All the English words are stemmed

Chinese	English	Prob.	Chinese	English	Prob.
塔	tower	0.8692	大教堂	cathedr	0.7312
	turret	0.0200		st	0.0475
	pinnacl	0.0198		iona	0.0231
	build	0.0048		dunblan	0.0161
	clock	0.0044		eli	0.0152
	squar	0.0042		durham	0.0147
	spire	0.0042		andrew	0.0143
	church	0.0028		elgin	0.0139
	transept	0.0026		dunkeld	0.0104
	hous	0.0023		transept	0.0098

The retrieval performance using statistical translation model for cross lingual retrieval is listed in Table 2 under the column entitled as 'Model-based'. For the purpose of comparison, we also run the simple translation-based approach, which applies the online translation system to translate each Chinese query into an English query. The results of this translation-based approach are also included in Table 2 under the column entitled as 'Translation-based'.

As indicated in Table 2, the approach based on the statistical translation model performs substantially better than the simple translation-based approach in terms of almost every metric. In particular, the major difference between these two approaches lies in the region when only the top retrieved documents are examined. For example, when only the first five documents are examined, the precision for the translation-based approach is only 28.8%, while the precision for the approach based on statistical translation model is 41.6%. This fact is further confirmed by the precision results for the low recall points. For example, when systems recall 10% of the relevant documents, the precision for the translation-based approach is only 37.4%, while the precision for the model-based approach is above 50%. Thus, we conclude that the proposed approach is a better way of utilizing the online translation system for cross lingual information retrieval than the simple translation-based approach.

Table 2. Retrieval results for both the translation-based approach and the approach based on the statistical translation model

Recall@	**Translation-based**	**Model-based**
0.0	0.638	0.680
0.1	0.374	0.521
0.2	0.367	0.432
0.3	0.328	0.392
0.4	0.290	0.338
0.5	0.261	0.301
0.6	0.225	0.265
0.7	0.203	0.239
0.8	0.171	0.194
0.9	0.141	0.153
1.0	0.099	0.106
Avg Prec.	0.245	0.293
Prec@		
5 doc	0.288	0.416
10 doc	0.260	0.344
100 doc	0.150	0.161

3 Interactive Image Retrieval: User Relevance Feedback

Compared to example-based image retrieval, text-based image retrieval provides an intuitive and natural means for users to specify their information needs and expectations. However, text queries also face many challenges [8]. One major problem concerns both the sparsity and inconsistency of textual descriptions [12]. The words used to describe an image or a similar image vary from one user to another. Furthermore, the textual descriptions are usually short. This vocabulary variation and the conciseness of textual descriptions make it difficult for the traditional text retrieval to work effectively for image retrieval.

To address this problem, we are currently in an on-going investigation on user relevance feedback (URF) in image retrieval. Here, user relevance feedback is motivated by the success of pseudo relevance feedback (PRF) in information retrieval [10]. The difference between URF and PRF is that, in URF we introduce users in the loop to do a sanity check on potential expanded terms. Instead of automatically expanding the query as in PRF, the URF presents a list of terms to users and ask them to choose relevant terms that can describe the target image. Only those terms chosen by the user will be used in query expansion.

Our hypothesis is that this type of feedback can take advantage of the conciseness of textual descriptions and consolidate the inconsistency of user textual queries. On one hand, the concise descriptions make it possible for the system to efficiently identify potential important terms. On the other hand, the system selected terms will remedy the difference between query term and image description. Furthermore, the sanity check from the user will improve the quality of query expansion, which will ultimately result in the improvement of final retrieval results.

As a first step in our investigation, we developed several strategies to select terms and conducted simulations to evaluate different strategies. We then implemented the best strategy for the real user study. In the user study, we compared the interface using URF with a standard interface that only allows users to interactively refine or expand their queries. However, out of our expectation, the results from user studies were not able to validate our hypotheses. In fact, the results indicate the current design and implementation of URF is not working. Therefore, in this section, rather than presenting a successful story (as much as we wish), we report our current investigation and discuss lessons learned from this experience that are useful for future investigation.

3.1 Term Selection

Term selection in URF is different from that in PRF. In URF, our goal is to find terms from descriptions that are related to the initial user query terms, however with large uncertainties as to whether they are relevant. As a first step, we investigated different strategies for term selection using simulation experiments. Simulation studies are important since they can provide some insights on whether a strategy can potentially work even before the expensive user studies are conducted. In these simulated experiments, the system first selects a list of ten terms based on different strategies. To simulate human behavior in identifying relevant terms from this list, the system picks terms that occur in the description of the target images. The picked terms, together with the initial query terms, will be sent to the backend retrieval engine. This process repeats until either the target image is found in the top N (currently, N = 20) retrieved images or the system reaches M iterations (currently, M = 10).

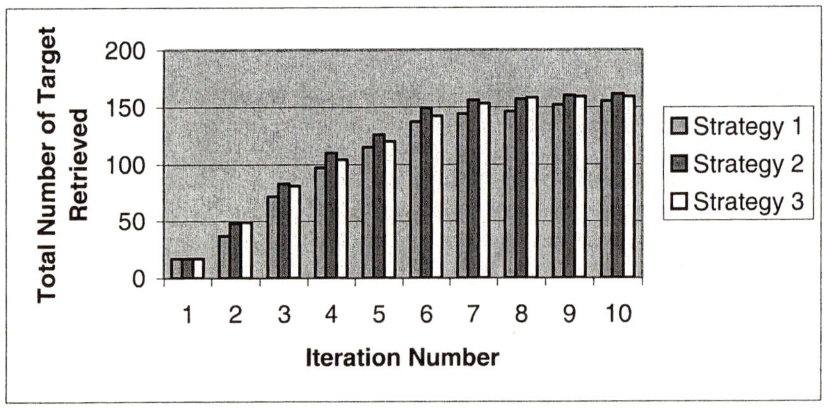

Fig. 1. Performance of three strategies at each iteration point

To generate the terms, we have experimented with different strategies. The first strategy measures the entropy of a term based on the top *N* retrieved results (called *Top Set* later) and/or the next *100-N* retrieved results (called *Bottom Set* later). The idea is that the term with higher entropy is more uncertain in terms of whether it describes user's interest. By asking user to confirm those higher entropy terms, the system can quickly narrow down the search space. The higher the entropy is, the higher the weight is given. We tried different combinations of retrieved results to calculate the entropy for a given term, specifically the following three strategies:

- Strategy 1: Higher weights are given to terms that have higher entropy from the Bottom Set and also occur less frequently in the Top Set.
- Strategy 2: Higher weights are given to terms with higher entropy from the Bottom Set.
- Strategy 3: Higher weights are given to terms with higher entropy from the Top Set.

In the simulation experiments, we randomly picked 200 images from ImageCLEF collection [4]. For each image, we provided an initial query. Then we applied the simulation process as described above to retrieve each image. Figure 1 shows the simulation results from three different strategies as to how many out of 200 images were successfully retrieved as top 20 results at each iteration point. Results indicate that there is no significant difference between three strategies. All three strategies are more effective at earlier iterations (from 1 to 6) than later ones in the simulation. At iteration 1, since no query expansion is used, all three strategies resulted in the same number of successful retrievals only based on the initial queries. Since the strategy 2 seems slightly better, we use the strategy 2 in our user study.

We have also experimented with the inverse correlation strategy and the synonym strategy. The idea for the inverse correlation strategy is that if a term is very correlated with a query term given by the user, then that term carries less information in identifying new images that might be of user's interest. Therefore, we give a lower weight to the terms that is highly correlated with a query term using a vector space model. The idea for the synonym strategy is that if a term is the synonym of a query term, then it could be very relevant. We want to give it a higher weight since it maybe just a different vocabulary expressing the same meaning. To test this synonym strategy, we used WordNet. However, our current simulations have not shown the effectiveness of these two strategies in term selection. Therefore, we did not include these two strategies in the user study.

Once one or more prompted terms are selected (either automatically by the system in the simulation or manually by the user in the user studies), those terms will be used to expand the initial query in further retrieval cycles. The retrieval model is based on a statistical language modeling approach using textual descriptions of images [11].

3.2 User Studies

To validate our hypothesis and evaluate the effectiveness of the current URF, we conducted a comparative study following the guidelines provided by the ImageCLEF interactive track.

3.2.1 Method

Eight subjects participated in the study and each of them was asked to search for 16 images from the Eurovision St. Andrew collection provided by ImageCLEF. The subjects were first asked to complete a screening questionnaire to elicit demographic data and data concerning searching experience. Then the subject was asked to use one interface to search eight images (one at a time). After using each interface, the subject was given a questionnaire to indicate how easy he feels about the search process, and how satisfied he is with a particular system. During the search, the system also automatically logged the information such as the original queries from the user, the system retrieved results, terms prompted by the system, and the time spent on searching, etc. When an image was found or when five minutes were run out, the search stopped. After searching all images using two different interfaces, each subject was asked to give an overall ranking of the two interfaces in terms of their overall satisfaction and systems' effectiveness of locating the target images.

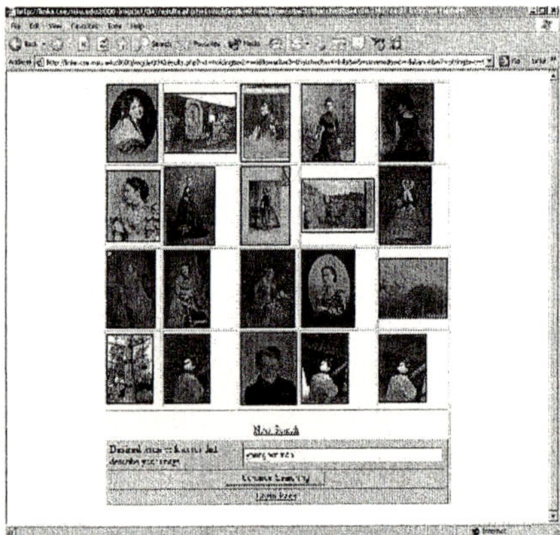

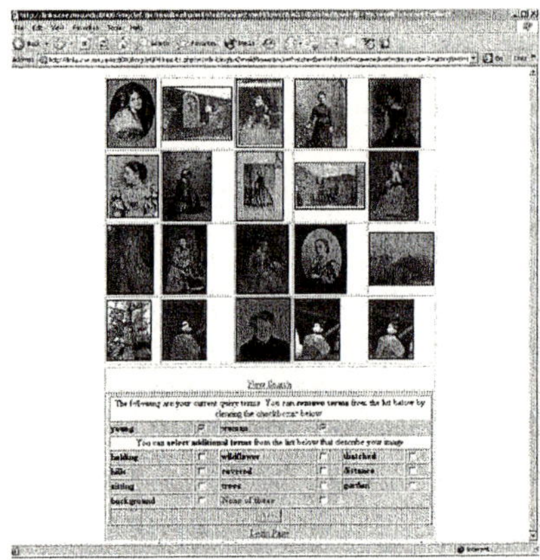

Fig. 2. (a) Standard Interface (b) Interface with URF

Two interfaces used in the study are shown in Figure 2. Figure 2(a) is a standard interface to be compared with, where users could refine or expand their queries using their own terms. Figure 2(b) is the URF interface. In the URF interface, in addition to ten terms prompted by the system for user feedback, the system also shows the query terms that are used so far for the retrieval. Users have choices to revise these query terms from previous iterations by "de-select" them from the list. This feature was designed so that the URF interface is comparable to the standard interface where users can freely add/remove their query terms at each iteration.

3.2.2 Evaluation Results

Unfortunately, after three users, we found some inconsistency in the system, so we had to discard the results from those three users. The results shown here are from five out of eight users. Table 3 shows the effectiveness for the two interfaces. The successful retrieval rate is calculated by dividing the number of target images that are shown in the top 20 retrievals by the total number of target images tried for that interface. Since the success rate for the interface B (with URF) is lower than the interface A (the standard interface), we conclude that the interface B is not effective based on the current design and implementation.

Table 3. Overall performance of two interface

	Standard Interface	URF
Successful Retrieval	0.575	0.175
Average time	0:48	1:57
Average number of interactions	2.43	3.57

3.3 Discussion

The failure with the current design points to several problems that need to be addressed in our future investigation. Users were involved in the loop to provide feedback for query expansion. However, one major problem is that many of those terms do not mean much to the user. Certainly, we hope that when a prompted term appears in the description of the target image, the user would pick that term (as in our simulation). However, from our studies, we found that even those terms appear in the description, the user still could not recognize them. This caused the big performance difference between the simulated experiments and the real user study. We feel that there are different classes of terms. Some classes of terms are much easier to identify than the others. For example, "background" and "substantial", both terms occurred in the description of a target image. However, it was very hard for users to recognize them since they did not directly match any salient features conveyed by the image. On the other, the term "bridge" would be easier for the user to recognize. It would be ideal if the system can only prompt to the users those key terms that could mean something to the user. Thus, it would be interesting to study how users respond to these different terms based on the salient features and semantic content presented in an image and how to identify those significant terms from the retrieved results. Only with such an understanding, is it possible to build a potentially effective URF.

In additional, as in the traditional text retrieval, the term mismatching is another problem for image retrieval. For example, suppose among the ten terms prompted by the system, the user chooses the term "road". Even this term does describe some object in the target image, this term will not be effective if the term "street" is used in the description, rather than the term "road". Therefore, in order to effectively use URF, the system needs to have a capability of handling this type of mismatching caused by variations of terms.

Because of the time limitation, here we only briefly describe some very preliminary observations and problems. We certainly need more in-depth analysis on our collected data. Although the current experiment is not successful, what we have learned from this experience can help us focus on specific issues identified. We believe URF still has a potential in interactive image retrieval. For example, instead of only allowing URF as in our current interface, we can consider adding URF to a standard interface. However, before that happens, first of all, we need to reach a better understanding of user cognitive models on describing image content and its implication in user relevance feedback.

4 Conclusion

In this report, we examined two important issues associated with cross language image retrieval and interactive image retrieval:

1) How to improve the accuracy of information retrieval given that only an online translation system is available;
2) How to enhance text-based image retrieval using the user relevance feedback (URF).

Our empirical results with cross language retrieval have indicated that an employment of statistical translation model is effective, even when the parallel corpus is created automatically by an online translation system. Our preliminary study with interactive image retrieval has illustrated that to make user relevance feedback effective for text-based image retrieval, a carefully designed procedure of automatic term selection is critical. In particular, the selected terms should be able to not only distinguish certain images from others, but also be consistent with the users' perception of images. Thus, more in-depth investigation is needed to reach a better understanding of user cognitive models on describing image content and its implication in user relevance feedback.

References

1. Ballesteros, L. and W.B. Croft. *Phrasal Translation and Query Expansion Techniques for Cross-Language Information Retrieval.* in Proceedings of the 20th annual international ACM SIGIR conference on Research and development in information retrieval. 1997.
2. Ballesteros, L. and W.B. Croft. *Resolving Ambiguity for Cross-Language Retrieval.* in Proceedings of the 21th Annual International ACM SIGIR Conference on Research and Development in Information Retrieval. 1998.
3. Brown, P., et al., *The Mathematics of Statistical Machine Translation.* Computational Linguistics, 1993. **19**(2): p. 263-311.
4. Clough, P., M. Sanderson, and N. Reid. The Eurovision St Andrews Photographic Collection. http://ir.shef.ac.uk/imageclef2004/guide.pdf.
5. Federico, M. and N. Bertoldi. *Statistical Cross-Language Information Retrieval Using N-Best Query Translations.* in Proceedings of the 25th Annual International ACM SIGIR Conference on Research and Development in Information Retrieval. 2002.
6. Gao, J., et al. *Improving Query Translation for Cross-Language Information Retrieval Using Statistical Models.* in Proceedings of the 24th Annual International ACM SIGIR Conference on Research and Development in Information Retrieval. 2001.
7. Hiemstra, D. and F.M.G.d. Jong. *Disambiguation Strategies for Cross-Language Information Retrieval.* in Proceedings of the Third European Conference on Research and Advanced Technology for Digital Libraries (ECDL). 1999.
8. Keister, L.H., *User Types and Queries: Impact on Image Access Systems.* ASIS, 1994: p. 7-22.
9. Lavrenko, V., M. Choquette, and W.B. Croft. *Cross-Lingual Relevance Model.* in Proceedings of the 25th Annual International ACM SIGIR Conference on Research and Development in Information Retrieval. 2002.

10. Mitra, M., A. Singhal, and C. Buckley. *Improving Automatic Query Expansion.* in Proceedings of SIGIR 1998. 1998.
11. Ponte, J.M. and W.B. Croft. *A Language Modeling Approach to Information Retrieval.* in Proceedings of the 21st annual international ACM SIGIR conference on Research and development in information retrieval. 1998.
12. Seloff, G.A., *Automated Access to Nasa-Jsc Image Archives.* Library Trends, 1990. **38**(4): p. 682-696.
13. Voorhees, E.M. and D.K. Harman, eds. *Proceedings of the Ninth Text Retrieval Conference (Trec-9).* 2000: Gaithersburgh, MD.
14. Voorhees, E.M. and D.K. Harman, eds. *Proceedings of the Ninth Text Retrieval Conference (Trec-10).* 2001: Gaithersburgh, MD.
15. Westerveld, T. and A.P.d. Vries. *Experimental Result Analysis for a Generative Probabilistic Image Retrieval Model.* in Proceedings of the 26th ACM SIGIR. 2003.
16. Xu, J., R. Weischedel, and C. Nguyen. *Evaluating a Probabilistic Model for Cross-Lingual Information Retrieval.* in Proceedings of the 24th Annual International ACM SIGIR Conference on Research and Development in Information Retrieval. 2001.

CLEF 2004 Cross-Language Spoken Document Retrieval Track

Marcello Federico[1], Nicola Bertoldi[1], Gina-Anne Levow[2], and Gareth J.F. Jones[3]

[1] ITC-irst, Italy
[2] University of Chicago, U.S.A.
[3] Dublin City University, Ireland
{federico, bertoldi}@itc.it, levow@cs.uchicago.edu, gareth.jones@computing.dcu.ie

Abstract. This paper summarizes the Cross-Language Spoken Document Retrieval (CL-SDR) track held at CLEF 2004. The CL-SDR task at CLEF 2004 was again based on the TREC-8 and TREC-9 SDR tasks. This year the CL-SDR task was extended to explore the unknown story boundaries condition introduced at TREC. The paper reports results from the participants showing that as expected cross-language results are reduced relative to a monolingual baseline, although the amount to which they are degraded varies for different topic languages.

1 Introduction

The CLEF Cross Language Spoken Document Retrieval (CL-SDR) track aims to evaluate CLIR systems for spoken document collections. The CLEF 2004 CL-SDR track once again takes as its starting point data prepared by NIST for the TREC 8-9 SDR tracks [1]. In particular, the task consists of retrieving news stories within a repository of about 550 hours of American English news. The original English short search topics were manually formulated in other languages, e.g. French or German, to form a CL-SDR task. Retrieval is performed on automatic transcriptions made available by NIST, and generated using different speech recognition systems.

For CLEF 2004, the CL-SDR task was extended to include the unknown story boundaries condition introduced in the TREC SDR evaluations. Whereas for the previous CL-SDR evaluation [2], the transcription was manually divided into individual story units, participants were this year provided only with the unsegmented transcripts. For each search topic, systems had to produce a ranked list of relevant stories, based on identifying a complete news show and a time index within the news show. In this way, relevance is assessed by checking if the provided time index falls inside the manually judged relevant stories. According to the NIST evaluation protocol, systems generating results corresponding to the same stories are penalized. In fact, successive time indexes falling in the same story are marked as non relevant results.

C. Peters et al. (Eds.): CLEF 2004, LNCS 3491, pp. 816–820, 2005.

2 Data Specifications

The document collection consists of 557 hours of American-English news recordings broadcast by: ABC, CNN, Public Radio International (PRI), and Voice of America (VOA) between February and June 1998. Spoken documents are accessible through automatic transcriptions produced by NIST and other sites, which participated in the TREC 9 SDR track. Transcripts are provided with and without story boundaries, for a total of 21,754 stories. For the application of blind relevance feedback, participants were allowed to use parallel document collections available through the Linguistic Data Consortium.

Queries are based on the 100 English topics in short format from the TREC 8 and TREC 9 SDR tasks, and the corresponding relevance assessments. For the CLIR task, the topics were translated by native speakers into Dutch, Italian, French, German, and Spanish. The existing SDR retrieval scoring software was used for the known and unknown story boundary conditions.

Of the available 100 topics, the first 50 (topic 074 to topic 123) were designated for system development, and the latter 50 (topic 124 to topic 173) for testing. Submission format and evaluation criteria followed the same conventions as those that were used at the 2000 TREC-9 SDR track[1].

The following evaluation conditions were specified:

- Primary Conditions (mandatory for all participants):
  - Monolingual IR on NIST transcripts, no parallel data.
  - Bilingual IR from French/German on NIST transcripts, no parallel data.
- Secondary Conditions (optional):
  - Bilingual IR from French/German, on NIST transcripts, with parallel data.
  - Bilingual IR from any language, any available transcript,with parallel data.

3 Participants

Two sites participated in the evaluation: University of Chicago (USA) and ITC-irst (Italy). A brief description of each system is provided.

3.1 CL-SDR System by University of Chicago

Runs were submitted for both the baseline English monolingual task and the French-English cross-language task, using only the resources provided by CLEF with no external resources.

Topic Processing. Topic processing aimed to enhance retrieval of the potentially errorful ASR transcriptions through pseudo-relevance feedback expansion. The baseline conditions required the use of only the CLEF provided resources. This restriction limited our source of relevance feedback to the ASR transcriptions, segmented as described below. For both the monolingual English and the

[1] See `http://www.nist.gov/speech/tests/sdr/sdr2000/sdr2000.htm`.

English translations of the original French topics, we performed the same enrichment process. We employed the INQUERY API to identify enriching terms based on the top 10 ranked retrieved segments and integrated these terms with the original query forms. Our hope was that this enrichment process would capture both additional on-topic terminology as well as ASR-specific transcriptions.

For the French-English cross-language condition, we performed dictionary-based term-by-term translation, as described in [3]. We employed a freely available bilingual term list (`www.freedict.com`). After identifying translatable multi-word units based on greedy longest match in the term list, we used a stemming backoff translation approach with statistically derived stemming rules [4], matching surface forms first and backing off to stemmed form if no surface match was found. All translation alternatives were integrated through structured query formulation [5].

Spoken Document Processing. This year the SDR track focused on the processing of news broadcasts with unknown story boundaries. This formulation required that sites perform some automatic segmentation of the full broadcasts into smaller units suitable for retrieval. Using an approach inspired by [6], we performed story segmentation as follows. First we created 30 second segments based on the word recognition time stamps using a 10 second step to create overlapping segment windows. These units were then indexed using the INQUERY retrieval system version 3.1p1 with both stemming and standard stopword removal.

Retrieval Segment Construction. To produce suitable retrieval segments, we merged the fine-grained segments returned by the base retrieval process on a per-query basis. For each query, we retrieved 5000 fine-grained segment windows. We then stepped through the ranked retrieval list merging overlapping segments, assigning the rank of the higher ranked segment to the newly merged segment. We cycled through the ranked list until convergence. The top ranked 1000 documents formed the final ranked retrieval results submitted for evaluation.

3.2 CL-SDR System by ITC-irst

The ITC-irst system for the CLEF 2004 CL-SDR task was based on the following three processing steps:

1. A collection of news segments is automatically created from the continuous stream of transcripts. Text segments are produced with a shifting time-window of 30 seconds, moved with steps of 10 seconds. Segments are also truncated if a silence period longer than 5 seconds is found.
2. The resulting overlapping texts are used as the target document collection for our text CLIR system [8].
3. Entries in the ranking list which correspond to overlapping segments are merged.

The implemented method works as follows. All retrieved segments of the same news show are sorted by their start time. The first retrieved segment is assumed as the beginning of a new story. If the second segment overlaps with the first, the two are merged, and the time extent of the current story is adjusted, and so on. If a following segment does not overlap with the current story, the current story is saved in a stack, and a new story begins. Finally, for all stories in the stack, only the segments with the highest retrieval score are considered. The process is repeated for all news show files with at least one entry in the rank list. The resulting list of non overlapping segments is then sorted according to the original retrieval score.

4 Results

Table 1 shows a summary of the participants results. For the primary condition, there is a considerable loss in retrieval effectiveness for cross-language relative to monolingual retrieval. This reduction in average precision varies between about 40% and 60%. These figures are larger than those observed for the known story boundary test condition in the CLEF 2003 CL-SDR task [2]. One possible explanation is the small size of the document segments used for the unknown story boundary condition. The combination of errorfully translated short topic statements with these inaccurately transcribed document segments may be responsible for this effect, where, since both are short, redundancy effects, which often help to compensate for transcription and translation errors in SDR and CLIR respectively, will often be very limited.

Table 1. Mean average precision statistics of submitted runs

Site	Source	Primary	Secondary
ITC-irst	Monolingual	0.306	0.359
	French	0.182 (-40.5%)	0.233 (-35.1%)
	German	0.158 (-48.4%)	0.205 (-42.9%)
	Italian	–	0.251 (-30.1%)
	Spanish	–	0.299 (-16.7%)
U. Chicago	Monolingual	0.296	–
	French	0.108 (-63.5%)	–

As we would expect based on previous work on SDR [2], the use of additional data resources produces an improvement in absolute retrieval performance figures in all cases, although the relative cross language reduction is still very large for all conditions except for Spanish topic translation.

5 Concluding Remarks

The participation of only two groups in the CL-SDR task at CLEF 2004 was disappointing. The comparative results for monolingual and cross-language retrieval in this paper illustrate that effective CL-SDR is a non-trivial task. Unfortunately, since the TREC SDR task, on which the CL-SDR task was based, has previously been investigated extensively both at TREC and in our own earlier CL-SDR investigations [2], it was probably not a sufficiently exciting challenge to encourage wider participation. However, we still regard CL-SDR as both an interesting research problem and a technology which, as with text CLIR, when sufficiently effective and robust may have significant practical applications.

For CLEF 2005 we plan to introduce a brand new CL-SDR task using on a new document collection taken from an entirely different domain, and using a more challenging set of topic languages. The initial task will be based on English documents, but we expect to extend this to more challenging document languages in future years.

References

[1] Garafolo, J. S., Auzanne, C. G. P., and Voorhees, E. M.: The TREC Spoken Document Retrieval Track: A Success Story. In Proceedings of the RIAO 2000 Conference: Content-Based Multimedia Information Access, pages 1–20, Paris, 2000.

[2] Federico, M. and Jones, G. J. F.: The CLEF 2003 Cross-Language Spoken Document Retrieval Track. In Proceedings of Workshop of the Cross-Language Evaluation Forum (CLEF 2003), Peters, C., et al. editors, pages 646-652, Lecture Notes in Computer Science (LNCS 3237), Springer, Heidelberg, Germany, 2004.

[3] Levow, G.–A., Oard, D. W., and Resnik, P.: Dictionary-Based Techniques for Cross-Language Information Retrieval. Information Processing and Management. In press.

[4] Oard, D. W., Levow, G.–A., and Cabezas, C.: CLEF Experiments at the University of Maryland: Statistical Stemming and Backoff Translation Strategies. In Proceedings of Workshop of the Cross-Language Evaluation Forum (CLEF 2000), Peters, C., editor, pages 176-187, Lecture Notes in Computer Science (LNCS 2069), Springer, Heidelberg, Germany, 2001.

[5] Pirkola, A.: The Effects of Query Structure and Dictionary Setups in Dictionary-Based Cross-Language Information Retrieval. In Proceedings of the 21st Annual International ACM SIGIR Conference on Research and Development in Information Retrieval, pages 55-63, ACM, 1998.

[6] Abberley, D., Renals, S., Cook, G., and Robinson, T.: Retrieval Of Broadcast News Documents With the THISL System. In Proceedings of the Seventh Text REtrieval Conference (TREC-7), Voorhees, E. M., and Harman, D., editors, pages 181–190, NIST Special Publication 500-242, 1999.

[7] Callan, J. P., Croft, W. B., and Harding, S. M.: The INQUERY Retrieval System. In Proceedings of the Third International Conference on Database and Expert Systems Applications pages 78–83, Spinger Verlag, 1992.

[8] Bertoldi, N., and Federico, M.: Statistical Models for Monolingual and Bilingual Information Retrieval. Information Retrieval, (7):51–70, 2004.

The Key to the First CLEF with Portuguese: Topics, Questions and Answers in CHAVE

Diana Santos and Paulo Rocha

Linguateca, Oslo node, SINTEF ICT, Norway
Diana.Santos@sintef.no, Paulo.Rocha@di.uminho.pt

Abstract. In this paper we report the work done by Linguateca in order to add Portuguese to two tracks of CLEF, namely the *ad hoc* IR and the QA tracks. We start with a brief description of Linguateca's aims and the way we see CLEF from the standpoint of Portuguese language processing. We then comment on several interesting problems that emerged during our work and offer some suggestions for improvement, and finally raise some possibly controversial points for discussion.

1 The Role of Linguateca

The creation of Linguateca (http://www.linguateca.pt/) originated from the realization that there were too few resources for the processing of Portuguese, and that the large language resource centres such as LDC or ELRA could not take a primary role in the deployment of such resources, given their world-wide priorities. In addition, there was little sense of community among practitioners of Portuguese language processing (PLP): the PLP community had scarcely met; groups were not only scattered around Portugal and Brazil, but they were located in different departments with different practices – linguistics, IR, AI, NLP...; there was no tradition of sharing results and comparing approaches. Therefore, Linguateca's main aims (which we call the IRE model) are to inform, create and disseminate resources and promote evaluation contests (or campaigns) dealing with Portuguese.

Linguateca thus concentrates on Portuguese. To improve PLP, we believe that one must start by studying the Portuguese language and comparing the state of the art of tools developed for Portuguese, in tasks that deal with Portuguese, evaluated by native speakers of Portuguese – a language-specific bias as emphasized in [1]. We have, therefore, created resources for Portuguese, such as the large annotated corpus CETEMPúblico [2] and the Floresta Sintá(c)tica treebank [3], and organized evaluation contests dealing with Portuguese only [4].

There is no contradiction, however, in Linguateca joining CLEF, the most international of all evaluation contests (at least as far as the number of different languages and participants from different countries are concerned), given that the primary aim of CLEF is to foster **crosslingual** information retrieval. Thus, whether to evaluate querying a multilingual collection in Portuguese, or querying a Portuguese collection in another language, CLEF is the place to go. Instead

C. Peters et al. (Eds.): CLEF 2004, LNCS 3491, pp. 821–832, 2005.

of copying or adapting something borrowed from another language to deal with Portuguese, we have added Portuguese, so that people primarily concerned with other languages may be encouraged to process Portuguese as well.

In any case, at present, for certain monolingual tasks, there would not be enough participants to organize one evaluation contest on its own: only two monolingual groups participated in the Portuguese QA task. Nevertheless, the QA@CLEF coordinators added Portuguese without too much work. This shows that joining a circle of international experts in order to define a particular task precisely is a sensible way to begin, even if one disagrees with some of the choices taken.

In fact, although we have publicly voiced the opinion that an all-Portuguese-speaking organization would give more weight to Portuguese-specific matters and more influence to participants dealing with Portuguese – and hence one should ideally start with Portuguese-only evaluation contests [5] –, this opinion must be weighed against the organizational relief of having general matters coordinated centrally.

Also, the only unbiased way to assess whether it was worthwhile for the Portuguese language processing community to participate in CLEF was to try it out, and we now believe it was worthwhile. This participation provided clear deadlines for building resources that otherwise would have taken us much longer to complete, and a lot was learned from working together with the teams for other languages.

As a result of our participation in CLEF, we have now released the CHAVE collection (www.linguateca.pt/CHAVE/), containing PÚBLICO newspaper's collection, the IR topics and relevance judgements, and the questions and answers created for the QA campaign.

2 Tasks

Portuguese was included in the Monolingual (non-English)/Bilingual/ Multilingual Information Retrieval (also called *ad hoc*) tasks and QA track. QA is, in fact, conceptually a more advanced IR task and the communities involved were different: not only the groups and systems that competed (at least for Portuguese) but the organizational apparatus and decisions.

The workload involved was also differently distributed: for IR, the topic creation and discussion was relatively light, but the evaluation of the results was demanding. On the contrary, the preparation and translation of the questions and answers, as well as finding justifications for them, represented the bulk of work for QA@CLEF, while evaluation was light and even intellectually rewarding.

In the following sections, we discuss in some detail our participation in each of the tracks. We avoid gory details and lengthy descriptions of issues which can only be fully apprehended by speakers of Portuguese (see [6] for this), trying instead to produce an interesting summary of our difficulties and remaining doubts, as well as provide some guidance to newcomers to the (CLEF) field.

2.1 IR Topic Preparation

The main issue in the ad-hoc topic preparation was to come up with information needs that could be both representative of natural topics of interest for a Portuguese speaker, and relevant for an international (European) observer as well.

International vs. National. According to the ad-hoc track coordinator's directives, a tripartite division should be aimed at: one third should cover international events (the world at large), another cover European news, and another third, language or country-specific subjects. This was a rule of thumb for suggesting initial candidates; then, all topics were checked by all language groups and a final common decision was taken, based mainly on coverage in different collections. It would be interesting to assess how the distribution of the final topics appears from each language standpoint.

In fact, as regards "internationality", it is not always clear whether some events are world-wide, European or just Portuguese (in fact, this does not depend on the event itself, but on its media coverage). It was an enlightening experience to check other groups' topics as well as to learn about the relative importance of the Portuguese topics that we expected to be reported elsewhere. There are studies on the relative impact of the Romance languages in the web as a whole [7], and we suggest doing something similar: to measure, for each foreign collection, the degree of "Portugueseness" to be expected. Unfortunately, we did not have access to the collections in the other languages at the time of topic preparation, so this must be postponed.

Another Classification of Topics. We suggest a different classification of topics: cyclic events; once-only events; states of broader events; impact measures; and atemporal subjects. Examples of the latter kinds[1] follow.

As for *states* (or sub-events) *of broader events*, "East Timor guerilla" or "civil war in Rwanda" can be considered as "states" of a larger war. The same is true for "Fight against AIDS in Africa" or "Russian-Finnish relations" (both subjects concerning a much larger period than 1995 alone).

Impact measures can be illustrated by topics such as: "Tourism information on the internet"; "Music in digital form"; "Prevention of human rabies in France"; "EU and the price of food". For this kind of topic, we are interested in how these subjects fare in news coverage in 1995, although the topic may have been raised by specific events taken up in (local) press. Nevertheless, a user may want to know about these topics in collections that cover other years.

Atemporal subjects are exemplified by: "Dam building", "The deaf and society", "Domestic fires" and, less straightforwardly, "Iranian cinema" or "Seal-fishing". One may argue that the latter can also be interpreted as states of a larger event (e.g. the whole history of Iranian cinema), or impact measures,

[1] For lack of space, we present only the topic titles, asking the readers to trust our judgement, although most of the title names, in isolation, could describe radically different information needs.

i.e., the user is looking for events concerning seal-fishing (like laws and debates) occurring in 1995. Still, we believe that searchers may be interested in knowing about seal-fishing or deaf people in society without a temporal grounding, while news covering "EU and the price of food" seems to make sense only at a particular time.

In any case, we suggest considering carefully whether these different kinds of topics, which we argue reflect different user needs, and consequently may even require different kinds of query applications, should have different evaluation practices (or not), and/or different forms of description (and narrative).

Different Answers in Different Collections. We believe considerably more attention should be given to this issue. To us, topics with different answers in different collections are the cases where CLIR and MLIR make the most sense from an arbitrary user's point of view: situations in which the addition of results provides genuinely more information. Apparently there were not many of these topics in this year's campaign[2], but the (related) QA@CLEF campaign provided good examples: take the case of "Name some X", with X "person charged of paedophilia", or "what is the masonry?", in which different facets – and facts – about this organization in different countries might be uncovered in a multilingual collection.

This illustrates the strikingly fuzzy borderline between IR and QA. QA can be seen as a request for more precision about a topic, and some topics were even stated as questions. In fact, Magnini *et al.* [8] even report that the original set of questions used in QA@CLEF 2003 was inspired by the topics of the previous year's ad hoc competition. Having prepared the material for both, we cannot help stressing how both tracks are conceptually the same, despite testing different types of systems.

Topic Wording. Although we have not received any specific instructions on this subject, we attempted to profusely word the topics, distributing paraphrases among title names, topic description and topic narrative in Portuguese.

Using as many synonyms and wording variants as possible, systems would get (almost) a synonym-expansion capability for free, if they used all material provided. For example, in topic C249 below, *dez mil metros* and *10.000 m* are alternative ways of stating "ten thousand meters" in Portuguese. And *campeã* (champion), *vencedora* (winner) and *venceu* (won) are closely related, but different ways of expressing the concept at stake.

[2] "Sports women and doping", "Sales of the Sophie's world book" and "Change of sex operations" are possible ones, but "Multibillionaires", although apparently possible to find everywhere, are not evenly distributed. Incidentally, and no matter their seemingly general character, atemporal subjects are not necessarily also a-locational: "Seal-fishing", and "Avalanche disasters" are not often discussed in Portuguese media, for geographical reasons, and the same applies to topics on bowling or haunted buildings, suggested respectively by the Finnish and British teams. Apparently, these are, for cultural reasons, simply uninteresting subjects to Portuguese readers of newspapers.

```
    <num> C249 </num>
    <PT-title> Campeã dos 10.000 metros femininos </PT-title>
    <PT-desc> Quem venceu os 10.000 metros femininos nos Mundiais de Atletismo
em Gotemburgo? </PT-desc>
    <PT-narr> Documentos relevantes devem nomear a vencedora da final dos dez
mil metros nos Mundiais de Atletismo em Gotemburgo. </PT-narr>
```

2.2 QA Preparation

Preparing the resources for the QA track presented another kind of challenge. Very briefly, our job was as follows: we had to create 100 natural Portuguese questions with answers, indicate an associated document where the answers could be found; translate them into English; and translate 600 other questions (with answers) from English (and/or from the original language) into Portuguese. Furthermore, for 100 of those we had to check the answer in our collection and provide it.

Each subtask was far from straightforward, the main challenges being: For our questions, (a) coming up with a set of not too difficult, natural questions with a straightforward answer; (b) identifying clearly the answer(s), finding all plausible answers in our collection; (c) providing a natural English translation with (if possible) the same presuppositions of the Portuguese one. For the questions coming from other groups (which we had both in English and in the original language), the main challenges were: (a) translating the question into Portuguese so that it made (some) sense to a Portuguese speaker; (b) translating the answers as close as possible to the answers found in our collection (in case there were any), and adding other answers (either more correct in case a wrong answer had been supplied, or more Portuguese-like as regards measures or spelling); and (c) in case no answer could be found in our collection, trying to provide suitable translations of both answers and questions.

What is a Natural Question?. A "natural" question is something that eludes a precise definition, and has often been discussed in the context of QA systems. In general, the solution is to stick to a particular user's model. We just mention here a few cases that we have not seen documented elsewhere.

If a given role is occupied by a woman, should the natural question be in the feminine or in the masculine (neutral in Portuguese if you don't know the gender)[3]? We decided to use the easier kind in our set, as shown in question `337 F PERSON Quem é a ministra do Ambiente alemã?`, where *ministra* is the feminine form. Curiously, all other groups used the masculine form in their translation of this question.

[3] In fact, the feminine form would only be natural if one knew the minister was a woman. This might have occurred if the word minister (in the feminine) had been mentioned before, and the user wanted to know who she was. A politically correct asker might use *Quem é o ministro ou ministra do Ambiente?* (who is the male minister or the female minister of the environment?) but we strongly doubt such users will ever amount to the majority of Portuguese speakers.

Another concern was the following: Should one use the informal way of posing questions in (European) Portuguese, or suppose that normal users of a QA system will not use it, given that it implies more typing? We tried to address this issue by using both ways. So, some questions were provided featuring the emphatic "é que", and others not.

Question Classification. In addition to coming up with questions, we had to classify them, according to the track instructions [12]. This turned out not to be as meaningful as expected. The classification was to be done according to the semantic category of the right answer (person, location, manner, object, measure...), but this in turn had little correlation with the linguistic properties of both question and answer.

In fact, questions `558 F OTHER Qual a nacionalidade do tenista Sergi Bruguera? SEARCH[espanhol]` and `582 F LOCATION De que país é a escritora Taslima Nasreen? SEARCH[Bangladesh]` are after precisely the same kind of information (What is X's nationality? and Which country is X from?), but have been classified differently.

Also, one might argue that, although question `688 F OTHER Qual o endereço da Livraria Barata? LING-940102-050 Av. de Roma, 11` asks for a postal address, classified as OTHER, an address is ultimately a linguistic specification of a LOCATION, and should thus be classified as such.

Conversely, some questions are classified as MANNER when one is looking for causes. "How does cancer begin?" can be interpreted as what is the cause (or what precedes what). Likewise, the most frequent kind of MANNER questions were related to <u>cause</u> of death.[4]

To further prove our point, note that other "manner" questions such as "How is indocyanine angiography performed?" have been rightly translated as "what is..." in a number of different languages, showing that the kind of answer is not a semantic invariant – or that there were problems with the "semantic" classification.

Definition questions – which were introduced in the 2004 campaign – are, in our opinion, especially tricky. Consider question `693 D PERSON Quem é Guilherme da Fonseca? LING-940127-152 juiz do Tribunal Constitucional` (Who is X? with answer = supreme court judge). This is the same as asking what is X's profession, which should then be classified as F OTHER...[5]

Therefore, we believe that a more objective way of classifying questions, such as the one presented in [9], is preferable. Alternatively, one could classify questions according to the kind of linguistic entity expected as answer, using categories like "proper name", "common name", "toponym", on a par with "definition" (which is a kind of answer, not a real world object).

---

[4] Not all answers to "How did X die?" had to do with cause. One was "In strange conditions"! Again, something rather hard to conceive as MANNER.

[5] Incidentally, in order to provide a more accurate answer, one should state "one (of several) judges". In other words, the indefinite article should not have been left out.

Presuppositions Abound. How many presuppositions should be allowed in a natural (as opposed to a tricky) question? Looking for the answer to question `327 F PERSON Como se chama a filha do líder chinês Deng Xiaoping?`, what is Deng Xiaoping's daughter called?, we found out that he had not one, but two daughters ("Deng Rong" in the original Dutch collection, and "Deng Nan" in ours). Apparently, therefore, this question was ill-posed.

In general, anyway, most questions presuppose that it is possible to share the referent with the reader, as we point out in the next section, on definitions.

More against "Definitions". Definition questions have always the lurking presupposition that there is no one (in the case of persons) or no other organization (in the case of organizations) bearing the same name. This is generally not possible to ascertain. In fact, asking who Fernando Gomes (the mayor of Porto in 1995) is, we found, in the very same collection, a reference to a football player of the same name. We leave the reader to try to find out how many organizations called GIA exist (in all languages covered in QA@CLEF).

A definition is the most complex question one can ask. To give answers to "what is the masonry?" or "what is indocyanine angiography?", one needs to be an expert in the field, and still consider carefully how to produce an appropriate rendering. Of course, if one is querying a collection of authoritative texts (and, especially, didactic material), it may be possible to automatically extract definition-like passages. But in a newspaper collection, it is doubtful whether more than `is-a` relations (which are not definitions) can be extracted.

The "definitions" as described by the CLEF organization have still other flaws:

1. They often overlap linguistically with factoid questions, cf. F(actoid) "Who is the pope?" D(efinition) "Who is João Paulo II?" In free text, it is often difficult to know whether linguistic expressions are attributive or appositive, and, in fact, in most cases both questions (and corresponding answers) make sense.
2. "Definitions" of a person are in fact requirements for a specific kind information: questions about the most prominent role of a particular person, the one that allows the use of the definite article, or questions about his profession and nationality (in case of artists).
3. "Definitions" of organizations are very often elicitations of the full name of something that is conveyed as an acronym, and should be called "expansions", or proper (anaphoric or cataphoric) antecedents.

Therefore, we propose giving more attention to the user's (or system's) goals in order to decide on what can sensibly be called a request for definition, as opposed to questions of the kind "Who occupies the *role* Y?"or "What *profession* does X have?" (which idiomatically is expressed by *Quem é X*?).

Getting Correct Answers: Articles, Gender and Redundancy. Another interesting observation is that it is not always obvious what the answer(s) to be claimed as the golden set should be, even if we are the question's authors. Should the answer be grammatically correct? In that case, prepositions are required in most cases, but they have consistently been left out. A more specifically Portuguese case is example 647: the proper name could have been preceded by the Portuguese article *a*, meaning "the Petrogal". This would, however, probably confuse the other groups in the translation task too much, and we expected that most participating systems would throw articles away anyway. (That this should not be done lightly is illustrated by the two possible distinct questions *O que são os EUA?* and *O que é a EUA?* – the first having as right answer *os Estados Unidos da América* (USA) and the second *a European University Association.*)

In example 558 above, there are also two ways of answering the question: either *espanhola*, modifying the feminine noun *nacionalidade* (nationality), or *espanhol*, masculine (modifying Sergi Bruguera). We used the second, since this was the form present in our collection.

Finally, another concern as to the proper specification of the golden answer is how much redundancy is acceptable. In the case of the first answer of `443 F MEASURE Que proporção do seu volume de negócios fez a HP na Europa? 1 SEARCH[um terço do volume de negócios do grupo] 2 SEARCH[35 por cento]`, *volume de negócios* was repeated in order to translate the original answer (which specified "of the group"). In `588 F MEASURE Quantos empregados tem o grupo Warburg? SEARCH[4.472 pessoas]`, on the other hand, the word *pessoas* (persons) in the answer about how many employees is quite uninformative.

Translation is Hard: Idiomaticness and Presuppositions. Not surprising, not every question we came up with was equally easy to render in English. In some cases, we simply made up what seemed to us the best translation, like "Party of National Solidarity" for *Partido da Solidariedade Nacional.*

In addition, not all presuppositions are easy to maintain: consider the possible question *Como se chamava a amante de Mussolini?* which could be appropriately rendered, in English, by "What was Mussolini's mistress called?". If one had used the expression "Mussolini's lover", however, the information that we were looking for a woman would be lost. On the other hand, since "minister" is gender neutral in English, it would have been advisable, for most questions, not to add gender, thus rendering both *ministra* and *ministro* as "minister".[6]

Translation of Ungrounded Arbitrary Fragments. The translation of other groups' questions, especially when there were no hits in our collection, or when the question seemed about unfamiliar subjects or contexts, also caused us problems. In question `293 F MANNER Como se garante a cobrança de sanções? SEARCH[pelo sistema de notificação de multas através de edictos]`, we had no idea of which kind of sanctions were mentioned, nor to whom the indeterminate *se* refers: government? tax authorities? sports club? Likewise, no clue was given as to who is supposed to pay them.

[6] Yet, one can easily conceive of questions which had to state gender: who was the first female president of Iceland? *Quem foi a primeira presidente da Islândia?*

Translating the answers that came with the questions was even worse. In fact, it was in general a major headache, not only because of the reasons already discussed, but because it was not evident why some of the answers (paraphrases) had to be translated at all. And the shorter the units, the more difficult to translate them. Consider `172 D ORGANIZATION O que é a Amnistia Internacional?`

```
1 SEARCH[grupo preocupado com os direitos humanos]
2 SEARCH[organização de direitos humanos sediada em Londres]
3 SEARCH[organização de direitos dos prisioneiros sediada em Londres]
4 SEARCH[um grupo privado de voluntários à escala mundial dedicado a
proteger prisioneiros políticos e outras vítimas de violações dos
direitos humanos]
```

Answer 3, for example, sounds awkward, while we could concoct more precise and interesting definitions of AI (if one were after one gold standard with the "right" answers in Portuguese).

Generally, we tried to match the most similar answer form(s) to the answers in our collection, and put those as "translations", since we did not see the point of doing literal translations that sounded far-fetched. Still, in many cases (especially in the cases of subjects not mentioned in the PÚBLICO collection), we had to engage in the translation of answers that did not really feel adequate, like in "Tell me a reason for teenage suicides", some of the answers to "Who are the Simpsons?", "How can you save energy?", "How do they plan to carry out family planning in Peru?", "What does the company Victorinox produce?". Example 480 shows how little informative, and possibly even erroneously translated, can be the result of this process. `480 F OBJECT Que produz a MCC?`

```
1 SEARCH[o automóvel Micro Compact Car]
2 SEARCH[o "carro urbano do futuro" de dois lugares]
3 SEARCH[o carro compacto Smart]
4 SEARCH[veículos]
5 SEARCH[Swatchmobile]
6 SEARCH[carro urbano]
```

In fact, MCC salespeople may come up with different ways of describing the products in Portugal. In addition, it seems totally arbitrary to keep in the translation the fact that in some cases the word "car" is used and in others not, just because it happened to occur that way in the original collection.

Irrelevant Questions. Finally, not all questions selected by the other groups make sense for Portuguese speakers to ask, as examples `174 F OTHER O que significa Forza Italia!? 1 SEARCH[Força, Itália!] 2 SEARCH[Força Itália]` and `202 F OTHER Qual o acrónimo da Amnistia Internacional? SEARCH[AI]` should make obvious. In [10], similar cases are mentioned for German.

In fact, one might want to ask about acronyms in another language, given that an international organization can have different acronyms (such as NATO and OTAN) in different languages. This raises, in any case, the question of whether one was supposed to translate the original "Amnesty International" as *Amnistia Internacional*, or not, in question 202.

3 Preparing and Using the Collection

The Portuguese collection, which we called CHAVE (the Portuguese translation of French *clef*) was created using the same texts (restricted to years 1994-1995) that were used to build the CETEMPúblico corpus (for a description of the building process, see [11]). In CETEMPúblico, for legal reasons, the documents were split into extracts of about two paragraphs each and shuffled so that no reconstruction of the full articles were possible. For CLEF, however, PÚBLICO allowed us to distribute the full texts, so our task was solely to adapt the original programs to the new format, while solving also some of the problems reported in [4]. A few cases, mostly having to do with the proper separation of documents, were impossible to solve automatically, and we had to perform a limited manual clean-up. We know that some minor imperfections still persist, though.

We ended up with a collection of 106,821 documents (348Mb). Ideally, each document contains a single article in the newspaper. However, some "articles", from sections like "Last news", gather several different short news about quite different subjects, which may harm the performance of some IR systems. The documents are only marked with date and kind of section (as provided by the newspaper). Neither titles nor authors have been marked as such, so they appear as free text, but, to help systems that rely on titles (and would thus filter authors), we also provided a list of probable authors at our website.

We had no IR system or QA engine available. We therefore encoded the collection in the IMS Corpus Workbench [12], a powerful suite of programs designed to deal with large corpora, efficiently handling several kinds of annotations. For each document we encoded an unique ID, composed from its date and section), and used the corpus query processor (CQP) to retrieve concordances showing the ID of the document they occurred in.

So, checking whether the topics proposed by the other groups existed in our collection was considerably simplified: For example, to find whether we had any document referring to Sosnovyj Bor, we would look for `"Sosn.+" "Bor"`, allowing for variations in orthography.[7] We could also check which documents referred to a minor earthquake in Nice in the dates provided.

For QA, CQP proved useful in no less than four stages: while searching for possible questions and their answers; while translating the other groups questions and their answers (checking the more usual Portuguese forms); while selecting the 100 additional questions among those, through searching for the translation

---

[7] As anyone dealing with real text is aware, there are often several spelling variants, even within a single language, especially if the texts have not been proofread. This is a problem particularly with less used foreign names: the Icelandic capital, Reykjavík, appears in six different forms in CETEMPúblico; similarly, Antwerp is often written as *Anvers* in texts whose original was published in French, despite having a name universally used in Portuguese, *Antuérpia*. Also common is the unstable use of the dash: prime minister can equally frequently appear as *primeiro-ministro* or *primeiro ministro*, and variable capitalization, e.g. "in Northern China" is rendered both as *no Norte da China* or *no norte da China*.

of the answers; and while evaluating the correctness of the answers provided by the participant groups.

4 Concluding Remarks

One aim of this paper was to describe some of the difficulties in creating the topics and the questions for the CLEF campaign of 2004, with a view to helping future groups when adding a new language, but also in order to suggest improvements for future editions. In fact, some of the ideas stated here, especially for what concerns QA may be relatively controversial, but we use this opportunity to stimulate discussion on the subject in the CLEF community.

Our main conclusion is that, in general, more reflection and study should be given to the process of selecting topics and questions, in order to maximize the utility of the collection. We feel it is extremely important to look at topics and questions really posed by actual users, also to ascertain how difficult and how frequent are the test data we have created, to eventually evaluate our work (and that of the CLEF organizers as a whole).

Having access to all collections, one might (collaboratively) study them and find out a) in which (subject) areas the information is conveyed by all languages, b) which areas exist where local information can be relevant for people of other languages, and c) areas (maybe the most interesting) where there is complementariness in the collections.

As regards QA categorization, we argued that the present classification does not seem very useful, especially because there may be different ways to look for the same information, and we also suggested removing definition questions, which seem to require a passage and hence are not good examples of QA with unique and consensual answers. We furthermore suspect that quite different subjects are asked by people looking at newspaper text, and some missing question types may be quite relevant. A case in point are confirmation questions[8] – people often want to confirm what they think they know, instead of asking about something they know nothing of.

We also suggest to integrating more closely the work for IR and QA: On the one hand, it would be interesting to submit all questions as IR topics and see whether IR systems could provide the documents where the answers could be found. Conversely, it would be interesting to create a set of questions from the topic description and/or narrative and look for them in the QA exercise. More integration between both tasks might shed light on the current state of the art of both kinds of systems.

Acknowledgements. We are grateful to José Vítor Malheiros and PÚBLICO for their material, and to Luís Costa and Nuno Cardoso for valuable comments on previous versions. We acknowledge grant POSI/PLP/43931/2001 from the Portuguese Fundação para a Ciência e Tecnologia, co-financed by POSI.

[8] Such as "Is Oslo the capital of Norway?", "Is Athens the first city where the modern Olympic games took place?", "Did James Joyce write *Finnegans Wake*?"

References

1. Santos, Diana: Toward Language-specific Applications. Machine Translation Vol.14 (1999) 83–112.
2. Santos, Diana, Rocha, Paulo: Evaluating CETEMPúblico, a free resource for Portuguese. In: Proceedings of the 39th Annual Meeting of the Association for Computational Linguistics. Toulouse, July 2001, 442–449.
3. Afonso, Susana, Bick, Eckhard, Haber, Renato, Santos, Diana: "Floresta sintá(c)tica": a treebank for Portuguese. In Rodríguez & Araujo (eds.): Proceedings of LREC 2002, Las Palmas, May 2002, ELRA, 1698–1703.
4. Santos, Diana, Costa, Luís, Rocha, Paulo: Cooperatively evaluating Portuguese morphology. In: Mamede et al. (eds.). Computational Processing of the Portuguese Language, 6th PROPOR, Springer (2003) 259–266.
5. Santos, Diana, Rocha, Paulo: AvalON: uma iniciativa de avaliação conjunta para o português. In: A. Mendes & T. Freitas (orgs.), Actas do XVIII Encontro da Associação Portuguesa de Linguística, Porto, October 2002, APL (2003) 693–704.
6. Rocha, Paulo, Santos, Diana: CLEF: Abrindo a porta à participação internacional em RI do português. In: Santos, Diana (ed.), Avaliação conjunta: um novo paradigma no processamento computacional da língua portuguesa, in print.
7. Latin Union: L4: The fourth study on Languages and the Internet. http://www.funredes.org/LC/english/L4.html.
8. Magnini, B., Romagnoli, S., Vallin, A., Herrera, J., Peñas, A., Peinado, V., Verdejo, F., de Rijke, M.: Creating the DISEQuA Corpus: a Test Set for Multilingual Question Answering. In: C. Peters (ed.), Working Notes for the CLEF 2003 Workshop, August 2003, Trondheim. http://clef.isti.cnr.it/publications.html.
9. Costa, Luís: First evaluation of Esfinge, a question-answering system for Portuguese. This volume.
10. Magnini et al.: Overview of the CLEF 2004 Multilingual Question Answering Track. This volume.
11. Rocha, Paulo, Santos, Diana: CETEMPúblico: Um corpus de grandes dimensões de linguagem jornalística portuguesa. In: M.G.V. Nunes (ed.). Actas do V Encontro para o processamento computacional da língua portuguesa escrita e falada. PROPOR2000, Atibaia-SP (November 2000), 131–140.
12. Christ, Oliver, Schulze, Bruno M, Hofmann, Anja, Koenig, Esther: The IMS Corpus Workbench: Corpus Query Processor (CQP): User's Manual. Institute for Natural Language Processing, University of Stuttgart, March 8, 1999 (CQP V2.2).

How Do Named Entities Contribute to Retrieval Effectiveness?

Thomas Mandl and Christa Womser-Hacker

University of Hildesheim, Information Science,
Marienburger Platz 22, D-31141 Hildesheim, Germany
mandl@uni-hildesheim.de
womser@uni-hildesheim.de

Abstract. The search for features in topics and queries relevant for the performance in information retrieval is an important strategy for system optimization. Named entities in topics are a significant feature contributing to the quality of the retrieval results. In this contribution, we present an analysis on the correlation between the number of named entities present in a topic formulation and the final retrieval quality for these topics by retrieval systems within CLEF. The analysis includes the results of CLEF 2004. We found that a medium positive correlation exists for German, English and Spanish topics. Furthermore, the effect of the document or target language on the retrieval quality is also investigated.

1 Introduction

Within the Cross Language Evaluation Forum (CLEF), various strategies are employed in order to improve retrieval systems. CLEF allows the identification of successful approaches, algorithms and tools in CLIR [1].

We believe that the knowledge and effort dedicated to large scale evaluation studies can be exploited beyond the optimization of individual systems. The amount of data created by organizers and participants remains a valuable source of knowledge awaiting exploration. Many lessons can still be learned from evaluation initiatives such as CLEF, TREC [2], INEX [3], NTCIR [4] or IMIRSEL [5].

Ultimately, further criteria and metrics for the evaluation of search and retrieval methods may be detected. This could lead to improved algorithms, quality criteria, resources and tools in cross language information retrieval [6]. This general research approach is illustrated in figure 1. The identification of patterns in the systems' performance for topics with specific items may lead to improvements in system development. For example, one analysis showed that topics can be automatically classified as monolithic, structured and diffuse by analyzing the similarity density of positive examples [7]. Another approach tries to identify the level of ambiguity of topics [8].

C. Peters et al. (Eds.): CLEF 2004, LNCS 3491, pp. 833 – 842, 2005.

Our current analysis concentrates on named entities within the topics of CLEF. Named entities frequently occur in CLEF as part of the topic formulation. Table 1 gives an overview.

Table 1. Name of named entities in the CLEF topics

CLEF year	Number of topics	Total number of named entities	Average number of named entities in topics
2000	40	52	1.14
2001	50	60	1.20
2002	50	86	1.72
2003	60	97	1.62
2004	50	72	1.44

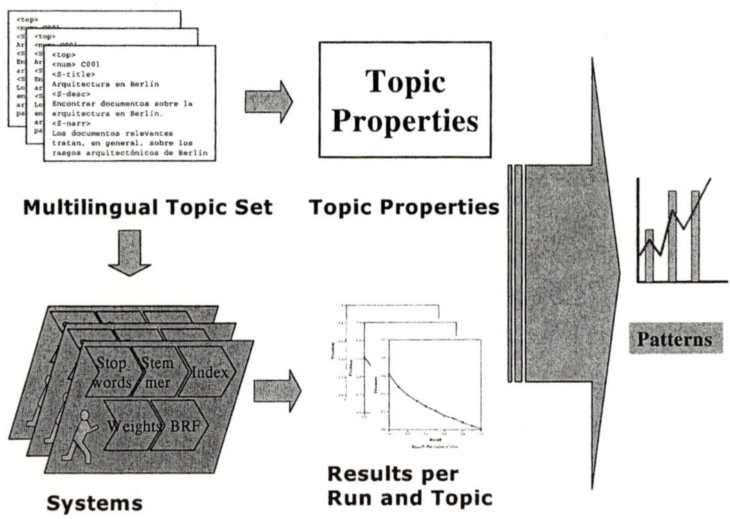

Fig. 1. Overview of the approach

The large number of named entities in the topic set shows that they are a subject worth studying. The large number may be due to the fact that the document corpus for CLEF consists of newspaper texts. We can also observe an increase of named entities per topic in 2002 compared to 2001. Because of the effect of named entities on retrieval performance [9], the number of named entities needs to be carefully monitored. Table 2 shows how the named entities are distributed over groups with different numbers of named entities and shows the tasks analyzed in this paper.

2 Named Entities in Topics and Retrieval Performance

In a previous study presented at CLEF in 2003, a correlation between the number of named entities present in topics and the systems' performance for these topics was shown [10]. In this paper, the analysis is extended to include Spanish as a topic language and several monolingual tasks. In our earlier analysis, the relation was shown for English and German. By including Spanish, the positive effect of named entities can also be shown for another language. By including monolingual tasks, we are able to compare the strength of the effect in cross- and monolingual retrieval tasks.

Table 2. Overview of named entities in CLEF tasks

CLEF year	Task	Topic language	Nr. runs	Topics without named entities	Topics with one or two named entities	Topics with three or more than three named entities
2002	Mono	German	21	12	21	17
2002	Mono	Spanish	28	11	18	21
2002	Bi	German	4	12	21	17
2002	Multi	German	4	12	21	17
2002	Bi	English	51	14	21	15
2002	Multi	English	32	14	21	15
2003	Mono	English	11	8	14	6
2003	Mono	Spanish	38	6	33	21
2003	Multi	Spanish	10	6	33	21
2003	Mono	German	30	9	40	10
2003	Bi	German	24	9	40	10
2003	Multi	German	1	9	40	10
2003	Bi	English	8	9	41	10
2003	Multi	English	74	9	41	10
2004	Multi	English	34	16	23	11

Named entities were intellectually assessed according a well balanced schema [11]. The performance of the systems was extracted from the appendix of the CLEF proceedings. The average precision for a topic is calculated as the average precision of all systems for a individual topic. From the average precision for a topic, we can calculate the average of all topics which contain n named entities. Figure 2, 3 and 4 show the average precision for topics with n named entities for tasks in CLEF 3 (2002), CLEF 4 (2003) and CLEF 5 (2004) respectively.

In the figures we can observe that monolingual tasks generally result in higher average precision than cross-lingual tasks. The average precision of the runs is higher, the more named entities are present in the topics.

The relation previously observed for German and English can also be seen for Spanish.

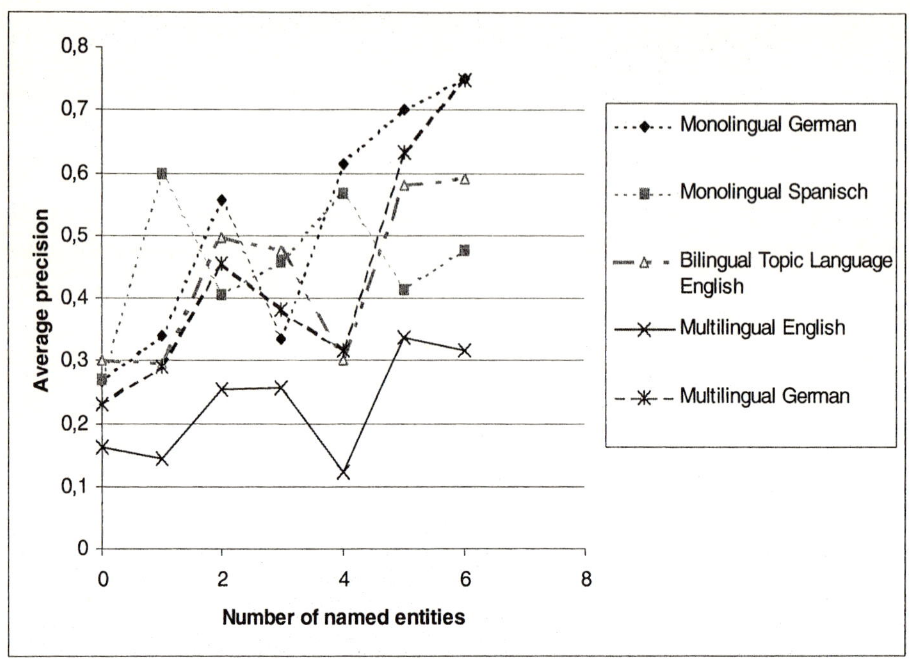

Fig 2. Average precision for topics with n named entities for CLEF 3 (in 2002)

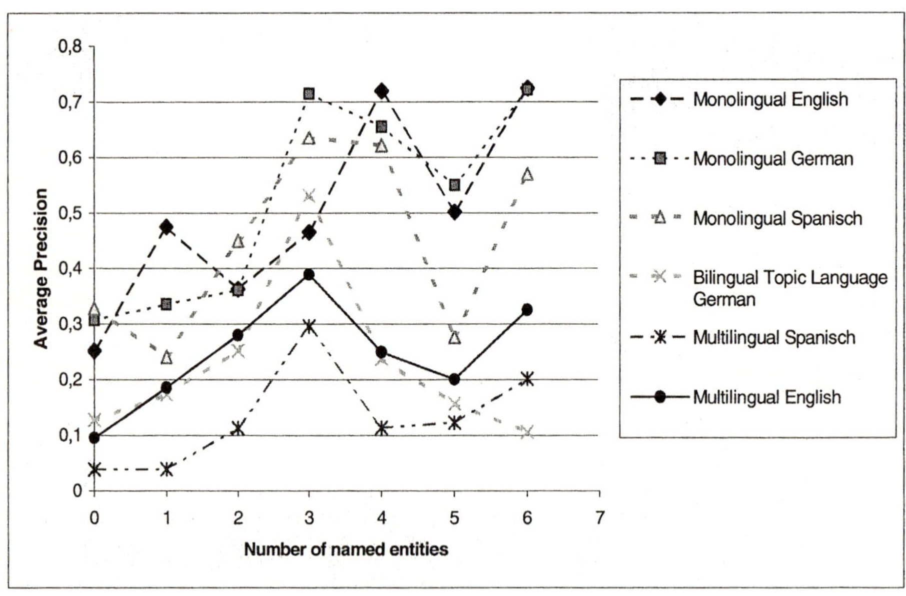

Fig. 3. Average precision for topics with n named entities for CLEF 4 (in 2003)

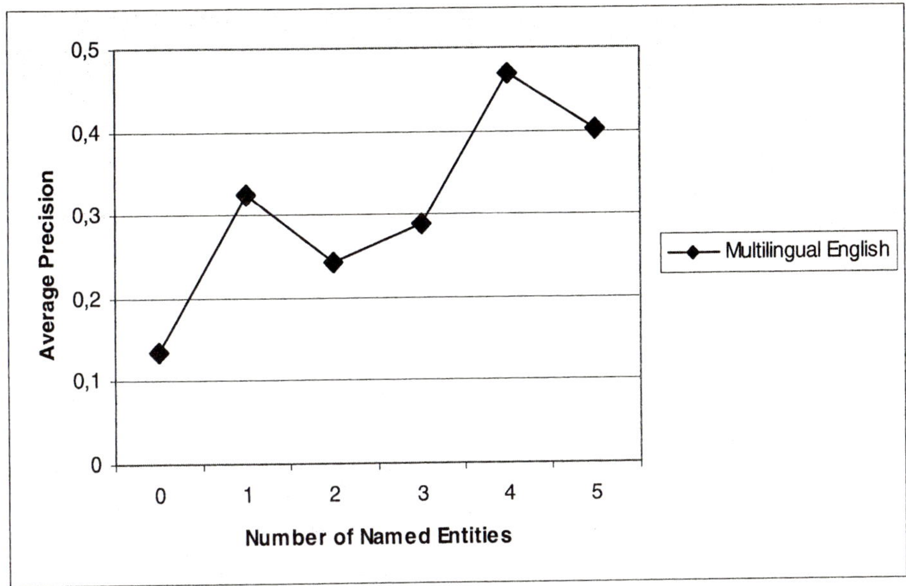

Fig. 4. Average precision for topics with n named entities for CLEF 5 (in 2004)

We also calculate the correlation between the number of named entities and the average precision per topic for each of the tasks. The results are presented in the tables 3 , 4 and 5.

Table 3. Correlation between the number of named entities in topic and the average system performance per topic for tasks in CLEF 3 (2002)

Monolingual German	Monolingual Spanish	Bilingual Topic Language English	Multilingual German	Multilingual English
0.449	0.207	0.399	0.428	0.294

Table 4. Correlation between the number of named entities in topic and the average system performance per topic for tasks in CLEF 4 (2003)

Monolingual German	Monolingual Spanisch	Monolingual English	Bilingual Topic Language German	Multilingual Spanish	Multilingual English
0.372	0.385	0.158	0.213	0.213	0.305

Table 5. Correlation between the number of named entities in topic and the average system performance per topic in CLEF 5 (2004)

Multilingual English
0.33

We can observe that the correlation is in most cases higher for the monolingual task. That would mean, that named entities help systems more in monolingual retrieval than in cross-lingual retrieval. However, English seems to be an exception in CLEF 4 (2003), because the correlation is almost twice as strong in the multilingual task.

3 Potential for Optimization Based on Named Entities

While the overall tendency to better retrieval quality can be shown some systems perform even better for topics with many named entities while others deliver better retrieval quality for the topics without named entities. The systems vary in their performance with respect to named entities. The performance of systems varies within the three classes of topics based on the number of named entities. We distinguished three classes of topics, (a) the first class with no proper names called *none*, (b) the second class with one and two named entities called *few* and (c) one class with three or more named entities called *lots*.

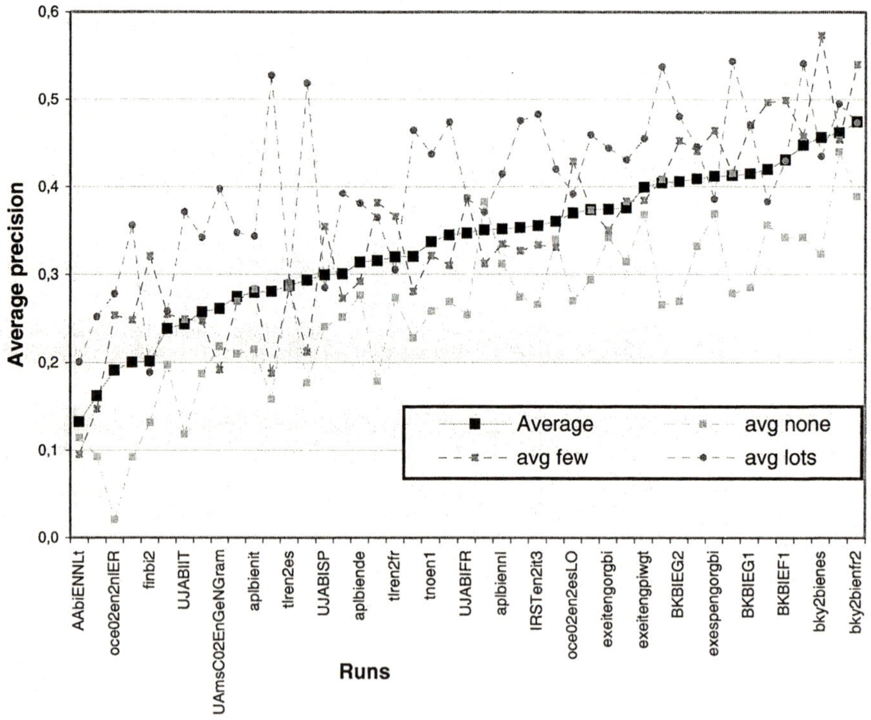

Fig. 5. Performance variation for runs in CLEF 2002 (task bilingual, topic language English)

The patterns of the systems are strikingly different for the three classes. Exemplarily, this effect is shown for one task in figure 5. As a consequence, there seems to be potential to improve system by fusion based on the number of named entities in a topic. Many systems already apply fusion techniques.

Based on our results we propose a simple fusion rule. First, the number of named entities is determined for each topic. Subsequently, this topic is channeled to the system with the best performance for this named entity class. The best system is a combination of at most three runs. Each category of topics is answered by the optimal system within a group of systems for that number of named entities. The groups were selected from the original CLEF ranking of the runs in one task. We used a window of five runs. That means, five neighboring runs by systems which perform similarly well overall are grouped and fused by our approach. Table 6 shows the improvement by the fusion based on the optimal selection of a system for each category of topics.

The highest levels of improvement are achieved for the topic language English. For 2002, we observe the highest improvement of 10% for the bilingual runs.

Table 6. Improvement through named entity based fusion

CLEF year	Run type	Topic language	Average. precision best run	Optimal average precision name fusion	Improvement over best run
2001	Bilingual	German	0.509	0.518	2%
2001	Multilingual	English	0.405	0.406	0%
2002	Bilingual	English	0.494	0.543	10%
2002	Multilingual	English	0.378	0.403	6.5%
2003	Bilingual	German	0.460	0.460	0%
2003	Bilingual	English	0.348	0.369	6.1%
2003	Multilingual	English	0.438	0.443	1.2%

This approach regards the systems as black boxes and requires no knowledge about the treatment of named entities within the systems. Considering the linguistic processing within the systems might be even more rewarding. Potentially, further analysis might reveal which approaches, which components and which parameters are especially suited for topics with and without named entities.

This analysis shows that the performance of retrieval systems can be optimized by channeling topics to the systems best appropriated for topics without, with one or two and with three and more names. Certainly, the application of this fusion on the past results approach is artificial and the number of topics in each subgroup is not sufficient for a statistically reliable result [12]. Furthermore, in our study, the number of named entities was determined intellectually. However, this mechanism can be easily implemented by using an automatic named entity recognizer. We intend to apply this fusion technique in an upcoming CLEF task as one element of the fusion framework MIMOR [10, 13].

4 Named Entities in Topics and Retrieval Performance for Target Languages

So far, our studies have been focused to the language of the initial topic which participants used for their retrieval efforts. Additionally, we have analyzed the effect of the target or document language. In this case, we cannot consider the multilingual tasks where there are several target languages. The monolingual tasks have already been analyzed in section 2 and are also considered here. Therefore, this analysis is targeted at bilingual retrieval tasks. We grouped all bilingual runs with English, German and Spanish as document language. The correlation between the number of named entities in the topics and the average precision of all systems for that topic was calculated. The average precision may be interpreted as the difficulty of the topic. Table 7 shows the results of this analysis.

Table 7. Correlation for target languages for CLEF 3 and 4

CLEF year	Task type	Target language	Number of runs	Correlation between number of named entities and average precision
2003	Mono	English	11	0.158
2002	Bi	English	16	0.577
2003	Bi	English	15	0.187
2002	Mono	German	21	0.372
2003	Mono	German	30	0.449
2002	Bi	German	13	0.443
2003	Bi	German	3	0.379
2002	Mono	Spanish	28	0.385
2003	Mono	Spanish	38	0.207
2002	Bi	Spanish	16	0.166
2003	Bi	Spanish	25	0.427

First, we can see a positive correlation for all tasks considered. Named entities support the retrieval also from the perspective of the document language. This results for the year 2002 may be a hint, that retrieval in English or German document collections profits more from named entities in the topic than Spanish. However, in 2003, the opposite is the case and English and Spanish switch. For German, there are only 3 runs in 2003. As a consequence, we cannot yet detect any language dependency for the effect of named entities on retrieval performance.

5 Outlook

In this paper a strong relation between named entities in topics and the performance of retrieval systems for these topics was confirmed. This finding allows us to formulate a hint for searchers and users of retrieval systems: Whenever you can think of a name related to your retrieval problem, consider including it in the query. In addition, our results encourage further analysis of other topic features. We are especially considering a part of speech (POS) analysis of the CLEF topics.

Furthermore, the results obtained need to be considered for the design of future evaluation studies. Topic construction is a crucial process for the success of an evaluation [14]. It also one important factor determining the adoption of scientific evaluation results in practice. Named entities need to be incorporated into the topics in a way that resembles real user behavior in the domain under question.

Acknowledgements

The first author was supported by a grant from the German Research Foundation (DFG, grant nr. MA 2411/3-1). We would like to thank Martin Braschler for providing the crucial data for our study. Furthermore, we acknowledge the work of several students from the University of Hildesheim who contributed to this analysis as part of their course work.

References

1. Braschler, M.; Peters, C.: Cross-Language Evaluation Forum: Objectives, Results, Achievements. In: Information Retrieval 2004 no. 7. pp. 7-31.
2. Voorhees, E.; Buckland, L. (eds.): The Eleventh Text Retrieval Conference (TREC 2002). NIST Special Publication 500-251. National Institute of Standards and Technology. Gaithersburg, Maryland. Nov. 2002. http://trec.nist.gov/pubs/trec11/t11_proceedings.html
3. Fuhr, N.: Initiative for the Evaluation of XML Retrieval (INEX) : INEX 2003 Workshop Proceedings, Dagstuhl, Germany, December 15-17, 2003. http://purl.oclc.org/NET/duett-07012004-093151
4. Oyama, K.; Ishida, E.; Kando, N. (eds.): NTCIR Workshop3 Proceedings of the Third NTCIR Workshop on research in Information Retrieval, Automatic Text Summarization and Question Answering (September 2001-October 2002) 2003 http://research.nii.ac.jp/ntcir/workshop/OnlineProceedings3/index.html
5. Downie, S.: Toward the Scientific Evaluation of Music Information Retrieval Systems. In: Intl Symposium on Music Information Retrieval. Washington, D.C., & Baltimore, USA 2003. http://ismir2003.ismir.net/papers/Downie.PDF
6. Schneider, R.; Mandl, T.; Womser-Hacker, C.: Workshop LECLIQ: Lessons Learned from Evaluation: Towards Integration and Transparency in Cross-Lingual Information Retrieval with a special Focus on Quality Gates. In: 4th International Conference on Language Resources and Evaluation (LREC) Lisbon, Portugal, May 24-30. Workshop Lessons Learned from Evaluation: Towards Transparency and Integration in Cross-Lingual Information Retrieval (LECLIQ). pp. 1-4
7. Evans, D.; Shanahan, J.; Sheftel, V.: Topic Structure Modeling. In: Proc. of the Annual Intl. ACM Conference on Research and Development in Information Retrieval (SIGIR '02) Tampere, Finland (2002) pp. 417-418
8. Cronen-Townsend, S.; Zhou, Y.; Croft, W.: Predicting Query Ambiguity. In: Proc. of the Annual Intl. ACM Conference on Research and Development in Information Retrieval (SIGIR '02) Tampere, Finland (2002) pp. 299-306

9. Mandl, T.; Womser-Hacker, C.: Analysis of Topic Features in Cross-Language Information Retrieval Evaluation. In: 4th International Conference on Language Resources and Evaluation (LREC) Lisbon, Portugal, May 24-30. Workshop Lessons Learned from Evaluation: Towards Transparency and Integration in Cross-Lingual Information Retrieval (LECLIQ). pp. 17-19
10. Mandl, T.; Womser-Hacker, C.: A Framework for long-term Learning of Topical User Preferences in Information Retrieval. In: New Library World 105 (5/6). 2004. pp. 184-195.
11. Sekine, S.; Sudo, K.; Nobata, C.: Extended Named Entity Hierarchy. In: Proceedings of Third International Conference on Language Resources and Evaluation (LREC 2002); Las Palmas, Canary Islands, Spain.
12. Voorhees, E.; Buckley, C.: The Effect of Topic Set Size on Retrieval Experiment Error. In: Proc. of the Annual Intl. ACM Conference on Research and Development in Information Retrieval (SIGIR '02) Tampere, Finland (2002) pp. 316-323
13. Hackl, R.; Kölle, R.; Mandl, T.; Ploedt, A.; Scheufen, J.-H.; Womser-Hacker, C.: Multilingual Retrieval Experiments with MIMOR at the University of Hildesheim. To appear in: Evaluation of Cross-Language Information Retrieval Systems. Proceedings CLEF 2003 Workshop. 2004 Springer [LNCS]
14. Womser-Hacker, C.: Multilingual Topic Generation within the CLEF 2001 Experiments. In: Peters, C.; Braschler, M.; Gonzalo, J.; Kluck, M. (eds.): Evaluation of Cross-Language Information Retrieval Systems. Springer [LNCS 2406] (2002) pp. 389-393

Author Index

Lecture Notes in Computer Science

For information about Vols. 1–3492

please contact your bookseller or Springer

Vol. 3626: B. Ganter, G. Stumme, R. Wille (Eds.), Formal Concept Analysis. X, 349 pages. 2005. (Subseries LNAI).

Vol. 3596: F. Dau, M.-L. Mugnier, G. Stumme (Eds.), Conceptual Structures: Common Semantics for Sharing Knowledge. XI, 467 pages. 2005. (Subseries LNAI).

Vol. 3587: P. Perner, A. Imiya (Eds.), Machine Learning and Data Mining in Pattern Recognition. XVII, 695 pages. 2005. (Subseries LNAI).

Vol. 3582: J. Fitzgerald, I.J. Hayes, A. Tarlecki (Eds.), FM 2005: Formal Methods. XIV, 558 pages. 2005.

Vol. 3580: L. Caires, G.F. Italiano, L. Monteiro, C. Palamidessi, M. Yung (Eds.), Automata, Languages and Programming. XXV, 1477 pages. 2005.

Vol. 3578: M. Gallagher, J. Hogan, F. Maire (Eds.), Intelligent Data Engineering and Automated Learning - IDEAL 2005. XVI, 599 pages. 2005.

Vol. 3576: K. Etessami, S.K. Rajamani (Eds.), Computer Aided Verification. XV, 564 pages. 2005.

Vol. 3575: S. Wermter, G. Palm, M. Elshaw (Eds.), Biomimetic Neural Learning for Intelligent Robots. IX, 383 pages. 2005. (Subseries LNAI).

Vol. 3574: C. Boyd, J.M. González Nieto (Eds.), Information Security and Privacy. XIII, 586 pages. 2005.

Vol. 3573: S. Etalle (Ed.), Logic Based Program Synthesis and Transformation. VIII, 279 pages. 2005.

Vol. 3572: C. De Felice, A. Restivo (Eds.), Developments in Language Theory. XI, 409 pages. 2005.

Vol. 3571: L. Godo (Ed.), Symbolic and Quantitative Approaches to Reasoning with Uncertainty. XVI, 1028 pages. 2005. (Subseries LNAI).

Vol. 3570: A. S. Patrick, M. Yung (Eds.), Financial Cryptography and Data Security. XII, 376 pages. 2005.

Vol. 3569: F. Bacchus, T. Walsh (Eds.), Theory and Applications of Satisfiability Testing. XII, 492 pages. 2005.

Vol. 3568: W.K. Leow, M.S. Lew, T.-S. Chua, W.-Y. Ma, L. Chaisorn, E.M. Bakker (Eds.), Image and Video Retrieval. XVII, 672 pages. 2005.

Vol. 3567: M. Jackson, D. Nelson, S. Stirk (Eds.), Database: Enterprise, Skills and Innovation. XII, 185 pages. 2005.

Vol. 3566: J.-P. Banâtre, P. Fradet, J.-L. Giavitto, O. Michel (Eds.), Unconventional Programming Paradigms. XI, 367 pages. 2005.

Vol. 3565: G.E. Christensen, M. Sonka (Eds.), Information Processing in Medical Imaging. XXI, 777 pages. 2005.

Vol. 3564: N. Eisinger, J. Małuszyński (Eds.), Reasoning Web. IX, 319 pages. 2005.

Vol. 3562: J. Mira, J.R. Álvarez (Eds.), Artificial Intelligence and Knowledge Engineering Applications: A Bioinspired Approach, Part II. XXIV, 636 pages. 2005.

Vol. 3561: J. Mira, J.R. Álvarez (Eds.), Mechanisms, Symbols, and Models Underlying Cognition, Part I. XXIV, 532 pages. 2005.

Vol. 3560: V.K. Prasanna, S. Iyengar, P.G. Spirakis, M. Welsh (Eds.), Distributed Computing in Sensor Systems. XV, 423 pages. 2005.

Vol. 3559: P. Auer, R. Meir (Eds.), Learning Theory. XI, 692 pages. 2005. (Subseries LNAI).

Vol. 3558: V. Torra, Y. Narukawa, S. Miyamoto (Eds.), Modeling Decisions for Artificial Intelligence. XII, 470 pages. 2005. (Subseries LNAI).

Vol. 3557: H. Gilbert, H. Handschuh (Eds.), Fast Software Encryption. XI, 443 pages. 2005.

Vol. 3556: H. Baumeister, M. Marchesi, M. Holcombe (Eds.), Extreme Programming and Agile Processes in Software Engineering. XIV, 332 pages. 2005.

Vol. 3555: T. Vardanega, A. Wellings (Eds.), Reliable Software Technology – Ada-Europe 2005. XV, 273 pages. 2005.

Vol. 3554: A. Dey, B. Kokinov, D. Leake, R. Turner (Eds.), Modeling and Using Context. XIV, 572 pages. 2005. (Subseries LNAI).

Vol. 3553: T.D. Hämäläinen, A.D. Pimentel, J. Takala, S. Vassiliadis (Eds.), Embedded Computer Systems: Architectures, Modeling, and Simulation. XV, 476 pages. 2005.

Vol. 3552: H. de Meer, N. Bhatti (Eds.), Quality of Service – IWQoS 2005. XVIII, 400 pages. 2005.

Vol. 3551: T. Härder, W. Lehner (Eds.), Data Management in a Connected World. XIX, 371 pages. 2005.

Vol. 3548: K. Julisch, C. Kruegel (Eds.), Intrusion and Malware Detection and Vulnerability Assessment. X, 241 pages. 2005.

Vol. 3547: F. Bomarius, S. Komi-Sirviö (Eds.), Product Focused Software Process Improvement. XIII, 588 pages. 2005.

Vol. 3546: T. Kanade, A. Jain, N.K. Ratha (Eds.), Audio- and Video-Based Biometric Person Authentication. XX, 1134 pages. 2005.

Vol. 3543: L. Kutvonen, N. Alonistioti (Eds.), Distributed Applications and Interoperable Systems. XI, 235 pages. 2005.

Vol. 3542: H.H. Hoos, D.G. Mitchell (Eds.), Theory and Applications of Satisfiability Testing. XIII, 393 pages. 2005.

Vol. 3541: N.C. Oza, R. Polikar, J. Kittler, F. Roli (Eds.), Multiple Classifier Systems. XII, 430 pages. 2005.

Vol. 3540: H. Kalviainen, J. Parkkinen, A. Kaarna (Eds.), Image Analysis. XXII, 1270 pages. 2005.

Vol. 3537: A. Apostolico, M. Crochemore, K. Park (Eds.), Combinatorial Pattern Matching. XI, 444 pages. 2005.

Vol. 3536: G. Ciardo, P. Darondeau (Eds.), Applications and Theory of Petri Nets 2005. XI, 470 pages. 2005.

Vol. 3535: M. Steffen, G. Zavattaro (Eds.), Formal Methods for Open Object-Based Distributed Systems. X, 323 pages. 2005.

Vol. 3533: M. Ali, F. Esposito (Eds.), Innovations in Applied Artificial Intelligence. XX, 858 pages. 2005. (Subseries LNAI).

Vol. 3532: A. Gómez-Pérez, J. Euzenat (Eds.), The Semantic Web: Research and Applications. XV, 728 pages. 2005.

Vol. 3531: J. Ioannidis, A. Keromytis, M. Yung (Eds.), Applied Cryptography and Network Security. XI, 530 pages. 2005.

Vol. 3530: A. Prinz, R. Reed, J. Reed (Eds.), SDL 2005: Model Driven. XI, 361 pages. 2005.

Vol. 3528: P.S. Szczepaniak, J. Kacprzyk, A. Niewiadomski (Eds.), Advances in Web Intelligence. XVII, 513 pages. 2005. (Subseries LNAI).

Vol. 3527: R. Morrison, F. Oquendo (Eds.), Software Architecture. XII, 263 pages. 2005.

Vol. 3526: S.B. Cooper, B. Löwe, L. Torenvliet (Eds.), New Computational Paradigms. XVII, 574 pages. 2005.

Vol. 3525: A.E. Abdallah, C.B. Jones, J.W. Sanders (Eds.), Communicating Sequential Processes. XIV, 321 pages. 2005.

Vol. 3524: R. Barták, M. Milano (Eds.), Integration of AI and OR Techniques in Constraint Programming for Combinatorial Optimization Problems. XI, 320 pages. 2005.

Vol. 3523: J.S. Marques, N. Pérez de la Blanca, P. Pina (Eds.), Pattern Recognition and Image Analysis, Part II. XXVI, 733 pages. 2005.

Vol. 3522: J.S. Marques, N. Pérez de la Blanca, P. Pina (Eds.), Pattern Recognition and Image Analysis, Part I. XXVI, 703 pages. 2005.

Vol. 3521: N. Megiddo, Y. Xu, B. Zhu (Eds.), Algorithmic Applications in Management. XIII, 484 pages. 2005.

Vol. 3520: O. Pastor, J. Falcão e Cunha (Eds.), Advanced Information Systems Engineering. XVI, 584 pages. 2005.

Vol. 3519: H. Li, P. J. Olver, G. Sommer (Eds.), Computer Algebra and Geometric Algebra with Applications. IX, 449 pages. 2005.

Vol. 3518: T.B. Ho, D. Cheung, H. Liu (Eds.), Advances in Knowledge Discovery and Data Mining. XXI, 864 pages. 2005. (Subseries LNAI).

Vol. 3517: H.S. Baird, D.P. Lopresti (Eds.), Human Interactive Proofs. IX, 143 pages. 2005.

Vol. 3516: V.S. Sunderam, G.D.v. Albada, P.M.A. Sloot, J.J. Dongarra (Eds.), Computational Science – ICCS 2005, Part III. LXIII, 1143 pages. 2005.

Vol. 3515: V.S. Sunderam, G.D.v. Albada, P.M.A. Sloot, J.J. Dongarra (Eds.), Computational Science – ICCS 2005, Part II. LXIII, 1101 pages. 2005.

Vol. 3514: V.S. Sunderam, G.D.v. Albada, P.M.A. Sloot, J.J. Dongarra (Eds.), Computational Science – ICCS 2005, Part I. LXIII, 1089 pages. 2005.

Vol. 3513: A. Montoyo, R. Muñoz, E. Métais (Eds.), Natural Language Processing and Information Systems. XII, 408 pages. 2005.

Vol. 3512: J. Cabestany, A. Prieto, F. Sandoval (Eds.), Computational Intelligence and Bioinspired Systems. XXV, 1260 pages. 2005.

Vol. 3511: U.K. Wiil (Ed.), Metainformatics. VIII, 221 pages. 2005.

Vol. 3510: T. Braun, G. Carle, Y. Koucheryavy, V. Tsaoussidis (Eds.), Wired/Wireless Internet Communications. XIV, 366 pages. 2005.

Vol. 3509: M. Jünger, V. Kaibel (Eds.), Integer Programming and Combinatorial Optimization. XI, 484 pages. 2005.

Vol. 3508: P. Bresciani, P. Giorgini, B. Henderson-Sellers, G. Low, M. Winikoff (Eds.), Agent-Oriented Information Systems II. X, 227 pages. 2005. (Subseries LNAI).

Vol. 3507: F. Crestani, I. Ruthven (Eds.), Information Context: Nature, Impact, and Role. XIII, 253 pages. 2005.

Vol. 3506: C. Park, S. Chee (Eds.), Information Security and Cryptology – ICISC 2004. XIV, 490 pages. 2005.

Vol. 3505: V. Gorodetsky, J. Liu, V. A. Skormin (Eds.), Autonomous Intelligent Systems: Agents and Data Mining. XIII, 303 pages. 2005. (Subseries LNAI).

Vol. 3504: A.F. Frangi, P.I. Radeva, A. Santos, M. Hernandez (Eds.), Functional Imaging and Modeling of the Heart. XV, 489 pages. 2005.

Vol. 3503: S.E. Nikoletseas (Ed.), Experimental and Efficient Algorithms. XV, 624 pages. 2005.

Vol. 3502: F. Khendek, R. Dssouli (Eds.), Testing of Communicating Systems. X, 381 pages. 2005.

Vol. 3501: B. Kégl, G. Lapalme (Eds.), Advances in Artificial Intelligence. XV, 458 pages. 2005. (Subseries LNAI).

Vol. 3500: S. Miyano, J. Mesirov, S. Kasif, S. Istrail, P. Pevzner, M. Waterman (Eds.), Research in Computational Molecular Biology. XVII, 632 pages. 2005. (Subseries LNBI).

Vol. 3499: A. Pelc, M. Raynal (Eds.), Structural Information and Communication Complexity. X, 323 pages. 2005.

Vol. 3498: J. Wang, X. Liao, Z. Yi (Eds.), Advances in Neural Networks – ISNN 2005, Part III. XLIX, 1077 pages. 2005.

Vol. 3497: J. Wang, X. Liao, Z. Yi (Eds.), Advances in Neural Networks – ISNN 2005, Part II. XLIX, 947 pages. 2005.

Vol. 3496: J. Wang, X. Liao, Z. Yi (Eds.), Advances in Neural Networks – ISNN 2005, Part II. L, 1055 pages. 2005.

Vol. 3495: P. Kantor, G. Muresan, F. Roberts, D.D. Zeng, F.-Y. Wang, H. Chen, R.C. Merkle (Eds.), Intelligence and Security Informatics. XVIII, 674 pages. 2005.

Vol. 3494: R. Cramer (Ed.), Advances in Cryptology – EUROCRYPT 2005. XIV, 576 pages. 2005.

Vol. 3493: N. Fuhr, M. Lalmas, S. Malik, Z. Szlávik (Eds.), Advances in XML Information Retrieval. XI, 438 pages. 2005.